ISBN 0-471-55079-5 (vol. 1)
      0-471-55075-2 (vol. 2)
      0-471-55076-0 (vol. 3)
      0-471-55078-7 (vol. 4)
      0-471-19330-5 (vol. 5)
      0-471-19331-3 (vol. 6)
      0-471-19332-1 (vol. 7)
      0-471-19329-1 (vols. 5, 6, 7)
      0-471-19328-3 (7-volume set)

Printed in the United States of America

10 9 8 7 6 5 4 3 2 1

HANDBOOK OF
Child and Adolescent Psychiatry

Joseph D. Noshpitz, Editor-in-Chief

VOLUME FIVE:

Clinical Assessment and Intervention Planning

SAUL ISAAC HARRISON AND SPENCER ETH

VOLUME EDITORS

John Wiley & Sons, Inc.
New York • Chichester • Weinheim • Brisbane • Singapore • Toronto

In Memoriam

Joseph D. Noshpitz, M.D.
1922–1997

DEDICATION

This set of volumes grows out of an attitude that reflects the field itself. To put it succinctly, the basic theme of child and adolescent psychiatry is hope. Albeit formally a medical discipline, child and adolescent psychiatry is a field of growth, of unfolding, of progressive advance; like childhood itself, it is a realm of building toward a future and finding ways to better the outcome for the young. But within the field, an even greater theme inspires an even more dominant regard. For, beyond treating children, child and adolescent psychiatry is ultimately about rearing children. This is literally the first time in human history that we are on the verge of knowing *how* to rear a child. While people have reared children since we were arboreal, they did it by instinct, or by cultural practice, or in keeping with grandma's injunctions, or by reenacting the memories, conscious and unconscious, of their own childhood experiences. They did what they did for many reasons, but never because they really knew what their actions portended, what caused what, what was a precondition for what, or what meant what.

At this moment in history, however, things are different. The efforts of researchers, neuroscientists, child developmental specialists—in short, of the host of those who seek to understand, treat, and educate children and to work with parents—are beginning to converge and to produce a body of knowledge that tells us what children are, what they need, what hurts them, and what helps them. Hard science has begun to study the fetus, rating scales and in-depth therapeutic techniques have emerged for the mother with the infant in her arms, increasing precision is being achieved in assessing temperament, in measuring mother/infant fit, and in detecting the forerunners of personality organization. Adolescence and the intricacies of pubertal transformation are being explored as never before. Indeed, a quiet revolution is coming into being: the gradual dissemination of knowledge about child rearing that, within a few generations, could well alter the quality of the human beings who fall under its aegis.

If children—all children—could be reared in a fashion that gave them a healthier organization of conscience, that preserved the buds of cognitive growth and helped these to flower (instead of pinching them off as so many current practices do), that could recognize from the outset any special needs a child might have in respect to impulse control or emotional stability—and could step in from the earliest moments in development with the appropriate tactics and strategies, anodynes and remedies, techniques of healing and practices of enabling to allow the youngster to better manage his or her inner life and interpersonal transactions—consider what fruit this would bear.

Today this is far more than a dream, far more than a wistful yearning for a better day to come. The beginnings are already accomplished, much of the initial work has been done, the directions of future research are becoming ever more evident. The heretofore cryptic equations of development are beginning to be found and some of their solutions to be discerned, the once-mystical runes are being read—and are here inscribed in page after page of research report and clinical observation.

Some of the initial changes are already well under way. As with all science first a process of de-mystification must occur. Bit by bit, we have had to unlearn a host of formulaic mythologies about children and about parenting that have been part of Western civilization for centuries.

We have indeed begun to do so. We have been able to admit to the realities of child abuse, first to the violence directed toward children and then to their sexual exploitation. And we have had to admit to children's sexuality. Simply to allow those things to appear in print, to become part of common parlance, has taken immense cultural energy, the overcoming of tremendous defensiveness; after all, such things had been known but not spoken of for generations. Right now the sanctity, the hallowed quality of family life, is the focus of enormous cultural upheaval. There is much to suggest that the nuclear family set in the bosom of a body of extended kin relationships that had for so long served as the basic site for human child rearing is no longer the most likely context within which future generations of our children will grow. The quest is on for new social arrangements, and it is within this milieu that the impact of scientific knowledge, the huge and ever-increasing array of insights into the nature of childhood, the chemistry of human relationships, the psychodynamics of parent-child interplay—in short, within the area of development that this work so carefully details—that we find the wellsprings of hope. As nursery schools, kindergartens, grade schools, and high schools become more sophisticated, as the psychiatric diagnostic manuals become more specific and more differentiated, as doctors become better trained and better prepared to address human issues with dynamic understanding, as what children need in order to grow well becomes ever more part of everyday cultural practice, the realization of this hope will slowly and quietly steal across the face of our civilization, and we will produce children who will be emotionally sounder, cognitively stronger, and mentally healthier than their parents. These volumes are dedicated to advancing this goal.

Joseph D. Noshpitz, M.D.
Editor-in-Chief

iv

PREFACE

Some 16 years ago the first two volumes of the *Basic Handbook of Child Psychiatry* were published, to be followed shortly by volumes III and IV, and then, in 1985, by the fifth volume. More than a decade has passed since that volume was released, during which time the field of child psychiatry has advanced at a remarkable pace. Indeed, it has even changed its name to be more inclusive of the teenage years. New advances in neuroscience, in genetics, in psychoanalytic theory, in psychopharmacology, in animal studies—new findings in a host of areas have poured out during these years. It is therefore necessary to revise the handbook, to reorganize it, to update many of the clinical accounts, and to bring it to the level where the active practitioner can use its encyclopedic format to explore the enormous variety of clinical possibilities he or she may encounter.

The focus of this work is on development. It is no exaggeration to look on child development as the basic science of child and adolescent psychiatry. Development is so vital a concern that in this revision, we have abandoned the classical way of presenting the material. Rather than following tradition, wherein development, diagnosis and assessment, syndromes, treatment, and so on are discussed for a variety of related topics, in these volumes the bulk of the material is presented developmentally. Thus, volumes I, II, and III focus on development and syndromes of infancy and preschool, of grade school, and of adolescence, respectively. Within each of these larger sections, the material on development comes first, followed by chapters on syndromes, conceptualized as disturbances of development. While syndromes are described in depth, they are discussed only within the framework of the developmental level under study. Volume IV, entitled "Varieties of Development," explores a host of ecological niches within which children are reared.

Volume V includes an unusually rich banquet of studies on the assessment and evaluation of children, adolescents, and their families. Volume VI reports on the basic science issues of the field and the current status of the various treatment techniques. Volume VII contains sections on consultation/liaison, emergencies in child and adolescent psychiatry, the prehistory of child and adolescent psychiatry, current cultural issues that impinge on young people, forensic issues involving children and youth, and professional challenges facing the child and adolescent psychiatrist.

The intention of the work is to be as comprehensive and as readable as possible. In an encyclopedic work of this sort, concerns always arise as to how much space to allot to each topic and to which topics should be covered. To deal with such questions, a number of readers reviewed each submission. One editor had primary responsibility for each section; a coeditor also reviewed submissions. Then the editor of another section reviewed the submissions, exchanging his or her chapters with the first colleague so that someone outside the section read each chapter. In addition, one editor reviewed all submissions with an eye to contradictions or excessive overlap. Finally, the editor-in-chief reviewed and commented on a large proportion of the materials submitted. In short, while the submission process was not juried, a number of readers reviewed each chapter. Each author was confronted with the in cumulative critiques and asked to make appropriate changes. Most did so cheerfully, although not always with alacrity.

The writing and review process lasted from about 1990 to 1996. For much of this time, a host of authors were busy writing, revising, and polishing their work. The editors worked unstintingly, suffering all the ups and downs that accompany large projects: many meetings, huge expenses, moments of despair, episodes of elation, professional growth on the part of practically all the participants (a couple of authors who never came through with their material may be presumed to have shrunk), profound disappointments and thrilling breakthroughs, lost causes that were snatched from the jaws of defeat and borne aloft to victory, and, ultimately, the final feeling that we did it!

I speak for all the editors when I say that it was our purpose and it is our earnest wish that these volumes make for better understanding of young people, greater access to knowledge about children and adolescents, a richer sense of what this field of human endeavor entails, and a better outcome for the growth, development, mental health, and happiness of all the young in our land and of those who would help them.

Joseph D. Noshpitz, M.D.
Editor-in-Chief

CONTENTS

SECTION I / Clinical Assessment

SECTION II / Decision Trees for a Sampling of Presenting Problems

Contents

SECTION III / Initiating Assessment

SECTION IV / Clinical History

Contents

SECTION V / Clinical Observation

Contents

SECTION VI / Concluding the Assessment Process

CONTRIBUTORS

THOMAS M. ACHENBACH, PH.D.
Professor and Director, Center for Children, Youth, and Families, Department of Psychiatry, University of Vermont, Burlington, Vermont.

NORMAN ALESSI, M.D.
Associate Professor, Department of Psychiatry, University of Michigan Hospitals, Ann Arbor, Michigan.

DENNIS A. ANDERSON, M.D.
Deceased. Formerly Assistant Professor of Psychiatry, Division of Child and Adolescent Psychiatry, Long Island Jewish Medical Center, Albert Einstein College of Medicine, New Hyde Park, New York.

L. EUGENE ARNOLD, M.ED., M.D.
Professor Emeritus of Psychiatry, Ohio State University, Columbus, Ohio; Specialist, Child and Adolescent Disorders Research Branch, Division of Clinical Research, National Institute of Mental Health, Rockville, Maryland.

WILLIAM ARROYO, M.D.
Child Psychiatry O.P.D., Los Angeles County-University of Southern California Medical Center, Los Angeles, California.

PETER ASH, M.D.
Department of Psychiatry, Grady Memorial Hospital, Atlanta, Georgia.

SARAH ATKINSON, M.D.
Staff Psychiatrist, Child and Adolescent Services, The Menninger Clinic, Topeka, Kansas.

MARION TAYLOR BAER, PH.D., R.D.
Associate Director, USC University Affiliated Program, Center for Child Development and Developmental Disabilities; Adjunct Associate Professor, Division of Community Health Services, University of California at Los Angeles School of Public Health, Los Angeles, California.

CHRISTIANE A. M. BALTAXE, M.D., PH.D.
University of California at Los Angeles (UCLA-NPI), Los Angeles, California.

JULES R. BEMPORAD, M.D.
Clinical Professor of Psychiatry, New York Medical College, Valhalla, New York.

DAVID I. BERLAND, M.D.
Clinical Professor of Psychiatry, St. Louis University School of Medicine; Private Practice, St. Louis, Missouri.

EFRAIN BLEIBERG, M.D.
Executive Vice-President and Chief of Staff, The Menninger Clinic, Topeka, Kansas.

MARK BLOTCKY, M.D.
Timberlawn Psychiatric Hospital, Dallas, Texas.

SUSAN J. BRADLEY, M.D., F.R.C.P.(C.)
Psychiatrist-in-Chief, The Hospital for Sick Children; Professor and Head, Division of Child Psychiatry, University of Toronto; Consultant Psychiatrist, Child and Adolescent Gender Identity Clinic, Clarke Institute of Psychiatry, Toronto, Canada.

JOEL D. BREGMAN, M.D.
Associate Clinical Professor of Psychiatry and Pediatrics, University of Connecticut School of Medicine, Farmington, Connecticut; Assistant Clinical Professor of Child Psychiatry, Yale University Child Study Center, New Haven, Connecticut.

SAUL L. BROWN, M.D.
Private Practice, Malibu, California.

LUCIENNE A. CAHEN, M.D.
Private Practice, Newton Centre, Massachusetts.

DENNIS CANTWELL, M.D.
Deceased. Formerly Professor of Psychiatry at the University of California at Los Angeles, UCLA-NPI, Los Angeles, California.

Contributors

AUDREY J. CLARKIN, PH.D.
Clinical Assistant Professor of Psychology in Psychiatry, Cornell Medical College, New York, New York; Director of Psychology, Scarsdale School System, Scarsdale, New York.

SUSAN COATES, PH.D.
Director, Childhood Gender Identity Center, St. Luke's-Roosevelt Hospital Center, New York, New York.

DEWEY G. CORNELL, PH.D.
Clinical Psychologist and Associate Professor of Education, Programs in Clinical and School Psychology, School of Education; Faculty Associate, Institute of Law, Psychiatry, and Public Policy, University of Virginia, Charlottesville, Virginia.

JANET M. DEMB, PH.D.
Assistant Professor of Psychiatry, Yeshiva University, Albert Einstein College of Medicine, Bronx, New York; Private Practice, Scarsdale, New York.

MINA K. DULCAN, M.D.
Chief of Child and Adolescent Psychiatry, Northwestern University Medical School; Head, Department of Child and Adolescent Psychiatry, Margaret C. Osterman Professor of Child Psychiatry, Children's Memorial Hospital, Chicago, Illinois.

MONIQUE ERNST, M.D., PH.D.
Senior Staff Fellow, Brain Imaging Center, National Institute on Drug Abuse, NIH, Baltimore, Maryland.

SPENCER ETH, M.D.
Vice-Chair and Clinical Director, Department of Psychiatry, Saint Vincents Hospital and Medical Center, New York, New York; Professor of Psychiatry, New York Medical College, Valhalla, New York.

JANET E. FISCHEL, PH.D.
Associate Professor of Pediatrics and Psychology, Director of Pediatric Medical Education, State University of New York at Stony Brook School of Medicine, Stony Brook, New York.

GREGORY K. FRITZ, M.D.
Director of Child and Family Psychiatry and Division of Child and Adolescent Psychiatry, Rhode Island Hospital; Professor of Psychiatry, Brown University School of Medicine, Providence, Rhode Island.

STEWART GABEL, M.D.
Chairman, Department of Psychiatry and Behavioral Sciences, The Children's Hospital; Associate Professor of Psychiatry and Pediatrics, University of Colorado Health Sciences Center, Denver, Colorado.

JAQUELIN GOLDMAN, PH.D.
Department of Clinical and Health Psychology, University of Florida, Gainesville, Florida.

DAVID B. GOLDSTON, PH.D.
Associate Professor of Psychiatry, Bowman Gray School of Medicine, Wake Forest University, Winston-Salem, North Carolina.

MAUREEN FULCHIERO GORDON, M.D.
Assistant Clinical Professor of Psychiatry, UCLA Neuropsychiatric Institute, University of California at Los Angeles School of Medicine; Private Practice, Child and Adult Psychiatry, Los Angeles, California.

JENNIFER J. GOULD, M.D.
Assistant Professor of Psychiatry, Emory University School of Medicine, Atlanta, Georiga.

NICOLA S. GRAY, B.S.
Medical Student, University of Pittsburgh School of Medicine, Pittsburgh, Pennsylvania.

SANDRA GREENE, MA, OTR
Private Practice, Occupational Therapy with Children, Santa Monica, California.

OWEN R. HAGINO, M.D.
Instructor, Psychiatry and Human Behavior and Pediatrics, Brown University; Child and Family Psychiatry, Rhode Island Hospital, Providence, Rhode Island.

SUSAN HAIMAN, MPS, OTR/L, FAOTA
Assistant Professor and Academic Fieldwork Coordinator, Philadelphia College of Pharmacy and Science, Division of Health Sciences, Department of Occupational Therapy, Philadelphia, Pennsylvania.

SAUL ISAAC HARRISON, M.D.
Professor Emeritus, University of Michigan, Ann Arbor, Michigan; Adjunct Professor of Psychiatry and Biobehavioral Sciences, University of California at Los Angeles, Los Angeles, California.

ROBERT L. HENDREN, D.O.
Professor of Psychiatry and Pediatrics, Director of Child and Adolescent Psychiatry, Robert Wood Johnson Medical School, Piscataway, New Jersey.

LUCIE HERTZ-PANNIER, M.D.
Visiting Fellow, Diagnostic Radiology Department, The Warren G. Magnuson Clinical Center, National Institute of Health, Bethesda, Maryland

MILTON HUANG, M.D.
Lecturer, Department of Psychiatry, Assistant Director, Psychiatric Informatics Program, University of Michigan Hospitals, Ann Arbor, Michigan.

STEVEN L. JAFFE, M.D.
Professor of Psychiatry, Emory University School of Medicine; Clinical Professor of Psychiatry, Morehouse School of Medicine; Medical Director of Child and Adolescent Services, Charter Peachford Hospital, Atlanta, Georgia.

Contributors

JOSEPH J. JANKOWSKI, M.D.
Associate Clinical Professor of Psychiatry and Pediatrics; Director of Child and Adolescent Residency Training and Triple Board Residency Program; Director of Consultation/Liaison Program for Child and Adolescent Psychiatry, New England Medical Center; Academic Appointment at Tufts University School of Medicine, Boston, Massachusetts.

MICHAEL S. JELLINEK, M.D.
Professor of Psychiatry and of Pediatrics, Harvard Medical School, Boston, Massachusetts.

PETER S. JENSEN, M.D.
Chief, Child and Adolescent Disorders Research Branch, Division of Clinical Research, National Institute of Mental Health, Rockville, Maryland.

ALLAN M. JOSEPHSON, M.D.
Professor of Psychiatry; Chief of Child, Adolescent, and Family Psychiatry, Department of Psychiatry and Health Behavior, Medical College of Georgia, Augusta, Georgia.

GREGORY JURKOVIC, Ph.D.
Associate Professor of Psychology, Georgia State University, Atlanta, Georgia.

NEIL KALTER, Ph.D.
Professor, Department of Psychiatry; Professor, Department of Psychology, University of Michigan, Ann Arbor, Michigan.

SANDRA J. KAPLAN, M.D.
Associate Professor of Clinical Psychiatry, Cornell University Medical College, New York, New York; Associate Chairperson, Department of Psychiatry for Child and Adolescent Psychiatry, North Shore University Hospital, Manhasset, New York.

DAVID KAUFMAN, M.D.
Adjunct Clinical Professor of Psychiatry, Department of Psychiatry, University of Rochester Medical School, Rochester, New York.

CHARLES R. KEITH, M.D.
Professor, Department of Psychiatry, Division of Child and Adolescent Psychiatry, Duke University Medical Center, Durham, North Carolina.

ROBERT A. KING, M.D.
Associate Professor of Child Psychiatry, Yale Child Study Center, Yale University School of Medicine, New Haven, Connecticut.

KATHERINE KIRKHART, M.A.
Doctoral Candidate, Department of Psychology, University of North Carolina at Greensboro, Greensboro, North Carolina.

RACHEL G. KLEIN, Ph.D.
Director of Psychology, New York State Psychiatric Institute; Professor of Clinical Psychology, Columbia University, College of Physicians and Surgeons, New York, New York.

MARKUS J. P. KRUESI, M.D.
Professor of Psychiatry, Head, Division of Child and Adolescent Psychiatry; Director, Institute for Juvenile Research, Department of Psychiatry, University of Illinois, Chicago, Illinois.

ELISSA LANG, MEd, MA, CRC
Director of Housing and Clinical Services, YWCA of White Plains and Central Westchester, White Plains, New York.

JULIE A. LARRIEU, Ph.D.
Assistant Professor of Psychiatry, Louisiana State University Medical Center, New Orleans, Louisiana.

GREGORY B. LEONG, M.D.
Chief of Mental Health and Behavioral Science Services Veterans Affair Outpatient Clinic, Columbus, Ohio.

JENNIFER LEVITT, M.D.
Assistant Professor, Division of Child and Adolescent Psychiatry, Neuropsychiatric Institute and Hospital, University of California at Los Angeles, Los Angeles, California.

LINDA J. LOTSPEICH, M.D.
Assistant Professor of Psychiatry and Behavioral Sciences, Stanford University School of Medicine, Stanford, California.

RICHARD E. MATTISON, M.D.
Associate Professor of Psychiatry (Child), Washington University School of Medicine, St. Louis, Missouri.

BRIAN J. McCONVILLE, M.D., M.B., Ch.B., F.R.C.P.(C.)
Director of Child and Adolescent Psychiatry Research, Professor of Child Psychiatry and Pediatrics (tenured), University of Cincinnati College of Medicine, Cincinnati, Ohio.

JANICE M. McCONVILLE, M.D., F.A.A.P., F.R.C.T.(C.)
Cincinnati, Ohio.

JAMES T. McCRACKEN, M.D.
Associate Professor and Director, Division of Child and Adolescent Psychiatry, Neuropsychiatric Institute and Hospital, University of California at Los Angeles, Los Angeles, California.

JOHN F. McDERMOTT, Jr., M.D.
Professor Emeritus, University of Hawaii School of Medicine, Honolulu, Hawaii.

ELI C. MESSINGER, M.D.
Associate Clinical Professor of Psychiatry, New York Medical College, Valhalla, New York; Director of Child and Adolescent Partial Hospitalization Program, Attending Psychiatrist, Metropolitan Hospital Center, New York, New York.

KLAUS MINDE, M.D., F.R.C.P.(C.)
Head, Division of Child Psychiatry, Professor of Psychiatry and Pediatrics, McGill University; Director, Department of Psychiatry, Montreal Children's Hospital, Montreal, Quebec, Canada.

FRANK MONCHER, Ph.D.
Assistant Professor of Psychiatry, Department of Psychiatry and Health Behavior, Medical College of Georgia, Augusta, Georgia.

PETER MUEHRER, Ph.D.
Chief of Youth Mental Health Program, National Institute of Mental Health, National Institutes of Health, U.S. Department of Health and Human Services, Rockville, Maryland.

ROBERT NADRICH, M.D.
Faculty Research Fellow, Developmental Neurobiology Unit, Division of Child and Adolescent Psychiatry, Department of Psychiatry, New York University School of Medicine and Bellevue Hospital Center, New York, New York.

MICHAEL W. NAYLOR, M.D.
Director, Adolescent Psychiatry Program, The Warren Wright Center for Adolescence, Stone Institute of Psychiatry, Chicago, Illinois.

JOSEPH D. NOSHPITZ, M.D.
Deceased. Dr. Noshpitz passed away in April of 1997. At that time, he was Clinical Professor of Psychiatry and Behavioral Science at George Washington University and had a private practice in Washington, D.C.

PATRICIA NOVAK, M.P.H., R.D., C.L.E.
Maternal-Child Health, Sierra Vista Regional Medical Center, San Luis Obispo, California.

BARRY NURCOMBE, M.D., F.R.A.N.Z.C.P., F.R.A.C.P., D.P.M.
Professor of Psychiatry; Director of Child and Adolescent Psychiatry, University of Queensland, Australia.

RICK OSTRANDER, Ed.D.
Chief of Child and Adolescent Psychology, Department of Psychiatry, Georgetown University, Washington, D.C.

BRADLEY S. PETERSON, M.D.
House Jameson Assistant Professor in Child Psychiatry, Yale Child Study Center, Yale School of Medicine, New Haven, Connecticut.

CYNTHIA R. PFEFFER, M.D.
Professor of Psychiatry, Cornell University Medical College; New York Hospital, Cornell Medical Center, Westchester Division, White Plains, New York.

DANIEL PILOWSKY, M.D.
Assistant Professor, Division of Child Psychiatry, Johns Hopkins Medical School, Bethesda, Maryland.

ELLIOT M. PITTEL, M.D.
Private Practice, Child and Adolescent Psychiatry; Consultant, Barron Assessment and Counseling Center, Boston Public Schools, Boston, Massachusetts.

RICHARD R. PLEAK, M.D.
Director of Education and Assistant Professor of Psychiatry, Division of Child and Adolescent Psychiatry, Long Island Jewish Medical Center, Albert Einstein College of Medicine, New Hyde Park, New York.

STEVEN R. PLISZKA, M.D.
Associate Professor and Chief, Division of Child and Adolescent Psychiatry, The University of Texas Health Science Center at San Antonio, San Antonio, Texas.

NAOMI RAE-GRANT, M.D.
Retired. Formerly Director of Treatment and Training Research, CPRI; Professor Emerita, Department of Psychiatry, The University of Western Ontario, London, Ontario, Canada.

HELEN REID, L.C.S.W.
Thalians Medical Center, Los Angeles, California.

RANDY M. ROCKNEY, M.D.
Assistant Professor of Pediatrics and Family Medicine, Brown University; Department of Pediatrics, Hasbro Children's Hospital, Providence, Rhode Island.

JAMES R. RODRIGUE, Ph.D.
Associate Professor, Departments of Clinical and Health Psychology and Pediatrics, University of Florida, Gainesville, Florida.

HENRY T. SACHS III, M.D.
Clinical Assistant Professor of Psychiatry, Brown University School of Medicine, E. P. Bradley Hospital, East Providence, Rhode Island.

JOHN SARGENT, M.D.
Director of Education and Research and Dean, Karl Menninger School of Psychiatry and Mental Health Sciences, The Menninger Clinic, Topeka, Kansas.

BARRY SARVET, M.D.
Medical Director, Behavioral Health Programs, Presbyterian Healthcare Services; Clinical Assistant Professor of Psychiatry, Division of Child and Adolescent Psychiatry, University of New Mexico School of Medicine, Albuquerque, New Mexico.

KAREN J. SAYWITZ, PH.D.
Associate Professor, University of California at Los Angeles School of Medicine, Los Angeles, California; Director, Child and Adolescent Psychology, Department of Psychiatry, Harbor-UCLA Medical Center, Torrance, California.

RONALD SEIFER, PH.D.
Associate Professor, Department of Psychiatry and Human Behavior, Brown University School of Medicine, Providence, Rhode Island; Director of Research, Division of Child and Adolescent Psychiatry (Brown Department of Psychiatry) and E. P. Bradley Hospital, East Providence, Rhode Island.

DANIEL J. SIEGEL, M.D.
Medical Director, Infant and Preschool Service, Clinical Facility, University of California at Los Angeles Division of Child and Adolescent Psychiatry, Los Angeles, California.

LARRY B. SILVER, M.D.
Clinical Professor of Psychiatry, Georgetown University Medical Center, Washington, D.C.

STUART M. SILVERMAN, M.D.
Assistant Professor, Department of Psychiatry, University of Hawaii School of Medicine, Honolulu, Hawaii.

MAE S. SOKOL, M.D.
Director, Eating Disorders Outpatient Clinic, The Menninger Clinic, Topeka, Kansas.

ARTHUR D. SOROSKY, M.D.
Clinical Professor of Psychiatry, Division of Child Psychiatry, University of California at Los Angeles Center for the Health Sciences, Los Angeles, California.

BONNIE L. SOROSKY, L.C.S.W.
Private Practice, Encino, California.

HANS STEINER, DR. MED. UNIV.
Professor of Psychiatry, Division of Child Psychiatry and Child Development, Stanford University School of Medicine, Stanford, California.

CARRIE SYLVESTER, M.D., M.P.H.
Associate Professor and Director of Education in Child and Adolescent Psychiatry, Northwestern University School of Medicine, Chicago, Illinois.

PETER E. TANGUAY, M.D.
Bingham Child Guidance Center, Louisville, Kentucky

LENORE C. TERR, M.D.
Clinical Professor of Psychiatry, University of California San Francisco School of Medicine, San Francisco, California.

PATRICK H. TOLAN, PH.D.
Professor of Psychology in Psychiatry; Director of Research, Institute for Juvenile Research, Department of Psychiatry, University of Illinois, Chicago, Illinois.

LUCILE M. WARE, M.D.
Children's Division, The Menninger Clinic; Faculty, Topeka Institute for Psychoanalysis, Topeka, Kansas.

SIDNEY H. WEISSMAN, M.D.
Professor of Psychiatry, Stritch School of Medicine, Loyola University, Chicago, Illinois.

KAREN C. WELLS, PH.D.
Associate Professor of Medical Psychology, Duke University Medical Center; Director of Family Studies Program and Clinic, Director of Internship Training, Duke University, Durham, North Carolina.

LOUIS JOLYON WEST, M.D.
Professor of Psychiatry, University of California at Los Angeles School of Medicine, Los Angeles, California.

GROVER J. WHITEHURST, PH.D.
Professor of Psychology and Pediatrics, State University of New York at Stony Brook, Stony Brook, New York.

SABRINA WOLFE, PH.D.
Co-Director, Childhood Gender Identity Center, St. Luke's-Roosevelt Hospital Center, New York, New York.

J. GERALD YOUNG, M.D.
Professor of Psychiatry, Division of Child and Adolescent Psychiatry, New York University School of Medicine and Bellevue Hospital Center, New York, New York.

CHARLES H. ZEANAH, M.D.
Professor of Psychiatry, Louisiana State University School of Medicine, New Orleans, Louisiana.

LORI ZUKERMAN, M.D.
West Valley Mental Health, Canoga Park, California.

Reader's Guide to Child and Adolescent Psychiatry (CAP) Clinical Assessment/Intervention Strategy Planning (CA/ISP)

Saul Isaac Harrison and Spencer Eth

Before we describe the format and suggest strategies for using the clinical processes sections of the *Handbook,* the "P" in "CAP" mandates linguistic precision. The terms *child* and *adolescent* require no explanation. But a sad relic of our field's rich traditions requires explanation that the word *psychiatry* is used in the clinical processes sections of the *Handbook* exclusively in its precise original meaning derived from the Greek words for mind and healing. In the clinical processes sections, psychiatry refers to knowledge and skills; it does not refer to professionals. It has become acceptable over the years for the several professions schooled in psychiatric processes to be designated as mental health professions. But that euphemism does not seem to do justice to the rich mix of biopsychosocial knowledge and skills that comprise CAP processes. Thus, in the pages that follow, references to child and adolescent psychiatry bespeak multidimensional, multidisciplined helping processes.

The foregoing explanation is necessitated by an unfortunate feature of our field's rich traditions. It denotes a deficiency of rational planning in the best interests of children, adolescents, and their families. It reflects, instead, a historical brew of economics, elitism, and politics combining to create and reinforce the formal educational and accreditational boundaries that delineate the several professions participating in CAP processes. Consistent with the arbitrary nature of the system we inherited, each of the professions possesses its own vertical career ladder with minimal, if any, horizontal permeability. For instance, if a nurse wishes to become a physician, the nurse is required to start afresh and be educated as if no knowledge or skills had been acquired in the process of qualifying and practicing as a nurse.

This section of the Handbook differs from other books about CAP clinical processes. The chapters in this volume describing facets of clinical assessment and intervention strategy planning (CA/ISP) can be thought of as a collection of

building blocks assembled to help the reader construct ever-improving CA/ISP processes. To maximize continuing utility, the reader will have to insert new information into these pages.

These building block chapters describe clinical assessment predicated on familiarity with normal development and psychopathology, which, along with other valuable information, are addressed in depth in other volumes of the *Handbook.*

The processes of clinical assessment and intervention strategy planning begin with attention to a variety of global clinical issues, such as nosology, vulnerabilities, strengths, communicating with youngsters and with families, statistical considerations, and ethical issues. These global chapters represent a conceptual foundation for the practical building block chapters that follow in this volume as well as in the treatments section of Volume VI.

After these overarching chapters there are a series of diagrammatic illustrations of clinical decision-making processes for a potpourri of presenting problems. The decision trees were designed to convey to the reader a sense of the range of clinicians' thought processes in their own styles. The intention is to inform the reader, via the equivalent of brief visits with esteemed clinicians, about a variety of presenting problems. Hence, the decision trees encompass a multiplicity of individual formats. Some are bare-bones diagrams while others encompass content that will enrich subsequent subsections devoted to clinical history and to observation/interview/mental status assessment. Consequently, those subsections do not have chapters focused on accident proneness or on runaway youngsters, for example, because of the comprehensiveness of the decision tree chapters devoted to those particular presenting problems.

The chapters that follow the initial conceptual overviews and the accumulated decision trees are assessment building blocks. There are a range of ways to use the collection of building blocks.

Indulge us for a moment by forgetting CAP clinical processes in order to think metaphorically and imagine that our intent is a tourist's study of American history via a scholarly tour of the National Mall in Washington, D.C. As we visit each monument, we would study all there was to know about it. Absent the inspirational aesthetics, such a comprehensive study tour could be thought of as the American historical monument equivalent of reading the clinical assessment/intervention strategy planning section from cover to cover.

Alternatively, different combinations of building block chapters can be assembled to fit individual youngsters with whom readers are involved clinically. Accumulated chapters might be assigned to students as a minitextbook focused on a specific youngster.

Each individual child and family confronts us, as clinicians, with a unique array of biopsychosocial issues. For example, a host of chapters pertain to 9-year-old José, born in Los Angeles to Central American refugees, who was brought to the clinic by his mother, without an appointment, the day after he had been apprehended by the police in the company of his baseball coach. José had been reported missing when he failed to return home following practice. After being taken into custody, José disclosed to the police that he had been kidnapped and sexually molested by the coach. José's parents are divorced. His father's whereabouts are unknown and his family subsists on his mother's earnings from cleaning homes. José has a history of asthma and hearing impairment, and has been bused to a public school special education class. In the waiting room, José is observed to be sitting in a corner with his head down and a pained expression on his face.

A clinician approaching José could be aided by reviewing several chapters. The chapter on communicating with children might be particularly useful with a child who may be reluctant to discuss a painful, embarrassing, traumatic event. Also, the chapters devoted to the sexual and health aspects of the clinical history and those regarding socioeconomic, cultural, educational and trauma aspects of the history could prove valuable. Chapters in the observation/interview/mental status assessment subsection devoted to family assessment as well as the culturally different child, the possibly abused child, the disabled child, the slow-learning child, the physically ill child, the traumatized child, the child of divorce, and assessment of children's competence to testify all might contribute specifically to the clinician's fund of knowledge and skills. Also, material in the chapters on physical examination as well as the one on speech, language, and hearing studies all might be useful.

Those practical building blocks designed to enrich José's clinical assessment are located in different parts of this volume, which is designed to be used in concert with the treatment chapters in Volume VI.

SECTION I
Clinical Assessment

1 / Types and Goals of Clinical Assessment

Mina K. Dulcan

The realm of clinical psychiatric assessment of children, adolescents, and their families is in a state of healthy ferment, as a search for empirical evidence and attempts at integrative models replace earlier patterns of learning by apprenticeship and almost religious adherence to a chosen theoretical orientation. Key guideposts along the way have been works of the Group for the Advancement of Psychiatry, including its Committee on Child Psychiatry's 1957 monograph, *The Diagnostic Process in Child Psychiatry,* and its 1974 classification of psychopathological disorders in childhood; Anna Freud's Diagnostic Profile (1962) and "Concept of Developmental Lines" (1963); and James Simmon's *Psychiatric Examination of Children,* first published in 1969 and now in its fourth edition (1987). Important structure has been added by the diagnostic manuals of the American Psychiatric Association, especially the third edition and its revision (1987) and the fourth edition (DSMIV) (1994). Moreover, the approach to assessment has been enriched by numerous seminal thinkers taking behavioral, family systems, biological, developmental, and cognitive approaches. The American Academy of Child and Adolescent Psychiatry has now developed Practice Parameters for the assessment of children and adolescents (AACAP 1995), infants and toddlers (AACAP 1997), and children who may have been abused (AACAP 1997), as well as guidelines for evaluation in the context of a custody dispute. (AACAP 1997).

Clinical assessment is the cornerstone of all child and adolescent psychiatry. Effective triage, treatment, and consultation all begin with a carefully tailored evaluation. In psychiatric research, whether the focus is on prevention, epidemiology, neurobiology, genetics, treatment outcome, or prognosis and natural history, the first step is appropriate assessment and diagnosis. The training of clinicians in the crucial and complex skills related to evaluation process and content often has been neglected. Training in conducting assessment and diagnosis is discussed in detail by Costello (1987).

Purposes and Goals of the Assessment

Clinical evaluations vary widely in their purposes and goals. The traditional model has been the scheduled outpatient assessment in a clinic or a practitioner's office, with the goal of developing and initiating a detailed, comprehensive intervention plan. Child and adolescent psychiatrists are called upon by or seek out many other settings where the purposes and goals of the evaluation may be quite different. Brief screenings of populations at high risk for psychopathology can identify children who are in need of intervention, among medically ill children, children of psychiatric patients, or victims of a natural disaster or urban violence. A crisis situation presenting in an emergency room or the intake center of a hospital may require a rapid evaluation and triage. Pediatricians, schools, and courts may request consultative evaluations, either of general functioning or to answer a specific question. Nor is assessment confined only to the beginning of the clinical process; rather it should be repeated at intervals in order to measure progress and to make midcourse corrections in intervention strategies. An assessment also may be conducted in the context of a research project, to discover the prevalence of disorder, specific phenomenology, biological correlates, suitability for a particular intervention, or treatment outcome.

3

Characteristics of the Clinical Assessment

DESIGNING AN ASSESSMENT

Every assessment presents a unique opportunity to draw on the clinician's creativity and sensitivity to individual differences with the aim of tailoring strategies and procedures to the specific mission and the presenting cast of characters. Although standardized protocols may be useful, there is no single "cookbook" for evaluation, especially in training and research settings. The complexity of children's abilities, symptoms, and developmental processes, and the multiple systems within which they live, require comprehensive attention to all dimensions and perspectives.

In the past, all too often a child received an assessment determined by the clinician's narrow training or by the agency's pet theory rather than an integrated view emphasized what was most relevant to that child's unique situation. Given the extreme paucity of objective data comparing types of assessment (detailed in Rutter, Tuma, & Lann, 1988), it is no longer acceptable to limit the collection of data and the formulation of recommendations for intervention to any single theoretical orientation. "Self-fulfilling prophecies are not acceptable substitutes for the application of inductive reasoning" (Cohen, 1979, p. 487). A clinician who is trained in only one model must be prepared to collaborate with others or to make referrals.

The structure and content of the assessment varies with the age of the identified patient, the type of psychiatric disorder, and the characteristics of the family. Logistic and administrative issues must be considered, such as the amount of time available to the family and to the clinician, the distance the family must travel, the pressure of waiting lists, limits on reimbursement, and the nature and agenda of the referring agent.

COMMON FEATURES

Although the types and goals of clinical assessment can be categorized according to multiple schemes, all share several characteristics. What-

ever the setting, the outcome is best when the clinician is able to establish an initial alliance with the child or adolescent, the family, and other systems that may be involved (e.g., school or pediatric ward). Parental feelings of guilt, shame, frustration, and failure are common, although rarely voiced, and the clinician must take care not to exacerbate them. Unfortunately, families often perceive the standard questions that constitute a psychiatric evaluation as critical or blaming. For an assessment to be maximally useful in planning intervention strategies and in maintaining the cooperation of the key players, efforts must be made to identify and acknowledge strengths as well as weaknesses, coping skills as well as failures, and protective as well as risk factors. Although the clinician may have a clear agenda for the assessment, if the questions and goals of the identified patient, family, and referring agency are not recognized and addressed, an otherwise excellent evaluation may have little value. The skilled clinician orients the youth and family to the purpose, structure, and anticipated product of the assessment along with eliciting their wishes and fears. Resistance, a feature of nearly all clinical situations, must be addressed in order to maximize success. (See Anderson & Stewart, 1983, for a discussion of managing initial resistance.)

Nearly all assessments include presenting problems, psychiatric history, developmental history, family and social histories, and observation and mental status examination of the identified patient. In most clinical situations, direct observation of interactions among family members is a key portion of the evaluation. A medical history, including past history, review of systems, nutritional status, medications, and family medical history, and a recent pediatric exam are essential parts of a comprehensive evaluation. Additional lab tests, neurological evaluations, and central nervous system tests such as electroencephalogram, computerized tomography, or magnetic resonance imaging may be obtained if there are specific indications.

Social and ethical issues commonly complicate the clinical assessment. The experienced clinician is cautious about labeling a child with a psychiatric diagnosis but is also aware that a label may be necessary for obtaining entry to or funding for services. In addition, a carefully made diagnosis actually may reduce stigma, by helping family members and school personnel understand that a child has a disability, replacing the more pejorative labels commonly used by laypersons, such as "bad," "lazy," "crazy," or "just doesn't care." On the other hand, in the current insurance climate, the use of a diagnosis to obtain services now may make the patient uninsurable in the future. Cultural factors, such as ethnic background, religious beliefs, and socioeconomic status, also must receive appropriate attention in the diagnostic process.

A key part of the evaluation is the identification of strengths in the youth, the family, and the community. The concept of healthy responses to developmental or situational stressors was first highlighted in 1966 by the Committee on Child Psychiatry of the Group for the Advancement of Psychiatry (1974). This committee urged specific attention to strengths in intellectual, social, emotional, and personal and adaptive functioning. It also focused on the importance of the developmental stage-appropriateness of behavior. Strayhorn (1983) advocates the assessment of "Psychological Health Skills," specific areas of competence or ability in the cognitive, emotional, and social domains. Compared to more traditional diagnoses or psychodynamic-based schemes, skills assessment has a number of advantages. It is more likely to translate directly into therapeutic strategies; it lends itself less to negative labeling of patients; and it is more easily operationalized for purposes of prevention of psychological disability and measurement of treatment outcome.

Every clinical assessment should yield a formulation in which the clinician integrates possible etiologic factors, considers the differential diagnosis, and identifies both targets to be addressed in treatment and areas in which further evaluation is needed. Depending on the context, the clinician next produces a plan for triage, for further evaluation, or for comprehensive intervention. Interventions may include a combination of individual, family, and/or group psychotherapy, pharmacologic treatment, behavior modification, psychiatric hospitalization, medical intervention, change of placement or custody, educational or vocational strategies, and adjunctive treatments, such as a camp or recreation program or matching with a Big Brother or Big Sister. Prognosis with and without treatment is estimated, and appropriate feedback is given to the youth, the family, and relevant professionals.

Assessment Types

Achenbach (1985) has delineated 4 major paradigms, or conceptual models, of assessment: medical (disease), psychodynamic (unconscious structures and processes), psychometric (standardized, norm-referenced dimensions), and behavioral (context-based observations). Supplementary approaches identified by Achenbach include developmental assessment (achievement of specified milestones), psychoeducational assessment (measurement of academic achievement, motivation, and learning disabilities), assessment of skills and competencies (by observation at home or school or while performing standardized tasks in the clinic setting, by self-rating, or from checklist reports from parents or teachers), assessment of social cognition, sociometric assessment (evaluation of an individual by his or her peers), assessment of family functioning, and ecological assessment (appraisal of physical, cognitive, or emotional characteristics of the child's home or school environment).

Alternatively, clinical assessments can be categorized by their purpose, theoretical underpinnings, format (site, duration, type and number of clinicians, persons assessed), or the techniques or instruments used. These characteristics form a multidimensional interactive matrix into which each type of evaluation can be placed.

Theoretical Underpinnings
of Assessment

Anna Freud (1962) devised the Diagnostic Profile to structure the psychoanalytic assessment of normal development and of childhood psychiatric disturbances. The profile includes reason for referral, description of the child, family background, personal history, and possibly significant environmental influences. The clinician assesses drive development (libido and aggression), ego and superego development, development of the total personality, regression and fixation points, conflicts, and general characteristics such as frustration tolerance, sublimation potential, attitude toward anxiety, and the balance of progressive developmental forces versus regressive tendencies. The profile is supplemented by 6 developmental lines, each of which addresses a particular area of ego functioning, self-care, or object relationships (Freud, 1963). Important data include the current status along each line, any regression along one or more lines, and the correspondence between lines. Laufer (1965) has extended the diagnostic profile into adolescence.

The phenomenological or Kraepelinian approach is seen in both the third revised and fourth edition of the *Diagnostic and Statistical Manual of Mental Disorders* (*DSM* IIIR and *DSM* IV) (American Psychiatric Association, 1987, 1994). The eventual goal is a taxonomy of empirically validated descriptive diagnostic or disease categories defined by operational criteria. Presumed etiology does not generally enter into this frame of reference, unless it can be demonstrated by experimental data (e.g., organic syndromes).

Family systems theorists deemphasize or actively avoid the use of individual psychiatric diagnoses, focusing on family dynamic issues. Different schools of family therapy, such as structural (Minuchin), multigenerational (Bowen), strategic (Haley, Palazolli), behavioral (Patterson), functional (Alexander), and psychoeducational, vary widely in their use of assessment techniques and intervention strategies.

Other important theoretical frameworks include ecological, neurodevelopmental, cognitive, and behavioral or social learning.

Assessment Format

Clinical evaluations differ in location, clinicians, time frame, participants, and sources of data.

The place in which an evaluation occurs is im-
portant for several reasons: Children and adolescents are much more variable than adults from one environment to another, and the setting of the evaluation also may determine other factors, such as the purpose, sources of data, degree of confidentiality, and potential recommendations. Psychiatric assessment of children and adolescents may occur in private offices, psychiatric clinics, family service agencies, psychiatric hospitals, pediatric clinics and wards, schools, group homes, youth detention centers, and juvenile and family courts. Home visits, although appearing costly in clinician time, may yield, in an efficient manner, crucial information about the child, family, and physical and social environment. These data are not obtainable in the office or clinic, especially for very young, physically disabled, or excessively anxious or withdrawn children, complex or deprived living situations, and family members who cannot be enticed into the clinic (Freeman, 1967).

The traditional triad of child psychiatrist, psychologist, and social worker originated in the child guidance clinics. A team approach has the advantage of bringing multiple perspectives, diverse skills, and additional stamina to the clinical problem. Disadvantages include inefficiency, expense, rigidity of roles, and the potential for lost data and dissention (Group for Advancement of Psychiatry, 1982). Flexibility and intensive collaboration are required for a team to function effectively. A more efficient arrangement assigns primary responsibility to a single clinician, with the opportunity and obligation to include others with specialized skills as needed.

Depending on factors just noted, the time frame of an assessment may be as brief as a single 1-hour consultation or screening or may extend over many hours and many weeks.

As indicated by availability or clinical needs, participants may include, in addition to the identified patient, 1 or both parents, stepparents, foster parents, siblings, other family members, teachers, probation officer, pediatrician, child welfare agency worker, or other professional who knows the child. Each informant will present a different picture of the child, in part because the information is filtered through the observer's own experience and agenda and in part because children's behavior and mood may differ dramatically from home to school to playground, or even from one classroom to another. In some cases, assessment in the context of the peer group is useful, such as a group diagnostic assessment in a clinic or psychiatric unit (especially for preschool children) or in the child's existing peer group at school. In addition to considering individual and family dynamics and characteristics, the clinician may assess the system in which the child is embedded, such as a school, group home, or pediatric ward. Information may be gathered by telephone conversations or by review of medical, psychiatric, or legal records.

Psychiatric Evaluation Techniques and Instruments

Selection of techniques and instruments to use in a specific assessment is influenced by all of the factors just discussed. In addition, the psychometric properties of an assessment measure or method should be taken into consideration. Reliability, or the reproducibility of results, is essential for an accurate assessment. Measures include immediate and delayed test-retest and interrater reliability. The validity of a technique addresses whether it really measures what it is supposed to measure and whether it measures something real and relevant. Unfortunately, in child psychiatric diagnosis, there is no "gold standard" (such as the autopsy in clinical medicine), so absolute validity is difficult to measure. Because of the complexity of the human condition, there exist multiple sources of variability or possible error in the assessment process. (See Young, Leven, Ludman, Kisnadwala & O'Brien, 1990, for more detail.) A great deal of variance is a result of the interview structure, such as which questions are asked, how they are worded, and in what order they are presented. The respondent may have memory lapses, may not understand the questions, or may have a personal agenda for the interview (e.g., not appearing "crazy" or avoiding hospitalization). Certain characteristics of the interviewer, such as age, sex, race, or ability to establish rapport with the patient, may affect the answers given. An obvious but often overlooked source of potential error re-

sults from illegibility of or omissions in the written report of the information obtained.

In the past, techniques were selected almost entirely according to the training and theoretical preference of the evaluator. Today it is increasingly likely that the methods employed will be selected according to their demonstrated advantages and disadvantages (see Achenbach, 1988, for more detail), the characteristics of the patient (e.g., age, diagnosis), and the purpose of the assessment. In most situations, in an attempt to obtain a comprehensive understanding and to minimize the disadvantages of any 1 method, combinations of techniques are used.

Clinical interviews offer the most flexibility, but clinician diagnoses are often unreliable. Interview techniques can be placed on a continuum of their degree of structure. The content of the nondirective play or verbal interview is determined by the child. The relative amounts of play and talk vary by age, developmental level, and verbal ability. In a semistructured interview the clinician uses an outline or defined list of topics. This may be completely informal or may pair an ad lib interview with a structured recording system. A pioneering example of the latter was the Clinical Data for Children system, developed at the Pittsburgh Child Guidance Center (Snyderman, Magnussen, & Henderson, 1979). The Kiddie SADS (Schedule for Affective Disorders and Schizophrenia for School-aged Children) is a semistructured research diagnostic interview in which the order and format are defined, some wording is provided, and the types of probes are specified. At the far end of the continuum of structure is the NIMH DISC (Diagnostic Interview Schedule for Children), a diagnostic interview that is completely scripted and is intended to be administered by trained lay interviewers in epidemiologic studies.

Family assessment methods focus on the context of the child's problems and can provide information on powerful family dynamics and on other individuals in the family. Unfortunately, few have been standardized by developmental stage or using normal families, and most are dependent on theoretical constructs that have not been solidly validated.

Rating scales are easy to use, inexpensive, cover a variety of both frequent and rare behaviors, and have high test-retest reliability. Norms can be developed on large samples of youth in the community. On the other hand, they reflect only the viewpoint of the single informant and do not typically generate diagnoses. A wide variety of general and syndrome-specific rating scales have been developed to gather efficiently standardized information from multiple informants (patient, parent, teacher, clinician). Rating scales are generally used as screens or as supplements to interview techniques.

Direct observation measures can be highly reliable, if observers are properly trained. They provide the most accurate numerical data are recorded on the rate and frequency of behaviors; thus the interaction between the subject and his or her environment can be depicted. Disadvantages of naturalistic observations include expense and inconvenience, although if a large number of similar observations are required, nonclinicians can be trained to carry them out. Observational methods cannot assess rare behaviors and internal emotional states.

Biomedical and psychobiological measures are useful in research and may indicate organic abnormalities, but normative developmental reference points are few, and connections with specific psychopathology are often obscure.

Computer programs have been developed to administer both rating scales (Sawyer, Sarris, & Baghurst, 1991) and questionnaires (Sawyer, Sarris, Quigley, Baghurst, & Kalucy, 1991) to parents and a structured interview (a modified Child Assessment Schedule) to children (Aiken et al., 1987). Both the DICA (Diagnostic Interview for Children and Adolescents) and the NIMH DISC have computerized versions that display the questions to the interviewer and allow for data entry during the interview. Rapidly improving computer technology provides greater speed, larger memory capacity, greater ease of use, and easily portable laptops at a more economical price. As clinicians and patients grow increasingly comfortable with computers, accelerated use of computers in both clinical and research settings can be anticipated.

Supplemental Assessment Techniques

Depending on the clinical needs and the resources available, a wide variety of additional techniques may be employed. Standard psychometric measures include tests of IQ and academic achievement. Questions regarding organic impairment may call for neuropsychological test batteries. Although projective tests, when administered by an experienced psychologist, may yield useful clues about the child's inner life, they have not been demonstrated to be valid instruments for the assessment of children's personality structure or psychiatric diagnosis, or for prediction of future adjustment (Klein, 1986). Computerized tests of attention (eg continuous performance test or CPT) and learning (eg paired associate learning or PAL) may be useful adjuncts. Specialized tests of speech, language, and hearing or genetic screening may be essential in the differential diagnosis of certain children and adolescents.

Future Directions

Experts continue to puzzle over how to integrate data from multiple informants (child, parent, teacher) or from different measures (interview, observation, rating scale) that invariably differ. Progress in determining the most efficient and accurate combinations of techniques for specific situations is eagerly awaited by both clinicians and researchers. Future advances in clinical assessment are inevitably tied to improvement in the diagnostic system. We are engaged in a process of repetitive "bootstrapping," in which more reliable and valid assessment methods interact with empirical data on psychopathology. Our task is to make full use of standardized and scientific methods while not losing clinical flexibility and creativity.

REFERENCES

Achenbach, T. M. (1985). *Assessment and taxonomy of child and adolescent psychopathology.* Beverly Hills, CA: Sage Publications.

Achenbach, T. M. (1988). Integrating assessment and taxonomy. In M. Rutter, A. H. Tuma, & I. S. Lann (Eds.), *Assessment and diagnosis in child psychopathology* (pp. 300–343). New York: Guilford Press.

Aiken, R. C., Jones, R. N., McMahon, W. M., Furia, L., Ferre, R. C., Latkowski, M. E., & Christensen, P. L. (October, 1987). *Research on a computer-assisted structured interview for inpatient children and adolescents.* Paper presented at the annual meeting of the American Academy of Child and Adolescent Psychiatry, Washington, DC.

American Academy of Child and Adolescent Psychiatry (1995). Practice parameters for the psychiatric assessment of children and adolescents. *Journal of the American Academy of Child and Adolescent Psychiatry, 34,* 1386–1402.

American Academy of Child and Adolescent Psychiatry (1997). Practice parameters for the psychiatric assessment of infants and toddlers (0–36 months). *Journal of the American Academy of Child and Adolescent Psychiatry, 36,* in press.

American Academy of Child and Adolescent Psychiatry (1997). Practice parameters for the forensic evaluation of children and adolescents who may have been physically or sexually abused. *Journal of the American Academy of Child and Adolescent Psychiatry, 36,* in press.

American Academy of Child and Adolescent Psychiatry (1997). Practice parameters for child custody evaluation. *Journal of the American Academy of Child and Adolescent Psychiatry, 36,* in press.

American Psychiatric Association. (1987). *Diagnostic and statistical manual of mental disorders* (3rd ed., rev.). Washington, DC: Author.

American Psychiatric Association. (1994). *Diagnostic and statistical manual of mental disorders* (4th ed.). Washington, DC: Author.

Anderson, C. M., & Stewart, S. (1983). *Mastering resistance: A practical guide to family therapy.* New York: Guilford Press.

Cohen, R. L. (1979). Basic concepts. In J. D. Call, J. D. Noshpitz, R. L. Cohen, & I. N. Berlin, *Basic handbook of child psychiatry* (Vol. 1, pp. 485–493). New York: Basic Books.

Costello, A. J. (1987). Assessment and diagnosis. In R. L. Cohen & M. K. Dulcan (Eds.), *Basic handbook of training in child and adolescent psychiatry* (pp. 67–76). Springfield, IL: Charles C Thomas.

Freeman, R. D. (1967). The home visit in child psychiatry: Its usefulness in diagnosis and training. *Journal*

of the American Academy of Child Psychiatry, 6, 276–294.

Freud, A. (1962). Assessment of childhood disturbances. *Psychoanalytic Study of the Child, 17,* 149–158.

Freud, A. (1963). The concept of developmental lines. *Psychoanalytic Study of the Child, 18,* 245–265.

Group for the Advancement of Psychiatry, Committee on Child Psychiatry. (1957). *The diagnostic process in child psychiatry.* New York: Author.

Group for the Advancement of Psychiatry, Committee on Child Psychiatry. (1974). *Psychopathological disorders in childhood: Theoretical considerations and a proposed classification.* New York: Jason Aronson.

Group for the Advancement of Psychiatry, Committee on Child Psychiatry. (1982). Collaborative therapy with children. In *The process of child therapy* (pp. 199–211). New York: Brunner/Mazel.

Klein, R. G. (1986). Questioning the clinical usefulness of projective psychological tests for children. *Developmental and Behavioral Pediatrics, 7,* 378–382.

Laufer, M. (1965). Assessment of adolescent disturbances: The application of Anna Freud's Diagnostic Profile. *Psychoanalytic Study of the Child, 20,* 99–123.

Rutter, M., Tuma, A. H., & Lann, I. S. (Eds.). (1988). *Assessment and diagnosis in child psychopathology.* New York: Guilford Press.

Sawyer, M. G., Sarris, A., & Baghurst, P. (1991). The use of a computer-assisted interview to administer the Child Behavior Checklist in a child psychiatry service. *Journal of the American Academy of Child and Adolescent Psychiatry, 30,* 674–681.

Sawyer, M. G., Sarris, A., Quigley, R., Baghurst, P., & Kalucy, R. (1990). The attitude of parents to the use of computer-assisted interviewing in a child psychiatry service. *British Journal of Psychiatry, 157,* 675–678.

Simmons, J. E. (1987). *Psychiatric examination of children* (4th ed.). Philadelphia: Lea & Febiger.

Snyderman, B., Magnussen, M. G., & Henderson, P. B. (1979). Standardized data collection. In J. D. Call, J. D. Noshpitz, R. L. Cohen, & I. N. Berlin, *Basic handbook of child psychiatry* (Vol. 1, pp. 657–675). New York: Basic Books.

Strayhorn, J. M. (1983). A diagnostic axis relevant to psychotherapy and preventive mental health. *American Journal of Orthopsychiatry, 53,* 677–696.

Young, J. G., Leven, L., Ludman, W., Kisnadwala, H., & O'Brien, J. D. (1990). Interviewing children and adolescents. In B. D. Garfinkel, G. A. Carlson, & E. B. Weller (Eds.), *Psychiatric disorders in children and adolescents* (pp. 443–468). Philadelphia: W. B. Saunders.

2 / Classification Systems and Nosology

Thomas M. Achenbach

Classification issues may seem remote from the needs of clinical practice. However, to advance clinical practice, we need conceptual frameworks within which to group the target phenomena and procedures for distinguishing among the groupings. This chapter presents issues that arise in efforts to construct useful groupings of children's behavioral/emotional problems. For brevity, I use the term *children* to include adolescents and *behavioral/emotional problems* to encompass a broad range of disorders for which children (and adolescents) are commonly referred for mental health services.

When we assess and group children's disorders, confusion often arises from variations in terminology. The term *diagnosis,* for example, is used in several different ways that may blur into one another. As expressed by a leading psychiatric diagnostician, diagnosis is the "medical term for classification" (Guzé, 1978, p. 53). A diagnosis in this sense is called a *formal diagnosis.* It is the sense in which the categories of the *International Classification of Disease (ICD)* by the World Health Organization (WHO, 1992) and the *Diagnostic and Statistical Manual (DSM)* by the American Psychiatric Association (APA, 1994) are diagnoses.

In a broader sense, diagnosis refers to a *diagnostic formulation,* which is defined as an "investigation or analysis of the cause or nature of a condition," and "a statement or conclusion from such an analysis" (Mish, 1988, p. 349). A diagnostic formulation typically involves integrating diverse data into a comprehensive picture of the case that may include hypotheses about etiology, prognosis, and the desirability of particular interventions. Although the formal diagnoses of the *ICD* and *DSM* type often are required for purposes of record keeping and third-party reimbursement, formal diagnoses do not provide a basis for planning interventions to the extent that diagnostic formulations do.

NOTE: This work was supported in part by NIMH grants MH40305 and MH46093 and W. T. Grant Foundation research grant 92-1458-92.

In addition to formal diagnoses and diagnostic formulations, diagnosis also refers to *diagnostic processes.* Diagnostic processes often imply not only gathering data but also "getting the feel of the case" by observing and interacting with the relevant people, trying out preliminary hypotheses, and evolving an overall impression.

When applied to such inadequately understood phenomena as the behavioral/emotional problems of childhood, the multiple denotations and connotations of "diagnosis" give it a slippery quality. Furthermore, the term *diagnosis* often carries an aura of clinical authority that may imply more than is really known about the target phenomena.

A more neutral term than diagnosis for the grouping of phenomena is *classification.* However, classifications can include groupings formed according to criteria that are extrinsic to the phenomena being classified. For example, children seen in a clinic can be classified according to the source of funding or the therapist who happens to treat them, but these classifications probably would not reflect the distinguishing characteristics of their disorders.

Taxonomy

To avoid the excess connotations of "diagnosis" and the overly broad meaning of "classification," I will use the term *taxonomy* in reference to systematic groupings of children's behavioral/emotional problems intended to reflect important distinctions among types or patterns of problems. The term *taxon* (plural *taxa*) refers to particular groupings within a taxonomy.

Multiple taxonomies may be applied to the same individuals and phenomena. For example, children referred for mental health services may be grouped according to a taxonomy of ability levels, ranging from Profoundly Retarded to Very Superior. Such a taxonomy could be based on IQ test scores in conjunction with developmental and social competence measures. The same children could be grouped according to patterns of behavior problems and according to the presence of identified physical abnormalities. Thus, for example, the same child might be classified in one taxonomy as moderately retarded, in a second taxonomy as manifesting a syndrome of aggressive behavior, and in a third taxonomy as having trisomy 21. Each of the taxonomies may be organized according to different principles, and each may be useful for different purposes. Three taxonomies of this sort are included as "axes" of the ICD-10 multiaxial system for children's disorders (WHO, 1996).

Each taxonomy may be organized according to different principles, and each may be useful for different purposes. As knowledge advances, taxa based on certain criteria may be superseded by taxa based on other criteria. Since 1959, for example, the cytogenetic identification of trisomy 21 has become the basis for a taxon that previously had been defined in terms of the physical stigmata of Down syndrome (Lejeune, Gautier, & Turpin, 1963).

For taxonomies to be useful, they must be *reliable*—that is, users must be able to assign the same phenomena consistently to the same taxa. The taxa also must be *valid*—that is, the criteria for the taxa must accurately mark important similarities and differences among phenomena. The similarities and differences deemed to be important depend on the functions to be served by the taxonomy and on the stage of knowledge about the phenomena to be grouped within the taxonomy. If specific etiologies are known, etiological similarities and differences often would be important bases for taxonomic distinctions. However, even if etiologies are known, they may not provide the only or the most useful basis for taxonomy. For instance, in the example of the child classified as moderately retarded, aggressive, and trisomy 21, knowledge of the child's cognitive level and behavior problem pattern, plus a variety of other characteristics, may be more useful than the trisomy 21 in applying previously gained knowledge to the education and treatment of this particular child. The trisomy 21, on the other hand, is useful as a signpost in relation to accumulated knowledge about the permanent nature of the condition, likely developmental course, and vulnerability to other conditions that often accompany it. The knowledge of trisomy 21 also may be useful as a marker for research into specific risk factors for this condition, as depicting the mechanisms by which it causes abnormal development, and as a point of departure in considering prevention.

For the taxonomy of some conditions, the specific etiology may be irrelevant. In bone fractures, for example, the location and nature of the fracture and accompanying injuries are usually more important than the specific etiological event.

Where little is known about specific etiologies, typical course, or optimal interventions, an important taxonomic function is to group phenomena in ways that will help to advance knowledge about them. One way in which taxonomy can help to advance knowledge is by providing groupings of individuals or disorders according to standardized criteria. These, in turn, may be found to mark important differences in etiology, course, or optimal intervention. If researchers consistently use standardized taxonomic criteria that reliably and validly mark differences, then relations between the criteria and possible differences in etiology, course, and responsiveness to treatment can be tested in a cumulative fashion.

Taxonomies also can have heuristic value. If a taxonomy reliably and validly reflects the actual co-occurrence of criterial attributes, the groupings thus formed may suggest underlying principles concerning etiology, course, or treatment responsiveness. Suppose, for example, that several patterns of problems are empirically identified. Suppose, too, that some patterns are found in only one age period or one sex. These findings would suggest differences in etiology or in the form of problems related to the age or sex of the child. Developmental studies could be used to determine whether the relations of particular patterns to age reflected *heterotopy* (Kagan, 1969), in which the same basic condition spawns different phenotypic manifestations at different ages, or whether the age differences are more likely to reflect fundamentally different disorders.

Assessment

If we construct taxonomic groupings, how can we determine which individuals should be assigned

11

to particular groupings? In order to assign individuals reliably and validly to a taxonomy, we must identify the features of those individuals that correspond to the criteria used to define the taxonomic groupings. The term *diagnosis* includes the process of identifying the distinguishing features of individuals. However, the multiple meanings of the term make it just as troublesome in reference to identifying distinguishing features as in reference to the construction of groupings. In keeping with the title of this section, the more neutral term *assessment* will be used for the process of identifying the distinguishing features of individual cases.

Each case has numerous distinguishing features, many of which may be unique. When planning intervention strategies, both the unique features and the specific permutations of features shared with other cases need to be taken into account. Assessment therefore must distinguish what is unique from what is more general; moreover, it must highlight features of the individual case that link it with previous cases from which knowledge has been gained.

To link an individual case reliably and validly with previous cases having similar features, assessment procedures must enable us to match the features of the case with the features that define taxonomic groupings derived from previous cases. To provide bridges between assessment and taxonomy, taxa should be *operationally defined* in terms of specific assessment procedures. Findings from those assessment procedures would, in turn, reveal which taxon the individual case resembles most closely. In other words, taxonomy and assessment should be linked, so that taxonomic groupings are defined according to particular assessment procedures. Conversely, the results of applying these assessment procedures to individual cases should tell us how to match the cases to particular taxa.

Linking Assessment and Taxonomy

Why should assessment and taxonomy be so closely linked? There are several reasons. One set of reasons relates to the improvement of clinical assessment. A second set relates to advancing our overall knowledge of children's behavioral/emotional problems.

IMPROVING CLINICAL ASSESSMENT

In assessing children's problems, we can choose from a vast array of procedures, including interviews with children, parents, and other collaterals; psychological and biomedical tests; physical examinations; rating scales; sociometrics; and direct observations of behavior. Only a few of the possible procedures are used in the assessment of most children. The subset of procedures actually employed to assess a particular child is governed by such factors as the questions to be answered, the child's developmental level, the setting in which the child is assessed, costs, funding sources, and the clinician's predilections.

Because not all procedures are useful or cost effective for all children, choices must be made from the array of all possible procedures. To maximize the utility and cost effectiveness of clinical assessment, we need to choose procedures according to how well they achieve the following aims

1. Tap all aspects of the child's functioning that are relevant to the questions to be answered.
2. Tap each aspect that yields reliable and valid data in the most cost-effective way.
3. Obtain data in a form that facilitates making decisions about interventions.
4. Provide a baseline against which to compare subsequent assessments in order to measure change.
5. Relate the case to administrative classifications that are used for record keeping and third-party reimbursement.
6. Relate the case to taxonomies that facilitate access to knowledge about the etiology, course, and treatment responses previously found for similar cases.

For certain kinds of disorders, such as mental retardation and disorders having known physical etiologies, assessment procedures for determining the presence or absence of the disorder are well established. The presence or absence of a particular disorder may, in turn, have important implications for prognosis and for some kinds of interventions, although numerous other factors also may be relevant to prognosis and the choice of intervention strategy.

Most children seen for mental health services

are not retarded, nor do their problems have identifiable physical etiologies. Instead, they manifest diverse behavioral/emotional problems that may not be intrinsically pathognomonic. In fact, many of the behavioral/emotional problems seen among children referred for mental health services also are seen among nonreferred children; hence, a basic question that arises is whether a referred child is actually deviant. If so, what are the specific areas of deviance? To answer these questions, we need to organize assessment data on behavioral/emotional problems into coherent form and to have a basis for determining what is within the normal range versus what is deviant.

Taxonomies that are closely linked to clinical assessment can help us choose and interpret assessment procedures. If taxonomies are designed to distinguish among syndromes of behavioral/emotional problems and to distinguish the clinical from the normal range, assessment procedures that are used to operationalize these distinctions should be applied to every case for which behavioral/emotional problems are to be judged. Clinicians also can use whatever additional assessment procedures seem appropriate for each case. However, a taxonomy that is operationalized in terms of specific assessment procedures could improve assessment, by ensuring that certain procedures are used across cases and across clinicians. It also could ensure that the same types of assessment and taxonomic questions are answered for most cases, in addition to whatever more idiographic questions need to be answered for each case. If the general assessment and taxonomic questions can be answered effectively in a standardized format, this would make it easier to separate the idiographic aspects of cases from the more nomothetic aspects, both of which are important for understanding individual cases. The goals listed previously for clinical assessment are not achievable through closer linkage of assessment and taxonomy alone; they also require advances in our knowledge of children's behavioral/emotional problems, as discussed in the following sections.

ADVANCING KNOWLEDGE

Systematic research on child psychopathology is still in an early stage. Any advance in our knowledge requires progress on several levels, including the conceptual, methodological, and taxonomic.

Each level can be viewed in terms of different paradigms, as outlined in the following sections.

Conceptual Paradigms: Research requires conceptual paradigms that generate researchable questions and provide guidelines for the possible answers. Examples of conceptual paradigms relevant to child psychopathology include psychodynamic, learning, developmental, genetic, and neuropsychiatric paradigms. Each of these conceptual paradigms may spawn multiple theories, as exemplified by the multiple psychodynamic, learning, developmental, genetic, and neuropsychiatric theories that have been presented at various times. Certain theoretical explanations for particular phenomena may come and go without affecting the overall paradigm. In fact, one function of conceptual paradigms is to facilitate the testing of competing theoretical explanations by providing common terms, variables, and ways of viewing relations among them.

Methodological Paradigms: Whereas conceptual paradigms embody terminology, concepts, and frameworks for conceptualizing phenomena, methodological paradigms embody sets of methods for assessing particular variables and the relations among them. Some methods may have originated with a particular theory or paradigm. The use of free association to infer unconscious thoughts and defenses, for example, originated with Freud's (1900/1953) psychoanalytic theory. However, methodological paradigms may cut across different conceptual paradigms. Statistical techniques, the operational definition of variables via measurement procedures, and criteria for reliability and validity are components of a methodological paradigm that can be applied to different conceptual paradigms and theories relating to children's behavioral/emotional problems.

Taxonomic Paradigms: Many different factors are likely to be associated with the etiology, course, and treatment responsiveness of children's behavioral/emotional problems. No single conceptual paradigm or theory is likely to embrace all the factors relevant to all the problems. Instead, different conceptual paradigms and theories may be helpful for understanding different factors. Similarly, different methodologies may be needed to test different factors and theories. Nevertheless, to advance knowledge, taxonomies are needed that will facilitate the testing and comparison of conceptual and methodological paradigms for dealing with various phenomena. Multiple taxonomies can be constructed to deal with similar phenomena, as illustrated in the following sections.

The Kraepelinian Taxonomic Paradigm

Nineteenth-century research produced major advances in knowledge of the biological basis for physical illness. The success of biological research into the causes of physical illness helped to foster a view of mental disorders as brain diseases (Griesinger, 1845/1867). In order to identify the specific brain disease responsible for each disorder, it was necessary to discriminate between different disorders. Numerous efforts therefore were made to describe symptom patterns hypothesized to represent different disorders. Some of these efforts focused on single disorders, while others aimed to construct more general taxonomic systems.

The most influential general system was published by Emil Kraepelin in 1883 and was continually revised until his death in 1926. Kraepelin initially based his efforts on the assumption that appropriate descriptions of symptoms eventually would lead to the discovery of a specific somatic etiology for each disorder (Kahn, 1959). However, by 1896 Kraepelin was using course and prognosis to distinguish between manic-depressive psychosis and dementia praecox (which Bleuler (1911/1950) renamed schizophrenia). People who recovered were judged to be manic depressive, whereas those who deteriorated were judged to have dementia praecox. By 1915 Kraepelin's taxonomy included a category of "psychogenic" disorders that comprised functional neuroses and traumatic psychoses. Personality disorders were placed in a separate category that occupied a border region between illness and common eccentricity.

ICD AND DSM

The overall structure of Kraepelin's system has continued to shape psychiatric nosologies such as the *ICD* and *DSM*. In *DSM-I* and *DSM-II* (APA, 1952, 1968), categories were specified in terms of a mixture of narrative description and inference. For example, *DSM-I* specified childhood schizophrenia as follows:

> Here will be classified those schizophrenic reactions occurring before puberty. The clinical picture may differ from schizophrenic reactions occurring in other age periods because of the immaturity and plasticity of the patient at the time of onset of the reaction. Psychotic reactions in children, manifesting primarily autism, will be classified here. Special symptomatology may be added to the diagnosis as manifestations. (APA, 1952, p. 28)

Adjustment reaction was the only other category for childhood disorders in *DSM-I*, but *DSM-II* added several behavior disorders of childhood and adolescence, as exemplified by Runaway Reaction: "Individuals with this disorder characteristically escape from threatening situations by running away from home for a day or more without permission. Typically they are immature and timid, and feel rejected at home, inadequate, and friendless. They often steal furtively" (APA, 1968, p. 50).

The assignment of individual cases to the categories of *DSM-I* and *DSM-II* depended on the user's interpretation of the meaning of each category, interpretation of the clinical picture presented by the case, and mental matching of the case to the *DSM* categories.

DSM-III: A major innovation of *DSM-III* was the definition of categories according to explicit criteria that must be met for a diagnosis to be made. For some categories, multiple features were listed and cutoffs were specified in terms of the number of features that had to be present to warrant assignment to the category. This approach was based on prior efforts to develop research diagnostic criteria (RDC) for distinguishing between major adult disorders for research purposes (Overall & Hollister, 1979).

DSM-III provided many new categories of childhood disorders that either had no counterparts in *DSM-II* or involved major changes in *DSM-II* categories. Although *DSM-III* provided explicit criteria for each childhood disorder, neither the choice of disorders nor the criteria rested on either previous research or on a lengthy clinical tradition of the sort on which many of the adult categories were based.

DSM-III-R: *DSM-III-R* made additional major

changes in the categories of childhood disorders. For example, the four types of *DSM-III* conduct disorders were replaced in *DSM-III-R* by Group and Solitary Aggressive types that actually were based on a single set of defining criteria. For some of the *DSM-III* categories that were retained, *DSM-III-R* made major changes in the defining criteria. In *DSM-III*, for example, Oppositional Disorder required the presence of only 2 out of 5 behaviors, each of which is quite common among children (e.g., violations of minor rules, temper tantrums, argumentativeness). In *DSM-III-R*, however, Oppositional Defiant Disorder required 5 out of 9 behaviors that were all specified as "often" (e.g., often loses temper, often argues with adults, often actively defies or refuses adult requests). It should therefore not be surprising that many children who met the *DSM-III* criteria for Oppositional Disorder or Conduct Disorder did not meet the *DSM-III-R* criteria for these disorders (Lahey et al., 1990).

DSM-IV embodies additional changes. For example, the criteria for Attention Deficit Hyperactivity Disorder (ADHD) were changed from the *DSM-III-R* list of 14 symptoms (with 8 required for diagnosis) to two separate lists of 9 symptoms each in *DSM-IV* (PA, 1994). A child who manifests at least 6 symptoms from one of the lists qualifies for ADHD, Predominantly Inattentive Type. A child who manifests at least 6 symptoms from the other list qualifies for ADHD, Predominantly Hyperactive-Impulsive Type. A child who meets criteria for both types qualifies for ADHD Combined Type.

RELIABILITY OF *DSM* CHILD CATEGORIES

The introduction by *DSM-III* of explicit features for defining each category and cut-off points for the number of features required for category membership represented potential advances over prior taxonomies in which clinical impressions were matched to vaguely defined categories. The *DSM-III* adult categories yielded better interclinician reliability than had been found previously. However, the interclinician reliability found for *DSM-III* child categories was considerably lower than that found for the adult categories (APA, 1980). Furthermore, the reliability of the *DSM-III* child categories was slightly lower than was true for *DSM-II* categories applied to the same

cases (Mattison, Cantwell, Russell, & Will, 1979; Mezzich, Mezzich, & Coffman, 1985). Other studies also have reported mediocre reliability for many *DSM-III* child categories, although reliability has been better for inpatients than for outpatients (Strober, Green, & Carlson, 1981; Werry, Methven, Fitzpatrick, & Dixon, 1983). At this writing, data are not available on the reliability of *DSM-IV* diagnoses of children.

Obstacles to Reliability: One reason why the *DSM-III* child categories may be less reliable than the adult categories is the fact that for the child disorders the prior research basis for both the choice of disorders and their defining criteria is much weaker than is true for the adult disorders. Unlike the adult disorders, the child disorders were not based on any RDC, because none had been developed.

A second reason for the poor reliability of the child categories may have been the lack of specific assessment procedures for determining the presence versus absence of each defining feature. Even though its criteria are more explicit than in previous editions, the *DSM* still does not specify assessment procedures that operationally define the criteria. The means for obtaining assessment data, combining different types of data, and deciding which defining features are present therefore may vary greatly among users of the *DSM*. This too could limit interclinician reliability.

The failure to define categories operationally in terms of specific assessment procedures may be less of a handicap for linking adult cases to the *DSM* categories than would be true for child cases, because data about adults' history and problems are obtained mainly from interviews with the adults themselves. Each clinician therefore would obtain data in a similar fashion from the same informant—the adult patient. Even reliance on the same single source of assessment data does not guarantee interclinician reliability, however, as differences among clinicians may affect what they elicit and observe in interviews, how they mentally weight and combine the data, and how they then fit the data to the defining criteria of each category. Nevertheless, variations in data obtained directly from adult patients themselves are relatively small compared to the variations in data arising in the course of assessing children.

Typically children are referred by adults who decide whether there are problems that require mental health services. Children's views of their own behavior may differ greatly from the views of their mothers, fathers, and teachers, who also may differ among themselves in what they report. Variations among informants' views are indicated by the modest correlations typically found among reports by different informants (Achenbach, McConaughy, & Howell, 1987).

Few children, especially at mental ages below 11, can adopt the role of a patient who dutifully reports symptoms and history in a clinical interview. Although adolescents may be cognitively more capable of reporting their symptoms and history, they also may be more resistant to revealing themselves in clinical interviews. Individual differences among clinicians may have greater effects for children than for adults on both the data obtained and how it is combined. This is true because clinician characteristics may have more influence on how children interact with the clinician and because more diverse multisource data must be mentally weighted, combined, and fitted to the defining criteria of each category. Furthermore, because the DSM defining criteria are not based on norms, the clinician must judge subjectively whether specific behaviors assessed in particular contexts actually deviate from the normal range for that child's age and sex. Considering the challenges of these information-processing tasks as well as the early stage of our knowledge, the modest reliability of the DSM child categories should not be surprising.

Studies of other Kraepelinian taxonomies also have yielded modest reliability for categories of childhood disorders. Examples include 2 studies of the ICD-9 (Gould, Shaffer, Rutter, & Sturge, 1988; Remschmidt, 1988); 2 studies of a system proposed by the Group for the Advancement of Psychiatry (1966) (Beitchman, Dielman, Landis, Benson, & Kemp, 1978; Freeman, 1971); and a study of a system proposed by a World Health Organization seminar (Rutter et al., 1975).

DIAGNOSTIC INTERVIEW SCHEDULE FOR CHILDREN

Efforts to operationalize the assessment of the DSM child categories have been made by developing structured interviews that ask children and their parents about the presence of the criterial features of each DSM category. These interviews have been modeled on the Diagnostic Interview Schedule (DIS; Helzer & Robins, 1988) that was developed for epidemiological research on the prevalence of adult disorders in the Epidemiological Catchment Area (ECA) studies (Eaton & Kessler, 1985). The most ambitious has been the Diagnostic Interview Schedule for Children, of which there have been several editions designed to be administered to children (DISC) and their parents (DISC-P; see Shaffer, et al., 1996).

Originally the DISC was intended to obtain yes-or-no answers to questions regarding each DSM criterial attribute. The questions were designed to be administered by lay interviewers separately to children and their parents. Computer algorithms then were used to determine whether the child met criteria for any DSM categories.

The most comprehensive research on the initial versions of the DISC led to the following conclusions (Costello, Edelbrock, Dulcan, Kalas, & Klaric, 1984).

1. Many DSM-III criteria could not be reliably scored as present versus absent. They were therefore scored as 0 = never, 1 = sometimes, 2 = often.
2. The DSM-III criteria for excluding certain disorders when they were "due to" other disorders led to logical contradictions that necessitated dropping these exclusionary criteria.
3. Lay and clinical interviewers could administer the DISC and score child and parent responses reliably.
4. Test-retest reliability for interviews with children was poor, especially because children tended to affirm many symptoms at the initial interview that they then denied at the second interview (Edelbrock, Costello, Dulcan, Kalas, & Conover, 1985). This is now known as the test-retest attenuation effect.
5. Categorization of children on the basis of the DISC showed little agreement with categorization of the same children on the basis of DISC-P interviews with their parents or with categorization based on complete clinical workups.
6. DSM-III criteria assigned large proportions of children to certain categories and the same children to multiple categories (e.g., 79% of clinic children qualified for Oppositional Disorder, 52% for one or more Conduct Disorders, and 46% for Attention Deficit Disorder).

Later editions of the DISC have been developed to take account of changes in the *DSM* criteria and to provide questions that are better adapted to the abilities of children and adolescents. However, many of the original problems persist (Costello, Burns, Angold, & Leaf, 1993; Shaffer et al., 1996). Furthermore, many of the DISC questions are not understood by children before age 12 (Breton et al., 1995).

The Multivariate Taxonomic Paradigm

Prior to the introduction of more differentiated categories for child and adolescent disorders in *DSM-II* (APA, 1968), the lack of attention to such disorders in official nosologies stimulated efforts to identify syndromes through statistical analyses of children's problems. Ackerson (1942), for example, computed correlations between pairs of problem items that were scored as present versus absent from clinical case histories. To derive syndromes from the correlations between items, Jenkins and Glickman (1946) identified pairs of highly correlated items and then added items that correlated highest with each member of the correlated pairs. This and other studies by Jenkins influenced some of the *DSM-II* child categories. However, the research data were case history reports, and the *DSM-II* committee based its categories on the committee's conceptions of disorders rather than on data obtained from the direct assessment of representative samples of children.

As computers became available, factor analysis and other multivariate methods have been used to identify syndromes of problems that tend to occur together. (The term *syndrome* is used here in its generic sense of a pattern of problems found to co-occur. In this usage, *syndrome* is neutral with respect to the possible nature and etiology of disorders.) The multivariate research has focused mainly on the common behavioral/emotional problems that account for most referrals for mental health services, rather than on relatively rare problems, such as those associated with autism. Numerous studies have reported syndromes derived from diverse samples of children scored on a variety of rating instruments by different kinds of informants, including parents, teachers, mental health workers, direct observers, and the children themselves. Despite the diversity of analyses and data, findings from numerous studies have converged on certain syndromes (reviewed by Achenbach, 1992, and Quay, 1986).

FEATURES OF THE MULTIVARIATE PARADIGM

The multivariate paradigm for constructing taxonomies of childhood disorders differs in several ways from the Kraepelinian paradigm. First, the multivariate paradigm starts with standardized data obtained on specific problems in large samples of children. Second, the data are quantified. The level of quantification can be as simple as scoring 0 for the absence of a problem versus 1 for the presence of the problem, although slightly more differentiated scores, such as 0 = not true, 1 = somewhat or sometimes true, and 2 = very true or often true, can make judgments easier and more reliable. Third, problem scores obtained on large samples of children are subjected to multivariate statistical analyses to identify syndromes of problems that tend to co-occur. The most common methods for identifying syndromes are factor analysis and its close cousin, principal components analysis, both of which derive groupings of mutually associated items from the correlations between pairs of items. However, multivariate methods such as cluster analysis also can be used to identify groups of cases that are similar with respect to profiles of scores on specific features or on syndrome scales that might themselves have been derived by multivariate analyses.

After syndromes have been derived via multivariate analyses, syndrome scores can be computed for individual children by summing their scores on each item of a syndrome. Various schemes for differentially weighting particular items also can be used. However, the added complexity of differential weighting usually has not yielded better results than obtained with unweighted item scores (Piacentini, Cohen, & Cohen, 1992).

Norms and cutpoints for discriminating between the normal and clinical range then can be constructed from the distributions of syndrome scores obtained by appropriate samples of children. For example, the distribution of syndrome scores obtained from a sample of nonreferred children representative of the general population can provide a basis for determining percentiles of the normal range. To reflect sex and age differences, separate distributions can be computed for children of each sex within particular age ranges. These distributions of syndrome scores also can serve as a basis for assigning standard scores, such as z scores or T scores, in order to create a common metric for multiple syndromes whose distributions of raw scores may differ greatly.

By comparing the distributions of syndrome scores obtained by demographically similar referred and nonreferred children, cutpoints can be identified that discriminate between the clinical and normal range. A particularly useful approach to identifying efficient cutpoints is via Relative Operating Characteristics (ROC) analysis (Swets & Pickett, 1982). Such analysis graphically displays the percent of cases that are correctly classified as deviant (true positives) in relation to the percent of cases incorrectly classified as nondeviant (false negatives) for various cutpoints. Cutpoints then can be chosen that optimize discrimination between the normal and clinical range. For some purposes, it may be desirable to set a relatively high cutpoint if the user wishes to minimize the proportion of normal children misclassified as deviant (false positives), at the risk of misclassifying larger proportions of deviant children as normal (false negatives). For other purposes, a user may choose a lower cutpoint in order to minimize false negatives while risking more false positives. By using distributions of syndrome scores obtained from actual samples of children considered to be normal versus deviant, we can optimize the choice of cutpoints to discriminate between normal versus deviant children. Table 2.1 summarizes the main features of the multivariate paradigm.

RELIABILITY OF MULTIVARIATE SYNDROMES

A child's standing on each multivariate syndrome is determined by the scores the child receives on the items of a particular assessment instrument completed by a particular informant. Interclinician reliability is therefore not a factor in determining the relation between a child's re-

TABLE 2.1

Main Features of the Multivariate Taxonomic Paradigm

1. Standardized data obtained on specific samples of children are used.
2. Data are quantified.
3. Multivariate analyses (e.g., factor analysis, principal components analysis) are used to identify syndromes; cluster analysis can be used to identify profile types.
4. Syndrome scores for individual children are computed by summing their scores on each item of the syndrome.
5. Norms are constructed from distributions of scores in representative samples of nonreferred children.
6. A common metric for different syndromes is constructed by assigning standard scores.
7. Cutpoints are selected that discriminate effectively between normal versus clinical samples of children (e.g., by using Relative Operating Characteristics analysis).

ported problems and taxa that are operationally defined as the sum of the scores for those problems. This does not mean that data from all sources relevant to a child will always agree, or that no clinical judgment is needed in drawing conclusions about multivariate taxa. As is discussed later, the clinical integration of multisource data is equally important for the multivariate and Kraepelinian paradigms. However, because standardized assessment data operationally define a child's standing on each multivariate syndrome, it is unlike the assignment of cases to Kraepelinian taxa on the basis of the clinician's judgment. Accordingly, there is no need to test interclinician reliability in the assignment of cases to multivariate taxa.

The main type of reliability relevant to the multivariate paradigm is test-retest reliability. Extensive data show good test-retest reliability for various informants' ratings of multivariate taxa over periods of a few weeks (e.g., Achenbach 1991b, c, d, e, 1997a, b; McConaughy & Achenbach, 1994). The scores for multivariate taxa thus maintain quite stable rank orderings over test-retest periods when the target problems probably are not changing much. Although parent and self-ratings for several taxa showed declines in problem scores from the first to the second ratings, these declines were much smaller than found on the DISC interviews with children (Edelbrock et al., 1985).

18

Other Views of Taxonomy

There are other taxonomic views of childhood disorders beside the Kraepelinian and multivariate approaches, although none has generated such systematic efforts to construct groupings of problems.

PSYCHODYNAMIC VIEWS

Anna Freud (1965) proposed a Developmental Profile based on the psychoanalytic theory of development. The profile consists of a listing of inferences about drives, ego and superego development, regressions, fixations, and conflicts. These inferences lead to categorizations such as the following:

1. In spite of current behavior disturbance, personality growth is within the wide range of "normality."
2. Symptoms are of a transitory nature and can be classed as by-products of developmental strain.
3. There is permanent drive regression to fixation points leading to neurotic conflicts.
4. There is drive regression plus ego and superego regressions that lead to infantilisms, borderline psychotic, delinquent, or psychotic disturbances (adapted from A. Freud, 1965, p. 147).

To simplify the Developmental Profile, Greenspan, Hatleberg, and Cullander (1980) proposed the Metapsychological Assessment Profile, which consists of 11 inferential assessment categories for rating children as good, fair, marginal, or inadequate. The categories include ego flexibility, superego functioning, affects, and defenses. Although ratings of such categories can be tested for reliability, Greenspan et al. presented only a single case example, with no reliability or validity data. Other publications on Anna Freud's approach also have consisted largely of case illustrations, with no reliability or validity data (e.g., Yorke, 1980).

BEHAVIORAL VIEWS

Despite their widespread applications to assessment and intervention, behavioral views have not spawned a taxonomic paradigm. Some proponents of behavioral views have implied that there is no important distinction between assessment and taxonomy and that standardized assessment of co-occurring behaviors is not a worthwhile goal (e.g., Nelson, 1983). Although other proponents of behavioral views have sought to identify clusters of behaviors (e.g., Wahler & Fox, 1980), there has been a continuing lack of behavioral concepts for aggregating co-occurring problems. As Kazdin (1983, pp. 84–85) put it:

Behavior therapy has no concept clearly analogous to that of a syndrome. Behavioral treatments are likely to focus on symptoms [target behaviors].... There is a lack of attention to the possibility that larger constellations of behavior may need to be assessed and treated.

Within behavior therapy, there is little appreciation for the fact that behaviors often come in packages or that constellations have been demonstrated empirically in many multivariate analyses. Behavioral assessment infrequently attempts to determine whether the target behavior for a given client is part of a larger scheme of behaviors, cognitions, and affects.

SERVICE-BASED CLASSIFICATIONS

Many agencies and institutions classify children for a variety of purposes. Some classifications are based on extrinsic variables, such as the source of funding or the therapist or treatment unit to which children are assigned, rather than on direct assessment of children's characteristics. Other classifications are based on judgments about the type of care required, owing to considerations such as risk of suicide or lack of self-help skills. Still others are administrative classifications based on regulations or laws for the provision of funding. Public Law 94–142, the Education of the Handicapped Act (1977, 1981; revised in the Individuals with Disabilities Education Act, 1990), for example, has given rise to administrative classifications in each state for determining eligibility for funding according to categories such as learning disabled (LD) and seriously emotionally disturbed (SED). Although the categories were not derived from assessment of actual children, schools are required to determine whether individual children meet the criteria for each administrative category. Research shows that children who have been administratively classified as learning disabled vs. seriously emotionally disturbed differ significantly in their scores on empirically derived syndromes of behavioral/emotional problems (McConaughy, Mattison, & Peterson, 1994). However, McConaughy et al. (1993) found that children classified as seriously emotionally disturbed are most deviant in respect to aggressive behavior, which the administrative classification does not officially recognize as a basis for SED eligibility.

Relations Between Kraepelinian and Multivariate Taxonomies

Although other approaches to taxonomy are important in particular contexts, the Kraepelinian and multivariate paradigms aspire to deal with more general taxonomic issues than do the other approaches. Before coming to grips with the general issues that must be addressed by any comprehensive approach, it is helpful to compare and contrast the current status of the Kraepelinian and multivariate paradigms.

DESCRIPTIVE RELATIONS BETWEEN KRAEPELINIAN AND MULTIVARIATE TAXA

The Kraepelinian categories of childhood disorders embodied in the *DSM* and *ICD* have been chosen and defined by committees. Multivariate syndromes, on the other hand, have been empirically derived from statistical analyses of behavioral/emotional problems reported by informants such as parents, teachers, clinicians, trained observers in natural settings, and children themselves. Even though their origins are quite different, there are descriptive similarities between several Kraepelinian and multivariate taxa. Table 2.2 lists taxa that have counterparts in both approaches.

Beside the descriptive similarities between Kraepelinian and multivariate taxa, research has demonstrated that, when *DSM* categories were operationalized via structured interviews, significant associations were found between *DSM* categories and scores on the empirically derived multivariate syndromes. This was true both for adolescents' self-reports on the DISC in relation to their self-ratings on the Youth Self-Report

(Weinstein, Noam, Grimes, Stone, & Schwab-Stone, 1990) and for parents' reports on the DISC-P in relation to parents' ratings of their children on the Child Behavior Checklist (Edelbrock & Costello, 1988; Gould, Bird, & Jaramillo, 1993). The relations to *DSM* syndromes were especially clear when cases were grouped according to whether they failed to meet criteria for a *DSM* category, were reported to have just enough features to qualify for a category ("mild diagnosis"), or had more than enough features to qualify for a category ("severe diagnosis").

Children who failed to meet the criterion for a *DSM* category had mean T scores of less than 70 (the cutpoint for the clinical range on the multivariate syndrome). Children who just met the criterion for a category had mean T scores equal to or greater than 70, and those who exceeded the criterion for a category had mean T scores well above 70 on the syndrome that was descriptively similar to the *DSM* category.

RELIABILITY COMPARISONS

The quantitative scoring of multivariate taxa lends itself to reliability analyses in terms of correlations and other quantitative statistics, although these taxa also can be analyzed categorically by dichotomizing syndrome scores at the clinical cutoff points or elsewhere. In their standard form, Kraepelinian taxa are purely categorical, in that each disorder is deemed to be present versus absent. This means that statistics for assessing agreements between categorizations typically are used to assess the reliability of Kraepelinian taxa.

A change in one criterial feature of a Kraepelinian category can make the difference between an individual qualifying or not qualifying for that category. In such taxonomy, the tendency for fewer problems to be reported at a second assessment than at an initial assessment thus can have a major impact on reliability. It also can lead to illogical findings. For example, when lifetime *DSM* diagnoses have been made from DIS interviews of (adult) subjects on 2 occasions 6 to 12 months apart, the subjects qualified for fewer diagnoses on the second assessment than on the first assessment, even though they had (obviously) lived longer by the second assessment (Helzer, Spitz-

TABLE 2.2

Approximate Relations Between DSM-IV and Multivariate Taxa

DSM-IV	Parent Reports	Self-Reports	Teacher Reports	Observer Reports
Social Phobia	Withdrawn	Withdrawn	Withdrawn	Withdrawn-Inattentive
Somatization Disorder	Somatic complaints	Somatic complaints	Somatic complaints	—
Generalized Anxiety Disorder	Anxious/depressed	Anxious/depressed	Anxious/depressed	Nervous-obsessive
Major Depressive Disorder	Anxious/depressed	Anxious/depressed	Anxious/depressed	Depressed
Dysthymic Disorder	Anxious/depressed	Anxious/depressed	Anxious/depressed	Depressed
Schizotypal Personality	Thought problems	Thought problems	Thought problems	
Psychotic Disorders	Thought problems	Thought problems	Thought problems	—
Attention Deficit-Hyperactivity Disorder	Attention problems	Attention problems	Attention problems	Hyperactive
Conduct Disorder	Delinquent behavior	Delinquent behavior	Delinquent behavior	—
Conduct Disorder	Aggressive behavior	Aggressive behavior	Aggressive behavior	Aggressive behavior
Oppositional Defiant Disorder	Aggressive behavior	Aggressive behavior	Aggressive behavior	Aggressive behavior
Gender Identity Disorder	Sex problems[a]	Self-destructive/ identity problems[b]	—	—

NOTE. Adapted from *Integrative Guide for the 1991 CBCL/4-18, YSR, and TRF Profiles* (p. 125), by T. M. Achenbach, 1991, Burlington: University of Vermont Department of Psychiatry. Copyright 1991 by T. M. Achenbach. Adapted with permission.
[a]For ages 4 to 11 only. See Achenbach (1991c) for details.
[a]For boys only. See Achenbach (1991e) for details.

nagel, & McEvoy, 1987; Robins, 1985; Vandiver & Sher, 1991; Wells, Burnham, Leake, & Robins, 1988). In fact, less than half the subjects who received lifetime diagnoses of major depression, dysthymia, or anxiety disorder at Time 1 received the same lifetime diagnosis at Time 2.

The decline in lifetime diagnoses was attributed largely to a decline in symptoms reported by subjects who had been just above the criterial threshold at Time 1 and who had then dropped below this threshold at Time 2. In a multivariate taxonomy, by contrast, changes of a small number of criterial features do not greatly alter an individual's standing with respect to particular taxa. Thus it is desirable to highlight the quantitative nature of the scores and to prevent small changes from making the difference between "sick" and "well." To do this, explicit borderline ranges can be demarcated between scores that are most clearly in

the clinical range and those that are most clearly in the normal range. Furthermore, if most children tend to change in the same direction (e.g., downward) from one assessment to the next, this tendency can be taken into account when using scores that are to be obtained over particular test-retest periods. Quantitative ratings also may produce better interjudge reliability than do categorical judgments, as has been found for assessments of personality disorders from case vignettes (Heumann & Morey, 1990).

Challenges to be Met

Taxonomies can play multiple roles with respect to childhood disorders. They can embody current knowledge about similarities and differences among particular kinds of problems. They also can contribute to knowledge by organizing diverse information and procedures into coherent frameworks that can guide research on the correlates, etiologies, outcomes, and interventions for particular problems. In dealing with individual cases, taxonomies can be the vehicles by which knowledge gained on previous cases is brought to bear. In addition, taxonomies can facilitate communication among clinicians about individual cases, between clinicians and agencies that must document services, and between agencies that serve overlapping populations. Funding for services also can be made more rational if administrative classifications are based on taxonomies of actual differences among children's problems.

Because taxonomies must serve multiple purposes, and because knowledge, concepts, and needs are continually changing, no taxonomy can be expected to permanently meet all needs. Instead, taxonomies should be regarded as provisional, subject to change and to displacement by other taxonomies as knowledge and needs change. To facilitate the improvement of taxonomies at this particular stage of knowledge, several challenges need to be dealt with, as discussed in the following sections.

ERRORS OF MEASUREMENT AND ASCERTAINMENT

Measurement: All procedures for measuring any variable are subject to error. Even such simple variables as people's height and weight do not yield exactly the same values each time they are measured. When a person's height is measured on multiple occasions, for example, variations may occur because of variations in the person's actual height, the way the person stands, the firmness with which the measuring instrument is pressed on the person's head, the fineness of the gradations on the measuring scale, the angle from which the gradations are read, and the accuracy of recording what was read. If the same person were measured by a different instrument with finer or coarser gradations and with someone else recording the data, a different distribution of scores is apt to be obtained.

Because multiple sources of variation may affect every measurement of a person's height, there is no way to determine the person's "true" height by any single measurement. Instead, if it is assumed that the errors are randomly distributed around the true height, the true height can be estimated as the mean of a large number of measurements. If multiple instruments are used, the true height may be estimated as the mean or some other parameter of the distributions of scores obtained from the different instruments.

Whether it is height or some other variable, the true score for the variable is not precisely captured by a particular measurement on a particular occasion, but it can be estimated from the obtained score or scores. Each measurement may be affected in different ways by all the possible sources of variation. Collectively, the variations from the true score are called *error of measurement*, although most of the variations are not due to actual mistakes. By taking account of the inevitable variations ("error") of measurement, statistical procedures can provide more accurate conclusions about both simple variables such as height and about more complex variables such as behavioral/emotional problems than if error of measurement is ignored.

Scores on the items that comprise a multivariate syndrome are analogous to repeated measurements of a variable such as height. The score obtained by a child on each item of a multivariate syndrome scale is a separate measurement of the variable represented by the syndrome scale. Each item may be subject to different errors of measurement. If these errors of measurement are assumed to be randomly distributed, the total score obtained from all the items of the syndrome scale can be used to estimate the child's true score on that syndrome, at least as measured by a particular instrument completed by a particular informant at a particular point in time. The child's true score may change from one occasion to another and also may differ according to the instrument and the informant who completed it. Consequently, more than just the variation among scores on individual items may be relevant to drawing conclusions about the child's standing in respect to a syndrome. Furthermore, because the concept of a syndrome as a set of co-occurring problems may not be fully defined by any one set of scores on a particular occasion, it can be viewed as a *hypo-*

thetical construct—that is, an inferred or theoretical entity that is used to help us understand certain phenomena but that may never be directly observed. In statistical terms, an inferred syndrome can be thought of as a *latent variable*— that is, a variable that can be captured indirectly by multiple measuring procedures but that is not completely defined by any one of them.

Errors of Ascertainment: Whereas "measurement" implies quantitative assessment, "ascertainment" implies determination of whether an entity is present or absent. In reference to formal diagnosis, the term *ascertainment* often is used in the sense of determining which category of a nosology a person's problems match. Nevertheless, ascertainment of conditions that are assumed to exist only in categorical, present-vs.-absent form raises the same problems of measurement error as does quantitative assessment of syndromes. For example, 4 previously cited studies all demonstrated *declines* in lifetime *DSM-III* diagnoses made from DIS interviews 6 to 12 months apart (Helzer et al., 1987; Robins, 1985; Vandiver & Sher, 1991; Wells et al., 1988). This counterintuitive decline in lifetime diagnoses was attributed largely to the decline in symptoms reported at Time 2 by people who had been just above the threshold of the diagnostic criterion at Time 1. Even though the *DSM* conceptual model implies that disorders are either present or absent, the diagnostic criteria involve measurement in the sense of determining the number of criterial features that are present. Furthermore, the judgment of each criterial feature implies quantification, as the interviewee and/or clinician must judge whether each criterial feature is severe enough to warrant being reported.

As an example, the *DSM-IV*'s 9 criterial features for major depressive episode start with: "depressed mood most of the day, nearly every day, as indicated either by subjective report . . . or observation made by others. . . . Note: in children and adolescents, can be irritable mood" (APA, 1994). To determine whether this feature is present, the diagnostician must take account of the sources of data, intensity, frequency, and change from previous functioning. For each child and adolescent, the diagnostician must consider whether irritable mood qualifies as an alternative to depressed mood. The diagnostician also must compare and weigh reports obtained both from the

child and from others, such as parents and teachers, who may disagree. The ascertainment task thus involves measurement error (or variation) analogous to the variations that affect measurement of people's height and quantitative scores on multivariate syndromes. Hence, when taxonomic decisions require a forced choice between present and absent, a very small amount of measurement error makes a very large difference in the decision.

Considering the diverse sources of variation (in judgments) of criteria for disorders such as major depression, dysthymia, and anxiety disorder, it should not be surprising that less than half the subjects who met DIS interview lifetime criteria for these disorders at one point in time no longer met DIS interview lifetime criteria 6 to 12 months later (Vandiver & Sher, 1991). Considering that the (adult) subjects themselves were the only sources of data in these studies, the problem could be much worse where multiple sources of data are relevant, as is generally true for children.

Dealing with Error: No measurement or ascertainment procedure can be entirely free of error. However, as Einhorn (1988, p. 65) put it, "the acceptance of error can lead to less error." If variations in measurement are documented and quantified, it may be feasible to reduce measurement error. Because such error cannot be eliminated entirely, our conceptual and statistical models should be designed to take account of these inevitable errors of measurement. If both the assessment process and the assignment of individual cases to a taxonomy are understood to incur measurement error (whether the underlying constructs or latent variables are quantitative or categorical), we can avoid such illogical outcomes as the large declines in lifetime diagnoses over repeated assessments of the same subjects.

Even if one firmly believes that disorders such as depression, dysthymia, and anxiety truly exist in present-vs.-absent form, use of a borderline range of critical attributes can explicitly mark cases that are "too close to call" because they are not clearly in either the normal or clinical range. Some DSM categories are defined "polythetically" by lists of criterial features. This makes it possible to quantify them directly by simply summing the number of features judged to be present. Thus, for example, *DSM-IV* defines ADHD in terms of 2 lists, each of which has 9 criterial features. A child may qualify for the diagnosis by having 6 features from the first list or 6 from the second list. If children are scored in terms of the number of features judged to be present on either list, their score can range from 0 to 9 on each list, or 0 to 18 on both lists combined.

However, in judging the presence of each feature, measurement error is inevitable; hence, the assessment of 8-year-old Ricky on different occasions, by different clinicians, or using different sources of data might yield scores of 5 or 6 on the first list. That is, either 5 or 6 features are judged to be present at the various assessments. On the occasions when 6 features were judged to be present, Ricky would be classified as having attention deficit hyperactivity disorder. Yet, on the occasions when only 5 features were selected, Ricky would be considered free of the disorder. The essential fact is that Ricky has a moderate number of features of ADHD. This sets him apart both from children who are more clearly classifiable as non-ADHD, because they have fewer ADHD features and from children who are more clearly classifiable as ADHD, because they have more ADHD features. If we defined a borderline range of 5 to 6 features, Ricky could be officially designated as borderline ADHD, which would avoid the errors of classifying him as either completely normal or clinically deviant with respect to attention deficit hyperactivity disorder.

If we carried quantification a step further, we could allow each criterial feature to be judged as 0 = not true, 1 = somewhat or sometimes true, and 2 = very true or often true of Ricky. Summing his scores on the criterial features would provide a total score that could be compared with distributions of scores for normal 8-year-old boys and boys judged to have ADHD. We could then determine where Ricky's score fell in relation to the distribution of scores for these 2 criterial groups. Rather than having to judge Ricky as ADHD vs. not ADHD on the basis of the a priori cutpoint of 6 features on either list, we could make use of the assessment data to determine much more precisely how Ricky compares with other boys.

Quantification of assessment data allows for error of measurement in drawing conclusions about individual cases. The multivariate approach to taxonomy employs statistics that assume the presence of measurement error, but Kraepelinian taxonomy also can take advantage of quantification to prevent unacknowledged measurement error from leading to illogical conclusions.

DEVELOPMENTAL VARIATIONS

Another challenge for taxonomy is to deal with the enormous changes in capabilities and functioning at different epochs of development that occur from birth to maturity. Many behaviors that are normal at one developmental period would be considered deviant if they occurred much earlier or later. Furthermore, different assessment procedures and sources of data are needed for different developmental periods. For example, structured psychiatric interviews such as the Diagnostic Interview Schedule for Children would not be appropriate for assessing preschool children, whereas for school-age children, teachers' reports and achievement tests become important sources of assessment data.

It is evident that major developmental changes occur in children's behavior, and that there are differences in the problems for which help is sought at different ages. Nonetheless, it is still an open question whether there is any underlying continuity in most disorders from early childhood through adolescence or adulthood. Whether there is underlying continuity or not, the developmental changes in phenotypic behaviors certainly require different assessment procedures and different ways of aggregating the assessment data into taxonomic groupings. Furthermore, in order to determine whether children's problems are more extreme than would be normal for their age, data are needed on large representative samples of children in order to construct norms for each age.

To take attention deficit hyperactivity disorder as an example, the prevalence of criterial features (e.g., "is often easily distracted by extraneous stimuli") will vary with age. Consequently, the proportion of children who meet a fixed criterion, such as 6 out of 9, may vary with the prevalence of each of the 9 ADHD features among children of that age. In order to identify children who are truly deviant, a different cut-off point may be needed for children of different ages, such as 8 criterial features to identify deviant 5-year-olds and 5 features to identify deviant 12-year-olds. If a borderline range or continuous scores are used, these too can be based on norms for a child's age and other relevant characteristics, such as the child's sex.

To make it easier for users, a similar metric can be constructed for each age by converting raw scores to standard scores. As an example, normalized T scores convert raw scores that may vary with age to a common scale, where a particular number represents the same percentile for each age group. If comparisons of scores for normal vs. deviant children show good discrimination between them at a particular percentile, such as the 90th percentile, the T score equivalent of that percentile ($T = 63$) can be used for each age group, even though the raw scale score that falls at the 90th percentile may differ among the age groups. Similarly, a particular range of T scores may be used to demarcate a borderline clinical range for all age groups, even though the raw scale scores in that range differ among the groups.

COMORBIDITY

Use of the Diagnostic Interview Schedule for Children to operationalize *DSM* criteria has revealed that many children and adolescents qualify for multiple diagnoses (Costello et al., 1984; Weinstein et al., 1990). Two studies of referred boys have shown that 96% of those who met *DSM-III* criteria for Conduct Disorder (CD) also met criteria for Oppositional Defiant Disorder (ODD) (Faraone, Biederman, Keenan, & Tsuang, 1991; Walker et al., 1991). Although *DSM* has provided rules whereby particular categories preempt other categories, the preemptory rules for children's disorders have been found to be too contradictory to be applied logically (Costello et al., 1984). It is possible that more advanced knowledge will yield preemptory rules that accurately reflect hierarchical relations among disorders, such that certain disorders are by-products of others. However, in the absence of such knowledge, the apparent comorbidity of many *DSM* disorders has become a source of confusion, as detailed by Achenbach (1991a) and Caron and Rutter (1991). Without valid and reliable criteria for distinguishing between disorders, it cannot be assumed that a child who meets criteria for 2 taxonomic categories actually has 2 different disorders. Instead, apparent comorbidity may occur as

an artifact of either assessment procedures or taxonomies that fail to distinguish clearly between disorders. For example, the Faraone et al. (1991) and Walker et al. (1991) findings that 96% of boys who met criteria for Conduct Disorder also met criteria for Oppositional Defiant Disorder begs the question of whether the disorders really are separate entities. If they really are separate entities, then independent external criteria are needed to substantiate their separateness. If they were physical illnesses, differences in tissue pathology or in pathogens could serve as validity criteria against which taxonomic criteria could be tested. However, in the absence of such firm validity criteria for discriminating between conduct disorder and oppositional defiant disorder, it hardly seems worth viewing them as separate categories, when their "comorbidity" seems to occur virtually by definition.

All approaches to taxonomy must cope with the inevitable co-occurrence of many kinds of problems. No existing taxonomy of children's behavioral/emotional problems is likely to be validated by the discovery of specific physical etiologies in the near future. An important task for taxonomy is therefore to capture the actual patterns of co-occurring problems. This is a more appropriate focus than drawing a priori boundaries between disorders and then concluding that the co-occurrence of problems from multiple categories implies the presence of multiple disorders. The finding that the defining features of conduct disorder and oppositional defiant disorder commonly co-occur, for example, could be used either to construct a taxon that includes their co-occurring features or at least to place them on a continuum from mild to severe or from younger ages to older ages.

Because the multivariate approach is intended to quantify associations among co-occurring problems, it can capture higher-order patterns that otherwise might be construed as separate disorders. If enough individuals share a pattern that comprises different kinds of problems, such as aggression and attention problems, this pattern may be used to define a taxonomic grouping, without implying that children who manifest it necessarily suffer from an aggressive disorder plus an attentional disorder. To distinguish between disorders that truly differ with respect to etiology, course, or treatment responsiveness, we need to organize assessment data flexibly enough to detect higher-order patterns that may provide a better basis for taxonomy than current categories or syndromes do.

INTEGRATING MULTISOURCE DATA

It is a truism that children do not identify themselves as needing mental health services. Nor can children be depended on to report their history and symptoms accurately to the clinician. Furthermore, children's behavior in the clinical setting may not be typical of their behavior in their home, school, or neighborhood. Consequently, adults, such as parents, teachers, and pediatricians, play a major role in deciding whether help is needed and in providing data about the child's functioning.

Meta-analyses of informants' reports of children's behavioral problems have yielded a mean correlation of 0.60 between reports by people who play similar roles with respect to the child (pairs of parents, pairs of teachers, pairs of mental health workers). Between pairs of informants who play different roles (e.g., parent vs. teacher, teacher vs. mental health worker), the mean correlation was 0.28. And between children's self-reports and reports by parents, teachers, and mental health workers, the mean correlation was .22 (Achenbach et al., 1987).

Agreement among informants is likely to be limited by several factors, including variations in children's behavior as it appears in different contexts, differences in the effects of each informant on the child's behavior in the presence of that informant, and differences among informants in how they perceive and report children's behavior. Because no one source of data is able to provide an accurate picture of children's functioning in all important contexts, multiple sources usually are needed. Because there may be only modest overlap in what is reported by different sources, integration of multiple sources of data raises challenges for all approaches to assessment and taxonomy. In *DSM-IV,* for example, what source of data should be used to decide whether each criterial feature of a category is present or absent? In the multivariate paradigm, what source should be used to derive syndromes and then to score individual children once the syndromes have been derived?

Cross-Informant Syndromes: Because the multivariate approach derives its taxa from data on actual samples of children, it has had to deal more directly with problems of variations among sources than has the Kraepelinian approach, which generally formulates taxa by a committee process. Although similarities have been identified in some taxa derived from different sources (Achenbach, 1992; Quay, 1986), recently a more rigorous approach to deriving taxa from multiple sources has been tried. This entails doing separate multivariate analyses of parent, teacher, and self-reports on parallel instruments scored for large clinical samples (Achenbach, 1991b). Separately for each instrument, core syndromes were identified that consisted of items that co-occurred for both sexes and multiple ages. The *core syndromes* derived separately from parent, teacher, and self-reports were then compared with one another in order to identify items that occurred together in reports by at least 2 of the 3 types of informants. These items were used to define *cross-informant syndrome constructs* that represented patterns of co-occurring problems evident to multiple informants.

To assess individual children in terms of the syndrome constructs, scales consisting of the items reportable by a particular type of informant were normed separately using ratings by each type of informant (parent, teacher, self) for a nationally representative nonreferred sample. To reflect sex and age variations, each scale has separate norms for each sex within particular age intervals, as rated by each type of informant.

Figure 2.1 summarizes the procedures employed, first for deriving cross-informant syndrome constructs from parent, teacher, and self-reports on clinical samples and then for constructing normed scales for assessing individual children in terms of the syndromes. The 8 syndromes derived in this way were designated as Aggressive Behavior, Anxious/Depressed, Attention Problems, Delinquent Behavior, Social Problems, Somatic Complaints, Thought Problems, and Withdrawn. A computer program is available for systematically comparing data obtained from parent, teacher, and self-ratings on these syndromes and all their constituent items (Achenbach, 1993).

Taxonomic Decision Tree: Whether syndromes are derived empirically from multivariate analyses or constructed in other ways, taxa that can be assessed by multiple sources offer possibilities for

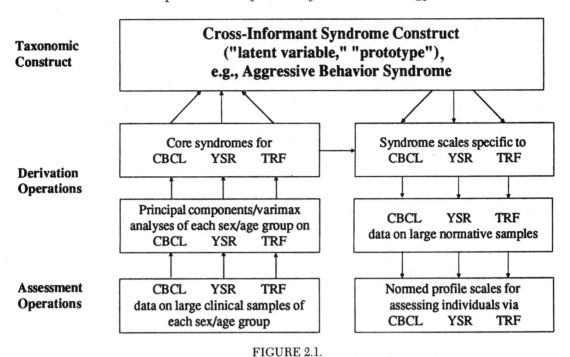

FIGURE 2.1.

Derivation of cross-informant syndromes from parent, self, and teacher-reports. CBCL = Child Behavior Checklist (parent reports); YSR = Youth Self-Report (self-reports); TRF = Teacher's Report Form (teacher reports). From Integrative Guide for the 1991 CBCL/4-18, YSR, and TRF Profiles *(p. 51), by T. M. Achenbach, 1991, Burlington: University of Vermont Department of Psychiatry. Copyright 1991 by T. M. Achenbach. Reprinted with permission.*

more explicit coordination of assessment data in relation to taxonomic decisions. Figure 2.2 illustrates a taxonomic decision tree that can be used to assign cases to taxa on the basis of multiple sources of data such as parents, teachers, observers, self-reports, and interviews. If we start at the top of the tree with data from any combination of sources, we then ask questions whose answers lead to the conclusions or additional questions indicated in each box. This process can make use of either categorical taxa that are defined as present vs. absent, or quantitative taxa on which cutpoints are imposed to distinguish between individuals who are considered deviant vs. nondeviant.

Conclusion

In this chapter, *taxonomy* refers to systematic groupings of children's behavioral/emotional problems intended to reflect important distinc-

tions among the types or patterns of problems. *Assessment* refers to the process of identifying the distinguishing features of individual cases. To link an individual case with previous cases having similar features in a fashion that is both reliable and valid, assessment procedures must enable users to match the features of the case with taxonomic groupings derived from previous cases. Reliable and valid taxonomies are needed both to advance knowledge and to improve clinical services.

Kraepelinian and multivariate paradigms were compared and contrasted as approaches to the taxonomy of child and adolescent behavioral/ emotional problems. Current versions of Kraepelinian taxonomy are embodied in the *DSM* and *ICD;* multivariate taxonomy is embodied in syndromes and profile patterns derived from statistical analyses of children's problem scores. Other approaches to taxonomy have not yielded such extensive efforts to construct groupings of children's problems.

There are descriptive similarities between several *DSM* categories on the one hand and syn-

27

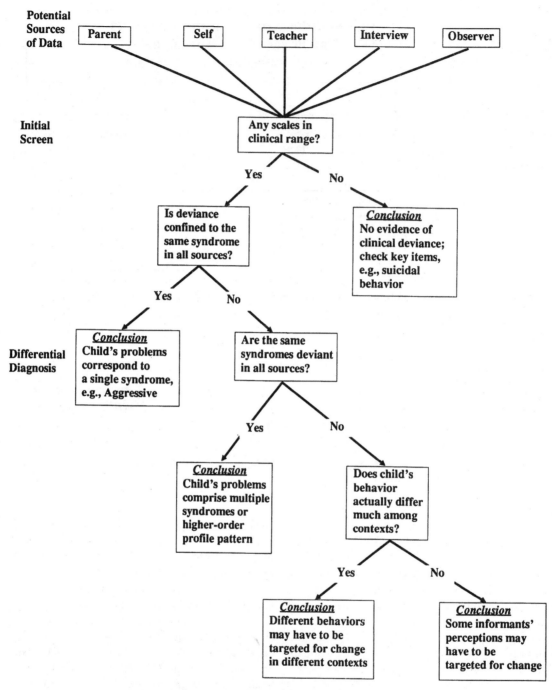

FIGURE 2.2.

Decision tree for making taxonomic assignments from multiple sources of data. From Integrative Guide for the 1991 CBCL/4-18, YSR, and TRF Reports *(p. 95), by T. M. Achenbach, 1991, Burlington: University of Vermont Department of Psychiatry. Copyright 1991 by T. M. Achenbach. Adapted with permission.*

dromes derived empirically via multivariate analyses on the other. Significant associations have been found between scores on multivariate syndromes and corresponding *DSM* categories that were operationally defined in terms of DISC interviews, especially when the *DSM* categories were quasi-quantified.

The test-retest reliability of children's structured self-reports is generally low, because children tend to report far more problems at Time 1 than at a Time 2 reassessment. Smaller declines in problems also are found in Time 2 reports by adult subjects and informants. This tendency to report fewer problems on a second occasion can

have large impacts on categorical taxa; indeed, it has led to illogical declines in *DSM* lifetime diagnoses between one assessment and another. Quantification of assessment and taxonomic criteria, even as coarse as the addition of a borderline category, can reduce anomalies arising from fluctuations in reported problems.

All approaches to taxonomy must contend with certain challenges, including the inevitable errors of measurement and ascertainment, developmental variations, comorbidity, and the integration of data from multiple sources. This raises challenges both for the derivation of taxa and for making decisions about individual cases.

REFERENCES

Achenbach, T. M. (1991a). "Comorbidity" in child and adolescent psychiatry: Categorical and quantitative perspectives. *Journal of Child and Adolescent Psychopharmacology, 1,* 271–278.

Achenbach, T. M. (1991b). *Integrative guide for the 1991 CBCL/4-18, YSR, and TRF profiles.* Burlington: University of Vermont Department of Psychiatry.

Achenbach, T. M. (1991c). *Manual for the Child Behavior Checklist/4-18 and 1991 Profile.* Burlington: University of Vermont Department of Psychiatry.

Achenbach, T. M. (1991d). *Manual for the Teacher's Report Form and 1991 Profile.* Burlington: University of Vermont Department of Psychiatry.

Achenbach, T. M. (1991e). *Manual for the Youth Self-Report and 1991 Profile.* Burlington: University of Vermont Department of Psychiatry.

Achenbach, T. M. (1992). Developmental psychopathology. In M. E. Lamb & M. H. Bornstein (Eds.), *Developmental psychology: An advanced textbook* (3rd ed.). (pp. 629–675). Hillsdale, NJ: Lawrence Erlbaum.

Achenbach, T. M. (1993). *Empirically based taxonomy: How to use syndromes and profile types derived from the CBCL/4-18, TRF, and YSR.* Burlington: University of Vermont Department of Psychiatry.

Achenbach, T. M. (1997a). *Guide for the Caregiver-Teacher Report Form for Ages 2–5.* Burlington: University of Vermont Department of Psychiatry.

Achenbach, T. M. (1997b). *Manual for the Young Adult Self-Report and Young Adult Behavior Checklist.* Burlington: University of Vermont Department of Psychiatry.

Achenbach, T. M., McConaughy, S. H., & Howell, C. T. (1987). Child/adolescent behavioral and emotional problems: Implications of cross-informant correlations for situational specificity. *Psychological Bulletin, 101,* 213–232.

Ackerson, L. (1942). *Children's behavior problems: Vol. 2. Relative importance and interrelations among traits.* Chicago: University of Chicago Press.

American Psychiatric Association. (1952). *Diagnostic and statistical manual of mental disorders.* Washington, DC: Author.

American Psychiatric Association. (1968). *Diagnostic and statistical manual of mental disorders* (2nd ed.). Washington, DC: Author.

American Psychiatric Association. (1980). *Diagnostic and statistical manual of mental disorders* (3rd ed.). Washington, DC: Author.

American Psychiatric Association. (1987). *Diagnostic and statistical manual of mental disorders* (3rd ed., rev.). Washington, DC: Author.

American Psychiatric Association. (1994). *Diagnostic and statistical manual of mental disorders* (4th ed.). Washington, DC: Author.

Beitchman, J. H., Dielman, T. E., Landis, J. R., Benson, R. M., & Kemp, P. L. (1978). Reliability of the Group for the Advancement of Psychiatry diagnostic categories in child psychiatry. *Archives of General Psychiatry, 35,* 1461–1466.

Bleuler, E. (1950). *Dementia praecox or the group of schizophrenias* (translation). New York: International Universities Press. (Original work published 1911.)

Breton, J. J., Bergeron, L., Valla, J. P., Lepine, S., Houde, L., & Gaudet, N. (1995). Do children aged 9 through 11 years understand the DISC Version 2.5 questions? *Journal of the American Academy of Child and Adolescent Psychiatry, 34,* 946–954.

Caron, C., & Rutter, M. (1991). Comorbidity in child psychopathology: Concepts, issues and research strategies. *Journal of Child Psychology and Psychiatry, 32,* 1063–1080.

Costello, A. J., Edelbrock, C., Dulcan, M. K., Kalas, R., & Klaric, S. H. (1984). *Report on the Diagnostic Interview Schedule for Children (DISC).* Pittsburgh, PA: University of Pittsburgh, Department of Psychiatry.

Costello, E. J., Burns, B. J., Angold, A., & Leaf, P. J. (1993). How can epidemiology improve mental health services for children and adolescents? *Journal of the American Academy of Child and Adolescent Psychiatry, 32,* 1106–1113.

Eaton, W. W., & Kessler, L. G. (1985). *Epidemiologic field methods in psychiatry. The NIMH Epidemiologic Catchment Area Program.* Orlando, FL: Academic Press.

Edelbrock, C. (1984, October). *Relations between the NIMH Diagnostic Interview Schedule for Children (DISC) and the Child Behavior Checklist and Profile.* Paper presented at the American Academy of Child Psychiatry, Toronto, Ontario.

Edelbrock, C., & Costello, A. J. (1988). Convergence between statistically derived behavior problem syndromes and child psychiatric diagnoses. *Journal of Abnormal Child Psychology, 16,* 219–231.

Edelbrock, C., Costello, A. J., Dulcan, M. K., Kalas, R., & Conover, N. C. (1985). Age differences in the reliability of the psychiatric interview of the child. *Child Development, 56,* 265–275.

Education of the Handicapped Act. (1977). *Federal Register, 42,* p. 42478. Amended in *Federal Register* (1981), *46,* p. 3866.

Einhorn, H. J. (1988). Diagnosis and causality in clinical and statistical prediction. In D. C. Turk (Ed.), *Reasoning, inference, and judgment in clinical psychology.* New York: Free Press.

Faraone, S. V., Biederman, J., Keenan, K., & Tsuang, M. T. (1991). Separation of DSM-III attention deficit disorder and conduct disorder: Evidence from a family genetic study of American child psychiatry patients. *Psychological Medicine, 21,* 109–121.

Freeman, M. (1971). A reliability study of psychiatric diagnosis in childhood and adolescence. *Journal of Child Psychology and Psychiatry, 12,* 43–54.

Freud, A. (1965). *Normality and pathology in childhood.* New York: International Universities Press.

Freud, S. (1953). The interpretation of dreams. In J. Strachey (Ed. and Trans.), *The standard edition of the complete psychological works of Sigmund Freud* (Vol. 4). London: Hogarth Press. (Original work published 1900).

Gould, M. S., Bird, H., & Jaramillo, B. S. (1993). Correspondence between statistically derived behavior problem syndromes and child psychiatric diagnoses in a community sample. *Journal of Abnormal Child Psychology, 21,* 287–313.

Gould, M. S., Shaffer, D., Rutter, M., & Sturge, C. (1988). UK/WHO study of ICD-9. In M. Rutter, A. H. Tuma, & I. S. Lann (Eds.), *Assessment and diagnosis in child psychopathology.* (pp. 37–65). New York: Guilford Press.

Greenspan, S. I., Hatleberg, J. L., & Cullander, C. C. H. (1980). A developmental approach to systematic personality assessment: Illustrated with the case of a 6-year-old child. In S. I. Greenspan & G. Pollock (Eds.), *The course of life: Psychoanalytic contributions toward understanding personality development. Vol. II: Latency, adolescence, and youth.* Washington, DC: Department of Health, Education, and Welfare.

Griesinger, W. (1867). *Die Pathologie und Therapie der psychischen Krankheiten.* Translated as *Mental pathology and therapeutics* by C. L. Robertson & J. Rutherford. London: New Sydenham Society. (Original work published 1845.)

Group for the Advancement of Psychiatry. (1966). *Psychopathological disorders in childhood: Theoretical considerations and a proposed classification.* GAP Report No. 62.

Guzé, S. (1978). Validating criteria for psychiatric diagnosis: The Washington University Approach. In M. S. Akiskal & W. L. Webb (Eds.), *Psychiatric diagnosis: Exploration of biological predictors.* (pp. 49–59). New York: Spectrum.

Helzer, J. E., & Robins, L. N. (1988). The Diagnostic Interview Schedule: Its development, evaluation, and use. *Social Psychiatry and Psychiatric Epidemiology, 23,* 6–16.

Helzer, J. E., Spitznagel, E. L., & McEvoy, L. (1987). The predictive validity of lay Diagnostic Interview Schedule diagnoses in the general population: A comparison with physician examiners. *Archives of General Psychiatry, 44,* 1069–1077.

Heumann, K. A., & Morey, L. C. (1990). Reliability of categorical and dimensional judgments of personality disorder. *American Journal of Psychiatry, 147,* 498–500.

Individuals with Disabilities Education Act. (1990). Public Law 101–476. 104 *Statutes,* 1103–1151.

Jenkins, R. L., & Glickman, S. (1946). Common syndromes in child psychiatry: I. Deviant behavior traits. II. The schizoid child. *American Journal of Orthopsychiatry, 16,* 244–261.

Kagan, J. (1969). The three faces of continuity in human development. In D. A. Goslin (Ed.), *Handbook of socialization theory and research* (pp. 983–1002). Chicago: Rand McNally.

Kahn, E. (1959). Emil Kraepelin. In B. Pasaminick (Ed.), *Epidemiology of mental disorders.* Washington, D.C.: American Association for Advancement of Science.

Kazdin, A. E. (1983). Psychiatric diagnosis, dimensions of dysfunction and child behavior therapy. *Behavior Therapy, 14,* 73–99.

Kraepelin, E. (1883). *Compendium der Psychiatrie.* Leipzig: Abel.

Kraepelin, E. (1896). *Compendium der Psychiatrie* (2nd ed.). Leipzig: Abel.

Kraepelin, E. (1915). *Compendium der Psychiatrie* (3rd ed.). Leipzig: Abel.

Lahey, B. B., Loeber, R., Stouthamer-Loeber, M., Christ, M. A. G., Green, S., Russo, M. F., Frick,

P. J., & Dulcan, M. (1990). Comparison of DSM-III and DSM-III-R diagnoses for prepubertal children: Changes in prevalence and validity. *Journal of the American Academy of Child and Adolescent Psychiatry, 29,* 620–626.

Lejeune, J., Gautier, M., & Turpin, R. (1963). Study of the somatic chromosomes of nine mongoloid idiot children (1959). In S. H. Boyer (Ed.), *Papers on human genetics.* Englewood Cliffs, NJ: Prentice-Hall.

Mattison, R., Cantwell, D. P., Russell, A. T., & Will, L. (1979). A comparison of DSM-II and DSM-III in the diagnosis of childhood psychiatric disorders. *Archives of General Psychiatry, 36,* 1217–1222.

McConaughy, S. H., & Achenbach, T. M. (1994). *Manual for the Semistructured Clinical Interview for Children and Adolescents.* Burlington, VT: University of Vermont Department of Psychiatry.

McConaughy, S. H., Mattison, R. E., & Peterson, R. L. (1994). Behavioral and emotional problems of children with serious emotional disturbance and learning disabilities. *School Psychology Review, 23,* 81–98.

Mezzich, A. C., Mezzich, J. E., & Coffman, G. A. (1985). Reliability of DSM-III vs. DSM-II in child psychopathology. *Journal of the American Academy of Child Psychiatry, 24,* 273–280.

Mish, F. C. (Ed.) (1988). *Webster's ninth new collegiate dictionary.* Springfield, MA: Merriam-Webster.

Nelson, R. O. (1983). Past, present, and future. *Behavioral Assessment, 5,* 195–206.

Overall, J. E., & Hollister, L. E. (1979). Comparative evaluation of research diagnostic criteria for schizophrenia. *Archives of General Psychiatry, 36,* 1198–1205.

Piacentini, J. C., Cohen, P., & Cohen, J. (1992). Combining discrepant diagnostic information from multiple sources. Are complex algorithms better than simple ones? *Journal of Abnormal Child Psychology, 20,* 51–63.

Quay, H. C. (1986). Classification. In H. C. Quay & J. S. Werry (Eds.), *Psychopathological disorders of childhood* (3rd ed., pp. 1–42). New York: John Wiley & Sons.

Remschmidt, H. (1988). German study of ICD-9. In M. Rutter, A. H. Tuma, & I. S. Lann (Eds.), *Assessment and diagnosis in child psychopathology.* (pp. 66–83). New York: Guilford Press.

Robins, L. N. (1985). Epidemiology: Reflections on testing the validity of psychiatric interviews. *Archives of General Psychiatry, 42,* 918–924.

Rutter, M., Shaffer, D., & Shepherd, M. (1975). *A multiaxial classification of child psychiatric disorders. An evaluation of a proposal.* Geneva: World Health Organization.

Shaffer, D. (1992). *Diagnostic Interview Schedule for Children, Version 2.3.* New York: Columbia University Division of Child Psychiatry.

Shaffer, D., Fisher, P., Dulcan, M., Davies, M., Piacentini, J., Schwab-Stone, M., Lahey, B., Bourdon, K., Jensen, P., Bird, H., Canino, G., & Reiger, D. (1996). The NIMH Diagnostic Interview Schedule for Children Version 2.3 (DISC-2.3): Description, Acceptability, Prevalence Rates, and Performance in the MECA Study. *Journal of the American Academy of Child and Adolescent Psychiatry, 35 (7),* 865–877.

Shaffer, D., Schwab-Stone, M., Fisher, P., Davies, M., Piacentini, J., & Gioia, P. (1988). *A revised version of the Diagnostic Interview Schedule for Children.* New York: Columbia University Division of Child Psychiatry.

Strober, M., Green, J., & Carlson, G. (1981). The reliability of psychiatric diagnosis in hospitalized adolescents: Interrater agreement using the DSM-III. *Archives of General Psychiatry, 38,* 141–145.

Swets, J. E., & Pickett, R. M. (1982). *Evaluation of diagnostic systems: Methods from signal detection theory.* New York: Academic Press.

Vandiver, T., & Sher, K. J. (1991). Temporal stability of the Diagnostic Interview Schedule. *Psychological Assessment, 3,* 277–281.

Wahler, R. G., & Fox, J. J. (1980). Solitary toy play and time out: A family treatment package for children with aggressive and oppositional behavior. *Journal of Applied Behavior Analysis, 13,* 23–29.

Walker, J. L., Lahey, B. B., Russo, M. F., Christ, M. A. G., McBurnett, K., Loeber, R., Stouthamer-Loeber, M., & Green, S. M. (1991). Anxiety, inhibition, and conduct disorder in children: I. Relations to social impairment. *Journal of the American Academy of Child and Adolescent Psychiatry, 30,* 187–191.

Weinstein, S. R., Noam, G. G., Grimes, K., Stone, K., & Schwab-Stone, M. (1990). Convergence of DSM-III diagnoses and self-reported symptoms in child and adolescent inpatients. *Journal of the American Academy of Child and Adolescent Psychiatry, 29,* 627–634.

Wells, K. B., Burnam, M. A., Leake, B., & Robins, L. N. (1988). Agreement between face-to-face and telephone administered versions of the depression section of the NIMH Diagnostic Interview Schedule. *Journal of Psychiatric Research, 22,* 207–220.

Werry, J. S., Methven, R. J., Fitzpatrick, J., & Dixon, H. (1983). The interrater reliability of DSM-III in children. *Journal of Abnormal Child Psychology, 11,* 341–354.

World Health Organization. (1992). *Mental disorders: Glossary and guide to their classification. International classification of diseases* (10th ed.). Geneva: Author.

World Health Organization. (1996). *Multiaxial classification of child and adolescent psychiatric disorders. The ICD-10 classification of mental and behavioural disorders in children and adolescents.* Cambridge, England: Cambridge University Press.

Yorke, C. (1980). The contributions of the Diagnostic Profile and the assessment of developmental lines to child psychiatry. *Psychiatric Clinics of North America, 3,* 593–603.

3 / Vulnerabilities, Risk Factors, Protective Factors, and Resilience

Naomi Rae Grant

Residents in training often express the concern that child psychiatry is more complicated than adult psychiatry because of the necessity to work with so many different people in the child's life in order to effect change. It is now clearly established that, for maximum effectiveness, interventions should be in as many spheres of the child's life as possible (Mzarek & Haggerty, 1994). In examining all the potential opportunities for intervention, the psychiatrist has to be concerned not just with the genetic, biological, and temperamental factors in the child but also with the family environment, including parent/child attachment and parenting practices. Beyond the family sphere, there needs to be concern with the community in which the family lives, the institutions with which the child comes in contact, and the interaction of all these domains. This chapter looks at the factors in these different arenas that predispose children to disorder (vulnerabilities and risk factors) and those that support and strengthen children to cope with stressors in the environment (protective factors and resilience), the possible mechanisms of interaction between these positive and negative factors, and the implications for assessment and intervention planning.

The Nature of Child/Parent Interactions

THE CONCEPT OF CAUSAL CHAINS

Lee Robins (1970) first described the concept of causal chains by which one situation or event leads to another which leads to an eventual outcome. For example, take the chain: depressed mother → unresponsive parenting → lack of language stimulation → language delay → learning difficulties. Intervention could be aimed at improving parental responsiveness by treating the

mother's depression or at strengthening the child's relationship with another responsive adult in the nurturing environment. Both would be preventive interventions for the child, whereas speech therapy for language delay or tutoring to correct a learning problem later on would come under the heading of treatment. Sameroff (1987) modified Robbins's concept of causal chains to include a bidirectional framework, reflecting not only the effect of the parent on the child but also the effect of the child on the parent. The individual child elicits a response from parents, which, in turn, changes the child's responses to them, and so on. How things turn out is a complex result of the interaction between child and environment at different points in time as parent and child each, in turn, affect the other and change the outcome. (See Figure 3.1)

THE SPECTRUM OF PARENT/CHILD TRANSACTIONAL FIT

Things go wrong in early parent/child interaction when the family environment is just not able to meet the needs of an individual child, either because the child is too impaired or temperamentally difficult, or because the parents lack responsiveness due to their own lack of nurturing, to psychiatric problems, or to environmental distress. Samaroff and Chandler (1975) described this as "the continuum of the caretaking casualty"; at one end of the continuum is an adaptive family environment that can meet the needs of the most distressed infant and at the other end is the disordered family environment that cannot meet the needs of the least distressed, most healthy, normal, temperamentally easy newborn. In between are the majority of average parenting environments that provide "good enough" parenting to allow the child to master early developmental tasks. Figure 3.2 presents the continuum of child-caring casualty.

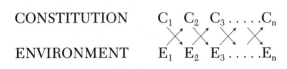

CONSTITUTION $\quad C_1 \quad C_2 \quad C_3 \ldots \ldots C_n$

ENVIRONMENT $\quad E_1 \quad E_2 \quad E_3 \ldots \ldots E_n$

TIME $\qquad\qquad\qquad\qquad\qquad\qquad \blacktriangleright$

FIGURE 3.1.

The transactional model of organism-environment reciprocity.

NOTE: From "Reproductive Risk and the Continuum of Caretaking casualty" (pp. 187–244), by A. J. Sameroff and M. J. Chandler, in *Review of Child Development Research* (Vol. 4), edited by F. D. Horowitz, M. Hetherington, & S. Scarr-Salopatek, 1975, Chicago: University of Chicago Press. Copyright 1975. Adapted with permission.

Examples of Adaptive and Maladaptive Family Environments

AN ADAPTIVE FAMILY ENVIRONMENT:

A family came with their youngest adopted daughter, who was having some difficulty in transferring her attachment from her foster parents, with whom she had lived for several years, to her newly acquired adoptive parents. During the course of taking the history, these adoptive parents recounted the story of their oldest adopted child, a boy who had come into their family at the age of 8 years. At that time, John was, as they described it, the size of a 4-year-old, a psychological dwarf. He had a haunted look about him and would cower under the bed or in closets, terrified of everything and everybody. They knew that John had had an extremely chaotic and depriving background, but they did not know how best to help him. Receiving very little advice from the social agency, they decided that the way to care for a child with such obvious distrust of adults was to reassure him with their constant presence. This they achieved by holding him, each taking turns night and day for a whole week. Subsequently they had gradually helped him to learn by breaking down each task into its component parts. They taught him to eat, to sleep at regular times, they toilet trained him, they taught him how to interact with other children and adults, and ultimately to read and write.

They had accomplished this series of developmentally graduated therapeutic tasks by discussing the events of the day together each evening and sharing the humor of the funny things that had happened during the day. They said that they had discovered that it was very important to start where the child was at developmentally and not where he was supposed to be chrono-

logically, and they planned together as to how to break down each learning task into its component steps. They also agreed not to carry over any displeasure in their attitude toward the boy that might have resulted from the problems of the day before. Each day they started over, expecting that it would be a better one than the last. By the time this family came for help with the question as to how best to assist their youngest adoptive daughter, John was 14 years old. He was in his first year of high school, he was functioning at grade level and doing well physically, emotionally, and intellectually—a remarkable tribute to an outstanding family environment.

A MALADAPTIVE FAMILY ENVIRONMENT:

By contrast another adoptive family was referred by the Child Welfare agency. The parents were clearly furious at the persistent non-attachment and non-compliance of their five-year-old son who had come into their household eight months earlier. They had a litany of complaints about his behavior, railed at his evident lack of trust in them and stated, firmly, that they could not tolerate such a difficult child in their family. The boy, an extremely articulate and intelligent child, was sad but responsive in the interview setting, he said, mournfully, "I want to be good, but there's a voice in my head, that I call 'ugly' that tells me not to trust them."

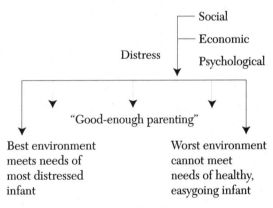

FIGURE 3.2.

Continuum of child-caring casualty.

NOTE: From "Reproductive Risk and the Continuum of Caretaking Causality" (pp. 187–244), by A. J. Sameroff and M. J. Chandler, in Horowitz FD, Hetherington M, Scarr-Salopatek S, eds. *Review of Child Development Research* (Vol. 4), edited by F. D. Horowitz, M. Hetherington, & S. Scarr-Salopatek, 1975, Chicago: University of Chicago Press. Copyright 1975. Adapted with permission.

The adoption failed and the boy, three failed foster homes and two group home placements later, was again brought for assessment. By this time he was aggressive, non-compliant and was, despite his superior intelligence, not learning in school.

It has become evident that adverse conditions in a growing child's environment do not necessarily always produce adverse outcomes. However, it is becoming increasingly clear that it is the number of risk factors and the combination of risk factors in the child and risk factors in the family environment that predisposes children to adverse outcomes. Children of at least average cognitive potential and those with an easy disposition are better equipped than are handicapped children to cope with life stresses. Such children are able to call forth the best from interested adults in their own family and outside the family, to resist models of family violence and to make good personal judgements and choose healthier life styles.

Risk Factors

Garmezy (1983) has defined risk factors as "those factors which, if present increase the likelihood of a child developing an emotional disorder in comparison with a randomly selected child from the general population." To qualify as a risk factor a variable must be associated with an increased probability of disorder and must antedate the onset of disorder. Variables that may constitute risk factors at one life stage may or may not put an individual at risk at a later stage of development. These factors can include biological and genetic attributes of the child, family factors, and community factors that impinge on the child and family environment.

RISK FACTORS IN THE CHILD

Risk factors in the child can lead to a state of vulnerability in which other risk factors may then impact, for example a prematurely born infant is more vulnerable and less likely to develop full cognitive potential than is a full term, healthy sibling in a suboptimal family environment. Other in-

nate risk factors which render the child vulnerable include adverse prenatal conditions such as smoking, drug or alcohol ingestion in pregnancy, developmental delay (late walking and talking) (Werner and Smith, 1982) and below average intelligence. Links have been shown between early language disabilities and later development of behaviour disorders. (Dattilo and Camarata, 1991). Children who are temperamentally difficult are more likely to show later behavioral problems than children who are less difficult. (Rietsma-Street, Offord and Finch 1985; Earls 1981). It is the combination of infant difficulty with family stress or dysfunction that has been found to contribute to later behaviour problems (Maziade et al 1989). Similarly, chronic illness and functional disability (Cadman et al., 1986) place a child at increased risk for externalizing disorder and chronic conditions affecting the central nervous system place a child at the highest risk (Rutter and Quinton 1977). It is not known whether this is due to the congnitive damage itself or through the resulting difficult temperament of the child.

RISK FACTORS IN THE FAMILY ENVIRONMENT

Family dysfunction (Quinton, Rutter, & Liddle, 1984), involves a number of different aspects, factors that have to do with family adversity, disruption, and stress; factors that interfere with the parent/child interaction; and factors that interfere with optimal parenting practices. Marital discord in families has been found persistently to predict disruptive behavior problems in boys, especially in combination with maternal depression (Rutter & Giller, 1983). The extent of discord and conflict between the parents, whether they are separated or not, is associated with risk for antisocial behavior (Hetherington, Cox, & Cox, 1985). The effects of witnessing parental violence have been clearly shown to predispose boys to use violence as a means of conflict resolution (Jaffe, Hurley, & Wolfe, 1990).

Factors that interfere with the development of parent/child relationships include parental alcoholism (Quinton et al., 1984); (maternal alcohol problems have been found to have the greatest effect on the behaviors of younger boys (Avison, 1992)) and parental psychiatric illness (Rutter & Quinton, 1984), especially maternal depression

(Avison, 1992). Poor maternal education has been found to correlate with poor school achievement but not with emotional disorder in children (Offord, Last, & Barrette, 1985). Dysfunctional parenting practices, especially harsh, erratic, and abusive forms of discipline, have been found to predispose to conduct disorder. Patterson, Reid, and Dishion 1992 have documented systematically how coercive behavior on the part of both child and parent combined with parental inconsistency creates negative reinforcement patterns in which child aggression and coercion are reinforced. These authors have demonstrated that the combination of inadequate supervision, parental criticism, harsh and inconsistent discipline, and rejecting attitudes toward a child have a specific effect in producing antisocial behavior in children.

COMMUNITY FACTORS

Community factors that impinge on children and their families include the impact of poverty (Offord et al., 1989). Low income has been found to be one of the most powerful risk factors for conduct disorder in young children (Offord, Alder, & Boyle, 1986; Kolvin, Miller, Fleeting, & Kolvin, 1988). Having a parent on welfare has been found to have a particularly detrimental effect on children, especially girls (Offord, 1987). Overcrowding (Rutter & Quinton, 1977) and living in subsidized housing (Rutter, 1981) also have been found to be risk factors for conduct problems (Hawkins et al., 1992). Poverty appears to have its effect due to the aggregation of risk factors, that is, the number of life stresses and daily hassles that inevitably have an impact on family interactions and relationships in a way that changes what Rutter has described as the "under-the-roof culture of the family."

Schools have been found to have the power either to enhance or detract from intellectual and social growth. Thus they can function as community risk or protective environments for children and adolescents.

Urban areas typically have higher rates of delinquency than do rural areas. Even within cities there is marked variation in crime rates by neighbourhood.

In early childhood it is evident that a positive family environment is able to protect children from the effects of the wider community environment; as the child grows older, the peer, school, and community effects become more powerful.

MULTIPLE RISK FACTORS

Adverse conditions in the environment do not always necessarily produce adverse outcomes. It is becoming clear that the *combination* and *number* of risk factors in the child and risk factors in the family environment that are likely to predispose children to negative outcomes. For example, Greenberg, Speltz, and Deklyn (1993) have suggested that there are 4 domains of risk that are interrelated to produce early-onset conduct disorder. These are contributions from the child's organic or temperamental difficulties; family factors such as family adversity, disruption, and stress; ineffective parenting and socialization of the child; and problems in the early parent/child relationships. Rutter and Quinton (1977) suggested that a 4-fold increase in the amount of stress in childhood produced a 24-fold increase in the incidence of later psychiatric disorder. Not all subsequent studies have replicated this exponential effect, but it is quite clear that the presence of multiple risk factors markedly increases the preponderance of adverse outcomes.

Sameroff (1987) found that families with 7 or more risk factors had children who scored 30 IQ points below families with no risk factors.

Resilience

Resilience has been described as the capacity for successful adaptation, positive functioning, or competence despite high-risk status, chronic stress, or following prolonged or severe trauma (Egeland, Carlson, & Sroufe, 1993). These authors view resilience in terms of a transactional process within an organizational framework. Developmental outcomes are determined by the interaction of genetic, biological, psychological, and sociological factors in the context of environmental support (Cicchetti & Schneider-Rosen, 1986).

Protective Factors

Rutter (1985, pp. 598–611) defined protective factors as "those factors that modify, ameliorate or alter a person's response to some environmental hazard that predisposes to a maladaptive outcome." Because protective factors modify risk factors, however, they do not necessarily foster normal development in the absence of risk factors. Research into protective factors is less well developed than risk factor research, and several conceptual and methodological issues remain to be resolved (Luthar 1993). There is evidence that a core set of individual characteristics and sources of support can buffer the effects of both biological and psychosocial risks during childhood (Mrazek & Haggerty, 1994). Protective factors can be considered as those within the child, the family, and the community.

CHILD FACTORS

Child factors include positive temperament (Rutter, 1985), above-average intelligence (Rutter, Tizard, & Whitmore, 1970), and measures of social competence, which include academic achievement, participation and competence in outside-school activities, and the ability to relate easily to others. Rae Grant, N. I., Thomas, H., Offord, D. R., & Boyle, M. H. et al. (1989) found that the ability to get along with teachers, parents, and peers and having friendships was strongly protective for adolescents. Children who are easy-going and responsive call forth the best not only from their parents but later from teachers, peers, and other adults in their environment. Above-average intelligence may allow a child not only to succeed academically but also to develop problem-solving skills. In adolescence having a sense of coherence and internal locus of control has been cited as a protective factor (O'Grady & Metz, 1987).

FAMILY FACTORS

Favorable family factors include supportive parents, family closeness, and adequate rule setting (Werner & Smith, 1982). A supportive relationship with even one parent was found to provide a substantial protective effect for children living in severely discordant, unhappy homes (Rutter, 1978). There is consistent evidence that the nature and quality of children's interaction with their parents affects their interpersonal behaviors, social competence, and school performance (Amato, 1989; Dornbusch, 1989). Smaller family structure with spacing of more than 2 years between siblings has been found to be protective (Werner & Smith, 1992).

COMMUNITY FACTORS

Community factors include the relationships that children develop outside the family with peers, significant other adults, and the institutions with which they come in contact. These have been found to have the potential to exert significant positive or negative effects. Good schools were found not only to affect academic achievement positively but also to reduce the rate of truancy and school dropout and juvenile court appearances for children in disadvantaged areas in inner London (Rutter et al., 1979).

In the Kauai Longitudinal Study, 3 clusters of protective factors were found to differentiate the resilient group from other high-risk children who developed serious and persistent problems in childhood and adolescence (Werner & Smith, 1992). These were: (1) at least average intelligence and temperamental attributes that elicited positive responses from family members and other adults; (2) good relationships with parents or parent substitutes; and (3) an external support system that rewarded competence and provided a sense of coherence.

HOW RISK AND PROTECTIVE FACTORS INTERACT

Anthony (1974) suggested a useful analogy to explain the interaction of vulnerability, risk, and resilience. Three dolls, one made of glass, one of plastic, and the other of steel, are each exposed to a blow of equal force from a hammer. The glass doll shatters, the plastic doll bears a permanent scar, and the third is unharmed and gives out a fine metallic sound. The glass doll is obviously fragile and at risk from external forces because of its constitution; it also could have been mishandled after leaving the factory but might have been neglected by its owner and thus have been exposed to being chipped or cracked. Accumulation of risk experiences may leave the doll in a heightened state of susceptibility. To carry the analogy further, Anthony suggested that one might imagine a protective coating of some sort being applied to the glass doll to reduce its vulnerability and protect it from further trauma.

It has been suggested that there are different ways in which risk and protective factors interact to produce competence in children (Garmezy, Masten, & Tellegen, 1984).

1. The *compensatory model*, stressors, risk, and vulnerability factors combine additively.
2. The challenge model, as long as stress is not excessive, it enhances competence in children.
3. The *protective model* suggests that protective factors modulate the negative impact of stressors as variables by improving coping adaptations, allowing the child to build competencies.

"The interaction of risk and protective factors is a balance between the power of the individual and the power of the social or physical environment. A balance is necessary throughout life, although different factors assume different degrees of importance at different developmental stages. Constitutional factors and family factors are most important during infancy and early childhood; interpersonal and community factors assume increasing importance during later childhood and adolescence (Werner & Smith, 1982)."

CONTINUITIES AND DISCONTINUITIES FROM CHILDHOOD TO ADULTHOOD

Parents may provide different kinds of environments for their children at different stages of their development. Some mothers, for example, are more comfortable and competent with their children as infants and can provide a safe secure, nurturing environment that allows the child to develop a secure attachment during the first year of life; however, they may get into difficulty once the child becomes a toddler, starts to explore, and begins to display the normal oppositional behavior typical in the second year of life. Conversely, a good family environment may deteriorate by reason of the onset of psychiatric disturbance in a parent or because of the presence of severe family stressors, such as unemployment, bereavement, or parental separation. Similarly, families that may

be stable and supportive for one child may be less so for a subsequent child because of changes in the family's life circumstances or because one child can be temperamentally more difficult or have a chronic disabling condition that makes him or her more difficult to look after. Situations can improve or deteriorate not only within the immediate family environment, but also between the child and the institutions with which he or she comes into contact; for example, some risk pathways may turn to more adaptive outcomes for individual children because of a positive school experience. Rutter and his coworkers found that some secondary schools in socially deprived neighborhoods were able to produce more positive, vocational, academic, and social outcomes for their students than were others (Rutter, Maughan, Mortimore, Ouston, & Smith, 1979). Similarly, in adulthood, having good social support—for example, a successful job or a supportive marital partner—can lead to good social and parenting functioning in a mother formerly at risk because she had grown up in an institutional environment (Rutter, 1989).

Outcomes, in summary, depend on the interaction of a number of factors:

- The number of stressors in the wider environment
- The number of stressors/risk factors in the family
- The vulnerability of the child
- The timing (i.e., the developmental stage in which a particular life experience occurs)
- The resilience of the child (protective attributes)
- Protective factors in the family environment
- Protective factors in the wider environment

Assessing Risk and Protective Factors

One important task during the assessment is to ascertain the number, timing, and quality of risk factors in the child, in the parent/child environment, and in the wider environment to which the child comes into contact and, similarly, to identify current and potential protective factors in each of these domains. In working with children and adolescents, the aim of intervention is to alter the balance of vulnerability, risk, and protective factors in a positive direction and thus to change the developmental trajectory for them. Not all risk factors need to be reduced; reducing even some in a multirisk situation will result in a more advantageous outcome. Conversely, increasing the number of protective factors either in the individual child or in the family environment or by increasing support systems available to the child outside the home, in school, and in the community is likely to improve the outcome. There is now a sizable body of literature on reducing risk and increasing protective factors at the community level which suggests that the situation for children and adolescents could be ameliorated by focussing on protective processes that bring about changes in children's interactions with others (Rae Grant 1996).

The evaluation of risk and protective factors during the assessment may be incorporated easily into the history and interview format. For example, in eliciting the developmental history, it is important to assess the risk attributes (child risk factors) during the prenatal, perinatal, and postnatal periods that might have put the child at risk. These include both biological and temperamental factors.

Was this pregnancy planned or unplanned? Did the parents accept the pregnancy, even if it was unplanned? How did this color their attitude to the developing fetus? Were there obstetric or psychological complications during the pregnancy? Did the parents abuse substances such as tobacco, alcohol, or prescription or street drugs either immediately before or during the pregnancy?

What was the length of pregnancy? Was it premature or full term? Was it uneventful or complicated? What was the status of the newborn infant? Were there any difficulties in establishing breathing? Was the infant transferred to a neonatal intensive care unit? If premature, was the infant ventilated? If so, for how long? Were there complications of prematurity? If so, how many and over how long a period of time? An infant may recover despite severe complications of prematurity but if it is severely ill over a prolonged period, the mother may not be able subsequently to regard the infant as healthy (Minde et al., 1983). Were there cerebral complications? These put an infant at risk for adverse development especially in a family environment that is compromised for other reasons. (Rutter et al., 1970).

The following case example illustrates the interaction of several risk factors.

CASE EXAMPLE

John A's mother, a primipara, developed acute abdominal pain during the third month of her pregnancy. Her mother, with whom she always had had a conflictual relationship, advised her not to have the surgery that had been recommended, on the grounds that her child might be born brain damaged. She reluctantly agreed to surgery, and the remainder of the pregnancy and delivery passed uneventfully. Within 6 days of the baby's birth, however, she returned to her pediatrician demanding that he examine John to ascertain why the infant refused to settle and would not sleep. The irritable, restless infant never slept for more than an hour at a time, would arch his back when picked up, and screamed incessantly. Over the course of the next 2 years, Mrs. A was repeatedly told by different pediatricians that she was an "overanxious mother" and that her child was physically healthy. What was not identified was the problematic interaction between the anxious, first-time mother and the irritable child that led to a dysfunctional attachment.

Child risk factors in this situation included both biological, and temperamental difficulties. Factors in the mother included her initial anxiety as a first-time mother together with her memory of the prophecy by her own mother that the child would be brain damaged. A severely negative mother/child interactional pattern was established that led to lack of attachment on the part of the infant and subsequent aggressiveness, poor peer relationships, and noncompliance from earliest childhood.

At 2 years of age John was admitted to the care of the Children's Aid Society when his exhausted mother could no longer care for him. The receiving home to which he was then taken refused to keep him longer than 2 hours because of his destructive and totally uncontrolled behavior. He was then admitted to a pediatric unit for observation, where he created havoc by running around the ward, attacking other children, pulling out intravenous lines, and resisting all efforts by the nursing staff to corral him with blows and bites to their shins.

Symptoms of attention deficit hyperactivity disorder including impulsivity, restlessness, impaired concentration, and inattentiveness were readily apparent as were symptoms of reactive attachment disorder with inability to trust others, wariness, and refusal to sleep. It was only after 2 years in foster care that John finally slept through the night.

TEMPERAMENT

In eliciting information about the child's temperament, it should be determined whether the infant quickly developed rhythms of eating and sleeping or if there were early difficulties.

Once the infant had developed a routine pattern of feeding and sleeping, was this an easygoing infant or one who responded poorly to changes of routine or reacted adversely to new situations? Was this a stubborn, difficult child? Parents may have more difficulty with one child than others in the sibship because of difficult temperamental characteristics. Sometimes parents react angrily toward temperamental or physical characteristics in a child that remind them of themselves as children or of disliked attributes of the spouse.

Displaying a difficult temperament in early childhood has been found to place a child at risk for disorder, particularly in a family with other stressors. Maziade, Cote, Bernier, Boutin, and Thivierge (1989) have emphasized that temperamental difficulty at 7 years can strongly predict difficulties at 12 if this is combined with dysfunction in the family.

An example of the interaction of difficult temperament in a child in interaction with his family may illustrate such a transaction.

CASE EXAMPLE

Jason, a 6-year-old, made life very difficult for his family because of his apparently inborn, pessimistic outlook on life. Whatever the family planned to undertake, Jason would always be sure that something would go wrong. A promised picnic would turn into a disaster because on the ride there, Jason would complain that there were sure to be bugs that would bite him or wasps that would get into the food. The parents berated Jason for his negative attitude and urged him to count his blessings, but this only made him more negative. These conversations frequently ended in temper outbursts on Jason's part, which further interfered with the family's enjoyment of an activity.

In the assessment the parents were asked whether Jason was like any relative in temperament. His father replied, in a surprised tone of voice, that he was indeed very similar to an uncle of his. Once the parents recognized that Jason was pessimistic by temperament and was not setting out to be difficult, they soon were able to relax and learn not to allow his negative attitude to spoil family activities. By remaining calm and reassuring in their attitudes, they gradually were able to show

Jason that, in fact, his dire predictions were not borne out and that he had it within his ability to cope if things were, on occasion, not the way he would like. Jason's tantrums abated, he relaxed and became more responsive, which, in turn, made his parents more appreciative of his evident intelligence and dry sense of humor.

How did the child's subsequent development progress? Were motor, sensory, language, and social skills development within normal limits? How did this child's development compare with that of the siblings? A history of delay in walking and talking may be correlated with later development of psychiatric disorder.

CHRONIC ILLNESSES AND
FUNCTIONAL IMPAIRMENTS

A chronic illness or functional limitation may put a child at risk of psychiatric disorder (Cadman et al., 1986). Such conditions impact not only on the child's self-image but interfere with normal individuation and with sibling and peer relationships, for example.

CASE EXAMPLE

Jenny, age 12, had sustained a severe back injury following a fall from a horse at age 8. Her almost constant back pain caused her to be irritable and difficult, which led to criticism from her parents and interfered with her image of herself as an athlete. She felt that she was different from her peers, a disappointment to her father, a keen horseman himself, and a nuisance to her mother.

For young children under the age of 6, acute or chronic illnesses may be complicated by the trauma inherent in hospitalization experiences. A history of more than 1 hospitalization lasting more than 1 week puts them at risk for disorder later in childhood. Young children do not understand the reasons for hospitalization and painful procedures and may hold their parents responsible for those events or may feel that they are being punished for some misbehavior. Daily visiting or parents being allowed to stay at the hospital with their child go a long way to reduce the effects of these stressors. However, parents with other children at home may feel torn between their wish to remain with the child patient and their concern for and guilt about the other children at home.

SCHOOL HISTORY

How did the child settle into day care or kindergarten? Were there difficulties with separation? How long did these continue? How did the child get along with peers and the teacher? Were there any problems in kindergarten?

Problems should be elicited both in the behavioral as well as in academic areas. Children who fail first grade are at significant risk for later psychiatric disorder (Offord, Last & Barrette et al.). Learning problems often underlie other areas of difficulty, either because the child attempts to hide the fact that there are academic difficulties by acting up or because a third factor may be responsible for both learning and behavioral problems. The child who has problems in learning is at increased risk for externalizing disorders; conversely, children who do well in school may be protected to some extent from the negative effects of adverse family factors (Rutter et al., 1970).

SEPARATIONS

The history should include reports of any separations from the family for more than brief holiday periods with relatives. Children who have been taken into care of the local children's authority are at greater risk for disorder, particularly if they were not visited frequently by their parents or if they remained in care over a prolonged period of time (Rutter & Quinton, 1977). Young children may interpret the placement as an abandonment by their parents or may fear subsequent abandonment as a punishment for bad behavior. The following case example presents this kind of situation.

CASE EXAMPLE

Johnny, age 6, suddenly began to be inattentive in school, often appearing to be in a daydream during which he looked sad. He also had developed an insatiable appetite, stealing lunches from his first-grade school friends. At home, usually described as a loving and obedient child, he became noncompliant, slept badly with nightly bingeing, and became quite demanding of his mother. When referred by his school teacher for assessment, his mother revealed that she had been in a violent, abusive relationship from which she had escaped with 3 children under the age of 3. Only 20 years old at the time, she had placed her 3 children in care and subsequently had agreed for the younger 2 to be adopted. A year later Johnny was released to her care. She established a home for him and reported that her relationship with him appeared to be a good one until the recent onset of his unusual behaviors. In the assessment interview, Johnny revealed that he was sad and angry; he thought often about his little brother and sister and wondered where they had gone. He said he had thought that his mother might give him away for adoption as she had the others. He reported that he had only just recently begun to worry about these events. It appeared likely that he was now cognitively of an age to feel that the loss of his siblings was permanent. The risk factors were further increased by the mother's experience of her own chaotic childhood as the youngest of 10 siblings. She had run away from home at the age of 12 and after 2 failed group home experiences had been "on the streets" for 2 years before entering the abusive relationship with Johnny's father.

SEXUAL HISTORY

What has the child's exposure been to adult sexuality? Has the child been sexually abused? If so, by whom and over how long a period of time? How was this disclosed? How did the parents react? What followed after the disclosure? The child who is believed and emotionally supported by at least 1 parent is less at risk for subsequent psychiatric disorder.

CASE EXAMPLE

Joan, age 12, disclosed to her mother that she had been sexually abused on several occasions by an adolescent male baby-sitter 3 years earlier. Her father was outraged but supportive of her, but her mother appeared, at first, to show very little reaction. A few weeks later her mother became severely depressed and was admitted to a psychiatric unit for a brief period during which she disclosed her own, formerly repressed, childhood sexual abuse. Joan felt deserted by her mother, became increasingly withdrawn from her family and friends, did poorly in school, and was subsequently referred to a children's mental health center by her teacher when her written homework revealed a strong suicidal preoccupation.

Two years later, following prolonged individual therapy, Joan's mother was finally able, in a family session, to tell Joan how sad she had been that she had not been able to protect her from the abuse and how she now understood Joan's anger at her lack of support.

Girls who have been sexually abused are at greater risk for subsequent abuse. Boys who have been sexually abused may, in turn, abuse other children when they reach adolescence. A history of childhood sexual abuse often is elicited as one underlying risk factor in many different psychiatric disorders, including anxiety disorders, depression, posttraumatic stress disorder, dissociative disorders, and borderline personality disorders.

FAMILY HISTORY

A good family history will include details about the parents, their ages, occupations, and details of their families of origin. Inquire as to what they remember about their own childhood. Can they empathize with their children? Do they like this child? Can they say anything positive about the youngster? Does this child remind them of themselves as a child?

Parents who can remember nothing of their own childhood are possibly at risk for parenting their own children. Such total repression of childhood events has been found to correlate with very severe trauma to offspring in early childhood (Main & Hesse, 1990). This is not to say that parents who were not well parented cannot overcome such difficulties; they may have gone to tremendous lengths, knowing that they are at risk, to improve their parenting skills. Such parents may model themselves, for example, on a friend whose interaction with their own children they appreciate or on a relative whom they admired in childhood; they may have read a great deal about parenting and have attended parenting courses. If they have a supportive spouse who was well parented, they are likely to do quite well. The history of an attachment difficulty in childhood may predispose parents to having difficulties in attaching to their own children, particularly those who are temperamentally difficult, chronically ill, or whose appearance reminds them too poignantly of themselves as children. Parents who were physically abused as children may bend over backward not to physically abuse their own children; however, having been brought up on corporal punishment, they may find their repertoire of child management techniques limited or may fail to intervene and set limits for children because they are afraid of succumbing to abusive reactions. Poor relationships with their own parents put parents at risk of establishing inadequate relationships with their own children. The difficulty is likely to be not only in the past but to continue into current family situations because parents who have not resolved their relationship with their own parents are left without extended family support.

The work history of both parents is of importance in terms of the meaning that their jobs have for them. Thus it is important to inquire about job satisfaction, hours of work, feelings about being away from the children because of work schedules. It has been found that having a job is a protective factor for mothers who can work in positions that they enjoy; being forced to work because of the family's financial situation does not serve as a protective factor. For a young mother who feels guilty about being away from her children and forced into the job market, employment may be an added risk rather than a protective factor. In some families where both parents work shifts and alternate their hours to avoid the necessity for day care or baby-sitting, family schedules, interactions with children, and work schedules appear at times to be so precariously balanced that if any additional stress occurs, the system falls apart.

CASE EXAMPLE

Kevin, age 5, was brought to the clinic initially because of his dramatic behavioral reaction to his parents' separation. At first his mother found his difficult behavior hard to understand in light of the fact that she felt relieved by the separation, was now able to pay more attention to Kevin, and felt that he should be glad that the tense atmosphere, punctuated by frequent quarrels, had given way to a more peaceful, consistent routine, particularly as she and her husband had been working long hours every week to try to salvage their joint business, which subsequently failed. Kevin, however, reacted negatively to the loss of his father, the move necessitated by his mother's financial position, the change of school, and loss of his friends and his favorite afterschool activities. Within a year, as in the usual course of events, Kevin's behavior improved. Being an intelligent child, he rapidly made up his lost ground at school and he once again developed friends in the neighborhood. His mother was once more surprised, however, when his behavior again deteriorated and he showed evidence of repressed rage that erupted at times under minor provocation. The rage always erupted in response to decreased attention from her—she had taken another job, which required very long hours and much homework—or to his father's reduced visits because of a new romantic interest in his life. This child, already at risk by reason of his early childhood punctuated by inadequate parental attention, had reacted negatively to

41

the multiple stressors that followed on his parents' separation and was quick to react to any additional life stress. His mother was encouraged to keep a log so that she could record periods of improvement and regression in Kevin, which she reluctantly did. It became apparent that his difficult behavior correlated either with changes in the amount of attention that she was paying to him or to the advent of other additional stresses in his environment. She came to understand that it was absolutely essential that she ensure regular individual time with Kevin and a consistent routine, and that she and her ex-husband communicate about Kevin's emotional status. Kevin's father was helped to recognize his son's need for support and attention. The parents were able to add some other supportive factors into the environment. Kevin was enrolled in after-school activities at which he excelled, and he was very positively reinforced by both parents for his increasing prowess at swimming and hockey.

MARITAL HISTORY

It is important to get a good history of the parents' marriage, their relationship over the years, and the attitude of each parent to the other. Do they respect each other? Does each portray a depreciating attitude toward the other that children may then project onto all males or females? Is their relationship one in which there are frequent recriminations and fights? Being in a discordant family is a markedly stressful experience for children and is a risk factor for disorder (Rutter, 1978).

Is the relationship a violent one in which one or other parent is physically abused? If children witness the father being violent toward the mother, they are at risk for repeating these behaviors; boys may identify with the aggressive father and girls may identify with the victim mother (Jaffe, Hurley, & Wolfe, 1990). Have there been separations in the marriage? If so, for how long? Did the absent parent visit the children during that time? Where there other partners? If so, for how long and how many? Partners who may not to have appeared to be particularly emotionally significant for the remaining parent may have been important parent substitutes for the children, and their loss may need to be mourned and understood in the same way as the loss of a parent.

Each stage of family transition—separation, divorce, remarriage—poses significant difficulties for children, which they will experience differently depending on their age and sex, their rela-

tionship with the custodial and absent parent before and during the separation, and their own ability to understand the situation. In general, small children react very negatively to the separation of their parents, whereas adolescents may appreciate more readily the nature of the difficulties in their parents' relationship. Conversely, small children will accept a stepmother or stepfather more readily than adolescents who frequently have extreme difficulty in so doing (Hetherington et al., 1985).

Arriving at Conclusions about the Risk/Resiliency Equation

George Albee (1979) suggested that the incidence of disorder was equal to the child's innate vulnerabilities plus the number of stressors in the family and community environment, divided by the amount of resilience in the child and coping competency plus protective factors in the family and community environment. So far this equation has not been converted into mathematical terms; nor has a computer algorithm been developed that could evaluate the strengths of the various factors and come up with a degree of risk or resilience for an individual child. Such methods certainly would be helpful in assessing the degree of risk and the potential strength or resilience of the child and for suggesting angles or levers for intervention using these factors. It is probable, as Rutter has pointed out, that some risk factors are transactional—that is, the presence of one increases the likelihood of the presence of another—some are additive, and some are possibly multiplicative—that is, the sum increases geometrically rather than summatively (Rutter & Quinton, 1977). There seems to be a measure of agreement among authors that 4 or more risk factors certainly will be correlated with the onset of disorder. Sameroff (1987) has suggested that 7 or more will be correlated with a decrease in intelligence in the children. However, the degree of risk needs to be balanced with a measure of the child's individual resilience and the presence of protective factors in the family and the community environment. The relative weighting of individual, family, and community factors will change in importance as the child

Points of possible intervention

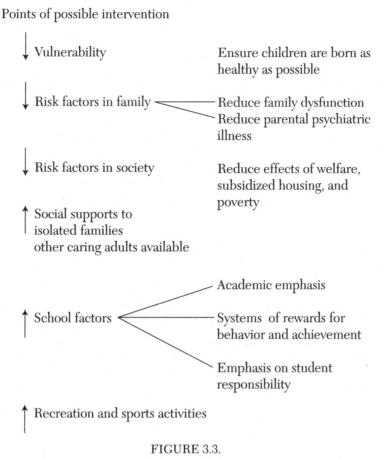

FIGURE 3.3.

Points of possible intervention

NOTE: From "Primary Prevention" (p. 919), by N. I. Rae Grant, in *Child and Adolescent Psychiatry: A Comprehensive Textbook* edited by M. Lewis, 1991, Baltimore, MD: Williams & Wilkins. Copyright 1991. Reprinted with permission.

grows; thus, in infancy, prenatal or perinatal biological factors may place a child at risk; however, if there is a sufficiently supportive, responsive family learning environment, the effects of these risk factors will be minimized (Maziade et al., 1989).

In a similar fashion, good intelligence and an easy disposition may allow a child to develop resilience, even in a markedly adverse family environment (Werner & Smith, 1992). Such a child may call forth very positive responses from other adults, school teachers, and peers.

It is suggested that a list of the biopsychosocial factors for each stage of development in infancy, preschool, school age, and adolescence be developed and that all the possible protective and risk factors be evaluated during the assessment process.

Intervention Strategy Planning

The aim of intervention should be, as far as possible, to reduce risk and increase protective factors in the child, the child's family, and the community environments. Is it possible, for example, to change the child by reducing his or her individual vulnerability or to change the parent's attitude toward the child by reframing the nature of the child's difficulties, thereby improving the parent/child interaction? Referring the parents to a support group for parents with children with similar problems may not only assist in their better understanding of the child's difficulties but also provide them with a strong support group for them. Possible points of intervention are shown in Figure 3.3.

FAMILY ADVERSITY, DISRUPTION, AND STRESS

The family's basic needs for employment, safe housing, and adequate food need to be met before other interventions are planned. Parents cannot give their children adequate care and responsive attention when these needs are not attended to.

Marital discord is a risk factor that needs therapeutic attention. Violent interactions need to be dealt with as an urgent matter, and aggressive partners must be referred to the appropriate agency for group treatment.

If one or other of the parents have psychiatric problems, these should be identified and referral sought for appropriate treatment and support. Psychoeducational support to the spouse and older children will be an important aspect of overall intervention planning.

It is possible to provide a more consistent, stable environment for a preschool child by improving the parents' parenting practices. Parent training groups that target consistency, positive reinforcement, and management of defiant behavior may obviate the development of antisocial behavior later in childhood (Patterson, Chamberlain, & Reid, 1982). Parent/child interaction also may be improved by giving parents some suggestions for age-appropriate activities in which to involve their child. The child's interactions with other children can be improved by social skills or anger management training so that the child feels better about him-/or herself and less enraged. Social skills training may be a necessary prerequisite to involvement in outside school activities, activities that might allow a child to develop competencies and thus improve self-esteem. These things will not happen if the child is immediately expelled from a sports team or scout group due to difficult behavior. Similarly, a change of school may be indicated if a child has previously developed such a bad reputation with teachers and peers that no amount of change on the child's part will change their negative attitude toward him or her. Collaboration with the school is an essential component of therapeutic work with a child. Besides strategies for managing behavioral difficulties, reframing school personnel's understanding of the child and ensuring that any underlying learning disability has been addressed and that the child's assets and deficits identified are prerequisites to the development of a prescriptive educational program as much as are strategies for managing behavioural difficulties. Such suggestions in addition to the appropriate employment of the usual therapeutic modalities may go a long way in changing the negative balance for the individual child and thus ultimately the developmental trajectory.

REFERENCES

Albee, G. W. (1979). Primary prevention. *Canadian Mental Health, 27,* 5–9.

Amato, P. R. (1989). Family process and the competence of adolescents and primary school children. *Journal of Youth and Adolescence, 18,* 39–53.

Anthony, E. J. (1974). The syndrome of the psychologically invulnerable child. In E. J. Anthony & C. Koupernik (Eds.), *The child and his family: Children at psychiatric risk* (Vol. 3, pp. 99–121). New York: John Wiley & Sons.

Avison, W. R. (1992). *Risk factors for children's conduct problems and delinquency: The significance of family milieu.* Paper presented at the annual meeting of the American Society of Criminology, New Orleans, LA.

Cadman, D., Boyle, M. H., Offord, D. R., Szatmari, P., Rae-Grant, N., Crawford, J. W., & Byles, J. A. (1986). Chronic illness and functional limitation in Ontario children: Findings of the Ontario child health study. *Canadian Medical Association Journal, 135,* 761–767.

Cicchetti, D., & Schneider-Rosen, K. (1986). An organizational approach to childhood depression. In M. Rutter, C. Izard, P. R. Read (Eds.), *Depression in young people: Developmental and clinical perspectives* (pp. 71–134). New York: Guilford Press.

Dattilo, J., & Camarata, S. M. (1991). Facilitating conversation through self-initiated augmentative communication treatment. *Journal of Applied Behavior Analysis, 24,* 369–378.

Dornbusch, S. M. (1989). The sociology of adolescence. In W. R. Scott & J. Blake (Eds.), *Annual review of sociology* (pp. 223–259). Palo Alto, CA: Annual Reviews.

Earls, F. (1981). Temperament characteristics and behavior problems in three-year-old children. *Journal of Nervous and Mental Disease, 169,* 367–373.

Egeland, B., Carlson, C., & Sroufe, L. A. (1993). Resilience as process. *Development and Psychopathology, 5,* 517–528.

Garmezy, N. (1983). Stressors of childhood. In N. Garmezy & M. Rutter (Eds.), *Stress, coping and development in children* (pp. 43–84). New York: McGraw-Hill.

Garmezy, N., Masten, A., & Tellegen, A. (1984). The study of stress and competence in children. *Child Development, 55,* 97–111.

Greenberg, M. T., Speltz, M. L., & DeKlyn, M. (1993). The role of attachment in the early development of disruptive behavior problems. *Development and Psychopathology, 5,* 191–214.

Hawkins, J. D., Catalano, R. F., Morrison, D. M., O'Donnell, J., Abbott, R. D., Day, L. E. (1992). The Seattle Social Development Project. Effects of the first four years on protective factors and problem behaviors. In J. McCord & R. Tremblay (Eds.), *The prevention of antisocial behavior in children.* New York: Guilford Press.

Hetherington, E. M., Cox, M., & Cox, R. (1985). Long-term effects of divorce and remarriage on the adjustment of children. *Journal of the American Academy of Child Psychiatry, 24,* 518–530.

Jaffe, P. G., Hurley, D. J., & Wolfe, D. (1990). Children's observations of violence: 1. Critical issues in child development and intervention planning. *Canadian Journal of Psychiatry, 35* (6), 466–470.

Kolvin, F. J., Miller, J. W., Fleeting, M., & Kolvin, P. A. (1988). Social and parenting factors affecting criminal-offence rates: Findings from the Newcastle thousand family study (1947–1980). *British Journal of Psychiatry, 152,* 80–90.

Luthar, S. S. (1993). Annotation: Methodological and conceptual issues in research on childhood resilience. *Journal of Child Psychology and Psychiatry, 34,* 441–453.

Main, M., & Hesse, E. (1990). Adult lack of resolution of attachment—trauma related to infant disorganized/disoriented behaviour in the Ainsworth Strange Situation: Linking parental states of mind to infant behavior in a stressful situation. In M. T. Greenberg, D. Ciccheti, & M. Cummings (Eds.), *Attachment in the preschool years: Theory, Research and Intervention* (pp. 339–426). Chicago: University of Chicago Press.

Maziade, M., Cote, R., Bernier, H.; Boutin, P.; Thivierge, J. (1989). Significance of extreme temperament in infancy for clinical status in pre-school years: 1. *British Journal of Psychiatry, 14,* 535–543.

Minde, K., Whitelaw, H., Brown, J., et al. (1983). Effect of neonatal complications in premature infants on early parent-infant interaction. *Developmental Medicine and Child Neurology, 25,* 763.

Mrazek, P., & Haggerty, R. J. (Eds.). (1994). Reducing risks for mental disorders. Frontiers for preventive intervention research. Washington, DC: Institute of Medicine, National Academy of Sciences.

Offord, D. R. (1987). Prevention of behavioural and emotional disorders in children. *Journal of Child Psychology and Psychiatry, 28,* 919.

Offord, D. R., Alder, R. J., & Boyle, M. H. (1986). Prevalence and sociodemographic correlates of conduct disorder. *American Journal of social psychiatry, 6,* 272–278.

Offord, D. R., Boyle, M. H., Fleming, J. E., Munroe Blom, H., & Rae Grant, N. I. et al. (1989). *Ontario Child Health Study: Summary of selected results. Canadian Journal of Psychiatry, 34,* 483–491.

Offord, D. R., Last, J. M., & Barrette, P. A. (1985). A comparison of the school performance, emotional adjustment and skill development of poor and middle class children. *Canadian Journal of Public Health, 76,* 174–178.

O'Grady, D., & Metz, J. E. (1987). Resilience in children at high risk for psychological disorder. *Journal of Pediatric Psychology, 12,* 3–23.

Patterson, G. R., Chamberlain, P., & Reid. (1992). See ref. Lewis chapter.

Patterson, G. R., Reid, J. B., Dishion, T. J. (1992). *Antisocial boys. Oregon Social Learning Center.* Eugene, OR: Castalia Publishing Co.

Quinton, D., Rutter, M., & Liddle, C. (1984). Institutional rearing, parenting difficulties and marital support. *Psychological Medicine, 14,* 107–124.

Rae Grant, N. I. Primary prevention. 88 in Textbook of child & Adolescent Psychiatry. 1996. 2nd edition. M. J. Lewis (Ed.) Williams & Wilkins.

Rae Grant, N. I., Thomas, H., Offord, D. R., Boyle, M. H. (1989). Risk, protective factors, and the prevalence of behavioral and emotional disorders in children and adolescents. *Journal of the American Academy of Child and Adolescent Psychiatry, 28,* 262–268.

Reitsma-Street, M., Offord, D. R., & Finch, T. (1985). Pairs of same-sexed siblings discordant for antisocial behaviour. *British Journal of Psychiatry, 146,* 415–423.

Robins, L. N. (1970). Follow-up studies investigating childhood disorders. In E. H. Hare & J. K. Wing (Eds.), *Psychiatric epidemiology.* London: Oxford University Press.

Rutter, M. (1978). Family, area and school influences in the genesis of conduct disorders. In L. A. Herson & M. Berger (Eds.), *Aggression and antisocial behaviour in childhood and adolescent* (pp. 95–114). London: Pergamon Press.

Rutter, M. (1981). Stress, coping and development: Some issues and some questions. *Journal of Child Psychology and Psychiatry, 22,* 323–356.

Rutter, M. (1985). Resilience in the face of adversity: Protective factors and resistance to psychiatric disorder. *British Journal of Psychiatry, 147,* 598–611.

Rutter, M. (1989). Pathways from childhood to adult life. *Journal of Psychology & Psychiatry, 30,* 23–51.

Rutter, M., & Giller, H. (1983). Juvenile delinquency: Trends and perspectives. New York: Penguin Books.

Rutter, M., Maughan, B., Mortimore, P., Ouston, J., & Smith, A. (1979). Fifteen thousand hours: Secondary schools and their effects on children. Cambridge, MA: Harvard University Press.

Rutter, M., & Quinton, D. (1977). Psychiatric disorder:

Ecological factors and concepts of causation. In H. McCurck (Ed.), Ecological factors in human development. Amsterdam: North Holland Publishing.

Rutter, M., & Quinton, D. (1984). Parental psychiatric disorder: Effects on children. *Psychological Medicine, 14*, 853–880.

Rutter, M., Tizard, J., & Whitmore, K. (1970). Education, health and behaviour. London: Longman.

Sameroff, A. J. (1987). Transactional risk factors and prevention. In J. A. Steinberg & M. M. Silverman (Eds.), Preventing mental disorders: A research perspective (p. 76). Rockville, MD: U.S. Department of Health and Human Services.

Sameroff, A. J., & Chandler, M. J. (1975). Reproductive risk and the continuum of caretaking casualty. In F. D. Horowitz, M. Hetherington, & S. Scarr-Salopatek (Eds.), *Review of child development research* (Vol. 4, pp. 187–244). Chicago: University of Chicago Press.

Werner, E. E., & Smith, R. S. (1992). *Overcoming the odds: High risk children from birth to adulthood.* New York: Cornell University Press.

Werner, E. E., & Smith, R. S. (1982). *Vulnerable but invincible: A longitudinal study of resilient children and youth.* New York: McGraw-Hill.

West, D., & Farrington, D. (1982). *Delinquency: Its roots, careers and prospects.* London: Heinemann Educational.

4 / Communicating with Children

Janet M. Demb and Saul Isaac Harrison

Speaking with Children

When an adult engages in a conversation with another adult, there are shared expectations: If one asks a question, the other will answer; if one speaks, the other will listen or perhaps feign interest; neither will run around wildly during the exchange, and neither will whip out a game for solitary play. Shared conventions make for an easier exchange between adult and adult than between adult and child. When confronted with an adult who wishes to converse, a young child may simply take off in search of Mother; an older child may answer a question that is apparently different from the one posed or sit silently and fiddle with coat buttons; an adolescent may focus on the music on his headset with apparent disregard for everyone and everything else. The challenge of interviewing a child is a familiar one; many have watched a skilled talk show host chat easily with a wide variety of adults, only to be undone by a terse or silent child from whom words cannot be teased. Moreover, it is not only grown-ups who find this burdensome. Saint-Exupéry's Little Prince spoke eloquently: "Grown-ups never understand anything by themselves and it is tiresome for children to be always and forever explaining things to them."

When the exchange between child and adult occurs in a clinical context, the problem is compounded. As a rule, the child is involved because the parents have identified a problem and not at all because the child is interested in seeking help. Typically, the child is either not aware of or denies distress and perceives no problem. In an effort to assist clinicians confronted with the challenge of communicating with the young, this chapter explores some of the barriers to communication between clinicians and children.

INDIRECT COMMUNICATION

Young children tend to be referred to mental health practitioners because of academic difficulties, behavior problems, poor peer relations, or a specific symptom, such as encopresis. Unlike adults, who voluntarily seek help, children *are sent.* Thus, a question such as "Why are you here today?" often elicits a blank stare, an effort at distraction, or a denial of the existence of the presenting problem. Physicians are taught in medical school to greet patients by asking about the chief complaint; with a child, however, all too often such a direct approach is fruitless. To establish the kind of rapport with a child that will allow for the gathering of necessary information, a great deal more can be achieved by indirection. To illustrate:

John is 7 years old, and almost every day, his teachers have been sending notes about him to his parents. The complaints are that he disrupts his class by clowning or walking out of the room, that he does not follow directions and talks out of turn, and that he seldom brings homework to class. His parents have scolded him repeatedly and have denied him television privileges—with only transitory improvement. Now he is being threatened with retention in the second grade.

Enter John. He is a boy who looks his age, clean, but with his shirt partially untucked. He separates easily from his parents in the waiting room and sits down hesitantly in the office. At first he sits quietly, but soon he begins to kick softly at his chair and to fidget with the pages of the interviewer's desk calendar. He catches himself, reaches into his pocket, and takes out a plastic wrestler; he places it on his lap and proceeds to reposition its arms.

What are the possible interventions at this juncture? Telling John to sit still and not fidget would clarify whether he can follow such a suggestion, and for how long. Unfortunately, it would make John feel that the clinician was criticizing him, perhaps much the way he feels in the face of similar remonstrances at home or at school. The clinician might, alternatively, ask John why he fidgets, why he does not do his homework, or why he clowns around in class. Most likely John would shrug his shoulders in response, because he would not know the answers. Moreover, although the intent of the clinician's "why" is to understand what motivates behavior, the message received by the child very likely would be "you shouldn't!" (Harrison, 1964). Children rarely experience *why* questions as sincere inquiries; almost always, they mean don't do a certain behavior again. They have never experienced being asked *why* they got an A or hit a homerun. But they have been "asked" *why* they failed or struck out. Since feeling criticized or admonished will not help the interviewer to develop a clinical alliance, asking a "why" question will not advance the goal of learning from John what only he can communicate. A critical clinical challenge is to discover a fruitful medium of communication.

Instead, by taking a lead from John and meeting him at his level, the clinician directs the interview along a potentially more productive route. The inquiry is directed toward his wrestler, and presently John reveals that he has a large set of toy wrestlers at home, he enjoys watching wrestling on television with his father, but he does not aspire to become a wrestler himself. Following his lead, the clinician poses more questions, and John speaks of his desire to take a karate class and his belief that his parents would not consent to this. While on the subject of martial arts, it is easy to ask John if other kids ever fight with him. This is a much more acceptable question than asking if he starts fights with other children, for it respects his need to maintain his psychological defenses. In fact, John seems glad to have been asked and reveals that not only do other kids fight with him but that they call him names and get him into trouble with his teacher. Moreover, the teacher never takes his side. The clinician is hitting pay dirt and goes with the flow. Continuing to follow John's lead, the clinician asks what names the kids call him. With uncomfortable hesitation and with eyes averted John says that he is called "retard." (The labels youngsters attach to their peers can be informative, since children are often curiously sensitive to their peers' problems. A boy who avoids rough-and-tumble play may draw the title "sissy" while the slow or learning disabled child may be labeled "retard.") John talks a bit about how he responds to teasing, and, when he is finished, the interviewer returns to John's earlier comment about his teacher taking the side of the other children by asking if that kind of thing ever happens at home. John is not at all hesitant in describing the many ways in which his mother takes the side of his younger brother, elaborating with considerable energy about incidents in which he feels that he has been blamed unjustifiably for what his little brother has done.

Thus far we have described a single interview, but much of what has been outlined would apply equally well to a series of assessment interviews or to therapeutic contacts. The clinician's position of neutrality, open nonjudgmental interest, and acceptance of the child with whatever behavior and defenses he brings will allow the clinical process to move ahead.

Clinical Opportunities

A child who overheard the tardy clinician tell a secretary he had been "delayed" later asks the professional the meaning of that word. The clinician could follow the virtually universal adult inclination to educate the young by defining this word; however, by doing so, the clinician would have missed a clinical opportunity to explore the boy's thoughts. The child guessed that "delayed" meant that the tardy clinician had injured a child with his big Mercedes and was late because he had taken the screaming, bleeding youngster to the emergency room.

Similarly, a clinician's inability to understand a child's use of language can be turned to clinical advantage. The late Margaret Mahler used to illustrate this point by relating one of her initial clinical efforts in English following her migration to the United States. In response to her empathic expressions of interest, the young boy continued to refer to her as a "stinkpot." Mahler's dictionary-assisted efforts at comprehension proved futile. Enlisting the boy's assistance in defining the word led eventually to the clinically significant recognition that his repeated verbal assaults had been designed to fend off his unacceptable longing to be protected and comforted.

Clinically relevant information can stem from serendipitous events in the environment. The barking of a dog, for example, can lead to a disclosure about a wish for a pet, a discussion about wanting to be a veterinarian, the description of how an abusive father had acted toward a pet, or the recollection of having been bitten and a subsequent fear of dogs.

Confidentiality

Returning to John, a significant clinical decision must be made about what the clinician should share with the child regarding what has been communicated by parents as well as what the clinician should share with parents regarding what has transpired with the child.

John's parents told us that their son may have to repeat second grade. As with any sensitive, pos-

sibly "secret" information (e.g., an impending divorce, the illness of a family member), it is important to explore with parents, caregivers, and/or teachers whether the child is aware of information, lest we rudely surprise a child or betray the implied trust of the adult who provided background material. If John's parents had made it clear that the boy is aware that his promotion is in question, after establishing rapport, this can be injected matter-of-factly at an appropriate point in the interview—"your mom and dad told me that you may have to repeat the second grade." Such an honest and forthright statement allows the clinician to explore with John his feelings and fantasies without devoting time needlessly to eliciting anew from the child what the examiner already knows. On the other hand, there may be times when it is important to evoke from a child what has already been described by adults, in order to access what is in fact the child's perspective—for example, in this case John's version of his behavior toward his little brother.

There are times that children will be eager for the interviewer to advocate their case with the parents; at the same time youngsters may be inhibited by fears of reprisal should the parents be told what they have said. If the interviewer is unsure about how a child might react, he or she can pose a simple question, such as "Would it be okay with you if I talked to your mom and dad about how you feel about your _____? (It should be noted that material elicited from the child should not be presented to parents as if the clinician has naively accepted the child's side. Doing so could alienate the parents, thereby diminishing the clinician's capacity to help the child.)

Clinical impressions about such factors as parental quality, the youngster's characteristic level of trust/suspicion, and the nature of the parent-child relationship are of considerable importance. They allow the clinician to determine how to articulate basic ground rules in the contact with a child. It must be clear to the child that the clinician will treat what is said confidentially, unless potential danger obligates the clinician to inform parents lest harm result from information being withheld.

It is wiser to communicate too much about confidentiality to a child rather than too little. If a clinician does not address the need to share information about potential danger until actual danger is present, he runs the risk of losing the trust of a child who may see this breach of confidentiality as a broken promise.

Meaning and Management of Silence

Despite the clinician's openness, interest, acceptance, and willingness to follow the child's lead, there are times when a child will remain silent. How the clinician then proceeds stems from his or her sense of the source of the child's reluctance to communicate verbally. Might the silence represent elective mutism or perhaps an effort to conceal a speech problem? Or does it bespeak shyness, embarrassment, anxious terror, or a shameful fear of revelation fueled by a determination to suppress undesired thoughts or feelings? The possibilities encompass passive-aggressive oppositionalism on the one hand and the quietude of peaceful reflection or love on the other. The child may storm out of the office, perhaps because he or she is being faced with issues too troubling to be addressed. Or perhaps for similar reasons, the child may absorb him- or herself in some repetitive and mindless game. Not every child will oblige by bringing his or her own toys conveniently to the clinical setting, and the clinician must search creatively for ways to help the child to share information that is not readily forthcoming.

Any clinician who has sat in quiet frustration with an uncommunicative child or listened for what can feel like an eternity to the sound of her own voice has wished for some magic with which to penetrate a child's silence. Asking a child to draw a picture of a person may not only help to loosen up the lines of communication but will serve also as some indication of his fine motor and cognitive skills (Koppitz, 1968). Beyond the objective aspects of the picture, a drawing can be used as an opener to further discussion via exploring what the figure is doing, thinking, feeling, and so on. Although the child is talking about what has been drawn, his presentation simultaneously conveys what he is thinking and feeling, thereby enriching assessment and therapeutic processes (Di Leo, 1973).

Winnicott's *Therapeutic Consultation in Child Psychiatry* (1971) offers examples of engaging children by making drawing into an interactive activity. He developed the "squiggle game" in which a child begins a drawing, which is then elaborated by the interviewer, and vice versa. A child is thus both led and followed down a path to territory that had been inaccessible to words alone.

The silent child engrossed in doll play is communicating without words. Fruitful communication can be facilitated by the clinician articulating what is transpiring in play (not unlike the running commentary of sportscasters who describe verbatim what all can see).

Providing small dolls and furniture and observing how the child plays with these can be invaluable. Does the child initiate play or wait for permission from the clinician? Does the child play interactively, allowing the clinician into the proceedings? Is the play spontaneous or rigid and unimaginative? Does the child seem to enjoy playing, or is the process wooden, repetitive, and joyless? Does the child play in a manner expected from a much younger child? Is the play material used appropriately, that is, are the chairs used for sitting and the beds for sleeping, or are the articles treated with disregard for their symbolic properties and perhaps tasted, sniffed, or stacked? Are the themes aggressive in content, with much crashing of objects and injury to the dolls, or are more nurturing themes played out? Just as the clinician asks questions following the lead of a child who talks about life experiences, and just as the clinician asks about the pictures a child draws, it is important to question doll play when necessary: What are those dolls over there doing? Allowing the child to communicate through dolls affords him or her the freedom to express thoughts and feelings that might otherwise be impossible to acknowledge.

There is clinical merit in leaving the child's play idiom undisturbed and not translating it into current experience. Thus the clinician does not tell the child that the doll's feelings are indeed the child's lest that interrupt the flow of communication. This, however, does not hold true in those instances in which a child's reality testing is deficient. In such cases, the clinician may need to shore up the child's ability to distinguish reality from fantasy via explicit distinctions between make-believe and reality or, in extreme instances, by discouraging the playing out of fantasies that are already too real.

Additional suggestions about the use of dolls and puppets are available in Millar (1968) and Woltmann (1951).

Sometimes a child can be coaxed out of an unproductive silence into constructive interaction by the clinician's handing the child a written note, saying, for example: "You look sad, are you?" In that context, a child may have the courage to write about a worry before being able to verbalize the "unspeakable" possibility of a parent's drug abuse or terminal illness (Demb, 1993).

Anthony (1964) provides descriptions of ways in which a clinician can enter the child's world of play, for example, by taking on roles assigned by the child. By participating in playing out a child's conflicts and fantasies, the clinician gains an understanding of the child and simultaneously allows the child both to abreact some of his or her pain and to feel understood.

Telling a story by child and clinician taking turns and building on what the other has said can be both enjoyable for the child and informative to the clinician. Gardner (1971) describes a variety of other ways in which mutual storytelling games can be used to enhance communication with children.

With an older child whose language is limited because of an impairment or whose intelligence is more generally limited, a forced-choice technique involving yes-or-no responses can be used to gather information, while a simple comment such as "I bet you felt sad" can build an empathic bridge between child and clinician. Indeed, even children who are facile with language benefit from the clinician assigning words to feelings—in contrast to adults, who would be offended by being told they are angry while expressing that feeling.

Board games such as checkers can provide the backdrop against which issues of competition can be explored. Such activities provide a setting that allows a child to feel safe in the presence of a clinician without being overwhelmed by the pressure to speak. Within this nonthreatening context, surprising and unrelated material sometimes will emerge. More directive games can be used with children, either individually or in groups. In Creative Therapeutics' Talking, Feeling, and Doing Game (1973), for example, children spin a counter and advance their tokens around a game board in return for responding to questions about what makes them the most angry or what their most frightening experience was.

Clinical Mistakes

Whether drawing, playing with dolls or puppets, writing, storytelling, playing board games, or simply talking, the goal remains the same: to understand the child and to use that understanding constructively. In the spontaneity of clinical encounters, however, it is not uncommon for clinicians to utter communications that would not pass their own thoughtful threshold of acceptability. The bad news is that we all make mistakes. The good news is that such errors can be corrected and accompanied by apologies, which simultaneously model for the youngster the benefits to be derived from acknowledging mistakes and the prosocial renewing contribution of pursuing redemption. For example, in the course of an extended discussion, the clinician's empathic interest had enabled a 12-year-old girl to talk for the first time about the death of her grandmother. Soon the girl communicated that she did not attend school for a year following the grandmother's demise. The clinician had been moved deeply during the earlier discussion; now, in response to the girl's admission of a year's truancy and influenced by a combination of weariness and the eager anticipation of a forthcoming vacation, he blurted out "that was some long vacation." It was only after apologizing and recognizing that it must have been a very difficult year for her and far from a vacation that the clinical communication returned to its earlier productive course.

Physical Setting and Interview Sequence

Just as clinicians have different interviewing styles, they also furnish their offices differently. Some prefer an austere setting with little more than perhaps paper, pencil, and a dollhouse at hand. Others prefer a rich array of games, toys, construction paper, paint, glue, and scissors along with dolls and puppets, both racially and, perhaps anatomically correct. There are no right or wrong styles, but certain setups can prove to be a better match for certain children. For example, a hyperactive 4-year-old might devote an entire 45-minute interview to moving frenetically from one toy to another, with the clinician having little more than a disordered office when the interview is over. By contrast, an inhibited 3-year-old in the same setting may disregard all but a single doll, which may be held quietly and rocked for the entire interview unless interrupted from this reverie in an effort to achieve a more productive exchange. Older children and adolescents may feel uncomfortable in the presence of "babyish" things; it is therefore useful to maintain a certain flexibility in the office arrangements and to conceal what is not needed at that time.

Just as the clinician follows the lead of the child in conducting an interview, so too must the clinician sometimes follow the child's lead in deciding the sequence and participants that will best serve the clinical goal. At childhood's two extremes, different strategies tend to maximize the fruitfulness of clinical communication. With the very young it is often wisest to meet with the child and parent(s) or other caregiver simultaneously. Young children benefit from the supportive presence of familiar adults. The parent(s) may leave after the young child develops comfort with the clinician. Similar strategies apply to older children burdened with separation anxiety. In adolescence, on the other hand, the clinician should consider carefully whether to meet initially with the youngster, the parent(s), or the entire family. The challenge to the clinician is avoiding being cast in the role of a parental agent while at the same time striving to be the youngster's professional ally without alienating the parents.

Beyond noting that scene and sequence should be considered in the context of advancing the goal of understanding the youngster, there are no hard and fast rules governing sequence any more than there are precise rules about how best to furnish the interview room. Other chapters discuss developmental influences on clinical assessment/intervention strategy planning processes and provide suggestions to enhance the quality of the assessment interview and mental status assessment of youngsters. To maximize the utility of that information, the clinician must strive to establish a communicative bridge with the young patient.

REFERENCES

Anthony, E. J. (1964). Communicating therapeutically with the child. *Journal of the American Academy of Child Psychiatry, 3*, 106–125.

Creative Therapeutics. 1973. *The talking, feeling and doing game: A psychotherapeutic game for children.* Cresskill, NJ: Author.

Demb, J. (1993). The written word in psychotherapy with a latency age girl. *Journal of the American Academy of Child and Adolescent Psychiatry, 32* (5), 1028–1031.

Di Leo, J. (1973). *Children's drawings as diagnostic aids.* New York: Brunner/Mazel.

Gardner, R. A. (1971). *Therapeutic communication with children: The mutual storytelling technique.* New York: Jason Aronson.

Greenspan, S. I. (1992). *Infancy and early childhood: The practice of clinical assessment and intervention with emotional and developmental challenges.* Madison, WI: International Universities Press.

Harrison, S. I. (1964). Communicating with children in psychotherapy. *International Psychiatry Clinics, 1*, 39–52.

Koppitz, E. M. (1968). *Psychological evaluation of children's human figure drawings.* New York: Grune & Stratton.

Millar, S. (1968). *The psychology of play.* Hardsmondsworth: Penguin.

Saint-Exupéry, A. (1943). *The little prince.* New York: Reynal & Hitchcock.

Winnicott, D. W. (1971). *Therapeutic consultations in child psychiatry.* New York: Basic Books.

Woltmann, A. G. (1951). The use of puppetry as a projective method in therapy. In H. H. Anderson & G. L. Anderson (Eds.), *An introduction to projective techniques and other devices for understanding the dynamics of human behavior.* New York: Prentice Hall, pp. 606–638.

5 / Communicating with Adolescents

Robert L. Hendren and Barry Sarvet

Much like the developmental phase of adolescence, communication with adolescents can be interesting, enlightening, and fun; or it can be challenging, frustrating, and discouraging. Adolescence is a time of rapid growth and change. At one minute, adolescents are using higher-level abstractions to communicate from an almost mature body; the next minute they are seeking childlike reassurance that their support system is still there for them. This is confusing not only for the adult attempting to communicate with the adolescent; it also is confusing for the adolescent who is struggling with a changing body and mind and with changing relationships to their environment. Successful communication with an adolescent, therefore, is facilitated by flexibility, openness, genuine interest, and a sense of humor.

The interview with an adolescent usually is improved when based on an understanding of the developmental position of adolescence between childhood and adulthood. As Chapter 4 describes, the purpose of the communication between a clinician and a child usually occurs at the request of a parent or the school. The young child is not in the therapist's office of his or her own volition. The communication of a younger child is in the present; it is direct and action-oriented. On the other hand, the communication of an adult with a clinician is usually initiated by the adult, and the area to be worked on is identified by the prospective patient. The communication with an adolescent usually does not begin so clearly. The adolescent is aware of the ostensible reason for being with the clinician; however, ambivalence and dependency conflicts may result in unclear communication. There is often a period of "checking out" the clinician. Only after this period of testing occurs does more direct communication usually become possible.

Prior to meeting with the adolescent and his or her family, it is important to consider the purpose of the communication. Is this meeting to determine the appropriateness of hospitalization or to make an evaluation for ongoing care? Will others have access to the report? How long will the clinician have to gather the information? The purpose of the communication should be reviewed with both the adolescent and the family. The clinician and the adolescent should agree about the purpose and format of the communication as soon as possible; then their decisions should be reviewed with both the adolescent and the family. However, in terms of building a relationship, there are instances where mentioning the presenting problem at the outset may be counter-productive. For example, if the problem is very embarrassing, it might be more strategic to wait until after an initial rapport is established before attempting to discuss the specific behavior. Consider the following case.

CASE EXAMPLE

Referred by his father and stepmother for defiant behavior, uncommunicativeness, and declining school performance, Robert is a 16-year-old Caucasian male, in the 11th grade, whom the parents describe as being opposed to seeing a therapist. Robert's parents requested an initial consultation without him. When they were asked for their rationale for meeting without Robert, they explained that Robert would probably be unwilling to come to the meeting. When advised that it was necessary to include Robert in the first consultation, the parents halfheartedly agreed to attempt to bring him. Robert came quite readily and, although sullen in the presence of the parents, later, when he was with the clinician alone, he was quite eager to communicate.

In arranging the first meeting, the clinician must decide whom to see in the interview and when. Often it is useful to arrange a series of meetings with various combinations of the involved persons, such as the adolescent and parents, the adolescent alone, the parents alone, and the entire family, including siblings. It is a reasonable policy, not without exceptions, to see the adolescent along with the parents first, then proceed to see the adolescent alone. A meeting with the parents alone first may lead to the adolescent feeling that the adults are banding together, leaving the youth in a vulnerable position. This situation can result in greater difficulty communicating with the adolescent. If the parents have matters to discuss regarding the adolescent, it is important that they share this information when their child is present. However, unless the adolescent has requested the meeting with the clinician, seeing him or her without the parents may not reveal all the information essential to understanding the reason for the visit. It is important to attend to the thoughtful maintenance of boundaries to ensure that the adolescent's privacy and personal integrity are properly respected.

When an adolescent is in conflict with his or her parents about the need to see a clinician, the youth might resist coming to the interview and the parents may need consultation on how they might best address this reluctance. One effective method is to advise the parents that the young person's presence is necessary to understand the problem as perceived by the family. The parents also may be advised that the adolescent is likely to be anxious about coming to such a meeting. The youngster may be reassured by a general description of the interview process, including a statement that he or she would participate in the discussion regarding whether he or she and the family will need to return. The assurance that going for an evaluation is not committing to a longer-term process and that the young person will be included in the decision-making process often can convince the reluctant adolescent to try one meeting. After the youngster is in the office, the clinician's communication skills can make the idea of subsequent visits, should they be necessary, more palatable.

The adolescent's issues of privacy and confidentiality, wishes for autonomy as well as possible anger and resentment toward parents and authority figures need to be balanced against issues of safety, the need for the parents to set limits, the minor's legal status, and blatant or hidden dependency needs. The clinician's excessive reassurances about confidentiality actually may generate suspicion. A straightforward conveyance of a respectful attitude with an indication of the plan for communication with the parents is worthwhile. Discussing the plan to invite the parents' collaboration will implicitly reassure the adolescent about

confidentiality. If the clinician feels obliged to share a safety concern with parents, the adolescent should be informed of this intent directly.

The ease of communication with adolescents varies over time, with them appearing quite different from one meeting to the next, depending on anxiety, familiarity, and the vicissitudes of their lives. If a youth exhibits these shifts in communication, the clinician may want to consider more than one meeting with the adolescent in order to glean more knowledge about his or her behaviors and emotions.

Developmental Factors Influencing Communication

For the great majority of adolescents, the loosening of dependent emotional and practical ties to primary childhood figures is a central issue in their life. This loosening of ties may be stormy and filled with conflict; at times it may involve rejection, ambivalent engagement, or needy, demanding postures. During the interview, to the extent that the clinician is seen as akin to parental figures, the adolescent may assume a similarly rejecting or manipulative stance. On the other hand, the professional may be viewed not as a parental figure but as a resource from the outside world who offers an opportunity for transition toward a status of greater autonomy. More than likely, the clinician will be regarded in both ways, perhaps with one view or the other predominating at a given point in time.

To avoid highlighting the parental stance, the clinician should assume a calm, straightforward approach, neither especially nurturing nor especially clever or intuitive. An excessively nurturing style stimulates a fear of dependence and is likely to encourage the adolescent to regress. Also, using insights gained from experience in living or working with adolescents to make piercing, quickly intuitive comments about a youth's inner emotions may provoke early childhood fantasies of parental omnipotence. These, in turn, give rise to feelings of helplessness, which adolescents experience as a violation of their boundaries. This confusion within the adolescent can result in the communication becoming more of a contest than an exchange or, alternatively, a regressive "friendship." Let us consider Robert's case again.

When seen alone, Robert complained bitterly of his parents' intrusive and critical stance. However, he also reported using his father's car without permission, coming home long after curfew, and frequently being caught lying to his parents regarding his whereabouts. Confronting him about the way in which he invites his parents' intrusiveness with his untruthful behavior would have run the risk of creating a power struggle in respect to the communication. Instead, the clinician conveyed a sense of puzzlement over the irresponsible behavior. Robert was able to share in this puzzlement and became intrigued with his own motivations.

Depending on whether the youths are in early, middle, or late adolescence, there is variability in their ability to identify how they feel or what they believe. Sincere interest in their way of seeing the world is the key to learning about them. For example, an expression of interest in an adolescent's newly acquired philosophical views not only conveys a useful attitude of benevolent curiosity but also provides opportunities to appreciate his or her values, feelings, and cognitive functions.

Anxiety related to sexual impulses and bodily changes commonly complicates the relationship between the clinician and the young person regardless of the gender mix of the adult and adolescent. These complications are not usually explicitly sexual. For example, a young person may feel embarrassed or self-conscious with the interviewer and not be aware of the reason. It is difficult to predict at the outset of treatment whether a given adolescent may feel more comfortable with a clinician of a particular gender. An adolescent's fears of homosexual impulses, incestuous impulses, and parental jealousy and judgment may lead to painful states of anxiety during the interview; these can be exacerbated by behaviors that might be interpreted as seductive. When the professional tries too hard to engage an adolescent by conveying an excessive interest or by attempting to relate as if he or she is the adolescent's peer, there is a risk of appearing seductive. On the other hand, adolescents' anxieties about sexuality may be contagious and lead the clinician to the evasive path of avoiding the issue entirely, an equally unfruitful alternative. Questions about sexual experience and fantasy do not necessarily

lead to disruption in the relationship with an adolescent after the uncomfortable early stages of the interview and may allay anxieties by conveying to the young person that this aspect of his or her life can be discussed without the clinician being shocked or judgmental.

Important Clinical Components of the Interview

In interviewing an adolescent, the clinician must be flexible in order to facilitate the building of rapport and to allow a natural unfolding of information, including unforeseen issues. However, the interview may be structured around a basic plan to obtain the most comprehensive picture of the adolescent and the presenting problems. The structure also lends an orderly quality to the interview, thus reducing the adolescent's anxiety and fear of regression.

Skillful communication with an adolescent involves careful observation of his or her appearance, including stature, sexual development, physical anomalies, anxiety, attention, dress, and mannerisms. Data gleaned from the manner of relating include the adolescent's separation from the parents and from the clinician, friendliness, behavior, language and speech, and relationships to family, peers, and pets. These observations can help the clinician to identify key issues and themes early, and then to use these to guide the process and content of the communication. Let us consider Robert again.

Robert came to the first interview wearing a T-shirt proclaiming "Better living through chemistry." Initially, this alerted the interviewer to the possibility of drug usage. A casual comment about the slogan on the T-shirt lead to a rich discussion of Robert's identification with the culture of the 1960s and with his father's "hippie life" when he and Robert's mother were in college together.

The adolescent should be invited to present his or her understanding of the purpose of the meeting. The clinician should follow the discourse closely, and allow questions to emerge naturally from the points that the youth raises. It is helpful to ask for clarification and expansion of aspects of the adolescent's discourse. At the same time, the interviewer must avoid "the third degree" or rapid-fire questions. The clinician will need to allow the adolescent opportunities to tell his or her story but gently ask questions to avoid awkward silences. It is important to explore the various realms of the adolescent's life. Another avenue for learning about the adolescent is allowing him or her to be the teacher. For example, if the clinician does not feign familiarity with popular culture, the youth is given the opportunity to explain their view. Family life, peer relationships, school and work, special interests, and fantasies merit discussion. Although adolescents may be reluctant to share fantasies directly, in order to gain access to fantasy material, the clinician may inquire about dreams, beliefs, wishes, and activities involving the imagination, such as favorite stories, films, television viewing, music, and daydreaming. Even in the context of seemingly global difficulties, it is worthwhile for the clinician to show an interest in areas of success and enjoyment in the adolescent's life and to explore them thoroughly.

Adolescents often are surprisingly willing to engage in play if it is not presented in an infantalizing manner. Leaving a variety of play materials around the interview room, such as paper with crayons, playing cards, and a doll with changeable clothes can accommodate a reasonably wide range of play. Adolescents may gravitate to the play materials while at the same time disdaining them. Urging an adolescent to play may threaten his or her fragile sense of maturity or stimulate anxiety associated with regressive wishes. Quiet observance of the adolescent's interest or a gentle suggestion about engagement in a shared activity often works best.

The nature of the rapport established is the result of the clinician's response to the adolescent's emotions. Empathy for the adolescent's emotions can be an effective rapport-building skill. Suggesting a label for the emotion might begin with "It sounds like . . ." or "I wonder if . . ." and end with the inflection of a question. This allows the adolescent to correct an inaccurate guess (or deny a painful emotion) and conveys a desire to "get it right." It also verbally and nonverbally fosters the supportive collaborative partnership and legitimizes the adolescent's feeling. It is important that these suggestions be offered with an attitude of

positive regard and respect, and that they avoid placing a value judgment on the feeling.

The use of thoughtful commentary can convey a benevolent interest in the adolescent through the clinician's active involvement, thus motivating both the clinician and the young person to seek further understanding. Commentary may be in the form of a clarification or an interpretation; however, the clinician should avoid the risk of being too quick to offer an interpretation of linkages out of conscious awareness, which can make the adolescent more guarded. The commentary might also be offered in other ways—in the form of a summation or reflection; in the form of an association; or as a reminder to the adolescent of something said previously that is relevant to the current topic.

At the conclusion of the interview, the adolescent and the family should be asked for their reactions to it. An opportunity should be provided to ask questions, offer revisions, and address any area not already discussed. The adolescent should be told of the next possible step and be invited to participate in the formulation of recommendations. If a report to an outside person or agency is required, the content of this communication should be discussed with the adolescent and the parents.

Process of the Interview

Successful communication with adolescents is enhanced by paying close attention to the process of the interview. Process, as opposed to the actual verbal content, is the sensitivity and sensibility that evolves, often beneath the surface, during communication. It is evidenced by shifts in topics, interruptions in communication, body language, and in repetition or avoidance. The communication during the interview consists of language and nonverbal communication, including play. Questions invite speculation and imagination. These questions may be quite engaging to adolescents, who tend to be fascinated with their own thinking and imagination. Adolescents tend to scrutinize others carefully and may be quite sensitive to expressed interests and inferred intentions. In order to convey a benevolent interest, questions should avoid focusing on the negative. We return again to Robert.

During the interview, Robert tore up a piece of paper into smaller and smaller pieces, especially when talking about his parents. Toward the end of the meeting, Robert walked to a wastebasket near the clinician's desk and hurled the paper scraps into the container. The interviewer used this symbolic communication to ask further questions about the divorce of Robert's parents 2 years earlier.

The interviewer or the adolescent may respond to the other with a feeling going beyond what is actually known about the other person. These so-called transference and countertransference reactions describe how the clinician or the young person may react to the other based on important past experiences with other significant people rather than on the reality of the current transaction. This situation introduces a distortion that can disrupt the communication. These concepts are discussed in detail in other chapters. The adolescent often will associate the clinician with parents and with authority figures, despite the clinician's efforts to avoid this association. This association may occur even if the clinician is only slightly older than the adolescent. On the other hand, clinicians may either identify with the adolescent through reminders of their own adolescence or identify with the parents through the adolescent's challenge to authority. Overidentification with the parents can lead to engagement in unproductive power struggles with the adolescent. Overidentification with the adolescent can lead to behavior in the clinician that may appear to be seductive and overly eager to please. These feelings of identification also can lead to passivity in the clinician or to feelings of envy and competition. In most cases, these feelings are normal and acceptable when recognized, as long as they do not lead to disturbances in the relationship with the adolescent.

Special Challenges in the Clinical Process

THE UNCOMMUNICATIVE ADOLESCENT

Lack of communication is a common complaint among parents of adolescents; therefore, it is not surprising that this issue comes up during many clinical encounters. An adolescent who does not speak over the course of an interview presents an extraordinary challenge to the clinician. Such uncommunicativeness is usually derived from anxiety or anger, the source of which often can be observed through nonverbal cues. Questions should be framed and structured carefully, progressing from direct, nonthreatening questions to open-ended ones. An overly friendly approach should be avoided since the lack of communication may be related to conflicts about intimacy. When the uncommunicativeness is a manifestation of anger, the clinician may be lured into conflict with the adolescent, either by playing a waiting game or by attempting to set firm limits. This is a battle the clinician cannot win. Maintaining a steady, unruffled, inquisitive approach may be useful. Verbally acknowledging that the adolescent does indeed have control over involvement in the interview often is disarming.

In response to an uncommunicative adolescent, the clinician may become angry at the seeming lack of cooperation and challenge to sincere efforts to learn about him or her. Often recognition of these feelings of frustration can help reduce the mounting tension. When the feeling is overlooked, it may lead to a premature curtailment of the session or to retaliatory uncommunicativeness. Alternatively, the clinician may become overzealous, leading to an intrusive approach that the adolescent may experience as overbearing or frightening. It also may increase anxiety, resulting in the adolescent becoming even more uncomfortable. Prolonged silences are to be avoided. Efforts to engage the youth in some sort of expressive activity should be maintained. Alternative methods of expression, such as art materials, might be introduced to help the adolescent get started with verbal communication.

THE ADOLESCENT WITH "NO PROBLEM"

The adolescent with "no problem" is a variation on the uncommunicative adolescent. There usually is similar fear of exposing vulnerability. The adolescent also may be attempting to draw the interviewer into conflict with the parents, who are often portrayed as unduly concerned or overly critical. Assuming a nonjudgmental, naive attitude may be reassuring to an adolescent who may see the interviewer as an agent of the parents. Information the clinician learned from other sources may be introduced matter-of-factly without the adolescent feeling confronted. It is also helpful for the clinician to focus the interview on the adolescent's subjective experience rather than making it a fact-finding mission. The facts, whatever they may be, can be sought in other contexts. These adolescents will need proof that clinicians are concerned, primarily with helping them, not simply carrying out the parents' agenda. Therefore, with the "no-problem" adolescent, special attention to confidentiality is important. Informing the adolescent about what information will be conveyed to the parents is especially important in communicating with the guarded adolescent.

THE SEDUCTIVE ADOLESCENT

Seductive behavior by either a male or female adolescent may be frankly overt, or it may be quite subtle and veiled, manifested by a strong interest in the clinician. In response, a clinician may be tempted quickly to adopt a defensive posture, possibly including an observer or chaperone in the interview for medicolegal protection. While this may ultimately be considered necessary, such a defensive posture on the part of the clinician may stymie the interview process, convey a fear of the adolescent, and jeopardize confidentiality. Alternatively, an observer's presence could reassure the adolescent. Especially with seductive adolescents,

it is important for the clinician to establish and maintain appropriate boundaries early in the interview. The clinician must avoid even casual physical contact with the adolescent. Self-disclosure should be avoided as well. The interviewer may simply decline to answer personal questions during the interview or answer questions in a general, reassuring manner, thus acknowledging the question yet keeping the focus on the goal of the interview.

Conclusion

For the young person who is trying to make the transition from childhood to adulthood, adolescence is a confusing stage of development, even under the best of conditions. Therefore, it is not surprising to discover there are special issues to face while trying to communicate with an adolescent. All clinicians make mistakes during their communications with adolescents. It is important to view these mistakes as a path to a better understanding of good communication and interviewing skills; and, indeed, addressing these errors may lead to a deeper understanding of adolescents. It is hoped that the guidelines set forth in this chapter will help make encounters with adolescents an enjoyable, although still-challenging experience.

REFERENCES

American Academy of Child and Adolescent Psychiatry. (1995). *Practice Parameters for the Diagnostic Assessment of Children and Adolescents.* Washington, DC: Author.

Colby, A., & Kohlberg, L. (1987). *The measurement of moral judgment, Vol. 1: Theoretical foundations and research validation.* Cambridge: Cambridge University Press.

Erikson, E. (1963). *Childhood and society.* New York: W. W. Norton.

Fraiberg, S. (1955). Some considerations in the introduction to therapy in puberty. *Psychoanalytic Study of the Child, 10,* 264–286.

Freud, A. (1958). Adolescence. *Psychoanalytic Study of the Child, 13,* 255–278.

Freud, A. (1965). *Normality and pathology in childhood: Assessment of development.* New York: International Universities Press.

Freud, A. (1968). On certain difficulties in the preadolescent's relationship to his parents. In *The writings of Anna Freud* (Vol. 4, pp. 95–106). New York: International Universities Press.

Hendren, R. L., & Phelps, J. (1995). Communication and interviewing. In J. M. Wiener, N. A. Breslin (Eds.), *Behavioral sciences in psychiatry* (3rd ed., pp. 203–218). Philadelphia: Williams & Wilkins.

Piaget, J. (1952). *The origins of intelligence in children.* New York: International Universities Press.

6 / Engaging Parents in Clinical Processes

Saul L. Brown

Acknowledging the Need for Clinical Help

When parents become aware that all is not well with their child, they become more attentive to the stories they may have heard from friends or relatives about serious psychiatric disorders in children and they begin to seek out information about psychological dysfunction. As this evolves invasive and sometimes terrifying questions not uncommonly enter their minds: Could our child be autistic? Is the problem Attention Deficit Disorder? What about Tourette's, or an Obsessive Compulsive Disorder, or a predisposition to a Bipolar Disorder? Is our teenager suicidal? These and other diagnostic categories are no longer hidden away in psychiatric textbooks and medical journals. They have become a part of the current stream of information available to everyone, and parents with greater education or psychological sophistication are especially vulnerable to thinking of these possibilities and what the consequences might be for their own and their child's future. Along with this is the inevitable question, "What have we done wrong?" The fear of stigma may be extremely stressful for many parents.

Not all parents are affected in this way. Those who have benefited at some time from clinical help for themselves or who have been close to the positive experiences of friends or family members are likely to be less frightened and may even be optimistic about obtaining professional help for their child.

Finding Appropriate Help

With the decision to obtain professional help comes the uncertainty about where to find it. What kind of mental health professional is appro-

priate, and whom can they trust? Where should they go? While pediatricians and family physicians may have some suggestions, they are not always knowledgeable about the best resource for a specific problem. For the parents the route ahead often seems hazardous. Adding to this is the flow of commentaries about mental health clinicians in newspapers and magazines, on television, in films, stories, and novels, and in the varied opinions of relatives and acquaintances. Jokes and caricatures abound and may evoke new anxieties in the parents as they approach an initial meeting with a clinician.

Initial Expectations of the Clinical Process

CIRCUMSTANCES AFFECTING THE PARENTS' PARTICIPATION

The educational as well as the cultural and the socioeconomic background of the parents strongly influence how they perceive the clinical situation and what they expect from it. Those who seek educational guidance expect the clinician to be a benign teacher and believe they will receive specific advice. They may become openly or covertly disappointed if this is not immediately forthcoming. Alternatively, some who are from an authoritarian subculture may look for firm directive leadership and will not feel reassured by a clinician whose style is more subtle.

Many parents come to the clinical situation with the hope that a medication will resolve the problem and become confused and, in some instances, angry, if this is not offered. Others have exactly the opposite view and are automatically resistant to any suggestion of medication.

Those who have had prior contact with the mental health profession are likely to be aware that the help they will find for their child's problem may not necessarily begin with specific suggestions or advice from the clinician. Even so, most parents want to be told or even hope to observe what the clinician actually does with their child and become suspicious or intrusive if they are excluded from the sessions. This is a particularly sensitive issue for parents of adolescents, since, typically, adolescents are jealous of their privacy and expect confidentiality. It may be no less the case with younger children. Parents may resent being "left out" in those situations, while others believe their adolescent is "manipulating" the clinician by insisting on privacy.

For parents of children of all ages, the experience of sitting in a waiting room while something unknown is going on in the clinical office can be troubling. This is especially so for those who have their own inner problems with separation and at times may lead to an impulse to interrupt the clinical effort.

EXPECTING TO BE JUDGED

Interwoven with the parents' expectations are complex feelings that inevitably underlie their entry into this new experience. Sometimes these cause the parents to perceive reactions or attitudes in the clinician that may not be accurate. Embarrassment and an undercurrent of shame are not uncommon, especially in parents who have made great effort to do "all the right things." Some parents characterize the experience as feeling like a child who has been brought to the school principal. They expect the clinician will see their imperfections and make judgments of them. This is particularly so in situations when the parents have lost control and have acted out their rage. While this is not uncommon with adolescents whose repetitive rebellious or oppositional behavior has become disruptive to the functioning of the whole family, it also may occur in reaction to the stubborn assertiveness of 2- or 3-year-olds.

THE PARENTS' INNER FEELINGS

Parental Feelings of Having Failed: Depression is not an unusual state of feeling in parents coming to the clinical situation. It arises from the deep sense of helplessness that builds over time as they see that their child is not developing at the same pace as others of the same age and the problematic behavior is ongoing and unrelenting. Depression also often accompanies the parents' belief that they have failed to do "all the right things." It is particularly poignant in mothers who have needed to go to work or who have elected to pursue professional careers very early in their child's life, leaving much of the rearing to day care or employed caregivers, a not uncommon situation in single-parent households, but also is those in which both parents are deeply involved in their own careers or work demands.

The Need for Mutual Validation, Parent with Child: When the sense of pleasure and the mutual validation that arise from a warm reciprocity of good feeling between parent and child become disrupted for whatever reason, the end result is diminished self-esteem and emotional suffering for both. Each feels devalued by the other. An immediate and ongoing challenge for the clinician is to discover ways that can help them establish a continuous flow of mutual validation.

External Events: Less threatening to the parents' self-esteem are the problematic behaviors or the distress in their child that are related to a discrete event or situation, as with stress reactions to natural disasters—earthquakes, floods, hurricanes, fires, violence in school or the neighborhood—or from losses—as with the death of a beloved family member or friend or a cherished pet, or the departure of a longtime caregiver. These are definitively external to the parent-child relationship, and the parents usually do not feel as if they have caused the child's reactions.

Physical Dysfunctions: Nor do parents usually feel guilty when the child's problems are clearly a result of developmental lags or failures related to physical deficits. In those cases, while the pain in the parents is ultimately no less than in other situations, it may be less permeated by the sense of guilt. When guilt is dominant, it is usually because the parents feel they delayed too long in seeking help or did not tune into their child's feelings with sufficient understanding. For some parents, guilt relates to potentially harmful behaviors during the pregnancy such as substance abuse.

Autistic Behaviors, Attention Disorders, Attachment Avoidance, Evoking Discontinuity in the Parent-Child Relationship: The unpredictability of children with these kinds of severe problems

59

leads to recurrent major discontinuities of pleasureful and validating experiences between child and parent and creates in the parents an undercurrent sense both of helplessness and loss. These feelings may not become fully conscious in the parents until they are brought forth through contact with the clinical process; they may then result in a kind of delayed bereavement.

Parental Reactions Specific to the Very Young Child: For parents of infants or very young children, awareness of problematic behavior or failure in development may be brought to them by the staff of a sophisticated day care or nursery school or by the observations reported to them by the leader of a parent-child group or by an experienced caregiver. If this occurs too quickly or with insufficient sensitivity in a day care or nursery school, a not uncommon initial reaction from the parents may be to withdraw their child resentfully and seek another setting. In those situations it may take many months or even longer for the parents to face their need for help. By this time their feelings have become compounded with embarrassment and a sense of defeat. If the staff in those settings are trained in early childhood development, they usually are deeply understanding of how exquisitely sensitive the parents of very young children are to the notion that their child is imperfect; accordingly, the staff members learn to bring such views to the parents in slow stages.

Parent Defenses: Externalizing vs. Problem Solving

DISTRACTIONS FROM EMOTIONAL PAIN

The defenses in parents that evolve to protect them from a direct awareness of their painful feelings may mislead a clinician who is not attuned to what lies under their surface behavior. Externalizing the causes of the problem to outside sources is the most common way that parents may ward off their sense of being inadequate. Projection outward distracts not only from their feelings of self-depreciation, guilt, and shame, but also (and sometimes even more difficult to acknowledge) from their profound anger at a child who has over-

burdened them and caused them to feel defeated. This occurs most dramatically in reaction to adolescents who are rebellious, acting out, or oppositional. But it may occur as well with 2-year-olds whose willfulness is beyond the parents' ability to tolerate. Parents may be inclined to blame the teachers or the school system, the adolescent's friends, or the neighborhood. While there may be some truth in any of these, this kind of defense can lead to a long delay before the parents seek appropriate professional help.

PARENTS BLAMING EACH OTHER

Not infrequently the defense parents present is mutual blaming. Each become hypersensitive to the other's failings in dealing with their child. Again, this is more vividly the case with adolescents, but it may occur at all ages. When these parents come to the clinician, they may need some time to reorient themselves from the pattern of mutual blaming to a process of problem solving. Underlying dynamics in the marital relationship may need to be reworked by the parents before they can move to a shared problem solving orientation with the clinician.

The Initial Encounter with the Clinician

PARENT INSECURITY

Not all parents experience the level of distress described in the preceding commentary and may indeed be trusting of the mental health profession. Nevertheless most are extremely sensitive to how the clinician responds to them. Even within the first few minutes of a telephone conversation subjective reactions are formed. The unwary clinician may not keep in mind the power implicit in the professional role with parents and may overlook the extent to which he or she can validate or invalidate them. This is a particularly difficult with some parents who approach the clinical situation with a provocative attitude that overlies their great emotional vulnerability and self-doubt and may evoke a negative reaction in the clinician.

Exaggerated perceptions by the parents of the clinician's response to them may be reflective of their own personality and history, but also of their past experiences with people in authority. On the other hand, clinicians do vary in their personality and communicative styles and what parents perceive may not be simply a distortion. A more formal clinician elicits a different response from parents than does an informal one. Some parents may find the first more reassuring while others prefer the second. Ultimately it is the warmth and the genuineness they discern in the clinician that reassures most parents.

Some Psychodynamic Reactions in Parents

PROJECTION OF BLAME

Once their child is involved in the clinical process there is a great potential for parents to experience a variety of unsettling reactions. Not the least of these are profound shame and embarrassment over what they feel to be their failings as parents now open to an expert's view. Close to these are feelings of guilt. These feelings are especially powerful and disruptive for those parents who are extremely demanding of competence in themselves and who now anticipate criticism or judgment from the clinician.

DEFERRING TO A "MORE COMPETENT" PARENT

A particular difficulty for parents of very young children is the feeling that they are giving their child over to a "more competent" parent, i.e., the clinician. Ancient doubts from their own childhood about their competence may become reawakened and lead to a depressive reaction, sometimes obscured by overt competitiveness with the clinician. Their essentially unconscious competitiveness may lead them to miss appointments or forget to tell the clinician of an imminent vacation, or bring their child to appointments late, or fail to arrive on time to pick the child up, or even abruptly terminate the clinical intervention.

PARENTS' COMPETITION FOR THE GOOD PARENT

Parents who have experienced significant emotional deprivation in their own early years may react to the warmth and ease of the clinician with their child with longings for a good parent for themselves; in effect, they become unconsciously competitive with their child for the clinician's attention. This can evoke a distancing reaction from the clinician whose principal focus is on the child.

PARENTAL PROBLEMS WITH SEPARATION AND BOUNDARIES

Parents for whom boundaries in relationships have been problematic or who have had great difficulty with separation from a parent in their early childhood may find it difficult to take their child to a professional, even for the relatively short time of each clinical session. Such feelings sometimes can lead to a disruption of the process by the parent bringing the child late for the sessions or canceling sessions for trivial reasons.

PARENTAL ANGER TOWARD THEIR CHILD

The powerful feelings set off by adolescent oppositional behavior or conduct disorders may evoke deep anger in parents who hope to find an ally in the clinician.

FEELING EXCLUDED

The necessity for the clinician to develop a trusting relationship with the adolescent may cause some parents to feel left out and create an antagonism that can subvert the progress of the intervention. Something similar may evolve when a much younger child is involved in an intensive long-term intervention that does not include direct contact with the parents. These clinical situations demand great sensitivity and tact on the part of the clinician.

THE DYNAMICS OF THE MARITAL RELATIONSHIP

The balance of the marital relationship is sometimes affected by the involvement of the family with a new person—the clinician. An obvious example of this is when the parents' preoccupation with their child's problem serves as a means of avoiding direct confrontation of problems with each other. Other complex situations occur, for example, where a parent selects one child as a favorite with resulting parent-child misalliances. The over involvement with the child on the part of one parent may need to be addressed in order for the clinical work to progress. When the child becomes less an object of enmeshment in the parents' emotional conflicts, the unresolved issues between the adults may then become more directly felt. This sequence is not unusual when children reach adolescence, but can occur much earlier as well.

Validation and Fulfillment for Parents

Central in becoming a parent is the anticipation of creating a perfectly formed newborn infant. For those who are seriously committed to their roles as parents, the days and months and years of family life bring deep gratification to them as they experience the progressive growth of competence in their child. To a greater or lesser degree, parents always sense their child as a representation of themselves. Their child's imperfections inevitably are felt as their own. When disabilities or dysfunctions in their child appear early or evolve over time, the parents feel this as loss. They lose the perfect body and the successful function they had fantasied for their child, and they lose a deep internal validation of themselves as well.

When the problem in their child is severe or not totally reversible, a kind of bereavement takes place in the parents; while it may not always become conscious to the parents, it is essential for the clinician to understand this. As with all loss and bereavement, the pain is less when hope can replace it. If the sensitivity of the clinician succeeds in guiding parents through these profound issues of self esteem and of loss, the genuine working relationship that evolves from this gives hope to the parents and to their child.

SUGGESTED READINGS

Brown, S. (1978). *Functions, tasks, and stresses of parenting: Implications for Guidance in helping parents help their children*, L. E. Arnold (pp. 22–34). New York: Brunner/Mazel.

Brown, W., Thruman, S. K., Pearl, L. (1993). *Family-centered early interventions with Infants and Toddlers*, Baltimore: Paul H. Brokes.

Cooper, M. (1996). Obsessive-compulsive disorder: effects on family members, *American Journal of Orthopsychiatry* 66: 296–304.

Cunningham, C., Benness, B. B., & Siegel, L. (1988). Family functioning, time allocation, and parental depression in the families of normal and ADHD children. *Journal of Clinical Child Psychology 17*, 169–177.

McGregor, P. (1994). Grief: The unrecognized parental response to mental illness in a child. *Social Work 39*, 160–165.

Rodriques, J. R., Morgan, S. B., Geffken, G. (1990). Families of Autistic Children, *Journal of Clinical Psychology, 19*: 371–379.

Schnitzer, P. K. (1996). They don't come in, stories told, lessons taught about poor families in therapy. *American Journal of Orthopsychiatry, 66*: 562–581.

7 / Clinical Use of Interpreters

William Arroyo

Clinicians use various methods to understand patients' problems. The most widely used method is direct verbal communication. In child and adolescent psychiatry where the use of multiple informants is the rule, establishing several lines of communication is indicated. These include lines of communication among the clinician, the child, the family, and other informants.

Verbal communication between patient and doctor is predominantly influenced by culture. In the situation in which the physician and patient are not from the same culture, we can assume that at least 2 cultures will influence this complex interaction between the patient and the physician. The salient elements of this complex cross-cultural interchange include the language(s) spoken by the patient and the doctor, their health belief systems, the style of communication (including nonverbal elements), and the expectations of both the patient and the clinician. Often an interpreter is an important element of this complex interchange.

Role of the Interpreter

The limited body of psychiatric literature dealing with the role of the interpreter relates almost exclusively to the adult population (Marcos, 1975; Oquendo, 1996).

Interpretation is a complex process in which the denotative and connotative aspects of communication are conveyed from one source (or person) to another by some means, which in clinical settings is often an interpreter. The mere translation of the word or statements is often insufficient for the process of interpretation; the corresponding affect also must be conveyed (Marcos, 1975; Westermeyer, 1987). The interpreter's role often evolves into a complex one, one that extends beyond conveying verbal communication to the clinician. These roles relate to the relationships

between the interpreter and the other parties involved (Westermeyer, 1987), namely, the clinician, the family, and child. The quality of these various and different working relationships will determine in large part the outcome of the care provided. The interpreter often assumes the role of the primary contact person for the child and family and the cultural peer to the child's parents. The interpreter also may fill the role of service broker for other related services, such as health and education. Therefore, often the interpreter assumes a crucial role in the treatment team and acts in concert with the clinician. Thus the clinician needs to be aware of the quality of relationship between the interpreter and the family. Ideally the interpreter should be familiar with the clinician's own culture besides that of the family. The interpreter should be readily able to discuss the uniqueness of the cultural group especially as it pertains to help-seeking behaviors, the common idiomatic expressions of psychological distress within that particular group, socialization of children, and the roles of the different family members as prescribed by their particular culture. Often using the same interpreter by both the clinician and the patient in ongoing treatment is preferred, especially when good working relationships have been established.

The interpreter must adopt an approach to patients that is consistent with the clinician's role. For example, the interpreter must assume the empathic posture that ordinarily a clinician would convey in a clinical encounter. This is very different from the role of someone who has a very restricted function, for example, one who merely translates. As the use of an interpreter generally increases the amount of time expended in working with a patient, sufficient time must be allocated to achieve the treatment goal. Kline, Acosta, Austin, and Johnson (1980) concluded that despite the concerns and frustration noted by psychiatric residents in the use of interpreters, the patients themselves were generally pleased with the encounters, perceiving the residents as making a special effort to more fully understand their suffering via an interpreter.

Just prior to each session, often it is useful for the interpreter and the clinician to meet to discuss an agenda for the subsequent session; after the session, they should meet to minimize any distortions and misunderstandings, especially at the outset of the treatment of a particular family (Westermeyer, 1987).

The clinician must weigh various factors prior to deciding to use an interpreter. In the case of an immigrant child and a family, for example, the parents' degree of language fluency in the clinician's language separate from that the child's fluency must be determined. It is not uncommon for the young immigrant child to become much more fluent in the new language than the parents. An interpreter who shares the same primary language and culture is generally better than one who simply speaks the language. When a qualified interpreter is unavailable, although the practice of soliciting the identified patient or another family member as interpreter may be expedient, in general, it should be discouraged, for reasons to be discussed; there are infrequent exceptions to this guideline.

Interpreters often have widely divergent backgrounds, including training and fluency in the patient's primary language (Vasquez & Javier, 1991; Westermeyer, 1993). They may include professional staff, nonprofessional staff, volunteers, family members, friends, native-speaking telephone operators, and on rare occasions fully trained translators. The skills of an interpreter in clinical work are rarely assessed by a standard relevant to their important role.

Bilingualism

Three of the more salient issues relevant to bilingualism are the following. First, according to several authors, the period during which a patient learns the language that he or she uses in treatment has implications for that treatment (Buxbaum, 1949; Marcos & Alpert, 1976). These authors strongly suggest that both the cultural and developmental contexts of learning languages have special implications for psychotherapy; this

work is described primarily with reference to adult populations. For example, the words used to describe a particular traumatic event from childhood may have much more emotional resonance for the patient when described in the patient's primary language than in the language that learned after emigration. Oquendo (1996) opines that bilingual patients should be evaluated in both languages. This author, who is bilingual in Spanish and English, notes that in his clinical experience with a group of bilingual adolescents whose primary language is Spanish, the group shares more obvious emotional resonance when certain concepts are expressed in Spanish than in English.

Secondly, the degree of bilingualism often varies greatly within the same family. The monolingual novice clinician may conclude that an interpreter may not be useful in working with bilingual families whose secondary language is the same as his or hers. However, clinical experience indicates that a bilingual family periodically resorts to their primary language without fully interpreting these discussions to the treating clinician. Before a clinician decides whether to use an interpreter in the treatment of a bilingual family, the family should be given the option of including an interpreter. Usually family members agree not to have an interpreter and agree to speak in the clinician's language throughout the clinical sessions.

Thirdly, clinicians are cautioned (Marcos & Alpert, 1976; Pitta, Marcos, & Alpert, 1978) that bilingual patients in psychotherapy may resort to the use of their secondary language to defend against feelings that would be difficult to fend off if they spoke their primary language; Pitta, Marcos, and Alpert (1978) suggest that a bilingual clinician may be strategically more effective in this situation than a monolingual clinician who only speaks the patient's secondary language.

Potential Pitfalls

Nonprofessional staff who are not reimbursed for their interpretation skills often are reluctant to engage in this activity when their other duties await their return from lengthy interpretation sessions. Those who have not had special training in the terminology commonly used in psychiatry and are not familiar with cultural aspects relevant to the patient are less likely to describe adequately the condition with which a child presents and/or the response to a specific intervention. It is also not uncommon in many urban areas for interpreters to have a much lower level of fluency of the language as compared to the child and his or her family.

Clinicians often falsely assume that the designated interpreter and a patient who speaks the same language share all of the same cultural influences. The interpreter may in fact be of a different country of origin, different religion, and have divergent ideas about, for example, socialization of children and the constellation of symptoms with which the child presents based on a dissimilar cultural background. In another scenario, the interpreter and the patient may be from different social classes of the same country of origin and have unique perceptions of each other's social class that ultimately may interfere with the treatment process.

Five common errors made by untrained interpreters (Vasquez and Javier, 1991) are: omission, a process by which the psychiatrist's message is completely or partially deleted; addition, the tendency for the interpreter to include information that was not mentioned by the clinician; condensation, where the interpreter oversimplifies a message; substitution, whereby an interpreter replaces a meaning or concept by another one; and role exchange, the process by which the interpreter fully assumes the role of interviewer.

The use of a child or family member as the interpreter can be fraught with problems. In the case of a young bilingual child who is the identified patient, the psychiatrist may inadvertently encourage the child to assume a role of service broker. The child's parents may view the new role as a cultural breach and the psychiatrist as culturally insensitive. In another instance, a young bilingual adolescent referred for severe behavioral problems who serves as an interpreter for monolingual parents during an intake may, for example, purposefully minimize the severity of his behavioral problems when interpreting for the clinician.

Issues related to confidentiality also may be a problem, especially if the interpreter happens to be a member of the same local community as that of the family. If the child's parents determine that indeed they are of the same community, then they may be less willing to participate. The interpreter always must agree to honor confidentiality policies and procedures.

The interpreter must be able clarify for the clinician about the shortcomings of the interpretation to either the patient or vice versa. Some concepts and words cannot be adequately translated. Different languages may have few, if any, words to represent certain emotional and mental experiences (Westermeyer, 1993).

Early in the course of the clinical encounter, the interpreter should address the family's treatment expectations, especially in cases of newly immigrated families who are very unfamiliar with psychiatric care. Cultural customs that discourage the discussion of marital discord and other "secrets" with strangers, despite what appears to be relevant to the clinical encounter, may compromise the gathering of social history. Such customs should be honored, to be revisited at some future date; otherwise the family may cease treatment.

Medical histories of all immigrants should be comprehensive. During the first interview often there must be direct inquiry about common pediatric problems endemic to the country of origin, especially in regard to those that may have concomitant behavioral or psychological manifestations.

Clinicians should appreciate that several of the integral elements of a mental status examination, such as appearance, behavior, expression of affect, proverb interpretations, and most certainly language, are to varying degrees influenced by cultural factors (Hughes, 1993). The attempt to adequately determine the presence of psychosis by interviewing the patient in the patient's primary vs. secondary language (or vice versa) in adult bilingual patients has demonstrated contradictory results (Del Castillo, 1970; Marcos et al., 1973); similar studies have not been conducted with children and adolescents. A well-trained interpreter should help the clinician understand the cultural influences on the standard mental status examination.

Clinicians are cautioned against using an untrained interpreter during play sessions. Interpreters should have more specialized training in play and related areas before serving in this function. Most interpreters can readily elicit a child's favorite play or pasttimes.

Clinicians must consider their own emotional reactions that arise during the course of the care of a child and family from another country and presumably culture. Training models in cross-cultural issues and ethnic self-awareness to enhance the cultural competence (Cross, Bazron, Dennis, & Isaacs, 1989) of clinicians are discussed elsewhere (Moffic et al., 1987; Moffic et al., 1988); such models should be integrated into professional school curricula.

REFERENCES

Buxbaum, E. (1949). The role of the second language in the formation of the ego and superego. *Psychoanalytic Quarterly 18*, 279–289.

Cross, T., Bazron, B. J., Dennis, K. W., & Isaacs, M. R. (Eds.). (1989). *Towards a culturally competent system of care.* Washington, DC: CASSP Technical Assistance Center, Georgetown University Child Development Center.

Del Castillo, J. C. (1970). The influence of language upon symptomatology in foreign-born patients. *American Journal of Psychiatry, 127,* 242–244.

Hughes, C. C. (1993). Culture in clinical psychiatry. In A. C. Gaw (Ed.), *Culture, ethnicity, & mental illness* (pp. 3–42). Washington, DC: American Psychiatric Press.

Kline, F., Acosta, F. X., Austin, W., & Johnson, R. G. (1980). The misunderstood Spanish-speaking patient. *American Journal of Psychiatry, 137,* 1530–1533.

Marcos, L. R. (1975). Effects of interpreters on the evaluation of psycho-pathology in non-English-speaking patients. *American Journal of Psychiatry, 136,* 171–174.

Marcos, L. R., & Alpert, M. (1976). Strategies and risks in psychotherapy with bilingual patients: The phenomenon of language independence. *American Journal of Psychiatry, 133,* 1275–1278.

Marcos, L. R., Alpert, M., Urcuyo, L., Kesselman, M. (1973). The effect of interview language on the eval-

uation of psychopathology in Spanish-American schizophrenic patients. *American Journal of Psychiatry, 130,* 549–553.

Moffic, H. S., Kendrick, E. A., Lomax, J. W., Reid, K. (1987). Education in cultural psychiatry in the United States. *Transcultural Psychiatric Research Review, 24,* 168–187.

Moffic, H. S., Kendrick, E. A., Reid, K., Lomax, J. W. (1988). Cultural psychiatry education during psychiatric residency. *Journal of Psychiatric Education, 12,* 90–101.

Oquendo, M. A. (1996). Psychiatric evaluation and psychotherapy in the patient's second language. *Psychiatric Services, 47,* 614–618.

Pitta, P., Marcos, L. R., & Alpert, M. (1978). Language switching as a treatment strategy with bilingual patients. *American Journal of Psychoanalysis, 38,* 255–258.

Vasquez, C., & Javier, R. A. (1991). The problem with interpreters: communicating with Spanish-speaking patients. *Hospital and Community Psychiatry, 42,* 163–164.

Westermeyer, J. (1987). Clinical considerations in cross-cultural diagnosis. *Hospital and Community Psychiatry 38,* 160–165.

Westermeyer, J. (1993). Cross-cultural psychiatric assessment. In A. C. Gaw (Ed.), *Culture, ethnicity, & mental illness* (pp. 125–146). Washington, DC: American Psychiatric Press.

8 / Experimental Concepts in Clinical Assessment

Karen C. Wells

It is the nature of clinical work in psychiatry that a patient brings the clinician some complaint of maladaptive behavior or subjective misery and seeks treatment that will supply improvement or relief. With all best intentions, that patient is treated and is expected to get better. Often there is some discriminable improvement, and clinicians would like to attribute the improvement to the treatment. However, sometimes there is a nagging sense that the patient's improvement had nothing to do with the treatment provided. Having a good theory to back up the treatment is not completely reassuring. Science is full of examples of treatments, based on popular theories of the day, that were later proven to be ineffective.

Until recently, the only place to turn for validation of various psychiatric treatments was to reports of experiments using group comparison methods. There are now several large-scale controlled outcome studies examining the efficacy of a few of the major treatments in child psychiatry. For example, large-scale and very expensive group outcome studies demonstrate that stimulant medications improve symptoms of attention deficit hyperactivity disorder (DuPaul & Barkley, 1990). There are a limited number of other examples.

However, there are many problems in relying on group experimental methods to prove that given treatments actually work. First, for the clinician working from an office practice, the cost of large numbers of homogeneous patients assigned to different treatments is out of reach.

Second, there are ethical problems in withholding treatment (even treatment that has not been proven effective) from a group of patients seeking help. Third, even if the clinician was to conduct a group comparison-based experiment, it would be unwise to conclude that the results generalize to the individual patient sitting in the office. For example, group outcome studies show that 70% of patients with attention deficit hyperactivity disorder improve on stimulant medication and 30% do not (Conners & Werry, 1979). How does the clinician know if the specific patient will be an improver or a nonimprover? To the extent that he or she relies on group experimental methods, the answer cannot be known.

Finally, group experimental designs usually do not provide data on within-subject variation, that is, the fluctuations in the course of the patient's progress over time. While the scientist may not need this information to test a hypothesis, the clinician is vitally concerned with the course of progress. For example, by tracking treatment progress, the clinician can develop useful hypotheses about factors in the therapy or in the patient's life that are correlated with improvement and deterioration.

What practicing clinicians need is the ability to apply the concepts of the scientific method to the clinical decision-making process *with their own patients*. The concept of experimental control is essential to scientific analysis and is relevant to clinical decision making as well. It may be useful to review this concept in order to uncover alternatives to group experiments with their ethical, economic, and theoretical limitations.

In the simplest experiment, the researcher wishes to isolate the relationship between 2 variables. The aim is to show that when changes occur in Variable A, then changes also occur in a lawful and reliable fashion in Variable B. This demonstrates a causal relationship between A and B. In the process of demonstrating this relationship, the researcher must rule out alternative causal explanations for the observed relationship. An experiment with strong *internal validity* is one that tests the relationship between the variables under study while controlling the influence of other variables that might account for the observed events.

The clinician engages in a similar process when attempting to decide if a particular treatment is working. The goal is to conclude that the treatment (Variable A) creates improvement in some symptom (Variable B), and that other events in the patient's life are not responsible for the improvement. If clinicians had some method for ruling out extraneous life events as competing explanations for observed improvements, then they could attach greater confidence to their conclusions about therapeutic effectiveness.

What are some of the possible competing explanations for symptom improvement, or, in the parlance of the scientific method, what are the major threats to internal validity? The first threat is the effects of *history,* that is, events in the patient's world that impinge on him or her at the same time as the treatment and that mimic the effects of the treatment. For example, if a depressed patient who has been unemployed for 2 years finds employment the same week that pharmacological treatment for depression begins, it would be difficult to ascribe any observed improvement to the treatment. Without some method for ruling out the effects of the important historical event in the patient's life, the clinician cannot know what was responsible for the change.

A second class of threats to internal validity is *maturation:* processes occurring within subjects that change over time and that mimic treatment effects. It is especially important to consider developmental effects in child psychiatry. For example, if developmental decreases in oppositional behavior occurring in the 4- to 5-year-old coincide with the onset of treatment, disentangling the effects of treatment from the effects of development that would have occurred at that time anyway will be difficult.

A third threat to internal validity is the effects of *testing;* repeated assessment can produce changes that mimic treatment effects. For example, practice effects may produce improvement in test scores on a second or third administration of a test. In this event, practice effects become confounded with treatment effects, and it is impossible to determine whether the treatment produced the observed changes.

Fourth, *instrumentation* changes or shifts that occur simultaneously with treatment onset may obscure the effects of treatment. For example, when clinicians' ratings of improvement are used to quantify change, the standards that they use in judging improvement may drift over time. Changes in the measure of improvement over the course of treatment may result from changes in the clinicians' judgment standards rather than changes in the actual behavior of the patient.

Finally, another common threat to internal validity is the effect of *statistical regression.* Regression refers to the tendency for extreme scores on a measure to move toward the mean score when the measurement device is repeated. In this case, scores produced at the second testing would tend to be less extreme purely on statistical grounds that have nothing to do with a treatment effect. Thus changes due to treatment cannot be distinguished from the effect of scores reverting toward the mean (Campbell & Stanley, 1966).

Changes due to history and maturation effects present obvious problems to the clinician who wishes to judge the effectiveness of treatment. Changes due to the effects of testing, instrumentation, and statistical regression are just as troublesome for the clinician as for the researcher, since more and more clinicians are incorporating objective assessment methods (e.g., rating scales) into routine clinical practice.

Researchers historically have controlled for threats to internal validity by using group experimental designs employing control groups of patients who experience all the conditions that the experimental subjects experience *except* the treatment. Since control group subjects are exposed to the same competing explanations for change as the treated subjects, differences obtained between treatment and control groups are due, presumably, to the unique effects of the treatment. Random assignment to treatment and control groups is necessary to ensure that there are no systematic differences between the groups other than the treatment.

What clinicians need is a similarly effective method for controlling or ruling out competing explanations for therapeutic change, and, in particular, one that does not involve large groups of patients. Clinically oriented researchers have developed an array of methods for evaluating the effects of treatment in a single individual (Barlow & Hersen, 1973, 1984; Barlow, Hayes, & Nelson, 1983; Hayes, 1992; Kazdin, 1982). These methods combine the best features of individualized clinical management with experimental control and objective assessment. Since it is the response of the individual that is of ultimate concern to the practicing clinician, these methods can be used in clinical practice to assist clinicians in a valid decision-making process.

A variety of single-subject experimental designs control threats to internal validity and have been used in clinical settings. Despite differences in design elements, all single-subject designs share some essential features. First, each subject (or small set of subjects) serves as his or her own control by establishing baseline rates of target symptoms in the individual before (and sometimes after) treatment is instituted. This design feature eliminates the ethical dilemma of withholding treatment from large numbers of patients.

Second, target symptoms, whether cognitive, behavioral, physiological, or emotional, are clearly specified and precisely defined. Once symptoms are defined, there is repeated measurement throughout each phase of the design. Enough observations are collected in each phase to establish stability of response or, in the case of a trend, the direction of the trend. In this way, variability is observed rather than obscured as occurs in group designs.

Third, while statistical approaches to the analysis of single-subject data exist, the results typically are displayed graphically and inspected visually. In this way meaningful judgments about the magnitude and *clinical* significance of symptom changes can be made.

Classes of Single Subject Experimental Designs

THE A-B DESIGN

In the A-B design, there is an initial period of observation (the A phase) in which baseline or natural rates of symptom occurrence are measured, usually across several days. Baseline measurement continues until a stable pattern emerges, with at least 3 data points (i.e., 3 measurements of the symptom that is tracked) being required to establish a trend. After a baseline trend is established, a treatment is introduced (the B phase) while measurement continues as in Phase A. Again, at least 3 data points are needed to determine the level and trend of symptom occurrence under the treatment condition. The response to treatment is then compared to the baseline rate of response via visual inspection of the data.

The A-B design is not a true experimental design because it does not adequately rule out threats to internal validity. However, it is the building block for all of the true experimental single-subject designs. In addition, it is a clear improvement over the uncontrolled case study in that target responses are defined and measured repeatedly and the effects of treatment can be evaluated against baseline rates of symptom occurrence. All subsequent designs to be discussed in this section are true experimental designs that do rule out threats to internal validity.

THE A-B-A DESIGN

The A-B-A design is the simplest of the true experimental single-subject designs. In this design, a return to baseline conditions is instituted (i.e., treatment is withdrawn) in a final A phase following the treatment phase. If symptom occurrence returns to initial baseline levels, then experimental control has been demonstrated. That is, it is unlikely that the effects of history, maturation, and so forth would exert their influences in the same directions and at precisely the same times as with treatment administration and withdrawal.

Although the A-B-A design allows the clinician/ researcher to draw *causal* conclusions about the effects of treatment, it has the clinically undesirable feature of ending on a nontreatment phase.

The next design corrects this deficiency by ending on a treatment phase.

THE A-B-A-B DESIGN

The A-B-A-B design strengthens the probability that the effects observed with the introduction of treatment are due to the treatment and not to extraneous factors. It does this by providing 2 replications of the treatment. If symptom responses can in effect be turned off, turned on, and turned off again with the introduction, withdrawal, and reintroduction of treatment, then history, maturation, and other threats to internal validity become very implausible explanations for the pattern of results. The design, therefore, provides a very powerful demonstration of experimental control and has the advantage of ending on a treatment phase. Once control has been demonstrated, the clinician can extend the final B phase for as long as may be clinically indicated.

The withdrawal designs (i.e., A-B-A and A-B-A-B designs) are based on a premise of the reversibility of treatment; that is, that when the treatment is discontinued, the effects will revert to baseline levels. For that reason, they are most obviously appropriate for palliative treatments in which the therapeutic effect is dependent on the treatment continuing at least in the short run (as in the use of stimulant medications for attention deficit hyperactivity disorder). However, withdrawal designs have been used to establish initial control with treatments that are presumed to be curative in an initial, short-term A-B-A design. Once experimental control is established in the A-B-A design, a final long-term B phase is added so that the curative (nonreversible) effects of the treatment are achieved. For example, in an A-B-A-B evaluation of cognitive therapy, an initial baseline is established and then the patient is introduced to cognitive self-instructional methods. After a short-term B phase in which symptom reduction occurs, the patient is instructed to stop using the methods for a brief period (withdrawal phase). Following this short-term withdrawal phase (presumably achieved because the new cognitive strategies have not yet become permanently incorporated into the patient's solid cognitive schema), the patient is again instructed to utilize the cognitive control strategies and the therapy continues in a final long-term B phase.

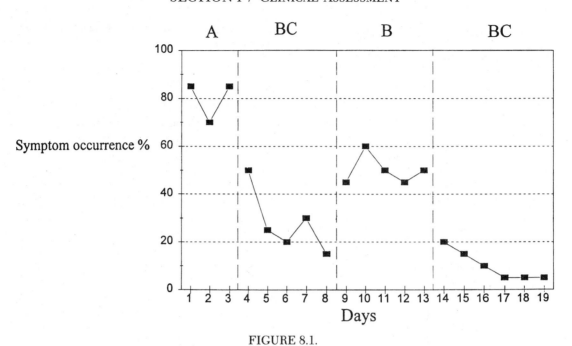

FIGURE 8.1.

A = baseline; B = parent training; C = stimulant medication.

VARIATIONS OF THE WITHDRAWAL DESIGN FOR STUDYING INTERACTION EFFECTS

The logic of the A-B-A-B design can be used when the question involves one or more treatment components in a multicomponent treatment regimen. For example, the hypothetical clinical study utilizing an A-BC-B-BC design depicted in Figure 8.1 examines the combined effects of stimulant medication and parent training for a child with attention deficit hyperactivity disorder. By systematically applying both treatment components—parent training and stimulant medication—withdrawing one, and then reapplying both, the combined effects of the 2 treatments can be evaluated experimentally and a valid conclusion can be drawn that for this child, a combination treatment is more effective than parent training alone. Although it would be tempting to conclude that parent training alone is more effective than no treatment (comparing the A and B phases), it is not possible to do this with certainty since there is no systematic application and withdrawal of parent training. To include this comparison in the clinical study, the clinician might have used an A-B-A-B-BC-B-BC design.

Other examples of withdrawal designs can be developed depending on the question of interest to the clinician. The main rules to follow in constructing withdrawal designs are to use withdrawal phases to demonstrate experimental control and to change only one variable at a time.

MULTIPLE BASELINE DESIGNS

Sometimes withdrawal designs may be unfeasible. For example, once an effective treatment has been found for an extremely harmful symptom, withdrawing the treatment may not be ethical. Likewise, some treatments, once applied, may not be reversible even in the short term. In these cases, the clinician/researcher can use a multiple baseline design. The multiple baseline design demonstrates experimental control by evaluating the effects of one treatment (or treatment composite) across a succession of target symptoms. One assumption of the multiple baseline designs is that the successive target symptoms are independent of one another—in other words, changes in one target symptom do not affect changes in other target symptoms.

The basic procedure is one in which baseline occurrence of a minimum of 3 symptoms is established. Treatment is then applied to the first symptom, while baseline conditions continue for the remaining symptoms. After symptomatic behavior stabilizes for the first symptom, the same treatment is then applied to the second symptom while baseline conditions remain in effect for the remaining symptoms. This procedure continues until all target symptoms have been treated.

The design demonstrates experimental control by showing that target symptoms change when and only when treatment is introduced. Threats to internal validity are ruled out by virtue of the *staggered* introduction of treatment across the baselines. If treatment were introduced *simultaneously* to all the baselines, the result would be a series of A-B designs and experimental control would be lost.

There are 3 classes of multiple baseline designs. In the *multiple baseline across behaviors* design, 3 or more different symptoms are targeted for measurement and intervention in the same patient. In the *multiple baseline across subjects* design, the same symptom is targeted in 3 or more subjects and treatment is introduced in sequential fashion to the subjects. In the *multiple baseline across settings* design, the same target symptom is measured across 3 or more different settings in the same patient. Treatment is introduced in sequential fashion across the 3 settings (e.g., Classrooms 1, 2, and 3 for a school-based treatment). In each case, experimental control is demonstrated when it is shown that changes in the baselines occur when and only when treatment is introduced; at that point causal conclusions about the effects of treatment can be drawn.

Figure 8.2 shows another hypothetical clinical study of a multiple baseline analysis of a teacher-implemented reinforcement program for improving behavioral symptoms in a child with attention deficit hyperactivity disorder. In the study, symptoms are first tracked across 3 different classrooms for this middle-school child. Then, in sequential fashion, Teacher 1, followed by Teacher 2, and finally Teacher 3 are taught to implement a reinforcement system in which the child receives checks on an index card on his desk every 10 minutes for displaying 3 prosocial target behaviors (e.g., stay in seat; raise your hand before blurting out; follow classroom rules). Reduction in symptoms occurs when and only when the program is implemented in staggered fashion across the 3 classrooms, clearly demonstrating the effects of the treatment and ruling out competing explanations for the observed effects.

THE SIMULTANEOUS TREATMENT DESIGN

Also known as the alternating treatment design, this is the only one of the single-case experimental designs that allows valid comparisons of different treatments in the same subject. Although some clinician/researchers have attempted to utilize the withdrawal design to compare 2 or more treatments (e.g., A-B-A-B-A-C-A-C), withdrawal designs do not control for order and sequence effects, such as carryover effects from one treatment to another. Therefore, the effects of sequence cannot be ruled out as an explanation for superior effects of the second treatment.

In the simultaneous treatment design, after baseline occurrence of a target symptom is established, 2 or more treatments are rapidly alternated within a single subject and measures are taken at each treatment application. Barlow and Hersen (1984) suggest that the order of treatments be determined randomly, thereby controlling for the effects of sequence. For example, a clinician interested in evaluating the comparative effects of response cost and positive reinforcement programs on the classroom behavior of a child with attention deficit hyperactivity disorder might measure symptomatic behavior in 2 classrooms across several days to establish their baseline occurrence. Then the 2 treatments are administered in random fashion across the 2 classrooms on consecutive school days. Since the clinician/researcher is interested in comparing the effects of the 2 treatments, the data would be plotted by connecting all the data points measuring the effects of response cost and then connecting all the data points measuring the effects of positive reinforcement. If the 2 resulting series of data points diverge, valid conclusions about the comparative effectiveness of the treatments could be drawn.

Conclusions

The issues that confront the clinician when attempting to draw conclusions about the effectiveness of psychiatric treatments are in many cases the same issues that confront the researcher who wishes to design an experiment that allows a valid assessment of the causal relationship between 2 or more variables. Single-case experimental designs

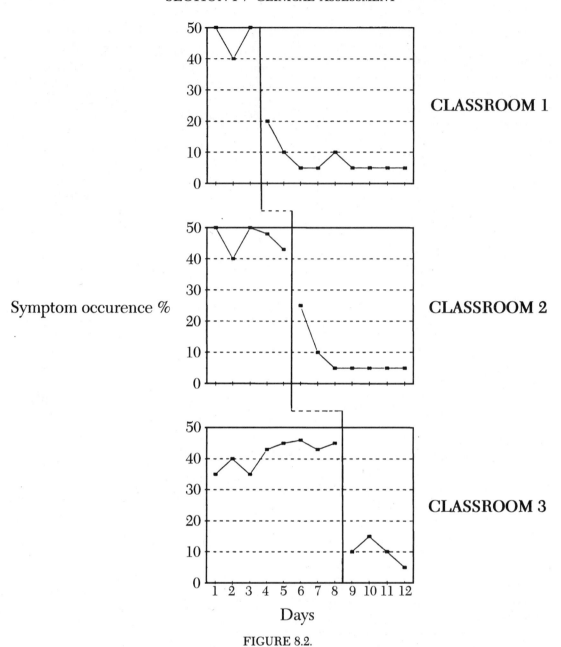

FIGURE 8.2.

*Analysis of a teacher-implemented reinforcement program for
improving behavioral symptoms in a child with ADHD.*

have the distinct advantage of allowing the clinician/researcher to rule out competing explanations for the apparent effects of treatments and to do so with only one subject or very small series of subjects. Because they also avoid the ethical dilemma of withholding treatment from real patients who present themselves for care, such studies also have a distinct advantage over group experimental designs that require untreated or placebo-treated groups to demonstrate experimental control. Finally, because they rely on visual inspection of the effects of treatment in the individual, judgments about effectiveness are often more clinically meaningful than in group designs that report statistically significant but clinically unimportant results.

Some of the often-stated disadvantages of single-subject designs compared to group designs are more apparent than real. For example, it is sometimes said that single-subject experimental designs have weak external validity (generalizability) compared to group designs. That is, the results from the single case cannot be generalized to a larger population. Indeed, researchers *would* want to replicate the effects on an *n* of 1 experiment across a number of patients in a systematic replication series in order to define the range and limits of generalizability. However, just because group experimental designs employ larger numbers of subjects, their results do not necessarily have greater generalizability. For example, if an experimental group of depressed subjects on treatment A shows a statistically greater improvement than a placebo-treated control group, the effect may be due to a small number of subjects in the treated group showing a large improvement, while the majority of treated subjects shows no improvement or even deterioration. In this case a small number of improvers carry the statistical effect even though a majority of the subjects were not helped by the treatment.

It would be unwarranted to generalize the statistically significant result from this study to the total population of depressed patients. And yet, because group designs obscure the individual's response to treatment in a group average, it is not possible to study particular individual patient characteristics that may be associated with improvement or deterioration. In addition, researchers and clinicians increasingly are aware that carefully composed group trials on highly select, homogeneous subject populations often are unrepresentative of the clinical populations about which such studies presume to generalize. A systematic replication series of single-subject experimental designs on similarly diagnosed patients highlights individual differences in response rather than averaging them out and allows a systematic exploration of the limits of generalizability.

Single-case experimental designs provide a mechanism for clinicians working in the world of clinical practice to draw valid conclusions about the effects of treatment on their patients. As objective assessment measures and computerized office practice become increasingly available to the clinician, the feasibility of conducting single-case designs in clinical practice is enhanced. The suitability of this approach should lead to more effective treatments being applied to patients and to important contributions to the knowledge base about how, when, where, and for whom psychiatric therapies work.

REFERENCES

Barlow, D. H., Hayes, S. C., & Nelson, R. O. (1983). *The scientist-practitioner: Research and accountability in clinical and educational settings.* Elmsford, NY: Pergamon Press.

Barlow, D. H., & Hersen, M. (1973). Single-case experimental designs: Uses in applied clinical research. *Archives of General Psychiatry, 29,* 319–325.

Barlow, D. H., & Hersen, M. (1984). *Single-case experimental designs: Strategies for studying behavior change* (2nd ed.). New York: Pergamon Press.

Campbell, D. T., & Stanley, J. C. (1966). *Experimental and quasi-experimental designs for research.* Chicago: Rand McNally.

Conners, C. K., & Werry, J. S. (1979). Pharmacotherapy. In H. C. Quay & J. S. Werry (Eds.), *Psycho-pathological disorders of childhood* (2nd ed.) (pp. 455–495). New York: John Wiley & Sons.

DuPaul, G. J. & Barkley, R. A. (1990). Medication therapy. In R. A. Barkley (ed.), Attention deficit hyperactivity disorder: A handbook for diagnosis and treatment (pp. 573–612). New York: Guilford Press.

Hayes, S. C. (1992). Single-case experimental designs and empirical clinical practice. In A. E. Kazdin (ed.), *Methodological issues and strategies in clinical research* (pp. 491–522). Washington, DC: American Psychological Association Press.

Kazdin, A. E. (1982). *Single-case research designs: Methods for clinical and applied settings.* New York: Oxford University Press.

9 / The Ethics of Consent and Confidentiality in Clinical Practice

Gregory B. Leong and Spencer Eth

The ethical code of psychiatry traces its history to the moral teachings of the Hippocratic tradition and to the ensuing centuries of modification. Under the more recent influence of Anglo-American jurisprudence and culture, in the mid-19th century the American Medical Association (AMA) promulgated ethical principles for the practice of medicine in the United States. Since then these principles have undergone continual reassessment and revision. Subsequently, the American Psychiatric Association (APA) adopted the AMA ethical principles with annotations especially applicable to psychiatry (APA, 1995b). The AMA ethical principles are in force for child and adolescent psychiatrists, regardless of whether they are members of the American Psychiatric or American Medical Association. Similar ethical codes operate for other professional disciplines.

There are currently 7 "sections" of the AMA ethical principles (APA, 1995b):

1. A physician shall be dedicated to providing competent medical service with compassion and respect for human dignity.

2. A physician shall deal honestly with patients and colleagues, and strive to expose those physicians deficient in character or competence, or who engage in fraud or deception.

3. A physician shall respect the law and also recognize a responsibility to seek changes in those requirements which are contrary to the best interests of the patient.

4. A physician shall respect the rights of patients, of colleagues, and of other health professionals, and shall safeguard patient confidences within the constraints of the law.

5. A physician shall continue to study, apply, and advance scientific knowledge, make relevant information available to patients, colleagues, and the public, obtain consultation, and use the talents of other health professionals when indicated.

6. A physician shall, in the provision of appropriate patient care, except in emergencies, be free to choose whom to serve, with whom to associate, and the environment in which to provide medical services.

7. A physician shall recognize a responsibility to participate in activities contributing to an improved community. (APA, 1995b, p. 2).

Over time, the APA has provided specific annotations and opinions to these guiding principles (APA, 1995a; 1995b). The clinical guidelines for the practice of child and adolescent psychiatry have been embodied in the "Principles of Practice of Child and Adolescent Psychiatry," adopted in 1982 by the American Academy of Child and Adolescent Psychiatry (AACAP). These can readily be seen to flow from the AMA/APA ethical principles (AACAP, 1982). While quite comprehensive, as medical ethics evolves, the APA annotations and opinions undergo frequent revisions. In the nature of things, many ethical issues arise in clinical practice; however, those that are most prominent and cogent to the clinical work with children and adolescents are concerns about consent and confidentiality that emerge from the evaluation and treatment of young patients. Accordingly, this chapter focuses primarily on these issues.

In considering moral issues, the 2 prominent modes of ethical analysis derive from the utilitarian and deontologic perspectives. The utilitarian view holds that ethical rules should be designed to produce optimal consequences, while the deontologic perspective posits that ethical principles serve moral duties and obligations. The practice of medicine depends on ethical principles stemming from both schools. Ethical analyses generally involve: (1) balancing beneficence and nonmaleficence within the domain of competing patient and societal needs, (2) respecting the demands of the patient's liberty interest, and (3) promoting the creation of social justice.

Legal Contours of Ethical Practice

Two standards for clinical practice coexist, namely the legal standard and the ethical standard. Legal standards derive from statutory and case law, while ethical standards flow from professional codes developed in a utilitarian-deontologic matrix. Although these 2 standards often overlap to a considerable extent, there are many instances in which a given behavior may be licit but not ethical for the child and adolescent clinician.

The boundary between legal and ethical behavior has become increasingly diffuse. In particular, confidentiality in the traditional sense has been considered an ethical duty, while the corresponding legal equivalent is privilege. Privilege, however, has a narrower focus; it is defined as the (patient's) power to insist on the privacy (confidentiality) of information communicated within the context of a special relationship, such as a psychotherapist-patient or physician-patient relationship, for purposes of legal proceedings. Because privilege does not specifically protect the privacy of information in extralegal situations, privacy or confidentiality laws have been enacted to cover these other settings. Thus, for instance, the traditional Hippocratic ethical principle of confidentiality has found codification in modern American law.

Violation of ethical (or legal) rules exposes the child and adolescent clinician to a civil liability action, licensure sanction, and/or ethics committee review by professional organizations. Ethically sound clinical practice is the best way to avoid the potential for such adverse actions.

Developmental Issues Relevant to Ethical Practice

The United States has established a bright line age requirement to demarcate minors (children and adolescents) from adults. Reaching a certain chronological age permits a person to obtain a driver's license, to marry, to vote, and so on. Hidden within this scheme is the legal presumption that at the requisite age (usually adulthood), a person has attained a relevant level of competence. However, although competency is legally viewed as a discrete event occurring on a particular birthday, functionally it operates as a continuous process involving cognitive, emotional, and social development. While it is easy to conceptualize children (those under age 12) as being incompetent or, in clinical terms, to lack rational decision-making capacity, the situation for adolescents (ages 13 to 17) is less clear. The majority of ethical dilemmas in clinical practice with children and adolescents arise as the child matures both cognitively and emotionally into adolescence. Historically, the equivalent of adult responsibility was generally conferred on persons at the point of biological maturation during puberty. Thus our modern concept of adolescence as a transitional phase presents ethical conundrums for the practicing child and adolescent clinician.

When discussing ethical issues, local state law must be considered, especially those statutes that define categories (such as an emancipated or mature minor who can receive treatment without parental consent) and other requirements (such as laws mandating reporting suspected abuse) that are applicable to both minors and adults. With both the developmental perspective and local legal regulations in mind, consent and confidentiality issues will be explored.

Consent Issues

Prior to undertaking an evaluation in a nonemergency situation, the child and adolescent clinician must ascertain who is the custodial and/or legal parent or guardian of the dependent child and adolescent. It is this adult who has a claim both to authorizing the evaluation and treatment and to accessing the record of the evaluation and treatment of the child or adolescent. Sometimes the child or adolescent is brought for evaluation by a noncustodial parent or resides with an individual who is not the authorized decision maker.

A long-standing component of the ethical practice of medicine has been obtaining the patient's permission prior to implementing clinical interventions. The 20th century has seen the evolution of the concept of informed consent in case and statutory law. For a consent to be informed and valid, sufficient information must be disclosed to the patient in order that the patient can render a voluntary and competent decision. Appelbaum and Grisso (1988) have proposed a clinician-friendly model of informed consent that incorporates sequential cognitive elements, notably the patient's: ability to communicate choices, understanding of relevant information, appreciation of the situation and its consequences, and ability to consider information rationally. In essence, a paternalistic model, in which the physician decided which treatments were best for the patient, has yielded place to a model in which the patient is offered various treatment options along with their likely outcomes and side effects, and selects the preferred modality.

Adolescents as a group pose the greatest dilemma for clinicians in terms of competence to give a valid consent. Adolescents often will have attained "adult" levels of competence, yet they generally are excluded from the legal authority to consent to treatment. In some situations, local law could permit short-term or emergency psychiatric interventions for adolescents. Undertaking psychiatric treatment for a willing patient would not seem to present an ethical problem. However, in cases where the parent did not authorize the treatment, the issue of who will pay for the services is then left unanswered.

Adolescents are less likely to seek psychiatric treatment than to decline such treatment, especially when arranged by one or both parents. In many jurisdictions the child's or adolescent's wish to refuse voluntary inpatient treatment may fall under legal or quasi-legal review. Even if such permission is not legally required, ideally the child and adolescent clinician would obtain permission from both the minor and the parents before undertaking nonemergency voluntary inpatient treatment. In the ambulatory care setting, treatment would require at least the assent of the minor, since there is no means by which to compel a patient to remain in outpatient treatment. Nonetheless, obtaining permission from the minor for treatment has ethical rationale as well as clinical utility.

Of special relevance to the clinician is consent for psychotropic medications. As a rule, these medications are less frequently prescribed for young people than for adult patients; nonetheless,

their use, particularly in the case of neuroleptics, merits careful consideration. Regardless of local law, the possibility of tardive dyskinesia dictates that informed consent should be obtained from both minor and custodial parent(s).

Confidentiality Issues

The potential ethical problems raised by confidentiality are similar to those pertaining to consent. Which persons are legally authorized to access the private therapeutic communications between child or adolescent patient and clinician may become a significant issue in the clinical process. Nonetheless, ethical practice may involve protecting the confidentiality of the therapeutic situation to the greatest extent possible. Providing confidential information to an unauthorized person is an error that can produce adverse legal and ethical consequences for the unwary clinician.

After completion of the comprehensive clinical assessment, the choice of an intervention strategy becomes clinically, legally, and ethically relevant. For child or adolescent patients receiving individual therapy, confidentiality issues are complicated, but not nearly as complex as is the case for family therapy. In individual psychotherapy, the legally responsible adult has the right of access to the communications between therapist and patient—the clinical record. However, as the patient matures cognitively, emotionally, and socially toward "adult" levels, the youngster's moral claim for confidentiality concomitantly increases. Even with less mature adolescents and children, confidentiality should be favored to the greatest extent possible as a deontologic means to foster autonomy. While not legally binding, establishing the boundaries for confidentiality at the outset of evaluation and treatment with both the child or adolescent patient and the parent(s) may prevent later disputes. Absent an emergency situation such as suicidality or homicidality, preservation of confidentiality is important. In particular, from a utilitarian viewpoint, it facilitates the child's or adolescent's participation in treatment.

Respecting confidentiality in the context of family therapy can be problematic. While the child or adolescent may be the only identified patient, for clinical purposes there are multiple patients. Any of the participants may request information about the family session. In this instance, as the laws governing confidentiality for group psychotherapy suggest, there may be no privilege granted to protect the privacy of each family therapy member. However, the clinician should establish ground rules for the entire family regarding the confidentiality of the sessions. While the personal and intrafamilial psychodynamics of the parent(s) and offspring will determine how the issue of confidentiality is managed, it is the clinician's responsibility to strive to protect this privacy.

In addition to informing the patient and parent(s) of the professional's ethical and legal duties involving confidentiality and its limitations, embedded in the discussion of confidentiality is an opportunity to educate the parents about such child or adolescent developmental issues as the growing need for autonomy. Moreover, these discussions present opportunities for the clinician to respond to a parent's curiosity or apprehension about what the child or adolescent patient may reveal about the parent. These conversations can serve to engage the parent in the subsequent therapeutic process.

Evaluations of the child or adolescent may be requested as part of child custody proceedings. These cases can arrive at the office or clinic de novo, but, to the consternation of the clinician, often will arise in the midst of ongoing treatment. Establishing ground rules prior to undertaking the evaluation and treatment of the child or adolescent may well reduce later problems; however, in the event that a child custody dispute involving the patient does arise, difficulties are all too likely. Child custody proceedings can erode the confidentiality of the clinical record. Clinicians may be privy to embarrassing and potentially deleterious information about the child or adolescent patient and others that has no bearing on the custody issue. If called upon by the court to disclose the record of a treatment case, the professional must exercise appropriate caution about what is disclosed. When serious doubt exists as to what can be withheld, the clinician should request a private (*in camera*) meeting with the judge in chambers to discuss the matter. When clinicians undertake from the outset to perform an evaluation involving a custody dispute, the limits of confidentiality should be delineated to all the involved parties

and especially to the child or adolescent patient in a developmentally sensitive manner.

Sexuality is an area fraught with a number of potential confidentiality conundrums. All jurisdictions have reporting statutes requiring professionals to notify the appropriate agency in cases of suspected child abuse or neglect. These statutes supersede the confidentiality of the treatment setting, and neither the patient nor parent(s) can prevent the report. Failure to report a suspicion of abuse or neglect subjects the clinician to potential civil liability or criminal sanction. Subsumed in this mandatory reporting is the especially emotionally charged issue of suspected sexual abuse of the child or adolescent. The alleged perpetrator also may be a child or adolescent. In virtually all instances of reporting, whether ultimately validated or not, the psychosocial consequences of the investigation for the alleged perpetrator and victim are profound.

Although many adolescents fall below the age of consent for mutually agreed upon sexual activity, the law cannot preclude such activity between one assenting adolescent and another. Nonetheless, no matter how mature the adolescent patient, if not at the age of consent, problems may arise when a parent insists on discussing the adolescent patient's sexual behavior with the clinician. Of particular concern are the common sexually transmitted diseases, especially the very real possibility of contracting the HIV virus. This has two faces: On the one hand are the therapeutic implications for the adolescent and parent arising from the issue of sexuality and sexually transmitted diseases, and on the other the legal mandate to report certain communicable diseases to the public health authorities.

While many of the sexually transmitted diseases have serious sequelae if untreated, infection with the HIV virus represents a special public health risk. When confronted with an HIV-infected patient who declines to reveal sexual contacts, there is no overriding ethical reason for the clinician to encourage preservation of absolute secrecy of this information. Indeed, both the utilitarian and deontologic perspectives converge to force the psychiatrist to disclose this information to the public health authorities. In such cases exploring the patient's resistance to disclosure would be clinically and ethically sound (Eth, 1988).

Whether approached from the patient's intrapsychic, family psychodynamic, and/or societal perspectives, adolescent pregnancy and abortion are always controversial topics. Therapeutically, addressing the emotionally laden decision to maintain or terminate a pregnancy is difficult enough without at the same time trying to satisfy the parental notification requirements regarding abortion that certain states have established. While in some cases parental notification may serve a therapeutic goal, in others the potential psychological harm of such disclosure may overshadow a parent's right to be informed. Child and adolescent clinicians may wish to consider these issues in advance of treating postpubertal youngsters. Alternatively, the clinician may work with a medical clinic in which the anonymity of the adolescent patient is preserved. The clinician then can concentrate on the therapeutic issue without having to be concerned that the confidentiality of the therapy will be jeopardized.

The clinician may encounter the more traditional type of third-party notification when a *Tarasoff*-type duty to protect situation arises during the evaluation or treatment of psychiatric patients. Since the California Supreme Court rendered its 1976 decision in *Tarasoff v. Regents of the University of California,* several other states have established a similar duty to protect (Mills, Sullivan, & Eth, 1987). A duty to protect arises for mental health clinicians when the patient poses a serious danger of physical harm to an identifiable person. When the child or adolescent patient presents such a threat, appropriate action calls for the clinician to take the necessary clinical steps to reduce the danger. The interventions may include breaching the confidentiality of the clinician-patient relationship to warn the threatened person or notify the police. In several jurisdictions the clinician is immunized against civil liability when he or she breaches confidentiality in the above manner and despite the warning harm befalls the intended victim (Appelbaum, Zonana,

Bonnie, & Roth, 1989). While such protection from legal liability may be reassuring, ethical dilemmas remain as overzealous warnings may trigger other adverse consequences.

Confidentiality could be virtually assured if information were not memorialized in the clinical record. In the case of records located in hospitals, in theory, access to such records is legally confined to professionals involved in the case. In reality, however, records may not be secure. In addition, computerization of records increases the likelihood of unauthorized access and underscores the desirability of preserving in the record only essential information for the proper care and treatment of the patient. However, it is not always easy to determine what documentation may be necessary for adequate care and for protection from future malpractice actions.

While records kept in the clinician's office may be more secure than charts located in the hospital, the same general principle holds of not recording embarrassing, sensitive material that not relevant to the patient's care and treatment. The increasing requirements for information by third-party payors in order to reimburse the cost of service reflect further intrusion into the sanctity of the clinical record.

Closing Remarks

Ethical issues frequently arise in clinical practice with children and adolescents. This chapter has explored consent and confidentiality. If the clinician cannot resolve an ethical issue alone by consulting the available principles and guidelines (AACAP, 1982; 1987; APA 1995a,b), then consultation with a knowledgeable colleague, including members of the ethics committees of professional organizations, is strongly recommended.

REFERENCES

American Academy of Child and Adolescent Psychiatry. (1982). *Principles of practice of child and adolescent psychiatry.* Washington, DC: Author.

American Psychiatric Association. (1987). Guidelines on confidentiality. *American Journal of Psychiatry, 144,* 1522–1526.

American Psychiatric Association. (1995a). *Opinions of the ethics committee on the principles of medical ethics with annotations especially applicable to psychiatry.* Washington, DC: Author.

American Psychiatric Association. (1995b). *The principles of medical ethics with annotations especially applicable to psychiatry.* Washington, DC: Author.

Appelbaum, P. S., & Grisso, T. (1988). Assessing patients' capacities to consent to treatment. *New England Journal of Medicine, 319,* 1635–1638; erratum (1989), *320,* 748.

Appelbaum, P. S., Zonana, H., Bonnie, R., & Roth, L. H. (1989). Statutory approaches to limiting psychiatrists' liability for their patients' violent acts. *American Journal of Psychiatry, 146,* 821–828.

Eth, S. (1988). The sexually active, HIV infected patient: Confidentiality versus the duty to protect. *Psychiatric Annals, 18,* 571–576.

Mills, M. J., Sullivan, G., & Eth, S. (1987). Protecting third parties: A decade after Tarasoff. *American Journal of Psychiatry, 144,* 68–74.

SUGGESTED READING

Benedek, E. P. (1992). Ethical issues in practice. In D. H. Schetky & E. P. Benedek (Eds.), *Clinical handbook of child psychiatry and the law* (pp. 75–88). Baltimore, MD: Williams & Wilkins.

Geraty, R. D., Hendren, D. L., & Flaa, C. J. (1992). Ethical perspectives on managed care as it relates to child and adolescent psychiatry. *Journal of the American Academy of Child and Adolescent Psychiatry, 31,* 398–402.

Group for the Advancement of Psychiatry. (1989). *How old is old enough? The ages of rights and responsibilities.* New York: Brunner/Mazel.

MacBeth, J. E. (1992). Legal issues in the psychiatric treatment of minors. In D. H. Schetky & E. P. Benedek (Eds.), *Clinical handbook of child psychiatry and the law* (pp. 53–74). Baltimore, MD: Williams & Wilkins.

Munir, K., & Earls, F. (1992). Ethical principles governing research in child and adolescent psychiatry. *Journal of the American Academy of Child and Adolescent Psychiatry, 31,* 408–414.

O'Rourke, O. P., Snider, B. W., Thomas, J. M., & Berland, D. I. (1992). Knowing and practicing ethics. *Journal of the American Academy of Child and Adolescent Psychiatry, 31,* 393–397.

Shields, J. M., & Johnson, A. (1992). Collision between law and ethics: Consent for treatment with adolescents. *Bulletin of the American Academy of Psychiatry and the Law, 20,* 309–323.

SECTION II
Decision Trees for a Sampling
of Presenting Problems

10 / Disruptive Behavior

Patrick H. Tolan and Markus J. P. Kruesi

Once a child has been referred because of a disruptive behavior or with symptoms such as inattention, hyperactivity, or aggressivity, the clinical assessment/intervention strategy planning must proceed along 2 lines of inquiry: evaluation of symptoms and the presence of other psychiatric disorders, and assessment of the important parameters, apart from psychopathological symptoms, that will indicate what intervention methods, intensity, and foci are the most apt and plausible. Figure 10.1 presents the decision tree for disruptive behavior.

A. *Assessment.*

A.1. *Assessment of Symptoms and Diagnoses.* Disruptive behavior is the most frequent presentation in child mental health services. Symptom and diagnostic assessment for the disruptive child or adolescent requires multiple information sources. Data concerning the child, family/parent/surrogate, and the school are generally all required. No laboratory or psychological measures are pathognomonic for this diagnosis. However, laboratory measures, such as drug screens, may be helpful in differential diagnosis and treatment planning. Variation by source in noting the presence and type of symptoms is frequent. Parent, teacher and child accounts may differ. For example, teachers or parents may not report depressive symptoms the child experiences. Standardized teacher and parent rating scales often are useful both in initial assessment and in monitoring response to treatment. Very low scores can rule out a disruptive disorder, but high scores cannot confirm this diagnosis since they can result from other causes. Agreement of information from multiple sources and evidence of cross-situational problems are the strongest indicators of a need for treatment. Symptom constellation, history, duration, and functional impairment are the constituent determinants of whether the symptoms constitute an appropriate target for intervention. Environmental, cognitive, physical examination, and medical history data are used in treatment planning.

A.2. *Intervention Assessment.* Intervention assessment is guided by evaluation of 4 basic aspects: child characteristics, family history and functioning, motivation, and resources and constraints.

B. *Child Characteristics.*

In addition to symptom types and severity, there are a number of child characteristics relevant to intervention planning. These include: the child's *cognitive characteristics* including intelligence level, social perspective, reasoning, and problem-solving skills; the youngster's *neurologic integrity;* and his or her *academic* and *emotional functioning,* including the presence of anxiety about the behavior, emotional responsiveness to others, and extent of anger experienced when frustrated. For disruptive behavior problems, low intelligence (below 85) is related to a poorer prognosis and may indeed lessen the child's response to social problem-solving and anger management interventions. High intelligence offers a better prognosis. For problems of inattention/hyperactivity, pharmacologic responses may differ if mental retardation is present. The extent of hostile bias in the interpretation of others' motives, particularly those of authority figures and peers, can indicate the necessity of cognitive problem-solving and social skills training as well as the likely rate of progression of family intervention. The responsiveness to direction, feedback, and reinforcement for attending can indicate the need for direct cognitive help in addition to parent behavior management training.

Comorbidities are common. Low academic achievement and learning disabilities also suggest a poorer prognosis and may complicate treatment progress. In addition to determining the presence of coexisting affective and anxiety disorders, emotional functioning evaluation is important. The presence of anxiety, especially moral conflict about the dubious behavior, suggests a better prognosis; indeed, it may be the instance in which individual psychotherapy in addition to family therapy is most clearly indicated. In contrast, the absence of any

Child's behavior is a problem

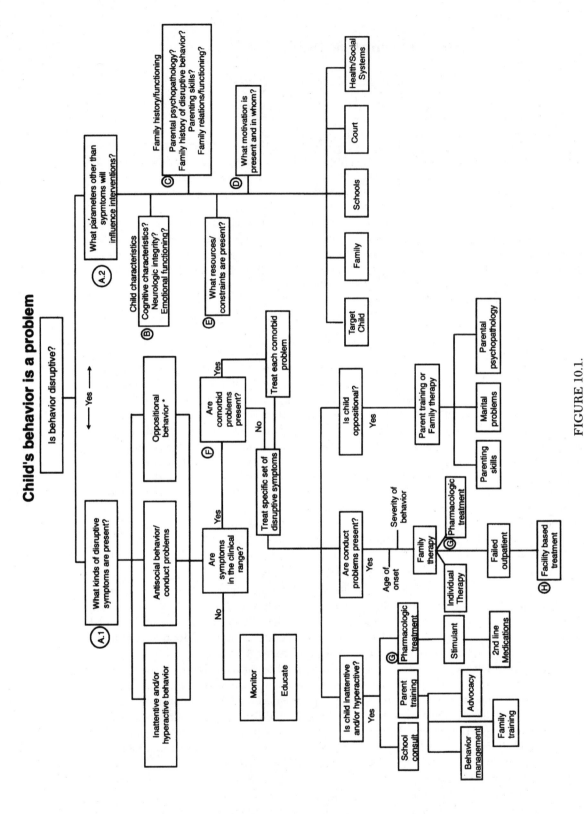

FIGURE 10.1.

Child's behavior is a problem.

*Oppositional behavior is distinguished from other antisocial behavior in the child's apparent intent to express opposition to a parent or other authority figure. Generally, these are less severe behavior problems than are observed in conduct disorders.

anxiety or any hint of moral quandary bodes un-favorably for prognosis. It indicates that interven-tion should focus almost entirely on developing a tightly monitored, carefully constructed, and well-coordinated reward and response cost system (e.g., lots of positive reinforcers) related to increasing behavioral compliance. Also, this absence indi-cates a need to direct greater attention to moni-toring the relationship among involved social sys-tems (e.g., school, family, courts, social service) as well as to a careful scrutiny of intervention prog-ress. Individual therapy focused on social skills and cognitive attributions also may be needed in such cases. The presence of stronger anger reac-tions in regard to conflict or frustration indicates the necessity of including anger management in-tervention as a pre- or corequisite to the family and other interventions.

C. *Family History and Functioning.*

The disruptive disorders are often familial. In addition, the characteristic ways the family func-tions are often major concomitants or contribu-tors to such a disorder and are usually the primary target of intervention. It is important to assess 4 related but distinct areas in regarding the family influence when planning intervention: (1) paren-tal psychopathology; (2) familial history of disrup-tive disorders; (3) parenting skills; and (4) current family relations and functioning. A particularly critical issue in regard to parental psychopathol-ogy is the presence of antisocial personality or such other conduct problems as substance abuse in the parents. These relate to a poorer prognosis as well as more feeble motivation for intervention, a weaker response to intervention efforts, and less likely maintenance of intervention accomplish-ments. Parental, particularly maternal, depression also may contribute to the occurrence of disrup-tive disorders.

Parental psychotherapy and/or pharmacother-apy may be needed as pre- or corequisites. Parent-ing skills that are critical in regard to intervention are the use of consistent rules and discipline methods, monitoring the child's behavior and whereabouts, and the avoidance of harsh disci-plinary tactics. In some cases, these skills have never been developed; in other cases, the parents possess them but have not applied them to the tar-get child. If the skills have never been learned, then training is needed in monitoring the child's

behavior and in the consistent use of a rational discipline system and related methods. If parent-ing skills are present but are not used, then inves-tigation of and intervention to remove the impedi-ment to the use of these skills are needed. This may require parental psychotherapy, marital ther-apy, or parental pharmacologic treatment. In in-stances where the stresses of life impede the use of skills the parents possess, social support and re-source development are indicated. In many cases it may be that the parents have become disillu-sioned and no longer believe that parenting can affect this child's behavior; such parents need emotional support as well as technical advice about how to apply the methods persistently and improve their effectiveness. Dysfunctional family functioning characteristics often are co-occurrent with parenting skills problems. Such family prob-lems also can both co-occur with disruptive disor-ders as well as act as precipitants of conduct and disruptive disorders. Characteristics such as low intrafamilial cohesion and support, poor organiza-tion of family roles, and high conflict with poor conflict resolution skills are regularly associated with an increased risk for disruptive behavior and poor prognosis. When these family characteristics seem to be an outgrowth of the strain of the dis-ruptive disorder on family relations, a psychoedu-cational approach is needed that is oriented to-ward managing the chronic problem and limiting its negative impact on the family. In addition, par-ticularly in regard to children with attention defi-cit hyperactivity disorder, the parent(s) will need preparation to educate successive teachers and otherwise advocate for their child. In cases where disturbed family functioning appears to be the cause of the disruptive behavior or at least contri-butes to maintaining its degree of difficulty, tech-niques need to be applied that can shift family interaction patterns toward improving conflict resolution, support, organization, and cohesion.

D. *Motivation.*

Even more than is the case with most interven-tion planning, in planning for disruptive disorders, the motivations for intervention are key. Most fre-quently, such referrals are instigated by difficult-ies with behavior in school or involvement with the juvenile justice or social service systems. Thus external pressure and involvement of multiple sys-tems is almost inevitable. Child and parent motivation may vary from grave concern for the child's well-being and/or the social offensiveness of the behaviors at one extreme, to practical interest in responding to the external pressure, to no motivation except that coerced by others on the other extreme. Similarly, the range of motivations and the interest level expressed by the other involved systems can vary. The motivations of all the involved systems can heavily influence which resources can be utilized, which constraints must be respected, and which intervention components are practical. In particular, the intervention relationship may become constrained by the conflicting motivations and interests among the child, family, and referring agents.

E. *Resources/Constraints*.

In planning intervention for disruptive disorders, among the necessary considerations are social and economic resources and constraints. Neighborhood and school conditions, legal considerations, residential and family makeup stability, and parental social and economic resources all influence which intervention components can be tried, which will be applied, whether they have some impact or not, and whether the impact lasts. Progress from the array of intervention tactics (parenting, family cognitive/behavioral, and pharmacological components) will depend on adequate access to needed social, educational, and economic resources and stability in family makeup and residence. Disruptions and disappointments in intervention services can be particularly deleterious for disruptive disorders. Hence the quality of services available and affordable to the family and how comprehensive an intervention can be coordinated are important practical considerations. Many times the referral for disruptive behavior occurs because of problems that increasingly provoke the oversight of the social service, educational, or legal systems. This situation can bring needed resources to bear, but also can seriously constrain intervention options. Practical planning necessitates including consideration of these concerns in designing interventions; one of the goals is to minimize unexpected societal intrusions.

F. *Comorbidity*.

In epidemiologic samples, comorbid psychiatric disorders appear in 30 to 60% of disruptive behavior disorders. The comorbidity can involve both other psychiatric problems and medical and psychosocial conditions. Non-comorbid conduct disorder is more apt to be found in epidemiologic or juvenile justice samples compared to mental health facilities. Generally, comorbidity worsens prognosis and requires more comprehensive treatment. Antisocial behavior significantly worsens the prognosis of those with inattention and/or hyperactivity. Relative to an individual with conduct disorder alone, suicide risk is increased for a youngster with conduct disorder comorbid for substance abuse and depression. Compliance with treatment of a medical condition, for example, diabetes, often is compromised by the presence of a disruptive disorder. In general, the simultaneous presence of another disorder requires at once direct treatment of that problem, closer monitoring, and greater patience about progress on the part of the parents and teachers.

G. *Pharmacologic Treatment*.

Pharmacologic treatment is directed at symptom amelioration but is not curative. Primarily, the choice of medication is based on the quest for symptom relief. However, refractory symptoms or the attempt to prevent a more restrictive placement may warrant consideration of an additional medication trial. For inattention/hyperactivity, stimulants are usually the first-line treatment, with antidepressants and clonidine as second-line strategies. However, when stimulant abuse by the patient or parent is likely, when nondisruptive comorbidity is present, or when poor risk/benefit results are seen with stimulants, nonstimulant alternatives may be preferred. In the absence of relative contraindications or comorbidity with a nondisruptive behavior, trials of different stimulants should be carried out before moving to any second-line medications. Conduct disorder does not require pharmacologic treatment, although some individuals with this condition may benefit. Comorbidity is the most frequent indication for pharmacologic treatment in conduct disorder. Aggression that is distressing to the child (egodystonic) and/or failure of other treatment modalities may warrant a trial use of medication. It has been suggested that affectively driven aggression is more likely to respond to pharmacologic treatment than that which is predatory or instrumental. Studies do not yet provide clear distinctions. Studies to clarify risk/benefit ratios of pharmacologic treatment for oppositional symptoms in the absence of attention deficit disorder are not available at present.

H. *Facility-based Intervention.*

Intervention strategy planning aims at using a least restrictive environment. However, even when multimodal treatment is aggressively pursued in the home, there will be individuals who experience an insufficient response. Danger to others and/or self and/or the failure of treatment at a less intensive level of care are indications for facility-based treatment (e.g., inpatient, partial hospital, or residential treatment). Comorbidity such as substance abuse or absence of a family or family surrogate also may necessitate facility-based treatment.

REFERENCES

American Academy of Child and Adolescent Psychiatry Work Group on Quality Issues. (1992). Practice parameters for the assessment and treatment of conduct disorders. *Journal of the American Academy of Child and Adolescent Psychiatry, 31* (2), 4–7.

American Academy of Child and Adolescent Psychiatry Work Group on Quality Issues. (1991). Practice parameters for the assessment and treatment of attention-deficit hyperactivity disorder. *Journal of the American Academy of Child and Adolescent Psychiatry, 30* (3), 1–3.

Hanish, L. D., Tolan, P. H., & Guerra, N. G. (1995). Treatment of oppositional defiant disorder. In M. Reineke, F. Dattilio & A. Freeman (Eds.), *Cognitive therapy with children and adolescents: A casebook for clinical practice* (pp. 62–78). New York: Guilford Press.

Kruesi, M. J. P., & Lelio, D. F. (1996). Disorders of conduct and behavior. In J. Weiner (Ed.), *Diagnosis and psychopharmacology of childhood and adolescent disorders* (2nd ed.) pp. 401–448. New York: John Wiley & Sons.

Tolan, P. H., & Loeber, R. (1993). Antisocial behavior. In P. H. Tolan & B. J. Cohler (Eds.) *Handbook of clinical research and practice with adolescents* (vol. 13, pp. 307–331). New York: John Wiley & Sons.

11 / Shyness and Fearfulness

Richard E. Mattison

Figure 11.1 presents the decision tree for shyness and fearfulness.

A. Shyness may be not so much a pathological symptom as the forerunner of a personality trait; Chess and Thomas have described shyness as characteristic of slow-to-warm children; Kagan states that it is present in inhibited children. A family history of such personality types may be helpful in this determination. Shyness also can commonly accompany a speech or language disorder. If suspected, a good developmental history followed by appropriate testing should prove useful.

B. Specific fears may be normal at different developmental ages, especially related to cognitive maturation. Infants and 2- to 3-year-old children are commonly afraid of sudden sensory stimulation, strangers, or separation, while 4- to 5-year-olds frequently fear the dark or animals. Older 6- and 7-year-old children normally may have fears of imaginary figures such as ghosts or monsters. As youngsters mature to 8 years and older, their fears become more realistic, such as death, illness, and social competence.

C. Chronic shyness or fearfulness in a dysfunctional child or adolescent may be indicative of an anxiety disorder. However, since a good deal of anxiety commonly accompanies certain non-anxiety disorders, differential diagnosis must be comprehensive. Shyness actually may take form as

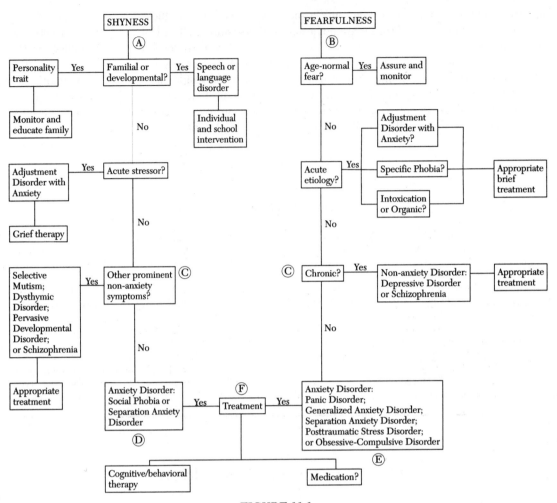

FIGURE 11.1.

The shyness and fearfulness decision tree.

a persistent refusal to talk, as in selective mutism, as the generalized withdrawal of dysthymic disorder, or as the social impairment of a pervasive developmental disorder or schizophrenia. Fearfulness often can appear in a depressive disorder or manifest itself as paranoia in schizophrenia.

D. The circumstances of chronic shyness can help distinguish between 2 possible anxiety disorders. In social phobia the patient is distressed by social situations involving scrutiny or the exposure to unfamiliar people. In contrast, children with separation anxiety disorder are distressed upon separation from home or major attachment figures.

E. The nature of the chronic fearfulness helps to determine which anxiety disorder may be present. A child with posttraumatic stress disorder suffers a major trauma followed by ongoing reexperi-ences, numbing, and arousal symptoms. Panic disorder includes fear of the reoccurrence of a panic attack, and obsessive-compulsive disorder involves distress over obsessional thoughts and/or compulsive behavior. Generalized anxiety disorder includes excessive worry and/or pervasive anxiety, while separation anxiety disorder focuses on fear of separation from a major attachment figure. Overall, comorbidity is common.

F. Except for phobias, adequate treatment studies for child and adolescent anxiety disorders are limited. Therapeutically, cognitive/behavioral approaches with the child and family appear to be the most promising. For good presentations of such techniques, refer to Kendall et al. (1991) and McDermott, Werry, Petti, Combrinck-Graham, and Char (1989). Except for the use of selective seritonin reuptake inhibitors clomipramine and fluoxetine in obsessive-compulsive disorder, the usefulness of selective seritonin reuptake inhibitors, tricyclic antidepressants, benzodiaze-

pines, and antihistamines in childhood anxiety disorders is not yet clear (Berstein, Borchardt, and Perwein, 1996). Pending future research, such medications should be used with caution.

REFERENCES

Berstein, G. A., Borchardt, C. M., & Perwein, B. A. (1996). Anxiety disorders in children and adolescents. A review of the past 10 years. *Journal of the American Academy of Child and Adolescent Psychiatry, 35,* 1110–1119.

Kagan, J., Reznick, J. S., & Snidman, N. (1988). Biological bases of childhood shyness. *Science, 240,* 167–171.

Kendall, P. C., Chanshy, T. E., Freidman, M., Kim, R., Kortlander, E., Sessa, F. M., & Siqueland, L. (1991). Treating anxiety disorders in children and adoles-

cents. In P. C. Kendall (Ed.), *Child and adolescent therapy: Cognitive-behavioral procedures* (pp. 131–164). New York: Guilford Press.

McDermott, J. F., Werry, J., Petti, T., Combrinck-Graham, L., & Char, W. F. (1989). Anxiety disorders of childhood of adolescence. In American Psychiatric Association, *Treatment of psychiatric disorders* (Vol. 1, pp. 401–446). Washington, DC: Author.

Thomas, A., Chess, S., & Birch, H. G. (1968). *Temperament and behavior disorders in children.* New York: New York University Press.

12 / **Unhappiness**

Jules R. Bemporad and Stewart Gabel

Unhappiness is a generalized mood or feeling state that conveys a lack of appropriate pleasure from one's existence plus a sense of evanescent or persistent displeasure. As is true for any mood state, unhappiness may vary in degree, may be transient or chronic, and may appear justified or irrational to an outside observer. While commonly seen in psychiatric practice, unhappiness, by itself, is not a diagnosis; it is better conceptualized as a symptom indicative of other underlying or related problems. Treatment of "unhappiness," therefore, is directed toward those difficulties that produce this disagreeable mood. In some instances, these difficulties may be external, such as in the case of a child who is chronically abused, and intervention aims at amelioration of the environmental stress. In other instances, unhappiness may result from internalized modes of processing experience that are unrealistic and distorted. For example, chronically dysphoric children may mistakenly believe that they will be rejected by peers

or fail in any endeavor, resulting in a limitation of pleasurable activities, a low self-regard, and a loss of interest in age-appropriate relationships. Ultimately, this will culminate in a self-generated state of unhappiness. In these instances, treatment seeks to correct those personality distortions that beget the troubled inner state and prevent individuals from obtaining a normal sense of satisfaction from their existence.

In these cases, changing the environment may still be necessary; since, however, the causes of the dysphoria reside in the children's own dysfunctional mode of processing experience, more extensive treatment is required. Therefore, remediation is directed at correcting this maladaptive and incorrect way of judging self and others.

When children's "unhappiness" is so severe or profound that it interferes with their everyday school performance, relationships with friends or family, and the usual interest in or enjoyment of age-appropriate activities, a mood disorder should

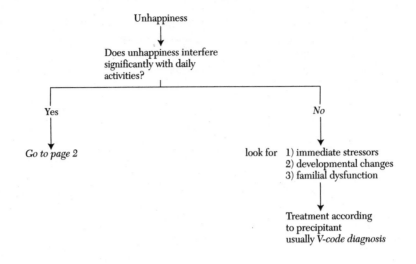

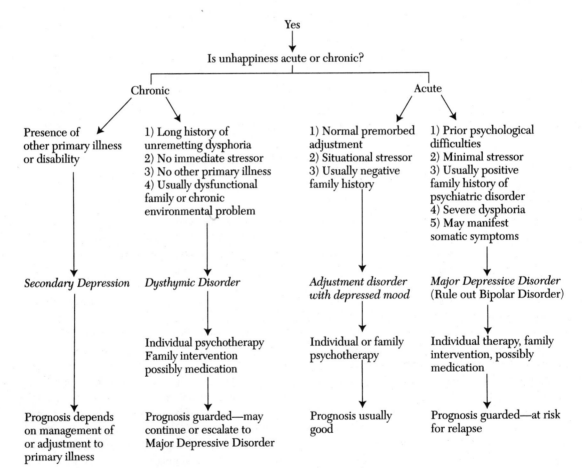

FIGURE 12.1.

Unhappiness.

be suspected. Often there may be associated symptoms, such as difficulties with sleeping, problems concentrating, disturbances in appetite, and a lessening of energy level. Children with true mood disorders, in contrast to those with adjustment disorders, usually present histories of long-standing psychological difficulties preceding the onset of their disorder. Often they come from dysfunctional families in which physical and/or psychological abuse is frequent. A parent of such a child also may have suffered from a mood disorder. Therefore, true mood disorders in children offer evidence for possible genetic, environmental, or neurobiological etiological factors.

In addition, conditions that preclude children obtaining gratification from their everyday life, such as a chronic physical illness, or that hamper them from succeeding in esteem-building pursuits, such as a learning disability, may predispose to depressive disorders. These "secondary" depressions may reach the severity observed in primary mood disorders.

Unhappiness also may be an indicator of health rather than psychopathology as children progress through developmental stages that increase both their cognitive awareness of their environment and the demands made on them by that environment. The normal perturbations during maturation have been called "developmental crises" (Group for the Advancement of Psychiatry, 1966) and include: 8-month anxiety of the infant, separation anxiety of the toddler, normal phobias of the preschool child, the rigid conscientiousness of the school-age child, and the bewilderment of the adolescent. Other expected instances of unhappiness that occur throughout development may be termed "situational crises." These indicate that particular events, such as loss of a loved one or the restrictions imposed by physical illness, may elicit dysphoric responses that are understandable and necessary to the psychological integration of the experience.

Finally, temperamental factors that may find different degrees of expression in various households may predispose certain children to a quiet, emotionally restricted, and, perhaps, gloomy constitution. While far from proven, constitutionally based modes of reactivity may color individuals' manner of interacting with their surroundings and of processing experience.

Whatever the underlying reasons for unhappiness, developmental differences have a strong effect on its clinical manifestations.

When unhappiness is a presenting problem, the decision tree depicted in Figure 12.1 emphasizes important aspects of the evaluation. Except for the concept of the "healthy reaction" to developmental or situational crises described by the Group for the Advancement of Psychiatry (1966), other terms are consistent with those used in the *Diagnostic and Statistical Manual of Mental Disorders,* fourth edition (American Psychiatric Association, 1994). Those unhappy children who present with prior histories of healthy functioning, whose families appear relatively free from marital discord or parental psychopathology, and who have experienced a significant environmental stressor are usually suffering from an adjustment disorder with depressed Mood. In contrast, unhappiness that is so severe or chronic as to interfere with a child's everyday functioning and is accompanied by ancillary symptoms of depression usually indicate that the child has a true mood disorder, either Major Depressive Disorder, Dysthymic Disorder or Depressive Disorder NOS, (APA, 1994) particularly when there is also a history of prior psychological difficulties, a dysfunctional family, or parental psychopathology.

REFERENCES

American Psychiatric Association. (1994). *Diagnostic and statistical manual of mental disorders* (fourth edition). Washington, DC: Author.

Group for the Advancement of Psychiatry. (1966). Psychopathological disorders in childhood: Theoretical considerations and a proposed classification. Report No. 62. New York: Author.

13 / Difficulty with Academic Performance

Larry B. Silver and Rick Ostrander

A decision tree for children and adolescents presenting with problems relating to academic performance involves a preliminary screening followed by a fuller assessment of the child or adolescent, the family, and the environmental and cultural issues. (See Figure 13.1.)

A. Preliminary Screening.

The preliminary screening frequently is done by telephone. The clinician should attempt to clarify 3 issues: (1) the purpose of the contact; (2) what information needed for the assessment is already available; and (3) what additional information will be needed. In addition, information is obtained about the child or adolescent, the family, and the school. Based on this screening process, the clinician will be able effectively and efficiently to start the evaluation process.

To clarify the *purpose of the contact,* the clinician should identify who made the contact, why it was initiated, and what might have precipitated the contact at this time. Of equal importance, the clinician should learn who else is concerned; for example, the classroom teacher, other school professionals, and so on. In addition, it is important to ascertain whether there is any validation for the concerns; for example, report cards, teacher reports, school conference reports, and school or private educational or psychological evaluations.

To clarify *what information needed for the assessment is already available,* the clinician should learn if observations or psychological, educational, or other evaluations have been done and by whom. In addition, the clinician should gain preliminary information about the child or adolescent by asking if there have been difficulties in areas outside that of academic performance and by asking general questions about the family and family functioning. General questions about the child's or adolescent's friends, the neighborhood, and the school might alert the clinician to other possible areas of concern.

Based on this preliminary information, the clinician should be able to *identify what other information will be needed to carry out the evaluation.*

Will the child or adolescent need to be seen? Will the family need to be seen as a whole or the parents first and then the family? Will specific medical, psychoeducational, or neurological studies be necessary? Will more information about the community or the school be important?

With this screening information, the clinician should be able to: (1) develop an assessment plan, prioritizing what needs to be done and in what order; (2) initiate requests for any consultations that will be necessary by the end of the assessment (medical, neurological, or other consultations; psychoeducational or other evaluations) and start the process for completion of any rating scales by parents or teachers; and (3) schedule the initial sessions.

B. Child or Adolescent Evaluation.

Difficulties in academic performance can be related to a range of psychiatric, medical, and/or cognitive factors. In order to determine the primary source of academic difficulties, the evaluation should involve a comprehensive examination of the individual's psychiatric, medical, and psychoeducational status.

B.1. The *psychiatric evaluation* should clarify whether psychopathology is present. If it is, it is useful to determine first if the problems relate to a Disruptive Behavioral Disorder, Attention Deficit Hyperactivity Disorder, or to other psychiatric disorders. Oppositional Defiant Disorder, Conduct Disorder, and Attention Deficit Hyperactivity Disorder have a high incidence of comorbidity with academic difficulties. The full assessment should seek to clarify if the identified disorder is causing the difficulty with academic performance or is secondary to this difficulty. A diagnosis of disruptive behavioral disorder or Attention Deficit Hyperactivity Disorder can result in a student being unavailable for learning or so disruptive as to cause removal from the classroom. The frustrations and failures caused by a learning disability can find expression in the form of an Oppositional Defiant Disorder or a Conduct Disorder. In some cases, the Disruptive Behavioral Disorder can co-

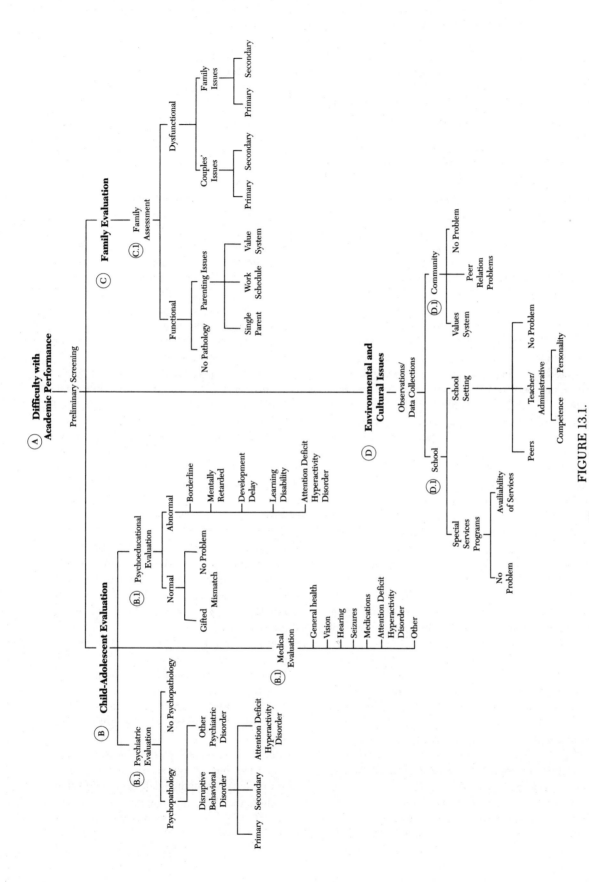

FIGURE 13.1.

Decision tree for youths exhibiting difficulty with academic performance.

exist with a learning disability, each contributing to the academic problems. Students with Attention Deficit Hyperactivity Disorder will have difficulty with attending and possibly with processing information. In addition, many also have a learning disability.

Internalized disorders, such as a depression or anxiety disorder, may result in an uncharacteristic disinterest in or avoidance of school requirements. If one of the internalized disorders is present, it is important to clarify if it is primary or secondary to the academic difficulties. The cognitive, motor, and language deficits plus the social deficits associated with a pervasive developmental disorder may result in the individual being unavailable for learning and in academic difficulties.

B.1. The *medical evaluation* is necessary to assess the influence of health factors on the individual's availability and ability to learn. Problems in acquiring academic content can be significantly affected by undiagnosed visual or hearing deficits. Generally poor health can influence the stamina, motivation, and/or concentration needed to focus adequately on academic demands. Students with chronic medical disorders (asthma, diabetes, etc.) may miss many days of school. Medications might cause sedation or other side effects that make the student less alert and available.

Early developmental stresses can result in focal or global deficits in neurological development. An undiagnosed seizure disorder, especially petit mal and partial complex seizures, may result in difficulties in general cognitive functioning, memory, and attention.

With adolescents, it is important to assess the possibility of substance abuse. Alcohol and drugs will have an impact on both attitude toward school and cognitive functioning.

B.1. The evaluation of *cognitive, academic, and neuropsychological functioning* is critical in any assessment concerning academic problems. The results of this psychoeducational assessment will indicate the parameters of the individual's academic and cognitive liabilities while also identifying strengths. In some instances, borderline cognitive development or mental retardation may be the primary explanation for the academic difficulties. Borderline cognitive development is reflected by a generally flat and low-average profile on intelligence tests (IQ of 70 to 85). Mental retardation is reflected in significant impairment in

both cognitive functioning (IQ below 70) and adaptive functioning.

In other instances, however, low scores on indices of cognitive functioning may be somewhat ambiguous and may represent artificially delayed scores on cognitive measures. This finding is particularly true with preschool children where rapid and uneven developmental changes can lead to considerable variability in findings arising from measures of intellectual functioning.

Learning disabilities are another prevalent explanation for children experiencing academic difficulties. These disabilities typically are reflected by a significant discrepancy between average or better cognitive abilities and low academic functioning. Appropriate psychoeducational assessments should reveal the magnitude of this discrepancy as well as the nature of the processing deficits. This assessment also can be useful in targeting appropriate interventions.

The results of psychoeducational testing can identify instances where the child's or adolescent's capabilities are mismatched with the school program. For example, a gifted student, assigned to a classroom that fails to challenge him or her, can become bored. Alternatively, a student with average intellectual ability may be unable to keep up in a school where the majority of students are of above-average ability or where unusually high academic standards must be met.

C. *Family Evaluation.*

C.1. The family evaluation must include an assessment of the parents and of the family. A judgment must be made about in what order to do these assessments. The first clinical question is whether the family is found to be functional or dysfunctional. If the family is seen as functional, the clinician should clarify that there is no evidence of individual psychopathology, or that there are "normal" parenting issues that might be contributing to the presenting problems. If there is no evidence of psychopathology, alternative explanations must be considered that do not relate to family issues.

Evidence of "normal" parenting issues might relate to time and energy stress on a parent or on both parents, or might relate to family values concerning education. A single parent might feel overwhelmed with responsibilities for the family plus the need to work, and thus have little time or energy to offer the children. Even in 2-parent

94

families, one or both parents might feel so extended by work demands that little time or energy is available for the children. The clinician might learn that education is not a high priority for this family, and that a possible issue to be considered is the difference between the school's expectations and those of the family.

If the family is found to be dysfunctional, the clinician must assess if this dysfunctionality is caused by problems with one parent, issues between the parents, and/or broader family difficulties. If stress between the parents results in parenting or marital problems, the clinician should seek to clarify whether these problems are primary or whether they arise secondary to the presenting problems. That is, might the parenting or marital stress be contributing to or causing the child's or adolescent's academic difficulties, or are the child's or adolescent's academic difficulties and reactions to these difficulties bringing stress to bear on the parents?

The assessment might reveal that one parent is having psychological problems that are contributing to the couple's and/or the family's stress. If there is family dysfunction, the clinician must discern, if possible, what the difficulties are. Further, the clinician must clarify whether the family dysfunction is contributing to or causing the child's or adolescent's academic difficulties, or whether the child's or adolescent's academic difficulties and reactions to these difficulties are causing the family stress and dysfunction.

D. *Environmental and Cultural Assessment.*

Academic difficulties are typically attributed to cognitive deficits or behavioral problems within the child or adolescent. Yet environmental factors involving the school and/or community also can contribute to such difficulties. The clinician should be aware of the impact social, cultural, or institutional problems can have on learning. In many instances, such an awareness is developed over time in the process of conducting clinical practice in a community. Data collection within this context is accomplished through formal and informal observations of the school system and the cultural milieu. Through ongoing interactions with the community and with the school system,

a clinician may develop an appreciation for the community values and the general programmatic resources provided by the school. With this understanding as a backdrop, the clinician can conduct a more direct assessment of how specific environmental or school considerations can affect a given individual.

In respect to *school considerations* as such, a child or adolescent with special needs may be further impaired because the range of services offered by the school system is inadequate for his or her needs. For example, a child's learning disabilities may require special accommodations and services in a specific program; yet the school may not have allocated sufficient resources to provide either the program or the services. School program effectiveness also can be influenced by such interpersonal considerations as the competence and personality of the teachers or administrators. A specific individual may have insufficient knowledge concerning a particular psychiatric condition or may have insufficient training to address a particular problem effectively. Although less common, a more troublesome influence on learning can emerge when a teacher exhibits biases or personality difficulties that affect his or her ability to teach.

In addition to problems associated with school personnel, the degree to which peers value academic success can motivate or discourage students from reaching their academic potential. An assessment of school-based interpersonal conflicts and alliances can provide valuable insights concerning what influences learning.

While the school exerts a more direct influence on learning, the *community's influence* is less direct, although no less profound. For example, the value system of some communities includes very high expectations for academic accomplishment; other communities view academic success as largely unobtainable. Similarly, inappropriate peer pressure can minimize or degrade the importance of academic performance and success. Within more affluent communities, unusually high academic expectations can place unrealistic pressure on a student who has average intellectual capabilities.

14 / Sleep Difficulty

Michael W. Naylor

Assessment of the Sleep Complaint

Children or adolescents with sleep disorders typically present with one or more types of sleep complaint: difficulty falling or staying asleep (insomnia), excessive daytime sleepiness, or abnormal behaviors arising during sleep (parasomnias). These sleep complaints are not exclusive and may coexist.

INSOMNIA

Insomnia is a common sleep problem affecting children of all ages. In evaluating the chief complaint of insomnia, specific information relating to environmental conditions; alcohol, drug, or medication use; the presence of a psychiatric or medical illness; sleep-related respiratory disturbances such as apnea, wheezing, or snoring; abnormal sleep-wake patterns; sleep hygiene; recent stressful events; struggles around or recent alterations in the bedtime routine; and subjective arousal associated with bedtime may help establish the correct sleep disorder diagnosis.

An assessment of the sleep environment is necessary for all patients who present with complaints of insomnia. The patient and his or her parents should be asked about the amount of noise in the sleep environment, the sleep surface, the ambient temperature, and level of lighting in the sleep environment. Even patients who deny that their sleep is affected by noise demonstrate polysomnographic evidence of sleep disruption upon exposure to noise. Ambient temperature either above or below thermoneutrality leads to an increased amount of wakefulness and Stage 1 sleep and decreased rapid eye movement (REM) sleep, even when sleep onset is unaffected.

Acknowledgment: I would like to thank Melanie Banas, M.D., and Kathleen M. Kaminski, B.A., for their valuable assistance in the preparation of this manuscript.

Alcohol, caffeine, nicotine, and illicit drug use must be assessed. Alcohol causes severe sleep disruption during the second half of the night due to metabolism of the alcohol. Chronic alcohol abuse can produce long-lasting changes in sleep patterns. Caffeine also produces significant sleep disturbance, even in those who deny difficulties. Nicotine dependency may lead to nocturnal awakenings in heavy tobacco users. Cocaine, amphetamines, barbiturates, and opiates are associated with marked disruption of sleep architecture. Since many commonly used medications have deleterious effects on sleep or wakefulness, a history of current medication use is often informative. Specific inquiry about nonprescription medications is necessary since patients often fail to include over-the-counter preparations when listing current medications. Cold preparations, appetite suppressants, and caffeine-containing stimulants are commonly used over-the-counter drugs that disrupt sleep.

The history of current or past medical and psychiatric illnesses and surgical procedures must be obtained. Anxiety disorders, acute psychosis, and mood disorders, for example, often are accompanied by severe sleep disruption. Seizure disorders, illnesses accompanied by pain, asthma, Tourette's disorder, and migraine headaches are examples of medical problems that may cause or contribute to disturbed sleep. The effects of these disorders on sleep may be direct, mediated through the effects of the illness or the associated symptoms on sleep mechanisms, or indirect, mediated by the pharmacologic effects of the medications used to treat the medical condition. Head trauma may lead to the postconcussion syndrome, often accompanied by disrupted sleep continuity.

A history of difficulty falling asleep, difficulty awakening at the desired time, sleepiness in the morning and early afternoon, and normal sleep in the absence of social obligations raises the diagnostic possibility of delayed sleep phase syndrome. In evaluating the "insomnic" child, the parents' belief about what constitutes a normal night's sleep for a child must be assessed. Concurrent questions about how many hours of sleep the child actually needs to feel rested and to be able to meet academic, social, and familial demands may establish a mismatch between the parents' expectations and the child's needs. This is particularly true for those children who appear to be short sleepers.

A history of transient sleep difficulties accompanying an acute stressor is characteristic of the diagnosis of adjustment sleep disorder. Although the sleep disturbance typically is transient and resolves with resolution of the stressor, there may be a history of repeated episodes.

In preschool and early grade-school children, the history of inadequate enforcement of bedtime routines by the primary caregiver may lead to delayed settling and refusal to go to bed at the appropriate time. Specific inquiry should be made about nighttime fears, which may also cause delayed sleep onset.

Normal infant sleep is characterized by intermittent nocturnal arousals and occasional difficulties settling. Parents, unaware that the problems are normative and time limited, may respond by rocking their child to sleep. The infant's rapid transition to sleep conditions lead the parent to believe that it was the rocking that lulled the infant to sleep. After repeated trials, the infant associates sleep onset with rocking and may develop severe sleep-onset difficulties when not rocked. Furthermore, even if a child falls asleep with the rocking, he or she may awaken when it stops, requiring repetition of the routine until transition to a deep stage of sleep is complete. Well-meaning parents also may condition arousals through nocturnal feedings. There is no physiologic need for nocturnal feedings after the infant reaches 2 to 3 months of age; when feedings continue after this age, nocturnal arousals are reinforced. At its extreme, nighttime feedings are associated with hourly awakenings and may prevent the appearance of a more mature circadian pattern.

A less common cause of sleep disturbance in the pediatric age group is psychophysiologic insomnia. This diagnosis is supported by a history suggesting that the sleeper has learned to associate the sleep environment with difficulty falling asleep. The child is overconcerned about his or her inability to sleep and "works hard" to fall asleep, further complicating his or her difficulties. The child may report falling asleep quite easily during monotonous activities or in novel sleep environments that have not been associated with increased arousal and sleeplessness. A pattern of lifelong insomnia that cannot be explained by psychological factors or medical or psychiatric conditions should alert the clinician to the possible diagnosis of idiopathic insomnia. Often dating back to birth, idiopathic insomnia generally is accompanied by impaired daytime functioning due to fatigue. A history of attention deficit hyperactivity disorder or dyslexia is common in children with this diagnosis. Probably caused by abnormal sleep-inducing or sleep-maintenance mechanisms, idiopathic insomnia has been associated with decreased serotonergic neurotransmission. Rarely diagnosed in childhood, idiopathic insomnia is one of the few indications for pharmacotherapy in children with difficulty falling or staying asleep. Figure 14.1 depicts the approach to the sleepless child or adolescent.

EXCESSIVE SLEEPINESS

Sleep in toddlers and school-age children is generally very efficient, and excessive sleepiness in these age groups is almost always abnormal. When present, sleepiness in this age group may be difficult to identify since it may present as behavioral changes, such as irritability or hyperactivity. In adolescents, however, sleepiness during the day is common and is mediated by a variety of social and developmental determinants.

Careful examination of symptoms accompanying sleep or extreme sleepiness may shed light on the etiology of the sleep complaint. Specific information relating to the child's or adolescent's sleep hygiene, sleep/wake pattern, alcohol and drug use, sleep environment, medical and psychiatric history, sleep-related respiratory problems, the presence of cataplexy, cyclicity of symptoms, and the association between the sleepiness and the adolescent's menstrual cycle is necessary to diagnose the chief complaint of excessive daytime somnolence.

Information pertaining to the sleep/wake schedule may provide the clinician with sufficient information to establish the diagnosis. A discrep-

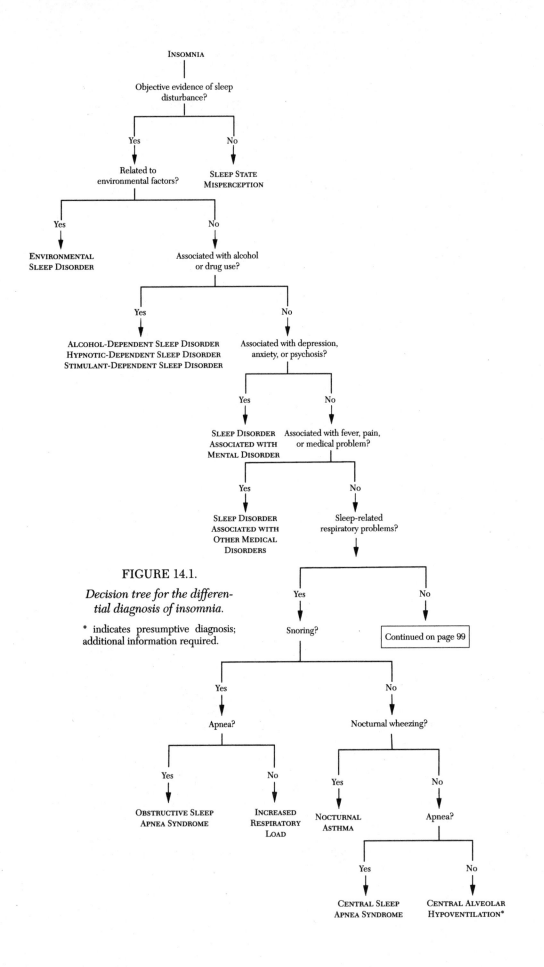

INSOMNIA

Objective evidence of sleep
disturbance?

Yes — Related to environmental factors?
No — SLEEP STATE MISPERCEPTION

Related to environmental factors?
Yes — ENVIRONMENTAL SLEEP DISORDER
No — Associated with alcohol or drug use?

Associated with alcohol or drug use?
Yes — ALCOHOL-DEPENDENT SLEEP DISORDER / HYPNOTIC-DEPENDENT SLEEP DISORDER / STIMULANT-DEPENDENT SLEEP DISORDER
No — Associated with depression, anxiety, or psychosis?

Associated with depression, anxiety, or psychosis?
Yes — SLEEP DISORDER ASSOCIATED WITH MENTAL DISORDER
No — Associated with fever, pain, or medical problem?

Associated with fever, pain, or medical problem?
Yes — SLEEP DISORDER ASSOCIATED WITH OTHER MEDICAL DISORDERS
No — Sleep-related respiratory problems?

Sleep-related respiratory problems?
Yes — Snoring?
No — Continued on page 99

Snoring?
Yes — Apnea?
No — Nocturnal wheezing?

Apnea?
Yes — OBSTRUCTIVE SLEEP APNEA SYNDROME
No — INCREASED RESPIRATORY LOAD

Nocturnal wheezing?
Yes — NOCTURNAL ASTHMA
No — Apnea?

Apnea?
Yes — CENTRAL SLEEP APNEA SYNDROME
No — CENTRAL ALVEOLAR HYPOVENTILATION°

FIGURE 14.1.

Decision tree for the differential diagnosis of insomnia.

° indicates presumptive diagnosis; additional information required.

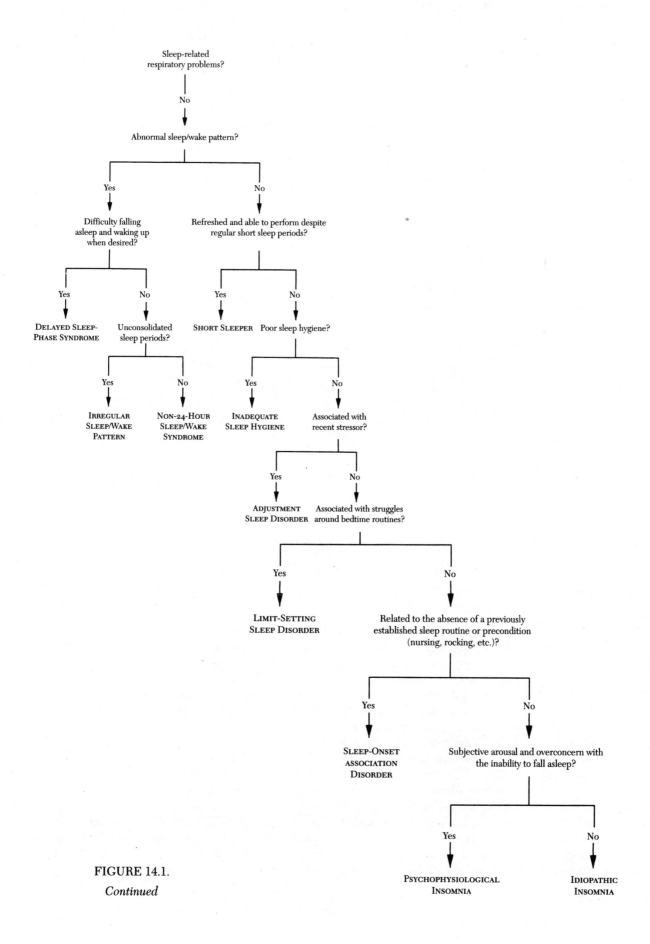

FIGURE 14.1.

Continued

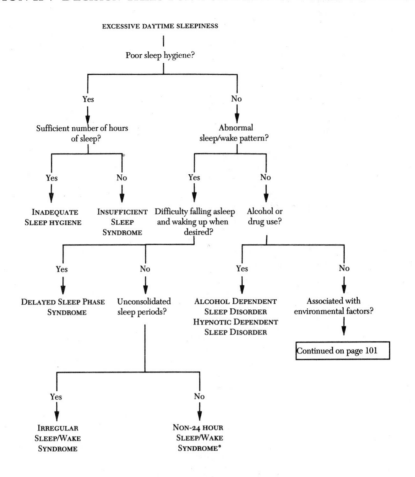

FIGURE 14.2.

Decision tree for the differential diagnosis of excessive daytime sleepiness.

° indicates presumptive diagnosis; additional information required.

ancy between the amount of sleep obtained and the amount of sleep previously obtained or the amount of sleep desired; short nocturnal sleep times; rapid sleep onset; and longer sleep on weekends or holidays suggest the diagnosis of insufficient sleep syndrome. Sleepiness in the morning and early afternoon accompanied by a history of difficulty falling asleep and difficulty awakening at the desired time suggests the diagnosis of delayed sleep-phase syndrome.

Alcohol, several drugs of abuse, and numerous prescription medications may cause sedation. Alcohol use or abuse may intensify snoring and obstructive sleep apnea in adolescents by causing relaxation of the genioglossus muscle during sleep. Adolescents who drink heavily on the weekend

may complain of excessive daytime sleepiness primarily on weekend and Monday mornings due to the extreme sleep disruption caused by the alcohol. Antihistamines, nonprescription sedatives, and cold preparations are commonly used over-the-counter drugs that also may cause excessive sleepiness.

A variety of medical conditions may contribute to the development of sleepiness via their association with obstructive sleep apnea, including hypothyroidism, acromegaly, Cushing's syndrome, allergic rhinitis, and some of the mucopolysaccharidoses. Information about tonsillectomy, cleft palate repair, and orofacial surgery is essential in patients with suspected obstructive sleep apnea syndrome. Depression often is associated with ex-

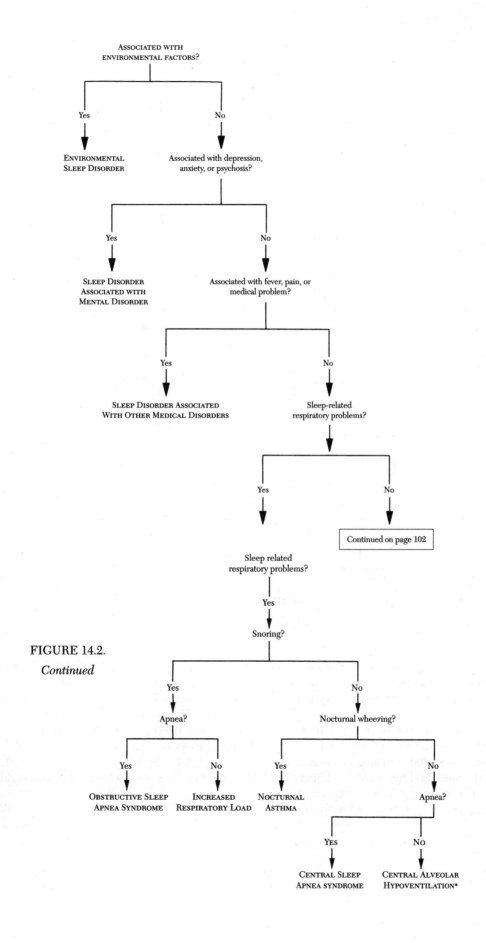

ASSOCIATED WITH
ENVIRONMENTAL FACTORS?

Yes

No

ENVIRONMENTAL
SLEEP DISORDER

Associated with depression,
anxiety, or psychosis?

Yes

No

SLEEP DISORDER
ASSOCIATED WITH
MENTAL DISORDER

Associated with fever, pain, or
medical problem?

Yes

No

SLEEP DISORDER ASSOCIATED
WITH OTHER MEDICAL DISORDERS

Sleep-related
respiratory problems?

Yes

No

Continued on page 102

Sleep related
respiratory problems?

Yes

Snoring?

FIGURE 14.2.
Continued

Yes

No

Apnea?

Nocturnal wheezing?

Yes

No

Yes

No

OBSTRUCTIVE SLEEP
APNEA SYNDROME

INCREASED
RESPIRATORY LOAD

NOCTURNAL
ASTHMA

Apnea?

YES

No

CENTRAL SLEEP
APNEA SYNDROME

CENTRAL ALVEOLAR
HYPOVENTILATION*

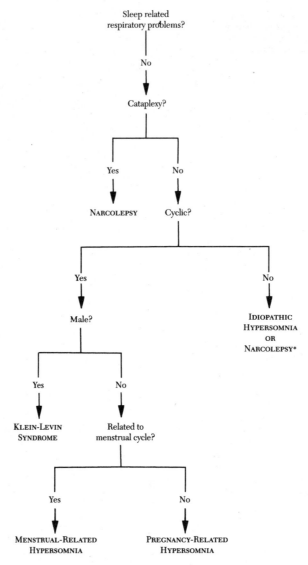

FIGURE 14.2.

Continued

cessive sleeping, especially among adolescents. The presence of snoring, gasping during sleep, and episodes of apnea suggests the diagnosis of obstructive sleep apnea.

A history of sleep paralysis (loss of muscle tone preceding sleep onset), cataplexy (sudden loss of muscle tone associated with laughter, exercise, or intense emotions), and hypnogogic hallucinations (vivid hallucinations preceding sleep onset) are highly suggestive of narcolepsy. A history of recur-

rent episodes of hypersomnia in adolescent males with hypersexuality, binge eating, and disinhibited behaviors suggests the diagnosis of Kleine-Levin syndrome. The association of recurrent hypersomnia and the menstrual cycle in adolescent females supports the diagnosis of menstrual-associated sleep disorder. Figure 14.2 presents a decision tree for assessing the sleepy child or adolescent.

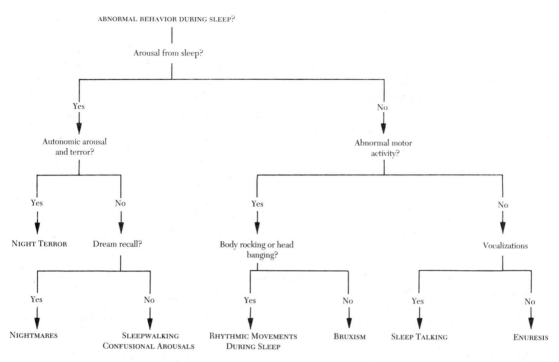

FIGURE 14.3.

Decision tree for the differential diagnosis of abnormal behaviors during sleep.

Parasomnias

Parasomnias are abnormal behaviors, physiological events, or sensations that arise at sleep onset, during sleep, during sleep/wake transitions, with sleep stage transitions, or during confusional arousals from sleep. In most instances these behaviors do not cause subjective problems for the sleeper who often is unaware of the problem. The referral usually is initiated by the patient's parents who themselves are disturbed by the patient's abnormal sleep behavior.

Specific attention should be paid to descriptions of motor behavior, vocalizations, and mental status during these episodes and their relationship to sleep onset and time of the night. The patient's recall of the episode also must be assessed. Sudden arousals during the first third of the night accompanied by screaming, behavioral evidence of terror, intense autonomic discharge, and inconsolability, followed later by lack of dream recall, slow return to full awareness of the environment, and amnesia together typify sleep terrors. Sleepwalking and confusional arousals are less severe presentations of sleep terrors without the associated autonomic arousal. Episodes of sudden arousal from sleep during the last half of the night accompanied by anxiety, dream recall, and full alertness upon arousal are characteristic of nightmares.

Questions about other motor behaviors during sleep should be pursued. Grinding or clenching of the teeth during sleep suggests the presence of bruxism. Rhythmic, stereotypical movements of large muscle groups such as head banging, body rocking, and body rolling are diagnostic of rhythmic movement disorder. Rhythmic vocalizations often accompany this diagnosis. Nocturnal enuresis (involuntary urination during sleep) is followed by feelings of shame and embarrassment. The afflicted child or adolescent may be reluctant to offer such information, and the clinician must routinely ask about such problems. The assessment of parasomnias during sleep is schematized in Figure 14.3.

Conclusion

Sleep disorders are fairly common in the pediatric age group and are especially prevalent in children and adolescents who present to the child psychiatry clinic. Diagnosis of the sleep complaint often presents a difficult clinical challenge given the numerous diagnoses that must be entertained and because of the patient's inability to describe events that occur during sleep or during arousals from sleep. A thorough history and physical examination, however, usually will suggest the most likely diagnoses that can then be either confirmed or excluded by appropriate diagnostic procedures. Fortunately, most sleep disorders respond well to treatment once the correct diagnosis is established and the appropriate intervention made.

REFERENCES

American Psychiatric Association. (1994). *Diagnostic and statistical manual of mental disorders* (4th ed.). Washington, DC: APA Press.

Diagnostic Classification Steering Committee. (1990). *International classification of sleep disorders: Diagnostic and coding manual.* Rochester, NY: American Sleep Disorders Association.

Faber, R. (1985). *Solve your child's sleep problems.* New York: Simon and Schuster.

Guilleminault, C. (Ed.). (1987). Sleep and its disorders in children. New York: Raven Press.

Hauri, P. J. (1992). *Current concepts: Sleep disorders.* Kalamazoo, MI: The Upjohn Company.

Kryger, M., Roth, T., Dement, W. C. (Eds.). (1994). *The principles and practice of sleep disorders medicine* (2nd ed.). Philadelphia: W. B. Saunders.

Sheldon, S. H., Spire, J. P., & Levy, H. B. (1992). *Pediatric sleep medicine.* Philadelphia: W. B. Saunders.

15 / Appetite Disturbances: Anorexia and Hyperphagia

Hans Steiner

Loss of Appetite or Anorexia

Appetite is the desire for food and drink, especially for preferred nutritive substances. Appetite is based on simple hunger but goes beyond it, containing mental and social elements that elaborate and shape the basic drive for food (Hoeberl and Novin, 1982). Assessment of a child's appetite should be obtained during all psychiatric assessments, as this area may contain some of the most succinct and important indicators of the presence of pathological development. Appetite disturbances may take many forms. Anorexia—loss of appetite—is the most common appetite disturbance in childhood, but some variants of this disturbance, such as anorexia nervosa, emerge for the first time during puberty.

DEVELOPMENTAL ASPECTS OF ANOREXIA

Food intake in the newborn is governed only by hunger; this lasts until approximately 3 months, when food preferences begin. Appetite develops in response to and under the influence of multiple social and cultural factors. Food is one of the first and most important means of communication between child and caregiver. Because food has such tremendous reinforcing value, it does not take long for food and ministrations centered on food to assume many excess significances, which remain strongly and permanently paired with desiring food. At the same time, many biological processes affect a person's desire for food as well, especially those associated with illness. Thus this whole area of functioning is of prime importance to those who are interested in assessing the development of the child.

Anorexia accompanies a wide variety of acute and chronic pediatric and psychiatric illnesses across childhood and adolescence and should be carefully assessed in terms of differential diagnosis (Tunnessen, 1988; Oski et al., 1990; Ziai, 1983). It should be kept in mind that at any age, there is considerable normal variability among children in terms of their tendency to lose their appetite in reaction to stress or illness. Such variants are most likely either constitutionally determined or learned very early; they are accordingly very difficult to change. In terms of temperament, a tendency to lose one's appetite seems to appear more often in individuals who are somewhat anxious, inhibited, tend to be shy and withdrawn, and who appreciate a strong routine in their daily activities.

SYNDROMES MOST COMMONLY ASSOCIATED WITH LOSS OF APPETITE

Loss of appetite is the most frequent appetite disturbance accompanying most acute and chronic pediatric illnesses (Green and Richmond, 1986). Furthermore, anorexia is a significant side effect associated with many medications that are routinely prescribed in the treatment of these illnesses. Loss of appetite may accompany a wide range of psychiatric problems (Steiner, 1996), most commonly disturbances of affect and mood, and is commonly present during abuse of drugs, many of which suppress appetite (such as cocaine and other stimulants). Adjustment disorders, posttraumatic stress disorders, schizophrenia—especially those forms where the symptomatic delusions involve food—conversion disorders, and dissociative disorders all may be accompanied by some degree of anorexia. Weight loss associated with these disorders may be dramatic enough to mimic anorexia nervosa. Classical eating disorders such as anorexia nervosa do present a loss of appetite, but usually not until quite late in the development of weight loss. Early in the course of this condition, conscious control of hunger and appetite is much more common. Not to be forgotten, of course, are appetite-suppressing drugs such as stimulants and street drugs, which can lead to chronic loss of appetite and weight loss. For iatrogenically induced losses of appetite, any of the medications used for treatment of acute and chronic childhood illnesses and certain psychiatric

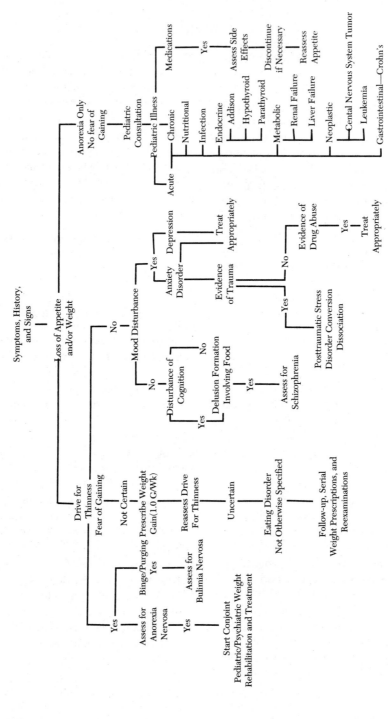

FIGURE 15.1.

Decision tree for anorexia.

medications, such as selective serotonin reuptake inhibitors and stimulants, must be considered.

TREATMENT AND MANAGEMENT OF ANOREXIA

Given the wide variety of problems that can appear with loss of appetite, it is important to entertain an adequate differential diagnostic list and proceed with appropriate caution. As a long list of acute and chronic illnesses can affect appetite, any serious loss of appetite (extending over several meals and/or leading to loss of hydration and weight) needs to be assessed in consultation with a pediatrician. In general, biologically based loss of appetite tends to recede rather rapidly when given appropriate treatment and management. Persistence of the symptoms indicates a need to reconsider the etiology and perhaps to focus more on the psychosocial aspects of the child's life. Since major and persistent loss of appetite can have profound and immediate impact on weight, body composition and functioning, and growth patterns, such disturbances should be handled in conjunction with a pediatrician. Ongoing pediatric evaluation of nutritional status, eating patterns, growth curves, and endocrine function is essential for any child, but during times of disturbance of the crucial energy-supplying process of eating, surveillance should be intensified to weekly or even twice-weekly contact. In most cases appropriate treatment of the underlying disturbances leads to normalization of eating at all ages and is the preferred mode of action. Only rarely is medication indicated to selectively stimulate (such agents as phenothiazines or cyproheptadine) or inhibit (by means of appetite suppressants) appetite. Medications alone usually are insufficient to correct appetite disturbances; most underlying syndromes call for a carefully coordinated approach of nutritional prescription and supervision, behavioral intervention in the home or school, and family and individual treatment (Steiner, 1996; Steiner, 1997a, 1997b).

Constant Hunger or Hyperphagia

Appetite disturbances may exist as hyper- or polyphagia. Overeating may be continuous or episodic (binge eating). Under the influence of uncontrollable hunger, the individual consumes large quantities of food in one sitting and does not halt food intake even after internal signals of satiety. Problems of this kind can assume grotesque proportions, such as when quantities in excess of tens of thousands of calories are consumed; very often these problems are complicated by secondary forms of pathology, such as eating nonnutritive substances, various forms of purgation, and clandestine pathological behavior needed to sustain the habit—the sneaking and stealing of food (Steiner, 1996).

DEVELOPMENTAL ASPECTS OF HYPERPHAGIA

As loss of appetite, hyperphagia appears in the context of multiple acute and chronic pediatric and psychiatric illnesses across childhood and adolescence and requires careful differential diagnosis (Oski et al., 1990; Ziai, 1983). Hyperphagia is most common in the context of certain specific disorders that may appear at both extremes of the developmental spectrum—during the preschool years and in adolescence. Hyperphagia in the preschool years most often leads to obesity and accompanies certain forms of mental retardation. The hyperphagia typical of bulimia nervosa typically begins in early puberty. At any given time, though, hyperphagia might be induced by either an acute or chronic pediatric illness, or, iatrogenically, by the administration of treatment regimens or medications that induce appetite increases.

SYNDROMES MOST COMMONLY ASSOCIATED WITH HYPERPHAGIA

Hyperphagia is most commonly associated with the following pediatric diagnoses: obesity, mental retardation (such as Prader-Willi), hyperthyroidism, diabetes mellitus, cystic fibrosis, Kleine-Levine syndrome, hypothalamus lesions due to pituitary tumors, craniopharyngiomas, central nervous system leukemia, encephalitis, the Laurence-Moon-Biedl syndrome, pinealomas, and porencephaly. The most common psychiatric syndromes accompanying hyperphagia are bulimia nervosa, abuse of psychoactive drugs (such as marijuana or rebound after use of stimulants and cocaine), atypical depression, premenstrual syndrome, and psychosocial dwarfism. It is impor-

HYPERPHAGIA

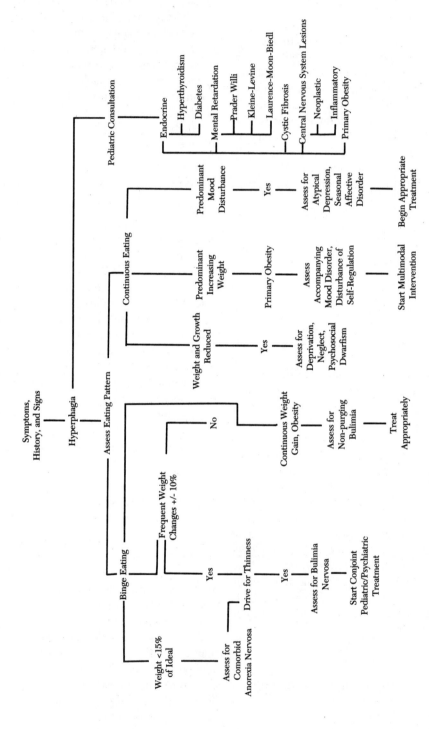

FIGURE 15.2.

Decision tree for hyperphagia.

tant to remember that there are some forms of nonpurging bulimias that usually result in obesity. Some bizarre eating may accompany the pervasive developmental disorders, but this occurrence is more rare. The iatrogenically induced hyperphagias are varied and need to be ruled out. They can either be the result of treatment regimens that require that patients eat large amounts of food to maintain their health, such as in cystic fibrosis or in the aftermath of a burn injury, or they are the direct result of some medications necessary for treatment, such as insulin, thyroid medication, phenothiazines, tricyclics, or some antiallergic medications such as cyproheptadine, to name just a few of the common ones.

TREATMENT AND MANAGEMENT OF HYPERPHAGIA

As in the treatment of loss of appetite, it is important to entertain an adequate differential diagnostic list and proceed with appropriate caution.

Again, the assessment of hyperphagia requires close collaboration with the child's pediatrician to rule out complex causes of the problem. Hyperphagia usually leads to weight gain and, in terms of medical stability, does not present all the immediate problems of loss of appetite. But it is possible that some of the overeating leads to secondary problems such as purgation, which can then rapidly involve acute medical problems such as esophageal tears, dehydration, and hypokalemia. Thus, even after adequate diagnostic evaluation has been performed by the pediatrician and child psychiatrist, it is to be expected that an appropriate amount of ongoing pediatric supervision of the child will be necessary to determine problem patterns and to assess progress. In contradistinction to loss of appetite, rapid treatment of problems of hyperphagia is much more difficult. Behavioral interventions and psychopharmacological management both should be considered actively, but, in most cases, neither is curative, and relapse rates after treatment remain high.

REFERENCES

Hoeberl, B. G., & Novin, D. (Eds.). (1982). *The neural basis of feeding and reward*. Brunswick, ME: Haer Institute for Electrophysiological Research.

Green, M., & Richmond, R. (1986). *Pediatric diagnosis* (4th ed.). Philadelphia: W. B. Saunders.

Oski, F., De Angelis, C. D., Feigen, R. D., & Warshaw, J. B. (1990). *Principles and practice of pediatrics*. Philadelphia: J. B. Lippincott.

Steiner, H. (ed) (1996). *Treating Adolescents*. San Francisco: Jossey-Bass.

Steiner, H. (ed.) (1997a). *Treating School-age children*. San Francisco: Jossey-Bass.

Steiner, H. (ed) (1997b). *Treating Pre-School Children*. San Francisco: Jossey Bass.

Tunnessen, W. W. (1988). *Signs and symptoms in pediatrics* (2nd ed.). Philadelphia: J. B. Lippincott.

Ziai, M. (1983). *Bedside pediatrics*. Boston: Little, Brown.

16 / Substance Abuse

Steven L. Jaffe and Jennifer J. Gould

Figure 16.1 presents a decision tree for substance abuse.

Additional Considerations

I. Full psychiatric evaluation is needed because substance abuse frequently coexists with one or more psychiatric disorder (especially mood disorders, behavior disorders including attention deficit hyperactivity and conduct disorder, and anxiety disorders)

II. Failure of treatment usually indicates that a more advanced stage of use was actually present. Treatment modalities of this more advanced stage are then indicated.

III. Adolescents usually do not need detoxification because of the following:
   A. Adolescents tend to be in better physical condition than adults.
   B. Adolescents tend to use multiple drugs.
   C. Marijuana, LSD, and cocaine, which are frequently used by adolescents, do not require detoxification.
   D. Heavy alcohol abuse is often episodic without the development of physical addiction.

IV. Although rare in adolescents, physical addiction to alcohol, sedatives, or minor tranquilizers can have life-threatening withdrawal symptoms and necessitates detoxification.

V. Pharmacologic treatment for substance-abusing adolescents is used mostly to treat the comorbid psychiatric disorders.

Treatment Modalities for Stages of Use

1. **Education** helps adolescent and parents learn about alcohol and drugs and their detrimental effects. Excellent information and pamphlets for distribution may be obtained at no charge from the National Clearinghouse for Alcohol and Drug

SUBSTANCE ABUSE

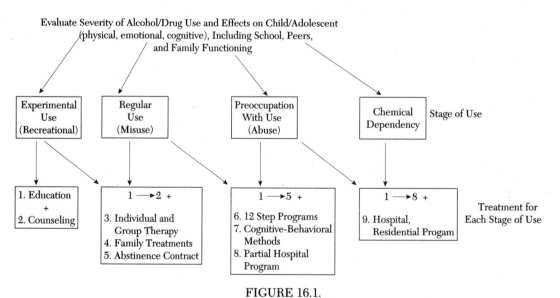

FIGURE 16.1.

Decision tree for substance abuse.

Information Publications Catalog (1–800–729–6686).

2. **Counseling** includes talking with the adolescent about his or her life and drug use.

3. **Individual and group therapy** should be performed by a mental health professional.

4. **Family treatments** include specific theory-based (i.e., structural or functional) treatment, multifamily therapy, and behavioral therapies, such as Parent Management Training and contracting.

5. An **abstinence contract** is a written agreement not to use drugs, to have regular urine drug screens, and to abide by home rules (privileges and consequences) as developed by the parents and the adolescent.

6. Participation in a **12-Step Program** requires attending regular meetings of Alcoholics Anonymous or Narcotics Anonymous; establishing a sponsor, and working the steps.

7. **Cognitive/Behavioral Methods** of coping include drug- and alcohol-related methods that teach refusal skills, coping with urges, managing using thoughts, handling emergencies, and handling a lapse; communication skills methods teach nonverbal ways of coping, assertiveness training, and negotiation/conflict resolution; problem solving, anger, and negative mood management; relaxation training and time management skills; and relapse prevention.

8. Attendance at a **partial hospital program** during the day or evening includes therapy groups, family programs, individual therapy, creative activities, and school.

9. A **hospital program** provides acute and intermediate level of care.

A **residential program** provides a long-term, intermediate level of 24-hour care and a therapeutic program.

17 / **Suicidal Behavior**

Cynthia R. Pfeffer

Figure 17.1 presents the decision tree for suicidal tendencies.

A. Suicidal tendencies that are nonfatal in children and adolescents involve a spectrum including suicidal ideation, suicide threats, and suicide attempts (Pfeffer, 1986). Suicidal tendencies are complex states whose evaluation necessitates review of risk and protective factors. Risk is associated with severity of the type of suicidal tendency, that is, ideation or acts, and other elements, such as severity of suicidal intent, degree of planning, and level of lethality of act. Other risk factors include:

1. Affects and psychiatric diagnoses such as depressive symptoms, aggressive behavior, psychiatric disorders especially those affecting mood, disruptive tendencies, schizophrenia, and the presence of substance abuse (Pfeffer et al., 1991, 1993).

2. Interpersonal problems. These may stem from family discord and involve parents in the form of parental psychopathology or situational problems such as parental conflict, separation or divorce, or they may derive from problems with peers and others (Pfeffer, Normandin, & Kakuma, 1994).

3. Adaptive skill problems such as poor impulse control, hopelessness, poor reality testing (Pfeffer, 1986).

4. Past developmental experiences involving physiological problems or interpersonal traumas involving abuse (Deykin, Alpert, McNamarra, 1985).

These factors should be evaluated by means of interviews with the child or adolescent, with parents, and with others and by review of medical and school reports (Jacobsen et al., 1994).

B. Suicidal intent, degree of planning for a suicidal act, and lethality of a suicidal act are correlated factors (Robbins & Alessi, 1985). For example, the presence of a high suicidal intent—that is, the intense desire to kill oneself—is significantly correlated with high degree of lethality of a suicidal act—that is, the high probability that the suicidal act will cause death or serious injury. These factors are important indicators of the likelihood of future suicidal act and of injury.

C. An important protective factor is the pres-

SUICIDAL TENDENCY

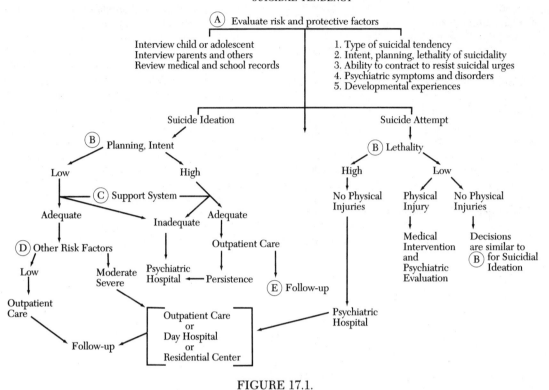

FIGURE 17.1.

Decision tree for suicidal tendency (ideation or act).

ence of a supportive network to provide immediate discussion or actions to delay a suicidal act (Pfeffer, 1989). Such a support system also functions to enhance the youngster's adaptive skills by maintaining a consistent, structured, and nonstressful atmosphere. Discussion with people in the support network can involve developing alternative approaches to coping with problematic circumstances, assistance in adequately and objectively appraising situations, and improved ways of maintaining adequate levels of impulse control. The ability of the child or adolescent to make a commitment or a contract to resist acting on suicidal urges is an important protective factor, especially during diagnostic or therapeutic work.

D. Other risk factors, especially psychiatric symptoms and disorders, may be chronic and severe (Pfeffer et al., 1991). Alleviation of the severity of these factors is essential and may be effected by means of various interventions, such as individ-

ual, family, and group psychotherapy and psychopharmacology. Administration of these treatments may occur in a psychiatric hospital, residential treatment, psychiatric day hospital, or psychiatric outpatient setting (Pfeffer, Peskin, & Siefker, 1992). The use of these settings is determined in part by the severity of risk factors and the intensity of treatment needed to ameliorate the level of risk. A treatment network that provides easy accessibility to an appropriate treatment setting is essential.

E. When most risk factors are reduced and risk for recurrence of suicidal tendencies is low, treatment may be terminated. However, follow-up is advisable to identify early signs of intensification of risk. Education of the child or adolescent and the parents about how to recognize signs of risk factors is part of the treatment termination process.

REFERENCES

Deykin, E. Y., Alpert, J. J., & McNamarra, J. J. (1985). A pilot study of the effect of exposure to child abuse or neglect on adolescent suicidal behavior. *American Journal of Psychiatry, 142,* 1299–1303.

Jacobsen, L. K., Rabinowitz, I., Poppr, M. S., Solomon, R. J., Sokol, M. S., & Pfeffer, C. R. (1994). Interviewing prepubertal children about suicidal ideation and behavior. *Journal of the American Academy of Child and Adolescent Psychiatry, 33* (4), 439–452.

Pfeffer, C. R. (1986). *The suicidal child.* New York: Guilford Press.

Pfeffer, C. R. (1989). Life stress and family risk factors for youth fatal and nonfatal suicidal behavior. In C. R. Pfeffer (Ed.), *Suicide among youth: Perspectives on risk and prevention.* Washington, DC: American Psychiatric Press. pp. 143–164.

Pfeffer, C. R., Klerman, G. L., Hurt, S. W., Lesser, M., Peskin, J. R., & Siefker, C. A. (1991). Suicidal children grow up: Demographic and clinical risk factors for adolescent suicide attempts. *Journal of the Amer-* ican Academy of Child and Adolescent Psychiatry, 30 (4), 609–616.

Pfeffer, C. R., Klerman, G. L., Hurt, S. W., Kakuma, T., Peskin, J. R., & Siefker, C. A. (1993). Suicidal children grow up: Rates and psychosocial risk factors for suicide attempts during follow-up. *Journal of the American Academy of Child and Adolescent Psychiatry 32* (1), 106–113.

Pfeffer, C. R., Normandin, L., & Kakuma, T. (1994). Suicidal children grow up: Suicidal behavior and psychiatric disorders among relatives. *Journal of the American Academy of Child and Adolescent Psychiatry 33* (8), 1087–1097.

Pfeffer, C. R., Peskin, J. R., & Siefker, C. A. (1992). Suicidal children grow up: Psychiatric treatment during follow-up. *Journal of the American Academy of Child and Adolescent Psychiatry 31* (4), 679–685.

Robbins, D. R., & Alessi, N. E. (1985). Depressive symptoms and suicidal behavior in adolescents. *American Journal of Psychiatry, 142,* 588–592.

18 / Bizarre, Odd, and Eccentric Behavior

Peter E. Tanguay

Two major categories of disorders should be considered when a child or adolescent is reported as being "odd" or "bizarre." The first is pervasive developmental disorder, and the second includes the psychoses of adulthood: schizophrenia, manic disorder, and major depressive disorder with psychosis. Sometimes a child who has been physically or sexually abused or an adolescent with dissociative identity disorder may present with fleeting hallucinations and possible thought disorder; however, the nature of this situation should become apparent as the evaluation progresses (Terr, 1991).

Pervasive developmental disorders always begin in early childhood, whereas schizophrenia, manic disorder, and psychotic depressions are rare in prepubertal children (Russell et al., 1989). It is very rare for children with pervasive developmental disorder to develop schizophrenia or manic disorder later in life.

In the past 15 years, we have come to recognize that deficits in social communication skills play a role in pervasive developmental disorder, and we also have become aware that the symptoms of pervasive developmental disorder can range from severe to mild (Piven et al., 1997). Autism represents the most severe form and Asperger's disorder a less severe form. "Odd" and "eccentric" behaviors in children may represent even milder forms of the disorder, ones in which the child's problems primarily center around an inability to understand the rules of social communication. These rules include understanding what others may be thinking, maintaining a give-and-take conversation, and reading the social communication cues encoded in facial expression, in gestures, and in tone of voice. Children who have such handicaps may appear "weird" to their peers, "off the wall," or bizarre.

Children with pervasive developmental disorder should have their hearing tested, although today it is rare for deaf children to be misdiagnosed as having this disorder. Chromosome testing for

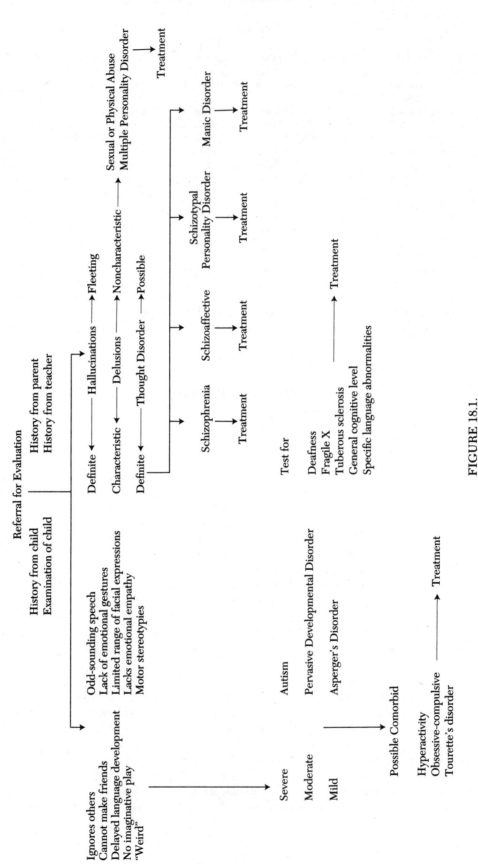

FIGURE 18.1.

Bizarre, odd, and eccentric behavior decision tree.

fragile X syndrome also may be considered, especially if the child has the large ears and prominent jaw usually seen in fragile X syndrome. Pervasive developmental disorder must be differentiated from childhood disintegrative disorder, Rett's disorder, and from the behavioral manifestations of tuberous sclerosis (Smalley et al., 1992).

Children who have pervasive developmental disorder may have associated language and cognitive handicaps; it is therefore important that their intelligence and language be formally evaluated.

The symptoms of schizophrenia and manic disorder are generally the same in adolescents as they are in adults. In those rare cases of childhood-onset manic disorder, it has been reported that bouts of intense irritability are seen rather than recurrent episodes of elation. Bouts of irritability coupled

with episodes of dysphoria may suggest early onset bipolar disorder. Onset of a manic disorder may be very difficult to diagnose in children who are 8 to 12 years of age (Bowring & Kovace, 1992). If a history reveals quite normal development to age 5 or 6, then the symptoms are not the late manifestations of pervasive developmental disorder. If the child has been diagnosed with severe attention deficit hyperactivity disorder, it may be difficult to determine whether the development of more bizarre symptoms in late childhood is a marked exacerbation of the symptoms of that disorder or the early manifestations of a thought disorder characteristic of mania. Trials of appropriate antimanic or antipsychotic medication may be helpful in deciding the issue.

REFERENCES

Bowring, M. A., & Kovace, M. (1992). Difficulties in diagnosing manic disorders among children and adolescents. *Journal of the American Academy of Child and Adolescent Psychiatry, 31,* 611–614.

Piven, J., Palmer, P., Jacobi, D., Childress, D. & Arndt, S. (1997). Broader Autism Phenotype: Evidence from a Family History Study of Multiple Incidence Autism Families. *American Journal of Psychiatry, 154*:185–190.

Russell, A. T., Bott, L., & Sammons, C. (1989). The phenology of schizophrenia occurring childhood.

Journal of the American Academy of Child abd Adolescent Psychiatry, 28, 399–407.

Smalley, S., Tanguay, P., Smith, M., & Gutierrez, G. (1992). Autism and tuberous sclerosis. *Journal of Autism and Developmental Disorders, 22,* 339–355.

Tanguay, P. (1990). Early infantile autism: What have we learned in the past 50 years? *Brain Dysfunction, 3,* 197–207.

Terr, L. (1991). Childhood traumas: An outline and overview. *American Journal of Psychiatry, 148,* 10–20.

19 / Enuresis

Gregory K. Fritz and Randy M. Rockney

A. Enuresis is clinically defined as involuntary voiding of urine at least twice a week occurring after the age at which voluntary control is expected (4 to 6 years) (Rutter, 1985).

B. The extent and pattern of urinary incontinence symptoms should be elucidated and discussed. Important points are whether the bedwetting is primary (child has never been consistently dry through the night) or secondary (child has had a period of at least 6 months to one year of nocturnal dryness); is there daytime as well as nighttime wetting?; does the child have associated constipation or soiling?; has the child ever had a urinary tract infection or symptoms to suggest urological

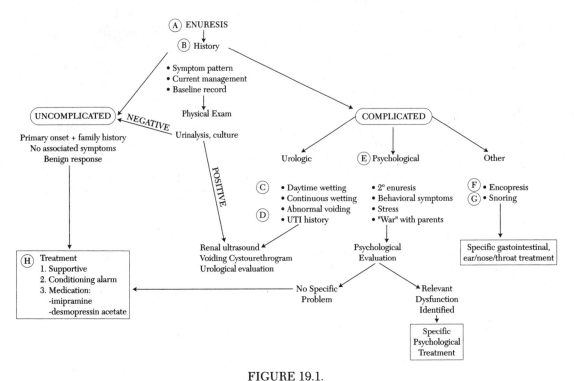

FIGURE 19.1.

Decision tree for enuresis.

dysfunction? [see D]. It is also important to discuss what the parents have tried to do to eliminate the problem; whether there have been any previous medical evaluations; and what, if any, medical treatments have been attempted, the duration of any attempted treatments, and the results. A baseline symptom calendar (a record of wet and dry nights) can be helpful in establishing an accurate picture of symptom frequency and the subsequent response to therapy.

C. Daytime continence is usually attained before nighttime continence. Infrequent daytime enuresis associated with the younger (less than 5 years) child's being absorbed in play activity must be distinguished from frequent daytime incontinence or constant dribbling.

D. Abnormal voiding symptoms include posturing, straining, poor stream or discomfort on urination.

E. Psychosocial problems directly causing enuresis (as opposed to co-occurring with or resulting from the symptom) are relatively rare. Enuresis can be assumed to be of psychological origin when a previously dry child begins wetting during a period of stress (parental divorce, out-of-home placement, school trauma, hospitalization, etc.). At an early age, control struggles between parent and child may settle on urination patterns as a "battlefield"; this struggle serves to maintain the enuresis symptom as the child matures. In the uncommon instance where family disorganization or neglect has resulted in a failure to toilet train the child, the symptom is seen to have a psychosocial etiology (Foxman, 1986).

F. Fecal soiling or fecal retention may accompany the symptom of enuresis 15% of the time; it is usually more distressing to the parent and child than the enuresis. For this reason we recommend treating the symptoms in stepwise fashion—first the fecal and then the urinary incontinence, thus replicating the usual developmental progression of attaining continence.

G. Upper airway obstruction leading to sleep apnea and associated enuresis may be manifested by snoring. In one series of patients, surgical removal of the obstructing tonsils and adenoids led to improvement or complete cure of the enuresis.

H. Except for supportive approaches which include education, demystification, journal keeping, fluid restriction, night lifting, etc., only the conditioning alarm and two medications, imipramine and desmopressin acetate (DDAVP), have been demonstrated to be superior to placebo in a number of trials. The choice of one over another is made on an individual basis, taking into account family structure, patient preferences, and previous experiences (Moffatt, 1996).

REFERENCES

Foxman, B., Valdez, R., & Brook, R. (1986). Childhood enuresis: Prevalence, perceived impact, and prescribed treatments. *Pediatrics, 77*, 482–487.

Moffatt, M. E. K., Nocturnal Enuresis: A Review of the Efficacy of Treatments and Practical Advice for Clinicians. (1997). *Journal of Developmental and Behavioral Pediatrics, 18* (1), 49–56.

Shaffer, D. (1985). Enuresis. In M. Rutter & L. Hersov (Eds.), *Child and adolescent psychiatry: Modern approaches* (pp. 465–481). London: Blackwell Scientific Publications.

20 / **Encopresis**

Randy M. Rockney and Owen R. Hagino

Figure 20.1 presents a decision tree for encopresis.

A. The etiology of encopresis is most often multifactorial, and the constellation differs from child to child. A useful framework for thinking about the development of fecal soiling posits critical stages in the potentiation of encopresis from infancy to early school years (Levine, 1983). In Levine's conceptual framework, factors that may potentiate encopresis during infancy and toddlerhood include anatomical, physiological, and social mechanisms. During later years, psychological processes, psychiatric symptoms (attention deficits, impaired task persistence, anxiety), and broader social stresses play a greater role in exacerbating and maintaining encopresis. Regardless of the specific etiologic factors involved, the usual final common pathway takes the form of fecal retention, the consequent loss of sensation of rectal distention, and overflow incontinence.

B. Certain features are common to most children with encopresis. Questioning the child and his or her parent about these features can be reassuring because of the implicit acknowledgment of how frequently the disorder is encountered. Also, asking the child and parent about the common features provides a natural lead-in to a discussion of the many day-to-day issues facing encopretic children and their parents. It is important to elicit and discuss 2 historical features that frequently are the source of conflict between encopretic children and their parents. The children often hide their soiled underwear, an expression of denial and shame, which usually serves only to increase the parent's aggravation. Also, most children with encopresis have lost the ability both to sense rectal fullness and to appreciate, by smell, that they have soiled themselves. Again, these are difficult points for parents to grasp and common sources of aggravation.

C. Routine psychiatric consultation for encopresis does not appear to be warranted since children suffering from this disorder have no higher rates of concurrent psychopathology or behavior problems than their peers (Gabel, et al., 1986).

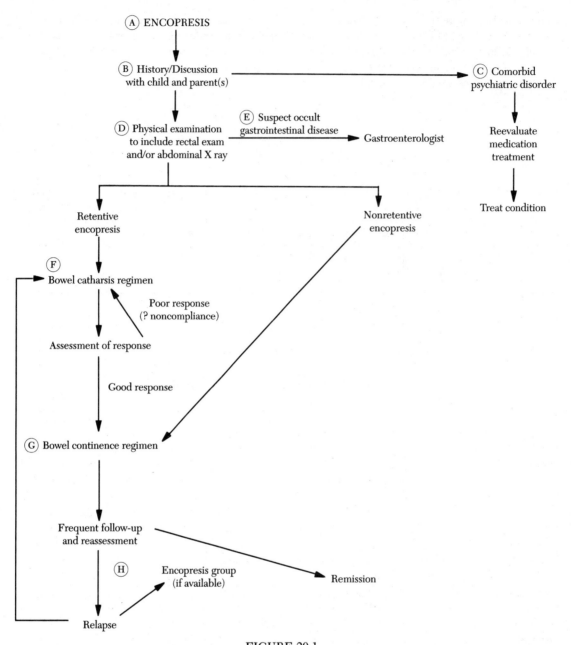

FIGURE 20.1.

Decision tree for encopresis.

However, when cognitive delays are known or suspected, psychological consultation should be obtained in order to assist in providing developmentally appropriate interventions. Psychological and/or psychiatric consultation is indicated for any child in whom a psychiatric condition comorbid with encopresis is known or suspected. This is es-

pecially true in cases of attention deficit hyperactivity disorder, since this condition appears to occur at a higher rate in encopretic boys. Psychiatric consultation is also necessary when children with encopresis are receiving psychotropic medications (e.g., heterocyclic antidepressants, serotonin reuptake inhibitors, phenothiazines), which

118

alter gastrointestinal motility and thus may exacerbate or ameliorate the problem of soiling. The prescribing physician may wish to consider alternative medications.

D. A standard physical examination including a rectal examination is necessary. The presence of fecal retention can be determined either by rectal examination or by plain abdominal radiography. The former is quicker, cheaper, and does not expose the child to radiation. The latter may be indicated in situations in which the child is not willing to allow a rectal examination or if that examination is best deferred because of concern that the examination itself may be traumatic (e.g., when the child has suffered sexual abuse). Whether the radiograph plays a role in demystification or patient education has not been determined (Rockney, et al., 1995).

E. Diagnosing encopresis usually is not difficult, although clinicians must, as specified in the definition of the disorder, differentiate it from other pathologic causes of stool retention and overflow. These include Hirschsprung's disease, congenital or traumatic anorectal malformations, smooth muscle disease, and spinal cord injury or malformation. If doubt exists, the child should be referred to a pediatric gastroenterologist to consider anal manometry or rectal mucosal biopsy.

F. There is no universal agreement on the best approach to the management of encopresis. Most interventions, however, involve a combination of bowel catharsis and behavior modification. One approach to bowel catharsis involves 4 consecutive 3-day cycles of treatment, each cycle consisting of an enema (day 1), a suppository (day 2), and a laxative tablet (day 3). Alternatives to this approach include daily enemas for 3 to 7 days depending on the output of feces or a high dose of mineral oil (up to 1 ounce per year of age twice a day). However, despite the unpopularity of enemas, mineral oil is even less acceptable to children.

G. When bowel catharsis has been satisfactorily achieved, usually by parent report of abundant fecal production and decreased episodes of soiling, a bowel continence maintenance program should be initiated. The goals of this program are no soiling and regular (at least every other day) soft bowel movements. To achieve these goals, a printed list of suggestions can help the child acquire bowel control. In the long run, the main determinants of bowel continence are good bowel habits and a diet conducive to fecal regularity. In subsequent follow-up visits, the parents and the clinician may individualize the specific regimen for each child, selecting from the menu of suggestions those interventions that are most helpful and acceptable to the child and parent.

H. A more rigorous approach using group behavioral therapy involving both children and parents often is effective for difficult-to-treat patients (Stark, et al., 1990).

REFERENCES

Gabel, S., Hegedus, A. M., Wald, A., Chandra, R., & Chiponis, D. (1986). Prevalence of behavior problems and mental health utilization among encopretic children: Implications for behavioral pediatrics. *Journal of Developmental and Behavioral Pediatrics, 7* (5), 293–297.

Levine, M. D. (1983). "Encopresis." In M. D. Levine, W. B. Carey, & A. C. Crocker (Eds.), *Developmental-behavioral pediatrics* (pp. 586–595). Philadelphia: W. B. Saunders.

Rockney, R. M., McQuade, W. H., Days, A. L. (1995). The Plain Abdominal Roentgenogram in the Management of Encopresis. *Archives of Pediatrics and Adolescent Medicine, 149,* 623–627.

Stark, L. J., Owens-Stively, J., Spirito, A., Lewis, A., & Guevremont, D. (1990). Group behavioral treatment of retentive encopresis. *Journal of Pediatric Psychology, 15* (5), 659–671.

21 / School Refusal

Rachel G. Klein

Figure 21.1 presents a decision tree for school refusal.

A. School refusal is on a spectrum of severity, from resistance to going to school, to partial absence, and to complete refusal. The prevalence of school refusal is not known, but the severe form, complete school avoidance, is believed to be uncommon. The behavior has the main advantage of being objective, and its identification poses little problem. When there is doubt about the exact nature, such as onset, severity, and frequency, school records are valid sources of information.

B. Some children do not overtly refuse to attend school. Rather, they act upon the refusal without communicating their intent. This pattern characterizes children who truant. Truants lie about their whereabouts when they are not in school. They

avoid school because it holds little interest for them and because they find its task demands unpleasant. They would rather spend their time elsewhere. When truancy is suspected, school information is critical, since the youngsters may lie about it, and parents are not always aware of the truancy. Truancy usually occurs in the context of a conduct disorder and represents one aspect of the disorder's antisocial adaptation. It is the only form of school refusal that is more prevalent in boys than girls. The conduct disorder needs to be treated with active family involvement.

C. Anxiety disorders are frequent among children who refuse or resist school, especially among young children (preadolescents). Children with anxiety disorders rarely state explicitly that they are uncomfortable in school. Typically they claim

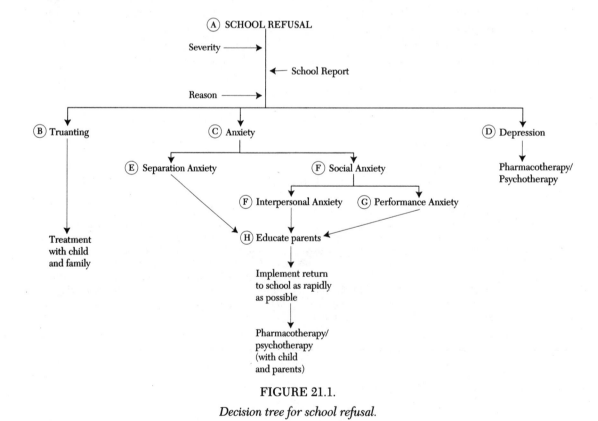

FIGURE 21.1.

Decision tree for school refusal.

not to feel well and report somatic complaints, the most common is gastrointestinal distress (Gittelman, 1986).

D. Adolescents who suffer from major depression may refuse to go to school. Their refusal stems from loss of interest in school, inability to mobilize themselves, or both.

E. Young children (preadolescents) who refuse to go to school almost always do so because of separation anxiety. This is less often the case in adolescents. For such children, school can be an especially difficult separation from the home or parents since the school schedule does not allow them freedom of movement (Hersov & Berg, 1980). Therefore, they are hemmed in for a fixed period without access to home or parent. To avoid this intolerable situation, severely separation-anxious children may refuse to attend school or will do so only if the mother stays in school. Separation anxiety may be missed or misunderstood when children express a fear of a specific event, such as the school bus, but not of being in school per se. However, these fears can be distinguished from specific phobias by their specific relationship to school. Separation anxiety may be difficult to elicit from adolescent boys, who often deny separation anxiety, which they view as a shameful weakness. The presence of separation anxiety in these children may need to be inferred from their pattern of avoidance in a variety of situations and their difficulty in functioning when not accompanied by a trusted companion.

F. Older children (adolescents) with school refusal may suffer from severe social anxiety. They find it difficult to be exposed to the possibility of being called on in class or to interact with peers. They feel self-conscious and are afraid of social embarrassment.

G. On occasion, social anxiety will take the form of performance anxiety, and children and adolescents will refuse to go to school because of concerns about their academic performance. In such cases, school refusal tends to be restricted to days when tests are given or the child is scheduled to give a presentation. Interpersonal and performance anxiety may co-occur (Klein, 1994).

H. Most parents and school personnel are not aware of the reasons that lead to a child's school refusal. Part of the treatment involves informing parents and school personnel of the nature of the child's difficulties. Treatment will depend on the cause of the refusal. Psychosocial and psychopharmacological interventions exist for each underlying anxiety disorder associated with school refusal. Parents and school need to be involved in the treatment (March, 1995).

REFERENCES

Gittelman, R. (Ed.). (1986). *Anxiety disorders of childhood*. New York: Guilford Press.

Hersov, L., & Berg, I. (Eds.). (1980). *Out of school*. London: John Wiley & Sons.

Klein, R. G. (1994). Anxiety disorders. In M. Rutter, E. Taylor, & L. Hersov (Eds.), *Child and adolescent psychiatry: Modern approaches* (3rd ed., pp. 351–374). Oxford: Blackwell Scientific Publications.

March, J. S. (Ed.). (1995). *Anxiety disorders in children and adolescents*. New York: Guilford Press.

22 / Lying

Efrain Bleiberg and Sarah Atkinson

Figure 22.1 presents a decision tree for lying.

A. Parents frequently report lying as a problem behavior. Lying always occurs in a relational context as it involves, by definition, children's misrepresentation of either external events or internal states in order to deceive the listener (Paniagua, 1989). This definition implies both a capacity to differentiate reality from fantasy and an intention to deceive. Young children often make up stories and tell tall tales. The clinical literature has emphasized that children under 4 or 5 years of age may blur the distinction between reality and fantasy and thus lack the capacity to differentiate between lying and telling the truth. Developmental research (Emde & Buchsbaum, 1990), on the other hand, questions this assumption by demonstrating that normal children, as young as 2, can clearly recognize and get involved in pretend activities and distinguish them from nonpretend interactions.

The frequency of lying in childhood and adolescence remains elusive. Most children will lie occasionally to avoid punishment, deny responsibility, protect their privacy, or avoid hurting someone else's feelings. It becomes a clinical concern only when lying turns into a persistent pattern of coping and relating. Lying as a primary presenting problem occurs in approximately 5% of children seen by mental health professionals. Lying may be associated with significant problems in children's lives, such as physical and/or sexual abuse or parental conflict. Lying at an early age can be a harbinger of other problematic behaviors at later ages, such as stealing, truancy, drug use, aggression, fire setting, and other antisocial behaviors. Lying also suggests a heightened risk for the development of severe psychopathology in late adolescence or adulthood, including antisocial personality disorder or borderline personality disorder. Finally, lying can be a symptom of serious childhood psychopathology, including oppositional defiant disorder and conduct disorder.

B. Children with mental retardation as well as psychotic children and those with pervasive developmental disorders may have difficulty differentiating fantasy from reality or may misinterpret events and communications. Psychosis by definition involves a disturbance in reality testing; this condition is present in disorders such as schizophrenia, schizoaffective disorder, or bipolar disorder, which are rarely seen before puberty. These children's "lies" occur in the context of manifestations of thought disorder, such as looseness of associations, flight of ideas, or delusional thinking and perceptual distortions, such as hallucinations. When they intentionally lie, psychotic children's lies appear fantastical, dreamlike, and only tangentially associated with particular events. Family history may reveal genetic loading for schizophrenic or mood disorders. Psychiatric evaluation and psychological testing give evidence of the characteristic signs and symptoms of these disorders.

Children with mental retardation, autism, and pervasive developmental disorder often misinterpret complex situations or symbolic communications and may construe their experiences into distorted accounts that appear to be lies. Psychometric assessment of intelligence and psychiatric evaluation of language, communication, and interpersonal relationships clarify the diagnosis and the true nature of the "lies."

C. Family circumstances may induce children to lie. Lying is associated with absence of parental warmth and honesty, parental and maternal rejection, lack of parental supervision, single and unhappy parents, disharmonious homes, and parental untruthfulness (Stouthamer-Loerer, 1986). Parents engaged in custody disputes or marital conflict may subtly or overtly pressure children to distort reality in an effort to secure financial gain, inflict punishment on the other spouse, or gain advantage in custody battles. Parent counseling is indicated in these instances. Various other family circumstances, such as parental unemployment, a pronounced drop in family income, illness—particularly psychiatric illness or other conditions associated with a high degree of stigmatization—or

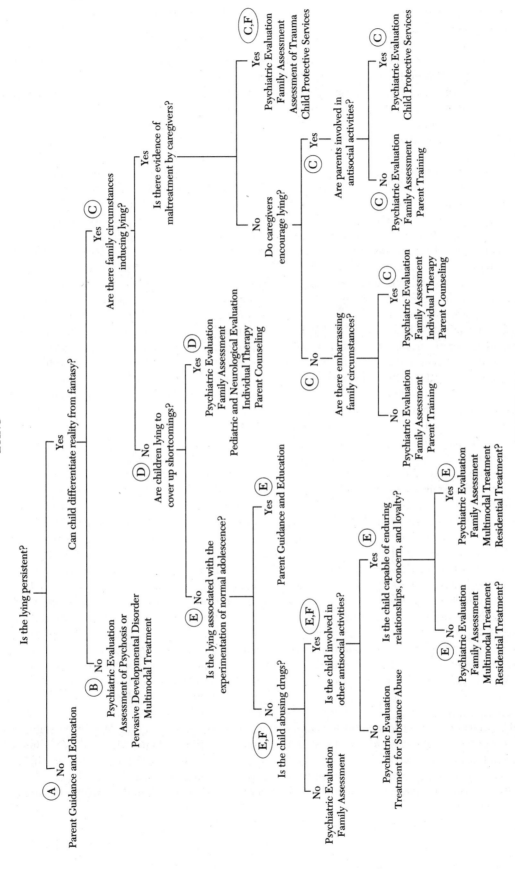

FIGURE 22.1.

Lying decision tree.

incarceration of a family member, tend to evoke ridicule or rejection from peers. Under such circumstances, children may lie to distance themselves from the embarrassing situation. Parents also may coerce children to lie in order to cover up physical and/or sexual abuse, spousal abuse, or parental engagement in other forms of criminal behavior. Various forms of deception, including marital infidelity and tax evasion, may be established patterns designed to avoid conflict, gain advantage, or, more generally, be woven into the very fabric of family relationships and adaptations.

Parental responses to children's lying can reinforce the lying. Punishment tends to be less effective as a deterrent, and, by enhancing children's engagement with otherwise disinterested or unavailable parents, it can reinforce the very behavior it was meant to eliminate. Ineffectual parenting is an indication for parent training.

Parents or other significant adults can be members of cults or gangs that compel children to share in idiosyncratic or antisocial belief systems; these may include systematic lying to protect the group, cover up illegal activities, or challenge conventional morality and authority.

Sensitive inquiry into the family's belief system, past and current events and circumstances within the family, and patterns of family interaction, particularly around discipline and truthfulness, may reveal the source and function of children's lying. In evaluating the family situation, particular attention must be given to parents' views about lying and their responses to their children's lying and, above all, to the physical and emotional safety of the children. Assessment of the home environment, particularly in cases when children's safety may be at risk, may require the intervention of children's protective services.

D. Children's inability to measure up to expected levels of academic, athletic, or social performance may prompt them to fall into patterns of repetitive lying in an effort to deal with the real or imaginary demands of parents, teachers and peers. Children with attention deficit hyperactivity disorder, learning disorders, or limited intellectual capacity often struggle mightily to keep up with their peers academically and socially. Parental expectations of high academic, social, or athletic achievement may compound these children's difficulties—even of those only minimally lim-

ited—thus promoting children's reliance on lies to cover up their shortcomings. Physical disabilities, malformations, or chronic illnesses also can impair children's adaptive efforts and accomplishments. Subtle disabilities, such as very mild cerebral palsy or a mild developmental disorder may be undiagnosed, yet burden the affected children with their peers' scorn and their own chronic frustration. Likewise, children disfigured by trauma or congenital abnormalities often experience rejection or are subjected to demeaning name-calling. These various groups of children are at risk of becoming seriously demoralized and giving up on their efforts to master reality's adaptive challenges. They may retreat instead to the creation of elaborate stories that may explain their difficulties, evoke sympathy from others, secure attention, or create for them an alternative reality where gratification, success, and self-esteem are more easily within their grasp. Thorough assessment of these factors requires a careful evaluation of children's physical and cognitive development and functioning; this may include psychological, psychometric, and neuropsychological testing, speech and hearing evaluation, psychoeducational testing, and pediatric and neurological evaluations.

E. The developmental and psychosocial tasks of adolescence strain the adaptive capacities of both normal youngsters and of those afflicted with psychiatric disorders. The passage through adolescence is marked by a proneness to embarrassment and shame, acute self-consciousness, and painful questions about self-esteem and self-worth. Biological, cognitive, emotional, sexual, and psychosocial changes impose a complex array of adaptive demands that adolescents often feel ill-equipped to master. Adolescents are uncertain about who they are, feel torn between regressive and progressive trends, and lack a clear road map to guide their transition into adulthood. Relentless psychosocial and developmental pressures demand that they separate from the family, find an independent niche in the world, and engage in sexual and emotional intimacy.

For adolescents lying may become a strategy to avoid or minimize shame triggered by feelings of inadequacy. Lying also can constitute an effort to cover up the forbidden activities adolescents routinely experiment with in their search for identity and relationships. For example, adolescents will lie repeatedly to hide the truth about where they have been, whom they were with, and what they were doing when experimenting with drugs, alcohol, or sexual intercourse, or when they become involved with other youths engaged in antisocial activities. The key clinical differentiation is between the normal experimentation of adolescence and the manifestations of adolescent psychopathology. Normal adolescents may engage in squabbles and conflicts but nonetheless maintain basically good relationships with their parents. Experimentation with drugs and alcohol does not evolve into dependency on these substances to maintain a sense of identity or self-esteem, or a key to sustain peer relationships. Sexual experimentation stops short of promiscuity, maintains a realistic level of self-protection, and occurs in the context of stable, caring relationships. Lying and other violations of family rules and values are accompanied by clear signs of remorse. Last, but not least, normal adolescents can construct plans for the future that match their inherent talents, characteristics, and the realities of their physical and social world. By pursuing their plans, they enhance their competence, self-esteem, and adaptation, thus lessening their need to lie. By contrast, adolescents with conduct disorder, oppositional disorder, or borderline personality disorder are not troubled by lying or taking advantage of others and lie systematically to cover up serious drug or alcohol abuse, promiscuity, and/or involvement with cults or gangs. These youngsters' lying reinforces an illusory sense of power and control, which for them replaces the efforts to achieve real competence and improved adaptation. Antisocial youngsters have limited capacity for enduring relationships, concern for others, or loyalty. Borderline children are moody, clingy, irritable, and prone to emotional storms. Indications of a developing personality disorder point to the need for multimodal treatment that includes individual and family therapy, pharmacotherapy, and often day treatment or residential treatment.

F. Children who experienced chronic physical and sexual abuse as well as those exposed to particularly overwhelming traumatic events, such as witnessing parental homicide or rape, are at risk for posttraumatic stress disorder and/or dissociative disorders. These children may confabulate to fill gaps in their memory. On the other hand, when experiencing a dissociative state, these children may appear to be "making up" stories. Likewise, youngsters with significant problems of drug abuse may experience blackouts and cognitive impairment accompanied by confabulation. Glue and aerosols in particular cause memory impairment. A detailed inquiry into children's knowledge and use of drugs is important in all instances of seemingly volitional lying. Identification of other symptoms of posttraumatic stress disorder and/or dissociative disorder, such as recurrent traumatic dreams, traumatic reenactments, numbing of general responsiveness, altered sense of the future, persistent symptoms of hyperarousal, depersonalization experiences, or confusion about personal identity are highly suggestive of exposure to trauma.

REFERENCES

Emde, R., & Buchsbaum, H. (1990). Didn't you hear my mommy: Autonomy with connectedness and morale self emergence. In D. Cicchetti and M. Beeghly (Eds.), *The self in transition: Infancy to childhood* (pp. 35–60). Chicago: University of Chicago Press.

Paniagua, F. A. (1989). Lying by children: Why children say one thing, do another? *Psychological Reports, 64,* 971–984.

Stouthamer-Loerer, M. (1986). Lying as a problem behavior in children: A review. *Clinical Psychology Review, 6,* (4) 267–289.

23 / Stealing

Efrain Bleiberg and Sarah Atkinson

Figure 23.1 presents a decision tree for stealing.

A. Stealing is a relatively common problem behavior reported by parents, teachers, and/or the authorities. Because of its covert nature, the very presence of stealing defies reliable identification. Arguments about "yes, you did it," "no, I didn't," loom large in the clinical presentation. An operational definition of stealing thus cannot be based on certainty about whether children inappropriately take something that belongs to someone else. Instead, stealing can be practically defined as children possessing something the origin of which they cannot account for (Seymour & Epston, 1989) or possessing anything other than that which specifically belongs to them (Patterson, 1982). This definition, of course, fails to encompass the thefts that are overlooked because "plausible" explanations, such as "finding," "borrowing," or "receiving a gift," are accepted.

A review of surveys of stealing in children reveals a marked gender difference. Parents report stealing as a problem in approximately 10% of all boys and 2.5 to 5% of all girls. Stealing, along with other covert antisocial behaviors such as lying and fire setting, are antecedents of delinquency. Nonconfrontive stealing, defined as theft without direct contact with the victim, is a sensitive predictor of subsequent academic failure, delinquency, and serious psychopathology (Farrington, 1973; Patterson, 1982, 1986; Robins, 1978), particularly oppositional defiant disorder, conduct disorder, borderline personality disorder, and antisocial personality disorder. Stealing in adolescents often is associated with other problematic behaviors and/or symptoms such as promiscuity, eating disorders and substance abuse.

Appraisal of the significance and severity of stealing are hindered by the lack of developmental norms (Miller & Klungness, 1989). Isolated incidents of stealing are not necessarily indicative of psychopathology or maladjustment. Adolescents often report a history of petty theft during childhood (Belson, 1976). Petty theft in preschool children generally is tolerated and, in and of itself, of little clinical relevance, as the concepts of ownership, concern for others, and permission to use other's personal property are not well established (Hartup, 1974; Renshaw, 1979). On the other hand, peers and adults are far less tolerant of stealing after children enter school or when it turns into a persistent pattern.

B. Children who steal from peers and strangers almost invariably steal from their families and are at much greater risk both to become a threat to society and to develop serious psychopathology than those who steal solely from family members (Stumphauzer, 1976). Several factors in children's environment impact the likelihood of stealing. Children who are part of a social and family context that condones, values, or ignores stealing learn that this behavior is acceptable and even desirable as they identify with peers and adults who steal. A strong association exists between the criminal records of parents and close friends and children's criminal behavior (Patterson, 1982). Participating in stealing activities with a gang or peer group can become the currency with which children purchase acceptance, status, and affiliation. Once children acquire reputations as thieves, nondelinquent adults and peers tend to reject them or withdraw from them, increasing these youngsters' dependency on the delinquent group and further reducing reinforcement for pro-social behavior. Thus it is important to assess the social environment and the extent to which the stealing is confined to group activities.

Caregivers' responses to their children's stealing is a crucial variable in maintaining and reinforcing or extinguishing this behavior. Parents of stealers characteristically are detached, harsh or inconsistent in disciplining, and poor at monitoring their children. These parents generally fail to track and apply consequences to their children's behavior, either pro-social or antisocial, and provide minimal support for appropriate social behavior. There is little involvement between parents and children except for highly charged emotional and physical exchanges brought about by children's

126

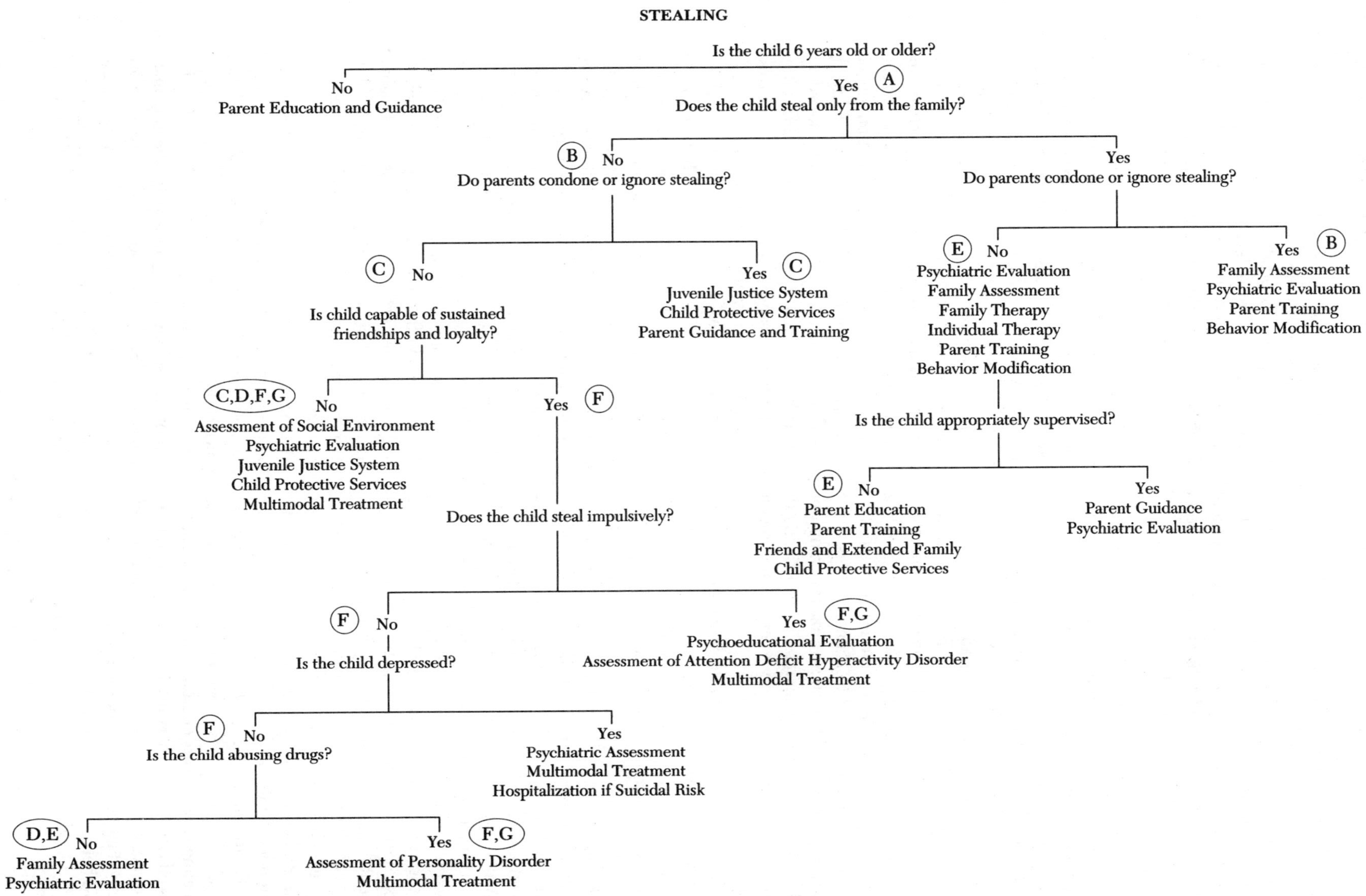

STEALING

Is the child 6 years old or older?

No — Parent Education and Guidance

Yes — (A) Does the child steal only from the family?

No — (B) Do parents condone or ignore stealing?

Yes — (A) Do parents condone or ignore stealing?

Do parents condone or ignore stealing?

Yes — (B) Family Assessment
Psychiatric Evaluation
Parent Training
Behavior Modification

No — (E) Psychiatric Evaluation
Family Assessment
Family Therapy
Individual Therapy
Parent Training
Behavior Modification

Is the child appropriately supervised?

Yes — Parent Guidance
Psychiatric Evaluation

No — (E) Parent Education
Parent Training
Friends and Extended Family
Child Protective Services

No — (B) Do parents condone or ignore stealing?

Yes — (C) Juvenile Justice System
Child Protective Services
Parent Guidance and Training

No — (C) Is child capable of sustained
friendships and loyalty?

Yes — (F) Does the child steal impulsively?

No — (C,D,F,G) Assessment of Social Environment
Psychiatric Evaluation
Juvenile Justice System
Child Protective Services
Multimodal Treatment

Yes — (F,G) Psychoeducational Evaluation
Assessment of Attention Deficit Hyperactivity Disorder
Multimodal Treatment

No — (F) Is the child depressed?

Yes — Psychiatric Assessment
Multimodal Treatment
Hospitalization if Suicidal Risk

No — (F) Is the child abusing drugs?

Yes — (F,G) Assessment of Personality Disorder
Multimodal Treatment

No — (D,E) Family Assessment
Psychiatric Evaluation

FIGURE 23.1.
Stealing decision tree.

misbehavior. Thus stealing, along with other antisocial behaviors can become a vehicle to decrease parental detachment and secure some degree of attention. In any assessment of children's stealing it is essential to evaluate parents' child-management skills, as significant deficiencies point to parent training and behavioral management as critical components of treatment.

D. Children's inability to demonstrate concern for their peers serves to differentiate those youngsters on the way to develop a narcissistic or antisocial personality disorder.

These children fail to sustain friendships, extend themselves to others, or show much loyalty even to their accomplices in antisocial activities. When they steal they attempt to cover it up and worry about being caught, blamed, or punished, but not about being wrong. Rather than holding themselves responsible for the consequences of their behavior, they tend to blame circumstances and other people. They show a narrow range of affect and are typically concrete, egocentric, rigid, and limited in their capacity to experience much joy or regret.

E. Stealing restricted to the home foreshadows less serious psychopathology in terms of overall adjustment but points to specific transactional patterns within the family system and/or psychological meanings that the stealing behavior may have for children. Parents can subtly—even unconsciously—encourage their children's delinquency (Johnson & Szurek, 1952). Children steal from caregivers or siblings to test relationships (Winnicott, 1953), attempt to remedy feelings of deprivation and abandonment, or express hostility, envy, and rivalry. Children's stealing may be associated with the absence of developmentally appropriate supervision. Children with developmental lags may require levels of supervision that overwhelm the parents' or caregivers' resources. An assessment of inadequate supervision points to parental education and the enlistment of friends, extended family, and social agencies. Assessment of family interaction patterns and of individual psychodynamic issues, particularly in instances of stealing that appears circumscribed and bound to specific settings or persons, is important. Circumscribed stealing may point to family therapy and individual therapy in addition to parent training and behavioral management.

F. Children with attention deficit hyperactivity disorder may steal impulsively. Their delinquent behavior initially springs from a propensity for immediate translation of affects, wishes, or needs into action. The central feature of their subjective life is a distortion of the experience of intention. Their actions "happen" to them instead of resulting from their choice. The world appears as a disconnected set of temptations and frustrations, possibilities for immediate gain and satisfaction, or obstacles for gratification. As a result of such experiences, their inner life is barren and undifferentiated and they often confuse thought, feeling, and action. Their concreteness and egocentricity interferes with planning and abstraction and forms the basis for their difficulty in learning from experience. In the diagnostic assessment they present a history of pervasive overactivity, inattentiveness, and impulsivity. Of particular significance is the association of attention deficit hyperactivity disorder with a developmental reading disorder and/or other learning disorders, which compounds these children's difficulties generalizing and abstracting, increases their frustration with schoolwork, and adds to the pull of antisocial activities. Careful assessment of school records, academic history, and psychoeducational evaluations are critical to determine the need for special educational approaches aimed at these children's specific cognitive and learning problems. A diagnosis of attention deficit hyperactivity disorder complicated by serious conduct problems, such as stealing, requires a multimodal treatment that includes pharmacotherapy, parental counseling on behavior management and effective parenting, information about the nature of the children's strengths and weaknesses, and individual therapy often combining cognitive behavioral approaches with supportive psychodynamic interventions designed to improve children's ability to communicate with words feelings of anger, frustration, and sadness, to enhance their self-esteem, and to acquire a more realistic view of their capacities and opportunities. Group therapy and family therapy also can become valuable additions to these children's treatment.

G. Theft of money or stealing objects for the purpose of selling them anticipates serious maladjustment. Such behavior raises suspicion of involvement with delinquent groups and/or substance abuse. Delinquent peers and immersion in a life permeated by drug abuse pave the way for the transition from impulsive or peer-pressured stealing to a personality disorder. Cold, remorseless children who are exploitive, intimidating, manipulative, and violent are at great risk of crystallizing an antisocial personality disorder. They often hold others in contempt or perceive them as worthless, inept weaklings—tools to be manipulated or objects to be utilized. Abuse and neglect within chaotic, violent, drug-abusing environments figure prominently in these children's development. Assessment of the presence of physical and/or sexual abuse requires the intervention of child protective services. An antisocial pattern suggests the need for a multimodal treatment program that may include day treatment or long-term residential care.

Children on the way to developing a borderline personality disorder are moody, irritable, and explosive as well as needy and clinging. To maintain a sense of well-being and identity they require a constant stream of "supplies": other people's attention, sex, drugs, or food. When such supplies are not forthcoming they panic, become enraged or transiently psychotic. Their delinquent behavior often is associated not only with desperate efforts to secure "supplies" and counter feelings of emptiness but also with difficulties that arise from drug abuse and their dependency on other delinquents. In borderline youngsters a broad genetic vulnerability to mood disorders, impulse control problems, and/or learning disorders interacts with a broad array of developmental problems, including early parental loss, sexual and physical abuse, and parental discouragement of separation and autonomy. The presence of signs and symptoms of a mood disorder, particularly when linked with a positive family history, points to the indication for mood-stabilizing medication. Borderline symp-tomatology, however, requires a multimodal treatment that often involves residential treatment.

Numerous studies (Kovacs et al., 1984; Puig-Antich, 1982) have documented the coexistence of conduct disorders and depression. Although they feel depleted and deprived, depressed conduct-disordered children typically reject or sabotage offers of help or support. Genetic studies (Weissman et al., 1987) lend qualified support to the role of genetic transmission in the etiology of depressive disorders in children. A biologically based proneness to irritability, aggression, and depression probably is linked with psychological and psychosocial factors in establishing the link between depression and conduct disorder. Freud (1916/1963), described people—including children—who engage in criminal behavior to appease their sense of guilt and confirm their badness. Some children, said Freud, commit theft or arson and become quiet and content only after being punished.

Evoking punishment with stealing and other delinquent behaviors also ensures a responsive from otherwise indifferent or exhausted caregivers. Thus stealing and other conduct problems may become the currency of relatedness every bit as much as they represent a protest against neglect, an effort at self-nurturance, a search for punishment, or an expression of a biologically based predisposition to depression and mischief. Signs and symptoms of depression, such as sleep and appetite disturbances, depressed or irritable mood, fatigue or loss of energy, and suicidal ideation, point to the possible indication for antidepressant medication as an element in a comprehensive treatment plan. Hospitalization is indicated, of course, when suicide risk is substantial or cannot be ruled out.

REFERENCES

Belson, W. A. (1976). Juvenile stealing: Getting the record straight. *Bulletin of the British Psychological Society, 29,* 113–116.

Farrington, D. P. (1973). Self-reports of deviant behavior: Predictive and stable? *Journal of Criminal Law and Criminology, 64,* 99–110.

Freud, S. (1963). Some character-types met with in psychoanalytic work. In J. Strachey (ed. and trans.) *The standard edition of the complete psychological works of Sigmund Freud* (Vol. 14, pp. 309–333). London: Hogarth Press. (Originally published 1916.)

Hartup, W. W. (1974). Aggression in childhood: Developmental perspectives. *American Psychologist, 29,* 336–339.

Johnson, A. M., & Szurek, S. A. (1952). The genesis of antisocial acting out in children and adults. *Psychoanalytic Quarterly, 21*, 323–343.

Kovacs, M., Feinberg, T., Crouse-Novak, A., Paulauskas, S., Finkelstein, R. (1984). Depressive disorders in childhood. *Archives of General Psychiatry, 41*, 229–237.

Miller, G. E., & Klungness, L. (1989). Childhood theft: A comprehensive review of assessment and treatment. *School Psychology Review, 18* (1), 82–97.

Patterson, G. R. (1982). *A social learning approach to family intervention: Coercive family process.* Eugene, OR: Castalia Publishing Co.

Patterson, G. R. (1986). Performance models for antisocial boys. *American Psychologist, 41*, 432–444.

Puig-Antich, J. (1982). Major depression and conduct disorder in prepuberty. *Journal of the American Academy of Child Psychiatry, 21*, 118–128.

Renshaw, D. C. (1979). Stealing and school. *The Pointer, 21*, 9–13.

Robins, L. N. (1978). Sturdy childhood predictors of adult antisocial behavior: Replications from longitudinal studies. *Psychological Medicine, 8* (4), 611–622.

Seymour, F. W., & Epston, D. (1989). An approach to childhood stealing with evaluation of 45 cases. *Australian & New Zealand Journal of Family Therapy, 10* (3), 137–143.

Stumphauzer, J. S. (1976). Elimination of stealing by self-reinforcement of alternative behavior and family contracting. *Experimental Psychiatry, 7*, 265–268.

Weissman, M. M., Gammon, D., John, K., Merikangas, K., Warner, V., Prusoff, B., Sholomskas, D. (1987). Children of depressed parents: Increased psychopathology and early onset of major depression. *Archives of General Psychiatry, 44*, 847–853.

Winnicott, D. W. (1953). Transitional objects and transitional phenomena. *International Journal of Psycho-Analysis, 34* (2), 89–97.

24 / Temper Tantrums

Saul L. Brown and Helen Reid

Temper tantrums are episodic outbursts of intense anger expressed through crying and accompanying body movements including thrashing about, flailing of arms, kicking, and occasionally attacking the parent or caregiver by scratching or biting. While the tantrum may be preceded by some initial milder outburst or tearful protestations, these almost immediately rise to a single dominant crescendo of crying or screaming that may continue from a minute or two to several minutes or even longer. Typically there is an extended period of sobbing and negativity. While antecedent events such as frustration of the child's expressed wishes are usually the obvious cause, tantrums may occur seemingly without provocation. The intensity of the outburst often is surprising to parents or seems to them far greater than the situation warrants. Once the expression of anger approaches a crescendo, it is usually impossible for parents or caregivers to arrest it.

Tantrums in Children Under Three Years of Age

Temper tantrums in children from approximately 14 months to 3½ years of age are expectable and essentially normal; parents often are relieved to learn this. When the tantrums recur several times a day, or have continued over several days, or if they last for more than a few minutes and the child cannot be calmed, a specific stress may be at work. The parents may not have recognized this, and a careful exploratory review with them about the current situation should then take place. This level of assessment can occur in the course of an extended telephone consultation. When parents seem unable to accept the developmental normality of tantrums for this age group, or when they show a defensive or even a punitive reaction, additional assessment is indicated. Similarly, if there is evidence, in the initial inquiry, of developmental lags or deficits or of unusually stressful recent

ASSESSMENT OF TEMPER TANTRUMS
UNDER THREE YEARS

Frequent or Prolonged Episodes?

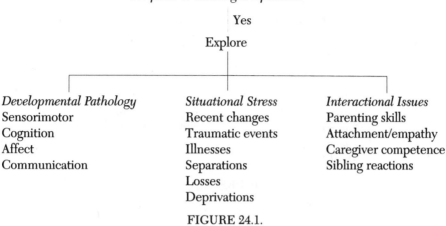

FIGURE 24.1.

Temper tantrums—under three years—decision tree.

events, extended evaluation is appropriate. Assessment begins with a carefully supportive but detailed exploration of current parent-child and family relationships and recent events in the family.

Tantrums in Children Three Years and Over

We assume that a prior pediatric evaluation for specific medical pathology already has taken place. Recurrent, severe, frequent, or long-lasting tantrums during which the child is very difficult to console merit an extensive assessment. While this may begin with an initial extended telephone inquiry, a meeting with the parents is indicated, often followed by a series of meetings with the child and parents. At least one interview should include the siblings. In some situations other significant caregivers for the child should be included.

DIFFERENTIATION OF POTENTIAL CAUSES

Three potential causes of tantrums should be differentiated: those caused by developmental de-

lays or deficits, by problematic parenting and family interactions, or by situational stresses and deprivations.

Developmental Deficits or Delays: Tantrums may be indirect reactions to the stress upon the child and parents resulting from developmental disorders, or they may be direct symptoms of those disorders. Examples are pervasive developmental disorder; attention deficit disorder with or without hyperactivity; obsessive compulsive syndrome; Tourette's disorder; Asperger's disorder; autism or autistic features.

Problematic Parenting and Family Interaction: These include early attachment problems; limited parenting skills relating especially to managing aggressive behaviors; severe sibling rivalry; provocative behaviors such as teasing or ignoring or excitatory behaviors; punitive or restrictive attitudes; abusive behaviors; parent substance abuse; and poorly defined structure and role functions.

Situational Stresses and Deprivations: These can involve family disruptions such as divorce or chaotic behavior; parents unable to provide consistent age-appropriate daily care because of financial, physical, or environmental limitations; foster care or multiple placements away from parents.

ASSESSMENT OF TEMPER TANTRUMS
THREE YEARS AND OLDER

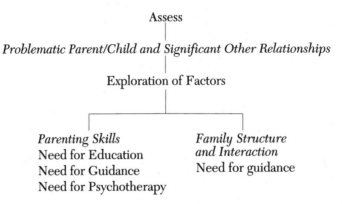

FIGURE 24.2.

Temper tantrums—three years and older—decision tree.

The Assessment Process

The assessment of temper tantrums needs to be done with the parents in an exploratory and supportive fashion, giving them full opportunity to express their frustration, helplessness, and even anger. When feasible, an extended telephone consultation may precede the office meeting. The value of this lies in alerting the parents to factors that may be affecting the family while helping them with their great discomfort about feeling powerless with their child. The basic orientation of the assessment is a contextual one, in which multiple factors that might provoke tantrums are reviewed.

CHILDREN UNDER THREE YEARS

Even while reassuring parents about the normalcy and even desirability of occasional tantrums in this age range, certain typical precipitating possibilities should be reviewed with them. Among these are: frustration of the child's need for mastery and control or for gratifying desires; reactions to departures of significant others; reactions to loss of favored objects or of significant caregivers; reactions to overexcitation by adults or sibling; and reactions to unexpected changes. Often par-

ents are unaware of how certain events are affecting their child and they can be quite relieved to have these brought to their attention.

CASE EXAMPLE

A 2½-year-old suddenly began having frequent severe tantrums. In the extended telephone inquiry with the mother, she was asked if there had been recent changes in the family. Almost casually she told of the recent abrupt departure of a housekeeper who had been a constant caregiver for the child since birth. The mother was helped to understand this as a separation and loss reaction for the child and encouraged to talk with him about it and share photographs of the housekeeper. To her amazement, he attacked the photo and wept. She responded empathically and shortly the tantrums abated.

CHILDREN OVER THREE YEARS

The Tantrums: Parents are asked to describe the tantrums in detail. How long do they last and what are the accompanying behaviors? Is there biting, kicking, physical or verbal attacks on others, breath holding, head banging, or self-attack? Exactly how do the parents or siblings or caregivers respond? If the child attends day care or nursery school, how does staff respond? Are punitive

ASSESSMENT OF TEMPER TANTRUMS
THREE YEARS AND OLDER

Behaviors Associated with Developmental Delays or Deficits

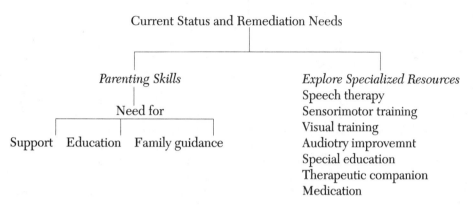

FIGURE 24.3.

Temper tantrums—three years and older—decision tree.

actions or threats or isolation used? If so, by whom? What finally calms the child?

History and Context: A detailed developmental history is necessary, but it need not be fully accomplished in the initial parent interview. There is ample opportunity to complete this in subsequent contacts. Historical data that come forth spontaneously in the course of meetings with the parents are often more illuminating than a linear history since the parents' affective expressions as they review events may be at least as relevant as the factual information itself.

In taking the history, it is essential to address the following points: a description of the child's tantrums in the past; when they occurred and how they were dealt with. Other information that is important are details about the child's use of transitional objects in past and currently and the parents' reaction to them; data about medical or surgical procedures including anesthesia—what occurred and what treatments or procedures were used, how the child was prepared for these, and the child's emotional reactions during and after; traumatic events other than medical, such as sudden departures of significant others, deaths, losses, or injuries. Parental illnesses that have limited their availability to be involved with the child

should be explored. Family disruptions or environmental stresses need review.

Parent-Child Relationship and Family Interactions: How parents relate to the child's self-assertion and aggression; the quality of warmth and sensitivity to the child; how limits are set; attitudes about discipline; exactly how parents respond to tantrums in others, themselves, and the child all must be examined. How have parents calmed the child in the past? Are the parents allied in their approach to the tantrums? What is the role of siblings?

Caregivers: Who they are and how competent are they? Exactly how do they respond to the tantrums? Information should be obtained from day care and nursery school workers.

Family Observations: Among other significant items are: the emotional maturity of the parents, their sophistication and/or intuitive wisdom about young children. Their own problematic behavior patterns as they reveal them in the interviews are of signal importance. Possibilities include overt emotionality; temper outbursts; open hostility; teasing; invasive or controlling behaviors; timidity or ambivalence about limit setting; unclear communication; irregularity about time and schedules; poorly organized sleeping and eating arrangements; constrictive, punitive, or blaming attitudes; casual arrangements for the child's safety; unclear messages about arrivals and departures of adults and siblings.

The Child's Behavior: The child's level of interactional and social maturity can be discerned in meetings with both the child and the parent. Developmental lags or deficits of central nervous system function may be evident. In the course of 1 or 2 meetings the following may be observed: developmental delay in speech; poor ability to focus attention; overexcitation with problematic impulse regulation; limited frustration tolerance; "strange behaviors" suggestive of atypical ego functions or autism; extreme negativity; and obsessive-compulsive tendencies. Evidence of problematic self-integration that may relate to persistent tantrums includes: oppositional tendencies; anxiety; shame; self-depreciation; defensive omnipotence or overassertiveness.

Focal Assessments

The assessment process may require supplementary focal evaluations. These may include developmental neurologic study; psychologic testing; consultation from specialists in speech therapy; special education; and sensory motor training. Refined hearing tests also may be indicated.

Moving From Assessment to Intervention

Recommendations may be made for conjoint parent-child meetings, for family therapy, for intensive parent guidance, for special school placement, for employment of a therapeutic companion, or for individual psychotherapy. Selective combinations of these are not unusual. Typically, tantrums that are primarily or predominantly related to neurophysiologic dysfunction, such as attention deficit disorders with or without hyperactivity, or to severe obsessive-compulsive disorders, benefit from medication. Parents may require an extended period of consultation before accepting the use of medication. The child needs careful preparation to understand the purpose of the medication if it is instituted.

25 / Speech and Language Disorders

Lori Zukerman and Dennis Cantwell

Communication disorders in children and adolescents can be classified into speech disorders (those disorders affecting the production of speech) and language disorders (those disorders that affect the child's ability to encode or decode meaning in ways that are consistent with the rules of the child's linguistic community) (Synder-McLean & McLean, 1987).

Speech disorders can be further classified into articulation disorders (substitution of one sound for another, e.g., "fing" for "thing"; distortion of a sound, e.g., a distorted [s] due to a lisp; or omission of a sound, e.g., "mik" for "milk"); fluency disorders (stuttering or cluttering), and voice disorders (characterized by inappropriate pitch, volume, nasality, or breathiness). Language disorders can be further classified into receptive language disorders (impairment in understanding language), expressive language disorders (impairment in expression of language), and pragmatic language impairment (inappropriate use of language for communication and disregard for the rules of social language).

Broadly speaking, speech and language impairments may have either an organic or a functional/developmental etiology. Examples of organic etiologies of speech disorders include articulation disorders resulting from neurologic damage (dysarthria) or abnormal voice quality due to cleft palate. Examples of organic etiologies of language disorders include those associated with brain injury (e.g., infarct or head trauma) or a seizure disorder. The diagnosis of a developmental speech or language disorder, by definition of the fourth edition of the *Diagnostic and Statistical Manual of Mental Disorders* (American Psychiatric Association [hereafter cited as APA], 1994), requires that the communication disorder is not due to a pervasive developmental disorder, defect in hearing acuity, mental retardation, defect in the oral speech mechanism, or neurologic disorder. Some speech and language problems may be associated with syndromes such as mental retardation or hearing impairments, or with childhood psychiatric syndromes such as schizophrenia, mania, depression, anxiety disorders, autism, or other pervasive developmental disorders. Additionally, children with developmental speech and language disorders are at risk for future learning disorders (reading more frequently than math) and psychiatric disorders (Cantwell & Baker, 1987).

Figure 25.1 presents a decision for a speech/language problem.

A. A knowledge of normal speech and language development is essential before speech and language problems can be assessed. The first step in assessment is to obtain a communication history from the child's parents, including medical, developmental, social, environmental, and family history. Pregnancy, birth, infancy, or childhood medical problems such as anoxia, Rh incompatibility, congenital infections, hyperbilirubinemia, apnea, recurrent ear infections, exposure to ototoxic drugs, high fevers, and infectious diseases are risk factors for hearing impairment (Cantwell & Baker, 1987). Abnormal, inconsistent, or unusual responses to sounds may suggest hearing impairment or deficits in auditory processing (Cantwell & Baker, 1987). A history of the child's speech and language development, including descriptions of early vocalizations, characteristics of pitch, milestones, manner of verbal and nonverbal communication, triggers for communication, and intelligibility (by family as well as strangers) should be obtained. Social, environmental, and family fac-

tors may influence speech and language development. These include family size, family history of speech or language problems, the amount of time family members spend talking with the child, day care arrangements, the number of languages spoken in the home, and the ages and language backgrounds of playmates. Psychosocial risk factors associated with delayed speech development include low socioeconomic status, large family size, late birth order, twinship, and bilingual background (Cantwell & Baker, 1987).

B. The majority of speech and particularly language problems during childhood are longstanding in nature. Although they may tend to be recognized more often during the school years, careful history may reveal early signs of communication impairment.

C. Any sudden change in communication and/or loss of previous function may be a presenting feature of an acute medical or psychiatric problem, and warrants immediate medical and mental status evaluation. Abnormal physical, neurologic, or mental status findings may necessitate the need for further workup, including psychiatric evaluation, blood studies, brain imaging studies, or electroencephalogram. Examples of acute medical or neurologic syndromes that may have associated speech or language impairments include delirium, seizures, or acute brain infarct. Psychiatric syndromes often manifested by sudden change in speech and language functioning include psychotic disorders, mood disorders, anxiety disorders, and elective mutism. Recent history of behavioral changes associated with these disorders will help clarify the diagnosis.

D. Any child suspected of having a long standing speech or language problem should have an evaluation of hearing. Depending on the degree of hearing impairment, articulation, prosody, voice quality, language comprehension, and expression may be affected.

E. An informal assessment of the child's pragmatic skills can be performed by observation of the child's verbal and nonverbal communication. This can provide information not only about the child's language skills and deficits, but it may also provide information about the child's behavior that may be helpful in identifying specific psychiatric disorders.

F. The majority of children with mental retar-

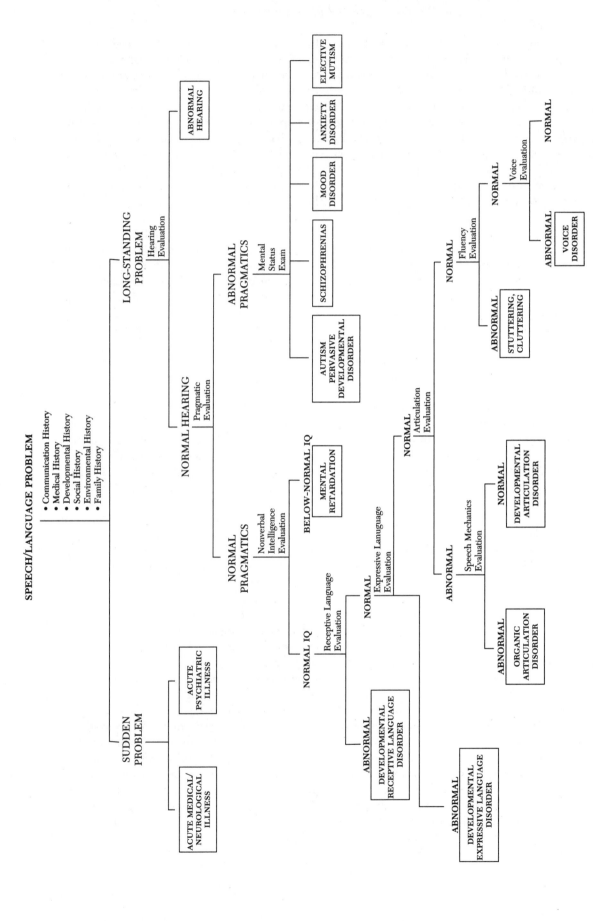

FIGURE 25.1.

Speech/language problem decision tree.

dation will have some impairment in speech or language. Assessment of nonverbal IQ can be helpful in distinguishing those children with mental retardation and its associated speech and language impairments from those with normal IQ who also have a speech or language disorder. Even a child with mental retardation whose language delay is greater than his or her overall cognitive delay, however, would be considered to additionally have a specific language disorder.

G. Although the degree of language impairment may be quite varied, impairment in both verbal and nonverbal communication (from no language, to inability to name objects or use abstract terms, to monotonous tone of voice, to minimal or inappropriate facial expression or gesture) with a history of impaired reciprocal social interaction and restricted repertoire of activities and interests may suggest pervasive developmental disorder or autism (APA, 1994). The presence of delusions, hallucinations, and/or disturbances in affect and form of thought (sometimes characterized by illogical speech, poverty of content of speech, incoherence, blocking) may suggest a diagnosis of schizophrenia or related disorders (APA, 1994). There also may be characteristic changes in speech or language associated with mood disorders: loud, pressured, rapid speech with jokes, puns, and clanging, or hostile, angry tirades accompanied by elevated, expansive, or irritable mood may be suggestive of mania (APA, 1994). Poverty of speech, slowed speech, monotone, or muteness with a history of neurovegetative symptoms may be suggestive of major depression (APA, 1994). Refusal to speak in one or more social situations despite the presence of receptive and verbal language abilities and nonverbal modes of communication (e.g., gestures or drawings) suggests a diagnosis of elective mutism (APA, 1994).

H. If acute medical, neurologic, and psychiatric illnesses have been ruled out and evaluation for hearing impairment and mental retardation is unrevealing, a formal speech and language evaluation should be done to clarify the nature of the child's developmental communication problem. Impairments in language comprehension (e.g., deficits in understanding language concepts, vocabulary, grammar, or syntax) suggest a diagnosis of developmental receptive language disorder. Impairments in expressive language (deficits in vocabulary, word usage or grammar) suggest a diagnosis of developmental expressive language disorder. Disorders of articulation with normal speech mechanism suggest a diagnosis of developmental articulation disorder; disorders of fluency suggest a diagnosis of stuttering or cluttering; abnormalities in voice quality suggest a specific voice disorder.

None of the developmental speech and language disorders is mutually exclusive; More than 1 disorder may be present in a particular child. Likewise, medical, neurologic, or psychiatric disorders do not exclude the existence of a speech or language disorder. Given the high rate of comorbidity, it is essential that a comprehensive assessment be done on any child presenting with a speech or language disorder.

REFERENCES

Cantwell, D. P., & Baker, L. (1987). *Developmental speech and language disorders*. New York: Guilford Press.

Diagnostic and statistical manual of mental disorders (Third edition–revised). (1987). Washington, D.C.: American Psychiatric Association.

Snyder-McClean, L., McLean, J. E. *Effectiveness of early intervention for children with language and communication disorders*. In: Guvalnick, M. J., Bennett, F. C. (Eds.) (1987). *The effectiveness of early intervention for at risk and handicapped children*. New York: Academic Press.

26 / Language Delay

Janet E. Fischel and Grover J. Whitehurst

There is enormous variation in the rate at which language develops in young children. Perhaps this is why language problems are among the most common of parental concerns in the preschool years. By 24 months of age, the typical child has a single-word vocabulary of at least 100 to 200 words and is beginning to produce 2-word combinations; many children are even further along in language development. However, a significant percentage of children have little or no productive vocabulary by 24 months. A similarly wide range of language development is present at later points in the preschool period. Careful attention should be given to the presenting symptom of delayed language in preschoolers. Although many such children are manifesting nothing more than normal variation in development, for others language delay reflects one or more impairments that are associated with significant later problems.

Types of Language Delay

Language delay is described as *primary* when it is the focus of concern in an otherwise apparently healthy and normally developing child. When more global developmental delays or abnormal development is present, the language delay should be defined as *secondary*. This would be the case, for example, in children with pervasive disorders, such as mental retardation or autism, which cut across virtually all areas of development. While the language deficit in such instances is important to evaluate, the treatment and prognostic implications differ substantially from cases in which the delay is primary. In instances of primary language delay, the clinician should remain alert to associated problems such as inability to attend/hyperac-

Preparation of this manuscript was supported by grants to the authors from the U.S. Administration on Children and Families (90CD095701) and to author Whitehurst from the Pew Charitable Trusts.

tivity or conduct difficulties. These may require dual diagnosis and a focus of treatment addressing the *comorbidity* of the language and psychiatric disorder.

Within the diagnosis of primary language delay, it is important to distinguish between *primary expressive delay,* which refers to delay that is exclusive to the production of language—that is, a limited expressive vocabulary compared with age norms—vs. *primary receptive-expressive delay,* in which the child has deficits in both understanding and production of language. The other major category of early language problems are phonological in nature—stuttering and articulation. These are usually called speech problems and are not the focus of this chapter.

Essentials of Assessment

As shown in Figure 26.1, the clinician's assessment of language delay in 2- to 5-year-olds should include an initial assessment, with careful history and screening of current language status, in order to determine whether formal diagnostic procedures and referrals to other specialists are advisable. This would be the case if other medical or developmental conditions exist that might preclude consideration of the language delay as primary—conditions such as mental retardation, autism, or hearing impairment. Most of the initial assessment can be based on information obtained from the child's primary caregiver and should address the following issues:

1. Family history of language or reading problems (which are typically present in children with delayed language in the late preschool period but may not be present in younger children with language delay)
2. Whether the child's problem extends to understanding the language of others or appears to be

LANGUAGE DELAY

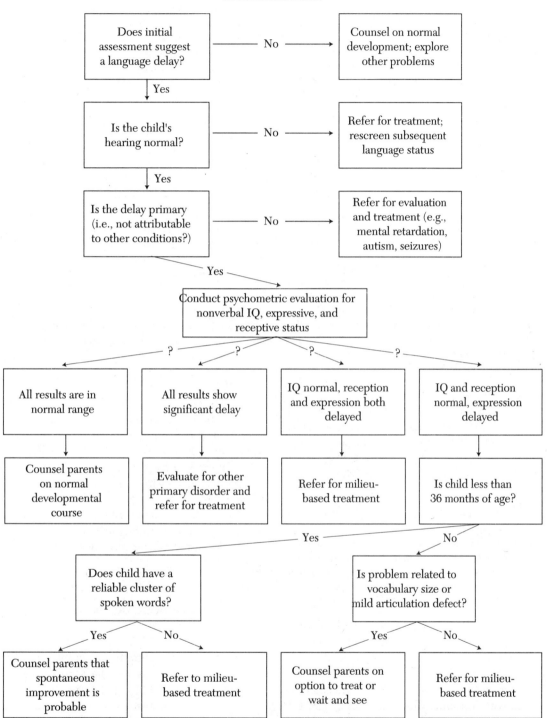

FIGURE 26.1.

Decision tree for language delay in children between 24 months and 5 years of age.

limited to producing language (receptive-expressive difficulties are associated with a much higher risk of later problems than exclusively expressive difficulties)

3. History of middle ear infections (children with frequent bouts of middle ear infections during the toddler period may have expressive delays that resolve more quickly than children whose delay is due to more central impairments)

4. Problems in hearing (which can directly produce language delays and should be formally assessed in any child with serious language delay)

5. Presence of oromotor problems, such as difficulty in chewing, or other soft neurological signs (which may warrant fuller neurological evaluation)

6. Presence of delay in nonlinguistic developmental milestones (which may indicate the presence of mental retardation or other problems to which language delay is secondary)

7. Unusual patterns of language development in the home (minimal adult-child verbal interaction may not provide sufficient stimulation for normal language development)

8. Degree of delay, if any, in pragmatic abilities (children who can communicate successfully with gesture, pantomime, or pointing are likely to have a more limited and self-correcting problem than those children who have communicative as well as linguistic difficulties)

9. Previous pattern of linguistic development (children who started talking normally and then stopped, without associated neurological trauma, or those who talk only in selective circumstances are likely to have a psychiatric disorder to which the language delay is secondary)

10. Gender (male preschoolers are disproportionately represented in samples of children with language delay)

11. The child's age (language delay occurs in a progressively smaller proportion of children across the preschool years and is increasingly problematic as it persists)

To expand the last point, for a nontalking child under 24 months who can understand simple sentences and is normal in other areas of development, there is probably no reason for concern. The vast majority of these children will catch up in expressive vocabulary by 36 months of age. The same is true for children between 24 and 36 months if they reliably produce a small cluster of single words (Fischel et al., 1989). Children between 24 and 36 months of age who speak no words at all, older children with very limited vocabularies, or children of any age who appear to lack age-appropriate comprehension of adult language deserve full and formal evaluation.

In the formal psychometric evaluation of language delay, it is critical to obtain separate information on expressive skill, receptive skill, and nonverbal IQ. The essential findings of primary expressive delay are that nonverbal IQ is normal and receptive skills are normal but expressive skills are substantially below normal. The essential findings of primary receptive-expressive delay are that nonverbal IQ is normal but both receptive skills and expressive skills are substantially below normal. The psychometric instruments should include standardized tests of language skill and nonverbally measured intelligence. The *Expressive One Word Picture Vocabulary Test—Revised* (Gardner, 1990), the *Peabody Picture Vocabulary Test—Revised* (Dunn & Dunn, 1981), and the *MacArthur Communicative Development Inventory* (Fenson et al., 1993) are useful for expressive and receptive assessment, particularly for children in the younger age range of 24 to 48 months. A nonverbal IQ test, such as the *Leiter International Performance Scale* (Leiter, 1976), allows a general assessment of intellectual status without language bias. Comparison of performance vs. verbal scale scores on standardized tests of intelligence such as the *Stanford-Binet Intelligence Scale* (Thorndike, Hagen, & Sattler, 1986) can be used to detect the gap between nonverbal intellectual skills and language skills. However, these tests usually lack the separation of scales within the language field to distinguish between expressive delay and receptive-expressive delay.

Treatment Decisions

Treatment decisions follow from considerations of the nature of the disorder and the age of the child, as previously discussed. There are a variety of treatment approaches available (Whitehurst, 1994). The treatment considered most efficacious is one in which the problem is addressed in the context of the child's everyday environment. This can include a speech/language professional who involves the family in a parent-guided treatment program or a school-based program in which the child's language needs are specifically addressed in the context of social interaction and preacademic learning. Milieu-based treatments such as these are more likely to offer naturalistic opportunities for generalization of learning and reinforcement of new skills. Least favored is the traditional episodic office-based treatment, because it lacks a conduit of generalization to the everyday interactions of language comprehension and language use. The clinician is best guided by the severity of delay, the age of the child, and other risk factors, such as conduct disorders. Children under 36 months of age with primary expressive delay are likely to show spontaneous improvement to the normal range by 4 or 5 years of age without treatment (Paul, 1996; Rescorla, Roberts, & Dahlsgaard, 1997; Whitehurst & Fischel, 1994), although they may experience a phase of articulation delay after a period of rapid vocabulary catch-up (Whitehurst et al., 1991). Further, they may be at increased risk of later syntactic problems, or weakness in other verbally related abilities such as reading achievement, short-term memory, processing, or word retrieval, but there is little evidence to date that these problems, when they occur, are sufficiently severe to be clinical in nature

(Fischel & Payne, 1995; Paul, 1996; Rescorla, 1993). Children with substantially delayed receptive language or children whose language delay is secondary to other conditions should be referred for treatment regardless of age. Children over 36 months of age with continuing expressive delay raise more complicated issues with respect to their need for treatment. Many of these children will show spontaneous improvement without treatment and will suffer no long-term effects, but many may not, depending in part on subtleties in the nature and severity of their expressive delay. Of concern to parents and clinicians alike is the briefer time available to await spontaneous improvement before elementary school begins, if therapy is not the option chosen. Thus some professionals are likely to recommend treatment for all these children. Other professionals differentiate between children with milder basic expressive deficits (problems of vocabulary size or articulation errors) and those with broader communicative concerns or more severe syntactic expressive deficits in the 3- to 5-year-old age range, recommending treatment for the latter group only, because problems with the syntax or coherence of expressive narratives are much more problematic than problems that are restricted to vocabulary size or articulation.

REFERENCES

Dunn, L. M., & Dunn, L. M. (1981). *Peabody Picture Vocabulary Test—Revised*. Circle Pines, MN: American Guidance Service.

Fenson, L., Dale, P. S., Reznick, J. S., Thal, D., Bates, E., Hartung, J., Pethick, S., & Reilly, J. S. (1993). *The MacArthur Communicative Development Inventory*. San Diego: Singular Publishing Group.

Fischel, J., & Payne, A. (1995). Children with severe specific expressive language delay: School achievement in second grade. *Society for Research in Child Development Abstracts, 10,* 396.

Fischel, J. E., Whitehurst, G. J., Caulfield, M. B., & DeBaryshe, B. (1989). Language growth in children with expressive language delay. *Pediatrics, 82,* 218–227.

Gardner, M. F. (1990). *Expressive One-Word Picture Vocabulary Test—Revised*. Novato, CA: Academic Therapy Publications.

Leiter, R. (1976). *Supplement to general instructions for the Leiter International Performance Scale*. Chicago: Stoelting Co.

Paul, R. (1996). Clinical implications of the natural history of slow expressive language development. *American Journal of Speech-Language Pathology, 5* (2), 5–20.

Rescorla, L. (1993). Outcomes of toddlers with specific expressive language delay (SELD) at ages 3, 4, 5, 6, 7, & 8. *Society for Research in Child Development Abstracts, 9,* 566.

Rescorla, L., Roberts, J. & Dahlsgaard, K. (1997). Late talkers at 2: Outcome at age 3. *Journal of Speech, Language and Hearing Research, 40,* 556–566.

Thorndike, R. L., Hagen, E. P., & Sattler, J. M. (1986). *Stanford-Binet Intelligence Scale* (4th ed.). Chicago: Riverside Publishing Company.

Whitehurst, G. J. (1994). Treatment of children with

language disorders. *British Journal of Clinical Psychology, 33,* 579–581.

Whitehurst, G. J., & Fischel, J. E. (1994). Early developmental language delay: What, if anything, should the clinician do about it? *Journal of Child Psychology and Psychiatry, 35,* 613–648.

Whitehurst, G., Smith, M., Fischel, J., Arnold, D., & Lonigan, C. (1991). The continuity of babble and speech in children with specific expressive language delay. *Journal of Speech and Hearing Research, 34,* 1121–1129.

---

27 / Accident-Proneness

Mae S. Sokol and Nicola S. Gray

Accidental injuries are the most important cause of morbidity, mortality, and disability during childhood and adolescence. Accidents account for more deaths among children ages 1 to 14 years than the next 5 most common causes. In highly industrialized countries, approximately 35% of all deaths in children ages 1 to 14 years are due to accidents. It is further estimated that for each child who dies from an injury, 70 more were hospitalized for the treatment of an injury (Department of Health, 1980, 1982); and for every hospitalization for injury, there are at least 9 injuries requiring outpatient medical attention (McGee & Silva, 1982). Langley (1984) and others have explored the relationship of injuries to demographic and psychosocial factors.

Certain children are described as accident-prone by parents, pediatricians, and others. This implies that these children have a variety of traits that increase their risk of having accidents. These traits include lack of motor coordination, hyperactivity, inattention, and impulsivity. The term *clumsy child syndrome* also has been used by some to describe children with impaired development of sensorimotor coordination that cannot be attributed to focal neurological deficits (Gordon & McKinley, 1980; Gubbay, 1975). Sleepiness is also associated with increased risk for accidents, especially in adolescents (Carskadon & Dement, 1987).

Few objective studies have explored the relationship between the prevalence of accidents and these various cognitive, physical, and behavioral factors. A relationship does appear to exist, however, between psychosocial stress and injuries. Accidents tend to occur more frequently when there is family or environmental stress.

Accidents appear to occur with increased frequency when the caregiver is tired or ill, or when children are in the care of someone other than the primary caregiver. In general, when a child has repeated injuries, it is important to evaluate for the presence of family stress. Similarly, when environmental stress is known to be present, it is important to educate the child and family about injury prevention. (For discussions of injury prevention, see Ehrlich, Hulstyn, & d'Amato, 1992; Gordon & McKinley, 1980; Grossman & Rivara, 1992; and Paulson, 1983.)

The possibility of child abuse or neglect always must be considered as a cause of repeated injury. Special attention should be given to cases in which repeated injuries are not commensurate with the history given by the child and/or parents.

"Accident-proneness" is a diagnosis of elimination; that is, before ascribing repeated injury to accident-proneness, various other possible causes need to be ruled out by history taking and physical and mental status examination. Figure 27.1 presents a decision tree for accident-proneness. Please note that this is only a partial listing of possible causes of accident-proneness. Also, the categories of possible causes are not mutually exclusive.

A. Neurological Disorders.

Seizure Disorders. Involuntary motor and/or sensory activity is, among other things, one of the manifestations of a seizure. A seizure may occur

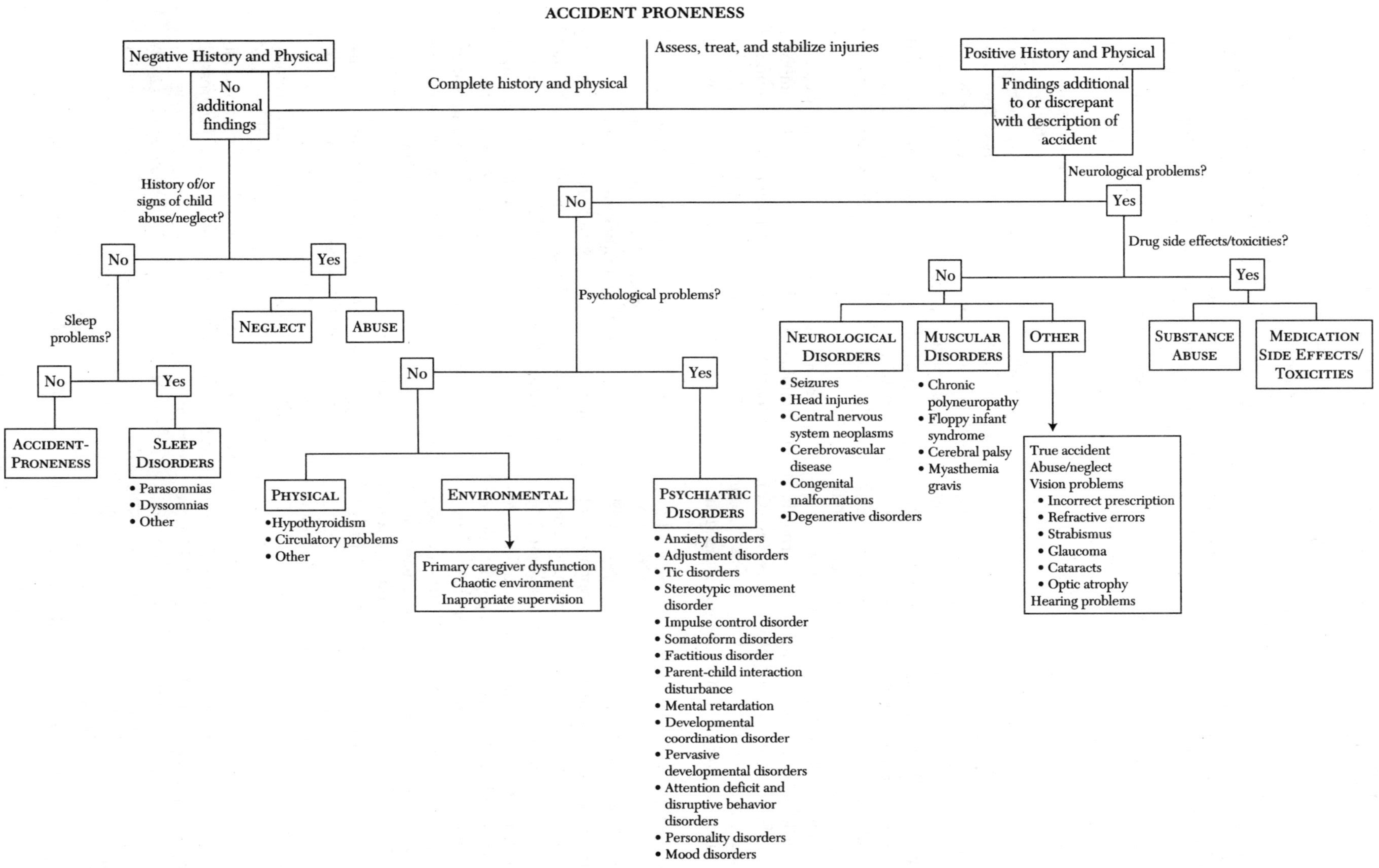

ACCIDENT PRONENESS

FIGURE 27.1.

Accident-proneness in children decision tree.

after a transient metabolic, traumatic, anoxic, or infectious insult to the brain. The incidence is higher in children than in later life. Repeated seizures without evident time-limited cause justify the label of epilepsy. The key to the diagnosis of epilepsy is the history; events prior to, during, and after the seizure can help classify the seizure. Every case of suspected seizure disorder warrants an electroencephalogram. However, a seizure is a clinical phenomenon: An electroencephalogram showing eleptiform activity may confirm and even extend the clinical diagnosis, but it cannot make the diagnosis. An increased blood creatine phosphokinase (CPK) level and a history of a prodromal and/or postictal state are also clinical findings that suggest the diagnosis of a seizure. Other studies are used selectively. Signs of an injury resulting from a seizure may include a pattern of injuries that suggest there was no attempt to break the fall, a bitten tongue, or a report of an altered state of consciousness at the time of the "accident."

Febrile seizures are defined as occurring between the ages of 3 months to 5 years, fever of 38.8 degrees C, and non–central nervous system infection. Greater than 90% are generalized and brief (less than 5 minutes) and occur early in an OMPA (otitis media, pharyngitis, adenitis) illness. Meningitis must be ruled out.

Head Injuries. Whenever the cause for the head injury is not readily apparent, nonaccidental trauma should be suspected. Symptoms of a moderately severe head injury usually resolve in 1 to 2 days, although vertigo and some alteration in behavior, mood, and concentration persist for several days. Some children will experience relatively protracted problems regarding attention, concentration, headaches, and school performance after seemingly mild or moderate head injury. From 3 to 5% of children with a history of severe head injury have severe long-term neurological deficits, and another 5 to 6% have moderate long-term deficits.

Neoplasms of the Central Nervous System. Twenty percent of childhood cancers are primary brain tumors. The incidence of primary brain tumors among children under the age of 15 is between 2.1 and 2.5 per 100,000 population. In children over the age of 2 years, approximately 65% of brain tumors are *infratentorial,* and, regardless of histologic type, frequently present with gait disturbance, incoordination, multiple and often asymmetric cranial nerve deficits, and nystagmus. Specific neurologic manifestations of *supratentorial tumors* are dictated by the location of the tumor. *Pseudotumor cerebri* is a condition characterized by increased intracranial pressure in the absence of an identifiable intracranial mass or hydrocephalus. Clinical manifestation are those of increased intracranial pressure, including decreased level of consciousness, blurred vision, double vision, developmental delay, and visual field loss. Although the precise cause is usually not known, the condition has been described in association with a variety of inflammatory, metabolic, toxic, and connective tissue disorders. The diagnosis of pseudotumor cerebri is one of exclusion. Clinical manifestations of *spinal cord tumors* include gait disturbance, pain, and bowel and bladder dysfunction in association with abnormal muscle stretch reflexes, weakness, and sensory loss.

Cerebrovascular Disease. Because many conditions leading to childhood stroke result in emboli, multifocal neurologic involvement is common. Physical examination of the patient should be aimed not only at identifying the specific deficits related to impaired cerebral blood flow but also at seeking evidence for any predisposing disorder. Retinal hemorrhages, splinter hemorrhages in the nail beds, cardiac murmurs, in addition to signs of trauma are especially important clinical findings. Cardiac, vascular, or hematologic disease and intracranial disorders should be considered. Initial studies should include complete blood count, lipid profile, and electrocardiogram. Additional laboratory tests should be carried out with particular attention to disorders involving the heart, blood vessels, platelets, red cells, hemoglobin, and coagulation proteins.

Congenital Malformations of the Nervous System. In general, the diagnosis of neural tube defects is obvious at the time of birth. However, *Arnold-Chiari malformation type I* may remain asymptomatic for years; in older children and young adults, it may cause progressive ataxia, paresis of the lower cranial nerves, and progressive vertigo.

Central Nervous System Degenerative Disorders. These include spinocerebellar degeneration disorders, extrapyramidal disorders, and hereditary sensory and autonomic neuropathies.

Spinocerebellar degeneration disorders may be

hereditary or may occur in sporadic distribution. *Friedreich's ataxia* is a recessive disorder characterized by onset of gait ataxia or scoliosis before puberty, becoming progressively worse in the first 2 years of life. Light touch and position sensation as well as reflexes are reduced. Dysarthria becomes progressively worse. *Dominant ataxia* occurs with varying manifestations among members of the same family. Ataxia occurs first, and progression continues with opthalmoplegias, extrapyramidal tract, and motor neuron degeneration. Only 10% of cases have childhood onset and their course is more rapid. Associated findings permit identification of other *miscellaneous recessive ataxias*. These include ataxia-telangiectasia (telangiectasia, immune defects) and Wilson's disease (Kayser-Fleischer rings in eye). Neuropathies such as Charcot-Marie-Tooth disease also produce ataxia.

Extrapyramidal disorders are characterized by the presence in the waking state of one or more of the following features: dyskinesias, athetosis, ballismus, tremors, rigidity, and dystonias.

Sydenham's postrheumatic chorea is characterized by rapid involuntary movements of the limbs and face and variable degrees of psychological disturbance. Although the disorder follows infections with beta-hemolytic streptococci, the interval between infection and chorea may be greatly prolonged; throat cultures and antistreptolysin O (ASO) titers may be negative. The diagnosis usually is not difficult. Tics, drug-induced extrapyramidal syndromes, Huntington's chorea, and Wilson's disease as well as other rare movement disorders usually can be ruled out on historical and clinical grounds. Sydenham's chorea is a self-limiting disease that may last from a few weeks to months.

Transient tics of childhood last from 1 month to 1 year and seldom need treatment. The trunk and extremities often are involved, and there can be twisting or flinging movements. Many children with tics have a history of encephalopathic past events, "soft signs" on neurological exam, and school problems. *Gilles de la Tourette's disorder* is a chronic disorder of multiple fluctuating motor and vocal tics, with onset in childhood, lasting more than a year, and with absence of other recognizable causes for tics. Tics evolve slowly, new ones being added to or replacing old ones. Partial forms are common.

Hereditary sensory and autonomic neuropathies include at least 5 clinical entities, all characterized by progressive loss of function that predominantly affects the peripheral sensory nerves. B. Muscular Disorders. (For review, see Patterson & Gomez, 1990.)

Chronic polyneuropathy. Polyneuropathy, usually insidious in onset and slowly progressive, occurs in children of any age. The presenting complaints are chiefly disturbances of gait and easy fatigability in walking or running and, slightly less often, weakness or clumsiness of the hands. Pure sensory neuropathies show up as chronic trauma; the patient does not feel minor trauma and burns to the fingers and toes. Known causes of polyneuropathy include: (1) toxins (e.g., lead, arsenic, mercurials, vincristine, and benzene); (2) systemic disorders (e.g., diabetes mellitus, chronic uremia, recurrent hypoglycemia, porphyria, polyarteritis nodosa, and lupus erythematosus; (3) "inflammatory states" (e.g., chronic or recurrent Guillain-Barre syndrome and neuritis associated with mumps or diphtheria); (4) hereditary, often degenerative conditions; and (5) the hereditary sensory or combined motor and sensory neuropathies. Laboratory diagnosis of chronic polyneuropathy is made by measurement of motor and sensory nerve conduction velocities; electromyography may show a neurogenic polyphasic pattern.

Floppy Infant Syndrome. This syndrome often presents in young infants as "frog posture" or other unusual positions at rest and, in older infants, as a delay in motor milestones. Hypotonia is a frequent presenting complaint in neuromuscular disorders but also may accompany a variety of systemic conditions or may be due to certain disorders of connective tissue. Clinically, there are 2 groups: a paralytic group in which there is a significant lack of movement against gravity and a nonparalytic group in which there is floppiness without significant paralysis.

Cerebral Palsy. This is a term of clinical convenience for disorders of impaired motor functioning and posture with onset during pregnancy, birth, or the first year of life. These disorders are basically nonprogressive and vary widely in their causes, manifestations, and prognosis. The most obvious manifestation is impaired function of voluntary muscles.

Myasthenia Gravis. This is an uncommon disease. Essentials of diagnosis include: (1) weak-

145

ness, chiefly of muscles innervated by the brain stem, usually coming on or increasing with use (fatigue); (2) a positive response to neostigmine and adrophonium; and (3) acetylcholine receptor antibodies in the serum (except in the congenital form).

C. Vision Problems.

Visual difficulties that cause a decrease in visual acuity are frequently a problem in children. A child's vision changes with time and needs to be monitored accordingly.

Incorrect eyeglass prescriptions are a frequent problem.

Refractive errors include myopia, hyperopia, astigmatism, and anisometropia.

The diagnosis of *Strabismus* (*"lazy eye"*) frequently is made by simple inspection. If there is questionable or only slight deviation, the diagnosis is established by the corneal light reflection technique or the cover test. Strabismus can cause a decrease in depth perception and (rarely) diplopia.

Glaucoma is a condition in which elevated intraocular pressure is related to the development of a characteristic optic neuropathy and a loss of visual function. The susceptibility of the optic nerve to pressure damage varies greatly from person to person.

Cataracts may be congenital or secondary to ocular trauma or associated with systemic diseases such as diabetes mellitus, galactosemia, atopic dermatitis, Marfan's syndrome, or Down syndrome. The associated reduction in vision varies considerably according to the location and extent.

The etiology of *optic atrophy* is complex. Disorders associated with optic atrophy in infants and children include the following: *hereditary* (e.g., primary optic atrophy, Leber's optic atrophy); *heredodegenerative* (e.g., mucopolysaccharidoses I–VI, abetalipoproteinemia, Charcot-Marie-Tooth disease, acute intermittent porphyria, retinitis, pigmentosa syndromes); *developmental* (e.g., glaucoma, posttraumatic hydrocephalus, postpapilledema); *infectious/inflammatory* (e.g., syphilis, acute viral illness, optic neuritis); *demyelinating* (e.g., spinocerebellar degeneration, multiple sclerosis); *compressive* (e.g., optic nerve glioma, meningioma, fibrous dysplasia, Graves disease, pituitary adenoma); and *toxic/nutritional* (e.g., lead, methanol, chloramphenicol, ethambutol, vitamin B12 deficiency, thiamine deficiency, folate deficiency).

D. Hearing Problems.

Hearing impairment can be inherited as an isolated trait or as part of a recognizable syndrome. In addition, there is a broad spectrum of acquired causes. In most cases, hearing impairment is subtle and can easily evade detection. Dysfunctional behavioral patterns and/or impaired social interaction secondary to hearing problems may be incorrectly ascribed to disorders such as autism/pervasive developmental disorder or mental retardation. Infectious diseases known to be associated with hearing loss include mumps, measles, bacterial meningitis, and congenital cytomegalovirus and toxoplasmosis.

E. Medication Side Effects/Toxicities.

Seizure medications, especially dilantin and barbiturates, can have neurologic side effects. Sedation can increase the risk of accidents and is a common side effect of such *psychotropic medications* as antihistamines, antidepressants, and neuroleptics. Adverse effects of *neuroleptics* (medications with dopamine-antagonist properties) that may increase the risk of accidents include medication-induced movement disorders, including parkinsonism, acute dystonia, acute akathisia, and tardive dyskinesia. *Psychostimulants* can cause increased impulsivity or hyperactivity as side effects, leading to accidents.

F. Substance Abuse.

Substance abuse is a frequent cause of accidents among adolescents in particular. Common consequences of drug and alcohol use include somatic symptoms, blackouts, trauma and accidental injury, impulsive behavior, motor vehicle accidents and near misses, and visits to the emergency room for intoxication or overdose. A thorough history, urine toxicology screen, and a breathalyzer test should all be part of the workup in cases of suspected substance abuse.

G. Other Physical Causes.

Early symptoms of *hypothyroidism* include lethargy and fatigue.

Circulatory problems can cause accident-proneness. Inadequate cerebral blood flow can lead to recurrent weakness, dizziness, syncope, and disturbances of consciousness. Causes include inadequate vasoconstrictor mechanisms, hypovolemia, mechanical reduction of venous return, reduced cardiac output, and arrhythmias.

Other causes of weakness and faintness can include an altered blood flow to the brain (e.g., hypoxia, anemia, hyperventilation, hypoglycemia) and physiological changes due to emotional disturbances, anxiety attacks, and hysterical seizures.

H. Sleep Disorders.

Parasomnias are undesirable physical night-time attacks that are disorders of arousal from deep non–rapid eye movement sleep. They include night terrors (pavor nocturnus), sleepwalking (somnambulism), nocturnal seizures, and nightmares.

Dyssomnias are a group of primary disorders of sleep initiation, sleep maintenance, or excessive sleepiness. These disorders are characterized by abnormalities in the amount, quality, or timing of sleep. The sleep disturbance (or associated daytime fatigue) can cause clinically significant functional impairment and increase the risk of accidents.

Sleep disorders also may be related to another mental disorder (often a mood or anxiety disorder), a general medical condition, or be substance- or medication-induced.

I. Child Abuse and Neglect.

Note. The possibility of nonaccidental trauma should be suspected when multiple sites of injury or injuries at different stages of healing are present. To diagnose child abuse and neglect, the clinician must take a complete history and assess physical and radiologic/laboratory findings.

The medical diagnosis of *physical abuse* is based on the presence of a "discrepant history." The history offered by the caregiver and/or child does not accord with the clinical findings. The discrepancy may exist because there is no history, partial history, changing histories over time, or simply an illogical or improbable history. *Emotional abuse* may cause nonspecific symptoms in children. Loss of self-esteem or self-confidence, sleep disturbances, somatic symptoms (e.g., stomachaches, headaches), or hypervigilance may be presenting symptoms or complaints. The American Academy of Pediatrics (1991) has published guidelines for the evaluation of child *sexual abuse* by primary care physicians. Neglect of children is not easily documented on history. *Physical neglect*, which must be differentiated from the effects of poverty, will be present even after the provision of adequate social services to families in financial need. Neglectful parents appear unable to recognize their children's physical or emotional states. Indications of physical neglect include broken toys, developmentally inappropriate toys, or inappropriate clothes or shoes (poorly fitting or not protecting against the weather). The history offered in cases of *failure to thrive* often is discrepant with physical findings as well. In such cases, out-of-home placement is usually followed by a dramatic height and weight gain. The hallmark of cases of *Munchausen syndrome by proxy* is that children have repeated visits to health care providers for unexplained illnesses.

The physical findings of physically abused children include bruises, burns, lacerations, scars, bony deformities, alopecia, dental trauma, and, in the case of head or abdominal trauma, findings consistent with these injuries. The bruises of physically abused children are sometimes patterned (e.g., belt marks, looped electric cord, or oval grab marks), and usually are found over the soft tissue areas of the body. Toddlers or older children who sustain accidental bruising usually do so over bony prominences. *Any* bruise in an infant not yet developmentally able to be mobile should be viewed with concern. Burns also may exhibit pathognomonic features. Scald burns in stocking or glove distribution, immersion burns of the buttocks, and cigarette burns are most common. The absence of splash marks or a pattern consistent with spillage is helpful in differentiating accidental from nonaccidental burns.

It is important to realize that children who are victims of sexual abuse may have no physical findings attributable to the abuse. Similarly, some nonspecific abnormalities of the genital and rectal regions do occur and, in the absence of a history, mean little or nothing. Children who present with the symptoms and signs of sexually transmitted diseases should be strongly suspected of having been sexually abused. Children with *nonorganic failure to thrive* often have an absence of subcutaneous fat in the cheeks, buttocks, and extremities. Children with Munchausen syndrome by proxy present with the physical findings of whatever illness is fictitiously induced. Reported presentations include dehydration from intentionally induced diarrhea or vomiting, sepsis from injection of contaminated materials, and poisoning.

Certain radiologic findings are strong indicators of physical abuse: Examples are metaphyseal corner or bucket handle fractures of the long bones in infants, spiral fractures of the long bones in nonambulatory infants, and multiple fractures of

147

the ribs or long bones at different stages of healing. Computed tomograph or magnetic resonance imaging findings of subdural hemorrhage in infants is highly correlated with abuse, especially since the advent of infant seat restraint laws. Ultrasound is useful in the delineation of abdominal injuries in children. Coagulation studies may be useful in children with many bruises at different stages of healing. Several recent reviews have discussed the differentiation of physical abuse from osteogenesis imperfecta. The radiologic findings are different in most cases, but there may be variants that are difficult to diagnose. The laboratory evaluation of sexually abused children should be modified depending on the history of the type of contact and the epidemiology of these infectious agents in the community. Abnormal somatomedin levels, growth hormone levels, and thyroid function tests that normalize after a short period of hospitalization, along with a complete blood count, urinalysis, and serum electrolyte panel are screening tests for children with suspected failure to thrive. The best test for this condition, however, is placement in a setting in which the child can be fed "ad lib" and the weight monitored. The diagnosis often is made by placing the child away from the inimical environment and observing subsequent catch-up growth.

J. Psychiatric Disorders.

Note. The reader is referred to the fourth edition of the *Diagnostic and Statistical Manual of Mental Disorders* (American Psychiatric Association, 1994) for complete diagnostic criteria and clinical findings of the following psychiatric disorders.

The essential feature of *mental retardation* is significantly subaverage general intellectual functioning (an IQ of approximately 70 or below) that is accompanied by significant limitations in adaptive functioning in at least 2 of the following skill areas: communication, self-care, home living, social/interpersonal skills, self-direction, use of community resources, functional academic skills, work, leisure, health, and safety. The onset must occur before 18 years. The risk of accidents increases when these individuals engage in activities that are not commensurate with their level of functioning.

The essential feature of *developmental coordination disorder* is marked impairment in the development of motor coordination. The manifestations of this disorder vary with age and development. For example, younger children may display clumsiness and delays in achieving developmental motor milestones. Older children may display difficulties with the motor aspects of assembling puzzles, running, playing ball, and printing or handwriting. Lack of coordination often continues through adolescence and adulthood.

Pervasive Developmental Disorders include autistic disorder and childhood disintegrative disorder. Autistic disorder is uncommon but is the most severe of these disorders. Autistic children often display peculiar interests, bizarre responses to sensory stimuli, repetitive stereotypic motor behaviors, odd posturing, impulsivity, aggressiveness, and self-injurious behavior. Rates of this disorder are 4 to 5 times higher in male than females. Childhood disintegrative disorder is characterized by a marked regression in multiple areas of functioning after the first 2 years of life (but before age 10). Clinically significant loss of previously acquired play or motor skills often occurs.

One of the features of Rett's disorder is the development of multiple specific deficits, including problems in the coordination of gait or trunk movements, following a period of normal functioning after birth. Rett's disorder typically is associated with severe or profound mental retardation and has been diagnosed only in females.

Attention deficit and disruptive behavior disorders include attention deficit hyperactivity disorder and conduct disorder. Attention deficit hyperactivity disorder is a clinical syndrome characterized by symptoms of inattention and impulsivity. Gayton, Bailey, Wagner, and Hardesty (1986) studied and confirmed the relationship between it and "accident-proneness" for both girls and boys. Conduct disorder is characterized by a repetitive and persistent pattern of behavior in which the basic rights of others or major age-appropriate societal norms or rules are violated. Aggression is a common symptom.

Personality disorders often cause accident-proneness. For example, individuals with borderline personality disorder may engage in self-mutilating or suicidal behaviors. They also may display impulsivity in areas that are potentially self-damaging (e.g., substance abuse, reckless driving).

Mood disorders can cause accident-proneness. Lethargy and tiredness, self-deprecating thoughts or statements, thoughts of death or suicide, somatic complaints (particularly headache and stomachache), irritability, and quick temper are among the many clinical manifestations of depression in children and adolescents. In addition, adolescents have the propensity to avoid the pain of depression through substance abuse or other excitement-seeking behaviors. Bipolar disorder is characterized by periods of abnormally and persistently elevated, expansive, or irritable mood and heightened levels of energy and activity. The poor judgment associated with manic episodes predisposes to dangerous and impulsive activities.

Anxiety disorders can cause accident-proneness. Signs and symptoms of anxiety in children often include psychomotor manifestations such as motor restlessness and hyperactivity, sleep disturbances, and decreased concentration.

Adjustment disorder can cause accident-proneness. When faced with stress, children can manifest many different symptoms, including changes in mood, changes in behavior, and physical complaints.

Tic disorders, such as Tourette's disorder, are characterized by multiple motor tics and at least 1 vocal tic. Commonly associated symptoms are hyperactivity, distractibility, and impulsivity.

Stereotypic movement disorder is characterized by repetitive, seemingly driven, and nonfunctional motor behavior that markedly interferes with normal activities or results in self-inflicted bodily injury.

Impulse control disorders are characterized by aggressiveness and impulsivity.

Somatoform disorders include conversion disorder, somatization disorder, hypochondriasis, somatoform pain disorder, and body dysmorphic disorder. A number of reports have pointed to the increased association of conversion symptoms with sexual overstimulation or sexual abuse.

The essential feature of *factitious disorder* is the intentional production of physical or psychological signs and symptoms in order to assume the sick role. The presentation may include fabrication of subjective complaints, self-inflicted conditions, exaggeration or exacerbation of preexisting general medical conditions.

Disturbances in parent-child interaction can cause accident-proneness. Primary caregiver dysfunction is defined as a failure to provide parenting functions because of parental vulnerability or disability, with the result that the parent is unable to meet the caregiving or developmental needs of the child.

REFERENCES

American Academy of Pediatrics. (1991) Guidelines for the evaluation of sexual abuse of children. *Pediatrics, 87,* 254.

American Psychiatric Association. (1994). *Diagnostic and statistical manual of mental disorders* (4th ed.). Washington, DC: Author.

Anglin, T. M. (1995). Adolescent substance abuse. In W. W. Hay, J. R. Groothuis, A. R. Hayward, & M. J. Levin (Eds.), *Current pediatric diagnosis and treatment.* Norwalk, CT: Appleton and Lange.

Carskadon, M. A., & Dement, W. C. (1987). Sleepiness in the normal adolescent. In C. Guilleminault (Ed.), *Sleep and its disorders in children.* New York: Raven Press.

Clark, R. B. (1995). Psychosocial aspects of pediatrics and psychiatry. In W. W. Hay, J. R. Groothuis, A. R. Hayward, & M. J. Levin (Eds.), *Current pediatric diagnosis and treatment.* Norwalk, CT: Appleton and Lange.

Daroff, R. B. (1994). Dizziness and vertigo. In K. J. Isslebacher, E. Braunwald, J. D. Wilson, J. B. Martin, A. S. Fauci, & D. L. Kasper (Eds.), *Harrison's principles of internal medicine.* New York: McGraw-Hill.

Department of Health. (1980). *Hospital and selected morbidity data, 1979.* Wellington: National Health Statistics Center.

Department of Health. (1982). *Mortality and demographic data, 1979.* Wellington: National Health Statistics Center.

Ehrlich, M. G., Hulstyn, M., & d'Amato, C. (1992). Sports injuries in children and the clumsy child. *Pediatric Clinics of North America, 39* (3), 433–449.

Ellis, P. P. (1995). The eye. In W. W. Hay, J. R. Groothuis, A. R. Hayward, & M. J. Levin (Eds.), *Current pediatric diagnosis and treatment.* Norwalk, CT: Appleton and Lange.

Gayton, W. F., Bailey, C., Wagner, A., & Hardesty, V.

(1986). Relationship between childhood hyperactivity and accident proneness. *Perceptual and Motor Skills, 63,* 801–802.

Goldson, E. (1995). Behavioral disorders and developmental variations. In W. W. Hay, J. R. Groothuis, A. R. Hayward, & M. J. Levin (Eds.), *Current pediatric diagnosis and treatment.* Norwalk, CT: Appleton and Lange.

Gordon, N., & McKinley, I. (Eds:). (1980). *Helping clumsy children.* London: Churchill Livingstone.

Greensher, J. (1984). Prevention of childhood injuries. *Pediatrics, 74,* 970–975.

Grossman, D. C., & Rivara, F. P. (1992). Injury control in childhood. *Pediatric Clinics of North America, 39* (3), 471–485.

Gubbay, S. S. (1975). *The clumsy child. A study of developmental apraxic and agnosic ataxia.* Philadelphia: W. B. Saunders.

Krugman, R. D. (1995). Child abuse and neglect. In W. W. Hay, J. R. Groothuis, A. R. Hayward, & M. J. Levin (Eds.), *Current pediatric diagnosis and treatment.* Norwalk, CT: Appleton and Lange.

Langley, J. (1984). Injury control—psychosocial considerations. *Journal of Child Psychology and Psychiatry, 25* (3), 349–356.

Ludwig, S., & Kornberg, A. F. (Eds.). (1992). *Child abuse: A medical reference* (2nd ed.). London: Churchill Livingstone.

Martin, J. B., & Ruskin, J. Faintness, syncope, and seizures. In K. J. Isslebacher, E. Braunwald, J. D. Wilson,

Martin, J. B., Fauci, A. S., & Kasper, D. L. (Eds.). (1994). *Harrison's principles of internal medicine.* New York: McGraw-Hill.

Menkes, J. H. (1995). *Textbook of child neurology.* Baltimore, MD: Williams & Wilkins.

Moe, P. G., & Seay, A. R. (1995). Neurogenic and muscular disorders. In W. W. Hay, J. R. Groothuis, A. R. Hayward, & M. J. Levin (Eds.), *Current pediatric diagnosis and treatment.* Norwalk, CT: Appleton and Lange.

Patterson, M. C., & Gomez, M. R. (1990). Muscle disease in children: A practical approach. *Pediatrics in Review, 12* (3), 73–82.

Paulson, J. A. (1983). Accidental injuries. In R. E. Behrman & V. C. Vaughan III (Eds.), *Nelson's textbook of pediatrics* (12th ed., pp. 261–263). Philadelphia: W. B. Saunders.

Rivara, F. P. (1995). Developmental and behavioral issues in childhood injury prevention. *Journal of Developmental and Behavioral Pediatrics, 16,* 362–370.

Rudolph, A. M., Hoffman, J. I. E., & Rudolph, C. D. (1996). *Rudolph's pediatrics.* Stamford, CT: Appleton and Lange.

Schwartz, M. W., Charney, E. D., Curry, T. A., & Ludwig, S. (1990). *Pediatric primary care: A problem oriented approach.* Chicago: Year Book Medical Publishers.

28 / No Friends

Audrey J. Clarkin

During childhood and adolescence, the absence of friends is an adverse situation and possible risk factor for other difficulties (Kupersmidt, Coie, & Dodge, 1990). The clinician's task is to pursue the presenting complaint of "no friends," assess its duration and related causes, and plan a targeted intervention to alleviate the distressing condition. Historical factors such as parental bonding, sibling relationships, early nurturance, gender, temperament, intelligence, and social experiences as well as contemporary issues such as age, socioeconomic level, cultural group, school, outside social opportunities, and available role models are all relevant and contribute unique aspects for each individual.

Current studies on children estimate that 6 to 11% of elementary school age children can be described as having no friends. The estimates for specific subgroups, such as children with a learning disability (Gresham, 1988) or mild retardation (Taylor, Asher & Williams, 1987), are even higher.

Isolation from peers as a single factor can place a child at risk for other problematic behaviors, such as school dropout.

Although physical or social immaturity can result in inadequate peer interactions, emphasis for treatment should be on 2 subgroups of children with no friends: the rejected (who can be labeled *externalizers*) and the neglected (who can be classified as *internalizers*) (Achenbach & Edelbrock, 1983).

The child's individual behavior determines so-

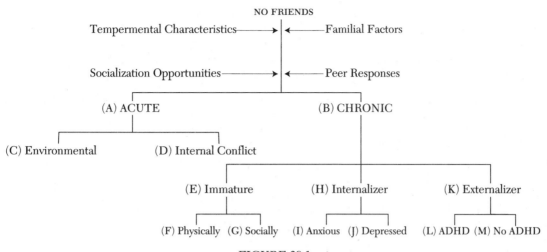

FIGURE 28.1.

No friends decision tree.

cial acceptance/rejection. Once rejected, this negative group reaction pervades and changes the child's self-image.

Decision Tree for Differential Treatment Planning

Figure 28.1 provides significant foci of evaluation related to specific interventions as the clinician gets to know the child or adolescent. Children with friends are acceptable to peers. Children without friends can be either neglected by agemates or rejected by them. Another approach is to regard the condition of no friends as either (A) acute or (B) chronic. Children who suffer acute loss of friends can be responding to the pressure of (C) environmental events (e.g., geographic move, parental divorce). Interventions include support and social manipulation (e.g., play dates with other peers, group socialization), which can be helpful for children suffering from temporary and immediate lack of friends. (D) Current internal conflict relates to disrupted here-and-now social relations (e.g., jealousy and loss of a best friend, or resentment toward a newborn sibling). These children often can resolve their immediate distress by brief therapy or family therapy.

The three clusters of children who chronically have no friends are the immature, the internalizers, and the externalizers. Children who are (E) immature either (F) physically or (G) socially often are unacceptable to peers. Children who are small and significantly undersize need time to grow and parental reassurance that it will happen. For children who are socially/emotionally immature, play dates with chronologically younger but developmentally appropriate children and structured social activities with adult monitoring—such as scouts, chess clubs—are recommended to enable them to develop confidence and positive relationships.

Children whose inhibitions prevent them from interacting positively with peers—(H) internalizers—are isolated from and neglected by age mates. Internalizers can be regarded, on evaluation, to be either predominantly (I) anxious or (J) depressed. Anxious children need programmed and progressive desensitization and social skills training that includes role playing and rehearsal. depressed children benefit from psychotherapy and, possibly, medication.

Children who actively provoke peers to reject them—(K) externalizers—exhibit negative and often aggressive social behavior. Externalizing children must be evaluated for the presence or absence of attention deficit hyperactivity disorder. For (L) externalizers with attention deficit hyperactivity disorder, treatment includes medication, behavior management, and family counseling. For

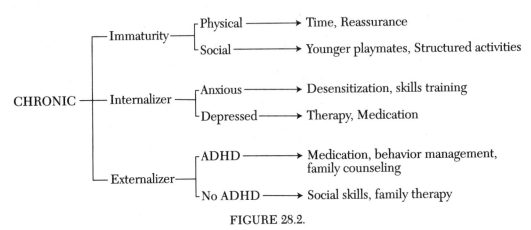

FIGURE 28.2.

Suggested interventions for no friends.

(M) externalizers without attention deficit hyperactivity disorder, social skills training and/or family therapy is effective.

A number of patterns of behavior need to be explored for children with no friends; the emerging information can be classified in terms of onset, duration, contributing factors, locus of control, level of social skills knowledge and practice, self-control, motivation, coping strategies, support systems, and subjective reactions. Studies dealing with peer rejection (Asher & Coie, 1990) and with the development of prosocial behavior (Eisenberg & Mussen, 1989), provide clinicians with a framework to understand the condition of no friends. These studies also suggest intervention strategies to help children with different developmental responses to the lack of friends. See Figure 28.2.

REFERENCES

Achenbach, T. M., & Edelbrock, C. S. (1983). *Manual for the Child Behavior Checklist and Revised Child Behavior Profile*. Burlington: University of Vermont, Department of Psychiatry.

Asher, S. R., & Coie, John D. (Eds.). (1990). *Peer rejection in childhood*. New York: Cambridge University Press.

Eisenberg, N., & Mussen, P. H. (1989). *The roots of prosocial behavior*. New York: Cambridge University Press.

Gresham, F. (1988). Social competence and motivational characteristics of learning disabled students.

In M. C. Luang, M. C. Reynolds, & H. J. Walberg (Eds.), *Handbook of special education: Research and practice* (Vol. 2, pp. 283–302). Oxford: Pergamon Press.

Kupersmidt, J., Coie, J., & Dodge, K. (1990). The role of poor peer relationships in the development of disorder. In S. R. Asher & J. D. Coie (Eds.), *Peer rejection in childhood* (pp. 253–273). New York: Cambridge University Press.

Taylor, A., Asher, S., & Williams, G. (1987). The social adaptation of mainstreamed, mildly-retarded children. *Child Development, 58*, 1321–1334.

29 / Runaway Behavior

John Sargent

Figure 29.1 presents a decision tree for runaway behavior.

A. It is essential that the presenting complaint be identified and addressed in the evaluation. Accurate and complete history is often difficult to obtain and should be sought in an organized fashion. Often many systems, including family, the child or adolescent, child welfare, juvenile justice, police, and extended family, foster family, or peers and their families may be involved. Differing points of view, competing agendas, and strong feelings, including significant antagonisms, may be present and may complicate information gathering and problem definition.

B. The evaluating clinician *must* obtain history of the child's custody and living situation. Doing so may require painstaking effort and marked attention to detail so that gaps in the story are not left unfilled and all uncertainties about custody are clarified. Social service or legal consultation may be necessary. Very often, children or adolescents and others are evasive in discussing this information. The clinician also will need to be aware of state laws concerning capacity of an adolescent to consent to treatment. Statutes defining age of majority vary from state to state; individual states may have regulations that lead to different ages of consent for medical and psychiatric treatment. Also the clinician should be aware of the legal requirements for considering a minor adolescent "emancipated" and thus able to consent independently for treatment.

C. Comprehensive medical evaluation is highly desirable in reviewing the status of runaway children and adolescents (Adams, 1992). Acute and chronic conditions may be present and require emergent as well as long-term treatment. Sexually transmitted diseases, HIV, malnutrition and its sequelae, complications of substance use including intoxication and addiction, physical trauma, poorly treated chronic illnesses, pregnancy, and, increasingly, infectious diseases such as tuberculosis have been identified in runaway youths. The longer the runaway episode, the more likely these conditions may be present. Many of these conditions are also chronic and subacute and may lead only to vague or nonspecific symptoms.

D. A wide range of psychiatric disorders must be considered in evaluating runaway adolescents. (Tomb, 1991). Psychotic disorders are not uncommon, both schizophrenia or bipolar disorder. Suicidality is frequent. Substance abuse or dual diagnosis is also common. Posttraumatic stress disorder, dysthymic disorder, or major depressive disorder are also common. Disruptive behavior disorders and learning disabilities, severe academic problems, and mild mental retardation also are encountered frequently. Adolescent precursors of personality disorders also are found among runaway teenagers. Evaluation warrants active consideration of these possibilities, assessment of safety, plans for further diagnostic study, and assessment of acute and chronic treatment needs.

E. Physical and sexual abuse are common occurrences in the immediate and long-term history of runaway youths. The evaluating clinician must inquire about these possibilities in a gentle fashion and be prepared for emotional distress in discussing these issues. The clinician should have specific guidelines for reporting abuse and be aware of the procedures for reporting abuse to state authorities and of facilities and resources to document or corroborate allegations. The clinician also should expect that violence and abuse may have precipitated a runaway episode; family members may believe the violence to have been warranted by the child's behavior. Extremes of emotion and severe interpersonal conflict and mistrust may be present in these situations.

F. An ambulatory intervention strategy may involve many systems and professionals. The child or adolescent and involved family members will need to know who is in charge of treatment, what the problems to be addressed are, what the goals might be, and what treatment will consist of. The involvement of associated systems, such as child welfare, juvenile justice, pediatric health care, and the school, should be clearly specified as the plan for intervention is reviewed.

153

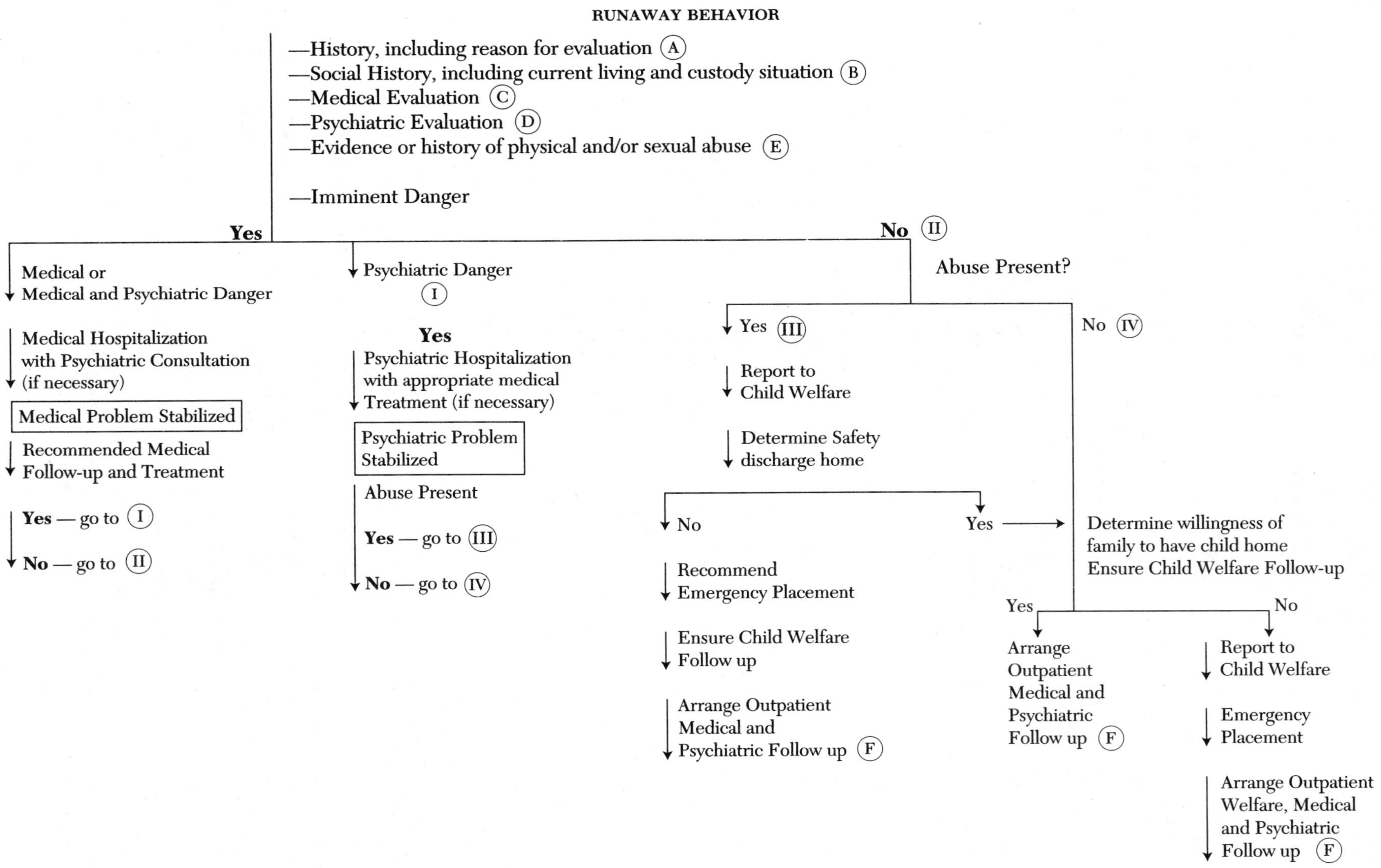

RUNAWAY BEHAVIOR

—History, including reason for evaluation (A)
—Social History, including current living and custody situation (B)
—Medical Evaluation (C)
—Psychiatric Evaluation (D)
—Evidence or history of physical and/or sexual abuse (E)

—Imminent Danger

Yes

Medical or
Medical and Psychiatric Danger

Medical Hospitalization
with Psychiatric Consultation
(if necessary)

Medical Problem Stabilized

Recommended Medical
Follow-up and Treatment

Yes — go to (I)
No — go to (II)

→ Psychiatric Danger (I)

Yes

Psychiatric Hospitalization
with appropriate medical
Treatment (if necessary)

Psychiatric Problem
Stabilized

Abuse Present

Yes — go to (III)
No — go to (IV)

No (II)

Abuse Present?

Yes (III)

→ Report to
Child Welfare

→ Determine Safety
discharge home

No ──→ Recommend
Emergency Placement

→ Ensure Child Welfare
Follow up

→ Arrange Outpatient
Medical and
Psychiatric Follow up (F)

Yes ──→

No (IV)

Determine willingness of
family to have child home
Ensure Child Welfare Follow-up

Yes ──→ Arrange
Outpatient
Medical and
Psychiatric
Follow up (F)

No ──→ Report to
Child Welfare

→ Emergency
Placement

→ Arrange Outpatient
Welfare, Medical
and Psychiatric
Follow up (F)

FIGURE 29.1.

Runaway behavior decision tree.

REFERENCES

Adams, G. R. (1992). Runaways. In S. B. Friedman, M. Fisher, & S. K. Schonberg (Eds.), *Comprehensive adolescent health care* (pp. 795–800). St. Louis: Quality Medical Publishing.

Tomb, D. A. (1991). The runaway adolescent. In M. Lewis (Ed.), *Child and adolescent psychiatry: A comprehensive textbook* (pp. 1066–1071). Baltimore, MD: Williams & Wilkins.

---

30 / Involuntary Movements

Bradley S. Peterson

Clinicians evaluating and treating children and adolescents for emotional or behavioral problems frequently observe that a child exhibits any of a variety of unusual movements that are said to be either entirely involuntary or are otherwise suppressed voluntarily only briefly. Many of these movements are benign and transient, while others are more chronic and debilitating. Some are iatrogenic, due to the use of medications often intended to treat the child's presenting problems. Occasionally the movements may be the manifestation of serious, even life-threatening, disease. Stress and anxiety worsen all movement disorders and therefore are especially likely to be seen in child psychiatry clinics. It is imperative that clinicians be able to recognize when these movements are benign, when they warrant further attention and possible treatment within the field of child psychiatry, and when they need to be referred for more specialized neurological evaluation.

Components of the Evaluation

The evaluation of these movements depends critically, and often solely, on taking a thorough medical history and assessing carefully the quality and somatic distribution of the movements. Elements of the medical history that are particularly relevant include the onset and duration of the movements, their temporal patterning (whether continuous, episodic, constant, or fluctuating), their proximal temporal antecedents, and the patient's neurologic and psychiatric family history, medication use, and comorbid medical and neuropsychiatric illnesses.

General Classification Scheme for Involuntary Movements

Involuntary movements can be regarded as being entirely involuntary or as being temporarily, but not indefinitely, suppressed or inhibited. This generalization is not ideal, however, because often very young children are poorly able to verbalize the degree to which they can suppress their movements. Movements that are not under any appreciable degree of volitional control include: *tremor,* which are rhythmic, oscillatory movements of the extremities or head that are rapid (4 to 8 cycles per second) and of low amplitude; *choreoathetosis,* which consists of random, writhing movements of the trunk or axial musculature (chorea), or wriggling, wormlike movements of the digits (athetosis); *ballismus,* a violent, irregular flinging of the arms or legs; and *myoclonus,* brief, rapid contractions of a muscle producing movements at a joint (Berg, 1994).

Movements that can be voluntarily suppressed

This work was supported in part by grants grants MH49351, MH18268, MH30929, NIH RR06022, HD03008, MH01232, and by grants from the Tourette's Syndrome Association (TSA), the Charles A. Dana Foundation, and the National Alliance for Research on Schizophrenia and Depression (NARSAD).

for at least a brief period of time include: *akathisia,* an extreme motor restlessness, usually of the lower extremities, that is uncomfortable when sitting and thus often leads to frequent pacing; *tics,* rapid, darting, purposeless movements most commonly involving musculature of the head and neck and less commonly of the trunk and extremities; *compulsions,* behaviors resulting from an intense need, pressure, drive, or urge to perform the act, often repetitively, and which if prevented or inhibited produces anxiety; and *stereotypies,* repetitive, often rhythmic fragments of normal behavior that typically are simultaneously self-stimulating and anxiety-reducing.

When an involuntary movement has been classified according to the above-listed scheme, further clinical or laboratory assessment often can provide information that will yield either a diagnosis or enough information to discern whether more expert consultation and evaluation are required. (See Figure 30.1.) With this additional clinical information, obtained largely from the history and physical assessment, each classification can be further specified.

A. Tremors.

Tremors are subclassified according to whether they occur at rest or with sustained posture (with "action"). A resting upper-extremity tremor is best observed while the child is seated, with elbows supported on the child's knees and forearms dangling between them. A resting tremor will moreover disappear during voluntary movement of the upper extremities. An action tremor, in contrast, is best evaluated with the child's arms outstretched, palms facing upward.

Tremors, particularly *action tremors,* are not uncommon in childhood and usually are a benign condition. When they occur in the context of a family history of a similar tremor, usually manifested as a front-to-back head nodding and vocal tremor, they likely represent benign essential tremor. If too disruptive during periods of stress-induced exacerbation, beta-adrenergic blocking agents can be symptomatically helpful. Persistent action tremor occurring in the absence of a family history can be due to use of medications such as tricyclic agents, lithium, caffeine, stimulants, or bronchodilators, or to medical conditions such as endocrinopathies (hyperthyroidism), or to other physiologic conditions, especially fatigue and anxiety.

Resting tremors generally signify basal ganglia dysfunction. When occurring in conjunction with motoric slowing (bradykinesia), paucity of movement (akinesia), and rigidity, the tremor is parkinsonian. In children, the most common cause of parkinsonism is the use of neuroleptic medication. Onset of tremor and other parkinsonian symptoms after initiation of neuroleptic medication or after a dose increase should raise suspicion of this cause, and improvement of the parkinsonism with either antiparkinsonian medications or neuroleptic dose reduction is diagnostic. Resting tremor in childhood due to other causes is rare and include juvenile onset Parkinson's disease or parkinsonism as a component or sequela of other neurologic disorders, such as encephalitis or head trauma (Cummings, 1992). Neurologic consultation is then indicated.

B. Choreoathetosis.

The most common childhood form of chorea is typically noted in the elementary school years during a neurologic examination for some unrelated problem (e.g., seizures, attentional problems, or headaches). A mild chorea can be seen in the extended arms of normal children and rarely causes any degree of dysfunction. This benign chorea typically improves with age and disappears by adolescence. Occasionally another mild chorea that is familial can cause mild motor dysfunction, but it is nonprogressive and thus is referred to as benign familial chorea.

A choreiform disorder that is important for clinicians in child psychiatry to recognize is neuroleptic-induced tardive dyskinesia. Tardive dyskinesia typically produces a prominent choreoathetosis primarily of oral-buccal-lingual (mouth, cheeks, and tongue) musculature, but it also can affect muscles of the trunk and extremities. A history of prolonged medication exposure (typically 6 months or more) in the presence of chorea should raise clinical suspicion. Often transient tardive dyskinesia is seen upon rapid discontinuation of neuroleptic medication. If tardive dyskinesia is suspected, every effort should be made to reduce the dose of neuroleptic medication and, if at all possible, to discontinue it entirely. Tardive dyskinesia often will attenuate or disappear completely within several months of discontinuing neuroleptic medication. Persistent or worsening choreiform movements after neuroleptic withdrawal warrant a more detailed neurologic evaluation.

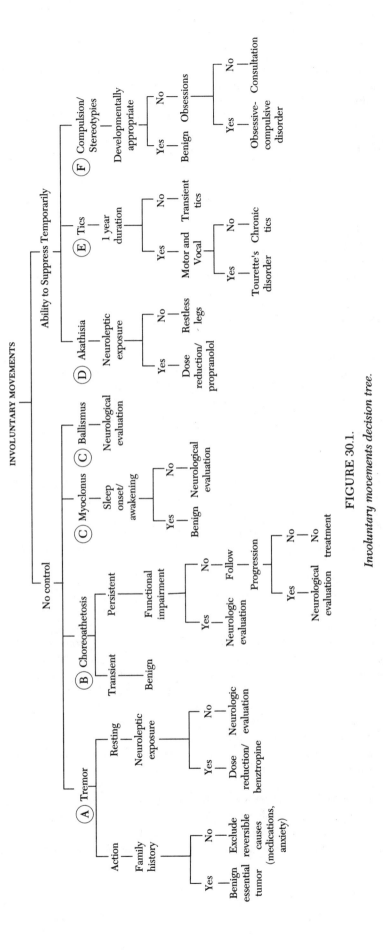

FIGURE 30.1.

Involuntary movements decision tree.

Other persistent choreas that cause functional impairment should receive prompt neurologic evaluation. The differential diagnosis will include Sydenham's chorea, which is a sequela of streptococcal infections that cause rheumatic fever. Although relatively rare in the current age of antibiotic therapies for streptococcal pharyngitis, evidence of a cardiac murmur on physical examination or a history of rheumatic fever should raise clinical suspicion of Sydenham's. Antibody titers for anti-DNAase B and antistreptolysin O should be obtained, although often these titers have decreased by the time chorea appears. Other choreas include the juvenile form of Huntington's disease, an autosomal dominant genetic disorder producing a relentlessly progressive decline in motor and cognitive functioning that can appear as early as 5 years of age. A family history of a progressive chorea is usually evident. Choreiform movements also can be seen in Lesch-Nyhan and Hallervorden-Spatz syndromes, porphyria, Friedreich's ataxia, Wilson's syndrome, and a host of other relatively uncommon medical and neurologic illnesses of childhood (Berg, 1994).

C. Myoclonus and Ballismus.

The most common form of myoclonus in childhood is sleep myoclonus, and is seen shortly after falling asleep or before awakening. Sleep myoclonus may first appear or increase in frequency during a period of emotional stress. It is self-limited in duration and requires no treatment. Myoclonus occurring while the child is awake or in the context of other neurologic symptoms or illnesses (such as a seizure disorder) requires neurologic evaluation. Ballismus is an uncommon symptom in children, and it warrants neurologic evaluation regardless of the time or context in which it occurs. Ballismus generally signifies dysfunction of the subthalamic nucleus or other basal ganglia nuclei.

D. Akathisia.

Akathisia commonly occurs in children as a side effect of neuroleptic use. Discontinuing the neuroleptic or changing to another agent usually will produce improvement. Symptomatic relief often can be achieved with beta blockers or clonazepam. Akathisia that occurs in a context other than neuroleptic administration probably represents the benign restless legs syndrome, although a neurologic evaluation to exclude underlying medical or neurologic abnormality (Tarsy, 1992) is recommended.

E. Tics.

Motor tics are rapid, darting, purposeless movements usually affecting face, head, and neck musculature and less often affecting the trunk and extremities. Vocal tics are rapid, repetitive, often meaningless sounds emitted from the mouth, throat, or nose. Typical motor tics might include eye blinking, nose twitching, facial grimacing, head jerking, and shoulder shrugging, while typical vocal tics could include throat clearing, sniffing, snorting, coughing, grunting, humming, screeching, and even syllables or whole words. Tics usually begin in early childhood, and an onset that is clearly in adolescence or later probably warrants a neurologic evaluation. Up to 20% of normal elementary school-age children exhibit tics that will resolve spontaneously within several months and therefore do not require treatment. Older children and adolescents often will report that tics are preceded by an experience of discomfort in, or an urge to move, the body region in which the tic will occur. Capitulating to the urge provides only temporary relief before another premonitory urge and tic appear.

Motor tics that recur or persist may represent chronic multiple tic disorder, and if they occur in conjunction with vocal tics, they probably represent Tourette's disorder. Evidence for the presence of comorbid obsessive-compulsive disorder or attention deficit hyperactivity disorder should be sought. Although medications can be helpful for tics, the decision of whether medication is indicated is a complex one that depends on the developmental and psychosocial context in which they occur (Peterson, 1996). Consultation from clinicians experienced in the treatment of tic disorders should be considered.

F. Compulsions and Stereotypes.

Compulsions typically have in common with tics the subjective experience of a compelling urge to perform a certain behavior. Unlike the rapid, darting and purposeless quality of tics, compulsions are of much longer duration than a tic, they are much more purposeful appearing and goal directed, and they can be inhibited or delayed more readily (albeit with much attendant discomfort and anxiety). They thus appear and are experienced as more voluntary behaviors, although younger children have difficulty in making this distinction and often indicate that the movements and behaviors are not under their control. While compulsions in any given child typically manifest as any number of goal-directed behaviors (hand washing, grooming, checking, ritualized routines), most commonly stereotypies involve just one repetitive behavior (rocking, head banging, hair pulling) that may be more rhythmic and that is usually less goal directed than are compulsions.

Compulsive behaviors that do not interfere significantly with school performance or relationships are common in the later elementary school years. Stereotypies are also a part of normative development, and rocking or head banging in an infant who otherwise is cognitively and motorically on track developmentally usually will subside with time. Compulsions that occur in conjunction with obsessions and that together produce impairment of function warrant a diagnosis of obsessive-compulsive disorder. Stereotypies often are seen in children with mental retardation, autism, or developmental delays, and stereotypies occurring in the context of a child with subnormal intelligence or other developmental delays should receive special attention.

REFERENCES

Berg, B. O. (1994). Movement disorders. In B. O. Berg (Ed.), *Child neurology: A clinical manual* (2nd ed., pp. 307–318). Philadelphia: J. B. Lippincott Co.

Butler, I. J. (1992). Movement disorders of children. *Pediatric Clinics of North America, 39,* 727–742.

Cummings, J. L. (1992). Parkinson's disease and parkinsonism. In A. B. Joseph & R. R. Young (Eds.), *Movement disorders in neurology and neuropsychiatry* (pp. 195–203). Boston: Blackwell Scientific Publications.

Peterson, B. S. (1996). Considerations of natural history & pathophysiology in the psychopharmacology of Tourette's syndrome. *Journal of Clinical Psychiatry, 57* (suppl. 9), 24–34.

Tarsy, D. (1992). Restless legs syndrome. In A. B. Joseph & R. R. Young (Eds.), *Movement disorders in neurology and neuropsychiatry* (pp. 397–400). Boston: Blackwell Scientific Publications.

SECTION III
Initiating Assessment

31 / The Initial Encounter

Robert A. King

As the introductory phase of the assessment, the initial encounter has several explicit goals: (1) to introduce the clinician and the family to each other; (2) to explicate the reasons for the parents' (and/or child's) seeking evaluation; (3) to clarify the "ground rules" of how the evaluation will proceed; and (4) to begin the evaluation (King & Noshpitz, 1991). In addition, the clinician has the important implicit task of forming an alliance with the child and parents in order to facilitate the frank communication of relevant information during the assessment and to promote their cooperative engagement in whatever interventions are recommended.

The collaborative work of the initial interview also has a potentially therapeutic element. The parents (and child, if present) have the opportunity and task of spelling out what they consider most important about the child's perceived difficulties. The clinician, in turn, will begin the complementary work of inquiring along the line that seems most relevant. The initial encounter thus provides a beginning opportunity for the family members to reconsider their attitudes, perceptions, and feelings about the child's difficulties as well as to attain a measure of relief in sharing their concerns with a sympathetic professional.

Preliminary Contact

The practical arrangements and logistics of the assessment will vary with the clinical setting. Although many assessments will take place as scheduled appointments in an outpatient clinic or clinician's office, others may occur in a variety of

This chapter is adapted in part from R. A. King, Work Group on Quality Issues (1995), Practice parameters for the psychiatric assessment of children and adolescents. *Journal of the American Academy of Child and Adolescent Psychiatry, 34* (10), 1386–1402.

settings, such as schools or residential treatment centers. The encounters may take place as unscheduled or emergency evaluations in walk-in clinics, hospital wards or emergency departments, or detention centers. Scheduled assessments usually are preceded by an intake phone call in which the parents (or other referring adult) may describe the presenting problem briefly; the time, date, and place of the first appointment are set; and practical issues of fee or insurance coverage are discussed.

One of the most important preliminary issues to be resolved is who will attend the first meeting. During the course of the assessment, the clinician will want to meet with the parents and child separately as well as together. The separate meetings provide an opportunity for both the child and parents to speak frankly; meeting with the parents and child together provides an opportunity to observe their interaction and to assess how they formulate and discuss the problem together. The practical arrangements of how these interviews are ordered or combined, however, varies with the case and clinical setting. For preschoolers or school-age children, one or more initial parent interviews without the child usually is appropriate before the child is seen either alone or with the parents. In contrast, usually it is best to include the adolescent in the initial interview, either with or without the parents. Excluding the adolescent may potentially undermine the clinical alliance by casting the clinician as the parents' agent in the patient's eyes (King & Schowalter, 1996). The parents' thoughts and preferences concerning the question of the child's presence at the initial meeting should be discussed and a decision made. If the child is to attend, the clinician should discuss with the parents how the child is to be prepared for the appointment.

For children in intact families, if at all feasible, the clinician should insist on the presence of both parents. For children living in other family arrangements, the question of whether a particular noncustodial parent, stepparent, or other adult should attend the first meeting should be discussed in the initial phone contact.

The First Meeting—The Nature of the Presenting Problem

After introductions, the first job is to clarify the reasons and context for the referral. In other words, who is concerned about the child and why? What has led to the decision to seek help at this particular time? Save for some adolescents, the chief complaint and impetus for referral usually come from the adults in the child's life, such as parents or teachers, rather than directly from the child. The child's own understanding of the reason for the evaluation and his or her motivation and ability to cooperate in it may be variable.

If the child is present, often it is useful for the clinician to start by asking "What did your mom and dad tell you about why they wanted you all to come in to see me today?" Children's responses provide some insight into their perception of why they are there as well as their and their family's language for discussing the problems (e.g., "Because I'm bad at school" or "Because of my ADHD.") This approach also conveys from the start an interest in the child's point of view and helps to involve the child as an active participant in the assessment, rather than as merely a passive audience to the parents' concerns. Even when a child denies knowing anything about why he or she is there, the clinician's asking next "Is it all right if I ask your mom and dad what they told you?" helps to involve the child at least tacitly in the process.

As most clinical referrals originate with the parent(s) rather than child, the parents' account of the child's presenting difficulties is of paramount importance. In addition to factual information about the child's current symptoms and functioning, the initial interview also aims to elucidate the meaning and impact of the child's difficulties on the family as well as the parents' attitude toward the referral and assessment process. This interview thus provides the initial opportunity to foster an alliance with the parents around the goals of

identifying and helping the child's difficulties (Leventhal & Conroy, 1991). To this end, it is especially important to identify the parents' implicit and explicit attitudes, expectations, and concerns about the evaluation.

The question of who is concerned about the child and why may require clarification. On the one hand, parents may have a clear consensus about the child's perceived difficulties and the need for evaluation. In some cases, however, the parents may disagree sharply with each other about the nature or severity of the problem or the advisability of seeking help. In still other cases, parents may convey the message that they are not there fully of their own accord. This is especially the case when the impetus for referral is attributed by them to some third party or agency. ("The school said he was acting up in school and we should come here to have him checked out.") Possible sources of such divergent perspectives of the child are discussed in Chapter 37. Whatever their origin, however, when such disagreements are apparent, it is important to explore each parent's attitudes and feelings about the referral and the proposed assessment. The indifference or significant opposition of one or both parents poses a serious obstacle to obtaining a full picture of the child as well as to the implementation of any intervention recommendations that may stem from the assessment. Such opposition or uninvolvement limits the information available from the parents. Furthermore, when, as is often the case, this parental attitude is communicated covertly or overtly to the child, the child's willingness to participate fully is often also impaired. Understanding what common ground, if any, exists about the child's problems or the need for help is thus essential. Furthermore, when sharp disagreements exist between the parents or between the parents and the school (or others involved in the child's care), these disagreements are likely to have a significant impact on the child's functioning in these different settings. Hence, explicating these disagreements is also a crucial component of the assessment process.

Epidemiological studies find that many children in the community are *never* brought for help despite problems as severe as those who are referred to clinical attention. Understanding the context and dynamics of the decision to seek help is thus a crucial component of the assessment.

Moreover, the child's difficulties may have been present for a considerable time before help is sought. It is therefore important to explore how the decision came to be made to seek help *at this particular time.* For example, the decision to seek help may have been prompted by an exacerbation of the child's symptoms; alternatively, there may have been a decrease in the parents' tolerance for these difficulties (perhaps due to the intrusion of other life stresses or the loss of important supports), or some third party—a teacher or relative, perhaps—may have prompted or encouraged the referral.

Interview Techniques

In the initial interview, the clinician uses a variety of interview techniques to elicit information. These tactics, in turn, influence the type and quality of information obtained. To establish rapport and to avoid narrowing the focus prematurely, the parents should be given an opportunity to tell their story in their own fashion. The clinician may then supplement this information by seeking gently to clarify details. Specific questions (e.g., "When did that start?" "Who lives at home?") are most useful for obtaining factual and chronological data, while information about feelings and relationships are better elicited by more open-ended, indirect queries (e.g., "Tell me more about that" or "How did that make you feel") (Cox, Hopkinson, & Rutter, 1981; Cox, Rutter, & Holbrook, 1988; Rutter & Cox, 1981). (For a review of methodologic studies comparing different interview approaches, see Cox, 1994.)

The dual goals of gathering information and establishing rapport are complementary. Parents are most likely to be nondefensive and forthcoming with a clinician whom they perceive as trustworthy, interested, understanding, and nonjudgmental. The interviewer maintains an empathic stance that is neither aloof nor overly familiar. The child's and family's situation and concerns are discussed in terms that are comprehensible to them and free of jargon. It is important to learn the family's own terms for describing the child's behavior, especially if these are idiosyncratic or culture-specific (see King & Cohen, 1994). For example,

a child or family may not understand a question regarding "compulsions" or "tics" but may respond to a question put in their own terms, such as "habits" or "movements."

In fact, the hazards of using jargon or technical terminology lie not only with the clinician. Especially in an age of popular self-help books and articles, parents or child may describe the presenting problem in such terms as "It's his ADHD," "I have OCD," or "I think she might have a chemical imbalance." Even when such diagnostic formulations prove accurate, they often serve to impede rather than advance the clinician's task of obtaining a clear and detailed description of the child's behavior and feelings. We should heed Wittgenstein's caution against "the bewitchment of our intelligence by words." It is usually helpful to explain "That's certainly something for us to think about, but different people can mean different things by those terms. Let's start out by talking about what Johnny actually does or feels."

Expectations and Anxieties

Sooner or later the clinician should ask, "Were there some specific ways you were hoping we could help?" Some parents may bring to the assessment strong preset notions about what is to be done or not done. These often concern medication; parents may say "I think she needs to be on Prozac; I don't want her to have to suffer like I did before I went on it" or "I don't want to be told that he needs to be on Ritalin; I don't believe in those medications." Other expectations or agendas may include the attribution or refutation of blame. When parents are in conflict, one or both may want the clinician as a partisan who will declare the other parent at fault. Alternatively, the parent may seek support for his or her view that the teacher or school is to blame for the child's difficulties. Regardless of the appropriateness of such expectations, it is useful to communicate directly about them, as they will have a powerful influence on the progress and outcome of the assessment and on the fate of any recommended interventions.

Occasionally a child will be brought to assessment by a parent with a rigid preconceived agenda. For example, the parent may insist that the clinician confirm that the child has been abused or has an undiscovered medical illness. Alternatively, the parent may demand that the clinician agree that there is nothing wrong with the child. The clinician's firm statement that he or she can undertake only to do a careful assessment and give the family his or her best professional advice is often insufficient for the disgruntled parent. Despite the best efforts to understand and address these peremptory agendas, not all such situations are workable.

The clinician also must be alert to the often unspoken anxieties, hopes, and expectations that the child and family bring to the encounter. For most parents, bringing a child for help is no easy matter; usually it is the end product of much soul-searching and worry. Our children are the repositories of our dearest hopes (and often our darkest fears) for ourselves. While a parent may rationally conclude that seeking consultation is reasonable and necessary, it is nevertheless always painful to admit that one's child (or oneself) is in need of help. Submitting one's child and one's parenting to professional scrutiny stirs many anxieties as well as positive expectations of help, even in the most enlightened parents.

Some parental anxieties may concern the child's possible diagnosis or prognosis. For example, is the child's uneven development a sign of autism or retardation? Do his facial grimaces portend a disabling tic disorder? Is her moodiness a harbinger of a serious depression or suicide? Other parental anxieties may be guilty ones. Is failed child rearing or transmitted heredity somehow to blame for the child's difficulties? Is the child fated to share the parent's (or other relative's) own painful struggle with depression, anxiety, or psychosis? Does the parent feel his or her relationship to the child recapitulates some distressing aspect of the parent's own early family experience?

The clinician may not be able to address these questions fully, perhaps not until a later phase of the evaluation. However, the clinician must convey his or her interest in hearing the parents' worries and private speculations, without brushing them off dismissively or with false reassurances. The clinician may need to acknowledge the limits of knowledge about etiology or prognosis in individual cases. (Parents often seek a psychiatric assessment only after years of nagging concerns

unrelieved by well-meant but inappropriate reassurances. For example, many parents of children with autism report having sought help from the child's first year of life on, only to be told not to worry, that the child would "grow out of it.")

While inquiring carefully about various areas of difficulty, the tenor of the inquiry should convey the clinician's appreciation that the child is not merely a troubled bearer of symptoms. A focus on the child's (and family's) adaptive strengths, talents, and resources is crucial both in order to obtain a full picture of the child and in supporting the child and family in the difficult task of self-revelation.

Observing the Family's Interactive Style

The initial interview provides an opportunity to observe how the parents (and child, if present) interact. In the course of describing what has brought them to seek help, what is the affective tone of family members' interchanges? How do the parents talk to each other? In what configuration does the family seat itself; in particular, next to whom does the child sit? How do the parents respond to the child's comments or signs of distress, restlessness, or puzzlement?

The family's style of relating to the clinician also should be noted. There may be marked differences in the cultural or linguistic backgrounds of the family and clinician. In that event, the impact of this on the participants' rapport and mutual understanding should be considered. Some assessments are undertaken at the behest of a third party (e.g., court, school, or social agency) that will use the findings as the basis for administrative decisions. In such instances, it is important to explore the family's attitude toward the evaluation.

The clinician should pay careful attention to his or her own emotional responses to the family. Does the clinician feel welcomed into the family's discourse, or is the family guarded or antagonistic? Does the clinician experience a sense of struggling against an undercurrent of chaos, helplessness, or depression? These responses can provide potentially important diagnostic information and cues to the conduct of the assessment. If the family's response to the clinician (or vice versa) is intensely negative, the clinician may need to decide, after due reflection, whether to proceed further with the assessment. Whatever their origin, if such feelings seem likely to compromise the clinician and family's ability to work together productively, the family should be helped to find another clinician.

Financial Arrangements, Confidentiality, and Contact with Other Informants

By the end of the initial interview, several practical matters should be addressed. Assuming the parties are agreed that the assessment is to go forward and that the clinician is the appropriate person for the task, issues of fees, payment, confidentiality, contact with other informants, and how the assessment is to proceed need to be spelled out in explicit detail.

FEES AND PAYMENT

Although a few parents may regard it as evidence of venality, most welcome the clinician being clear about fees, payment arrangements (e.g., how phone calls, review of records, written reports, and the like will be charged for) and whether he or she participates in whatever insurance coverage the family may have.

CONFIDENTIALITY

The ground rules concerning confidentiality should be spelled out. The usual expectations (embodied as well in legal and ethical requirements) are that information will not be divulged to a third party without a parent's written permission. Where the legal or institutional context raises questions about these boundaries, this should be addressed early in the initial session. (For example, if the assessment is court ordered or is part of a protective services evaluation, it should be made clear with whom the findings will

be shared.) With adolescents, there are special considerations regarding the extent to which confidentiality can be promised. In particular, there are occasions when the occurrence of safety-endangering behavior may need to be shared with the parents (King & Schowalter, 1996). (See Chapter 5.)

PRIOR CLINICAL CONTACTS

Prior assessments and intervention attempts should be inquired about in the initial interview. The fate of these earlier interventions (and the child and family's attitudes toward them) may provide insight into the hopes, concerns, and disappointments with which the family is approaching the current assessment. The evaluator should contact and request information from other relevant informants, such as school, primary medical care providers, and previous diagnosticians or therapists, and they, in turn, should be given written permission to release such data. A parent may object to contact with a specific school or prior therapist, and this, of course, must be honored; at the same time, however, it is useful to clarify the reasons for the objection.

Preparation of the Child

If the child has not been included in the initial interview, the parents should be helped to think through how to prepare the child for his or her first meeting with the clinician. This is best done by the parents seeking to create a context of shared, nonpunitive concern, with sensitivity to the possibility that the child may fear embarrassment or perceive the consultation as punishment for bad behavior. In most cases, the child is likely to be aware of many of the concerns that have prompted the assessment. The parents might be encouraged to tell the child something like "We know you've been having a hard time at school (or feeling upset and sad, or having trouble with friends) so we are going to see Dr. _____, who is used to helping kids with that sort of problem to see if he can help figure out what would help." For younger children, explanatory terms, such as a "feelings doctor" or a "talking doctor" who helps children with problems and worries, may be useful. (If accurate, younger children may be reassured that there will be no needles or shots.)

Closing the Initial Interview

The family should be asked if there are any additional issues that need to be taken up at the first meeting; if there is no time to deal with these in the initial session, they should be noted as topics to be taken up at subsequent sessions. In closing the first interview, it is often useful for the clinician to restate briefly the major themes and questions that have been raised and to review how the evaluation will proceed—the date of the next appointment, who will attend, what reports are to be forwarded to the clinician, what phone contacts with the family or informants are planned in the interim. This helps to convey the sense that the assessment is a process and that there is work to be done even between the sessions—the work of reflection as well as of information gathering.

REFERENCES

Cox, A. D. (1994). Interviews with parents. In M. Rutter, E. Taylor, & L. Hersov (Eds.), *Child and adolescent psychiatry: Modern approaches* (3rd ed., pp. 34–50). Oxford: Blackwell Scientific Publications.

Cox, A., Hopkinson, K. D., & Rutter, M. (1981). Psychiatric interviewing techniques: II. Naturalistic study: Eliciting factual information. *British Journal of Psychiatry, 138,* 283–291.

Cox, A., Rutter, M., & Holbrook, D. (1988). Psychiatric interviewing techniques: A second experimental study: Eliciting feelings. *British Journal of Psychiatry, 152,* 64–72.

King, R. A., & Cohen, D. J. (1994). Psychotherapy with children and adolescent with neuropsychiatric disorders: ADHD, OCD, and Tourette's syndrome. In J. M. Oldham and M. B. Riba (Eds.), *Review of Psychiatry* (Vol. 13, pp. 519–539). Washington, DC: American Psychiatric Press.

King, R. A., & Noshpitz, J. D. (1991). *Pathways of growth: Essentials of child psychiatry, Vol. 2: Psychopathology.* New York: John Wiley & Sons, Inc.

King, R. A., & Schowalter, J. (1996). The clinical interview of the adolescent. In M. H. Wiener (Ed.), *Textbook of child and adolescent psychiatry* (2nd ed.) (pp. 89–93). Washington, DC: American Psychiatric Press.

Leventhal, B. L., & Conroy, L. M. (1991). The parent interview. In M. H. Wiener (Ed.), *Textbook of child and adolescent psychiatry* (pp. 78–83). Washington, DC: American Psychiatric Press.

Rutter, M., & Cox, A. (1981). Psychiatric interviewing techniques: I. Methods and measures. *British Journal of Psychiatry, 138,* 273–282.

32 / Assessment of Dangerousness

Joseph J. Jankowski

Dangerousness is defined as a state of mind in which the patient potentially can inflict injury on him- or herself or on others. The clinician's role is to determine how the patient's dangerousness might be expressed and when. Assessment and intervention strategies will depend on the patient's past history of dangerousness and comorbid psychiatric problems. Potentially dangerous patients can be encountered in any clinical setting. In our society clinicians provide an important service by assessing these patients, but doing so can be challenging.

Categories of Dangerousness

In assessing dangerousness, it is necessary to be familiar with its major categories and to appreciate the clinical factors that affect these categories (Holinger, 1979). The major categories of dangerousness include homicidality, suicidality, fire setting, accidents, and assaultiveness. Empirically derived specific clinical factors are related to each category. These factors help clinicians assess how likely patients are to be dangerous and what their potential to act on or express that dangerousness might be at a given time. Currently there is no algorithm available to rank-order these factors to obtain an intensity score, but they are helpful in clinical decision making.

Each factor with its pertinent variables and sex ratio of incidence are as follows:

HOMICIDALITY

Variables: father behaves violently, homicidally; parental psychopathology (maternal psychiatric hospitalization); parent(s) condone/encourage murderous assault; severe physical abuse by parent; attempted suicide; prior physical assaults; serious neurological impairment (seizures, head injury); psychiatric disorders (schizophrenia, mental retardation, organic brain disorders); language disorders; inability to develop empathy (Lewis et al., 1988; Lewis, Shanok, Grant, & Ritvo, 1983; Myers, Scott, Burgess, & Burgess, 1995; Sargent, 1962).

Sex Ratio Incidence: 4.1 male to 1 female; (Lewis, Shanok, Grant, and Ritvo, 1983, pg. 150): 5.5 male to 1 female; (Lewis et al, 1988, pg. 583).

SUICIDALITY

Variables: past suicide attempts/threats; seriousness of the attempt; homicidal behavior; parent or other family member with suicidal attempts/completions; availability of firearms; prior dangerous acts (e.g., accidents, injuries); peers who have attempted or were successful at committing suicide; psychopathology (major depression, bipolar disorder, conduct disorder), schizophrenia, substance abuse; considers suicide as an escape (An-

drews & Lewinsohn, 1992; Brent, Perper, & Allman, 1987; Brent et al., 1988; Shaffer, 1988).

Sex Ratio Incidence: *Attempted-* 1 male to 4 female; *Completed-* 5 male to 1 female; (Kalogerakis, 1992).

FIRE SETTING

Variables: parental psychopathology; rejection of child by father; abandonment by parents; fire used as punishment/discipline by parent; physically abused in the home (beatings, burnings); witnessed violence in the home (stabbing, shooting, beatings); history of burns (burned by parent, smoke inhalation, burned in a fire at home); psychiatric diagnosis (schizophrenia, mental retardation); neuropsychiatric impairment; problem with psychosexual development; rage of child; repeated placements out of the home (Justice, Justice, & Kraft, 1974; Kaufman & Heims, 1961; Ritvo, Shanok, & Lewis, 1983).

Sex Ratio Incidence: 5 male to 1 female; (Jacobson, 1984).

ACCIDENTS

Variables: maternal psychopathology (major depression); psychosocial dysfunction occurring during increased personal or family stress; psychiatric disorder of patient (conduct disorder, attention deficit hyperactivity disorder), substance abuse; very aggressive behavior; prior history of physical injury (Bijur, Stewart-Brown, Golding, Butler, & Rush, 1983; Husband & Hinton, 1972; Langley, McGee, Silva, & Williams, 1983).

Sex Ratio Incidence: 2.27 male to 1 female; (Jaquess, and Finney, 1994).

ASSAULTIVENESS

Physical Factors: Variables: parental assaultiveness; paternal violence directed at child; maternal psychiatric hospitalization; seizures; neurological dysfunction; psychopathology (conduct disorder); suicidal behavior (Goldberg & Wilensky, 1976; Lewis, Shanok, Pincus, & Glaser, 1979b; Pfeffer, Solomon, Plutchick, Mizruchi, & Weiner, 1985; Stewart and Leone, 1978).

Sex Ratio Incidence: 3.3 male to 1 female; (Pfeiffer, et al, 1985, pg. 778).

Sexual Factors: neuropsychiatric problems; psychiatric symptoms (psychotic, depressive, paranoid, illogical thought process); psychopathology (posttraumatic stress disorder, substance abuse, conduct disorder); neurological issues (abnormal electroencephalogram, seizures); learning disability (below grade level for reading); other assaultive, violent acts; violent antisocial behavior since early childhood; physically abused by mother and father; witnessed extreme violence, especially toward mother; sexually abused by males and/or females (Lewis, Shanok, & Pincus, 1979a; Rubinstein, Yeager, Goodstein, & Lewis, 1993).

Sex Ratio Incidence: There is little literature on juvenile female assaulters. Among male assaulters, 21.8% of incarcerated juveniles are sexual assaulters. (Lewis, et al, 1979a, pg. 1196).

Process of Assessment

During the assessment of dangerousness, as data are obtained about the patient and family, the clinician needs to keep these categories in mind. While data are being collected, it is recommended that the clinician meet with the child/adolescent and parent(s) together as a group for an initial interview. Doing so increases the reliability for reporting incidents. Through the overlapping accounts of experience, a better chronicling of life events and a more accurate relating of potentially dangerous interactions or issues in the family and/or environment can be obtained. Dangerousness can be discussed with the child and family in this context more easily, and data that might otherwise be overlooked may be more likely to be provided.

Joint interviews also are helpful in engaging the child and parent(s), thereby enhancing treatment compliance. The follow-up of potentially dangerous patients assumes special significance since it might avert a possibly catastrophic event. A dangerousness assessment therefore assumes a very high priority, beginning in the initial interview.

After meeting with the child/adolescent and parents together, additional interviews are conducted with the patient and the parent(s) separately. During all the interviews, issues related to dangerousness are discussed as directly as the patient, parents, and clinician can tolerate. Here the

attitudes of the clinician about dangerousness play an important role. How sensitive is the clinician to dangerousness? Is the clinician likely to over- or underreact to a patient's dangerous behavior depending on his or her own prior experiences?

During the assessment for dangerousness, the clinician should consider the following questions in establishing a database about a potentially dangerous patient:

1. *How reliable is the information provided by the patient?* Will the patient discuss details about a potential act? Is he or she openly giving information to the examiner or withholding information? How open is he or she regarding events of his or her own life? Does the patient deny known facts or misrepresent them?

2. *Is the patient deliberate vs. impulsive in regard to potentially dangerous acts?*
   a. *How much planning or thinking about a dangerous act has occurred?* How long has the patient been thinking about this plan? Has he or she seriously been planning to carry out a dangerous act—acquiring weapons or pills, site selection, timing? Has he or she been gaining information about weapons, techniques, others who performed such an act?
   b. *How impulsive is the patient?* Does he or she make decisions rapidly, lose control easily, have a past history of impulsive acts? Does he or she act first and think about it later?

3. *How does the patient deal with anger?* Is the patient an angry person? Does he or she have certain trigger points for anger or action? Is anger projected onto others? Are angry feelings turned inward or outward toward others?

4. *Which current personal intrapsychic or psychosocial issues play a role in a patient's dangerousness?* How much affect or energy is attached to a potentially dangerous act? Does the patient have an unreasonably negative view of a potential victim or event? Does he or she misrepresent the intent of others? Has he or she experienced a traumatic or dangerous event as a perpetrator or victim? Is empathy lacking? Do unreasonable political or racial views exist? Is the patient a loner? Does he or she belong to a gang? Is substance abuse present? Has he or she had a prior psychiatric disorder, with or without treatment? Is he or she depressed, paranoid, anxious, psychotic?

5. *Which past events in the life of a patient play a role in the development of dangerousness?* Has he or she experienced losses, separations, or

deaths? Is there a history of physical/sexual abuse? Has he or she threatened, attempted, or actually injured anyone or him- or herself? Have any friends, peers or relatives been injured or killed accidentally or purposefully by themselves or others?

6. *In which type of academic or social/recreational activities does the patient participate?* Is there access to guns or other weapons? Does he or she enjoy paintball (a controlled war game using rifles that fire paintballs)? Is the patient involved in wrestling, boxing, or other potentially physically injurious sport? Does he participate in high-risk sports (motorcycle racing, bungee jumping, skydiving)? Does he or she belong to a gang, unusual religious sect, antisocial peer group, or extremist political group? Is he or she an avid collector of weapons or books/magazines concerning violence or weapons?

7. *What are the family/environmental issues regarding potential for the development of dangerousness?* Do any family members have guns or weapons? Are there weapons in the patient's home? Has there been a history of suicide or homicide in the family or environment? Is there a history of violence or abuse in the family or environment? Is the environment at high risk for potential violence (drive-by shootings)? Does the family have extreme religious or political views? Is there a history of criminality in the patient or family? Is there a history of serious psychiatric disorder in the family?

8. *Is the patient aware of his or her own potential dangerousness?* Is the patient aware of the danger in carrying a weapon (gun, knife) or making a Molotov cocktail or bomb? Is he or she aware of the potential of injuring someone when carrying a concealed weapon into a public building (school, stadium, subway)? Does he or she understand the fine line between self-protection and dangerousness? Is the patient aware that if by participating in dangerous behavior—dealing in drugs or being a drug courier—he or she can be injured or killed? Does the patient use words to express or diminish affect or anger that potentially might indicate that he or she would commit a dangerous act?

9. *How serious is the actual or potentially dangerous event?* Is it life-threatening or injurious? Is it harmful psychologically? Does the patient conceptualize the event as life-threatening?

10. *How likely is the dangerous event to happen?* Is the patient talking about or threatening to commit the act? Has something happened that potentially might trigger off the event? Have reactions developed more rapidly in the patient's mind than he or she can integrate? Has this event been the culmination of many complex issues related to family, peers, work, school, or romantic involvements? Has this patient been involved in dangerous behavior previously? If so, what type? Is it potentially harmful or destructive to a person, place, or object?

11. *Can you contract with the patient to diminish or alleviate the dangerousness?* Is the patient reliable enough to contract for safety? Can he or she understand contractual terms? Will he or she agree to speak first to a third party in the event that he or she has an urge to commit a dangerous act?

Levels of Dangerousness

The patient's level of dangerousness can be assessed by determining whether the dangerousness potential is acute, intermediate, or chronic.

ACUTE DANGEROUSNESS

The level of acute dangerousness refers to individuals who are about to become dangerous immediately. They have a past history of abuse or serious personal affronts that makes them vulnerable, and an otherwise innocuous event can trigger them into instant action. They are about to carry out a dangerous act immediately or in the very near future, having perceived an affront, deprivation, or perceived attack on themselves. The presence or availability of a weapon is more likely to place a patient at this level.

CASE EXAMPLE

A 16-year-old boy threatens to murder his mother, father, and sister with a gun. He has been physically abused by his father for the past 10 years and, for the past 3 years, has been treated for temporal lobe seizures with symptoms of rage attacks. His father was arrested for assault and battery and substance abuse. The patient was diagnosed previously as suffering from attention deficit hyperactivity disorder with a specific reading disability. His mother has had several psychiatric hospitalizations and a diagnosis of major depression. The patient was involved with shoplifting, petty thievery, and injuring a pet dog. He shows no remorse for past crimes or for the possible death of his parents and sister. The precipitating event that elevated his potential dangerousness to an acute level included an argument about the use of the family truck. The patient recently received his driver's license and wanted more access to the vehicle than his parents allowed. He felt entitled to use the truck and was mimicking his father, who previously bullied and threatened others with harm to get his way. He was becoming rageful at both parents for depriving him of the truck, just as he felt they had deprived him of other things when he was younger. He became physically aggressive with them and was brought to the emergency room by the police. Upon searching his bedroom, a gun and bullets were found.

This boy is at high risk for acutely precipitating a dangerous act, given his experience of being abused, witnessing violence at home, the presence of temporal lobe seizures, maternal psychiatric illness, lack of empathy for others, and his own criminality. The precipitating event of restricting his use of the family truck resulted in his becoming acutely dangerous. If there were no precipitating event and no presence of guns, he would be considered at an intermediate level of dangerousness. However, the presence of a gun, bullets, and overt verbal threats place him at the acutely dangerous level.

INTERMEDIATE DANGEROUSNESS

Patients who are at an intermediate level of dangerousness reveal less intensity in their potential for acute dangerousness. This reduction in intensity is demonstrated by a diminished seriousness of the event(s) (talks about fighting rather than killing), reduced intensity of psychodynamic aspects (feels deprived but not loss or rage), less serious prior threats (attacks a peer verbally instead of physically), psychiatric diagnoses with less potential for violence (posttraumatic stress disorder, substance abuse), not overtly violent with weapons (reads magazines about guns but does not own them). Included in this group are individuals who may be tipped over into becoming acutely dangerous given proper circumstances.

CASE EXAMPLE

Patient is a 14-year-old boy who is obsessed with guns. He reads magazines about weapons and keeps a scrapbook listing the pictures and specifications of many assault weapons. His major interest is playing paintball (a war game using paintballs as bullets) so he can "stalk his prey." He verbally attacks classmates; however, he once hit a classmate on the head with a broom handle because of being teased. He was arrested on 2 occasions during Halloween for destroying property. After being evaluated by several psychiatrists, he was diagnosed as a borderline personality disorder. Neurological evaluation revealed no positive findings. He spoke about a mass murderer not being efficient enough in utilizing his bullets to kill as many people as he could. His mother was diagnosed with major depression and is receiving outpatient psychotherapy and medication. His father, a professional who is rarely home, had been physically abused as a child. His maternal grandparents are Holocaust survivors, and he states that his interest in guns is a reaction to protect himself as his grandparents could not. "If anyone touches me, I will kill them." Patient has no guns at home. He has tried to acquire a pistol but the shopkeepers would not sell him one. He has tried without success to get one by mail order. At this point he seems content to read and talk about guns but not own one. Given a specific stimulus he could become acutely dangerous.

This boy reveals considerable potential for perpetrating a violent act, but he is not acutely dangerous at this time. He has a special interest in guns and has wanted to obtain one. He was involved in several overtly aggressive acts, in particular, assaulting a peer and destroying property. In the past, he spoke about dangerous activities but did not act on them. He carries a diagnosis of borderline personality disorder and has developed a unique personal protective attitude that involves his maternal grandparents being victims of the Holocaust. It appears that if he were provoked by aggressive acts on the part of others and had a weapon, he could become acutely dangerous. However, at this point, he is at an intermediate level of dangerousness.

CHRONIC DANGEROUSNESS

A patient is considered chronically dangerous when the following is present: lowered seriousness of event(s) (e.g., guns at home belong to father who is a police officer), psychiatric diagnoses indicating chronicity (e.g., attention deficit hyperactivity disorder, pervasive developmental disorder, learning disorder), parental psychopathology (e.g., major depression, bipolar disorder, substance abuse), past history of abuse/neglect (e.g., father verbally but not physically abuses patient and others in the home). These patients are often bullies who verbally threaten, intimidate, or engage in physically or sexually abusive behavior in a repeated fashion.

CASE EXAMPLE

Patient is a 17-year-old boy who is a senior in high school. He feels inferior to others because of his learning disability and placement in special classes. He was diagnosed as having a pervasive developmental disorder at age 5. Recently he became angry at his peers and several adults in his community to the point of verbally threatening them with physical harm. He cannot stand being teased at school or in his community. At one point he said, "I will kill them if they keep teasing me. I can't stand it any more." He abuses alcohol and marijuana. He reveals several delinquent acts—driving to endanger while intoxicated and causing an auto accident with bodily harm to others. He has no ready access to weapons and is not obsessed with them. His mother was psychiatrically hospitalized for major depression on one occasion. He has no prior history of suicide attempts.

This patient has a chronic psychiatric problem (pervasive developmental disorder) that contributes to his vulnerability in coping with stressors in his environment, such as being teased by his peers. He has verbally threatened to kill his peers if they do not stop teasing him, abuses substances, and has had 2 auto accidents involving alcohol abuse. However, he has no guns or other weapons and has not assaulted anyone. He is chronically at risk to carry out a dangerous act but is less likely to do so than a patient at the acute or intermediate level of dangerousness. However, he maintains his level of chronic dangerousness with fluctuations depending on external and/or internal stimuli.

Patients can shift from one level of dangerousness to another depending on precipitating events. The reasons for such a shift are patient-specific but usually involve an event perceived as an affront, deprivation, or attack or an anger-provoking incident resulting in loss, frustration, or rage. Potentially dangerous patients usually do not remain static, often changing levels depending on environmental, interpersonal, and intrapsychic factors.

Protective Factors

During the assessment of a patient's potential for dangerousness, it is important to assess protective factors that might be relevant in a shift toward becoming acutely dangerous or be utilized during an intervention. Such protective factors include the following.

FAMILY STABILITY

Families can provide supervision, nurturance, support, trust, and protection, which are valuable in helping protect or avert a patient from becoming dangerous at an acute or intermediate level.

FAMILY SENSITIVITY AND RESPONSIVITY TO POTENTIAL DANGEROUSNESS

Families can make certain that weapons are not at home and arrange for intervention as needed. It is important that they acknowledge and identify their child/adolescent as being a person who may be potentially dangerous so that intervention can take place.

SUPPORTIVE SOCIAL ENVIRONMENT

Community expectations for nonviolence, nonacceptance of violence, and support and concern for others are helpful in diminishing the development of dangerousness in a child or adolescent. Pfeffer et al. (1985, p. 779) note that "the existence of a social network tends to inhibit or enhance assaultive behavior in children in different populations." Support from schools and community programs, such as sports teams and musical programs, can help increase self-worth, improve esteem, and decrease feelings of worthlessness.

PSYCHIATRIC TREATMENT

Treatment of psychiatric disorders in patients and parents can be an ameliorating factor in the onset and expression of dangerousness. For example, parents receiving psychotherapy and psychoactive medication for major depression may become capable of more effective interventions for a child who is becoming potentially dangerous. Psychotherapy and psychopharmacologic treatment for patients can help with improved mood stabilization as well as interpersonal, social, and academic functioning, thereby lessening the onset of potentially dangerous behavior.

ASSESSMENT AND TREATMENT OF NEUROLOGICAL AND NEURO-PSYCHIATRIC PROBLEMS

The treatment of neurological issues, such as seizures, can both improve the patient's psychiatric functioning and diminish dangerousness. Intervention with learning or neuropsychiatric problems can avoid the kinds of cognitive distortions that might lead youngsters to misinterpretation about themselves and others. Also, treatment of these disorders can lead to decreased impulsivity, overaggressiveness, and dangerousness.

CHANGING ENVIRONMENT AND EXPERIENCES

The absence of physical/sexual abuse, neglect, and victimization by violence helps the individual to mature developmentally without the reactive experiences or residua of trauma. Intervening with children/adolescents who have had such experiences can break the cycle of revictimization and improve self-worth. The placement of a child in a therapeutic foster home, away from an abusing caregiver, may be helpful in reducing the impact of continuing trauma.

Forensic Issues

As part of the assessment of dangerousness, the clinician must know when to take action to protect the intended victim(s), including the patient him- or herself. The clinician is expected not only to warn the intended victims but also to protect them (Tarasoff II). Doing so may result in patients being detained against their will or committed to a secure psychiatric facility during the assessment phase (Appelbaum, 1985).

At times this decision is difficult to make because the patient may talk about or express a variety of dangerous-sounding threats or references but will not have done anything specific to lead to such a restrictive intervention. Therefore the

evaluator must attempt to determine whether the patient is dangerous at an acute, intermediate, or chronic level. If the patient is acutely dangerous, the evaluator must take steps to protect both the patient and/or the intended victims and, to that end, override patient confidentiality and hospitalize the patient. If the patient is at an intermediate level of dangerousness, close follow-up is required. Confidentiality may or may not need to be broken and the intended victims might or might not need to be notified. With such patients, the decision to breech confidentiality or notify intended victims or family members will depend on the clinician's judgment. Since a patient's movement from an intermediate to an acute level of dangerousness can be difficult to predict, the evaluator must be careful to arrange follow-up. If the evaluator feels uncomfortable with the patient and is concerned that the shift from intermediate to acute might occur soon, confidentiality must be broken and the intended victim or family member notified.

Sites of Evaluation

The most common sites for the initial evaluation of potentially dangerous patients are emergency rooms, clinicians' private offices, schools, and the courts. In evaluating a child or adolescent suspected of dangerousness, the specific advantages and problems inherent in each of these sites are as follows.

EMERGENCY ROOM

The patient often arrives in a crisis state accompanied by parents who want a rapid resolution—either discharge the child home or send him or her to a hospital. Obtaining a clear history of dangerousness can be difficult because of the overemphasis on the crisis, which may not initially indicate the patient's dangerousness potential (e.g., running away from home). Other patients brought to the emergency room might present with concerns about suicide or have had an overt suicide attempt. The need to make a thorough and accurate clinical decision is great. If there remain unanswered questions and an unknown dangerousness potential, the clinician might have the patient sent to an acute residential unit for an extended evaluation. An acute residential unit is less staff and programatically intense than an inpatient unit but does provide for observation, evaluation, and crisis management.

CLINICIAN'S PRIVATE OFFICE

Most patients seen at a clinician's private office, if potentially dangerous, are usually at the intermediate or chronic level and are well known to the clinician. A major problem develops, however, if these patients become acutely dangerous. In this setting a clinician is less able to manage such patients because of the lack of other provider supports (e.g., security) and the inability to restrict or restrain them. Private offices do not lend themselves to secluding and committing patients. As a result, the private practitioner must arrange to transport such patients to an emergency room as soon as possible.

SCHOOLS

School personnel frequently underreport and underestimate a patient's capacity for dangerousness. As a result, a relatively minor complaint from school staff should alert the clinician to see any patient with a potential for dangerousness. For example, the staff confiscates a knife or razor blade from a student. If such patients are seen at the school, the clinician must be prepared to have them transported to an emergency room using an ambulance and police escort, if needed. It is not safe to continue assessing them at the school where there are no means to manage them. Continued dialogue may further incite or provoke them to flee the premises.

COURTS/JAILS

Clinicians often are asked to see patients in the court setting where they may be highly dangerous to themselves or others. Although the setting might be staff intensive and very restrictive, it is not prepared to manage such patients clinically. A substantial number of patients commit suicide while in jail or in the court system. The extreme restrictiveness without clinical support adds to patients' feelings of hopelessness and despair. As a

result, it is necessary to remove such patients from jail and admit them into a locked inpatient psychiatric facility.

In addition, patients in the court system who are dangerous at an acute or intermediate level must be managed carefully so that they do not injure or kill fellow prisoners who share common facilities. In the face of the stresses of the court system, especially when incarcerated, those who are dangerous at an intermediate level are more likely to escalate into the acutely dangerous category.

Age at Onset of Dangerousness

It is important for the clinician to determine the age at which dangerous behavior began. Although it is poorly understood or accepted, young children can behave in very dangerous ways. In the *London Times* and *Chicago Press* there were recent reports of children ages 7 to 10 who were arrested because of murder or aggravated assault with intent to kill or seriously injure. In another instance, videotapes were taken in public of adolescents severely beating peers and threatening to kill them. In both of these situations, professionals as well as the public at large were surprised by the participants' youthfulness. It is clear that dangerousness needs to be considered in a developmental context.

Dangerousness can first present as a clinical feature when children are moving around by themselves in an independent fashion and might inadvertently act in a dangerous manner. This generally begins at 10 to 12 months of age. In most instances the parents or caregivers need to be protective of their baby's behavior up to approximately 3 years of age. From 12 months to 3 years, accidents can happen, such as falling out of windows, eating poisonous substances, and strangulation on drapery cords or the cords of coat jackets. During these years, the central cause of dangerousness is generally one of questionable supervision by the parent/caregiver.

When children are about 3 years old, they are ready to enter preschool and begin their public socialization experiences. At that time they are exposed to frustrations of primary drives and may, at times, strike out and injure a sibling, peer, or teacher. By the age of 5, it is expected that the child will have begun to internalize and integrate some of the basic rules and expectations of society (teachers/parents/other adults) as he or she enters kindergarten. Those who have problems with accepting socialization principles tend to become bullies or injurious to peers, siblings, and others. If this continues unchecked during the ages of 7 to 10, the possibility of more dangerous behavior in adolescence increases (Bijur, Golding, & Haslum, 1988; Fine, McIntire, & Fain, 1986; Stewart, DeBlois, Meardon, & Cummings, 1980).

Role of the Evaluator

Evaluators are expected to assess dangerous patients as a means of protecting both society and the patient, which thereby places a clear burden on them. An evaluator's effectiveness depends on how reliable the patient is in providing personal information, the clinician's experience in understanding this information, and how well ancillary sources—schools, families, courts—provide a more complete picture of the patient.

As the evaluation proceeds, the clinician must be aware of the patient's potential threat to self, to others, and to the evaluator. An evaluator may be able to contract with patients at an intermediate or chronic level to avoid acting out their impulses. This, however, cannot be done with acutely dangerous patients.

The evaluator must keep in mind the patient's threat to self and others and must warn potential victims and/or maintain the patient in a safe area as needed. Being judicious and careful when evaluating such patients is essential. Additionally, dangerous patients can escape detection or act so that their seriousness is not appreciated if the clinician is hurried. Such evasion also will succeed if a clinician has a psychological block regarding diagnostic material presented during the assessment. If any questions arise regarding dangerousness, especially at the intermediate or chronic levels, it is best to err on the side of being safe and to extend the evaluation by utilizing a psychiatric inpatient unit or an acute residential unit. The extended di-

agnostic assessment in a well-staffed, secure, controlled environment could be immensely helpful in stabilizing the patient psychiatrically and maintaining the safety of both the patient and others until the assessment phase is completed.

At times, clinicians recognize that their patient is becoming increasingly dangerous to a level that is disquieting. Given the nature of the established treatment relationship with the primary therapist, it may be difficult for that therapist to accept or evaluate the patients' dangerousness potential directly. In such cases, patients would be best served by a separate evaluator who can assess their potential dangerousness more objectively.

If an ongoing therapy patient or family member becomes acutely dangerous, they should be seen by a separate evaluator in the context of an emergency services program. Clinicians must be aware that a patient's dangerousness or that of a family member may become directed or projected onto themselves. Therapists could become the target of the dangerous person and their lives might be in jeopardy. Dangerous patients might stalk, repeatedly telephone, or harass the therapist prior to actually committing a dangerous act. If this happens, the psychotherapist must inform the security services or police and speak to an attorney about obtaining a restraining order. Requesting consultation with a clinician who performs evaluations on dangerous patients can be very beneficial.

Conclusion

The psychiatric assessment of dangerousness in children and adolescents is highly complex and must include psychosocial, interpersonal, neuropsychological, pediatric, parental, behavioral and community elements. Behavioral categories of dangerousness include homicidality, suicidality, fire setting, accidents, and assaultive behavior (physical/sexual). Additionally, empirically derived factors relate to each of the behavioral categories. There is, as expected, much crossover of these factors between categories.

Joint interviews with the child/adolescent and parents are useful to the process of assessment. It is essential to establish a database about a potentially dangerous patient and to determine levels of dangerousness by utilizing definitions of acute, intermediate, and chronic.

Protective factors—those that might help avoid dangerousness from becoming manifested—are important in assessing potential for dangerousness. They give the clinician a perspective on utilizing countervailing factors that can neutralize or prevent the expression of dangerous behavior.

Forensic issues in working with potentially dangerous patients include liability, privilege, and confidentiality. The site of the evaluation must be considered in regard to its ability to provide a secure setting.

Age of onset of dangerousness is important for clinicians to understand so they can integrate early developmental aspects of dangerousness with current findings.

In the role of protecting society, evaluators may place themselves in a threatening position, especially if the dangerous patient escapes detection or the clinician has a psychological block regarding dangerousness or violence. Clinicians need to have heightened awareness and ability to cope with and protect themselves when evaluating dangerousness in patients. Psychotherapists are particularly vulnerable to not being aware of their patient's dangerousness potential because of their patient's dangerousness potential, because of the transference issues which intensify during psychotherapy and, at times, interfere in the therapist's objectivity. They should feel free to obtain needed consultation from expert clinicians or attorneys. If possible, dangerous patients should not be evaluated in the home, office, school, or court settings. It is preferable to have them evaluated in an emergency room where security and containment are possible.

REFERENCES

Andrews, J. A., & Lewinsohn, P. M. (1992). Suicidal attempts among older adolescents: Prevalence and co-occurrence with psychiatric disorders. *Journal of the American Academy of Child and Adolescent Psychiatry, 31,* 655–662.

Appelbaum, P. S. (1985). Tarasoff and the clinician: Problems in fulfilling the duty to protect. *American Journal of Psychiatry, 142,* 425–429.

Bijur, P. E., Stewart-Brown, S., Golding, J., Butler, N. R., & Rush, D. (1983). Behavioral correlates of severe accidental injuries in children birth to five. *Pediatric Research, 25,* 93A.

Bijur, P. E., Golding, J., & Haslum, M. (1988). Persistence of occurrence of injury: Can injuries of preschool children predict injuries of school-aged children? *Pediatrics, 72,* 707–712.

Brent, D. A., Perper, J. A., & Allman, C. J. (1987). Alcohol, firearms and suicide. *Journal of the American Medical Association, 257,* 3369–3372.

Brent, D. A., Perper, J. A., Goldstein, C. E., Kolko, D. J., Allan, M. J., Allman, C. J., & Zelenak, J. P. (1988). Risk factors for adolescent suicide. *Archives of General Psychiatry, 45,* 581–588.

Fine, P., McIntire, M. S., & Fain, P. R. (1986). Early indicators of self-destruction in childhood and adolescence: A survey of pediatricians and psychiatrists. *Pediatrics, 77,* 557–568.

Goldberg, L., & Wilensky, H. (1976). Aggression in children in our urban clinic. *Journal of Personal Assessment, 40,* 73–80.

Grossman, D. C., and Rivara, F. P. (1992). Injury control in childhood. *Pediatric Clinics of North America, 39:3,* 471–485.

Holinger, P. C. (1979). Violent deaths among the young: Recent trends in suicide, homicide, and accidents. *American Journal of Psychiatry, 136,* 1144–1147.

Husband, P., & Hinton, P. E. (1972). Families of children with repeated accidents. *Archives of Diseases of Children, 47,* 396–400.

Jacobson, R. (1984). The subclassification of child firesetters. *Journal of Child Psychology and Psychiatry. 26,* 771.

Jaquess, D. L. and Finney, J. W. (1994). Previous injuries and behavior problems predict children's injuries. *Journal of Pediatric Psychology, 19,* 86.

Justice, B., Justice, R., & Kraft, I. (1974). Early warning signs of violence: Is a triad enough? *American Journal of Psychiatry, 131,* 457–459.

Kaufman, I., & Heims, L. (1961). A reevaluation of the psychodynamics of firesetting. *American Journal of Orthopsychiatry, 31,* 123–136.

Kalogerakis, M. G. (1992). Emergency evaluation of adolescents. *Hospital and Community Psychiatry, 43,* 620.

Langley, J., McGee, R., Silva, P., & Williams, S. (1983). Child behavior and accidents. *Journal of Pediatric Psychology, 8,* 181–189.

Lewis, D. O., Lovely, R., Yeager, C., Ferguson, G., Friedman, M., Sloane, G., Friedman, H., & Pincus, J. H. (1988). Intrinsic and environmental characteristics of juvenile murderers. *Journal of the American Academy of Child and Adolescent Psychiatry, 27,* 582–587.

Lewis, D. O., Shanok, S. S., & Pincus, J. H. (1979a). Juvenile male sexual assaulters. *American Journal of Psychiatry, 136,* 1194–1196.

Lewis, D. O., Shanok, S. S., Pincus, J. H., & Glaser, G. H. (1979b). Violent juvenile delinquents: Psychiatric, neurological, psychological and abuse factors. *Journal of the American Academy of Child Psychiatry, 18,* 307–319.

Lewis, D. O., Shanok, S. S., Grant, M., & Ritvo, E. (1983). Homicidally aggressive young children: Neuropsychiatric and experiential correlates. *American Journal of Psychiatry, 140,* 148–153.

Myers, W. C., Scott, K., Burgess, A. W., & Burgess, A. G. (1995). Psychopathology, biopsychosocial factors, crime characteristics, and classification of 25 homicidal youths. *Journal of the American Academy of Child and Adolescent Psychiatry, 34,* 1483–1489.

Pfeffer, C. R., Solomon, G., Plutchick, R., Mizruchi, M. S., & Weiner, A. (1985). Variables that predict assaultiveness in child psychiatric inpatients. *Journal of*

the American Academy of Child Psychiatry, 26, 775–780.

Ritvo, E., Shanok, S. S., & Lewis, D. O. (1983). Firesetting and nonfiresetting delinquents: A comparison of neuropsychiatric, psychoeducational, experiential, and behavioral characteristics. *Child Psychiatry and Human Development, 13,* 259–267.

Rubinstein, M., Yeager, C. A., Goodstein, C., & Lewis, D. O. (1993). Sexually assaultive male juveniles: A follow-up. *American Journal of Psychiatry, 150,* 262–265.

Sargent, D. (1962). Children who kill—a family conspiracy? *Social Work, 7,* 35–42.

Shaffer, D. (1988). The epidemiology of teen suicide: An examination of risk factors. *Journal of Clinical Psychiatry, 49,* 36–41.

Stewart, M. A., & Leone, L. (1978). A family study of unsocialized aggressive boys. *Biologic Psychiatry, 13,* 107–117.

Stewart, M. A., DeBlois, C. S., Meardon, J., & Cummings, C. (1980). Aggressive conduct disorder of children: The clinical picture. *Journal of Nervous and Mental Disease, 168,* 604–610.

SECTION IV
Clinical History

33 / Psychiatric History

Mina K. Dulcan

The psychiatric history consists of the presenting problems and their history, past episodes, and the review of psychiatric symptoms. Although the developmental history, family assessment, social history, observation and mental status assessment, and specialized psychological and somatic tests are all important components of a complete evaluation, the psychiatric history is the essential core of the psychiatric evaluation of a child or adolescent. In particular, it provides the specific data for making a psychiatric diagnosis. As more precise treatments (such as pharmacotherapy and targeted models of psychotherapy) are developed, the psychiatric history and the resulting diagnosis will become increasingly crucial for developing a comprehensive intervention strategy.

Historical Development

HISTORY OF ATTEMPTS TO STRUCTURE CLINICAL INTERVIEWS

Until relatively recently, the recommended style for psychiatric interviewing was determined by psychoanalytic practitioners, who recommended unstructured, nondirective techniques that would allow significant data on conflicts, fantasies, drives, and defenses to come to light. Although appropriate to the context of exploratory psychotherapy, these interviews were unreliable and incomplete in unpredictable ways—and hence unsatisfactory for diagnostic purposes. In addition, supposedly nondirective techniques actually influence the patient to a significant degree, mediated by the interviewer's conscious or unconscious encouragement of certain types of information and discouragement of others (Cox & Rutter, 1985).

The 1960s saw the development of the first semistructured clinical interview of parent and child. Prior to that standard practice included an unstructured discussion with the parent and nondirective play sessions with the child. The new format was composed of a free conversation with the child, followed by systematic questioning on specified topics (fears, worries, unhappiness, irritability, temper outbursts, and peer relationships) (Rutter & Graham, 1968) and a semistructured interview with the parent (Graham & Rutter, 1968). This flew in the face of the conventional wisdom (which prevailed in some circles through the 1980s) that it was not only not useful but was, in fact, harmful to ask children direct questions about psychiatric symptoms. More than that, it was felt that attempts to structure an interview would result in the inhibition of the parent's emotional expression. Subsequent research has demonstrated that even community youths who are not referred patients but are subjects in epidemiologic surveys can well tolerate a detailed, highly structured, and directed psychiatric interview (Lewis, Gorsky, Cohen, & Hartmark, 1985; Shaffer, D., Fisher, P., Dulcan, M. K., Davies, M., Piacentini, J., Schwab-Stone, M. E., Lahey, B. B., Bourdon, K., Jensen, P. S., Bird, H. R., Canino, G., Regier, D. A. (1996). The NIMH Diagnostic Interview Schedule for Children Version 2.3 (DISC-2.3): Description, acceptability, prevalence rates, and performance in the MECA study. *Journal of the American Academy of Child and Adolescent Psychiatry, 35,* 865–877).

Another early attempt to improve the consistency of psychiatric histories was the development of a structured recording system to guide and accompany the unstructured clinical interview. The Pittsburgh Child Guidance Center, site of pioneering efforts in the study of the psychiatric assessment of children and adolescents, developed a system for the recording of evaluation data based on principles of clinical decision making in selecting treatment interventions (Henderson,

Magnussen, Snyderman, & Homann, 1975). Subsequently, a number of clinical settings have developed more phenomenological, symptom-based, standardized data recording systems. Unfortunately, none has been rigorously evaluated or shared in multiple clinical settings.

Components of the Psychiatric History

REASONS FOR REFERRAL AND PRESENTING PROBLEMS

Relatively early in the history of child psychiatry, Kanner (1957) noted that a given symptom might serve a number of different purposes. The possible functions of a symptom include: an admission ticket to the clinic for the child or the parent, an alert that there is a problem, or access to finding out what is wrong and correcting it. A child's or adolescent's symptom may have multiple meanings as a signal of something wrong with the child, the family, or even the school or neighborhood. A given behavior may provide a safety valve for the youth or family, irritate parents or teachers, and/or resolve a conflict for the identified patient or the family. The experienced clinician investigates the meaning of each symptom to both the child and the family.

The timing of a referral may have as much or more to do with the environment as with the severity of the symptoms. It is important to discover who initiated the referral and why now. How did the family come to this particular agency or clinician? What are the reactions of family members to the prospect of an evaluation?

HISTORY OF THE PRESENTING PROBLEMS

The history is the least structured part of the assessment, and it involves obtaining the story in the parents' and child's own words. Cox and Rut-

ter (1985) advocate a problem-solving approach to taking the psychiatric history. Based on the interaction between the clinician's experience and knowledge of psychopathology and data gathered from the child and family, hypotheses regarding the nature, meaning, and etiology of the problems are developed, explored, and tested. Throughout, a balance is needed among obtaining objective data, building rapport, and discovering feelings and attitudes.

Nurcombe and Fitzhenry-Coor (1987) describe psychiatric history-taking by experienced clinicians as "the result of flexible, focused, economic, and deductive detection" (p. 479). The process of clinical reasoning is used to observe patterns from clinical cues, to generate hypotheses, and to formulate a plan of inquiry composed of questions, each of which has 1 of 5 purposes:

- to substantiate a favored hypothesis
- to exclude a diagnostic alternative
- to further explore an important diagnostic issue
- to gather more data on expected prevalent or serious conditions for the particular clinical situation
- when uncertain, to temporize, to allow additional information to emerge

Nurcombe and Fitzhenry-Coor's (1987) curriculum for teaching diagnostic interviewing suggests attention to the following 7 issues:

- Predisposition—physical or psychosocial factors leading to vulnerability
- Precipitation—nature and severity of antecedent stressors and their interaction with predisposition
- Pattern—how do physical and emotional symptoms fit together?; do they fit one or more clinical diagnoses?; what do they communicate, and to whom?
- Perpetuation—what factors maintain the disorder?
- Presentation—why? why now?
- Prognosis
- Potentials—physical, psychological and emotional strengths, and how they could be used to support recovery

History-taking requires probes regarding apparent precipitants; how symptoms developed;

child, parental, and teacher attitudes toward the symptoms; informal intervention strategies and their results; and potential stressors in the family, school, and neighborhood. Specific, concrete examples of behaviors are most useful, including frequency, severity, and environmental and emotional context. Events that immediately precede behaviors (antecedents) and follow them (consequences) are elucidated. The clinician inquires regarding what exacerbates and ameliorates the symptoms. The time course and pattern from initial onset are detailed, and an attempt is made to distinguish patterns that may be sporadic, waxing and waning, or steadily increasing or decreasing in severity. In addition to those mentioned spontaneously, inquiries are made regarding any associated symptoms.

A time line is helpful in organizing data; it graphically relates calendar years (beginning with conception) to the age of the child, symptoms, major life events, changes in family and environment, and treatment episodes.

A detailed description of prior evaluations and treatment is essential, including the methods and results of assessment; any psychotherapy, with type, frequency, duration, and effects; medication, specifying exact doses, schedule, compliance, and beneficial and adverse effects; and hospitalization or environmental changes (e.g., classroom interventions or moves, custody changes) and their outcomes.

REVIEW OF PSYCHIATRIC SYMPTOMS

This section of the psychiatric history requires a thorough knowledge of potential psychopathology, expectable correlates and syndromes, and the most current diagnostic system (currently the fourth edition of the *Diagnostic and Statistical Manual of Mental Disorders*). The interviewer uses informed and organized questioning but avoids "leading the witness." Both parent and youth are questioned regarding general categories of symptoms, with positive replies followed up in detail regarding the nature and course of the symptoms and any resulting interference with developmental progress or impairment in function-

ing in the family, at school, or with peers. Areas of inquiry include:

- Relationship with parents and peers
- Worries, fears, anxieties, separation behavior (in relation to developmental level)
- Suicidal thoughts and actions
- Obsessions, compulsions
- Depression/irritability and associated symptoms
- Symptoms of thought disorder (disorganization) or psychosis (hallucinations, delusions)
- Conduct symptoms—aggression, stealing, lying, tantrums, defiance, disobedience
- Patterns of eating and sleeping
- Enuresis, encopresis
- Activity level, attention span, impulsivity
- Tics, habits, mannerisms, rituals
- Substance use/abuse

Although somatic symptoms are covered in the health history, they may represent stressors and/or psychiatric symptoms, and should be integrated with the psychiatric history.

Sources of the Psychiatric History

IMPORTANCE OF MULTIPLE SOURCES IN THE ASSESSMENT OF CHILDREN AND ADOLESCENTS

Far more than for adults, for a child or adolescent, multiple informants often are crucial to the assessment process. Each observer has access to a unique portion of the youngster's feelings and behavior, and each (including the identified patient) has an idiosyncratic perspective on the situation and specific motivations for disclosing or concealing information.

INFORMANT CHARACTERISTICS

Children: Prior to adolescence, children are less reliable reporters than their parents, especially children younger than age 10 years. In test-retest protocols, young children show a dramatic reduction in symptoms from first to second interview. When comparing children's reports from one interview to the next, behavior and conduct symptoms are more stable than are mood and anxiety symptoms (Edelbrock, Costello, Dulcan, Kalas, & Conover, 1985). In taking a psychiatric history, it is essential to consider the stages of cognitive and emotional development. Young children have a limited ability to understand and verbalize abstract concepts such as emotions and time. Children are particularly poor reporters of age of onset and duration. Their accounts of the present are generally more accurate than of the past.

Parents: Parents are the most important informants regarding their child's psychiatric history, although they are by no means immune to gaps in knowledge and to distortions in memory or in reporting. Chess, Thomas, and Birch (1966) compared previously recorded data to the history gathered when 33 of the subjects in the New York Longitudinal Study presented for clinical assistance. One of the most striking findings was the clinicians' inability to classify parents correctly as either accurate or unreliable historians. Parents who appeared to be well organized and confident in their reports were frequently less accurate than those who seemed scattered or doubtful. Over a third of the parents demonstrated one or more of the following types of distortions:

- Retrospective conformity to a theory of causation
- Denial or minimization of a prior problem
- Inability to recall relevant past parental behavior
- Blaming the child for behavior previously fostered by the parent

Maternal depression or other psychopathology can alter reports of child behavior by increasing the mother's perception of child maladjustment and by disrupting parenting skills, leading to actual increases in noncompliance (Chilcoat & Breslau, 1997; Forehand, Lautenschlager, Faust, & Graziano, 1986). In an analog study, mothers in a high-stress condition rated neutral child behavior described in a vignette as significantly more deviant than when they were in a low-stress condition. Mothers of psychology clinic patients were more likely to rate vignettes describing neutral child behavior as inappropriate than were mothers of control children (Middlebrook & Forehand, 1985).

Teacher Reports: Teacher reports are virtually essential for the preschool and elementary school child. They are crucial because of the importance of school as a test of developmental progress and the significance of academic and social skills for success in adult life. In general, compared to parents, teachers have more training and much broader experience with children on which to base observations. Teachers often are involved in the referral and assessment of children for special services. With entry into middle school, however, and increasingly in junior high and high school, regular classroom teachers are unlikely to know an individual youth well, and their reports are less useful.

Although teachers are not affected by the family dynamics, experienced clinicians are aware that when completing rating scales or reports on their students, teachers may harbor a variety of hidden (or not so hidden) agendas. This situation is especially apparent in the assessment for attention-deficit/hyperactivity disorder. One teacher may be determined to produce a high enough score to remove a troublesome child from his or her class, while another may deliberately underestimate problems because of objections to special class placement or unwillingness to "give up on" a child. Attitudes toward the use of medication may skew teacher reports dramatically; at times, in order to obtain accurate information, this may even require the use of double-blind, placebo-controlled trials.

More experienced teachers tend to rate the same sample of behavior as less symptomatic than do less experienced teachers (Sonis & Costello, 1981). Experience with the Teacher Report Form of the Child Behavior Checklist (Achenbach, 1991b) has shown that special education teachers rate the same children as less disturbed than do regular class teachers, probably due to a mixture of a higher teacher threshold for judging psychopathology and an actual difference in the child's behavior in the special class setting.

AGREEMENT AMONG INFORMANTS

It has been repeatedly demonstrated that when evaluating a child's or adolescent's symptomatology, reports from different informants disagree. This lack of agreement is presumed to be due to a combination of factors. Differences exist among observers in their standard for the range of normal; this causes the same behavior to be observed or reported differently. For example, from videotaped samples of child behavior, child psychiatrists and psychologists rated symptoms of activity level, motor behavior, perseveration, uncoordination, and fidgetiness as less severe than did pediatricians and teachers (Sonis & Costello, 1981). To a much greater extent than for adults, the behavior of children and adolescents actually differs from one situation to another (e.g., school vs. home) and even when with the mother and father or with different teachers. Finally, types of informants vary in their access to information. Covert behaviors such as stealing or self-induced vomiting may be hidden from all adults, some behaviors may be restricted to home or to school, and internal states and experiences (e.g., mood or hallucinations) are known only to the patient, unless he or she chooses to report them.

In evaluating child and adolescent emotional and behavioral problems, the reports of similar informants (e.g., 2 teachers) correlate more closely than reports from pairs of informants in different roles (e.g., parent/teacher, child/parent) (Achenbach, McConaughy, & Howell, 1987). There is greater consistency between child (6 to 11 years old) and adult informants than between adolescents and adults.

Parent-child agreement is higher for behavior and conduct symptoms and factual information than it is for affective or "neurotic" symptoms. The degree of agreement increases with the age of the child until adolescence. In general, teenagers reporting about themselves describe more alcohol and drug use, stealing, truancy, fears, obsessions, depression, suicidal ideation, hallucinations, and delusions than do their parents reporting about them. On the other hand, parents report more relationship problems, school difficulties, medical problems, aggression, and disobedience. Parents are more accurate informants than children on past history, treatment history, observable behavior problems, overt conduct symptoms, ADHD, and oppositional behavior.

Parents and teachers typically report more symptoms of ADHD and oppositional defiant disorder than do children, but there is rarely external validation as to who is "correct." In one recent study, parent and teacher reports of disruptive behavior problems more accurately predicted future poor outcome measures (external validity criteria) than did child reports (Loeber, Green, Lahey, & Stouthamer-Loeber, 1991).

Developmental Issues in Diagnosing Children and Adolescents

There are good reasons why the evolution of diagnostic categories in young people has lagged behind similar work with adults. Many childhood disorders (e.g., enuresis, encopresis, oppositional defiant disorder, and specific developmental disorder) are characterized by behaviors that would be normal at an earlier age, rather than by symptoms that are always pathological, such as true hallucinations. In addition, normal children and adolescents may manifest some of the behaviors characteristic of disorders such as oppositional defiant disorder, conduct disorder, and attention deficit hyperactivity disorder. What distinguishes the pathological is the inappropriateness of the behavior for the child's age and sex and/or the frequency, intensity, or persistence of the behavior. The context within which symptoms arise and how they cluster are important in distinguishing a healthy reaction from an adjustment disorder or a psychiatric disorder. The clinician must have expert knowledge of the range of normal development in children and adolescents, both to identify variations from normal and to assess whether psychiatric disorder has interfered with the achievement of social, cognitive, or emotional developmental milestones. Detailed knowledge of the natural history of disorders is also essential, since typical symptoms differ with age.

Methods of Collecting Psychiatric History Data: Indications and Research Evidence

RELIABILITY AND VALIDITY

One of the most troublesome aspects of the psychiatric history has been the variability of information from one time to the next or from one interviewer to another. The gathering of data on psychiatric symptoms is complex, and a wide variety of potential sources of variability have been identified (Costello, 1987). Variables related to the method of data collection include: the topics that are covered; the way questions are worded; the skill of the interviewer in phrasing questions, observing responses, and formulating follow-up questions; the setting of the interview, and the informant's expectations regarding both the purpose of the interview and what will be done with the information. Repeated questioning may induce a change in the informant's threshold for reporting symptoms. Although it seems like a simple matter, differences in the recording of information can be dramatic, especially in unstructured formats. In transforming historical data into diagnoses, variability can occur in the categories used, the criteria applied, and the interpretation given to ambiguous criteria. As noted, different informants typically supply inconsistent data. Finally, actual change over time may occur, through spontaneous remission or exacerbation, as an effect of the interview itself, or as a result of treatment.

Reliability is the measure of reproducibility from one time to another (test-retest) or from one observer to another (interrater). (For a detailed discussion of reliability in diagnostic interviewing, see Costello, 1989.) Young children appear to be less reliable on retest than are adolescents or parents (Edelbrock, Costello, Dulcan, Kalas, & Conover, 1985).

Validity measures how closely the results of an instrument or technique resemble the "truth," or the real value, of what is being measured. Unfortunately, since there is no "gold standard" in psy-

chiatric diagnosis, validity has been difficult to assess. Typically, clinical "experts" are used, although it has been demonstrated repeatedly that clinician diagnosis is highly unreliable. This problem may be reduced to some degree by using a best estimate or consensus of experts, using all available information, using diagnostic criteria checklists and explicit rules for making decisions and for resolving disagreements among the experts. The most stringent test is predictive validity—correlation of a diagnosis with treatment response or prognosis. In any case, the validity of an instrument or procedure can be no better than its reliability, although reliability can be excellent and validity poor.

INTERVIEW STYLE

In the 1960s, Rutter's group at the Maudsley Hospital began a series of studies on the efficacy and acceptability of psychiatric interview techniques for children and their parents (Graham & Rutter, 1968; Rutter & Graham, 1968). A later project (Cox, Hopkinson, & Rutter, 1981; Hopkinson, Cox, & Rutter, 1981; Rutter & Cox, 1981) investigated the effects of different styles of interviewing parents of children referred to a psychiatric clinic. More open-ended questions and less interviewer talking yielded more talkative informants and more expression of feelings, but a directive style using specific probes and requests resulted in more precise and complete data than did a free-style open-ended interview. Double questions (e.g., "Does he steal or truant?") led to ambiguous answers, while multiple-choice probes (e.g., "Was it once a day, once a week, or once a month?") led to improved focus and precision.

The Maudsley team then developed 4 contrasting model interviewing styles, based on both naturalistic observations and on recommendations of various experts for proper interview techniques. The models represented all possible combinations of high- and low-directive fact-seeking, and high and low exploration of emotions. Active, fact-oriented techniques yielded more complete symptom reports, without interfering with the expressions of emotion. Mothers had no overall preference for a particular style, although a few mothers strongly preferred each of the 4 (Cox, Holbrook, & Rutter, 1981; Cox, Rutter, & Holbrook, 1981; Rutter, Cox, Egert, Holbrook, & Everitt, 1981).

Clinicians typically use an unstructured interview style; albeit flexible, it is highly idiosyncratic and dependent on the skills of the individual interviewer. This style is vulnerable to omissions and distortions resulting from the interviewer's inexperience, lapses in memory, incomplete training, or theoretical biases. Experienced clinicians develop an informal skip structure of questions that is efficient but may miss data if symptom patterns are unexpected or if the clinician has a blind spot or lapse of concentration. Unstructured clinical interviews are prone to premature closure. They typically yield fewer diagnoses than does a more structured assessment method.

In the usual clinical setting, the inquiry moves from more general, open-ended to more specific, close-ended questions, seeking examples, then using specific probes to obtain detailed information. Probes must be carefully worded to avoid introducing distortion into the answers. Cox and Rutter (1985) suggest, for example, frequency probes first using widely spaced time intervals (e.g., several times a day or once every few months), then narrowing down the choices. It is important to avoid negatively phrased leading questions, such as "He doesn't use drugs, does he?" Wording of probes can minimize social desirability effects (e.g., asking "How often do you feel angry with your son?" rather than "Do you ever feel angry . . . ?")

SEMISTRUCTURED AND STRUCTURED INTERVIEWS

Assessment instruments are discussed in detail elsewhere in this volume. (See also Costello, 1987; Edelbrock & Costello, 1988; Gutterman, O'Brien, & Young, 1987; Orvaschel, 1989).

Semistructured Interviews: Semistructured interviews, such as the Schedule for Affective Disorders and Schizophrenia for School-Age Children, or Kiddie-SADS (KSADS) and the Interview Schedule for Children (ISC), consist of an outline for areas to be covered, specified in more or less detail. They may include model probes, but the wording of questions can be changed to fit the situation. For the most part, questions refer only to the present, except as needed to assess duration and onset criteria for diagnosis. However, the K-SADS-E (epidemiologic version) does assess life time symptoms. The interviewer integrates parent and child reports (and optionally data from school or clinical records) in making summary ratings.

The advantages of the semistructured over the structured interviews or rating scales include greater flexibility and better coverage of the presenting complaint and history of psychiatric illness; they also provide greater reliability and more complete coverage of symptoms than do unstructured interviews. The disadvantages of the semistructured approach include the requirement for an experienced clinician, specifically trained in the use of the interview. This, in turn, implies greater expense and increased interviewer-generated variance than is true for structured interviews.

The Diagnostic Interview for Children and Adolescents (DICA) and the Child Assessment Schedule (CAS) are transitional forms between the structured and semistructured interview that provide the exact wording of questions but require the application of clinical judgment to code responses and score behavioral observations.

Structured Interviews: Structured interviews such as the National Institute of Mental Health's Diagnostic Interview Schedule for Children (DISC), are like a script. Questions to be asked are selected by a predetermined skip structure, according to the subject's replies to stem questions. The focus is on present psychiatric symptomatology, except where past history is required to make a diagnosis. The DISC is designed to be administered by lay interviewers after relatively brief training and is therefore practical for use in epidemiologic field studies. The interviewer has minimal discretion, other than to use common sense. Scoring is relatively automatic, and diagnoses are made by computer algorithm.

The increased structure has the advantage of reducing interviewer-introduced variability. Compared to a questionnaire, a structured interview is more personal, with a greater potential of motivating an informant to cooperate. Limited reading ability is not a problem. If a question is not understood, there is a chance to explain, and if an answer is ambiguous or too general, the interviewer can clarify or ask for more detail. On the negative side, the interview may sound artificial or stilted, and the language may be too simple or too complex for certain respondents. A completely preplanned sequence of questions cannot respond to unique individual concerns and is therefore more suited for research than for clinical purposes. Because no clinical judgment is allowed, unless diagnostic criteria are clearly operationalized it is difficult for the computer algorithm to reproduce clinical reality.

RATING SCALES

Questionnaires and rating scales are covered in detail elsewhere in this volume. (See also Barkley, 1990; Edelbrock, 1987, for reviews and references). Rating scales are available for parents, teachers, children and adolescents, and clinicians. Some, such as the Child Behavior Checklist (Achenbach, 1991a), cover a wide range of psychopathology, while others, like Kovacs' Child Depression Inventory, focus on a single diagnostic area. (See Aman, 1993 and Kutcher, 1997, for compendia of symptom rating scales.) As supplements to a psychiatric history interview, rating scales have many advantages. They are simple, economical, and efficient in professional time. The broad range scales are multidimensional and assist in obtaining a fuller description of the patient and in preventing a too-narrow focus on a single diagnosis. Rating scales can be used to gather detailed descriptive information on specific behaviors or to assess infrequent behaviors that would be missed in an interview or observation. Although reports are still filtered through the rater's attitudes and experience, compared to an unstructured interview, these questionnaires can increase the objectivity of reporting. Rating scales typically have age- and sex-graded norms. They are therefore useful in distinguishing psychopathology from behaviors that are normal at low frequency or at certain developmental stages. Rating scales also can compare the behavior that is generating parent or teacher complaints to an external standard. Rating scales are especially efficient for gathering data from teachers.

Checklists and rating scales are less useful in gathering data on past psychiatric history, since they typically focus only on the present or on the past 6 to 12 months. Also, few are keyed to diagnostic categories.

In the clinical setting, rating scales are useful in that they help focus parental reports and the subsequent clinical discussion. They can compare quantitatively the reports of 2 parents, a parent and teacher, or a parent and child.

Unresolved Issues and Future Directions

Many challenges remain in the assessment of the psychiatric history. Reliability and validity of existing techniques remain suboptimal. Children under the age of 10 years are especially problematic. In an effort to address this age group, Achenbach and McConaughy have developed and are testing the Semistructured Clinical Interview for Children (SCIC), a protocol for the multiaxial assessment of children ages 6 to 11 by an experienced clinician.

Improved validity of assessment measures requires a more satisfactory standard of comparison than simple clinician diagnosis, one perhaps to be found in biological, neuroimaging, or genetic tests, or in the results of long-term follow-up studies. The integration of data from multiple informants remains a knotty problem, as does the almost universal finding of a decrease in reported symptoms from a first to a second interview. Whose report at what time represents "the truth"? Finally, the psychiatric history is linked inextricably to the diagnostic system, where much empirical work remains to be done.

REFERENCES

Achenbach, T. M. (1991a). *Manual for the Child Behavior Checklist/4–18 and 1991 Profile.* Burlington: University of Vermont Department of Psychiatry.

Achenbach, T. M. (1991b). *Manual for the Teacher's Report Form and 1991 Profile.* Burlington: University of Vermont Department of Psychiatry.

Achenbach, T. M., McConaughy, S. H., & Howell, C. T. (1987). Child/adolescent behavioral and emotional problems: Implications of cross-informant correlations for situational specificity. *Psychological Bulletin, 101,* 213–232.

Aman, M. G. (1993). Monitoring and measuring drug effects. II. Behavioral, emotional, and cognitive effects. In J. S. Werry and M. G. Aman (eds): *Practitioner's Guide to Psychoactive Drugs for Children and Adolescents,* pp. 99–159. NY: Plenum.

Barkley, R. A. (1990). Behavior rating scales. In R. A. Barkley (Ed.), *Attention deficit hyperactivity disorder: A handbook for diagnosis and treatment* (pp. 278–326). New York: Guilford Press.

Chess, S., Thomas, A., & Birch, H. G. (1966). Distortions in developmental reporting made by parents of behaviorally disturbed children. *Journal of the American Academy of Child Psychiatry, 5,* 226–234.

Chilcoat, H. D. (1997). Does psychiatric history bias mothers' reports? An application of a new analytic approach. *Journal of the American Academy of Child and Adolescent Psychiatry, 36,* 971–979.

Costello, A. J. (1987). Structured interviewing for the assessment of child psychopathology. In J. D. Call, R. L. Cohen, S. I. Harrison, I. N. Berlin, & L. A. Stone (Eds.), *Basic handbook of child psychiatry* (Vol. 5, pp. 143–153). New York: Basic Books.

Costello, A. (1989). Reliability in diagnostic interviewing. In C. Last & M. Hersen (Eds.), *Handbook of child psychiatric diagnosis* (pp. 28–40). New York: John Wiley & Sons.

Cox, A., Holbrook, D., & Rutter, M. (1981). Psychiatric interviewing techniques: VI. Experimental study: Eliciting feelings. *British Journal of Psychiatry, 139,* 144–152.

Cox, A., Hopkinson, K., & Rutter, M. (1981). Psychiatric interviewing techniques: II. Naturalistic study: Eliciting factual information. *British Journal of Psychiatry, 138,* 283–291.

Cox, A., & Rutter, M. (1985). Diagnostic appraisal and interviewing. In M. Rutter & L. Hersov (Eds.), *Child and adolescent psychiatry: Modern approaches* (2nd ed., pp. 233–248). Oxford: Blackwell Scientific Publications.

Cox, A., Rutter, M., & Holbrook, D. (1981). Psychiatric interviewing techniques: V. Experimental study: Eliciting factual information. *British Journal of Psychiatry, 139,* 29–37.

Edelbrock, C. (1987). Behavioral checklists and rating scales. In J. D. Call, R. L. Cohen, S. I. Harrison, I. N. Berlin, & L. A. Stone (Eds.), *Basic handbook of child psychiatry* (Vol. 5, pp. 153–164). New York: Basic Books.

Edelbrock, C., & Costello, A. J. (1988). Structured psychiatric interviews for children. In M. Rutter, H. Tuma, & I. Lann (Eds.), *Assessment and diagnosis in child psychopathology* (pp. 87–112). New York: Guilford Press.

Edelbrock, C., Costello, A. J., Dulcan, M. K., Kalas, R., & Conover, N. C. (1985). Age differences in the reliability of the psychiatric interview of the child. *Child Development, 56,* 265–275.

Forehand, R., Lautenschlager, G. J., Faust, J., & Graziano, W. G. (1986). Parent perceptions and parent-child interactions in clinic-referred children: A preliminary investigation of the effects of maternal depressive moods. *Behavior Research and Therapy, 24,* 73–75.

Graham, P., & Rutter, M. (1968). The reliability and validity of the psychiatric assessment of the child: II. Interview with the parent. *British Journal of Psychiatry, 114,* 581–592.

Gutterman, E. M., O'Brien, J. D., & Young, J. G. (1987). Structured diagnostic interviews for children and adolescents: Current status and future directions. *Journal of the American Academy of Child and Adolescent Psychiatry, 26,* 621–630.

Henderson, P. B., Magnussen, M. G., Snyderman, B. B., & Homann, J. (1975). A clinical decision-making model for child psychiatric intervention selection. *Psychological Reports, 37,* 923–934.

Hopkinson, K., Cox, A., & Rutter, M. (1981). Psychiatric interviewing techniques: III. Naturalistic study: Eliciting feelings. *British Journal of Psychiatry, 138,* 406–415.

Kanner, L. (1957). *Child psychiatry* (3rd ed.) Springfield, IL: Charles C Thomas.

Kutcher, S. P. (1997). *Child and adolescent psychopharmacology,* Appendix VI: Symptom assessments. Philadelphia: Saunders, pp. 405–468.

Lewis, S. A., Gorsky, A., Cohen, P., & Hartmark, C. (1985). The reactions of youth to diagnostic interviews. *Journal of the American Academy of Child Psychiatry, 24,* 750–755.

Loeber, R., Green, S. M., Lahey, B. B., & Stouthamer-Loeber, M. (1991). Differences and similarities between children, mothers, and teachers as informants on disruptive child behavior. *Journal of Abnormal Child Psychology, 19,* 75–95.

Middlebrook, J. L., & Forehand, R. (1985). Maternal perceptions of deviance in child behavior as a function of stress and clinic versus nonclinic status of the child: An analogue study. *Behavioral Therapy, 16,* 494–502.

Nurcombe, B., & Fitzhenry-Coor, I. (1987). Diagnostic

reasoning and treatment planning: I. Diagnosis. *Australian and New Zealand Journal of Psychiatry, 21,* 477–483.

Orvaschel, H. (1989). Diagnostic interviews for children and adolescents. In C. Last & M. Hersen (Eds.), *Handbook of child psychiatric diagnosis* (pp. 483–495). New York: John Wiley & Sons.

Rutter, M., & Cox, A. (1981). Psychiatric interviewing techniques: I. Methods and measures. *British Journal of Psychiatry, 138,* 273–282.

Rutter, M., Cox, A., Egert, S., Holbrook, D., & Everitt, B. (1981). Psychiatric interviewing techniques: IV. Experimental study: Four contrasting styles. *British Journal of Psychiatry, 138,* 456–465.

Rutter, M., & Graham, P. (1968). The reliability and validity of the psychiatric assessment of the child: I. Interview with the child. *British Journal of Psychiatry, 114,* 563–579.

Sonis, W. A., & Costello, A. J. (1981). Evaluation of differential data sources: Application to the diagnostic process in child psychiatry. *Journal of the American Academy of Child Psychiatry, 20,* 597–610.

34 / Genetic, Prenatal, and Delivery History

Linda J. Lotspeich

A full genetic, prenatal, and obstetrical history should be standard practice in child psychiatry. There are a number of reasons why such a complete history is important. First, there may have been prior complications that have a direct effect on the child's current problems. These complications could include in utero exposure to drugs such as alcohol or cocaine, anoxia at birth, or prematurity, to mention just a few. Second, the parents may have concerns about specific events of conception, pregnancy, or childbirth; they may fear that these events were the cause of their child's psychiatric disorder. For example, a mother may recall a difficult labor and delivery and wonder if that was the cause of her child's hyperactivity. The clinician can help to relieve the parents of guilt or worry associated with such events. It is important when taking the genetic, prenatal, and obstetric history to focus not just on the information but also on the emotional emphasis placed on events during this time. Frequently this part of the history is reviewed with the parents in a cursory fashion, simply to ensure that there were no serious medical complications; often too little time is spent in learning about the parent's expectations, guilt, and worries.

There are well-demonstrated correlations between certain prenatal or delivery complications and the later appearance of developmental disorders. However, in many cases a direct causal connection between an untoward prenatal event and the disorder will be missing. A principal reason for this is that conditions such as attention deficit hyperactivity disorder, pervasive developmental disorders, mental retardation, and learning disabilities most often are caused by a combination of environmental and genetic factors. Because of the many factors at work in a given case, the importance of any single factor is usually impossible to determine. For example, a number of careful studies have looked for causative associations between prenatal or perinatal complications and autism. The controls in these studies have been extensive, and the many factors examined have included delivery abnormalities, meconium-stained amniotic fluid, low Apgar scores, bleeding in pregnancy, maternal viral illness, and advanced maternal age. Of 26 factors examined, bleeding in pregnancy was the only factor even somewhat correlated with autism. In general, these studies indicate that although certain problems of pregnancy may increase the risk of autism, these problems are not specific to autism, nor are they useful as predictors of autism. These studies along with other neurobiological studies of autism are reviewed in Lotspeich and Ciaranello (1993).

This chapter reviews the major topics of conception, genetics, fetal brain development, prenatal history, and obstetric history, with an emphasis on their impact on psychiatric evaluation of children with developmental or behavioral disorders. Our reasons for emphasizing these topics should be readily apparent. Nontraditional methods of conception have resulted in novel and ambiguous situations that must be weighed in effective psychiatric counseling. Also, an effective psychiatric evaluation requires a basic knowledge of normal fetal brain development, as this provides a basis for understanding and explaining to parents how congenital defects may arise from genetic errors or environmental influences. Finally, an appreciation of the prenatal and obstetrical history may be very important, for instance, in the event of a significant degree of anoxia at birth.

Conception

Taking the history of conception calls for sensitivity, since society has strong values regarding the

This work was begun with Roland Ciaranello, M.D., who died on December 15, 1994. This author is grateful for Dr. Ciaranello's mentorship. The work was supported by the grant from the National Alliance for Research on Schizophrenia and Depression (NARSAD) and from the Scottish Rite Benevolent Foundation's Schizophrenia Research Program.

conditions under which conception takes place. Asking the parents if this was a planned conception insinuates that, if it was not, then the parents and particularly the mother was irresponsible; already a judgment has been made about their ability to properly parent a child. Thus it is best to use a phrase, such as "Was there anything special or unique about your child's conception?"

For some families, the parents' feelings about the child's conception can reflect an important aspect of the parent-child interaction. For example, a couple seriously considered aborting a fetus because the pregnancy was unexpected. The pregnancy came late in the life of the parents, after their other children were well into their teens. The parents had different opinions regarding this decision. The parents chose to have the child, and when the boy was 3 or 4 years old they learned that he had severe mental retardation. These parents felt that a "damaged" child was their punishment for wanting the abortion, and this guilt affected their ability to adjust and cope with their child's mental retardation. Every time they were called by the school with complaints about the child's disruptive behavior, they felt solely responsible for their child's suffering. Identifying this guilt and helping the parents cope and develop a guilt-free relationship with their child could make a powerful positive change in the quality of their lives and of their child's life.

With today's technologies, conception can take place in a number of alternative ways: for instance, through a surrogate mother, or by use of donor sperm and in vitro fertilization. A common method is the use of donor sperm, where the sperm donor (the biological father) generally remains anonymous. Sometimes the sperm of a male with low fertility is added to that of donated high-fertility sperm; then, unless genetic testing is done, paternity is even more uncertain. This sort of ambiguity may well have an impact on how the parents feel about their child. There are also families where a male relative—for example, the father's brother—donates sperm, so that the child's genes will come from both parents' families. This too may complicate the parents' relationship with the child, since there are 2 fathers: a biological father and a social one.

For adoptive parents, the idea of conception is related to their decision to adopt a child and the adoption process. Parents whose children are adopted have a variety of experiences. Some, such as gay couples, always have known that they could not conceive their own child. Others have spent years struggling to conceive a child before finally adopting. Some adoptive parents may meet their adopted child immediately following birth and may know a great deal about the genetic and other history of the biological parents. Other times they may meet their adopted child years after birth and know little or nothing about circumstances of birth. These differences in experience and expectation can have a profound effect on the parent-child bond when a psychiatric problem is in question.

It is not clear at this time how these alternative forms of conception will impact children and society at large, but certainly new and different issues will arise as a consequence. Information on conception is frequently significant in the medical history. Most likely the greatest effect of this information will come from the parents' own feelings about conception and what they communicate to the child either directly or indirectly.

Genetics

In deciding to have a child, most couples give at least some thought to the possibility that their baby might have a genetic disorder or chromosomal anomaly. This is especially true if there is a family history of a genetic disorder (such as fragile X syndrome or neurofibromatosis) or if the mother-to-be is older than 35 years and is concerned she may have a child with Down syndrome. In these cases some couples consult a genetic counselor to evaluate their risks and explore their options. Other couples, who are not overtly at risk, may learn of a genetic or chromosomal disorder during routine prenatal ultrasonography. Reviewing the history of such testing or of concerns about genetic problems can be valuable, so we will briefly describe the tests of ultrasonography, amniocentesis, and chorionic villus sampling.

Ultrasonography is an increasingly routine part of pregnancy monitoring. Ultrasound imaging is useful for determining the age and sex of the fetus, and many congenital defects also are identifiable as early as the middle of the first trimester.

Such defects include limb defects, abnormal genitalia, achondroplasia, neural tube defects, and fetal heart defects. These defects are sometimes the result of a genetic disorder. A suspicious sonogram can lead to a definitive genetic diagnosis through evaluation of fetal cells and chromosomes, with cells obtained either by amniocentesis or chorionic villus sampling.

Amniocentesis is the transabdominal removal and examination of amniotic fluid, usually at 16 weeks of pregnancy or later. From this fluid fetal cells for karyotyping can be recovered and biochemically tested. Karyotype analysis can determine sex and, more important, can identify common aneuploidies, such as translocations, trisomy 21, or less common chromosomal abnormalities. Some single-gene defects (such as cystic fibrosis and fragile X syndrome) may require fetal DNA testing, using specific probes. Amniocentesis may be suggested if there is a strong family history of a genetic disorder, for mothers age 35 or older, or as a result of a suspicious ultrasound scan.

Similar information can be obtained by examining cells from chorionic villi sampling. This testing is still in limited use due to a small risk of fetal damage or miscarriage. Its main advantage is that it can be used as early as the ninth week of pregnancy, usually when a serious problem is suspected and abortion is an option.

A good deal can be learned about the risk of Down syndrome and neural tube defects without invasive techniques, by evaluating maternal serum at specific times during pregnancy. Abnormally high levels of alpha-fetoprotein in maternal serum indicates the strong likelihood of a neural tube defect, while an abnormally low level may signal Down syndrome. Additional testing then must be done to rule out either condition. Thompson, McInnes, and Willard (1991) review medical genetics.

Fetal Brain Development

Although links between events in fetal development and later behavioral problems are generally tenuous, it is still valuable to have an appreciation of the timing of specific events in fetal brain development. For example, an infection or toxin may have a deleterious effect on the fetus at one stage of development and little effect at an earlier or later stage. Rubella exposure, for instance, has a great potential for damaging the fetus during the first and second trimesters but has relatively little effect during the third trimester, when organs are already developed. On the other hand, in utero exposure to alcohol is deleterious to fetal development at any stage of the pregnancy.

Since psychiatric disorders are based on brain pathology, this review of fetal development focuses on fetal brain development. During the first trimester, the neural plate is formed in the first 18 to 21 days. This event is followed immediately by development of the neural tube, which bulges, flexes, and develops cavities so that, by the end of the first trimester, structures are present that will soon become cerebral hemispheres, midbrain, brain stem, cerebellum, and spinal cord. Thus a fundamental event of neural development in the first trimester is formation of the basic brain structures. The first cortical neurons appear at about 6 weeks. Characteristic neuronal cell layers begin to form, and myelination begins in the spinal cord at 12 weeks. As we might anticipate, first-trimester injuries to the fetal brain usually result in aborted fetuses or gross neuroanatomical defects, such as anencephaly. Most teratogens, whether drugs, medications, or in utero infections, have their most potent effects at this stage.

In the second trimester, the main themes are neuronal development, neuronal migration, and increase in neuronal cell number. The characteristic cell layers of the cortex form, the brain increases greatly in size, and, toward the end of the second trimester, folding of the cortical surface results in formation of the important sulci. Myelination is intense in both second and third trimesters and continues after birth. Chemical toxins, such as alcohol, heavy metals, and hexachlorophene, can interfere with myelination. Mice with mutational defects in myelination have motor abnormalities that give some clue about the consequences of abnormal myelination; this is reflected in the lab names for such mutations, for instance "shiverer" and "trembler."

In the third trimester, neuronal and glial cell growth continues, and the brain grows larger without much additional cellular migration. Arborization and synapse formation is pronounced and, indeed, continues well into postnatal life.

Once again, alcohol exposure during the third trimester has toxic effects on brain development; some maternal complications, such as poorly controlled maternal diabetes, also can produce developmental abnormalities. Sadler (1995) provides more detailed information on development of the fetal brain.

Prenatal History

When taking a prenatal history, a long list of complications that could affect the developing fetal brain and thus lead to developmental and psychiatric disorders must be considered. Many of the children seen clinically for learning disabilities, hyperactivity, behavioral outbursts and poor attention span have histories of prenatal exposure to recreational drugs, such as alcohol, cocaine, and heroin. Another central concern should be any history of prenatal infections that could have had a deleterious effect on brain development. Insults to fetal brain development also can occur because of such maternal complications as gestational diabetes and preeclampsia/eclampsia. The prenatal history should seek to uncover any abnormal results from diagnostic studies done during pregnancy, such as amniocentesis or ultrasound studies. As with conception, the clinician will want to be attentive to any specific thoughts or concerns that the parents may have regarding the pregnancy and its relationship to the child's current problems. Some of the more common complications that can predispose an infant to a psychiatric illness will be reviewed in this section.

ALCOHOL AND OTHER DRUGS

Maternal consumption of alcohol during pregnancy can produce behavioral changes and mental retardation in the child. Of all the types of fetal damage resulting from intrauterine exposure to recreational drugs, those resulting from alcohol exposure are perhaps the best understood. Recognition of this problem is relatively recent; only since the 1970s has it been recognized that alcohol can produce characteristic developmental symptoms in the fetus. Intrauterine exposure to alcohol produces a spectrum of symptoms, collectively known as fetal alcohol syndrome. Fetal alcohol syndrome is estimated to occur in 0.3 to 1.0 of every 1,000 births, and additional children will show milder effects. Children with the syndrome frequently are seen for learning disabilities, hyperactivity, impulsivity, inattentiveness, poor judgment, and/or oppositional behaviors. Such children characteristically have growth retardation, dysmorphic features, and developmental delays along with their behavioral disturbances. Growth retardation usually persists throughout life. At birth they will be small for gestational age, and some will develop failure to thrive in infancy. The growth retardation affects height, weight, and head circumference (microcephaly). The most recognizable dysmorphic facial features include absent philtrum, thinned upper lip, hypoplastic midface, epicanthal fold, and low-set ears. On psychological testing, such children usually will have cognitive delays ranging from mental retardation to specific learning disabilities. In addition to fetal alcohol syndrome, there are milder disorders known as fetal alcohol effect and alcohol-related birth defects. With most teratogens, the first trimester is the critical exposure period; alcohol is no exception. However, any alcohol exposure, particularly the high blood levels produced by binge drinking, can damage the developing fetal brain during the second and third trimesters as well. Coles (1993) reviews fetal alcohol syndrome.

Many children with intrauterine exposure to recreational drugs are exposed to more than one drug. Since this is a fairly common occurrence, it is difficult to determine the effects of exposure to a single drug. Other than alcohol, recreational drugs associated with developmental and behaviors problems include cocaine (Plessinger & Woods, 1993) and, to a lesser extent, heroin. When evaluating a child for learning disorder, attention deficit hyperactivity disorder, or oppositional disorder, the practitioner should focus on the prenatal history for any exposure to these recreational drugs.

Medications also can be teratogens. Among the more recently discovered teratogens are isotretinoin, used in treatment of acne. Prenatal exposure to isotretinoin can result in brain malformations, thymic hypoplasia, and heart defects. Anticonvulsants such as carbamazapine and phenytoin may cause growth retardation of the fetus. Another anticonvulsant, valproic acid, is known to cause spina bifida, facial anomalies, and developmental delays in exposed fetuses. With both drugs and medications, the fetus is most at risk during the first trimester; this is unfortunate, as a woman may not be aware she is pregnant until the damage has been done. Damage to the developing brain from teratogen exposure during the second and third trimester is probably more subtle, although it undoubtedly occurs. In only a few situations can the exact mechanism of teratogenicity be specified or the critical stage of brain development identified. Behrman (1992) provides a list of other potentially teratogenic medications.

INTRAUTERINE INFECTIONS

Intrauterine infections are less of a problem now than in the past because of the availability of vaccines and sophisticated methods of early detection. TORCH is a mnemonic for the most frequent serious intrauterine infections; it stands for T—toxoplasmosis; O—other, such as syphilis; R—rubella; C—cytomegalovirus (CMV); and H—herpes. Most infants infected in utero with toxoplasma are asymptomatic; however, as many as 10% may have serious central nervous system manifestations, such as seizures. Toxoplasmosis may produce developmental disorders if symptomatic infants are not treated at birth. Congenital rubella is now a rare disorder, because the vast majority of women of child-rearing age are immune to the rubella virus as a result of natural immunity or vaccination. The characteristic symptoms of congenital rubella are the result of organ defects such as cardiac anomalies, cataracts, hearing loss, seizures, and central nervous system sequela ranging from mild learning problems to mental retardation and autism. Cytomegalovirus, like toxoplasmosis, is symptomatic in only 10% of infected infants. Its common sequela are pneumonitis, retinitis, and, in some cases, meningoencephalitis. Usually there are no significant long-term effects of congenital cytomegalovirus infections. Herpes virus infection prior to or during birth results in eye and skin lesions and, in a few cases, produces an encephalitis that may be lethal or may cause developmental delays later in life.

In most cases the symptoms of congenital infection are present at birth or during the infant's first year of life and are readily observable; thus, when it does occur, a record of congenital infection normally will be available in the medical history of a child with a developmental or psychiatric problem. Complications that are most likely to have developmental and psychiatric consequences are hearing impairment and visual impairment. Behavioral and cognitive delays also may be the result of congenital infections. Sever et al. (1992) provide a review of TORCH infections.

MATERNAL CONDITIONS — MEDICAL COMPLICATIONS

Several maternal conditions during pregnancy can present special risks to the developing fetus and may be correlated with developmental delays. Among the most important are preeclampsia and congenital diabetes. Preeclampsia occurs in 8 to 10% of pregnant women. It is recognized by elevation in blood pressure and proteinuria, usually during the third trimester. There is a risk of early delivery, but timely recognition and treatment generally lead to a favorable outcome. If poorly controlled, preeclampsia may progress to severe preeclampsia or eclampsia (convulsions and/or coma), which may result in prematurity and/or delivery of a low-birthweight baby. Preeclampsia is reviewed in Rudolph, Hoffman, and Rudolph (1996).

A percentage of women enter pregnancy with active diabetes or develop diabetes during pregnancy. Uncontrolled hyperglycemia during pregnancy results in fetal hyperglycemia and hyperinsulinism, leading to both an increase in fetal body size and abnormalities in organ development. Possible fetal complications include cardiomyopathy, congenital anomalies, and neural tube defects. Because of their size and organ dysmaturity, these large infants are at high risk of birth and perinatal complications, including asphyxia, hypoglycemia, and hypocalcemia. In the past, with no treatment, gestational diabetes commonly resulted in brain damage and poor psychomotor development related to birth trauma. However, attention to maintenance of a normal glucose level throughout pregnancy can eliminate these problems almost completely. When not properly controlled, maternal hyperglycemia in the second and third trimesters may result in ketone body formation, which is strongly correlated with abnormal neonatal behavior, poor infant development at 2 years, and low intellectual performance at 4 years. Maternal diabetes and its effects on the fetus are thoroughly reviewed in Rudolph, Hoffman, and Rudolph (1996).

Many factors lead to growth retardation in utero, resulting in a fetus that is small for gestational age (SGA). SGA can be defined in 2 ways. The most stringent includes infants who are at least 2 standard deviations below normal gestational weight (roughly the lowest 5%). A more relaxed and inclusive standard focuses attention on the lowest 10%. However, most morbidity is confined to infants who fall into the first or stringent category. A cohort of such infants was followed for 8 years; 25% were found to exhibit symptoms of minimal brain dysfunction (hyperactivity, short attention span, poor fine motor coordination, and learning disabilities), and 30% had speech defects. These problems were not predicted by other risk factors but were predictable solely on the basis of low weight for their gestational age. Rudolph, Hoffman, and Rudolph (1996) provide additional information on SGA.

A great diversity of factors can lead to growth retardation; among the preventable ones, smoking is by far the most important. Other factors include poor nutrition, hypertension, drug addiction, chromosomal defects, dysmorphic syndromes, infections, metabolic disorders, multiple gestation, chronic illness, hypoglycemia, placental problems, and environmental toxins. However, regardless of the factors at work, the timing of growth retardation seems to be critical, with earlier effects being most persistent. For instance, slowing of fetal head growth before 34 weeks' gestation is associated with short stature but normal developmental status, while slowing of head growth before 26 weeks is associated with poor motor and performance skills as well as short stature.

Delivery History

Today, delivery is usually an uncomplicated experience to be celebrated by both the parents and the extended family. Yet despite the medical advances that have removed much of the anxiety from childbirth, there are still some perinatal complications that can have an effect on the infant on into childhood. These complications include premature delivery and fetal distress due to a variety of factors.

Prematurity has been defined in a number of ways. For our purposes it is defined as gestation of less than 37 weeks or a birthweight of less than 2,500 grams (5.5 pounds). Innovations in neonatal medicine have enabled premature infants as young as 24 weeks to survive. With many more premature infants surviving, some are presenting with developmental and psychiatric disorders secondary to complications related to their prematurity. For instance, follow-up studies of premature infants born at 26 weeks or later, weighing 1,000 to 1,500 grams (2.2 to 3.3 pounds) revealed that, by 3 years of age, 80% were normal, about 5% had developed cerebral palsy, and 10% had developmental delays. Some mechanisms of central nervous system damage are reasonably well understood. For instance, cerebral palsy and developmental delays frequently are due to intraventricular hemorrhage. Premature infants can develop visual impairments secondary to retinopathy of prematurity. This retinopathy is caused by the toxic effects of oxygen treatment. A further 1 to 3% of premature infants will have a hearing impairment as a result of severe hypoxic encephalopathy, persistent pulmonary hypertension, ototoxic drugs, or some combination of these. Thus prematurity, especially extreme prematurity, is a recognized risk for hearing impairments, visual impairments, developmental delays, and cerebral palsy. Rudolph, Hoffman, and Rudolph (1996) and Escobar, Littenberg, and Petitti (1991) provide more information on prematurity.

Modern medicine has developed many techniques for monitoring, preventing, and managing fetal distress. Fetal distress usually takes the form of hypoxia and circulatory instability. It may occur prior to birth, due to placental insufficiency, or during delivery. A major concern is that untreated fetal distress will result in brain impairment manifesting itself as cerebral palsy, mental retardation, or other developmental and behavioral abnormalities in the child. In the obstetrical history the term *normal spontaneous vaginal delivery* frequently is used to indicate that there was no deviation from the natural course of events. However, often some medical intervention is performed to aid the delivery or to treat potential fetal distress. For example, pitocin is used to induce labor if it is taking too long or if the dates are postterm. Forceps and vacuum extraction also are used to quicken the pace of the last stage of delivery; they may be used if fetal distress is a concern or if difficult and prolonged. About 15% of deliveries require cesarean section. Indications for cesarian section are fetal distress necessitating emergency delivery, as for example in the case of abruptio previa. Cesarian sections also are performed for breech positions, failed induced deliveries, or if there is a previous history of cesarian section. Obstetrical practices differ, and so even when a history is positive for nonspontaneous delivery, it may be impossible to determine the seriousness of these events without the actual delivery room records. Behrman (1992) provides a more extensive review of fetal distress and its causes.

Fetal asphyxiation often results in meconium-stained amniotic fluid. Asphyxiation apparently stimulates the fetus to pass meconium into the amniotic fluid; in severe cases, the fetus may gasp and aspirate the meconium. When an infant is born with stained amniotic fluid, there is risk of aspiration unless fluids are sucked from the pharynx prior to baby's first breaths. If meconium is not removed in time, meconium aspiration pneumonia may result. About 10 to 20% of births after 34 weeks' gestation are notable for meconium staining, but only a small percentage of these result in aspiration. When it occurs, aspiration of meconium is a clinically weighty matter for both preterm and term infants, as witnessed by the fact that 80% of preterm infants with meconium aspiration show evidence of previous intrauterine infection and about 80% of term infants with aspiration show evidence of undernutrition. Most infants with meconium present at birth do not aspirate, and these infants develop normally. Behrman (1992) provides a more complete discussion of meconium aspiration.

Apgar scores are measurements of motor activity, grimace from nasal catheter, skin color, heart rate, and respiration rate recorded at birth usually at 1 minute postdelivery and again at 5 minutes postdelivery. The scores are on a scale of 0 to 10, and they usually represent the degree of infant hypoxia and acidosis. Low scores of 0 to 3 are strongly correlated to the need for immediate infant resuscitation. There is, on the other hand, little correlation between Apgar scores and later appearance of developmental and psychiatric disorders. Cerebral palsy, a disorder that historically has been associated to birth asphyxia, is only slightly correlated with low Apgar scores. There are many children with cerebral palsy who had normal Apgar scores (8 to 10), and many normal children who had Apgar scores between 0 to 3. Thus Apgar scores provide only minimal predictive information for developmental and psychiatric disorders. Rudolph, Hoffman, and Rudolph (1996) review prenatal asphyxia studies.

Conclusion

The problem of directly linking prenatal and perinatal events to child psychiatric diagnoses remains both difficult and uncertain. Nonetheless, some useful insights have emerged. In the case of fetal alcohol exposure, there is a well-documented correlation between exposure to alcohol and fetal neurological damage. Most cases of this syndrome seem to be associated with chronic or binge drinking; however, because the precise pattern is unknown in all cases, minor alcohol consumption during pregnancy is discouraged. Regarding the effects of other recreational drugs on the fetus, serious cocaine abuse has been associated with hyperactivity. With teratogenic medications, sometimes very specific correlations can be made, such as those between growth retardation and neural tube defects in fetuses exposed to anticonvulsants. Fetal and congenital infections may produce long-term consequences, but the fetal effects of infection usually are recognized and treated at birth and seldom surface unsuspected at a later time. Congenital infection is most likely to be manifested as damage to vision and hearing, but cognitive delays are also possible. Similarly, the fetal effects of maternal disease, such as preeclampsia/eclampsia or gestational diabetes, almost always are recognized at birth. Fetal involvement is recognized as growth retardation, prematurity, abnormally high or low birthweight, or abnormal organ development. Babies who experience growth retardation in utero or who have low birthweight are clearly at increased risk of developmental abnormalities, and the risk of abnormalities increases with increasing degrees of prematurity or growth retardation.

A thorough psychiatric history should allow the clinician to identify the most important genetic, prenatal, and obstetric events. Even when there is no obvious event in the prenatal and delivery history to suggest the etiology of a child's disorder, a discussion with parents on the uncertain state of knowledge in this area is an important part of parent education.

REFERENCES

Behrman, R. E. (1992). *Nelson textbook of pediatrics* (14th ed.). Philadelphia: W. B. Saunders.

Coles, C. D. (1993). Impact of prenatal alcohol exposure on the newborn and the child. *Clinical Obstetrics and Gynecology, 36,* 255–266.

Escobar, G. J., Littenberg, B., & Petitti, D. B. (1991). Outcome among surviving very low birthweight infants: A meta-analysis. *Archives of Disease in Childhood, 66* (2), 204–211.

Lotspeich, L. J., & Ciaranello, R. D. (1993). The neurobiology and genetics of infantile autism. In R. Bradley (Ed.), *International review of neurobiology* (pp. 87–129). New York: Academic Press.

Plessinger, M. A., & Woods, J. R. (1993). Maternal, placental and fetal pathophysiology of cocaine exposure during pregnancy. *Clinical Obstetrics and Gynecology, 36,* 267–277.

Rudolph, A. M., Hoffman, J. I. E., & Rudolph, C. D. (1996). *Rudolph's pediatrics* (20th ed.). Stamford, CT: Appleton and Lange.

Sadler, T. W. (1995). *Langman's medical embryology* (7th ed.). Baltimore, MD: Williams & Wilkins.

Sever, J. L., Ellenberg, J. H., Ley, A. C., Madden, D. L., Fuccillo, D. A., Tzan, N. R., & Edmonds, D. M. (1992). Perinatal TORCH infections identified by serology: Correlation with abnormalities in the children through 7 years of age. *International Journal of Epidemiology, 21,* 285–292.

Thompson, M. W., McInnes, R. P., & Willard, H. F. (1991). *Thompson & Thompson: Genetics in medicine* (5th ed.). Philadelphia: W. B. Saunders.

---

35 / Neonatal and Infancy History

Klaus Minde

The detailed exploration of the developmental history of our patients' very early lives is important for a number of reasons. Early biological insults often affect the later motor, cognitive, and socioemotional functioning of a child; the awareness of such traumata may allow the clinician to link past events with presenting concerns (Casaer, de Vries, & Marlow, 1991; Minde, Perrotta, & Hellmann, 1988).

The period of infancy also stands out as an especially decisive part of a child's life since it is at that time that the representations or fantasies the parents-to-be have about their future children meet the reality of the "baby as is" and need to be dealt with (Brazelton & Cramer, 1990). The interpretations given the events of this period are often crucial for an understanding of the inner workings of a particular set of parents or a specific family. For example, in a study of very prematurely born twin infants, Minde, Perrotta, and Corter (1982) found that at 2 weeks of age, some 85% of all parents had developed a preference for 1 of their infants. Although the infants at that time weighed only approximately 1,200 grams, their parents had already decided which of the twins was going to be a survivor or a success in life (e.g., a professor) and who would be a loser (e.g., a thief). More important, in more than half of the cases these early judgments remained unchanged during the ensuing 4 years; indeed, they were associated with significant differences in parental behaviors toward the children and in the number and type of behavioral difficulties these youngsters showed at age 4 (Minde et al., 1989).

Finally, discussing the beginnings of an infant's life usually touches on strong memories within parents. The birth and the early weeks of a baby's life that follow usually cause highly significant transactions within a family's development; these, in turn, are important determinants for the quality of the later parent-child relationship. In our experience, the sharing of such memories is often much valued by parents and can significantly aid the consolidation of a collaborative relationship between the clinician and the patient's families. In fact, it is very useful to allow parents to give the clinician a detailed narrative of the birth and early weeks of the identified patient. For example, the clinician can inquire how mother knew that it was time to go to the hospital, who brought her there, how was she received by the hospital staff, what the obstetrician or pediatrician said about the baby at the time of birth, and so on.

Taking the History

Overall, the developmental history includes a detailed exploration of all developmental aspects of the young child's life—his or her biological, cognitive, and socioemotional milestones, early behavioral organization, degree of individuation, special strengths and vulnerabilities as well as responses to previous stresses.

PHYSICAL, COGNITIVE, AND EMOTIONAL MILESTONES

See Table 35.1. Here the clinician seeks to learn when the child first sat alone; could stand, walk, or ride a tricycle; showed a first smile; evidenced the first recognition of self as a separate person; displayed stranger anxiety; became aware of self

as being a boy or girl; when he or she began to use the form "I" when talking about self; and when he or she first seemed to respond to the feelings of others.

Norms for milestones today are understood in a more flexible manner than was true in the past. For example, parents should be told that children are expected to roll over between 2 and 5 months, sit by self from 5 to 7 months, stand alone for 2 seconds between 10 and 12 months, and walk well between 11 and 14 months. The ability to talk is likewise subdivided by asking caregivers when the infant could say 1 or 2 intelligible words (9 to 14 months), had a vocabulary of 6 words (13 to 20 months), could construct a short sentence such as "mommy come here" (18 to 24 months) and could name 1 color (27 to 42 months).

In terms of emotional milestones, stranger anxiety appears from 6 months onward and decreases after age 12 to 15 months. However, infants vary

TABLE 35.1

Milestones in Infancy

Behavior	Age Range (months)	Average Age (months)
Sits with support	1–5	2.3
Sits alone 30 seconds	5–8	6.0
Stands up holding to furniture	6–12	8.6
Stands alone	9–16	11.0
Walks alone	9–17	11.7
Walks up stairs alone with both feet on each step	18–30	25.1
Laughs	1–4	1.6
Imitates speech sound	3–8	5.0
Combines syllables	5–9	6.2
Says 3 words	11–18	13.4
Combines words	17–25	19.5
Regards own hands	1–4	2.2
Feeds self	5–7	5.8
Waves bye-bye	6–14	7.7
Helps in house	12–14	14.1
Washes and dries hands	19–36	21.0

greatly in the intensity of this special fear, and some show virtually no stranger anxiety at any time during infancy.

By 15 to 18 months, children recognize themselves in the mirror and know who they are. They will show this by trying to rub a red mark off their nose if it has been placed there before they looked in the mirror. By that time they also develop a sense of their gender, which in turn allows them to begin to explore how boys and girls differ, both anatomically and in their social roles. Hence the physical and cognitive milestones cited later always should be interpreted within the whole perspective of the child.

What is the significance of achieving a specific milestone earlier or later than other children of the same age? In general, the clinician should be concerned about major delays (e.g., a child who does not yet walk at 20 months) but be cautious in interpreting the early attainment of a biological or cognitive milestone as a sign of superior intelligence. As will be recalled, there is virtually no correlation between the overall motor developmental achievement of an infant and his or her intelligence later in life. However, serious delays that cannot be traced to specific deprivations, such as hospitalization or foster home placement, may well indicate global intellectual delay.

EARLY BEHAVIORAL ORGANIZATION

The concept of early behavioral organization is based on the recognition that infants show individual differences in the way they regulate their state (i.e., activity pattern, breathing, startle responses, etc.). Some infants can calm themselves easily from birth onward and early in life develop regular patterns of sleeping, eating, or affective organization. Others appear to have difficulty in processing sensations (inflow) or motor output (outflow) and remain disorganized without sensitive handling (De Gangi, DiPietro, Greenspan, & Porges, 1991). It follows that this varying ease of self-regulation can affect an infant's ability to adjust to caregivers and environment.

To assess this function, clinicians are interested in learning how the baby organizes or regulates adaptive, physiological, sensory, attentional, and motor or affective behaviors. Each of these processes can be over- or underregulated. In practice, clinicians want to know whether the infant or young child could be consoled easily and what methods have to be used to do so; whether the baby could console him- or herself and how was that achieved; what the infant's general activity level was; how regular he or she was in sleeping, walking, and eating; how adaptable or reactive the child was to new stimuli and how able to attend to his or her surroundings. A recently published diagnostic classification system for infants from 0 to 3 years, published by the National Center for Clinical Infant Programs (1994) has provided clinicians with a good outline for assessing the regulatory functions of young children.

INDIVIDUATION OVER TIME

The degree of individuation the child has shown over time involves his or her general level of perceived independence and involvement with other adults, siblings, and other peers.

SPECIAL STRENGTHS AND VULNERABILITIES

A child's special strengths and vulnerabilities may relate to individual gifts or talents, such as being musical or particularly well coordinated, or liking to be with people. This area also encompasses specific temperamental traits such as extreme shyness, a vulnerability to specific physical illnesses, and taking much time to adjust to novelty, such as changes in routines, a new house, or new people.

RESPONSE TO PREVIOUS STRESSES

Prior stresses would include medical illnesses or hospitalizations, a brief parental absence, or the death of a sibling. In all these cases, clinicians also would want to know how caregivers have supported the infant and the effect this has had on the child's competence.

Each of these factors have been shown to contribute to the later social and cognitive competence of children, as exemplified in studies by Werner and Smith (1982), Bornstein and Sigman (1986), and Chess and Thomas (1989). For example, children with an easy temperament and good behavioral organization seem to have a far easier time withstanding adverse socieoeconomic conditions, especially if at the same time they have a close relationship with one or more adults (Werner & Smith, 1982). Likewise, there is now good evidence that the ability to maintain good attention to environmental stimuli in early infancy significantly predicts later intellectual functioning (Bornstein & Sigman, 1986), whereas the date of achieving specific motor milestones does not correlate with later intelligence. Finally, the clinician often can use the developmental history to assess the impact particular environmental events may have had on the infant's growth and development. For example, the association of a developmental regression with the birth of a sibling or with mother's return to work can provide important clues about the strengths and vulnerabilities of a family

and may help the clinician to choose a more appropriate intervention later on.

The clinician may wonder how comprehensive a list of milestones should be obtained from the family. This depends somewhat on the nature of the child's problem. If a parent is concerned about the youngster's overall ability to play and get along with other children, the clinician initially may spend less time on the basic motor and cognitive milestones and more time in elucidating data pertaining to the child's emotional development. If the child has trouble learning, a closer scrutiny of cognitive milestones is obviously in order.

More detailed information regarding the developmental evaluation of infants and their families can be found in Chapter 59.

REFERENCES

Bornstein, M., & Sigman, M. (1986). Continuity in mental development from infancy. *Child Development, 57,* 251–274.

Brazelton, T. B., & Cramer, B. G. (1990). *The earliest relationship.* Reading, MA: Addison-Wesley.

Casaer, P., de Vries, L., & Marlow, N. (1991). Prenatal and perinatal risk factors for psychosocial development. In M. Rutter & P. Casaer (Eds.), *Biological risk factors for psychosocial disorders* (pp. 139–174). Cambridge: Cambridge University Press.

Chess, S., & Thomas, A. (1989). Issues in the clinical application of temperament. In G. A. Kohnstamm, J. E. Bates, & M. K. Rothbart (Eds.), *Temperament in childhood* (pp. 377–386). New York: John Wiley & Sons.

De Gangi, G. A., DiPietro, J. A., Greenspan, S. I., & Porges, S. W. (1991). Psychophysiological characteristics of the regulatory disordered infant. *Infant Behavior and Development, 14,* 37–50.

Minde, K. K., Perrotta, M., & Corter, C. (1982). The

effect of neonatal complications in same-sexed premature twins on their mother's preference. *Journal of the American Academy of Child Psychiatry, 21,* 446–452.

Minde, K., Perrotta, M., & Hellmann, J. (1988). Impact of delayed development in premature infants on mother-infant interactions: A prospective investigation. *Journal of Pediatrics, 112,* 136–142.

Minde, K., Goldberg, S., Perrotta, M., Washington, J., Loijkaset, M., Corter, C., & Parker, K. (1989). Continuities and discontinuities in the development of 64 very small premature infants to 4 years of age. *Journal of Child Psychology and Psychiatry, 30,* 391–404.

Werner, E. E., & Smith, R. S. (1982). *Vulnerable but invincible: A longitudinal study of resilient children and youth.* New York: McGraw-Hill.

Zero to Three: Diagnostic Classification of Mental Health and Developmental Disorders of Infancy and Early Childhood. (1994). National Center for Clinical Infant Programs. Washington, DC.

36 / Preschool History

Klaus Minde

The developmental history of the preschool period follows the same format as that used for infants. Thus, the clinician is interested in exploring the biological, cognitive, and socioemotional aspects of the patient's development.

Nevertheless, some developmental achievements at this stage of life are particularly relevant for the later psychosocial functioning of the child and, for this reason, deserve especially detailed exploration.

Possibly the most important developmental event during the preschool years is the almost simultaneous onset of locomotion and symbolic representation, both in play and language, which occurs during the second and third year of life. These new skills offer toddlers novel opportunities for exploration and experimentation. Children now can decide on their own when and where to go, and they can argue with their parents if the adults try to interfere in their activities (Mahler, Pine, & Bergman, 1975). The challenge for the child is to consolidate this new freedom without losing the feeling of security that the parental presence provides (Lieberman, 1992). This can be a difficult task as it involves 2 basic motivational systems, attachment and exploration (Bowlby, 1982). While the freedom to explore is enhanced by a secure attachment to the primary caregivers, overconfidence also can easily lead to frustration, anxiety, a sense of failure, and sometimes, to danger and injury. For this reason, it is the parents' task to balance their protective behaviors with those of "letting go" in such a way as to allow the child to explore the world without fear. Thus children should be encouraged to become autonomous and independent yet retain the sense that they are protected and nurtured by those who care for them. The clinician should inquire about these issues and note how parents taught their children this interpersonal approach to reality—helped them to develop patterns of compromise and priorizing that leave them with the ability to "give and take" for the sake of an important relationship.

The attainment of a capacity for compromise and mutuality often is helped by further aspects of development that become evident at that time. During the third year, we see a definite decrease in children's undirected aggression and a concomitant increase in their prosocial behaviors (Cummings, Hollenbeck, Iannotti, Radke-Yarrow, & Zahn-Waxler, 1986). Thus, 3-year-old children fight less than those age 2, because now they are able to put themselves into someone else's shoes, that is, they can experience empathy (Maccoby, 1980). This is particularly likely to be noted in the home, but it also occurs with friends and strangers.

The clinical relevance of these new cognitive constructs and the associated developmental changes cannot be overemphasized. (See Table 36.1 for a list of more concrete milestones for the preschooler). On the one hand, this new ability enables children to be concerned about others and is an important prerequisite for establishing mutually satisfying relationships later in life. On the other hand, delays and distortions in the development of empathy often provide the first clues about possible defects in the capacity of a youngster to modulate affect or aggression and tell the clinician a great deal about the strategies some caregivers used in directing their children along the path toward socialization.

Finally, their increasing autonomy also allows children more opportunities to compensate for problematic caregivers, since children now often attend nursery school, have friends in the neighborhood, and may spend time with other adults. The degree to which such relationships can compensate for difficulties between parents and their children is not clear, although there is good evidence that a positive school experience can ameliorate early cognitive deprivation or unsatisfactory caregiving relationships (Rutter, 1989).

An important aspect of this compensatory ability has to do with the preschooler's new cognitive and language achievements. During the third year, children realize that they cannot do and be

TABLE 36.1

Milestones from 2 to 5 Years

Behavior	Age Range (months)	Average Age (months)
Throws ball over head	17–34	19.5
Balances on each foot 2 seconds	33–50	37.0
Goes downstairs alternating feet	36–48	38.0
Speech all understandable	24–54	28.0
Understands 4 prepositions	36–62	39.0
Uses 3 to 4-word sentences	36–48	41.0
Understands prepositions	33–58	39.0
Knows 3 adjectives	36–66	40.0
Puts on shirt	27–40	31.0
Can brush teeth alone	30–58	37.0
Plays board or card games	32–57	38.0
Draws a person with 6 parts	48–66	60.0

everything. Thus they cannot run as fast as Mom and Dad, and they are unable to have a penis and give birth to a baby at the same time. On the other hand, their ever-increasing control over their body and the associated toilet training gives them a far more solid sense of their own separateness. As they now also understand a great deal of what others tell them, and as their own speech becomes increasingly understandable, they become capable of learning how to negotiate with peers or parents to tackle everyday problems.

Despite these cognitive advances, however, for the preschooler, parents and other caregivers remain the most important sources of support and security. Parents must pay attention to how the child may be feeling and must put these feelings into words to build a solid road to their eventual partnership. Preschoolers also should be secure in knowing about their parents' basic positive regard for them, as this provides them with the needed solid base on which they can build their relationship with the world. This and other challenges of toddlerhood have been vividly described by Lieberman (1993).

In practice, these considerations mean that the clinician should inquire about the toddler's sense of exploration and affect. For example, does a child staying close to mother show a restriction in the range of exploration as well as a constriction of affect?; or does he or she show general recklessness and get into accidents? How does he or she approach the task of toilet training? Does a child empathize with other children or animals (e.g., on *Sesame Street* or in the nursery)? Is a child oversolicitous of the mother, suggesting a need to comply so as to ensure her presence and continuing care?

Compensating factors also can show themselves in the interplay between the child's temperament and his or her caregiving environment. Evidence suggests that early on, active and outgoing children may be seen as problematic by their parents, as they require more direct care and parental structuring. As a result, however, when they enter school, they will experience more socializing activities from adults around them and end up showing more prosocial behaviors than less active children (Manning, Heron, & Marshall, 1978).

The clinician who takes a developmental history at any age must be aware of the internal representations parents have formed about any of their children's achievements or abilities (Zeanah & Anders, 1987). Thus it is important to inquire whether parents saw a child's temper tantrums as deliberately staged performances to make them angry, or whether they could acknowledge the tantrums to be a reflection of the struggles their child had in consolidating a sense of independence and attachment. The parents' personal history often can help here. For example, mothers who were abused during childhood may anticipate a similar fate for their children, and, as a consequence, will not permit them to engage in normal exploratory behaviors. Such ingrained parental attitudes are powerful determinants of children's future development and often are a primary target of later treatment efforts.

In summary, toddlerhood heralds the beginning of formal socialization. Along with that, it often gives evidence of the first clinical signs of a dysfunctional relationship between children and those around them. For more information regarding the developmental evaluation of preschoolers and their families, see Chapter 59.

REFERENCES

Bowlby, J. (1982). *Attachment and loss. II: Attachment* (2nd ed.). New York: Basic Books.

Cummings, E. M., Hollenbeck, B., Iannotti, R., Radke-Yarrow, M., & Zahn-Waxler, C. (1986). Early organization of altruism and aggression: Developmental patterns and individual differences. In C. Zahn-Waxler, E. M. Cummings, & R. Iannotti (Eds.), *Altruism and aggression: Biological and social origins* (pp. 165–188). Cambridge: Cambridge University Press.

Lieberman, A. F. (1992). Infant-parent psychotherapy with toddlers. *Development and Psychopathology, 4,* 559–574.

Lieberman, A. F. (1993). *The emotional life of the toddler.* New York: Free Press.

Maccoby, E. (1980). *Social development.* New York: Harcourt Brace Jovanovich.

Mahler, M. S., Pine, F., & Bergman, A. (1975). *The psychological birth of the human infant: Symbiosis and individuation.* New York: Basic Books.

Manning, M., Heron, J., & Marshall, T. (1978). Styles of hostility and social interactions at nursery, at school, and at home. In L. A. Hersov, M. Berger, & D. Shaffer (Eds.), *Aggression and antisocial behaviour in childhood and adolescence* (pp. 29–58). Oxford: Pergamon Press.

Rutter, M. (1989). Pathways from child to adult life. *Journal of Child Psychiatry and Psychology, 30,* 23–52.

Zeanah, C. H., & Anders, T. F. (1987). Subjectivity in parent-infant relationships: A discussion of internal working models. *Infant Mental Health Journal, 8,* 237–250.

37 / History of School-Age Children

Robert A. King

In taking a clinical history, the clinician strives to obtain a picture of the child's problems over time. The goal of this effort is to understand the symptoms' meaning and function in relation to the factors in the child and environment that influence them (Cox & Rutter, 1985). A given symptom, such as a temper tantrum, act of theft, or hallucination, may have quite disparate meanings, functions, and clinical implications in different children (Freud, 1965). To draw the necessary distinctions, the interviewer must assess the antecedent circumstances, immediate precipitants, behavioral concomitants, and consequences of the problem behavior as well as the broader developmental and family context in which the symptoms occur. Thus, beginning with the initial contact, history taking and diagnostic formulation are reciprocal rather than separate processes. The clinician continually formulates and tests tentative hypotheses that guide the questions and diagnostic possibilities to be explored in the interview; in turn, the parents' and child's responses shape the clinician's evolving differential diagnosis. As a result, it is not possible to specify a universally applicable algorithm for history taking. The specific sequence and focus of inquiry will vary with the nature of the presenting symptoms and the details of the individual case. Clinical experience and judgment guide the decision as to both which screening questions are most effective in determining whether significant difficulties or vulnerabilities are present in given areas and where further inquiry is indicated.

In taking a developmental history, it is important for the clinician to inquire about the child's strengths, talents, and areas of superior adjustment as well as his or her difficulties and vulnerabilities. This approach conveys the clinician's wish to understand and appreciate the child as a whole person. By thus supporting the parents' and child's self-esteem, the clinician may help reduce the often unspoken anxiety (and attendant defensiveness) that only bad things will be discovered. (See Chapters 31 and 60.) Furthermore, in addi-

This chapter is adapted in part from R. A. King et al. (1995), Practice parameters for the psychiatric assessment of children and adolescents. *Journal of the American Academy of Child and Adolescent Psychiatry, 34* (10), 1386–1402.

tion to promoting the nascent therapeutic alliance with family and child, it is an essential part of diagnostic formulation and intervention planning to amass information about factors that may ameliorate or compensate for the child's areas of vulnerability.

Sources of Information

For the school-age patient, the parents are likely to be the principal source for much of the developmental history. To begin with, the school-age child will not have reliable information concerning many aspects of the developmental or family history; in addition, however, defensiveness and lack of a mature capacity for self-observation may limit the child's ability to offer a description of his or her behavioral difficulties. On the other hand, in respect to inner feelings, subjective experiences, and attitudes, only the child can provide this uniquely important information.

Clinical experience and methodologic studies concur that parents are more likely than school-age children to report disruptive or externalizing behaviors such as restlessness, inattention, impulsiveness, oppositionality, or aggression, or certain specific symptoms such as enuresis or tics (Herjanic & Reich, 1982). Conversely, children may be more likely to report anxious or depressive feelings and symptoms (including suicidal thoughts and acts) of which the parents may be unaware (Kashani, Orvaschel, Burk, & Reid, 1985). Information from the child is essential to assess his or her feelings and attitudes about present and past events. Furthermore, the child may be the only source of information regarding certain events, such as sexual abuse.

In general, the reliability of children's reports of specific symptoms increases with age; children under 10 years of age tend to be less reliable reporters of symptoms than their parents (Edelbrock, Costello, Dulcan, Kalas, & Conover, 1985). Parents are usually more accurate reporters of chronological information than are children (Orvaschel, Weissman, Padian, & Lowe, 1981). Even when parents' and child's recollections concur, however, they may not agree with contemporane-

ous accounts of past events (such as nursery school records) (Robins, 1963; Yarrow, Campbell, & Burton, 1970).

In addition, mothers' and fathers' accounts may not always agree completely, either with each other or with those of other observers, such as teachers.

These discrepancies (termed *informant variance* in methodologic studies) may arise for a variety of reasons. Informants may differ both in the type and the amount of time they spend with the child as well as in the setting or context in which they observe the child. This is particularly important when the child's symptoms are situation-specific (occurring only at school or only at home). (When symptoms such as anxiety or hyperactivity and distractibility occur across multiple settings, they may carry a different clinical significance than when noted in only one setting [Schachar, Rutter, & Smith, 1981]). Fathers and mothers often differ in the activities and roles that they share with their child. Divorced and reconstituted families provide sources of even greater discrepancies.

Informants also differ in how they perceive or evaluate the behaviors they do observe. The experienced grade-school teacher or parent of several children has a broader normative standard against which to compare a given child's development than do the parents of an only child. Each observer's judgments regarding the child's behavior also are influenced by the biases and standards stemming from that individual's own personal, family, and cultural experiences and background. Parental psychopathology also can distort the reporting of the child's symptomatology (Jensen, Traylor, Xenakis, & Davis, 1988).

It follows, then, that disagreements or discrepancies between different informants' accounts of the child's behavior or personality do not necessarily imply that one observer is "right" while another is "wrong." Such divergences, however, do underline the importance of drawing on multiple informants to obtain a full and accurate picture of the child's past and present. Thus, information and reports from teachers, family members, and other clinicians often are essential in supplementing the information provided by parents and child. In some cases, direct observation of the child at home or in class can provide invaluable additional information.

Areas of Inquiry and Their Significance

There is no single invariant order in which to take a developmental history. In some cases, the clinician will want to elicit systematically the history and details of the chief complaint or present illness, returning only later to explore other aspects of the child's developmental history. In other cases, inquiries about the presenting complaint will lead immediately to other important areas concerning the child's or family's history and functioning. In all areas of history taking, the clinician is interested in both the objective facts of the child's development and the emotional significance of these various facets of the child's life to the parents and child.

HISTORY OF THE PRESENTING PROBLEM

With respect to each aspect of the presenting problem, it is necessary to inquire about the onset, frequency or intensity, duration, and circumstances in which the problematic behavior occurs and the attitudes of the parents, child, and others toward the problem. A systematic account of specific instances of the problematic behavior should be elicited (Cox & Rutter, 1985). The extent of functional impairment caused by the child's difficulties should be assessed by inquiring as to the degree of the child's distress, interference with social and academic activities, deleterious effects on the child's overall development, and the impact of the child's symptoms on others (Cox & Rutter, 1985).

It is also important to hear what explanations and theories (implicit or explicit) the parents and child have considered regarding the child's problems. The details of prior attempts at diagnosis and intervention should be obtained along with the parents' and child's attitude toward and responses to these interventions. It is usually helpful, with the appropriate consent, to obtain the records of such interventions or to speak directly with prior clinicians and assessors.

HISTORY OF OTHER ASPECTS OF DEVELOPMENT

In addition to focusing specifically on the presenting complaint, it is necessary to obtain a detailed history of the child's physical, cognitive, linguistic, social, sexual, recreational, and emotional development and family background. The clinician is interested in the significance of these various aspects of the child to the parents in terms of their own hopes, fears, expectations, and life circumstances. Even when parents cannot provide a precise chronology of the child's early history, they may be able to compare the child's development to that of siblings or relate it meaningfully to important family events. Particular attention should be paid to changes or discontinuities in the child's developmental progress or level of functioning.

Other chapters in this volume describe in detail the assessment of the child's perinatal and early development as well as specific functional domains. The remainder of this chapter will address the realms of development of particular importance to the school-age child.

Cognitive and School Functioning: Beginning with the preschool years, the child's pattern of cognitive strengths and weaknesses, including verbal and attentional skills, should be surveyed.

Successful participation in school requires a broad array of competencies that go beyond the cognitive, verbal, and attentional realms. These include: the ability to separate from parents and to attend school regularly, interpersonal skills with peers and teachers, motivation to learn, tolerance for frustration and delay of gratification, compliance with authority, and ability to accept criticism. Thus, in taking the child's educational history, it is necessary to address these social and emotional as well as the intellectual aspects of school participation. A sequential history should be taken of day care centers, preschools, and schools attended by the child, including the reasons for any changes.

In addition to inquiring as to the adequacy of the child's academic progress in various subject areas, it is important to investigate the child's ability to sustain concentration, exclude distracting stimuli, and persevere with classwork and homework. Executive and organizational skills, such as remembering assignments, pacing long-term projects, and remembering books and supplies, also require assessment. The child's ability to accept responsibility for his or her school work performance, rather than deflecting blame for shortcomings onto teachers, parents, or classmate, is another important dimension.

When the child's school behavior or academic progress is among the problem areas, school records, including any standardized testing, should be reviewed. Direct information gathering from the child's teachers or other school personnel is usually desirable.

Peer Relations: The quality of peer relations is an important litmus test for many aspects of the child's functioning. School-age children are sensitive (yet harsh) judges of each other's social skills, attentional and intellectual capacities, impulsivity, and control of aggression. (Experimental studies show that school-age children can distinguish between videotapes of unfamiliar age peers with and without attention deficit hyperactivity disorder and between medicated and unmedicated hyperactive children. Similarly, grade schoolers with attention deficit hyperactivity disorder are distinguished by the low level of their classmates' sociometric ratings (Whalen, Henker, Castro, & Granger, 1987)).

It is thus important to inquire as to the extent and quality of the school-age child's friendships (including age and gender preferences). What is the quality of participation in and enjoyment of informal and organized peer activities? Does he or she have one or more best friend? How do they get along? Does the child get invited and go to peers' houses for play dates, birthday parties, or sleepovers? Are the youngster's own social overtures accepted and reciprocated? What interests, activities, and personality traits does the child's circle of friends share? If the child has difficulty making or keeping friends, what are the apparent sources of this difficulty, as seen by the parents and child?

Family Relationships: The child's relationship to individual family members and his or her place in the overall family system should be assessed. It is also important to inquire about the impact of changes in the family constellation, such as births; deaths; parental separations, divorce, or remarriage; and changes in caregiving arrangements, custody, or visitation. The quality and style of parental discipline and limit-setting should be as-

sessed as well as the child's response to such interventions. How cooperative is the child and to what extent does he or she comply with family rules and expectations (implicit and explicit)? Does the child have specified chores or responsibilities (such as practicing an instrument) or an allowance?

Physical Development and Medical History: The details of the developmental history for the perinatal, infancy, and preschool years are covered in Chapters 34, 35, and 36.

Aspects of the physical developmental history relevant to the school-age child include: gross and fine motor development (especially as manifested in writing, drawing, and physical activities such as throwing, catching, bike riding, etc.); lapses in toilet training and the attendant circumstances; eating behavior and attitudes; and sleep patterns and disturbances. Precocious or lagging physical growth or signs of pubertal maturation should be noted.

Systematic inquiry should be made regarding medications, allergies, illnesses, hospitalizations, serious injuries (especially those involving the head), and operations as well as the child's reactions to these events and their impact on his or her health and activities.

Specific inquiry also should be made about the occurrence of tics, motor mannerisms or stereotypies, difficulties with hearing or vision, unusual sensory sensitivities, or alterations or loss of consciousness. All relevant medical reports should be obtained and reviewed.

Emotional and Personality Development: Assessment of this domain includes a history of the child's mood and affect regulation; style of attachment and reaction to separations; vulnerability to anxiety; and adaptability to new, challenging, or frustrating situations.

The assessment of mood elicits information about the child's prevailing mood as well as any history of periods of depression, as manifested by the developmentally relevant signs and symptoms of depression. In the school-age child, these may include irritability, listlessness, and vague somatic complaints. Although overt suicide attempts are uncommon in school-age children, inquiry should be made about the occurrence of suicidal ideation or gestures.

Specific inquiry also should be made about the presence of excessive anxiety, including its apparent initial precipitants and current evokers, degree of pervasiveness, and extent of associated distress or functional impairment. Is the child able to tolerate age-appropriate separations from the parents, such as play dates and sleepovers, or, for older school-age children, overnight camp? How does the child adapt to new or unfamiliar situations? Does the child seem excessively heedless or lacking in appropriate caution?

The occurrence of any unusual fears, excessive shyness or withdrawal, and obsessive or compulsive symptoms also should be explored. In preschoolers, some degree of rituals (especially at bedtime) and insistence on sameness is normative; however, persistence of these areas into the school years is more pathological and requires assessment (King & Noshpitz, 1991). Unusual or circumscribed preoccupations, especially when not meaningfully shared with others, also deserve further exploration. The child's regulation of aggression is a critical factor in development. Under what circumstances, if any, does he or she become angry or aggressive—or fail to display appropriate anger? What form does it take, and what are its consequences for the child in terms of his or her own reaction or that of others? Does the child verbalize homicidal, suicidal, self-injurious, or self-defeating impulses? Is the child overly aggressive or too fearful of anger? If so, how has this affected his or her social relationships? Is the child cruel to pets or younger children? Is he or she deliberately destructive or involved in fire play?

By the school years, the child's temperamental style and characteristic coping patterns are usually discernable. These include such elements of behavioral style as activity level; regularity of biological functions; attitude and adaptability to new situations; intensity of reactions; predominance of positive vs. negative mood; and persistence, impulsivity, and distractibility (Chess & Thomas, 1984). It is important to assess the goodness of fit between the child's and parents' styles. The child's capacity for insight and sense of humor are also important adaptive capacities.

Development of Conscience and Values: This area of assessment examines the stage and quality of the child's moral development. Given his or her age, is the child's conscience excessively harsh, lax, or preoccupied with specific issues? Is it effective in helping the child to conform behavior to the expectations of family and society, or does the child appear to lack remorse for transgressions? Does the child display a pattern of theft, lying, dissimulating, or blaming others? Does the child express particular religious, ethical, or cultural concerns; how do they relate to the values of the family?

Although such issues loom larger in adolescence, does the child have important goals and aspirations? If so, how realistic are these and how do they relate to the family's values and expectations?

Interests, Hobbies, Talents, and Avocations: What are the child's interests and what does he or she like to do for fun alone, with peers or family members? How much television does the child watch, and what supervision do the parents provide regarding violent or overstimulating programs? Does the child have areas of special interest or talent? If so, how have these been regarded or responded to by the family, school, and peers? What impact, if any, have the child's difficulties had on his or her enjoyment and involvement in usual recreational activities?

Unusual Circumstances: Has the child been exposed to traumatic circumstances, such as sexual or physical abuse, family substance abuse, family or community violence, or natural disaster? If so, what was the nature of the child's exposure; the immediate and subsequent response of the child, caregivers, and other adults; and the risk of the child's continued exposure?

ASSESSMENT OF FAMILY AND
COMMUNITY BACKGROUND

A picture of the family and community background is essential to a complete diagnostic assessment of a child. Much of this material may emerge spontaneously in the course of exploring other issues; specific inquiry, however, also may be necessary.

Parents or Caregivers: When the child resides with his or her biological or adoptive parents, an assessment must be made of who the parents are both as individuals and as a marital and parental couple; this includes their individual and joint strengths, weaknesses, and areas of conflict or difficulty. If the child is adopted, in foster care, or residing with relatives other than the biological parents, the history and circumstances of these living arrangements must be reviewed.

Beginning with the child's conception, what

have the parents' attitudes, involvement, and re-actions to the child been? To what extent do they agree or disagree about the care and management of the child and in their hopes, fears, and expectations concerning the child? How have the parents' own developmental histories with their families of origin and subsequent experiences shaped their responses to the child?

What are the parents' ethnic and religious backgrounds, and are they a source of conflict? What language is spoken by the parents and/or by the child? Is the interviewer familiar with that language or culture and its terms relevant to the child's and family's situation?

What are the parents' education, occupation, and financial resources? Are there economic or geographical limitations that are likely to influence the intervention options available to the family?

What other immediate family members and persons live in the home, and what is their relationship to the child? What are the various boundaries and alliances within the family, and how does the child fit into the family system?

The modes and effectiveness of family communication and problem solving should be assessed. How does the family deal with issues of separation or disagreement? What is the prevailing emotional tone of the family, especially as it impinges on the patient; is it, for example, tense, anxious, critical, or supportive? Does either parent suffer from substance abuse or other psychiatric disorder? Are there episodes of violence or sexual abuse between family members? Have there been significant stresses impinging on the family as a whole or on individual members, such as moves, migration, illness, accidents, job loss, and/or legal difficulties?

Community: What is the community or neighborhood in which the family lives, and how do they relate to it? What are the family's religious and ethnic identifications? How congruent are they with the demographics of their neighborhood? What is the family's involvement with civic, community, and religious activities (and to what extent does the child participate)? What are the neighborhood's resources (e.g., recreational and academic), and what are its adverse circumstances (e.g., poverty, poor housing, high rates of crime, or urban violence)? How prevalent are the child's difficulties among other children in the community? How is this sort of difficulty or the use of mental health services regarded in the community?

FAMILY MEDICAL AND PSYCHIATRIC HISTORY

It is essential to inquire about family members' past and current history of medical and psychiatric disorders that have potential environmental or genetic consequences for the child. Examples of such disorders include, but are not limited to, psychotic and affective disorders (including suicide), anxiety disorders, tic and obsessive-compulsive spectrum disorders, alcohol or substance use, attentional deficit disorder, learning and developmental disabilities and delays, antisocial personality disorder, and metabolic and neurologic disorders. When any such disorders have been present in family members, inquiry should be made as to the impact of the symptoms or resulting hospitalization or incarcerations on the child.

OPEN-ENDED INQUIRY

Even with a detailed outline, it is not always possible to anticipate all of the relevant lines of inquiry. Therefore, often it is useful for the clinician to conclude the history taking by asking the parents and child if anything that has not been discussed would be important to know to get a full picture of who they are and of what has been giving them difficulty. Doing so provides an opportunity to introduce or explore areas that have been omitted or need further elaboration.

REFERENCES

Chess, S., & Thomas, A. (1984). *Origins and evolution of behavior disorder: From infancy to early adult life.* New York: Brunner/Mazel.

Cox, A., & Rutter, M. (1985). Diagnostic appraisal and interviewing. In M. Rutter & L. Hersov (Eds.), *Child and Adolescent Psychiatry: Modern Approaches* (2nd ed., pp. 233–248). Oxford, England: Blackwell Scientific Publications.

Edelbrock, C., Costello, A. J., Dulcan, M. K., Kalas, R., & Conover, N. C. (1985). Age differences in the reliability of the psychiatric interview of the child. *Child Development, 56,* 265–275.

Freud, A. (1965). *Normality and pathology in children.* New York: International Universities Press.

Herjanic, B., & Reich, W. (1982). Development of a structured psychiatric interview for children: An agreement between child and parent on individual symptoms. *Journal of Abnormal Child Psychology, 10,* 307–324.

Hodges, K. (1993). Structured interviews for assessing children. *Journal of Child Psychology and Psychiatry, 34,* 49–68.

Jensen, P. S., Traylor, J., Xenakis, S. N., & Davis, H. (1988). Child psychopathology rating scales and interrater agreement: I. Parents' gender and psychiatric symptoms. *Journal of the American Academy of Child and Adolescent Psychiatry, 27* (4), 442–450.

Kashani, J. H., Orvaschel, H., Burk, J. P., & Reid, J. C. (1985). Informant variance: The issue of parent-child disagreement. *Journal of the American Academy of Child Psychiatry, 24,* 437–441.

King, R. A., Work Group on Quality Issues. (1995). Practice parameters for the psychiatric assessment of children and adolescents. *Journal of the American Academy of Child and Adolescent Psychiatry, 34* (10), 1386–1402.

King, R. A., & Noshpitz, J. D. (1991). *Pathways of growth: Essentials of child psychiatry, Vol. 2: Psychopathology.* New York: John Wiley & Sons.

Orvaschel, H., Weissman, M. M., Padian, N., & Lowe, T. L. (1981). Assessing psychopathology in children of psychiatrically disturbed parents: A pilot study. *Journal of the American Academy of Child Psychiatry, 20,* 112–122.

Robins, L. (1963). The accuracy of parental recall of aspects of child development and child rearing practices. *Journal of Abnormal Social Psychology, 66,* 261–270.

Schachar, R., Rutter, M., & Smith, A. (1981). The characteristic of situationally and pervasively hyperactive children: Implications for syndrome definition. *Journal of Child Psychology and Psychiatry, 22,* 375–392.

Whalen, C. K., Henker, B., Castro, J., & Granger, D. (1987). Peer perceptions of hyperactivity and medication effects. *Child Development, 58,* 816–828.

Yarrow, M. R., Campbell, J. D., & Burton, R. V. (1970). Recollections of childhood: A study of the retrospective method. *Monographs of the Society for Research in Child Development, 35* (5), 1–83.

38 / Puberty and Adolescence

Carrie Sylvester and Sidney Weissman

Structuring the Assessment

The first step in assessing a new patient is understanding from whom, how, and why the referral was made and whether the need for assessment is urgent. For example, is the patient perceived to be a danger to self or others? If the adolescent is not the individual who first contacted you, you also will need to decide how he or she is to be engaged in the assessment. Who will inform the adolescent and/or the family that a psychiatric assessment is needed? Usually the parents or guardians tell the adolescent of the reason for the consultation and the arrangements for it. They may, nevertheless, desire guidance as to how to communicate that to their child. It is important to help parents anticipate common responses such as the idea that only "crazy" people see a psychiatrist or other mental health professional, that the aim is to lock the adolescent up somewhere, or that the parents are planning to use the consultation simply to exert control. Parents may need and/or appreciate support in communicating the need for an assessment with concepts such as seeking help to alleviate psychological discomfort or pain, trying to understand difficulties in maintaining progress in academic or other pursuits important to the adolescent, or working together to reduce family discord. For court-ordered assessments, usually the court is responsible for advising the adolescent and the family, but the clinician may have an opportunity to express exactly what he or she wishes to have communicated depending on the nature of the problem as well as the professional's role.

Parents are interviewed about their child either with or without the adolescent present. Although we explore obtaining essential information regarding an adolescent from the parent's perspective, with some, especially older, adolescents, the optimal alliance is formed by seeing them first after minimal initial contact with parents. Interviewing parents apart from their child provides as opportunity to obtain a second view of the adolescent's behavior. The interview with parents can yield important developmental information that the adolescent could not provide and additional information regarding him or her, can clarify the reason for the assessment, and can provide a check on what he or she reported. The independent interview of the parents either before or after the adolescent is not, however, simply a means of confirming the reliability of data already obtained. The parental interview also provides a powerful means to learn about the parents and the patient's family situation. It is important to note if one or both parents attend as well as reasons for attendance or absence. The clinician can learn something about the life story of each parent and learn how they relate in the interview. What is the quality of the parental alliance in working with their child (Weissman & Cohen, 1985)? Are they similarly committed to the child's care and needs? What kind of relationship do they have? Indeed, seeing the parents together is similar to an assessment in couples' therapy, but the issue is focused less on the marital relationship and more on the adolescent's behavior and the impact the parental alliance or relationship has on the adolescent. If, however, their marital relationship dominates the assessment, that information may be crucial to successful treatment planning.

Assessment of the family as a basis to proceed with the interview of the adolescent includes parental marital history. In the case of divorce, it may be necessary to see each parent separately. In

these cases, knowledge of the existence or lack of a parental alliance is crucial to planning a successful evaluation and intervention. At times, stepparents and other significant adults will need to be interviewed. If the parents are divorced, the clinician must learn about both the specifics of family living arrangements and how they were developed. In cases of joint custody, the clinician should ask how joint custody was decided and the specific living and sleeping arrangements, paying special attention to the impact on school and other activities and peer relationships.

Pubertal Onset and Growth Differences

Inquiry about the adaptation of the adolescent and family to differences in the timing of pubertal development and maintenance of normal linear growth provides an approach to learning quite a lot about the meaning of having children grow up in a particular family. As a clinician asks questions about these various issues, he or she should note the manner in which parents approach adolescent physical development. For example, are they matter-of-fact or do they seem vague and almost in denial of the changes that their child has been undergoing? Few data exist regarding the meaning of the biological events of puberty to adolescents and their parents, but available evidence suggests that the experience is viewed as both positive and negative (Offer & Schonert-Reichl, 1992).

The clinician should inquire as to whether the adolescent experienced particularly early or late onset of visible pubertal changes. How did parents respond to concerns raised by such variations in development? There is wide variation in onset of puberty; some 9-year-old girls exhibit noticeable linear growth acceleration and breast development. Boys typically have onset about 2 years later. Boys who mature early are thought to be at an advantage because height is highly valued for males in many cultures. They may, however, have a mixed experience, because later-maturing adolescents have a smoother growth curve leading to the elongated body habitus favored for men and women in many cultures (Wilson, Kraemer, & Ritter, 1987). If onset has been early for a girl, was there evidence of increased peer difficulties, greater risk for mood and anxiety difficulties, or poorer school achievement (Tobin-Richards, Boxer, & Petersen, 1983)? Were the parents aware of the difficulty that appearing different from many classmates was causing their child? Has the rounder body habitus typical of the early-maturing girl caused her to have eating difficulties (Smolack, Levine, & Gralen, 1993)?

As implied earlier and discussed in detail in Volume 3 of this *Handbook* on adolescence, a pubertal stage rather than age is clearly a more accurate reflection of the biological events of puberty. Pubertal stages can be gauged by asking about growth spurt, appearance of secondary sexual characteristics including breast development and axillary hair, and onset of menses or nocturnal emissions. The importance of this line of inquiry can be introduced by explaining that the hormonal events of puberty influence the predominant symptoms of or onset of certain disorders. For example, a recent study of the onset of panic disorder with careful pubertal staging demonstrated that rates in girls were not accounted for by increasing age but appeared related to increasing sexual maturity (Haywood, Killen, Hammer, 1992). In framing questions, the clinician should remember that adolescents who are especially immature and short in stature as well as unlike their familial growth patterns are more likely to have a history of some significant physiological insult or to be currently chronically ill. Psychological difficulties thought to be due to the difference in linear growth may be aggravated by or primarily due to stigmata of the insult or chronic illness that caused the short stature.

When asking about menarche, the clinician should take both sides of the family into account. It is common for mothers to become concerned when a daughter's pubertal development, as highlighted by this event, is different from her own, even if it is entirely consistent with numerous paternal relatives. Nevertheless, menarche at a time that is inconsistent with family history can provide a clue as to nonpsychiatric medical causes of mental disorder, such as hyperthyroidism and hypothalamic or pituitary tumors (Litt, 1983). It is well known that vigorous aerobic exercise associated with very lean body mass may delay menarche and cause early osteoporotic changes in otherwise healthy-appearing young girls. Parental information about family interests and the adolescent's early interests will help clarify whether such activities, including ballet and gymnastics, are symptomatic of an eating disorder or body-dysmorphic disorder or were selected by an emotionally healthy girl with familial later onset of puberty and the associated lean, elongated body type (Malina, 1983). Boys who become involved with wrestling or body building are also at risk for eating disorders, so gender-specific questions about growth and development should be asked.

Parents of both boys and girls should be asked about past or current concerns about variations in breast development. Boys often are quite troubled by gynecomastia and girls by significantly uneven breast development in the middle stages of puberty (Blyth, Simmons, & Bulcroft, 1981). It is more frightening to those who do not realize that gynecomastic is frequently unilateral and that although areolar enlargement persists for life, breast tissue regresses in about 18 months. Have the parents noted the adolescent trying to avoid situations where the breast development would be more apparent? Have they sought consultation if it has persisted or is interfering with important activities? The answers to these questions will give a sense of parental sensitivity to their child's developmental needs.

Relationships

RELATIONSHIPS WITH ADULTS

It is important explicitly to explore relationships with adults including parents, adult relatives with whom the adolescent has contact, teachers, employers, and any other significant adult figures. The clinician should ask who the most significant adults are and what they mean to the patient. Most normal adolescents turn to parents; disturbed adolescents tend to turn to peers (Offer, Howard, Schonert, & Ostrov, 1991). Parents serve as a major emotional buffer for most adolescents in traumatic or emergency situations (Frey & Rothlisberger, 1996). Are specific people seen as helpful with special problems, or is the same individual always selected? Such inquiry as to the quality of relationships with adults is, therefore, a basis for assessing the degree to which an adolescent is being provided with and is making appropriate use of mature supports and role models at home and in the community. A late 20th-century view of adolescent development is that a deficit in those relationships is a risk factor for psychopathology (Offer & Schonert-Reichl, 1992).

FAMILY RELATIONSHIPS

When exploring relationships with siblings, the clinician should remember that relationships with half siblings and stepsiblings also can be important in blended families. If the patient has siblings, their position in the family should be noted. Who is living in the home should be determined. Particular attention should be paid to unrelated adults or individuals who demand extra care and attention from the adolescent's parents. Whether family members such as stepsiblings or half siblings are living elsewhere and the circumstances leading to their absence from the home should be determined.

RELATIONSHIPS WITH PEERS

In dealing with peers, does the adolescent have friends? What are their ages? With what age and gender peers is the adolescent most comfortable? Are there a few exclusive relationships, or is most time spent in a group? The clinician should ascertain specifically what the adolescent actually does with friends. As with other age groups, general statements such as "I have lots of friends" can be misleading. Peers are a major source of social support during a typical adolescent's daily activities. Frey and Rothlisberger (1996) carefully studied adolescent social supports and confirmed the extensive social support network of normal adolescents. Although adults are very important, most adolescents reported having twice as many peers in their close social support network. Friends were seen as important in daily activities and social integration, but not as important as adults in times of extreme stress. Further, only about 25% of adolescents studied admitted to lacking a single confidential and reciprocating friendship. It is noteworthy that 6 times as many boys as girls said that they lacked such relationships outside of the family during adolescence. Thus, although the ex-

tent of boys' and girls' social networks were similar, boys tended to depend less on peers for intensive emotional support in their daily lives. Clinicians should assess both the extent and the quality of peer relationships with these gender differences in mind.

In discussing peer relationships the clinician should, where appropriate, explore gang/criminal involvement. If the adolescent is involved in a gang, it is important to understand his or her role in the gang's organization and the potential for criminal activity. Involvement with appropriate youth or religious groups also helps characterize the adolescent's social supports. Of course, the unique issues of each patient determine the amount of time spent exploring each type of relationship.

SEXUAL RELATIONSHIPS

Although most of the issues of sexuality are discussed privately with an adolescent patient, it is useful to ask parents if they have any concerns about their child's sexuality. Adolescence is a time of consolidation of sexual identity with regard to both sexual orientation and expression of gender identity. These issues are addressed by the adolescent in family and cultural contexts that may allow relatively open exploration or that may rigidly deny, suppress, or repress orientations or identities that are viewed as deviant or abhorrent. Having some sense of parental concerns can prove invaluable in approaching the adolescent whose parents have very strong personal views contrary to their child's identity.

Responsibilities

Children who grow through successful adolescence to have high self-esteem are the beneficiaries of accepting, involved, affectionate parents who are noncoercive disciplinarians while setting high standards (Leff & Hoyle, 1995; Maccoby, 1980). Discussing how varied responsibilities are addressed is a method of learning about parenting style and how closely it approximates that ideal. Here responsibility does not refer simply to a specific task in the home. What is important for the clinician to learn is the adolescent's ability to carry out sustained tasks that involve a number of different areas of functioning. These include school, employment, and household tasks in addition to care for siblings, offspring, other family members, or pets. In each of the areas addressed, it is useful to obtain descriptive performance data. Where appropriate, the adolescent's report can be compared to adult reports of the youth performing the same tasks. When adolescent and parent are seen together, differences in perception can be explored as well as how adolescent and parent resolve disagreements. The clinician needs to learn how the adolescent carries out the tasks in relation to their perceived appropriateness. It is also useful for the clinician to learn how the adolescent experiences each task or situation. For example, what is the meaning of school? How does the adolescent appreciate life experiences? It is essential to compare the adolescent's competency in carrying out tasks with his or her chronological and developmental ages.

School

Critical early developmental information usually is obtained from parents and includes information about genetic and perinatal factors that are related to presence of learning problems. The adolescent's experience of the current and past school settings should be discussed, with information gathered on how performance this year compares with the previous year and the impact of performance on career goals. All aspects of school performance, including attendance, evaluations, and special placement or tutoring, should be explored. The clinician should ask if anything is interfering with attendance and determine whether the adolescent is gainfully employed, including such jobs as baby-sitting and helping in a family business. Is the work interfering with homework and social development? Parental corroboration of this information is needed when an adolescent is unwilling to reveal behavior such as poor attendance or fighting in school.

Inquiries about expectations and perceptions about the junior high school and high school experience should be based on an appreciation of the difficulties quite normal adolescents encounter. Have the parents visited the adolescent's school and met with the teachers? Are school personnel aware of the adolescent's difficulties; what is their perceived attitude? The clinician must inquire about the size of classes and the number of students in the adolescent's school. Is it a public school or a private school? How selective is the school? Are there serious discipline or safety problems in the school? Is there intense academic or social competition in the school? In the United States, there has been a trend toward putting both early adolescents and those in high school in very large, impersonal, collegiate-style school environments without much critical assessment of their impact on most youngsters' developmental needs. Entry into junior high school where adolescents between 12 and 14 years of age are grouped together has been implicated in decreased self-esteem and destabilizing of self-image even in high-functioning early adolescents (Simmons, Blyth, & Van Cleve, 1979). Further, early-maturing girls have been found to adjust better when elementary school lasted through eighth grade, when they are typically 13 to 14 years old at exit, rather than when they enter junior high school in seventh grade (Blyth et al., 1981). The parents' impression of a large school as a rich resource may not match that of an adolescent, who feels unsupported in the environment (Holland & Andre, 1994).

Conclusion

Although we have addressed obtaining information from the adolescent's parents, adolescents also may be interviewed with their parents at any time during the assessment process. Medical history usually is reviewed in a joint interview, and the impact of illness is discussed in the interview of the adolescent. A joint interview is necessary when treating adolescents who are believed to be at considerable risk of harming themselves and may be helpful where there is difficulty establishing a clinical alliance with the youth. In most clinical circumstances, the clinician must not serve as an advocate of either a parent or an adolescent, and he or she must be careful to be and appear neutral in a joint interview—to function as a care provider concerned about the best interests of the adolescent patient. The joint interview addresses a number of concerns, including whether parents and adolescents have a common understanding of

the problem or of the reason the adolescent was referred for the evaluation. It also reduces the potential for distortion by or to the absent parties when presenting a plan for further evaluation or treatment.

REFERENCES

Blyth, D. A., Simmons, R. G., & Bulcroft, R. (1981). The effects of physical development on self-image and satisfaction with body-image for early adolescents. In R. G. Simmons (Ed.), *Research in community and mental health* (Vol. 2, pp. 43–73). Greenwich, CT: JAI Press.

Frey, C. U., & Rothlisberger, C. (1996). Social support in healthy adolescents. *Journal of Youth and Adolescence, 25,* 17–31.

Haywood, C., Killen, J. D., & Hammer, L. D. (1992). Pubertal stage and panic attack history in sixth- and seventh-grade girls. *American Journal of Psychiatry, 149,* 1239–1243.

Holland, A., & Andre, T. (1994). The relationship of self-esteem to selected personal and environmental resources of adolescents. *Adolescence, 29,* 345–360.

Leff, S. S., & Hoyle, R. H. (1995). Young athletes' perceptions parental support and pressure. *Journal of Youth and Adolescence, 24,* 187–203.

Litt, I. F. (1983). Menstrual problems during adolescence. *Pediatrics Review, 4,* 203–212.

Maccoby, E. (1980). *Social development.* New York: John Wiley & Sons.

Malina, R. M. (1983). Menarche in athletes: A synthesis and hypothesis. *Annals of Human Biology, 10,* 1–24.

Offer, D., Howard, K. I., Schonert, K. A., & Ostrov, E. (1991). To whom do adolescents turn for help? Differences between disturbed and non-disturbed adolescents. *Journal of the American Academy of Child and Adolescent Psychiatry, 30,* 623–630.

Offer, D., & Schonert-Reichl, K. A. (1992). Debunking the myths of adolescence: Findings from recent research. *Journal of the American Academy of Child and Adolescent Psychiatry, 31,* 1003–1014.

Simmons, R. G., Blyth, D. A., & Van Cleve, E. F. (1979). Entry into early adolescence: The impact of school structure, puberty, and early dating on self-esteem. *American Sociology Review, 44,* 948–967.

Smolack, L., Levine, M. P., & Gralen, S. (1993). The impact of puberty and dating on eating problems among middle school girls. *Journal of Youth and Adolescence, 22,* 355–368.

Tobin-Richards, M. H., Boxer, A. M., & Petersen, A. C. (1983). The psychological significance of pubertal change: Sex differences in perceptions of self during early adolescence. In J. Brooks-Gunn & A. C. Petersen (Ed.), *Girls at puberty* (pp. 127–154). New York: Plenum Press.

Weissman, S. H., & Cohen, R. S. (1985). The parenting alliance and the adolescent. *Adolescent Psychiatry, 12,* 24–45.

Wilson, D. M., Kraemer, H. C., & Ritter, P. L. (1987). Growth curves and adult height estimates for adolescents. *American Journal of Diseases of Childhood, 141,* 565–573.

39 / Temperament and Personality

Ronald Seifer

Temperament and personality as observed in children and adolescents can represent an extremely broad range of individual and social functions. The more clearly articulated domain is that of temperament, as defined in the tradition of Thomas and Chess (1977). From this perspective,

temperament is identified as the individual's behavioral style. Briefly, behavioral style refers to the way in which an individual conducts the variety of everyday activities. Aspects of success, motivation, or specific content are not of concern in the assessment and evaluation of temperament.

Temperament constructs currently are useful in both research and clinical contexts, although they are still plagued by many conceptual difficulties, including outstanding definitional issues, specific usage in clinical settings, and the place of infant behavioral style in the adaptation of developing families.

Background

The current approach to the field of temperament research may be traced back to the work of Thomas and Chess that began in the late 1950s (Thomas, Chess, Birch, Hertzig, & Korn, 1963). At that time, they attempted to define characteristics of individuals that were presumed to be important to infant and child development. This was in contrast to the prevailing environmentalism manifest in psychodynamic and learning theory approaches to development. What has set this temperament approach apart from other constitutional theories of development is that it always has emphasized the dynamic interactions ("fit") between individual constitution and developmental context. More recently, alternatives have emerged to the behavioral-style approach to temperament. The 2 most notable of these alternatives are the biobehavioral regulation approach of Rothbart and Goldsmith (Goldsmith & Campos, 1982; Rothbart & Derryberry, 1982) and the typology approach of Kagan (Kagan, Resnick, & Gibbons, 1989). Characteristics of these three approaches are described in the following text.

BEHAVIORAL STYLE

Behavioral style refers to *how* an individual behaves, in contrast to that person's *motivation, success,* or the *specific content* of the behavior. The early work of Thomas and Chess yielded 9 dimensions of temperament that continue to be widely used: activity, rhythmicity, approach (to novel stimuli), adaptability (to repeated presentations), intensity of behavior, mood, persistence, distractibility (which changes from soothability in infants to level of attention to background stimuli in older children), and threshold to stimulation. These dimensions range from simple descriptions of behavior (such as activity level) to complex descriptions of change over time in response to new situations (such as adaptability).

The basic assumptions that underlie this approach are that (1) aspects of style constitute important individual differences in behavior, (2) these behavioral styles are relatively stable over time, and (3) these stylistic aspects of behavior generalize across situations.

BIOBEHAVIORAL REGULATION

The biobehavioral approach to temperament assumes that there are 4 basic regulatory processes important in everyday interactions with one's environment: regulation of arousal, response to fear-inducing stimuli, adjustment to environmental limitations, and modulation of affect. The evaluator, then, is concerned with examining behavioral indicators of these processes. The specific behaviors observed are of interest primarily because they provide insight into otherwise non-observable internal regulatory activity (Goldsmith, 1996).

From this perspective, temperament behaviors always are interpreted in a conditional framework. That is, what are the environmental constraints operative when the behaviors were observed? This distinction from the behavioral-style perspective is important because it implies more situational specificity in the expression of temperament behaviors (Kochanska, et al., 1996).

TYPOLOGY

Many potential typologies could be applied to the domain of temperament. One approach has been to classify individual children as difficult versus easy based on the 9 Thomas and Chess dimensions (Carey & McDevitt, 1978; Thomas et al., 1963). This approach, however, is intended more as a summary of a large set of behavioral information than as a statement about the nature of individual children.

A stronger approach to temperament typology is found in Kagan's theory of behavioral inhibition (Kagan et al., 1989). Kagan asserts that there is a small group of children (10 to 20%) who exhibit a well-defined syndrome of extremely shy, inhibited behaviors in response to novel situations. Further, this behavioral pattern is strongly linked to underlying nervous system properties. Individual differences outside of this extreme range are not of interest, as the focus is on identifying individual children who fit this particular category.

Developmental Considerations

All of the different approaches to temperament share a bias that dimensions or types of temperament persist across a broad span of development. These theories are not insensitive to developmental change. Rather, they attempt to identify common processes that are manifest across different developmental periods, even though they may be expressed in vastly different specific behaviors. With 1 notable exception (Buss & Plomin, 1984), assessment batteries typically include a series of instruments that measure temperament at different points in development.

An important developmental consideration to keep in mind is that the bulk of the work in temperament has addressed the infancy and early childhood periods, with some substantial bodies of work conducted with older, school-age children. Relatively little work has been done with adolescents.

Goals and Objectives of Temperament Assessment

Within clinical practice, temperament assessments seek to understand whether behavioral-style characteristics of children shed any light on the etiology and maintenance of specific disorders. Such assessments are not well suited to the identification of diagnosable disorders as defined in current nomenclature.

Many clinical conditions have been related to variations in children's temperament (Carey, 1985). The best-known associations are the studies that have linked early temperament to later behavior problems, which are usually externalizing

in nature and of relatively mild to moderate severity (Bates & Bayles, 1988; Graham, Rutter, & George, 1973; Thomas & Chess, 1977). Temperament is also an important factor in children's school performance. Activity level, persistence, distractibility, and general difficulty have been related to IQ, grades, classroom behavior, and interaction with teachers (Keough, 1989; Martin, 1989). Behavioral inhibition has been associated with risk for anxiety disorder (Rosenbaum et al., 1988). Difficult temperament also has tended to accompany higher rates of physician visits, accidents, abdominal pain, sleep disturbance, and absences from school.

Perhaps more important than the documented relations between temperament and specific disorders is the fact that temperament is one component of family adaptation. The theoretical work of Thomas and Chess clearly indicates how temperament interacts with parental expectations and behavior to influence developmental trajectories. Relatively little empirical investigation of such transactions has been carried out, but the findings thus far do support their ideas. For example, Maziade (1989) reports that the combination of difficult temperament and dysfunctional family behavior control is a better predictor of behavioral disorder outcome than temperament alone.

Instruments and Assessment Technology

Three basic methods are used to assess temperament in infants and children: (1) parent or teacher report questionnaire, (2) direct observation of the child, and (3) structured parent interview. Obviously, the questionnaire approach is the most economical and has been the method of choice in the vast majority of work on temperament. However, serious questions about the utility of this approach have been raised. (See the discussion in the next section.) Several methods for direct observation are available for home and laboratory, but they are used mostly during the infancy and early childhood years. Parent interviews were the method used in Thomas and Chess's New York Longitudinal Study; today, however, they are chiefly of historical significance and are rarely used.

Perhaps the most widely used instruments are those developed by Carey and associates for infants (Carey & McDevitt, 1978), toddlers (Fullard, McDevitt, & Carey, 1984), and 3- to 7-year-old children (McDevitt & Carey, 1975). These instruments share in common the use of the 9 scales that were originally developed by Thomas and Chess in the New York Longitudinal Study. The questionnaires contain between 95 and 100 items each. Individual items are scored by parents on 6-point scales that range from *almost never* to *almost always*. Each individual item describes a behavior (sometimes very specific, sometimes of a more general class) and a style of response associated with that behavior; for example, "The infant accepts new foods right away, swallowing them promptly." The individual items do not specify specific time frames, specific contexts (the implicit context in most questions is the home), or detailed descriptions of behavior.

Bates and colleagues have developed the Infant Characteristics Questionnaire, a series of temperament instruments designed for use with children 6 months to 2 years of age (Bates, Freeland, & Lounsbury, 1979). The instruments contain between 24 and 32 items at the different ages. Unlike other instruments based on the New York Longitudinal Study approach, the Bates instruments do not have the same set of scales at each assessment period. The most consistent scale at all 3 ages is the one of infant difficulty. There is also some degree of overlap on scales for unadaptable (to events and people) and dull-unexcitable. Other scales measure regularity (6, 24 months), persistence (13 months), and noncuddly/unstoppable (24 months). Most individual items require parents to make generalizations about specific classes of behavior; for example, "How well does your baby typically respond to being in a new place?" The response scale is different for each item, but in all cases has 7 points that range from positive to negative types of response: for example, *very easy* to *difficult;* or *a great deal, really loves it* to *very little, doesn't like it much*. Some items on the scales specify detailed descriptions of behavior, response sets in counts of individual

behavior, or detailed description of context, but most items are of a more general nature.

Another set of instruments that are based on the New York study are the Dimensions of Temperament Surveys (DOTS), which have both parent-report and self-report versions (Lerner, Palermo, Spiro, & Nesselroade, 1982). The instruments were developed to cover the age range from preschool through college. The 5 scales on the instruments are activity level, attention span/distractibility, adaptability/approach, rhythmicity, and reactivity. The first 4 scales have labels (or combinations) that correspond with the ones on the New York study; the fifth scale contains items related to that study's dimensions of activity, intensity, and threshold. The response scale on all instruments is *true* vs. *false*. The 3 instruments (child [parent report], child [self-report], and adult [self-report]) all contain the same 34 items.

Buss and Plomin (1984) developed the EAS Questionnaire, a set of instruments to be used as a self-report (adults), teacher-report, or parent-report measure from infancy to adulthood. The EAS acronym refers to the 3 scales on the instruments: emotionality, activity, and sociability. Each instrument has 20 items, with a great deal of overlap in the 2 child instruments. The items are very general in nature, with little reference to specifics of behavior, context, or time frame; for example, "Child is very sociable." All require the informant to make broad generalizations. The items for the parent- and teacher-report instruments are scored on a 5-point scale that ranges from *not characteristic or typical of your child* to *very characteristic or typical of your child*. For the adults, the scale is the same with the referent being *you*.

Rothbart (1981) developed a parent-report scale to assess temperament in children during the first year of life. The instrument contains 87 items. Scales include activity level, smiling and laughter, fear, distress to limitations, soothability, and duration of orienting. This is the most behaviorally specific of the parent-report measures and most clearly specifies context and time frame—for example, "During the last week, how often did the baby protest being put in a confining place (infant seat, playpen, car seat, etc.)?" The items are scored by the parent on a 7-point scale of frequency ranging from *never* to *always*. Goldsmith (1987) has developed an extension for preschool-age children.

218

The common features of these questionnaires are: (1) they are parent-report measures (although some have self-report versions); (2) all require generalizations about children's behavior over a time period, although that time frame is almost always unspecified (phrases such as "usually" or "during feeding" are characteristic of the instruments rather than an emphasis on "during the past 24 hours" or "in the previous month"); and (3) they share some core constructs in common (e.g., most instruments rate activity, adaptability to people and events, and quality of affect).

Despite these similarities in approach to the problem of measuring individual differences in temperament, definite differences among the instruments influence which should be used in a specific setting. The most obvious differences are in the size of the instruments and the age groups to which they apply. The shortest instrument is the Buss and Plomin EAS, which contains 20 multiple-choice items, compared with the Carey instruments, which contain up to 100 items. In general (although there is certainly not a one-to-one correspondence), the trade-off in using shorter instruments is in decreased behavioral, contextual, and time-frame specificity. However, there is no clear evidence that the instruments with more specific items are necessarily better measures of temperament than others (Goldsmith, Rieser-Danner, & Briggs, 1991). With respect to age-appropriateness, only one family of instruments is designed to be used from infancy through adulthood—the Buss and Plomin EAS. Lerner et al.'s Dimensions of Temperament Surveys also have a wide age range but cannot be used with infants. Note that these 2 sets of instruments with large age range are both relatively small in terms of the item-set size and the number of temperament dimensions measured.

A less obvious difference in the instruments involves whether they hypothesize a single set vs. multiple sets of temperament dimensions over their specified time frame. For example, the Carey instruments and the Lerner et al.'s ones, both derived from the New York Longitudinal Study framework, determined at the outset that all forms would have the same set of scales (although the Dimensions of Temperament Survey scales do not exactly match the New York Study framework). In contrast, the Bates ICQ instruments vary from form to form on the scales in-

cluded. However, there is still a large conceptual overlap in the various versions.

OBSERVATION METHODS

Current observational methods to assess temperament require highly structured protocols and detailed scoring procedures. Garcia-Coll and colleagues report a 20-minute laboratory sequence where progressively intrusive stimuli (e.g., putting a hat on the baby, a large toy that has intense light and sound effects) are presented to 3- to 9-month-old children. Summary scores include positive, negative, approach, and inhibition (Garcia-Coll, Halpern, Vohr, Seifer, & Oh, 1992). In a similar vein, Kagan has laboratory procedures that index behavioral inhibition when challenging stimuli are presented (Kagan et al., 1989). Goldsmith and Rothbart's (1990) Laboratory Assessment Battery battery assesses fear, anger-frustration, joy-pleasure, interest-persistence, and activity. Seifer and Sameroff have developed procedures designed for use in the home during the first year of life. Multiple observations are used to derive scores for mood, approach, activity, intensity, and total difficulty (Seifer, Sameroff, Barrett, & Krafchuk, 1994). All of these observation methods are expensive to administer in terms of assessment time, laboratory space, equipment, and scoring time. Thus they are best suited to clinical or research protocols where temperament is a central concern.

Reliability and Validity of Temperament Assessments

An important consideration in deciding whether to use a specific instrument is the degree to which it has been demonstrated to measure what it claims to measure as well as the consistency of those measurements across time and across individuals. In the case of all temperament instruments, this is a nontrivial issue that is currently under much debate.

The major temperament questionnaires and laboratory assessments have good internal psychometric properties (i.e., scale reliabilities are typically 0.70 or above). Test-retest reliabilities over short periods are typically 0.50 to 0.90 for questionnaires. Direct observations of behavior generally have cross-time correlations of 0.20 to 0.50, but the time intervals in these studies are typically a month or more. A detailed review is provided by Hubert, Wachs, Peters-Martin, and Gandour (1982). Recently Seifer et al. (1994) demonstrated high reliability coefficients (0.60 to 0.80) when sets of 8 observations were aggregated.

Despite demonstrations of reliability, there is little evidence that parent reports correspond to direct observations of behavior (Seifer et al., 1994). Most studies that have compared parent reports with observations of children have been restricted to either home or laboratory settings and a time frame of a few days or a week. These studies uniformly have found small to moderate relationships between parent reports and observational measures (i.e., correlations in the 0.20 to 0.50 range). Those criticizing parent-report methods have emphasized that these observations should yield more substantial relationships with temperament instruments, while others have claimed the observations are inadequate to test the validity hypotheses.

A related issue is whether parents' reports of their children's temperaments reflect more their own concerns than their children's behavior. Those questioning the validity of parent reports have noted that measures of parental anxiety, beliefs about children in general, prenatal conceptions of their own child, or social status explain more variance in temperament measures than do observations of actual child behavior (e.g., Vaughn, Bradley, Joffe, Seifer, & Barglow, 1987). Bates and Bayles (1984) argued that parent report instruments contain both objective child behavior and subjective parent cognition components, and that these have the potential for being empirically distinguished.

Clinical Standards, Decision Making, and Intervention Strategy

Since temperament has been investigated primarily within a research context, there is little guid-

ance available with respect to the establishment of specific standards. The closest approximation to a standard is the identification of difficult children using algorithms associated with the scales on the New York Longitudinal Study. The other approaches yield only judgments based on whether individuals score toward the extreme of normative distributions or not. Thus the clinician is left with decisions based on percentile ranks rather than any demonstrated sensitivity or specificity of these identification decisions.

Results of temperament assessments are better suited to the task of intervention planning and strategy. Information about temperament obtained from questionnaires can provide information about (1) parents' or teachers' representations of individual children, (2) specific types of contexts that may be more or less well suited to an individual's behavioral style, or (3) behavioral-style components that may interfere with particular treatment options. Perhaps the best way to think about using temperament assessments in clinical settings is in a hypothesis-generating mode. In this way specific results may form the basis for planning initial interventions, which are closely monitored and updated, around issues related to children's behavioral style.

The fact that clinical utility of temperament assessments is not very advanced should not discourage clinicians from utilizing the valuable information they produce. The early stages of a person's development may be the time when temperament issues are most salient but least recognized. For example, problems with feeding or sleeping may be intimately tied to an infant's temperament. Children who are irritable, who respond strongly to novel stimuli, who respond with great intensity, or who do not adapt well over time may present difficulties for parents who are attempting to manage daily regulatory tasks. Often interventions can be offered that increase parents' awareness of the individual differences in their infant. These interventions can provide adaptive strategies for the parents that successfully ameliorate such developmental perturbations.

Likewise, specific qualities of children may create difficulties later in life. For example, children who are easily aroused and apprehensive in the face of novel situations may develop difficulties in social integration with peers or teachers in school settings. In particular, such qualities may be most problematic when children are first entering a new setting or making a transition between settings. Heightening the awareness of parents and teachers about the qualities of an individual child and providing more structured situations where children can successfully overcome their initial apprehensions can substantially improve the extent to which some temperamentally inhibited children can be integrated into larger social settings (Cameron & Rice, 1986; Carey & McDevitt, 1995).

There also have been some efforts to use information about temperament in a preventive way. Early assessment tactics were used to identify infants with temperament profiles of extreme degree. Anticipatory guidance techniques then could be used to prepare parents for difficulties that might emerge as well as to provide strategies for interacting with temperamentally difficult children.

In sum, while there is no established one-to-one connection between temperament measurement and identification of clinical cases, nor between temperament and specific treatment options, there are many ways that temperament may be applied in clinical practice. In particular, temperament may be an important variable to examine when investigating parent-child interaction problems surrounding identified child behavior or adjustment disorders.

Unresolved Problems and Issues

Two basic unresolved issues exist in the field of temperament assessment. The most critical is whether the parent-report questionnaire method provides information about actual child behavior that is in fact useful. These questionnaire data may serve as predictors of child outcome, but their predictive value may lie more in the informants' attitudes and beliefs than in the child's be-

havior. The second unresolved issue is in the area of decision making. No useful standards allow for the identification of individual children who manifest clear difficulties in the area of behavioral style.

Future Directions

Three future directions in which temperament assessment may proceed might well be of direct benefit to the clinical process. The first lies in the domain of measuring specific child behavior. One way to do that is to develop well-standardized and economically feasible methods of direct observation for application in individual cases. A second approach is to develop improved parent or teacher report methods. These must be both substantially related to actual child behavior and at the same time tend to minimize the subjective component attributable to the informant.

A second future effort will be in the area of clinical decision making. As more clinical practitioners use temperament assessments, appropriate standards will need to be developed. These will sensitively and specifically identify children who have the kinds of temperament profiles that are important to consider in the context of diagnosis and treatment.

The final future direction is in the application of family adaptation models that involve temperament and other child characteristics. Assessments of individual behavioral styles probably will prove to be of little use unless they are embedded in the family context in which they arose. The extent to which specific profiles of behavior fit in with individual families' expectations, beliefs, appraisals, affective responses, and behavioral/cognitive adaptations to those profiles will provide a much richer set of information than is currently available. This, in turn, will allow for better identification and treatment of childhood disorders.

REFERENCES

Bates, J. E., & Bayles, K. (1984). Objective and subjective components in mothers' perceptions of their children from age 6 months to 3 years. *Merrill-Palmer Quarterly, 30,* 111–132.

Bates, J. E., & Bayles, K. (1988). The role of attachment in the development of behavior problems. In J. Belsky & T. Nezworski (Eds.), *Clinical implications of attachment* (pp. 253–299). Hillsdale, NJ: Lawrence Erlbaum.

Bates, J. E., Freeland, C. A., & Lounsbury, M. L. (1979). Measure of infant difficultness. *Child Development, 50,* 794–803.

Buss, A. H., & Plomin, R. (1984). *Temperament: Early developing personality traits.* Hillsdale, NJ: Lawrence Erlbaum.

Cameron, J. R. & Rice, D. C. (1986). Developing anticipatory guidance programs based on early assessment of infant temperament: Two tests of a prevention model. *Journal of Pediatric Psychology, 11,* 221–234.

Carey, W. B. (1985). Interactions of temperament and clinical conditions. *Advances in Developmental and Behavioral Pediatrics, 6,* 83–115.

Carey, W. B., & McDevitt, S. C. (1978). Revision of the Infant Temperament Questionnaire. *Pediatrics, 61,* 735–739.

Carey, W. B., & McDevitt, S. C. (1995). *Coping with children's temperament: A guide for professionals.* New York: Basic Books.

Fullard, W., McDevitt, S. C., & Carey, W. B. (1984). Assessing temperament in one- to-three-year-old children. *Journal of Pediatric Psychology, 9,* 205–216.

Garcia-Coll, C. T., Halpern, L. F., Vohr, B. R., Seifer, R., & Oh, W. (1992). Stability and change of early temperament in preterm and fullterm infants. *Infant Behavior and Development, 15,* 137–154.

Goldsmith, H. H. (1987). *Toddler Behavior Assessment Questionnaire.* Eugene: University of Oregon Press.

Goldsmith, H. H. (1996). Studying temperament via construction of the Toddler Behavior Assessment Questionnaire. *Child Development, 67,* 218–235.

Goldsmith, H. H., & Campos, J. (1982). Toward a theory of infant temperament. In R. N. Emde & R. J. Harmon (Eds.), *The development of attachment and affiliative systems* (pp. 161–193). New York: Plenum Press.

Goldsmith, H. H., & Rothbart, M. (1990). *The laboratory Temperament Assessment Battery (Version 1.3; Locomotor Version).* Eugene: University of Oregon Press.

Goldsmith, H. H., Rieser-Danner, L. A., & Briggs, S. (1991). Evaluating convergent and discriminant validity of temperament questionnaires for preschoolers, toddlers, and infants. *Developmental Psychology, 27,* 566–579.

Graham, P., Rutter, M., & George, S. (1973). Temperamental characteristics as predictors of behavior disorders in children. *American Journal of Orthopsychiatry, 43,* 328–339.

Hubert, N. C., Wachs, T. D., Peters-Martin, P., & Gandour, M. J. (1982). The study of early temperament: Measurement and conceptual issues. *Child Development, 53,* 571–600.

Kagan, J., Resnick, J. S., & Gibbons, J. (1989). Inhibited and uninhibited types of children. *Child Development, 60,* 838–845.

Keough, B. K. (1989). Applying temperament research to school. In G. A. Kohnstamm, J. E. Bates, & M. K. Rothbart (Eds.), *Temperament in childhood* (pp. 451–462). New York: John Wiley & Sons.

Kochanska, G., Murray, K., Jacques, T. Y., Koenig, A. L., & Vandegeest, A. (1996). Inhibitory control in young children and its role in emerging internalization. *Child Development, 67,* 490–507.

Lerner, R. M., Palermo, M., Spiro, A., & Nesselroade, J. R. (1982). Assessing the dimensions of temperamental individuality across the life span: The Dimensions of Temperament Survey (DOTS). *Child Development, 53,* 149–159.

Martin, R. P. (1989). Activity level, distractibility, and persistence: Critical characteristics in early schooling. In G. A. Kohnstamm, J. E. Bates, & M. K. Rothbart (Eds.), *Temperament in childhood* (pp. 451–461). New York: John Wiley & Sons.

Maziade, M. (1989). Should adverse temperament matter to the clinician? An empirically based answer. In G. A. Kohnstamm, J. E. Bates, & M. K. Rothbart (Eds.), *Temperament in childhood* (pp. 421–436). New York: John Wiley & Sons.

McDevitt, S. C., & Carey, W. B. (1975). The measurement of temperament in 3–7 year old children. *Journal of Child Psychology and Psychiatry, 19,* 245–253.

Rosenbaum, J. F., Biederman, J., Gerstern, M., Hirshfeld, D. R., Meminger, S. R., Herman, J. B., Kagan, J., Reznick, J. S., & Snidman, N. (1988). Behavioral inhibition in children of parents with panic disorder and agoraphobia. *Archives of General Psychiatry, 45,* 463–470.

Rothbart, M. K. (1981). Measurement of temperament in infancy. *Child Development, 52,* 569–587.

Rothbart, M. K., & Derryberry, D. (1982). Theoretical issues in temperament. In M. Lewis & L. T. Taft (Eds.), *Developmental disabilities: Theory, assessment, and intervention* (pp. 383–400). New York: Spectrum Publications.

Seifer, R., Sameroff, A. J., Barrett, L., & Krafchuk, E. (1994). Infant temperament measured by multiple observations and mother report. *Child Development, 65,* 1478–1490.

Thomas, A., & Chess, S. (1977). *Temperament and development.* New York: Brunner/Mazel.

Thomas, A., Chess, S., Birch, H. G., Hertzig, M. E., & Korn, S. (1963). *Behavioral individuality in early childhood.* New York: New York University Press.

Vaughn, B. E., Bradley, C. F., Joffe, L. S., Seifer, R., & Barglow, P. (1987). Maternal characteristics measured prenatally predict ratings of temperamental "difficulty" on the Carey Infant Temperament Questionnaire. *Developmental Psychology, 23,* 152–161.

40 / Speech, Language, and Communication

Christiane A. M. Baltaxe

Adequate speech, language, and communication skills are necessary for a normal, happy life. The importance of these skills to overall well-being generally comes to light only when problems arise. Delays or impairment in speech, language, and communication can vary in severity from slight delay to a complete inability to communicate.

In order to assess a child's language abilities, the clinician must ascertain speech, language, and communication milestones and the level of linguistic function reached by the youngster, an important and integral aspect of taking a developmental history. General questions to ask relating to developmental language milestones include when the child started to talk and said his or her first words, could put 2 and 3 words together, and started to talk in sentences. When bilingualism is part of the picture, the clinician also needs to question when these languages were acquired. The parameters of their use are also important, as is the determination of the relative competency of the child in both languages (Gavillan-Torres, 1984).

Parents are generally the key source for a developmental history. The precise delineation of the child's achievement of developmental speech, language, and communication milestones depends on the parents' recollection and accuracy. Obviously recollections become dimmer as the time interval from the initial event increases. Accuracy also may be subject to such factors as parental involvement with the child, presence of other siblings, and a variety of other factors. Diaries on language behavior may be an important source in substantiating the information in the developmental history, as may videotape recordings—in particular, those where verbal interactions of the child with others are recorded. It is of interest that parents tend to be less accurate about the time the child reaches language milestones compared to motor milestones (Majnemer & Rosenblatt, 1994).

The history of the development of speech, language, and communication generally falls into one of the following patterns: normal onset and devel-

opment; delayed onset but normal patterns of development; delayed onset but deviant patterns; normal onset with subsequent loss (with or without reacquisition); and lack of language development.

Even when development is reported as normal, deficits still may exist. The reasons for this discrepancy may be that the parents are not fully aware of what constitutes normal development. In addition, certain language deficits may emerge only as the child reaches school age (Wiig & Semel, 1984).

The clinician needs to be aware that although youngsters may have serious problems with school performance and social functioning, underlying language and communication problems may go undetected for long periods of time (Cohen, Davine, Horodesky, Lipsett, & Isaacson, 1993). It may depend on the clinician's skill to interpret indirect manifestations as to whether possible delays or deficits exist. A wide range of indirect manifestations of linguistic deficits include behavioral and emotional problems, issues of self-confidence, academic failure, poor peer interaction, and having few friends. Often a communication problem exists when the parents report the child is acting up at home or in school, is too self-conscious when speaking, or is defensive or withdrawn, or acts silly when he is faced with specific linguistic demands. Poor school performance and poor grades also may be indications of a language delay or deficit. When parents or the school report forgetfulness about homework and that the child is easily distracted, it may be an indication of an underlying language processing deficit. Also, when parents report that the child does not listen, is obstinate, and does not follow directions, this may be due to their child's poor auditory processing of language.

Questions about the child's peer relationships may reveal that that youngster appears to miss social cues at home, in school, and with friends and has few or no friends. Lack of self-confidence and extreme sensitivity to task performance also may be indicators of poor communication skills

(Beitchman, Hood, Rochon, & Peterson, 1989; Cantwell & Baker, 1991; Wiig & Semel, 1984).

The clinician's first indication of a potential problem in the child's current linguistic function is a parental report of a history of no development, delayed or deviant development, or uneven acquisition of speech-language milestones. While delays and deficits in speech may disappear over time, other deficits, such as delay in reaching an appropriate level of language, deficits in the use of language in social communication, and faulty auditory processing tend to persist.

Relevant background information helps the clinician establish the relative strengths and weaknesses of the child's speech, language, and communication and identify the forces that maintain or worsen his or her linguistic skills. Early identification is the key to early intervention as well as to the prevention of other problems (Lahey, 1988). Therefore, it is crucial that the clinician understand the significance of both the direct and indirect manifestations of speech-language-communication problems as they appear in the child's history. This type of information is also crucial for intervention planning. It forms the basis for the well-based program of intervention strategies and its success. Issues include prioritizing problems identified as well as type of intervention approaches to be taken. For example, before social skills training and language intervention can succeed, a youngster with hyperactivity disorder may need pharmacological intervention to bring hyperactivity and poor attention under control.

For the clinician to identify delays and deficits in a child's speech-language-communication, he or she must:

1. Understand the differences among the components of speech, language, and communication. When delay or deficit occurs, such knowledge will help answer the question of which of the domain—speech, language, or communication—is affected and help identify those functions of a more serious nature.
2. Be familiar with a child's developmental stages of speech, language, and communication. Doing so will help answer the question of whether, when delays are present, normal or deviant steps in development have taken place. It also will help to establish the child's linguistic strengths and weaknesses.

3. Be familiar with the relationship of language function to other areas of development. Such knowledge will help answer the question of whether delays or deficits in speech, language, and communication occur in isolation or are part of a larger pattern.
4. Be familiar with risk factors that may be responsible for possible delays or impairment. The issue of risk factors addresses the possible etiology of the existing linguistic problem and may be useful in the prevention of other problems in the future.

Speech, Language, and Communication

In clinical practice and in common parlance, the terms *speech, language,* and *communication* often are used interchangeably, even though they are distinct but interrelated domains with different developmental timetables. When problems arise or are suspected, each of these 3 domains carries a different predictive value with respect to comorbidity, age, prognosis, and intervention strategies (Baker & Cantwell, 1987; Baltaxe, 1997; Baltaxe & Simmons, 1990; Beitchman et al., 1996; Beitchman, Hood, & Inglis, 1990).

Speech is the motor component of communication. Speech involves the coordination of oral neuromuscular action to produce spoken language. Speech can be defined operationally as including articulation of speech sounds, fluency of speech production, prosody—that is, the intonation and stress patterns of speech—and such vocal characteristics as voice quality, resonance, pitch, and loudness. In spoken language these parameters of speech are coarticulated.

Speech problems, for example, are likely if the parents report that the child is unintelligible, pronounces words incorrectly, sounds nasal, has a halting way of speaking, or speaks in a monotone.

Language as opposed to speech is defined as an arbitrary system of symbols and rules used as a code for representing and conveying messages. Language involves 2 major functions: reception (i.e., understanding, or receptive language) and expression (i.e., communicating, or expressive language). Specific areas of language include vocabulary and grammar and, in its silent form, reading and writing.

Language is composed of several subsystems that in child language development have separate but interrelated schedules of development. These subsystems include the phonological, morphological, semantic, and syntactic systems.

The phonological system relates to the rules governing speech sounds and their combination—for example "play" but not "lpay" in English—as opposed to the articulation of speech sounds. (Even though it is part of the language component as a system of rules, the phonological component, in clinical practice, usually is treated within the speech component underlying articulation.)

The morphological system relates to the rules governing the internal organization of words—for example, "walk-walk-ed," but not "break-breaked," "apple-apple-s," and "child-children," but not "child-child-s."

The semantic system relates to the rules governing the meaning of words and their combination—for example, "married man" but not "married bachelor," and not "colorless green ideas sleep furiously."

The syntactic or grammatical system relates to the rules governing the internal organization of sentences and their relation to each other—for example, word order in English, as in "the child ate the cake" but not "ate the cake the child."

The clinician should anticipate a language problem when the parents report that a child has only a small or inadequate vocabulary, shows inadequate growth of vocabulary, does not know how to express him- or herself, consistently uses wrong grammar, reverses word order, or does not seem to understand others well enough.

AUDITORY LANGUAGE PROCESSING

Auditory language processing refers to the linguistic and cognitive capacity for processing language that is heard. Various component skills have been hypothesized, including selective attention, auditory attention, discrimination of speech vs. background noise, discrimination of individual speech sounds from other speech sounds and nonspeech sounds, auditory discrimination of speech from ambient background noise, memory

for auditory information, sequencing of auditory information, and cognitive information processing (Barch & Berenbaum, 1994; Kelly, 1995; Wiig & Semel, 1984).

Auditory processing of language is a concept that is closely associated with receptive language skills. The clinician, however, should not confuse the former with the latter. In the most general sense, receptive language skills or linguistic comprehension refers to the ability to interpret and make sense of spoken and written language (Miller & Paul, 1995). Receptive language and auditory processing are different in scope and require different intervention strategies (Kelly, 1995; Miller & Paul, 1995).

When a youngster has difficulty following directions or 2- and 3-step commands; is unable to repeat a series of numbers, unrelated words, or sentences, or retell a story, an auditory language processing problem may be present.

Social communication refers to the use of language in a social context (pragmatics). It involves a sender, a message, and a receiver. Communication in a social context includes verbal and nonverbal elements simultaneously. Nonverbal communication involves facial expression, gestures, body movement, eye contact, and body space. Social communication requires both a linguistic and a situational context. The message, the receiver, and contextual variables can impact on any specific communicative event. Variations in communication may be due to age, sex, education, state of mental or physical health, dialect, and ethnic or social group of either speaker or listener. The same speaker may vary language depending on the social situation or specific language function (Baltaxe, 1993; Baltaxe & Simmons, 1988; Bernstein & Tiegerman, 1985; Walker, Schwarz, Nippold, Irvin, & Noell, 1994).

The use of nouns to signal new information and of pronouns to signal old information in English is an example of the use of pragmatic rules in language that are fundamental in social communication (e.g., The *farmer* plowed the fields and then *he* fed his animals). The use of polite and familiar forms of address is another example of important pragmatic rules.

The clinician needs be aware of whether the child is using inappropriate language with respect to topic, situation, or context.

Stages of Language Development

The normally developing child does not merely speak an incorrect or garbled version of adult language. Child language has its own characteristics with its own patterns and gradually evolving system. The rules for each of the subsystems of language (phonological, morphological, syntactic, and semantic) are acquired in an orderly and predictable progression of steps as are the rules for social communication. For example, an English-speaking child will produce "boon" for "spoon" at an early stage of phonological development. At the morphological level, the young child produces "brok-ed" for "broken" and "eat-ed" instead of "ate" because he or she has not yet acquired the idiosyncratic morphological past tense marker for irregular verbs. At the semantic level "dada" may refer to a generic male rather than to "father" early in development. At the syntactic level, "baby sleep" may signal "the baby is sleeping," a grammatical form that develops later (Gleason, 1989).

When language development is delayed, phonological forms such as "boon" appear at a later stage in the child's language. The child eventually will acquire the adult pattern, demonstrating that he or she follows a normal but delayed pattern of development. However, producing "oon" for "spoon" is not a normal substitution; the developmental phonological pattern is deviant. Likewise, the grammatical pattern "sleeping is the baby" is also deviant because it does not follow the sequential rules of English. Thus we see that in the latter cases the language deficit is more complicated than just delayed development. When deviant patterns are reported, it is likely that there may be other physical or neurological problems, such as a hearing loss or other physical and neurological involvement (Shipley & McAfee, 1992).

Most basic language development takes place between the ages of 9 months and 4 years, although the development of certain subcomponents may require more time. Developmental speech and language milestones are not reached uniformly in all areas. While the acquisition of most basic sentence types is complete by the age of 4, the phonological system is not expected to be fully developed until the age of 7. Sounds acquired late involve thrusting the tongue forward (e.g., /th/ as in "think" and "the") or raising the tongue without touching the palate (/r, s, z, sh, j, ch/ as in "red," "sit," "zebra," "share," "jet," and "church"). In addition, certain combinations of sounds, such as triple consonant clusters as in "split" and "street," develop late. Thus the child uses basic sentence types correctly before the complete system of sounds of the language is mastered.

When parents report concern about a lack of mastery in sound production in a very young child, the clinician needs to be aware of the patterns of early and later sounds in phonological development. When parents report telegraphic speech in a 5-year-old, the clinician also needs to know that this grammatical pattern should have been attained 2 years earlier.

Growth of the semantic component, including vocabulary and understanding of abstract linguistic concepts, continues into adolescence and adulthood. In addition to expanding the vocabulary, the child has to learn the semantic features of a word and the restrictions in the use of each word. Comprehension and expression of abstract language is one of the later areas of development and does not emerge before the child reaches about 6 to 8 years of age. Delays or problems with abstract language function can be identified only in later childhood years or in adolescence. Abstract language includes the ability to use and understand relational terms; concepts of time, space, and quantity; secondary and multiple meanings of words; idioms; and metaphors. The use of language in abstract reasoning and in making judgments and drawing inferences from what is said are applications of metalinguistic knowledge that continue to evolve in adolescence and even in adulthood. Metalinguistic knowledge involves an individual's ability to distance him- or herself from language and to view it as a tool (Wiig & Secord, 1985). Deficits in abstract language function cannot be identified in an early developmental history. Later they are "hidden" problems, less obvious to direct observation, but they become detrimental to social communication and school performance (Wiig & Secord, 1985; Wiig & Semel, 1984).

In a child's or adolescent's developmental history, problems with abstract language may become evident in comments made about her social communication. Such comments may include that "She fails to understand the fine nuances of language" or "He is very literal in his interpretations of what is said to him," and that the youngster has difficulties making judgments and decisions.

The ability to use abstract language generally is impaired when there is a history of early language delay, in pervasive developmental disorders, in schizophrenia, and in mental retardation (Baltaxe, 1997; Baltaxe & Simmons, 1995; Wiig & Semel, 1984).

Parents also may report that the child appears to have problems finding the right words to express him- or herself. Especially in the older child, the clinician should be alert to word-finding or word retrieval problems. Word-finding difficulties often can be identified through hesitations and long response latencies or long pauses in a conversation, groping for words, reformulating what is intended to be said, circumlocutions, and using word approximations and similar-sounding words as well as gestural communication. When this type of behavior is reported in the developmental history, follow-up questions should be considered. Word-finding difficulties can be expected to occur with neurological conditions, such as seizure disorders, and with abnormal electroencephalograph findings, but also with learning disabilities and with language disorders in general. Word-finding difficulties also may exist because of depression, use of drugs, in some metabolic conditions, and with attention deficit hyperactivity disorder (Baltaxe & Simmons, 1990; Wiig & Becker-Caplan, 1984).

Developmental stages also occur in auditory language processing (Levinson & Sloan, 1980). Deficits in auditory language processing almost always occur with language disorders, although they can exist independently (Wiig & Semel, 1984). Deficits in auditory processing are common in children with attention deficit hyperactivity disorder. When language delay is not also present, auditory processing deficits generally are not identified early on. Children with unidentified problems in auditory language processing may be considered uncooperative and obstinate, and their failure to follow instructions often may be interpreted as an intentional act rather than attributed to an underlying problem. Parents frequently feel relief and may even change their attitude toward the child when auditory processing deficits are identified as part of the problem. Deficits in auditory language processing are detrimental to school achievement and social interaction. Such deficits should be anticipated from such comments as "The child does not remember, does not follow instructions, is forgetful in schoolwork, only completes part of the work, does not follow through with a task, does not listen, is not obedient, acts out or withdraws," and so on.

Social communication or pragmatics is the interface between linguistic, cognitive, emotional, and social development (Bates, 1976). Delays or impairment in any one of these areas impacts social communication. While the rules of social communication begin to be acquired early, as children get older, the "right type" of social interaction becomes increasingly important in order for them to be accepted by their peer group. Thus by the age of 2 to 3 children are able to express basic feelings, respond to questions, and introduce new topics in an interaction. By the age of 4 years children have become aware of some of the rules that govern conversation and are able to make comments, requests, and greetings appropriate to the situation. Children also begin to be able to translate feelings such as anger and sadness into the appropriate linguistic form fitting a particular conversational partner or setting. By that age youngsters also can interpret the feelings of others, obtain clarification when there is a conversational breakdown, and ask for details.

Children with language delay may be limited in these skills.

In the course of linguistic development, children must learn how to provide relevant background information to the listener, relate a coherent narrative, and sequence events in time. Youngsters also must learn to establish a conversational topic, maintain and switch topics appropriately, and introduce new topics using the grammatical conventions of language. They must learn to take turns in a conversation and adjust conversation to the listener and the situation. Nonverbal behavior, such as gestures, body language, and space as well as eye contact appropriate for the topic, the conversational partner, and the situation, also must be acquired.

Youngsters may have problems in the development of any one of these areas; pragmatic skills may be delayed or they may be deviant and not fit any normal pattern at any age.

The clinician must be alert to social communication problems when parents report that the child has difficulties with turn-taking behaviors and rambles on and on, has difficulty listening, and constantly interrupts. Parents also may report they often do not know what a child or adolescent is talking about, or that she does not talk much, always wants to be in control of the conversation, talks back constantly, provides inappropriate or irrelevant information, and other similar comments.

In the school years, language skills are closely associated with academic achievement and educational success. In the classroom, children must master oral language to be successful. Other important classroom skills are associated with auditory language processing skills and abstract language skills. They include being able to interpret directions, follow instructions, and make inferences from what the teacher says—that is, understand the implied meanings of what is said. Language skills also facilitate other areas of learning, such as understanding mathematical concepts and solving problems. Getting along with peers and teachers in the classroom also requires important social communication skills.

Delays or deficiencies in the use of abstract language, auditory language processing, and social communication, therefore, can have detrimental effects in an educational setting. There is also a close relationship between a language disability and a learning disability (Bashir & Scavuzzo, 1992; Wiig & Semel, 1984).

While speech problems, such as articulation problems, disappear over time, language deficits tend to persist (Baker & Cantwell, 1987; Beitchman et al., 1996; Hall & Tomblin, 1978; Weiner, 1985). Problems in language function generally are more difficult to identify in older children because of the more subtle manifestation of the problem. Since basic grammatical skills develop early, a delay in language might manifest itself only in a child's use of simple, less complex sentence structure, having a smaller vocabulary, or other difficult-to-detect deficits such as abstract language function and word-finding problems. The clinician will have to use specific linguistic assessment measures to identify the actual extent of such delays. When language impairment is present in older children, auditory processing skills, and pragmatic deficits generally can be also expected.

Relationship of Speech-Language-Communication to Other Areas of Development

The acquisition of speech, language, and communication is interrelated with the acquisition of other skills, including motor, cognitive, social, and emotional. The clinician needs to know that the developmental stages of speech-language-communication are synchronized with developments in these other skills and may even be predicted on the basis of accomplishments in these other areas. For example, children's first expressive words parallel their motor behavior of standing and walking with assistance. When attainment of gross or fine motor skills is delayed or impaired, speech also may be delayed as one aspect of general motor delay or impairment, such as in cerebral palsy.

The development of various linguistic forms also parallels the development of various corresponding cognitive stages. For example, single-object play is associated with single-word utterances, and the development of complex pretend or symbolic play is associated with multiword utterances, while cognitive development relating to constructive play such as sequencing, proximate and functional space, linearity, and hierarchicality parallel the acquisition of spatial, temporal, and causal linguistic units in language development (Cromer, 1981; Westby, 1980). Delay in the cognitive area may signal delay in the language area and vice versa.

Language function, in particular abstract language skills, is important in concept formation, problem solving, reasoning, and thinking. A delay or impairment in language may be an early warning sign to possible later difficulties in these cognitive areas. In turn, reported impairment or delay in these areas also may be an indicator of possible deficits in language function.

Risk Factors for Speech, Language, and Communication Problems

Discrepancies in speech-language development may occur for a variety of reasons. They may signal specific language delay without being associated with other delays or impairment, or they may be associated with impairment in any of the areas mentioned earlier. Delays or abnormalities in the development of speech, language, and communication may be the direct result of hearing problems, vision problems, generalized motor problems, mental retardation, physical abnormalities of the speech mechanism, brain damage due to trauma or neoplasms, or other central nervous dysfunction (Murdoch, 1991). Risk factors associated with speech and language delay also may be related to such medical factors as complications during the mother's pregnancy and delivery, low birthweight, metabolic disorders, genetic conditions or predisposition as well as environmental deprivation. Other risk factors include such general factors as sex, socioeconomic class, family size, and birth order. There is a significantly greater incidence of language disorders in boys than in girls. Language delay is also significantly associated with developmental psychopathology (Baltaxe & Simmons, 1990; Beitchman et al., 1990; Cantwell & Baker, 1991). In most cases, however, no obvious cause for the speech or language disorder can be demonstrated (Bernstein & Tiegerman, 1985; Lahey, 1988).

Children who have a history of chronic otitis media may be delayed in language development, in particular in vocabulary acquisition, as well as in the acquisition of prelinguistic patterns of vocalization. Children with a hearing loss will have difficulty hearing at specific frequencies. The articulation pattern of these children is affected by the sounds they cannot hear or hear with distortion, and depends on degree of loss and the speech frequencies affected. The child whose mother contracted rubella or was exposed to ototoxic drugs during pregnancy may have a congenital hearing loss or deafness and consequently also experience problems associated with language comprehension and expression (Northern & Downs, 1991; Stoker & Ling, 1992). Chil-

dren who are visually impaired or who are blind do not have the opportunity to acquire language in the context of both auditory and visual stimuli. This may be reflected not only in the timing factors of language onset but also in the pattern of language acquisition. For example, blind children may have difficulties in the acquisition of reference, in particular pronoun reference and their statements and comments may lack precision. (McConachie & Moore, 1994). Children with cerebral palsy may show delayed speech because of generalized motor involvement impacting the use of spoken language, although language comprehension may be intact and develop on time (Love, 1992). An inner-city child or a child living in poverty with insufficient early language stimulation may show evidence of environmental deprivation in delayed language and the quality of language skills. Inadequate prenatal medical care also places the child at greater risk for developmental problems (Byrd & Weitzman, 1994). The bilingual child, exposed to 2 languages, may experience a temporary delay in 1 or both languages (Miller, 1984). When there is a family history of a language-learning disability, a child may display a similar disability (Bashir & Scavuzzo, 1992). A child with a seizure disorder may have language delay or impairment (Tuchman, 1994). Certain genetic disorders, such as tuberous sclerosis (Hunt, 1993) and Down syndrome (Van Borsel, 1996), are associated with language delay and impairment, and genetics may play a role in language impairment in general (Bishop, North, & Donlan, 1995; Ludlow & Cooper, 1983; Tomblin & Buckwalter, 1994).

The clinician must be alert to the possibility of speech, language, or communication problems when any of the above factors are reported.

Speech-language delay or deviance also must be expected with certain types of psychopathology, such as the pervasive developmental disorders. Such delays must be ruled out in other disorders including the learning disorders, attention deficit (hyperactivity) disorder and the disruptive behavior disorders, elimination disorders, especially enuresis, and emotional disorders including selective mutism, re-active attachment disorder of infancy and early childhood and the anxiety disorders, movement disorders such as Tourette's disorder, psychosis, early onset schizophrenia, and schizophrenia spectrum disorders, as well as the affective disorders. Speech-language-communication problems have been significantly associated with these disorders as well (Baltaxe & Simmons, 1990; Baltaxe, 1997; Beitchman et al., 1990, Beitchman et al., 1996; Cantwell & Baker, 1992).

Case Examples on the Manifestation of Speech-Language Deficits

SPEECH, LANGUAGE, AND COMMUNICATION:

Kevin: Kevin, a 10-year-old boy, is brought to clinical attention with the primary complaint that in school he has difficulties writing and completing homework assignments. Kevin also takes too long expressing himself. His classmates call him stupid, and Kevin has become withdrawn.

In the course of ascertaining Kevin's developmental history, the clinician establishes that there was a slight delay in reaching the developmental language milestones. There also was a slight delay in reaching the developmental motor milestones. Kevin's mother reports that she had a difficult birth.

Several thoughts present themselves immediately. Does Kevin have a speech, a language, and/or a social communication problem? Since Kevin did not talk early on, did he comprehend what was said to him? How did Kevin communicate? Did he use nonverbal communication such as gestures and eye contact? Did Kevin vocalize early in development? Has his hearing been checked? Was there chronic otitis media? Today, how does the youngster function in nonverbal cognitive areas? Can other risk factors in the developmental history be identified? Is there a relationship between motor delay and speech/language delay in Kevin's early development and/or difficulties in writing and expressing himself now?

Follow-up questions and assessment revealed that Kevin had diminished vocalizations, did not have chronic otitis media, was not hearing impaired, understood what was said to him early in development, communicated through gestures, and had good eye contact. Kevin also was not cog-

nitively delayed based on nonverbal testing, nor was he delayed in current language function receptively or expressively. However, he needed more time to express himself. Neurological examination revealed that the youngster had slight cerebral palsy and a speech motor problem but not a language problem. Developmentally then, Kevin had a speech delay that affected his language expression and social interaction with his peers.

This example shows that linguistic delays may be related to the speech component alone, which in turn is related to a general motor component. In Kevin's case, the motor speech problem had a neurological substratum.

Delays and impairment in speech in children are more common than delays or deficits in language. Generally, they are also not related to organic factors. In other cases, however, both language and speech may be delayed. This is a common pattern when delay is associated with hearing disorders and/or general cognitive delay and some types of psychopathology. Speech-language delay also may exist independently without obvious evidence in other areas. Expressive language may be impaired, with comprehension being intact; in a few cases expressive language may appear intact but comprehension is poor. However, the clinician needs to know that the more common pattern is that when language is impaired, both receptive and expressive language are affected. Delay in language often is seen with attention deficit hyperactivity disorder, behavior disorders, and emotional disorders such as posttraumatic stress disorder and elective mutism, but also Tourette's disorder as well as with learning disabilities (Baltaxe, 1997; Baltaxe & Simmons, 1990).

Some language delay also may be associated with bilingualism. It is important to identify the order in which the 2 languages were acquired. In the case of simultaneous exposure to both languages, the child may use vocabulary and grammar from both languages, as if it were 1 system, only gradually differentiating the 2 systems. A great number of variables are associated with bilingualism. Frequently 1 language is spoken at home with the family and to express emotion, while the other language is used in school and for other public functions. Given normal intelligence and sufficient exposure or stimulation in a language, the bilingual child can be expected to catch up in language skills. In considering the possibility of a communication deficit, often it is difficult to differentiate the effects of bilingualism from actual speech-language deficits. A contrastive analysis approach is helpful in which assessment is performed in both languages and the results for the 2 languages are compared. The effects of bilingualism must be separated from actual deficits by differentiating transfer features of 1 language to the other from those of actual deficits.

DELAY IN ONSET WITH DEVIANT PATTERNS

Adam: Adam, a 5-year-old youngster, is brought to clinical attention. Adam's parents are concerned about his language behavior. Adam often does not make sense when he communicates. When Adam talks at all, it is in a singsong tone. There are no problems with his articulation. Adam seems to be using stereotypic phrases, and his sentences are not always grammatically correct. Often Adam does not seem to understand what is said to him. Although at home Adam plays alongside his younger sister, Jennifer, he avoids other children in nursery school.

Adam's developmental history demonstrates that speech-language onset was delayed.

The clinician needs to consider several follow-up questions to clarify the following points: Does Adam have normal hearing? Does the youngster understand what is said to him? If so, how much does he understand? Could Adam have auditory processing problems? Did he vocalize as a baby? Does Adam initiate conversation with others? How is his nonverbal communication, such as eye contact and use of gestures? What is Adam's cognitive level?

Further assessment showed that Adam's articulation was within normal range but that his prosody was disturbed as was fluency, characterized by starts into false sentence patterns and reformulations of sentences. The child's language level appeared to be delayed, and there were general difficulties with social communication. Adam's hearing and auditory processing were normal. Gestures, facial expression, and eye contact were poor. Adam also was cognitively delayed. The assessment pointed to the presence of autism, a pervasive developmental disorder, with a deviant pattern of communication in some areas but not in others. In this case articulation was normal (Schopler & Mesibov, 1985).

Deviant patterns of speech in autism can include voice, fluency, articulation, and prosody abnormalities. Voice may have an abnormal quality. Pitch may be too high or too low and pitch range too narrow. The sentences produced may resemble those of a younger child, but at the same time may show unexpected characteristics, such as errors in word order and echolalia. There also may not be a direct relationship between the meaning of what is said and what is referred to. Language may be used idiosyncratically. There may be an overuse of stereotypic patterns, a lack of comprehension, as well as deficits in social communication, which may include a lack of eye contact and of gestures. Similar delays and deviance in some or all of the above areas also have been reported for other pervasive developmental disorders not otherwise specified, such as childhood disintegrative psychosis and early-onset schizophrenia, and schizotypal personality disorder (Baltaxe, 1997; Baltaxe & Simmons, 1995; Lord, 1985). Deviant patterns also are associated with hearing disorders and are reflective of the type and degree of loss (Stoker & Ling, 1992).

NORMAL ONSET OF SPEECH, LANGUAGE, AND COMMUNICATION AND SUBSEQUENT LOSS

Stacy: Stacy is a 6-year old girl referred to the clinician with a presenting problem of sudden language loss, anxiety, and low frustration tolerance.

Developmental history reveals that Stacy recently had a serious case of chicken pox with a high temperature. Stacy's language function as well as frustration level had been normal prior to her illness. Stacy's hearing, at least prior to her illness, was normal. Follow-up questions included: Is this a speech, language, or communication problem? Does Stacy have a hearing loss? How does she communicate now? Does the youngster understand what is said to her? Does Stacy have an auditory processing problem?

Linguistic assessment and further information revealed that Stacy did not seem to understand unless she also saw what was being talked about. When Stacy tried to speak at all, her few expressive words appeared incomprehensible. There was difficulty with repetition and a groping for words. Stacy used gestures to communicate. Hearing testing revealed a slight bilateral hearing loss. Her electroencephalogram was abnormal. Groping behavior and poor repetition were evidence that Stacy had an apraxia of speech, a disturbance in the speech-motor patterns resulting from neurological damage and an inability voluntarily to select, direct, organize, and/or sequence the speech musculature, also characterized by an inability to execute volitional speech movements (Hodge, 1994).

A pattern of normal onset and subsequent loss can occur with childhood diseases, lesions, or trauma. These may include encephalitis and chicken pox, cerebral vascular accidents, the onset of seizures. An abnormal EEG may be one of the associated manifestations in a history of normal onset and subsequent loss. The above pattern described for Stacy may be seen with Landau-Kleffner syndrome, brain tumors, or trauma to the head. Landau-Kleffner syndrome is sometimes also associated with a hearing loss (Landau & Kleffner, 1957). When language is reduced or lost due to the disorders mentioned, nonverbal communication is generally intact or grossly intact. This is not the case for autism, where initial normal onset and subsequent loss is also one of the patterns of language development. In autism this pattern also may be associated with an abnormal electroencephalogram or a seizure disorder. When severe or global hearing impairment occurs later in childhood or adolescence, a gradual deterioration of speech and language function may occur.

DIFFICULTIES IN SPEECH, LANGUAGE, AND COMMUNICATION IN LATER CHILDHOOD AND ADOLESCENCE

Troy: Troy, a 15-year-old youngster, has a presenting complaint of increasing school failure including reading difficulties. Troy also had oppositional behavior at home and acts like a wise guy in school, with truancy behavior.

Troy's developmental history reveals that early language and communication milestones were normal. Troy said his first words at about 1 year and 2-word combinations at about 18 months of age, and started walking at 12 months. Parents report that Troy was forgetful, easily distractible,

and that he had a short attention span. While initially there were no school problems, as time progressed and the work got harder, school problems also increased.

Follow-up questions revealed that Troy did not always seem to remember what was said to him and that sometimes he seemed to take what was said to him quite literally. Troy also appeared to have hesitations in his speech pattern and sometimes did not use quite the right words.

Further follow-up and assessment revealed that Troy had auditory processing problems, abstract language difficulties, and word-finding difficulties. Troy's social communication also revealed poor strategies. All these are linguistic deficits that may be seen in adolescents with or without a delay in reaching early developmental language milestones described earlier in this chapter.

Conclusion

The focus of this chapter was to place speech, language, and communication into the framework of a child's developmental history, clearly a key domain in that context. The clinician's ability to ask more specific questions about language acquisition, its use, and its function becomes a valuable asset, as does familiarity with stages of language development and the ability to identify areas of possible asynchrony of developmental language stages with stages in other areas of development. The type of general and specific questions asked about language development in the course of taking a developmental history will depend on the clinician's knowledge and understanding of the components of speech, language, and communication; their development and their function; and the associated risk factors and the warning signs as they relate to the area of language itself or as they are evident from other areas of function. Inasmuch as deficits in language also may represent essential or associated features of developmental psychopathology, information about language and its function becomes even more important in the developmental history of a child assessed for psychopathology.

REFERENCES

Baker, L., & Cantwell, D. P. (1987). A prospective psychiatric follow-up of children with speech/language disorders. *Journal of American Child and Adolescent Psychiatry, 26,* 546–553.

Baltaxe, C. (1993). Pragmatic language disorders in children with social communication disorders and their treatment. *Neurophysiology and Neurogenic Speech and Language Disorders, 3* (1), 2–9.

Baltaxe, C. (1997). Communication behaviors associated with psychiatric behaviors. In T. Ferrand & R. L. Bloom (Eds.). *Organic and neurogenic disorders of communication* (pp. 51–83). Boston: Allyn & Bacon.

Baltaxe, C., & Simmons, J. Q. (1988). Pragmatic deficits in emotionally disturbed children and adolescents. In J. Schiefelbusch & L. Lloyd (Eds.), *Language perspectives: Acquisition, retardation, and intervention* (pp. 223–253). Austin, TX: Pro-Ed.

Baltaxe, C., & Simmons, J. Q. (1990). The differential diagnosis of communication disorders in child and adolescent psychopathology. *Topics in Language Disorders: Children and Adolescents with Emotional and Behavioral Disorders, 10* (4), 17–31.

Baltaxe, C., & Simmons, J. Q. (1995). Speech and language disorders in children and adolescents with schizophrenia. *Schizophrenia Bulletin, 21* (4), 125–140.

Barch, D., & Berenbaum, H. (1994). The relationship between information processing and language production. *Journal of Abnormal Psychology, 103,* 241–250.

Bashir, A., & Scavuzzo, A. (1992). Children with language disorders: Natural history and academic success. *Journal of Learning Disabilities, 25* (1), 53–65.

Bates, E. (1976). *Language and context: The acquisition of pragmatics.* New York: Academic Press.

Beitchman, J. H., Brownlie, E. B., Inglis, A., Wild, J., Ferguson, B., Schachter, D., Lancee, W., Wilson, B., & Mathews, R. (1996). Seven-year follow-up of speech/language impaired and control children: Psychiatric outcome. *Journal of Child Psychology and Psychiatry and Allied Disciplines, 37* (8), 961–970.

Beitchman, J. H., Hood, J., & Inglis, A. (1990). Psychiatric risk in children with speech and language disorders. *Journal of Abnormal Child Psychology, 18* (3), 283–296.

Beitchman, J. H., Hood, J., Rochon, J., & Peterson, M. (1989). Empirical classification of speech/language impairment in children II: Behavioral characteristics. *Journal of the American Academy of Child and Adolescent Psychiatry, 28,* 118–123.

Bernstein, D., & Tiegerman, E. (1985). *Language and communication disorders in children.* Columbus, OH: Charles Merrill Publishing.

Bishop, D. V. M., North, T., & Donlan, C. (1995). Genetic basis of specific language impairment: Evidence from a twin study. *Developmental Medicine and Child Neurology, 37,* 56–71.

Byrd, R. S., & Weitzman, M. L. (1994). Predictors of early grade retention among children in the United States. *Pediatrics, 93* (3), 481–487.

Cantwell, D. P., & Baker, L. (1991). *Psychiatric and developmental disorders in children with communication disorder.* Washington, DC: American Psychiatric Press.

Cohen, N. J., Davine, M., Horodesky, N., Lipsett, L., & Isaacson, L. (1993). Unsuspected language impairment in psychiatrically disturbed children: Prevalence and language and behavioral characteristics. *Journal of the American Academy of Child and Adolescent Psychiatry, 33* (3), 595–603.

Cromer, R. (1981). Developmental language disorders: Cognitive processes, semantics, pragmatics, phonology, and syntax. *Journal of Autism and Developmental Disorders, 11,* 57–74.

Gavillan-Torres, E. (1984). Issues of assessment of limited English proficient students and of truly disabled in the United States. In N. Miller (Ed.), *Bilingualism and language disability* (pp. 131–154). San Diego: College Hill Press.

Gleason, J. (1989). *The development of language* (2nd ed.) Columbus, OH: Charles Merrill Publishing.

Hall, P., & Tomblin, B. (1978). A follow-up study of children with articulation and language disorders. *Journal of Speech and Hearing Disorders, 43,* 227–241.

Hodge, M. (1994). Assessment of children with a developmental apraxia of speech: A rationale. *Clinics in Communication Disorders, 4* (2), 91–101.

Hunt, A. (1993). Development, behavior and seizures in 300 cases with tuberous sclerosis. *Journal of Intellectual Disability Research, 37,* 41–51.

Kelly, D. (1995). *Central auditory processing disorder.* San Antonio, TX: Communication Skill Builder.

Lahey, M. (1988). *Language disorders and language development.* New York: Macmillan.

Landau, W., & Kleffner, F. (1957). The syndrome of acquired aphasia with a convulsive disorder in children. *Neurology, 7* (8), 523–530.

Levinson, P., & Sloan, C. (Eds). (1980). *Auditory processing and language.* New York: Grune & Stratton.

Lord, K. (1985). Autism and the comprehension of language. In E. Schopler & G. Mesibov (Eds.), *Communication problems in autism* (pp. 257–282). New York: Plenum Press.

Love, R. (1992). *Childhood motor speech disability.* New York: Macmillan.

Ludlow, C., & Cooper, J. (1983). *Genetic aspects of speech and language disorders.* New York: Academic Press.

Majnemer, A., & Rosenblatt, B. (1994). Reliability of parental recall of developmental milestones. *Pediatric Neurology, 10,* 304–308.

McConachie, H., & Moore, V. (1994). Early expressive language of severely visually impaired children. *Developmental Medicine and Child Neurology, 36* (3), 230–240.

Miller, J., & Paul, R. (1995). *The clinical assessment of*

language comprehension. Baltimore, MD: Paul H. Brooks.

Miller, N. (1984). Bilingualism and language disability. San Diego: College Hill.

Murdoch, B. (Ed.). (1991). *Acquired neurological speech/language disorders in childhood.* London: Taylor & Francis.

Northern, J. L., & Downs, M. (1991). *Hearing in children* (4th ed.). Baltimore, MD: Williams & Wilkins.

Schopler, E., & Mesibov, G. (Eds.). (1985). *Communication problems in autism.* New York: Plenum Press.

Shipley, K., & McAfee, J. (1992). *Assessment in speech-language pathology.* San Diego: Singular Publishing Group.

Stoker, R., & Ling, D. (1992). (Eds.). Speech production in hearing impaired children and youth [Monograph]. *Volta Review, 94.*

Tomblin, J. B., & Buckwalter, P. R. (1994). Studies of genetics of specific language impairment. In R. Watkins & M. Rice (Eds.), *Specific language impairment in children* (pp. 17–34), Baltimore, MD: Paul H. Brooks.

Tuchman, R. (1994). Epilepsy, language, and behavior: Clinical models in childhood. *Journal of Child Neurology, 9* (1), 95–102.

Van Borsel, J. (1996). Articulation in Down's syndrome adolescents and adults. *European Journal of Disorders of Communication, 31* (4), 415–444.

Walker, H., Schwarz, I., Nippold, M., Irvin, L., & Noell, J. (1994). Social skills in school-age children and youth: Issues and best practices in assessment and intervention. *Topics in Language: Pragmatics and Social Skills in School-Age Children and Adolescents, 14* (3), 70–82.

Weiner, P. (1985). The value of follow-up studies. Topics in Languages Disorders. *Language Impaired Youth: The Years between 10 & 18, 5* (3), 78–92.

Westby, C. (1980). Assessment of cognition and language abilities through play. *Journal of Language, Speech, and Hearing Services in the Schools, 11,* 154–168.

Wiig, E. H., & Semel, E. (1984). *Language assessment and intervention for the learning disabled* (2nd ed.). Columbus, OH: Charles Merrill Publishing.

Wiig, E. H., & Becker-Caplan, L. (1984). Linguistic retrieval strategies and word-finding difficulties among children with language disabilities. *Topics in Language: Neurolinguistic Approaches to Language Disorders, 4* (3), 1–18.

Wiig, E. H., & Secord, W. (1985). *Test of language competence* (expanded ed.). Minneapolis: Psychological Corporation, Harcourt Brace Jovanovich.

41 / Health History

Hans Steiner

The occurrence of medical illness and disability profoundly influences child development. (Further detailed information is available in Chapter 24 in Volume 4 of this *Handbook.*) There is more information in "Treating Adolescents, School Age Children and Pre-School Children" (Steiner, 1996, 1997a, 1997b). Any comprehensive investigation of a child's development therefore must include intensive and extended study of the child's history of illness. Of equal importance is a detailed account of nutritional habits and status, as nutrition significantly influences mental health and growth patterns. Such an investigation naturally will lead to an exploration of a child's concept of illness, health-related behaviors, and capacity for compliance. A similar history also should be obtained from the family; the younger and more dependent the child, the more important is such a history, as it is the parents who will supervise or perform the bulk of prescribed treatment. More often than not, information gathered in this way will be of considerable significance for assessing and predicting compliance with prescribed psychiatric treatment. Such information is invaluable in treatment planning, as many psychiatric problems are complex, ambiguous, and abstract, and their treatment tends also to be complex, multimodal, and prolonged. Predicting that the patient will encounter difficulties following through with psychiatric treatment is often a useful strategy in facilitating compliance at critical points, when a variety of factors threatens adherence to treatment.

Definitions

Acute illness may be defined as any illness lasting less than 3 months per year and necessitating less than 1 month in the hospital per year. *Chronic illness* has been defined by Pless, Cripps, Davies, and Wadsworth (1989) as a "physical, usually non-fatal condition which lasts longer than three months in a given year or necessitates a continuous period in hospital of more than one month" (p. 747). Additionally, the condition must be of sufficient severity as to interfere in some degree with a child's activities. *Disability* is defined as a stable form of impairment of either cognitive or physical functioning, most often the result of a chronic illness, chronic trauma, or a birth or genetic defect (Feinstein & Berger, 1987). *Nutritional status* refers to the child's intake of food and fluid as well as body composition. The child's nutritional requirements are fluid and dynamic, changing as a function of continued growth and development. Needs change as a function of body size, activity, and state of health (Colon, 1990).

Developmental Factors that Interact with the Occurrence and Reporting of Disease

At different ages, different issues modify a child's and family's experience of illness and injury. For the infant, illness and hospitalization threaten to disrupt attachment processes. Separation from the parent, the appearance of strangers who perform painful ministrations with parental sanction, disruption of regular feeding and sleeping schedules, and strong emotional reactions in the parents all can generate potential problems. Much will depend on the adequacy of the parents' response during medical diagnosis and management, and how well parents are able to provide relief and support for each other. The child's understanding of disease is mediated predominantly through the parent. In the preschooler, magical thinking and egocentricity prevail. Illness is not a chance occurrence; it is a retribution for things done—or imagined to have been done—wrong. Children of this age understand the situation well enough to anticipate hurt, even when there is no immediate prospect of pain, and panic often ensues. Usually treatment involves restriction of movement or some limitation of gratification; for children, this is further evidence of punishment. Children's anger usually is directed at parents for exposing them to such circumstances; only in dysfunctional support systems does this anger spill over toward the treatment team and result in interference with health care.

A different problem arises with school-age children. Since they are able to reason concretely, sometimes idiosyncratic ideas about bodily functioning are concealed beneath a reasonable and cooperative facade. The thinking of children of this age usually restricts the view of disease causation to only 1 cause; thus they reduce complex health issues to a single factor. Concrete interpretation of procedures and treatment can lead to anxiety and panic, which disappear when appropriate explanations are forthcoming.

Adolescents have all the cognitive equipment of adults with which to understand the situation appropriately but sometimes refuse to act in accordance with their understanding, brushing off serious health concerns as a threat to newfound autonomy and freedom. Often patients test doctors' predictions; when predictions do not come true, adolescents take this as evidence that everything the doctor said is nonsense, and therefore they need not comply with treatment. This fact is especially salient for adolescents with chronic illness, who usually begin prolonged periods of noncompliance in their early teens. Cognitively, adolescents can comprehend complex causes for illness, but emotionally, adolescents do not weigh and incorporate into their behavior the impact of illness on, for instance, social development. Parental supervision and enforcement must be delivered with some sensitivity to avoid control struggles and further injury to threatened autonomy. An additional issue of great importance, although not necessarily immediately and openly discussed, is the impact illness and treatment has on the maturing body. An adolescent can be unusually concerned with, for example, a small facial scar, convincing him- or herself of its deleterious consequences for life. Imagine the horror such a youngster experiences at the suggestion of a Herrington rod implant, a cast, or a lifelong regimen of obesity-inducing immunosuppressants. Extensive testing of limits around treatment is the rule rather than the exception and calls for much patience and persistence on the part of health care providers. An issue that emerges in full force for the first time in this age group is the development of risky habits that are directly related to most adolescent morbidity and mortality. Some risk-taking is appropriate to the age and is part of normal development. Adolescents have to test the limits of their capabilities and powers; indeed, at this stage of development, the complete absence of risk-taking would signal problems with successful mastery. But for the most part, such experimentation is not too destructive and occurs relatively infrequently. Most parents and primary care physicians are well attuned to the dangers of alcohol, drug use, and smoking, and are appropriately mindful of and watchful for these behaviors. However, other forms of behavior signal unnecessary risk-taking and are sometimes not regarded in the same way by parents and primary care physicians, and yet are common areas of experimentation. This group of behaviors includes reckless and drunken driving, immoderate sports activities, promiscuous and unprotected sex, and bearing a child without the necessary prerequisites for support and parenting. Given the frequency with which they occur, over-the-counter drug use for weight control, purgation and dieting, and excessive aerobic exercise might be considered in this context as well. Very often, such risk-taking is more common in adolescent girls and is actively concealed from parents and primary care physicians, even from those who have known patients for a long time. These adults often greet the revelation of such behavior with surprise and incredulity. Indeed, all too often, the child psychiatrist is in the unique position of being able to approach this topic (i.e. risk taking) most effectively. Adolescents do not have to maintain the illusion of a "good image" during the psychiatric examination, as there has been no prior relationship. Excessive risk-taking often is juxtaposed with a paradoxical overconcern about special areas of health care—

hair cleanliness and dental appearance are good examples—to which attention is meticulously given.

Frequency and Occurrence of Problems in Different Age Groups

At any given time, in any population, between 6 and 10% of children and adolescents suffer from chronic illness and disabilities (Millstein & Litt, 1990). In addition, children up to age 12 are the most likely age group to suffer from acute illness, with youngsters of adolescent age the next most likely (Children's Defense Fund, 1986). Illness and injury interfere with schooling: The average child and adolescent misses 5 days of school per year, suffers restricted activities on 9 days, and is in bed an average of 4 days. Hospitalization occurs in 6.4% of children and adolescents, with an average 5-day hospital stay. Patterns of acute illness and injury vary between children and adolescents. While children are more likely to suffer from illness, adolescents are most likely to suffer from injury, either self- or other-inflicted. Adolescent health problems by and large relate to faulty health behavior and bad habits, while children suffer most often from disease.

For adolescents with chronic illness, the following disorders occur with decreasing frequency: mental disorders (32%), respiratory disorders (21%), and disorders of the musculoskeletal system (15%) (Newachek, 1989). Given these figures, the child psychiatrist must be prepared to consider acute and chronic pediatric diseases in the differential diagnosis of each patient evaluated. A practitioner who sees 10 children per day sees at least 1 child afflicted by illness, chronic or acute. This fact is important for many reasons. Psychiatric symptoms in children often mimic symptoms of pediatric disorders; accordingly, psychiatric symptoms may be expressions of undiagnosed pediatric illness. Neither patient nor parent is fully able to cooperate in the difficult task of making a differential diagnosis. Acute illness and its treatment increase the stress experienced by a child or parent who is already disturbed and may worsen a mental disorder. During a time of acutely increased demands, a marginally adjusted family may behave neglectfully or even abusively. The interventions necessary for treatment of acute illness often are complex and thus poorly understood; this in itself could lead to trauma in the child. Traumatization occurs more frequently in those patients who have a history of poor adjustment and premorbid dysfunction. Chronic illness and disability seem to affect children and parents negatively over long periods of time, leading to adjustment and economic problems as well as to interpersonal difficulties (Pless & Nolan, 1991). Thus, even when a child's symptoms are primarily psychiatric at first glance, a detailed history of illness is important. All psychiatric assessments should include a review of the pediatric record of growth and development.

Specific Areas to be Investigated

In addition to the youngster's complete health care record (which should document acute and chronic illnesses, growth patterns, immunization status, and possible and potential disabilities), the child psychiatrist should obtain the following information.

GENERAL HEALTH CARE

How adequate has been the supervision of nutrition, growth, and development? What kind of advice have parents sought from the pediatrician? How adequate was the advice, how well was it applied? Have they had extensive experience with tertiary care systems? For what reasons? How do they describe the care they have received so far? How do they characterize the health professionals with whom they have dealt? Have they had any experiences with psychiatry? How do those experiences compare with their experience with other medical specialists? The goal here is to obtain a general sense of the child's and family's health care experience and the family's conceptualization of health care—whether it is realistic or unrealistic—and the extent of their knowledge about the health care system.

CURRENT HEALTH STATUS

Is the youngster currently suffering from an illness? Is the review of systems negative? How has the child reacted to illness in the past? Is there any history of physical trauma? What were the circumstances? What is the family's former and current health status? Has the youngster ever been hospitalized? How long and for what? Has there been any prolonged period of separation? If so, how was it handled by the family and the child? Were there any procedures that were unusual, invasive, or hurtful, and did they result in traumatization? How did the child, family, and health care staff handle this? How often is the child seen by a pediatrician?

In this section the clinician should clarify the details of the child's health status. It is important to look for evidence that acute or chronic illness has taken some emotional toll on child or family. It is necessary to determine if the family has maintained a good working relationship with health care personnel, or if this was disrupted in some significant way that would affect current treatment.

NUTRITION AND GROWTH

Is the youngster eating and drinking age appropriately? Is he or she growing and developing as expected? Were there any periods of growth delay? Periods of excessively low or high weight? Periods of accelerated growth? Any precocious maturation, as in precocious puberty and early menses? Any disproportionate development (e.g., head circumference)? What is the current stage of the youngster's pubertal maturation? What is the Tanner stage? Has the child been appropriately prepared for bodily maturation; if so, by whom? What is his or her immunization status? Any history of allergies or unusual reactions? The aim with these questions is to get a sense of how effective the family was in obtaining routine health care and how it handled normative transitions. In particular, it is necessary to determine if there is evidence of disregard or even neglect of certain difficult health care issues.

HEALTH CARE BELIEFS AND BEHAVIOR

How does the family conceptualize illness? Has this conceptualization changed significantly? Is it easy and appropriate for the family to see themselves as collaborators with the treatment team? Is there evidence of parental over- or under-involvement? Did the child ever suffer from illnesses that medical staff could not explain? Did these episodes recur? Do the parents have unusual knowledge of certain illnesses? Do parents and child have unusual beliefs about illness and health care? Do they reject certain aspects of allopathic medicine? Have they sought help from homeopathic or other kinds of medicine? Did this result in a detrimental outcome, or was it seen as helpful? Have parents and child been cooperative in prior treatment? For how long? How complex was the treatment regimen? Is there any evidence of discharges against medical advice? Have there been frequent changes in health care providers? Is there evidence for denial and acting out by noncompliance with treatment recommendations or ignoring potentially lethal consequences of health-related behavior by either parent or child? Is there evidence for either under- or overutilization of health care? Has there ever been any accusation of or reporting of child neglect because of insufficient supervision of the child's treatment? What is the child's and family's expectation of the youngster's future health status? Is this realistic, overly optimistic, or pessimistic? Are there any religious prohibitions concerning medical intervention? How appropriate and realistic are these?

This section clearly deals with the most sensitive material in the developmental health history. By putting it toward the end of the history, the clinician ensures that adequate time has been allotted for rapport formation. Here the clinician seeks to obtain a sense of the more irrational and sometimes outright damaging distortions that the child, family, or both exhibit in approaching health care. In this section, particular attention should be paid to material pertaining to the diagnosis of Munchausen's by proxy or plain neglect. In Munchausen's by proxy, a parent who appears very concerned actually is making the child ill, inducing illness under the guise of concern for the child's physical health. Usually the syndrome involves profound distortions of reality on the part of both child and parent, distortions maintained even in the face of overwhelming evidence. Attachment problems usually are evident, and in many cases the parent is successful in inducing all kinds of inappropriate treatment of the child from

even very experienced pediatric and other medical practitioners. A milder form of this problem finds expression as illness exaggeration, where the parent's ministrations to the child are not as lethal and unremitting. In such instances, reality-testing reassures parent and child rather than causes them to disappear, as is typical of Munchausen's-by-proxy cases. The child whose physical health has been neglected usually presents many health problems, diffuse, general, and multifaceted; parallel to this, the child's capacity for attachment is weak to nonexistent. All these forms of parent-child disturbance must be thought of and explored as a child is examined for normal development and physical health status.

IMPACT OF ILLNESS ON SOCIAL AND ACADEMIC DEVELOPMENT

Has illness resulted in prolonged absence from school? If so, how has this affected the youngster's grades? What about peer relationships; how does the child present his or her illness or disability to peers? Have school staff been helpful, or is there tension about the child's special needs? Is the child appropriately placed in a general classroom, or should there be special arrangements? Is there any evidence that the youngster is being ostracized or victimized because of illness? In sum, it is essential to explore the broader impact of illness on the child's development and family life as well as to pursue the clarification of issues of secondary and/or primary gain from illness.

Conclusion

Exploring the physical health of a child or adolescent should be a normal part of any child psychiatric assessment. The practitioner should not merely review existing pediatric records, as there are many reasons why the primary care physician may not be privy to all relevant information. The most common and prevalent barrier is time limitation—the average medical assessment of a child lasts less than 10 minutes. The child psychiatrist usually has much more time available as well as the necessary interviewing skills, which make exploring uncharted territory and sensitive areas possible. In the course of such an investigation, it should not be surprising if new information comes to light that will allow the child psychiatrist to make concrete suggestions for further medical inquiry. Such an active role in the assessment of the whole health of the patient is an appropriate task for the modern child psychiatrist, one that allows him or her to be a full partner in children's health care.

REFERENCES

Children's Defense Fund. (1986). *Building health programs for teenagers.* Washington, DC: Author.

Colon, A. R. (1990). Nutrition. In M. Ziai (Ed.), *Pediatrics* (pp. 117–124). Boston: Little, Brown.

Millstein, S. G., & Litt, I. F. (1990). Adolescent health. In S. Feldman & G. Elliott (Eds.), *At the threshold. The developing adolescent* (pp. 431–456). Cambridge, MA: Harvard University Press.

Feinstein, C., & Berger, K. (1987). The chronically ill or disabled child. In J. D. Noshpitz (Ed.), *Basic handbook of child psychiatry, Vol. 5: Advances and new directions* (pp. 91–96). New York: Basic Books.

Newacheck, P. W. (1989). Adolescents with special health needs: Prevalence, severity and access to health services. *Pediatrics, 84,* 872–881.

Pless, I. B., Cripps, H. A., Davies, J. M., & Wadsworth, M. E. J. (1989). Chronic physical illness in childhood: Psychological and social effects in adolescence and adult life. *Developmental Medicine and Child Neurology, 31,* 746–755.

Pless, I. B., & Nolan, T. (1991). Revision, replication and neglect—research on maladjustment in chronic illness. *Journal of Child Psychology and Psychiatry, 32,* 347–365.

Steiner, H. (ed.): *Treating Adolescents.* San Francisco: Jossey-Bass, 1996.

Steiner, H. (ed.). *Treating Preschool Children.* San Francisco: Jossey-Bass, 1997.

Steiner, H. (ed.): *Treating School Age Children.* San Francisco: Jossey-Bass, 1997.

42 / Nutrition Assessment

Patricia Novak and Marion Taylor Baer

Developmental delays or psychiatric disorders may predispose a child to nutritional deficiencies. Factors negatively influencing nutrition such as pica, altered feeding behaviors, or use of psychopharmaceuticals are common to this population (Ekvall, 1993). Conversely, nutrition can influence behavior; for example, iron deficiency anemia can give rise to behaviors similar to attention deficit hyperactivity disorder (Pollitt, 1983). A nutrition assessment, completed by a registered dietitian trained in pediatrics, can identify nutritional factors that may contribute to or result from the child's disorder.

A nutrition evaluation typically involves 4 main areas: anthropometric, dietary, clinical, and biochemical assessments (Underwood, 1986). When feeding skill development appears impaired, a feeding assessment also should be included (Ekvall, 1993).

Anthropometry

Growth, as determined by measurements over time of height or length (birth until 24 to 36 months), is considered the best objective measure of a child's nutritional status. If basic nutritional needs are not met, growth will not occur in a predictable, linear manner.

When assessing growth, measurements need to

be taken at regular intervals and plotted on standardized, age- and sex-appropriate growth charts (National Center for Health Statistics 1976). The ideal is a normal growth rate rather than a hypothetical ideal, such as growth along the 50th percentile. Serial measurements are required to determine the severity of weight changes in eating disorders or stunting due to stimulant use (Scott, 1992). When evaluating cases of failure to thrive, a characteristic rate decline occurs for weight for age, followed by a decrease in length for age. If intervention is not initiated, the rate of head circumference growth may show a corresponding decline indicating impaired brain development. Other considerations for analysis include genetic variations (e.g., height of parents), medical diagnoses (e.g., prematurity or disabilities), and social conditions associated with poor growth (Ekvall, 1993).

In order to analyze body composition, additional anthropometric measurements frequently are made. These include arm circumference and fat-fold measurements. In conjunction, these measurements allow calculation of muscle mass, protein, and fat stores (Garrow, 1982). Bioelectrical impedance and underwater weighing also are used clinically to estimate body fat; these, however, require more costly equipment and may not be appropriate for children. Estimates of muscle mass and fat stores are warranted when poor weight/height gains indicate low stores of one or the other, as in anorexia nervosa or attention deficit hyperactivity disorder (Scott, 1992). These estimates also aid in determining the degree of obesity or in monitoring weight loss/gain. (Ekvall, 1993). Anthropometric deviations may reflect either normal variation or signs of pathology. Therefore, anthropometry must be combined with dietary or biochemical indicators.

Dietary Assessment

Dietary assessment identifies both limitations and excesses (Persson, 1984). In addition, it frequently exposes information regarding the family dynamics and economics as well as the child's developmental skills (Steiner, Smith, Rosenkranz, & Litt, 1991). Dietary information typically is obtained through a 24-hour recall, 3- to 7-day food record, or a food frequency report. While the 24-hour recall is prone to memory and estimation inaccuracies, it is easy to administer and provides immediate information. A 3- to 7-day food record kept as a running account of food consumed provides more complete and accurate information. Food records also can include mealtime behavioral observations. The limitations of a food record include: inability to maintain or return the record and the potential for change in dietary intake as a result of the recording process (Persson, 1984). A food frequency report screens the child's general diet, alerting the clinician to gross excesses or deficiencies (Zulkifi & Yu, 1992).

In-depth nutrient assessment usually makes use of a computer database system to determine nutrient content of foods consumed. Databases vary in the number of foods included and the completeness of nutrient values listed for foods. All nutrient assessments, therefore, need to be considered as estimates (Lee, 1995). Estimates of dietary intake are compared to recommendations for specific nutrients. These recommendations, such as the Recommended Dietary Allowances (RDA) are designed to serve as a general measure of adequacy for healthy population groups and not as indicators of the optimum intake for an individual. Clinically, they can only be used to assess the level of risk of inadequate nutrient intake for any individual. Finally, while dietary evaluation will estimate the level of consumption for a given nutrient, it cannot indicate the amount of that nutrient that actually is absorbed and utilized.

Clinical Assessment

Clinical assessment includes the medical examination of the child to determine if abnormalities in appearance or behavior could be related to malnutrition. This includes examination of hair, skin, mouth, eyes, nails, musculature, affect, and vital signs (Underwood, 1986). When calcium status is in question—as in cases of anorexia or long-term use of anticonvulsants, radiography is also warranted to determine the degree of bone calcification (Mycek, 1984; Pomeroy, 1989). Drugs such as anticonvulsants, monoamine oxidase inhibitors, or stimulants can alter nutritional status either directly by disturbing metabolism or indirectly by changing taste sensitivity or appetite (Mycek, 1984). Most clinical signs of malnutrition, such as dry skin or cracked lips, are nonspecific and may indicate some other pathology or even normal individual variation; they must therefore be confirmed by concurrent dietary or biochemical signs of malnutrition (Underwood, 1986).

Biochemical Assessment

Hematological and urinary analyses are useful in nutrition assessment, as they are objective and can estimate nutrient storage and/or function (Underwood, 1973). As with all assessment parameters, these tests have limitations. A biochemically detectable deficiency may occur well after functional status has been affected; for example, low hematocrit occurs after iron deficiency anemia has produced a decrease in red blood cell capacity. Laboratory tests are invasive and may produce equi-

vocal results with regard to nutritional status, as abnormal blood or urinary values may have other etiologies. Therefore, biochemical tests usually are conducted as a secondary level of assessment, after dietary, clinical, or anthropometric assessments have indicated the need for further evaluation (Pi-Sunyer, 1984).

Reassessment

Nutritional status is not static. Formal assessment should occur on a regular basis to coincide with major developmental changes in the infant and toddler, and every 6 months to 1 year for older children, depending on the level of risk. Frequent evaluation is critical in cases with long-term medication use, where nutritional rehabilitation is essential to the treatment process; this is especially the case with eating disorders or with the use of clinically modified diets, such as ketogenic or weight-control diets (American Dietetic Association, 1995).

REFERENCES

American Dietetic Association. (1995). Position of the American Dietetic Association: Nutrition services for children with special health care needs. *Journal of the American Dietetic Association, 95,* 809–812.

Ekvall, S. W. (1993). Nutrition assessment and early intervention. In S. W. Ekvall (Ed.), *Pediatric nutrition in chronic diseases and developmental disorders: Prevention, assessment and treatment* (pp. 41–77). New York: Oxford University Press.

Garrow, J. S. (1982). New approaches to body composition. *American Journal of Clinical Nutrition, 35,* 1152–1157.

Lee, R. D., Nieman, D. C., & Rainwater, M. (1995). Comparison of eight microcomputer dietary analysis programs with the USDA Nutrient Data Base for Standard Reference. *Journal of the American Dietetic Association, 95,* 858–867.

Mycek, M. J. (1984). Interaction of drugs with foods and nutrients. In M. D. Simko, C. Cowell & J. A. Gilbride (Eds.). *Nutrition Assessment: A comprehensive guide for planning intervention,* Rockville MD: Aspen Publication.

National Center for Health Statistics (NCHS): National Center for Health Statistics Growth Charts (1976). In *Monthly Vital Statistics Report 25* (3), Supplement (HRA) 76–1120. Rockville, MD: Health Resources Administration.

National Research Council. (1990). *Recommended Dietary Allowances, 10th ed.* Washington DC: National Academy of Sciences, NRC.

Persson, L. A. & Carlgren, G. (1984). Measuring children's diets; Evaluation of dietary assessment techniques in infancy and childhood. *Int J Epidemiol 13,* 506–517.

Pi-Sunyer, F. X. & Woo, R. (1984). Laboratory Assessment of Nutritional Status. In M. D. Simko, C. Cowell and J. A. Gilbride (Eds). *Nutrition Assessment—A comprehensive guide for planning intervention.* Rockville, MD: Aspen Publishers, Inc.

Pollitt, E., Viteri, F. E., Saco-Pollitt, C., Leibel, R. L. (1982). Behavioral effects of iron deficiency anemia in children. In E. Pollitt & R. L. Leibel (Eds) *Iron Deficiency: Brain Biochemistry and Behavior.* New York: Raven Press. pp. 195–208.

Pomeroy, C. & Mitchell, J. E. (1989). Medical complications and management of eating disorders. *Psychiatric Annals 19*, 438–485.

Posner, B. M. (1992). Comparison of techniques for estimating nutrient intake: The Framingham Study. *Epidemiology 3*, 171–177.

Scott, B. J., Artman, H. & St.Jeor, S. T. (1992). Growth Assessment in children: a review. *Topics in Clinical Nutrition 8*, 5–31.

Steiner, H., Smith, C., Rosenkranz, R. T., & Litt, I.

(1991). The early care and feeding of Anorexics. *Child Psychology and Human Development, 21*, 163–167.

Underwood, B. (1986). Evaluating the nutritional status of individuals: A critique of approaches. *Nutrition Review, 44* (Suppl.), 213–224.

Zulkifi, S. N., & Yu, S. M. (1992). The food frequency method for dietary assessment. *Journal of the American Dietetic Association, 92*, 681–685.

43 / Assessment of Gender and Sexual Development in Children

Susan Coates and Sabrina Wolfe

An assessment of gender and sexuality as a part of any comprehensive psychiatric evaluation of a child always should be carried out in the context of a comprehensive evaluation of the family. The function and significance of gender and sexuality in a child's experience will be constructed within the framework of its meaning in the child's family. Families differ greatly in the degree to which gender and sexuality are preoccupying concerns and differ as well in the positive and negative attribution made to each. Moreover, both the family and the child can appropriate gender and sexuality for managing a variety of anxieties that have been experienced as intolerable or traumatic. Thus, the child's behavior will not be understandable unless it is considered within the context of his or her particular family.

In taking a psychosexual developmental history pertaining to the first 5 to 6 years of life, 3 areas are focused on: (1) the child's comfort and discomfort with his or her own gender; (2) the child's awareness of and interest, both positive and negative, in his or her own genitals and in those of others; and (3) the child's ability to integrate and contain sexual-sensual feelings in an intact body schema without the use of either compulsive rituals or aggressive intrusion on the body boundaries of others.

The psychological and interpersonal processes governing the development of gender and sexuality result in a great deal of variation. However, extremely rigid stereotypical cross-gender or same-

gender behavior or compulsive sexual behavior accompanied by negative feelings about his or her own gender or sex is usually a signal of significant suffering in the child and significant disturbance in the child's primary attachment relationships—with parents, important caregivers, and siblings—and accordingly always should be evaluated from this standpoint.

In assessing the child's gender and sexuality, it is essential that the clinician understand the complexity of the child's sense of sexuality and gender in a developmental context (Coates, 1997). The first 5 to 6 years of life is a period of rapid development in these domains, and there is a good deal of unevenness in the rate at which the component aspects of each develop. By the end of this period children ordinarily will have consolidated a sense of their own gender as a positively valued aspect of the self. Typically, they also will have consolidated a basic body schema that will include and accommodate a degree of sexual/sensual pleasure, vitality, and excitement as positively valued aspects of the self. Thus, during the school-age years, most children will have established characteristic patterns relating to their sense of gender and sexuality.

The 2 domains, gender and sexuality, become interwoven in complex ways at multiple levels of development throughout life. Some of that integration begins in infancy and continues, with notable transformations and consolidations, in the preschool, school-age, and adolescent years. However, we do not yet understand how these integrations occur or what the mechanisms are. Nevertheless, in assessing the child, the clinician should keep the domains conceptually distinct.

Infant Assessment

For both parents and physicians, at birth the external genitals are the hallmarks of gender categorization: This is a boy or this is a girl. From the moment the sex is determined, the child will develop in a gendered world with expectations directed at him or her based on the parents' knowledge of the child's gender and the meaning of gender in their own life and their social world. Infants appear to have a preverbal appreciation of gender difference. By 6 months infants can discriminate between female and male faces and voices, and by 15 months toddlers can identify pictures of girls and boys. In the first 2 years of life infants identify with and readily imitate the activities and mannerisms of persons of both genders. By age 2 children can use verbal labels to identify adult females and males; by 2½ they can use verbal labels to identify their peers and their own gender.

The known sex differences between boys and girls that are presumptively innate are few and quite relative. Infant boys in aggregate are more reactive to stress, are more irritable and difficult to soothe, and may be more reactive and vulnerable to the impact of maternal depression. The clinician can elicit from the parents their own attitudes about the child's gender, the child's temperament, and whether they are happy or disappointed with this particular child. In general, however, in listening to the parents' report about the infant's gender, the clinician should bear in mind that the parents are schematizing what they observe about the child's temperament and proclivities according to their own values and preconceptions about gender.

The capacity for sexual-sensual arousal begins early (Serbin & Sprafkin, 1987). Erections in boys have been observed in utero via sonograms, and lubrication has been documented in infant girls; these facts indicate that the sexual response system is ready to function at birth or at least in the

first months of life. Behavior that appears to be similar to adult orgasm has been observed in infants of both sexes.

Children's interest in the visual and tactile exploration of their own genitals generally first emerges in the second half of the first year of life. Their vital interest in their body grows out of a vitalized emotional connection to their primary caregivers. Very little, if any, masturbation occurs in institutionalized infants deprived of attachment relationships, in contrast to infants raised at home. In family-reared children, masturbation during the first year of life is typical, although usually it is only in the second year that a distinctively sexual excitement begins to become differentially observable. Typical is Kleeman's (1965) observation of an 11-month-old boy who would grab at his penis, rub it with a bottle, or squeeze it together with his testicles and move them around. At this early age it was not easy to distinguish his exploratory interest in his penis from his exploratory interest in other objects and parts of his body. By 15 months this same boy's interest in his penis had a distinct masturbatory character of self-stimulation, with self-absorption and mounting excitement plainly evident. Roiphe and Galenson (1981) similarly report observing masturbatory activity in the second year accompanied by a preoccupied, faraway look in the child's eyes; the inference is that the activity is already beginning to be accompanied by internal fantasy. During the first 18 months, and sometimes for a period afterward, masturbatory activity may accompany other sensuous activities such as sucking, which at times can take on similar qualities of self-absorption and excitement. Observations have been made indicating that even very young children sometimes may transiently direct these various behaviors toward preferred adults and do so in a way that suggests concomitant sexual-sensual excitement.

Instances of active masturbation in infants under 1 year of age have been reported. Masturbation in young infants often is unexpected and can be sufficiently difficult to recognize that it becomes confused with abdominal cramps and other conditions, including seizures. Infant masturbatory episodes may feature stereotyped posturing with tightening of the thighs or mechanical pressure applied to the pudendum accompanied by intermittent quiet grunting, irregular breathing, and facial flushing. Several cases have been described in the literature where this kind of activity has been misinterpreted as indicating an alteration of consciousness secondary to epilepsy. Although sexual abuse has been reported in some cases, active early infant masturbation also may rarely occur in conditions of neglect. In girls, it can occur in the context of perineal discomfort secondary to yeast vaginitis.

In assessing infants and children under the age of 2, the clinician should ask the parents if the child has an interest in his or her genitals and plays with them. Further inquiry is warranted if the parents' reply indicates either excessive masturbation or the absence of any interest whatsoever.

Toddlers

Most observers of children's sexuality identify the period of about 16 to 24 months in both boys and girls as a time when a marked increase in genital interest occurs (Roiphe & Galenson, 1981). For boys the pattern of masturbatory activity tends to remain the same thereafter. In girls, however, following an efflorescence during this period, it is not uncommon for masturbation to decrease or drop out completely or be replaced by indirect techniques of masturbation, such as using thighs, pillows, or rocking horses to masturbate. By age 2 children can recognize their own genitals by pointing to the one that is "like me" when presented with dolls with female and male genitals (de Marneffe, 1997).

Children's failure to develop any interest whatsoever in their genitals usually occurs in a context of extreme abandonment and neglect, although, paradoxically, occasionally the same conditions can lead to compulsive interest in sexual activity as a form of self-soothing. Compulsive and intense interest in their own genitals also frequently occurs in the context of sexual overstimulation and/or sexual abuse, which we will return to later. The clinician should ask the parents not only whether children play with their genitals but also whether children prefer to do this alone or in the presence of other people, and whether objects are incorporated in the masturbatory activity. For example, the parents can be asked if the child places objects

in her vagina or his or her anus. They also should be asked whether the child intrudes on the body boundaries of other children, by aggressively trying to touch others' genitals.

During the second half of the second year, children's interest in their own genitals ordinarily will be joined by an interest in the anatomical differences between the sexes. Both boys and girls will be interested in penises and vaginas and who has them. The clinician should ask whether the child is curious about other people's bodies, both adults and children, and how this curiosity is expressed. In addition, the parents should be asked how sexual curiosity was handled in their family of origin when they were growing up and how they handle it in their own child. Finally, the parents should be asked if the child appears to have any particular anxieties relating to his or her body.

Although children become interested in the genitals of others at this age, this does not constitute the basis for the concurrent emergence of children's understanding of their own and others' gender. Initially these domains do not appear to be integrated; they become so only over time. Herzog (1996) has demonstrated that at about 15 months, children can identify pictures of girls and boys and apply the correct verbal labels. Research from many different disciplines has converged in pointing to the period between 1 and 3 years as the time when gender identity first begins to emerge. Kohlberg (1966) has discussed this period in terms of children's dawning cognitive abilities. Similarly noting that it coincides with the emergence of language development, Money and Ehrhardt (1972) have identified this as the sensitive period for gender development—the time during which this aspect of the self ordinarily becomes established; thereafter it becomes progressively more resistant to change. And Mahler, Pine, and Bergman (1975) have argued that the achievement of gender identity follows upon the consolidation of self- and object-representations at the end of the rapprochement stage of development.

The development of a sense of one's own gender thus appears to be inextricably bound up both with the emergence of language and with the dawning appreciation of the self as an autonomous agent with wishes and desires that are separate and distinct from those of the primary caregivers. The emergence of a verbal conception of self occurs simultaneously with the capacity verbally to categorize boys and girls; as soon as children can identify pictures of themselves, they also can categorize children by sex (Lewis & Brooks-Gunn, 1979). This fact suggests that emergence of the sense of self is closely linked with the construction of gender as a meaningful category.

Before children can accurately label self and other according to gender, they pass through an undifferentiated stage: They believe they can be and do all things (Fast, 1984). Thus toddler girls may announce that they will grow a penis and toddler boys may declare that they have a baby in their stomach just like Mommy. One 4-year-old boy, while sitting in his mother's lap, touched her breast and said, "Mom, when I grow up will I have muscles like this?" She said, "No, boys have penises and girls have breasts." He looked at her intently and said, "Mom, you're wrong, I'm going to have both." In general, in very young children, penis envy is no more common in girls than the wish to have breasts and give birth to a baby is in a boy. Many children experience some degree of loss when they realize the limits that their body imposes on their experience: that is, boys do not become pregnant and girls do not have penises (Fast, 1984). Some children whose self-esteem is fragile can encounter difficulty in negotiating the transition from the undifferentiated stage to a gendered sense of self, particularly if the issue of loss is already charged for them.

In assessing gender development during the ages 18 months to 3 years, the clinician should ask the parents if the child can tell the difference between boys and girls, if the child can correctly identify his or her own gender, and if the child seems content with his or her own gender. The parents also should be asked about the child's play, whether he or she prefers to take the male or female role, and whether the child imitates people of the same sex, the other sex, or both.

A flexible degree of cross-gender behavior is typical at this age. What is clinically significant, and warrants more intensive assessment even at this early age, is where a child appears intensely dysphoric about his or her gender coupled and extremely preoccupied with the clothes and activities of the other gender. Behavior occurring in this extreme form may be indicative of a transient reaction due to severe family stress, or it may mark the onset of a gender identity disorder (Coates, 1992).

Sexual curiosity and interests continue to develop along with gender in toddlers and preschool children. Toilet training becomes possible in the third year, as children develop increasing physical control over their bodies. Depending on the relationship with the parents, toilet training can be simple, uneventful, and a source of pride in mastery for children. Alternatively, it can become the focus of struggles over autonomy and a ready arena for expressing ongoing conflicts in the child-caregiver relationship. In general, toilet training leads both parents and child to become newly focused on the child's body, and this in turn may further stimulate the child's interest in his or her body and its capacities.

At about the same age as toilet training becomes instituted, children also begin to develop a curiosity about the processes of birth and where babies comes from. This phenomenon has been well studied; it is clear that children pass through a sequence of cognitive-developmental stages (Bernstein & Cowan, 1975). At first their conceptions are highly artificial—"babies come from the baby store"—or based on other more familiar bodily processes—"the baby comes out the doodoo hole"—or animistic—"the sperm goes into the mommy and makes each egg safe so if there's a bump they won't break." Education and socialization have been shown to have an impact on the rate at which children arrive at an understanding of the processes of conception, gestation, and birth, although by the same token the literature abounds in anecdotal reports of children misconstruing information in wonderfully fanciful ways owing to their cognitive immaturity. By age 7 to 8, some 30% of children will still give artificial or animistic explanations. Noteworthy is the fact that while gestation and giving birth become quickly ascribed to "mommies" and thus linked to gender role, in very young children the process of procreation is not ordinarily connected to sexual feelings.

The Preschool Years

The early preschool years are a period in which there is an efflorescence of sexual curiosity, while during the later preschool years, children begin to consolidate a gendered sense of self. Both domains will begin to become more integrated when children reach the school years; gender and sexual interests then gradually become intertwined as children are progressively more able to imagine themselves in romantic relationships.

The task for assessment during the preschool years is essentially to evaluate the child's progress in the 2 developmental domains of gender and sexuality, both of which display a great deal of individual variation. In general, the clinician should be knowledgeable as to the expectable degree of variation in both domains, while understanding that flexibility and curiosity are indications of health. Conversely, the clinician should be alert for indications of intense anxiety related to bodily functions, of compulsive, rigid, and/or markedly aggressive behavior in the area of sexuality, and of intense dysphoria in the area of gender.

In this realm, clinical assessment must reckon with a degree of cognitive immaturity in children. Once children are able to identify their own gender and that of their peers, for the majority this ushers in an increased interest in associating with their own gender. Yet even though children at this age can label by gender accurately and show an investment in their own gender, the category of gender is exceedingly concrete. It continues to lack a depth of meaning until the child arrives at a further understanding of gender stability, gender constancy, and the fact that the genitals are the defining attribute of sex categorization. Children's understanding of gender is progressively reconstructed and reorganized and becomes progressively more abstract as they move through the Piagetian cognitive-developmental stages (Kohlberg, 1966).

Gender stability refers to the ability to appreciate that one is born a boy or a girl and will remain a boy or a girl when one is grown up. *Gender constancy* refers to the understanding that a change in one's external appearance, clothes, or activities does not change one's gender categorization (i.e., wearing girls' clothing does not transform a boy into a girl). These cognitive differentiations must in turn become integrated with the understanding that the defining attribute of being a boy or a girl is one's genitals and not one's activities, mode of dress, outward appearance, or any other culturally derived emblem of gender.

Research has identified a period of development when the understanding of gender, although present and affectively laden, is nonetheless cognitively immature. Many 4- to 6-year-olds may exhibit confusion when asked whether a change of activities will lead to a change of gender (gender constancy) or whether they will always be or have always been the same gender (gender stability). When it is acquired, knowledge of the anatomical differences between the sexes appears to play a significant role in stabilizing these cognitive structures.

Although knowledge of anatomical genital differences may stabilize cognitive structures pertaining to gender, the linkage between genitalia and gender categorization is not necessarily automatic (Bem, 1989). This fact can be seen in the frequent idiosyncratic responses of children at early ages. For example, when asked how to tell the difference between boys and girls, a 3-year-old who knew that boys have penises and girls have vaginas said, "Boys burp and run faster." Another 4-year-old, similarly knowledgeable of genital differences, told his teacher that he had gone to a pet shop the day before with his father and saw 2 girl cats and 2 boy cats. When the teacher asked him how he knew which was which, he said, "My dad turned them over and I think he read the print." Even seasoned clinicians are startled by how difficult it is for children to develop the stable conceptions of sex and gender that adults take for granted. From the young child's perspective, genitals are not relevant for categorization as one sex or the other.

As noted earlier, the known sex differences between boys and girls that are presumptively constitutional are few and quite relative. Although there is a wide range of individual variation in children as toddlers, in the aggregate boys are somewhat bolder and more physically aggressive than girls, and they are more active explorers of their environment. In particular, they show a preference for rough-and-tumble play and playfighting. Moreover, once a child selectively prefers same-gender peers, he or she becomes progressively more socialized into masculine and feminine stereotypes and acquires differential patterns of managing interpersonal conflict. (See Maccoby, 1990.) For boys in particular, during the ages 3 to 6, peer group socialization plays an important role in the consolidation of gender role behaviors (Fagot, 1993). The clinician should be aware that a child's adoption of behaviors related to gender is largely the result of socialization (including the child's own contribution to it through particular proclivities and fantasies), not of innate differences and the degree of variation of expressed differences within each gender is considerable. For example, some girls are more physically active than some boys and some boys are more interested in nurturing activities than some girls.

Some degree of stereotypical cross-gender interests continues to be nearly universal in preschool children but diminishes markedly between the ages of 4 to 6. The frequency of stereotypical cross-gender behaviors is low for both boys and girls after age 3, although, in our culture to be sure, some children have a greater sense of gender flexibility than others.

Occasionally more compulsive yet still transient patterns of cross-gender identification may be observed in young children in response to familial stress. For example, in the face of severe family stress brought about by a sudden maternal depression or by a paternal heart attack, a boy may take to dressing compulsively in Mommy's clothes and saying that he wants to be, or is, a girl. Such behavior can indicate significant anxiety in the child, as would any other symptom, such as an obsessional preoccupation or phobia. Not infrequently cases are seen where the behavior spontaneously diminishes once the family crisis has passed. In other cases, direct intervention with the parents is sufficient to help them become more emotionally available to the child or to respond more appropriately to the child's developmental needs. Direct intervention with the child also may help to address the child's distress while helping him or her to develop a range of strategies for managing anxiety more effectively. Clinical experience suggests that 3 to 6 months is the outside limit for spontaneous remission of such transient but compulsive, crisis-related cross-gender identifications; where they persist longer, they almost invariably indicate a significant disturbance in the family, in the child's capacity to regulate affect, in the child's developing sense of self, and in the child's attachment relationships.

Gender identity disorder is relatively rare, with onset during and just after the sensitive period of gender development (roughly ages 18 months to 4 years of age). It is characterized by intense dysphoria regarding the child's given gender coupled with a compulsive and preoccupying wish to become the other gender that is manifest in the child's identifications, play, dress, and preferred activities. Children with this disorder need to be evaluated for concomitant psychiatric disorder as well; usually they are anxious about separation, are troubled by depression, often are emotionally isolated, and can have marked difficulty dealing with their own and others' aggression. It is important to note that any and all of these issues may be masked on initial presentation. This is particularly true for a subgroup of boys with Gender Identity Disorder who are often role-reversed in terms of parenting, who are highly attuned to parental affect, and who serve as containers of their parents' affect rather than the parents' serving as theirs. Accordingly, once their preoccupations have become a parental concern, these boys often will suppress their compulsive behavior's in an effort to try to help their parents regulate their own affect. In the course of evaluating boys, it is not uncommon for parents to report that as soon as they made an appointment to have the child seen, but before they came for an appointment, the child's cross-gender preoccupations markedly decreased or seemed to disappear. In an extended evaluation involving psychological testing, interviewing, and observation of play, however, if the child's problems have been long-standing rather than fleeting and transitory, the preoccupations with gender nearly always emerge. The assessment should focus on the child's sense of self and self-worth and on his or her capacity to manage affect, including separation anxiety, depression, and anger. In collateral interviews with the parents, which are essential to the assessment, the clinician should be alert to the high probability of parental psychopathology and of familial stress experienced by one or both parents as traumatic. It is not at all uncommon to find unresolved traumatic experiences even from childhood that are linked to gender in the parents' experiences. An understanding of the significance of gender to the family is crucial in planning family interventions to heal the suffering in the family and the child. A differential diagnosis must be made between gender identity disorder and gender atypicality.

Despite extensive research, no chromosomal or hormonal abnormalities have been discovered in children with gender identity disorder. Accordingly, an endocrine evaluation is not warranted.

The significance of Gender Identity Disorder in regard to later sexual orientation and adult gender identity is a matter of current research. Unfortunately, longitudinal studies of boys with this disorder largely have focused on sexual orientation as the principal outcome measure rather than on the children's well-being in terms of feelings of self-worth, personal vitality, and creativity. Longitudinal research to date (see Zucker & Bradley, 1995) suggests that roughly half to two thirds of boys with the disorder will later develop a homosexual orientation, while a sizable minority of boys will be heterosexual. In addition, a small but significant fraction of boys will be intensely gender dysphoric well into their adolescent years and may wish or seek transsexual surgery. However, in no individual case is it possible to predict the later outcome during early childhood. It must be emphasized that while retrospective studies of adult homosexual men (Bell, Weinberg, & Hammersmith, 1981; Saghir & Robins, 1973) indicate that a large majority were gender "nonconforming" as children—for example, interested in solitary and/or artistic pursuits, and/or avoidant of rough-and-tumble play—only a very small minority appear to have met the criteria for having had a Gender Identity Disorder. No systematic follow-up studies of girls with childhood Gender Identity Disorder have been carried out.

Conceptually distinct from Gender Identity Disorder but sometimes conflated with it by the lay public is gender atypical interests (Coates & Wolfe, 1995). Approximately 10 to 15% of children have a sensitive, shy, and behaviorally inhibited temperament. Unlike the great majority of boys, those with an inhibited temperament usually have an aversion to rough-and-tumble play. Many also have an esthetic sensibility and develop interests in art or music that are not considered stereotypically masculine. Comparably, in girls, approximately 10 to 15% will have a strong interest in athletics and prefer rough-and-tumble play. The clinician should be aware that such children represent temperamental variations, and their proclivities have nothing to do with suffering, except insofar as they lead children to become scapegoated.

Children who vary temperamentally from their peers and who do not conform to prevailing gender stereotypes are not infrequently scapegoated by peers. The clinician should be alert to this possibility occurring both to children with atypical gender interests and to those with gender identity disorder. In addition, children with gender atypical interests sometimes must contend with parental censure and/or pressures based on the parents' own attitudes toward gender. By contrast, in families where a child develops a gender identity disorder, the parents most often powerfully encourage the child's cross-gender behavior either overtly or covertly, at least until neighbors or teachers identify it to them as potentially problematic.

During the preschool years, a significant degree of gender stereotypy in the conception of gender is typical for all children. Young children tend to think in quite concrete terms and form categories on an all-or-none basis. Despite the efforts of some parents to encourage unisex or androgynous conceptions, many children, owing to the immaturity of their cognitive abilities and to the presence of cultural stereotypes, will pursue gender stereotypes with a remarkable intensity. Thus most children in this culture learn to associate masculinity with aggression and fighting (Fagot, 1993; Kohlberg, 1966), regardless of their parents' attitudes. Beyond that, children may absorb a host of preconceptions about gender roles and occupations, sometimes in ways that are remarkably at odds with their own direct experience in the family. One 4-year-old girl, who tested in the superior range of intelligence and whose mother was a practicing physician, responded to a set of questions about gender roles by asserting that only boys could be doctors and only girls could be nurses.

In the individual interview with a child, his or her sense of self and feelings of self-worth need to be evaluated along with the child's attitude toward gender and the experience of gender identity. Gender identity is an aspect of self-concept, and its assessment is best accomplished in the context of an overall assessment of self-development and capacity for affect regulation. Thus in a comprehensive evaluation, the simple screening questions "Is it better to be a boy or a girl?" and "Why?" and "If you could change anything about yourself, what would you change?" are helpful in ascertaining children's feelings about their own gender.

Children's sexual development should be evaluated in interviews with the parents. An initial question about a child's interest in sexuality can be followed-up with questions concerned with the degree of the child's absorption, possible anxiety about bodily intactness, and the kind of limits the parents place on sexual behavior in the home. Any aggressive sexual behavior by a child always warrants further evaluation. In taking a history of a child's sexual development from the parents, the following questions, flexibly used when needed, have proved consistently useful.

1. How does your child express an interest in his penis/her vagina?
2. How often does your son/daughter play with his penis/her vagina?
3. Does he/she do it alone or when other people are around?
4. When does it happen? At home, school, playing with other children, watching TV, going to sleep, or when upset, etc.?
5. Does he/she stimulate his penis/her vagina with an object?
6. Does your child put objects into her vagina or into her/his anus?
7. Does your child try to harm his/her genitals?
8. Does he/she often masturbate in front of others?
9. Is your son often worried that his penis is or could be damaged?
10. Is your daughter preoccupied with a concern that her vagina is or could be damaged?
11. Is your child interested in or curious about other people's bodies (or show any interest whatsoever)? Adults or children? How often?
12. Is he/she involved in sex play with other children? Does your child often touch children's sexual parts? How often? Under what circumstances? With other children's consent or not?
13. Does your child imitate adult sexual behavior?

Parent replies should be assessed against an understanding of typical patterns. Sexual curiosity and interests are common in preschool children and are expressed in a variety of ways, including showing their own genitals to adults and to other children; touching their own genitals and those of other children; touching their mother's breast and their father's penis; masturbating with their hand; trying to look at people undressing; and undressing in front of others. It is not at all uncommon for these sexual behaviors to occur either in the context of mild curiosity or with apparent experienced excitement.

Young children usually are curious about the genitals of the other sex. Extreme lack of interest and curiosity about sexuality may suggest inhibition or anxiety in this domain and must be understood in the context of the meaning of sexuality to the family. Sexual interest in young children typically increases during the preschool years, appears to level off during the school years (although most children continue to have an interest in sexuality), and increases again during the prepubescent years (Friedrich, Grambsch, Broughton, Kuiper, & Beilke, 1991). Persistently high levels of observed sexual behavior continuing and/or increasing into the school-age years is atypical. Despite the fact that sexual curiosity and sexual behavior in preschool children are typical, very high levels of sexual interest and behavior in early and later childhood tend to be correlated with behavior problems in the child and with sexual overstimulation by the parents. At any age level, extreme preoccupation with sexuality in its more aggressive forms (e.g., grabbing at other children's genitals or trying to harm his or her own genitals) should raise the question of whether child abuse may be occurring.

A minimum degree of transient anxiety in connection with the genitals and with the body in general also is common. From about the age of 15 months on, children begin to develop a positively valued schema of their own genitals (de Marneffe, 1995). As development proceeds further and they begin to become more attentive to anatomical differences, this positive valuation is joined by curiosity. However, their curiosity also may be transiently connected to anxieties about bodily intactness in general, which emerges once children begin to regard themselves as bounded objects in space. It is not uncommon for children to fear that they could lose life or limb down the drain of a bathtub or in the toilet. These concerns may become manifest in various preoccupations, including concerns about the genitals and their functioning, as children mature. Further, children's research in the domain of anatomical differences between the sexes is compounded by the fact that their child's cognitive understanding of the permanence of objects has not yet developed adequately; thus, for some children, various transformations of their own body, both wanted and unwanted, may seem eminently in the realm of the possible.

Later on in the preschool years, fantasies and concerns about the body form a fertile field in children's imaginations for symbolizing various anxieties associated with stresses in their lives or in the family system. These concerns can take the form of castration anxiety, which children may express fairly directly or which they may allude to indirectly in play or drawings. In assessing fears of this kind, the clinician should be alert to the degree to which they are well integrated into a fantasy narrative that promotes mastery of anxiety. In its extreme forms, anxiety about the genitals also can become a vehicle for expressing and symbolizing more basic concerns, such as separation anxiety or the threat of annihilation. Such intense anxiety often follows in the wake of early loss, surgical intervention, witnessing a person severely bloodied in an accident, family violence, or other experiences that leave children with a heightened vulnerability in the area of body intactness and/or in the stability of self- and object representations.

Another phenomenon that may emerge during the preschool years is fetishistic behavior. Such behavior can be distinguished from the use of transitional objects, such as a teddy bear or blanket for purposes of self-soothing, by the fact that it is more ritualistic and compulsive. Fetishistic behavior typically takes as its focus either wearing or holding on to mother's undergarments. Children as young as 2 years of age have been known to insist on sleeping in their mother's panty hose. Fetishistic behavior, especially in school-age boys, may be employed either for self-soothing or for generating a degree of sexual-sensual arousal in compulsive, ritualistic enactment. Boys who engage in this form of fetishistic behavior are usually unremarkably masculine and these behaviors are not used to support or construct a cross-sex identification.

The School Years

Roughly during the period of 5 to 7 years, many children enter into a phase that can aptly be characterized as the "family romance"; at this time children use their burgeoning imaginative capacities to experiment with various roles and relationships. It is not unusual for them to imagine themselves as rivals to one parent for the attentions and affections of the other parent of the other sex, although most often this theme is expressed only in a derivative way in play fantasy. Then, too, siblings, teachers, or peers also may be included in these romances. Cognitively, these phenomena reflect children's dawning ability to imagine complex scenarios in the context of a narrative sense of self. The ability to cope with both dyadic and triadic relationships, which heretofore may have been expressed in sibling rivalries, is also involved. Another factor is children's ability to recognize that an important part of the parents' life is being kept from them and will remain inaccessible.

The specific resolution that a child creates for this initial imaginative foray into the domain of erotic and rivalrous relationships will reflect: the child's temperament, the child's experience of the preexisting relationship with the parents, the parents' own relationship with one another, and the child's level of emotional integration and capacity for fantasy elaboration. The way in which the child resolves this stage will become one of the important contributors to how he or she experiences eroticism and rivalry when these become important in later development.

During the school-age years children's understanding of gender roles ordinarily continues to be highly stereotypical until the various cognitive and affective structures mediating gender are consolidated. After age 7 a notable increase in the flexibility of gender concepts is observable, as children's thinking becomes less sex-role stereotypic (Serbin & Sprafkin, 1987). Children at this age are more likely than younger children to state that both sexes can participate in activities that are traditionally considered highly sex-role stereotyped, although gender segregation in interests and in preferred activities remains high.

Not until adolescence when children can acquire the capacity for formal operations and significantly higher levels of abstraction do they become able to experiment fully with multiple identifications. It is at this age that multiple identifications with role models from both genders which are always a part of the child's experience can become integrated in a more complex and personally authentic identity.

In the school-age years, as in the preschool years, extremely rigid gender stereotypy in behavior or fantasy (whether of the same gender or of the other gender) is potentially problematic and should alert the clinician to evaluate further. Clinical experience suggests that in some cases of extremely hypermasculine behavior in boys or extremely hyperfeminine behavior in girls, the child has developed a rigid and highly stereotypic gender identification in the face of loss, abuse, or other trauma. The clinician should be alert to the possibility that such extreme same-sex role stereotypy continuing into the school years may reflect underlying psychological conflicts that need to be addressed. In boys it is often associated with marked anxiety and/or aggressiveness of a kind that may be an indicator of psychological dysfunction. With girls it is often associated with anxiety and depression.

The consolidation of gender identity continues apace during the school years, during which time peer socialization continues to exert a major influence on attitudes and identifications. Typically, although not exclusively, same-gender role models come to be preferred as identification figures; though in our culture girls more flexibly will take role models from both genders. Boys in particular who significantly deviate from peer expectations regarding gender behavior, either on the basis of temperament or for other reasons, unfortunately often will experience significant degrees of social ostracism, with all the negative impact on the developing sense of self that this may entail.

Sexual interests continue into the school years in both genders. Most authors have noted a diminishment in the range and intensity of sexual behaviors as compared to the preschool years, but some have argued, plausibly, that children simply become more adept at keeping their activities and interests to themselves and away from parents and other adults. Certainly the achievement of a sense of a privacy is one of the developmental tasks associated with this period of development. Not until after age 7 are the majority of children observed to be shy about undressing in front of others (Friedrich et al., 1991).

Incest occurring in the home may lead to hypersexuality in the child (Yates, 1982). Sexual aggression of one child toward another at any age, inserting objects into the vagina or anus in school-age years, or attempts physically to harm one's own genitals are extremely rare behaviors. On clinical grounds, such behaviors raise questions about whether sexual abuse of the child is occurring (Cosentino, Meyer-Bahlburg, Alert, Weinberg, & Gains, 1995; Friedrich, Beilke, & Urquiza, 1987; Friedrich et al., 1991), or whether other significant pathology is present. Such behaviors always indicate a need for further evaluation.

Conclusion

Gender identity, sensuality, and sexuality are deeply rooted in children's experiences with primary caregivers. Gender constructions and sexual preoccupations can be appropriated by both parents and children for managing a wide variety of anxieties and for consolidating various defenses against whatever is experienced as intolerable and/or traumatic (Goldner, 1991). Extreme stereotypic cross-gender behavior, extreme and rigid gender conformity, and extreme lack of interest in or preoccupation with sexuality indicate underlying difficulties in a child's attachment relationships as well as in the development of the self. They always merit an evaluation in this context.

REFERENCES

Bell, A. P., Weinberg, M. S., & Hammersmith, S. K. (1981). *Sexual preference: Its development in men and women.* Bloomington: Indiana University Press.

Bem, S. L. (1989). Genital knowledge and gender constancy in preschool children. *Child Development, 60,* 649–662.

Bernstein, A. C., & Cowan, P. A. (1975). Children's concepts of how people get babies. *Child Development, 46,* 77–91.

Coates, S. (1992). The etiology of boyhood gender identity disorder: An integrative model. In J. W. Barron, M. N. Eagle, & D. L. Wolitzky (Eds.), *Interface of psychoanalysis and psychology.* (pp. 245–265). Washington, DC: American Psychological Association.

Coates, S. W. (1997). Is it time to jettison the concept of developmental lines? Commentary on de Marneffe's paper "Bodies and Words." *Gender and Psychoanalysis, 2,* 35–53.

Coates, S., & Wolfe, S. (1995). Gender identity disorder in boys: The interface of constitution and early experience. *Psychoanalytic Inquiry, 15* (1): 6–38.

Cosentino, C. E., Meyer-Bahlburg, H., Alert, J., Weinberg, S., & Gains, R. (1995). Sexual behavior problems and psychopathology symptoms in sexually abused girls. *Journal of the American Academy of Child and Adolescent Psychiatry, 34,* 1033–1042.

De Marneffe, D. (1997). Bodies and words: A study of young children's genital and gender knowledge. *Gender and Psychoanalysis, 2,* 3–33.

Fagot, B. I. (1985). Changes in thinking about early sex role development. *Developmental Review, 5,* 83–98.

Fagot, B. I. (1993, June). *Gender role development in early childhood: Environmental input, internal construction.* Paper presented at the International Academy of Sex Research, Pacific Grove, CA. (Annual.)

Fast, I. (1984). *Gender identity: A differentiation model.* Hillsdale, NJ: Analytic Press.

Friedrich, W. N., Beilke, R. L., & Urquiza, A. J. (1987). Children from sexually abusive families: A behavioral comparison. *Journal of Interpersonal Violence, 2,* 391–402.

Friedrich, W. N., Grambsch, P., Broughton, D., Kuiper, J., & Beilke, R. L. (1991). Typical sexual behavior in children. *Pediatrics, 88* (3), 456–464.

Goldner, V. (1991). Toward a critical relational theory of gender. *Psychoanalytic Dialogues: Journal of Relational Perspectives, 1,* 249–272.

Herzog, E. W.(1996). *Learning gender labels at 15, 18, and 21 months.* Ph.D. dissertation, Tufts University.

Kleeman, J. (1965). A boy discovers his penis. *Psychoanalytic Study of the Child, 20,* 139–265.

Kohlberg, L. A. (1966). A cognitive-developmental analysis of children's sex-role concepts and attitudes. In E. E. Maccoby (Ed.), *The development of sex differences.* Stanford, CA: Stanford University Press. pp. 83–171.

Lewis, M., & Brooks-Gunn, J. (1979). *Social cognition and the acquisition of self.* New York: Plenum Press.

Maccoby, E. E. (1990). Gender and relationships: A developmental account. *American Psychologist, 45* (4), 313–320.

Mahler, M., Pine, F., & Bergman, A. (1975). *The psychological birth of the human infant.* New York: Basic Books.

Money, J., & Ehrhardt, A. (1972). *Man and woman, boy and girl: The differentiation and dimorphism of gender identity from conception to maturity.* Baltimore, MD: Johns Hopkins University Press.

Roiphe, H., & Galenson, E. (1981). *Infantile origins of sexual identity.* New York: International Universities Press.

Saghir, M. T., & Robins, E. (1973). *Male and female homosexuality: A comprehensive investigation.* Baltimore, MD: Williams & Wilkins.

Sandberg, D. E., Meyer-Bahlburg, H. F. L., Ehrhardt, A. A., & Yager, T. J. (1993). The prevalence of gender-atypical behavior in elementary school children. *Journal of the American Academy of Child and Adolescent Psychiatry, 32,* 306–314.

Serbin, L. A., & Sprafkin, C. H. (1987). A developmental approach: Sexuality from infancy through adolescence. In J. H. Geer & W. T. O'Donohue (Eds.), *Theories of human sexuality.* New York: Plenum Press. pp. 163–195.

Yates, A. (1982). Children eroticized by incest. *American Journal of Psychiatry, 139* (4), 482–485.

Zucker, K., & Bradley, S. (1995). *Gender identity disorder and psychosexual problems in children and adolescents.* New York: Guilford Press.

44 / Assessment of Sexual and Gender Development in Adolescents

Susan Bradley

Gender Development

Gender identity is defined as the inner conviction of being male or female, and *gender role* as the behaviors and activities that are considered stereotypically masculine or feminine. Gender development in adolescence can be seen as an extension and elaboration of processes begun in childhood. In this regard it is a part of the overall task of adolescence, that is, to evolve an identity about various aspects of the self. Preoccupation with body image is a normative phenomenon in adolescence; in particular, it plays an important part in the working out of gender and sexual issues. This process also is affected by previous experiences and relationships that have contributed to a person's sense of gender identity and role, by relationships and experiences in adolescence, and by other factors, such as cognitive and emotional development.

Although a person's gender identity typically is established by ages 3 to 5, the physical, social, emotional, and sometimes political challenges of adolescence can cause an individual to reevaluate both gender identity and, more often, gender role. Most of these challenges do not cause fundamental shifts in gender identity but may cause individuals to question their own adequacy as male or female. Compared to more mature age mates, late-maturing and obese adolescents may feel less gender-adequate, specifically in heterosocial situations. The resulting self-doubt can lead adolescents to withdraw from social situations and thus interfere with opportunities to affirm their gender adequacy. Adolescents with self-esteem difficulties may generalize their feelings about themselves to include a devaluing of their gender self. In some instances, this, in turn, may result in a reduction of same-sex interest and behaviors; in other cases it can lead to a defensive intensification of those same interests and activities. Chronic physical illness that affects development, strength, or physical appearance may produce significant concerns about body image accompanied by a sense of gender inadequacy.

As they confront pubertal changes, those adolescents who have experienced earlier conflicts about gender identity may find these conflicts renewed. The onset of breast development and menarche in girls who have nurtured a private fantasy of being male, may cause them to experience intense distress as the reality of their bodily development confronts their fantasied self. Similarly, muscle development and facial hair growth in an adolescent male with underlying fantasies of being female can cause a resurgence of gender conflict. Intense crushes on same-sex peers are quite normative and nonstressful for adolescents who are comfortable about themselves. The same phenomena may cause adolescents with an insecure or uncertain gender identity to experience marked gender confusion and an intensification of cross-gender wishes. Both experience and fantasy may affect the resolution of intrapsychic dilemmas, as the individual attempts to work out a co-

herent sense of self. Involvement in relationships that affirm a person's gender self can reduce confusion, while, alternatively, relationships that promote valuing of the other gender may intensify and consolidate cross-gender wishes. Some isolated adolescents who spend much time daydreaming or fantasizing about themselves as the other sex may elaborate a well-structured and seemingly immutable self-image that is largely cross-gendered.

Cognitive development, specifically the capacity to abstract, allows adolescents to entertain and explore various aspects of gender role and identity. Those adolescents whose capacity to explore gender roles and aspects of gender identity is limited either by the concreteness of their thinking or by anxiety (which forecloses exploration) may come to a premature determination of both their identity and their role behavior.

Assessment of Gender Development

The assessment of gender in adolescence involves inquiry about general identity issues as well as role behaviors. Questions such as: "How do you feel about yourself?" "What are you good at?" and "What are you not so good at?" often are good introductions to more specific inquiry.

Certain adolescents evince feelings, manifest behavior, or report a background that might interfere with a positive sense of themselves as males or females. There may be an earlier history of cross-gender behavior or interests, of sex abuse, or of chronic and disfiguring physical illness or illness that would interfere with physical strength and engagement in sports for boys. In all such instances, more specific inquiry is warranted. The following questions are useful prompts to further discussion depending on the adolescent's responses.

QUESTIONS FOR BOYS AND GIRLS

- Do you find yourself unhappy about your body? If yes, in what way?
- How did you feel about your body when you developed more hair under your arms, in your crotch?

QUESTIONS FOR BOYS

- How did you feel about your body changing when your penis began to grow?
- Do you sometimes think you're not as strong as or good at sports as other boys, or do you sometimes feel like a wimp compared to other boys?
- Do you ever have dreams/daydreams in which you imagine that you are a girl? If yes, what would be better about being a girl?
- Do you sometimes imagine that everything would be better in your life if you could be stronger or more like other boys?

QUESTIONS FOR GIRLS

- How did you feel about your body changing when your breasts began to grow?
- Do you often think you are not as attractive or not as comfortable as other girls in social situations?
- Do you ever have dreams/daydreams in which you imagine that you are a boy? If yes, what would be better about being a boy?
- Do you sometimes imagine that everything would be better in your life if you were more attractive or more like other girls?

For those few adolescents evidencing cross-gender interests or preoccupations, specific inquiry about wishes to be of the opposite sex are appropriate. If the adolescent indicates some preoccupation with cross-gender wishes, the evaluator can inquire about how intense or prolonged these wishes have been. Has the adolescent acted upon these wishes, that is, passed as the opposite sex? Has the adolescent changed his or her body in any way to conform more to looking like the opposite sex? For example, did a boy shave his legs or wear makeup? If the wishes are intense or prolonged or if the adolescent has been passing as a member of the opposite sex, referral to a specialist for a more thorough gender identity assessment is warranted. (See Zucker and Bradley, 1995, for more information.)

Sexual Development

As noted, sexual development in adolescence is a continuation of processes begun in childhood. The prepubertal child typically has experienced crushes, talked about love and marriage, and may even have begun more overt sexual behaviors (Broderick & Fowler, 1961). Adolescence, however, marks the emergence and partial consolidation of the individual as a sexual being, physiologically, psychologically, and interpersonally.

Pubertal changes that begin in late childhood signal to the adolescent and to others the development of this person as a physical sexual being. These changes begin earlier in girls than boys (Chilman, 1980; Dyk, 1993) and are accompanied by hormonal changes, some of which correlate with the individual's increasing interest in sexual issues (Udry, 1990). For most adolescents, there is a typical sequence of sexual behaviors, beginning with kissing, dating, and petting, and leading eventually to sexual intercourse (Miller, Christopherson, & King, 1993). The sequence of feelings and fantasies that accompany this development is slightly less clear but includes crushes and falling in love. The onset of dating, which for most adolescents signifies a formal beginning of heterosexual behavior, also appears to influence the timing of the behaviors that follow. Over the last 50 years, sexual activity in adolescence has begun earlier with succeeding cohorts (Hofferth, 1990).

Girls begin their sexual experience earlier than boys. By midadolescence, however, boys tend to catch up in terms of overall sexual experience. In late adolescence, somewhat more boys than girls are sexually active (Schofield, 1965). Those adolescents who begin dating at an early age are more likely to experience coitus at a relatively earlier age. The timing of this sequence also is affected by pubertal development, socioeconomic status, gender, and possibly ethnic factors as well. Early-maturing males are more likely to begin their overall sexual activity earlier than later-maturing males (Udry, 1990). Black males; males and females from families of low socioeconomic status, from families without a consistently available parent, and from single-parent families; and females who have been sexually abused are all more likely to be sexually involved at a younger age (Chilman, 1980). Earlier data suggesting that black females are more sexually active than white females seem less significant when socioeconomic status has been controlled for (Wyatt, 1990). Cultural factors also affect the age of onset of sexual activity. Those cultures that closely monitor adolescents' activity may provide a less permissive environment for their sexual involvement (Hotvedt, 1990).

Sexual behaviors occur in the context of relationships for both males and females. For early adolescents, some of those relationships may be with same-sex peers and may be termed homosexual behaviors (Fay, Turner, Klassen, & Gagnon, 1989). For the majority of these adolescents, this homosexual activity does not constitute an enduring aspect of their sexual identification but may be reported as a period of sexual exploration. Understanding the meaning of the behavior to the adolescent as well as a history of earlier cross-gender behavior may help the clinician and adolescent clarify whether early homosexual activity is likely to be part of a more enduring homosexual identification.

Although males tend to have more sexual partners than females, both sexes value the traditional notion of sex within a loving relationship. Boys, however, are more likely than girls to consider sex in a casual relationship as acceptable, and more boys are likely to define themselves as sexual adventurers, that is, seeking many partners (Sorensen, 1973). The number of partners also is related to age of first intercourse, with more partners associated with earlier age of first intercourse (Miller et al., 1993); however, black males report more lifetime partners than do white or Hispanic males (Miller et al., 1993). Sonenstein, Pleck, and Ku (1991) concluded that the racial differences between black and white males in terms of the number of lifetime sexual partners was due to the fact that black males began having intercourse at an earlier age than whites.

Most individuals do not find their first experience with intercourse highly pleasurable (Schofield, 1965). However, once begun, most adolescents continue to engage in sexual behaviors with varying degrees of frequency, depending on the availability of partners and privacy. The development of sexually interactive behavior as a mutually pleasurable activity may take time and, especially for females, may not be achieved during adolescence (Sarrel & Sarrel, 1990).

Factors affecting sexual activity in adolescence are both biological and psychosocial. The androgenic hormone upsurge that accompanies puberty in both sexes appears to initiate sexual interests and, for males, to influence the likelihood of the individual's engaging in intercourse. In females, however, although androgen levels also correlate with the onset of sexual interests, coitus appears to be more determined by psychosocial factors (Udry, 1990). Peer influence, such as sexual behavior of friends, appears to be more instrumental in white females, whereas in black females, the stage of pubertal development appears to be more important (Udry, 1990).

Some physical conditions may affect sexual interest and willingness to engage in sexual behaviors. Congenital adrenal hyperplasia in females appears to result in a later onset of heterosocial and heterosexual interests and a greater homoerotic interest (Dittmann, Kappes, & Kappes, 1992; Erhardt, 1979; Money & Schwartz, 1977). Chronic physical illness may affect the development of sexuality in many ways. Physical disability may interfere with the capacity to engage in intercourse in traditional ways and may prevent adolescents from exploring alternative ways of developing a sexual self. Further, for such adolescents, overprotection by parents and extreme dependency, self-esteem issues, and body issue concerns may cumulatively lead them to avoid social interaction and may interfere with the development of their sexual experience. Ostracism and rejection by peers continue to be real issues for many adolescents with disabilities (Greydanus, Gunther, Demarest, & Sears, 1990). Similarly, sensory disabilities may interfere with the process of achieving a comfortable identity as a sexual person (Evans & Lee, 1990).

The use of contraceptives in adolescence has become more commonplace with the campaign against AIDS. However, early in their sexual experience, the majority of adolescents still do not use adequate protection against both pregnancy and sexually transmitted diseases (Hofferth, 1990). Accurate and up-to-date figures are difficult to obtain, but estimates from population surveys of adolescents in 1988 indicated condom use of 54% at first intercourse (Sonenstein, Pleck, & Ku, 1989). As adolescents mature, the figure for overall contraception appears to improve and approaches that for young adults (Hofferth, 1990).

Most adolescent males acknowledge masturbation as a frequent activity; somewhat fewer adolescent females admit that they masturbate (Chilman, 1980). Many adolescents continue to experience guilt and shame over masturbation despite exposure to sexual education in this area.

Concerns about homosexuality may arise in the context of general concerns about the self. Depression and low self-esteem may lead to social withdrawal and failure to develop comfort in heterosexual relationships. This situation can lead an adolescent to question his or her sexual orientation, especially in the context of a crush on a same-sex peer. Exploration of erotic fantasy and earlier cross-gender history may help clarify whether the adolescent is moving in a homosexual direction or is experiencing these worries simply as part of a larger state of self-doubting. (For a more extensive discussion, see Zucker and Bradley, 1995.)

Assessment of Sexual Behaviors & Orientation

The assessment of sexuality depends on the adolescent's social and cognitive development. Questions need to be framed in language that the adolescent understands. In reasonably mature adolescents it is appropriate to begin with "Are you sexually active?" However, it is often more tactful to ask younger adolescents:

Do you date?
Have you held hands or kissed?
How far have you gone with a boy/a girl?
Have you had sex? If so, with whom? How did it feel? Were you worried about having sex? What made you worry?
Has anyone ever forced sex on you when you didn't want it?

Inquiries about contraception may be more straightforward:

Do you use any kind of protection when you have sex? If so, what do you use? If not, why not?

Issues about number of partners may reveal risk-taking behaviors.

How many persons have you had sex with? (If the report is of numerous partners, the adolescent should be asked the following.) How careful are you about using protection? What do you understand about sexually transmitted diseases? Have you engaged in high-risk behaviors, such as anal intercourse?

When the person is not reporting sexual behaviors, concerns about sexual development and sexual orientation can be inquired about by first asking about crushes. Assuming the adolescent understands the word *crush,* the interviewer can ask: "Whom did you first have a crush for?" After finding out about various crushes, the examiner may ask whether the youngster ever had a crush on someone of the same sex. This can be followed up with: Have you ever had sexual feelings about someone of the same sex? Have you ever acted on those feelings? If the individual acknowledges feelings of attraction toward same-sex individuals, the examiner can ask whether he or she also is attracted to opposite-sex individuals. Again, asking about what kinds of actual sexual experiences the individual may have had will complete the inquiry.

Assessment of sexual concerns in an adolescent often is easier if the interviewer asks directly and frankly about sexual matters. Questions such as "What or who do you think about when you masturbate?" may reveal more than "Do you masturbate?" Sometimes inquiry about friends and their sexual activities will allow the clinician to find out whether the patient sees him- or herself as similar or different. This can be used to explore worries or concerns about sexual involvement, including use of contraception and concerns about AIDS. However, many adolescents initially will deny concern about themselves, revealing their worries only later, in the course of a therapeutic relationship. Careful inquiry regarding concerns about pregnancy and homosexuality may be particularly important in suicidal adolescents. Frank discussions about sexual issues with adolescents with disabilities or chronic illness may permit them to regard their feelings as normal and to be more comfortable voicing them. However, as with adults, comfortable discussion of sexual issues continues to require a sensitive and patient approach; even with the most tactful inquiry, however, many patients may fail to reveal their concerns.

Adolescents may exhibit paraphilic interests and behaviors, the most common of which is transvestic fetishism. The fourth edition of the *Diagnostic and Statistical Manual of Mental Disorders* (American Psychiatric Association, 1994) defines transvestic fetishism as a disorder occurring in a heterosexual male in which the individual experiences sexually arousing urges, fantasies, or behaviors involving cross-dressing. Most typically the adolescent is brought for assessment when female undergarments have been found in his possession. Inquiry into when and how the adolescent has used the garments may reveal fetishistic behavior, although many adolescents are unable or unwilling to discuss their behaviors in this area. (For a more complete assessment of transvestic fetishism, see Zucker and Bradley, 1995.)

Conclusion

In conclusion, clinical assessment of gender and sexual issues in adolescents requires a knowledge of normal and abnormal adolescent development in these areas. Further, it requires a sensitive but frank interviewing style that conveys the message that discussion of such issues, despite feeling awkward, is important. Learning how to discuss sexual and gender issues with adolescents, in an empathic fashion, can be rewarding as it will lead to improved clinical care.

REFERENCES

American Psychiatric Association. (1994). *Diagnostic and statistical manual of mental disorders* (4th ed.). Washington, DC: Author.

Broderick, C. B., & Fowler, S. E. (1961). New patterns of relationships between the sexes among preadolescents. *Marriage and Family Living, 23,* 27–30.

Chilman, C. S. (1980). *Adolescent sexuality in a changing American society: Social and psychological perspectives.* Washington, DC: U.S. Department of Health Education and Welfare, Public Health Service, National Institute of Health.

Dittmann, R. W., Kappes, M. E., & Kappes, M. H. (1992). Sexual behavior in adolescent and adult females with congenital adrenal hyperplasia. *Psychoneuroendocrinology, 17,* 153–170.

Dyk, P. H. (1993). Anatomy, physiology, and gender issues in adolescence. In T. P. Gullotta, G. R. Adams, & R. Montemayor (Eds.), *Adolescent sexuality* (pp. 35–56). Newbury Park, CA: Sage Publications.

Evans, N. W., & Lee, M. (1990). Sensory disability and adolescent sexuality. In M. Sugar (Ed.), *Atypical adolescence and sexuality* (pp. 57–86). New York: W. W. Norton.

Fagan, P. J., & Anderson, A. G. (1990). Sexuality and eating disorders in adolescence. In M. Sugar (Ed.), *Atypical adolescence and sexuality* (pp. 108–126). New York: W. W. Norton.

Ehrhardt, A. A. (1985). Psychosexual adjustment in adolescence in patients with congenital abnormalities of their sex organs. In H. L. Vallet & I. H. Porter (Eds.), *Genetic mechanisms of sexual development.* New York: Academic Press. (pp. 473–483).

Fay, R. E., Turner, C. F., Klassen, A. D., & Gagnon, J. H. (1989). Prevalence and patterns of same-gender sexual contract among men. *Science, 243,* 338–348.

Greydanus, D. E., Gunther, M. S., Demarest, D. S., &

Sears, J. M. (1990). Sexuality of the chronically ill adolescent. In M. Sugar (Ed.), *Atypical adolescence and sexuality* (pp. 147–157). New York: W. W. Norton.

Hofferth, S. L. (1990). Trends in adolescent sexual activity, contraception, and pregnancy in the United States. In J. Bancroft & J. M. Reinisch (Eds.), *Adolescence and puberty* (pp. 217–233). New York: Oxford University Press.

Hopwood, M. J., Kelch, R. P., Hale, P. M., Mendes, T. M., Foster, C. M., & Beitins, I. Z. (1990). The onset of human puberty: Biological and environmental factors. In J. Bancroft & J. M. Reinisch (Eds.), *Adolescence and puberty* (pp. 29–49). New York: Oxford University Press.

Hotvedt, M. E. (1990). Emerging and submerging adolescent sexuality: culture and sexual orientation. In J. Bancroft & J. M. Reinisch (Eds.), *Adolescence and puberty* (pp. 157–172). New York: Oxford University Press.

Miller, B. C., Christopherson, C. R., & King, P. K. (1993). Sexual behavior in adolescence. In T. P. Gullotta, G. R. Adams, & R. Montemayor (Eds.), *Adolescent sexuality* (pp. 57–76). Newbury Park, CA: Sage Publications.

Money, J., & Schwartz, M. (1977). Dating, romantic and non-romantic friendships and sexuality in 17 early-treated adrenogenital females, aged 16–25. In P. A. Lee, L. P. Plotnick, A. A. Kowarski, & C. Migeon (Eds.), *Congenital adrenal hyperplasia* (pp. 419–431). Baltimore, MD: University Park Press.

Sarrel, L., & Sarrel, P. M. (1990). Sexual unfolding in adolescents. In M. Sugar (Ed.), *Atypical adolescence and sexuality* (pp. 18–43). New York: W. W. Norton.

Schofield, M. (1965). *The sexual behavior of young people.* London: Longmans.

Sonenstein, F. L., Pleck, J. H., & Ku, L. C. (1989). Sexual activity, condom use and AIDS awareness among adolescent males. *Family Planning Perspectives, 21*, 152–158.

Sonenstein, F. L., Pleck, J. I. T., Ku, L. C. (1991). Levels of sexual activity among adolescent males in the United States. *Family Planning Perspectives, 23* (4), 162–167.

Sorensen, R. C. (1973). *Adolescent sexuality in contemporary America.* New York: World Publications.

Udry, J. R. (1990). Hormonal and social determinants of adolescent sexual initiation. In J. Bancroft & J. M. Reinisch (Eds.), *Adolescence and puberty* (pp. 70–87). New York: Oxford University Press.

Wyatt, G. E. (1990). Changing influences on adolescent sexuality over the past forty years. In J. Bancroft & J. M. Reinisch (Eds.), *Adolescence and puberty* (pp. 182–206). New York: Oxford University Press.

Zucker, K. J., & Bradley, S. J. (1995). *Gender and psychosexual problems in children and adolescents.* New York: Guilford Press.

45 / Assessment of Conscience Development

Charles R. Keith

All major theories of human development attempt to explain the personal evolution of moral judgment and its crystallization into a conscience. Likewise, any systematic clinical assessment always involves explicit and implicit study of the patient's morality—that is, the beliefs about what is good and bad, and how these morals interdigitate with perception, behavior, and feelings about the self.

Two central themes pervade theories about moral development. One theme is that the child and adolescent create their inner morality through a series of increasingly complex epigenetic, cognitive stages by which the events of the world are morally processed and through which moral decisions are made (Lickona, 1976). Kohlberg and his associates, working within a Piagetian cognitive-developmental framework, have outlined explicit stages of moral conceptualizations used by children and adolescents to organize and process moral decision making (Colby, Kohlberg, Gibbs, & Lieberman, 1983). Kohlberg's theory has generated a tremendous amount of research and will be described in more detail later. Psychoanalytic developmental theory also emphasizes how a child's moral development evolves from early stages involving magical thinking and primitive, harsh injunctions to a more tolerant, less harsh, and more reality-based morality of normal adolescence. However, the stages of psychoanalytic developmental theory are less explicit than

the Kohlbergian stages and have not generated much empirical research.

A second theme weaving through moral development theorizing is that the child learns morality via reward and punishment; eventually these learning experiences and the perceptions of parental and societal moral values are internalized into a structure called the conscience. Behaviorism (Eysenck, 1976), social learning theory (Emler & Hogan, 1981), and psychoanalytical developmental theory (Tyson, Tyson, 1990) all have emphasized the role of learning, internalization, and identification with parents' moral values as crucial steps in the creation of an internal moral gyroscope.

All developmental theories note that moral beliefs do not coalesce into a unitary, cohesive whole but instead are a variable, often confusing and contradictory collection of dos and don'ts. All theories (or at least some of their theorists) warn that moral beliefs can change, weaken, or strengthen, depending on the social context of the moral decision-making process. Milgram's (1964, 1965) and Bandura, Underwood, and Fromson's (1975) classic studies often are used to illustrate the fragility of moral beliefs. In these studies, normal research subjects administered painful "shocks" to dummy subjects when rewarded to do so by researchers. The dummy subjects were actors who screamed in pain and begged the research subjects not to administer further shocks. Even though upset, the research subjects often continued to administer shocks despite their saying that they did not believe it was right to do so. Indeed, history abounds with examples of individuals and groups committing immoral acts that are not at all consonant with their moral values (Carroll & Rest, 1982).

On the other hand, it is a common clinical experience that moral beliefs can be tenacious and impervious to external manipulation, plunging a child or adolescent into guilty self-recrimination, which, in turn, could lead to depressions of psychotic proportions and suicide.

A clinically useful perspective for assessing the conscience is that of Brenner (1982), who, working from a psychoanalytic perspective, describes how every action and thought pattern involves the superego, that is, a moral decision. A thought or action is either good, and permissible, or bad, and worthy of punishment. Punishment is most commonly in the form of guilt and lowered self-esteem. Brenner makes the interesting point that it is therefore incorrect to say that a superego or conscience has "lacunae" or is absent. Moral decision making is always present, in every thought and action, at the conscious, preconscious, or unconscious level.

Another clinical perspective useful in assessing the conscience is to keep in mind that moral beliefs are one part of a complicated sequence. This begins with perception and the comparison of perceptions with a person's moral beliefs; i.e. that is, is it right to "see" what is there? One or more action plans are then conceptualized. Further moral evaluations help decide which action plans are acceptable and which are unacceptable. It is only when this preliminary decision work is done that an action plan might finally become the approved one that is then carried out in reality. Of course, these multiple moral decisions determining perception and action sequences usually are made automatically and out of awareness (Rest, 1983).

Although we must be cautious in making mind-brain leaps, it is probably safe to say that the conscience has its biological basis in the extensive development of the human frontal lobe cortex. It has been known for a long time that individuals with frontal lobe brain damage characteristically have difficulty making high-level moral decisions. The conscience, as a crystallized collection of moral

beliefs, continually is reinforced by the basic need to adapt to one's social group in order to survive. Thus the clinician often assesses how well a patient's moral belief system is in tune with both the patient's social group and the society in which it is imbedded. Clinically, we know that many forces can sweep away part or all of this moral belief system and its connections with perception and behavior. These forces include anxiety-flooding, intoxication, and organicity.

The assessment of the child's or adolescent's moral beliefs is primarily a study of conflict. Most presenting symptoms involve a clash of belief systems. Consider the following case example.

CASE EXAMPLE

At the request of the local court counselor, because of persistent shoplifting, a 14-year-old boy was brought to the outpatient clinic by his mother for an evaluation. The mother divorced the boy's biological father 6 years previously because of the father's persistent difficulties with the law, including incarcerations for breaking and entering. Among the many reasons for the divorce was that the mother did not want her children, including the current patient, to be exposed to the father's criminal behavior patterns. History revealed that when the father was out of jail and in the home, he had many positive involvements with his children.

Thus it was not surprising when our 14-year-old patient readily spoke of conscious loyalty conflicts between his mother and father. This external loyalty mirrored the patient's internalized clashes between the 2 sets of parental moral values. The one involved his father's conscious moral stance that it was all right to steal and rob in order to take from those who are rich and who have material possessions in order to give to those who are in hardship, including one's own family. The mother's moral system viewed stealing and robbing for any reason as repugnant. The patient was further conflicted by the fact that, following his release from prison, mother had accepted father back into the home. Furthermore, the patient was aware of societal laws and their moral underpinnings involving the wrongness of stealing. He could verbalize that it is generally wrong to steal. He recognized that if people stole without restraint, they could not live together in an orderly society. He thus could mirror the moral philosopher's position, that society's stability depends on the majority having similar moral beliefs so that everyday functions can be carried on without a police officer being on every corner. He also was quite involved in peer group activities, which mirrored his own internalized and familial moral conflicts. Some of his peers believed that it was morally justified to steal and encouraged him to join them in shoplifting forays. He felt the need to identify with this group, as he yearned to be closer with and identified with them and his father. On the other hand, the majority of his peer group, particularly those in his school setting, made it quite clear that stealing was wrong and unacceptable. Thus the patient's symptom of shoplifting involved at least 5 and probably more interacting, yet conflicting, moral belief systems that brought about considerable guilt at the very moment that he was stealing clothing items from the store shelves. This is an example of how clinicians must be humble and cautious in making early diagnostic generalizations about a patient's conscience. Diagnostic statements that the conscience is weak or absent can quickly become damning pejoratives and shed little, if any, light on the complexities and struggles experienced by the patient. Thus clinicians face a daunting task to bring the complicated, multilayered mental processes and belief system's involved in the conscience into a workable, helpful treatment formulation.

Assessment of the Conscience

The following perspectives are useful in the assessment of the conscience.

The developmental perspective is crucial in the evaluation of moral beliefs. The foundation of morality begins in the first year of life as the infant molds its behavior to the wishes of the caregivers (Emde, Biringer, Clyman, & Oppenheim, 1991). For example, biting a caregiver usually occurs only once due to the stern reaction of the pained adult. The cessation of protest crying upon going to sleep and the general molding of sleep patterns after the adult's wishes are other examples of early foundations of morality, that is, of doing what is good according to the caregiver and not doing what is bad and frowned upon.

Adults' limit-setting of a 2-year-old's aggression and motor activity become even more clearly part of the early conscience. The normal harshness of the conscience of the 5-year-old child has long been noted.

A crucial developmental task of the elementary school years is for the child to soften these Draconic, internal moral edicts, so that by age 10 to 12 the child can genuinely apologize for wrongdoing. The less harsh superego of the preadolescent child provides a more normal entry into puberty and early adolescence; the advent of adolescence brings with it a revision and questioning of familial moral beliefs. This challenge, in turn, makes it possible for the youth to achieve a more healthy adolescent independence.

Early primitive superego beliefs normally are poorly integrated with other personality functions, so that the young child's behavior must be shored up by external structure and support. As the child progresses through the early school years into adolescence, there is increasing stability of moral beliefs with improved integration with other areas of personality functioning, so that the older normal youth has an internalized, stable moral gyroscope.

In normal adolescence, basic moral beliefs acquired through early development remain essentially untouched by the developmental process. This provides a personality with firm foundation, which in turn permits the adolescent to experiment with new conscious and preconscious moral beliefs that can be deliberately turned against parental moral values (Keniston, 1970). This psychodynamic developmental scheme provides a yardstick for assessing the conscience.

Kohlberg's Moral Judgment Stages

Kohlberg's moral judgment stages parallel the above-described psychodynamic developmental scheme.

In Stage I (approximate ages 3 to 6), the child submits to the caregiver and believes that breaking a caregiver's rule will and should bring pain and punishment. This morality has been called the "morality of obedience."

In Stage II (early elementary school years, ages 7 to 9), the child can conceptualize instrumentality and the gains to be had from following agreed-upon rules. Breaking mutual rules is bad and worthy of punishment.

In Stage III (late elementary school years, ages 10 to 12), the child can cognitively grasp the "morality of interpersonal concordance"; grasping this concept depends on the ability to conceptualize and anticipate the needs and feelings of others, and to act accordingly, in order to get what one wants and to have the pleasure of being accepted and getting along with others.

Stage IV (ages 12 to 15) marks the onset of the cognitive stage of formal operations. The youth now can conceptualize and abstract broader moral issues, particularly the importance of social law and order. This has been called the "morality of law and duty." The youth now can cognitively grapple with the clashes between an individual's wishes and the needs of the larger society.

Kohlberg and his associates have described more advanced stages of moral judgment involving abstract, philosophical concepts of due process and social interactions. These later stages appear to be largely dependent on advanced levels of schooling rather than on the more basic developmental processes that underlie the 4 stages.

A vast amount of research has been carried out on these Kohlbergian stages, much of it by asking children and adolescents to discuss standardized moral dilemmas. The stages are sequentially invariant, always appearing in the listed order. In advanced, industrialized societies, more individuals reach Stage IV than in simpler, agrarian, societies; there individuals rarely, if ever, develop beyond Stage III. Psychopathology is inversely correlated with the stage of moral judgment; mental illness appears to damage the forward movement of moral judgment stages. However, the correlation is far from perfect, so that, for instance, some youths with severe conduct disorder can discuss moral dilemmas using Stage IV concepts.

The clinician must keep in mind that the conscience is a large collection of often conflicting beliefs, only a few of which are available to the patient's conscious or preconscious awareness. This basic principle provides a warning to the clinician, who might otherwise be tempted to make initial, global diagnostic statements about the patient's consciously stated morality.

Paradoxically, a patient often experiences this collection of moral beliefs as a unitary object in the mind. This object can be described as a devil, judge, or monster who talks to the patient (i.e., the voice of conscience) and orders him or her to carry out self-destructive acts. This concretized conscience is experienced as above and/or behind the patient—as an internalized replication of the child's physical disparity with adult authority figures. Many normal and mildly disturbed youths talk with and receive reprimands from these concrete images; doing so does not necessarily imply psychotic thinking.

Transgression of moral beliefs leads initially to separation anxiety in the toddler and to guilt in the preschool, oedipal, elementary school-age child, and adolescents. This painful anxiety and guilt are coped with by defensive maneuvers such as repression and by turning affect into the opposite which can lay snares for the unwary clinician. A guilty child can state defiantly that he does not care that he has struck and hurt another person. The more the clinician pushes for some expression of remorse, the louder become the patient's shouts that he doesn't care that another person was hurt. This common clinical situation, which also occurs frequently within the school and family, usually is caused by a "denial of guilt." In fact, the child actually may hit the person again in order to prove to self and to others that he indeed does not feel guilty, nor has he suffered a fall in self-esteem.

Although almost everyone agrees that the content of a child's and adolescent's moral beliefs comes from parental and societal moral values, it is often forgotten that these inner beliefs are not exact replications of external belief systems. The identification with the parents' moral values and their internalization within the child is a transformative process. In the younger child, this process involves egocentric, magical modes of thinking; it usually leads to inflation of the external moral values, making them more harsh on the self and others than intended by the parents and external authorities. In the 1920s and 1930s the attempts to raise guilt-free children by never punishing or saying no ran aground on these shoals.

It should be remembered that the process of

clinical assessment begins by establishing a non-judgmental position; it is from this standpoint that the clinician listens to the youth's story as told through play and words. Thus an identification process is initiated involving the patient internalizing the clinician's more benign, nonharsh, non-sadistic conscience. This is probably the principal pathway to account for the common clinical finding that some children and adolescents obtain rapid remission of presenting behavior problems and/or affective disturbances as they go through the evaluation process. Sometimes these initial rapid changes are dismissed too readily as "transference cures." Instead, they demonstrate that the child's and adolescent's overly harsh, poorly integrated moral belief system is amenable to change.

Because of the complexities of assessing moral beliefs, a straightforward, simple, mutually agreed upon framework for assessing the conscience has never emerged in the field. Mental status exams, with their questions and logical sequencing, may include queries about the patient's social judgment. However, whether a patient's social judgment is poor or adequate may tell us very little about his or her moral beliefs and their workings in the mind. Some social-cognitive clinicians such as Selman (1976) present standardized moral dilemmas to their patients in order to assess cognitive, moral reasoning development. For instance, the following is an example of a moral dilemma presented to children ages 4 through 10.

Holly is an 8-year-old girl who likes to climb trees. She is the best tree climber in the neighborhood. One day while climbing down from a tall tree, she falls off the bottom branch but does not hurt herself. Her father sees her fall. He is upset and asks her to promise not to climb trees any more. Holly promises.

Later that day Holly and her friends meet Shawn. Shawn's kitten is caught up in a tree and can't get down. Something has to be done right away, or the kitten may fall. Holly is the only one who climbs trees well enough to reach the kitten and get it down, but she remembers her promise to her father.

In this dilemma, Holly has to decide whether to help Shawn by rescuing the kitten or to obey her father's injunction not to climb trees.

Can the child assume the temporary role of Shawn or Holly and empathize with her plight? Can the child imagine how Holly's father will feel if he were to know that Holly faced this dilemma?

What would the child him- or herself do if faced with Holly's predicament?

Through such probing and open-ended questions, the clinician can assess the child's social-cognitive level of moral decision making. Such presentation and analyzing of standardized dilemmas has not caught on in child psychiatry. Clinicians may present moral dilemmas to their child and adolescent patients, constructing the situations out of information from the patient's history and family milieu. This method has the advantage of being closer to the patient's life experience but has the disadvantage of not being standardized through research.

These various perspectives on assessing moral development have immediate treatment implications. For instance, cognitive-developmental clinicians following Kohlberg's model have utilized a discussion of Kohlbergian moral dilemmas with groups of patients. Follow-up studies on these time-limited discussion groups show positive results, even when the subjects have considerable levels of psychopathology (Arbuthnot & Gordon, 1986). Cognitive-behavioral clinicians work actively with moral issues through discussions with patients concerning following the rules, being fair to one another, and how to empathize with others (Selman, 1976). Psychodynamic psychotherapists treating families, parents, and individual children and adolescents identify and interpret harsh, inconsistent, or poorly integrated moral beliefs that become visible in either the interpersonal or the intrapsychic spheres and which result in excessive guilt, depression, or self-destructive behaviors.

Conclusion

Many child and adolescent psychopathologies have at their heart either a relative failure to develop age-appropriate conscience functioning (e.g., the conduct disorders) or, conversely, a conscience that becomes excessively harsh, as in the depressions and suicidality. Appreciation of the stages and vicissitudes of normal conscience development are thus central to the diagnosis and treatment of much of childhood and adolescent psychopathology.

REFERENCES

Arbuthnot, J., & Gordon, D. A. (1986). Behavioral and cognitive effects of a moral reasoning development intervention for high-risk behavior-disordered adolescents. *Journal of Consulting and Clinical Psychology, 54* (2), 208–216.

Bandura, A., Underwood, B., & Fromson, M. D. (1975). Disinhibition of aggression through diffusion of responsibility and dehumanization of victims. *Journal of Research in Personality, 9,* 253–269.

Brenner, C. (1982). The concept of the super-ego: A reformulation. *Psychoanalytic Quarterly, 32,* 507–527.

Carroll, J. L., & Rest, J. R. (1982). Moral development. In B. B. Wolman (Ed.), *Handbook of developmental psychology* (pp. 434–451). Englewood Cliffs, NJ: Prentice-Hall.

Colby, A., Kohlberg, L., Gibbs, J., & Lieberman, M. (1983). A longitudinal study of moral judgment. *Monographs of the Society for Research in Child Development, 48* (1–2), 1–96.

Emde, R. N., Biringer, Z., Clyman, R. B., & Oppenheim, D. (1991). The moral self of infancy: Affective core and procedural knowledge. *Developmental Review, 11* (3), 251–270.

Emler, N. P., & Hogan, R. (1981). Developing attitudes to law and justice: An integrative review. In S. Brehm, S. Kassin, & F. Gibbons (Eds.), *Developmental social psychology* (pp. 299–314). New York: Oxford University Press.

Eysenck, H. J. (1976). The biology of morality. In T. Lickona (Ed.), *Moral development and behavior: Theory, research, and social issues* (pp. 108–123). New York: Holt, Rinehart and Winston.

Keniston, K. (1970). Student activism, moral development, and morality. *American Journal of Orthopsychiatry, 40* (4), 577–592.

Lickona, T. (1976). Critical issues in the study of moral development and behavior. In T. Lickona (Ed.), *Moral development and behavior: Theory, research, and social issues* (pp. 3–27). New York: Holt, Rinehart and Winston.

Milgram, S. (1964). Group pressure and action against a person. *Journal of Abnormal and Social Psychology, 69,* (2), 137–143.

Milgram, S. (1965). Some conditions of obedience and disobedience to authority. *Human Relations, 18,* 57–76.

Rest, J. D. (1983). Morality. In P. H. Mussen (Ed.), *Handbook of child psychology* (Vol. 3, pp. 556–629). New York: John Wiley & Sons.

Selman, R. L. (1976). Social-cognitive understanding. In T. Lickona (Ed.), *Moral development and behavior: Theory, research, and social issues* (pp. 299–316). New York: Holt, Rinehart and Winston.

Tyson, P., Tyson, R. L., *Psychoanalytic Theories of Development: An Integration.* New Haven: Yale University Press, 1990.

46 / **Assessment of Cognitive Processes**

Daniel J. Siegel

This chapter describes an approach to the psychiatric assessment of the cognitive processes of children and adolescents. Its intention is to provide a useful framework for the clinician in how to think about those mental processes that are the basis for what we think of as "cognition." For an account of specific tests, individual assessment instruments, or particular diagnostic categories, it may be more efficient to refer to the chapters in the *Handbook* that focus on those topics.

A basic premise of this neurobiological approach to the assessment of cognition is that *the mind and the psyche emanate from the interface between neurobiological processes and human relationships.* When we speak of assessing cognition, we are talking about evaluating the mental processes of an individual human being, those that constitute the "psyche," defined, according to *Webster's Dictionary,* as (1) the human soul; (2) the intellect; (3) psychiatry—the mind considered as a subjectively perceived, functional entity, based ultimately upon physical processes but with complex processes of its own: it governs the total organism and its interaction with the environment.

The content of this approach can seem at times

very abstract and almost too theoretical. Once mastered, however, clinicians have found these ideas extremely useful with practical clinical applications. I shall present the material in the first person and address you, the reader, in the second person ("you") in order to help make the material less abstract. I will use examples from everyday life and from clinical encounters in order to provide illustrations of the concepts. By drawing on a wide variety of academic disciplines, including the fields of anthropology, cognitive psychology, developmental psychology, computer science, linguistics, and neurobiology, this chapter is by its nature a synthetic overview rather than a comprehensive review. I have tried to avoid using jargon from these various disciplines of cognitive science. However, this chapter may offer unfamiliar concepts that require a new vocabulary. Italics will be used when a basic idea is labeled with a name, making it more accessible for later reference.

What Is Cognition?

A general view of cognition comes from the *information processing* approach: input (stimuli) → processing (cognition) → output (observable behavior). *Cognition* thus refers to any process that does something with input and/or influences output. Cognitive science is a multidisciplinary field that studies the nature of mental processes from various academic perspectives. Although old distinctions implied that cognition was equivalent to thought, new conceptualizations are much broader and encompass processes ranging from logic to emotion.

During the initial clinical interviews, you as the evaluator will need to obtain information from a variety of sources, including the child, parents, observations of the parent and child interacting, teachers, school reports, and findings from formal testing and diagnostic assessment tools. This multilayered approach to information gathering allows you to gain insights into how the child functions in different settings.

As you sit with the child and parent during the interview, you will be able to utilize observations

of spontaneous behavior, verbal output to specific questions, affective reactions, and nonverbal bodily responses. Each of these is an example of cognitive output. When we aim our focus at the evaluation of cognition, we are taking on a broad task. How can the evaluation process even begin to conceptualize cognition if it means everything between input and output?

You sit with a boy who gazes back at you. You may say, "Tell me about your home." The child looks away. Then you add, "Who lives at home with you?" The child turns toward you and begins to tell you about his mother, father, dog, and goldfish. He does not tell you about his younger brother, with whom he is always in conflict. His mind has avoided the uncomfortable emotion that might be activated if he brought his brother into the story, an omission mediated either by an automatic nonconscious or intentional conscious process.

What just occurred? Your brain created an output of a statement "Tell me about. . . ." His ears received the vibrations of the air at the tympanic membrane (input), his auditory nerve responded with impulses into the brain, and he began to process the input (cognition) creating linguistic *representations* in his auditory cortex. He then turns away (perhaps because he did not understand your statement or because the emotions it evoked were too intense and one way of regulating his emotional state is to diminish eye contact with you). You ask a more specific question. He returns to looking at you and gives you a verbal output. In this case, his output is to begin to tell you a *story* about his life. The story will be woven from many layers of cognition from memory and emotions to his perceptions of your expectations and those of his listening parents.

In this brief transaction, we can see that even the simplest event contains massive amounts of cognitive processing. What determines the child's output (response) to your question? How did the words you used in the question evoke this particular reaction? What does the child do to compose the story he is about to tell?

These are fundamental questions in every clinical encounter. To answer them, we need to examine both the cognitive processor involved—the brain in the body—and the context in which the processing occurs—the social setting.

Neurobiology and Cognition

The brain is considered by many to be one of the most complex things in the universe. It achieves this status first by the density of intricately organized interacting units contained within its small space. There are over 100 billion neurons in the brain. Each neuron connects to a range of from a few to 10,000 other neurons at synaptic junctions. Thus there are trillions of synapses. The function of these neurons is to send electrical impulses down the long axons to release a substance at the synaptic cleft that then excites or inhibits the subsequent postsynaptic neuron.

The brain functions as a complex *parallel processor*. Neurons are set up in small clusters or nuclei, larger groups, circuits, and systems. These groupings connect to one another in both linear and parallel fashions, creating a weblike structure called a *neural network*. The functioning of the system is in the on-off patterns of neuronal activation that create a *neural net activation profile*. Function emerges from structure. Given the number of synaptic connections, the estimated number of possible profiles is on the order of 10 to the millionth power, or 10 times 10 one million times. The cognitive processing of the brain is thought to reside in the way this neural net processor takes in stimuli (such as verbal or visual input), transforms it via various and complex neuronal responses to the initial activations, and then produces a network response leading to output, such as bodily motion, emotions, or words.

A neural net activation profile refers to the potential combination of on-off patterns within the possible set of network activity. Thus the activity of the brain's billions of neurons, determined by trillions of synaptic inhibitory and excitatory connections, allows for nearly infinite (10 to the millionth power) combinations of profiles. The *state* of the system refers to the activity of these components at a given time. The neural net activity can be described in both space and time dimensions with the added complexity of the kinetics (timing) of change in the system's state. A useful mathematically derived theory about such a system is called the *nonlinear dynamics of complex systems*. This view predicts 3 principles that seem to be quite applicable to cognition and the human brain: (1) spontaneous self-organization, (2) innate movement toward increased complexity, and (3) recursive (repeating) patterns of organization. Modern views of development emphasize the importance of *self-regulatory processes* that help the individual organize internal functions. Development involves progressively increasing complexity in its various domains (motor, emotional, intellectual, social). Neurobiological studies demonstrate the recursive nature of the brain's function in that processes appear to be distributed in the system as a whole rather than in 1 isolated localization.

A clinical implication of this self-regulation can be seen as you observe or listen to the history of abrupt shifts in mental state within the child. From the earliest days of the child's life, the connection between parent's and child's state allows for the child to attain smooth transitions. Watch closely for how these states shift from moment to moment, as seen in changes in facial expression, bodily posture, tone of voice, and content of speech, and how you can correlate these with social interactions.

Representations and Processes

With all of this given complexity, how can we—as scientists or clinicians—begin to unravel what goes on inside the minds of human beings? Some basic ideas from cognitive science have proven quite helpful; these utilize the notions of representations, processes, and structures to conceptualize the transformational activities of the mind. A *representation* can be thought of as a neural net profile of activation that is symbolic for something, either external or internal. Thus when you look at a picture of the Eiffel Tower, your brain's visual processing system creates a pattern of activation that has the internal image of the tower. If you then close your eyes, you may be able to evoke a visual memory of the tower by reactivating a similar neural net profile representing that image. Functional brain imaging scans suggest that the parts of the brain we use for initial registration of a stimuli are similar to those that we use to recall the same visual input.

A cognitive *process* is thought to be a pattern of action of the neural net on representations that alters their form, makes new associations, and creates new representations. Cognitive processes thus act on representations as a form of input and create new ones as their output. Noting similarities and differences is an example of a cognitive process. A cognitive *structure* is a highly complex process with a repeated pattern of action. An example would be long-term memory in which items must have conscious attention in order to be processed into certain forms of permanent memory storage. Even a representation is a dynamic process that stems from the changing activation of neurons. There is nothing concrete or static in cognition.

Representations are highly interwoven with other representations and various forms of cognitive processes. The term *dispositional representation* (see Damasio, 1994) captures this idea that symbols, such as that of the Eiffel Tower, will have cognitive connections to other representations—such as the emotions you may have felt visiting the tower for the first time, knowledge you may have about the history of architecture, or about the French, or France, or baguettes, or the last French film you saw. How are these linkages made? A basic principle, called Hebb's hypothesis, states that neurons which fire together at one time will tend to fire together in the future. Associations link elements together by general similarities (within the same category of French) and by unique elements of timing (your various feelings at the time you were at the tower).

A hierarchy of *meaning* is established by the emotional value connected to representations. The amygdala is thought to be the brain location responsible for the assignment of this meaning by establishing a sense of importance to stimuli that are then laid down in memory. The emotional meaning of events and the *value-laden memory* (see Edelman, 1992) connected to them is created by the limbic portion of the brain. One view holds that it is the body's response to stimuli, encoded in the brain as a *somatic marker* (see Damasio, 1994), that registers the emotional meaning of that event. In this way the brain is "embodied": Bodily responses are both regulated and monitored by the brain and then represented in the brain (as a somatic marker) and simultaneously woven into other aspects of cognition within dispositional representations.

This view of cognition puts an end to old debates about how the brain is distinct from the body. Close examination of the way the brain learns and remembers also puts an end to the historical dichotomies of nature vs. nurture and biology vs. experience. The brain, its function and structure, is shaped by genetics *and* experience. The infant is born with inherent characteristics of his or her nervous system, such as intensity of reactions, regularity of biological rhythms, sensitivity to the environment, and response to change or to novel situations. As the infant grows, there is a dying back of the huge number of neurons present at birth—a process called *pruning*. Experience-dependent growth determines which neurons remain and also leads directly to the development of new axonal branches and the establishment of new synaptic connections. Learning involves the growth of new synaptic junctions and alteration in the strength of these connections. Thus experience shapes the architecture of the brain; the brain enables experience to occur. Experience is biology.

Another dichotomy that begins to have only academic and historical value is the distinction between hot and cold cognitive processes. In research it is important to keep conditions as stable as possible and endeavor to alter only 1 variable at a time in order to have causal attribution to the controlled changes. To accomplish this, initial studies of cognition utilizing an information-processing perspective attempted to omit emotions from their focus of study. It now appears clear, however, that emotions commonly play a central role in cognitive processes ranging from rational decision making to memory retrieval. The term *cold* is used to refer to such processes as sensation, perception, attention, memory, and metacognition. The term *hot* refers to emotions and their regulation, social cognition, and autobiographical narrative.

As you evaluate a child, the complexity of representations will become evident to you as you follow the child's spontaneous speech and responses to your questions. Some children may have access to specific forms of representations, such as verbal or perceptual. Others may have awareness of sensory representations but be less capable of putting these into words. The notion of "shared representational worlds" refers to the concept that some of these cognitive representations are available to be mutually attended by 2 people.

Specific Cognitive Processes

SENSATION, PERCEPTION, AND ATTENTION

Sensation is considered as the registration of input from the body or the external world in a form that is given no "signal value"—that is, it is experienced directly with little filtering from prior experience. (It is processed from a bottom-up rather than a top-down perspective.) *Perception* is the transformation of sensation utilizing processes that categorize and generalize patterns from prior experience. When you "see" the Eiffel Tower and recognize it as such, this is considered a perception. As children develop, they attain progressively more sophisticated perceptual processes. Some disorders directly affect the ability to perceive in certain modalities, such as visual or auditory perceptual deficits.

Attention is thought to direct the flow of energy—labeled as the arrows—in an information-processing model. There are various aspects of attention, including *focal attention,* in which conscious effort is extended to focus a "spotlight" of attention on a stimulus, internal or external. Focal attention requires the ability to filter out extraneous factors and the capacity to sustain attention over time. These latter areas are abnormal in many children with attention deficit hyperactivity disorder. *Nonfocal attention* is quite different from focal attention and is able to scan the environment for gestalt features and stimuli with signal value, such as your name or signs of danger (e.g., "fire").

When you conduct an evaluation, you may notice that one child efficiently uses attentional resources to focus a "spotlight" of attention on an object or process. In contrast, another child may have a more random allocation process, seen as a quickly shifting focus of attention to stimuli other than those being mutually attended by you and the child. Sources of this distraction may be external—via perceptions—or internal—via sensations. Thus you may sense that the child has a bombardment of off-task representations (perceptual and sensory) that attract attentional processes away from the main subject of discussion.

FORMS OF PROCESSING: SERIAL AND PARALLEL

Two types of processing have been described. *Serial processes* are linear, rate-limited, energy-consuming processes that usually can occur only one at a time. Focal attention, language use, and consciousness are examples of serial processes. How energy resources are allocated to allow for a prioritizing of the use of serial processes is an executive function that develops slowly during the first years of life. This executive function appears to be underdeveloped in children with attention deficit hyperactivity disorder.

Parallel processes, by contrast, occur simultaneously, are fast, low-energy-consuming processes that can occur at the same time as other parallel or serial processes. Most of the brain's processes are in a parallel mode, including nonfocal attention, mental state regulation, mental models, and metacognitive processes. This parallel nature of cognition explains why the vast majority of mental processes occur outside of serial consciousness, which is the common basis for our awareness of internal and external processes.

During the evaluation phase, you may find that some children are extremely unaware of parallel processes while others follow the flow of these processes and disregard the linearity of serial processes. At the extreme, this latter situation might appear to an outside observer as a form of scattered thought or outright tangential thinking. Understanding the internal meaning of such parallel processes can provide a clue to underlying emotional issues in the child's life.

LOGICOSCIENTIFIC AND NARRATIVE MODES OF PROCESSING

Another distinction in cognitive processing is that between the narrative mode of thought and the paradigmatic or logicoscientific mode. Children first develop the narrative mode in which the world is understood in story form, including the internal experiences and external activities of characters in their lives. By 18 months, children demonstrate the presence of this mode of cognition, which is experience and context dependent. Narrative includes 3 main genres: schematic, fictional, and autobiographical. In the evaluation process, you will notice both children and parents telling narratives woven from all 3 of these genres. Indeed, stories are a common form of communication across all human cultures by people of all ages. Play is filled with narratives in which children blend the major forms of stories revealing the themes that play a central role in their lives. Narratives both record history and help determine future action. In this way, autobiographical stories can help the clinician understand how an individual is cognitively making sense of the world and how this view is influencing his or her behavior.

In contrast, the paradigmatic mode develops later and is experience and context independent, utilizing logic and concepts as the basis for manipulating more abstract cognitive representations. Even after the development of this logicoscientific mode, people rely on narrative processing to explore the subjective lives of others and of themselves.

Children's lives are filled with stories in the form of play and direct storytelling. During the evaluation process, the blend of autobiographical, schematic, and fictional genres of narrative allows stories to be a rich resource for understanding the important themes of a child's life.

CONSCIOUS AND NONCONSCIOUS PROCESSES

When we ask patients what they remember, what they feel, or what they are aware of, we are asking them to evaluate their conscious access to representations in their mind. Representations of memories, feelings, or perceptions can exist outside of consciousness. In fact, most mental processes are outside of conscious awareness. The study of consciousness is a wide field with numerous theories into the nature of its neurobiological substrate and the various aspects of its subjective experience. Several forms of consciousness have been described.

A clinically useful view is that of primary and secondary (higher-order) consciousness. (See Edelman, 1992.) In this view, the simultaneous neural net activation of sensory and categorical representations within their respective neuronal centers leads to a here-and-now experience of *primary consciousness*. Awareness of a picture of the Eiffel Tower (without naming it) is an example of primary consciousness. When a name is given, the linguistic neuronal groups are activated and resonate with the categorical groups leading to a *secondary or higher-order consciousness*. This language-dependent form of consciousness is thought to transcend the prison of the present and allow for conscious reflections on the past and the future. Higher-order consciousness allows me to write these words and for you to read them.

During the evaluation process, it is important to remember that patients have varying degrees of ability to put words to their internal experiences. Thus there may be a primary consciousness for certain representations—such as feelings, thoughts, or perceptions—but an inability to put words to them (and therefore, in this view, either to reflect on their history or consciously to alter their future action). Helping patients find words to describe their experience may allow them both to share their experience with another person and to transform the nature of consciousness and the neurological ability to process those representations.

COGNITIVE REPRESENTATIONS: LINGUISTIC, PERCEPTUAL, AND SENSORY

As you sit with your patients and their families and discuss what they experience, you may find that 3 layers of representations are used in their descriptions. These layers have been used to define a 3-part division of mental processes into sensory, perceptual, and linguistic representations. The first 2 forms of representations are defined as *analogic;* the last form, as *digital.* Some authors argue that the right hemisphere processes analogic representations, whereas the left hemisphere specializes in linguistic, digital representations.

Interestingly, the right hemisphere contains a more integrated somatosensory system registering the state of the body. This bodily representation, part of a somatic marker, is thought to form the basis for emotions in the brain. It may be for this reason that emotions often are felt as sensations or experienced as perceptions or bodily impulses; words are a long way—both conceptually and hemispherically—from this proposed analogic basis for emotional experience.

Dispositional representations contain the linkages between these 3 forms of cognitive representations. As you evaluate your patient, keep in mind that each person will hear your questions in a unique way based on the individual meanings contained within the dispositional representations that are activated in response to your words. This is part of the neurological basis of the idiosyncratic meaning each of us brings to our perceptions and responses to the world.

As you listen to the child and parents tell about their lives, keep a watchful eye on the form of representations they tend to use in communication. You will encounter significant differences within and between families, differences that can inform you about the limitations of family members' abilities to share their internal worlds—with each other or with a potential therapist.

MEMORY: IMPLICIT AND EXPLICIT

In asking your patient about what he or she remembers, you are referring to a specific form of memory called *explicit memory.* This is the form of memory in which an event has been encoded with focal attention, registered into storage, and, when retrieved into consciousness, has the internal sensation of something being recalled. This form of memory actually does not develop well until into the second year of life. After this time, children do have the ability to recall, explicitly, what they have experienced. The phenomenon of *childhood amnesia* refers to both this period before the onset of explicit memory and to the few years afterward in which a child, after the age of about 5 years, does not have explicit recall of the years before.

The medial temporal lobe, including the hippocampus, is necessary for explicit memory processing. The hippocampus is not fully functional until after the second year of life, a fact that explains the first period of childhood amnesia. It

is not known why the few years after this period, which are in fact accessible at the time, are later no longer explicitly retrievable in most individuals.

From the beginning of an infant's life, another form of memory is active. *Implicit memory* refers to behavioral, perceptual and emotional learning that is present from birth and throughout the life span. Recollection of an implicit memory involves a behavioral or emotional response and does not include the sense of something being recalled. The medial temporal lobe does not appear to be directly involved in implicit memory. Brain regions responsible for motoric (basal ganglia) and emotional (limbic system) responses are thought to be the site for implicit memory encoding, storage, and retrieval.

When clinically assessing how experiences have affected children during the first 5 years of life, it is important to remember—explicitly—that although children usually will not be able to describe what occurred, they will demonstrate the learning that occurred through their emotional and behavioral responses. Repeated patterns of response and transference reactions may have their root in the implicit memory system.

Views of memory utilize the concepts of encoding, storage, and retrieval. *Encoding* is the way in which the neural net is affected by a stimulus and then processes it into representational form. *Storage* is the probability that a neural net activation profile will be activated again in the future. There is no "storage closet" in the brain. Experience affects the neural net directly through learning that occurs by the creation of new and altered strengths of synaptic connections. This associational nature of learning and memory is explained by Hebb's hypothesis; neurons that fire together, wire together. Memory *retrieval* is the activation of a neural net profile similar to that activated at the time of encoding. Retrieval does not physically get something out of a storage space—but is the activation of potential neuronal patterns by cues (internal and external) that are linked to the associational network and serve to initiate an activation process within the network as a system. When representations are reactivated or "retrieved from storage," they often become a part of *working memory* in which they can be focally attended and consciously processed. Retrieval thus can act as a "memory modifier" in that this processing in working memory can lead to new associations and characteristics of the representation as it "returns to storage" with its new probability of reactivation in this altered neural net profile form.

During the evaluation process, children and adults may become filled with recollections of the implicit and explicit variety. You will notice patients becoming overwhelmed by emotions, images or behavioral impulses that may reflect implicit recollections being activated by specific cues during the interview. These implicit recollections will not be experienced as "something remembered" but will feel "real in the moment." Your understanding of this process can help patients tolerate previously unbearable emotional states by linking an understanding of how the present becomes flooded by memories. Making explicit memory available to form a coherent story of what these intense implicit recollections represent can begin to occur even during the evaluation process.

MENTAL MODELS

Part of the learning that occurs throughout life involves the registration of representations of experience that are contrasted and compared to prior representations. From this generalization process emerges a complex cognitive process or structure called a *mental model*. A mental model, or schema, is a neural net process that is derived from past experience, shapes present perceptions, and influences future action. Mental models encode the patterns of experience and then allow the mind rapidly to interpret present experience in order to anticipate the future. The inherent survival value in such a generalization process would be crucial in a hostile environment, allowing for predators to be perceived quickly and avoided.

During the evaluation process, patients will reveal their mental models to you by how they respond, not by what they directly are consciously able to describe of their experiences. Mental models are always nonconscious. When they enter awareness, they become concepts or perceptions—useful, but not actually mental models. We can detect models only by the shadows they cast on our pa-

tient's verbal and nonverbal responses. Understanding the nature of these shadows is our task as clinicians.

METACOGNITION

In addition to generalizing on the patterns of representations, as in mental models, the mind is also capable of creating representations of its own processes. This process is termed *metacognition*. Rapid metacognitive development occurs between the ages of 2 and 9 years. During the evaluation process, you may encounter some of the basic dimensions of metacognition, including the appearance-reality distinction in which children learn that what they perceive may be different from external reality.

Specific metacognitive capacities include representational diversity and representational change in which the child realizes that what he or she experiences may be different from what another person experiences, and that what is thought one day may be different the next day, respectively. Children also begin to learn that they may have 2 emotions about the same person and that emotions bias their perceptions. Developmental phase as well as individual differences determine the level of metacognitive capacity.

As patients move through the evaluation and therapy process, they gradually may develop more elaborated forms of self-reflection. For many patients, the ability to represent their own cognitive processes, the essence of metacognition, can be a crucial achievement that will last a lifetime. For some, inhibited metacognitive ability may have served an adaptive function to avoid awareness of intolerable life situations.

EMOTIONS AND STATE OF MIND

Emotions are complex processes involving the body and the brain, the self, and other people. Emotions influence all cognition, from attention and perception to decision making and remembering. Emotions affect cognition with or without the involvement of consciousness. One way to conceptualize the essence of emotion is as the brain's way of appraising the significance, or meaning, of stimuli from the outer or inner world. The brain has specific regions within it which are arousal/appraisal centers whose purpose is to respond to input by creating increased activation or arousal within various neuronal circuits. As this process occurs, there is an initial activation which signifies, "pay attention, this is important!" A second phase is the evaluation of the hedonic tone of the arousal: "this is good, or this is bad." A third aspect is the specific elaboration of the arousal/appraisal in which the quality of the emotional activation is further differentiated leading to the experience, conscious or nonconscious, of categorical emotions such as fear, anger, sadness, joy, surprise or shame. Emotions are thus the mind's way of determining meaning.

The brain is embodied. This means that the registration of changes in the body's state of arousal directly establishes the individual's emotional state. This is an automatic process, not requiring consciousness. Thus emotions can affect mental processes even if they are out of awareness. The brain's representation of bodily state, called a somatic marker, also can be activated independently of present bodily response in the emotional recollection of a memory and the establishment of an emotional state.

Mental activity can be organized by what is called a *state of mind*. A mental state is the clustering of neuronal activations into repeatable patterns, including characteristic features of emotions, perceptual biases, mental models, behavioral response style, and memory. These state-dependent mental processes can be activated rapidly when a particular state of mind is instantiated (made active). For example, if you see a patient in a fearful state of mind, she may feel frightened, bias her perception of the world toward things being threatening, have mental models activated of events being attacking toward her, respond behaviorally in a defensive fashion, and have increased probability of recalling—both explicitly and implicitly—events from the past that were frightening.

States of mind constantly organize our internal experience and external behavior. Learning about how your patient regulates the shifts in states of mind is important in evaluating his or her capacity for *self-organization,* a fundamental property of each of us as complex organisms.

During the evaluation process, you may first get a sense of a patient's emotional state by what *you* feel in your own body and mind. Nonverbal cues, often subtle and fast, can be perceived without your own conscious awareness. Your own emotional/bodily reaction forms a response to such cues. Noting these feelings in yourself and becoming consciously aware of what bodily changes are occurring in the patient—changes in posture, movement, facial expression, tone of voice, eye contact—will help you incorporate your patient's emotional state into your evaluation process.

AFFECT REGULATION AND SELF-ORGANIZATION

The mind is a complex system. Recent views of the nonlinear dynamics of complex systems capable of chaotic behavior suggest that the brain functions as a dynamical system. The term *nonlinear* indicates that small changes in input can lead to dramatic—and, in the longterm, unpredictable—changes in output. It is this amplification of response that helps explain the idiosyncratic nature of mental processes and human behavior. Part of this system's function is to have a process of self-organization. One of the basic forms of self-organization of the system is in the area of affect regulation, a process that develops during the first 2 years of life and appears to arise from the experience-dependent maturation of an area of the brain called the orbitofrontal cortex (Schore, 1994).

Early patterns of interaction with attachment figures in the infant's life allow for the attunement of the child's and caregiver's emotional states. These repeated patterns of connection allow for the infant to develop a tuning process with the caregiver's state of mind that is then thought to become an autonomous self-regulating process by the second year of life.

One view of this *attunement* process is that when caregiver and infant are aligning their emotional states, the child has the activation of an "accelerator" system, the sympathetic branch of the autonomic nervous system. (See Schore, 1994.) When there is a rupture in attunement, the "brake" system—the parasympathetic branch of the autonomic nervous system—is activated. The reconnection following such a rupture, as occurs intentionally during limit-setting, followed by redirection of the child's energy and attention, allows for a balance between the child's accelerator and brakes. In this view, it is the regulation of the 2 branches of the autonomic nervous system that constitutes the fundamental basis of self-regulation.

This perspective can provide helpful insights into the developmental origin of affect and behavioral regulation. For example, in parent-child dyads in which limit-setting is inconsistent or infrequent, the child is not given the opportunity to develop a brake system. In these children, behavioral impulses may go unchecked and emotions can go beyond tolerable levels quickly without a smooth transition back toward a stable state. In dyads where parents utilize repeated and prolonged periods of ruptured connections, especially with hostile limit-setting, the child may experience emotional states of shame and humiliation; these are counterproductive to the child's development of a mature affect and behavioral regulation system. In this view, parental misattunement at a time of heightened need for alignment produces a sudden shift from an "accelerator" to a "brakes" mode: the parasympathetically mediated shame state. The addition of parental hostility at the time of disconnection leads to a toxic state of humiliation.

In your evaluation of the child, it is important to remember that the match between the child's inborn temperament features with the expectations of the caregivers is an important predictor of the child's future developmental progression. How the child and parent establish emotional connections and repair their inevitable ruptures can help you see how these transactions shape the child's developing regulatory systems.

As these interpersonal transactions continue, the child encodes patterns of interactions as *representations of the self with other people*. These dyadic representations may be essential in the growing child's developing sense of self. By age 2, a process called *evocative memory* is thought to be in place in which the child elicits the sensory representation of the self with an attachment figure in order to help regulate his or her internal emotional state. Evocative memory may thus be used as a self-soothing cognitive process. In a sense, these forms of self-representations are a cognitive form of internal transitional object.

SOCIAL COGNITION

The study of social cognition focuses on the mental processes involved in social interactions, including empathy, interpersonal communication, relationship schema, perceptual biases, and group behavior. Social cognition is thought to depend on the ability of the mind to form representations of other individuals' mental lives. This capacity permits the perception and interpretation of others' internal states, such as beliefs, desires, attentional focus, emotions, thoughts, and intentions. Social cognition is a vital process essential for understanding, and attempting to predict, others' behavior.

One perspective on social cognition views these processes as a form of "mind-reading" that relies on 4 basic mechanisms. (See Baron-Cohen, 1995.) *Intentionality detection* allows for the child to interpret contextual cues in order to estimate the intentional stance of another person. An automatic human process, perhaps fundamental to narrative, is that people will attribute intentionality even to inanimate, moving figures or geometric shapes. *Eye gaze detection* permits the evaluation of the direct focus of another's visual attention on the child, thus establishing an alert signal that some form of interaction with the other may be imminent. Direct eye contact appears to be crucial in the normally sighted individual's development of affect regulation. *Shared attentional mechanisms* allow for the child to detect the object of interest to another person. This capacity allows for joint referencing, the frequent social interaction within which 2 individuals attend to a common object or activity. *Theory of mind* is a term used to describe the ability of the child to represent the complex subjective experience or intentional stance of other people, including their feelings, desires, and memories.

Social cognitive deficits may be seen to various degrees in several conditions during childhood. A primary social cognitive deficit has been characteristically described in children with right-hemisphere lesions and in those with autistic disorder. One view (see Baron-Cohen, 1995) suggests that autistic children have an abnormal shared attentional mechanism and theory of mind emanating from a neurophysiological dysfunction in the orbitofrontal cortex, the part of the brain central to the regulation of affect and for social cognition.

Other views (see Sigman, 1994) highlight the complex route to socioemotional understanding that may be disrupted at various points. This pathway includes the perception of one's own emotional responses; attention to and perception of the vocal, facial, and behavioral displays of others; awareness of others' emotional responses; understanding others' views and desires; and the understanding of beliefs and a theory of mind. Language is a highly social cognitive process that also has its developmental pathway disrupted in children with autism.

During the evaluation process, you will sense your "connection" with the child first as an emotional openness the child may have to relating. This availability is not the same as social cognition but can be impaired in children who are withdrawn or are hesitant to be vulnerable to strangers. In children who have a significant deficit in social cognitive abilities, you may determine that their sense of personal space boundaries is not clear, that they violate basic rules of communication (such as considering the listener's perspective in offering details, allowing for a give-and-take, and having the ability to share attention to the focus of conversation), and that they seem to be "off" in considering that you or anyone has their own "subjective experience."

NARRATIVE

The narrative mode of cognition is a crucial way in which the child learns about the world. *Coconstruction of narrative* refers to the cross-cultural finding that families create stories together. These emerging narratives help shape the child's experience of reality. An in-depth view into the neurobiology of stories also suggests that narratives utilize various forms of cognitive representations, from analogic (sensory and perceptual) to digital (linguistic). In this way, narratives serve to recruit both right- and left-hemispheric processing in an increasingly complex tapestry that

both emotionally and logically explores social reality. Narratives also draw on both implicit and explicit memory in establishing the themes that organize their structure.

In the evaluation process, the stories your patients tell can be seen as a reflection of these numerous important aspects of their mental life. Narratives—emerging in art, play, storytelling, and recollections—can reveal how the mind is attempting to organize the many layers of mental processes contained both within and outside of conscious awareness. Narratives also establish a link among past experiences, present perceptions, and the anticipation of future events. Listen carefully to the revealing details and themes of your patients' stories.

An Integration of Cognitive, Developmental, Emotional, and Social Neuroscience

Developmental studies suggest an interrelationship among the domains of attachment, emotional regulation, memory, and narrative processes. It appears that patterns of relationships have a direct influence on the capacity for self-regulation, especially that of emotions. The dyadic process of discussing the contents of a child's memory leads to a more fully developed language system and the increased accessibility of explicit memories for experiences. Attachment studies reveal that parent-child dyads that have an emotionally distant pattern of relating, one that does not involve focusing on the child's internal experience, may have a paucity of autobiographical narratives. Interestingly, the parents of these dyads also reveal a lack of autobiographical recall for childhood experiences. The nature of this deficit in narrative processing is yet to be elucidated.

Developmental studies of early social referencing suggest that, in an ambiguous situation, the child looks to the parent to know how he or she should feel and behave. The child thus is absorbing the emotional communication with the parent.

273

Overall, secure attachments appear to provide the foundation essential for a child to explore the world and regulate his or her behaviors and emotional state. Secure attachments emerge from relationships with parental sensitivity and responsivity to the child's needs. Parents who demonstrate an interest in the inner experience of their child are most likely to create a secure attachment. Communication in these pairs is said to be collaborative in which each member responds contingently to the signals of the other.

These and other studies suggest that the brain has *experience-dependent maturation,* that is, it requires certain forms of stimulation in order for it to develop properly. Cognitive processes come directly from the neurobiological activity of the brain, which has been shaped by experiences, especially those in the social world. It is within this perspective that mental activity—the essence of the mind and the psyche—can be seen to emerge from the interface of interpersonal relationships and neural processes. The evaluation of cognition thus must incorporate an assessment of these emotionally meaningful relationships and the fundamental processes that make up the mental life of the child.

As we sit as clinicians with children and their families, we are embarking on an important observational task requiring us to see across the dimensions of time and space into the complex and changing processes of human minds. This role is both a challenge and a privilege. It is our responsibility to attempt to incorporate perspectives ranging from the importance of cultural factors in the social development of children to the molecular mechanisms underlying neuronal activity. Viewing the brain as a complex dynamical system allows us to begin to understand how the mind regulates itself by altering its own internal components and attuning itself to the states of other individuals. These self-organizational processes move the mind toward increasing complexity as the child develops.

This brief overview has provided just a sample of the ideas of a developmental neuroscience approach to the psychiatric evaluation of cognition. It is important to remember that in minding the brain we must not lose our minds. For each of us in the mental health field, clinical evaluation and treatment offers us an opportunity to consolidate our identity in the integration of cognitive, developmental, emotional, and social neuroscience.

REFERENCES

Sensation, Perception, and Attention

Flavell, J., Miller, P. H., & Miller, S. A. (1993). *Cognitive development* (3rd ed.). Englewood Cliffs, NJ: Prentice Hall.

Kosslyn, S. M. (1994). *Image and brain: The resolution of the imagery debate.* Cambridge, MA: MIT Press.

O'Mara, S., & Walsh, V. (Eds.). (1994). The cognitive neuropsychology of attention. *Cognitive Neuropsychology, 11,* 96.

Osherson, D. N., & Smith, E. E. (Eds.). (1990). *Visual cognition and Action: An Invitation to Cognitive Science* (Vol. 2). Cambridge, MA: MIT Press.

Forms of Processing: Serial and Parallel

McClelland, J. L., & Rumelhart, D. E. (Eds.). (1986). *Parallel distributed processing: Explorations in the microstructure of cognition* (Vols. 1 and 2). Cambridge, MA: MIT Press.

Morris, R. G. M. (Ed.). (1989). *Parallel distributed processing: Implications for psychology and neurobiology.* Oxford: Clarendon Press.

Logicoscientific and Narrative Modes of Processing

Bruner, J. (1986). *Actual minds, possible worlds.* Cambridge, MA: Harvard University Press.

McCabe, A., & Peterson, C. (Eds.). (1991). *Developing narrative structure.* Hillsdale, NJ: Lawrence Erlbaum.

Ochs, E., & Capps, L. (1996). Narrating the self. In W. Durham, E. Valentine Daniels, & B. Schieffelin (Eds.). (1996). *Annual review of anthropology,* Palo Alto, CA: Annual Reviews. pp. 19–43.

Conscious and Nonconscious Processes

Greenwald, A. G. (1992). New look 3: Unconscious cognition reclaimed. *American Psychologist, 47,* 766–799.

Kihlstrom, J. F. (1987). The cognitive unconscious. *Science, 237,* 1445.

Marcel, A., & Bisiach, E. (Eds.). (1988). *Consciousness in contemporary science.* New York: Oxford University Press.

Cognitive Representations: Linguistic, Perceptual, and Sensory

Edelman, G. (1992). *Bright air, brilliant fire.* New York: Basic Books.

Perner, J. (1991). *Understanding the representational mind.* Cambridge, MA: MIT Press.

Posner, M. I. (Ed.). (1989). *Foundations of cognitive science.* Cambridge, MA: MIT Press.

Memory: Implicit and Explicit

Ceci, S., Bruch, M. (1993). Suggestibility of the child witness: A historical review and synthesis. *Psychological Bulletin, 113,* 403–439.

Christianson, S. A. (Ed.). (1991). *Handbook of emotion and memory.* Hillsdale, NJ: Lawrence Erlbaum.

Fivush, R., & Hudson, J. A. (Eds.). (1990). *Knowing and remembering in young children.* New York: Cambridge University Press.

Nelson, K. (1993). The psychological and social origins of autobiographical memory. *Psychological Science, 2,* 1–8.

Schacter, D. L. (1992). Understanding implicit memory: A cognitive neuroscience approach. *American Psychologist, 47,* 559–569.

Schacter, D. L., Tulving, E. (Eds.). (1994). *Memory system 1994.* Cambridge, MA: MIT Press.

Squire, L. R. (1992). Declarative and non-declarative memory: Multiple brain systems supporting learning and memory. *Journal of Cognitive Neuroscience, 4,* 232–243.

Mental Models

Horowitz, M. J. (Ed.). (1991). *Person schemas and maladaptive interpersonal patterns.* Chicago: University of Chicago Press.

Johnson-Laird, P. N. (1982). *Mental models: Towards a cognitive science of language, inference and consciousness.* Cambridge, MA: Harvard University Press.

Metacognition

Flavell, J. H., Green, F. L., & Flavell, E. R. (1986). Development of knowledge about the appearance-reality distinction. *Monographs of Social Research and Child Development, 51,* 212.

Main, M. (1990). Metacognitive knowledge, metacognitive monitoring, and singular (coherent) versus multiple (incoherent) models of attachment: Findings and directions for future research. In M. T. Greenberg, D. Cichetti, & E. M. Cummings (Eds.), *Attachment in the preschool years: Theory, research, and intervention* (pp. 161–182). Chicago: University of Chicago Press.

Metcalfe, J., & Shimamura, A. P. (1989). *Metacognition: Knowing about knowing.* Cambridge, MA: MIT Press.

Emotions and State of Mind

Damasio, A. R. (1994). *Descartes error: Emotion, reasoning and the human brain.* New York: Putnam.

Fonagy, P., Steele, M., Steele, H., Moran, G., Higgitt, A. (1991). The capacity for understanding mental states: The reflective self in parent and child and its significance for security of attachment. *Infant Mental Health Journal, 12,* 201–218.

Siegel, D. J. (1996). Cognition, memory and dissociation. *Child and Adolescent Psychiatric Clinics, 5* (2), 509–536.

Frith, U., & Happe, F. (1994). Autism: Beyond "theory of mind." *Cognition, 50,* 115.

Sigman, M. (1994). What are the core deficits in autism? In S. H. Broman & J. Grafman (Eds.), *Atypical cognitive deficits in developmental disorders: Implications for brain function.* Pp. 139–157. Hillsdale, NJ: Lawrence Erlbaum.

Trevarthen, C. (1993). The self born in intersubjectivity: The psychology of infant communicating. In U. Neisser (Ed.), *The perceived self: Ecological and interpersonal sources of self-knowledge* (pp. 121–173). New York: Cambridge University Press.

Affect Regulation and Self Organization

Beebe, B., & Lachman, F. (1994). Representation and internalization in infancy: Three principles of salience. *Psychoanalytic Psychology, 11,* 127–166.

Cicchetti, D., & Tucker, D. (1994). Development and self-regulatory structures of the mind. *Development and Psychopathology, 6,* 533–549.

Globus, G., & Arpaia, J. P. (1993). Psychiatry and the new dynamics. *Biological Psychiatry, 35,* 352–364.

Schore, A. N. (1994). *Affect regulation and the origin of the self: The neurobiology of emotional development.* Hillsdale, NJ: Lawrence Erlbaum.

Siegel, D. J. *Emotional Connections.* Guilford, New York: In Press.

Narrative

Coles, R. (1989). *The call of stories: Teaching and the moral imagination.* Boston: Houghton-Mifflin.

Nelson, K. (Ed.). (1989). *Narratives from the crib.* Cambridge, MA: Harvard University Press.

Vitz, P. G. (1990). The use of stories in moral development: New psychological reasons for an old educational method. *American Psychologist, 45,* 709–720.

White, M., & Epston, D. (1990). *Narrative means to therapeutic ends.* New York: W. W. Norton.

Social Cognition

Baron-Cohen, S. (1995). *Mindblindness: An essay on autism and theory of mind.* Cambridge, MA: MIT Press.

47 / Social Communication

Peter E. Tanguay

Definition of Social Communication

Although we may think of "human communication" in terms of spoken language, linguistic studies indicate that vocabulary (the semantic aspect of speech) and grammar (the syntactic aspect) carry only a part of the information that humans exchange with each other. In addition to the semantic/syntactic domain, social communication encompasses other equally important domains. These include prosody, facial expression, gestural expression, and pragmatic skills or understanding.

PROSODY

Prosody is the melody of speech. Prosodic information is conveyed by changes in tone of voice, changes in the rate and rhythm of speech, and modulations in the volume of our speech. Prosody not only tells the listener about the feelings of the speaker but can encode other information, even that which is grammatical in nature; for example, in English, a rising pitch toward the end of a statement signifies that the speaker is asking a question. Irony also can be encoded by tone of voice to indicate to the listener that the speaker intends the opposite of what the words imply.

FACIAL EXPRESSION

Izard, Huebner, Risser, McGinnes, and Dougherty (1980) found that by 2 months of age or earlier, children display 4 basic facial expressions of emotion: interest, joy, sadness, and anger. As early as 4 to 6 months of age, infants also have been shown to be capable of learning to use facial expressions in response to maternal social cues.

During social interactions, we frequently scan the facial expressions of our listeners, looking, for instance, to check whether our audience is "getting the message" or if, instead, they are showing the puzzled expression of one who does not understand. Higher primates have a rich repertoire of facial expressions for interpersonal communication. A story was told to me by a young man on the staff of a well-known primate research center in Africa that illustrates the strength of facial expression signals, even between species. The young scientist said that his parents came to visit him one week, and owing to the large numbers of visitors, it was necessary to house them in a nearby corrugated-iron shack. He warned his father, "You probably will be visited in the morning by one of the alpha males. Don't worry, he means no harm, but if you want him to go away just look at him and suddenly raise your eyebrows sharply. That's an aggression signal." Sure enough, the next morning the gorilla did come, towering outside the shack and peering into it. The father, who had bushy eyebrows, placed himself in front of the gorilla and suddenly shot his eyebrows up. The gorilla shouted, "Whoops," turned, and dashed up the hillside as fast as he could go.

GESTURAL EXPRESSION

Three types of gestures are recognized in the literature. There are *instrumental gestures,* such as holding one's hand out front, palm facing forward, meaning "stop," or beckoning with one's hand to tell another person to approach. A second form of gesture is *social gesture,* which is culturally diverse and must be learned. Social gestures in European and American culture include shaking hands to indicate friendliness and goodwill, waving "bye-bye," and "blowing a kiss." A third form of social gesture is *emotional gesture.* Emotional gestures are often spontaneous, and while they may be greatly modified through learning, they may in part be innate. They include covering one's face in embarrassment or shrugging one's shoulder (and looking puzzled) to indicate disbelief. At times it may be difficult to decide whether certain gestures are social or emotional, and some may be a bit of both. Still, the concept can be useful in helping to understand the development of gestural communication.

PRAGMATIC SKILLS OR UNDERSTANDING

Pragmatics have been defined as the social rules of communication. They encompass skills such as knowing how to start a conversation, how to continue a conversation, and how to end a conversation in a socially empathic way. They also include knowing how to pitch a spoken message to meet the current needs and expectations of the listener. Another aspect of pragmatics is *theory of mind*. Theory of mind is the understanding that others have minds, that they have thoughts, and that their thoughts may be different from ours. It implies that a speaker will read all possible social communication signals being sent by the listener in order to gain an understanding of what the listener's relevant thoughts may be at that moment.

The Precursors of Social Communication in Infancy

As recently as 40 years ago, it was supposed that to an infant, the world must be a buzzing, inchoate, confusing cacophony of sounds, tactile sensations, and sights. Early in the century psychoanalytic theory hypothesized that a "stimulus barrier" existed to protect the infant from what might otherwise be a damaging overload of sensory input. We know today that neither of these beliefs is true. From studies carried out in the past 30 years we have learned that the young infant comes into the world with a surprising set of behavioral propensities and capacities designed to propel him or her into the realm of social communication as rapidly as possible (Karmiloff-Smith, 1995; Locke, 1993). Learning to master certain elements of social communication is one of the most important tasks in the infant's first 18 months of life.

Within a few hours of birth, infants can recognize their mother's voice. Ockleford, Vince, Layton, and Reader (1988) alternately stimulated infants who were less than 24 hours of age with recordings of their mother's voice and with the voice of female controls matched for age. The infant's orientation to a particular voice was measured using changes in heart rate. The children oriented to their mother's voice but not to the voice of a stranger. Infants also were found to show a discriminative response to their father's voice. Since the infants had not had an opportunity to hear their mother's voice in the short time since they were born, it was deduced that they had become familiar with her voice in utero. It is well known from animal studies that environmental sounds can be perceived in utero.

In a similar experiment, DeCasper and Spence (1986) had pregnant women recite a particular speech passage aloud each day to their fetus during the last 6 weeks of pregnancy. Shortly after birth, the infants were tested using an operant-choice procedure to determine whether the sounds of the recited passage were more reinforcing to them than the sounds of a novel passage. The previously recited passage was more reinforcing. The reinforcing nature of the 2 passages did not differ for a group of control subjects.

Infants can discriminate their mother's face from the face of a stranger shortly after birth (Field, Cohen, Garcia, & Greenberg, 1984). The subjects in this study averaged 45 hours of age. Infants were presented with the face of their mother, and an observer, blind to the study's hypothesis, recorded the neonate's visual fixation time on the mother's face. Infants were tested until their visual fixation time showed they had habituated to the stimulus. They were then presented with the face of a stranger. The infants looked significantly longer at the stranger's face, suggesting that they recognized this stimulus as novel.

Not only do infants appear to recognize faces, but they appear to have an at least rudimentary understanding of what a "normal" face should look like. Goren, Sarty, and Wu (1975) report a study of newborn infants who were examined at a mean age of 9 minutes. The infants were held in the experimenter's lap and presented with 4 moving stimuli: a schematic of a normal face, of a moderately scrambled face, of a very scrambled face, and of a blank. Many children followed the normal face as it moved. They followed the normal face to a significantly greater degree than they followed the scrambled faces, and they followed the scrambled faces more than the blank face. The authors concluded that there is an inborn propensity to identify faces and to follow them and that this ability is present at birth. Work in a similar vein by Field and her coworkers suggests that neonates are capable of discriminating happy, sad, and surprised facial expressions (Field et al., 1983). The infants appeared to fixate on the mouth, or alternately the mouth and eye regions, rather than eye regions alone. The investigators also found that differential mimicry of mouth movements occurred more frequently than mimicry of eye movements.

In what may be the most counterintuitive finding of all, infants appear capable of "imitating," again in a rudimentary fashion, certain facial expressions. This observation was initially reported by Meltzoff and Moore (1977). Infants between 12 and 21 days of age were studied. It was found that they could imitate such facial expressions as lip protrusion, mouth opening, and tongue protrusion. The authors argued that conditioning and innate releasing mechanisms did not appear to underlie this behavior. Their observations have been verified by many investigators since. In one study Field and her colleagues (1983) showed that infants could imitate certain facial expressions as early as a few hours after birth.

Although infants can be expected to engage in such behaviors only when they are in an optimal state of arousal, the presence of these behaviors emphasizes the extent to which infants come into the world prepared to engage in social communication. It also underlines the importance of interpersonal contact between the child and his or her caregivers from the first days of life. Such parental activities as looking at, talking, and holding their infant are very important, as they may act as initial organizers of later social communication development.

Development of Social Communication Behaviors in the First 6 Months of Life

The first 6 months of life are important for the development of a wide range of social communication behaviors. In a review article, Tronick (1989) concluded that infant emotions and emotional communication are far more organized in the first half of the first year than had been thought. Infants display a variety of discrete emotional expressions that are appropriate to the nature and content of events. They appreciate the emotional meaning of their caregivers' affective displays. The emotional expression of the infant and caregiver function to allow them to mutually regulate their interactions.

Studies have revealed how mother-child social interactions may drive the child's learning of social communication skills. Haith, Bergman, and Moore (1977) studied 3- to 5-week-old, 5- to 7-week-old, and 9- to 11-week-old infants as they scanned an adult's face. Three types of faces were offered: a stationary face, a moving face, and a talking face. A dramatic increase in face fixations occurred between 5 and 7 weeks for all conditions. Talking produced an intensification in the infant's scanning of the eye area in the 2 older groups. While 3-month-old infants may not know what cues to look for in facial expressions, the fact that they scan faces intently suggests that they are at least in a position to begin to learn what facial expressions mean.

Laboratory studies (Stern, Jaffe, Beebe, & Bennett, 1975) have found that by 4 months of age, an infant's head and body movements, tone, gaze, facial expressions, and vocalizations come together during social interactions to form recognizable complex expressive acts. During play sessions, mothers and their 3- to 4-month-old infants may vocalize simultaneously or in a turn-taking manner.

In response to their infant's increasing social communication development, caregivers modify their own communication behaviors toward the child. Stern, Spieker, and MacKain (1982) report that mothers use specific pitch contours to signal specific messages when talking to their prelinguistic infants. The infants were 2, 4, and 6 months of age. Rising contours were used when the infant was not visually attending and the mother wanted eye contact. Sinusoidal and bell-shape contours were used when the infant was gazing and smiling at the mother and she wanted to sustain the behavior.

Mothers expect specific feedback in their social interchanges with their infants. Murray and Trevarthen (1986) arranged for mother-infant pairs to interact with each other via a video system. They could see each other's faces and hear each other's voices. In half the instances mothers were shown a videotape of their interacting baby, the tape having been made on a previous trial. Mothers were not told that what they were seeing was a recording. The mother's baby talk varied markedly between live and replay sequences. In the latter instances, mothers were puzzled at the "unresponsiveness" of their infants and worked hard to get the interaction going again.

Some of the most dramatic instances of mother-infant play are seen when mothers use a form of communication called "motherese" to structure play. Stern's report (1974) is among the most graphic. Mothers set out at certain times of the day to engage in intensive emotional play with their infants, even when the latter are as young as 3 months of age. They begin by bringing infants to an optimal level of arousal, calming the infants if they are too aroused or stimulating infants if they are underaroused. Once the mother deems that her baby is at the optimal arousal level, she begins to play "games" with the child. In these games, the mothers use exaggerated facial expressions, exaggerated prosody, and exaggerated gestures. The infants, over time, learn a rich and complex repertoire of responses. The exercise appears to be a veritable learning lab for social communication in early childhood (Kuhl, et al. 1997).

In contrast to normal infants who can use both auditory and visual cues as their mothers engage them in motherese, deaf children must rely on facial and gestural cues. For a mother who speaks American Sign Language (ASL) to her infant, there is a potential conflict between affective facial signals and specific ASL facial grammatic cues. A study by Reilly and Bellugi (1996) has shown that in the first 18 months of life, infants focus primarily on affective facial cues. It is not until they reach their second birthday that they begin to attend to the grammatical cues.

In assessing the infant's social communication skills, it can be particularly helpful to observe mothers and their infants engaging in play together. By 6 months of age the child should be alert and responsive to adults with whom he or she is familiar and should be capable of good eye contact and at least rudimentary interactional play.

Development of Social Communication Skills Between 6 and 24 Months of Age

Social communication phenomena studied in children 6 to 24 months old have included that of mutual gaze (Barratt, et al., 1992). Mothers may gaze for extraordinarily long periods of time at their 6-month-old babies. In the first year of an infant's life, mothers are responsible for initiating mutual eye contact. Between the baby's first and second year, there is a shift in this locus of responsibility. Mother's initiation of gaze decreases over time, while the infant's initiation increases dramatically.

During this time, mothers are also teaching their children about prosody. One study that focused on this phenomena (Fernald & Mazzie, 1991) examined the manner in which women used prosodic emphasis in telling stories to their 14-month-old children, in contrast to how they would use prosody with adults. The investigators employed a picture book in which 6 target items were chosen as the focus of attention. Prosodic emphasis was measured both acoustically and subjectively. In speech to infants, mothers consistently used exaggerated pitch peaks to signal a target, whereas in their speech to adult controls, the mothers' prosodic emphasis was more variable. The authors suggested that the use of exaggerated pitch peaks may facilitate speech processing for infants.

Scaife and Bruner (1975) examined referential communication in infants. As early as 2 to 4 months of age, 30% of infants were found to follow another person's line of gaze. By 11 to 14 months, 100% of infants did so. In the upper age group, the infants engaged in true referential communication, looking where the experimenter was looking, then looking back to the experimenter again.

By 15 months of age, there is evidence that children may understand "theory of mind" (Sorce, Emde, Campos, & Klinnert, 1985). The investigators used an apparatus known as a visual cliff: a Plexiglas plate atop 2 boxes set 2 feet apart. The child was placed on the Plexiglas at the edge of the "cliff," and his or her subsequent behavior was observed. Unlike younger children, 14-month-old children know immediately to look to the face of their mother who is seated on the opposite side of the cliff. If their mother looks happy, he or she will cross, but if mother looks worried or alarmed, he or she will stay put.

By 18 months of age, children have a remarkable repertoire of social communicative behaviors. They are eager, even driven, to play "baby games" such as pat-a-cake and peek-a-boo with adults, and especially with their caregivers. They point with a finger or arm to indicate interest. In another few months they will be on the verge of learning social gestures such as "bye-bye," and by 30 months they will expand their social communication horizons to begin interacting with other children. Eckerman, Davis, and Didow (1989) have found that between 16 and 32 months, imitations of a peer's nonverbal actions are the primary forms of child-to-child behavior. Such actions increase with age. They found that the use of words to direct a peer also increased with age but remained infrequent even at 32 months.

In summary, it appears that except for spoken language, 2-year-old children are already equipped with a rich repertoire of social communication skills. Learning these skills has been one of the most important tasks of their early life.

Assessment of Social Communication Skills

THE FIRST 20 MONTHS OF LIFE

In assessing a child's social communication skills, clinicians should inquire about a number of specific behaviors. When asking about these, the parents should provide concrete examples from the recent past, a practice that should enable clinicians to gain a sense of the depth of feeling that may be attached to the behaviors in question. Questions include:

1. When you come into a room where your child is playing or sitting in her high chair, does she vocalize, gesture to you, or follow you about with her eyes? If she is free to crawl or toddle, does she come to you with appropriate gestures and vocalizations? Does she hold up her arms to indicate she wishes to be picked up?
2. When you return home after an absence (or to the day care program at the end of the day), how does he react to your return? Does he run to the door to greet you and use voice as well as gesture and eye contact to indicate his excitement?
3. If she wishes to get your attention, how does she go about getting it? Does she point to indicate her focus of interest, and does she use referential communication, looking toward the object, vocalizing with jargon or words (if the child is over 18 months of age), and looking back toward you? Does she point things out to you and vocalize about them while you are driving in a car or while on a walk?
4. Is he curious about new toys, objects around the house, objects he sees outside the home?
5. Does she, or has she at some time in the past, responded enthusiastically to the popular baby games, such as tickle-tickle, peek-a-boo, and patty-cake? Has she demanded you play them with her over and over again, perhaps chortling with glee each time?

Clinicians can gain a good understanding of the child's ability to participate in social communication by asking the mother to play with the child, as she would do at home. For children under 12 months of age, this may mean playing with the child using "motherese." With older infants it may mean play involving baby games. Watching their interaction will enable clinicians to understand the role of both mother and child and the degree of feeling and creativity each brings to the play.

FROM THE SECOND TO THE FIFTH YEAR

For children younger than 18 to 24 months, inquiries in regard to social communication focus on the parents, siblings, close relatives, or other everyday caregivers. After approximately 24 months, clinicians can begin to extend their view to another set of interactional partners, namely other children whom the child may encounter at the park, mother-and-me programs, or in preschool and kindergarten. Younger children may not be able to participate in all of the activities to be described, but between 36 and 48 months of age they should be starting to do so. Questions of importance include:

1. Is he interested in other children? How does he try to approach them? If he is 4 or 5 years old, does he observe the activities of stranger children and try to imitate them as he attempts to join into their group play?
2. Has she learned to play the usual children's games, such as ring around the rosie, the wheels on the bus, and London Bridge is falling down? Can she play tag, hide-and-seek, or musical chairs? Does she know the rules of these games?
3. When he plays with other children, does he get caught up in the excitement of the game or event and show his excitement with suitable tone of voice, gesture, and facial expression? What happens when he attends a birthday party? Does he understand the pragmatics of a birthday party: when you open the presents, when you sing the birthday song, and what you do to the burning candles?
4. Does she show emotional empathy? If you, or his brothers or sisters, were very upset and crying, how would she react to this? Would she use appropriate vocal expression of empathy as well as gestures, such as patting the other person or putting her arm around them? Conversely, does she come to you for comfort when she has hurt herself, or if her feelings have been hurt?
5. Does he show you things he is interested in or things he has made in school? Does he ever tell you about things that happened at school or at home while you were away?
6. How does she play with toys? Does she use toys in an imaginative way, creating scenes that mirror what older children or adults might do? Does she use objects in a pretend way, pretending to drink from an empty cup, or talk on a toy telephone? After age 4, can she join into imaginative games with other children whom she sees on a regular basis?

By 5 years of age, children should be eager and active participants in nursery school activities, able to interact with other children. Shy children may do so with only a smaller group of good acquaintances, but all children should be able to do so to some degree.

AFTER 5 YEARS OF AGE

After 5 years of age, children should be adept at using spoken language and be ready to begin to form more specific friendships as well as understand the rules of the kindergarten class and of the playground. Five-year-olds are only beginners in

this regard, but by 8 years of age children should be well along in such areas. Several major questions and issues should be addressed, mostly with the child's parents and teachers.

1. Can the child engage in reciprocal conversation? Does she know to tailor her conversation to encompass a listener's interests? Does she quickly grasp the topic of conversation and join in with appropriate remarks? Does she use appropriate changes in tone of voice (rate, rhythm, and intensity) to emphasize her verbal conversation? Does she use appropriate gestures?
2. Does he have friends, other children with whom he shares ideas, interests, and activities? By the age of 9 or 10, children should have one or more "best friends," with whom they share even closer relationships. There are many reasons why some children may not have friends, for which a lack of ability to engage in social communication may not necessarily be relevant. Children may lack the opportunity to make lasting friendships because of family chaos and frequent moves, they may be too aggressive and undersocialized, or they may be depressed or anxious.

AFTER 12 YEARS OF AGE

Deficits in social communication usually are cast into prominent relief by the time children reach puberty and when they begin high school. Teenagers' conversations and communications are complex and require participants who are able to grasp quickly the nuances of colloquial expressions and slang, and who can speak with a facile and automatic repertoire of body language, meaningful glances, and changing tone of voice. Even children whose ability to react empathically and to send signals through appropriate facial expression, gesture, and prosody may fail to understand the pragmatics of communication (Baron-Cohen, 1995). They may seem odd to others, they seem "off the wall," even bizarre to other children and to adults. Usually they are desperate for friends and fail to realize why they are having difficulty making friends.

In addition to getting a history of an individual's social communication skills, clinicians can, in their evaluation of children and adolescents, gauge the degree to which the person can sustain a conversation and use appropriate gestures, facial expression, and tone of voice. They can identify whether the person understands what interests peers may have and whether the person can see him- or herself as others see him or her.

Conclusion

Understanding the degree to which a person has social communication skills is as important as understanding the person's level of vocabulary and grammar skills, overall cognitive ability, motor ability, and ability to learn in the classroom. In past years, assessment of social communication was not a usual part of history-taking and mental status examination. This is unfortunate, because only when social communication disabilities are identified will the family and school be likely to take appropriate action in helping the person with the disability. Children and adolescents with social communication disabilities often are misunderstood by teachers and even by parents. Adults may recognize that something is amiss, and they often, in my clinical experience, psychologize endlessly about the nature of the problem, often reaching wildly incorrect conclusions. "He's stubborn, and he's doing this on purpose to humiliate me," "He's doing this because his parents have not taught him good manners," "He's spoiled rotten and his parents are to blame," or, simply, "He's weird—get him out of here now." Teenagers are often intolerant of deviation, and many times they will ostracize a peer who has social communication problems or tease and scapegoat him or her. Knowing why such a person behaves bizarrely can make a world of difference in how parents or teachers respond, even if it may not have such a salutary effect on peer responses.

REFERENCES

Barratt, M., Roach, M., Leavitt, L. (1992). Early channels of mother-infant communication: pre-term and term infants. *Journal of Child Psychology and Psychiatry, 33,* 1193–204.

Baron-Cohen, S. (1995). *Mindblindness.* Cambridge, MA: MIT Press.

DeCasper, A. J., & Spence, M. J. (1986). Prenatal maternal speech influences newborn's perceptions of speech sounds. *Infant Behavior and Development, 9,* 133–150.

Eckerman, C. O., Davis, C. C., & Didow, S. M. (1989). Toddlers' emerging ways of achieving social coordinations with a peer. *Child Development, 60,* 440–453.

Farran, D., & Kasari, C. (1990). A longitudinal analysis of the development of synchrony in mutual gaze in mother-child dyads. *Journal of Applied Developmental Psychology, 11,* 419–430.

Fernald, A., & Mazzie, C. (1991). Prosody and focus in speech to infants and adults. *Developmental Psychology, 27,* 209–221.

Field, T. M., Cohen, D., Garcia, R., & Greenberg, R. (1984). Mother-stranger face discrimination by the newborn. *Infant Behavior and Development, 7,* 19–25.

Field, T. M., Woodson, R., Cohen, D., Greenberg, R., Garcia, R., & Collins, K. (1983). Discrimination and imitation of facial expressions by term and preterm neonates. *Infant Behavior and Development, 6,* 485–489.

Goren, C., Sarty, M., & Wu, P. (1975). Visual following and pattern discrimination of face-like stimuli by newborn infants. *Pediatrics, 56,* 544–549.

Haith, M., Bergman, T., & Moore, M. (1977). Eye contact and face scanning in early infancy. *Science, 198,* 853–855.

Izard, C. E., Huebner, R. R., Risser, D., McGinnes, G., & Dougherty, L. (1980). The young infant's ability to produce discrete emotional expressions. *Developmental Psychology, 16,* 132–140.

Karmiloff-Smith, A. (1995). The extraordinary cognitive journey from fetus through infancy. *Journal of Child Psychology and Psychiatry, 36,* 1293–1313.

Kuhl, P., Andruski, J., Chistovich, I., Chistovich, L., Kozhevnikova, E., Ryskina, V., Stolyarova, E., Sunberg, U., & Lacerda, F. (1997). Cross-language analysis of phonetic units in language addressed to infants. *Science: 277,* 684–686.

Locke, J. L. (1993). *The child's path to spoken language.* Cambridge, MA: Harvard University Press.

Meltzoff, A., & Moore, M. (1977). Imitation of facial and manual gestures by human neonates. *Science, 198,* 75–78.

Murray, L., & Trevarthen, C. (1986). The infant's role in mother-infant communication. *Journal of Child Language, 13,* 15–29.

Ockleford, E. M., Vince, M. A., Layton, C., & Reader, M. R. (1988). Responses of neonates to parents' and others' voices. *Early Human Development, 18,* 27–36.

Reilly, J. & Bellugi, U. (1996). Competition on the face: affect and language in ASL motherese. *Journal of Child Language, 23*: 219–39.

Scaife, M., & Bruner, J. (1975). The capacity for joint visual attention in the infant. *Nature, 253,* 265–266.

Sorce, J., Emde, R., Campos, J., & Klinnert, M. (1985). Maternal emotional signaling: Its effect on the visual cliff behavior of 1-year-olds. *Developmental Psychology, 21,* 195–200.

Stern, D. (1974). The goal and structure of mother-infant play. *Journal of the American Academy of Child and Adolescent Psychiatry, 13,* 402–421.

Stern, D. N., Jaffe, J., Beebe, B., & Bennett, S. L. (1975). Vocalizing in unison and in alteration: Two modes of communication within the mother-infant dyad. *Annals of the New York Academy of Sciences, 263,* 89–101.

Stern, D. N., Spieker, S., & MacKain, K. (1982). Intonation contours as signals in maternal speech to prelinguistic infants. *Developmental Psychology, 18,* 727–735.

Tronick, E. Z. (1989). Emotions and emotional communication in infants. *American Psychologist, 44,* 112–119.

48 / Family History

Allan M. Josephson and Frank J. Moncher

A thorough understanding of family history is an essential element of the assessment of the mental disorders of children and adolescents. Family history informs the clinician's formulation of clinical problems and furthers the goal of treatment planning.

Family history, like an individual's history, illuminates the present as it describes the past. Carefully collected, it tells a cogent story that clarifies the context of a child's current disorder and earlier development. At times, family history can offer a compelling explanation regarding the reason for clinical presentation. Understanding family history also prepares for the future in that history tends to repeat itself. Parents tend to re-create the experience of their family of origin or, contrastingly, parent in a manner diametrically opposed to the pattern of their own parents. In each instance, reviewing family history is the key to understanding such patterns. Family history also includes the area of biologic transmission of genetically influenced characteristics, such as temperament. Genetic history has been dealt with in Chapter 34. This chapter focuses on the family history as it refers to the formative influence of significant life events and family experiences on child and adolescent behavior and emotional development.

Family history is relevant to a young person's presenting complaint and can be categorized into predisposing, precipitating, and maintaining events. Predisposing historical events refer to ongoing family interactional experiences that, through repetition and the encoding processes of memory, become internalized in the youngster's mind. When such mental structures do not foster adaptation, they can predispose to difficulty.

Nancy, a 12-year-old only child, has had a close relationship with her mother and now relates to the environment in a dependent manner. She views adults as she has experienced her mother—always available and always supportive. This behavioral expectation of others, based on her life experience, predisposes her to difficulties in assertive functioning and is associated with her academic difficulty midway through the seventh grade.

Precipitating or acute factors, such as parental divorce or a major geographic move, may be relevant in the onset of a youth's disorder or may be a significant developmental stressor. Family factors can maintain problems, and this category is related to, but slightly different from, predisposing factors. Here the clinician gathers history of family interaction that maintains or perpetuates a problem previously generated. It is possible for a family factor, such as parental overprotectiveness, to be a predisposing risk factor and also be a factor that is maintaining a current problem. In Nancy's case, her dependent behavior is maintained by her father's frequent absences from the home, influencing her mother to rely excessively on the girl for emotional support.

The family history should be gathered with an attitude of objectivity with respect to the family's role in the onset and maintenance of psychopathology. Family interactions and parental choices can give rise to individual child psychopathology, respond to child psychopathology, or involve a combination of these 2 directional effects. For example, a young boy's oppositional and disruptive behavior may be the result of intrusive, inconsistent parenting practices or, in contrast, his parents' inconsistencies may be the result of their frustrating experiences in parenting an impulsive, inattentive child. Determinations regarding such directional effects are part of an accurate formulation that prepares for effective family treatments. The clinician who gathers family history should not make a priori judgments with respect to the family's role in the evolution and maintenance of disorders, as such judgments will preclude the gathering of all the relevant family history and are the function of the case formulation.

Sources of Family History

Family information comes from a variety of sources. The most thorough way to gather family history is by interviewing individual family members. This can be done with all members present, termed a conjoint interview, or through the separate interview of parents and children. This process is facilitated by the use of general survey instruments covering aspects of family demographic history and specialized instruments such as a family genogram. The genogram is a drawing made in conjunction with the family that identifies the facts and relationship patterns of 3 or more generations of family members (McGoldrick & Gerson, 1985). The content of the genogram allows a family history to be seen in longitudinal context, beyond the presenting complaint, and can assist in uncovering information such as "the child who did not survive" or the relative with severe emotional disturbance. It helps illuminate past events, address parental concerns, and objectify family experience. A genogram provides an overview of family structure, may identify vulnerable individuals, and can point toward influential family beliefs. Figure 48.1 presents an example of a genogram.

Several aspects of family history can be ascertained from this data source. The children in the family do not have the same father, and they each have significant psychiatric problems. The youngest 2 children are a product of a relationship that has never been formally committed. The indication that the youngest son currently lives with maternal grandparents is an important observation (indicated by dotted line).

The daughter's father, Jack, abandoned the family when Cathy was pregnant, and little is known of his history. It is important to note that Cathy chose to keep his last name and passed that name along not only to their child but also to her sons through a different relationship. The sons' father, Barry, is the youngest of 4 brothers, whose father died during his childhood. He has a history of problems both in school and in social adjustment and continues to abuse substances. The mother, Cathy, is the youngest of 3 sisters whose biological father was incarcerated much of her life for serious crimes and whose mother is described as an intrusive woman. Cathy's stepfather is described as a verbally abusive man to both her and the grandchildren. Cathy herself has a history of difficulty achieving in life and of being exposed to traumatic events.

A time line is a simple yet graphically useful instrument. (See Figure 48.2.) A time line is a chronological mapping of important events—family moves, family illness, and alterations in family structure. The visual portrayal allows critical events to be placed in chronological historical context. The time line often brings understanding of precipitating and predisposing historical factors related to a child's or adolescent's clinical problems. Taken together, the time line and the genogram allow an assessment of the family's current family life cycle stage and past alterations in family structure.

The time line reveals that Heather has had marked difficulties since entering adolescence. Psychiatric hospitalizations, problems with the law, unplanned pregnancy, and divorce are sequential events indicating her pervasive dysfunction. Episodic family crises such as intermittent parental

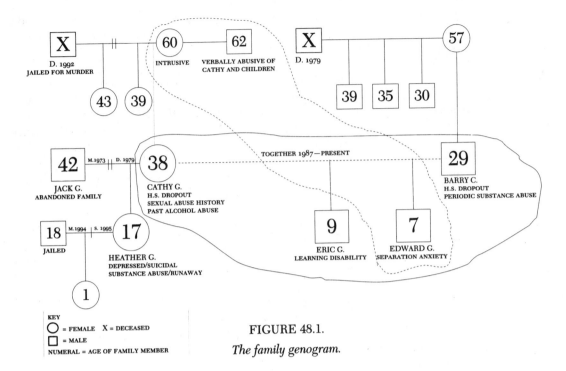

FIGURE 48.1.

The family genogram.

substance abuse and parental separations are revealed by the time line.

A family's historical report should be supplemented by ancillary contacts. These can include history from other professionals who have evaluated family members, either medically or psychiatrically, as well as information from schools, local child welfare agencies, social service agencies, and the courts. These sources often provide valuable information the family either sees as unimportant or is unable or unwilling to communicate clearly to the clinician. In most instances parents must give their consent for clinicians to gather history from these other sources.

Factors Influencing Accuracy of Family History

The informants will vary in the accuracy of their historical data commensurate with their age and their cognitive ability. Children's reports of early family experience may, in fact, not be based on

their memories but may merely be a recitation of other family member's descriptions. The length of time an individual is part of the family is particularly important in blended families, where even adults may repeat history they have heard but not personally experienced (Visher & Visher, 1988).

The most challenging problem in assessing the significance of family history is the discrepant presentations of data offered by children, parents, and those who are outside the family (Cox, 1994). These differences range from factual inconsistencies and the expected different perspectives on what is important (Mosher and Schreiber, 1997) to frank incompatibilities. Determining how these discrepant presentations can be reconciled is an important task of the clinician. History is most useful when each member of the family has his or her view considered. It is not uncommon for some history to be known by some family members and not known by others. This can be related to age-appropriate differences, such as parents knowing facts of which children have no knowledge. At other times, this differential awareness of family history can have dynamic underpinnings, such as insecure parents fearful of revealing to their child that he or she was adopted.

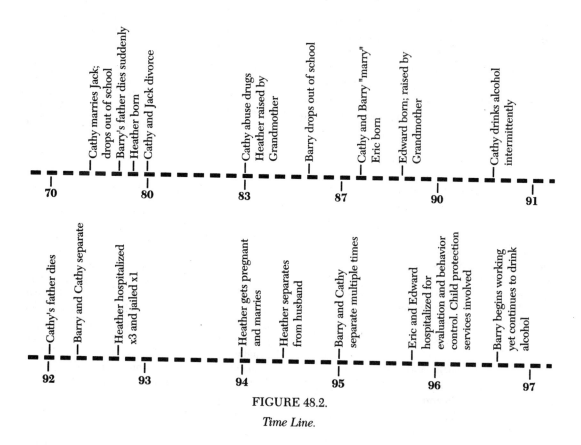

FIGURE 48.2.

Time Line.

The Data of Family History

The facts of family constellation should be the starting point for any review of family history. Demographic data such as the composition of the family, the ages of each of its members, and the duration of the parents' relationship and/or marriage are all basic. In families where remarriages have occurred, custody arrangements such as visitation contacts should be described. Regular contact with extended family members or others, such as a parent's boyfriend or girlfriend, also should be considered. Other individuals not formally part of the family but interacting with it on a regular basis could be included in the historical review with the nature of their relationship described.

The following description of family history data is organized into 3 interrelated categories: parent history, marital history, and family unit history. Building on these basic data, we then describe

family developmental and family interactional history, both current and enduring, which further completes the understanding of family history.

PARENT HISTORY

While the onset of children defines a family, family history begins with an understanding of what influences the formation of family, specifically the developmental histories of each of the parents and the history of the marital relationship. Because this process is developmental and progressive, individual parent histories and marital histories are here described as the early stages of the family history.

What type of person is each parent? In order to answer this with confidence, the clinician needs to have a systematic developmental history of each parent, most typically derived from their descriptions of experiences in their family of origin. Such history informs an understanding of parental strengths and weaknesses, or personality functioning, which mediates parental role functioning. Most parents' adaptive and maladaptive parenting strategies have been influenced significantly by how their parents reared them. Essential parent functions, such as the nurturing of children and setting appropriate limits on their behavior, are carried out successfully to the degree parents' own developmental tasks are successfully mastered.

Wendy L., a 34-year-old single mother, presented to the clinic because of her inability to control her 8-year-old son, Rodney. Her individual history included a fear that she would never be a good parent, something that she heard from her mother, an intrusive woman who withheld affection. During the interview, she tearfully described her marriage to, and subsequent divorce from, a very dominant man. Wendy's pervasive fear was that her son's difficulties were evidence that she was not a good parent. She had particular difficulty when her son challenged her, refused her requests, and said, "You are stupid; you don't know what you're doing." This behavior only confirmed what she had always believed.

A formal psychiatric and medical history of both parents should be obtained, including data regarding previous diagnoses and treatments. The presence of a psychiatric disorder in either parent suggests an increased likelihood the disorder will be transmitted to the children, whether through genetic or experiential mechanisms.

It is also important to gather historical data relevant to a parent's pervasive personality functioning. The developmental demands and needs of children tend to unmask, or give insight into, the nature of parental personality structure. The term *goodness of fit* describes a balance between the demands and expectations of the environment, including a parent's personality, and the child's capacities, motivations, and style of behaving (Chess & Thomas, 1984). Goodness of fit is conducive to a child's emotional stability; poorness of fit is associated with clinical problems.

Johnny, an active, assertive 7-year-old, was not a behavior problem for his teachers; on the other hand, his parents had a great deal of difficulty with his behavior. He was the firstborn to Larry and Alice, both of whom were in their 30s at the time of his birth. Alice was a quiet, submissive woman who had difficulty asserting herself. Larry was a dominant, somewhat impulsive male who made decisions quickly and had no tolerance for lack of order in the home. Johnny's activity significantly stressed each parent, albeit in different ways. His mother could not consistently set limits on Johnny's excessive activity while his father overreacted to Johnny's natural spontaneity.

History in other areas can provide valuable information. A parent's history of frequent job changes, several marriages, and legal difficulties, particularly in combination, is relevant to parenting efforts. A parent's responses to the patient or sibling of the identified patient may be similar to behavior observed in other venues and independently confirm a suspected problem in personality functioning.

Roger, a 44-year-old accountant, is described by his wife as "very self-centered." She complains that "his career is all that matters" and that he is insensitive to the feelings of others. His previous marriage had ended after his wife, apparently lonely, had an affair with someone who had befriended her. His children find him aloof and unavailable. Roger was fired from several jobs because his subordinates found him arrogant and demanding. When the family presented to the clinic for assessment, the clinic personnel experienced him as rude and haughty when he complained about intake procedures.

The parents' relationship history with others gives a clue about social skills and assists clinicians in understanding how these skills would affect parenting. Other relevant history includes history of medical disorder, educational achievement, vocational and socioeconomic status as well as any legal or financial difficulties. These demographic facts allow the clinician to achieve a full perspective of the strengths of the parent as a person, a perspective that should never be omitted. Parental strengths also can be defined experientially. Courage in the face of adversity, revealed by the lengthy illness of a child or the sudden death of a spouse, and fidelity and commitment, revealed by an enduring marriage and fulfilling personal relationships, are examples such strengths.

MARITAL HISTORY

The marital history is a logical continuation of the individual parent history. After an historical profile emerges for each parent, the question arises: What led these 2 individuals to decide to marry or have children together? A chronologic review of the relationship history begins to answer these questions: How did the couple first meet? What attracted them to each other? What were their expectations of marriage or their relationship? Through such probes, the clinician is able to consider how the choice of marital partner facilitated strengths and perpetuated weaknesses in the marriage.

Cathy and Barry have problems parenting their two young boys, age 8 and 6, who have disruptive behavior problems. While Cathy and Barry have never legally married, their relationship is of 8 years' duration and they continue to reunite after numerous separations. At the initiation of their relationship, Barry was attracted to Cathy's independent nature, which allowed him to separate emotionally and physically from his mother. Cathy was physically attracted to Barry and was pleased that her disfiguring scars, related to a childhood burn injury, did not prevent her from being attractive to him. Barry's limited cognitive skills placed him at risk for employment difficulty, and Cathy seemed more capable in handling the couple's financial matters. Over time, this apparent complementarity in roles has become a liability. Barry feels Cathy is controlling and demeaning, not just merely helping with decisions, while Cathy feels Barry is excessively dependent, not just showing his devotion.

Clues to problems in the marriage often can be gleaned from early marital history. Prior relationship history, especially marriages, often sheds light on the timing of a subsequent marriage and choice of partner. Such historical data are important in that early relationship patterns tend to repeat themselves in the current marriage and are relevant to treatment planning.

A thorough marital history includes data on strengths of the marriage, level of marriage satisfaction, and comfort with roles. One indication of the strength of a marriage is how successfully a couple has negotiated the stages of the family life cycle, both anticipated challenges, such as children entering formal schooling, and unanticipated ones, such as childhood illness. History of such events and family responses to them reveal marital resources.

These marital resources are the basis for parenting responses. Parents tend to re-create the experience of their family of origin by, for example, either conferring a stable environment for their children or continuing a cycle of neglect and unavailability. In some cases, families tend to have

significant counterresponses to such histories. Individuals who come from families with an overriding negative factor, such as familial alcoholism, can overrespond and totally avoid all alcohol use. These observations will be developed further as we consider the history of the family as a unit.

HISTORY OF THE FAMILY AS A UNIT

The Family Life Cycle: Clinicians must recognize that the family traverses its own series of developmental stages, termed the family life cycle (Combrinck-Graham, 1985), and gather history relevant to this cycle. These stages bear some correspondence to development of individuals yet emphasize the collective experience of the family as a unit.

In the newlywed period, the couple must strengthen the marital subsystem. In this task, each partner clarifies and reshapes influences from his or her family of origin. Adjusting to a new, intimate relationship can be simultaneously exhilarating and taxing. The couple's tasks range from a reconsideration of their family-of-origin behavioral patterns, such as defining their own view of the enjoyable family vacation, to a reevaluation of attitudes, such as the definition of male and female roles in a marriage and family.

It is important for the marriage to have begun to address some of these issues because, with the advent of children, parenting tasks begin to dominate family life. During the early childhood stage, parents need to be readily available to their children for nurture and support, provide consistent limit-setting on their behavior, and mentor them in the tasks of learning. As children move into adolescence, parents tend to shift from unilateral limit-setting to negotiating rules. The family should facilitate the adolescent's contact with the world outside of the family. As children reach the legal age of majority and move out of the home, parents and adolescents simultaneously experience a sense of achievement and a feeling of loss. These normal yet strongly ambivalent feelings are an opportunity for intensive self-evaluation of all family members.

This description of the family life cycle presents a healthy progression through the different phases of family development. History obtained from families will illuminate the successful task mastery of some transitions and incomplete task mastery at others, which may be associated with the problems that have brought a child to clinical attention.

Jason and Emilie, parents in their late 20s, were having difficulty managing the behavior of their 2 young children. Historical inquiry revealed a problem in early family development, specifically the newlywed stage. The pregnancy of their first child was unplanned and welcomed unequally by each parent. The couple's lack of consensus on parenting issues seemed rooted in the fact that Emilie desired the pregnancy while Jason did not.

The family history gathered becomes measured against the backdrop of the typical transitions of the family life cycle. The events of the family life cycle can be categorized into anticipated and unanticipated events. Anticipated events, experienced by most families, include such things as managing routine childhood illnesses and children graduating from high school. Unanticipated events, experienced only by some families, range from the more commonplace events, such as divorce and single parenthood, to rare situations, such as the life-threatening illness of a family member. If unanticipated events have occurred, a thorough history of their antecedents and effects is indicated. The clinician must consider how changes, such as divorce and remarriage or single parenting, alter the typical family life cycle. The family history should be thorough, delineating the new relationships of blended families and how these situations affect the development of children.

The stage of the family life cycle suggests the direction for historical inquiry. For example, questions asked of young parents regarding their first child would differ from those directed toward more experienced parents who are bringing their third child to the clinic. History obtained from a family with children under the age of 8 years covers parental functions of nurturance, limit-setting, and facilitating early success experience for children. Historical questions of a family with several teenagers focuses on issues of separation, independence, sexual matters, and early vocational concerns. The nature of demands placed on parents differs widely according to the ages of their children, and the family history gathered should reflect this fact.

Economic Factors: History regarding family financial status is important because such factors powerfully determine clinical involvement. Basic life necessities—food, clothes, shelter, and transportation—must be provided for optimal child development. They are also a necessary, if not sufficient, prelude to effective involvement in the clinical setting. In many cultures, the affordability of health care is a major concern of the family. An extremely common factor, which the history must assess, is the financial strain of single parenting, often worsened by the noncustodial parent's lack of financial support. (See also Chapter 50.)

Sociocultural Factors: The family's life cycle should be understood from the perspective of its cultural heritage. The clinician cannot be expert in all cultural matters but must be aware of the likelihood of culturally related differences in child rearing and the family life cycle, and reflect this awareness in the gathering of the family history. The family history should include an awareness that the family's religious position or worldview may be the decisive factor in determining some of the family's behavior regarding parenting and child care. Related to this, the clinician should elaborate history that describes how the family relates to the community at large and by this history attempt to determine whether the family is an integral part of the community or isolated from it. (See also Chapter 52.)

DEVELOPMENTAL REGULATION

The emotional, social, and physical tasks inherent in child and adolescent development evolve in an interactional context. In healthy development, the family regulates a child's successful negotiation of these developmental tasks. Regulation implies an equilibrium between inhibiting and facilitating actions by caregivers that either foster or impede a child's adaptation (Anders, 1989). In health, this regulation by caregivers applies not only to the psychological processes of development, such as a move toward autonomy, but to physical well-being, such as an unanticipated illness.

The family history should include information

that illuminates the process of regulation, which we will now consider in more detail. History in this framework attempts to link the family's responses to a child at various stages of development with the child's subsequent emotional and cognitive development. In addition to recognizing the types of regulatory functions and dysfunctions, the clinician needs to recognize basic aspects of individual child development in gathering this type of history.

An appropriate, or balanced, regulation implies a sensitive attunement to a child's developmental need. For example, a sensitive, shy child will thrive developmentally with active, encouraging parenting responses. An energetic, impulsive child will do better with a firm, empathic limit-setting response. A teenager with self-doubt would benefit from a parent regulatory response that assists independent activity but stops short of performing functions for the adolescent.

Families with clinical problems tend to have various problems in regulation, or dysregulations. *Overregulation* and *underregulation* refer to excessive or deficient responses to developmental need.

Jenny's family overregulated her developmental need for nurturance and support. As an infant she was picked up whenever she appeared distressed and was fed whenever she cried. As a toddler she had difficulty with separation and was somewhat overweight. She could not tolerate stressful new situations, such as entering day care, without her mother readily available to soothe her.

Jeremy, age 4, was referred for evaluation of aggressive behavior. He was about to be removed from his day care setting because of his aggression toward other peers and his attempt to bite a child care worker. History revealed that Jeremy's family underregulated his need for limit-setting. His mother stated, "It's so difficult to see him upset; I want to do anything to keep him happy." The father traveled frequently and was unavailable to assist with parenting.

Inappropriate regulation implies the family's responses are appropriate for one developmental stage but inappropriately applied to the current stage.

Roger, age 7, did not like his teacher or the school cafeteria's food. His parents discussed these problems with him and offered to give him a choice of which school he would attend. This method of negotiation, appropriate for handling an adolescent's concerns, was inappropriate for school-age Roger.

Irregular regulation refers to the family that is consistent in one domain of functioning, such as facilitating an adolescent's hygiene, but inconsistent in another, such as monitoring an adolescent's choice of friendship.

Allen, age 15, was in frequent conflict with his parents about the state of his room. They complained about the clothes he wore, the unkempt state of his room, and his inability to clean up after himself in a shower. This excessive parental monitoring of self-care was contrasted with their lack of comment when he returned home after curfew, walking unsteadily, with alcohol on his breath.

Essential historical data in assessing the family's regulation of child's development can be gathered by asking the following questions: How has the family responded to their child's need for nurturance, support, and encouragement? How has the family provided appropriate structure and set limits on unacceptable behavior? How has the family facilitated the child's entry into the outside world of socialization and peers? How has the family responded to their child's need to achieve in academic, musical, athletic, and other pursuits? Finally, how has the family responded to the adolescent's need to be a separate, autonomous individual? A key component of competent regulation of each of these developmental needs is a high level of parental involvement in the child's life. A family history should elicit the extent to which parents are involved in each of these areas.

Parental differences, or skew, in their approach to regulation often contributes to clinical presentations. We should consider whether history suggests parents coordinate their responses to the developmental needs of their children, or whether one parent regulates development in a consistent pattern and this effort is undermined by the behavior of the other parent.

Will, an active 8-year-old, was impulsive and distractable. He tended to be demanding, and his mother often gave into these demands. While she was aware of this pattern, whenever she solicited her husband's assistance in controlling Will, he tried to set limits but did so in a belligerent manner. This frightened Will, who went to his mother for comfort. A pattern evolved whereby mother overprotected Will and father, in an effort to foster Will's independence, became increasingly hostile toward both of them. Mother's overregulation and father's underregulation of Will's need for an effective attachment to parent figures was associated with clinical problems.

From a psychodynamic perspective, a history of family regulatory processes also informs the manner in which transactions in the family contribute to mental functioning of the child, adolescent, and parent (Reiss, 1989; Scharff & Scharff, 1987). These historical data allow the clinician to see that the parents' internalization of their past family interactional experience is an influential factor in many of their repetitive interactions with their children. They also allow the clinician to see that subsequent development of the child's internal world is shaped by these family interactions. The significance of such history lies in the support it lends to the intergenerational transmission of clinical problems.

Jane, 47 years of age, related a history of being adopted by a family that was somewhat neglectful. From the early days of her first marriage, she wondered about her parenting capabilities. She compensated by trying to "be friends" with her first 2 children, who resisted her hovering behavior. Karen, her third child and first from a second marriage, was of a passive temperament and, "from the moment of conception," Jane enjoyed a special close relationship with Karen. Jane's unsatisfying marriage predisposed her to overinvolvement in her child's life. As Karen became an adolescent, her dependency was unmasked. The challenges of adolescence were not easy; Karen assumed others would be as attentive, dutiful, and worshipful as her mother. Karen's eating disorder occurred in the context of this developmental stressor.

From a behavioral perspective, the clinician should inquire about a history of specific, pathogenic parental behaviors. Research consistently has shown that certain parental behaviors are associated with clinical problems and impede emotional development (Rutter & Rutter, 1993). Clinicians should inquire about: coercive and inconsistent discipline practices; negative parental mood; poor problem-solving skills; inflexibility

and overcontrol; and general stresses such as marital discord and a partner's substance abuse. Because of their high impact, history investigating the possibility of any of these problematic behaviors would have relevance for treatment planning.

FAMILY INTERACTIONAL HISTORY AND THE CHILD'S PRESENTING PROBLEMS

Acute Events: It is not uncommon for the history of a child's presenting problem to be associated with specific interactional sequences. Noncompliance, aggression, and self-harm often arise out of interaction with individuals and family members. This acute interactional history may be essential in understanding the precipitation of clinical problems.

Fifteen-year-old Deandra took an overdose of her mother's pain medication after she returned from school. Without her parents' knowledge, her boyfriend had stayed part of the previous night in her bedroom. When her stepfather discovered them together, he became angry and ordered the boy out of the house. Deandra withdrew to her room and closed the door. She was sullen the next morning, went to school but left early to come home and take 9 pills in a suicide gesture. The history of this acute event was accompanied by history of similar interactions in which Deandra's anger was triggered by parental limit-setting.

Chronic Events: In gathering the history, clinicians must attempt to see if the descriptions of family interactions associated with the acute events are similar to family interactions that have occurred on a chronic basis.

Fourteen-year-old Amanda, an only child, was admitted to a psychiatric unit after she ripped a telephone off the wall and threw it at her mother. Her mother, a single parent for over a decade, had requested that she return home at a specified curfew time. Amanda felt the time was too early and got into an argument with her mother. As mother restated her position, Amanda threw the phone. Six months earlier Amanda had struck her mother and fractured her hand. Further family history revealed that the mother had regularly attempted to appease Amanda. Any distress that Amanda felt as a young girl was accompanied by her mother's attempt to remove that distress and to create peace in the family. Amanda's entitled, self-serving behavior had prevented the formation of long-term peer relationships and was associated with depression.

FAMILY HISTORY RELEVANT TO ENDURING FAMILY CHARACTERISTICS

In contrast to the examples just discussed, enduring family characteristics, or chronic patterns of interaction, may not be related specifically to a presenting problem or acute event. Even so, the family's general characteristics remain the context for clinical problems, and history relevant to these characteristics should be considered. Such history can be categorized in 3 areas: family structure, family communication, and family belief.

Family Structure: Family structure refers to the typical organizational and transactional patterns and hierarchies that exist between individuals within the family (Minuchin & Fishman, 1981). Family health is associated with flexibility and adaptability, where transactional patterns are stable but can shift when circumstances dictate that change is needed. Pathology often is associated with a family's inflexibility or, contrastingly, their lack of structured relationships.

Andrew Jones, a 13-year-old boy and the first adolescent in the family, was creating significant stress for his family by challenging most family rules and expectations. At the time of clinical evaluation related to suspected drug use, he had been denied extracurricular activity for 2 weeks because of his poor grades; that had been extended to 8 weeks due to a shoplifting incident. The family was considering extending his "grounding" for 6 months. This rigid, unyielding pattern of behavioral consequence exemplifies the inflexible, maladaptive family.

The Gooding family, trying to manage 9-year-old Joshua, gave a history of such flexibility that it could be described as chaotic. Joshua's father impulsively and harshly set limits, being critical of Joshua for minor behavior transgressions; mother undermined father and gave in to Joshua's demands. Collectively, Mr. and Mrs. Gooding were very inconsistent in responding to Joshua.

A second aspect of family structure is the dimension of *cohesion,* which is a balance between connectedness and separateness. In cohesive families, members can be emotionally related to each other but not to the extent that they lose their own independence. Clinical problems are associated with familial overinvolvement, or enmeshment, and underinvolvement, or disengagement.

Michelle, age 14, was having difficulty with early adolescent emancipation. She stated, "I can't get upset about anything or express my anger because it will upset my mother. When she's in tears I just feel awful." Her mother had emotionally invested much of her life in Michelle and her activities and, while Michelle had received benefits from the special attention, it had ill-equipped her for independent functioning.

Angel, a 16-year-old, was brought by her single mother to the clinic for anxiety symptoms related to a history of being sexually abused. The history revealed that Angel's mother had been emotionally unavailable due to depression and substance abuse during Angel's childhood and early adolescence. In both of these situations, Angel had stayed with extended family members, yet mother did not know Angel was repetitively sexually abused during that time. The history obtained about Angel's family and her early development suggests a disengaged, distant family structure.

Family structure also includes the concept of *boundaries* that define family roles. Boundaries differentiate between the needs and role expectations of parents, siblings, and sibling groups; protect members from intrusions within the family; and help define interactions with other groups outside the family, such as schools and neighbors. Examples of boundary definition include, but are not limited to: the marital subsystem will have privacy from children; the parents will have authority over the children; a child will not be in alliance with the parent; parents do not scapegoat children; parents will be autonomous and differentiated from family of origin; and power and privilege will be balanced between husband and wife. The family as a unit will have semipermeable boundaries with the community; that is, the community is able to observe and influence the family but not intrude upon it unduly. As clinicians gather family history related to boundary function, they must be aware that the pathology of boundary dysfunction can include rigid, diffuse, or misaligned boundaries.

Jason, a 15-year-old male, was irritated because his parents answered the phone with "This is the Joiner residence, God loves you!" The Joiners, a family of strong religious faith, had rigid expectations of Jason's behavior and a rigid boundary definition between family and the nonreligious community. Jason was embarrassed by his family's overt religious proselytizing and made every effort to ignore the family's rigid demarcation of individuals based on religious interest.

Colin and Janice, 2 professionals, had a child-centered family. The history of their enduring family interaction suggested that 9-year-old Donna and 5-year-old Lisa seemed in control of family's emotional life. Any time they were distressed, their parents acted in a way to decrease this distress. At the time of clinical presentation, mother was sleeping with Donna and father was sleeping with Lisa because neither child reportedly could get to sleep without a parent's presence. This history revealed that the expected privacy of the marriage and boundary between parent and child was nonexistent or, at the very least, diffuse.

Linda and Brian were engaged in a tenuous marital relationship. Their 2 young boys frequently were drawn into their conflict. Jared, age 10, often was the go-between between mother and father. When Jared's behavior was disruptive and his father attempted to set limits, he would appeal to his mother, who would then criticize his father's harshness. The history revealed this coalition, or adultlike relationship between mother and son, to be harmful to Jared's development as well as the parents' marital relationship.

Family Communication: Family communication refers to the verbal and behavioral interactions by which family members impart information to each other about their individual needs and about their perceptions of others in the family. The main components of family communication reviewed in the family history are clarity of communication, types of emotional expression, and problem-solving capacities.

Family communication should be clear and consistent with respect to individual's expectations of each other and family rules. Factual information should be accompanied by affect congruent to the message conveyed. Clear communication fosters trust, which allows differences of opinion to be voiced without fear of loss of relationship. Families with clinical problems often present with confusing or contradicting communication patterns.

Emma, a 36-year-old mother of 2 teenagers, bitterly complained about her husband's "inability to communi-

cate." She stated that he frequently expressed a desire to set limits on his children but then did not follow through. She also described that his children never knew when to take him seriously. He frequently joked when the situation required a clear communication of displeasure. History gathered from Jim, her husband, revealed that he felt there were no problems in the family.

A history of healthy emotional expression reveals families that are able to openly share a range of feelings that are communicated with trust, respect, warmth, and are heard with tolerance. Any communication that blocks the expression of feelings sets a climate of mistrust and criticism.

The evaluation of Karen's family, a young girl who had anorexia nervosa, revealed a history of Mrs. Jones's feeling threatened by any expression of anger by her children. This seemed related to her view that angry children are frustrated children, which indicated she had failed as a parent. This history of repressed and suppressed emotion was gathered primarily from Karen who did not feel comfortable expressing this in the presence of her mother.

A history of the family's ability to solve problems completes the family communication review. The family should agree that problems exist, negotiate differences and conflicts, be reciprocal in their interactions, and use new information. Problems emerge when families tend to have multiple individual perceptions of problems and are unable, or unwilling, to perform the tasks necessary to assist family coping. Families that are ineffective at solving problems often are characterized by having one or more decision makers who communicate poorly and are either authoritarian or indecisive.

The Darby family shared a history of unsuccessful problem solving. Mrs. Darby wanted her husband to make more decisions in the family. Mr. Darby was an ineffective, passive man who would attempt to make independent decisions, only to postpone them until he could consult with his wife. She disliked this pattern, maintaining that she felt "everything falls to me." When father was particularly indecisive, their 3 young children tended to control the family. At clinical presentation, the 2 oldest children, Michael and John, were openly defiant of their father, which threatened him further.

Family Beliefs: The *family belief system,* or shared construction of reality, refers to the fact that families have a type of memory function that goes beyond the beliefs and memories of each of its members. This domain typically includes aspects that have to do with family functioning across the generations. The clinical history should ascertain if such beliefs, often termed family myths or family legacies, exist. If the history indicates they are present, clinicians must review whether these beliefs guide decisions and actions in the family across generations. These family beliefs may be adaptive or maladaptive, depending on their content, the interpretation the family gives them, and the impact they have on family functioning (Goolishian & Anderson, 1992).

The Jacobson family described an extended family history of very few divorces. While Mr. and Mrs. Jacobson were aware of several unhappy marriages that tended to stay together for reasons that were unclear, they were convinced that the family belief that "couples should stick together" was important in the enduring marriages of many family members. The family history revealed a family belief that couples can solve their problems if they remain together, and a strong religious tradition that further empowered this belief.

The Manol family, on the other hand, included a lengthy history of several fathers who were neglectful, abusive, and ultimately abandoned their families. Jane Manol, the mother of 2 children and recently divorced, described her own troubled childhood during which her own father left her mother for another woman. She remembers her mother's subsequent depression and belief that "men are not worth the trouble." Jane's own dating and marital relationship had been similar to that of her mother's, and her 2 sisters also had marriages which "did not work out." Jane was becoming concerned that her 13-year-old son had negative feelings toward women.

Conclusion

The complete family history should allow a clinician to determine the assets and liabilities of the individual parents, their marriage, and the family as a unit. The clinician should have gathered past history that predisposed a child to clinical problems, current family history that may have precipitated problems, and ongoing family factors that have maintained problems. History related to family processes will include interactions specifically related to the presenting complaint and family interactions specifically associated with chronic problems. Pervasive and enduring family characteristics may not be specifically associated with clinical problems yet often provide a context for their development. The clinician also should review history relevant to areas of family structure, family communication, and family belief. Finally, the family is the developmental setting; it can effectively regulate a child's development or impede the child's development through aberrations in the regulating process.

The significance of family history lies in its ability to facilitate a diagnostic statement regarding the family's role in a child's or adolescent's mental disorder. The data of the family history are the basis for evaluating whether the family's behavior is actively contributing to the problem, whether the family's behavior is predominantly a response to a disordered child, or a combination of both elements. The family history is also significant to the extent that it aids the clinical formulation and the treatment plan. Family history is important whether formal treatment interventions include family treatment or whether the family's involvement is limited to supporting other treatment interventions with a child or adolescent.

REFERENCES

Anders, T. (1989). Clinical syndromes, relationship disturbances, and their assessment. In A. Sameroff & R. Emde (Eds.), *Relationship disturbances in early childhood: A developmental approach.* (pp. 125–144) New York: Basic Books.

Chess, S., & Thomas, A. (1984). *Origins and evolution of behavior disorders: From infancy to early adulthood life.* New York: Brunner/Mazel.

Combrinck-Graham, L. (1985). A model of family development. *Family Process, 24,* 139–150.

Cox, A. (1994). Interviews with parents. In M. Rutter, E. Taylor, & L. Hersov (Eds.), *Child and adolescent psychiatry: Modern approaches* (pp. 34–50). London: Blackwell Scientific Publications.

Goolishian, H., & Anderson, H. (1992). Strategy and intervention versus nonintervention-A matter of theory? *Journal of Marital and Family Therapy, 18,* 5–15.

McGoldrick, M., & Gerson, R. (1985). *Genograms in family assessment.* New York: W. W. Norton.

Minuchin, S., & Fishman, H. C. (1981). *Family therapy techniques.* Cambridge, MA: Harvard University Press.

Mosher, L., & Schreiber, J. (1997). Family therapy. In A. Tasman, J. Kay & J. Lieberman (Eds.), *Psychiatry,* (pp. 1439–1451). Philadelphia: W. B. Saunders.

Reiss, D. (1989). The represented and practicing family: Contrasting visions of family continuity. In A. Sameroff & R. Emde (Eds.), *Relationship disturbances in early childhood: A developmental approach* (pp. 191–220). New York: Basic Books.

Rutter, M., & Rutter, M. (1993). *Developing minds: Challenge and continuity across the life span.* New York: Basic Books.

Scharff, D., & Scharff, J. (1987). *Object relations family therapy.* Northvale, NJ: Jason Aronson.

Visher, E., & Visher, J. S. (1988). *Old loyalties, new ties: Therapeutic strategies with stepfamilies.* New York: Brunner/Mazel.

49 / Peer and Adult Relationships

Audrey J. Clarkin

Any clinical evaluation of a child must be founded on a study of the youngster's social relations, their development, and their quality. For the well-adjusted individual, successful interpersonal skills contribute to a positive self-image. From a clinical viewpoint, many relationship difficulties lead to symptomatic behavior. As a child grows up and moves out of the family, it is developmentally appropriate for him or her to attach him- or herself to peers and friends. Especially among adolescents, social life, with its successes and failures, can lead to ecstasy at one moment and suicidal ideation the next.

Interpersonal adjustment correlates with current functioning, both social and academic, and can be used as a predictor for later psychological health/disturbance (Wentzel, 1991). Moreover, the nature of the relationship that the child is able to form with the therapist is probably predictive of the success of the child in forming meaningful relationships in general.

The quantity and quality of peer and adult relationships that the child or adolescent has attained are important elements in a clinical assessment. Long standing social patterns and ongoing adjustment to new social demands reveal the individual's level of social competence (Hubbard & Coie, 1994). Peers can be defined as those individuals who are close in age or level of maturity, who are not related, and with whom the child or adolescent interacts. Adults refer to significant grownups including parents, relatives, neighbors, caregivers, and teachers. Assessment is the study of a sample of typical behavior that reveals the individual's cognitive and/or affective level of functioning.

The earliest relationship is between the child and the mother. Research indicates that when attachment is secure, the child is encouraged to explore the environment and to move toward peers. In contrast, if parents and peers are not available, the consequences of such deprivation take form as aggressive and avoidant behavior (Rubin, Chen, & Hymel, 1993). As the child becomes older, other adults and a wide range of age mates play an important role as models, motivators, and companions. The child's social development is understood from the history of such attachments.

Children relate differently with age mates than they do with adults. Peers connote equality of status and similarity of interests, goals, and activities. Skills learned with and from peers are different from those acquired by way of adult instruction. In childhood, friendships serve many purposes. They enhance self-worth; provide opportunities for intimacy, support, and affection; promote a sense of alliance; and offer companionship (Furman & Robbins, 1985).

Content of Social Assessment

Clinical assessment of social development can be pursued from different vantage points, both theoretical and empirical. The construct *social competence* includes all those interpersonal responses that prove effective; such responses maximize the positive aspects of interactional experience for the child or adolescent within given situations. Social competence can be conceptualized as including both adaptive behavior and social skills, each emphasizing different aspects of social behavior (Gresham, 1985). Adaptive behavior includes independent functioning skills, physical and language development, and academic competencies. Social skills involve specific interactional behaviors, self-related behaviors, and task-related behaviors.

AREAS OF ASSESSMENT

There are at least 5 salient areas of social assessment. These include the relationship between the child and (1) parents, (2) siblings, (3) classmates, (4) peers and friends, and (5) peer group. While each of these areas of social relationships should be pursued, the method of examining each may be different. For example, the relationship between the child and parents can be assessed by (1) asking the child in a clinical interview to describe the interactions from his or her point of view, (2) observing the child interact with the parents in a conjoint interview, and (3) in an interview with the parents that excludes the child, asking them to describe the relationship from their perspective.

QUALITIES OF RELATIONSHIPS

Immaturity: Physically immature children are obviously smaller, shorter, and can weigh less than their age mates. Their size and stature set them apart from age mates and can contribute to feelings of insecurity, unacceptance, and isolation. For these children, expectations need to be modified as they take time to mature. Socially immature youngsters are those who, for a variety of reasons—parental overprotection, shy or insecure temperament, limited opportunities for socialization—are not as competent as their peers in interpersonal situations. When they are with same-age peers, these children behave inappropriately for they have not yet reached the same developmental level. On the other hand, their silliness or choice of games or way of interacting sometimes offers them social success with younger children. Often these children only require time, patience, and exposure. Sometimes more structured intervention, such as modeling and direct coaching, is indicated to help them achieve appropriate social behaviors.

Withdrawal: The essence of the internalizing dimension of childhood difficulties is withdrawal. The loneliest children are those who are unable to approach a peer and who do not know how to enter a group or be part of a group activity. Besides shyness (Engfer, 1993) their behavioral withdrawal can reveal strong emotions of anxiety and depression, which may account for their social difficulties.

Aggression and Disruption: Children who have the most difficulty initiating and maintaining peer relationships and friendships are those who exhibit aggression and disruption (Coie & Koeppl, 1990). These children are seen as bothersome, interfering, and obnoxious. Not only do they fail to make friends, but they provoke nonacceptance and rejection from their peer group.

Strengths: Every clinician knows that the child's assets—cognitive, social/emotional, and behavioral—will be instrumental in diminishing symptoms and problems. For that reason, it is important for the clinician to inquire about the child's interests, achievements, and progress and to utilize that information in setting up goals and a treatment plan (Ramsey, 1991). A youngster who "sees" himself as smarter than his age mates, but who has an interest in chess, might be challenged to join a chess group where players are matched not by age but by ability. The consequence could be positive interactions that improve the child's self-image and confidence and enable him to try other structured activities, such as scouts or a stamp/coin collecting group. An aggressive child who has a good sense of humor can be encouraged to handle frustrating, annoying situations by making a joke of them rather than reacting with hostility and physical force. An insecure, lonely child who is kind and has artistic talent but has trouble with same-age peers might derive pleasure and satisfaction from teaching a younger child. One of the clinician's goals must be to ascertain the child's positive attributes and to build on them.

CONCEPTUAL AND METHODOLOGICAL ISSUES

The first task is to specify the various types of horizontal relationships that children might have —acquaintance, playmate, teammate, classmate, friend or sibling—and to find out how these contacts develop and change over time. Another aspect is to determine how different types of interactions serve different purposes (such as that of companion, comforter, coach, playmate, or confidant). The availability of social contacts is another dimension, as is the quality and consequences of such contacts in settings such as school, family, neighborhood, and the larger community.

Individual friendships and group acceptance can be regarded as 2 distinct kinds of interactions that offer children different opportunities for social learning. Some children can succeed in having 1 or 2 friends and still not achieve social acceptance in a group. Because the capacity to relate to another as a friend is more critical than group inclusion, clinicians need to assess friendship patterns separately from group contacts and to inquire into their numbers, quality, and complexity, not just currently but over time.

Adult relationships imply a vertical attachment, where the older person is in charge and presumably instructing or controlling the actions and reactions of the younger person. The earliest experiences within the family, including maternal bonding and parental modeling, will affect how the child will interact with other grown-ups in respect to establishing identity and dealing with authority.

ASSESSING THE HISTORY OF SOCIAL DEVELOPMENT

Assessment of children's social development requires an appreciation the stages of normal growth, where problematic behavior can exist but will not necessarily persist—for example, temper tantrums at age 2. Children can exhibit symptomatic behavior that is reactive. Thus some children, on entering new situations, experience extreme anxiety that dissipates quickly as they adapt; such behavior may appear, for example, with a move to a different neighborhood. Sometimes symptoms get transformed with age or when parental reactions intensify, and thus lead to a referral. Generally children and adolescents are seen for evaluation when adults, either parents or teachers, have not been able to correct behavior that they view as a cause for concern. Seldom does the young child recognize the intensity of distress that requires attention. With increased cognitive and social/emotional maturity, children are better able to accept and sometimes to ask for help.

Social relationships affect development as the child responds to the opportunity to share, to compare, and to change vis-à-vis others, whether an age mates or adults. At the same time, cognitive and emotional development offers new and rewarding skills with which to relate to others. It is critical to be aware of the interaction of these 2 dimensions: development and social relations.

The clinician needs to evaluate the social experiences that the child and adolescent has had, both within and outside of the family. Data from correlational, longitudinal, and experimental studies indicate that positive family and peer interactions can and do have positive effects on children's personality, social behavior, and academic achievement.

Risk and Protective Factors

Risk factors are those that lead directly to disorder; protective factors are those that ensure adjustment (Rutter, 1987). Usually situations are complicated, and the clinician needs to examine the interaction between vulnerability and protective processes. Some potential risk factors that have been examined include chronic and severe maternal psychiatric dysfunction, abusive and ineffective parenting, family stress, and low socioeconomic level.

As an example, consider a 9-year-old girl who, as a result of her parents' divorce, has just moved to a new school where she has no friends. Her mother has returned to work full time, leaving the girl in charge of her 6-year-old brother each day after school. Given current family financial hardship, an anxious 9-year-old with unsatisfactory past peer connections who is extremely distressed both by the loss of her father and the burden of a difficult younger brother, the scenario is hopeless. On the other hand, a supportive extended family, which includes a resourceful and warm, caring mother with two well-adjusted children, is introduced, then the change in environment and the loss of father can be managed.

Loss, whether it is the temporary illness of a loved one, a physical move to a new location, or the more permanent loss inherent in divorce or a death, can impede social development. Studying the situation from the child's perception, the clinician must deal with the significant people, the degree of attachment, and the circumstances of the rupture. Often the child is unaware of the loss that has triggered the distress, and the clinician assists by linking words and feelings to the events. Sometimes the child sees the parent's reaction to a loss as a withdrawal of affection; this, in turn, may contribute to the child's problem.

Social development can be impeded from 2 directions: parental dysfunction and the child's impairment. Exploration of the parents' social history, a review of parental self-reports, and observation of parent-child interactions can provide the clinician with a picture of the parents' level of social adjustment. Family cohesion and warmth, the temperamental attributes of the child or adolescent, and the availability and use of support systems are protective factors (Garmezy & Rutter, 1988). The immediate task for the clinician is to determine the problem, its extent, intensity, and prognosis. The goal of assessment is to evaluate in order to intervene. The clinician needs to identify critical factors before planning intervention strat-

egies and to establish a baseline for evaluating both the process and the outcome of a given intervention. In an effort to alleviate distress and improve social functioning, the clinician's task is to make an informed judgment about the best possible route to determine the problem areas and to specify the intensity, duration, and extent of the difficulties within a developmental framework.

ASSESSMENT DIFFICULTIES

Assessment difficulties are of 2 types: those encountered in research and those faced by the clinician evaluating an individual child. We will consider both. Accurate evaluation of social behavior presents problems with validity and reliability. Many behaviors are situation specific, so the evaluator needs to determine what role the circumstances of the study play. Does the child have the social knowledge, does the child utilize this knowledge, is the child properly motivated to act, and are the circumstances and environment favorable for the given behavior?

Histories of adult psychiatric patients have established the long-range implications of childhood social disturbances (Crockett, 1988). Adult loneliness and lack of emotional closeness have been connected to long-standing childhood social patterns, including overdependency on the mother and failure to develop close peer attachments (Valliant, 1977). However, retrospective reports of early friendships can be distorted by time and subjective impressions. Contaminating factors include the possibility of subjective bias, insufficient evidence, and overgeneralization. Accuracy of assessment can be improved by using multiple methods, such as data from more than 1 setting and input from more than 1 person.

Future Directions in
Social Assessment

Assessment of social history is a first step in helping children and adolescents change unsatisfactory patterns and derive more satisfaction from peer and adult contacts. Research that would assess and explore patterns of highly socially competent children could offer not only specifics of how positive relationships originate and progress but also strategies to assist less skillful children to manage interactions. We now recognize that peer relationships contribute a unique and critical component to social-emotional development, but we have not yet developed techniques to implement these tenets in a formal way to make the journey more successful for young people.

Recent studies have begun to delineate specific components (Doll, 1996). Peer rejection, aggression, and low peer acceptance have been cited as risk factors for subsequent social maladjustment. Parker and Asher (1987) predict such at-risk behaviors as dropping out of school, criminality, and psychiatric disturbance from early findings of seriously disturbed social relationships. Results show that a lack of peer acceptance can predict school dropout, and aggressiveness can predict criminality, but we cannot generalize to other maladaptive outcomes.

Studies need to focus on how particular types of peer interactions contribute to specific forms of maladaption. Generalized instruments are not as helpful as those that address specific aspects of social acceptance, such as empathy, perspective-taking, or alternative solutions. Multiple measures provide a more accurate assessment.

Failure to consider developmental factors in assessing children's social skills leaves a major gap in our knowledge of children's behavior. Critical issues to be addressed include which specific social skills are most important at what age, how males and females differ in their perceptions and practices, and how social skills are modified by learning, maturation, and environment.

METHODS OF SOCIAL ASSESSMENT

Clinical assessment can take many forms, from fleeting observational impressions to systematic recording, from a psychiatric interview to the use of standardized instruments. In each instance, the goal is to obtain knowledge about the subject. For researchers, assessment is necessary for measuring change in social behavior. For clinicians and teachers, assessment can determine whether the goal of intervention is to develop new behaviors or to influence the environment so that the child can improve behaviors and skills that are present but not practiced.

Researchers and clinicians utilize the following social behavior assessment methods: sociometrics, ranking, rating by others, behavioral roleplays, self-report, naturalistic observations, and self-monitoring. Different modalities have been utilized for assessing social development and social behavior: interviewing, observation, informant reports, self-reports, and situational role-plays. Not only the type of assessment technique but the social situation where the interaction occurs affect the results (Ollendick & Hersen, 1984), indicating the importance of multiple assessment methods.

For selection-diagnostic purposes, sociometrics, ratings by others, self-report, and behavioral role-play are more useful, while for intervention purposes, behavioral interviews, naturalistic observation, and self-monitoring provide the antecedent, sequential, and consequent conditions detailing social behavior. Numerous procedures can assist in understanding a child's social history. Table 49.1 considers them in typical sequence and suggests their specific contribution.

By speaking directly to the child or adolescent, the clinician can utilize information that the subject presents to explore both current and past social history. The interview provides a face-to-face exchange with an opportunity to note nonverbal responses as well as immediate reactions which reveal the individual's level of social skill with excesses and deficits if they exist. The clinician is dependent on the responses of the interviewee who can avoid, camouflage, or mislead him or her. Without input from others who know the individual, relevant information can be omitted or distorted.

Communication with Children and Adolescents: Several guidelines are available to help clinicians talk with children and adolescents at an appropriate social level. A social scale (Bigelow & LaGaipa, 1980) based on essays written by children in grades 1 to 8 describes 9 dimensions that emerge with friendships as children progress through 3 developmental stages:

Stage 1: common activities, evaluation, propinquity
Stage 2: character admiration
Stage 3: acceptance, loyalty and commitment, genuineness, common interest, and intimacy

TABLE 49.1

Assessment Procedures of Social History and Their Relevance in Intervention Evaluation

Procedure	Focus and Yield
1. Mental status exam	Cognitive strengths necessary for social interactions
2. Family interview	Social skills in family context; parents and sibs as models for social behavior
3. Intellectual and educational assessment	Capacity for understanding, for drawing inferences
4. Personality inventories	Interpersonal traits
5. Behaviorally based tests	Social interactions in specific situations and under certain conditions
6. Projective techniques	Fantasies of self and others; defenses
7. Neuropsychological assessment	Level of hyperactivity, impulsivity, and/or distractability

Another developmental guide for expected appropriate interactions that suggests intervention strategies is based on a relatively universal and orderly 5-stage sequence (Selman, 1980).

Stage 1 (characteristic of children ages 3 to 7) involves physical interaction where friends are valued for their material and physical attributes and defined by proximity.
Stage 2 (ages 4 to 7) proceeds to 1-way assistance.
Stage 3 (ages 6 to 12) offers 2-way concern and cooperation that serves self-interests.
Stage 4 (ages 9 to 15) is based on intimate, mutual relationships.
Stage 5 (ages 12 and older) involves autonomous interdependent friendships.

In open-ended interviews, Selman identified 6 critical issues for interviewers to pursue: making friends, closeness, trust, jealousy, conflict, and ending friendships. He utilized social dilemmas to probe not only what the child would do but the reasoning behind the child's choice. Furman and Bierman (1983) studied young children's (age 4 to 7) conceptions of friendships via interviews, a picture recognition task, and a forced-choice rating. Their study substantiated increased affection and prosocial support as children matured. Youniss (1980) offers another assessment model for social development and adjustment. He asked subjects (ages 6 to 13) to tell brief spontaneous stories showing that they liked someone, showing someone that they were that person's friend, and showing kindness.

DIRECT OBSERVATION

Direct observation of behaviors can differentiate adaptive from nonadaptive interactions and can help to describe and identify youngsters who exhibit social awareness, sensitivity, and appropriate responses from those who do not. Observational studies can be utilized with all ages. As early as 6 months, a child initiates social contact by smiling, eye contact, and vocalizing. Many observational studies focus on the overt behavior—conversations in dyadic interactions. Such reports can be completed by professionals, such as a psychiatrist, psychologist, social worker, teacher, or by parents and other adults who have contact with the child. Behavioral observations that use trained observers and specific code categories can be introduced to provide objective data and identify antecedents and consequences, for example, cursing rather than generalized aggression.

Clinical assessment of childhood and adolescent dysfunction has improved significantly due to 3 recent advances. First, diagnostic interviews have been standardized to identify homogeneous psychiatric disorders and for subtyping alternative disorders (Edelbrock & Costello, 1988). Second, dimensional scales of psychopathology are available that permit evaluation of different dysfunctions and specific symptom clusters. These, such as the Child Behavior Checklist (CBCL, Achenbach & Edelbrock, 1983) can be completed by parents, teachers, and children and used to differentiate types of social problems. Third, instruments and observational techniques are widely used for specific disorders that interfere with social interactions, such as depression (Reynolds, 1985), attention deficits (Connors, 1997), and impulsivity (Kendall & Wilcox, 1979).

A more empirical approach is to understand social relationships by focusing on outcomes, contents, and processes. There has been an increasing interest in assessing children's actual social behavior (Michelson, Sugai, Wood, & Kazdin, 1983). Correlational and retrospective studies suggest a positive relationship between children's early social success and their adjustment later in life. Findings suggest that socially incompetent children are at greater risk for academic difficulties, for delinquency, and for manifesting physical and verbal aggression. Causal relationships still need to be explored; it will take more longitudinal research to establish generalizability across age, gender, culture groups and different settings.

Direct observation often is used as a method of evaluating social behavior. Two strategies used to assess interpersonal behavior among children and adolescents include naturalistic observation and analogue observation. In naturalistic observation, the frequency, duration, and quality of specified target behaviors are recorded. Different coding systems have been developed for noting the interaction between the individual and others, such as peers, teachers, and parents. In order to understand social interactions among children and adolescents, 2 conversation coding systems were developed (Parker & Gottman, 1989) to categorize information. MICRO indexes dyadic social processes and examines the following 8 social processes: self-disclosure, gossip, mindreading, exploration of similarity, exploration of differences, affect, conflict, and humor. MACRO codes specific dyadic social processes and evaluates each occurrence for interactional success or failure. The findings that emerged established 3 distinct age groupings for social interactional patterns. Each age cluster—young children (ages 3 to 7), latency-age children (ages 8 to 12), and adolescents (13 to 18)—displayed distinctive organization and content. It was found that fantasy play declined with age, that self-disclosure increased as children moved toward adolescence, and that the presence of an adult did not disrupt conver-

sations in early childhood but did interfere in middle childhood. These findings help the clinician to establish a baseline from which to determine the appropriateness of children's social behavior. Expectancy bias, observer reactivity, and reliability are methodological issues in naturalistic observation.

When observation occurs in contrived situations, the procedure is inherently limited because the situation is not real. Role-play sets up typical social situations appropriate for the child's age and sex and allows the child to act them out. Although role-play is vulnerable to faking or failure if the child is unmotivated, it is useful to evaluate social excesses or deficits. The Social Skills Test for Children (SST-C, Williamson, Moody & Granberry, 1983) is the most extensively researched. It offers 30 social scenes, including giving help, giving praise, and being assertive, and is appropriate for children of elementary school age. The social validity of role-plays must be questioned because normative information is lacking.

INFORMANT REPORTS

Depending on the informant—child, parent, teacher, or observer—reports can differ significantly. In one study (Weissman, Orvaschel, & Padian, 1980), mothers' reports about their children did not correlate with the children's reports about themselves, suggesting the need to obtain information from both self and other. Asking children about their social interactions is a valuable source of children's expectations for friendship. If the goal is to describe actual interaction, however, it is not a substitute for observation. Based on socioeconomic level and culture group, wide variations exist among persons and groups as to what constitutes appropriate social development and behavior. Informant reports can include self-ratings and reports by peers, teachers, parents, and significant others who are acquainted with the subject. Most informant reports are geared to identifying problematic social behavior. One of the most widely used standardized measures is the Walker Problem Behavior Inventory (Walker, 1970), which consists of a total score and 5 subtests: acting out, withdrawal, distractability, disturbed peer relations, and immaturity. The Child Behavior Checklist (Achenbach & Edelbrock,

1983) assesses overall psychopathology and offers forms that can be completed by parent, teacher, and child. Studies show that the checklist differentiates children on the basis of depression, conduct disorder, hyperactivity, and social dysfunction. Another scale widely used with parents and teachers is the Revised Behavior Problem Checklist (Quay & Peterson, 1983).

The advantage of ratings are they are easily administered and can be helpful in identifying socially incompetent children. Nevertheless, reliability is inconsistent, and these informant reports often do not identify specific social deficits or excesses.

Several specific measures of social interpersonal behavior include the Matson Evaluation of Social Skills with Youngsters (MESSY, Matson, Rotatori, & Helsel, 1983), which consists of a 62 item self-report and a 64-item teacher report. The self-report scale provides 5 factors: appropriate social skills, inappropriate assertiveness, impulsiveness/recalcitrance, overconfidence, and jealousy/withdrawal. The teacher scale yields 2 factors: inappropriate assertiveness and appropriate social skills. Scores correlate highly with independent teacher and parent ratings of children's social skills.

Two broad-based measures of social skills have been developed for adolescents. The Adolescent Problems Inventory (Freedman, Rosenthal, Donahoe, Schlundt, & McFall, 1978) for males offers 44 items and the Problem Inventory for Adolescent Girls (PIAG, Gaffney & McFall, 1981) has 52 items. Both scales have been shown to be reliable and valid.

The Tross-C developed by Clark, Gresham, and Elliott (1985) is based on items from other empirically derived scales that predict peer acceptance. Specifically designed to identify school social problems, the Tross-C provides the following subscales: academic performance, social initiation, cooperation, and peer reinforcement.

The Taxonomy of Problematic Social Situations (Dodge, McClaskey, & Feldman, 1985) asks elementary school teachers to identify situations that were actually problematic. The resulting problems were presented to children identified by teachers and peers as either socially well adjusted or socially maladjusted. Factor analysis revealed the following 5 problem cluster areas: peer group entry, response to provocation, response to failure, meeting social expectations, and meeting teacher expectations. The Taxonomy of Problematic Social Situations (TOPS) involves a role-playing interview and a scoring system focused on the child's cognitive perspective. This test is useful in identifying social incompetence by specifying skill deficits in situational contexts.

SOCIOMETRIC MEASURES

In addition to the formal tests listed in Table 49.1, investigators have utilized sociometric techniques, including peer nomination and peer ratings. Sociometrics often is used to identify the competent in contrast to the incompetent child within a structured group setting—such as a classroom or a team. With the peer nomination technique, children are asked to name best friends and/or those peers with whom they would most like to play or work. A child's sociometric score is based on the number of nominations. Both positive and negative nominations can be included. Children complete peer rating scales by specifying how much they like or would want to be with the individual, or by how much they dislike and would not want to associate with a particular peer. Older youngsters often use a 5-point Likert-type scale, while younger children are given a 3-point scale. In both cases, every child in the group is rated by every peer.

Peer nomination commonly is used to assess peer relationships. This form of sociometric evaluation typically asks children to name classmates with whom they would most like to play or work. A child's score is computed as the number of nominations received. Several variations have been used. With younger children, pictures are used. Sometimes negative nominations are sought. A second type of sociometric evaluation is the Peer Rating Procedure. The child responds to the question "How much would you like to play with a given child?" in reference to all classmates. Obviously, this approach is more time-consuming and requires greater discrimination. A third type of sociometric method is the Peer Assessment Procedure, where the child is given the opportunity to rate particular children on similarity to a specific characteristic. Again, this strategy is time-consuming and raises the question of parental consent, especially when negative behaviors such as aggression are being assessed.

In an effort to understand the complexities of social interaction, an Interpersonal Negotiation Strategies (INS) Model based on a triangle of cognitive testing, personality tests, and behavioral ratings has been developed (Yeates, Schultz, & Selman, 1990). Its goal is to specify the links among intellect, affect, and behavior independent of the clinician's interpretive skills.

The clinician needs to differentiate children who appreciate an appropriate social skill but do not utilize it (due to circumstances or to the particular situation) from those who have never acquired the skill.

Assessment Concerns of the Clinician

GUIDELINES FOR ASSESSMENT

What are some of the problems the individual clinician faces in assessing a child? The following questions can serve as guidelines to assist the evaluator:

1. Will the child cooperate and talk with a stranger? Is the child motivated to share what is troubling him or her?

The interviewer must assume a calm, gentle, and supportive manner but also needs to convey a sense of competence and a planned, clear procedure during the assessment. By establishing oneself as helper and problem solver, the evaluator encourages the youngster to describe situations and relationships that are difficult and/or problematic.

2. Is the child's behavior in the clinician's office representative of behavior in other settings, such as at home and in school?

Some intellectually precocious children might spend a great deal of time interacting with adults on an adult level, whereas their more infantile peers might, in their dependency, prefer to spend much time attached to adults. Both types will appear to be very comfortable during the interview. It is critical for the interviewer to probe peer relationships, both in structured (i.e., school, camp) and unstructured settings (neighborhood, play-

ground). The interviewer can then compare the child's self-report with information obtained from other sources of information, such as parents and teachers.

3. Are the child's levels of self-awareness, of cognitive ability, and of language skills limited, thereby restricting communication with the assessor? If so, what information must be obtained from others (parents, teachers, and peers)?

The clinician should be familiar with critical developmental milestones. A preschooler will be egocentric in both language and in the way experiences are described. By the third grade, many youngsters can appreciate not only their own emotional reactions but also the different responses of others. Sometimes the interviewer will need to use specific questions (e.g., who, what, when, where, why?) to help the child focus and deal with troublesome experiences. Another technique is to present what-if situations that would be typical of the age, and then have the child describe how to handle them. Asking children to illustrate by drawing how they felt or what happened also can be useful, especially when the child's receptive and expressive language is not developmentally appropriate.

4. Does the child know the necessary social skills but is not using them?

Some children have social skills but do not use them in specific situations, whereas others are deficient in these skills across all situations. The interviewer can probe this question in 2 ways: first, by asking the child to describe a recent peer interaction that did not work out the way the child wanted; and second, by providing the child with a what-if situation and examining the response.

5. Does the child's current environment make it difficult to behave appropriately? If so, how can that environment be assessed?

The environment includes home, school, and any other relevant locations; it includes as well what is happening in those locations, such as conflict, illness, or divorce. The evaluator needs to elicit the child's perceptions of how the environment is contributing to any current emotional upset and interpersonal difficulty. The interviewer can compare the child's perceptions of these environments with information obtained from parents, teachers, and, when appropriate, peers.

6. Is the child's inappropriate social behavior

TABLE 49.2

Decision-Making Variables to Consider in Treatment Planning

SUBJECT VARIABLES			
Diagnosis	Symptom Severity	Supports	Personality Traits
Neurotic	Mild	Intact family	Persistence
Psychotic	Moderate	Extended family	Motivation
	Severe	Church	Intelligence
		School	Temperament

ASSIGNMENT VARIABLES			
Setting	Format	Technique	Duration/Frequency
School	Individual	Dynamic	Brief
Clinic	Group	Cognitive	Extended
Day hospital	Family	Behavioral	Time-limited
Inpatient			

an indication of more serious psychopathology or not?

In some instances it will be immediately evident to the interviewer that the child's unsatisfactory social interactions are symptoms of more serious pathology that require further exploration, either with psychological assessment or in psychotherapy. In some instances, informants will indicate more critical problems by the intensity and duration of the child's behavior at home or in school.

7. Does the family constellation—parent and sibling interactions, expectations, and demands—contribute to the child's social problems?

The clinician will probe in what way and to what extent the child sees the family contributing to the current difficulties. A family interview with the clinician will provide a view of the actual interactions between family members and the child, and this can be compared to the child's previous self-report.

8. Is the child motivated to change?

First of all, the child must be aware that there is a problem. It is a good prognostic sign if the child thinks and feels that change can occur. The clinician must pinpoint where on the continuum of change the child currently stands and encourage active change from that point. There are some youngsters who, for a variety of reasons—perhaps cognitive level or defensiveness—at the moment are not willing or cannot deal with the present dif-

ficulties. The clinician offers these children assistance but realizes that they are not able to accept it at this time. Other alternatives might include working with the parents or family, delaying direct intervention with the child, or setting up a follow-up appointment with the parents to get an update on the problematic behavior.

The Clinician's Internal Decision-Making Process

The clinician evaluating children and adolescents needs an overall schema for relating assessment material to intervention strategies (Coie, 1985). If appropriate treatment is to be selected, the assessment process must lead to those recommendations. The clinician needs to have a cognitive model that is directed toward a treatment of choice based on multiple variables as represented in Table 49.2.

The clinician's schema for intervention would include prior social history, family functioning, school performance and progress, current stresses, support network, and motivation for change.

The greater the number of single negative factors, the more likely it is that the child will experience difficulties with prosocial behavior. Children with low impulsivity, good social skills, but poor current peer relations are the most likely to respond to brief interventions. Perhaps a situational or developmental stimulus caused the temporary upset, and it could be addressed in brief treatment. Youngsters who are shy and inhibited, who find change difficult to deal with, and who lack both spontaneity and the courage to initiate new relationships require a more focused, goal-oriented intervention. Whether offered within the school setting or in outside time-limited counseling, it would stress social skill training and the building of self-esteem. Those children who are impulsive yet cognitively aware of how to proceed,

and who can appreciate others' points of view, need to be taught how to delay action and problem-solve. In contrast, those children burdened with high levels of aggression, deficits in social skills, and a history of unsatisfactory peer relations are most at risk for continued and future maladjustment and require the most intensive extended intervention. When they are a threat to themselves or others, a day hospital or inpatient placement is indicated. In trying to predict and improve the child's adjustment, it is imperative for the clinician to determine personal traits as well as current and past relationships with peers and adults.

REFERENCES

Achenbach, T. M., & Edelbrock, C. S. (1983). *Manual for the Child Behavior Checklist and Revised Child Behavior Profile.* Burlington: University of Vermont, Department of Psychiatry.

Bigelow, B., & LaGaipa, J. (1980). The development of friendship values and choice. In H. C. Foot, A. J. Chapman, & J. Smith (Eds.), *Friendship and social relations in children* (pp. 15–44). New York: John Wiley & Sons.

Clark, L., Gresham, F. M., & Elliot, S. N. (1985). Development and validation of a social skills assessment measure: The TROSS-C. *Journal of Psychoeducational Assessment, 4,* 347–358.

Coie, J. D. (1985). Fitting social skills intervention to the target group. In B. H. Schneider, K. H. Rubin, & J. E. Ledingham (Eds.), *Children's peer relations: Issues in assessment and intervention* (pp. 141–156). New York: Springer-Verlag.

Coie, J. D., & Koeppl, G. K. (1990). Adapting intervention to the problems of aggressive and disruptive rejected children. In S. R. Asher & J. D. Coie (Eds.), *Peer rejection in childhood* (pp. 309–337). New York: Cambridge University Press.

Connors, K. C. (1997). *Connors' Rating Scales-Revised.* New York: Multi-Health Systems, Inc.

Crockett, M. S. (1988). Self-reports of childhood peer relationships of psychiatric and non-psychiatric subjects. *Issues in Mental Health Nursing, 9,* 45–71.

Dodge, K. A., McClaskey, C. L., & Feldman, E. (1985). A situational approach to the assessment of social competence in children. *Journal of Consulting and Clinical Psychology, 53,* 344–353.

Doll, B. (1996). Children without friends: Implications for practice and policy. *School Psychology Review, 25,* 165–182.

Edelbrock, C. S., & Costello, A. J. (1988). Structured psychiatric interviews for children. In M. Rutter, A. H. Tuma, & I. S. Lann (Eds.), *Assessment and diagnosis in child psychopathology* (pp. 87–112). New York: Guilford Press.

Engfer, A. (1993). Antecedents and consequences of shyness in boys and girls: A 6-year longitudinal study. In K. H. Rubin & J. B. Asendorpf (Eds.), *Social withdrawal, inhibition and shyness in childhood* (pp. 49–79). Hillsdale, New Jersey: Lawrence Erlbaum Associates.

Freedman, B. J., Rosenthal, L., Donahoe, C. P., Jr., Schlundt, D. G., & McFall, R. M. (1978). A social-behavioral analysis of skill deficits in delinquent and non-delinquent adolescent boys. *Journal of Consulting and Clinical Psychology, 46,* 1448–1462.

Furman, W., & Bierman, K. L. (1983). Developmental changes in young children's conceptions of friendship. *Child Development, 54,* 549–556.

Furman, W., & Robbins, P. (1985). What's the point? Issues in the selection of treatment objectives. In B. Schneider, K. Rubin, & J. Ledingham (Eds.), *Children's peer relations: Issues in assessment and intervention* (pp. 41–54). New York: Springer-Verlag.

Gaffney, L. R., & McFall, R. M. (1981). A comparison of social skills in delinquent and non-delinquent adolescent girls using a behavioral role-playing inventory. *Journal of Consulting and Clinical Psychology, 49,* 959–967.

Garmezy, N. (1985). Stress resistant children: The search for protective factors. In J. E. Stevenson (Ed.), *Recent research in developmental psychopathology* (pp. 213–233). Oxford: Pergamon Press.

Garmezy, N., & Rutter, M. (Eds.). (1988). *Stress, coping, and development in children.* Baltimore, MD: John Hopkins University Press.

Gresham, F. M. (1985). Conceptual issues in the assessment of social competence in children. In P. Strain, M. Guralnick, & H. Walker (Eds.), *Children's social behavior: Development, assessment and modification* (pp. 143–173). New York: Academic Press.

Hubbard, J. A., & Coie, J. D. (1994). Emotional correlates of social competence in children's peer relationships. *Merrill-Palmer quarterly, 40,* 1–20.

Kendall, P. C., & Wilcox, L. E. (1979). Self-control in children: Development of a rating scale. *Journal of Consulting and Clinical Psychology, 44,* 852–857.

Matson, J. L., Rotatori, A. F., & Helsel, W. J. (1983). Development of a rating scale to measure social skills in children: The Matson Evaluation of Social Skills in Children (MESSY). *Behavior Research and Therapy, 21,* 335–340.

Michelson, L. D., Sugai, D. P., Wood, R. P., & Kazdin, A. E. (1983). *Social skill assessment and training with children.* New York: Plenum Press.

Ollendick, T. H., & Hersen, M. (1984). *Child behavioral assessment: Principles and procedures.* New York: Pergamon Press.

Parker, J. G., & Asher, S. R. (1987). Peer relations and later personal adjustment: Are low-accepted children at risk? *Psychological Bulletin, 102,* 357–389.

Parker, J. G., & Gottman, J. M. (1989). Social and emotional development in a relational context: Friendship interaction from early childhood to adolescence. In T. J. Berndt & G. W. Ladd (Eds.), *Peer relationships in child development* (pp. 95–132). New York: John Wiley & Sons.

Quay, H. C., & Peterson, D. R. (1983). *Interim manual for the Revised Behavior Problem Check List* Coral Gables, FL: University of Miami.

Ramsey, P. G. (1991). *Making friends in school. Promoting peer relationships in early childhood.* New York: Teachers College Press.

Reynolds, W. M. (1985). Depression in childhood and adolescence: Diagnosis, assessment, intervention strategies and research. In T. R. Kratochwill (Ed.), *Advances in school psychology* (Vol. 4, pp. 133–189). Hillsdale, NJ: Lawrence Erlbaum.

Rubin, K. H., Chen, X. & Hymel, S. (1993). Social-emotional characteristics of withdrawn and aggressive children. *Merrill-Palmer Quarterly, 39,* 518–534.

Rutter, M. (1987). Psychosocial resilience and protective mechanisms. *American Journal of Orthopsychiatry, 57,* 316–331.

Selman, R. L. (1980). *The growth of interpersonal understanding: Developmental and clinical analyses.* New York: Academic Press.

Valliant, G. E. (1977). *Adaptation to life.* New York: Little, Brown & Co.

Walker, H. M. (1970). *Problem Behavior Identification Checklist.* Los Angeles: Western Psychological Services.

Weissman, M. M., Orvaschel, H., & Padian, N. (1980). Children's symptom and social functioning self-report scales. *Journal of Nervous and Mental Disease, 168,* 736–740.

Wentzel, K. R. (1991). Relationship between social competence and academic achievement in early adolescence. *Child Development, 62,* 1066–1078.

Williamson, D. A., Moody, S. C., & Granberry, S. W. (1983). Criterion-related validity of a role-play social skills test for children. *Behavior Therapy, 14,* 466–481.

Yeates, K. O., Schultz, L. H., & Selman, R. L. (1990). Bridging the gaps in child-clinical assessment: Toward the application of social-cognitive developmental theory. *Clinical Psychology Review, 10,* 567–588.

Youniss, J. (1980). *Parents and peers in social development: A Sullivan-Piaget perspective.* Chicago: University of Chicago Press.

50 / Socioeconomic Factors

Eli C. Messinger

Any evaluation of a child includes an assessment of the social factors at play in the child's life. The evaluator goes beyond delineating the child's psychopathology to consider the influences of the extended family, the neighborhood, housing conditions, cultural and religious traditions, the parents' work life, and other social forces. Thus the social history gives a picture of the child's total life situation.

This picture is of use in 2 ways. First, adverse social forces often contribute to the genesis of psychopathology. Dangerous neighborhood conditions, for example, can generate anxiety, which may contribute to a generalized anxiety disorder. The baby who grows up in a house with lead-based paint can ingest that lead and develop brain damage with consequent learning and behavioral problems. Second, intervention planning should take realistic consideration of the human and financial resources available to the family.

Antecedents and Conceptual Frameworks

Child psychiatry in the United States had its origins in the juvenile justice system, and its earliest practitioners therefore were concerned with the child's social environment. In his account of the origins of the child guidance clinic from the juvenile court, William Healy, who established the first such clinic in 1909, noted that information was obtained about home conditions, companionships, school career, and the like (Healy and Bronner, 1948).

The tendency in adult psychiatry has been to focus narrowly on the patient as an isolated individual; the family and social histories are rendered as backdrop to the account of psychopathological symptoms. The field of child psychiatry, however, with its origins in the child guidance clinics, has traditionally highlighted the influence of the parents, the family system, and the community. In recent years the increasing number of children from other cultures who require evaluation and treatment and the ideological influence of the multicultural movement have sensitized child psychiatrists to the cultural dimensions of assessment and treatment (Canino & Spurlock, 1994). Here we outline several conceptual frameworks that join individual development, family functioning, and the social milieu.

THE FAMILY AND SOCIALIZATION

The family is the chief socializing force in human society. Even in societies in which the family typically lives in a separate household, the nuclear family is nevertheless always part of a kinship system, which, in turn, links it with the larger social structure and culture. The family is entrusted with the vital task of socializing the child in accordance with society's norms, values, and mores in order to transmit these to the next generation.

For the clinician, the question that arises from this perspective is: To what extent does the family accomplish this purpose? Are the family's mores in sync with society's values or at odds with them? For instance, does the family work in concert with the school, or is there a clash of values? Conversely, does the school recognize and respect the distinctive values and life-style of the student's family?

THE EXTENDED FAMILY

The extent and quality of the ties to the extended family should be explored in the social history. Do they see themselves as a close or distant family? On what occasions does the extended family gather together? How is the time spent? Are these occasions pleasant and congenial or tense and quarrelsome? Does the child gravitate toward a favorite aunt, uncle, or godparent? Does the child play a particular role or have a special designation, e.g., nickname, in the family constellation? The clinician should ask to see home movies, photos, or family memorabilia.

The child's relationships with grandparents are usually less ambivalent than those with parents. Grandparents can offer grandchildren companionship, toys, stories, outings, and other treats without being taxed by the everyday burdens of parenting, and disciplining; in return, they often receive unalloyed affection. Relationships with cousins, on the other hand, are typically intense with a mix of friendship and companionship, on the one hand, and envy and competition, on the other.

SETTING THE BOUNDARIES BETWEEN THE FAMILY AND THE OUTSIDE WORLD

Families draw the boundaries separating them from the larger world and also utilize the broader culture in differential ways (Handel, 1967). For instance, children of Jehovah Witnesses are not permitted to celebrate the Christmas holidays or birthdays. Do the children feel a heightened sense of the family collectivity or, conversely, resentment for the exclusion from popular activities that their age mates participate in?

Families with a paranoid style isolate themselves away from their social surround, including professionals who wish to help. Consider this case example.

Walter is a paranoid schizophrenic adolescent whose mother tended to mistrust the sincerity and motives of the professionals and school personnel involved in her son's care. She actively discouraged the intensive case manager brought in to assist the family with its concrete service needs, turned off the phone to cut off communication with outsiders, and complained frequently that her son was being mistreated. The psychiatrist worked hard to keep open the channels of communication with the mother, to explain the intentions of the personnel who interacted with her son in realistic terms, and to point out her son's developmental needs for companionship and social activities.

In the normal family, the child observes parents socialize with a variety of friends, relatives, and neighbors. In the paranoid family, by contrast, the community is defined as malevolent and the child learns to distrust "outsiders."

SOCIAL CLASS

Social class differences make their weight felt in many spheres of the child's development. These differentials extend beyond material resources. As the titles *Hidden Injuries of Class* (Sennett & Cobb, 1973) and *Worlds of Pain* (Rubin, 1976) suggest, shame and self-doubt often are associated with lower-class and blue-collar status in this highly competitive society. These feeling-tones may color family life. A sense of personal failure undercuts the parent's confidence as a role model. Rubin wrote:

Such parents, believing that they haven't "made it," feel unsure of themselves, their worth, and their wisdom—a perception that often is shared by their children. No words are necessary to convey these feelings. Children know. They know when their teachers are contemptuous of their family background, of the values they have been taught at home. They know that there are no factory workers, no truck drivers, no construction workers who are the heroes of the television shows they watch. They know that their parents are not among those who "count" in America. And perhaps most devastating of all, they know that their parents know these things as well. (1976, p. 55)

Parents do not raise their children in a vacuum; they have a sense of what opportunities the adult world is likely to hold open—or shut—for their offspring. Lower-class families may restrict their expectations for educational success and vocational advancement for their children. These diminished expectancies themselves can act as barriers or limits. Other poor families, to the contrary, inspire their children to strive that much harder.

Description of Process

The social history attempts to construct a wide-ranging description of the child and family's social situation, and to account for how it came to be that way. The social history is an effort to answer 2 broad questions: What is the objective social situation faced by the child and the family? How do the family members attempt to negotiate and deal with that social situation—how do they mobilize their individual and joint resources to meet the challenges, dangers, and opportunities that confront them?

The social history can be organized around the topics of place, moves, migration, and the extended family.

PLACE

A good place to begin the interview with children is to ask where they live. In addition to opening the door to the socioeconomic realities that impinge upon the children's lives, their responses give information about cognitive functioning, communication skills, and phase-specific developmental concerns. Do children know their address, the streets that bound the area where they reside, the name of their neighborhood?

The conversation leads easily into issues of travel: "How did you travel today from your home to the office?" Do children know directions such as east and west, uptown and downtown? How do the children in their locale get around—bike, bus, car pools? Do the children go on excursions with peers? Are the children able to travel unaccompanied, and are they permitted to do so?

From this kind of everyday conversation, the clinician can gauge how extensive or confined is the life territory that the children occupies and how well they navigate it. The clinician also gains impressions concerning the developmental appropriateness of parental supervision. How do the parents resolve the perennial dilemma of encouraging independence without sacrificing concerns about safety? The social history maps the "ecological space" occupied by a child or adolescent.

Emotional life is rooted to the place where the person resides. People live emotionally where they live in actuality. Thus a child's sense of security rests in large measure on having roots in a stable residence. Consider Patty.

Patty, an early adolescent, was subjected to frequent, unplanned changes in residence throughout her childhood as her mother lurched from one love relationship to another and moved from one job to the next. As a consequence, Patty is chronically anxious, particularly about entering new situations. In a group context, she typically sees herself as an outsider and feels unwanted; she positions herself in a marginal role. This social position is true to her actual life experience of never having had time to settle into the numerous peer groups she could associate with only transiently.

MOVES AND MIGRATION

Families routinely should be asked when they last moved, for what reasons, the attitude of each member of the family about the move, and how the move in fact worked out for each family member.

A family's move from one nation and culture to a distant and foreign place of residence and mode of life obviously carries greater import than a local move. The uprooting and loss involved in transnational migration almost inevitably evokes a mourning process. For parents, this mourning process affects their parenting. This is especially true when their children are in the separation-individuation process and are thus paralleling the parents' experience of separation (Koplow & Messinger, 1990).

In the new land, a new language is spoken. But not everyone in the family learns this new language; often the older members of the family cling to their mother tongue. This can lead to a "linguistic incompatibility" between grandparents and parents, who retain their native tongue, and the younger generation, who readily master the dominant idiom (Canino & Spurlock, 1994).

Other cultural incompatibilities may make themselves evident in the evaluation process. Within Puerto Rican families that move to the mainland, the handling of aggression is a controversial issue and might lead to a youngster being referred for psychiatric attention. Canino and Spurlock write:

Assertiveness, competitiveness, and independence, which are valued by American parents, contradict the core values of Puerto Rican culture, especially that of *respeto*, which literally means respect and which implies a special consideration for older people. The more acculturated Puerto Rican children may be too assertive in the eyes of their parents, who perceive them as *presentao*, that is, as crossing "the boundaries of respect and distance that govern new relationships and behavior in the presence of adults and older people" (1994, p. 17).

THE EXTENDED FAMILY

The larger family often gathers for Sunday dinner; at holidays and religious rituals such as Thanksgiving or Bar Mitzvahs; and to celebrate birthdays, anniversaries, and graduations. The following questions will be revealing about the extended family (as well as cultural and religious practices): On what occasions does the whole family get together? At whose home? Who organizes the gathering? Whom does your child associate with? What are his or her favorite activities?

The grandparents are usually the most important figures in the extended family for the child, both in terms of direct care and symbolically. In a surprisingly large proportion of cases, especially in this era when both parents work, the grandparents also care for the child on a daily basis. When this is the case, the evaluator can invite the grandparents for an interview.

An aunt or uncle can stand in for a mother or father. In the African American as well as other cultures, godparents as well as "aunts" and "uncles" can play an active role in the life of the child; they are considered members of the family despite the absence of blood ties. Similarly, a parent's "significant other," particularly someone who lives in the household, becomes the object of considerable emotional attachment and/or rivalry for the children. If it is agreeable to the parent, the significant other can be invited to join the family evaluation. The continuing emergence of new family forms challenges the evaluator to be flexible and creative.

A useful distinction can be made between the externally integrated and the externally isolated family group (Ackerman & Behrens, 1956). The externally integrated family has contact with extended family, participates in the life of the community, and has friends. The externally isolated family, to the contrary, has little contact with members of the extended families, is isolated from the community, and does not have friends. The pattern of isolation potentiates the development of psychopathology and makes initiating intervention strategies more difficult.

Exploring How the Worlds of Work Life and Family Intersect

The sharply increased participation of married women, including mothers, in the labor force has sparked renewed interest in the intimate links between work and family life. The evaluator needs information about these connections in order to appreciate fully the situation of the child within the family system and to devise practical intervention plans. As noted by Piotrkowski and Gornick: "Family life is structured, in part, by the regular absences of family members engaged in work for which they are paid. Increasingly, family members go their separate ways each day—parents off to their respective workplaces, children to school or to substitute caregivers. Such work-related separations are part of the invisible background of everyday family life" (1986, 268).

Two demographic trends evident in the United States underscore the importance of this area of inquiry. First, since 1960, married women, married women with children, and, most dramatically, married women with young children, have joined the workforce in increasing numbers. Rather than remaining home from work until their children are enrolled in school or grown, they now stay in the labor force out of economic necessity or preference. Second, an increasing divorce rate has resulted in more single-parent families headed by an employed mother.

The employment of parents entails the regular interruption of face-to-face contact between family members. To judge the psychological impact of these interruptions, the evaluator needs to inquire into the specifics of the parents' work situation and the child care arrangements. Do the parents offer the child rituals to mark these departure and return events, for example, waving to the departing parent from a certain window? It is important to inquire about the arrangements for the preschool child during the workday. Are the parents satisfied with the supervision offered by the child care workers, the adequacy of the physical setting, and the quality of the program offered? Are the arrangements stable and reliable, or do the parents have to worry about their dependability? For the school-age child, are there after-school programs or safe playgrounds? Is a relative or family friend available to supervise the child? Alternatively, are conditions safe for the latchkey child?

Two variables mitigate the impact of work-induced separations. First, if parent and child can speak with one another by phone, information can be transmitted, and the child hears the parent's reassuring voice. Phone accessibility at work is related to occupational status: While professionals, executives, and some office workers can phone home during the workday or can be reached by phone in case of emergency, this is generally not true for factory and service workers. Second, control over work hours allows for adaptation to the day-to-day needs of children related to illness, birthday parties and play dates, school events, and the like. Again, professionals and executives as well as those who work "flex-hours" can modify their hours, while blue-collar and service workers cannot. Thus the 2 variables that mitigate the impact of work separations are largely dependent on social class status.

The sheer number of hours worked also makes a difference for the children. The extraordinarily long hours put in by parents who are pursuing demanding professional or fast-track business careers detracts from home life. Sad to say, many doctors' children suffer because of the demands of professional training. Many working-class mothers strive to move up the occupational ladder by combining college or technical study with both paid work and parenting. The result is a tight, demanding schedule that can take its toll on children and parent alike. Consider this case example.

A divorced Haitian immigrant mother managed to keep off welfare by working as a home health aide. In addition, the mother attended evening college class in pursuit of a more remunerative career. However, her 11-year-old son was prone to ferocious rages in which the boy sought revenge against those he felt had offended him. The mother was able to arrange for reliable, capable child care in the evenings. But neither she nor the boy could face up to the emotional distress that her absences imposed. The anger her absences generated in the boy was displaced to the schoolyard, where he engaged in repeated battles.

Other-than-ordinary work schedules typically create even more distressing separations for children than do the usual 9 to 5 jobs. Schedules of weekend work, shift work involving evening or night hours, and rotating shifts (e.g., for nurses and doctors in training) disrupt the rhythms of family life.

Information about work schedules should be gathered because they set the time boundaries for family-based activities. Does the father's work schedule allow for daylight time to play catch in the park with the children? If the parents' work schedules do not mesh, the whole family cannot gather for dinner. Extraordinarily late work hours infringe on precious evening time, including time for supervision of homework.

Upon returning home, the working parent is called upon to change his or her mental set from job preoccupations to domestic concerns plus meet the immediate needs of children who are hungry for attention—and all at once. The returning parent, tired and drained, needs time for decompression from the pressures of work and a respite from demands on him or her. Yet the children, who operate in a different time frame, want immediate attention for their pent-up needs.

In addition the typical working mother faces a mountain of domestic chores upon her return home; she is not given the luxury of putting her feet up. How much time and energy she then can muster to meet the needs of the children will depend on the help she gets for these domestic chores from her partner, the older children, or paid domestic help. As husbands rarely make a

significant contribution, the typical working wife or employed single parent engages in a day-by-day juggling act to meet the competing demands of children, work life, and household chores. It is important for the clinician to ask how she manages this juggling act—and whether this leaves her any time for herself. She will appreciate this interest.

Stress in the workplace spills over into home life. The older children can be asked: Do your parents sometimes come home from work tense? Do their jobs occasionally get in the way of family life? The parents too can be posed such inquiries as: How does your job affect your family life? Are there tensions between your work obligations and your family obligations? Conversely, how do parents protect their families from the long arm of the job?

While some parents choose at-home paid work in order to minimize conflicts between work and family obligations, this arrangement actually can create difficulties in that the parent is at home yet not accessible to the children.

Dual-earner families now constitute almost two-thirds of all 2-parent families. Most U.S. families today require 2 incomes to stay afloat. However: "The dual-earner family is a team short of players: These are really three-job families (if we count housework and childcare), and with children there are simply not enough hands to do the work" (Piotrkowski & Hughes, 1993, p. 200).

Parents who lose a job tend to blame themselves rather than see it as the consequence of an economic downturn. Clinicians therefore can anticipate increased emotional as well as financial strain throughout the family system with economic downturns.

Welfare families are burdened with shame in this society. The stigma attached to welfare seeps through to the children, who have to handle the taunts of other children, the embarrassment of shopping with food stamps or receiving free or reduced school meals, and perhaps most important, their parents' own shame.

But shame about being poor is not confined to welfare recipients; it extends to blue-collar and service workers and their spouses. The breadwinner (usually construed as the male) considers himself a failure because his family is not "making it." This leads him to question his own worth as a person and the wisdom he can transmit to his children. The children pick up this negative self-evaluation. These children receive messages from the larger society that deprecate their family's way of life, and their own parents confirm this devaluation.

In sum, the complete evaluation will encompass the impact of work and income on the family system and its influence on parent-child relationships. The family should be approached as an open social system that is embedded in a larger socioeconomic system.

Erik Erikson (1963), developing theory in the psychoanalytic tradition, emphasized the adolescent's need for social anchoring and social definition. He posited the choice of vocation as not only a practical decision but an essential ingredient of identity formation; without it the youth is vulnerable to the syndrome of identity diffusion.

The sources of data include interviews with the patient, family, and members of the extended family, such as grandparents, and a visit to the neighborhood and home. (See Chapter 63, "The Home Visit.")

Organizing Data

The family's class position is a key structure. Information concerning ethnicity, race, religion, country of origin, and language spoken in the home is routinely presented at the beginning of the psychiatric evaluation as essential demographic data. Information concerning social class should be similarly introduced. This could include neighborhood of residence and type of abode; the size of the family income and its security over time; the occupations of both parents and their educational backgrounds; and the family's self-identified class status.

The social history as it concerns socioeconomic factors can be organized around several issues:

- Does the child live in a nuclear family, with members of the extended family, or within a household that includes nuclear family plus members of the extended family or others?
- Which psychosocial stressors does this child face—whether directly or as a member of the family sys-

tem, whether objectively or symbolically? What dangers impinge on this family system by virtue of its history and its current socioeconomic circumstances? For many inner-city families, for example, random street violence and the ready availability of illicit drugs are preeminent dangers. The families engage in practices to buffer the children from these dangers, such as keeping the children indoors and closely supervised. These practices will, in turn, have consequences for social and recreational experience.
- What material, social, and interpersonal resources and skills are available to this family? A well-connected family may find it easy to help a teenager get a summer job. Contrariwise, the decline of inner-city communities means that fewer professionals and successful businesspeople live in the community to serve as role models, offer advice and to provide jobs for young people.

Contributions to Intervention Strategy Planning

The realistic assessment of the socioeconomic situation of the patient's family permits the evaluator to make more sensible recommendations for intervention. Does the family have the financial resources necessary for long-term or multiple services? Is there help available to take a young child to and from various offices? Does the family need concrete services prior to, or concomitantly with, professional services? An intensive case manager can help an overtaxed, multiproblem family by locating and coordinating services. Some mental health professionals consider attention given to concrete needs as simply a diversion from psychological issues. But most parents appreciate the professional's concern about their everyday problems and are then more receptive to a discussion of psychological issues.

Planning for the social, educational, and psychiatric needs of the child who lives within an isolated or paranoid family is especially challenging. The clinician has to address the family's lack of trust before it will accept the services of outsiders. This calls for considerable tact as well as sensitivity to the family's many fears.

Economic, Ethical, and Social Issues

The economic pressures on many families are growing. Real family income is declining; more working families are slipping below the official poverty line; and, increasingly, both parents work as an economic necessity rather than a personal choice. More than 14 million children in the United States are living in poverty (Sherman, 1994). For youths, the scarcity of jobs—especially jobs that are meaningful, challenging, and offer a chance for advancement—casts a shadow over adolescent development. The situation is particularly bleak for minority youths.

The mental health profession, in the main, has become sensitized to countertransference attitudes based on ethnicity, race, and religion. However, the obstacles toward elimination of comparable attitudes toward "poor patients" remain strong. The term *poor patients* refers both to those who are impoverished and to those who, largely for reasons of social class, fail to adhere to the conventions of the "good patient"—keeping appointments, persevering in a lengthy evaluation, and providing the expected information. Uneasiness about social class makes it difficult for the evaluator judiciously to weigh the influence of social class on patient behavior. Two errors are possible: The evaluator can incorrectly ascribe difficulties in the evaluation process to the family's low social class standing, when, in fact, more specific psychopathological processes are at work. Or, conversely, the real constraints imposed by lack of funds and lack of social confidence can be overlooked.

Unresolved Problems and Issues

A well-developed theoretical model for the complex interweaving, and reciprocal influences, of the biological, psychological, and sociohistorical dimensions of the course of human life is lacking. Erikson made a promising and imaginative start in his concept of stages over the full course of human development, each of which "has a special relation to one of the basic elements of society" (1963, p. 250).

The work of cultural anthropologists has shown that the developmental processes of childhood are molded by the particular culture in which they are embedded. Similarly, the work of social historians has shown that childhood is shaped by the historical period in which it occurs (Aries, 1962). There is no way for clinicians to step outside these cultural and historical constraints. Professional judgments regarding normal development vs. psychopathology undoubtedly reflect such ideological influences. Our only recourse is to try to be conscious of our own biases.

The increasingly multicultural character of the population of the United States places a special responsibility on American mental health practitioners. When making an assessment, they must give heed to the diversity of family life, value orientations, and child-rearing practices.

Future Directions

Several theoretical issues deserve further thought:

How can family systems studies that rigorously explore "the family's psychosocial interior" be joined with an equally rigorous exploration of the cultural, economic, and political forces that impinge upon and shape family life?

Should mental health professionals continue to see the isolated nuclear family as the modal structure of "the family" or, alternatively, consider the household unit or the extended family as "the family," that is, the fundamental social unit for the rearing of children? Is the very term *the family,* which implies only 1 form, too confining, abstract, and prescriptive?

From a methodological standpoint, how can clinicians incorporate more holistic and naturalistic ways of studying children in families? How can professionals move toward a more ecological appreciation of the child in his or her social and physical setting?

314

REFERENCES

Ackerman, N. W., & Behrens, M. L. (1956). A study of family diagnosis. *American Journal of Orthopsychiatry, 26,* 66–78.

Aries, P. (1962). *Centuries of childhood.* New York: Random House.

Canino, I. A., & Spurlock, J. (1994). *Culturally diverse children and adolescents: Assessment, diagnosis, and treatment.* New York: Guilford Press.

Erikson, E. H. (1963). *Childhood and society* (2nd ed.). New York: W. W. Norton.

Handel, G. (1967). Introduction. In G. Handel (Ed.), *The psychosocial interior of the family* (pp. 1–8). Chicago: Aldine Publishing Co.

Healy, W., & Bronner, A. (1948). The child guidance clinic: Birth and growth of an idea. In L. Lowrey and V. Sloane (Ed.), *Orthopsychiatry 1923–1948,* New York: American Orthopsychiatry Association.

Koplow, L., & Messinger, E. (1990). Developmental di- lemmas of young children of immigrant parents. *Child and Adolescent Social Work, 7,* 121–134.

Piotrkowski, C. S., & Gornick, L. K. (1986). Effects of work-related separations on children and families. In J. Bloom-Feshbach & S. Bloom-Feshbach (Eds.), *The psychology of separation* (pp. 267–295). San Francisco: Jossey-Bass.

Piotrkowski, C. S., & Hughes, D. (1993). Dual-earner families in context. In F. Walsh (Ed.), *Normal family processes* (2nd ed.) Chapter 6, 185–207. New York: Guilford Press.

Rubin, L. B. (1976). *Worlds of pain: Life in the working-class family.* New York: Basic Books.

Sennett, R., & Cobb, J. (1973). *The hidden injuries of class.* New York: Vintage Books.

Sherman, A. (1994). *Wasting America's future: The Children's Defense Fund report on the costs of child poverty.* Boston: Beacon Press.

51 / **Legal Factors**

Dewey G. Cornell

Juveniles commit offenses at approximately twice the rate of adults, and accordingly, many adolescents are referred for evaluation because of participation in delinquent or antisocial activities. In 1995 there were more than two million juvenile (under age 18) arrests, comprising approximately 18.3% of all arrests in the United States (Federal Bureau of Investigation, 1996). The peak age for property crime is 16 and the peak age for violent crime is 18 (Federal Bureau of Investigation, 1996; Siegal & Senna, 1988). Despite an overall drop in violent crime in recent years, juvenile violence is substantially higher than it was a decade ago and continues to outpace violent crime by adults (Federal Bureau of Investigation, 1996; Snyder & Sickmund, 1996). For example, from 1986 to 1995, although adult homicide arrests declined .3% juvenile arrests for murder increased 89.9% (Federal Bureau of Investigation, 1996).

Approximately 27% of all males will come in contact with law enforcement by their eighteenth birthday (Snyder & Sickmund, 1995). It is now well accepted that although most adolescents who come to the attention of the juvenile justice system do so only once, a small group (approximately 5 to 10%) of chronic offenders commit numerous offenses and account for over half of all serious juvenile crimes (Snyder & Sickmund, 1995). The earlier a youth commits a serious violent crime, the more likely he or she will persist in criminal behavior into adulthood. From this perspective, it would be naive for a well-meaning clinician to avoid detailed inquiry into the delicate subject of illegal or antisocial behavior. Moreover, many juveniles are referred by judicial or social service authorities with specific concerns about the juvenile's previous antisocial behavior. In these cases, a comprehensive social history that includes a detailed account of delinquent and antisocial behavior is essential.

Furthermore, arrest statistics understate the extent of juvenile antisocial behavior. Many

315

youths commit crimes that do not lead to their arrest. Still other youths engage in noncriminal, but nonetheless clinically noteworthy, rule-breaking or disruptive behavior, such as fighting and lying. Self-report studies reveal that most high school-age males acknowledge one or more instances of each of the following: fighting, shoplifting, vandalizing property, being truant, and using alcohol and illegal drugs (Hindelang, Hirschi, & Weis, 1981; Siegel & Senna, 1988; Snyder & Sickmund, 1995).

This chapter addresses issues related to general clinical evaluations but raises some specific concerns relevant to forensic evaluations. Inquiry into delinquent or antisocial behavior leads the clinician from the familiar territory of mental health concepts and psychological symptomatology into the less familiar, more subjective and value-laden arena of legal concepts and judicial decision making. Youths increasingly are referred by the legal system to address issues such as transfer to adult court, amenability to treatment, competency to confess or stand trial, criminal responsibility, and sentencing recommendations. Clinicians are strongly advised to be familiar with the legal principles and standards that underlie forensic referrals for such matters (Benedek & Cornell, 1989; Melton, Petrila, Poythress, & Slobogin, 1997). Furthermore, clinicians should be aware of the roles that their own social and political values, implicit theories of crime, and attitudes toward authority in general and the legal system in particular can play in evaluating social history data and formulating conclusions.

A history of aggressive crimes—sex offenses, assaults or murder, brutal treatment of young children or animals—poses special problems for the interviewer attempting to maintain rapport and empathize with a youth. Skilled psychotherapists who readily and comfortably investigate a patient's sexual or aggressive fantasies may experience strong emotional reactions to youths who have acted out such fantasies and who, moreover, may relate them in gruesome detail. Interviewers must guard against colluding with a resistive youth through defensive avoidance of aggressive material; yet in other cases they must resist the temptation to assume a voyeuristic attitude in response to a boastful, and possibly mendacious, young offender.

Description of Process

A social history is obtained in the course of a clinical interview with the juvenile, but the clinician should give strong consideration to obtaining information from collateral sources, such as court records and family interviews. Often it is useful to compare independent accounts provided by the juvenile with those of other individuals, such as peers, witnesses, or victims. Occasionally it is helpful to bring a parent into the interview with the juvenile in order to confirm and extend the young person's recollections. Naturally, the clinician must weigh the impact of such procedures on rapport with the youth. It is important for relationship-building that the clinician convey a sense of trust and acceptance to the juvenile; at the same time, inexperienced clinicians should be aware that young offenders who successfully deceive a clinician will not develop reciprocal trust and acceptance.

In forensic evaluations, it is imperative to review the police report of the instant offense; often it is desirable to contact any witnesses to the juvenile's alleged criminal behavior. A complete account of the offense is essential to understanding the circumstances and motivation associated with the crime.

CASE EXAMPLE

Ronald was a 16-year-old charged with attempted rape of a 21-year-old woman, Ms. Johnson. According to the police report, Ronald broke into Ms. Johnson's apartment sometime in the afternoon and waited until she came home that night. Wearing a mask, he threatened her with a knife. When the victim resisted, there was a brief scuffle and then the boy fled the house. During the scuffle the boy's mask came off, so that Ms. Johnson recognized him as the younger brother of a former boyfriend. During the court-ordered clinical evaluation, Ronald initially denied involvement in the rape and insisted that the woman identified him by mistake. Because Ronald had no record of prior offenses, he was likely to receive a modest sentence with no provision for mental health treatment.

Ms. Johnson had given her account several times to the police, but she was willing to be interviewed again in order to assist in Ronald's evaluation. Ms. Johnson reported details that either she had neglected to tell the police or that had been omitted from the report. She knew from her former boyfriend that Ronald had a "crush" on her, and she often had observed him walking by her apartment.

When asked about the assault, Ms. Johnson recalled that Ronald had been wearing one of her nightgowns when he attacked her. In the course of the struggle his mask came off, and to her surprise, he stopped his assault when she called out his name. He cried for several minutes, calmed down, and then left the apartment at her suggestion. Finally, Ms. Johnson reported that her phone bill indicated that while in her apartment prior to the assault, Ronald must have made a series of 1–900 telephone calls to sex hot lines.

When presented with the information obtained from Ms. Johnson, Ronald made a complete confession of his involvement in the attempted rape. He revealed a history of coercive sexual fantasies and a strong attraction to women's clothing. Several months prior to the offense he had attempted to molest a young neighbor girl. Based on this evaluation, the clinician was able to make a strong case to the court that Ronald receive specialized treatment for a sexual disorder as part of his sentence.

The list of possible antisocial behaviors to cover in a social history is extensive and must be adjusted to fit the needs of individual cases. As part of a comprehensive social history, the inventory of delinquent or antisocial behavior by a juvenile offender should include status offenses, substance abuse, property crimes, violence, and sexual behavior.

STATUS OFFENSES

Status offenses are relatively minor offenses that are illegal only because of the juvenile's age. Status offenses vary from state to state; typically they include: school truancy, running away from home, disobeying parents, sexual misconduct, and the use of alcohol or tobacco. Many studies demonstrate that most juveniles commit these offenses at least once; these behaviors signal more serious problems when there is a consistent pattern of offending that is likely to have a deleterious effect on the juvenile's personal safety or healthy development (Siegal & Senna, 1988; Snyder & Sickmund, 1995).

SUBSTANCE ABUSE

Adolescent substance use is commonplace, but no less serious a cause for concern. Substance use is associated with increased risk for a wide range of negative outcomes, including automobile-related injuries and other forms of accidental injury, depression and suicide, interpersonal violence, and other delinquent acts (Anglin, 1993; Hawkins, Catalano, & Miller, 1992). Clinicians should avoid dismissing substance use as normative because even "normal" levels of use can be excessive and have potentially adverse consequences. According to nationally representative results of the Youth Risk Behavior Survey administered to high school students in 1993 (Kann, et al., 1995), nearly half of all students in grades 9 to 12 had consumed alcohol in the 30 days preceding the survey, and 30% reported binge drinking (defined as five or more drinks on one occasion). Nearly one-third of students had used marijuana, 5% had used cocaine, and 1.4% had injected illegal drugs during their lifetime.

The clinician should be familiar with the currently popular drugs in the community and the local terminology used to designate them and describe their effects. Many adolescents will deny any use of drugs or, if pressed, glibly concede to "trying it one time" in the hope that a limited admission will satisfy the interviewer. If the clinician doubts the adolescent's sincerity, he or she can express some skepticism in a friendly but persistent manner. The clinician should not be surprised if a third or fourth question, posed immediately or asked later in the interview, elicits a contradictory acknowledgment of routine drug use.

In addition, the clinician should be sensitive to the fact that many juveniles play a role in the drug distribution system and may be induced by older dealers to assist in sales transactions by holding money or drugs, or by serving as a scout for police. One 14-year-old matter-of-factly remarked that he quit his summer job at McDonald's when he concluded that he could make more than his entire summer's earnings in one good night selling crack; for the same reason, he saw little reason to return to school the next fall.

Although underage drinking is a pervasive status offense that infrequently leads to court intervention, the clinical significance of alcohol abuse should not be overlooked.

CASE EXAMPLE

Fourteen-year-old Jason was referred for outpatient evaluation because his mother and stepfather found him to be increasingly rebellious at home and were distressed to learn that he was failing the ninth grade. During the family interview, Jason was very quiet and passive. He sank back into his chair and seemed to ignore what his concerned parents had to say. Psychological testing revealed average to above-average intellectual abilities but considerable evidence of depression, social anxiety, and poor self-esteem. When asked open-ended questions about his feelings and concerns, Jason seemed unusually nervous and was reluctant to elaborate his thoughts.

Later in the evaluation, Jason became more relaxed and cautiously agreed to talk if asked "specific questions" rather than face more questions about his feelings. The clinician responded by altering his more open-ended, indirect approach to a more direct and structured format focusing on social history. He proceeded through a series of concrete questions, such as "Have you ever cut classes at school?" and "Do you like to drink beer or other kinds of alcohol?" Step-by-step, in response to these questions, Jason acknowledged that he had been skipping school once or twice a week for several months. Jason almost always went home, where he liked to drink a beer or two before his parents came home from work. He did not smoke marijuana because he knew his parents would smell it in the house. He was afraid of trying other drugs.

Once the topic of alcohol was broached, the clinician was able to inquire further about the circumstances of Jason's drinking. Jason often drank alone in the evenings while listening to music in his bedroom. He started drinking sporadically one year ago. He estimated that he had been drinking up to 6 beers a day, 3 to 4 days per week, for the past 2 months. He stole money from his parents and paid an older acquaintance to buy his beer. He did not think he had a drinking problem because he "knew" that alcoholics drank every day. He liked to drink alone in his room because he could "relax and unwind and not think about things." After revealing this information, Jason was able to discuss the feelings of anxiety he experienced around his peers, which kept him from making friends. He also described the feelings of anger and distress he experienced concerning his parents' constant marital disputes.

As reflected in this example, the clinician should go beyond simple facts about the nature and extent of alcohol or drug use to include careful assessment of the attitudes, circumstances, and motives associated with substance use. A social history is not merely a compilation of facts; it is often a means of identifying unanticipated problems, moving the evaluation into heretofore unexplored territory, and discovering important clinical issues.

PROPERTY CRIMES

Juveniles account for more than 1 in 3 arrests for property crimes, including such offenses as larceny, burglary, and auto theft (Federal Bureau of Investigation, 1996). The clinician also should inquire about forms of stealing that rarely come to the attention of authorities, such as theft from parents, siblings, neighbors, and peers. Minor incidents of shoplifting may escalate into a regular pattern, particularly in the context of a supportive peer group that rewards the youth with praise and camaraderie after a successful expedition. Burglary may be encouraged by adults who request specific items such as televisions, videocassette recorders, computers, and guns—either for personal use or for sale.

VIOLENCE

Violent felonies are more common among young adults in their late teens and early 20s than among juveniles. Nevertheless, violent crimes by juveniles, especially homicide, have escalated dramatically since the mid-1980s (Cornell, 1993). Juvenile homicide has nearly tripled, and increasingly involves adolescent males using handguns to kill acquaintances (Cornell, 1993). Patterns differ for boys and girls. Homicides by girls have increased to a lesser degree, and girls are more likely to use a knife than a firearm, and to kill victims under the age of 13 (Loper & Cornell, 1996).

Adolescence is the critical period for the emergence of violent behavior (Eron, Gentry, & Schlegel, 1995). Even milder forms of aggressive behavior constitute a serious clinical as well as social problem. Many longitudinal studies of school-age and even preschool-age children followed into their late teens convincingly demonstrate that childhood aggressiveness is a surprisingly stable psychological trait, perhaps second only to intelligence in consistency over time (Olweus, 1979).

Unfortunately, there are no standard, generally accepted guidelines or parameters for obtaining an adequate history of aggressive behavior. However, clinicians should attempt to survey the frequency and severity of the adolescent's physical aggression from early childhood to the present. Sometimes topics such as fighting or bullying are best introduced by starting with questions about the adolescent's own experiences being attacked or bullied by others. Once the topic of fighting in self-defense has been introduced, the skillful interviewer can broaden the focus to include other acts of aggression. Particular attention should be paid to the use of weapons, the infliction of any physical injuries, and fighting initiated as part of a group activity. In addition to fighting, the clinician should cover cruelty toward animals, fire setting, vandalism, bullying, and verbal abusiveness. An important clinical and theoretical distinction can be made between reactive or hostile aggression in response to frustration and goal-directed, instrumental aggression that in extreme forms can be associated with predatory or psychopathic behavior (Berkowitz, 1993).

The clinician should choose several incidents for detailed inquiry and analysis. It is important to identify the psychological vulnerabilities that may predispose the adolescent to aggression, such as poor problem-solving or verbal communication skills, impulsivity or hyperactivity, primitive object relations, or social skills that lead to provocative or irritating behavior (Keith, 1984; Lochman & Dodge, 1994). Aggressive behavior is learned and encouraged through role modeling and exposure to media violence (Berkowitz, 1993; Eron, Gentry, & Schlegel, 1994), so the youth's exposure to such sources should be surveyed. In addition, clinicians should carefully assess the youth's own history of victimization or abuse; although most abuse victims do not become offenders, many if not most offenders have been victims of physical, sexual, or emotional abuse (Widom, 1989).

Many adolescents will offer the excuse that they fight only when provoked or threatened. However, these adolescents may be overly sensitive to perceived threat or insult (Keith, 1984; Lochman, & Dodge, 1994). Also, adolescents who have learned to enjoy their aggressive behavior may fail to volunteer ways that they precipitate fights or instigate provocation with threatening behavior of their own. In some cases, clinicians may be able to identify adolescents with sadistic tendencies, as revealed in their choice of young, relatively helpless victims and their apparent excitement or pleasure in the infliction of pain.

SEXUAL BEHAVIOR

Perhaps no interview topic is more challenging to broach than adolescent sexual behavior. Nevertheless, clinicians should be prepared to inquire if a youth is sexually active, and if so, to survey the nature and extent of sexual behaviors. Delinquent sexual behavior spans the full range from status offenses to criminal violence and accordingly the purpose of inquiry may vary from identifying a need for health education to early detection of a young sex offender. A survey of juvenile correctional facilities (Morris, et al., 1995) found that 62% reported onset of sexual intercourse by age 12 and 89% by age 14. Those with multiple sexual partners had increased incidence of sexually transmitted disease and pregnancy. Many adult sex offenders committed their first offense in adolescence, and recognition of the need to identify and treat adolescent sex offenders has grown substantially in recent years (Becker & Hunter, 1997). Techniques for careful evaluation and assessment of youthful sex offenders (Becker & Hunter, 1997) include review of possible victimization experiences, sexual fantasies, and various forms of paraphilic behaviors.

Developmental Considerations

Asking a juvenile to recount his or her history of various illegal or antisocial behaviors usually places strain on the interview relationship. The interviewer must lay the groundwork for conducting this section of the social history by carefully explaining the purpose of the evaluation at the outset and working to build and maintain rapport throughout the interview. Interviewers should clarify their role in any ongoing legal proceedings and make clear any limitations on confidentiality (Melton, Petrila, Poythress, & Slobogin, 1997).

Despite the clinician's best efforts, most children and many adolescents will lack a well-differentiated conception of the clinician's role and may tend to perceive him or her as a surrogate police officer or accusatory parent who is going to judge and condemn rather than try to understand their past behavior. Interviewers might try explicitly acknowledging and disavowing this perception; in addition, they can express empathy for the juvenile's frustration, stress, or personal point of view at the time of various incidents or offenses. The clinician should be sensitive to feelings of guilt, shame, disappointment, or rage that inhibit complete accounts of events.

It is best to inquire about past offenses or other antisocial behavior in a straightforward and matter-of-fact manner. Hesitation, prefacing apologies, euphemistic phrases, and indirect inquiries can have the unintended effect of signaling interviewer anxiety or a judgmental attitude. The interviewer should begin with specific questions that focus on concrete behavior rather than attempt to elicit the adolescent's feelings or motivations. In addition to adolescents' reluctance to acknowledge painful feelings, many youths with a history of antisocial behavior have verbal deficits and considerable difficulty articulating feelings and motives. Discussion of feelings and motives can develop later in the interview after the "facts" have been established and the youth is reassured by the clinician's empathic and nonjudgmental reactions.

Finally, it is important to consider the developmental impact of a family history of antisocial behavior. The juvenile's father or mother, older sibling, cousin, or other important person may have a criminal record, and this may influence the juvenile's attitudes and behavior. For an adolescent seeking sources of masculine identification, an uncle who is feared and respected in the neighborhood because he "did time" for a major felony may be a source of admiration rather than a bad example.

CASE EXAMPLE

Eighteen-year-old Jackson was charged with murder-for-hire after he beat a man and set fire to his house. Jackson had recently married, lost his job, and was desperate for money. He had an official record of school truancy, runaways, and assault, but in his interview he also reported an extensive history of theft and burglary. His attitudes toward illegal behavior were profoundly influenced at age 8, when his father started taking him along on regular expeditions to break into cars and garages in order to steal items they could sell to supplement the family income.

Goals and Objectives

The most obvious objective is to obtain a complete and accurate account of the juvenile's previous antisocial behavior, but, considered in isolation, this information is of limited value. It is important to investigate the motivations and circumstances surrounding the juvenile's behavior, and simultaneously to assess the individual strengths and vulnerabilities revealed by the youth's account; this information both provides a contextual basis for assessing the risk for future antisocial behavior and points toward specific intervention needs. Indications of individual strengths include existence of empathic or caring relationships, remorse for the victims of crime, some degree of psychological insight into personal motivation, an ability to acknowledge personal weaknesses and the need for change, and work and social skills that indicate a potential to develop more adaptive ways of functioning.

Instruments and Associated Technology

Numerous scales and surveys have been devised to elicit information about an adolescent's history of antisocial behavior (Brodsky & Smitherman, 1983; Sattler, 1997), but the clinician should be cautious in expecting any of these instruments to be more than an adjunctive or supplementary source of information, one that must be followed up in the clinical evaluation. Self-report scales have proven satisfactory for research purposes when administered to groups of anonymous research subjects (Cornell & Loper, in press; Hindelang, et al., 1981; Siegel & Senna, 1988). However, these instruments may not have adequate reliability and validity for use with individual clinical subjects, particularly serious offenders facing charges. Instruments that have been validated on clinical samples would be a valuable contribution to this area.

Careful, thorough clinical interviewing remains the most important means of gathering social history information. Sattler (1997) has produced a very comprehensive compilation of interview topics, questions, and procedures to use in interviewing children and their families, although again validational studies are needed. One promising interview-based instrument is the Psychopathy Checklist (Hare, 1991), which was derived from Cleckley's (1976) classic conception of the criminal psychopath. Based on social history data obtained from a semi-structured interview and review of available patient records, the Psychopathy Checklist is designed to identify self-centered, impulsive individuals who lead an irresponsible lifestyle that often involves deceiving, manipulating, or harming others. There are extensive validational studies with adult offenders and a smaller number with adolescents (Salekin, Rogers, & Sewell, 1996; Stafford, 1997).

many of the same reasons they might join more prosocial groups such as the Boy Scouts or Girl Scouts: gangs offer to members a sense of identity, belonging, and mutual support; perceived status and respect from peers; and opportunities for recreation and excitement which they otherwise lack (Spergel, 1995; Taylor, 1990).

No aspect of the youth's social history occurs outside a social and cultural context that is heavily influenced by family heritage and ethnic identity (Eron, Gentry, & Schlegel, 1995). In an increasingly multicultural society, clinicians must strive to improve their understanding of youths from diverse backgrounds and cultures or risk making serious errors in assessment and treatment planning (Dana, 1996).

Economic, Ethical, and Social Issues

Sociologists have long contended that juvenile delinquency is largely a consequence of nonindividual factors, such as socioeconomic deprivation or cultural differences in values and attitudes (Quay, 1987). Even if one rejects this position as overlooking important psychological and biological factors (Wilson & Herrnstein, 1985), it remains important to consider the influence of social and cultural factors on antisocial behavior (Eron, Gentry, & Schlegel, 1995). For example, many adolescents participate in antisocial activities through involvement in neighborhood gangs. Youth gangs have grown dramatically in number and size during the 1990s, and can be found in virtually all major cities as well as many smaller cities and even some rural areas (Spergel, 1995).

Criminal gangs can be characterized on a continuum of organizational sophistication ranging from informal, scavenger gangs that coalesce intermittently to commit acts of violence or theft, to moderately organized gangs with territorial claims, to highly organized, profit-oriented groups with formal leaders and roles (Taylor, 1990). Youths may join gangs in order to enhance their opportunities to engage in antisocial activities such as selling drugs or engaging in violent acts. More broadly, however, youths join gangs for

Unresolved Problems and Issues

There are no established clinical procedures or widely accepted instruments designed specifically to obtain a comprehensive social history of antisocial behavior. Ideally, the content and focus of such methods should be relevant to current understanding of the etiology and development of antisocial behavior and should assist in identifying intervention strategies (Quay, 1987).

However diligently and skillfully the clinician collects information about a juvenile's history of illegal or antisocial behavior, he or she also must be sensitive to the social, political, and ethical issues that influence how such information is valued and interpreted for both clinical and nonclinical purposes. The social history of the youth with antisocial behavior often plays a critical role in assessing that youth's amenability to treatment and dangerousness to the community, often the key issues to legal authorities. Under these circumstances, the clinician's role may extend beyond or even conflict with the traditional ones of health care provider or patient advocate—for example, in forensic evaluations of juveniles charged with capital murder. In many cases the demands of social policy and the exigencies of dispositional decision making exceed current scientific knowledge about the meaning and significance of juvenile antisocial behavior.

REFERENCES

Anglin, T. M. (1993). Psychoactive substance use and abuse. In M. I. Singer, L. T. Singer, & T. M. Anglin (eds.) *Handbook for screening adolescents at psychosocial risk* (pp. 41–83). New York: Lexington Books.

Becker, J. V., & Hunter, J. A. (1997). Understanding and treating child and adolescent sex offenders. *Advances in clinical child psychology, 19,* 177–197.

Benedek, E., & Cornell, D. (Eds.) (1989). *Juvenile homicide.* Washington, D.C.: American Psychiatric Press.

Berkowitz, L. (1993). *Aggression: Its causes, consequences, and control.* Philadelphia: Temple University Press.

Brodsky, S. L., & Smitherman, H. O'N. (1983). *Handbook of scales for research in crime and delinquency.* New York: Plenum Press.

Cleckley, H. (1976). *The mask of sanity (5th ed.).* St. Louis, MO: Mosby.

Cornell, D. (1993). Juvenile homicide: A growing national problem. *Behavioral Sciences and the Law, 11,* 389–396.

Cornell, D. G., & Loper, A. B. (in press). Assessment of violence and other high-risk behaviors with a school survey. *School Psychology Review.*

Dana, R. H. (1996). Culturally competent assessment practice in the U.S. *Journal of Personality Assessment, 66,* 472–487.

Eron, L. D., Gentry, J. H., & Schlegel, P. (1995). *Reason to hope: A psychological perspective on violence and youth.* Washington, D.C.: American Psychological Association.

Federal Bureau of Investigation (1996). *Crime in the United States: Uniform crime reports, 1995.* Washington, DC: U.S. Department of Justice, The Federal Bureau of Investigation.

Hare, R. D. (1991). *The Hare Psychopathy Checklist—Revised.* Toronto, Canada: Multi-Health Systems.

Hawkins, J. D., Catalano, R. F., & Miller, J. Y. (1992). Risk and protective factors for alcohol and other drug problems in adolescence and early adulthood: Implications for substance abuse prevention. *Psychological Bulletin, 112,* 64–105.

Hindelang, M. J., Hirschi, T., & Weis, J. G. (1981). *Measuring delinquency.* Beverly Hills, CA: Sage Publications.

Kann, L., Warren, C. W., Harris, W. A., Collins, J. L., Douglas, K. A., Collins, M. E., Williams, B. I., Ross, J. G., Kolbe, L. J. (1995). Youth risk behavior surveillance—United States, 1993. *Morbidity and Mortality Weekly Report, March 24, 1995, 44, No. SS-1,* 1–66.

Keith, C. R. (Ed.) (1984). *The aggressive adolescent: Clinical perspectives.* New York: Free Press.

Lochman, J. E., & Dodge, K. A. (1994). Social-cognitive processes of severely violent, moderately aggressive, and nonaggressive boys. *Journal of Consulting and Clinical Psychology, 62,* 366–374.

Loeber, R. (1982). The stability of antisocial and delinquent child behavior: A review. *Child Development, 53,* 1431–1446.

Loper, A., & Cornell, D. G. (1996). Homicide by adolescent girls. *Journal of Child and Family Studies, 5,* 323–336.

Melton, G. B., Petrila, J., Poythress, N. G., & Slobogin, C. (1997). *Psychological evaluations for the courts: A handbook for mental health professionals and lawyers.* New York: Guilford.

Morris, R. E., Harrison, E. A., Knox, G. W., Tromanhauser, E. (1995). Health risk behavioral survey from 39 juvenile correctional facilities in the United States. *Journal of Adolescent Health, 17,* 334–344.

Olweus, D. (1979). Stability of aggressive reaction patterns in males: A review. *Psychological Bulletin, 86,* 852–875.

Quay, H. C. (Ed.) (1987). *Handbook of juvenile delinquency.* New York: John Wiley & Sons.

Salekin, R. T., Rogers, R., & Sewell, K. W. (1996). A review and meta-analysis of the Psychopathy Checklist and Psychopathy Checklist—Revised: Predictive validity of dangerousness. *Clinical Psychology: Science and Practice, 3,* 203–215.

Sattler, J. M. (1997). Clinical and forensic interviewing of children and families. San Diego: Jerome M. Sattler, Publisher, Inc.

Siegel, L. J. & Senna, J. J. (1988). *Juvenile delinquency* (3rd ed.). New York: West Publishing.

Snyder, H. N., & Sickmund, M. (1995). *Juvenile offenders and victims: A national report.* Washington, DC: Office of Juvenile Justice and Delinquency Prevention.

Snyder, H. N., Sickmund, M., & Poe-Yamagata, E. (1996). *Juvenile offenders and victims: 1996 update on violence.* Washington, DC: Office of Juvenile Justice and Delinquency Prevention.

Spergel, I. A. (1995). *The youth gang problem: A community approach.* New York: Oxford University Press.

Stafford, J. E. (1997). Psychopathy as predictor of adolescents at risk for inpatient violence. Unpublished doctoral dissertation, University of Virginia.

Taylor, C. S. (1990). *Dangerous society.* East Lansing: Michigan State University Press.

Widom, C. S. (1989). Does violence beget violence? A critical examination of the literature. *Psychological Bulletin, 106,* 3–28.

Wilson, J. Q., & Herrnstein, R. J. (1985). *Crime & human nature.* New York: Simon & Schuster.

52 / Cultural and Religious Issues

Peter Muehrer

By the year 2000, African Americans, Latinos, Asian Americans, and American Indians/Alaska Natives collectively will comprise almost one third of the U.S. population. Thus the special needs of children and adolescents from these growing groups will increasingly challenge our mental health services delivery system. Assessment is an integral part of the foundation upon which effective intervention is based; it becomes challenging regardless of who is the focus. Because of their extreme diversity, however, assessment can be even more complex with racial/ethic minority groups. For example, as a group, Latinos have ties to several distinct nations and an even wider array of cultures in the Caribbean basin, Central America, and South America. Asian Americans are people from approximately 40 distinct nations and cultures that extend from southeast Asia to Japan. American Indians and Alaska Natives include over 300 different tribes (recognized by the federal government) distributed across 278 reservations and 209 Native villages (although more than half of these individuals now live in urban settings). Such diversity means that assessment procedures developed primarily for European Americans may not be valid for cultural minorities.

Another prominent feature in the lives of many people (regardless of cultural background) is their religious or spiritual commitment; this is often overlooked in both clinical assessment and intervention. Although most Americans report that they belong to some organized religious institution, less than half of mental health professionals report such membership (Bergin & Jensen, 1990; Gallup, 1985). Furthermore, only a minority of mental health professionals believe that religious or spiritual issues play an important role in intervention. Religious or spiritual beliefs, however,

may constitute a core feature of one's identity and can be an important predictor of behavior (Koltko, 1990). Furthermore, such beliefs may be central to topics frequently explored during intervention with children and adolescents, including death of a loved one, parental divorce, emerging sexuality, and birth control methods, to name just a few.

Religious and spiritual beliefs can play a special role in the development of cultural minority children and adolescents. Among African Americans, for example, religious institutions serve as a buffer against the destructive force of racism by strengthening family and moral authority, status in the African American community, leadership development, and social ties (Staples, 1978). Membership in the Roman Catholic Church, and thus the influence of its doctrines, is widespread throughout the Latin world. Among American Indians and Alaska Natives, spiritual beliefs of oneness and harmony with the natural world affect behavior in most aspects of life. Thus inattention to religious or spiritual beliefs may limit clinical assessment of a young person's fundamental view of the self, interpersonal relationships, and society more broadly. This, in turn, may lead to the implementation of incomplete or inappropriate interventions.

Unique aspects of clinical assessment with each of America's 4 principal cultural minority groups merit detailed examination, as does the complex role of religious or spiritual beliefs in mental health. Salient cross-cultural and religious issues are highlighted in this chapter. Several readings are recommended at the end of the chapter for more detail on clinical assessment with a particular minority group.

It always must be remembered that regardless of the cultural origin of those being evaluated, principles of sound clinical assessment in general must be applied. Other chapters in this volume provide more information on the fundamentals of sound clinical assessment.

The views expressed in this chapter are those of the author and do not necessarily reflect the official policies of the National Institute of Mental Health or the United States Department of Health and Human Services.

General Recommendations

Experts in the area of clinical assessment with cultural minority youth have offered a number of suggestions (Sattler, 1988).

Clinicians must acknowledge and minimize their own stereotypes about cultural minorities so that these biases are not reflected in assessment interpretations. If clinicians find that they cannot minimize their own prejudices, ethics require that the child be referred to another clinician who can.

Test results, classroom performance, medical and family history, and cultural patterns must be considered carefully before recommending special education classes for children who have a limited command of English.

Tests requiring substantial understanding of English should be supplemented with nonverbal performance tests in order to assess a minority child's level of cognitive functioning. Whenever possible, in addition to tests in English, alternative test forms in the child's primary language should be used. A case example may help to emphasize the importance of this point.

CASE EXAMPLE

Martina, age 12, and her family recently moved to the southwestern United States from Mexico. She was referred to a local practitioner for assessment because of her parents' and teachers' concerns about her elevated anxiety related to performance in a new school, including persistent withdrawal from peer interactions in school. Martina had been a gregarious child and had always performed well academically in Mexico. Part of the assessment included an examination of her cognitive abilities in order to determine both an appropriate treatment plan and proper placement in the local schools in order to foster academic performance and satisfactory social development. Martina's performance in English on the Reading subtest of the Wide Range of Achievement Test (Jastak & Jastak, 1978) indicated a 3rd-grade level of English verbal skill, while her performance in English on the Verbal Scale of the Wechsler Intelligence Scale for Children-Revised (WISC-R) (Wechsler, 1974) was in the low normal range. Her cognitive abilities as measured on the WISC-R Performance Scale and the Leiter International Performance Scale (Leiter, 1948), a nonverbal test, however, were in the superior range. Complementing assessment data related to emotional and social functioning, the nonverbal cognitive data suggested that Martina could per-

form very well in her new school given appropriate language training and encouragement from her parents and teachers. These data helped to assuage both Martina's anxiety about the transition and her parents' concern for her, and facilitated her subsequent performance, both academically and socially.

The importance of being able to speak the child's native language or dialect fluently whenever possible is obvious and cannot be overstated.

It is important to recognize that minority youths have a range of diagnoses and presenting problems as wide as any other group of children and adolescents. Similarly, their cultures provide as diverse a range of opportunities and limitations as those provided by European American culture. Thus clinical assessment should become a foundation for an appropriately wide range of interventions (Gray, 1989).

In the course of clinical assessment, ideally, information is obtained both from the child or adolescent as well as from such knowledgeable informants as parents, siblings, teachers, and peers. Investigators have noted, however, that information from diverse sources frequently differs, with fairly low correlations (near 0.25) between child and parent reports, child and teacher reports, and child and mental health professional reports (Achenbach, McConaughy, & Howell, 1987). Thus different conclusions might be reached depending on the source of information. This reflects the fact that a child's behavior may vary across situations, contexts, and informants (Kazdin, 1988). This is especially true for cultural minority youths, who frequently must move between majority and minority contexts (Triandis, 1989). Assessment should describe and elaborate, rather than hide, these differences. Consider James.

CASE EXAMPLE

James, age 13, is an African American student whose family recently moved to a school district populated primarily by European American and Latino families. He was referred to an examiner because his parents and teachers were concerned that he was not performing at a level consistent with his above-average scores on standardized achievement tests. In particular, his teachers reported that James was underperforming in areas involving mathematics and did not readily engage in group recreational activities. The teachers indicated that James seemed poorly motivated and that he often failed to try to solve problems, saying "I'm just not as smart in math as the other kids." In contrast, James's parents reported to the examiner that James had shown persistently conscientious efforts at maintaining his before-school job delivering newspapers and handled the related financial accounting very capably. Furthermore, James had been of considerable assistance to his grandparents, who owned a grocery store in their previous neighborhood, assisting with inventory-taking and helping tally the daily store income. James had been active in several community social groups appropriate to his age before the move to a new school district. These divergent accounts of James's math and social competencies helped the examiner coordinate better communication between James's parents and teachers, who, with James, developed a plan of academic activities that capitalized on his numerous intellectual and social skills. After a few months, James became not only one of the better academic performers in his class but a leader at organizing peer activities as well.

Furthermore, clinical assessment is valuable to the extent that it is accurate and relevant to the practical needs of those seeking intervention. That is, it is useful only if reliable and valid. Although many techniques developed primarily for the majority population have adequate psychometric properties, their reliability and validity with minorities remain largely unknown. Very few standardized assessment techniques are available in languages other than English. More research is needed to establish reliability and validity when standardized assessments are conducted in minority populations and to develop sound instruments in the languages spoken by these populations.

Assessment Validity with Cultural Minority Groups

In undertaking clinical assessment with cultural minority youths, a concern of particular importance is "ecological validity." That is, information must be relevant to their everyday environments and social contexts so that appropriate interventions may be implemented. Ecological validity rests on the premise that human behavior is determined through person-environment relationships; these, in turn, change over time and across con-

texts (Sameroff, 1986). Demands, constraints, and resources presented by the cultural environment influence behaviors, cognitions, and emotions. The notion of person-environment relationships is especially pertinent to clinical assessment with cultural minority children and adolescents; such youngsters often must function in a variety of majority and minority contexts each day. Thus sensitivity to the meaning of fundamental constructs within a particular cultural community lays a foundation for clinical assessment that is ecologically valid. Unfortunately, the meaning of such constructs is not always equivalent from culture to culture.

Thus a critical consideration in ethnocultural assessment is "equivalence," that is, the extent to which constructs may be considered relevant and applicable to cultural groups other than the mainstream culture in which they were developed (Marsella & Kameoka, 1989). Four types of equivalence must be considered—linguistic, conceptual, scale, and norm. "Linguistic" equivalence refers to the extent to which the content and grammar have a similar denotative meaning across cultures. Complex concepts such as those embedded in the definitions of many mental disorders often cannot be translated adequately. For example, Americans associating to the word *depression* replied with words reflecting internal subjective referents, such as "blue, sad, down, despair, dejection." Japanese associating to the closest equivalent in their language, *yuutsu,* replied with external referents such as "mountains, rain, storms, dark." These findings raise questions about the denotative meaning of depression for the two groups. Similarly, asking Chinese youth whether they "enjoy" life may lead to misinterpretations of their mental health status, since life in the Chinese-Confucian philosophy is to be endured or suffered—it is not meant to be enjoyed (Yu, 1989).

To minimize misinterpretations in clinical assessment caused by language difficulties, at the least clinicians must note the child's language proficiency and discuss possible limitations of the results. A 5-point rating scale might be useful: (1) the child exclusively speaks a language other than English; (2) predominantly speaks the other language but also speaks some English; (3) speaks both the other language and English with equal ease; (4) predominantly speaks English but also speaks some other language; and (5) speaks English exclusively (DeAvila & Duncan, 1976). Furthermore, when instruments are translated from English into another language, techniques such as "back translation" can help to maintain denotative and connotative meanings (Karno et al., 1987). In back translation, a sentence or word is translated from language A to language B by 1 person and then translated back into language A by another person to ensure that the translation was accurate (Marsella & Kameoka, 1989). All back-translation techniques emphasize the importance of making sure that what is translated is equivalent in the different languages.

Related to linguistic equivalence is "conceptual" equivalence, which more closely refers to the connotation of terminology. For example, the word *dependence* has a very negative connotation in Western society, implying immaturity, excessive needs for nurturance and support, and personal incompetence. In Japan, however, dependency, or *amae,* has a positive connotation because the Japanese value conformity rather than individuality, which threatens the collective identity of that culture (Yu, 1989). Thus Japanese children in the United States may experience conflict if conformity is emphasized at home while independence is encouraged at school.

Even basic inquiries such as "How may we help you?" or "What problems are you experiencing?" may not have conceptual equivalence with minority children and their parents (Bauman & Adair, 1992). For example, some African American and Latino mothers with sick children usually do not ask others for help directly, which implies failure to function independently, but instead make their needs known to a trusted individual with whom they have a reciprocal relationship. The mothers receive support from people in their social network who understand their situation and offer help without being asked. The word *problem,* as used by these mothers, indicates a specific challenge that needs a solution, such as how to do laundry in public washing machines when it means leaving children alone. The words they use to describe the psychological impact of their children's illness are "difficult," "hard," or "hardship." Clinicians must listen carefully to the language that minority children and their families use to describe difficulties in their lives and incorporate that language into assessment procedures whenever feasible. Language typically used with the majority population may have different denotative and connotative meanings for cultural minority groups.

"Scale" equivalence is a third important consideration. In Western culture, young people frequently are exposed to various interview and survey formats and very early in life come to scale events by how much they "agree" or "disagree" with them. But these formats may be unfamiliar to children not reared in the West. For example, such children may not be accustomed to selecting from among limited options. They also may be inclined out of social propriety to give an answer that they believe will please the interviewer or examiner.

Finally, "norm" equivalence refers to the need to refrain from applying normative standards developed within 1 cultural group to another cultural group. Cultures differ in behavioral expectations and standards, so if a child or adolescent is judged against standards that are not culturally relevant, it is obvious that deviancy will be a considerable risk. Nevertheless, if minority children are to succeed in the majority culture, they must acquire the skills that will permit such success (Sattler, 1988). It is always critical, however, for clinicians to make explicit which norms are being used and for which purposes. The next case example emphasizes this important point.

CASE EXAMPLE

Midori is a first-generation Japanese American adolescent mother seeking treatment for postpartum depression. Her first child, a daughter, is 6 months old. Midori has experienced persistent thoughts of suicide and has considered killing her daughter just before killing herself. The clinician examining Midori is familiar with the phenomenon of *oyako-shinju,* or parent-child suicide, which accounts for about 3 to 4% of all suicides in Japan (Takahashi, 1992). The clinician therefore knows that the Japanese show considerable sympathy toward a mother who has not been able to find any other recourse but to commit suicide with her child: "according to Japanese logic, the suicidal mother cannot bear to leave the child to survive alone; she would rather kill the child because she believes that nobody in the world would take care of it, and that the child would be better off dying with her. Japanese people feel that such a suicidal mother does not actually murder her child, but she kills a part of herself: to kill her child means to kill oneself" (Takahashi, 1993, p. 7). Thus, applying traditional Japanese normative expectations to the potential problem of mother-child suicide, the clinician is able to obtain a richer understanding of Midori's postpartum emotional experiences and help devise a treatment plan that respects these norms while offering solutions that do not result in death for Midori or her child.

Ethnic Identity and Clinical Assessment

The extent to which nonequivalence poses problems for assessment with minority youths depends on the children's "ethnic identity," or the degree to which they embrace traditional cultural attitudes, values, and behavioral practices (Marsella & Kameoka, 1989; Phinney, 1990). Too often, clinicians assume that the youngster they are interacting with is the normative representative of a particular ethnic group. Although some children and adolescents may behave according to traditional cultural patterns, others may be highly assimilated to the mainstream culture. It is critical that clinicians determine whether particular children and their families use traditional language, food, dress, religious practices, or social organizations. With respect to scale equivalence, in particular, a child who has attended American schools for several years may be quite familiar with our interview, survey, and test formats. Thus asking him or her to express level of "agreement" or "disagreement" with items may not be as problematic as, for example, with recent immigrants. Nevertheless, ethnic identity can significantly color clinical presentation, so attention to its potential effects is critical during assessment.

Further research will be required to develop assessment techniques that reliably and validly measure equivalence and ethnic identity in various cultural minority groups. Until such techniques become available, clinicians must take great care to determine the personal meaning of affective labels—especially internal vs. external referents for mood states—and related behaviors. It is also critical to determine the degree to which a particular child or adolescent identifies with traditional cultural beliefs and practices.

Religious/Spiritual Social History and Clinical Assessment

Regardless of cultural background, religious or spiritual commitment can play a central role in how people view themselves, their communities, and, more broadly, the nature of society and their role within it. These views may strongly influence the cognitive, behavioral, and emotional aspects of interpersonal interactions as well as the coping strategies employed, both by adults and by children and adolescents (Strommen, 1984). Yet religious or spiritual views often are ignored in clinical assessment and intervention. Consequently, critical information about a young person's current difficulties and possible resources for resolving them remain unavailable to clinicians. This section begins with an overview of the discrepancy between the high prevalence of religious/spiritual beliefs and the low frequency with which they are assessed. Potential negative consequences of inattention to them are explored. A brief examination of such beliefs as coping mechanisms follows. Finally, strategies for determining the extent of a young person's religious/spiritual commitment are presented.

Religious beliefs are widespread in American society. Gallup surveys indicate that 95% of Americans believe in a God or Universal Spirit (Gallup, 1985). Eighty-seven percent report that they pray, and 86% state that religious views are very important or fairly important in their lives (Gallup, 1987). Among 425 clinicians surveyed in a national sampling, 80% indicate a religious preference (including traditional organized religions, agnosticism, and atheism) (Koltko, 1990). Compared with 84% of the public at large, 77% of clinicians try to live according to their religious beliefs. Many clinicians, however, appear to express their spiritual views in noninstitutional, personal ways. For example, when asked whether they "seek a spiritual understanding of the universe and one's place in it," 68% replied affirmatively; only 44% endorsed having a "religious affiliation in which one actively participates."

Given the prevalence of religious beliefs both among the population at large and among the clinicians surveyed, it is somewhat surprising that only 29% of these clinicians believe that religious

327

matters are important for treatment with all or many of their clients (Bergin & Jensen, 1990). Furthermore, religious views may influence major life issues frequently examined during intervention with children and adolescents—for example, parental divorce or death, emerging sexual identity and activity, abortion, guilt or remorse as features of depression, and the presence or absence of religious proscriptions of suicidal behavior. Thus failure to address religious views may diminish assessment validity and shadow the efficacy of subsequent intervention.

Furthermore, many adolescents may not seek help from a mental health professional at all, because they fear their religious or broader cultural values will not be respected. Instead, they turn to clergy for assistance in resolving emotional difficulties (Veroff, Kulka, & Douvan, 1981). Historically, some mental health theorists have viewed religion quite negatively. Freud, for example, called religion a "universal neurosis," an opinion that has been echoed by some adherents to his theories (Braun, 1982). Ellis, creator of Rational-Emotive Therapy (RET), maintained that "the elegant therapeutic solution to emotional problems is to be quite unreligious and have no degree of dogmatic faith that is unfounded or unfoundable in fact. . . . The less religious they are, the more emotionally healthy they will tend to be" (Ellis, 1980, p. 637). Some clinicians have misinterpreted behavior normative for a client's religious community as pathological, while others have suggested that clients violate central religious values (Greenberg, 1987; Moench, 1970, 1985; Spero, 1983).

Regardless of clinicians' personal views on religion, they must recognize that these suggestions may threaten some clients' sense of identity and integrity (Bergin, Stinchfield, Gaskin, Masters, & Sullivan, 1988). Although some changes in values may be therapeutic, a negative appraisal of the client's core values may be harmful. While the identification and modification of "irrational beliefs" are central to cognitive/behavioral approaches such as Rational-Emotive Therapy, for example, it is essential that these beliefs be examined within the context of the religious community to which the client belongs.

In contrast to negative appraisals of religious beliefs, several writers note that these beliefs can be an important part of an young person's adaptive coping response. The fact that organized religion has served as a refuge from racism and a source of social support for African Americans has already been mentioned (Staples, 1978). Not unlike meditation or relaxation techniques, some individuals might employ prayer as a method of stress management (Meyer, 1988). Almost 1 in 5 Puerto Rican Roman Catholics facing emotional problems seeks social support from traditional healers and spiritists as well as from conventional mental health professionals (Hohmann et al., 1990). Regardless of clinicians' own religious views, they must recognize that for large numbers of people, values adopted by a community of believers over several generations probably play an important adaptive role (Koltko, 1990). Clinical assessment can be used to explore this role and help plan interventions accordingly.

Thus, as with all aspects of culturally appropriate clinical assessment, clinicians must familiarize themselves with a client's religious beliefs. This requires clinicians to know (1) the major teachings and personal dilemmas typically experienced in the client's religious orientation, and (2) the specific details of that client's religious commitment (Koltko, 1990; Meyer, 1988). This second point is especially critical because, like members of any group, adherents to a particular religious orientation can be quite diverse. Furthermore, subgroups of adolescents, such as young women, unmarried sexually active youths, and gay/lesbian youths may take exception to certain official religious teachings. Another subgroup, former members of a religious group who consider themselves "lapsed" or nonpracticing, may nonetheless retain some values espoused by the group and live accordingly.

Several writers have suggested that when assessing someone's religious commitment, there are at least 8 elements to consider: (1) frequency of church attendance; (2) number of church-related activities attended; (3) agreement with theological precepts of a religion or with an ecclesiastical policy; (4) frequency of reference to sacred writings; (5) self-reports of intensity of religious identification; (6) personal devotional practices; (7) ways that religious beliefs are incorporated into daily decisions; and (8) formal church membership (Basset et al., 1981; Gorsuch, 1984). While numerous instruments with adequate reliability and validity have been developed for research with adults, none is used frequently in child and adolescent clinical assessment (cf. Strommen, Brekke, Undewager, & Johnson, 1972).

Others have begun to explore empirically core components of noninstitutional spirituality (Elkins, Hedstrom, Hughes, Leaf, & Saunders, 1988). These components include: (1) a view that life transcends what can be perceived by human senses; (2) a meaning and purpose in life; (3) a mission in life; (4) regard for life as sacred; (5) appreciation for material goods without seeking ultimate satisfaction from them or substituting them for frustrated spiritual needs; (6) altruism; (7) idealism aimed at improving the world; (8) awareness of the tragic realities of human existence, such as pain, suffering, and death; and (9) improved relations with oneself, others, and nature as a result of spiritual commitment. Further research is needed to develop reliable and valid instruments to measure these constructs.

A clinical interview is currently the principal means of gathering information on religious and spiritual commitment. At the very least, religious affiliation and/or fundamental spiritual beliefs should be included in the list of personal background information. Clinicians may follow through as appropriate with inquiries about the influence of religious/spiritual commitment in the child's or adolescent's life. The broad areas just discussed may guide such inquiry.

Finally, as with cultural minority youths, it is critical that clinicians recognize and minimize any stereotypes they may have about someone with deep religious/spiritual commitments. If they feel that personal prejudices might interfere with their objectivity, they must refer the religious child or adolescent to another clinician without such bias.

Conclusions

Sound clinical assessment requires ongoing and comprehensive collection of information. Multiple methods should be used to gather data from multiple sources. When cultural minority children and adolescents are the focus of clinical assessment, ecological validity is critical. Linguistic, conceptual, scale, and norm equivalence as well as the ethnic identity of the young person are important considerations. Until reliable and valid measurement techniques are developed, clinicians must be careful to interpret assessment data with these issues in mind.

Similarly, the development of reliable and valid techniques for assessing religious or spiritual commitment will require further research. It is clear, however, that religious/spiritual beliefs are important to most Americans and can influence many of the fundamental life decisions that typically are explored in the course of clinical intervention. Thus it is critical that clinicians inquire about such beliefs during assessment and remain respectful of them throughout the course of intervention.

REFERENCES

Achenbach, T. M., McConaughy, S. H., & Howell, C. T. (1987). Child/adolescent behavioral and emotional problems: Implications of cross-informant correlations for situational specificity. *Psychological Bulletin, 101*, 213–232.

Basset, R. L., Sadler, R. D., Kobischen, E. E., Skiff, D. M., Merrill, I. J., Atwater, B. J., & Livermore, P. W. (1981). The Shepherd Scale: Separating the sheep from the goats. *Journal of Psychology and Theology, 9*, 335–351.

Bauman, L. J., & Adair, E. G. (1992). The use of ethnographic interviewing to inform questionnaire construction. *Health Education Quarterly, 19* (1), 9–23.

Bergin, A. E., & Jensen, J. P. (1990). Religiosity of psychotherapists: A national survey. *Psychotherapy, 27* (1), 3–7.

Bergin, A. E., Stinchfield, R. D., Gaskin, T. A., Masters, K. S., & Sullivan, C. E. (1988). Religious life styles and mental health: An exploratory study. *Journal of Counseling Psychology, 35*, 91–98.

Braun, J. A. (1982). Ethical issues in the treatment of religious persons. In M. Rosenbaum (Ed.), *Ethics and values in psychotherapy* (pp. 131–160). New York: Free Press.

DeAvila, E. A., & Duncan, S. E. (1976). A few thoughts about language assessment: The Lau Decision reconsidered. *Proceedings of the National Conference on Research and Policy Implications, Lau Task Force Report*. Austin, TX: Southwest Educational Development Laboratory.

Edelbrock, C. S., Costello, A. J., Dulcan, M. K., Conover, N. C., & Kalas, R. (1986). Parent-child agreement on child psychiatric symptoms assessed via structured interview. *Journal of Child Psychology and Psychiatry, 27,* 181–190.

Elkins, D. N., Hedstrom, L. J., Hughes, L. L., Leaf, J. A., & Saunders, C. (1988). Toward a humanistic-phenomenological spirituality: Definition, description, and measurement. *Journal of Humanistic Psychology, 28,* 5–18.

Ellis, A. (1980). Psychotherapy and atheistic values: A response to A. E. Bergin's "Psychotherapy and religious values." *Journal of Consulting and Clinical Psychology, 48,* 637.

Forehand, R., Lautenschlager, G. J., Faust, J., & Graziano, W. G. (1986). Parent perceptions and parent-child interactions in clinic-referred children: A preliminary investigation of the effects of maternal depressive moods. *Behavior Research and Therapy, 24,* 73–75.

Gallup, G. (1985). *Religion in America.* Princeton, NJ: The Gallup Report, No. 236.

Gallup, G. (1987). *The Gallup poll: Public opinion 1986.* Wilmington, DE: Scholarly Resources.

Gorsuch, R. L. (1984). Measurement: The boon and bane of investigating religion. *American Psychologist, 39,* 228–236.

Gray, B. (1989). Psychotherapy with minority clients: Black clients. In P. Muehrer (Ed.), *Research perspectives on depression and suicide in minorities* (pp. 68–73). Rockville, MD: National Institute of Mental Health.

Greenberg, D. (1987). The behavioral treatment of religious compulsions. *Journal of Psychology & Judaism, 11* (1), 41–47.

Hohmann, A. A., Richeport, M., Marriott, B. M., Canino, G. J., Rubio-Stipec, M., & Bird, H. (1990). Spiritism in Puerto Rico: Results of an island-wide community study. *British Journal of Psychiatry, 156,* 328–335.

Jastak, J. F., & Jastak, S. (1978). *The Wide Range of Achievement Test* (rev. ed.). Wilmington, DE: Jastak Associates.

Karno, M., Hough, R. L., Burnam, M. A., Escobar, J. I. (1987). Lifetime prevalence of specific psychiatric disorders among Mexican-Americans and non-Hispanic Whites in Los Angeles. *Archives of General Psychiatry, 44(8),* 695–701.

Kazdin, A. E. (1988). The diagnosis of childhood disorders: Assessment issues and strategies. *Behavioral Assessment, 10,* 67–94.

Kleinman, A., & Good, B. (1985). Culture and depression: Introduction to the problem. In A. Kleinman & B. Good (Eds.), *Culture and depression—Studies in the anthropology and cross-cultural psychiatry of affect and disorder* (pp. 1–33). Berkeley, California: University of California Press.

Koltko, M. E. (1990). How religious beliefs affect psychotherapy: The example of Mormonism. *Psychotherapy, 27* (1), 132–141.

Leiter, R. G. (1948). *Leiter International Performance Scale.* Chicago: Stoelting Co.

Marsella, A. (1980). Depressive experience and disorder across cultures. In H. Triandis & J. Draguns (Eds.), *Handbook of cross-cultural psychology, Vol. 6: Psychopathology* Boston: Allyn and Bacon.

Marsella, A., & Kameoka, V. (1989). Ethnocultural issues in the assessment of depression and suicidality. In P. Muehrer (Ed.), *Research perspectives on depression and suicide in minorities* (pp. 40–51). Rockville, MD: National Institute of Mental Health.

Meyer, M. S. (1988). Ethical principles of psychologists and religious diversity. *Professional Psychology: Research and Practice, 19* (5), 486–488.

Moench, L. A. (1970). Guilt: A psychiatrist's point of view. *Dialogue: A Journal of Mormon Thought, 5* (3), 50–55.

Moench, L. A. (1985). Mormon forms of psychopathology. *Journal of the Association of Mormon Counselors and Psychotherapists, 11* (1), 61–73.

Phinney, J. (1990). Ethnic identity in adolescents and adults: Review of research. *Psychological Bulletin, 108,* 499–514.

Sameroff, A. J. (1986). Environmental context of child development. *Journal of Pediatrics, 109,* 192–200.

Sattler, J. M. (1988). Assessment of ethnic minority children. In *Assessment of children* (3rd ed., pp. 563–596). San Diego: Author.

Spero, M. H. (1983). Religious patients in psychotherapy: Comments on Mester and Klein (1981) "The young Jewish revivalist." *British Journal of Medical Psychology, 56,* 287–291.

Staples, R. (1978). Black family life and development. In L. Gary (Ed.), *Mental health: A challenge to the black community* (pp. 73–94). Philadelphia: Dorrance and Company.

Strommen, M. P. (1984). Psychology's blind spot: A religious faith. *Counseling & Values, 28,* 150–161.

Strommen, M. P., Brekke, M. L., Undewager, R. C., & Johnson, A. L. (1972). *A study of generations.* Minneapolis, MN: Augsburg Publishing.

Takahashi, Y. (1992). *Clinical evaluation of suicide risk and crisis intervention.* Tokyo: Kongo-Shuppan Publishers. [In Japanese]

Takahashi, Y. (1993, May 26). *Recent trends of suicide in Japan and strategies for suicide prevention.* Paper presented to the United Nations/World Health Organization Interregional Experts meeting, National Strategies for Suicide Prevention, Calgary, Alberta, Canada.

Triandis, H. C. (1989). The self and social behavior in differing cultural contexts. *Psychological Review, 96*(3), 506–520.

Veroff, J., Kulka, R. A., & Douvan, E. (1981). *Mental health in America.* New York: Basic Books.

Wechsler, D. (1974). Manual for the Wechsler Intelligence Scale for Children—Revised. New York: Psychological Corporation.

Yu, E. (1989). Assessment issues with Asian Americans. In P. Muehrer (Ed.), *Research perspectives on depression and suicide in minorities* (pp. 56–59). Rockville, MD: National Institute of Mental Health.

RECOMMENDED FURTHER READING

General

Betancourt, H., & Lopez, S. R. (1993). The study of culture, ethnicity, and race in American psychology. *American Psychologist, 48* (6), 629–637.

Ogbu, J. (1992). Understanding cultural diversity and learning. *Educational Researcher, 21* (8), 5–14.

Sattler, J. M. (1988). Assessment of ethnic minority children. In *Assessment of children* (3rd ed., pp. 563–596). San Diego: Author.

Zuckerman, M. (1990). Some dubious premises in research and theory on racial differences: Scientific, social, and ethical issues. *American Psychologist, 45,* 1297–1303.

For African Americans

Allen, L., & Majidi-Ahi, S. (1989). Black American children. In J. T. Gibbs & L. N. Huang (Eds.), *Children of color: Psychological interventions with minority youth. The Jossey-Bass social and behavioral science series* (pp. 148–178). San Francisco: Jossey-Bass.

Cross, W. E., Jr. (1991). *Shades of black: Diversity in African-American identity.* Philadelphia: Temple University Press.

Gibbs, J. T. (1990). Mental health issues of black adolescents: Implications for policy and practice. In A. R. Stiffman & L. E. Davis (Eds.), *Ethnic issues in adolescent mental health* (pp. 21–52). Newbury Park, CA: Sage Publications.

Jones, R. T., & Herndon, C. (1992). The status of black children and adolescents in the academic setting: Assessment and treatment issues. In C. E. Walker & M. C. Roberts (Eds.), *Handbook of clinical child psychology* (2nd ed). (pp. 901–917). New York: John Wiley & Sons.

For American Indians and Alaska Natives

Manson, S., Walker, R., & Kivlahan, D. (1987). Psychiatric assessment and treatment of American Indians and Alaska Natives. *Hospital and Community Psychiatry, 38* (2), 165–173.

LaFromboise, T. D., & Low, K. G. (1989). American Indian children and adolescents. In J. T. Gibbs & L. N. Huang (Eds.), *Children of color: Psychological interventions with minority youth. The Jossey-Bass social and behavioral science series* (pp. 114–147). San Francisco: Jossey-Bass.

For Asian Americans

Lee, E. (1988). Cultural factors in working with Southeast Asian refugee adolescents. Special issue: Mental health research and service issues for minority youth. *Journal of Adolescence, 11* (2), 167–179.

For Latinos

Burnam, M., Hough, R., Karno, M., Escobar, J., & Telles, C. (1987). Acculturation and lifetime prevalence of psychiatric disorders among Mexican Americans in Los Angeles. *Journal of Health and Social Behavior, 28,* 89–102.

Canino, G., Bird, H., Shrout, P., Rubio-Stipec, M., & Bravo, M. (1987). The Spanish Diagnostic Interview Schedule: Reliability and concordance with clinical diagnoses in Puerto Rico. *Archives of General Psychiatry, 44,* 720–726.

Karno, M., Hough, R., Burnam, M., Escobar, J., Timbers, D., Santana, F., & Boyd, J. (1987). Lifetime prevalence of specific psychiatric disorders among Mexican Americans and non-Hispanic whites in Los Angeles. *Archives of General Psychiatry, 44,* 45–701.

Rogler, L. H., Cortes, D. E., & Malgady, R. G. (1991). Acculturation and mental health status among Hispanics: Convergence and new directions for research. *American Psychologist, 46,* 585–597.

53 / Occupational Assessment

Susan Haiman and Sandra Greene

Occupational assessment is based on a model that conceives of humans as integrated systems in which there is a constant dynamic interaction between 3 aspects of performance: *performance components, performance areas,* and the *performance context.* Performance components are the distinct skills required to accomplish most tasks. They are the basic building blocks of performance, such as fine motor coordination, problem-solving ability, sensory processing, and self-expression. Performance areas include the activity or occupational spheres of self-care, school/work performance, and social and recreational engagement. This might include performance of hygiene activities, eating and diet management, school behavior, and pursuit of age-consonant play. Context refers to the environment in which performance is expected to take place. This includes the physical and sociocultural environment as well as the developmental life cycle phase of both the child and his or her caregivers.

Occupational role performance is a way to describe how well a given child or adolescent is able to meet the complex physical, social, and emotional demands of being student, sibling, son/daughter, grandchild, worker, volunteer, and religious participant. A person may have more than one occupational role simultaneously, and the role may shift in importance over time. In addition, the tasks of each role may change as the person develops. For example, as a child moves from preschooler to student, less time is spent in free play and more time in the structured arena of the elementary school.

Occupational assessment and intervention with children and adolescents addresses the problems in daily living that these young people experience when normal role performance is difficult or impossible due to the full gamut of psychiatric illness. Or it may provide the contextual support in the environment that facilitates normal role performance whenever possible. For example, when problems with auditory information processing makes long periods at a classroom desk difficult, a schedule change allowing for engagement in gross motor activity may be necessary for one child, while another child would benefit from "independent study" time in the school library.

Occupational Assessment of Children

A wide range of structured observation, interviews with parents and patients, standardized tests, and checklists/inventories are appropriate for assessment of children and adolescents. These might include standardized evaluations assessment of structured and free play, social behavior, sensory processing (such as sensitivity to touch), visual perceptual and coordination as well as developmental and adaptive functioning. For example, the assessment of a 4-year-old diagnosed with pervasive developmental disorder would include standardized developmental tests: tests of sensory, perceptual, and motor development; observation of play and social interaction; as well as interviews with caregivers about the child's play patterns. With an older child with conduct disorder, the same standardized testing might be used, but assessment would expand to include an interview with the child focusing on play, social and community skills, and interest checklists. Whenever possible, observation of the child with peers is also desirable to reveal performance strengths as well as deficits.

Occupational Assessment of Adolescents

Assessment of adolescents may include a review of the patient's history, current behavior and performance related to social skills, cognitive skills, time management, and school performance. Adolescents are able to participate in self-reports related to daily or weekly routines, assessments of occupational roles, interest exploration, and vocational exploration. For example, in the Barth Time Construction adolescents are asked to complete a colorful graph of how they spent their time during the week preceding the assessment. The assessment assigns color code to each of a range of activities, including television, drug use, time spent on grooming, eating, work/school, hobbies and doing "nothing." Done individually, the assessment opens the door to exploration of time management, interests, and areas in which the adolescent can identify the desire to change. When done in a group, valuable information about peer relationships and social skills can be gained. Such was the case when in a group of adolescents completing the assessment together, one said to the other, after seeing his time chart, "God, look how much time you spend doing drugs!"

Conclusion

Assessment may be either a formal standardized event or it can be ongoing and informal. The outcome of the assessment always should be interpreted in relation to the youngster's participation in the routines and occupations of daily living. Occupational interventions will not focus on the causes of impairment but on the impact of impairment and disability on the youngster's current and future performance. Thus the question in assessment is not "What do the voices say to you?" but "How do the voices get in the way of your being able to do what you want to do each day?"

The range of standardized assessment tools is vast. In the following abbreviated list, tests are grouped according to performance components, performance areas, and performance context. (For detailed information, refer to Asher, 1996.)

PERFORMANCE COMPONENTS

DiGangi-Berk Test of Sensory Integration (Berk and DiGangi, 1983)
Sensory-Integration and Praxis Tests (SIPT) (Ayres, 1989)

PERFORMANCE AREAS

Adolescent Role Assessment (Black, 1976)
Interest Checklist (Matsutsuyu, 1967; Rogers, 1988)
Jacobs Pre-vocational Assessment (Jacobs, 1991)
Scoreable Self-Care Evaluation
Test of Playfulness (Bundy, 1993)

PERFORMANCE CONTEXT

National Institute of Health Activity Records (ACTRE) (Gerber and Furst, 1992)
Occupational Performance History Interview (OPHI) (AOTA, 1989)

REFERENCES

Allen, C. K. (1985). *Occupational therapy for psychiatric diseases: Measurement and management of cognitive disabilities.* Boston, MA: Little, Brown.
Asher, I. E. (1996). *Occupational therapy assessment tools: An annotated index-second edition.* Bethesda, MD: American Occupational Therapy Association.
Ayres, A. (1989). *Sensory integration and praxis tests.* Los Angeles, CA: Western Psychological Services.
Berk, R. & DiGangi, G. (1983). *DiGangi-Berk test of*

sensory integration. Los Angeles, CA: Western Psychological Services.

Black, M. (1976). Adolescent role assessment. *American Journal of Occupational Therapy, 30,* 73–77.

Bonder, B. (1995). *Psychopathology and function.* Thoroghfare, NJ: Slack Inc.

Bundy, A. (1993). *Test of playfulness.* Fort Collins, CO: Department of Occupational Therapy, Colorado State University.

Gerber, R. & Furst, G. (1992). Validation of NIH activity record: a quantitative measure of life activities. *Arthritis Care Research, 5,* 81–86.

Hemphill, B. (Ed). (1996). *Mental health assessment in occupational therapy.* Thoroghfare, NJ: Slack.

Jacobs, K. (1991). *Occupational therapy: Work-related programs and assessment,* second edition. Boston, MA: Little, Brown.

Kielhofner, G., Henry, A., & Whalens, D. (1989). *Occupational performance history interview.* Bethesda, MD: American Occupational Therapy Association.

Kramer, P. & Hinojosa, J. (1993). *Frames of reference for pediatric occupational therapy.* Baltimore, MD: Williams and Wilkins.

Matsutsuyu, J. (1967). The interest check list. *American Journal of Occupational Therapy, 11,* 179–181.

Reilly, M. (1974). *Play as exploratory learning: Studies of curiosity behavior.* Beverly Hills, CA: Sage Press.

Rogers, J. (1988). *The NPI interest checklist.* In B. Hemphill (Ed.), *Mental health assessments in occupational therapy.* Thoroghfare, NJ: Slack.

54 / Vocational Assessment

Elissa Lang

Change within the workplace is occurring at a staggering pace. Over the span of a relatively few years, we have seen the shift from a manufacturing to a service industry base, from the United States occupying a dominant international position in trade to having competitive difficulties. We see advances in technology changing the nature of jobs. And we see changes in the work force, with demographic trends reflecting greater diversity.

—P. WEHMAN, 1993, P. 3

In A.D. 172 Galen, the Greek physician, said that "employment is nature's best physician and is essential to human happiness" (Dunton, 1940, p. 27). Work was recognized early both as "a means of rehabilitation, and as an end in itself, evidence of wellness and citizenship" (Robinault & Weisinger, 1978). "The inherent human drive toward competence" supersedes age, race, gender or disability (Sternberg & Kolligan, 1990, p. 14). Relevant vocational measurement tools for children and young adolescents continue to be scarce. However, increasingly sophisticated theories of vocational development provide important guidance for parent, child, educator, or clinician about the successful lifelong transition from home to school to work.

Vocational Psychology

Vocational psychology is the study of human behavior in relation to work (Walsh & Osipow, 1995). As a clinical science, it provides empirical measurement of interest, ability, and traits. As a developmental science, it acknowledges vocational behaviors as identifiable components of a lifelong process. Vocational choice requires a planned synthesis of empirical, developmental, and environmental data culminating in an occupational selection that affords the greatest chance of success and satisfaction.

The discussion of vocational development is aided by maintaining a clear distinction between *occupation*—what one does—and *career*—the course of work, education, activity pursued over a period of time.

Occupational or vocational psychology employs a differential psychology approach to occupation that states that people in various occupations can be identified according to *aptitudes, interests,* and *personality traits* that contribute to success and satisfaction in the work. This *occupational model* prompted the development and use of psychometric tools (U.S. Department of Labor, 1967) to measure the characteristics of people and determinants of success in various occupations. This descriptive matching of the aptitudes of new workers with the standards of entry level jobs made possible the measurement of occupational interest patterns (Super & Bohn, 1970). A "good match" was thought to predict future job success and satisfaction. Although ground-breaking, the occupational model of success left out issues of cultural background, training, socioeconomic status, job availability and attainment, human malleability and mobility, job market and technological changes, vocational development, and family support. However, tests of known occupational validity, such as the Strong-Campbell Interest Inventory, Kuder Preference Interest Inventory, General Aptitude Test, Self-Directed Search, Edwards Personal Preference Schedule, and Meyers-Briggs Type Indicator, used by a well-trained counselor, have been shown to promote better vocational counseling results (Crites, 1969; McCrory, 1991).

Intelligence, achievement, and literacy tests for children and adolescents often are used in conjunction with occupational inventories (Bracken & Fagan, 1990). The wholesale use of such tools without informed counseling in clinical and educational settings, especially for students without family support or coordinated efforts, has caused frustration and misunderstanding about their true value. When they are properly used and integrated from kindergarten to grade 12 in school-to-work programs, they yield consistently high rates of success (Cunanan, 1994).

Career psychology refers to the clear concept of vocational *development* rather than difference alone. A career is a sequence of positions held by an individual over the course of a lifetime. It implies continued progress in the person's vocational life. Moves may be vertical, lateral, direct, indirect, initiated, imposed, systematic, or haphazard. Progress is not always "up a career ladder," but progressive achievement implies that moves made at any one point in a career always are related to positions occupied earlier in the career. The distinction between occupation and career is illustrated by the engineering student who eventually may work as a production engineer years later *versus* an auto worker who not only will never move

to an engineering position but whose mechanical/manual dexterity aptitudes have been replaced by technology.

The role and significance of family are highlighted in career psychology because careers begin before actual employment and are shaped by parental background through its determination of exposure to occupations and educational opportunities, by aptitudes and interests, and by educational attainments (Rogers, Toole, & Brown, 1991).

VOCATIONAL DEVELOPMENT

Vocational development is best understood by an examination of the successive approximations toward work that occur at recognized life stages.

Super, Crites, Hummel, Moser, & Overstreet (1957) and Osipow and Fitzgerald (1996) provide the clearest delineation of vocational development occurring throughout the life span. These vocational life stages include growth (0–14), exploration (15–24), establishment (25–44), maintenance (45–64), and decline (65+). The growth and exploration substages are discussed in Table 54.1.

Of note is the importance of early recognition of ability, interest, and emerging self-concept evident even at 1 to 2 years of age. Provision of opportunities for varied task exposure and recognition of consistent age- and role-relevant capacities form the foundations for future vocational choice and satisfaction. Although task performance is more fragmented at 0 to 2 years, splinter abilities such as interesting color choices, unusual block arrangements, running fast, social ease, strength, memory, experimentation with different foods, taking things apart, concentration level, keen eyesight, language, and the like are evident to those looking for the emerging individual.

Play activities are the precursor for future success in leisure, social, and work endeavors. The PreSchool Play Scale and Play Skills Inventory provide excellent measures of sensation, motor activity, perception, intellect, attitudes, and relation to environments. Activities of daily living or the developmental tasks related to home and self-independent tasks are important indicators for degrees of independence in learning and performance. The Activities of Daily Living and the

TABLE 54.1

Stages of Early Vocational Development

Life Stage	Behavioral Indicators of Vocational Growth
GROWTH (0–14 yr)	Self-concept, a major determinant of vocational choice and success, begins through identification with key family, school, and local figures. Need and fantasy are dominant followed by increased importance of interest and capacity as social participation and reality testing occur.
Fantasy (4–10):	Role-play of mom, dad, and familiar uniformed workers (police, doctor, fire chief) is common; task choices based on preference (ability) emerges as early as 2 years and results by 10 years in "I'm good at . . ."
Interests (11–12):	Personal likes and dislikes become dominant in aspirations and activities; ideas develop about what child can do, likes to do, is expected to do and what others do. "I like/don't like to do . . ."
Capacity (13–14):	Known abilities carry more weight as jobs and training are considered. "I'd like to be . . ."
EXPLORATION (15–24)	Self-appraisal, real role experimentation and occupational exploration occur in school, leisure, social, and part-time work activities. "I think I can be . . ."
Tentative (15–17)	Tentative choices based on needs, interests, capacities, values, opportunities are made and tried out in fantasy, discussions, courses, work, etc. "I'm going to be . . ."
Transitional (18–21)	Reality considerations weigh heavily with entry into labor market or training and attempts to implement a self-concept. "I am . . ."
Trial (22–24)	A beginning job is found and tried out as a lifework in a seemingly appropriate field. "I will/won't continue to be . . ."

Time-Oriented Record are helpful measures. The Miller Assessment for Preschoolers (MAP) provides early detection of potential learning, sensory, motor, cognitive, or social dysfunction related to school readiness. The Wechsler Preschool and Primary Scale of Intelligence (WPPSI-R) provides early intelligence measures for nondisabled children. The Wechsler Intelligence Scale for Children—Third Edition (WISC-III) considers performance of children with learning disabilities, attention deficit hyperactivity disorder, language disorders, dyslexia, deafness, and severe emotional disturbance.

Vocational Measurement

Clinical appraisal cannot substitute for a comprehensive evaluation of vocational potential. *Career decision making* is a complex process of self-discovery and definition that begins with an accurate measurement and a psychodynamically informed understanding of an individual's unique composite of aptitudes, values, interests, personality traits, social/behavioral modes, experiences, opportunities, wishes, and vocational maturity.

The intersection of measured vocational components and natural determinants is called career or vocational choice.

VOCATIONAL COMPONENTS

An *aptitude* is a measure of general intelligence and implies the overall capacity to learn certain behaviors more easily than others. Individual learning differences exist in varying degrees and are normally distributed. Learning variance exists within each occupational cluster and among all occupations where aptitudes cluster in the middle with a few outliers at the extremes. Aptitudes can

336

be simple or complex. Simple aptitudes involve a single ability or a consistent constellation of abilities. For example, verbal reasoning and numerical reasoning are simple aptitudes. In *Frames of Mind: The Theory of Multiple Intelligences,* Dr. Howard Gardner (1983) challenges the use of only verbal and numerical reasoning as overall intelligence indicators by postulating that all aptitudes are both ability in themselves *and* pathways for learning all other subjects. He adds interpersonal, intrapersonal, and bodily kinesthetic abilities to the traditional list. Abstract reasoning and spatial visualization or spatial judgment are also simple aptitudes indicating dimensional capacity. Manual dexterity is a constellation of motor aptitudes. Fine manual or finger dexterity is independent of gross manual or arm-and-hand dexterity. Perceptual speed and accuracy measures speed, accuracy, and attention to detail.

Complex aptitudes are those abilities that do not appear to comprise discrete and unitary characteristics. Complex aptitudes such as medicine, art, music, or mechanics are composites of simple abilities that enable particular skill learning and competence.

Aptitudes are needed to learn and master specific occupational tasks. The General Aptitude Test Battery (GATB) is the gold instrument for adolescent and adult assessment of verbal, numerical, abstract, spatial, mechanical, and perceptual aptitude. Other vocational aptitude instruments include the Career Ability Placement Survey (CAPS) and the Wisconsin Career Information System (WCIS). The Perdue Pegboard measures gross and fine motor ability. Music, artistic, and medical aptitudes are measured by synthesis of the complex aptitude composites. No standardized instruments to measure interpersonal or intrapersonal aptitudes are available at this time.

MOTIVATION

Motivation, in vocational development, is defined in terms of values and interests. Interests are the activities and objects through which a person seeks to enact values. Values are the objectives that people seek. Values may be achieved through more than 1 activity, and different ways of viewing an activity have bearing on continued pursuit. In-

terests determine the direction of vocational effort, stability, choice, and completed training. Values determine occupational choice, satisfaction, and extent of self-realization.

Edward Strong, G. F. Kuder (1954), and J. P. Guilford provided the early framework for modern interest measurement as a vocational determinant. Together they identified interests that differentiate men and women in 1 occupation from another and fields of interests that are homogeneous and independent of each other. Osipow and Fitzgerald (1996) provide the most comprehensive survey and evaluation of the major theories of career development.

The Work Values Inventory measures adolescent and adult vocational values. These include: altruism, esthetics, creativity, intellectual stimulation, independence, achievement, religion, prestige, management, economic return, security, surroundings, supervisory relations, associates, variety, and way of life.

The Strong Vocational Interest Inventory (SVIB), Self Directed Search (SDS), Kuder Interest Inventory, California Occupational Preference Survey (COPS), Wisconsin Career Information System (WCIS), Career Decision Maker (CDM) and Meyers-Briggs Indicator all provide vocational interest information. Commonly measured vocational interests are: scientific, mechanical, outdoor, social service, clerical, computational, persuasive, literary, business, artistic, musical, legal, and technical.

ACHIEVEMENT

Fundamental differences in aptitudes and motivation contribute to achievement, or what a person does, becomes, or obtains through attributes and effort. The routinely substantiated and validated importance of achievement lies in the fact that past achievement is a predictor of future success (Thorndike & Hagen, 1961). Achievement has a significant place in the vocational development of children and adolescents in that interests, values, achievement, development, and even inborn aptitudes can be affected by the experiences to which an individual is exposed. *Aptitude* development is now known to be crucial for the mastery of a field but not for success. Motivation determines the direction of the vocational effort more than the degree of success resulting from the effort. Interests may affect task or course selection and completion but do not affect achievement. Interests do affect job satisfaction. Workers with vocational interests most similar to the members in that occupation show the highest satisfaction levels and tend to remain in that occupation for longer periods.

Achievement is usually measured by the Wide Range Achievement Test (WRAT).

PERSONALITY

Personality traits and styles also play a role in work choice and success. The Minnesota Multiphasic Personality Inventory diagnostic scales that discriminate modes of behavior characteristic of normal individuals also show differences between occupational groups. Personality traits predict job satisfaction through choice of occupation and job environment and identify style of work behavior.

Holland (1992, p. 30) postulated that "individuals select occupations and job environments that well suit their personality types." His studies led to the identification of 6 major life orientations distinguishable by occupation. The Edwards Personal Preference Schedule (EPPS) and the Meyers-Briggs measure vocational personality traits for realistic (scientific), intellectual, social, conventional, enterprising, and artistic types.

Self-concept has special relevance for the adolescent's vocational choice since "an individual chooses the kind of work/occupation which represents the characteristics he/she sees in him/her self" (Super, 1957). Early stability in vocational choice is the exception rather than the rule in vocational development. The installation of an accurate self-concept based on realistic knowledge of and experience with personal aptitudes, abilities, opportunities, values, and needs may be the single most important proactive strategy available to foster career success. Self-concept is a primary determinant of vocational choice and self-estimated occupational success. The Coopersmith Inventory is often used to assess self-concept.

CAREER MATURITY

In the same way that achievement levels at one point in time predict future levels, the extent to which an individual's vocational goals are clear cut at one time predicts clarity later on. This developmental step is particularly crucial between eighth grade and 2 years post–high school. The linkage of vocational coping behavior continues throughout the vocational life span. The ability to cope with the tasks of vocational development as compared with others faced with the same tasks is called career or vocational maturity. Compared to aptitudes such as intelligence and spatial visualization, the uneven and irregular process of vocational maturity makes it much less stable than other traits.

Landmark longitudinal studies opened the door for career development as a primary postulant in occupational success and satisfaction (Super, Kowalski, & Gotkin, 1967). Issues such as the occupations preferred while in school, achievement in age-appropriate school tasks as measured by grades and activities, realism of reasons for and numbers of job changes, self-estimated occupational success, global ratings of career floundering or stability behaviors, readiness for vocational planning, and socioeconomic status all emerged to add clarity to the complex multidimensional process of career development.

The Career Maturity Inventory (CMI) is used to measure readiness for vocational planning, decision making, stability, floundering, problem solving, and adjustment ability.

The School-to-Work Opportunities Act (1994, 1995; see Hershey & Rosenberg, 1996) provides federal support for the creation of state and local systems to insist on partnerships among educational institutions, employers, career/guidance professionals, labor and industry organizations, teachers, parents, clinicians, mentors, and others. The act underscores the critical need for coordination and communication from as early as kindergarten in order to facilitate opportunities for human competence among those who follow us.

REFERENCES

Bracken, B., & Fagan, T. (Eds.). (1990). Intelligence: Theories and Practice (4th ed.). Monograph: *Journal of Psychoeducational Assessment.* Tennessee: University of Memphis.

Crites, J. (1969). *Vocational psychology.* New York: McGraw-Hill.

Cunanan, E. (1994, December). The MAGIC model. Brief. National Center for Research in Vocational Education, Office of Special Populations (OSP), 6(2). Urbana-Champaign: University of Illinois at Urbana-Champaign.

Dunton, W. (Ed.). (1940). *Occupational therapy and rehabilitation.* Baltimore, MD: Williams & Wilkins.

Gardner, H. (1983). *Frames of mind: The theory of multiple intelligences.* New York: Basic Books.

Hershey, A., & Rosenberg, L. (1996). *School-to-work implementation progress: The state perspective in early 1996.* Princeton, NJ: Mathmetica Policy Research.

Holland, J. (1992). Making vocational choices: A theory of vocational personalities and work environments. Odessa, FLA: Psychological Assessment Resources, Inc.

Kuder, G. F. (1954). Expected developments in interest and personality inventories. *Education and Psychological Measurements, 14,* 265–271.

McCrory, D. J. (1991). The rehabilitation alliance. *Journal of Vocational Rehabilitation, 1* (3), 58–66.

Osipow, S. H., & Fitzgerald, L. F. (1996). *Theories of career development* (4th ed.). Boston: Allyn & Bacon.

Robinault, I., & Weisinger, M. (1978). *Selected approaches to vocational rehabilitation: Community resources: Multifaceted model for the mentally ill.* New York: International Classification of Diseases Rehabilitation and Research Center, Research Utilization Laboratory.

Rogers, E. S., Toole, J., & Brown, M. A. (1991). Vocational outcomes following psychosocial rehabilitation: A longitudinal study of three programs. *Journal of Vocational Rehabilitation, 1* (3), 21–29.

Sternberg, R., & Kolligian, J. (Eds.). (1990). *Competence considered.* New Haven, CT: Yale University Press.

Super, D. E. (1957). *The psychology of careers.* New York: Harper & Row.

Super, D., & Bohn, M. (1970). *Occupational psychology.* Belmont, CA: Wadsworth Publishing.

Super, D., Crites, J., Hummel, R. C., Moser, H. P., Overstreet, P. L., & Warnath, C. F. (1957). *Vocational development: A framework for research.* New York: Teachers College, Columbia University Bureau of Publications.

Super, D., Kowalski, R., & Gotkin, E. (1967). *Floundering and trial after high school.* Cooperative Research Project No. 1393. New York: Teachers College, Columbia University.

Thorndike, R., & Hagen, E. (1961). *Measurement and evaluation in psychology and education.* New York: John Wiley & Sons.

U.S. Department of Labor. (1967). General Aptitude Test Battery. Section III 19962 Development. Washington, DC: Author.

Walsh, W. B., & Osipow, S. H. (Eds.). (1995). *Handbook of vocational psychology* (2nd ed.). Hillsdale, NJ: Lawrence Erlbaum.

Wehman, P. (Ed.). (1993). Introduction to business and marketing. *Journal of Vocational Rehabilitation, 3* (4), 3.

55 / Educational Issues

Rick Ostrander and Larry B. Silver

The focus of this chapter is on the special aspects of obtaining a social history when educational problems and academic difficulties are part of the presenting problems. The process begins with the initial intake contact and may continue throughout the evaluation. The process of the evaluation follows that described in Chapter 13.

Initially, a thorough history of the presenting problems will help to clarify if these problems began at a specific time or after a specific event, or if they evolved over a period of time. Were any interventions tried? If so, what type and for how long? Were these efforts within the school program or done privately by the family? Were the interventions successful?

Assessment of the Child or Adolescent

The child's or adolescent's current level of functioning should be compared both to the accepted norms for the age and to the parents' level of expectation. Unrealistically high parental expectations for academic success may magnify academic difficulties. Unusually low or no parental expectations for academic success might result in not encouraging the child or adolescent to reach potential academic levels. It is important for the clinician to determine whether the parental expectations are consistent with those of others who are involved with the student, such as teachers and health or mental health professionals.

Information should be obtained about each year of school, starting with the earliest preschool experiences. Did this child or adolescent show any difficulties with social adjustment or with mastering the academic expectations during any given school year? Did he or she relate well to teachers and to peers? Were there behavioral problems? Has he or she been retained for a year, repeating a grade? If so, why? Has this student been suspended or expelled from school? This information may clarify the severity of the problems as well as factors that might have contributed to or exacerbated them.

Changes in schools can be disruptive. Has this student been enrolled in several schools? If so, why? Have other changes in teachers, grade placement, or schools affected academic performance or behavioral/emotional status? It is not uncommon for changes in teachers to result in a positive or negative change in the child's attitude and performance. Repeated changes in school typically have a negative effect on academic and social functioning (Homes & Matthews, 1984).

A consistent behavioral, social, or academic finding across teachers, schools, and/or grades suggests that a given individual's problems are related to inner-child variables such as cognitive, personality, or psychiatric considerations. In contrast, inconsistency in function across school, grade placements, or teachers suggests that the individual's problems are significantly affected by variability in development or in the environmental context (Martin, 1986).

If the social history suggests that the difficulties are related to environmental circumstances, further explorations of these areas are indicated. Is there a relationship between the onset of the difficulties and any significant changes in the life of the individual or of his or her family? An illness or death of a family member; a separation, divorce, or remarriage; birth of a sibling; a move; or other stresses can influence academic performance (Silver, 1993).

It is equally important to attempt to clarify whether the presenting emotional, behavioral, or family problems are primary or secondary. That is, do those problems appear to be the cause of or a contributing factor to the academic difficulties, or are the academic difficulties causing or contributing to these problems?

DEVELOPMENTAL HISTORY

A review of the child's or adolescent's developmental history is essential. Through the history provided by the parents as well as by reviewing follow-up information obtained from relevant physicians or past records, evidence of a developmental delay might be clarified. Such delays might be very relevant to understanding current academic difficulties. These explorations should not be limited to aspects of motor and language development but also should include a history of cognitive development and psychosocial development. Information concerning memory, attention, reasoning, development of academic skills, comprehension, interpersonal relationships, and skills may be very helpful in shedding light on a developmental delay or a developmental disability, a factor that could be contributing to or causing the academic difficulties. Since parental reports concerning developmental issues are often unreliable, information from other sources is helpful. When exploring developmental progress, parents could be encouraged to compare the identified child with an age-appropriate sibling or peer.

The child's or adolescent's behavioral and emotional characteristics should be explored relative to several factors. Early temperament is one such dimension; another is the individual's ability to establish an equilibrium by adapting to the environment and to demands. Evidence from birth onward of difficulty in obtaining and maintaining such an equilibrium is often found with children who later show evidence of a developmental disability.

The history of how the motor, language, or cognitive areas developed often provides clues to the possible origins of current difficulties. A child with a delay in gross or fine motor development later might show problems with the kinds of motor skills required in school (such as the fine motor skills needed to write). A child with a delay in language development often can be identified by age 2½ to 3 and can then receive speech-language therapy. For many, this delay is the first evidence of an underlying language disability. By age 5 or 6 a receptive and expressive language disability is readily identified. By the third grade—and typically earlier—problems with such language-based learning tasks as reading comprehension and written language are all too evident. Difficulty with appropriate development of play as reflected in the choice and use of play objects and interactive play may be the earliest clues of such cognitive problems as inability to perform sequencing, abstraction, organization, and memory.

MEDICAL HISTORY

Information should be obtained about previous medical illnesses or procedures. Information arising from direct discussions with the family physician or from copies of medical records is useful. Have there been any health problems that might explain changes in school behavior or performance? A special focus should be on information relating to vision and hearing. Is there a history of a seizure disorder? Might the student have diabetes, asthma, or other diseases that have resulted in frequent absences from school? Is he or she on medication and, if so, are there side effects that might affect the ability and availability to learn?

A full history of pregnancy and delivery is essential. Although a direct relationship between difficulties during these times and academic difficulties is not fully established, the presence of complications during these critical periods would suggest that the child or adolescent might have a neurological dysfunction that, in turn, might be the cause of or a contributing factor to the academic difficulties.

CONCLUSIONS

The data obtained from the social history along with the information obtained from observations, clinical interviews, and the mental status examination should lead to several basic conclusions. First, does the child or adolescent have a psychiatric disorder? If the answer is no, the reasons for the academic difficulties might be clarified through the other areas of assessment. If yes, is the difficulty due to a disruptive behavioral disorder (oppositional defiant disorder, conduct disorder), attention deficit hyperactivity disorder, or another psychiatric disorder?

If there is psychopathology, the clinician must decide whether the identified disorder is primary or secondary. Does the psychopathology contribute to or cause the academic difficulties? Alternatively, might the psychopathology be secondary to the academic difficulties, with their predictable sequence of frustrations and failures, plus the impact they have on individual and family functioning? The clinician must bear in mind that a psychiatric disorder can be exacerbated by family dysfunction or stress created by the school environment.

Each answer to the preceding array of questions helps the clinician clarify the cause(s) for the presenting problems. Usually the full picture is not clear until the complete set of medical and psychoeducation assessments are completed.

Assessment of the Family

The relationship between family stress and/or dysfunction and school-related problems is now well established. However, even in relatively well-functioning homes, the nature of family interactions, attitudes, and parenting practices might influence school functioning. The complex interaction between family characteristics and academic problems should not be viewed as a simple linear relationship whereby family variables lead to academic problems. Academic difficulties experienced by the child or adolescent are equally likely to influence and be influenced by the family environment.

The assessment should include a study of each

parent, the couple, and each sibling. This family assessment should result in an impression or conclusion that either there is family dysfunction or that the family is functioning well.

FAMILY DYSFUNCTION

The family history should include both immediate and past factors that may currently or might previously have affected the child's or adolescent's school behaviors and academic performance. Couples', marital, or family stress or dysfunction impinges on each individual in the family and makes each vulnerable to emotional, behavioral, or academic difficulties.

Each parent should be assessed. A parent with an emotional disorder may create a home environment that makes functioning difficult for all family members. In particular, because of this stress, the children might become unavailable for school and learning. If the parent is currently ill, the relationship to the child's or adolescent's academic difficulties may be apparent. However, a parent might have experienced a depression, psychotic episode, or other disorder at an earlier time. Parental psychopathology, and the resulting disruption in the family, may compromise the degree to which a child is available to learn. This disruption in the child's learning may in turn limit skill acquisition. The resulting deficits might explain the current academic problems.

There is a considerable overlap between disruptive behavioral disorders associated with academic difficulties and family dysfunction (Patterson, 1986). It is particularly useful to determine if the family exhibits high levels of marital discord, and whether serious degrees of overt family conflict are reported. Further, is there a tendency for similar conflicts to arise through abrasive exchanges between the family and the school? Is the father underinvolved in the parenting of the child or adolescent? Have the parent-child interactions involved an escalating cycle of negative exchanges? Is there a history of noncompliance and inconsistent parenting? These family variables are among the most prevalent characteristics associated with a diagnosis of conduct disorder and, to a lesser extent, oppositional defiant disorder (Patterson, 1986). When these family variables predate the academic difficulties, the clinician should consider the family dysfunction to be the cause of or a contributing cause to the academic difficulties.

While family dysfunction can contribute to academic difficulties, it is also possible that academic difficulties create stress within the family, so much so, indeed, that they result in family dysfunction (Silver, 1993). Parents might have different expectations or styles of "correcting" the problem. One might be firm and strict, the other understanding and permissive. Homework might become a battleground, both between the child or adolescent and parents and between the parents. The increased stress caused by the academic problems might create sibling conflicts as well.

In addition, the child's or adolescent's academic difficulties might mask problems between the parents. A parent might request the evaluation of a son or daughter in an effort to seek help for marital or family problems. Alternatively, the youngster may generate problems to keep the parents focused elsewhere than on their mutual recriminations.

OTHER FAMILY FACTORS

A dysfunctional family can have a profound impact on a child or adolescent, and, in particular, on the young person's availability and ability to learn. Even in a family assessed as functioning well, other family issues could affect an individual's academic performance .

The family's socioeconomic level can influence a student's availability for learning as well as convey negative messages about the importance of learning. The quality of schools and of education also may be involved in such issues.

What are the educational and vocational accomplishments of the parents? Such issues affect the value placed on education by the family, such that educational accomplishments are highly valued, not considered important, or not valued. It is helpful to compare the family's valuation of education in light of the child's or adolescent's intellectual abilities and academic accomplishments. For example, a child with modest intellectual abilities might have difficulty meeting the expectations of parents who are themselves high achievers and want their children to achieve. In contrast, if academics are not valued by the family, a student judged to be underachieving by teachers may never meet school expectations. As an example, some families emigrated to the United States from rural parts of certain Central American countries where educational opportunities were limited and where it was important for each child to leave school and go to work as early as possible. These parents might not feel that school success is important; instead, reaching an age when the adolescent can leave school and go to work is what counts.

Divorce causes stress for all family members (Heterington, Cox, & Cox, 1982). After a divorce, often the children live with a primary parent (usually the mother) and visit with the other parent. Over time, it may appear that the single-parent family is now functioning. Yet the divorce might still affect the child or adolescent psychologically and continue to contribute to academic difficulties. The loss of a father through divorce appears to have a particularly significant influence on a child's academic confidence; this is especially true with boys (Heterington et al., 1982). It is important, therefore, not only to evaluate the temporal relationship of a divorce to the onset of academic difficulties but also to explore residual problems resulting from a divorce that took place at an earlier time in the life of the child or adolescent.

Following a divorce, the emotional health of the primary parent is particularly important. This parent still might be overwhelmed, angry, and/or depressed, thus being less available to each child. The economic level of the new, single-parent family is frequently much lower than that of the previously intact family. Not only might the single parent be overwhelmed and forced to work long hours, but the type of living arrangements, neighborhood, and lifestyle might be equally reduced from what had been their status before the divorce.

An intact and functional family might have difficulty with parenting issues relating to children's cooperation and compliance. At home, noncompliance might take the form of a youngster failing either to complete assigned chores, go to bed on time, or get to school on time. This noncompliance might be related to parental psychopathology (Patterson, 1986) or stress; however, it also might relate to family values or to an absence of a shared philosophy on child rearing. A parent might interact with the child in an ineffective manner. Such ineffective parenting might result in a child never recognizing the value associated with compliant behavior, which might in turn give rise to difficulties in the classroom.

In school, noncompliance might limit the degree to which the child or adolescent is available for learning (Patterson, 1986). The child might fail to compete assignments essential for adequate academic attainment. A child might fail to engage in teacher-directed seat work or to take turns in class discussions. The net result translates into school failure or, at best, underachievement.

To evaluate the degree to which noncompliance affects school performance, often it is useful to determine the degree to which the child is compliant at home. Is the child typically obedient in response to parental requests? Does he or she complete homework? Chores?

Another variable to consider with a family that appears to be functioning well is the time and energy each parent can devote to being a parent, especially, in this case, to being available for school-related activities. One or both parents might work long hours because of either financial need and/or career demands. A parent might bring home work that takes up every evening. Under such circumstances, there is little time or energy to invest in being a parent.

With some 2-parent working families, the children are dropped off at a preschool program by 7:00 to 7:30 A.M. and picked up at 6:00 to 6:30 P.M. By the time the family arrives home, the children are as tired and unavailable for school-related activities as are the parents.

Assessment of the Community and School

THE COMMUNITY

To understand a child or adolescent fully, the clinician must have some grasp of that youngster's total world. This understanding goes beyond the family and includes the neighborhood, the fuller community, and the school (Ostrander, 1993). School experiences focus on specific classrooms and teachers. Yet the general atmosphere and philosophy of the school are of equal importance. So, too, are the general atmosphere and philosophy of the community and its members.

Information from the parents plus the clinician's own knowledge and experiences can be used to put together a picture of the local neighborhood and the fuller community. What are the main cultural influences? Is the neighborhood safe? Are children considered important? Are education and educational success considered important? In some socioeconomic groups, doing well in school is considered critical to improving one's future. In other groups, doing well in school may be considered irrelevant, or even elitist.

What about other children and adolescents in the neighborhood or community? Is going to school and doing well valued, or is it unimportant? Might the general value system among peers be that of school indifference or school defiance? If the child or adolescent being assessed tries to achieve in school, might he or she be seen as different or be rejected by peers?

THE SCHOOL

Information about the school is of great importance. Does the child or adolescent go to a school that places great importance on learning? Is there considerable pressure to succeed? Or is the school philosophy one of indifference, where no one is expected to do well, and where goals are not high? The school principal and other administrators can set the tone for the school. Teachers can be excited about teaching or "burned out." Perhaps family members want their son or daughter to do well, but the general nonverbal message by the staff or by peers in the school is one of indifference to academic success.

Some children and adolescents go to a parochial school or to a school where all students are of the same sex. Some schools have students from multiple ethnic backgrounds, where many different languages are spoken. Each school offers special characteristics that should be considered during the evaluation. Some schools have a dual curriculum, one in English and one in another language. This bilingual demand may contribute to the stress experienced by the student being evaluated.

Difficulties in school may relate to the teacher's style of teaching or personality. Is he or she competent? Might the school problems relate to the teacher's ability to teach or style of relating to the students? Might the teacher be under personal stress or have an emotional problem? Might there be a personality conflict between the teacher and the child or adolescent being evaluated?

If the individual being evaluated has been identified as having a disability, for example a learning disability and/or Attention Deficit Hyperactivity Disorder, are the appropriate services and professionals available? All public schools are expected to provide necessary services for students with special needs; however, private schools may not have such services. If services are available, are they adequate in quality and quantity? It is not uncommon to see that a student has been identified as having a disability and then to find that minimal or inadequate services are provided. On paper, the services needed may appear to be adequate, but if examined closely, they are not effective. "Going to a resource room for special help for a learning disability three times a week" might, in reality, mean spending 30 minutes 3 times a week in this room along with 5 or 7 other children, no one of whom receives individual attention.

If a child or adolescent has a disability, the classroom teacher must be knowledgeable about the disability as such; about the requisite specific accommodations in the classroom, the curriculum, and the teaching style; and about the necessary compensatory skills that need to be taught. Sometimes a student is identified as having a disability and for part of the day, receives services outside the classroom. Yet in the regular classroom, the teacher continues to teach as if the student had no problems, criticizing or grading down work that is considered inadequate. There should be professionals within the school system who work with the regular classroom teacher. Has such help from the school psychologist, special education consultant, speech and language pathologist, or others been available?

Also of importance is the classroom itself. Is it contained and structured or open and unstructured? Are the curriculum and style of teaching appropriate? Are there adequate teaching materials?

344

Reaching Conclusions Following the Assessment

The process involved in assessing a child or adolescent with academic difficulties requires an understanding of the individual, the family, the school environment, and the community; in brief, it is complex. As the clinician obtains the history relating to each of these areas, certain constellations appear to be ruled out, while others remain as possible factors or contributing factors.

Based on the findings, a formal clinical assessment can be done, including necessary medical, psychological, or educational evaluations. The information from the history and the clinical assessment should result in a diagnosis or diagnoses.

It is unusual to find 1 specific problem as the cause for the presenting academic difficulties. To add to this confusion, sometimes the individual or family problems are not causing the academic difficulties but are a result of the emotional stresses experienced by the individual, the parents, and the family because of the academic difficulties.

Even if the individual or family problems are considered secondary to a primary academic difficulty, these problems may need to be addressed as well. In short, all possibilities must be considered.

Finally, understanding the variables involved that appear to be central to explaining the academic difficulties will allow for a comprehensive treatment plan utilizing appropriate interventions.

REFERENCES

Heterington, E. M., Cox, M., & Cox, R. (1982). Effects of divorce on parents and children. In B. Lamb (Ed.), *Nontraditional families* (pp. 233–288). Hillsdale, NJ: Lawrence Erlbaum.

Homes, C. T., & Matthews, K. M. (1984). The effects of non-promotion on elementary and junior high school pupils: A meta analysis. *Review of Educational Research, 45,* 225–236.

Martin, R. P. (1986). *Assessment of personality and behavioral problems.* New York: Guilford Press.

Ostrander, R. (1993). Clinical observations suggesting a learning disability. *Child and Adolescent Psychiatric Clinics of North America, 2,* 249–263.

Patterson, G. R. (1986). Performance models for antisocial boys. *American Psychologist, 41,* 432–444.

Silver, L. B. (1993). The secondary emotional, social, and family problems found with children and adolescents with learning disabilities. *Child and Adolescent Psychiatric Clinics of North America, 2,* 295–308.

56 / Trauma History

Lenore Terr

Posttraumatic stress disorder depends on the occurrence of a known traumatic event—one that is life-threatening, involves physical injury, or is threatening to the physical integrity of the individual or someone he or she is with. Although the definitions of trauma change slightly as new professional committees consider what would be traumatic for anyone—adult, child, or infant (e.g., American Psychiatric Association, 1980, 1987, 1994)—one point remains key to all of the definitions: There must be a traumatic event or events in order to make the diagnosis of posttraumatic stress disorder.

In assessing the "traumatic event," the clinician

often encounters a problem. Children come for evaluation from adoption agencies, foster homes, war zones, scenes of torture and/or neglect. In these instances, there may be little to no available history and few, if any, historians. In situations in which the child's guardians or parents are perpetrating the serious abuses or neglectful acts themselves, the parental histories likely will not match the extent of the children's injuries, malnutrition, or growth failures (Kempe, Silverman, Steele, Droegmueller, & Silver, 1962). Some children—as in the post–Vietnam War baby "market" and the Chinese baby adoption program—come with no relevant histories at all. Thus although it is important for clinicians to consider traumatic "event(s)" to be keys to the diagnosis of posttraumatic stress disorder, some of these events must be inferred from discussions with third parties, such as foster parents, agency workers, hospital nurses; implied in the behaviors of the child him- or herself; and researched by the consultant from legal documents, old newspaper accounts, medical examinations, and accounts from neighbors, teachers, and siblings.

A second problem arises when we go about applying such definitions as "life-threatening" or "bodily harm" to the various traumatic events of early childhood. Very young children do not fully understand "life" and "death," so they cannot comprehend threats against their lives as such. They often do not comprehend the kinds of bodily damage that occur with various actions (i.e., the 2-year-old who runs out into the street). In fact, other issues, such as fear of the loss of care, of the loss of parents, and of further fear, often pose more of a threat to infants and young children than the fear of death and/or of bodily harm. For example, in the Chowchilla schoolbus kidnapping of 1976, 23 children, ages 5 to 14 at the time of their mass abduction, feared separation from loved ones, death, and further frights (Terr, 1979). Only 1 child in that group feared bodily harm.

To children, events well beyond what would have been expected in an ordinary childhood may qualify as traumatic. Such events might include witnessing a miscarriage, witnessing adults having sex, witnessing an attack by 1 parent against the other, or coming home from school to find the household furniture and a parent gone. Trauma in childhood also has something to do with the conditions under which the youngster is living. In a war zone, homes may be found vacated as a matter of course. In a peaceful period, such an event might be devastating.

In considering the nature of "traumatic events" in infancy and in childhood, therefore, the definitions of such events must be modified to take into account the child's social situation and developmental level at the time of the event.

In assessing the effect of traumatic events, abuses, and neglectful situations in the lives of children, clinicians must recognize that all traumas and neglectful acts are external to the child. They create internal biological responses (McLeer, 1992), but the origins for these are psychological. Mind and brain changes after extreme outside events lead to biological cycles of response. But in assessing a traumatized youngster, mental health professionals must understand the original, external etiology and the way that this pathogen impacted the particular child. As clinicians, we must do all that we can to know the event and to know the child. What context did the child apply to the event? And what corrections did the child attempt to pursue?

The Child's History

DIRECT HISTORIES OF TRAUMA OCCURRING PRIOR TO THE AGE OF 3

Children over the ages of 2½ to 3 are usually able to tell the story of a very recent traumatic event (Terr, 1988). They are not, however, able to give the complete stories of very old traumas. It appears that a certain amount of hippocampal and medial-thalamic development is necessary before full verbal (explicit or declarative) memories of old traumas can fully be registered, stored, and retrieved (Terr, 1994). Over the years, psychological researchers have found that, for distant national traumas, such as the assassination of President John F. Kennedy, or for more ordinary events, nontraumatic ones, such as the birth of a younger sibling, children's memories do not take complete and retrievable form until sometime in the fourth to fifth year of life (Pillemer & White, 1989). This does not mean, however, that the assessing professional would choose to omit asking the child for a description of the "best" and the "worst" thing(s) that have ever happened in his or her experience. If the child remembers any fragments of an old traumatic event, these fragments may be recounted in response to a "worst" question.

After these general questions are asked, if mental health professionals already know that the traumatic event in question has to do with something specific—for instance, a baby-sitter—it would be acceptable to ask the youngster to name current baby-sitters and to go backward and name other ones from the past. Often the child can no longer remember the key baby-sitter. Then it would be acceptable to inquire if the child has any memories of each baby-sitter whom he or she has named and memories of any other ones that have not been named. The point here is that the questioning of a child must consistently present several possibilities or an entirely open-ended possibility for answers. It is important to provide considerable room for the child's open-ended response. Opposites or a group of possibilities may be asked, but interviewers always must be extremely careful in approaching a child about a supposed traumatic event in infancy or toddler life.

An examination for trauma is not identical to a verbal history of trauma. Certain behaviors, fears, nightmares, modes of play, attitudes about the future, reflect the child's nonexplicit, nonverbal remembrances of an early traumatic event. These behaviors may imply the event but do not provide a full narrative of it. Unfortunately for the children who have nothing but implicit, nonverbal memories of a traumatic situation, all that they can "tell" of these events will be through their behaviors and symptomatologies. In certain instances, therapists will have to help to make plans for such children entirely on the basis of nonverbal histories. Children must be taken as they present—and sometimes the only people who can shed light on children who have no verbal memories of old traumas are past therapists, medical practitioners, investigating detectives, or reporters who covered the story for a newspaper. The mental health clinician must coordinate each of these interpretations. Consider this case example.

CASE EXAMPLE

Beth Amelia came to my office at the age of 2. She was in the process of being adopted from a small agency. The prospective adoptive parents had been told

nothing about the child; thus they could not ascertain whether she had been traumatized. In coming to her permanent foster home to pick her up, they found the 2-year-old eating her dinner off the floor. When Beth Amelia first viewed her new, adoptive father, she screamed in terror. That night, when her new mother tried to bathe the child and wash her hair, Beth Amelia screamed as if she were being murdered. The child hollered repeatedly during the night. She could not stand to be touched.

An assessment of the child was attempted. The child's actions, although seeming posttraumatic, could not be tied to a particular event or events. A thorough physical examination and a full set of X rays were normal. Although I advised the parents not to adopt Beth Amelia (she appeared to be very seriously affected), the prospective parents went through with the adoption procedures and, when she was 4 years old, applied again to me for help.

At the present time, Beth Amelia is 15 years old. I have followed her at various times, although no thoroughly effective treatment program has ever been found. One large clue, however, turned up. When she was 5, Beth Amelia's foster mother made the local television news for having killed her boyfriend—a man, she said, whom she had found sexually abusing her daughter during her bath. Since this man had been a boyfriend for some time, it was likely that Beth Amelia's screams at men, shampooing, and baths originated with sexual attacks by him.

Beth Amelia currently attends a boarding high school for "difficult" children. She has never let herself trust her family or show much affection, yet she clings to them with infantile insistence. She shows some promise of more mature attachments to peers or to the parent substitutes at school, but at present, this is not fully adequate. In addition to her posttraumatic stress disorder, her reactive attachment disorder (most likely from trauma and neglect in infancy [Bingham & Harmon, 1996; Zeanah, Mammen, & Lieberman, 1993]) still affects her. Each of these problems apparently evolved from neglectful and traumatic foster care. There is no way to know how Beth Amelia would have turned out had these social factors not intervened.

DIRECT HISTORIES OF TRAUMAS OCCURRING OVER THE AGE OF 3

Traumas occurring beyond the age of approximately 36 months are not blocked from the child's explicit or declarative memory unless the defenses against memory are used—repression (purposely or inadvertently putting an event out of mind), dissociation (failing to fully register an event due to willful or inadvertent inattention), splitting (attributing an event to a "bad" side of the self or a "bad" side of a significant person), displacement (focusing attention away from the event to another situation), and others—are employed to stop remembrance. (See Vaillant, 1992, for more complete explanations and examples of the various defenses.) With exceptions, most of these defenses are reserved for ongoing or repeated, expected traumatic events, in which the child anticipates and prepares to dampen or mute physical and/or emotional pain. Children have described such forms of dissociation as "escapes" to other planets or vivid imaginings of pleasant scenes in order to block incoming memories (Terr, 1991). They have described purposeful suppression of thoughts, leading to eventual repression (Terr, 1994). Of course, some traumatic events are accompanied by head injury or delirium in which organic amnesias occur. But for singly occurring, terrifying events happening after age 3, most children are able to remember. These event memories may be completely true or generally true with false detail. If a child makes up the story of an event, the memories may be entirely false or false with true detail.

The child is asked open-ended questions about the event during the assessment: "Tell me about what happened that time you went to the hospital," for example, or "Can you talk to me about your accident? I'd like to hear all about it." The therapist goes on to ask for open-ended expansions of the story. "I know it's hard," for example, "but I need to know more about the person who grabbed you. Tell me everything you can remember about that person and about that day and what happened."

After children supply as detailed a story as they can—frequently, in robotish fashion, but often with agitation, a visit to the bathroom, a check in the waiting room for parents, some occasional weeping or expressions of rage—mental health professionals are obliged to gather specific information that has not yet been clarified. "Exactly what did the man do to you?" "What body part did he use on you?" "What part of your body did he do things to?" If the child has no words for it, interviewers can draw an outline of a child-size body and ask the child to draw in the spot or indicate what occurred. Sometimes it is helpful to have

children make a map of the scene, mark themselves with an X or O, and then mark in the other people who were there, while telling the clinician the story. Maps for the older child and simple diagrams for the younger child are particularly useful aids in eliciting stories of terrible events. Neural connections have been found in the hippocampus that process information having to do with spatial sense (Gustafsson & Wigström, 1990). These very active pathways are near to or identical with the ones that handle explicit memory.

Aids in taking traumatic histories from children should be considered with extreme caution. Hypnosis or amytal interviewing is not recommended because of children's high suggestibility and their extraordinary eagerness to please adults. (See Ceci and Bruck, 1995.) Suggestive questioning must be avoided with children. Such ideas as "Did he kiss you?" "Did he put his hands in places where he shouldn't?" may be established in the minds of the adults assessing a supposedly sexually abused child—but if the sex abuse did indeed occur, the child must be encouraged to tell the story without hints. Full disclosures from children remain a problem, however, because many youngsters cannot tell their story without first being given some clue as to what the story will be about (Saywitz, Goodman, Nicholas, & Moan, 1991). The assessing therapist must be careful with these clues or props to stories. Although their use is debatable (Yates & Terr, 1988), anatomically explicit dolls have been considered by California courts to be too suggestive to be the basis of courtroom testimony (*In re Amber B. and Teela B.*, 1987 and *In re Christine C. and Michael C.*, 1987). These dolls signal that the interviewer wants to know about sexual things.

In talking to children directly about their traumas, the professional must not omit taking a complete history of nontraumatic matters as well. Developmental, educational, and other diagnostic possibilities must be skimmed in any assessment. They will be inquired about more deeply if the child gives a positive response.

A child's history also includes an exploration of signs and symptoms, except when the child is too young to relate a history of these. In matters having to do with trauma, children are often better assessors of their own symptoms than are their parents (Terr, 1979).

Parents' Histories

HISTORIES FROM PARENTS WHO ARE NOT SUSPECTED OF PERPETRATION OF TRAUMA OR NEGLECT

Many children are traumatized or harmed through no fault of their parents. Some of these experiences may have occurred in natural circumstances—tornadoes, hurricanes, fires, and the like. Others may have occurred entirely accidentally. Still others may have been instigated by individuals far removed from the child's own family. Although the trauma may be external to the parents' control, as in an earthquake, parents' narratives are often guilt-ridden and full of defenses, such as denial. People who have given birth to a perfect baby usually have difficulty tolerating the idea that something beyond their personal control came along to make this child imperfect. Bearing all of this in mind, it may be necessary to gather history from other individuals who are third parties to the child's ordeal—and it becomes all the more important to also gather histories directly from the child. Often an acknowledgment of the parents' sense of guilt can be helpful in eliciting the story.

It is a tactical decision whether to separate the 2 parents in eliciting histories of a childhood trauma. It is also a tactical decision whether to hire a translator for parents with limited facility in the clinician's language. In one instance, a father who spoke better English than his wife translated what she said in a way that made her seem negligent and violent. On the next occasion, when she spoke through a neutral translator, the husband's interpretation was found to be biased.

Many times children's traumas have occurred out of their parents' view. In these instances it is still important to take a full history. Parents are aware of their children's behaviors and fears; it is necessary to ask about all of this, even though the child already may have supplied history regarding these symptoms. Ordinarily parents are far more aware than children of behavioral reenactments, even though the parents often miss the linkages of this behavior to the trauma. Parents notice characterological changes, such as extreme passivity or loss of lovingness, in their children and readily reveal these; while the children do not.

In addition to the history of the trauma, a history of the child's development, other childhood disorders, and the parents' current and past functioning as well as family functioning is necessary. All of these factors figure into a full understanding of the child's condition and how it is being handled at home. It is also very important to learn how the child's trauma-related behaviors are being handled by each parent. Do they agree? What are they doing and what have they done previously in response to their child?

HISTORIES FROM PARENTS SUSPECTED OF CAUSING TRAUMA

Unfortunately, a large amount of childhood trauma and neglect is perpetrated by parents. At times parents invent stories of childhood trauma and neglect in the course of contentious divorces, custody determinations, and dysfunctional relationships (Benedek & Schetky, 1985). True trauma occurs in many homes in which the nontraumatizing parent plays a complicitous role by denying that any harm is coming to his or her child. And the number of children who, every year, are physically battered, sexually misused, or grossly neglected in their own homes by their own parent(s) is indeed staggering.

A definition of child abuse, as put forward by a team from the University of Colorado that helped to define this condition (Kempe et al., 1962), included the fact that abused children have signs of injuries that do not correspond to what the children's parents offer as explanations. Thus, in taking histories from parents whose children show the wounds, scars, and internal changes of physical or sexual abuse, histories cannot be accepted at face value. On the other hand, the loss of personal liberties or the loss of the child to the family is a potentially devastating consequence of any abuse. The therapist must take a very careful and documented history (with handwritten word-for-word notes). These notes may become written evidence in a legal proceeding. They also may become part of a crucial history that determines where and with whom the child will live.

The history of the child's physical and/or emotional condition is taken in full from the possibly abusing parents. Often the parents are seen one at a time to establish if their narratives are consistent. It is helpful to see each parent, even when one is accusing the other. However, such assessments often have to take place without the cooperation of the accused parent.

In cases of possible abuse or neglect, it is important to ascertain if either parent holds unrealistic or exaggerated attitudes toward the child. Frequently, in parental abuse, displacements of rage, sexuality, or personal helplessness come from the offending parent toward the child (e.g., "she is a witch," "he is too dependent on me," "he is more destructive than my other children" [Galdston, 1965; Terr, 1970]). Clinicians also may become aware of the protectiveness of a parent toward an offending "significant other" or a stepparent. Whenever possible, clinicians should ask to see any significant partners so that the full family network can be assessed. (For further information on family interviewing and child abuse assessments, see Chapter 62 and 67.)

In intrafamilial assessments for abuse or neglect, siblings often play a key role in exposing the problems. Frequently they have experienced the problems themselves or have observed them directly. It is important to see siblings—sometimes the ones nearest in age, sometimes the ones of the same sex, sometimes all of them—in order to help to determine the nature and the extent of the traumatic events.

All 50 states require that suspected sexual or physical abuse be reported. Although the reporting laws vary, they are relatively uniform in that a suspected (not proven) case is to be reported. The physician should inform parents that a report will be filed, that it is mandated, not voluntary, and that the investigating authorities will be the ones to decide whether to pursue the matter further. It is hoped that the assessment of the child will be complete or virtually complete at the time of this legally mandated report. Thus, whenever possible, a child's assessment for intrafamilial trauma or neglect should be accomplished within a few days. If a child with suspected abuse or neglect is dropped from the assessment process, a report should be filed.

Third-Party Histories

Often the professional must gather histories from people other than the child's parents. Occasionally the police or the prosecuting attorney's office already has gathered such information and will make it available to the assessing clinician. Occasionally there are neighbors' reports, reports from eyewitnesses, or newspaper accounts about the child's plight. Although none of these third-party accounts will establish a child's history as the "truth," they are very helpful in establishing what in general happened to the child.

Traumatized adolescent or adult children and their parents often are eager to assist in the process of making third-party reports available. Doing so may offer such a person a renewed sense of competence to do something active in his or her best interests. An adult, named Felice, for instance, was able to visit the police and the district attorney of her old hometown in order to learn what ultimately happened to her kidnapper and sexual molester (from her midchildhood). She learned that he had been a serial rapist who was caught and incarcerated 2 years after the incident that had involved her. Felice found that this information-seeking marked a turning point in her recovery.

Clinicians must insist that agencies dealing with children give them full information on these children. This insistence must come, on an individual basis, from all clinicians. It also must be accomplished through political action. Clinicians need full histories of children in order to assess them completely. Nothing could fill this need better than full and complete histories from the agencies that have assessed and cared for these children in the past.

REFERENCES

American Psychiatric Association. (1980). *Diagnostic and statistical manual of mental disorders* (3rd ed.). Washington, DC: Author.

American Psychiatric Association. (1987). *Diagnostic and statistical manual of mental disorders* (3rd ed., rev.). Washington, DC: Author.

American Psychiatric Association. (1994). *Diagnostic and statistical manual of mental disorders* (4th ed.). Washington, DC: Author.

Benedek, E. P., & Schetky, D. H. (1985). Allegations of sexual abuse in child custody and visitation disputes. In D. H. Schetky & E. P. Benedek (Eds.), *Emerging issues in child psychiatry and the law.* New York: Brunner/Mazel. (Chapter 11, pp. 145–156.)

Bingham, R. D., & Harmon, R. J. (1996). Traumatic stress in infancy and early childhood: Expression of distress and developmental issues. In C. R. Pfeffer (Ed.), *Severe stress and mental disturbances in children* (pp. 499–532). Washington, DC: American Psychiatric Press.

Ceci, S. J., & Bruck, M. (1995). *Jeopardy in the courtroom: A scientific analysis of children's testimony.* Washington, DC: American Psychological Association.

Galdston, R. (1965). Observations on children who have been physically abused and their parents. *American Journal of Psychiatry, 122,* 440–443.

Gustafsson, B. & Wigström, H. (1990). Long-term potentiation in the hippocampal CA1 region. *Progress in Brain Research, 83,* 223–232.

In re Amber B. and Teela B. (1987), 191 Cal. App. 3rd 682.

In re Christine C. and Michael C. (1987) 191 Cal. App. 3rd 676.

Kempe, C. H., Silverman, F. N., Steele, B. F., Droegmuller, W., & Silver, H. K. (1962). The battered-child syndrome. *Journal of the American Medical Association, 81,* 17–24.

McLeer, S. V. (1992). Post-traumatic stress disorder in children. In G. Burrows, M. Roth, & R. Noyes, Jr. (Eds.), *Handbook of anxiety 5: Contemporary issues and prospects for research in anxiety disorders.* New York: Elsevier. (Chapter 17, pp. 329–352.)

Pillemer, D., & White, S. (1989). Childhood events recalled by children and adults. *Advances in Child Development and Behavior, 21,* 297–340.

Saywitz, K. J., Goodman, G. S., Nicholas, E., & Moan, S. (1991). Children's memories of physical examinations involving genital touch: Implications for reports of child sexual abuse. *Journal of Consulting and Clinical Psychology, 59,* 682–691.

Terr, L. C. (1970). A family study of child abuse. *American Journal of Psychiatry, 127,* 125–131.

Terr, L. C. (1979). Children of Chowchilla: A study of psychic trauma. *Psychoanalytic Study of the Child, 34,* 547–623.

Terr, L. C. (1988). What happens to the memories of early trauma? A study of twenty children under age five at the time of documented traumatic events. *Journal of the American Academy of Child and Adolescent Psychiatry, 27,* 96–104.

Terr, L. C. (1991). Childhood traumas: An outline and overview. *American Journal of Psychiatry, 148,* 10–20.

Terr, L. C. (1994). *Unchained memories: True stories of traumatic memories, lost and found.* New York: Basic Books.

Vaillant, G. (Ed.). (1992). *Ego mechanisms of defense: A guide for clinicians and researchers.* Washington, DC: American Psychiatric Press.

Yates, A., & Terr, L. C. (1988). Anatomically correct dolls: Should they be used as a basis for expert testimony? *Journal of the American Academy of Child and Adolescent Psychiatry, 27,* 254–257.

Zeanah, C. H., Mammen, O. F., & Lieberman, A. F. (1993). Disorders of attachment. In C. H. Zeanah (Ed.), *Handbook of infant mental health* (pp. 332–349). New York: Guilford Press.

57 / **Disabilities History**

Henry T. Sachs III

Children and adolescents may present with a broad range of disabilities that can have mild to catastrophic effects on their development. These disabilities place young people at greater risk of psychopathology (Matson & Barrett, 1993). Often disabilities present special challenges to the clinician eliciting a presenting problem and clinical history for a given child or adolescent. However, a thorough history incorporating issues specific to developmental disabilities provides essential information in formulating an appropriate treatment plan (Szymanski, 1980). Forethought, creativity, and patience are necessary characteristics of a clinician's interactions with youths with disabilities and their families.

Preparation

Frequently a youngster with developmental disabilities has had previous cognitive, medical, educational, and/or physical assessments. Knowledge of the child's current level of functioning allows the clinician to prepare for an initial interview that will be both productive and appreciated by the child or adolescent and the caregivers. (See also Chapter 73.)

Interview

Whenever possible, interviews of youngsters with disabilities should take place in a spacious, well-lit room with minimal distractions and developmentally appropriate toys and activities. Competent sign language interpreters, augmentative communication devices, room for a wheelchair, and the like should be available as needed.

An adolescent who has the cognitive and physical abilities to meet alone with the clinician should be given that opportunity. However, in many cases, caregivers will join the patient in the interview. Whenever appropriate, the child should introduce the caregivers and describe their role in his or her life.

Many children with disabilities will have communication or cognitive limitations that slow the interview process. However, including them in the interview process is time well spent. In children with cognitive or receptive language delays, the clinician must speak at developmentally appropriate levels without being infantilizing. This usually means short, simple questions asked in a slow, jargon-free manner after good eye contact is established. The interviewer must not assume that the youngsters understand questions and must

check in frequently with them on their understanding of the situation. Special attention should be given to orienting the children to the purpose of the interview and what can be expected (Sigman, M. 1985).

For youngsters with cognitive delays, concrete answers must be interpreted carefully. As an example, it is not unusual for clinicians to misinterpret children's reports of "hearing voices." The clinician should look carefully at such statements and attempt to clarify if the patient actually is having auditory hallucinations. The choice of words may be the result of immature language development, poor insight, and/or substitution of symptoms. The clinician always must assess patients' statements and concerns at their developmental age, not their chronological age. These young people may have great difficulty in assessing their own affective status. Anxiety often is misinterpreted as inattention, hyperactivity, mania, or irritability. Sadness often is expressed in aggression toward self or others. (See also Chapter 73.)

Frequently children with disabilities have experienced numerous social failures and rejection. Even within clinical settings they are often ignored as clinicians and caregivers talk for them. It is important to begin the interview process addressing them in a nonthreatening, open, respectful manner. They should be given the opportunity to feel comfortable with the setting (Hurley, 1989).

Chief Complaint and History of Presenting Problem

While many components of obtaining a chief complaint and history of presenting problem for youngsters with developmental disabilities are similar to the process used with other youngsters, the emphasis may be somewhat different. Mood, thought, or behavioral concerns must be put in the context of the child's or adolescent's disabilities and developmental level. His or her cognitive, language, social, and motor skills should be carefully reviewed. What were the youngster's level of functioning and baseline behaviors immediately prior to onset of problematic behaviors, or were the behaviors always present?

While changes in situation and environment have an impact on all youngsters, the effect of change on those with limited adaptive skills may be more pronounced. For some of these young people, routine provides the structural cues for the day. Even slight changes can cause significant confusion and frustration.

Clinicians must be sensitive to the patient's developmental level, not age, when considering the impact of change. Did any environmental or personal changes occur around the time of symptom onset? This may include moves, class or teacher changes, changes in parents' work schedule, or siblings leaving home. For example, a 13-year-old with moderate mental retardation and mild cerebral palsy became increasingly aggressive in school and destructive at home when her older sister, who always shared her bedroom, left home for college. With assistance eventually she was able to express verbally this loss and the behaviors ceased.

Young people with disabilities are very susceptible to medical issues. Have there been changes in psychiatric or nonpsychiatric medications, including over-the-counter medication? Has there been an exacerbation of any medical conditions? Has there been any changes in bowel habits? Otitis media and constipation often present as behavioral changes in nonverbal children. Recent surgeries or hospital stays may lead to regressed behaviors.

The regularity of difficulties should be reviewed. In one case, a 5-year-old nonverbal, autistic child began crying and becoming increasingly irritable each day at 3:30 P.M., and it lasted until supper. Hypothesizing that this behavior may be related to hunger, a larger snack was given at 3:00 P.M., and the symptoms resolved. Concrete or nonverbal pubertal females may have monthly difficulties related to the physical discomfort of menses, which they cannot understand nor describe. Children may be stressed by environmental factors that occur on a periodic or regular schedule. An example is the 7-year-old with cerebral palsy and limited hearing who becomes aggressive at home each Tuesday morning to avoid the scheduled class trip, which is very anxiety-provoking.

A thorough description of problematic behav-iors is essential. Antecedent events should be reviewed in detail. Are problematic behaviors environmentally specific? What is the family's or caregiver's response to these behaviors? This information will assist in planning behavioral interventions.

Social History

In addition to the standard question around the chief complaint and history of presenting problems, certain topics always should be reviewed in gathering the history of young people with disabilities (Matson & Mulick, 1991). While their academic progress is important, the type of class they are in, the ranges of disabilities of peers, and how they and their classmates are perceived by the school at large may be more significant. Children with developmental disabilities may be in self-contained classrooms or integrated into non–special education classrooms with in-class or resource support. Each of these settings places different demands on the children.

School officials often struggle to create appropriate peer groups in the special education classroom. Children functioning at significantly higher or lower levels than their peers may have greater difficulty. One 14-year-old girl with significant congenital abnormalities and moderate mental retardation was the only verbal student in her class. She engaged in life-threatening self-injury on a daily basis while in class and physically assaulted her parents each day as they prepared her for school. After she was moved to a class with appropriate verbal peers—and with no other changes being made—all self-injury ceased immediately and her affect was bright each morning as she got ready for school.

Social stresses across environments is another important topic. This issue grows in significance as children enter adolescence. Nondisabled children often accept young children with developmental disabilities as peers in the neighborhood and school. Adolescence heralds a period of decreased tolerance for differences. As children with mild to moderate cognitive delays or physical disabilities become increasingly aware of their limitations in comparison to same-age peers, those same peers become increasingly distant and intolerant. Children with disabilities often become socially isolated or targeted by peers. This situation may be exacerbated by difficulties in mastering age-appropriate milestones such as dating, achieving in athletics, having a job, and getting a driver's license. Low self-esteem, social isolation, and limited adaptive skills often result in worsening depression and even suicidal ideation. Conversely, the young person may respond to changes in peer relations by attempting to "fit in" with adolescents who take advantage of the patient's limited insight and judgment. This situation can lead to educational, social, or legal problems as well as substance abuse.

Clinicians should review with patients their current social situation. How do they spend their free time? How many friends do they have in school or at home? How are they treated by classmates and other children in the neighborhood? What is their response to this treatment?

Youngsters with disabilities comprise a population that is at increased risk of sexual and physical abuse as well as neglect. These issues should be addressed carefully with patient and caregivers. Many of these young people struggle with physical and sexual development without the accompanying maturity in social skills.

Also, patient's and family's perception of the limitations their disability places on them is significant. Disabilities can be seen as challenges or burdens by patients, their families, and friends. Setting and meeting reasonable goals for success and working to overcome challenges have beneficial effects on self-esteem and resilience. Young people and families overwhelmed by a disability often fail to engage appropriate services and become frustrated easily. Their ability to engage in the assessment and future treatment in a therapeutic fashion may be limited. Asking specific questions about the impact of the disability on patient and family is helpful. Often observation of patient and family interactions during the session gives the most accurate assessment of how they are coping with the disability.

Finally, the clinician should have an understanding of the inconveniences associated with a child's disabilities (e.g., how much assistance is needed in activities of daily living, what are the travel restrictions, how frequent are medical appointments, etc.).

Past Developmental History

Emphasis should be placed on developmental milestones (Harris, J. C., 1995). When, if ever, did the child walk, speak, or engage in reciprocal interactions? Has there been constant progression, a regression, or has a plateau been reached in cognitive, language, social, and motor functioning? Deterioration in previously achieved milestones may reflect metabolic disorders affecting neurological functioning or significant environmental stressors. Such cases will require further clarification and will impact on treatment planning.

Previous services and their effectiveness should be reviewed. Sometimes services are removed prematurely and deterioration occurs. In other instances, appropriate services were never identified.

Family Psychiatric and Medical History

Young people with developmental delays are at increased risk for psychiatric disorders (Matson & Barrett, 1993). However, these disorders often present in an atypical fashion. Knowledge of disorders present in the family may resolve some ambiguities. For example, a 9-year-old with mild mental retardation and autism is very distractible, hyperactive, and sleeps poorly. A trial with stimulants is not successful. A more careful review of the family history reveals bipolar disorder. Lithium is started, and the symptoms decrease markedly.

Sleep regulation is a significant problem in this population and should be carefully assessed (Stores, 1992). Sleep disturbance is correlated with compulsive, impulsive, and self-injurious behaviors in youths with developmental disabilities. Families suffering from chronic sleep deprivation have less tolerance for behavioral difficulties and are less likely to implement beneficial environmental changes.

Family histories of mental retardation or other developmental delays may indicate chromosomal or metabolic disorders. Genetic counseling may be appropriate in these situations.

Family medical history also can be helpful. Allergies and sinusitis often are heralded by behavioral changes in developmentally delayed youngsters. Asthma and migraine headaches are other examples of disorders that may be incorrectly identified and mistreated. For example, a minimally verbal 16-year-old presents with 4 months of periodic "psychotic" behavior characterized by withdrawal, chasing "unseen objects" in his right visual field, a "right bloodshot eye," and a reddening of his right ear lasting 1 hour. Additional neuroleptics increased the frequency of these episodes, and an electroencephalogram was normal. After a strong family history of migraine headaches was noted, a diagnosis of migraine equivalents was made and appropriate treatment was begun.

Other Sources

For some youngsters with severe disabilities, the only source of information will be knowledgeable caregivers. Family members may be the only caregivers, but frequently special educators, special program or residential staff members, or members of interdisciplinary clinical teams are involved in the treatment of youths with disabilities. These people often are very knowledgeable. Receiving permission to speak with these clinicians, service providers, and educators is important.

The observations of those who provide the greatest amount of direct care to the youngster are valuable. Even with children who participate

in the interview process, reviewing their statements and clarifying inconsistencies or missed topics with caregivers is necessary. They can explain the patient's daily activities and living arrangement and put many of the child's statements into a broader context. They also provide much-needed information on developmental history, previous evaluations, and family history.

It is helpful to have the youngster leave the room for at least part of the history taking with caregivers. Clinicians often underestimate the receptive language abilities of youths with disabilities. Caregivers may be more attuned to this issue and feel uncomfortable discussing some issues in the patient's presence. Often the presenting complaint or specific clinical questions come from the caregivers, not the patient.

Conclusion

Children and adolescents with disabilities should be active participants in the history-gathering process. Their participation ensures a broader understanding of the presenting issues for the clinician. Clinicians often feel uncomfortable interacting with children with disabilities. Approaching each youngster with dignity, openness, and understanding increases the likelihood of a successful session. Incorporating assistance and information from other sources enhances the information a clinician will obtain.

REFERENCES

Harris, J. C. (1995). Developmental Neuropsychiatry, Vol. II (pp. 3–17). New York: Oxford University Press.

Hurley, A. D. (1989). Individual psychotherapy with mentally retarded individuals: A review and call for research. *Research in Developmental Disabilities, 10,* 261–275.

Matson, J. L., & Barrett, R. P. (1993). *Psychopathology in the mentally retarded* (2nd ed.). Boston: Allyn and Bacon.

Matson, J. L., & Mulick, J. A. (1991). *Handbook of mental retardation* (2nd ed.). New York: Pergamon Press.

Sigman, M. (1985). Individual and group psychotherapy with mentally retarded adolescents. In M. Sigman (Ed.), *Children with emotional disorders and developmental disabilities* (pp. 259–275). Orlando, FL: Grune & Stratton.

Stores, G. (1992). Annotation: Sleep Studies in Children with a Mental Handicap. *Journal of Child Psychology & Psychiatry., 33:* 1303–17.

Szymanski, L. (1980). Individual psychotherapy with retarded persons. In L. Szymanski & P. Tanquay (Eds.), *Emotional disorders of mentally retarded persons.* Baltimore, MD: University Park Press.

SECTION V
Clinical Observation

58 / Observation, Interview, and Mental Status Assessment (OIM): Parent(s)

L. Eugene Arnold and Peter S. Jensen

Observation, interview, and informal (or formal) mental status examination of the parent(s) can yield four categories of useful information:

- Information about the parent-child relationship.
- Information about the parent's functioning, which forms part of the child's environment, either supportive or stressful or some combination of stressful and supportive.
- Information about the parent-parent relationship, another important part of the child's environment, perhaps inseparable from parental functioning, and a source of either strength or stress or both.
- Clues about the child's problems: what psychopathological tendencies a child may have inherited and what symptoms the child has learned to manifest.

The Parent-Child Relationship

The quality of a child's relationship with significant adults, especially parents, is one of the most important risk/protective factors in a child's life (e.g., Bronfenbrenner, 1985; Kimchi & Schaffner, 1990). What the parent says about the relationship with the child may be entirely different from what is observed when the two are together, but both can be useful in assessing the parent-child relationship. What the parent says about it may reflect the parent's wish and/or parenting ideal, and thus offers evidence of what the parent strives for. It is also possible that what the parent says is more true of the day-to-day relationship than what is observed in the artificial situation of the interviewing room. It is therefore useful to inquire (if the parent does not volunteer it) whether the child's behavior is any different at the evaluation than at home.

CASE EXAMPLE

Ten-year-old Mike was being evaluated for obsessions about dirt and handwashing compulsions. While his mother was describing his usual behavior as affectionate, well-behaved, and respectful, Mike was taking verbal potshots at her, including one childish obscenity; he kicked at her purse, even after she attempted to correct him. On inquiry, the mother explained that Mike was very resistant to coming; he was embarrassed that his friends might find out he is seeing a shrink and think he is crazy. His embarrassment was aggravated by his mother's description of his characteristic good behavior, because his peer group was very sensitive about anybody being a "goodie-two-shoes." Subsequent observation of Mike and his mother proved her verbal description more accurate than the initial observation. The mother's explanation saved the clinician from the pursuit of an erroneous behavior disorder diagnosis.

Some additional questions to elicit the parent's view of the parent-child relationship would include, for example: How has his problem affected you? How does it feel having him in the family? Describe his relationship with you, or in a more leading fashion: Is he a pleasant child to have around? Is he easy to enjoy? Is he an affectionate child? What do you do together that's fun? How do you manage his behavior? How does he respond to your discipline? Is he honest with you? Has he lived up to your expectations?

The concept of "goodness of fit" (Henderson, 1913; Thomas et al., 1968) between a child's temperament and the parent's temperament/personality/values can be useful in several ways: (1) as an organizer of elicited information; (2) as a guilt-resolving explanation of friction in the parent-child relationship; and (3) as an introduction to eliciting information about the parent's (and child's) temperaments and their similarities and differences. Sometimes relationship problems can arise because the parent and child are so alike in temperament, and sometimes because they are so different; this depends on which traits are at issue and what values the parent puts on them. A parent-child dyad where both have high activity levels is likely to get along better than a dyad where one person is very active and one phlegma-

TABLE 58.1

Diagnostically useful indicators of the parent-child relationship that can be observed in parent and child behaviors at initial evaluation. Although for simplicity the child behaviors are listed on the left, the initiative can arise from either member of the dyad. Most of the interactions should be considered circular.

Child Initiative/Response	Parent Initiative/Response
Child leans or snuggles against parent.	Parent pats or strokes child affectionately or reassuringly.
Child looks toward parent before answering question.	Parent speaks for child. -or- Parent encourages child to answer for self.
Child asks parent for help with interview question.	Parent supportively jogs child's memory. -or- Parent belittles child for not remembering. -or- Parent orders child to "speak up." -or- Parent takes responsibility for answer.
Child interrupts.	Parent tolerates interruption, perhaps reinforces with attention or response. -or- Parent reprimands or corrects child's interruption.
Child erotically strokes or touches parent.	Parent erotically strokes or touches child. -or- Parent tolerates child's erotic advances submissively. -or- Parent reinforces child's erotic advances. -or- Parent sets appropriate limits.
Child demands candy or other item from parent's pocket or purse. -or- Child respectively requests candy or other item. -or- Child tantrums when refused request. -or- Child gets into parent's purse or pocket after being told "no."	Parent at first refuses, then submits. -or- Parent refuses firmly and sticks to it. -or- Parent consistently indulges every request of child. -or- Parent ignores child's legitimate request or question.
Child ignores parent's direction or question.	Parent offers child treat to "distract" from misbehavior. -or- Parent ignores child's misbehavior.
Child negotiates with parent.	Parent negotiates with child.
Child initiates most interactions.	Parent initiates most interactions.
Child clings to parent.	Parent is oversolicitous about child.
Child tries to shut parent up.	Parent is reluctant to state chief complaint in front of child. -or- Parent divulges inappropriate material in front of child.

tic. On the other hand, a dyad where both are stubborn is likely to have more conflict than if one is stubborn and the other adaptable. These examples should not lead to a conclusion that goodness of fit is determined by whether the traits are good or bad by some objective standard: the connotation of the last example could be changed entirely by substituting "firm" for "stubborn" and "wishy-washy" for "adaptable" and it would be just as true. Nevertheless, the cultural and other values the parents (and child) place on the traits do influence the fit. For example, a parent who subscribes to "macho" cultural values might find a

son's aggressiveness admirable, while a more genteel parent would find it offensive.

Although the parent's verbal description of the relationship with the child is important, the observed actions are likely to speak more accurately as well as more loudly than the parent's disclaimer. Table 1 lists some observed parent-child interactive behaviors that shout to the observer.

Inspection of Table 1 demonstrates that observed behaviors can carry either a positive or a negative sign (and sometimes even a neutral one). There can be normal behaviors reflecting a basically healthy parent-child relationship, or at least a relationship that is healthy in some aspects. On the other hand, observed behaviors can reflect varying degrees of pathology in the relationship and possibly also in the mental status of parent or child or both. Further, they can indicate such risk factors as overindulgence, overcoercion, eroticization, or rejection or such protective factors as warm support or respect for autonomy.

Table 1 may at first convey the impression that the child initiates and the parent reacts or responds. This seems to stand on its ear the outmoded clinical assumption that the parent acts on the child as a *tabula rasa* and is responsible in a unilateral fashion for the resulting relationship. This counterpoint may serve a debunking purpose; however, attributing all relationship responsibility to the child is no more realistic than attributing it all to the parent. The apparent primacy of child initiative is mainly an artifact of the column placement, with the child's behaviors placed on the left and the corresponding parent behaviors on the right. If the columns were reversed, the impression would be largely reversed also. In reality, the observed parent and child behaviors are points in a continuing cycle. While somebody must have started the cycle somewhere in the past, it is often impossible at the time of evaluation to attribute the primary responsibility with any certainty. In any event, for the cycle to continue, both parties must keep the ball bouncing.

However, this does not imply that the responsibility should always be divided equally. The impression of the child having the main initiative in the relationship may well be accurate for many child psychiatric syndromes, because the child's symptoms may tyrannize both child and parent. A good example is the series of classical studies by Barkley et al. (e.g., 1979) demonstrating significant changes in the mother-child relationship when a hyperactive child is effectively medicated with a stimulant. A parent who is observed to be hostile, rejecting, overdirective, or coercive may not be so endogenously, only reactively.

STEPPARENT-CHILD RELATIONSHIP

Considering that half of American children experience parental divorce, that the majority of single parents remarry (or just marry), and that children who experience the stress of parental di-

vorce and remarriage are at higher risk for some child psychiatric disorders, a very high proportion of children coming for mental health evaluation can be expected to have stepparents. In many cases the spouse of a custodial parent takes a stronger parenting role/relationship with the child than the noncustodial original parent. Naturally, everything discussed above about observation of natural/adoptive parents with the child applies equally to stepparents. There are, however, some additional considerations to keep in mind when assessing the stepparent-child relationship. These are discussed in detail by Fast and Chethick (1978). Among the many points they make are the following:

- Stepparents have three roles with the child: parent, stepparent, and nonparent friend, with frequent confusion as to which role is valid at the moment.
- Traditionally, the stepparent image carries strong negative connotations that impose psychological burdens on the relationship: much effort is wasted trying to disprove this unfair negative image, and the "need" to disprove it often holds the stepparent to an unrealistic standard of parenting perfection that no natural parent could be expected to attain.
- Paradoxically, the better a stepparent does, the more the child may feel (out of loyalty to the original parent) honor-bound to reject the attachment to the stepparent. Therefore, care must be exercised in the interpretation of any hostility manifested by the child toward the stepparent.
- Because of the weakening of the incest taboo, adolescents may feel a special need to keep a stepparent of the opposite sex at a distance. The stepparent may either be puzzled by this, misinterpret it, or share the psychological need for distance and reinforce it.

Such issues should be explored by observation and open-ended questions.

The Parent's Mental Status

In the course of taking the history about the child's problem and the family background, a good bit of information about the parent's mental status can easily be gathered. Certainly things like rate and rhythm of speech, appearance, demeanor, pessimistic or optimistic outlook, cognition, com-

TABLE 58.2

Parental diagnoses and symptoms affecting the child's diagnosis, prognosis, and/or treatment planning.

Parental Diagnosis	Genetic Loading	Psychosocial Effect on Child	High Abuse Risk
Alcoholism	+	+	+
Drug Abuse	?	+	+
Depression	+	+	
Mania	+	+	+
Anxiety	+	+	
Personality Disorder	+	+	+
Schizophrenia	+	+	?
Somatization/Hypochondriasis	?	+	Munchausen by proxy

pulsiveness, and anxiety will be rather apparent. This can readily be fleshed out with a few questions such as: How has all of this affected you? How are you managing with all of these problems in the family? and Do you have enough energy to keep up with all this? One of the most important parent syndromes to check for is depression because (1) it has a high prevalence; (2) it has a profound impact on the child; (3) it has been suspected to influence the parent's perceptions of the child (reported on rating scales, structured interview, and clinical history); and (4) it is a highly treatable problem that often goes undiagnosed. Most signs of depression can either be observed during history taking or easily elicited by questions such as those above.

Although a formal, comprehensive mental status exam of the parent is not always required, the trend among many experts is toward making this a routine part of a comprehensive child evaluation, often by means of a structured interview administered by a psychometrist. As a minimum, it is often possible to have parents complete a simple self-report symptom inventory on themselves. When such procedures are made a routine part of the overall assessment, even experienced clinicians may be surprised to discover that many parents who seem calm and asymptomatic as they describe their child's problems are themselves quite symptomatic. Systematic assessment procedures and screening tools for parents may provide information that becomes exceptionally useful in de-

fining risk and protective factors, determining the scope of the child's difficulties, and optimizing a treatment plan. Parents seldom balk at such procedures, as long as they are done empathically and with explanation about the value for the child's treatment. There are several valid reasons that can be offered to the parents: Many psychiatric disorders are genetic, and it can help in diagnosing the child's symptoms if the more clear-cut adult manifestations in parents or other relatives can be defined. Furthermore, if the parent or other relative has been successfully treated with a certain drug, there is a good chance that if the child has the same disorder, the child will respond to the same treatment; therefore, treatment is also facilitated. In addition, even if the child does not have the same disorder, it helps in understanding the child and in planning treatment for the child if there is a clear understanding of what kind of personal strengths the parent has to support the child and the treatment efforts. Table 2 summarizes some of these considerations.

Many enlightened parents come to the evaluation expecting that they themselves will also be evaluated. In a substantial minority of cases, this is actually the parents' hidden agenda; in Leo Kanner's famous terms, the child is the "ticket of admission" to treatment for the parent. Although the parent's mental state is not usually the cause of a child's mental health problem, it is not unheard of for a child's symptoms to remit when the parent is prescribed an antidepressant.

CASE EXAMPLE

Jill's mother had a sad appearance and broke into tears when describing Jill's problems. She was somewhat slow moving and slow talking, and further inquiry elicited other signs of depression. The evaluator explained to the mother that she would need all of her energy and strength to help Jill recover, and that therefore it was important to pay some attention to her own depressive syndrome. At this the mother brightened somewhat and said, "Well, actually I had been planning to ask you to recommend someone for me to see."

In his book on child interviewing, Greenspan (1981) includes an extensive chapter on interviewing parents. Salient among the points he makes are the following:

- Be warm, available, and expectant rather than structured and interrogative at the beginning. Give the parents a chance to structure the situation for themselves, since they obviously had their reasons for bringing the child. If they verbalize an expectation of being questioned, plead ignorance: "I don't know where to begin. I'd like to hear from you first" (Greenspan, 1981, p. 173). If they seem too anxious to begin, empathize supportively with how difficult it is to organize one's thoughts in such a situation. After about 20 minutes unstructured or self-structured, the interviewer can begin structuring to fill in gaps in the information.
- Note the parents' "natural associative trends," which may be clues to how they feel about you, the interview, or the clinical setting. One does not need to be on a couch or even defined as a patient to have inner—perhaps even unconscious—feelings, concerns, beliefs, and attitudes hinted at by choice of words or topic, inflection, sequence of content, linkages, flow of associations, segues, and other metacommunication. Explore salient leads and facilitate unfolding of such associations when appropriate. If parents show (or possibly even verbalize) strong affect, reflect or inquire about this in an open-ended, supportive way.
- Observe the interaction of the two parents: synergistic or undermining? supportive or hostile? dominant-passive or teamlike? parallel disregard or mutually responsive?
- Be alert for different perceptions/descriptions of the child's problem by the parents. These may be clues to not only family dynamics, but also the child's psychodynamics. Sometimes a child will show different symptoms to one parent than to the other.
- Relate the parents' personality traits and perceptions of the child to the child's developmental stage

and needs. What may be helpful at one stage could be detrimental at another. For example, "smothering" might be fine for an infant, but catastrophic for a toddler or teenager.
- In the structured history taking, begin with the family tree and progress through the prenatal experience and each developmental stage. Elucidate the child's task mastery at each stage and the parent's response to the child's efforts/progress.

Examination of Parent-Parent Relationship

The quality of the parent-parent relationship is another important risk/protective factor for the child. As with the parent-child relationship, what is observed about the parent-parent relationship may be different from what the parents say about it, and what they say may occasionally be more accurate than what is observed, even though observations are generally more trustworthy.

Differing parental perceptions/descriptions of the child's problems may not necessarily reflect marital disharmony. Differences in perception could also result from different experiences of the two (or more) parents. Such experiential differences are especially likely when parents work different hours and have contact with the child at different times of day or are divorced and have contact with the child at different times of the week or under different circumstances (school days versus holidays and weekends). Even when both parents are at home simultaneously, the child may treat them differently, or may behave differently in father's "territory" (e.g., garage, workshop, barbecue pit) than in mother's (e.g., kitchen, laundry room, sewing/crafts room). Nevertheless, the possibility should be explored that such differences in perception may hint of deeper disagreements. Both observations of parental interaction and answers to specific (preferably open-ended) questions should be tapped to formulate an assessment of the relationship.

While we routinely interview the parents separately from the child, we have often found it valuable to have a brief interview with each parent separately. Not uncommonly, this yields rich new data, as each parent feels free to share his own outlook without the need to reconcile it into a single parental consensus viewpoint. Separate interviews of the two parents are facilitated if, when appointments are originally scheduled, the referring parent is advised that whether or not they are married, both parents should attend the meeting. Separate information from both parents is especially useful when there is marital conflict or separation/divorce. Under separate interviewing circumstances, the clinician can more readily obtain assessments of existing marital problems and their potential impact on the child, as well as a picture of each parent's interactions with the child from the other parent's point of view.

If one of the parents fails to attend the evaluation, this is a matter of considerable import, especially if both parents were asked to be present at the time of appointment scheduling. Such an absence of one parent may reflect a practical division of labor, but is more likely to be due to unilateral neglect/disinterest, disagreement about the child's need for psychiatric evaluation, or a manipulation by the parent who is present. Even divorced or never-married parents who are cooperating for the child's welfare often arrange to bring the child together. It is therefore important to inquire about the absence in a nonaccusatory fashion, such as "What prevented Dave's father from coming today?" If the attending parent says that the absent one refused to come, it is usually useful to offer to call the absent one directly and invite him. In a surprising proportion of such cases, the present parent decides that this is not necessary—she thinks she can get Dave's father to come—and manages to produce him at the next appointment. In other cases the present parent gladly accepts the offer, in which event the clinician must be sure to follow through. Rarely will the absent parent refuse a nonblaming telephone invitation directly from the doctor couched in terms of how important it is for Dave to get his father's (or mother's) input into the treatment plan. Regardless of outcome, the clinician's offer of valuable professional time and effort to bring in the absent parent imparts a useful therapeutic message.

STEPPARENTS

The relationship between stepparents and natural (or infant-adoptive) parents is often as important in determining the quality of the child's home

environment as is the relationship between the two original parents. Is there cooperation or competition? If cooperation, is it harmonious/enthusiastic or grudging? If competition, is it resentful, or guilt motivated ("It's my job and no one else should have to do it"), or insecurity driven ("I'm afraid he'll forget I'm his real father (mother)")? Do the original parents welcome the additional parenting help for the sake of the children or try to keep stepparents in their place, perhaps objecting if the children address stepparents as "Dad" or "Mom"? Do the stepparents feel comfortable in the parenting role or apologetic and deferential to the original parents? Do they relish the opportunity to be part of the child's life or consider it a necessary evil that came with the marriage? Are they grateful to the original parents for this opportunity or resentful that they "have to deal with a problem child that someone else created"? Do they mainly respect or criticize the original parents?

If both parents remarry, this not only doubles the number of parent figures in the child's life, but also sextuples the number of parent-parent relationships, creates four potential parental triangles, and multiplies by 17 the number of possible triangles involving the child (considering a coalition of two or three parents as a unitary potential party to a triangle). If there are subsequent divorces and additional remarriages, perhaps after adoption by one of the stepparents, the child can accumulate an amazingly complex network of parent figures. Each of these may or may not feel a continuing commitment to the child, but the child often feels some continuing attachment to all of them. Therefore the relationship of current parents to previous stepparents is worthy of note. Are previous stepparents still welcome in the child's life, even if not in the parent's life? If so, are they available for interview?

Clues to the Child's Disorder

One of the ways that observation of the parent can diagnostically clarify the child's disorder was mentioned above: the possibility of genetic loading making the child's diagnosis a phenocopy of the parents'. Other possible reasons for the child's dis-

TABLE 58.3

Missildine's (1962, 1983) Concept of Mutual Respect Parenting Imbalances. Causation can be either direction, and often involves vicious cycles. The diagnostic importance is the greater-than-chance linking of specific child behaviors to specific parental behaviors.

Parental Pathogen (or response to child)	Child Reaction (or eliciting stimulus to parent)
Overdirection and/or overcoercion	Dawdling, forgetfulness, resistance, stubbornness, passive-aggressiveness, lack of initiative
Oversubmission	Demandingness, tantrums, impulsiveness
Perfectionism	Perfectionism, excessive striving, self-devaluation
Seductiveness	Seductiveness, often with guilt or hostility
Overindulgence	Passivity, lack of motivation
Oversolicitude and/or anxiety about child	Anxiety, fears
Neglect	Shallow relationships, impulsiveness, attention-getting misbehavior
Rejection	Bitterness, hostility, and/or clinging, insecure attachment
Hypochondriasis	Somatic anxieties and complaints
Distrust	Self-devaluation, untrustworthy behavior
Punitiveness	Punishment-inviting behavior, retaliatory longings

order to mimic a similar disorder in the parent include role modeling and identification. For whatever reason, the child's symptoms may well be a confusingly manifested form of a disorder that the parent shows more clearly and convincingly.

We need, however, to consider another way in which observation of parents can yield clues to the child's problems. This involves an understanding of Missildine's (1962, 1985) concept of parental pathogens or parenting imbalances. Although this concept does not apply to every case, indeed probably not to the majority, it does seem to fit some cases. These cases will leap to the attention of a clinician who is familiar with the short list of "parental pathogens" in Table 3. These might be considered parental risk factors that predispose or correspond to the respective kinds of child psychopathology.

CASE EXAMPLES OF PARENTAL PATHOGENS AND CORRESPONDING CHILD PSYCHOPATHOLOGY

When Tom and his father were picked up from the reception room for the initial evaluation, Tom's father began urging him to hurry up and put away the toys he had been using. Father's repeated encouragement to hurry took on a quality of nagging, to which Tom responded with slower and slower compliance. As they walked down the hall to the interview room, the clinician thought of oppositional disorder as a diagnostic possibility to be explored. When asked about the chief complaint, Tom's father said, "He won't do anything he's asked, or if he does, it's as slow as molasses."

As 6-year-old Jim's mother was explaining the chief complaint, Jim laid his head against one of her breasts and began stroking the inside of her thigh. She seemed oblivious to this and made no move to limit his inappropriate activity. Inquiry about sleeping arrangements disclosed that Jim slept in mother's bed and father slept on the couch. Jim's symptoms gradually subsided after he was ordered into his own bed and the parents were referred for marital counseling.

Nine-year-old Mary's mother insisted on speaking with the clinician before the joint interview. She began telling about the chief complaint of Mary's nightmares and phobic symptoms, which had begun when a neighbor had been robbed at knifepoint 3 weeks earlier. When asked why she needed to tell about this alone, she said that she did not want to upset Mary by talking about it in front of her. Further inquiry revealed that mother herself had been extremely upset about crime occurring so close in their own neighborhood; she had refused to talk about it with the children when they asked.

In many cases the causal direction may well be more from child to parent than in the direction implied by Missildine's term "parental pathogens." The linkages between parental attitude and child behavior/symptom are often vicious circles. Therefore, Missildine in his later writings drifted away from the parental pathogen terminology and talked more about "mutual-respect imbalances"—that is, imbalances in the parent-child relationship deviating from the ideal of mutual respect (Missildine, 1985). This change reflects the general trend in professional thinking over the past three decades, which has moved away from habitually viewing parents as causes of children's psychiatric problems. Nevertheless, in those cases characterized by such an imbalance, observation of the parent may quickly and efficiently provide a clear understanding of the child's problem.

The above notwithstanding, it is important that the clinician avoid predetermined notions about causality. It would be easy for a clinician who deals with a child for only 50 minutes per week to assume that somehow the source of the child's difficulties lies in some parental failure. Although our etiologic assumptions are sometimes unwitting, parents are very sensitive to the notion of blame, and no single dynamic is as likely to poison the working alliance. Most parents come to us already blaming themselves, and they often need to be unburdened of this in order to maximize their capacities as parents. Unfortunately the history of our discipline has too many examples of mistaken etiologic assumptions (e.g., "refrigerator parents" and autism) that parents are at fault. Humility about our own ability to understand and "know" the cause of a child's condition is a necessary prerequisite for compassionate, effective work with parents.

REFERENCES

Barkley, R. A., & Cunningham, C. E. (1979). The effects of methylphenidate on the mother-child interactions of hyperactive children. *Archives of General Psychiatry, 36*, 201–208.

Bronfenbrenner, U. (1985). The parent-child relationship and our changing society. In L. E. Arnold (Ed.), *Parents, children, and change* (pp. 47–57). New York: Macmillan/Free Press.

Fast, I., & Chethik, M. (1978). Stepparents and their spouses. In L. E. Arnold (Ed.), *Helping parents to help their children* (pp. 292–303). New York: Brunner/Mazel.

Greenspan, S. I. (1981). Interviewing the parents. In: *The clinical interview of the child* (pp. 172–192). New York: McGraw-Hill.

Henderson, L. J. (1913). *The fitness of the environment*. New York: Macmillan.

Kimchi, J., & Schaffner, B. (1990). Childhood protective factors and stress risk. In L. E. Arnold (Ed.), *Childhood stress* (pp. 475–500). New York: John Wiley & Sons.

Missildine, W. H. (1962). The mutual respect approach to child guidance. *American Journal of Diseases of Children, 104*, 116–121.

Missildine, W. H. (1985). Restoring the balance in child rearing. In L. E. Arnold (Ed.), *Parents, children, and change*. New York: Macmillan/Free Press. pp. 59–66.

Thomas, A., Chess, S., & Birch, H. G. (1968). Stress: Consonance and dissonance. In *Temperament and behavior disorders in children* (pp. 138–139). New York: New York University Press.

59 / Observation, Interview, and Mental Status Assessment (OIM): Infants and Preschool Children

Klaus Minde

The key to assessing infants and toddlers is to appreciate the rapid growth or change which takes place during this period (Minde & Benoit, 1991). In the past, this developmental advance was felt to be primarily biologically determined (Gesell, 1929). However, a sizable body of research has clearly demonstrated that development results from transactions between biological and interpersonal determinants (Sameroff & Chandler, 1975). In a psychiatric assessment of infants and toddlers, therefore, the aim of the clinician is to obtain a database that allows for a diagnostic understanding of both the infants and the people caring for them. Furthermore, as relationships between the young child and its caretakers can both either support and/or compromise development, the evaluation of these relationships becomes a significant source of information regarding the infant's current and future functioning (Minde & Minde, 1986). The assessment of their quality is accordingly an essential aspect of the clinician's task.

As can be seen, evaluating infants, their families, and their mutual relationships requires special skills and sensitivities. On the one hand, clinicians must learn about a complex network of functions, each reflecting a mixture of biological, cognitive, and socioemotional endowments. On the other hand, the examiners must be able to evaluate the significance of these functions within the infant and its milieu and attain an ability to demonstrate them to the caretakers. Finally, the clinicians must be comfortable delving into the inner life of an infant's caretakers and assess to what degree their subjective feelings or "internal representations" influence their actual caretaking style (Bretherton, 1985; Zeanah & Anders, 1987). In summary, to be experts in diagnosing strengths and difficulties in young children, clinicians need to be experts in normal child development and be profoundly aware of the relationship life of adults. The present chapter provides an outline for assessing young children within their family context. This includes measures of the children's developmental status, the quality of their relationships with primary caregivers, and ways in which one can assess caretaking competence.

The Process of Assessment

Psychiatric assessment of an infant or preschooler and his/her family consists of

- A clinical interview with one or more caregivers to obtain an appropriate history of the presenting problems as well as a family and developmental history of both child and family;
- A clinical infant or preschooler assessment;
- A parent-child relational assessment; and
- An assessment of the parenting skills of the primary caregivers.

The material obtained from such an investigation must then be integrated in a dynamic fashion and a treatment plan developed.

THE CLINICAL INTERVIEW WITH THE PRIMARY CAREGIVERS

This interview is usually the first encounter between the clinician and the child's caretakers. Most parents of young children are anxious and concerned about meeting a specialist whom they need to see because "they cannot manage their youngster." They frequently feel that they have failed as parents right from the start, and they may experience this "failure" as proof of their inferiority or incompetence. Hence, the first aim of an evaluation should be to establish a good working alliance between parents and clinician. This will assure the parents of the clinician's respect and allow the interview to become as much a mutual discovery of the past as it is active in the present (Hirshberg, 1993).

The format of the initial clinical interview obviously varies from clinician to clinician. Some find it useful initially to talk to the parents alone. This allows them to tell their story without interruptions and gives them a sense of being an important partner in the evaluation process. It also makes it easier for the clinician to probe gently in areas where parents may be defensive and may otherwise use their children's presence to legitimize avoidance.

If the parents do bring the child along, one can begin assessing the parent-child relationship at that point. In practice, one should let the parents know at the outset that they should do whatever they need to do in order to care for their child. The interviewer should also be careful not to resume the interview too quickly after the parents have interrupted the conversation to attend to their child. Such sensitivity allows the parents to alternate attention between the interviewer and the child in a way they find comfortable.

The style of interviewing varies widely among individual clinicians; indeed, there is good evidence that different techniques will elicit similar information from the parents of young children. However, recent studies have shown that factual historical data can best be obtained by direct questions (Cox et al., 1981). Feelings and opinions, in contrast, are elicited more easily when the interviewer asks open questions such as "What does Michael do when you go away?" or uses inferences or interpretations (for example, "This must have reminded you of your father's anger at you") and linkages ("Having him cry all the time must have made you feel sad") (Hopkinson et al., 1981). Such indirect and synthesizing remarks are probably helpful because they suggest to parents that they have been understood, that the interviewer shares their sentiments, and that the interviewer can therefore be trusted.

There has been some concern about the extent to which the retrospective nature of a parent's report on his/her childhood family environment is reliable and therefore valid. This can be a potentially serious problem in a clinical interview which deals with both objective and subjective judgments about the parent's own past relationships. As early parental experiences are felt to be vital

for understanding the transactional themes which determine the present parent-child relationship, the clinician needs to be aware of the possible limitations of the clinical interview as a means of obtaining valid information (Lyons-Ruth et al., 1989).

Robins et al. (1985) have recently examined this issue of reliability of recall. They questioned whether biased recall may occur, which would then be used to explain the current problem status of a family member. In their study, two groups of sibling pairs were interviewed, one in which one sibling was a psychiatric patient with a diagnosis of depression or alcoholism, and another in which both siblings were psychiatrically well. The authors found that there was an agreement of 70% on all factual background questions and that this held true independently of the psychiatric status of the informant. The group also reported agreement ranging from 77% to 91% between childhood clinic records and adult responses regarding family stability. In a qualitative assessment of parental acceptance or rejection in childhood, Parker et al. (1979) have also reported good agreement between the accounts given by depressed patients and by their siblings or parents.

This suggests that in general, the childhood events and feelings presented by parents of preschool children are reported with some accuracy. Furthermore, dynamic theory suggests that feelings and sentiments expressed by parents about their own upbringing will have relevance for their relationship with their child even if they cannot be fully confirmed as accurate (van IJzjendoorn, 1995).

The content of the clinical interview should be made up of factual information, encompassing data about the family, the identified parent, and the child's particular condition as well as clinical opinions. The factual database should include identifying information about patient and family, source of referral, reason for referral, history of current difficulties, family history, developmental history, and the clinician's assessment of the child.

The opinions are usually expressed in the formulation. It is here that clinicians try to make sense of the variety of data presented to them by adding a personal judgment to the story of Jane or John. Their conceptualization usually reflects their own theoretical position; in the nature of things, it may be disputed by others who might use the same factual data to arrive at a different clinical opinion.

Identifying Data: These data should include the patient's and caretaker's names, address, telephone number, age, sex, and race, as well as the legal status of the child (e.g., natural child, adopted, or foster child).

Reason for Referral: This should include a short description of the concerns that led to the referral, the persons who hold them, and their reasons.

History of Current Difficulties: The history describes the patient's problems, their detailed course and severity, how they were first noted, possible precipitating events, what makes the problems worse or better, what caretakers and others have done to help, what has in fact been achieved, and how family members or other important caretakers understand the problems.

Family History: The family history should have data on:

1. The personal life experiences of parents and/or present caretakers. This includes information about their own parents and siblings and the number and identities of adults they lived with from birth onward. Such a historical narrative will yield information on parental deaths, separation or divorce, and any interval of placement in out-of-home care. The interviewer should also inquire about the parents' education and occupational career, any family medical or psychiatric conditions, and their medical history.

In assessing the parents' past and present relationships with their own parents and other important role models, we are interested in learning about (a) the structure and supervision provided by their parents; (b) the amount of family conflicts present during their childhood; (c) the number of and satisfaction with peer relationships; (d) the quality of school experiences in respect to both academic issues and relationships with teachers; and (e) overall parental warmth and the types of punishment used in their own families. All of these parameters have an established validity in predicting how parents will deal with their own children and can be reliably ascertained during a clinical interview (Minde, 1991; Quinton and Rutter, 1988).

2. The identifying data and personal life experiences of the identified patient's siblings. This in-

cludes any separations they have had from primary caretakers and their reactions to them, the presence of illnesses and the relationship of the siblings to the identified patient.

3. Information about characteristics of other important caretakers (or caretaking institutions) such as grandparents, babysitters, day care center personnel, professionals within the court system or children's aid society, and the sensitivity of these caretakers to the infant's needs.

4. At times standardized measures may be used to assess specific aspects of parental mental health. Measures that are useful in this connection are inquiries about parental depression (Zimmerman et al., 1986), life event questionnaires (Coddington, 1972), or measures of general anxiety (Rutter, 1970).

Developmental History: This includes a detailed exploration of all developmental aspects of the biological, cognitive, and socioemotional life of the infant and young child. Areas to be covered should include (1) physical, cognitive, and emotional milestones; (2) the child's early behavioral organization; (3) the degree of individuation the child has achieved over time; (4) special strengths and vulnerabilities the child displays; and (5) the child's response to previous stresses. A more detailed discussion of this area can be found in Part I of this volume.

THE CLINICAL CHILD ASSESSMENT

This assessment deals with the developmental status of the infant and toddler. Since one important reason for bringing a child to a mental health clinic is the caregiver's concern about disturbances or delay in a child's development, such an assessment is an important component of a comprehensive evaluation. Since developmental delay in young children may also be a reflection of a depressed or otherwise compromised caretaker (Lyons-Ruth et al., 1989), such an assessment may also highlight interactional difficulties. This is one of the reasons why a developmental assessment is best conducted with the parents' collaborative participation. This arrangement also allows the parent to comfort and reassure the young child, and observe him perform on the tasks given by the examiner.

This shared observation can be most valuable

for several reasons. To begin with, these young children are not challenged during an assessment by separation from their familiar caretakers. More than that the examiner will demonstrate the strengths and/or weaknesses of the child's performance, and so help the parents come to a more realistic perception of their infant's abilities (Field, 1982). Parents will also witness and partake in a sensitive interchange between their youngster and another adult. Such an encounter can potentially teach them something about ways to interact with young children and possibly also be an introduction to strategies that may modify, or at least manage, particular behavioral deviations. Shared observations also facilitate later communication of the diagnostic formulation by the clinician.

Finally, the parents' presence in this situation allows the examiner a view of the parent-child interaction. Facets of this interaction may center around the parents' ability and/or wish to provide emotional support to the child; their possible intrusiveness in the testing situation; or their reactions to the displays of particular behaviors of the child toward the examiner. This will often allow the clinician to combine the parent-child relational assessment with an overall developmental evaluation. However, for the purpose of clarity, we will discuss the assessment of the young child's developmental skills and emerging capacities and the quality of the parent-child relationship separately.

The developmental assessment includes the following components:

- Obtaining information about the child's past development and health;
- Engaging the child to participate in a structured or semistructured task that assesses specific developmental skills;
- Assessing the child's behavior during a formal testing procedure and observing her coping ability;
- Possibly observing the child in different settings such as the office, at home, or in a day care environment.

Details about obtaining a developmental history are discussed in chapters X and Y.

There are a number of developmental assessment instruments available which have been described in recent texts on infant psychiatry (e.g., Clark et al., 1993; Minde & Minde, 1986). However, these tests do not predict future outcomes (Kopp & McCall, 1982), and should therefore be used only as descriptive measures for the current functioning of the infant or toddler.

In addition, it must be stressed that the use of most structured test materials requires the tester to be specifically trained and experienced in their use. Substantial training is necessary in order to administer some of the commonly cited instruments such as the Neonatal Behavioural Assessment Scale (Brazelton, 1984) or the Stanford Binet Intelligence Scale; this limits their value for the general clinician.

Other developmental tests (e.g., Bayley Scales of Infant Development, or Griffith Mental Development) are less difficult for the clinician to master. Both these tests can be used to examine an infant's or toddler's current strengths and weaknesses. However, their outdated standardization and the inherent limitations of infant tests do not allow results from these measurements to be used for predicting possible future functioning of an individual patient.

In spite of these shortcomings, an infant's performance on the latter tests can be clinically useful because they are given in a structured situation in which the clinician can assess the quality as much as the quantity of the child's work. Questions such as, How does 2-year-old Daniel react when he does not know an answer? Can he rejoice when he has mastered the task? How does he cope or compensate for apparent shortcomings? Can he relate to the examiner as a trustworthy person, or does he see him as an adversary? can all be addressed within that structure. Such tests also serve as an excellent assessment of the child's general neurological integration. Thus, the clinician can assess the muscle strength, tone, symmetry in coordination, and ease of movements in a way which allows her to gain more useful information about central nervous system (CNS) functioning than would be possible during a conventional neurological examination. Other behavioral functions, normally subsumed under the mental status examination (such as attention span, modulation of impulses, the ability to organize material and activities), can also be observed during the testing sessions and often add significant diagnostic data. Indeed, Bornstein and Sigman (1986) and Ruff et al. (1990) have reported that attention and visual processing skills are strongly associated with later measures of cognitive capabilities and IQ.

A further advantage of using developmental tests to evaluate a young child is that it allows the youngster to form a relationship with the examiner by "doing things" with her, which most of these little ones find interesting. This is compatible with some of the dominant themes of the preschooler's existence—that of experimenting, exploring, and being active. The adult's participation in such activities, therefore, is far less threatening for a young child than being with a strange adult who tries to learn things about defenses or secret feelings. In fact, clinical experience suggests that the play sessions that follow developmental assessments have a far richer quality, since both partners know each other already. The clinician can then use these sessions to probe into areas still unclear to her in a more goal-directed fashion.

Play Interview: Children of about 18 months of age or older can be assessed in more formal play sessions. Play interviews are generally unstructured, and the young child can choose freely what to play and do. Toys offered to a child should cover a wide variety of themes. There should be some dolls for presenting a family and other people, preferably a doll's house with furniture, maybe even dishes and cutlery, animals, a few small cars and certainly plasticine, crayons, and paper. It is also important to have some potentially frightening animals, such as a lion or tiger, among the cows, sheep, and pigs, as well as puppets or dolls that represent authority figures or danger (such as a policeman or fireman). It is also useful to have two telephones and a doctor's kit in the playroom, so that the examiner can be an active partner in the play sequence.

For children under the age of three, it is essential that most of the toys look realistic because their sense of abstraction is not yet sufficiently developed to permit the use of, for example, a block for a telephone or a car.

In the play sessions, the clinician can usually make inferences about the child's inner life, his conflicts, desires, fears, and wishes, as well as about their possible source. She can also assess the child's coping strategies, defensive functions, modes of affective expression, and ability to form a relationship with the examiner.

It should be stressed that since the purpose here is investigative, such diagnostic play is different from the general play the clinician may engage in with children in therapy. For example, during therapy the clinician may want to stop or intervene when Mary repeatedly plays out a gruesome murder scene, in order to reinforce the concept of a caring and regulated environment. However, during an assessment play period, the clinician may not attempt to calm an overexcited youngster, but may simply comment that all the people and animals get killed here.

Play sessions for infants under 18 months normally consist of observing their spontaneous play with toys and possibly engaging them in games such as peekaboo or patty-cake. While the ability to pursue symbolic play sequences does not usually develop before 24 months, younger children will nevertheless exhibit a wide range of behaviors, both toward their parents and the clinician, and thus provide important information about their concept of their world and their general comfort or discomfort with it.

PARENT-CHILD RELATIONAL ASSESSMENT

The quality of the parent-child interaction is a critical factor in a young child's developmental functioning, and therefore needs to be carefully assessed. Furthermore, directly observable interactive behaviors can reflect the presence and type of parental subjective experiences which may affect the child's overall development positively or negatively. This means that the clinician should try to differentiate the extent to which an observed interaction between a parent and a child occurs only within a specific context (i.e., is a true interaction) as against the extent to which it reflects a more persistent underlying parental attribution (i.e., is a marker of the overall relationship between the two partners). Relationships tend to be less amenable to change, and behaviors reflecting them are more longstanding, consistent, and routinized patterns of interaction. Such behaviors are also often based on intergenerational continuities (Fonagy et al., 1991; Lieberman, et al., 1991).

How Can the Clinician Best Learn About the Parent-child Relationship?: The setting within which the interview takes place is of primary importance. It is useful to have a small room available that contains a few appropriate toys and is carpeted so that both adults and children can sit or move on the floor. The clinician then invites the parents to play or interact with the child as they see fit and observes the ensuing interactions for 15 to 25 minutes.

Since the parents have already spent some time with the clinician, they usually feel comfortable with this arrangement. It is also advisable to videotape the interactions. The tape can be used as a stimulus for discussions later on and to open the door for treating possible infant-caregiver relationship disturbances (McDonough, 1993).

While there are many parameters which help the clinician in structuring his observations, six domains of functioning suggested by Emde (1989) appear most relevant and inclusive. They are (1) attachment, including those aspects of behavior which deal with the child's and caretaker's emotional or physical closeness and/or availability to each other and their ability to separate from each other and/or the caretaker's support of the child's overall individuation; (2) vigilance and protection, reflecting behaviors of the caretakers which assure the physical safety of the child; (3) play: its style and symbolism; (4) teaching and learning; (5) power, control, and discipline; and (6) regulation of emotion or affect, including the expression and communication of emotion.

The attachment relationship. The clinical assessment of the infant-parent attachment is based on Bowlby's (1982) concept that attachment is a "system" composed of behaviors which keep the infant and primary caretaker in close proximity. It also includes the cognitions and affects that operate to organize and select these behaviors. How this proximity is maintained depends on the age of the child, the amount of stress the child experiences, and the attitude the caretaker shows toward the child. For example, a 5-month-old baby may simply raise her arms to have mom pick her up, while an 18-month-old in distress may run to mother, calling out, and actively climbing onto her lap. The clinician will look out for such things as the pleasure the caregiver shows in being with the child, and the depth and range of affect displayed and the parents' ability to understand and sympathize when the child wants to change from one activity to another. Families may have also developed private games between caregivers and children marking a personal style of parent-child attachment. The clinician looks for the degree to which the infant seeks physical comfort or visual

contact (also called social referencing) (Campos & Stenberg, 1981) from the parents, and the way they handle these approaches. While most parents provide the appropriate emotional support to their children at such points, some parents seem unresponsive and appear disinterested, while others are highly intrusive and seemingly preoccupied with making things easier for their children and/or directing them without considering the child's interest and abilities. The clinician will also look for how freely the child explores the available toys and how the parents encourage this, and if there is a difference in how the child relates to father and mother. The clinician may also enquire about separations and how they are tolerated by the infant, and attempt to elicit the parents' thoughts about why the child engages in specific actions.

Vigilance and protection. This is best assessed by observing whether the parents appropriately intervene when the child gets into potential trouble (e.g., climbs up a chair or gets entangled in other obstacles). It is equally important to observe whether the toddler shows either excessive caution or undue recklessness in dealing with toys and equipment. Parents may be either overly anxious about the child's safety or careless and lacking in awareness. The clinician might also want to know whether the child has had accidents in the past, and how the parents understand such an event.

Play. Play is the work of young children. By playing they discover the outer reality and develop their inner world. Parents have an important role to play here. However, they often turn the play into a teaching session, overwhelming a young child with concrete instructions (e.g., naming colors or shapes) or concentrating on testing or exhibiting diverse achievements to the examiner, rather than following a youngster into her world so that they may all experience it together.

It is equally important to observe the child's contribution to the parent-child play activity. Can she make use of symbolic play themes (e.g., put a baby to bed or feed a doll) when she is cognitively able to do so, and what is the content of the play?

If parents do not engage in playing with their children on their own, it is helpful for the clinician to ask them directly to do so. If this does not seem to be successful or possible, the clinician may advise the parents simply "to imitate the child and see what happens." Such a strategy commonly gives parents a chance to observe their children's play in a more sensitive fashion. Children will often respond to the parents' sudden "availability" and relate to them in a much more appropriate and direct way. Interactive changes like this can be pointed out during later video replays and often mark the beginning of productive therapeutic work.

It should be stressed again that by learning how the caregivers interpret the child's play behaviors and how they understand these connections, the clinician gains a good entry into dealing with possible relationship disorders (Lieberman, 1992).

Teaching and Learning. The variety, spontaneity, and richness of an environment have long been seen as vital ingredients of the child's later emotional and cognitive functioning (Ramey et al., 1984). Recent studies have also shown that, especially from the second year onward, an environment which provides both multiple types of play material and a stimulus shelter, where children can escape for quiet moments alone, becomes the best predictor for later cognitive functioning (Gottfried & Gottfried, 1984). This means that teaching and learning are related to the caregiver's understanding of when actively to teach, when to provide support, when to give distance, and when to leave a child to her own devices. In observing parents with their young children at play, the clinician should watch for this dynamic interplay, which is so important in helping the child develop a sense of mastery.

A related factor, a major building block in creating this sense of mastery, is the caretaker's ability or willingness to provide a social "scaffold" for the child's learning experiences, especially as they relate to ongoing attention and ongoing action (Bruner, 1985). For example, in the peekaboo game, the mother first hides and then uncovers herself, while later the child does the hiding and uncovering. Similarly, mothers play very different games with 6- and 12-month-old children (Gustafson et al., 1979). Early games are typically geared to the infant's more passive role (being bounced), while later "roll the ball" or "peekaboo" games stress the active role the child can take in these interactions. This implies that caregivers scaffold the acquisition of skills in their children, first, by constraining the free variation of their infant's behavior (through stage setting and getting

attention) and then by channeling their approximations of the new skill into its optimal form (by holding out hands, leaning forward, encouraging). Most parents perform the specific scaffolding practices seemingly automatically (Papousek & Papousek, 1987); it is obvious, however, that these practices vary with the development of the infant. However, their presence seems to reflect an important aspect of the teaching strategies used by sensitive caregivers.

Toward the end of the parent-child relationship assessment, it may be useful for the clinician to attempt to teach the youngster one small skill. If the child can learn, for example, how to build a tower or get a special doll undressed, it will allow the clinician to (1) determine how best to approach the child or how much encouragement the child needs and (2) provide feedback to the parents about teaching strategies which may be more appropriate for their youngster.

Discipline. The parents' regulation of their own and their children's behavior is an important aspect of the dyad's relationship. The strategies parents use to control their children have long been seen as important predictors of children's later social and intellectual competence (Maccoby & Martin, 1983). In addition, developmental researchers have identified a number of clearly demarcated styles of discipline which lead to differential patterns of competence and adjustment in later life (Steinberg et al., 1991). In particular, there is now a professional consensus that parents can obtain control through imposing hostile, rejecting, authoritarian, harsh discipline; through an authoritative parenting style; or by using a generally permissive style. One can well imagine that a harsh authoritarian type of discipline does not easily allow children to express their thoughts and feelings. As a result, in early childhood, such children may become passively hostile and, later, aggressive adults. Children who are raised in a permissive fashion tend to be sensitive and caring later on, but are likely to have difficulties in organizing and disciplining themselves, for example, they may underachieve academically. In contrast, children who have grown up in families with an authoritative discipline style, which is characterized by clearly presented parental expectations coupled with warmth and support, will do well academically and show sophisticated social skills (Steinberg et al., 1991).

Parents display these interactive patterns early in their children's lives by the way they present themselves to the infant (e.g., as calm and in control versus passive, overwhelmed, or tense and angry) and how they deal with routine parenting challenges. For example, a child who refuses to clean up at the end of a session may demonstrate a caregiver's overall discipline style.

Here again, it useful to have the clinician test how children who get in trouble with their caregivers react to a different way of getting them to follow instructions. If they readily change in their behaviors, a modification of the parents' style may be comparatively easy.

Regulation of emotion. This is a crucial area of relationship functioning, since the emotions or affects experienced in any interaction will determine its later psychological significance within the parent-child relationship (Emde, 1989). Early in life, children have limited self-regulatory capacities; hence, the parents' ability to help them to organize their behavior at that time provides an important experience of tension release and some degree of mastery over the world. Parents will usually increase their children's self-regulation by learning about their individual characteristics and by building on their strengths to aid them in achieving harmony and regulation. In practice, this could mean that a child's parents may have developed an intimate knowledge of little Mary's preferred sleeping position early in life, know how she prefers to be held and calmed, and the position most conducive to interesting her in the world. Other parents will have little interest in or knowledge about such things and may differ greatly in the affect they display toward their children from activity to activity. Some children may also be quite clear in how they signal their feelings and emotions. For those who communicate less well, the parents' ability to soothe and regulate the infant's behavior may be more difficult but also far more important for the infant's future development. In assessing these patterns, it is useful to differentiate between caretakers who respond inappropriately because they do not see or experience the needs of the child, and those who perceive these needs but cannot act because of personal problems or limitations (e.g., depression or overwork). Some parents may also show a transient inability to perceive and/or respond to their children's needs because of fatigue or other environmental stresses.

It is also recognized that the private meanings given to emotions and feelings in others are powerful determinants of our responses to others, and that relationships reflect these private meanings most directly. For example, the crying of a child may be seen as a willful attempt to hurt the mother or as a sign that the youngster is simply overtired (Zeanah & Benoit, 1995).

Finally, it is important to recognize that the behavior of young children with the same person can vary and depends on the overall context. Thus John may behave very differently toward his mom in the presence or absence of his dad or the clinician. This makes it important, before instituting any remediation, to consider the infant's relationship style when within the context of the family and when out in wider society.

Parent-Child Interaction Relationship Measures: As for the developmental assessment of children, there are now measures that can provide a comprehensive and valid assessment of parent-infant interactions. In a recent chapter by Clark et al. (1993), six such measures are described, of which, unfortunately, only two, the HOME (Caldwell & Bradley, 1978) and the PBP (Bromwich, 1983), can be used without extensive training. The HOME measures factors related to the child's home environment. For example, there is an assessment of the mother's responsivity and acceptance of her child, a measure of her ability to organize the child's physical environment and to provide toys and other stimulation. This scale, which has been used as, among other things, an assessment tool for home stimulation programs, does not provide much qualitative information. The parent behavior progression (PBP) is a checklist of 17 reported or observed behaviors (Bromwich, 1983). It was developed by a social worker who worked with premature infants, and hence contains items important for the cognitive as well as the affective development of infants and toddlers.

ASSESSMENT OF PARENTING SKILLS

Much of the information obtained during the assessment process described in the previous sections of this chapter obviously relates to the primary caregiver's ability to meet the young child's developmental needs. Yet the overall assessment of this capacity, which consists of so many different tasks and requirements, remains a difficult task. As was previously noted, it ranges from providing basic shelter, food, and warmth to an infant, to recognizing that Jonathan is not merely a small adult but needs some special emotional consideration before he can participate in the little games with which an infant attempts to challenge the world. Further complexities in measuring parenting abilities arise because a mother's care may be "good enough," to use a phrase by Winnicott (1960), during the first 6 months of a child's life as she enjoys the seemingly unlimited giving of comfort to the young infant. However, this mother may resent the same infant's increasing demands for separation and individuation later on.

Children are also differentially equipped to cope with a marginal environment; some may "make do," while others wither helplessly. The phenomenon of discontinuity in development can also work for or against a given child. For example, by becoming mobile and acquiring language, an older toddler may find substitute sources of stimulation and aids to cognitive growth that were not accessible to him before (Minde & Minde, 1986).

Another kind of challenge is presented by those infants who, because of traumatic biological or emotional life events, require special handling, techniques which are not usually part of a mother's repertoire of caretaking practices. Here a failure to provide developmentally appropriate caretaking may reflect the parents' ignorance of the "right way" of handling their child rather than their particular psychological or psychosocial limitations. For example, early on, prematurely born children usually need a more directive handling style, as they often have difficulties in overall CNS organization (Minde et al., 1980). Thus, in such a situation, we may confront a purely interactive difficulty and not a relationship problem. Finally, as was mentioned before, caretakers vary not only in their specific strengths but also in their day-to-day competence.

When we seek to assess parenting competence, what then should we look for in the parents of young children? We suggest that parents be rated on five general and relatively stable dimensions

that contribute to their interpersonal interactions regardless of the child's developmental stage (Minde & Minde, 1986). These are

- general emotional and physical health,
- self-esteem,
- general coping and adaptation skills,
- child-rearing attitudes and,
- a willingness and/or ability to provide developmental encouragement.

Assessment of the parents' past and present emotional and physical health was discussed in an earlier section of this chapter. The Malaise Inventory, a 20-item questionnaire developed by Rutter (1970) from items of the Cornell Medical Index, is a useful tool in assessing physical manifestations of parental anxiety, depression, or abnormal thought processes.

Self-esteem can often be estimated only from incidental statements of the parents. For example, a mother may say, "Michael doesn't listen to me, nor does anyone else in the family;" father may remark, "I would be so happy if Marilyn would smile at me just once a week." Both of these statements may be a reflection of low self-esteem and should alert the clinician to search for other signs of self-deprecation.

General coping and adaptation skills can be assessed by inquiring how previous stresses have been managed. When they are directly asked about them, parents will often report such data quite accurately. It should be remembered that there are many ways of coping with difficulties, ranging from complete denial to active working through. The final rating of coping skills will be based on the effectiveness of these strategies rather than on the type of defense or coping mechanism used.

Authoritarian or democratic attitudes toward parenting can be assessed by evaluating the decision-making process in a family. This can be done by asking how other children in the family behave and are managed during the parent-child relationship assessment. If there is a history of placement of a sibling or of family conflicts with other children, one may want to explore how, by whom, and about what are decisions made in the family, and how they are accepted by the children. As was discussed in a previous section, families may function in a primarily authoritarian or indulgent way. However, few families subscribe totally to one mode of disciplining. It is also important to establish how well specific interaction patterns seem to work. For example, in the interaction between handicapped and developmentally delayed children and their caregivers, more directive management patterns are likely to be found (Kogan, 1980; Minde et al., 1980). Moreover, it appears that for such children, more direct guidance and a less democratic management style may be developmentally appropriate.

The willingness of parents to provide developmental encouragement does not refer only to their ability to "stimulate" an infant. In fact, parents who are withdrawn and unavailable to their children can also be intrusive and hyperstimulating, or can shift between the two modalities. Both extremes tend to be maladaptive and may undermine the expression of the child's phase-expected capacities.

In addition to these general ratings, it has also been useful to inquire about the routines of an average day of the young child and his family. This can provide the examiner with a sense of the stresses the family faces and simultaneously afford the possibility of assessing the family's support systems and child-rearing attitudes. One can also observe the caretaker's response to the clinicians as professionals and as people, noting their predominant mood and thinking style. Such observations can help predict the caregiver's readiness and/or ability to engage with clinicians in a therapeutic relationship and may forecast the likelihood of influencing the parent-infant relationship.

Conclusion

In this chapter, we have examined the basic variables that make up an evaluation of an infant or young child and her family. The various types of information obtained must then be integrated into the child's story. No test or interaction observation should ever be put to clinical use without this synthesis of all the data. The final summary or formulation should also address the strengths and weaknesses of the family, the child, and the social matrix, the family's expectations of the clinician's assessment and possible treatment, and list those factors that may perpetuate the present problems or help to eliminate them.

REFERENCES

Bornstein, M., & Sigman, M. (1986). Continuity in mental development from infancy. *Child Development, 57,* 251–274.

Bowlby, J. (1982). *Attachment and loss. Vol. II: Attachment* (2nd ed.). New York: Basic Books.

Brazelton, T. B. (1984). *Neonatal Behavioral Assessment Scale.* Philadelphia: J. B. Lippincott.

Bretherton, I. (1985). Attachment theory: Retrospect and prospect. In I. Bretherton & E. Waters (Eds.), *Growing points of attachment theory and research. Monographs of the Society for Research in Child Development, 50,* 3–35. Serial no. 209.

Bromwich, R. (1983). *Parent behavior progression: Manual and 1983 supplement.* Northridge, CA: Center for Research Development and Services, Department of Educational Psychology, California State University.

Bruner, J. S. (1985). Vygotsky: A historical and conceptual perspective. In J. V. Wertsch (Ed.), *Culture, communication and cognition: Vygotskian perspec-* *tives, communication and cognition: Vygotskian perspectives* (pp. 21–34). New York: Cambridge University Press.

Caldwell, B., & Bradley, R. (1978). *Manual for the Home Observation for Measurement of the Environment.* Little Rock: University of Arkansas.

Campos, J. J., & Stenberg, C. (1981). Perception, appraisal, and emotion: The onset of social referencing. In M. Lamb & L. R. Sherrod (Eds.), *Infant social cognition* (pp. 273–314). Hillsdale, NJ: Lawrence Erlbaum.

Clark, R., Paulson, A., & Conlin, S. (1993). Assessment of developmental status and parent-infant relationships: The therapeutic process of evaluation. In C. H. Zeanah (Ed.), *Handbook of infant mental health* (pp. 191–209). New York: Guilford Press.

Coddington, R. (1972). The significance of life events as etiological factors in the diseases of children. *Journal of Psychosomatic Research, 16,* 17–18.

Cox, A., Hopkinson, K., & Rutter, M. (1981). Psychiatric interviewing techniques II. Naturalistic study: Eliciting factual information. *British Journal of Psychiatry, 138*, 283–291.

Emde, R. N. (1989). The infant's relationship experience: Developmental and affective aspects. In A. J. Sameroff & R. N. Emde (Eds.), *Relationship disturbances in early childhood* (pp. 33–51). New York: Basic Books.

Field, T. M. (1982). Infants born at risk: Early compensatory experiences. In L. A. Bond & J. M. Joffe (Eds.), *Facilitating infant and early development.* Hanover, NH: University Press of New England.

Fonagy, P., Steele, H., & Steele, M. (1991). Maternal representations of attachment during pregnancy predict the organization of infant-mother attachment at one year of age. *Child Development, 62*, 891–905.

Gesell, A. (1929). *Infancy and human growth.* New York: Macmillan.

Gottfried, A. W., & Gottfried, A. E. (1984). Home environment and cognitive development in young children of middle-socioeconomic-status families. In A. W. Gottfried (Ed.), *Home environment and early cognitive development: Longitudinal research.* Orlando, FL: Academic Press. pp. 57–115.

Gustafson, G., Green, J., & West, M. (1979). The infant's changing role in mother-infant games: The growth of social skills. *Infant Behavior and Development, 1*, 301–308.

Hirshberg, L. M. (1993). Clinical interviews with infants and their families. In C. H. Zeanah (Ed.), *Handbook of infant mental health* (pp. 173–190). New York: Guilford Press.

Hopkinson, K., Cox, A., & Rutter, M. (1981). Psychiatric interviewing techniques III. Naturalistic study: Eliciting feelings. *British Journal of Psychiatry, 138*, 406–415.

Kogan, K. L. (1980). Interaction systems between preschool handicapped or developmentally delayed children and their parents. In T. Field (Ed.), *High-risk infants and children: Adult and peer interaction* (pp. 227–247). New York: Academic Press.

Kopp, C. B., & McCall, R. B. (1982). Predicting later mental performance for normal, at risk, and handicapped infants. In P. B. Baltes & O. G. Brim (Eds.), *Life-span development and behavior* (Vol. 4, pp. 33–61). New York: Academic Press.

Lieberman, A. (1992). Infant-parent psychotherapy with toddlers. *Development and Psychopathology, 4*, 559–574.

Lieberman, A. F., Weston, D. R. and Pawl, G. H. (1991). Preventive intervention and outcome with anxiously attached dyads. *Child Development, 62*: 199–209.

Lyons-Ruth, K., Zoll, D., Connell, D., & Grunebaum, H. (1989). Family deviance and family disruption in childhood: Associations with maternal behavior and infant maltreatment during the first two years of life. *Development and Psychopathology, 1*, 219–236.

Maccoby, E., & Martin, J. (1983). Socialization in the

context of the family: Parent-child interaction. In E. M. Hetherington (Ed.), P. H. Mussen (Series Ed.), *Handbook of child psychology, Vol. 4: Socialization, personality and social development* (pp. 1–101). New York: John Wiley & Sons.

McDonough, S. (1993). Interaction guidance: Understanding and treating early infant-caregiver relationship disturbances. In C. H. Zeanah (Ed.), *Handbook of infant mental health* (pp. 414–426). New York: Guilford Press.

Minde, K. (1996). The effect of disordered parenting on the development of children, 2nd edition. In M. Lewis (Ed.), *Child and adolescent psychiatry: A comprehensive textbook* (pp. 398–410). Baltimore, MD: Williams & Wilkins.

Minde, K., & Benoit, D. (1991). Infant psychiatry: Its relevance for the general psychiatrist. *British Journal of Psychiatry, 159*, 173–184.

Minde, K. K., Marton, P., Manning, D., & Hines, B. (1980). Some determinants of mother-infant interaction in the premature nursery. *Journal of the American Academy of Child Psychiatry, 19*, 1–21.

Minde, K., & Minde, R. (1986). *Infant psychiatry: An introductory textbook.* Beverly Hills, CA: Sage Publications.

Papousek, H., & Papousek, M. (1987). Intuitive parenting: A dialectic counterpart to the infant's integrative competence. In J. D. Osofsky (Ed.), *Handbook of infant development* (2nd ed., pp. 669–720). New York: John Wiley & Sons.

Parker, G., Tupling, H., & Brown, L. (1979). A parental bonding instrument. *British Journal of Medical Psychology, 52*, 1–10.

Quinton, D., & Rutter, M. (1988). *Parenting breakdown: The making and breaking of intergenerational links.* Brookfield, VT: Gower.

Ramey, C. T., Bryant, D. M., Sparling, J. J., & Wasik, B. H. (1984). A biosocial systems perspective on environmental interventions for low birthweight infants. *Clinical Obstetrics & Gynecology* 27(3): 672–92.

Robins, L. N., Schoenberg, S., Holmes, S., Ratcliff, K., Benham, A., & Works, J. (1985). Early home environment and retrospective recall: A test for concordance between siblings with and without psychiatric disorders. *American Journal of Orthopsychiatry, 55* (1), 27–41.

Ruff, H., Lawson, K., Parrinello, R., & Weissberg, R. (1990). Long-term stability of individual differences in sustained attention in the early years. *Child Development, 61*, 60–75.

Rutter, M. (1970). Psychological development: Predictions from infancy. *Journal of Child Psychology and Psychiatry, 11*, 49–62.

Sameroff, A., & Chandler, M. (1975). Reproductive risk and the continuum of caretaking casualty. In F. D. Horowitz, E. M. Hetherington, S. Scarr-Salapetek, & G. M. Siegel (Eds.), *Review of child development research* (Vol. 4, pp. 187–244). Chicago: University of Chicago Press.

Steinberg, L., Mounts, N., Lamborn, S., & Dornbush, S. (1991). Authoritative parenting and adolescent adjustment across various ecological niches. *Journal of Research on Adolescents, 1,* 19–36.

van IJzjendoorn, M. H. (1995). Adult attachment representations, parental responsiveness, and infant attachment: A meta-analysis on the predictive validity of the adult attachment interview. *Psychological Bulletin, 117,* 387–403.

Winnicott, D. (1960). The theory of the parent-infant relationship. *International Journal of Psycho-Analysis, 41,* 585–595.

Zeanah, C. H., & Anders, T. F. (1987). Subjectivity in parent-infant relationships: A discussion of internal working models. *Infant Mental Health Journal, 8,* 237–250.

Zeanah, C. H., Benoit, D. (1995). Clinical applications of a parent perception interview in infant mental health. Child & Adolescent Psychiatric Clinics of North America. *Infant Psychiatry, 4,* 539–554.

Zimmerman, M., Coyvell, W., Coventhal, C., & Wilson, S. (1986). A self-report scale to diagnose major depressive disorder. *Archives of General Psychiatry, 43,* 1076–1081.

---

60 / Observation, Interview, and Mental Status Assessment (OIM): School-Aged Children

Robert A. King

The Unique Contributions of the Child Interview

The goals of the child interview are to assess directly the child's psychological functioning and to hear the child's own views of the presenting problem and the details of events, thoughts, and feelings relevant to it. Although there is considerable debate regarding the reliability, validity, and clinical utility of various approaches to the child interview (Angold, 1994; Feinstein, 1982; Rutter and Graham, 1968), there is general consensus that the direct interview of the child provides crucial assessment information that cannot be obtained from other sources. Parents may not be aware of or may discount the child's feelings, degree of distress, or perception of various events. In some cases, the child may have previously unshared secrets regarding abuse, sexual or antisocial activities, suicide attempts, or collusive family dynamics. Certain symptoms, such as compulsions,

premonitory urges, obsessive or suicidal thoughts, or hallucinations, may be apparent only to the child. The presence or significance of other symptoms, such as tics or a thought disorder, may become apparent only by the direct scrutiny of the clinician.

Beyond these assessment goals, an additional aim of the child interview is to establish rapport with the child in order to facilitate the child's cooperation in the assessment and with whatever recommendations for intervention may be made as a result of the evaluation. To this end, it is helpful for the child to experience the clinician in these initial encounters as an empathic, knowledgeable adult who is interested in understanding and helping the child.

Within these broad goals, there are many varieties of child interviews, depending on the nature of the presenting problem, the clinical setting, and the purpose of the assessment. (See Chapter X on Types and Goals of Clinical Assessment.) Thus the scope, focus, duration, setting, and predominant techniques employed will vary depending on whether the assessment is an emergency department evaluation of a suicide threat, a pediatric ward consultation of a regressed or uncooperative child, a forensic custody evaluation, an investigation of alleged child abuse, or the evaluation of a child who is academically underachieving, anxious, or manifesting tics.

This chapter is adapted in part from King, R. A., Work Group on Quality Issues (1995, 1997), Practice parameters for the psychiatric assessment of children and adolescents. *Journal of the American Academy of Child and Adolescent Psychiatry,* 34(10): 1386–1402. (Reprinted in *Journal of the American Academy of Child and Adolescent Psychiatry,* 36 (Supplement), (in press, 1997).

Special Considerations in the Child Interview

The goal of the child interview is not merely to gather information but also to establish rapport with the child (which in turn facilitates both information gathering and cooperation with recommended interventions). In shaping the interview, therefore, the clinician remains sensitive to issues of tact, timing, and context and the need to protect the child's self-esteem (King & Noshpitz, 1991). In their initial contact, the clinician helps the parents plan how best to prepare the child for the first interview; the parents are encouraged to explain to the child in understandable, nonpejorative terms why the child is going to see the clinician and what to expect (e.g., "You and the doctor will have a chance to play and talk together about the problems you [or we] have been having together with _____, so the doctor can help figure out what might help").

The clinician is aware, however, that even with the most thoughtful preparation, many children (like many adults) still approach the initial interview with unspoken, sometimes not fully formulated assumptions or anxieties. For example, children may fear that the doctor will read their mind; judge, punish, or force them to reveal embarrassing things; or do other scary things to them.

In conducting the child interview and interpreting its findings, the characteristic lability of children must also be born in mind. When tired, sick, hungry, or apprehensive in unfamiliar situations, children often fall back to more immature ways of behaving and may become silly, oppositional, shy, withdrawn, or clingy. As a result, a single initial interview may not accurately reveal the child's optimal or characteristic level of functioning. For example, a child with attention deficit-hyperactivity disorder may be on his best behavior in an initial, brief, or relatively structured interview in the office setting, especially if the child is at pains to avoid imagined disciplinary consequences. Restless, inattentive, or oppositional behavior may emerge only over time in subsequent interviews or on observation of the child in the classroom setting. In contrast, the highly anxious child may be apprehensive to the point of near muteness or inability to separate from the parent. It may be only over several interviews (perhaps with mother or father in the room at first) that the child feels secure enough to engage with or confide in the clinician. Thus, more than one interview is often desirable to place the child sufficiently at ease to obtain a representative and valid picture of the child's views and characteristic behavior. Even with multiple visits, it is important to bear in mind that the demand characteristics of the one-to-one office visit may elicit different behavior than that observed in the classroom or home. For example, physicians, parents, and teachers often assess the same child quite differently depending on whether the child is seen in the office, at home, or in the school (Schachar et al., 1981). (For more on the notion of informant variance see Chapter X on the Developmental History of the School-age Child.)

Components of the Child Interview

The components of the child interview are often conceptualized under two headings: history taking and the mental status assessment. *History taking* refers to the inquiry into the major areas of the child's life and functioning, past and current, including (but not limited to) the presenting problem. The *mental status assessment* refers to the assessment and description of the child's behavior and functioning as manifested in the interview situation itself. In actual practice, however, history taking and the mental status assessment usually proceed simultaneously rather than being clearly distinguishable segments of the interview. Thus, as the clinician notes the child's explicit response to a given question about the child's life (such as what does the child like to do for fun? or how does the child get along with other kids at school?), the clinician is also noting the child's emotional tone; attitude toward the examiner; vocabulary, syntax, prosody, and articulation; style of conceptualizing a response; etc. Conversely, while observing the school-age child draw a picture, in addition to gathering data on the child's cognitive and visual-motor abilities, the clinician may obtain important information regarding the child's feelings and fantasies about his life situation or significant events,

379

as well as the child's attitude toward his own work efforts (e.g., self-denigrating, perfectionistic, slapdash).

We will begin by detailing the areas to be assessed in the mental status assessment of the child and the history taking from the child, then turn to the technical issues of how best to order and conduct the interview in order to elicit this information.

The Mental Status Assessment

As with all aspects of the child psychiatric assessment, the mental status assessment of the school-age child is based on a developmental perspective that draws upon the clinician's knowledge of the range of normal and abnormal development as manifested during the school years. As will be discussed below, the data on which the mental status assessment is based may emerge spontaneously in the course of the interview or it may require explicit inquiry or elicitation. In whatever order the interview proceeds, the clinician should keep in mind the following aspects of the child's appearance and functioning to be observed, assessed, and recorded (Hill, 1985; King et al., 1995, 1997; King and Noshpitz, 1991; Lewis, 1996; Simmons, 1987):

- *Physical appearance,* including physical development, presence of minor congenital anomalies, style of hair and dress, cleanliness, and other indications of parental attentiveness (or its lack) to the child's physical appearance and hygiene.
- *Manner of relating to examiner and parents,* including ease of separation. How confiding or guarded does the child seem toward the clinician? Is the child eager to please or impress, flirtatious, quick to make excuses or minimize, passively withholding, or openly defiant? Are there discernible reactions toward the clinician's physical appearance, gender, or ethnicity (especially if different from that of the child)? How does the child's behavior toward the examiner compare to that observed or reported toward the parents or other adults?
- *Affect.* What is the child's predominant mood and how wide a range of emotion is apparent during the interview? Is the child's mood appropriate or incongruous?

- *Coping mechanisms.* As manifested toward the clinician, expressed in play, or described by the child in relation to important others, do the child's dependent longings, sexual interests and impulses, and aggressive feelings seem age appropriate in their intensity, object, and mode of expression? In what ways and with what success does the child control or modulate such urges (e.g., by finding alternative or socially permissible means of satisfying them)? How does the child cope when anxious or frustrated?
- *Orientation to time, place, person* refers to whether children are accurately aware of the date, where they are, and who they are. This can be evaluated by asking the child "What is the year? season? date? day? month" or "Where are we?" (name of building, town, state, country").
- *Motor behavior* including activity level, coordination, and presence of unusual motor patterns (e.g., tics, compulsions, or stereotypies, such as hand-flapping or twirling); evidence of cerebral dominance (preferred hand, foot, eye, ear).
- *Quality of thinking and perception,* including presence of hallucinations, delusions, thought disorder, flight of ideas; adequacy of hearing and vision.
- *Speech and language,* including reading and writing. What is the articulation, inflection, and rhythm of the child's speech? How rich, limited, or idiosyncratic is the child's vocabulary? How fluent is the child in the language spoken at home and that of the larger community?
- Overall *intelligence* and fund of knowledge.
- *Attention, concentration, impulsivity.* Does the child attend to an activity or topic of discussion or jump from activity to activity? Does the examiner have to set frequent physical limits? Does the child appear distracted by outside noises?
- *Memory.*
- *Neurologic functioning.*
- *Judgment and insight,* especially concerning the presenting problem; this is most usefully judged after the child has had the opportunity to develop some rapport with the clinician, as the child's initial impulse may be deny or minimize the parents' presenting concerns.
- *Preferred modes of communication.* Is the child open to talking directly about the presenting problems and the significant aspects of the youngster's life, or is the child more comfortable with indirect modes of expression such as play or drawing?

Although the clinician will usually want to assess all of these areas of the mental status assessment, the emphasis and detail given to the different elements may vary with the setting and presenting problem. (For example, in an agitated, potentially delirious child on a pediatric ward, particular attention should be paid to the child's orientation, alertness, memory, verbal coherence, neurological functioning, and the possible presence of hallucinations.)

HISTORY TAKING

In general, the history-taking component of the child interview concerns the child's account of the same domains reviewed in taking the developmental history with the parents, with due consideration for the child's age-related limitations of memory, conceptual ability, and knowledge. (See Chapter 37 on the Developmental History of School-Age Children.)

One area of specific inquiry concerns the child's functioning in the major adaptive realms of family, peers, school, and recreation. The clinician seeks to elicit the child's interests, strengths, weaknesses, and feelings concerning each of these realms. History taking also includes explicit inquiry, in developmentally appropriate terms, concerning the presence of specific psychopathological symptoms (such as those of depression, anxiety, psychosis, or disruptive behavior). (See the sections on assessment of major realms of functioning and inquiry about psychopathological symptoms below for details.)

In addition to the directly observable behavior of the child and the child's account of family, school, and social life, the clinician is also interested in inferring a picture of the child's personality organization. This assessment includes such less directly observable aspects as the child's sense of self (including areas of perceived competence or inadequacy, identifications, gender identity, body image and concerns), fantasy life, conscience and values, and characteristic patterns of perceiving self in relation to others. [See Freud (1965) and Greenspan and Greenspan (1991) for various schemas of profiling these features.]

Specific Child Interview Techniques

In conducting the child interview, the clinician must blend a range of techniques to fit the nature of the problem being explored and the individual child's developmental level and emotional style. These basic techniques include interactive play and projective techniques and direct discussion.

DIRECT DISCUSSION

Direct discussion or inquiry about the presenting problem and other aspects of the child's life requires tact, as well as attention to the child's level of cognitive and linguistic development. The goal of such discussion is more than completing a yes-or-no checklist concerning the presence or absence of various psychopathological signs or symptoms. Rather it is to obtain a picture of how children see their world and function in it—their attachments and antipathies, pleasures and anxieties, and strengths and weakness, including those difficulties that have brought them for evaluation.

In phrasing questions, it is important to use language that is comprehensible to the child [for more details see Lewis (1974)]. Technical vocabulary or overly abstract or complex questions may confuse the child. Leading, closed, or overly concrete questions often yield unproductive responses. For example, yes-or-no questions (e.g., "Do you get along with your brother?") may elicit little more than a monosyllabic response to the dichotomy posed by the adult; in contrast, open-ended or descriptive questions often elicit a richer picture of how children think and feel about their world (e.g., "What sort of guy is your brother?" or "Tell me about your last play-date with Danny.") School-age children's sense of time may be idiosyncratic and is usually not measured in abstract units such as weeks or months. If establishing the specific chronology of events or symptoms is important, it is usually better to phrase questions in terms of the child's personal time line, such as "Did that happen before or after your birthday?" or "Have you had trouble with that since school got out?" [For a review of empirical studies of the effects of various interview styles see Hill (1985) and Cox and Rutter (1985).]

In addition to developmental, linguistic, or cognitive limitations, other response biases may influence school-age children's responses to questions. Although questions are often needed to initiate or focus discussion, too heavy reliance on a question-and-answer format may inadvertently encourage a constricted, reactive mode of response focused on objective facts rather than a more expressive conversation. Young children may be acquiescently inclined to give what they perceive to be socially desirable responses to questions; older children are often loathe to acknowledge, even to themselves, sad or vulnerable feelings (Glasbourg and Aboud, 1982). As a result, children may be quick to deny anger, embarrassment, or unhappiness. A thoughtful and empathic demeanor on the clinician's part helps to convey that the clinician is genuinely interested in how the child feels rather than seeking a conventional response. Although it is wise to avoid leading questions, it may be helpful to give implicit permission for the expression of a feeling ("Some kids might feel mad if that happened to them; how about you?") or to comment on an unverbalized affect ("You looked sad as you were telling me about that.") Probing a bland, but equivocal response may also be useful. For example, in response to an "Okay, I guess," the clinician may ask, "Sounds like you're not quite sure."

While encouraging a tone of frank discussion of problem areas, it is important to do so in a way that protects the child's self-esteem. Since many children are prone to seeing their symptoms as shameful or guilty failings, they are more likely to be candid when the clinician is able to discuss issues in nonjudgmental terms as difficulties or problems rather than as transgressions. Since the assessment asks the child to be frank about areas of difficulty, it is important to provide a context that also permits a chance to talk about their strengths. For example, in inquiring about school, it may be useful to begin by asking, "Tell me the parts of school you like best" before going on to ask "Are there subjects [or classmates or teachers] that give you trouble?" or "What are the rough spots at school?" To the socially isolated child, it may be better to ask, "Do you sometimes have trouble making or keeping friends as much as you'd like? . . . What do you think the trouble is?," rather than "Do you have any friends?" (especially if the truthful answer to the latter is "no").

PLAY TECHNIQUES

Play with the school-age child can serve as an important supplement to direct discussion. In contrast to the potentially anxiety-producing face-to-face demands of the direct interview, play pro-

vides a more relaxed and less challenging mode of relating to the clinician or revealing concerns. Some children may find it easier to communicate in displacement, through the medium of play.

In addition to facilitating rapport and providing a measure of gratification, play can also yield important assessment data. Imaginative play, either directly with the clinician or through the medium of puppets or figurines, can provide useful inferential data about the child's concerns, perceptions, and characteristic modes of regulating affects and impulses (Cohen et al., 1987; Slade and Wolf, 1994; Solnit et al., 1993). In keeping with their individual style, clinicians differ in the degree and manner to which they join such play (as opposed to remaining a nonparticipatory observer who comments on or inquires about the various characters' motives or feelings). Whatever the clinician's degree of activity in the play, the goal is to facilitate the expressive elaboration of fantasy, without distorting the communication by unwarranted speculations or intrusive reactions. To make such play possible, the interview room should have a supply of human and animal figures or dolls and appropriate props. It is best for these to be simple ones. Overly elaborate figures become distractions in their own right, while stock characters (such as Barbie or Disney characters) run the risk of imposing their own specific story lines.

In addition to revealing the child's emotional concerns and style, the play component of the interview also provides valuable data for the mental status assessment, by virtue of the opportunity it provides to observe the child's coordination, attention span, speech, vocabulary, affective tone, level of conceptual sophistication, etc. For example, the absence of imaginative play or play that is very limited, concrete, and noninteractive may be evidence of pervasive developmental disorder.

Games such as cards, catch, or simple board games also provide an opportunity to place the child at ease, develop rapport, and learn something of the child's interpersonal style. (For example, is the child easily upset at losing, given to cheating, wary of competition, or protective of the clinician?) Some games, such as throwing a ball back and forth or war, are simple enough to permit meaningful concurrent conversation, while helping to discharge tension or to mute the interrogatory pressures of the encounter. As with toys, overly elaborate games, such as chess, should be avoided; games that demand much cognitive energy and concentration usually preclude discussion of issues relevant to the assessment and may become a vehicle for avoidance.

PROJECTIVE TECHNIQUES

Various projective techniques, formal and informal, can be used to complement unstructured imaginative play as a means of obtaining an indirect picture of concerns that the child may be reluctant or unable to report upon directly (Rabin & Haworth, 1960). In addition to opening up areas for further exploration, these techniques also introduce an element of playfulness and can help to place the child at ease.

Inviting the child to draw a picture is a common gambit, with the content either left up to the child or a specific request made (e.g., a person or the child's family doing something). The content and form of drawings provide a window on both the child's emotional concerns and intellectual and visual-motor development. For example, the relative size and placement or omission of family members in a family drawing may be an important nonverbal indicator of the child's perceptions or feelings about the family. Prominent aggressive or sexual themes may also reflect important preoccupations of the child. Similarly, self-depictions of the patient as nonhuman, grotesque, inconsequential, or of the opposite gender provide important clues concerning the child's self-image. Familiarity with the developmental norms for human figure details, such as limbs, joints, facial features, clothing, etc., provide the examiner of a useful rough estimate of intellectual maturity. Various systems have been developed for systematically assessing the cognitive and emotional aspects of children's drawings (DiLeo, 1970; Harris, 1963; Koppitz, 1968; Naglieri 1988; Naglieri et al., 1991; Thomas and Silk, 1990). As noted earlier, the child's behavior while drawing may also be revealing (e.g., throwing the picture away unfinished while protesting self-disparagingly or perfectionistically that it is no good).

Other common projective techniques are to ask the child what animal they would most or least like to be or whom they would take along if they were going to be on a desert island. Another use-

ful question is to ask what they would wish for if they could have three magic wishes—that they can wish to have anything they want, to have the world be any way they want, or to change themselves in any way they want (Winkley, 1982). Children's responses are often revealing. Some may needily or impulsively wish for material possessions, such as a videogame or a million dollars. Other responses may reveal longings to change painfully perceived circumstances, such as "for my mom and dad to get back together again," "not to have tics anymore or get teased about them," or "to have a mom who doesn't yell at me all the time." Still other children appear uncomfortable wishing for something for themselves, preferring instead to give seemingly altruistic responses, such as "no more poverty or wars." Children's responses can serve as the starting point for further exploration. For example, with the child who wishes for "a big house and lots of money," one can inquire about who else would live there and what would they do. For the child who wishes for "no more fighting in the world," one can inquire if there are some particular fights that they would especially like to stop.

Other gamelike interactive imaginative techniques are available as part of the clinician's armamentarium. The "squiggle" drawing game developed by Winnicott (1971) consists of the clinician drawing a curvy line and asking the child to turn it into a picture of something; the child then draws a curvy line that the therapist elaborates on, and so on, taking turns. In Gardner's (1985) mutual story-telling technique, the child is asked to tell an original story with a moral; the clinician surmises the story's dynamic meanings and, using the child's terms or characters, tells a story in response that elaborates alternative resolutions of the conflicts and themes expressed in the child's story. The Despert (1937) fables are a series of affectively evocative incomplete stories which the child is asked to complete.

Asking the child to tell about a dream or a book, movie, or TV program that they remember often provides information about the child's interests and preoccupations. (If the clinician is familiar with the plot, the distortions the child may introduce can be informative regarding the child's cognitive and emotional style.) Inquiring about what the child would like to do after finishing schooling also provides a window on the child's aspirations, values, and concerns, as well as those of the family.

Structure and Sequence of the Child Interview

While the clinician keeps in mind an overall map of the functional and historical areas to be covered in the child interview, the specific format and sequence of a given interview depends on the unique combination of the individual child, the nature of the presenting problem, and the clinician's preferred style. Thus, for example, the clinician must be familiar with and, at some point in the interview, inquire about the cardinal symptoms of depression, anxiety, and disruptive behavior disorders; when and how this is done, however, will vary from child to child. Some of choices and considerations that shape the structure of the interview are reviewed below.

BEGINNING THE INTERVIEW

Having greeted the child and gone together to the office or playroom, the clinician faces the choice of how to open the interview. Many clinicians choose not to begin by immediately addressing the presenting problem. Some clinicians, for example, remain quiet, permitting the child to look about the room and to begin playing or talking without further prompting or guidance (Greenspan & Greenspan, 1991). While this approach permits children to make what they will of the materials and the clinician's presence and provides information about how they handle situational anxiety, it may leave many children disoriented and uncomfortably uncertain as to the clinician's goals and intentions (Feinstein, 1982). Other clinicians choose to be more active in placing the child at ease, by inviting the child to explore the available play materials ("What looks interesting?") or opening the interview by inquiring about neutral or pleasurable topics ("Tell me about what you like to do for fun?").

Decisions about timing must rely on a sensitive reading of the child's cues. Some children find it more comfortable to begin with less threatening topics until they feel comfortable with the interviewer; others prefer to jump right into discussion of their problems.

Although it may be useful to establish some initial rapport around neutral or interesting topics before addressing the presenting problem, most children know that they have not come for a conventional social encounter. Hence it is important relatively early in the interview to review and clarify what the child believes or has been told about the purpose of the meeting. The topic can be introduced straightforwardly by asking, "What did your mom and dad tell you [or what do you know] about why they wanted you to come and see me today?" If the child has already met with the clinician together with the parents as part of an earlier clinical contact, the clinician should already have asked something similar at that time and indeed may have heard something of the child's view of the presenting problem and history in parallel with the parents' account. (See Chapter 31, The Initial Encounter and Chapter 62, The Family Interview.) If so, the interview with the child provides a chance to follow up the previous meeting by saying, "Last time, we got to hear what your mom and dad thought about things. Today, we have a chance to talk more about how things look to you." This might be followed up by asking, "Were there some of the things we talked about then that we should start with today?" In any event, asking what the child knows or thinks about why he has been brought to see the clinician serves several functions. It conveys an interest in the *child's* view of the matter and permits an opportunity to hear how the child describes or assumes responsibility for the problem (or repudiates it as someone else's concern). It also provides an opportunity to address misapprehensions and to frame the clinician's own understanding of what has prompted the assessment in terms that can be understood and acknowledged by the child.

ASSESSMENT OF MAJOR REALMS OF FUNCTIONING

As described in Chapter 37 on the developmental history of the school-age child, the clinician seeks to elicit a picture of the child's functioning in the realms of school, peers, family, and recreation. Although many of these same areas may be explored in greater detail in relation to the presenting problem, discussion of these areas provides an overall picture of the child's life and level of adaptation. The clinician can begin in each of these realms by asking for objective facts, such as Who lives at home with you? Whom do you like to play with (or hang out with?) What school do you go to? What grade are you in? or What do you like to do for fun? This can be followed up by probing for the child's more subjective attitudes: How do people in your family get along? Are there any problems at home? (or things people fight about, or things you get in trouble for, or things people at home do that you don't like?) The goal is, to as great an extent as possible, to open up a discussion of each of these realms rather than simply eliciting rote responses to a checklist of questions. (See the section on direct discussion regarding means of phrasing questions in ways least likely to threaten the child's self-esteem or to evoke defensiveness.)

Beginning with the child's recreational interests (What do you like to do for fun?) provides a nonthreatening opportunity to get to know the child (as well as his interests, capacities, and preoccupations) before delving into the potentially more stressful and problematic areas of social relations and academic accomplishment.

Family life may be explored by asking the child who lives at home, how the child gets along with each family member, and how family members get along with each other. The clinician can also inquire more specifically, "What sorts of things do you like to do with your dad [or other relative]?" or "What is your brother like?" In the case of nontraditional family structures or families of divorce or separation, the clinician may inquire about the history of the current arrangement and what sort of relationship the child maintains with the noncustodial parent(s).

INQUIRY ABOUT PSYCHO-PATHOLOGICAL SYMPTOMS

Although assessment of certain specific symptoms may be high on the clinician's agenda as part of the differential diagnosis of the presenting problem, it is important to screen routinely for the symptoms of common or major disorders; unless

systematically inquired about, such symptoms may go undetected. Thus, in addition to those symptoms touched on in the course of discussing the presenting problem, the clinician needs to inquire in developmentally appropriate terms about depressive symptoms (such as low self-esteem, anhedonia, and suicidal ideation or behavior), excessive anxiety or fears, obsessions and compulsions, hallucinations and delusions, and antisocial behaviors. For example, one should inquire, "Do you ever feel sad or grumpy a lot of the time?" or "Do you feel like crying often?" If the answer is positive, one can follow up concerning persistence ("Does that last for more than a few minutes?"), frequency ("Does that usually happen every week (or most days)?"), and context ("What sorts of things make you feel that way?"). To inquire about suicidal ideation, one can begin by asking, "Do you ever feel that life is so hard, you wish you weren't alive (or would be better off dead)?", following up with "Have you ever tried to hurt yourself (or done anything to try to make yourself dead)?" Exposure to potentially traumatic experiences can also be inquired about in developmentally appropriate terms by asking, for example, whether scary things have ever happened or been done to the child. (See also Chapter 71 on the Observation, Interview and Mental Status Assessment of Traumatized Youths).

MENTAL STATUS ASSESSMENT

Although some abnormalities or deficits may be apparent simply by observing the child in the course of play or history taking, other elements of the mental status may require explicit examination. The clinical interview cannot take the place of careful, standardized developmental, psychometric, language, or neurological assessment. Nonetheless, a brief semistructured evaluation asking for a drawing; copying a design; simple tests of orientation, recall, general knowledge, and language (e.g., naming three objects; repeating a phrase such as "No ifs, ands, or buts"; a three-stage command such as, "Take a piece of paper in your right hand, fold the paper in half, put the paper on the floor"; a writing sample, such as asking the child to write a sentence of their choice); and a brief screen of neurological soft signs requires only about 5 to 10 minutes, provides useful information on school-age children, and can be readily incorporated in a playful way into a clinical interview. [See Lewis (1996), Ouvrier et al. (1993), and Chapter 83, The Neurological Examination, for details.]

CLOSING THE INTERVIEW

Toward the end of the interview, it is often useful to ask, "We've talked about a lot of things; are there any other things it would be important for me to know about you?" Similarly, one may inquire, "I've asked you a lot of questions; do you have any questions you want to ask me?" The child should also be given some general sense of what will happen next. For example, the clinician might explain, "I'm going to think over what I've heard from you and your folks and meet again with them [and you] to talk about what might help with. . . . Are there any particular things I should be sure to mention or suggest?" If the clinician has indeed already developed a sense of what interventions might be helpful, this may be tentatively broached to the child, with due respect for the parents' right to hear and decide on the clinician's recommendations.

REFERENCES

Angold, A. (1994). Clinical interviewing with children and adolescents. In M. Rutter, E. Taylor, & L. Hersov (Eds.), *Child and adolescent psychiatry: Modern approaches* (third ed. pp. 51–63). Oxford: Blackwell Scientific Publications.

Cohen, D. J., Marans, S., Dahl, K., Marans, W., & Lewis, M. (1987). Analytic discussions with oedipal children. *Psychoanalytic Study of the Child, 42*, 59–83.

Cox, A., & Rutter, M. (1985). Diagnostic appraisal and interviewing. In M. Rutter & L. Hersov (Eds.), *Child and adolescent psychiatry: Modern approaches* (2nd ed., pp. 233–248). Oxford: Blackwell Scientific Publications.

Despert, J. L. (1937). Technical approaches used in the study and treatment of emotional problems in children. V: the playroom. *Psychiatric Quarterly, 11*, 677.

DiLeo, J. H. (1970). *Children's drawing as diagnostic aids.* New York: Brunner/Mazel.

Feinstein, C. B. (1982). The pros and cons of the unstructured child diagnostic interview. *Contemporary Psychiatry, 1*, 7–9.

Freud, A. (1965). *Normality and pathology in children.* New York: International Universities Press.

Gardner, R. (1985). The initial clinical evaluation of the child. In D. Shaffer, A. A. Ehrhardt, & L. L. Greenhill (Eds.), *The clinical guide to child psychiatry* (pp. 371–392). New York: Free Press.

Glasbourg, R., & Aboud, F. (1982). Keeping one's distance from sadness. *Developmental Psychology, 18*, 287–293.

Greenspan, S. I., & Greenspan, N. T. (1991). *The clinical interview of the child* (2nd ed.). Washington, DC: American Psychiatric Press.

Harris, D. B. (1963). *Children's drawings as measures of intellectual maturity: A revision and extension of the Goodenough Draw-a-Man Test.* New York: Harcourt Brace and World.

Hill, P. (1985). The diagnostic interview with the individual child. In M. Rutter & L. Hersov (Eds.), *Child and adolescent psychiatry: Modern approaches* (2nd ed., pp. 249–262). Oxford: Blackwell Scientific Publications.

King, R. A., Work Group on Quality Issues (1995). Practice parameters for the psychiatric assessment of children and adolescents. *Journal of the American Academy of Child and Adolescent Psychiatry, 34* (10), 1386–1402, 1995 (Reprinted in JAACAP, 36 (Supplement) Oct, 1997 in press).

King, R. A., & Noshpitz, J. D. (1991). *Pathways of growth: Essentials of child psychiatry* (Vol. 2). New York: John Wiley & Sons.

Koppitz, E. M. (1968). *Psychological evaluation of children's human figure drawings.* New York: Grune & Stratton.

Lewis, M. (1974). Interpretation in child analysis: Developmental considerations. *Journal of the American Academy of Child Psychiatry, 13*, 32–53.

Lewis, M. (1996). Psychiatric assessment of infants, children, and adolescents. In M. Lewis (Ed.), *Child and adolescent psychiatry* (2nd ed., pp. 440–457). Baltimore, MD: Williams & Wilkins.

Naglieri, J. A. (1988). *Draw a Person: A quantitative scoring system manual.* San Antonio, TX: The Psychological Corporation.

Naglieri, J. A., McNeish, T. J., & Bardos, A. N. (1991). *DAP: SPED, Draw a Person: Screening procedure for emotional disturbance, examiner's manual.* Austin, TX: Pro-ed.

Ouvrier, R. A., Goldsmith, R. F., Ouvrier, S., & Williams, I. C. (1993). The value of the Mini-Mental State Examination in Childhood: A preliminary study. *Journal of Child Neurology, 8*, 145–148.

Rabin, A. I., & Haworth, M. R. (Eds.) (1960). *Projective techniques with children.* New York: Grune & Stratton.

Rutter, M., & Graham, P. (1968). The reliability and validity of the psychiatric assessment of the child: I. Interview with the child. *British Journal of Psychiatry, 114,* 563–579.

Schachar, R., Rutter, M., & Smith, A., (1981). The characteristics of situationally and pervasively hyperactive children: Implications for syndrome definition. *Journal of Child Psychology and Psychiatry, 22,* 375–392.

Simmons, J. E. (1987). *Psychiatric examination of children* (4th ed.). Philadelphia: Lee & Febiger.

Slade, A., & Wolf, D. P. (Eds.). (1994). *Children at play: Clinical and developmental approaches to meaning and representation.* Oxford: Oxford University Press.

Solnit, A. J., Cohen, D. J., & Neubauer, P. B. (1993). *The many meanings of play: A psychoanalytic perspective.* New Haven, CT: Yale University Press.

Thomas, G. V., & Silk, A. M. (1990). *An introduction to the psychology of children's drawings.* New York: New York University Press.

Winkley, L. (1982). The implications of children's wishes—research note. *Journal of Child Psychology and Psychiatry, 23,* 477–483.

Winnicott, D. W. (1971). *Therapeutic consultations in child psychiatry.* London: Hogarth Press.

61 / Observation, Interview, and Mental Status Assessment (OIM): Puberty, Adolescents, and Young Adults

Sidney Weissman and Carrie Sylvester

Setting the Stage

For all new adolescent patient referrals, you will need to determine if you wish to see the adolescent first, the parents first, the parents and the child together, or, on occasion, school counselors or others either first or as part of the assessment. There is no one correct sequence. Rather than conceptualizing a correct sequence, it is more helpful to conceptualize the process involved in determining the sequence. Informed consent is, of course, first obtained from the parents in their child's presence by either the clinician or a member of the support staff, unless there is an emergent need for evaluation because of obvious danger to self or others (Myers, 1982). Even in such circumstances, efforts to obtain informed consent must be initiated and those efforts documented. Older adolescents who initiate the request for individual treatment and adolescents who are particularly suspicious of parental efforts at control are usually best seen initially alone. Parents can be further involved with older adolescents, as needed, to obtain information and their support for the treatment plan. With a younger, but suspicious adolescent, you can stress confidentiality while discussing the importance of reviewing certain factual information with parents. You may work with the adolescent to acknowledge the parental interest that led them to seek help for their child. In cases where there is no obvious advantage, it can be informative to have both parents and adolescent come to your office and ask them how they wish to begin. After reviewing the options, you can observe how they proceed. In this way, you will make direct observation about how the identified adolescent patient and the family solve a defined problem. Again, be particularly sensitive to the situation where parental intrusiveness and control are such that seeing the adolescent alone for a significant part of the first stages of assessment would facilitate engagement. If such issues become apparent, gently encourage the option of moving next to spending time with the adolescent. Observe cues as to whether a separate interview with the adolescent at that time is raising undue anxiety in the parents, which can be explored as a first part of your subsequent time with them.

The clinical situation will frequently determine the sequence in which the information is obtained. If, as noted above, you have offered the adolescent and parents the option of how to begin and they cannot agree, this fact must be noted and eventually understood as you conceptualize their difficulties, but the clinician must proceed. The clinician's decision on how to proceed will be based on all of the data available at that moment. The first consideration remains, however, using a route that will best engage the adolescent in the assessment.

The Interview

OTHER ASPECTS OF ENGAGEMENT

Each of us has a unique style, but certain personal characteristics warrant special consideration. It is crucial to maintain a genuine, adult interest in the adolescent. Pay close attention to your own tendencies to identify more strongly with the adolescent or with the parents. A clinician of the same sex may be useful for some adolescents, but there has been sufficient controversy about gender bias in psychotherapy to make it important to assess the issue in the context of individual and family issues (Barak and Fisher, 1989). The sexual orientation of the clinician is also a consideration, with some evidence that similar sexual orientation facilitates a therapeutic alliance (Liljestrand et al., 1978). Racial, ethnic, or cultural differences or similarities between patient and therapist may impact the diagnostic process. Greater differences possibly lead to somewhat reduced diagnostic accuracy, at least initially, while not apparently having as great an impact on empathic understanding over time in therapy (Martin, 1993; Turner and Armstrong, 1981). Thus it is important to take these issues into account throughout the evaluation process and particularly to reserve diagnostic closure in situations where the evaluating and treating clinician is least like the adolescent in any of the aforementioned characteristics.

Adolescents must feel safe and secure (Katz, 1990). They should be presented with an outline of the assessment process and the specific time demands. They must be told what the rules are for confidentiality early in the interview. For example, are there any circumstances under which you would divulge to the parents or anyone information regarding what you were told? It is helpful to most adolescents to learn that the rules of confidentiality for adults in circumstances of danger to self or others and for insurance purposes are essentially the same as the rules of confidentiality for children and adolescents (Moore, 1994; Myers, 1982). This may also be a time to briefly explore any concerns the adolescent may have about excessive parental curiosity and how you might work together to not alienate parents while preserving reasonable confidentiality. In the case of divorce, be clear to the adolescent how you would communicate to custodial and noncustodial parents and stepparents. Early in the interview, the clinician must learn the adolescent's view of the reasons for seeing a clinician. A point related to confidentiality and trust is that some adolescents will refuse to talk about the reasons for an evaluation. Other adolescents will tell you one thing early on, but later reveal reasons that are viewed as shameful until greater comfort with the process and the clinician is achieved.

If parents are interviewed separately and an adolescent does not see a need for an evaluation or has a view that differs from the individual requesting the assessment, it is appropriate to pursue the differences in a nonjudgmental manner. There is considerable literature indicating that children and adolescents are more reliable and valid than parents in communicating about their internalizing symptoms (Hodges et al., 1990; Verhulst & Van der Ende, 1991). For this reason, troublesome disagreement about symptoms of a disruptive behavior disorder may require attention. It is important, however, to approach the task of understanding such areas of disagreement carefully so as to avoid escalating family discord or the adolescent's sense of being disbelieved or misunderstood. Thus some judgment as to the urgency of clarifying these issues is crucial to the ability to engage in many adolescents in treatment.

OBTAINING ESSENTIAL INFORMATION

When interviewing an adolescent, family member, or appropriate party, it is essential to obtain special information needed to respond to the referral question. The process must, nevertheless, assure obtaining essential information about the adolescent and the family after having determined the stated reason for the evaluation. Does the adolescent see a difficulty as internally or externally caused? When did the adolescent first think that a problem existed or was told that help was needed? How is the difficulty interfering with the adolescent's functioning or causing difficulty for the adolescent? A review of current psychiatric symptoms and of current or past treatment efforts must be obtained. Family medical history including psychiatric disorders and substance abuse must not be omitted. Some of this information is well known to older adolescents and other information can be obtained in the adolescent's presence so that it is learned by the adolescent. Exploration of special abilities, for example, athletics, music, or art, expands the view of the adolescent and can provide opportunities for an adolescent who is feeling quite upset about the process to relax and talk about an area that is a source of pride or to begin to express distress at loss of interest in a previously pleasurable activity.

NONPSYCHIATRIC MEDICAL PROBLEMS

General health, with special reference to appetite, weight, energy, and changes in sleep patterns, should be ascertained. Any chronic illnesses including epilepsy or diabetes, past surgery, major accidents, or loss of consciousness should be noted. Asking about the age of onset of chronic disorders will set the stage for learning whether the adolescent has adapted to limitations over time or has become excessively dependent. Sensitively explore if new demands for independence are being placed on an adolescent whose parents are becoming less able to manage the physical requirements of caring for an adult-size individual with physical limitations. It is helpful to assess the degree to which other aspects of establishment of identity are being or have been addressed in early and middle adolescence. In other circumstances, the most important limitations to a chronically ill adolescent may be those that affect full expression of sexuality, including procreation, so that late adolescence is the time of greatest adaptive stress.

If the adolescent has visible differences, assess the degree of resilience when encountering others who are insensitive and rude at a time when much of the adolescent work of establishing a stable identity is in progress. The clinician must also obtain a sense of the adolescent's understanding of the constraints imposed by an invisible or nearly invisible chronic condition and of his ability to address the responses of others. Invisible or nearly invisible conditions, such as cardiac limitations or diabetes, can be particularly difficult in early adolescence when a sophisticated understanding of the unseen and a more mature future orientation are lacking in self and peers. This can be compounded by less support from those who would quickly come to the rescue of a more obviously impaired adolescent struggling with visible constraints. The degree of support provided by both family and peers is crucial, and lack of support from either will impair the adolescent's adjustment and outcome (Smith et al., 1983).

ASSESSING CAPACITY FOR ABSTRACT THOUGHT

Although increased use of abstract reasoning is considered by many to be a hallmark of adolescence, only about two-thirds of an adult college population and one-third of other adult samples show solid use of formal operations (Jahnke & Blanchard-Fields, 1993). Routine mental status examination tasks will not provide the kind of information about approach to the world that is the basis for a sophisticated understanding of an adolescent's psychology because, even with partial attainment of abstract reasoning, adolescents may become more introspective and go through a period of intense interest in their own thoughts and inner lives. Sensitive clinical inquiry into an adolescent's idea of being uniquely observed, or having an "imaginary audience," and the idea of being specially exempt from consequences of behavior, or a "personal fable," can add a new dimension to assessment and treatment of a variety of behaviors and attitudes that seem self-destructive or at least to be interfering with achievement (Elkind, 1967). Whether these ideas are modified and eventually extinguished primarily by the development of formal operational thinking or by increased interpersonal experience and understanding remains a topic of investigation and discussion (Jahnke & Blanchard-Fields, 1993). The degree to which the adolescent has moved from concrete syllogistic thinking to more formal propositional logic will also be a basis for assessing the development of a sense of well-formed personal identity and the capacity for moral reasoning based on voluntary compliance with ethical principles (Erikson, 1963; Kohlberg, 1964). This is in contrast to a sense of dependent, diffuse, or other-directed identity based more on cognitive processes using concrete operations. Concrete operations leads to a use of rigid authority-directed morality similar to a younger child.

SEXUALITY

A particularly sensitive, critical area that must be explored with each adolescent relates to sexual behavior. How this will be approached depends upon the age of the adolescent as well as the reason for the assessment. A matter-of-fact, nonjudgmental manner with the adolescent alone in the context of general questions about health and risk-taking behaviors is usually well-received if the clinician is comfortable with these issues. Approaching sexual topics in such a manner may also serve as entrance to discussion of some issues that have been troubling to an adolescent who is having difficulty confiding to parents, however well meaning.

It is important to know the sexual orientation of patients in addition to whether or not they date or are sexually active. Frequency of sexual activity is also significant. If they are sexually active, do they or their partners use any contraception? Most specifically, is the adolescent or partner consistently using condoms appropriately to reduce the risk of contracting AIDS? The risk for sexually transmitted disease is relatively high in the immature female genital tract of adolescents less than 18 to 20 years of age. That information may not have been taught and should be addressed in interactions between physicians and adolescents. Nevertheless, tendencies to succumb to peer pressure or to have a limited sense of personal vulnerability are more important in determining whether an adolescent will engage in unprotected sexual activity.

If a girl has been pregnant, determine whether the pregnancy was the result of forcible or statutory rape and if she delivered or had an abortion. Clinicians must not assume that adolescent pregnancy is the result of consensual sex between adolescents. The documented difference between maternal and paternal ages for adolescents in the United States indicates that a sizable minority of adolescent girls are impregnated by men who are at least 6 years older and thus are adult men

(Guttmacher Institute, 1994). Women who had a physical, emotional, or mental limitations during childhood were twice as likely as those without such limitations to have been victims of sexual abuse, so history of pregnancy or sexually transmitted disease should raise the index of suspicion when such vulnerable adolescents are seen (Moore et al., 1989). If the pregnancy was terminated, at what stage of pregnancy did the abortion occur, who supported her in the decision, and was the decision congruent with her beliefs? If a girl delivered, how has she dealt with the child and coparent? If a boy is a father, similar questions are relevant.

SUBSTANCE ABUSE

It is important to obtain a history of any substance use starting with tobacco and alcohol. Knowing the age of first use, frequency of use, circumstances of use, and whether used to intoxication is essential information. Inquire about perceived parental attitudes toward tobacco, alcohol, and marijuana. Tobacco is now well known to be an important gateway drug. Its use is illegal in adolescence, and it has the highest lifetime morbidity and mortality of all addictive substances. Marijuana use in adolescents has risen in the 1990s. This may be due to increased parental permissiveness of marijuana use because of their own frequently benign use histories (Stoil, 1996). The use of inhalants or parenterally administered agents should be explored when any other behaviors indicate risk for such.

Mental Status Examination

APPEARANCE AND BEHAVIOR

In your initial contacts with adolescents and parents or guardians, a great deal can be learned about adolescents and their families from their appearances. Is the dress age and culturally appropriate? In multicultural areas, the clinician must be familiar with diverse standards of dress in different subgroups. One must also note the similarity or lack thereof between the clothing style of adolescents and parents. If they are discrepant, in what manner? In the interview, the clinician can learn if there is parental agreement that the adolescent's appearance is appropriate. If not, why not? Further, note responses that indicate the adolescent's self-assessment of appearance? How far to probe about these observations will again depend on each clinical situation. In noting the adolescent's use of or importance of clothes and cleanliness, it is crucial to carefully observe for gang symbols or any other characteristics indicating gang affiliation.

In observing the adolescent, also note the adolescent's physical stature. Is the stature appropriate for age and pubertal development? Are there any physical problems that can be observed? Are there any scars or other stigmata, or is there any indication of chronic medical illness? Are weight or excessive dieting and exercise potential problems and are they congruent with historical information?

SPEECH

The observation phase of a clinical assessment includes using auditory methods as well as visual ones. For example, do the patient and family members use the same language? Do they all have a command of the community's language? If not, what other language? Is the adolescent able to communicate in an effective language that each parent or guardian, if present, can understand? For example, do parents of a deaf child understand signing? Is the adolescent's speech well modulated, goal oriented, and appropriate to age and community? If there is evidence of a speech impediment or communication difficulty, speech and communication assessment and treatment should be noted in the history of school performance and placement.

MOOD AND AFFECT

Affect can be effectively inferred from observations during the general interview. Questions about worries, fears, boredom, losses, and sadness need to be routinely asked to explore the possibility of an anxiety or affective disorder. Simply asking about anxiety or depression is usually misunderstood by all but the most sophisticated adolescents.

THOUGHTS AND RISKS

Even a very brief exploration of the use of fantasy and of an adolescent's future goals provides a useful window on the adolescent's thoughts and thinking style. The clinician can create a fantasy experience and see how an adolescent deals with it. For example, if given $1,000,000, what would an adolescent do? If marooned on an island, who would they want to have with them? It is equally important to note an adolescent's inability to use fantasy. Examination of future goals, although related to fantasy, is approached differently. Does the adolescent have a sense of time and the ability to project into or imagine the future? Of course, here as elsewhere, it is important to be aware of and sensitive to ethnic and economic issues that impact on career planning. In light of each adolescent's external realities, one must ask if such plans are consonant with that adolescent's abilities.

The presence of symptoms of psychosis needs to be broached. If the presence of hallucinations or delusional ideation emerges, they must be explored in detail from a developmental and cultural perspective. Situations where they occur or worsen should be highlighted. The clinician must attempt to determine if a psychosis is the result of a general medical condition or a primary psychiatric disorder.

Suicidal and homicidal potential must always be ascertained. Denial of suicidal intent is not adequate assurance that the patient is not a suicide risk. Assessment of risk for dangerousness to self or others includes a history of impulsive acts and risk for intoxication. When the clinician is concerned about dangerousness, knowledge of meaning of death and its permanence is important. Extreme anxiety with poor performance heightens suicidal risk so that the adolescent's subjective experience of stress and hope for its reduction must be also discussed.

COGNITIVE ABILITY

The adolescent should be oriented to self, others, place, and date. It is necessary, at times, to assess cognitive performance prior to assessing the capacity for abstract thought. As described earlier, assessment of capacity for abstract thought needs to take into account that if this thinking style develops, it is variable in normal adolescents. It is also related to academic and cultural issues. A sense of the complexity of the adolescent's approach to the world is gathered throughout the interview. To estimate learning or achievement, a few questions to ascertain the fund of knowledge consistent with age and gender may be helpful. For an adolescent who has not performed well in school, pursuing their knowledge in areas of special interest is frequently helpful.

As with adults, tasks such as serial subtraction of 7 from 100 or 3 from 20 can be used, noting speed and accuracy to assess attention and concentration. It is wise to err on the side of cognitively simpler tasks to avoid humiliating and alienating a patient. Judgment in situations in which the adolescent would interact without adult supervision should be explored. Having done this, the clinician can explore the adolescent's insight into self and both personal and family situations.

Conclusion

At the end of the assessment, which includes parents where appropriate, it should also be possible, using all the data obtained, to develop a tripartite formulation addressing biologic, psychologic, and the social (e.g., family, school) factors which have impacted on the patient. From this, a multiaxial differential diagnosis using standard nomenclature can be derived. Once a preliminary diagnosis is made, a plan for obtaining further information to confirm the diagnosis or diagnoses and an initial treatment plan can be developed. Those should be directly communicated to the patient and the family and/or to the referring source in a manner dictated by the same considerations that determined the sequencing of the assessment interviews. Additionally, recommendations based on the results of forensic consultations may need to be communicated to the court as required.

REFERENCES

Barak, A. & Fisher, W. A. (1989). Counselor and therapist gender bias? More questions than answers. *Professional Psychology—Research and Practice, 20,* 377–383.

Elkind, D. (1967). Egocentrism in adolescence. *Child Development, 38,* 1025–1034.

Erikson, E. (1963). *Childhood and society* (2nd ed.). New York: W. W. Norton.

Guttmacher Institute. (1994). *Sex and America's teenagers* New York: Author.

Hodges, K., Gordon, Y., & Lennon, M. P. (1990). Parent-child agreement via a clinical research interview for children: The Child Assessment Schedule (CAS). *Journal of Child Psychology and Psychiatry and Allied Disciplines, 31,* 427–436.

Jahnke, H. C., & Blanchard-Fields, F. (1993). A test of two models of adolescent egocentrism. *Journal of Youth and Adolescence, 22,* 313–326.

Katz, P. (1990). The first few minutes: The engagement of the difficult adolescent. In S. C. Feinstein, A. H. Esman, J. G. Looney, G. H. Orvin, J. L. Schimel, A. Z. Schwartzberg, A. D. Sorosky, & M. Sugar (Eds.), *Adolescent psychiatry: Developmental and clinical studies* (Vol. 17, pp. 69–81). Annals of the American Society for Adolescent Psychiatry. Chicago: University of Chicago Press.

Kohlberg, L. (1964). Development of moral character. In M. L. Hoffman & L. W. Hoffman (Eds.), *Review of child development research* (Vol. 1, pp. 400–404). New York: Russell Sage Foundation.

Liljestrand, P., Gerling, E., & Saliba, P. A. (1978). The effects of social sex-role stereotypes and sexual orientation on psychotherapeutic outcomes. *Journal of Homosexuality, 3,* 361–372.

Martin, T. (1993). White therapists' differing perceptions of black and white adolescents. *Adolescence, 28,* 281–289.

Moore, K., Nord, C., & Peterson, J. (1989). Nonvoluntary sexual activity among adolescents. *Family Planning Perspectives, 21,* 110–114.

Moore, S. (1994). Confidentiality of child and adolescent treatment records. *Child and Adolescent Social Work Journal, 11,* 165–175.

Myers, J. E. (1982). Legal issues surrounding psychotherapy with minor clients. *Clinical Social Work Journal 10,* 303–314.

Smith, M. S., Gad, M. T., & O'Grady, L. (1983). Psychosocial functioning, life change, and clinical status in adolescents with cystic fibrosis. *Journal of Adolescent Health Care, 4,* 230–234.

Stoil, M. J. (1996, January/February). Why more teens are toking. *Behavioral Health Management, 8.*

Turner, S., & Armstrong, S. (1981). Cross-racial psychotherapy: What the therapists say. *Psychotherapy: Theory, Research and Practice, 18,* 375–378.

Verhulst, F. C., & Van der Ende, J. (1991). Assessment of child psychopathology: Relationships between different methods, different informants and clinical judgement of severity. *Acta Psychiatrica Scandinavica, 84,* 155–159.

62 / Observation, Interview and Mental Status Assessment (OIM): Family Unit and Subunits

Allan M. Josephson and Frank J. Moncher

The interview of a family unit and its subunits is an essential element of the psychiatric assessment of children and adolescents. A family interview reveals factors which predispose a child to emotional or behavioral problems as well as factors which may precipitate or maintain them. While establishing factors relating to pathology, the family interview also identifies resources for intervention within the family. The clinician's goal is to observe interactions between family members, assess the thoughts and emotions of each family member, and obtain history of the immediate clinical problem and general family functioning.

The family interview allows the observation of each family member in relation to the family as a whole, as well as their interactions involved with the identified patient. Seeing the child in the context of the family provides data relevant to both a specific clinical problem and to general family functioning. Family interviews reveal different aspects of history and behavioral functioning than that obtained from separate interviews with the child or parent.

CASE EXAMPLE

Fifteen-year-old Tim appears self-assured in the individual interview, but appears less competent when he is verbally abusive of his mother during the family interview. Similarly, Tim's mother vividly describes his pathology in the individual interview, but is observed as being part of the problem, when during the family interview, she reacts with disproportionate anger toward him.

In a process that begins from the moment of first contact with the family, the clinician compares the gathered observations and historical data with norms of group behavior and family development in order to determine which interactions may be contributing to the clinical problem.

A family interview expands the presenting complaint into the broader framework provided by multiple perceptions of the problems. It is common for other problems to emerge in the interview, necessitating a reorientation of assessment from the problems of one child to a broader evaluation of other family members, or the family as a whole.

In the above example, Tim's oppositional behavior is discovered to be related to a long history of his parents' marital conflict. Additional interviewing suggests that Tim's mother is very angry at his father, to whom Tim bears a resemblance. Furthermore, Reggie, Tim's younger brother, describes somatic complaints and anxiety symptoms.

Interviewing the family as a whole has several additional beneficial effects. A review of a broad range of family functioning lessens the potential scapegoating of the identified patient. Scapegoating occurs when a family implies all family problems are the result of a disordered child. In a family interview, the concerns of siblings can be identified and these observations can be utilized in developing a more comprehensive formulation. Evaluation of each parent's style can be directly observed as parents intervene with other children as well as the patient. By comparing a parent's responses to siblings with their response to the identified patient, puzzling complaints can be clarified.

CASE EXAMPLE

Mr. Baron is described as being aloof, distant, and uncaring by his teenage daughter. During the family interview, he is observed comforting his crying infant grandson. As the interview progresses, it appears his "distance" from his daughter is related more to his anger at her becoming pregnant than a pervasive personality characteristic.

In family interviews, statements from siblings can confirm or contrast parent statements about the identified patient. Younger siblings are often less defended and more open about family concerns. The likelihood of genuine and relevant affect being displayed by all members increases when an attempt is made to foster family interaction. In doing so, we experience firsthand what it is like to be a member of the family. Family interviews expose the differences between the family history as reported by mother, father, and the children. Such delineation of discrepancies often leads to an understanding of family structure, communication, and problems. Family events are viewed differently by each participant and a thorough family interview allows an elaboration of each individual perception. The interview also serves as a catalyst for engaging family members and providing effective interventions as each family member sees the potential benefit from changes in the family system as a whole, in addition to whatever benefits accrue to the identified patient.

Conceptual Background Relevant to Family Interviewing

Systems theory serves as the basis for many of the observations made during the family interview. Family systems theory is derived from general systems theory, the most widely acknowledged proponent of which is Ludwig Von Bertallanfy (1968). According to the general systems theory, any system attempts to maintain homeostasis, a type of stabilization in which numerous variables in the system are maintained within constant limits. In human physiology, homeostasis occurs when the heart rate increases in response to the lowering of blood pressure, in order to maintain adequate blood flow throughout the body. Applied to families, homeostasis implies that members of the family are in a type of relationship balance or equilibrium with each other. Members respond to others and others respond to them in ways that maintain this balance. This equilibrium is never static and is constantly being redefined. Thus families are always in a state of dynamic tension and constant self-regulation. Any attempt to shift equilibrium from within, or without, will re-

sult in resistance to change and a desire to maintain the status quo.

CASE EXAMPLE

Three-year-old Billy is in an overly close, dependent relationship with his mother, and resists attending day care. As therapeutic intervention fosters his emotional separation from mother, he begins to attend day care without distress at separation from her. His new found competence in peer activities is associated with an increased desire to attend day care, and an absence of anxiety. As he improves, resistance to change comes from his father and mother. Billy's independence has forced mother to deal with her self-esteem problems and unfulfilling marriage. His father, an emotionally distant man, is threatened by the dual task of assisting his son's development and meeting the emotional needs of his wife, who is now despondent that "Billy no longer needs me." These family shifts unmask father's own sense of ineffectiveness. From the systemic perspective, there will be a strong tendency for this family to revert to habitual, predictable ways of relating to each other which will perpetuate Billy's problem.

In this systemic view of child psychopathology, symptoms are not seen as residing within the child but as serving a purpose or function for the family system. A child's somatic symptoms, which result in his father canceling a business trip, may serve the function of strengthening a tenuous attachment to his father, or lessen anxiety about marital conflict which the child has been observing. The weight loss of a young girl with anorexia nervosa may have the purpose of maintaining close ties with a parent, as well as providing an anxious mother with a focus for her attention. In such instances, each family member is presumed to act in a way which would oppose symptomatic improvement in the identified patient. While maintaining this equilibrium, the family interaction becomes a shared coping mechanism by which members avoid the destabilizing effects of change. The systemic perspective enables the clinician to anticipate what events would take place if a child's symptoms were removed.

Systems theory has, in the last several decades, been generative of numerous family therapy approaches to treating child and adolescent disorders. These interventions have generated new information on family processes which can be utilized in performing the family interview, whether or not an actual family therapy intervention takes place. Salvador Minuchin (1974) formulated the structural model with its emphasis on understanding the hierarchy of roles in family relationships and the boundaries within the family and between the family and the external environment. Watzlawick, Jackson, Haley, and others developed the strategic approach which emphasized strategic solutions to immediate, "here and now" problems (see Stanton, 1981). Carl Whittaker was a main proponent of the experiential approach, which focused primarily on the immediate affective experience of the family members (Neill & Kniskern, 1982). In recent years, Barton and Alexander (1981) have focused on the functional role of maladaptive problems in the family, that is, what purpose the psychiatric symptom has in maintaining overall family functioning. Behavioral approaches to family assessment have become common; for example, the work of Patterson (1982) describing interventions with the conduct problems of children. Numerous reviews describe these individual schools of family therapy in great detail and will inform the reader interested in a particular perspective (Gurman & Kniskern, 1991; Sargent, 1997).

While the systemic perspective helps us understand the forces impacting the family as a whole, it does not focus on individual motivation and individual function, which also must be addressed when interviewing a family (Freedman and Combs, 1996). When problems resist change, the motivation of one individual should be considered as a possible cause. The clinician recognizes that certain symptoms are biologically mediated and reside within individuals. Further, progress in developmental research suggests intrapsychic life is strongly influenced by family relationships; the parents own relationship history, once internalized, subsequently affects their functioning, including parenting (Sameroff & Emde, 1989). The impact of the parent's developmental histories, marital history, and family interactional history on the child's mental life and self-development are important components of the family interview. This perspective, in addition to the systemic perspective, must be utilized for a thorough, complete family interview.

The Clinical Task of Family Interviewing

GOALS AND OBJECTIVES OF THE FAMILY INTERVIEW

The primary goals of the family interview are to gather relevant family history, including history of the family unit and of the individuals comprising the family, and to observe family interactions (see also Chapter 48, "Family History and Its Significance"). The family interview should occur in the context of a comprehensive assessment of a child or adolescent's problems.

It is possible the presenting complaint, such as oppositional behavior, attentional problems, or depressive affect, may spontaneously occur during the family interview. If so, we should delineate the functional significance of such symptoms by interacting with each family member. When such events do not occur naturally, the clinician should facilitate some interaction between family members in order to observe their reactions.

The interview must gather enough data to develop a formulation of family problems that allows the clinician to determine if, and how, these family factors relate to clinical problems. The data of the family interview must serve the goal of developing a rational way to approach intervention. This goal may be met by direct intervention with the family or merely soliciting their support for other interventions. A definite goal of the family interview is to develop an alliance with each family member which facilitates future clinical contact of any type.

In addition to these goals, the family interview should achieve specific objectives. The thoroughly conducted family interview (1) indicates which areas of family interaction need systemic and behavioral intervention; (2) identifies impediments to systemic and behavioral interventions; (3) reveals which areas of a child's or adolescent's delayed development have been influenced by family interaction; (4) identifies and predicts the emergence of other symptomatic family members; (5) suggests which areas of delayed parental development have predisposed to family interactional problems; and (6) helps determine whether the family is compensating for a child's disorder or is contributing to the child's disorder.

These goals and objectives described apply to a family interview which is a component of an initial, comprehensive clinical assessment of the child. An additional family interview may also be indicated during the course of individual interventions with the child or adolescent. Frequently, the goal in this instance is to ascertain factors related to a lack of clinical progress.

CASE EXAMPLE

For 15 months, 6-year-old Eric had been treated for Attention Deficit Hyperactivity Disorder. During this time, he had been treated with three different medications, cognitive behavioral play therapy, and had also received special education assistance. As his symptomatology persisted, the treating clinician requested a family interview. Heather, a 7-year-old sister, and mother's boyfriend attended the interview with Eric and his mother. While Eric's mother was well meaning, she was observed to be a passive woman who had trouble resisting Eric's firm temperament. Her boyfriend had a tenuous relationship with Eric and seemed to believe Eric's behavior was "his mother's problem." When he did attempt to intervene and structure Eric's impulsive, distractible behavior, he became harsh and negative. This mobilized Eric's mother's protectiveness. The interview also revealed that Heather had recently been refusing to attend school.

In this instance, the family interview revealed significant resistances to symptomatic improvement in Eric's clinical problems. These data were used to formulate the case differently and involve the family more directly to assist Eric, and Heather as well.

PREPARING FOR THE FAMILY INTERVIEW

Prior to initiating a family interview, it is important to review the available clinical data, determine the referral source, recognize who has identified a need for change, and understand whether other agencies and professionals are, or have been, involved with the family. The most common presentation requiring a family interview is a symptomatic child, but a family may present with a family problem and request a family interview and intervention. When the family presents with a symptomatic child, they may need an explanation of why all family members need to attend, as a common assumption is that the symptomatic child needs evaluating, not asymptomatic family members. It is typically sufficient to explain that while one child may be having difficulty, it is helpful to understand all family member's perspectives of the problem, and that it is common for one family member's difficulty to have an impact on all family member's lives.

The interview is best conducted in a casual setting in a room large enough to comfortably accommodate the family. Furniture or objects potentially harmful to younger children should be removed. Toys or games for younger children should be present to facilitate rapport with them and decrease their likelihood of interrupting the discussion among older children and parents.

The family interview can be expected to take from 1 to 2 hours, depending on the clinical situation, the ages of the children, and the number of family members involved. Certain factors may extend this period of time, such as the complexity of clinical problems and the number of symptom bearers involved, as it is not uncommon for one child to be the identified patient and another child or parent to appear more symptomatic. As the interview progresses, acute problems, such as suicidal ideation or intense disagreement around an issue, can prevent systematic gathering of background family history. At times such as these, another family interview should be scheduled. The complexity of a family interview may indicate the need to have more than one evaluator present. With two clinicians, one can be engaged in dialogue with a family member while the other clinician observes the family interactions and the behaviors of others present.

The use of video technology facilitates the breadth of this assessment. Closed-circuit television captures verbal and behavioral interactions which often escape an examiner's in vivo observation. The video record of complex family interactions is then available for review by the clinician only, or together with patient and family as part of a later therapeutic intervention. A useful tool and specialized component of family interviewing is the observation team, utilized most often in educational settings (Andersen, 1987). This term refers to a group of professionals, who either through a one-way mirror or over closed-circuit television, observe the interview and intermittently consult with the clinician. This consultation usually results in recommendations for further areas of clinical exploration. Both of these methods enhance the family interview by providing increased opportunities for observing subtle, multiple, and often simultaneous interactions.

THE PARTICIPANTS

All first-degree biological relatives who reside with the identified patient should be invited to the family interview. In addition to members of the immediate family, the interview should also include those who have regular interactions with the identified patient that the clinician judges to be influential, such as grandparents or other family members who have daily contact or parenting responsibilities. When family members meeting this latter criterion are numerous, it is necessary to have several meetings with these individuals to fully observe patterns of interaction and gather historical data. A noncustodial parent living apart from the child may be invited to the family interview when parents are recently separated and permanent custody is yet to be established. Children of divorced parents should be interviewed with the biological parent who has regular physical custody. In some instances a separate interview with the noncustodial parent who has regular visitation is indicated to provide a complete perspective on the child's problems. A joint interview with divorced parents and their biological children is generally contraindicated because it confuses younger children and reawakens past conflicts for older ones. Not uncommonly, some family members fail to attend when requested. This is often an opportunity to understand some of the family dysfunction which may be contributing to the presenting complaint.

CASE EXAMPLE

Brian does not attend a session related to the evaluation of his hyperactive, aggressive young son, resulting in a hypothesis that his unavailability is part of the difficulty; Ellie's teenage sibling does not attend a session related to 9-year-old Ellie's refusal to go to school, suggesting that the parents also have difficulty gaining compliance from the older child.

On the other hand, some families will bring individuals who are not requested to attend, and this information also enriches the clinical formulation.

CASE EXAMPLES

Nancy, a 14-year-old with anorexia nervosa, was seen for an evaluation. When the family interview was planned, her parents and younger brother attended, but also her grandparents, one aunt, and an uncle came because they "were very concerned about her." They were allowed to attend the session, and the history gathered from all members indicated an emotionally close family. While they were overtly supportive, it became clear that adolescent emancipation was seen as a type of betrayal of family unity.

Brent, a 15-year-old conduct disordered adolescent, asked his friend to come to the family interview. His single mother allowed his friend to come to the interview and to give his impressions of Brent's problem. It became clear to the interviewer that the ease with which a nonbiological relative became involved in the interview, suggested a vague definition of family and a lack of connectedness between blood relations.

While the primary goal remains that all family members attend the family interview, the clinician should interview all who actually arrive. The clinician should be very attentive to the absence of certain members and its meaning for the family. The absence of a member, most often a reluctant adolescent or parent, powerfully affects what happens in the session. A family interview with members missing, while less than optimal, can nonetheless serve as a catalyst for family change.

CASE EXAMPLES

Mr. and Mrs. Jacobs and their two younger children presented for a family interview without their adolescent child, Donald. The withdrawn behavior of young Tabitha was the stated reason for the visit. Midway through the interview, 8-year-old Eric blurted out, "I don't know why Donald didn't have to come. He always gets his own way." This led to a fruitful discussion between the parents regarding Donald's tyrannical behavior and their feelings of powerlessness to influence him.

Matthew, 15, refused to come for family assessment. Mrs. Jones wanted to cancel the appointment but the clinician encouraged her to come with her husband to discuss their problems. While the information gathered was incomplete because of Matthew's absence, the couple did describe their challenges dealing with their son's noncompliance and substance abuse. Mother tearfully described how she felt that her indulgence contributed to Matthew's inability to follow through with his commitments. This family interview served as a stepping stone for further sessions during which Matthew's parents developed a behavioral plan to expect more maturity from their son. Matthew became increasingly symptomatic later in the year and sought assistance on his own accord.

Marilyn, 34, brought Eric, her overactive, disruptive 9-year-old son and two other young children to the family interview. Eric's father was resistant to the idea and declined to attend the session, stating that he was busy. Marilyn was encouraged to explain to her husband that his involvement, at least for the evaluation, was thought to be important by the clinician. When this was unsuccessful, the clinician then attempted to personally contact the father. The clinician explained that in order to understand Eric's problem fully, and provide the most effective and appropriate care, the perspectives of all family members were important, particularly his. The clinician clarified that ongoing attendance might or might not be necessary, but it was essential that he attend on at least one occasion. This intervention resulted in the father presenting for the next interview.

While engaging distant fathers may be one of the most difficult challenges of the family interview, it is potentially one of the most fruitful endeavors as well.

Valuable information is obtained when whole family data are contrasted with that obtained from subunits. Symptomatic children often distract the interviewer from observing marital discord. Interviewing parents alone may provide an opportunity to observe overt marital conflict only suspected during the whole family interview. Seeing one parent with the children provides an opportunity to observe interactions more accurately reflecting family life in families where this is a common occurrence, such as the family where one parent is frequently absent due to out of town travel. On occasion it is useful to have an interview limited to siblings. Such an interview can allow more direct communication of the children's concerns about family life. In this instance, as with interviews of children alone, it is important to clarify what will and will not be kept confidential from parents. In such an interview, siblings may reveal, through their verbal report or their observable behavior, how they function when parents are not present. Any concerns about maltreatment or other family secrets may be more easily disclosed without parents present. Interviewing the identified patient alone can lead to important information and re-

veal characteristics, such as self assuredness, not readily apparent in a family interview.

CASE EXAMPLE

Marilyn, a 14-year-old girl being evaluated for depression, rarely spoke during a family interview. She attempted to respond to the examiner on several occasions but her mother elaborated her answers. She became more withdrawn throughout the interview. When seen alone, Marilyn was verbal, articulate, and able to describe an inner sense of anger at her mother's intrusiveness.

The Clinical Interview

THE GENERAL CLINICAL PROCESS

The family interview is a semistructured, systematic event in which the behavior of the clinician is as important as in any area of clinical work. The collaborative nature of the general psychiatric interview is heightened in the family interview. In this instance, the clinician is attempting to engage an often reticent child in a clinical setting, as well as several other individuals, some of whom may be unclear as to the reason for being present. Often parents come with a mixture of confusion and strong emotional feelings, including anger, despair, or guilt.

In response to this complex challenge, the clinician should be sociable in order to foster comfort, yet professional to complete the task at hand. An alliance must be sensitively forged with parents, although this does not necessarily translate to total support of all parental behaviors and attitudes. An empathic, yet objective appraisal is indicated because parental behavior and attitudes may contribute to the child's difficulty.

The clinical interview involves several different aspects which merge with each other until the family's concerns are fully heard and the family interactions fully explored. The interview should move smoothly so that by its termination, each member feels that they have been understood and each member understands their role in subsequent clinical involvement, if required. Wherever possible, the clinician conveys a sense of hope with respect to future family adjustment.

OVERVIEW OF CONDUCTING THE FAMILY INTERVIEW

At the beginning of the family interview, the clinician typically puts the family at ease in preparation for more formal interviewing (Haley, 1976). Each family member is addressed in an informal manner consistent with their developmental level, with the goal of establishing rapport. Asking children about school or recent holidays allows them an opportunity to talk without having to comment initially on what may be an emotionally charged presenting complaint. Inquiries about parents' work or casual topics, such as parking and traffic, can serve not only to ease tension but shows that the clinician is interested in the family's entire experience, not just the presenting complaint. As the interview begins, extra effort should be made to engage the individual appearing least interested in being present, often a disinterested sibling or a parent who is skeptical about psychiatric intervention. Every attempt is made to move seamlessly into a delineation of clinical problems. By asking open-ended questions the clinician conveys to the patient and parents that their perception of the problem is important and it allows the clinician to discern core concerns, family style, and family structure. We then proceed by gathering the needed data, while always encouraging the parents and child to spontaneously recount their view of situations.

Often a nondirective opening inquiry such as, "What is it that brings your family to the clinic today?" provides valuable information. In directing such a question to no one in particular, the clinician can observe who takes initiative in the family, at least in terms of the clinical concern, and possibly in other areas of family life as well. After seeing who responds first, it is important for each family member to be addressed and for their perspective on the presenting complaint to be obtained. During this process the clinician can assess how each individual relates to her. In this initial phase, core concerns may be accompanied by affect and this should be sensitively explored by the interviewer until its precipitants are completely understood. By following the family members lead, the clinician can avoid misleading data which result from too many preconceived questions, and can focus instead on areas most important to the family. The clinician must balance activity with passivity, being flexible enough to follow family member's cues, yet structured enough to gather complete data. While many families in distress will reveal some feelings and history easily, other relevant information may require a great deal of empathic listening in order to be gathered.

Many presentations to clinics involve an interactive problem as the presenting complaint such as a child's oppositional behavior, a child running away from home, or a suicide attempt occurring after a family conflict. These presentations naturally lend themselves to questioning about the family's attempts to solve these problems and a review of the interaction sequences associated with the problems. Interviews which emphasize "blow-by-blow" accounts of the conflict reveal important family patterns of interaction. In gathering these data, the clinician must contrast what happened with family members' attitudes and perceptions about what happened. In-session elaboration of how the family has attempted to solve past problems could be part of this interview strategy, including review of previous interactions with professionals. The history of successful problem resolution should be reviewed as well as discussing situations where problems remained unsolved. Through all this activity, the clinician notes the processes involved, both cognitive and affective, in the family's problem-solving sequence.

Through asking family members about the responses, behaviors, and feelings of each other, the clinician begins to understand how events have acquired specific meanings for each member and how these meanings differ. If a son challenges a father during the interview, along with inquiring about their experience with each other, the clinician can ask the mother, "What is happening between your husband and your son right now?" The clinician can also ask the mother, "What are you thinking and feeling?" This type of inquiry can be applied to current events in the interview as well as past historical events. The clinician can inquire of a father, "How did your life change after your wife's mother died?" and "How did this loss affect your wife?" This type of questioning has been described as circular questioning, referring to the fact that other individuals are asked for their descriptions of thoughts, feelings, and the behavior of others (Tomm, 1988). This often captures the differences in relationships the family experienced before and after the clinical problems began, and allows problems to be discussed such that they are perceived as something in which all members have an emotional investment.

Once the clinician has a clear view of the presenting problem and the family is comfortably engaged, a systematic inquiry into other areas can begin, guided by the understanding of the presenting complaint and its associated epidemiology. The family will already have been allowed an open-ended response to examiners' question, so this phase of the interview tends to be more directive. The areas to review include parent's individual history, marital history, and family unit history, as well as several key domains of family functioning: family structure, communication patterns, shared beliefs, and regulation of development. A detailed description of each of these areas is presented later in this chapter.

The focus for an inquiry can be directed by the fact that some childhood disorders have a typical family profile. Refusal to go to school often occurs in the context of familial overprotectiveness. Conduct problems are often associated with deficits and inconsistencies in parental limit setting, with coercive limit setting practices being especially common. Adolescents with anorexia nervosa often have problems with independence from parents. Physical abuse often occurs with parents who have limited impulse control, or who have been abused themselves. Discussion during this phase of the interview may include information which is inappropriate or uncomfortable for all family members to know, such as details about a parent's upbringing, and this discussion should occur in interviews with subunits of the family (parents, sibling groups).

This type of inquiry can be aided by the development of a family genogram. A genogram is a drawing made in conjunction with the family which identifies the facts and relationship patterns of three or more generations of the family (McGoldrick & Gerson, 1985). This drawing helps illuminate past events and parental concerns and serves to objectify family experience. It provides an overview of family structure, points toward potential family beliefs, and is a way to identify vulnerable individuals. In addition to providing important data, it is often a helpful way to engage family members who may have difficulty talking during the interview. (This genogram also appears in Chapter 48, "Family History and its

Significance." You may wish to refer back to that chapter for additional information.)

At any point in the family interview where a family member reports history from their own perspective, the family often begins to interact in ways which demonstrate the presenting complaint or other problems. Once a significant interaction is set in motion, the assessment of such interaction often takes precedence over further historical data gathering. Historical data can be gathered after the spontaneous interaction has subsided. This decision whether to continue to focus on the presenting problem of the child, gather associated aspects of family history, or focus on some immediate interactions which interrupted the flow of the interview is an important one. The clinical decision should in most cases be to pursue the most pressing issue for the family, being ever mindful of the presenting complaint. When a child's disruptive behavior is the presenting complaint and we observe the father losing his temper over a trivial comment by his son, we have the benefit of living with the problem as opposed to merely hearing about it. Similarly, we develop a clear understanding of the family when we observe a mother repeatedly answering questions which have been directed toward her child, a young girl, who appears anxious. These observations have clinical utility in that families tend to behave in the clinic as they do in natural settings.

CASE EXAMPLES

Amanda, 14, was referred for evaluation after she ripped the telephone off the wall and threw it at her mother during an argument. During the interview, Amanda, an only child living with her single mother, interrupted her mother repeatedly, constantly disagreeing with her mother's view of events. This seemed to escalate when the clinician encouraged mother to tell her story. Amanda became more hostile, muttered obscenities under her breath, and finally told her mother to "shut up."

Dr. French, a very successful nephrologist, reluctantly made time in his schedule to attend a family evaluation related to his son's hyperactive behavior. Ten minutes into the interview, his beeper sounded, requiring him to leave the room. This happened on three other occasions during the interview. Dr. French's repeated absences were distracting to his son and younger daughter and irritating to his wife, who became tearful at discussing their lack of family life related to her husband's career advancement.

The clinician should also note interactions which involve her directly. Parents and children will negotiate their relationship with the clinician utilizing the same adaptive and maladaptive strategies that occur in the family. Hypotheses about family functioning can often be confirmed when the clinician, as an outside observer, becomes involved in a problematic interaction with a family member.

CASE EXAMPLE

Dr. Jones heard from clinic staff that Mr. Smith, the father of a 14-year-old behaviorally disordered boy, was difficult. During the family interview, the father gave terse responses to most questions and appeared irritated at his 8-year-old daughter's activity level. The last segment of the interview was diverted from clinical concerns to Mr. Smith's verbal tirade of Dr. Jones regarding the administrative function of the clinic.

The initial family interview typically ends with a summary of the clinical problem, how the family does and does not relate to the problem, whether further family interviewing is needed to complete the assessment, and whether they are likely to be involved in any subsequent clinical contacts. We should answer questions and summarize family strengths at this point. If families are to be involved in any intervention, they are likely to return if the interviewer has met the family's expectations, been sensitive to each member's concerns, and conferred hope.

CLINICAL CHALLENGES IN
FAMILY INTERVIEWING

For many clinicians accustomed to understanding the symptoms and problems of individuals, a cognitive frame of reference shift is required to conduct an effective family interview. The simple act of sitting in an interview room with a group united by blood relations and history can be somewhat intimidating. The apparent lack of organization in the presentation of material, distracting noises and spontaneous discussion, and the need to attend to multiple individuals simultaneously can be difficult elements of the family interview for the clinician. Over time, through viewing the

family as a system not expecting to simultaneously understand what is going on with each individual member's mental function, the task becomes more manageable. Clinicians experienced in family interviews have noted that perplexing individual thoughts and feelings become more comprehensible when the family is interviewed. On the other hand, those accustomed to viewing the family as a system operating in a unified way may have difficulty detecting the individual motivation of family members (Nichols, 1987). Children and parents behave for reasons of their own apart from family functioning, and a family interview which disregards this notion can miss important data.

Practically, the challenge in conducting a family interview involves simultaneously gathering the facts of history and observing family interaction. Due to the number of individuals involved, this task is more difficult than concurrently observing and listening to the individual patient during an individual interview. In addition, the likelihood of an individual losing control is increased when the source of their frustration is present and a scenario is being reenacted, not just discussed. By maintaining a sense of calm and setting the structure for the interview, the clinician minimizes the probability of this occurring. If the emotions being expressed during a session appear to be escalating, having certain family members leave the room temporarily is at times indicated so that the interview can be completed.

Interviewing family subunits raises the issue of confidentiality. For younger children it is often important that parent's be aware of the issues that are a concern to the child. As the child moves into adolescence, these issues become more complicated and, generally, the adolescent's wishes for confidence are respected unless an issue of dangerousness precludes maintaining confidentiality. Gathering history and interviewing ex-spouses, common-law partners, and stepparents also raises legal issues. As a general rule, the clinician should be open to any individual offering history relevant to a child's condition, but should be careful about the information that is divulged. This is particularly important when we become involved with divorced biological parents of a child who may ask about information related to the ex-spouse's current family situation; while it is generally appropriate for them to have access to data regarding their child, information regarding an ex-spouse's family should not be disclosed.

Clinicians must carefully assess their own responses because these can influence what information is gathered. This truism, which pertains to all clinical contacts, is even more relevant to the elicitation of family and marital history because these data evoke powerful memories and feelings of the clinician's past and current family situations.

CASE EXAMPLE

Dr. Brown, recently divorced and in an unsatisfying custody situation, finds herself struggling to be objective when probing a tenuous marriage where father suggests he would fight strongly for the custody of his child.

While a potential liability, the clinician's thoughts and feelings about a family can be used to develop the diagnostic assessment and formulation. These data generated by the interview should only be used after a thorough self-assessment. Emotional responses the clinician has toward the family being interviewed typically reflect her own family of origin experiences and her current family experiences. The clinician must monitor them so they do not affect the conduct of the interview, but, with this caveat, the data can be helpful.

CASE EXAMPLES

While 15-year-old Kathy was interviewed with her single mother, the interviewer was feeling protective toward her. This was perplexing in that Kathy seemed to have her mother's availability in most instances and, in fact, mother seemed too available at times. As the interview proceeded, mother became angry at several points, and this appeared most intense when Kathy was expressing her own point of view. When Kathy was needy, her mother was nurturing toward her, but when she expressed her independence, it appeared that mother was quite rejecting.

A psychiatry resident, the mother of a young child, was interviewing an internal medicine resident and her two adolescent children, one of whom was depressed. The mother reported that she spent much time on her career and openly stated that her career was the most important thing in her life. While her first marriage was dissolved because of this dedication, this had not changed her perspective. The clinician was aware of her mixed feelings. On the one hand, she admired her col-

league's career success, desiring that of her own career. On the other hand, because her commitment to her young child was unequivocal, she felt saddened as she explored her adolescent patient's anger with respect to the emphasis her mother placed on her career. The psychiatry resident also felt confirmed in her decision to try to balance career and parenting.

SPECIAL CONSIDERATIONS IN FAMILY INTERVIEWING

Blended Families: It is common for reconstituted, or blended, families to present for a family interview. The most common routes for family reconstitution include divorce and the death of a parent. These two situations share similarities in that one biological parent is actively removed from day-to-day contact with the child. An important difference is that a divorced parent is often intermittently involved with the child's development. Even if visitation does not occur on a regular basis, the child is keenly aware of the parent's existence and has feelings—positive, negative, or both—about that parent. In postdivorce families the clinician must observe how the custodial parent speaks about the ex-spouse and how the children react to this discussion. The absence of a parent through death is an unalterable loss. As a result, the acceptance of the reality of parental absence is more straightforward, although the circumstances of death can affect its impact upon the family. Death by accident, death as a result of a prolonged illness, or death as the result of suicide or homicide have very different family dynamics, and the reactions of both the widowed spouse and the children should be probed and understood.

When divorced or widowed parents remarry, the resulting blended families face numerous issues, the evaluation of which is an important part of the interview. It is important for the interviewer to consider how children were prepared for their parent's remarriage. Did they have time to meet their potential stepparent? Was there a chance to gradually develop a relationship with this person? It is important to review whether, prior to marriage, the biological parent and stepparent reviewed the unique needs of the children. One must investigate what the biological parent expected from their new partner in terms of acceptance of their child. On the other hand, the stepparent's expectations for being a part of the parenting team raising a child they did not conceive should be explored.

Children of divorce frequently wish, either consciously or unconsciously, for reunification of biological parents. This can occur many years after a remarriage and the formation of a new, or blended, family. Such a wish can be accompanied by hostility toward the stepparent which frustrates family harmony. In this situation, the expectations, both verbal and nonverbal, that the biological parent has given the child regarding their relationship with the spouse should be reviewed.

When the blending of families results in children of two previous families becoming stepsiblings, the complexity of interactions can increase. Favoritism between a biological parent and a biological child and frank competition between stepsiblings and biological siblings for the affection of parents can be problematic. In addition, practical matters such as arranging visitation schedules and dealing with child support are all areas to explore with blended families (Visher & Visher, 1988).

Single-Parent Families: A good number of formerly married and widowed parents do not remarry. In single-parent families, including those with parents who have never married, the clinician must observe if the parent involves others, such as an extended family or an adult friend, in the daily life of the child. The demands of single parenting often mean that there are surrogate caretakers. The clinician must make every effort to inquire if such individuals exist and, if so, to include them as part of the assessment.

The interview should include an assessment of financial resources and time management. Single parents typically do not have enough of either. Often single parents are lonely and have a desire to reestablish a new, intimate relationship. The impact of these needs on the lives of children should be explored, as they can place a significant stress on the parent-child relationship or at times result in overlooking the child's developmental needs.

The number of children the single parent is raising and the sex of the children is also important. Children with the same-sex parent have a somewhat easier time moving into adolescence. Being with a same-sex parent facilitates the process of identification and the learning of age-appropriate and sex-appropriate role. Children who are raised by a parent of the opposite sex may feel increasingly misunderstood as adolescence proceeds. Similarly, parents may have difficulty identifying with the needs of an opposite-sex adolescent. Developing sexual interests and the need to develop independence combine to distance children from their parents, particularly a parent of the opposite sex. A clinical problem of increasing importance is that of single mothers trying to control the aggression of their adolescent sons. When young boys become physically larger than their mothers, the ability to behaviorally control them is often lost.

CASE EXAMPLE

Lance, 16, was admitted for evaluation of conduct problems including delinquency. A family interview was arranged and it became apparent that Lance was living at home while his mother had checked into a small motel. She felt she could no longer live in her home and be subjected to the physical threats of aggression by her son.

Cultural Considerations: The family's ethnicity and cultural background impact its views of normative family structure, communication style, belief systems, and child development. In terms of family structure, cultures differ regarding the appropriate level of involvement of extended family members. Some European and many South American, Central American, and Asian families have extended family involvements where grandparents, and even aunts and uncles, may live together. In contrast, the majority of North American families are typecast as nuclear families, with blended families and single-parent families being common variants, without significant extended family involvement. Despite these differences, families in each culture must flexibly adapt to the problems posed by a child's developmental needs and provide emotional support for their children.

In terms of communication, a range of emotional expression will be evident. Family emotional outbursts may be the norm for some ethnic groups, yet may appear out of control to others. Similarly, families in some cultures may be more comfortable with little emotional expression, yet the clinician may believe this to be blunted and defensive. Nonetheless, despite these stylistic differences, clarity and competent problem solving appear to be necessary elements of successful communication in families of all cultures.

403

Many family beliefs and values are culturally related. It is important to understand a family's religion, world view, or philosophy of life, especially when the presenting complaint involves issues intimately related to these ideas. When families grapple with the problems of premarital sex, birth control, substance use, divorce, and the delinquent behavior of children, they implicitly bring to this discussion their view of how life should be lived. It is important for the clinician to understand the characteristics of such a world view. If this world view is substantially different from that of the clinician, it may be useful to have the family explain these aspects of their culture to the clinician, who should respond in an accepting manner. This review facilitates joining with the family and can clarify some diagnostic issues. On occasion the interview may need to be conducted with someone from the family's culture or religion, in order for the clinician to clearly understand the family milieu within which the child is developing.

The Data of the Interview

We have reviewed the process of conducting the interview and the challenges to this type of assessment. We will now describe the specific elements of history and observation of family interaction which comprise the thorough family interview. Data must be organized to illuminate the history of the parents as individuals, the history of the marital relationship, and the history of the family as a unit. The effective family interview also reviews acute family interactional problems related to the presenting complaint and family interactional problems that have persisted over time. Furthermore, we should observe and document family interaction which may not be directly related to the presenting complaint but which reflects features of family structure, family communication, family beliefs, and parental regulation of child development. These elements cover the important aspects of family functioning.

THE FAMILY AND ITS SUBUNITS

The family as mother, father, and their immediate children functions as a unit, and yet each have

individual lives; the marriage itself has its own unique history. The history of extended family members is important in that it illuminates formative influences on the parents and reveals whether extended family members play a part in any ongoing interactional problems. To understand the family, we must assess each of its components as well as its functioning as a whole.

The Parents: After the family interview, we should be able to identify parents' strengths and weaknesses, their level of parenting skill, and their emotional investment in the parenting task. The clinician should have, at least informally, a mental status assessment of each parent and an awareness if any psychiatric disorders are present. A systematic developmental history of each parent provides an understanding of parental strengths and weaknesses, or personality functioning, which mediates successful parental role functioning. A particularly challenging part of the interview is attempting to determine whether parents' perceptions of their children's behavior and problems are accurate. Parents play a critical role in the gathering of the clinical histories and developmental histories of their children; however, they may not perceive problems accurately due to their own developmental background.

CASE EXAMPLE

Laura, a 36-year-old mother of three, was sexually abused as a younger child. She had several early marriages and problematic relationships with men and her current marriage was stressed by her infidelity. When her 8-year-old son was found in a situation of sexual experimentation with another young boy, she was convinced that he was being "raped" and that he would become homosexual. She did not appear to be aware that her own traumatic sexual experiences influenced her interpretation of her son's behavior.

Observation of a parent's physical and verbal interactions with their children provide clues to their own individual functioning and individual stage of development.

CASE EXAMPLE

Sarah, a 34-year-old single, twice divorced mother, appeared overly familiar with her adolescent daughter. During the family interview, she and her daughter, Sonia, joked together, even when discussing significant problems. Sarah had left home at the age of 16 to escape a restrictive environment. She related she had trouble "settling down" and seemed to have difficulty with her own sense of identity. She was unsure of the future of her current relationship with a male and whether she should quit her current job. She had trouble setting limits on Sonia, alternating between being overly strict and overly accommodating. She stated, "I just want Sonia to be happy." It appeared that Sarah's own unfinished developmental tasks of adolescence prevented her from effectively parenting an adolescent.

The Marriage: The family interview should delineate a marital history. Factors which led each parent to choose each other and to decide to marry, or have children, should be reviewed. The strengths of the marriage, specifically how each partner compliments the other, should be identified.

CASE EXAMPLE

The marriage of Nan, an outgoing, socially skilled woman, to Bob, an introspective, socially awkward male, seemed to be a poor match. Upon further inspection, however, her social skills allowed him to handle social situations he could not have handled without her. On the other hand, his reflective and careful review of situations led to sound financial decisions and aided management of their children, a source of encouragement to her.

Differences between marital partners can just as easily counteract a complement.

CASE EXAMPLE

Nancy, 35, had become pregnant with her first child at the age of 16. She ultimately had four children by three different marriages. Her youngest son, Sean, was noncompliant and seemed to control her. He was overly close to her, in part due to her protection of him from his abusive father, who had also physically abused her. Through the history of the marriage, her husband was dominant and controlling and she was submissive. The problems they had individually with each other were reflected in the problems they each had with their son, Sean. The young boy disliked and was fearful of his father and was belligerent and disrespectful of his mother.

The family interview allows us to consider the level of support the couple gives to each other. Many couples struggle with the relative absence of a partner due to work concerns. In addition, we can ascertain whether roles are clearly defined between father and mother and whether they are comfortable with each other's roles. Interview observations can often reveal conflicts in the marital subunit which preclude effective parenting.

CASE EXAMPLE

Barry and Cathy frequently argued. Cathy stated that Barry was irresponsible and did not follow through on his fatherly responsibilities. She also believed that he tended to use alcohol in excess. Barry believed Cathy was too close to their two young boys and frequently undermined his attempts to discipline them. This parenting rift mirrored their problematic marriage in which they had several separations. Their ineffective marital functioning made consistent limit setting of their young sons impossible.

The Family as a Whole: An important historical aspect of the family is described through the family as a whole being viewed as traversing a series of developmental stages in a life cycle (Walsh, 1993; Combrinck-Graham, 1985). We must be aware of the ages of the children and the unique demands of their developmental phase. Accurate family interviewing requires a knowledge, not only of the identified patient's individual developmental needs, but also the developmental needs of other family members. We should be aware, for example, that families with infants are dealing with issues of nurturance; those with toddlers are confronting issues of limit setting and the draining needs of constant observation; those with school-age children are working with issues of socialization and achievement; and families with adolescents are concerned about the imminent independence of their child with continuing evidence that they are not quite ready for complete emancipation. Some families give us a clear history of meeting the needs of children at certain developmental stages but of having difficulty with children during other stages. One example is the family which meets the needs of its children when they are dependent and in need of nurturance but has difficulty accepting their children's move toward independence. Such knowledge of the family life cycle allows the clinician to empathically relate to the family she is interviewing.

During the family life cycle, families experience transitions, some of which are anticipated and others which are unanticipated. Anticipated transitions in the family life cycle are experienced by most families and include events such as routine childhood illnesses and children graduating from high school. Unanticipated transitions are experienced by some families and include a wide range of experiences, from divorce and single parenthood, to life-threatening illness of a family member or the incarceration of a parent, and can have a definitive impact on children's development. The data in the following vignette is most helpful to the formulation when placed in the context of an alteration of the family life cycle.

CASE EXAMPLE

Mr. and Mrs. Byrd had a troubled marriage. Their several separations had influenced their ability to parent their five children, four sons and a daughter. The boys had all left the home prematurely and with a great deal of conflict. It appeared that Mr. Byrd was unavailable for modeling effective behavior for his sons because of his frequent absences. Mrs. Byrd was anxious and lonely during the separations and tended to get overinvolved with her children. The youngest child, Kristin, went to live with one of her brothers, Ken, when she was 16. This move was precipitated by her mother's intrusive behavior.

THE PRESENTING COMPLAINT

It is not uncommon for the history of the child's present problem or presenting complaint to directly involve family interaction. Oppositional behavior, running away from home, and suicide attempts are all events which may be precipitated by family interaction. It is the clinician's task, as he gathers relevant historical data, to observe the nature of family interaction. It is common to get a history of problematic family interaction associated with the presenting complaint and begin to observe some elements of such interaction during the interview. The clinician not only hears about the problem but begins to live with it. These data can be most useful in attempting to understand other historical reports which are not directly observed.

CASE EXAMPLES

Cindy, a 16-year-old patient with anorexia nervosa, came for a family interview with her mother, father, and brother, Edward, age 12, after the resolution of her acute symptomology. The interview revealed Cindy and her mother as the only verbal participants, with father and brother remaining essentially silent. Cindy's mother communicated, in a distressed manner, the need for Cindy to gain weight and remain healthy, while Cindy maintained she did not have a problem with her eating. When family eating patterns were reviewed, it became clear that the discussion in the interview was identical to that which occurred at home, which involved Cindy's refusal to eat, mother cajoling her to eat, and father remaining distant.

Alice, 14, had recently taken a small number of pills in an overdose attempt. The family interview with Alice, her grandparents, and her aunt triggered Alice's anger. She had been living with her grandparents throughout much of her life due to her biological mother's problems with substance abuse. Alice had always been a difficult child, but her anger was a recent event and seemed related to her grandparents reasonable restrictions on her behavior. During the interview, Alice was verbally abusive to her grandmother who appeared to be a quiet, well-meaning woman. Alice stated that her grandfather was mean to her and that her overdose attempt was a way "to get back at him" for his demeanor. Both grandparents said, "This is how she is at home."

In gathering past history of family interactions, the clinician frequently finds chronic family patterns that are similar to those associated with an acute presentation of clinical disorder. For example, in the case of Cindy, the clinician commented on the apparent overly close relationship she had with her mother and its likely negative effect on her parent's marriage. This mobilized reporting of the history that her parents had tried several weekend trips without the children. These trips had always been unsatisfactory in that when they returned, usually feeling refreshed, Cindy had either lost weight or demonstrated by her misbehavior that her parents needed to be near at hand.

PERVASIVE FAMILY FUNCTIONING

In addition to documenting historical data and observations related to the presenting complaint and parental and marital function, the family interview data must include observation of family interaction reflective of enduring family function.

This may be specifically related to the present problem, as has just been discussed, or serve as a context for the problem. In this latter instance, it may be less clear how family structure and interaction are related to the problem.

During the interview, the clinician gathers and organizes data in four domains of family functioning: structure, communication, family beliefs, and regulatory processes. In order to determine the relationship of these functions to clinical problems, each of these areas should be systematically evaluated. Once completed, the data gathered in these areas will reveal what family factors are related to clinical problems, what factors serve as a general context for problems, and what factors are unrelated to the problems of concern. Each area of family function will be described with relevant clinical vignettes illustrating the domain.

Family Structure: Family structure refers to the typical organizational and transactional patterns and hierarchies that exist between individuals within the family (Minuchin, 1974). Important components of the family structure are adaptability, cohesion, and the functioning of subsystems, specifically the clarity of boundaries between parents and children, families and their extended families, and the family and the larger community.

Data informing the adaptability of a family's structure would include observations and history of how flexible the family has been. Interview observations relevant to family flexibility would include noting the responses of parents to a child running out of the office during the interview, to a child interrupting those speaking, or to a child's response to an intrusive parent who is controlling the interview. Common historical examples of such adaptability include parents' abilities to shift work schedules related to an ill child, or the children giving up some of their attention in response to the birth of an infant. Adjustments required of each family member are often seen as necessary for family unity and may be temporary. Often families with clinical problems do not adapt. They are either too rigid, where the family is unable to change typical ways of interacting as children and life circumstances demand change, or too chaotic, where patterns and individual family roles constantly change. In rigid families, individual symptoms often appear to maintain a family's preferred interactional pattern.

CASE EXAMPLE

Marilyn, 34, bitterly complained about her husband, Will, and his immaturity. Will had dropped out of high school and was engaged in manual labor jobs throughout much of their marriage. With the birth of their children, Marilyn constantly complained about his frequent job shifts, his tendency to drink too much, and his impulsive style when limiting the children's behavior. She had gradually become close to all three children and conveyed the sense that she was the effective parent because of her superior intellectual skills. When Will became sober, was gainfully employed, and functioned more effectively with the children, Marilyn tended to undermine him because his personal growth was threatening her control over family life. The children continued to go to mother, treating father as an inconsequential family member, which resulted in Will withdrawing from the family.

Chaotic families present different problems for their children.

CASE EXAMPLE

Nancy, 37, had four different children by three different fathers. Her estranged husband, the father of two of her children, was occasionally abusive and frequently threatened to physically harm her. As a result, she left him and had engaged in frequent family moves. She supported herself through government assistance and some support from her extended family. Of her two older girls, one had recently become pregnant. Of her two younger children, one son was noncompliant. His absences in school seemed related in part to his learning difficulties and multiple family moves which affected his ability to adjust in school and in peer relationships.

The goal for these families would be a structure where transactional patterns are stable but where they can adapt when circumstances dictate that change is needed.

Family *cohesion* is an element of family structure which refers to the level of emotional closeness family members have with each other. Families functioning well will have a balance between relatedness and separateness, where individual family members can be emotionally related to each other without risking the loss of their own independence. These families demonstrate family health by supporting family members and sharing their pain when they have a distressing experience. Data about the handling of disappointing events in a family can be informative.

CASE EXAMPLE

Eric, 13, enjoyed playing baseball, but was not picked to play on his school team. He had practiced diligently and had hoped to be chosen. The day the team was announced, his father picked him up from school, recognizing his son's need for support. As Eric liked reading, his father went to a bookstore with him and bought him a book written by his favorite author. They discussed how they could work together to improve his skills.

Families who are cohesive also allow individuals to express their independence. They see such independence as a natural progression and not as abandoning loyalty to the family. Families with clinical problems may demonstrate patterns of being either too emotionally close, where individuals feel so intensely for each other that they are unable to experience their own feelings as unique, or too disengaged, where individuals have minimal emotional contact and are unaware of others' feelings.

CASE EXAMPLE

Lance, a 56-year-old lawyer in psychotherapy for depression, described his own parents as "never forgiving me for reaching puberty." His overly close family was supportive, but he never felt that he could be independent without betraying the family. He can remember his parents repeatedly asking, "Do you still love us?" during adolescence. In his own parenting, Lance felt that he had overcompensated in an effort to avoid recreating his past. His two children complained that he was disconnected to them and didn't seem to care.

Families may be actively disengaging to the point of being neglectful.

CASE EXAMPLE

Shelly, an active 32-year-old involved with her career, was called to school to take her 10-year-old son, Craig, to the doctor's for care of a wound which he received during an activity on the school playground. Craig had been the product of an unplanned pregnancy and seemed a constant source of frustration to her. During the suturing of the laceration, she responded to her son's distress with the comment, "Don't complain; this doesn't hurt and you know it." The clinic personnel were surprised by her seeming distance toward her child.

Further examples of interview observations that can assist in organizing data on family cohesion include observing an older child sitting in a parent's lap, observing transactions which follow a child's criticism of parents or parents' criticism of children, and noting how parents respond to the clinician asking questions of the child.

Family *boundaries* is a term used to define family roles. Boundaries differentiate between parents, siblings, and subsystem groups such as sisters or brothers. Boundaries protect family members from intrusions within the family and help define exchanges with other groups such as schools or neighbors who exist outside the family. Ideally, families will have boundaries between its subsystems that are permeable but clear. An example of such a boundary is the relationship between parent and child where the child feels free to tease a parent or question some of the parent's behavior, while at the same time maintaining respect for parental authority in decision making. Other data to summarize include, but are not limited to, the marital subsystem's privacy from children, the parental subsystem's authority over the children, any alliances between a child and a parent, each parent's relationships with their family of origin, and the balance between husband and wife in terms of decision making in the family. Interview data that could lead to understanding misaligned boundaries include observing who speaks for whom, who interrupts interactions between members, how private topics are handled, freely chosen physical seating arrangements during the interview, who is absent, who is unduly supportive of another, and how the family handles extended family relationships. In terms of the boundary between the family and the community, information regarding the families involvement in community activities, and the community's ability to observe the family without intruding upon it should be noted.

Boundaries in clinical families can be rigid, diffuse, or misaligned. The interview of the rigid family will often reveal one spokesperson, few creative responses to problem solving, and some emotional restriction. Boundaries in families with clinical problems can also be diffuse. In this case roles are unclear, and children are often confused as to whom they should relate.

CASE EXAMPLE

Carolyn and Ken experienced numerous separations. During the time of separations, Carolyn had trouble handling her two young sons, one of whom, Justin, would go to live with her mother. When she and Ken would reunite, she would attempt to have Justin return only to have this complicated by her quarrels with Ken and an inability to manage their other son, Jason. Justin became extremely confused about which set of rules he should respond to, those of his mother or his grandmother. Also, when Ken was in the home, Jason had difficulty responding to him because Jason felt he would leave again.

Clinical problems can be maintained because of misaligned family boundaries. In this situation, the clinician observes evidence of members in the family inappropriately relating to other members. Children serving as a sexual partner for a parent, children acting as parents toward their siblings, or one parent being emotionally closer to a child than a marital partner, are all examples of coalitions, or boundary violations, which can be toxic to child development.

CASE EXAMPLE

Tabatha and Karen were two daughters of a professional mother. The father and mother were divorced when they were young children, and they were cared for intermittently by extended family members as mother pursued her career in law. Consequently, they became very close to each other, and Tabatha, 2 years older than Karen, frequently acted as a parent. While they received much emotional support from each other, Karen was tiring of Tabatha's directives because, as she frequently stated, "You're not my mother."

A specific type of boundary misalignment, in which children are drawn into parental conflict, is that of triangulation. Triangulation refers to behaviors of a child which divert attention from an interactive process occurring between two other members, typically parents.

CASE EXAMPLE

During the family interview Jared and Melissa, parents of 6-year-old Daniel, begin to raise their voices at each other. As the conflict escalates, Daniel, who had been quietly playing with toys in the corner of a room, begins to make loud noises of his own. He knocks over a chair and throws wooden blocks throughout the interview room. At this point, both parents stop, pay attention to him, and help him pick up the blocks. Their verbal aggressiveness toward each other ceases.

The clinician should also consider the nature of boundaries between the family and the larger community, determining whether the family has memberships in other groups, or if it is isolated from others, relying solely upon itself for social support. In summarizing these data, the nature of the boundaries with the extended family should be reviewed. Also, the clinician should assess the boundaries between current family members and members from previously formed families. With divorce and the reconstitution of family boundaries, numerous boundary adjustments must take place.

CASE EXAMPLE

The Jones family had a rigid boundary between themselves and the community. Father and mother worked hard at low-paying jobs and had little time for outside involvement. They spent whatever free time they had with their children and they discouraged the childrens' involvement in extracurricular activities. When Colin became 16 years old, his parents thought he should work to add to the family income. His mother called prospective employers regarding the application process, stating, "Someone has to do his dirty work for him." The use of the term "dirty work" implied that involvement with the outside world was unpleasant but had to be done to procure employment. This obscured the excitement that most adolescents have at discovering new skills and abilities.

Communication: Family communication refers to the verbal and behavioral interactions by which family members impart information to each other about their individual needs and about their perceptions of others in the family. We will consider the following components of family communication in organizing data from the family interview: clarity, emotional expression, and problem solving.

Clarity refers to factual information being shared accurately and accompanied by affect which is congruent to the message conveyed. Families that function well communicate clearly and consistently with respect to expectations and

409

rules. This clear communication fosters trust which allows for differences of opinion to be voiced without fear of loss of relationship. Families presenting in clinics may communicate ambiguously.

CASE EXAMPLE

The Ware family included both biological parents and two boys, Neil, age 9, and Lorne, age 4. Father was employed as a lawyer, and mother was a nurse who had chosen to stay home to raise the children. The family was interviewed because of Lorne's sleeping problems and Neil's anxiety symptoms. As it turned out, both boys tended to have difficulty sleeping alone and either parent would sleep with them in an effort to get them to sleep. The parents presented as a caring and supportive family who would do anything to help their children. During the session, when the clinician directed the father to tell the boys he expected them to stay in their own bed, Mr. Ware did so with jocularity and affability. The fact that he and his wife were upset with the current situation was not conveyed to either the clinician or the children. The request was ignored and the boys went on playing.

Examples of family interview data that would lead to understanding this area include whether the clinician, as an outside observer, is able to understand the clinical issues as elaborated by the family and the family rules and expectations for behavior of the children. If lack of clarity exists in the interview, it is likely to exist in everyday family life. A classic example of ambiguous communication is double-bind communication, where the stated message instructs the recipient to perform two incompatible responses simultaneously (Bateson, Jackson, Haley, & Weakland, 1956).

A second vital aspect of communication to understand is *emotional expression*. A child's development is optimally enhanced in families which openly share a range of feelings communicated with trust, respect, warmth, and which are heard with tolerance. This includes feelings seen as positive, such as love and support, and feelings which are seen as negative, such as anger. During the session, it is important to note the presence or absence of feelings, and also how they are communicated. Families presenting to the clinic may tend to block the expression of feelings through several mechanisms. A child's expression of a negative emotion may be seen as threatening to parents, particularly those with low self-esteem. Constructive criticism offered by a parent may be perceived as too harsh. These families may have difficulty distinguishing the difference between holding children accountable for unacceptable behavior and blaming them inappropriately.

CASE EXAMPLE

Mary, the 13-year-old daughter of a single mother, was evaluated for dissociative symptoms. The initial family interview was noteworthy for bland emotional expression of both mother and daughter. Her mother had been sexually abused as a young person and had several traumatic marriages, including to Mary's father, who had been physically abusive toward her. Mary's mother soon became aware that Mary was a consistent source of support for her and developed an extremely close relationship with her. Mary eventually found that any expression of anger or disagreement with her mother sent her mother into a despondent state. She found that it was unacceptable to express any emotion, particularly anger, as it hurt her mother. Such expressions complicated her life by engendering feelings of guilt for having hurt her mother.

Interview data that would lead to an understanding of this dimension include observing the range of emotions expressed by each family member, the congruence between content discussed and affect expressed, differences between mother and father in handling emotion, and noting the responses of the family to a member initiating an emotionally laden topic. In the family interview the clinician can also assess the broader emotional ambience or general emotional climate of the family. This varies from incident to incident and day to day, but as a general rule family environments tend toward being either emotionally warm or hostile and critical. Supportive environments tend to be sensitive to the feeling state of each family member, whereas unsupportive family environments tend to be insensitive, even to blatant attempts of family members to communicate feelings.

A third component of communication to understand is the family's *problem-solving* ability. A family's ability to differentiate between major and minor problems is important, as major problems require the executive function of parents, whereas minor problems may be left up to children to solve for themselves as a growth-promoting experience. The degree to which families negotiate differences and conflicts, utilize reciprocal interactions in problem solving, and are able to use new information is also important to include in summarizing a family's problem-solving ability. Parents should listen to their children and be responsive to their emotional state, yet also appropriately exercise their authority. Parents should also be aware that each problem does not involve all family members equally and thus should review the problem with the individuals who have a prime stake in its resolution.

Families in the clinical setting will tend to have multiple perceptions of the problem, be unable to sacrifice toward common goals, and be unable, or unwilling, to assist family coping.

CASE EXAMPLE

Nine-year-old Jeff reports the problem as, "My mother yells too much." The mother believes "My child is self-centered and out of control," and the father may see "No problem."

Many of the families who are ineffective at solving problems have a decision maker who communicates poorly and is indecisive, weak, or authoritarian.

CASE EXAMPLES

Mr. and Mrs. Meyers had three children, ages 12, 9, and 7 years. The family was interviewed related to the conduct problems of the 9-year-old boy, who was oppositional and unruly in school. During the session, the parents were frequently interrupted by the children, who would comment on issues even when they were not asked. As the clinician began to pursue the problem of the children controlling the session, important history emerged. Many family problems were addressed by a "family vote," which often left the parents outnumbered. The clinician reassured the parents that the family was not a democracy and, while listening to children was important, they did not have to gratify their wishes.

A clinical interview with the Dodd family was characterized by father's control of the session. Fifteen-year-old Chris rarely spoke. When Chris's depression was discussed, his mother mentioned that no one in the family talked about problems, particularly her husband and her son. It was then revealed that her husband continued to use corporal punishment and this was becoming increasingly contentious. Chris's mother feared danger because Chris was approaching the size of his father. His father's response to this difficulty was, "This is how my father disciplined me and it worked." In this authoritarian approach to family problem solving, Chris's mother had proposed solutions but they were not considered because father rigidly adhered to his past experiences.

Since family problem-solving ability is related to the functioning of the marital relationship, it is useful to understand gender-related differences in problem-solving strategies, and whether the parents support each other in the perception of the problem and in their behavioral implementation of solutions. Specifically, it is important to summarize how the parents have negotiated setting limits on their child's behavior, the consequences related to unacceptable behavior, how persistently the parents implement the consequences, and how much they are in agreement in the implementation. If disciplinary consequences are unsuccessful, are approaches modified? At times, families may reward negative behavior or feel so overwhelmed that they relent. The parents are often aware of this inappropriate response but do not persist because they, as more than one parent has said, "Just want peace."

Family Belief Systems: Family belief systems refer to the fact that families have a type of memory function that goes beyond the beliefs and memories of each of its members. Family belief, or shared construction of reality, is a concept that relates to the family as a whole and its multigenerational functioning (Reiss, 1989). These beliefs are important for a clinician to review and understand in that they often guide repetitive patterns of family behavior across generations (Breunlin & Schwartz, 1986). To gather these types of data typically requires a series of contacts and it is often not immediately apparent to the clinician during an initial interview.

Family beliefs may be healthy and empowering or may be maladaptive and destructive, depending on their content, the interpretation the family gives them, and the impact they have on family functioning. The family interview may spontaneously result in narratives that illustrate beliefs that empower the family's continuity, such as a family tradition of heroism or parental sacrifice to enhance children's success. A destructive family belief would include such beliefs as "the women in the family choose abusive men." In this belief system, any marriage or relationship is seen as one that ultimately will be violated and terminated. Similarly, families may believe that adolescent girls will always be promiscuous and the best a family can do is hope the adolescent avoids pregnancy or sexually transmitted disease. (See also Chapter 48, "Family History and Its Significance".)

Family Regulation of the Developmental Process: The emotional, social, and physical tasks inherent in child and adolescent development evolve in an interactional context which facilitates the mastery of developmental tasks. The family is perhaps the most influential factor regulating the developmental process. In this context, regulation implies an equilibrium or balance between inhibiting and facilitating interactions between caretaker and child (Anders, 1989). This regulation applies not only to developmental processes, but also to those elements essential for a child's physical survival and to the management of unanticipated events such as a serious illness. Families which appropriately regulate a child's development are attuned to developmental needs and adapt their behaviors accordingly. These developmental needs vary according to age and temperament, as well as particular life situations. In some situations, children need a limit or restriction and in others they need encouragement to proceed. At times, children need to be protected and at other times they need to be left to defend themselves. A fundamental way a family regulates a child's needs emanates from the differing perspectives of mothers and fathers. When mothers and fathers effectively communicate, they are able to calibrate their regulating function. For example, if one parent is more permissive about a child's risk-taking activity and the other more conservative, the process of parental interaction can produce an appropriate regulatory response to a child's behavior.

When families get into clinical difficulty, there can be several patterns of regulatory dysfunction. *Overregulation* and *underregulation* refer to an excessive and deficient response to a developmental need.

CASE EXAMPLES

Wesley, a 14-year-old conduct disordered boy, was evaluated for theft. The family interview indicated that he had been supported at every point in his life. His father, a lawyer, had negotiated several settlements to prevent legal charges from being filed against him. Earlier in his life, most stresses in his environment were eliminated. His mother described a feeling that she did not like the sound of him crying as an infant and she believed, in retrospect, that she had overfed him. Whenever he was crying, she fed him and whenever he was upset, she removed the source of his discomfort. This overregulation of his need for attachment is associated with Wesley's sense of entitlement, assuming that others should always respond to his needs.

Six year old Vicky was adopted at 18 months of age by supportive, nurturing parents. The first year and a half of her life, however, was one of neglect and deprivation. On occasion, she had been left alone, unattended and without food, for several days. There was clear evidence that she had been sexually abused by her mother's drug abusing boyfriend. Her clinical problems were those of disruptiveness and panic when her mother would leave her with a babysitter, a consequence of the underregulation of her developmental needs early in life.

Overregulation and underregulation can occur in the context of limit setting as well.

CASE EXAMPLE

Joshua, a 6-year-old boy, was actively playing in a family interview while his parents were engaged in a vigorous discussion. Joshua's mother repeatedly told him to keep quiet without offering him alternatives to his play activity. At one point, exasperated, she told him to "shut up." Normal childhood spontaneity was seen as unacceptable by his mother and she overresponded to it.

Brian, a 9-year-old boy with hyperactive behaviors, was noted to have his mother's welfare check in his possession at school. When it was returned to his mother, she had a minimal emotional response. In session, this single mother had difficulty setting limits on Brian. When he tried to sit in her lap and caress her in a sexual manner, the interviewer drew attention to the behavior. Mother stated, "This is likely a side effect of the medication, isn't it?" In this case, Brian's testing of limits required more active regulation.

Inappropriate regulation refers to a parent's response, which while appropriate for one developmental stage, is inappropriately applied to the current stage. A father may attempt to discuss his reasoning with a 3-year-old child rather than merely setting a limit and ensuring compliance with his expectations. On the other hand, a father who sets a limit on an adolescent and states, "I'm your father, that's the end of it," is similarly demonstrating inappropriate regulation. An adolescents' cognitive development necessitates parents offering a rationale for their limits and behavioral expectations.

Irregular regulation refers to the family which is consistent in one domain of function, such as self-care, but inconsistent in another domain, such as socialization.

CASE EXAMPLE

Mr. and Mrs. Jones were in the clinic because of 14-year-old Aaron's disrespectful behavior, which had resulted in his being suspended from school. During the interview Mr. Jones constantly remarked on Aaron's wearing a hat indoors, chewing gum, and slouching in his chair, clearly irritated with these behaviors. However, when Aaron told his mother to "shut up" and called her ideas "stupid," no response was given.

This family pattern of intense involvement in one domain and neglect or inconsistency in another, seemingly more important domain is an example of irregular regulation.

Chaotic regulation refers to no discernible pattern of family response to developmental need. In families such as these, caretakers are inconsistent and frequently change. Families are unable to report on such things as school attendance, behavioral tasks, and self-care.

The clinician should be aware that regulatory patterns may, over time, shift from one type of regulation to another. Interview observations which can inform the dimension of family regulation include noting how the family responds to their child's nurturant needs, to the child's need for limits and developing internal self-control, to

the child's need for socialization, to the child's need for achievement and academic success, or to the adolescent's need for independence and individuation. An appropriate interview technique is to review these basic developmental needs, ask each participant's perspective on and reaction to them, and observe any behavior in the interview which would help categorize the regulation of a child's development.

Conclusion

The relevance of the family interview lies in the fact that the family is the primary context in which a child develops, and it remains an enduring influence on the child. When a child has a clinical problem, the perspective of the family is essential, whether the family appears to be contributing to the problem or is being affected by the problem. For legal, financial, and emotional reasons then, we must hear their perspective.

The family interview shares characteristics with effective clinical interviewing of individuals. It is important to gather the facts of history, observe behavioral and emotional responses, and convey a sense of being understood. The family interview poses additional challenges for clinicians because of the number of individuals involved and the physical distractions which may take place.

The family interview should gather the facts of history and the observations of family interaction in a thorough, systematic manner. These facts and observations should be gathered regarding the family and its subunits, the presenting problems and the fundamental areas of family function—structure, communication, beliefs, and regulation of development. At its completion, the relevant data should contribute to a comprehensive assessment and prepare for intervention. Whether a direct intervention takes place with the family or not, the family interview ensures that the family's perspective will be considered in all clinical interactions with the child.

REFERENCES

Anders, T. F. (1989). Clinical syndromes, relationship disturbances, and their assessment. In A. J. Sameroff & R. N. Emde (Eds.), *Relationship disturbances in early childhood: A developmental approach* (pp. 125–144). New York: Basic Books.

Andersen, T. (1987). The reflecting team: Dialogue and metadialogue in clinical work. *Family Process, 26,* 415–428.

Barton, C., & Alexander, J. F. (1981). Functional family therapy. In A. S. Gurman & D. P. Kniskern (Eds.), *Handbook of family therapy* (Vol. 1, pp. 403–443). New York: Brunner/Mazel.

Bateson, G., Jackson, D. D., Haley, J., & Weakland, J. (1956). Toward a theory of schizophrenia. *Behavioral Science, 1,* 251–264.

Breunlin, D. C., & Schwartz, R. C. (1986). Sequences: Toward a common denominator of family therapy. *Family Process, 25,* 67–87.

Combrinck-Graham, L. (1985). A model of family development. *Family Process, 24,* 139–150.

Freedman, J. & Combs, G. (1996). *Narrative therapy: The social construction of preferred realities.* New York: W. W. Norton.

Gurman, A. S., & Kniskern, D. P. (Eds.). (1991). *Handbook of family therapy* (Vol. 2), New York: Brunner/Mazel.

Haley, J. (1976). Conducting the first interview (Chapter One). In J. Haley *Problem-solving therapy.* San Francisco: Jossey-Bass. pp. 9–47.

McGoldrick, M., & Gerson, R. (1985). *Genograms in family assessment.* New York: W. W. Norton.

Minuchin, S. (1974). *Families and family therapy.* Cambridge, MA: Harvard University Press.

Neill, J. R., & Kniskern, D. P. (1982). *From psyche to system: The evolving therapy of Carl Whitaker.* New York: Guilford Press.

Nichols, M. (1987). *The self and the system: Expanding the limits of family therapy.* New York: Brunner/Mazel.

Patterson, G. R. (1982). *Coercive family process.* Eugene, OR: Castalia.

Reiss, D. (1989). The represented and practicing family: Contrasting visions of family continuity. In A. Sameroff and R. Emde (Eds.), *Relationship disturbances in early childhood: A developmental approach* (pp. 191–220). New York: Basic Books.

Sameroff, A., & Emde, R. (1989). *Relationship disturbances in early childhood: A developmental approach.* New York: Basic Books.

Sargent, J. (1997). Family therapy in child and adolescent psychiatry. *Child and Adolescent Psychiatric Clinics of North America.* pp. 151–171. Philadelphia: W. B. Saunders.

Stanton, M. D. (1981). Strategic approaches to family therapy. In A. S. Gurman and D. P. Kniskern (Eds.), *Handbook of family therapy* (Vol. 1, pp. 361–402). New York: Brunner/Mazel.

Tomm, K. (1988). Interventive interviewing: Intending to ask lineal, circular, strategic or reflexive questions. *Family Process, 27,* 1–15.

Visher, E., & Visher, J. (1988). *Old loyalties, new ties: Therapeutic strategies with stepfamilies.* New York: Brunner/Mazel.

Von Bertalanffy, L. (1968). *General system theory: Foundations, development, applications.* New York: George Braziller.

Walsh, F. (1993). Conceptualization of normal family processes. In F. Walsh (Ed.), *Normal family processes* (pp. 3–69). New York: Guilford Press.

63 / The Home Visit

Eli C. Messinger

The home visit is an important procedure for directly assessing the child's family, social, and physical environment. Although it literally takes us to where the child lives, it is too often neglected by mental health professionals.

What can be learned through a home visit that might be missed on the clinician's turf? First, the home visit might reveal inadequate care for the child in terms of nutrition; lack of separate sleeping space; and conditions that cast doubt on the safety, and orderliness of the home. Second, the character of the neighborhood is better assessed through direct observation than through the family's report. Third, the clinician can best learn about the spatial features of the home through direct observation—the sleeping arrangements; the size, design, and comfort of the living space. These direct observations of the child's environment, that is, housing, might, for example, raise the possibility of lead ingestion as a cause of the presenting symptoms.

Advantages, Contraindications, and Resistances

The home visit permits the clinician to observe family interactions in their natural and usual setting. Sceptics claim that the family will act its best under the unusual conditions of a home visit. In fact, families undergoing assessment will often, consciously or unconsciously, present their psychopathology more vividly. Perhaps their motivation is to ensure their acceptance as a patient. They are also communicating their problems and needs.

The home visit is a tangible sign to the child, and to the family, of the clinician's interest.

A home visit to a paranoid or litigious family is contraindicated because the family may feel spied upon, or can allege that boundary transgressions took place.

The fact that a home visit costs the clinician more time than a comparable office visit often serves as a rationalization for not doing a home visit. In fact, however, the resistance typically comes from another source, namely, the clinician's discomfort in functioning outside of the usual office setting. The office setting is more than a backdrop: It provides the clinician with the trappings of professional authority. Some clinicians feel uneasy in temporarily giving these up. However, once the clinician tries operating outside of the familiar office surroundings, he will discover the richness of information which the home visit provides.

Procedures

The request to make a home visit should be made early by the evaluator as a part of the assessment. The visit should be scheduled when most or all members of the family will be at home. It should never be made unannounced or without an explicit invitation from the family.

There are several advantages to two clinicians making the home visit together:

- No one person can possibly take in the multitudinous data afforded by a home visit; a pair of clinicians can pool their individual observations.
- The interactions with several members of the family, especially in the home setting, can stir up strong emotional reactions in the clinicians. Distortions are lessened if the two clinicians process their observations and reactions immediately following the home visit.
- The presence of a companion reduces security risks.
- The presence of a companion minimizes the risk of allegations of boundary violations.

The home visit brings information about the neighborhood, the design and furnishings of the home, and interpersonal relations within the family.

The Neighborhood

The clinician can invite the child to accompany him on the trip to the home. This puts the child in the role of guide and instructor. The clinician can, at the same time, assess the child's familiarity with the transportation system, and knowledge of directions and maps.

The clinician may encourage the child to speak about the significance of the various landmarks encountered during a walk through the immediate neighborhood. The child can point out, for example, favorite hangout spots, his school, the grocery store where the family shops, and the family's place of worship. For the city child, the neighborhood may be divided between safe and dangerous areas. The child may be willing to indicate these lines of demarcation which may be subsequently represented—in play or in talk—in the office.

The Design and Furnishings of the Home

The physical layout of the home tends to reveal the interpersonal relations within the family; there is a unity between a way of life and its setting. Several questions concerning spatial design should be addressed:

- Is the amount of space adequate for the members of the household? Levels of tension and of aggressivity are heightened when people are forced to live in overcrowded spaces. A parent's complaint that a child is "hyperactive" can sometimes actually mean that the child is getting underfoot in an overcrowded household. Do the children, especially the adolescents, have room for privacy?
- What statement is the family making about its social position through its home? The family typically announces its social class status—actual or wished for—through its home furnishings. It may also announce its religious and ethnic affiliations.
- How are boundaries marked and how well do they function? Do the children have a quiet, demarcated space in which to do homework or read? Does each child have a locale within the home which is considered his own, even if it is no more than a portion of a room? Are generational and gender boundaries clearly marked in terms of who sleeps where and with whom?
- Which room is of greatest emotional significance for this family? Often it is the kitchen as the site of food preparation and the mother's availability. In other families, the parental bedroom is the primary site of family drama, with the children coming and going during the night hours.
- How are power, authority, and affectional relations manifested in spatial terms? Which sibling has access to the choice seat in front of the television set? Who sits next to whom around the dining room table? Does the parent have the authority to enter the adolescent's bedroom without permission?

Family Interaction

The home visit affords the opportunity to observe the family's patterns of interaction in a natural setting. Observation of the family's characteristic modes of communication, role allocations, power relations, and emotional issues takes on greater authenticity when these are seen and heard where they are normally enacted.

REFERENCES

Kupersmidt, J. B., & Martin, S. L. (Feb., 1997). Mental health problems of children of migrant and seasonal farm workers: A pilot study. *Journal of the American Academy of Child & Adolescent Psychiatry* 36 (2): 224–232.

Volling, B. L., Youngblade, L. M., & Belsky, J., Jan., 1997. Young children's social relationships with siblings and friends. *American Journal of Orthopsychiatry* 67 (1): 102–111.

64 / The School Visit

Maureen Fulchiero Gordon

Children typically spend an average of 30 hours in their school environments. By translating therapy into the school milieu, clinicians have an important opportunity to significantly extend their work with patients. To achieve this goal, clinicians have available a process, which can be accomplished in three distinct phases. Formulation, the initial phase, is the development of a communication tool, a "blueprint," to facilitate work with the clinician, family, and school staff. The second phase, translation, has several specific aspects: initiating the school contact, developing a working relationship with the appropriate teachers, and devising a system for the teachers and clinician that ensures ongoing progress. The final phase, transition, entails clarifying long-term goals and creating procedures for carrying the work into the following school year.

Formulation

This phase involves devising a tool for effective communication. After making an initial assessment that therapeutic intervention is appropriate, the clinician takes steps to assign therapeutic goals for a child's treatment. Treatment can take the form of any of the options available to a clinician, including individual psychotherapy, family treatment, referral to a group situation, or outpatient clinic intervention programs. Although a clinician who is involved directly in the treatment process will have much more opportunity to intervene in the school situation, any clinician who evaluates a child and makes a disposition to a treatment program can take advantage of the school as an opportunity to extend the intervention.

Before approaching the school with any treatment plan, it is important to have a well-defined overview of the patient. An effective clinical assessment allows the clinician to formulate the goals for therapeutic intervention in a clearly out-lined and organized manner. Just as significantly, such an outline can be an effective way of describing the patient to others who are enlisted as partners in an effort to extend the child's therapy. The author finds one such formulation to be particularly helpful. It is the developmental "blueprint," which is often the most translatable and pragmatic tool for communication. This tool incorporates the principles of development as a context for understanding the significance of the problems presented by the child. In such a structure, the clinician divides information obtained about the child into seven developmental areas, or lines, which include physical, temperamental, cognitive, social, emotional, psychosexual, and moral. Information observed or reported about the child is categorized into the appropriate section. A treatment plan is then devised based upon addressing information in the child's evaluation that differs from normal standards of development. With such a clear, cohesive treatment plan, the clinician can easily communicate goals with a school's staff, parents, or other caregivers.

SAMPLE INFORMATION USED TO FORMULATE A DEVELOPMENTAL BLUEPRINT

Katy S., a 7-year-old child, was brought to the clinician by her professional parents, who were concerned about Katy. They reported that, although Katy is not a behavioral problem, she has begun to show poor attention in school, and does not seem motivated or particularly interested in activities, either at home or at school. In several areas of development Katy is noted to be age appropriate. She is a physically well-developed and well-coordinated child, showing no evidence of perceptual, language, or motoric difficulty. Katy is cognitively at least 6 months ahead of the majority of her peers. Socially, Katy is mature, in that she is peer oriented. She is even beginning to show some ability to factor peer approval and peer choices into her thinking and decision making. This is age appropriate, and even somewhat advanced for a 7 year old. Psychosexually, she has a clearly defined concept of herself as a little girl, with appropriate concepts of the differences in her relationships with her mother and father. In addition, Katy seems to be developing the social referencing concept of needing to work and cooperate with others. Morally, she appears to understand the importance of choice; and she bases this upon an awareness of her own needs. Temperamentally, however, Katy is immature in several respects. She is unassertive, demonstrating difficulty in expressing her needs as compared to the assertion average for children her age. Katy is also relatively nonverbal temperamentally, as compared to other 7-year-old girls. She is, in addition, not particularly goal directed. The clinician notes that her social maturity, which motivates her strongly for peer interaction, may actually be aggravating her temperamental delays.

Having organized the information into a developmental format, such as the "blueprint," the clinician can use the structure of this approach to communicate the steps of a proposed treatment plan to parents, to discuss goals in a clear and focused manner with teachers, and to monitor changes with school staff as well as parents. A clinician who attempts to make an intervention without having such an approach invites difficulties, including poorly directed discussions with teachers, difficulty assessing progress, and communication difficulties between family, clinician, and school. In attempting to make school a part of the treatment process, good communication is essential.

It should be noted that utilizing the school as an extension for therapy may also be appropriate for the clinician who makes the decision to refer a child outside of the clinician's office for treatment. Although the role of the clinician is much more limited in this situation, the initial involvement can be significant. When the clinician chooses to attempt to extend the benefits of a therapeutic assessment, without actually becoming the child's therapist, the initial phase in the process remains the same, while the second and third phases of the school intervention are eliminated. It is important to keep in mind that schools, whether understaffed and overcrowded or because of a high degree of commitment and dedication, are often grateful for the input of professionals who can help them understand the children who are entrusted to their care. By offering professional information that can be pragmatically incorporated into a classroom, a referring clinician, who does not continue to have a role in further treatment,

can make a difference—with one single, effective contact—in the way in which a school system perceives and works with a child.

Translation

There are important considerations in making information available to the school. Not only must the clinician be capable of translating clinical material to the school but the clinician must be knowledgeable concerning issues such as confidentiality, school process, and appropriate levels of intervention. There are two major aspects to translating information to properly extend therapy into a child's school situation.

STEP ONE: EFFECTIVELY INITIATING THE INTERVENTION

Just as laying a strong foundation is critical for building an enduring structure, laying the groundwork for the school contact is critical. In the initiation process, there are certain important principles to keep in mind. Ideally the child's parents or guardians are part of the initiation process. If the clinician is dealing with guardians, such as staff of a residential placement, it is equally important that the clinician work with the primary caregiver assigned to the child who is being treated. Educating parents and other caregivers as to the value, need, and mechanics of the intervention process can mean the difference between a successful translation and a mediocre intervention. For example, it is important that the parents understand the information that will be shared with the school environment. Parents are reassured when a clinician makes it clear that confidentiality and discretion will be used in providing information. Not all information should be made available to the school. Just as the patient's needs are paramount in making decisions and interventions in therapy, what is best for the child's well-being dictates the information that is shared by the clinician. In certain situations, for example, it is not important that the school know that a child's father had a previous marriage, which ended in a bitter divorce several years before he and the patient's mother married. It might be important, however, for the teacher to know that a child's father is a successful physician and her mother is an assistant district attorney. For a child whose family context is one of highly achieving academics, symptoms of poor motivation may be very significant. Knowing such information often helps a teacher to understand better a child's special problems. In the case of institutional involvement, a residential treatment facility for example, it is important that the facility's staff also understand the particular information being shared. Again, information is selective and the emphasis is on the clinician's understanding of what is important for the school to know about a particular child.

As the parents or guardians learn the nature of the intervention, they are likely to eagerly cooperate in requesting that their children's teachers contact the clinician. Ideally the parents or guardians of a child, rather than the clinician, should make such requests. This practice is preferable to the clinician's sending a written release of information—which can set a tone of tension and distance. More importantly, requests made by the family help the teachers feel that they are not violating confidentiality issues when they speak to the clinician. The teachers tend to be more comfortable sharing their feelings and observations when direct permission is elicited. In addition, teachers approached in this manner are predisposed to feel that a call from the clinician is a working together for the child's benefit, not a relegating of responsibility to the teacher for the child's well-being. Another common practice among therapists and other clinicians is to send an evaluation form in lieu of personal contact with either family or clinician. Teachers report that receiving such a form tends to elicit their sense of being burdened by more of the never-ending "paper trail." In such cases, teachers often answer with perfunctory, single-word responses which do little to help clinicians or their patients. The latter situation, in turn, adds a slight sense of alienation and defensiveness to the process. On the other hand, direct parental or guardian requests, followed by the teacher's initiation of the call to the clinician, frequently help to create a good working relationship and to encourage a teacher's further involvement.

Understanding the environment in which the teacher is functioning is another aspect of the initiation. Knowledge of the teacher's situation allows the clinician to appreciate the teacher's position. In elementary classrooms, for example, there is usually a homeroom teacher who carries ultimate responsibility for the children. Although teachers frequently have an investment in helping the "whole child," there is little or no support system to help them deal with nonacademic issues with individual children. They frequently want to help the whole child function. However, they are often left to their own devices when working with the individual child. In addition, teachers are often barraged by overly anxious parents, supervisors, and assorted visitors to the classroom—all of whom make demands upon them. Although, at times, the classroom work is shared by aides, the teacher is primarily responsible. In such an environment, homeroom teachers often welcome other professionals—but only if they appear to be helpful. In higher grades, teachers have a parallel sense of sole responsibility in the subjects for which they are responsible.

There are situations, unfortunately, which preclude a personal, less formal request. In some schools, the legal system has inserted itself into the process, by requiring written permission. It is then important that the therapist shift gears and follows the school's regimen in those cases. In general, the school's rules must be carefully considered. Schools are closed communities which operate with hierarchies, rules, and regulations. Clinicians must adhere to such standards if they are to be welcomed into the school milieu. In a second situation—one in which parents are not the caregivers—the clinician must also alter the preferable protocol. In these situations, a more formal approach is warranted. Written permission from the caregivers is very important. In addition, the clinician should be the person who initiates the teacher's involvement. Whenever two systems are involved—the school and residential treatment staff, for example—the need for the formality of written permission outweighs the benefits of a more informal approach.

STEP TWO: STRUCTURING SUBSEQUENT "WORKING" SCHOOL SESSIONS

"Working" sessions, which follow the initial contact, form the backbone of the intervention. It is during these times that the teacher and clinician work out the details of translating therapy into school situations.

The first "working call," which follows the initial contact between the teacher and the clinician, can be either a long phone discussion or a face-to-face meeting. Personal contact offers the opportunity for the clinician to see the school milieu directly, and to form an effective relationship with the teacher. A face-to-face meeting in the school takes much more of the teacher's available time. If a teacher appears overburdened during the initial call, it is often better to defer this in-school meeting until the teacher has had a chance to see the benefits of the interventions. One indicator that a teacher might be overworked is the teacher's taking an inordinate time to initiate the working call. Comments, as well, can demonstrate a teacher's attitude and state of mind. "There are so many children I'm not sure which day Katy has physical education." "I'm sorry to have taken so long to get back to you but. . . ." Such statements point to the likelihood that a teacher feels being overworked or overwhelmed.

During the first "working" contact, there are certain issues that can be anticipated. It is important that, during this first working meeting, some background of the child and the problems are discussed. It is good technique for the clinician to allow the teacher to begin by freely commenting on the child's situation. Some teachers, however, are uncomfortable with an open format. In those cases, the clinician can volunteer certain selective experiences with the child. This frequently focuses the teacher, who often becomes comfortable joining in with classroom experiences. By mutually sharing their experiences with the same child, the working relationship between therapist/ clinician and teacher begins.

AN EXAMPLE OF ISSUES AND EXPERIENCES THAT MIGHT ARISE IN A "WORKING SESSION"

Katy's situation demonstrates the way in which the working process can be successful. In this case, the meeting was done entirely on the telephone. The clinician learned that Katy's teacher was a young woman, in her early thirties, who readily responded when asked how she felt Katy was doing. She seemed more than somewhat concerned that Katy was not responding to her efforts. She confirmed that Katy was not particularly motivated in her work. She was not sure if Katy had an attention deficit disorder—she appeared distracted and somewhat uninvolved. She felt that Katy looked as if she had a problem being an "only child," which might account for her "shyness." She suggested that perhaps she "was only average in intelligence." Her tone implied that perhaps the parents were "overly concerned" or even "demanding." Throughout the call, the teacher repeated how much she was doing for "her" children and how little she understood of why Katy was not responding. The clinician could readily hear the seeds of frustration with Katy being sown. Another few months without intervention and, paradoxically, because of this teacher's true commitment and involvement with the children, Katy would likely become one of the teacher's failures. It is not uncommon to find that the most committed and the most dedicated teachers become the most easily frustrated when a child is not responsive to their heroic efforts. Appropriate and effective intervention turns this situation around and becomes effective preventative psychiatry.

During the "working" phone interview, Katy's clinician, in turn, used her developmental profile as an outline for explaining Katy's situation to her teacher. This technique explained the child's problems in the most productive, positive light. The clinician made a point of using specific examples of Katy's behavior to demonstrate that she is a cognitively gifted, nonassertive, nonverbal child. The clinician was able to point out, for example, that nonverbal children often appear less intelligent than highly verbal children. Ironically, the opposite assumption can be made as well: highly verbal children can be mistaken for gifted children with the erroneous expectations that would necessarily follow. The clinician also pointed out that Katy was not particularly goal directed; a fact which made her look mistakenly like a child with an attention deficit. Katy's clinician explained that her nonassertive behavior made her look socially immature; when in fact she was developmentally quite capable of forming appropriate peer relationships. The clinician further explained Katy's parents' concerns. Her teacher was reassured that they were not overly pushy parents; but parents who, in spite of their busy schedules, were involved with Katy in a real, parenting sense. In no way were they unhappy with the school situation. The clinician explained that they, in fact, appreciated anything the school could do to help them with their daughter. The clinician also gave the teacher specific examples of the interventions that had already been successful in the home situation. Katy's teacher was more than willing to help after that explanation. She pointed out to the clinician that she felt she understood much more about Katy and was eager to help.

Determining the number of subsequent working sessions is another aspect of this translation step. The frequency will depend largely upon the particular situation's goals, which have been established by the clinician. There are general principles to follow, however. It is helpful to allow the teacher to have adequate time to assimilate the information shared during the first working meeting. Ideally, however, it should be done within a few weeks. The teacher should be comfortable with the scheduling. It is always important to keep in mind that a teacher is generally responsible for many children, not just the one child being discussed. In situations where there are small classes, the timing of the intervention periods is not as critical. Especially in a crowded setting, the clinician must balance the time constraints of the busy teacher with the inherent need for work to progress in a timely fashion. Spacing working sessions has another important aspect. It has been the author's experience that most teachers will use the time in between the calls to observe the validity of the professional's observations. This time tends to accomplish two further purposes: it allows the teacher to confirm the validity of the clinician's observations, and it allows the teacher to become more expert in detecting the child's individual behavior in the context that has been presented by the teacher. Often teachers will intuitively begin the therapeutic intervention once the issues have been focused for them.

Although the process of translating therapy into the school situation is similar when working with elementary, middle school, and high school students, there are some issues that are important to remember when working with students in the upper grades. In dealing with adolescents, for example, it is especially important that the teacher and clinician respect the adolescent's heightened sense of privacy. For example, when a clinician goes into the school setting it is important that the adolescent be given some sense of control over the situation. Adolescents like to feel in charge of their environment. They like to know details such as when, with whom, and how the clinician is going to be working. They are also especially conscious of their peers' opinions. The cognitive phenomenon of adolescent thinking, termed "imaginary audience," results in an adolescent feeling that everyone is focused upon him. This attitude

heightens an adolescent's potential for "feeling different." A clinician must make sure the adolescent is in agreement and cooperative with the school interventions. Some adolescents prefer the therapist to remain "invisible." In this case, scheduling contact with the teacher for a time when the students have gone home, or in a more private part of the school, is extremely important. In younger children, who are used to adults making choices for them and taking care of them, this is much less significant. Younger children, in fact, often enjoy the therapist's presence as a status symbol with their friends. To many younger children, it adds to their sense that an important adult is intervening for them.

In both middle and high school situations, there is another aspect to consider. At this older grade level, there are most often advisers or counselors to whom a significant number of students are assigned. In approaching the school staff it is important that the counselor be made aware of the clinician's involvement. In order to maintain the primacy of the teacher, however, this is best done after a working relationship with the teacher has been established. In most school situations, the teacher's role is regarded with deference. Headmasters, as a rule, avidly defend their teachers' positions and support them in their requests. The cooperation of counselors, however, can be very important. They are potential facilitators in the work of the teacher and clinician. The case of one student Harry J., illustrates the way in which the counselor can become part of a valuable team approach. Harry is a 16-year-old young man, who has auditory and visual perception learning problems. He is referred to the clinician by his legal guardian, who is concerned about Harry's poor school performance and his antisocial behavior. Harry's counselor, at the joint request of his teacher and clinician, was able to arrange for Harry to take untimed tests in all of his classes. The untimed testing situation dramatically improved Harry's performance by reducing his anxiety, which in turn lessened the effect of his perceptual difficulties. Therapy with Harry was significantly helped by this particular intervention. Self-esteem issues, with which the student was struggling, markedly diminished. Harry's truancy and marijuana use stopped. In addition, Harry's counselor helped him by obtaining the forms that were essential for him to obtain permission for taking the college qualification examination in a special, untimed situation.

Follow-up meetings—those sessions which are arranged after the initial work has been outlined and is in progress—may be largely update discussions. However, it is not unusual for such conversations to become opportunities to further extensions of the previous working sessions. During follow-up meetings, it is not uncommon for the teacher to make spontaneous observations regarding the child. Teachers might volunteer, for example, that a child is not disinterested in her peers, as was the teacher's initial observation. Katy's teacher, for example, noticed that she was drawn to the most assertive of the little girls in the class. She had observed that Katy had not persevered in getting the little girl's attention whenever other children had competed for her attention. The teacher volunteered that it was possible to "see that Katy is not a shy child," as had been the teacher's initial impressions. Katy's teacher had become part of the therapeutic process.

By using pragmatic suggestions, in subsequent meetings, a clinician can remotivate a teacher's more deliberated, direct participation. The clinician should be a "good listener" to the teachers' comments. In one situation, for example, a teacher might note that a particular child is "doing better." In other situations, the teacher might continue to have a negative response to the child involved. "He's such a handful." "She's doesn't like math." It is appropriate at this point—but especially if the teacher makes generic comments—for the clinician to make additional specific recommendations. In the case of the child who is considered to be a handful, the teacher might be given some behavior-specific guidelines to follow and to observe. Questions to the teacher often help with focusing. During what activities is the child having the least difficulty behaving? Are there certain areas in which he shows real self-control? How is your classroom structured during the afternoon? In Katy's situation, for example, the recommendation was for the teacher to allow Katy to make verbal statements whenever the choice was between written or nonverbal communication. Such a directive stimulates verbal temperamental development and allows it to become maximally practiced. As with all development, stimulation

produces the maximum development within the range potentially available to the particular child. Inhibiting nonverbal while stimulating verbal behavior allows Katy to utilize her potential. Secondly, it was suggested to Katy's teacher that Katy be given small, clearly defined goals with rewards for each step in the goal process. This would allow her to reinforce goal-directed behavior which was inherently low. Thirdly, it was suggested that Katy be given a leadership role in relating to her peers. Usually teachers intuitively choose the assertive child for roles like room monitor, passing out papers, taking messages to other teachers, etc. A nonassertive child would not likely make her desire to do those things known, even though her desire is certainly the same as for an assertive child. It was also suggested that Katy be asked to make choices whenever possible so that she could practice assertive behavior. In the case of children who are overly deliberate and seem overly concerned about their work, the directive might be to attempt humor with the child, or to reward the child when work is handed in quickly. A teacher might actually interrupt a deliberate child with some instructions: Could you go and work on that bulletin board for me?

Directives work well to further a teacher's pointed interventions with older age groups also. For the socially immature child the teacher might encourage peer activity rather than allowing the child to volunteer for an activity that encourages teacher mentoring or solitary task performance. An adult-oriented 15 year old, for example, who works with the teacher adviser as writer for the school paper might be encouraged to cover a school activity as a "journalist." This moves the student into his peers' world and encourages more socially mature interactions. Suggesting to the teacher that, in as many situations as possible, a socially immature student be carefully paired with peers will stimulate peer interaction as well.

These situations are just a few of the many which lend themselves to using the school as an extension of the therapeutic process. Attention deficit disorder, with or without hyperactivity, depression, situational difficulties, and of course other developmental issues, such as cognitive, emotional, moral, and social immaturity, are particularly helped by this approach. School liaisons with children who have special problems, such as perceptual learning difficulties, physical disabilities, and major physical illnesses, are not only invaluable, but one might assert, are essential to help a child develop cognitively and socially, while dealing with the special issues surrounding the child's particular situation.

DEALING WITH SPECIAL WORKING SITUATIONS

Clinicians may become part of the process, at the working session level, phase 2, when the staff of a school itself is the referral source. This becomes a particularly common situation when the clinician has already been recognized by the school as valuable and competent in the school setting. Two situations are typical of the kinds of situations which involve school referrals.

INTERVENTION WITH A CHILD WHO IS *REFERRED BY THE SCHOOL* FOR POSSIBLE ATTENTION DEFICIT DISORDER AND SECONDARY EMOTIONAL ISSUES

Will is an 11 year old, in the second semester of fifth grade, who was referred to the clinician by the school staff because of distractibility and a "macho" style of interacting with peers. Recently his "tough" style had begun to take the form of obstinacy with his parents and, alarmingly, had extended to his new second semester substitute teacher. Will's behavior had been a problem all through school, but it had escalated with the new teacher, a young woman for whom this was her first primary teacher assignment. In this situation, the clinician discussed, with Will's new teacher, Will's need for a highly structured environment and the use of medication to deal with his attention deficit disorder. The clinician felt that the "macho" behavior was an imaginative defensive system devised by a very intelligent, highly creative aggressive, assertive, verbal child who had no idea why he had trouble concentrating. The obstinacy had occurred with his new teacher, who had instituted the strictest of rules with rather severe consequences in order to move into the school situation in the middle of the year. She had targeted Will because she felt he was a negative leader in the class. Use of medication, a highly structured but not punitive reward system, and clear rules with consequences—all of which were instituted in Will's school by his teacher and reinforced by the clinician in work with Will's parents resulted in almost immediate improvement. Will became a sterling student,

a leader in every way, and a role model for his sixth-grade peers. At home, his sibling situation dramatically improved as well.

INTERVENTION FOR A CHILD FOR WHOM THE SCHOOL SITUATION ITSELF HAS *GENERATED* THE PROBLEM

The situation of Danny O. demonstrates the special kinds of tasks which are characteristic when translating the therapy of a child with two special circumstances. The child has a significant, chronic physical illness, that affects his school performance and participation. Perhaps, more significantly, the school itself is part of the referring problem. Danny's difficulties actually began because of his teacher's attempts to create a therapeutic environment in the classroom to deal with Danny's illness. When Danny's psychologically minded teacher discovered that 8-year-old Danny had juvenile diabetes she decided to bring the class into the situation. She asked Danny during a "show and tell" period to talk to his classmates about his illness. The intervention backfired. The class made fun of Danny. Danny was especially upset with their new name for him, "Diabetes Man."

When Danny was seen by the clinician, he presented as significantly depressed and anxious as a result of the school situation. He had begun to avoid school by claiming that he frequently felt "sick." The clinician felt that developmentally he was mature in every way. However, this social ostracizing, which was new, made him see his illness in a new light. Intervention took the form of explaining to the teacher the developmental issue involved with the children he was teaching rather than Danny in particular. However, the process of intervention was done in exactly the same manner as it had been in the case of Katy and Will. The teacher was quite progressive in his thinking; however, he did not understand the development of children at this age. He had been a teacher of adolescents prior to his move to a new city. In adolescents, a teen with an illness can wear an illness like a badge of courage. In his classes, he had a 15-year-old girl who managed to elicit her class's admiration and support for her illness. Fifteen year olds often like to take on the adult, "I know more than the doctor" role. They can do it by actually becoming "experts" in their disease. The 15-year-old student had decided to make her illness the subject of a school project. Her classmates were very receptive of the student's presentation. They seemed in awe of her knowledge of the illness and were eager to know more. Many of the teenager's classmates turned in reports on the illness and had actually volunteered at the local Children's Hospital as a direct result of their classmate's situation. Several of her peers actually began to get involved with the teen's progress itself. They became solicitous of the student and even became attuned to her low blood sugar moods, her need for orange juice, etc.

The clinician's task was to explain the difference between the developmental issues of adolescents and pre-teenagers in terms of illness. Adolescents who think developmentally that they are adults and who are cognitively, socially, and morally idealistic frequently like to think in terms of control over illness. In younger children, who socially tend to group as leaders and followers, and for whom cognitive understanding of illness often resorts to magical thinking (Danny confided to his therapist that he felt sometimes that he got the illness because his last name started with the letter "M;" and he knew two other kids with M in their initials who also had diabetes), an illness can isolate a child or relegate him to a position of outcast, "the loser" group. In this age group the child can actually enhance his social status. However, the illness must be presented by an adult with adult authority, not by the student himself.

During the course of the intervention, the clinician helped Danny's teacher shift the illness from peer to adult focus. The clinician called the treating endocrinologist. Together they did a presentation for Danny's classmates. The connection between Danny and his doctors impressed the children. Danny's image was repaired as well as Danny's sense of control and self. The children, in direct contrast to adolescents, needed adults to teach them about the illness. The teacher played a direct role in the therapy within the classroom. A recommendation for Danny's teacher to shift leadership to adults paradoxically and predictably moved Danny back to his peers. Of course, if the adolescent child with diabetes had been the referral the approach which Danny's teacher had used would have been appropriate and would be the kind of model a clinician would suggest in that case.

The single most important aspect of all of the working sessions, which are a part of this second phase of intervention, is maintaining clear, positive and open communication throughout the therapeutic liaison between teacher and clinician. Keeping in mind the principles already described will help keep the teacher-clinician relationship focused and functional. One situation in particular is more vulnerable to failure, however. When work is being done solely by telephone conversations, the system tends to feel more informal. This lends itself to poor follow-up, unless the clinician keeps in mind the goals. This situation tends to occur especially when a child is doing well or has

difficulties which are not causing classroom difficulty. Teachers, often stretched in their responsibilities, fall prey to the "squeaky wheel" syndrome of paying more attention to the child in trouble. Children who are doing well tend to be low on the teacher's agenda. Whenever possible, arranging at least one short meeting at some point in the working relationship increases the effectiveness of the therapeutic extension significantly. Such a meeting is valuable, not only to reinforce the teacher's participation, but also to offer the therapist an opportunity to form a relationship with other school personnel as well. It is not uncommon for a teacher, at such an informal meeting, to suggest that the therapist meet the principle or director. This provides an opportunity for the therapist to begin the third and last phase of the process of extending therapy into the school situation by carrying the therapy into the following school term.

Having initiated the therapeutic intervention and successfully worked on therapeutic extensions with the school teachers and staff, the clinician and teacher will find that most often their goals are achieved. In each situation, however, it is important that the final phase in the intervention process be completed. The next phase is aimed at maintaining the progress that has been made.

Transition

Finally, therapeutic goals can be extended into the following school year. In most schools, whether public or private, shortly before the end of the school term it is customary for the teacher and principal to sit together and make recommendations for matching children with available teachers for the upcoming school year. This is a highly political issue in most schools, since it is common for certain teachers' reputations to precede them. The principle is often besieged with parents' requests to place their child in the popular teachers' rooms. As a result, principals often discourage or ban parental involvement in teacher selection. However, a clinician who has established a relationship with the school faculty is in a position to provide significant meaningful input concerning child placement. Principals are not likely to allow clinicians to actually name the teacher, but are usually grateful for their suggestions as to what type of teacher is best for their patients. A clinician, for example, might suggest that a child with learning disabilities be placed with a structured teacher who is kind but firm. Children with moral immaturity, or with impulsive temperaments, might be recommended to a teacher who is more mature and experienced with children rather than a more academically credentialed, but less experienced teacher. Children who have parents who are democratic in their disciplinary approach will do better with a teacher who is less strict, but clear. For these children an authoritarian teacher tends to be perceived as "mean" rather than strict. In Katy's situation, for example, a recommendation was made by the clinician to have Katy placed with a teacher who had a structured classroom but who allowed students to take active roles in the classroom situation. Without specific intervention, it is most likely that Katy would have been placed with the opposite type of teacher. As an unassertive child she would not have been placed in a classroom where assertion played a large role. As a non-goal-directed student she most likely would have been matched intuitively with a teacher who had a loosely structured classroom. Both teachers would have reinforced Katy's temperamental delays rather than stimulated their development. Harry, a student with learning difficulties, was placed, with input from his clinician, with teachers who were comfortable with his special needs. His teachers were the most flexible available. For example, they were teachers who permitted his tape recording of his classes or allowed him extra time for his in-class assignments. Will, a student with attention deficit disorder, was placed in classes with teachers who were tolerant of a wide range of student behavior, yet these teachers were clear with their academic goals and highly structured assignments. On the other hand, Danny, a child who was dealing with a physical illness, was placed in a classroom whose teacher placed much emphasis on class presentations, projects, volunteering in the community, and peer partnering, all of which allowed Danny to find outlets to deal with his illness in relationship to his peers.

It is important for the clinician, at the end of school year meeting, to reinforce an appreciation for the teacher and the school's help with specific examples of success that have been accomplished as well as work that remains to be done. It is also essential that clinicians make themselves available for passing on appropriate information to the next teacher. As teachers review their classroom roster, they frequently make comments to the prospective new teachers. Most often they describe circumstances particular to each student. It is important that the present teacher pass on comments about the "valuable" support system—the clinician and parents or guardians—that a particular child has available. This means support for the teacher as well.

Helping to establish a transition for the child in the situation where the same teacher will have that student the following year is somewhat different. The principle of continuity, however, remains the same. For example, the clinician and teacher might have an end of school year meeting and go over the progress made by the child. The clinician can reinforce updates on the child's progress and reinforce the teacher's awareness of goals. The student will be one year older as well. This means new developmental goals for the student. Having updated the developmental schema, the clinician can anticipate certain behaviors and can share them with the teacher as a way to reinforce the therapeutic alliance for the following year.

School Interventions that Indirectly Assist the Clinical Process

It is not uncommon for clinicians, who have established valuable and effective records in their work with specific patients, to be asked to help other children, or even the staff, in more generalized school situations. Clinicians who work well with the school might be asked to present their information at parent/teacher meetings, to participate in staff educational meetings, or to teach certain parts of the curriculum, in areas such as sex education. By participating in each of these educational formats, clinicians can establish certain precedents, including curriculum changes, that may benefit other students, including their future patients.

REFERENCES

Anglin, T., Naylor, K., & Kaplan, D. (1996). Comprehensive school-based health care: high school students' use of medical, mental health, and substance abuse services. *Pediatrics, 97,* 318–330.

Berndt, T. J. (1986). Children's comments about their friendships. In M. Perlmutter (Ed.), *Cognitive perspectives on children's social and behavioral development* (pp. 189–212). Hillsdale, NJ: Lawrence Erlbaum.

Chalfant, J. C., Pysh, M. V., & Moultine, R. (1979). Teacher assistance teams: A model for within building problem solving. *Learning Disabilities Quarterly, 2,* 85–96.

Eder, D., & Parker, S. (1987). The cultural production and reproduction of gender: The effect of extracurricular activities on peer-group culture. *Sociology of Education, 60,* 200–213.

Eder, R. A. (1989). The emergent personologist: The structure and content of 3½-, 5½- and 7½-year-old's concepts of themselves and other persons. *Child Development, 60,* 1218–1228.

Elkind, D., & Bowen, R. (1979). Imaginary audience behavior in children and adolescence. *Developmental Psychology, 15,* 33–44.

Feldlaufer, H., Midgley, C., & Eccles, J. S. (1988). Student, teacher, and observer perceptions of the classroom environment before and after the transition to junior high school. *Journal of Early Adolescence, 8,* 133–166.

Gallimore, R., & Tharp, R. (1990). Teaching mind in society: Teaching, schooling, and literate discourse. In L. C. Moll (Ed.), *Vygotsky and education* (pp. 175–205). New York: Cambridge University Press.

Gannon, S., & Korn, S. J. (1983). Temperament, cultural variations, and behavior disorder in preschool children. *Child Psychiatry and Human Development, 12,* 203–212.

Lindsay, P. (1984). High school size, participation in activities, and young adult social participation: Some enduring effects of schooling. *Educational Evaluation and Policy Analysis, 6,* 73–83.

Masten, A., Coatsworth, J., Neemann, J., et al. (1995). The structure and coherence of competence from childhood through adolescence. *Child Development, 66,* 1635–1659.

Minuchin, P. P., & Shapiro, E. K. (1983). The school as a context for social development. In E. M. Hetherington (Ed.), *Handbook of child psychology: Vol. 4. Socialization, personality, and social development* (4th ed., pp. 197–274). New York: John Wiley & Sons.

Phillips, D. A. (1987). Socialization of perceived academic competence among highly competent children. *Child Development, 58,* 1308–1320.

Stone, S. (1993). *Shaping strategy. Independent school planning in the '90's.* Stoneham, MA: Graphic Touch Publications.

Tharp, R. G., & Gallimore, R. (1988). *Rousing minds to life: Teaching, learning, and schooling in social context.* New York: Cambridge University Press.

Zigmond, N. Learning disabilities from an educational perspective. In G. Lyon, D. Gray, J. Kavanaugh, & N. Krasnegor (Eds.), *Better understanding learning disabilities* (pp. 251–273), Baltimore, MD: Paul H. Brookes.

65 / Observation, Interview, and Mental Status Assessment (OIM): Unwilling or Resistant

Mark Blotcky

In their daily practice, child clinicians deal with unwilling, resistant, and unproductive youth on a regular basis. Children and adolescents brought to professional attention are commonly unreceptive to their parents' concerns, recommendations, and exhortations, and many will not demonstrate the social courtesy of talking—even superficially—with the examiner. Most child psychiatrists become accustomed to exploring their own range of flexibility and tolerance of aberrant childhood behaviors. In general, the examiner's optimal posture is one of spontaneity and comfort, while conveying a genuine interest in the child and his experience. Further, there is an enjoyment of the child as a unique individual with his own story to tell, as only he can tell it. Experienced clinicians become accepting of and more comfortable with managing therapeutic impasses—even treatment failures—and it may be through this seasoning, in fact, that clinicians become more effective. The examiner's most facilitative attitude includes a commitment to the evaluation and therapeutic process, offering the child his best effort, and then, with as little interference as possible, allowing the child the opportunity both to discover and to reveal himself.

The role of seduction in the evaluation and treatment of children is the source of some debate, but clearly the relationship with the examiner must offer some hope for gratification and satisfaction. In the effort to conduct an adequate evaluation, the examiner attempts to engage the child, facilitate the child, or interest the child in a nondirected activity or exchange, including conversation, or via play, a more indirect exploration of his problem. Without this effort, many children will not or cannot be very cooperative or productive. Just as a therapist's cold, detached attitude can lead to a problematic interview, so can an overtly seductive or gratifying posture. Either can contaminate the clinician's ability to observe the child's baseline functioning in a comprehensible and meaningful way.

In addition, the techniques of child psychiatry embrace a large repertoire of devices to facilitate the development of rapport and the production of useful material. The squiggle technique (Claman, 1980; Winnicott, 1971) involves using paper and pencil. The clinician begins by offering the child a squiggle, asking the child to make a drawing out of it. The child is then encouraged to share a story or fantasy about the picture. In short, it is a projective technique stimulated by a nondescript scribble provided by the clinician. A variety of responses may then elicit further material. The mutual storytelling technique uses the simple structure of the child and clinician taking turns at beginning and ending short stories. As she comes to understand the child more deeply, the clinician may use the child's stories to communicate a therapeutic message to the child, for example, the universal and acceptable ambivalence children have toward their parents. The "Talking, Feeling, and Doing Game" (Gardner, 1990) is a board game with all the typical props, but with cards which ask the players to answer questions or to do something. Some of the topics are relatively conflict-free for most youngsters, while others are highly charged. The structured therapeutic game method (Kritzberg, 1975) uses concrete, gamelike devices and a structured procedure for eliciting

and processing fantasies. It too has a board and comes in two formats. While any of these tactics may be varied in their use and can often be successfully employed in the evaluation process, nothing substitutes for the core elements of a client-centered interview: empathy, genuineness, nonpossessive warmth, spontaneity, and immediacy.

There are a variety of structures for the evaluation of children and adolescents. These vary as to who should be seen, the initial instructions provided, the structure of the interview, and the availability of play materials. Here, developmental considerations are critical. This discussion addresses some of the more general aspects of evaluation outlined in the previous chapters as they specifically relate to the observation, interview, and mental status assessment of the unwilling or resistant child.

Context of the Interview and Nature of the Resistance

The context of an interview is critical and, specifically, may avoid or evoke resistance. Does the child understand the context, want help, and define his problems as his parents do? Are the expectations of child, parents, and other parties in conflict? What was the child told about the interview and its purpose? Is the evaluation at the request of the parents, the school, the Juvenile Department, or a judge? These issues of context are powerful influences in setting the stage for the OIM. It is, for example, quite common for a preadolescent child to be brought by his parents for evaluation without the nature of the evaluation being explained. The child is fearful of medical examination, needles, and the like, and is frightened, uncooperative, and stubborn. Once the child understands what the consultation is about and how it will take place, he commonly becomes less anxious and more cooperative with the process.

When the examiner encounters a particularly intractable, resistant, or stubborn child, a systematic consideration of the format of the interview, including the physical space, may be useful. The

427

design and furnishings of the examiner's office convey the atmosphere of the interview. Is the interview taking place in an appropriate milieu? Toys may be dangerously regressive to adolescents but reassuring and facilitative for many elementary school-age children. A nicely decorated, more formal office may be stifling and threatening for younger children, yet may offer a supportive adult structure for impulsive adolescents. Is the clinician's behavior reassuring, including his dress, tone of voice, choice of language, style, and balance of casual friendliness with a respect for the seriousness of the patient's feelings and situation? All are building blocks that establish rapport.

Matching or pacing the behavior of the patient—his posture, movements, rate of verbalization—also facilitates rapport. Likewise, using the patient's general language, choice of words, and style of speaking can be helpful, as long as it is not socially, culturally, or personally inappropriate for the examiner. Repeating the patient's words is a client-centered approach which, if not stilted or mechanical, can connect the examiner empathically with the child's experience. Choice of language must be appropriate for the child's age and developmental stage, and must reflect cognitive, educational, and cultural variation. Language should be easily understood, casual, and familiar. The examiner's mirroring verbalization and behavior promote human connectedness with the unwilling or resistant child.

Certain types of resistance stimulated by the patient's concerns about trust and loyalty can be avoided or minimized by the way an initial assessment is conducted. There are often advantages in seeing the younger child and parents together during the first session (or initial part of the first session) and gathering the history from them as a family. If the patient is an older adolescent, there may be greater advantage in conducting an individual interview before meeting with the parents. Through an initial family interview the examiner fosters an alliance with the family as a whole. The child hears just what his family's concerns are and how they are presented, knows what the clinician is aware of, and is made to feel she is a respected partner in the entire process. Further, the examiner gains rich data about the family system and notes particularly their emotional reactions and style related to the presenting problem. Is there support and concern, sharing and intimacy, or

blaming and guilt, anxiety and insecurity, projection and denial? In the course of the early contacts, if a workable coming together is to occur, discovering what the child and family expect of the examiner, of the assessment, and of the treatment is crucial. During the initial family interview, once the clinician has demonstrated respect for the child's own experience and the expectation that the child can tell his own story, the groundwork for a more open and productive individual interview is laid.

Early Contacts

Even prior to meeting the child, in the earliest contacts with parents or guardians, the tone of the evaluation is often set on the phone. It is here that the purpose of the evaluation is first conveyed and then negotiated. Oftentimes, parents inquire how the child should be informed about the reasons for the evaluation, exactly what will occur during the interviews, and how the child should be reassured and/or compelled to cooperate. The unwilling or resistant youngster may either be so terrified, defiant, or incorrigible that his parents do not know to proceed. It is helpful to suggest to parents that unless they have reason to believe otherwise, it is wise first to clarify honestly with the child their own purpose for seeking the evaluation, and then to give the child an accurate picture of how the evaluation will proceed. Depending on the child's age and symptomatology, this may be done anywhere from a week or so prior to the evaluation, up to (for the rebellious and out-of-control adolescent) an hour or so prior to the evaluation. The school-phobic child, the violent delinquent adolescent, as well as certain other youth may require the family to seek the support of relatives or extrafamilial adults such as counselors or neighbors, or on rare occasions to employ the legal system. In the later instance, an explicit description of the appropriate legal procedures, necessary telephone calls and paper work, along with considerable support are often necessary. Where such legal enforcement may be required, one may be dealing with such dangerous and resistant behavior in a child or adolescent that an inpatient evaluation becomes an important consideration. The importance of this kind of careful work prior to the first appointment should not be underestimated. It can have a significant impact on the child's attitude, behavior, and level of cooperation during the interview, and on the parents' as well. A mother called for consultation and therapy with her 15-year-old daughter; the mother described the youngster as very difficult, not likable, and having been in therapy since the age of 6. Her daughter was in her words "beyond help" and "unsalvageable." Responding to mother's negative attitude, the clinician asked, "Do you feel I might help her? You seem to have such little hope." This early intervention was the first step in an alliance with the mother, who ultimately developed more positive feelings for her daughter and participated in family sessions on a monthly basis.

Careful observation of waiting room interactions and separations provides important information. The unwilling or resistant child may appear comfortable at first, or may look panicky, tearful, angry, or sulky. He may dash to the door, curse, destroy the examiner's favorite plant, or dart wildly around the room. He may disconnect emotionally into "autistic" aloneness and be unable or unwilling to interact or respond. Rapid assessment is critical; children require immediate feedback. Behavior and affect can escalate very rapidly in the form of aggression, overwhelming anxiety, or stubborn silence. The intervention of choice is guided by the clinician's best current intrapsychic and interpersonal dynamic understanding of the child. Is there any danger to the child or therapist? Do limits need to be set for safety or psychological containment and security? Is the child overwhelmed? Does this behavior represent separation anxiety, fear of harm, disorganization, guilt, depression, nondefined rage, antisocial behavior, or simple situational anxiety?

In an effort to facilitate the free elaboration of material, unless evidence suggests otherwise, individual sessions with a child are best approached initially with client-centered techniques of empathy, reflection, clarification, and genuineness (Axline, 1969; Moustakas, 1973). Later the examiner may choose to provide more structure using direct inquiries or focused activities and tasks. Confronted with a nondirective interview with a minimum of structure, some children respond poorly and need a modified approach. But more often, an approach using clarifying responses and avoiding directives, educational offerings, criticism, interpretations, or confrontations enhances rapport and the establishment of a working relationship. Reflections and empathic declaratives are best offered with some tentativeness and are preferable as opening tactics rather than asking direct questions that may generate only a "yes" or "no" answer or a very brief response. A 10-year-old boy with symptoms of a mild pervasive developmental disorder initially produced almost no play or interview material. However, he responded moderately well with the structure and distance provided by the use of a tape recorder and a request to take part in a "radio interview" with the examiner playing disc jockey.

The examiner can learn much from allowing the child to tell his own story in his own way at his own pace and at his own depth. Relating to the child with the utmost respect, while shunning any hint of a disingenuous tone or infantilizing posture proves most effective. An attitude of interest and concern and "wondering" with the child is bolstered when the atmosphere conveys that only the child knows precisely her own experience. Clearly the child knows herself best, and her way of revealing herself to the examiner is part of who she is and this must be respected. The child's style of revealing herself is, of course, a crucial part of the data collected and is one reason the examiner struggles not to structure the early interactions. Skillful empathic observing, listening, and interacting are the basic foundation of good interviewing technique, especially with the unwilling patient.

Interview Styles

One classification of interview styles defines two poles on a dimensional construct—structured and unstructured. Using the former, the examiner provides questions about school, the child's three wishes, or her dreams of the future, asks the child to complete stories the examiner has begun, or directs the child to particular play materials or topics. Even using this more structured style, the examiner studies the more projective aspects of the material elaborated, the themes, associations, affects, and conflicts, and observes the child's relatedness with the examiner. For some children the structure may contaminate the data or prove stifling; with such youngsters, an unstructured or semistructured interview offers a considerable advantage. For others, structure may diminish anxiety; this can provide indispensable help in approaching the resistant or unproductive child with whom the clinician struggles simply to maintain an interchange.

With the unwilling or resistant child, the examiner is more concerned with developing greater depth in the material than with being terribly cautious about contamination. Interviewer influences on the material may be secondary to the need for establishing basic rapport and an interaction that fosters communication. In fact, in such a difficult clinical situation, the examiner can rapidly come to focus most of his attention on expanding the interaction and gaining access to clinical data. Interventions are adjusted with the aim of developing a sense of connectedness, rapport, and social comfort. Child therapists are keenly aware of how quickly an interview can go sour with a resolutely oppositional or passive youngster. A child's stubbornness can escalate all too rapidly as she forges an impenetrable wall of deepening defiance, fear, or anger. In this situation the examiner has a number of options that may be useful, including changing the topic, noting the child's discomfort, asking what can be done to alleviate it, moving from an interview format to play or vice versa, offering a soft drink or a walk, sharing something of the clinician's own experience, asking the child her favorite pastimes, inquiring about her three wishes, carefully assessing and then employing the use of humor, or even moving to a parallel activity in an effort to support the child's freedom to express herself with a lessened sense of pressure or expectation from the examiner.

Every assessment interview requires that the clinician meticulously observe the child's responses both for diagnostic meaning and for signs that the interview may be becoming derailed. Some children begin an interview with silence. Rapid assessment can minimize the risk of prematurely structuring the interview or remaining too unstructured. Structure may only provide the child something definitive to defy or to fear. A child's initial silence may reflect anxiety, which may respond well to remarks dealing directly with the situation, such as, "What's it's like for you to come see me?" or "This may be uncomfortable or strange for you." Such efforts are simply empathic reaches and may be even more facilitative when stated in declarative form, "You seem uncomfortable being here" or "You look like you're thinking about something."

The earliest stage of the examination should not be rushed, despite the clinician's growing sense of urgency. An extra measure of patience, empathy, reflection, and rapport building often pays off generously during the remaining time with the child. Discerning what is going on with the child helps the interviewer decide whether to move to a more structured or less structured approach, depending on which allows the child to be more productive.

The clinician relates with consideration of the child's developmental level of adaptation both cognitively and emotionally. The examiner should be supportive, noting areas of success, competence, and mastery. Further, it is helpful to reflect the uniqueness of the child and his experiences by demonstrating respect for the child's varieties of experiences, both adaptive and maladaptive. With a resistant child, material should be framed on the side of adaptation rather than in the service of increasing anxiety, so that the examiner offers, "You really like to feel in charge" rather than "You are afraid of being out of control." The former may lead to a collaborative exploration; the latter is more likely to result in a stubborn or negative response with a refusal to elaborate. Within a strong alliance, with more trusting and productive children, or in certain stages of psychotherapy, a deeper interpretation may be appropriate; as an opening tactic with well-defended and guarded patients, it risks a further stiffening of resistance. Clinicians must always be sensitive to where they are in their relationship with a child and respect the youngster's defenses.

The examiner should be painstakingly attentive to the nature of the child's responses, even to what seem to be innocuous, simple clarifications. Although clarification may be intended to connect material the child has already provided or to facilitate the elaboration of more information, it still may touch sensitive, painful, or anxiety-ridden material just below the surface and be experienced by the child as threatening or injurious. This may be reflected as the child switches themes or play materials, withdraws, becomes anxious, or otherwise signals an imminent breach in the relationship.

Silence is one of the most common obstacles in the OIM of children and adolescents. Even with youth who warm up and are quite productive later in the session, it is not unusual for an interview to begin unproductively. The clinician is well advised not to pressure the child with expectations or repeated requests, invitations, or seductions. A more low-key approach facilitates rapport and the development of trust without the risks of more bold and provocative interventions.

Assessment of the Resistance

Early on the clinician should consider what is causing the underproductivity. Other blatant resistances such as impulsive or disorganized play, disheveling the play room, and daydreaming to the exclusion of making contact with the therapist often tax the clinician's patience and determination to understand before intervening. Is the resistance due to mistrust, rage, fear, or a general inability to communicate or relate? The style of resistance may be one clue as to intrapsychic dynamics, but as a rule, when considered alone, it does not tell the whole story. Even in a brief interview, keen observation of all the data presented, along with clinical experience, can lead the examiner to a formulation that encompasses biological and constitutional factors, family relationships, intrapsychic dynamics, socioeconomic cultural influences, contextual variables, and the response to the interviewer. Is this child intellectually deficient, language impaired, hyperactive, psychotic, or deaf? What does the child perceive about the parents' attitude toward the assessment and the examiner? Is this family fearful of doctors or of any social contact? It is particularly fruitful to be reminded of the power of the family system. Are there important family secrets, critical historical incidents, illnesses, or deaths that have had a major impact on the family and the child? How reflective is the behavior seen in the interview of the child's general social behavior and level of functioning? Is the child who is terribly anxious in the interview usually fearful of adults, suspicious, or

oppositional, or is this behavior related to the evaluation.

The assessment of the resistance—tentative though it may be—guides the examiner's style of managing it, and there are a variety of approaches. The importance of rapidly deriving a formulation cannot be overestimated. The approach then flows from the "meaning" assigned to this resistance, though the intervention certainly does not need to confront, interpret, clarify, or observe this meaning for the child directly. A familiar model for management might be that of the traditional psychoanalytic approach to transference and other patient material in treatment. The clinician focuses first on conscious, more superficial, and ego-based material and later deals with unconscious, deeper, defended, superego-ridden or impulse-driven material. The alliance must be protected throughout, and there must be enough connectedness, support, and ego strength to make use of the interventions.

Techniques for Interviewing Resistant Children

Once the examiner has recognized the resistance, several approaches are useful with the resistant or unwilling child or adolescent: "exploring the immediate context," "developing a social interaction," and "displacing the material." Exploring the immediate context refers to an empathic investigation of the child's feelings about the evaluation itself while providing support and information freely. The evaluation is conducted in order to understand the child, and the examiner and child talk and play together. The examiner wants to help the child. At first contact, it may be useful to reassure the child that there will be no injections or physical examination, that his parents will await him in the outer office, and that they will be available as soon as the interview is completed. What was the child told about coming to the session? What thoughts about the presenting information were provided while the family members were together in the clinician's office? This open approach is very facilitative with many children, especially those fearful of the evaluation itself and separation from their parents.

Developing a social interaction one attempts to establish rapport through dialogue and interactions, particularly around conflict-free, less affect-laden, and more enjoyable or gratifying areas of the child's experience. Does she have hobbies or special interests? What does she enjoy doing and with whom? Where does she like to go—movies, shopping in the mall, skating, biking, dances, rock concerts, or sporting events? Who are her friends, and what do they like to do together? What are her favorite TV shows, books, and pastimes? Through open-ended questions and allowing the child to speak freely and wander however and wherever her associations lead, the examiner conveys interest in the child's experience and her acceptance of it. In addition, the examiner learns a great deal by following the associations and disruptions in both play and verbal productions.

The child's concerns, fantasies, underlying themes and symptoms are often best understood by allowing the child to express these feelings in displacement, for example, through play with puppets, dolls, and other toys. Intrapsychic dynamics often unfold best in a story told by a child or in his play with toys. These displaced fantasies may best be encouraged without interpretation. With psychotic children it may be wise to expect the child to own the productions himself. A number of children are unresponsive to open-ended broad inquiries and client-centered interventions. Playing together, "bull sessions," or simple direct questions may help them feel comfortable speaking or playing. The first session is decisive in developing an interaction and a level of comfort. With many children the clinician begins to play either in parallel or interactionally. Familiar games and toys may especially relieve young children, so the availability of checkers, balls, pencils, crayons and paper, jacks, blocks, pick-up sticks, and the like is useful. Puppets and dolls that allow for rich fantasy tales, but allow adequate psychological distance, are particularly useful. Similarly, the use of telephones or a tape recorder can provide a wonderful vehicle through which a child can distance himself from what he shares with the therapist. Clearly the choice of technique and materials is closely related to age and developmental phase.

Adolescents often use displacement, projection, and externalization, and this should be noticed more than confronted or interpreted in the early OIM. The examiner may do best just to collect information about the adolescent; it is well to keep in mind that considerable data may be obtained without pointing out the adolescent's responsibility for his own behavior. Allowing the patient to blame teachers, parents, and peers must be accepted for a time prior to wondering with the teenager about his own responsibility in these interactions and situations or his own capacity to gain better control and cope with these encounters in a fashion that would be more adaptive. Although requiring cautious judgment, humor may be useful as the examiner attempts to test the capacity of the adolescent's observing ego. Narcissistic injury is a serious risk, especially with the guarded, unwilling, resistant youth.

While a number of children tell their parents that they will not speak to the clinician, thankfully only a few actually maintain this position. Of those who do, a very small percentage display elective mutism, and the large majority exhibit oppositional defiant disorder, conduct disorder, severe depression, severe anxiety, a personality disorder, or psychosis. There is no substitute for unfaltering patience in the development of rapport and trust. No amount of charisma, seduction, gimmickry, charm, or technical skill will ensure that the clinician will develop an ongoing dialogue or will facilitate the elaboration of play material with the resistant patient. However, the clinician's ability to demonstrate that he can tolerate the tediousness of a difficult session, his own lack of control over what transpires, the patient's excruciating pain and depression—or whatever any given child needs from the interviewer—all may eventuate in the child's feeling safe within the assessment interview.

One should remember that errors of technique will be tolerated far better than lapses in humanism. It can be useful to explain the examiner's role or to remind the patient of the confidentiality of the interview. Tentatively offering hypotheses about why the child may not be willing to speak—such as a fear of criticism, built-up anger and resentment, or an exhausting and hopeless depression—can be useful. Ultimately, however, the clinician may be left with an understanding that the patient is not quite ready to talk or play (Blotcky & Looney, 1980). With adolescents, at times the examiner needs to demonstrate a sense of firmness and a willingness to endure dangerous threats, rage directed toward the examiner, and the like.

432

Further, clinicians working with adolescents must be comfortable bickering and arguing with them, since that is the adolescent's customary and routine way of carrying on dialogue both to gain and to communicate information. But adolescents, too, need the acknowledgment that they will become involved in the interaction at their own pace, and the examiner's patience must be demonstrated.

SPECIAL ISSUES WITH PRESCHOOL CHILDREN

The OIM of preschool children presents special problems. These are often related to their insecure, anxious attachment to a parent or related to a parent's difficulty in cooperating or separating. Infants are usually seen in evaluation seated on their mother' laps. Toddlers, however, are interviewed first in conjunction with taking a history from their mothers; thereafter a separation is essayed. This expectation may lead to tantrums, panic in both mother and infant, or an apathetic withdrawal. The examiner may have to delay the separation, entice the child's interest in an activity or toy, or restrain the toddler, depending on the clinical circumstances. It is never productive to overwhelm any patient with anxiety for more than a few moments, although this certainly occurs. In the face of separation, some children cannot soothe themselves, regardless of their own or their evaluators' efforts. The evaluation is then best served by inviting the mother back into the interview.

The special problems preschool children present during evaluation may also be due to the nature of their pathology, which can include developmental delays, mental retardation, pervasive developmental disorders, attachment disorders, and oppositional and/or anxiety disorders.

SPECIAL ISSUES WITH CHILDREN

A number of issues are particularly pertinent in the OIM of school-age children. They may be most accustomed to seeing unfamiliar adults in situations that are uncomfortable, and where they are either disciplined, criticized, or examined (e.g., visits with a principal or a physician). They experience a psychiatric evaluation similarly. Often they are brought to evaluation after the failure of pa-

rental discipline; commonly the parents have told their children that they are bad, crazy, or sick, and thus need to see a psychiatrist. Given this context, the clinician needs to clarify the purpose of the interview. This can be accomplished by guiding the family away from a lengthy plaintive report of negative behavior by means of inquiries that develop a broader understanding of the child.

A uniquely exasperating situation arises for the clinician when the child or adolescent suddenly leaves the office or playroom. This is not uncommon with the unwilling or resistant child. Following the youngster can be embarrassing, though management can involve simply talking in a general way with the parent and child about what has transpired, without asking the child for much in the way of explanation, confronting him, or in any way taking the chance of injuring him further. Often children who suddenly leave the playroom feel very threatened, controlled, humiliated, or enraged, and any pressure from the examiner in the playroom will be counterproductive. It makes sense for the examiner to leave some face-saving and negotiating room for the child, while attempting to reestablish the interview by offering a change in activities. For example, this may involve getting a cold drink, taking a break, taking a walk together, or when necessary, rescheduling.

One of the more perplexing dilemmas for the clinician is dealing with separation anxiety. Should the child be pushed to separate or should the parent(s) be invited in or allowed to remain in the office? After assessing the child and parent—the child for the level of anxiety and capacity to cope, and the parent for his ability to support the child's separation firmly—the better approach is more often emotional firmness rather than a "shove" to separate. Firmness failing, an effective intervention can be a friendly and supportive suggestion that separation need not be hurried and that much can be understood by remaining together a bit longer. After a rapid assessment (including age, developmental stage, level of anxiety, intrapsychic and family dynamics, and general clinical circumstances) the examiner may decide to divert the discussion to a less threatening topic or to collect more information about the separation process. Sometimes the routine assessment must be conducted in the parents' presence. In so doing, the clinician may learn a great deal about the parent-child relationship—their attunement, handling of power and control, level of anxiety, self-regulatory capacities, connectedness, and differentiation.

Children demonstrating disruptive, hyperactive, oppositional, or aggressive behavior are often seen for evaluation and pose special problems for the examiner. These children may be so defiant and stubborn that they defend against any kind of self-revelation while demonstrating a single-minded, demanding rage. They may be unfocused, disorganized, or so aggressive that they overwhelm the examiner. Their tyrannical and belligerent behavior can become so forceful as to require the examiner to sit between them and the door, or physically to restrain them from leaving the room, damaging property, or hurting either themselves or the examiner. The evaluation of these troubled children taxes even the most experienced and seasoned clinician. They may threaten the clinician's sense of competence, engender a sense of helplessness, and stimulate a perceived vulnerability to parental criticism. In a worst-case scenario, the interviewer must deal with a child who loudly shrieks and screams, escapes the office, and provokes sarcastic comments and a rash of embarrassing queries from suite mates. Again there is no substitute for the clinician's patience and determination to complete the examination, as demonstrated by firmly expecting the child to remain in the playroom and settle down. A calm, reassuring voice offering empathy with the child's overwhelming feelings and inviting him to take part in something semistructured and active, such as playing catch, throwing darts, building blocks, or coloring can be useful. Ultimately, inviting a parent to join the interview may be stabilizing, as is the case with the child suffering overwhelming anxiety at separation.

SPECIAL PROBLEMS WITH ADOLESCENTS

Interviewing adolescents requires thoughtful management of their ubiquitous struggles to balance longings for autonomy with their usually more defended dependency needs. This powerful and crucial developmental struggle around autonomy and dependence is often experienced as a delicately balanced state which makes for considerable lability. The style, tone, and general demeanor of the clinician must respect the exquisite nature of this developmental dilemma. The examiner validates the adolescent's newfound capacity to think abstractly and, especially, respects his ability to present his own life situation. An examiner who interviews the adolescent alone first, who explains confidentiality, and who emphasizes his respect for and the importance of the adolescent's own feelings will bolster the adolescent's sense of trust. There will be information the adolescent does not want to share, and the examiner may respond that the adolescent need not reveal anything that she does not want known until she is ready to do so. Explaining the nature and purpose of the interview is reassuring. The examiner may share openly the goal of seeking to help the teenager tell her own very personal story from her own point of view so that together they can try to understand what is going on in the youngster's experience. The examiner has some expertise about how a teenager's mind works, not expertise about how the patient should live his life. Describing the interviewer's position explicitly can be reassuring and effective.

Confidentiality can be an overriding concern for adolescents, and resistance may appear because of their fear surrounding it. As one guide, the examiner initially informs the adolescent that any detailed information is confidential. However, there is an exception. The parents or guardians will need to be told if it becomes necessary to protect the adolescent from danger to himself or others, or from making a major life decision that is permanent or terribly harmful. Even in such circumstances, the examiner will discuss any concerns with the teenager before making a decision to inform his parents. Dealing directly and openly with the adolescent's fantasies, fears, and desires about confidentiality can be important, and the examiner may need to take the lead by providing information.

Adolescents are quite vulnerable to narcissistic injury and the attendant emotional lability, and unfortunately, such an upheaval can fracture a developing working relationship. Clinicians cannot be too freely responsive, light-hearted, humorous, critical, or outspoken, lest the adolescent feel her thoughts or dreams are being dismissed or glossed over. Such slights or injuries can turn a potentially productive interview into a very difficult, unproductive one. Further, the examiner is well advised to observe the adolescent throughout an interview for evidence that suggests there may have been a perceived injury, so that it may be repaired quickly.

Certain dilemmas arise during the assessment of adolescents because they evidence critical behavior around the sensitive topics of sexuality, substance abuse, delinquency, suicide, and certain psychotic symptoms. Each of these requires early consideration, but their exploration may heighten resistance to the entire assessment process and should be timed with care. The decision to explore an adolescent's sexuality is developed as other information is gathered, rapport established, and the interview stabilizes. One productive approach to sexual material is to begin by inquiring about friends. Having gathered information about social relations, the clinician may then move to the teenager's romantic relationships by asking, for example, in a matter-of-fact way, "How is it going with girls?" Those relationships are first explored in general by asking whether the youngsters have been "dating" or been "romantic," and then by asking how the teenager has handled sexuality in those relationships. Discussing sexuality may include a sensitive exploration of homosexual fantasies and/or behavior. One approach with the adolescent boy might be, "Boys occasionally have warm, tender, or sexual feelings for other boys, or sometimes have physical interactions with each other that are confusing. Anything like this go on with you?" Within what contexts have sexual relationships developed? What kind of precautions have been taken? While sensitive topics, these issues are crucial and must be approached early, and often these questions are more comfortable for both interviewer and adolescent if dealt with during early data collection.

Inquiries about substance abuse and delinquency are terribly important, although they can result in angry defensiveness or stubborn silence because of the resulting narcissistic threat. Indeed, this often occurs with youth who are in fact involved in such dangerous behavior. Here also exploration of these topics is probably best handled directly and in a businesslike fashion by asking whether or not the adolescent has been involved in drinking alcohol or using other drugs and whether or not the adolescent has been involved in skipping school, damaging property, or other illegal behavior. It is useful to ask an adolescent "What is the most dangerous thing that has happened to you or with which you have been involved?" This may provide material that leads to inquiry about risk taking and antisocial behavior as well as suicidal ideation and behavior.

Sadness and depression, feelings of hopelessness and helplessness, suicidal ideation or behavior, all these are important in the OIM of the adolescent, yet all are sensitive topics. These topics are important with children as well, but are dealt with here because they are more frequently pressing with adolescents. Resistance can erupt because of a heightened sense of vulnerability or the projection of harsh self-criticism and feelings of depreciation. The adolescent should feel this exploration is supportive, that his feelings are being understood, and that he is not strange or odd because of his emotional responses or thoughts. Here too the possibility of narcissistic injury is great and should be guarded against lest the adolescent shut down during the interview.

With the very disturbed adolescent, an investigation of psychotic symptoms should be pursued with support and sensitivity. Explorations may include "Often when teenagers are really depressed they have unusual experiences such as hearing or seeing something that isn't there or that others don't see. Has anything like that happened to you?" or "When someone has been under as much stress or is as upset as you have been, it is not uncommon for them to have strange experiences in which they don't really feel like they are themselves, or things seem to have special meaning, or they become so sensitive that they are very suspicious. Do you feel this way?" Most adolescents accept such questions better than many clinicians might expect, and their responses, both in content and emotional style, provide critical information.

Conclusion

Children and adolescents are commonly unwilling and resistant to assessment and present some of the most problematic clinical situations. They are often stubborn, difficult to understand, taxing and upsetting, silent, frustrating to the examiner, and hard to turn around. Yet with perseverance, creativity, and great patience, rewarding results are possible. The clinician should be sensitive to and meticulously observant of the child's responses in order to guide his approach in facilitating the

OIM. Nevertheless, many children and adolescents will be difficult to interview, and the examiner should be accepting of this. Awareness of developmental, dynamic, family, sociocultural, contextual, and examiner factors is critical. Many developmental factors play a role; these include narcissistic vulnerability, conflicts around dependency and autonomy, sexuality, and the child's view of adults. The family's attitude and the context of the OIM include for whom the evaluation is done, the family's attitude toward the examination and examiner, the level of dystonic symptoms and pain, and the child or adolescent's level of understanding of the nature of the procedure. The examiner should structure the assessment and the OIM so as to optimize rapport, trust, engagement, and the production of material. The risk of contaminating the child's productions must be weighed against the risk of the child's moving into an intransigent, stubborn, silent, chaotic, or aggressive resistant posture which may require exorbitant time to rework or the transfer of the patient. Bold, aggressive, or other approaches that derive from a lack of patience and are not well considered can in fact cause such a breach with family and child that assessment may no longer be sought.

REFERENCES

Axline, V. M. (1969). *Play therapy.* New York: Ballantine Books.

Blotcky, M. J., & Looney, J. G. (1980). A psychotherapeutic approach to silent children. *American Journal of Psychotherapy, 24* (4), 487–496.

Claman, L. (1980). The squiggle-drawing game in child psychotherapy. *American Journal of Psychotherapy, 34* (3), 414–425.

Costello, A. (1991). Structured interviewing in *Child and Adolescent Psychiatry A Comprehensive Textbook* (Ed) Lewis, M. Baltimore: Williams and Wilkins (1991). pp. 463–471.

Gardner, R. A. (1990). *Psychotherapeutic approaches to the resistant child.* New York: Jason Aronson.

Kritzberg, N. I. (1975). *The structured therapeutic game method of child analytic psychotherapy.* New York: Exposition Press.

Moustakas, C. (1973). *Children in play therapy.* New York: Jason Aronson.

Winnicott, D. (1975). *Therapeutic consultations in child psychiatry.* New York: Basic Books.

66 / Observation, Interview, and Mental Status Assessment (OIM): Culturally Different from Clinician

Stuart M. Silverman and John F. McDermott

It is our purpose in this chapter to present an outline that will offer the clinician an approach to cultural factors and influences when engaging in the assessment of a patient from a non-Caucasian, non-Western culture. It goes without saying that the clinician should address each patient with an open mind and a willingness to accept and integrate different belief systems, traditions, and values into her basic diagnostic framework. It is vital for clinicians to understand and evaluate the effect of culture both on the expression of psychopathology and on the diagnostic process itself.

Culture may be defined as the accumulation of a shared pattern of values, roles, and behaviors that are accepted and transmitted by the family and cultural group in which children are raised (Herberg, 1989). Acculturation is a dynamic process that begins at birth and which adds increasingly complex layers to the individual biological core as one enters into the community and the larger society. Culture structures a distinct and consistent way of viewing the world, and includes but is not limited to ethnic or national groups (Ka'opua & Waldron, 1991; Kiev, 1964).

Psychopathology—Multicultural Assessment

Each culture has its own concepts of illness and its own ideas about etiology. When taken out of context, local explanations for common phenomena as viewed from a different cultural perspective can seem unusual, even bizarre. Nevertheless, in order to evaluate behavior, culturally specific folklore must be understood. Thus, it is clear that the diagnostic significance of any behavior cannot be adequately interpreted until one has taken into account such matters as cultural attitudes toward illness and the ways in which differing philosophies and value systems find expression in an individual's behavior.

For example, a child psychiatrist from a culture which values independence, autonomy, and achievement may be evaluating a youngster from another culture in which dependence and interdependence are prized and in which standing out or above other group members is considered deviant. Under these circumstances, the evaluator may view what are in fact the child's normal adaptive characteristics as a form of psychopathology. Furthermore, the child psychiatrist from the first culture may fail to see a youngster's subtle deviations from the pattern of normal development within the other culture. By the same token, a child psychiatrist from the second culture may have difficulty evaluating the dependence/independence conflicts in children from the first culture. The same tendency to over- or undervalue according to one's own cultural norms tends to produce other kinds of diagnostic errors as well. In another pair of cultures, one with a high degree of tolerance for motor activity in preschool and school-age children, the other with a low degree of tolerance for such activity, a diagnostic study would produce another form of culture clash in an assessment of normal development versus pathology.

Thus clinical assessment is influenced by culture. Nevertheless, despite these cultural differences, it appears that most clinicians agree about certain youngsters who are beyond the normal spectrum across all societies. This may reflect a common biological core to certain psychiatric conditions, but culture may then shape the expression of the condition. Although differences in expression may exist, symptoms of anxiety and depression, learning problems, and to some extent severe hyperactivity would be recognized almost everywhere as evidence of disorder. This would hold true as well for extended, gross breaks of contact with reality, and severe disruption or lack of development of interpersonal relationships. The importance of such disturbances and the society's tolerance for their presence would, however, vary considerably.

Cultural influences become apparent in the way problems are conceptualized. Ideas about the etiology of psychiatric disorder may involve an ingrained belief that the problem is due to a devil or spirit, breaking taboos, an imbalance of vital powers, or family stress in childhood. Historically humankind has looked outside itself for the cause of its problems, first to the supernatural world, and later to the natural surroundings and an imbalance in the relationship with them. Only in recent times have we looked to ourselves, first to somatic and then to social and psychic origins of disturbance; unfortunately, we have done so at the expense of completely disregarding outside influences. It is clear that cultural factors condition such basic decisions as which emotional and behavioral expressions are actually diagnosed as psychopathology and which are regarded as normal or as mere eccentricity (Waldron & McDermott, 1979).

Finally, it is important to understand the cultural frame of reference or the belief system of the family whose child is being evaluated. Several major conceptual frameworks will be considered here by way of illustration. These are non-Western frameworks that we shall call subcultures A, B, and C. Subculture A is marked by a belief in the existence of supernatural experiences that may be either religious in the conventional sense or nonreligious. Historically, such an outlook is often found in farming, fishing, and hunting societies that developed without the aid of modern technology. These are societies which had to find solutions to the overwhelming stresses that arise from natural forces. An understandable belief in the supernatural emerged as a way of making some kind of order out of chaos and giving people at least some sense of power in the face of overwhelming helplessness. These people learned that living in harmony with the earth and with nature allowed for a balance to occur which alleviated stress and diminished discomfort. Once they entered into American society, many people from these cultures held on to old, familiar ways of interpreting stresses and treating crises. Within such a community there is often an important figure (a priest, witch doctor, or holy man) who is believed to communicate with spirits for religious ceremonies and to receive instructions for dealing with the patient's problems. The causes of problems are usually perceived and interpreted as having to do with object intrusion, loss of the soul, spirit intrusion, sorcery, violation of taboos, or having "sinned."

In subculture B, the system of reference shifts from the supernatural to the natural, and the problem may be explained as a result of an imbalance or disharmony with the natural principles that rule the universe. This subculture is also concerned with the relationships of forces within the body and with certain somatic predispositions ascribed to the individual. Here again the child may be the victim of a projected identification; a particular physical or emotional characteristic, which was present at birth or earlier, now makes him the bearer of the problem in the family. These subcultures arise in societies that traditionally made use of fortune tellers, astrologers, physiognomists, or herbalists.

In subculture C, indigenous treatment systems have been based on problems related to a disequilibrium, insufficiency, or decompensation of the individual's psychosociological system. Emotional problems and mental illness are viewed as psychological reactions to external social maladjustment (Waldron & McDermott, 1979).

HISTORY TAKING

In work with children and families who belong to cultures different from the clinician's own, it is essential for the clinician to understand that culture's traditions, values, and belief systems, including views of behavior and healing practices. Part of history taking should include a "cultural history," in which beliefs, behaviors, customs, and symbolism, as well as traditional roles and functions within a family or subculture, are identified.

General areas of inquiry include such topics as language, religion, traditions, rituals, dreams, beliefs about death and dying, ceremonies and holidays, beliefs about the supernatural, discipline and family relationships, communication patterns, and learning styles. These can be woven naturally into history taking, and provide important, culturally determined background information for the evaluation of symptoms and the development of a diagnostic formulation. General approaches to minimize cultural barriers include (Ka'opua & Waldron, 1991)

- Allocate more time for patients from cultural backgrounds different from yours. Rapport is more complex and often takes longer to develop.
- Anticipate that past frustrations with the health care system in your own culture may make the patient and family initially guarded and resentful. Inquire directly about such past experiences and frustrations.
- Pay special attention to communication: the family's nonverbal, expressive style and use of and meaning of words.
- Expect differences of beliefs about: help-seeking behaviors, causes of illness (emotional or physical), death and dying, caretaking, and sexuality.
- Learn the strengths of a culture (e.g., in Latino cultures the value of respeto, demonstrating appropriate social respect) and integrate these when possible.
- Encourage the negotiation of any difference of opinion to ensure a workable plan.
- Be prepared to serve as an advocate for a patient who may not have the knowledge or experience to negotiate the health care system. Employ bridging providers and healers from other cultures and cultural consultants. If necessary, assist in connecting the patient with other resources.

As clinicians develop cultural sensitivity, they move through four stages (Ka'opua & Waldron, 1991):

1. Being totally unaware of differences in values between themselves and the patient.
2. Being resistant to cultural differences.
3. Becoming introspective and accepting these differences and values.
4. Becoming advocates for cultural sensitivity and competence.

Developing cultural competence is an active process that requires that the clinician consciously engage in understanding differences that constantly assess her own assumptions, expand and changes her perceptions, and, ultimately, adapt to and negotiate with patients from different cultures.

DEVELOPMENT

Clinicians assessing developmental norms must be aware of what is normal for a child within a specific culture. Questions that the clinician should ask herself are, Within this culture, what child-rearing practices are considered correct in order to raise "normal" children? What behaviors are stressed developmentally? What behaviors are discouraged? Are there certain developmental stages or "rites of passage" that are recognized in the majority culture? If so, what are they and has the child negotiated them successfully? The interviewer must always consider what is normal for a child from this culture, living in this region, under these circumstances. For example, Native American children are cited for their high rate of illiteracy and may be diagnosed as having developmental learning disabilities (Yates, 1987). Although Native American children achieve the same level of cognitive development as peers in the majority culture, they consistently score lower on the verbal scales of intelligence tests, despite the fact that their scores on the performance scales approximate the national norm (Cazden & John, 1971; Silk & Voyet, 1970; Yates, 1987). Native American children display difficulties with language, auditory association and memory, grammatic closure and auditory processing, reading, and verbal discrimination (Lombardi, 1970; McShane, 1980; Trimble, Goddard & Dinges 1977). On the other hand, they demonstrate impressive ability to memorize visual patterns, visualize spatial concepts, and formulate descriptions with special attention to visual detail and with graphic metaphors (Kleinfeld, 1974). In other words, Native American children have different sensory preferences for learning, are less analytic and verbally descriptive (Shuberg & Cropley, 1972), but are more wholistic, employing intuitive, "right-brain" functions to define their experiences (Witelson, 1971). Visual patterns, symbols, and metaphors are emphasized over auditory and grammatic skills. From the earliest developmental stages, Native American people employ visual and metaphoric techniques with their children. The ensuing poor reading and learning skills their youngsters display may merely reflect differences in their learning and teaching styles. A working knowledge of these differences in learning styles can avoid the trap of classifying alternative learning mechanisms as pathological. A sensitivity to different learning styles and varying methods of language acquisition may well lessen the incidence of psychiatric difficulties related to language disorders (Beitchman et al., 1986).

The Interview

CULTURAL HISTORY

In most non-Western cultural groups, extended family members play important, distinct and often different roles than in the traditional majority culture. In many cases, family or community elders, the spiritual or tribal leaders, may have a powerful influence over the family's decision-making process. These family or community elders may in fact have attempted intervention prior to encouraging the family to seek "outside" assistance. It is crucial for the clinician to gain knowledge of family roles, and of the extent to which they are based on a hierarchical and gender assigned system. What are the roles for males and females? Men may play the dominant roles in decisions about sex, having children, or size of the family for example. Women may be more passive than in the majority culture and may be expected to serve primarily in the role of child bearer. Such issues as abortion may be unspeakable (Ka'opua & Waldron, 1991). It is important to assess not only the degree of role flexibility, but individuality as well. Are decisions made by and for the family as a group, or is differentiation of individual autonomy fostered?

How a family expresses its problems is another important area. Is the orientation principally cognitive or affective? Are the problems discussed in an objective analytic fashion? What is the culturally acceptable expression of problems or affect for this individual? In some cultures, certain emotions are unacceptable or restrictions may exist regarding where, when, and to whom such emotions

439

may be expressed. Acceptability of self-disclosure varies from culture to culture. For example, Asian Americans may avoid confrontation, stress nonverbal communication, and refer to feelings only tangentially. In these, as well as other cultures such as some Native American communities, open expression of emotion is considered a sign of immaturity or weakness. In other cultures, the content being disclosed is not as significant as the emotional tone of the delivery (Flaskerud, 1989).

It is important to determine whether to interview the young patient separately or with the immediate or extended family. For instance, in some Native American cultures, it is more likely that patients will discuss problems individually rather than with their family present. It is uncommon for the whole family to discuss problems together (Attneave, 1979; Simmons, 1981). On the other hand, strong family ties in Mexican American or Asian families may encourage family group interviews (Serrano & Castillo, 1979). Just as African American and Asian American cultures tend to stress family and community cooperation in times of stress, Caucasians place greater value on individual problem solving (Ka'opua & Waldron, 1991).

Some cultures are past or present oriented, while others are future oriented. Those with a more present orientation may be unable or unwilling to focus on future plans, hopes, dreams, or long-term changes. In some cultures, it is almost considered taboo to express future goals or the wish to have a better life than one's parents had, for example, via higher education. In other cultures the attitude of "what's past is past" may suggest the notion that previous events have no bearing on what's happening now or what might occur in the future.

Religious customs, beliefs, traditions, spiritual practices, and symbolism are all crucial to the way in which a specific cultural group perceives signs and symptoms of illness. Emotional illness, which is less tangible than physical illness, may be attributed to intervention from the spirit world, a curse or spell placed on one person by another. Charms and amulets may be used to defend against them. In many Native American Indian religious ceremonies, spirits are summoned for worship or healing. Speaking in tongues, hearing voices, and seeing visions are all within the range of acceptability. Without knowledge of these cultural phenomena, a naive clinician may misconstrue them as "symptoms" of a psychotic process. Spirit realms are an integral part of the belief systems of many cultures and are frequently utilized to explain or treat both emotional and physical illness. These issues are often part of the history of the present illness, that is, how it started, and the family's view of its development. If neglected, an incomplete history of the illness, so crucial for accurate diagnosis, will result, as well as possible alienation of the family whose belief system is ignored. One may simply ask, "Can you help me understand your spiritual or religious beliefs?" The clinician should attempt to find out who the various therapeutic agents or healers are within a community and should try to speak with them or to involve them in the assessment. However, it may be unwise to do this without permission from the family or even the community authorities. Such native healers bear different names in different cultures—Ministers, Root workers, voodoo priests, and spiritualists. Some examples are Haitian: voodoo priests; Native American: medicine men/women and "singers"; Mexican: curanderos, sobradores, and palm readers; Puerto Rican: espiritiastas and santerios; Southeast Asian: herbalists, dukuns, diviner, and fortune tellers; Native Hawaiian: kahuna lapa'au and kahuna'ana'ana (Randall-David, 1989).

The following vignette illustrates the importance of cultivating an awareness of other belief systems and a willingness to integrate these when explaining symptomatology and when formulating a diagnosis and treatment plan.

CASE EXAMPLE

James, an adolescent youth, presented with a history of hearing the voice and seeing visions of his deceased great uncle who was a traditional healer. The voice would comment on his behavior, help him to make decisions, and would tell him that great uncle wanted his nephew to follow in his footsteps and become a healer. At times, James would appear to be speaking to himself and peers would often make fun of him. His school performance deteriorated and his concentration was impaired, especially when his great uncle was speaking to him. He would go to a specific sacred place each night and would regularly report seeing and speaking with his deceased great uncle. James reported feeling upset that the voices were so intrusive and at times kept him from concentrating, but that generally he was not afraid of the experiences. He began having nightmares and would dream about snakes biting him. He also reported intermittent episodes where he experienced "electricity" running through his body, tingling in his extremities, and sensations of heat running up and down his spine. After evaluation by a child psychiatrist, a recommendation was made to begin treatment with a neuroleptic. James' family decided to consult with a religious leader who noted that the youth had been chosen to serve a special role in the community and that it was his destiny. The symptoms that James was experiencing were attributed to an expected sequence of events that could occur in the course of one's "spiritual awakening." James was given assistance and support from religious leaders and the child psychiatrist and within one year the symptoms subsided. Although James remained "in contact" with his deceased great uncle, with alot of support he was able to integrate his experiences successfully. Eventually his school performance improved and good peer relationships were noted.

It is important to assess child-rearing practices and their impact on the shaping of behavior. The clinician should ask about disciplinary practices and whether these practices are culturally sanctioned. Who is the disciplinarian? Is discipline abusive, and by whose standards? This is naturally an extremely sensitive area, and it is important for the clinician to understand different practices, to be sensitive and diplomatic regarding alternative disciplinary tactics, but at the same time, to keep the child's emotional and physical well-being and safety as the first priority.

For the purpose of assessment, diagnosis, and treatment planning, the basic history of the illness and symptom development differ little from one culture to the next. However, how one obtains the information may differ from culture to culture. One should ponder constantly whether he is asking about symptoms in an appropriate and culturally acceptable way. Is the doctor speaking on a level that is comprehensible for the patient and family? The clinician can assess this by asking what the family members have heard the doctor say so far. The clinician should take the time to determine educational levels and fluency in English. It is important to be sensitive to the fact that certain key words or terms may have different meanings to this patient or family, and that terms other than those familiar to the clinician may be used to describe a symptom picture. In particular, the clinician must beware of cultural stereotyping. Although similarities may indeed appear to exist

among patients of a specific ethnic group, each patient and family must be viewed as a separate entity who may or may not adhere to a particular set of beliefs or practices. What is the family view and attitude regarding emotional illness and symptoms? The clinician should expect culturally specific beliefs about certain conditions. Some helpful questions include, What do you know about depression? How does it affect the mind and/or the body? How did your son/daughter get it? What do you think will make it better? How have you tried to help him with this problem? Who else has tried? Has anything you've done helped? Regarding suicide: What do you believe about a person taking their own life? Why does a person want to die or to kill himself? What would you do for a person who wants to die? What do you believe happens after death? Regarding sexuality, the clinician may ask whether sex is discussed in the family. Have you spoken to your child about sex? What have you told him/her? Is it acceptable for men to have sex with other men or women with other women? Regarding substance abuse: What does drinking or using drugs mean in your family? Are drugs commonly used as part of a religious ceremony? How common is alcohol or drug use among your family and friends? When do you use drugs? Who do you drink/shoot up with?

Learning about a family and its cultural setting sets the stage for a comprehensive evaluation of the child.

THE CHILD

Setting and General Approach: Before seeing the child, the clinician should ask the parents for suggestions about ways to make the child feel more comfortable. Remember that superimposed the clinician's status as a professional is the very real, even more concrete issue of the difference in the clinician's appearance from the adults in a child's family or community. Indeed, the doctor may be the first contact a child has had with a person of another race or color. The patient may be mistrustful, not only because the professional is a stranger, but because of the patient's parent's own fears or prejudices as well. The clinician should ask children and parents, "How do you feel about seeing a therapist who is white, black, etc.?"

The clinician should create an interview atmosphere that is comfortable, with relatively easy access to toys, games, and other props. A patient, nonjudgmental, nonaggressive interviewer will learn more from observation than from asking direct questions, especially before a verbal exchange has established rapport. The ability to communicate at the child's level of thinking and feeling is crucial. For example, getting down on your knees in order to approximate the child's height is often helpful in establishing rapport. If the family has been seen first, the patient may pick up their nonverbal messages about the doctor's acceptability. The first few minutes are generally crucial. If the clinician comes across as a potential friend and ally, much information will follow. When possible, there should be some ethnically correct dolls, figurines, or puppets available to bridge the cultural gap.

Mental Status Examination:

Appearance and behavior. In the interview with a child from another culture, it may be important to understand nonverbal communication. It becomes even more important to understand such communication if the child and the clinician do not speak the same language. Aside from information gathered from the family, it may be the only available form of interaction. For example, the child may avoid eye contact or smile at what seems to be inappropriate times. The interviewer should know whether direct eye contact is perceived as disrespectful by a particular culture. In some cultures, hand shaking is considered to be an intimate gesture, so that a firm hand shake of a well-intentioned interviewer may be perceived by the child as an inappropriately aggressive interaction. As with any interview, talking simply to fill silence is unnecessary. A passive, even silent interviewer may gather much more information than the enthusiastic clinician who asks a series of rapid-fire questions. Again, it is vital to be aware of patterns relating to strangers in a particular culture. In children from some American subcultures, a slow-to-warm-up pattern is to be expected. An extended period of time is needed before a comfortable exchange can be expected. A clinician from the dominant culture may first be perceived as a potential exploiter who will take advantage or cause harm. The presence of a bicultural interpreter in the interview setting may help bridge the gap and assist in expediting a personal relationship that overrides this initial perception. If the child continues to be fearful or suspicious, however, the clinician may need to see him on two or three different occasions to gather enough clinical information for diagnostic purposes.

Physical appearance should be noted, with appropriate consideration for ethnic physical characteristics and dress. Speech patterns may be slower than average, with a greater time lag between thoughts and sentences. Rate and range of speech may be diminished by the interviewer's standards, but may be well within the range of acceptability for the culture or subculture.

Orientation and perception. Not everyone uses the traditional Western calendar or counts time in the same way. Make sure when testing cognition or perception that the frames of reference from which you and the patient are working are similar. Do not assume that a child from a different American subculture knows the President of the United States. Instead, she would more likely know the name of the tribal governor or the date of the next tribal religious holiday. A youngster who has never been off a reservation or out of a shelter should be examined on his or her own geographic frame of reference before assessing broader aspects of orientation and general knowledge. Time and space may be measured quite differently in other communities, and it is wise for a bicultural provider to study these issues in order to develop a culturally relevant set of questions and an appropriate conceptual framework.

Mood and affect. One may conceptualize a spectrum of affective expression that extends across cultures and has a wide range of normal limits. Within a specific culture, it may not be acceptable to express some emotions, or there may be restrictions about when, where, and to whom these emotions may be expressed. In some American subcultures, affect is generally reserved; indeed, by western standards, sometimes it is seen as flat or constricted. In these cultures, this is a far less reliable indicator of schizophrenia or depression. Asian Americans, for example, may restrict affective expression with no direct references to feelings. Somatization is a more acceptable route of expressing emotions, through aches, pains, and concerns over digestion or elimination. In observing children, especially children from a different cultural background, the clinician should observe subtle facial expressions, behavioral reactions, and themes in play or artwork as clues to internal affective states.

The clinician should watch for the use of special symbols, especially those of religious or traditional significance, and try to find out what these symbols mean. In some cultures, storytelling and the use of metaphors may be a comfortable vehicle for conveying affects through displacement onto other figures. Again, knowledge of just what range of affect and its expression is acceptable for a specific cultural group will give the interviewer the tools to perform a reliable assessment.

Coping mechanisms. It is important to learn about the particular situations a child has been exposed to and how he or she has responded, for example, to school and peers. Does the family feel the child dealt with them adequately and in an acceptable fashion? Who can the child rely on in times of great stress or need? When the child is in distress, what makes him feel better? How has he been taught to handle problems by parents or caretakers? Does the patient have poor impulse control by conventional standards? by that of the child's own culture? Do the parents agree?

Last but not least, how is the patient coping with the interview? How does this compare to how the patient usually copes with stressful life events? Is the child aggressive or prone to temper tantrums when challenged? Is the child passive and compliant? Is there evidence of seductive or sexual behavior? Does the child seem too afraid, too neat, too "good," or in denial by the interviewer's standards?

Physical and neuromuscular. Muscle tone and coordination can be assessed through the use of play and art materials. Important questions include, Is this child of normal stature for her community? Are the facies abnormal? Is the head too small or too large? Are chromosomal or genetic anomalies frequently seen in this culture? Which ones? Is there inbreeding? Is there frequent abuse of specific substances (i.e., alcohol, cocaine) during pregnancy which have characteristic manifestations, for example, fetal alcohol syndrome, or effects? What is the normal diet for this culture? Is this child undernourished? Are hearing and vision normal? Is there bruising on the child's body? Is the child's gait normal or culturally influenced? How are developmental milestones assessed in a specific cultural group and has the child achieved them? In brief, the issues are those considered in any mental status assessment; in a culturally sensitive interview, however, certain dimensions are amplified.

Thought process and content. This area may cause the most difficulty across cultures. Thought processes may seem circumstantial or tangential, but in actuality they may simply be different from what one is used to. Speech content may be less than that characteristic of children from one's own culture, for example there may be more pauses. It is important not to fall into the trap of calling a particular style of thinking pathological because it is different from Western standards. The clinician should always ask the family or bicultural provider, "Do you feel that this way of thinking or speaking is normal for your son or for a child living in your community?" Information should also be sought from the patient's school and teacher.

There are cultures in which rituals, ceremonies and beliefs condone the use of substances for altered states of consciousness and/or for contact with the Spirit World as an acceptable means of healing and worship. Under such circumstances, one may encounter what are normally called hallucinations or delusions. If they are present, find out when the patient has these experiences and in what context. Are these so-called symptoms confined to a specific setting and do they occur intermittently, or are they pervasive, disturbing to the child, and acting to interfere with the child's ability to function? Again, the examiner should assess whether the family feels that these symptoms are within the range of acceptability. These extraordinary or supernatural experiences may be conveyed as well in play or art.

In many cultures, dreams are treated as very potent and powerful messages from spirits or guides and may be regarded as predictors of future events. In cultures which place great emphasis on dreams and dream expression, such accounts may serve as a gateway into the patient's thought processes, feelings, fantasies, hopes, fears, and wishes. It is always wise to tread lightly however, as some cultures view dreams as sacred and private. The proper approach is always a sensitive one. A patient's dreams and wishes may become accessible by utilizing play, art, music, storytelling, or even relaxation and visualization exercises. Indeed, altered states of consciousness may be comfortable for children from other subcultures and may provide previously unaccessible information. If possible, one should be well versed in various traditional and nontraditional techniques and practices—music, art, drama, dance, imagery, drumming, chanting, somatic therapies including forms of massage and therapeutic touch, herbalism, rituals around discipline, relaxation or meditation, dream work, animal rituals, spirits, clairvoyance, and spontaneous healing—to name a few, or work with someone who is familiar with them. One need not know how to utilize all of these modalities, and indeed in certain circumstances it may not be appropriate to utilize them. However, to have some knowledge and awareness of cultural therapeutic strategies *is* important and is the mark of a sensitive clinician.

Self-concept and identification. In certain cultures it may be shameful to talk about oneself in a positive way or to list one's positive attributes. For example, some Native American youth displaying low self-esteem may experience difficulty in expressing their assets and strengths, even their likes and preferences. It may be unacceptable to wish to be better than everyone else; indeed, individuals who do so are sometimes ostracized. Their desire to excel beyond others is viewed as a statement that they are dissatisfied with their lot.

If a culture emphasizes current reality to the exclusion of future orientation, it may be difficult to elicit future hopes, dreams, goals, or aspirations. It is important to learn to recognize expressions of self-concept and self-esteem through indirect rather than direct means—through play, storytelling, puppets, artwork, or whatever creative medium may be available. How does the child see herself in relation to other family members, to peers, to other community members? What are her relationships like? With whom does the patient identify? How does the child negotiate activities of daily living? What is her personal hygiene like? What are the family's/culture's views on bathing/washing? Have the child's habits changed in any way in the recent past? Is she proud of who she is and of her achievements, even though she may be reluctant to talk about them? Is she self-destructive? Again, one may need to be clever in assessing self-concept and approach this issue in a circuitous fashion in order to avoid causing shame, guilt, anxiety, or embarrassment. In other words, when questioning, always err on the side of temperance and sensitivity rather than interro-

gating in blunt, heavy-handed ways. Instead of using direct questioning, the clinician might ask a child to describe himself or his attributes through artwork or storytelling. Utilizing the technique of mirroring, for example, may be an effective and empathic way of getting to know a child through more intuitive or kinesthetic means that bypasses the threat of direct language.

IQ. Most standardized intelligence tests are designed to assess children from Western cultures. Children from other cultures may score poorly on these tests, even though their intelligence is normal. It is important to be aware of differences in information and knowledge base, as well as differences in learning styles, which may account for the poor test scores of a patient from a specific cultural group. Too often children are classified into categories and assigned pathological diagnoses which are incorrect. Not only can this be psychologically traumatic and damaging, but it may contribute to an overall sense of hopelessness, helplessness, and low self-esteem.

DIAGNOSTIC FORMULATION

Epidemiologic studies suggest that there is a common core to most psychiatric disorders, and that they occur across cultures and subcultures. Anxiety Disorders, Depressive Disorders, Psychotic Disorders, Attention Deficit Hyperactivity disorder, Eating Disorders, and Developmental Learning Disorders occur in every culture studied. However, the culture shapes the form of their expression and the presenting symptom picture. A newer phenomenon has emerged from cross-national studies of diagnostic prevalence—that of comorbidity. In other words, while the major psychiatric conditions are found in every culture, their frequency varies, and in addition, their patterns of comorbidity (more than one diagnosis occurring together) may present profiles that differ from culture to culture.

Finally, there is a common phenomenon which influences diagnosis that must always be considered in assessing children from minority subcultures. Learned helplessness and low self-esteem are universal psychological effects of prejudice toward minority groups. They may be incorporated into the personality of individual children of that culture and must be differentiated from true psychiatric disorders. They may not only mimic depression and internalizing disorders, for example, but may produce dysfunctional coping behaviors which may appear as externalizing disorders.

INTERPRETIVE INTERVIEW AND FEEDBACK

Once the assessment has been completed, it is appropriate to provide feedback to the patient and his/her family. It is always a good idea to explain to the child in developmentally appropriate terms what the problem is believed to be. As he does so, he could give the child time to respond and to ask questions. The child should be asked if there are specific things he does or doesn't wish the clinician to discuss with his parents. It is appropriate to tell the child what will be told to the family.

When meeting with the child and/or parents, the clinician may wish to have an interpreter or bicultural therapist or provider present. Questions about how the parents perceived the assessment process give the clinician insight into how it was negotiated both by the child and the family. The findings should be presented in a simple, concrete fashion with clear justifications for clinical impressions and suggestions for what might be helpful. The clinician may wish to offer several options, from watching and waiting, to specific interventions such as medication. The clinician should assess the family views toward these options. There may be particularly strong biases against the use of medication or hospitalization. A skillful diagnostician is always willing to work in conjunction with a "healer" from the family's community, and is open to alternative or concurrent solutions or plans. The clinician should not be invested in the family's acceptance of a particular treatment plan or suggestion. The family is asked in a sensitive way to repeat back what their understanding is of what has been presented. It is up to the clinician to take the initiative to learn about a family's culture rather than expecting to be taught. It is important to be instrumental in creating a sense of mutual respect, working with the patient and family as part of a cooperative team, and always looking for the best answers and solutions. It is not only the diagnosis and treatment program that matters, but the enriching and valuable experience of touching lives from other backgrounds in a helpful way.

Appendix

SUGGESTED KEY QUESTIONS AND CONSIDERATIONS WHEN INTERVIEWING CHILDREN AND FAMILIES FROM OTHER CULTURES

When speaking with the family, one might ask:

- Do you feel comfortable sharing your feelings about what it's like to talk with a person like me who is (white, black, asian, hispanic, etc.)?
- Have you sought help from a spiritual person or traditional healer in your community?
- How are roles the same or different for males and females in your culture?
- What are your culture's views on sexual practices including homosexuality? Abortion?
- Are important decisions made by the family as a group or by each individual for himself?
- Is it acceptable to express problems, feelings and emotions in your family and culture? To whom and how?
- Does your family prefer to discuss problems with a therapist as a group, together or would they prefer to meet individually with the therapist?
- Do individuals from your culture focus more on the present or on the future, e.g. plans? What about things that have happened in the past?
- How do individuals from your culture regard physical and emotional illness? How do they feel about it? Where do they think it comes from? What makes it better or worse?
- If you feel comfortable discussing this, can you help me to understand your religious customs, beliefs, traditions, and spiritual practices?
- How do you discipline your child? Are these practices shared by your culture?
- What do you believe about a person taking his or her own life? Why would someone want to do this? What do you believe happens after death?
- How do people in your family and in your culture feel about drinking or using drugs? Are medicines, herbs, or other substances used during religious ceremonies or for healing purposes?
- How do people express affection in your culture? How do people relate to one another socially? What does a proper greeting consist of?
- What are the common foods favored by your family? On special occasions such as holidays?
- Have you lived here for a long time or did you immigrate from somewhere else? What was that like? How has it been adjusting to a new culture? What language do you speak at home? In public? Do you

have relatives "back home?" Does your child have a close relationship with them? Has your child had difficulty adjusting to a new environment (i.e., peer relations, school)? What is the ethnic makeup of your community? What is your home like? What are stressful things about living in your community?

When speaking with the child, one may ask some of the above questions in developmentally appropriate language. In addition

- consider the use of a bicultural interpreter or a familiar face in the room with the child.
- Know how to greet or shake hands with a child from another culture (e.g. firm versus gentle versus avoidance of physical contact altogether).
- Be prepared for differences in clothing, facial appearance, and normal variations in rates and affective ranges of speech patterns.
- Regarding physical appearance: Is this child of normal stature for her community? Is the facies normal or abnormal? Is the head size and shape characteristic or is the head too large or small? Is the child well nourished? Are hearing and vision normal? What is the normal skin appearance (e.g. Mongolian spots)? Is there bruising on the child's body? Is the child's gait normal for her culture? Has the child achieved expected developmental milestones?
- Avoid direct eye contact if you are aware that this is culturally inappropriate.
- Avoid excessive talking and questioning. Be a witness and an observer. Learn to be fully present during the interview and consider that nonverbal exchange is of paramount importance. Be as nonthreatening and as unconditionally accepting as possible. Cultivate a sense of cultural boundaries. Know how and when to cross the line and when not to.
- Along nonverbal lines, have toys, games, and props available that a child might play with at home or in his community. Ask parents about these.
- Regarding thought process and content: Is this child's manner of thinking or speaking normal for his culture? As a child psychiatrist, how comfortable are you with altered states of consciousness? Can you incorporate this child's so-called extraordinary experiences and dreams into the treatment in an effective and sensitive manner? Are true hallucinations or delusions present, or are these a part of the child's religious/traditional belief system? What do the parents say?

- Be prepared for various ways of expressing emotion. Know that smiling is not necessarily an indicator of a happy mood, and that frowning or a "flat" expression is not necessarily an indicator of disapproval, irritability, or sadness. Know that in some cultures, emotions may manifest as physical symptoms. Affective states are highly variable and the clinician must cultivate an appreciation for subtleties and nuances.
- The child's general knowledge base may vary greatly. Never assume children know seemingly obvious facts about Western culture or history. For example, be aware of how children from other cultures measure time.
- Is it acceptable to speak about the future or is it important to stay focused in the present?
- How does the child cope with stress? What kinds of experiences are stressful? How has he/she been taught to handle such situations?
- Learn about religious practices and about major traditions, customs, and symbolism. Myths and metaphors may serve as powerful tools in allowing expression of problems or difficulties.
- What is it like for a child from this culture to speak about her positive attributes? Is it acceptable or inappropriate?
- How does the child perceive himself in relation to the family and community? What about friends? Relationships? Personal hygiene?
- Can you safely diagnose this child based on her own cultural norms? It is important to know what depressed, anxious, psychotic, traumatized, hyperactive, etc., states look like in a child from the specific culture being addressed.

REFERENCES

Attneave, C. L. (1979). The American Indian child. In J. D. Noshpitz (Ed.), *Basic handbook of child psychiatry, Vol. 1: Development* (pp. 239–248). New York: Basic Books.

Beitchman, J. H., Nair, R., Clegg, M., et al. (1986). Prevalence of psychiatric disorders in children with speech and language disorders. *Journal of the American Academy of Child Psychiatry, 25,* 528–535.

Canino, I. A. (1988). The transcultural child. In C. J. Kestenbaum & D. T. Williams (Eds.), *Handbook of clinical assessment of children and adolescents* (Vol. 2, pp. 1036–1037). New York: University Press.

Cazden, C. B., & John, V. P. (1971). Learning in American Indian children. In N. L. Wax, S. Diamond, & F. O. Gearing (Eds.), *Anthropological perspective on education*. New York: Basic Books.

Flaskerud, J. (1989). Transcultural concepts in mental health nursing. In J. Boyle & M. Andrews (Eds.), *Transcultural concepts in nursing care* (pp. 243–269). Glenview, IL: Scott, Foresman & Company.

Harwood, A. (Ed.). (1981). *Ethnicity and medical care*. Cambridge, MA: Harvard University Press.

Herberg, P. (1989). Theoretical foundations of transcultural nursing. In J. Boyle & M. Andrews (Eds.), *Transcultural concepts in nursing care* (pp. 4–58). Boston: Scott, Foreman/Little, Brown College Division.

Ka'opua, L., & Waldron, J. (1991). *Training for cultural competence in the HIV epidemic* [Produced through the AIDS Education Project and Hawaii Area AIDS Education and Training Center]. University of Hawaii, John A. Burns School of Medicine.

Kiev, A. (Ed.). (1964). *Magic, faith, and healing*. New York: Free Press.

Kleinfeld, J. S. (1974). Characteristics of Alaskan Native students. In *Alaskan Native needs assessment in education: Project ANNA*. Juneau: Juneau Area Office, Bureau of Indian Affairs.

Loof, D. (1979). Sociocultural factors in etiology. In J. D. Noshpitz (Ed.), *Basic handbook of child psychiatry* (Vol. 2, pp. 87–99). New York: Basic Books.

Lombardi, T. (1970). Psycholinguistic abilities of Papago Indian school children. *Journal of the Exceptional Child, 36*, 485–493.

McShane, D. (1980). A review of scores in American Indian children on the Wechsler Intelligence Scales. *White Cloud Journal, 1*, 3–10.

Murphy, J. M., & Leighton, A. H. (Eds.). (1965). *Approaches to cross-cultural psychiatry*. Ithaca, NY: Cornell University Press.

Powell, G. J. (Ed.). (1983). *The psychosocial development of minority group children*. New York: Brunner/Mazel.

Randall-David, E. (1989). *Strategies for working with culturally diverse communities and clients*. Washington, DC: Association for the Care of Children's Health.

Serrano, A. C., & Castillo, F. G. (1979). The Chicano child and his family. In J. D. Noshpitz (Ed.), *Basic handbook of child psychiatry* (Vol. 1, pp. 257–263). New York: Basic Books.

Shuberg, J., & Cropley, A. J. (1972). Verbal regulation of behavior and IQ in Canadian Indian and white children. *Developmental Psychology, 7*, 295–301.

Silk, S., & Voyet, G. (1970). Cross cultural study of cognitive development on the Pine Ridge Indian reservation. *Pine Ridge Research Bulletin, 11* (DHEW Publication No. HSM 80-69-430). Washington, DC: Indian Health Service.

Simmons, J. (1981). *Psychiatric Examination of Children* (3rd ed.). Philadelphia: Lea & Febiger.

Timble, J. E., Goddard, A., & Ninges, N. G. (1977). *Review of the literature on educational needs and problems of American Indians, 1971 to 1976*. Seattle, WA: Battelle Memorial Institute, Social Change Study Center.

Waldron, J. A., & McDermott, J. F. (1979). Transcultural considerations. In S. I. Harrison (Ed.), *Basic handbook of child psychiatry* (Vol. 3). New York: Basic Books.

Witelson, S. F. (1971). Developmental dyslexia: Two right hemispheres and none left. *Science, 195*, 309–311.

Yates, A. (1987). Current status and future directions of research on the American Indian child. *American Journal of Psychiatry, 144*, 1135–1142.

67 / Observation, Interview, and Mental Status Assessment (OIM): Possibly Abused

Sandra J. Kaplan

Child abuse and neglect are major public health problems confronted by child and adolescent clinicians and evaluators. In the United States, 514,200 children under 18 were reported as abuse or neglect victims in 1988, and 1,100 deaths were reported to have resulted from this abuse and neglect (U.S. Department of Health and Human Services, Study of the National Incidence and Prevalence of Child Abuse and Neglect, 1988).

Definitions

The following are definitions of child physical abuse, child sexual abuse, and child neglect reported in the U.S. Department of Health and Human Services study findings in the "Study of the National Incidence and Prevalence of Child Abuse and Neglect" (U.S. Department of Health and Human Services, 1988).

PHYSICAL ABUSE

Physical abuse is the infliction upon a child under 18 years of age of nonaccidental physical harm, causing injury or creating a substantial risk of causing death, disfigurement, impairment of bodily functioning, or other serious physical injury. Examples of serious injuries include loss of consciousness, cessation of breathing, broken bones, and extensive second-degree burns. Moderate injuries include the persistence in observable form of pain or impairment for 48 hours (e.g., bruises).

SEXUAL ABUSE

Sexual abuse is the sexual assault of a child under 18 years of age causing harm or injury to the child in the following ways: intrusion (i.e., penile penetration of the child's mouth, anus, or genitals), molestation with genital contact (e.g., fondling), or the obscene or pornographic photographing or depiction of children for commercial purposes, or prostitution of one's child.

CHILD NEGLECT

Physical Neglect: Physical neglect of a child under 18 years of age is manifested as refusal of or delay in health care (which reflects inattention to remedial health care needs); abandonment (e.g., desertion of a child without arranging reasonable care and supervision); expulsion (e.g., indefinite expulsion of the child from the home without arrangement for care by others, or refusal to accept custody of a returned runaway); inadequate supervision (e.g., a young child left unsupervised for an extended period of time), or other physical neglect (e.g., conspicuous inattention to avoidable hazards in the home; inadequate nutrition, clothing, or hygiene; or other forms of reckless disregard for the child's safety or welfare, such as driving with the child while intoxicated or leaving the young child in a motor vehicle).

Educational Neglect: Educational neglect is manifested as one of the following: permitted chronic truancy (e.g., habitual truancy averaging at least 5 days a month if the parent has been informed of the problem and has not attempted to intervene); failure to enroll a child in school (e.g., failure to enter or enroll a child of mandatory school age, causing the child to miss at least 1 month of school); or a pattern of keeping a school-age child home for nonlegitimate reasons, i.e., to work, care for siblings, etc.) an average of at least 3 days a month; inattention to special educational needs including refusal to allow or failure to obtain recommended remedial educational services, or neglect in obtaining or following through with treatment for a child's diagnosed learning disorder or other special education needs without reasonable cause.

Assessment

IDENTIFICATION OF THE PRESENCE OF RISK FACTORS FOR CHILD ABUSE OR NEGLECT RISK FACTORS

Assessment and recognition of child abuse or neglect should include the examiner's consideration of family violence risk factors. These include exposure of the alleged perpetrator to family violence (i.e., child abuse, child neglect, or domestic violence experiences during childhood; stressful events; young or single parenthood of the alleged perpetrator; low birth weight of an alleged child victim; four or more children closely spaced) (U.S. Department of Health and Human Services, 1988), family social isolation, a lack of empathy and of nonviolent conflict resolution by the family, and alleged perpetrator substance abuse or depression.

INTERVIEW OF THE CHILD

In order to facilitate disclosure of possible abuse or neglect, it is essential that the clinician

448

interview possible victims in the absence of the alleged perpetrator and in the absence of other family members. This is important because the possible perpetrator is most often a relative or close family contact; it should be part of the assessment whenever clinical judgment does not determine a contraindication.

Play Materials Which Facilitate Interviews with the Child Include:

I. For Preadolescent children,
   A. a dollhouse with family member dolls to facilitate the child's description of family sleeping arrangements, daily activities, and household members;
   B. anatomically detailed dolls of the same race as the child to facilitate the child's description of anatomical parts in order to enable possible sexual abuse disclosure;
   C. toy telephones for both child and clinician to facilitate ease of disclosure for preschoolers and early latency age children;
II. For both preadolescent and adolescent children,
   A. Drawing materials. The figure drawings of sexually abused children and adolescents may reveal sexual immaturity or hypermaturity, and/or gender identity confusion (Aiosa-Karpas, Karpas, Pelcovitz, & Kaplan, 1991).

Discussion of Anatomically Detailed Doll Use: Many field professionals utilize anatomically detailed dolls in the evaluation of child sexual abuse. Boat and Everson (1988) surveyed 300 professionals in North Carolina and found that use of the dolls ranged from 40% among law enforcement agencies, to 67% among mental health professionals, to 94% among child protective services agencies. Other surveys indicate high percentages of doll usage (Conte, Sorenson, Fogarty, & Rosa, 1991).

The child's interaction with the doll has frequently been thought to be persuasive enough to be interpreted as expert testimony in cases involving suspected sexual abuse (Ceci & Bruck, 1993).

Researchers have criticized the validity of the use of anatomically detailed dolls by maintaining that the dolls are suggestive and thus encourage children to engage in sexual play that may not be indicative of child sexual abuse (Terr, 1988). Nonabused children may choose to experiment with the doll in similar ways to abused children. Moreover, normative data on nonabused children's doll play do not exist, casting doubts on firm judg-

ments concerning children's abuse status based on doll play (Everson & Boat, 1994).

Although many professionals use the dolls, few receive instructions or manuals to evaluate doll play. Professionals may therefore differ in their assessments of the same behaviors in children. Others contend that the dolls, although not suggestive, do not aid in recognition of abuse (Goodman & Aman, 1990). Hence, clinicians must exercise great caution when evaluating child sexual abuse with anatomically detailed dolls, and we recommend that the clinician reserve utilization of these dolls for facilitation of children's labeling of their anatomical parts.

HISTORY TAKING FROM THE CHILD

Interviews of possibly abused or neglected children are conducted in order to facilitate disclosure of abuse or neglect. Such interviews need to include specific questions about the sources of any injuries and about child disciplinary methods and family conflict resolution strategies, including the use of weapons during arguments. Approximately 50% of child-abusing families also have ongoing domestic violence or spousal assault. Clinicians need to inquire specifically about spousal assault between parents in order to formulate accurate treatment plans, including spousal violence prevention.

Specific professional organizational clinical guidelines have been developed for child physical abuse, neglect, and sexual abuse assessments (American Academy of Child and Adolescent Psychiatry, 1988, 1990; American Academy of Pediatrics, 1988, 1991; American Medical Association, 1988, 1991, 1992; American Professional Society against Child Abuse, 1990; American Psychiatric Association, 1991).

These guidelines include information about adequate history, informants, types of abuse and neglect, types of clinicians, and examples of questions for abuse assessment.

THE CHILD SEXUAL ABUSE HISTORY

It is essential that clinician's use nonleading questions when interviewing suspected abuse victims about sexual abuse. Interviews (Boat & Everson, 1986) containing nonleading questions to use with children when inquiring about possible sexual abuse allegations are helpful guides. They serve to prevent the clinician from influencing abuse disclosure by suggestions, and thus impairing the legal documentation or prosecution of the sexual abuse case.

THE CHILD NEGLECT HISTORY

To obtain a history of child neglect, the clinician needs to ask questions of children and parents or other child guardians about child supervision schedules, the identities of child caretakers, school attendance, child medical care history, including specific medical providers, and child personal hygiene routines. It is important that during the assessment the clinician should take note of the adequacy of a child's nutrition, growth, attire, and housing (according to parental economic ability to provide housing) (Rosenzweig & Kaplan, 1995).

PHYSICAL EXAMINATIONS, ABUSE, AND NEGLECT

Physical Examination of the Possibly Physically Abused or Neglected Child: A physical examination is an important component of the assessment of the child or adolescent suspected of suffering such victimization; clinicians should recommend a physical examination for all children and adolescents thought to be abused or neglected. The American Medical Association "Diagnostic and Treatment Guidelines Concerning Child Abuse and Neglect" (1985) report the following as diagnostic physical findings: Characteristically, the injuries are more severe than those that could reasonably be attributed to the claimed cause (Council on Scientific Affairs, American Medical Association, 1985). Physical signs of abuse include: bruises and welts of the face, lips, mouth, ears, eyes, neck, head, trunk, back, buttocks, thighs, or extremities on multiple body surfaces or soft tissue forming regular patterns, often resembling the shape of the article used to inflict the injury (e.g., hand, teeth, belt buckle, or electrical cord); burns inflicted with cigars or cigarettes, especially on the soles, palms, back or buttocks; immersion burns (stocking or glove-like on extremities, doughnut-shaped on buttocks or genitals), or pattern burns resembling an electrical appliance

(e.g., iron, burner, or grill); fractures of the skull, ribs, nose, facial structure, or long bones, frequently with multiple or spiral fractures in various stages of healing; lacerations or abrasions; rope burns on wrists, ankles, neck, torso, palate, mouth, gums, lips, eyes, ears, or external genitalia; bruises of the abdominal wall; intramural hematoma of duodenum or proximal jejunum; intestinal perforation; ruptured liver or spleen; ruptured blood vessels; kidney, bladder or pancreatic injury; central nervous system injuries including subdural hematoma (often reflective of blunt trauma or violent shaking); retinal hemorrhage; or subarachnoid hemorrhage (often reflective of shaking). Guidelines Concerning Child Abuse and Neglect; JAMA 254:796–800, 1985).

Physical Examination of the Possibly Neglected Child: The following have been suggested as typical physical findings of neglected children by the Scientific Affairs of the American Medical Association (1985):

- Physical neglect: malnutrition, repeated pica, constant fatigue, poor hygiene, clothing inappropriate for weather or setting (American Medical Association, Council on Scientific Affairs, 1985).
- Medical neglect: lack of appropriate medical care for chronic illness, absence of appropriate immunizations or medications, absence of dental care, absence of necessary prostheses such as eyeglasses or a hearing aid, discharge from treatment against medical advice.
- Emotional neglect: delays in physical development and failure to thrive (American Medical Association, Council on Scientific Affairs, 1985).

The physical examination of a possibly sexually abused child is an important component of assessment of child sexual abuse. The American Academy of Child and Adolescent Psychiatry (1990) recommends that clinicians consider the following when a physical examination on a suspected sexually abused child or adolescent must be performed:

This medical exam gathers medicolegal evidence and treats any problems related to the abuse. It can be informative and can reassure the child or adolescent. Preferably, the examination should be performed by a pediatrician or family physician known to the child or by a pediatric gynecologist. The physician should know the ramifications of an examination carried out in this context. Such evaluations require special training in physical findings and of history taking in sexual abuse cases. Thus is it important to determine the qualifications of the physicians planning to do the physical exam. When possible, the child should be allowed to choose the sex of the examining physician. It is recommended that a trusted, supportive adult remain with the child during the evaluation.

Whenever there is the possibility of obtaining forensic evidence, the exam should take place promptly. If the child has been raped, or there is a possibility of acute trauma or infection, or the abuse occurred within 72 hours of the disclosure, the child should be examined as soon as possible in order to obtain forensic evidence. Preferably, the child should be seen in the physician's office rather than in an emergency ward. The genital study may be conducted in the context of an overall physical examination so as to de-emphasize the sexual aspect, and the child should be informed of what the physician is doing and be told afterwards what the findings are. It should be remembered that a negative genital exam does not rule out sexual abuse. The child's emotional state and degree of relaxation may affect the findings on both vaginal and rectal exams. If the child refuses to cooperate with the physical exam for reasons of trauma, consideration should be given to deferring the exam until such a time when, with benefit of counseling, the child is deemed able to cooperate.

If a child is already being evaluated by a mental health professional, the physician doing the physical exam should be sensitive to the child and minimize questions about the abuse so as to avoid contaminating the child's data and duplicating the interviews. An illustrated guide of physical findings in child physical and sexual abuse and neglect has recently been published (Kessler, 1991).

MENTAL HEALTH ASSESSMENTS OF CHILDREN AND ALLEGED PERPETRATORS

Mental health assessments should be conducted for all children suspected of being abused or neglected as well as for those suspected of abusing or neglecting them. The findings that emerge will enable effective treatment planning for the child and the adults involved in order to prevent further abuse and neglect. Clinicians should assess for sexualized behaviors, depressive symptoms and syndromes, substance abuse, posttraumatic stress disorder, and aggressive or

suicidal behavior in order to make specific recommendations for victim and perpetrator rehabilitation.

Psychopathology of Abused Children and Adolescents

Studies of psychiatric disturbances in child abuse victims have found these children to be impulsive, hyperactive (Williams & Finkelhor, 1990), depressed (Kaplan, Montero, Pelcovitz, & Salzinger, 1986), conduct disordered (Kaplan, Montero, Pelcovitz, & Salzinger, 1986; Kinard, 1980), and learning impaired (Kline & Christiansen, 1975). They are also reported to abuse substances (Kaplan, Montero, Pelcovitz, & Salzinger, 1986). Studies of child and adolescent psychiatric populations have often found the children to have histories of physical child abuse (Kashani, Beck, Hoeper, et al., 1987). Lewis (1985) and Lewis, Shanck, Pincus, & Glaser (1979) found that delinquent and violent adolescents also frequently had histories of physical abuse.

Salzinger, Kaplan, Pelcovitz, Samit, & Krieger (1984) found that maltreatment victims who had been referred for treatment, and to a lesser extent their siblings, showed significantly more conduct disturbance, hyperactivity, tension, and anxiety than did a nonmaltreated comparison group. Kaplan, Montero, Pelcovitz, & Salzinger (1986) found that abused children and adolescents were significantly more often diagnosed as having depression, alcohol abuse, conduct disorders, and attention deficit hyperactivity disorders than were a comparison group of nonmaltreated children and adolescents.

SUICIDE AND ABUSE

An association between abuse and suicide has been found in studies of both abused children and adolescents, and of adolescent suicide attempters. Self-mutilative behavior was reported in abused and neglected children by Green (1978). Deykin, Alpert, & McNamara (1985) reported that adolescents who attempted suicide had more often been reported as abuse victims than had nonattempters. Pfeffer (1988) reported high rates of child abuse in children who attempted suicide, and Kaplan, Montero, Pelcovitz, & Salzinger (1986) reported high rates of suicide attempts in adolescent runaways. Garbarino and Farber (1983, 1984) reported high rates of adolescent abuse in runaway youth. Child abusive behavior was found more often in mothers who attempted suicide than in a comparison group of nonsuicidal mothers (Hawton, Roberts, & Goodwin, 1985).

Psychopathology of Parents of Abused and Neglected Children and Adolescents

A number of mental disorders and symptoms have been described in perpetrators of physical abuse and neglect. In order to rehabilitate families and prevent repeated abuse, the following conditions should be considered by clinicians during assessment of possibly abusive families.

PARENTS OF PHYSICALLY ABUSED CHILDREN AND ADOLESCENTS

These parents have been found to have more diagnosed psychopathology than have nonmaltreating parents. In suburban abusive families, mothers have been more frequently diagnosed as having depressive disorders, while fathers, usually the perpetrating parents in this study, were more often found to be diagnosed with alcoholism, antisocial personality disorder, or an affectively reactive personality style. Mothers of maltreated children are more often diagnosed as drug abusers than mothers of maltreated adolescents (Kaplan, Pelcovitz, Salzinger, & Ganeles, (1983). Therefore, assessment by the clinician for parental affective disorders, substance abuse, and antisocial behavior are essential for parental rehabilitation and abuse prevention.

PSYCHOPATHOLOGY OF POSSIBLY NEGLECTFUL PARENTS

There have been very few studies of the mental health of neglectful parents. Aragona and Eyberg (1981) found them to use more direct commands, to offer less verbal praise or acknowledgment, and to be more critical when interacting with their children than nonneglectful mothers.

In Zuravin's (1988) study, maternal depression was more often associated with physical child neglect than with physical child abuse.

As mentioned earlier in this chapter, spouse abuse/domestic violence, to which children are often exposed, has been defined as a form of emotional neglect (U.S. Department of Health and Human Services, 1988). Parental perpetrators of spouse abuse have frequently been found to abuse substances (Kaplan, 1988). Their nonviolent spouses tended to suffer from depressive disorders (Kaplan, 1988). Again, regardless of the type of family violence or neglect, clinicians need to recognize adult depression and substance abuse and to plan specific interventions for these disorders.

PARENTS OF POSSIBLY SEXUALLY ABUSED CHILDREN

Parents of sexually abused children and adolescents display a wide range of emotional and social difficulties. Although incest perpetrators do not reveal a consistent pattern of psychological disturbance, relative to controls they do manifest a high incidence of personality disorders (Langevin, Handy, Day, & Russon, 1985), psychopathology (Williams and Finkelhor, 1990), alcohol and drug abuse, paranoia, depression, and anxiety (Williams & Finkelhor, 1990). There are far fewer studies of the nonperpetrating parent; however, the clinical literature on nonoffending mothers notes a high incidence of depression and suicide (Haugaard & Reppucci, 1988).

Deviant sexuality in parents places the child at greater risk of developing later sexual difficulties (Ryan et al., 1990). Some recent studies of incest perpetrators found deviant sexual arousal and behavior toward young girls and low levels of arousal toward adult females in some but not all perpetrators (Coons, Bowman, Pellow, & Schneider, 1989). A number of studies comment on the low level of sexual satisfaction of both parents of incest victims (Saunders, McClure, & Murphy, 1986). Thus, in sex abuse cases, clinicians should include specific assessments of parental sexual practices and preferences as well as evaluation for the affective disorders, substance abuse, and antisocial behavior.

Ancillary Studies and Materials To Be Obtained

Since studies of abused and neglected children have documented that they are frequently educationally impaired (Salzinger, Kaplan, Pelcovitz, Samit, & Krieger, 1984), psychological testing to screen for learning disabilities and mental retardation should regularly be considered by clinicians. In addition, with parental or other guardian permission, clinicians should request school attendance, achievement test, and grade records. This will provide a better understanding of the child's school functioning, educational neglect allegations, and time of cessation of such neglect, if it did occur.

Moreover, in order to be fully informed regarding the health and treatment needs of all parties, clinicians should request pediatric and other medical records, and records of any mental health or substance abuse treatment for both the child and the adult guardians. In addition, in order to provide adequate care for abused or neglected children, the clinician needs to understand, communicate, and case manage with all agencies involved in the care of these children and their families.

Many of these children and families have had contact with law enforcement, judiciary, social services, foster care, and violence protection and prevention advocacy groups, as well as with education and health care providers. In order to maximize the outcome for all abused children, the efforts made by all service providers need to be coordinated and understood.

Protection

During assessment of a possibly abused or neglected child, clinicians need to consider the protection needs of the child. All states in the United States have reporting requirements for health care providers who suspect abuse or neglect, and all have agencies responsible for investigating and documenting child abuse or neglect. When assessing a child, if the safety of the child is in question, the proper agencies should be contacted to provide protection for the child until the safety of the child's home can be determined. Clinician information is available from state agencies regarding protection and reporting procedures specific to practice location.

REFERENCES

Aiosa-Karpas, C., Karpas, R., Pelcovitz, D., & Kaplan, S. (1991). Gender identification and sex role attribution in sexually abused adolescent females. *Journal of the American Academy of Child and Adolescent Psychiatry, 30*, 2 266–271.

American Academy of Child and Adolescent Psychiatry. (1988, June 10). *Statement on corporal punishment in schools.* Washington, DC: Author.

American Academy of Child and Adolescent Psychiatry. (1990, December 14). *Guidelines for the clinical evaluation of child and adolescent sexual abuse.* Washington, DC: Author.

American Academy of Pediatrics. (1988a). Public disclosure of private information about victims of abuse. Washington, DC: Author.

American Academy of Pediatrics. (1988b). Religious exemptions from child abuse statutes. *Pediatrics, 81* (1).

American Academy of Pediatrics. (1991). Guidelines for the evaluation of sexual abuse of children committee on child abuse and neglect. *Pediatrics, 87* (2).

American Medical Association. (1985). Diagnostic and treatment guidelines concerning child abuse and neglect. *Journal of the American Medical Association, 254* (6), 796–800.

American Medical Association. (1988). Physicians and family violence: Ethical considerations council report. Report B (I-91).

American Medical Association. (1991, June). Diagnostic and treatment guidelines on child physical abuse and neglect. AA22: 90–407 20M.

American Medical Association. (1992, June). Diagnostic and treatment guidelines on child sexual abuse. AA22: 92–407 20M.

American Professional Society on the Abuse of Children. (1990, Spring). Guidelines for psychosocial evaluation of suspected sexual abuse in young children. *The Advisor.*

American Psychiatric Association. (1991, June 28). *Position statement on child abuse and neglect by adults.* Washington, DC: Author.

Aragona, J. A., & Eyberg, S. M. (1981). Neglected children: Mothers' report of child behavior problems and observed verbal behavior. *Child Development, 52* (2), 596–602.

Boat, B. W., & Everson, M. D. (1986). Using anatomical dolls. *Guidelines for interviewing young children in sexual abuse investigations*, Chapel Hill, NC: Dept. of Psychiatry. University of North Carolina.

Boat, B. W., & Everson, M. D. (1988). Use of anatomical dolls among professionals in sexual abuse evaluations. *Child Abuse & Neglect, 12*, 171–179.

Ceci, S. J., & Bruck, M. (1993). Child witnesses: Translating research into policy. Social Policy Report. Society for Research in Child Development. VII,3.

Conte, J. R., Sorenson, E., Fogarty, L., & Rosa, J. (1991). Evaluating children's reports of sexual abuse: Results from a survey of professionals. *American Journal of Orthopsychiatry, 61* (3), 428–437.

Coons, P. M., Bowman, E. S., Pellow, T. A., & Schneider, P. (1989). Post-traumatic aspects of the treatment of victims of sexual abuse and incest. *Psychiatric Clinics of North America, 12*, 325–335.

Deykin, E. Y., Alpert, J. T., & McNamara, J. J. (1985). A pilot study of the effect of exposure to child abuse and neglect on adolescent suicide behavior. *American Journal of Psychiatry, 142*, 1299–1303.

Everson, M. D., & Boat, B. W. (1994). Putting the anatomical doll controversy in perspective: An examination of the major uses and criticisms of the dolls in child sexual abuse evaluations. *Child Abuse & Neglect, 18* (2), 113–129.

Goodman, G. S., & Aman, C. (1990). Children's use of anatomically detailed dolls to recount an event. *Child Development, 61*, 1859–1871.

Haugaard, J. J., & Reppucci, N. D. (1988). *The sexual abuse of children*. San Francisco: Jossey-Bass.

Hawton, K., Roberts, J., & Goodwin, J. (1985). The risk of child abuse among mothers who attempt suicide. *British Journal of Psychiatry, 146*, 486–489.

Herjanic, B., & Reich, W. (1982). Development of a structured psychiatric interview of children: Agreement between child and parent on individual symptoms. *Journal of Abnormal Psychology, 10*, 307–324.

Kaplan, S., Montero, G., Pelcovitz, D., & Salzinger, S. (1986, July). *Psychopathology of abused and neglected children*. Paper presented at the International Congress of Child Psychiatry and Allied Professions, Paris, France.

Kaplan, S., Pelcovitz, D., Salzinger, S., & Ganeles, D. (1983). Psychopathology of Parents of Abused and Neglected Children. *Journal of American Academy of Child Psychiatry, 22*, 233–244.

Kashani, Beck, Hoeper, et al. (1987). Psychiatric disorders in a community sample of adolescents. *American Journal of Psychiatry, 144* (5), 584–586.

Kessler, D., & Hyden, P. (1991). Physical, sexual, and emotional abuse of children. *Clinical Symposia, CIBA-GEIGY, 43* (1).

Kinard, E. (1980). Emotional development in physically abused children. *American Journal of Orthopsychiatry, 50* (4), 689–696.

Kline, D., & Christiansen, J. (1975). *Educational and psychological problems of abused children, Final Report*. EPIC. Microfiche No. ED12104.

Langevin, R., Handy, L., Day, D., & Russon, A. (1985). Are incestuous fathers pedophilic, aggressive and alcoholic? In R. Langevin (Ed.), *Erotic preference, gender identity and aggression*. Hillsdale, NJ: Lawrence Erlbaum.

Lewis, D. (1985). Biopsy and social characteristics of children who later murder: A perspective study. *American Journal of Psychiatry, 142*, 1161–1167.

Lewis, D., Shanck, S., Pincus, J., & Giaser, G. (1979). Violent juvenile delinquents: Psychiatric neurological, psychological, and abuse factors. *Journal of the American Academy of Child Psychiatry, 18*, 307–319.

Pfeffer, C. (1988). Suicidal behavior among children and adolescents: Risk identification and intervention. In A. Frances & R. Hales (Eds.), Rev of Psych, 7, Washington, DC: American Psychiatric Press.

Rosenzweig, H., & Kaplan, S. (Eds.). (1995). *Child neglect in family violence: A guide for the mental health and legal professional*. Washington, DC: American Psychiatric Press.

Ryan, G., Law, S., Astler, L., Sandau-Christopher, D., Sundine, C., Dale, J., & Teske, J. (1990). *Understanding and responding to the sexual behavior of children: A perpetration prevention project*. Denver, CO: Kempe National Center, University of Colorado Health Center.

Salzinger, S., Kaplan, S., Pelcovitz, D., Samit, C., & Krieger, R. (1984). Parent teacher assessment of children's behavior in child maltreating families. *Journal of the American Academy of Child Psychiatry, 23* (4), 38–64.

Saunders, B., McClure, S., & Murphy, S. (1986). Final report: Profile of incest perpetrators indicating treatability—Part I. Charleston, SC: Crime Victims Research and Treatment Center.

Terr, L. (1990). Too scared to cry. New York: Harper & Row.

Williams, L. M., & Finkelhor, D. (1990). The characteristics of incestuous fathers: A review of recent studies. In W. Marshall, D. Law, & H. Barbaree (Eds.), *Handbook of sexual assault: Issues, theories, and treatment of the offender* (pp. 231–255) New York: Plenum Press.

Zuravin, S. J. (1988). Child maltreatment and teenage first births: A relationship mediated by chronic sociodemographic stress? *American Journal of Orthopsychiatry, 58* (1), 91–103.

454

68 / Observation, Interview, and Mental Status Assessment (OIM): Possibly Substance Abusing

Jennifer J. Gould and Steven L. Jaffe

The use and abuse of alcohol and drugs has increased in the adolescent population during the 1990s. Among severely emotionally disturbed teenagers, almost half have significant alcohol or marijuana abuse or dependency problems (Greenbaum et al., 1991). These facts indicate that the clinician should suspect alcohol or drug abuse in every adolescent he evaluates. At the same time, interviewing and evaluating the possibly substance abusing adolescent presents one of the most difficult challenges the clinician can encounter.

In evaluating the teenager, the clinician should be knowledgeable about the drugs teenagers use and the types of effects that may occur. The clinician can quickly obtain an education about drugs and latest "druggie language" by simply asking teenagers what their peers use and abuse and what names are used. Such personal experience the clinician may have had with alcohol and drugs should not be revealed except in exceptional circumstances. An attitude of concern, interest, and seriousness mixed with a little humor is often the best attitude.

Substance abusing youth often distort, minimize, or deny the existence or extent of their drug abuse and other problems. Therefore, information from parents, school personnel, and legal authorities is essential. Other family members, especially siblings, as well as concerned peers, are often important sources of information.

There are a number of specific risk factors which, if present, make it more likely that the presenting adolescent is abusing alcohol and drugs. A positive family history for chemical dependence is the most significant risk issue. Genetic factors as well as parental beliefs in the harmlessness of certain substances are important contributors. Individual factors that correlate with use of substances include poor self-esteem, low achievement, especially in school, aggressive or impulsive behavioral characteristics, a history of sexual or physical abuse, or the presence of a psy-

chiatric disorder, especially depression. The presence of any of these risk factors should heighten the clinician's suspicion of alcohol or drug abuse.

Another major signal that should alert the clinician's suspicion is when parents or the adolescent describe that their friends abuse alcohol or drugs. It is extremely unlikely that the evaluated adolescent is the only nonusing member of her peer group.

The degree of difficulty in interviewing the possibly substance abusing adolescent will vary with the motivation and openness of the adolescent. The drug abusing adolescent who knows he has a problem and comes willingly for help, although rare, does exist. It is much more common for the adolescent to appear because someone else (parent, judge, principal, etc.) requests the evaluation and the adolescent begrudgingly submits to the interview. This situation calls for the clinician's highest level of skill and patience.

In order to engage the adolescent in the interview process, it is usually most helpful to begin with a nonconfrontational approach. The first issue to clarify is the adolescent's understanding of why he is at the interview. The TV character Colombo portrays how the clinician may slowly investigate the presenting problem by asking clarifying questions; in similar fashion the clinician takes an initial position of confused ignorance. Current life circumstances including home, family, and school relationships and level of functioning are then explored. Peer relationships, leisure activities, employment, and self-perceptions are carefully reviewed. Lastly, the clinician reviews the adolescent's use of drugs and alcohol. Bell (1990) describes that she rarely asks the first drug-use question. She will spend the first or second hour of evaluation talking about what the adolescent views as problems in his present situations or in growing up. Drug use is then divulged spontaneously by the adolescent, who wants to see what the interviewer thinks of the drug use. A drug and alcohol use history can then be explored with the adolescent's active participation. Anglin (1987) recommends using the strategy of asking the teenager about what they ingest. The clinician asks questions first about dietary patterns (i.e., snack foods, whether they skip breakfast, etc.) and then questions about prescribed medications and their compliance with there use. Next the clinician asks about over-the-counter medications (including antihistamines to sedate and caffeine/ephedrine pills to stimulate), and finally substance abuse. Here questions move from tobacco to alcohol to marijuana, sedatives and stimulants, hallucinogens, cocaine, and opiates. Use of inhalants, which peaks in use in early adolescence, is also explored.

Bukstein (1995) states that evaluation of substance use behavior involves inquiring into patterns of use (onset, how often, agent, and route), negative consequences, context of use (time, place, peers), and control (attempts to decrease, use more than planned, etc.). Substance abuse involves direct negative consequences of use. Substance dependency involves negative consequences plus physical dependence (tolerance and withdrawal) and/or compulsive use. It is extremely important to explore the adolescent's high-risk behavior when she is under the influence of alcohol and drugs. This includes driving under the influence of alcohol, marijuana, or LSD or being in a car where the driver is on a substance. Because of their life-threatening nature, other high-risk behaviors such as unprotected sex or becoming intoxicated on substances (i.e., alcohol or ecstasy) in a social setting where the adolescent could be beaten or raped are extremely important to identify.

Evaluating negative consequences involves exploration with the adolescent and family members into how the adolescent functions at school, at work, and within the family and peer group. Other family members may be abusing substances and it is essential to identify these members. School failure is one of the most common signs of substance use/abuse. Marijuana use impairs concentration and short-term memory and leads to school work decline. Direct objective information from the school is often helpful. A change in peer group or loss of interest in previous activities like music or athletics often results from drug involvement. Legal contacts such as arrests and involvement with the juvenile justice system must, of course, also be ascertained.

Adolescents usually progress along a specific sequence of drug use, with fewer adolescents using the "harder" drugs (Kandel, 1975). They begin with beer, wine, and cigarettes and move to marijuana, sedatives and stimulants, high-proof alcohol, and then LSD. Cocaine and opiates are used last. Adolescents differ from adults in that they continue to use the drugs used in the first part of the sequence resulting in multiple drug use. Thus the typical adolescent drug abuser regularly smokes a pack of cigarettes per day, gets drunk and smokes marijuana a number of times per week, trips on LSD intermittently, and occasionally uses stimulants and cocaine. These combinations of use need to be carefully evaluated.

Evaluating the type, extent, course, and negative consequences of substance involvement allows the clinician to make tentative judgments as to the stage of drug involvement, including the following (MacDonald, 1984).

- Experimental or recreational use.
- Regular or instrumental use where drugs are used to induce pleasure or suppress uncomfortable emotions.
- Preoccupation with use.
- Chemical dependency.

Experimental use often begins in junior high school with the associated peer pressure to just "try" alcohol (usually beer), marijuana, or inhalants. The setting can be virtually anyplace (home, school, party) or simply "hanging out." After getting high on a small amount of a drug, the adolescent returns to a normal mood without difficulty. What has been learned, however, is that drugs can affect mood; now drug use is associated with activation of the pleasure centers of the brain.

Regular use often progresses to hard liquor, where drinking to get drunk serves as a means of coping or of seeking pleasure. Drinking now occurs mid-week, and as a tolerance develops more alcohol is required; missing school or work due to hangovers is not uncommon. Different drugs including hallucinogens and pills are tried and nonusing friends are dropped. Money may be stolen from the family to buy drugs, and lying ensues to cover drug use. Mood changes are rapid and interests change.

By the substance abusing stage, problems have arisen in many areas of the adolescent's life. Preoccupation with drug use results in failures at home, school, work, and play, often leading to le-

456

gal problems. Despite the negative inter- and intrapersonal consequences caused by or worsened by drugs, repeated use continues. Mood and behavior changes fluctuate due to drug cravings.

Substance dependence involves an increasing tolerance, more drug use (both frequency and amount), and/or harder drugs. Preoccupation with drug use intensifies, as do the problems in the adolescent's life. Attempts are made to cut down or quit; these fail, however, and use is now necessary simply to feel normal. Drug intake is now compulsive and out of control. Fortunately, most adolescents do not progress to stage 4; however, stages 1 through 3 can be seriously debilitating and potentially fatal. In fact, 80% of teenage deaths are due to accidents, homicides, and suicides, with 50% of these being drug or alcohol related.

Urine drug screens may be helpful in evaluations, but are not always valid. Many teenagers know that extreme hydration may dilute their urine sufficiently to give a negative test. Like EEGs, a positive test indicates the presence of an abnormality but a negative test does not rule it out. Resistance to providing a urine specimen by a teenager being evaluated usually indicates the teenager has something to hide. Adolescent drug screening usually will indicate marijuana usage, since marijuana remains in the system from 1 to 3 weeks. Most other drugs used will be present in the urine for 24 to 36 hours.

In addition to using multiple drugs, which may result in the diagnosis of multiple substance use disorder, the substance abusing adolescent often has multiple psychiatric disorders that must be explored. Studies demonstrate the presence of other comorbid psychiatric disorders in 40 to 90% of adolescents with substance abuse (Bukstein, Brent, & Kaminer, 1989; Jaffe, 1996). These include disruptive behavior disorders (Attention Deficit Hyperactivity Disorder, Oppositional Defiant Disorder, and Conduct Disorder), mood disorders (major depression, dysthymia, and bipolar), anxiety disorders (phobias and posttraumatic stress disorder), eating disorders (especially bulimia), and schizophrenia. These comorbid conditions may occur before, during, or after the drug abuse and each disorder makes the others worse. Separating out which of these is primary is often impossible. Clinically the adolescent must first get off the alcohol and drugs and then the comorbid disorders can be evaluated and treated.

In summary, in addition to the more usual techniques described in other chapters, special interview techniques and approaches are needed in evaluating the possibly drug abusing adolescent.

REFERENCES

Anglin, T. M. (1987). Interviewing guidelines for the clinical evaluation of adolescent substance abuse. *Pediatric Clinics of North America 34:* 381–398.

Bell, T. (1990). *Preventing adolescent relapse.* Independence, MO: Herald House Independence Press.

Bukstein, O. C. (1995). *Adolescent substance abuse,* New York: John Wiley & Sons.

Bukstein, O. C., Brent, D., & Kaminer, Y. (1989). Comorbidity of substance abuse and other psychiatric disorders in adolescents. *American Journal of Psychiatry, 146* (9), 1131–1141.

Greenbaum, P. E., Prange, M. E., Friedman, R. M., et al. (1991). Substance abuse prevalence and comorbidity with other psychiatric disorders, among adolescents with severe emotional disturbances. *Journal of the American Academy of Child & Adolescent Psychiatry 30:* 575–583.

Jaffe, S. (Ed.). (1996). *Adolescent substance abuse and dual disorders,* Child and Adolescent Psychiatric Clinics of North America, Philadelphia: W. B. Saunders. vol. 5 No. 1, pp. 1–261.

Kandel, D. (1975). Stages in adolescent involvement in drug use. *Science, 190,* 912–914.

MacDonald, D. (1984). Drugs, drinking and adolescence. *American Journal of Diseases of Children, 13* (8), 117–125.

69 / Observation, Interview, and Mental Status Assessment (OIM): Slow Learning

Larry B. Silver and Rick Ostrander

The focus of this section will be on integrating information from the clinical observations, interview data, and the mental status assessment of the child or adolescent who presents with academic difficulties. The process used to collect this information follows the "Decision Tree on Difficulties with Academic Performance" (see Chapter 13, Figure 13.1).

The parents are usually seen before the child or adolescent to learn more of their concerns and questions. The clinician should obtain a full developmental and educational history. The specifics of obtaining this history as it relates to children or adolescents experiencing academic difficulties are discussed elsewhere in this volume.

After establishing rapport, it is critical to clarify if emotional or behavioral problems are causing the academic difficulties, or if the reverse is true and the academic difficulties are causing the emotional or behavioral problems. Students with a disability that interferes with their ability to achieve academically experience failure, which in turn results in frustration, low self-esteem, and a poor self-image. These feelings and thoughts might be expressed through emotional or behavioral problems. Further, the parents may experience their child's frustrations and feel as if it is they who are incurring a failure. In addition, the special attention given the child or adolescent with academic difficulties might cause sibling conflicts. It is for this reason that the clinician must look beyond the presenting problems to clarify if the emotional or behavioral problems are primary or secondary contributors to the academic difficulties.

Assessment of the Child or Adolescent

When evaluating a child or adolescent who exhibits emotional or behavioral problems along with poor academic performance, it is essential that the clinician identify or rule out the most frequent causes for this pattern, namely, learning disabilities and/or attention deficit hyperactivity disorder (Silver, 1981, 1993b). When seeking data relating to these diagnoses, the information that this child or adolescent provides is essential (Ostrander, 1993). Thus a specific set of questions should be added to the standard assessment questions. In addition, it is helpful to review classroom and home work and to ask the individual to do a writing exercise or to read.

SYMPTOMS SUGGESTIVE OF A LEARNING DISABILITY

Learning disabilities (in contrast to academic difficulties in general) are caused by a central processing disorder. A thorough understanding of the nature of this central processing disorder is essential in order to know what questions to ask the parents, child or adolescent, and teachers, as well as in understanding the data from psychological, educational, and other tests and examinations (Silver, 1993b). In this model, it is understood that any learning task involves more than one process and that any learning disability can involve more than one area of dysfunction. However, breaking learning down into steps helps to clarify the process.

The first step in this processing model is input, by which information from the sense organs enters the brain. Once the information is recorded, what is received is processed and interpreted through a step referred to as integration. The information must then be stored and later retrieved through the next step, memory. Finally, the information must be communicated through language or muscle activities. This final step is called output. It is important for the clinician to understand both the input-integration-memory-output processing model and the terminology and concepts used by professionals in the field of education and special education. Thus details will be provided before moving on to questions that might be used to identify clinical cues of a possible learning disability.

Input Disabilities: Input is a central brain process and does not pertain to peripheral visual or auditory problems. This process of perceiving one's environment is referred to as perception. A child might have a visual and/or an auditory perception disability.

A child with a visual perception disability may have difficulty organizing the position and shape of what he sees. Inputs may be perceived with letters reversed or rotated; for example, "n" might look like "u"; the letters d, b, p, and q might be confused with each other. This confusion with position of input is normal until about age 6; after this age, however, it should no longer be seen. Another type of visual perception disability is a figure-ground problem. The affected child has difficulty distinguishing the significant figure from the other visual inputs in the background. Reading requires this skill; you must be able to focus on specific letters or groups of letters, and then track from left to right, line after line. Children with this disability might skip over words, read the same line twice, or skip lines when reading. Judging distances or depth perception is another visual perception task that can go awry. A child may misjudge depth and bump into things, fall off a chair, or knock over a drink.

A child with an auditory perception disability might have difficulty distinguishing subtle differences in sounds, and, misunderstanding what is said, respond incorrectly. Words that sound alike are often confused, for example, "blue" and "blow," "ball" and "bell," "can" and "can't." Asked "How are you?," a boy answers, "I'm nine years old." He thought he heard "old" instead of "are" or in addition to "are." Some children have difficulty with auditory figure-ground. A child might be watching television in a room where others are playing or talking, and a parent or teacher calls out to speak to this child. It might not be until the third sentence verbalized that the child begins to note the voice (figure) out of the other sound inputs (background). It appears that the child never listens or pays attention.

Some children with an auditory perception disability cannot process sound inputs as fast as normal people are able to. This problem is called an "auditory lag" or an "auditory processing problem." In order to understand, the child must focus on each part of the message heard for a fraction of a second longer than most people require. While doing this, the child must concentrate on what is being said as well. Gradually she falls behind and misses a portion of the message. Adults think the child is not paying attention or that the information is too advanced for the child's ability.

Integration Disabilities: Once information enters the brain it has to be understood. At least three steps are required to do this: sequencing, abstraction, and organization. The child or adolescent may have a disability in one or all areas, and the disability may relate more to either visual input or auditory input.

A child with a sequencing disability might hear or read a story, but, in attempting to recount it, start in the middle, go to the beginning, and then shift to the end. Eventually the story is told, but the sequence of events is incorrect. The same is true with writing. All of the information is written but in an incorrect order. Others might read or write words with a reversed sequence: "dog" for "god" or "no" for "on." Some children have difficulty using a sequence of facts. A sequence is memorized, such as the months of the year, but is then unavailable for use when single units of the sequence are needed. When asked what comes after August, the child cannot answer spontaneously but must go back to January and work up. A child might know the alphabet but cannot use the dictionary without continuously beginning with "a" and working up to the desired letter.

Abstraction refers to the ability to infer the proper meaning for a word as it is used in a specific context. A disability in this area results in confusing the specific meaning of a word or phrase when there are several possibilities. For example, the word "dog" would have a different meaning if used as "the dog" than it would if used as "you dog." Children with this disability miss the meaning of jokes. Jokes, as well as puns and idioms, are based on a play on words. These children and adolescents often take what is said literally and may appear paranoid at times.

The integration of information requires processing the constant flow of information plus the memory tracks stimulated by this information into a meaningful whole concept or body of information. Difficulties with organization, "disorganization," result in a student whose notes or reports, as well as notebooks, desk, locker, and bedroom are all disorganized. This student might have difficulty in structuring school material in such a way that it can be understood and learned.

Memory Disabilities: This storage and retrieval process can involve either short-term or long-term memory. Short-term memory is the process of retaining information for a brief time while attending to or concentrating on it. Long-term memory refers to the process by which a person stores information that has been repeated often enough so that it can be retained and easily retrieved.

Most children and adolescents with memory disabilities have short-term memory problems. Such a student may require many more repetitions to retain what the average child can recall after a few repetitions. Yet the same child usually has no problem with long-term memory, surprising parents by remembering details from years ago.

The short-term memory problem might involve information coming in visually, auditorily, or both. For example, a child might review a spelling list one evening and know it well, then the next day in school it is forgotten. Or, the child might stop midway through talking and say, "Oh, forget it." The child started to talk but forgot what he was saying partway through. Some may read a page and understand, read the next page and understand, etc. Then, at the end of the chapter, they realize that they have forgotten what they read.

Output Disabilities: Information is expressed by means of words, language output, or through muscle activity such as writing, drawing, gesturing, or motor output. A child or adolescent may have a language disability and/or a motor disability.

Two forms of language are used in communication: spontaneous language and demand language. Spontaneous language is initiated by the speaker, who has the opportunity of selecting the subject, organizing thoughts, and finding the correct words before speaking. In the demand language situation, someone else initiates communication, for example, by asking a question. In the course of responding it is necessary for the person who is questioned to simultaneously organize the relevant ideas, find the right words, and speak.

Children with language disabilities usually have no difficulty with spontaneous language. They may, however, have problems with demand language. The inconsistency can be striking. A child may constantly initiate conversations, may never keep quiet, and may sound very normal. Where a situation demands a response, however, the same child might answer, "Huh?" or "What?" or "I don't know." To gain time, the child may ask that the question be repeated or may not answer at all.

Difficulty coordinating groups of large muscles such as the limbs or trunk is called a gross motor disability. Difficulty performing tasks that require coordination of groups of small muscles is called a fine motor disability.

Gross motor disabilities may cause the child to be clumsy, stumble, fall, bump into things, or have problems with generalized physical activities like running, climbing, swimming, buttoning, zipping, or typing.

The most common fine motor disability is poor handwriting. The problem lies in part in an inability to get the many small muscles in the dominant hand to work together. Such children write slowly and often illegibly. They complain that their hand does not work fast and their hand gets tired. In addition to the mechanical aspect of writing, these individuals may have difficulty transferring thoughts onto the page. They might make errors in spelling, grammar, or punctuation, or they may use poor syntax. This is called a written language disability.

THE LEARNING DISABILITY PROFILE

The learning process is complex. This simple processing model for describing specific types of learning disabilities attempts to make the process understandable. Each individual with a learning disability will have a profile of learning abilities and disabilities. There is no one pattern of learning disabilities. Thus each student must be evaluated and understood individually.

By using the learning disabilities processing model, the clinician can ask questions that will suggest the possibility that the child or adolescent being evaluated has such a disability. If a learning disability is suspected, formal psychoeducational testing can clarify whether or not it exists. Initial questions might be general. Does the child like school? What types of work are easiest? Hardest? Is class work usually completed? What about homework? Specific questions can then be focused on basic skills and later on other skills needed in learning.

- Reading:
  —Do you like to read or do you have to read?
  —How well do you read?
  —Is it easier to read out loud or silently?
  —Do you guess at unfamiliar words or sound them out?
  —When you read, do you make mistakes like skipping lines or reading the same line twice? (suggesting a visual figure-ground problem)
  —Do you find that you can read the words, but that you do not always understand what you have read? (suggesting a reading comprehension problem)
  —Do you find that you can read each page, but by the time you finish the chapter or book you have forgotten what you have read? (suggesting a visual short-term memory problem)
- Writing:
  —How is your handwriting?
  —Does your hand get tired when you write? (suggesting a fine motor problem)
  —Do you find that you cannot write as fast as you are thinking? If so, do you sometimes overlap words because you are thinking of the next word but still writing the first word? (suggesting a fine motor problem)
  —Can you copy things off of the blackboard fast enough? Can you take notes in class fast enough? (suggesting a fine motor problem)
  —How is your spelling? grammar? punctuation? If poor, the examiner should ask for a sample. (suggesting a written language problem)
- Math:
  —Do you know your multiplication tables? Can you use them? (if not, suggesting a short-term memory or sequencing problem)
  —When you do math, do you make a lot of careless errors like write "21" when you meant to write "12," or do you mix up your columns or add

when you meant to subtract? (suggesting visual perception, sequencing, or organizational problems)

Other questions can focus on areas other than specific skills; for example, basic processing skills like sequencing, abstraction, organization, memory, and language as well as study skills and strategies.

- Sequencing:
  —When you speak or write, do you sometimes have difficulty getting everything in the right order? That is, do you start in the middle, go to the beginning, then jump to the end?
  —Can you tell me the months of the year? (Some will have difficulty doing this in the right order.) Fine, now what comes after August? (Once answered, ask how the child got the answer. Individuals with sequencing problems have to go back to January and move up.)
  —When using a dictionary, do you have trouble remembering whether the next letter is before or after the letter you are on? Do you have to go back to "a" and work your way up?
- Abstraction:
  —Do you understand jokes when your friends tell them?
  —Do you sometimes get confused when people seem to say one thing yet they tell you they meant something else?
- Organization:
  —What does your notebook look like? Is it a mess with papers in the wrong place or falling out?
  —What about your desk? Locker? Is your room at home always a mess?
  —Do you have difficulty organizing your thoughts or the information you are learning?
  —Do you have trouble taking in a lot of information and putting it together into a concept you can use?
  —Do you find that you can read a chapter and answer the questions at the end of the chapter, but that you are still not sure what the chapter is about?
  —Do you lose things? Forget things? Do your homework but somehow forget to turn it in?
  —Do you have trouble planning your time so that everything gets done on time?
- Memory:
  —Do you find that you can learn something at night and then go to school the next day and realize that you have forgotten what you learned?
  —When talking, do you sometimes know what you want to say, but halfway through you forget what you are saying? If this happens, do you have to

cover up by saying something like, "Oh, forget it" or "It's not important?"

- Language:
  - —When the teacher is speaking in class, do you have trouble understanding or keeping up? (suggesting a receptive language problem)
  - —Do you sometimes misunderstand people and thus give the wrong answer? (suggesting a receptive language problem)
  - —When people are talking, do you find that you have to concentrate so hard on what they are saying that you sometimes fall behind and have to skip quickly to what they are saying now to keep up? (suggesting a receptive language problem)
  - —When the teacher speaks a lot in class, do you get lost and have trouble following? (suggesting a receptive language problem)
  - —Do you sometimes have trouble organizing your thoughts when you are speaking? (suggestive of an expressive language problem)
  - —Do you sometimes know what you want to say before you start to speak but find that the wrong words come out or you can't find the word you want? (suggestive of an expressive language problem)
- Study Skills and Strategies:
  - —Are you good at organizing your homework or studying for exams so that it is done correctly without an excess of time?
  - —Do you find that the way you studied for a test covered the right materials so that you were prepared?
  - —Do you know the best way for you to learn each subject area?

SYMPTOMS SUGGESTING ATTENTION DEFICIT HYPERACTIVITY DISORDER

A child or adolescent with attention deficit hyperactivity disorder (ADHD) may be hyperactive, distractible, and/or impulsive. The clinical history should be obtained from parents, child or adolescent, and teachers. Such an account should clarify first if one or more of these behaviors is present. Since anxiety, depression, and learning disabilities might result in the same behaviors, the evidence needed to suspect ADHD is that the history of these behaviors is both chronic and pervasive (Silver, 1992). That is, the behaviors have been there throughout the individual's life and the behaviors are observed by everyone who interacts with the individual.

Again, appropriate questions help clarify which

of the behaviors are present. Examples of questions to ask include

- Hyperactivity:
  - —Would anyone describe you as fidgety? That is, is it hard for you to sit still without tapping your fingers or playing with something? Do you wiggle in your chair? Do you find that it is hard to sit without having to get up and down a lot?
- Distractibility:
  - —Are you able to stay on task when you want to? If not, what seems to distract you? For example, when you are trying to work in class or do your homework, what distracts you? (Explore if the distractions are primarily sounds or movements/ visual stimuli.)
  - —If you are working in class and the teacher is whispering to another child, or if someone is walking in the hall, does that distract you?
  - —If you are working in class are you distracted by things seen out the window or pictures or people moving?
- Impulsivity:
  - —Would anyone see you as not being able to think before you talk or think before you act? For example, do you interrupt the teacher or parents? Do you call out without raising your hand? Do you get into trouble because you do not stop to think before you do things?

BEHAVIORAL ASSESSMENT OF THE CHILD OR ADOLESCENT

During the psychiatric evaluation, the principle informant is the child or adolescent. In a behavioral assessment, however, the principle informants are the significant others who are directly associated with the youngster's academic activities. Moreover, in a behavioral assessment, information from parents, teachers, and other school personnel is particularly critical (Ostrander and Silver, 1993).

Initially the purpose of this assessment is to identify the immediate environmental factors that may contribute to academic difficulty. The essential focus of a behavioral assessment is a detailed understanding of the functional relationship between a child's academic difficulties and environmental influences. This requires interviews with both the parents and the child plus information from teachers and other school personnel obtained by interviews, telephone calls, and/or rating scales.

Initially, the mission of these interviews should be to identify the behaviors that are most central to the academic failure. For some children, this could reflect the associated features of ADHD or of a learning disability. In others, the targeted behaviors might reflect noncompliance or oppositionality that extends to the academic domain and involves task avoidance or refusal (Ostrander and Silver, 1993).

After the targeted behaviors are identified, it is important to determine how environmental considerations affect these behaviors. Particular attention should be directed to understanding the antecedents (the conditions under which the problem occurs) and consequences (how parents, teachers, or peers respond to the behaviors). With children or adolescents who have a learning disability, one is likely to discover that particular subject areas or learning situations are frequent antecedents for the targeted behavior. For example, the child may complete math assignments quickly and accurately while having significant difficulty with reading assignments. For oppositional children or adolescents, the academic noncompliance may be inadvertently reinforced by teachers or parents. For example, as punishment, the teacher or parent may require the child to stay in from recess, when in fact the child enjoys the extra teacher attention. Moreover, oppositional children will likely display this negativistic tendency in situations that are unrelated to the academic enterprise.

In addition to understanding those environmental influences that may impact upon learning, the behavioral assessment can also determine the parameters of the targeted behavior. Through interviews and behavioral recording, the frequency, intensity, and duration of the targeted behavior can be recorded. In the process, a baseline is established. Baseline data not only allow for determining the relative effectiveness of subsequent interventions, but can also demonstrate how variations in the problematic behavior affect academic functioning. For example, one might determine that the rate of completing math homework from week to week is related to a similar variability in weekly test performance on math tests. By understanding the functional linkages between academic failure and specific targeted behaviors (such as task avoidance or noncompliance) the clinician can identify specific behaviors that can be changed and/or modified.

In essence, the focus of the behavioral assessment is to identify specific environmental influences that are central to academic failure. From this analysis, specific behavioral interventions can be targeted to alter those environmental influences that contribute to academic difficulties.

MEDICAL ISSUES

Relevant medical history is obtained from the family physician as well as from the parents. Current information on the child's physical status can also be obtained from the family physician.

The clinician notes relevant history and reflects on possible relationships to the presenting problems. For example, a history of frequent middle ear infections in infancy and early childhood, especially when associated with effusion, may delay the attainment of speech milestones. It can then be suspected as a contributing factor in some types of language delay. A history of febrile seizures or of a head injury might raise the question of organicity and its possible impact on academic difficulties.

Current chronic conditions such as diabetes, arthritis, or asthma may result in the child or adolescent being on medications that interfere with learning. In addition, these individuals may miss many days of school, a factor that may contribute to the presenting difficulties.

The Psychoeducational Evaluation

The psychoeducational evaluation can serve several purposes. At its most basic level, the assessment can provide an objective index of a child's intellectual abilities and academic capabilities.

This evaluation should include a formal assessment of perception, reasoning, comprehension, language, attention, memory, and retrieval (Satler, 1988). There should be a global measure of intelligence that reflects a range of verbal and nonverbal cognitive components. A comprehensive psychological assessment should include measures of academic functioning. Depending on the nature of the academic difficulty, these assessments should include evaluations of written expression, basic reading skills, reading comprehension, math calculation, and math reasoning. These, in turn, should be supplemented by measures of oral expression and listening comprehension (Satler, 1988). Additionally, assessment of behavioral and emotional functioning should be included as part of the evaluation.

With these data in hand the clinician should be aware of focal or generalized deficits in intellectual or academic functioning. These intellectual or academic characteristics should then be compared to the reason for referral. For example, immediate memory or visual-spatial deficits have been linked to respective difficulties in phonic analysis and math computation. In other instances, the child or adolescent may exhibit global deficits in intellectual, academic, and/or adaptive functioning, characteristics associated with a diagnosis of mental retardation.

From this information the clinician can determine the degree to which causal linkages can be established between the child's learning style and the reason for referral. If causal linkages between cognitive style and the reason for referral appear to be direct, for example, the assessment data show the child to be of at least average intelligence but to have learning disabilities, it might be concluded that the academic difficulties are due to the learning disability. If the causal linkages are less direct and cannot primarily be explained by intellectual or cognitive considerations, the clinician would have to look for other explanations for the difficulties.

In the case of a child with mental retardation, the psychoeducational assessment can supplement other studies of cognitive functioning. The data may provide an objective assessment of strengths and adaptive functioning.

The psychoeducational evaluation will also identify specific global or cognitive and academic strengths and weaknesses. Children who manifest academic and intellectual abilities that are uniformly within the average range do not typically experience academic problems. When the psychoeducational assessment yields such unremarkable findings, one must consider alternative explanations for the academic difficulties, such as family, school, or cultural considerations (Ostrander, 1983). If the child or adolescent manifests uniformly superior intellectual and academic functioning, the clinician must consider the possibility that the student is experiencing transitory or chronic underachievement due to a lack of stimulation and possible boredom.

The child or adolescent who displays uniformly low-average scores (IQ scores ranging from 70 to 85) will likely experience difficulty in school (Satler, 1988). In schools that have a social and cultural climate that particularly values academic and intellectual accomplishments, the significance of relatively modest intellectual functioning may become exaggerated.

Children and adolescents with low-average intellectual and academic functioning pose a particular challenge for the clinician. Such individuals do not exhibit the global or specific intellectual or academic deficits that would make them eligible for special education services. Their IQ scores may range from 71 to 84. Under school guidelines, the student must have an IQ of 70 or lower to be eligible for mental retardation services, and must have an IQ of 85 or higher to be eligible for services under the category, learning disability. Nonetheless, these youngsters clearly need some type of special help and accommodations. In such instances, the problem is often thought to be related to family, child, or environmental issues. Parents may blame the school for not identifying the child as having a learning disability. The administrator may blame the classroom teacher for not providing an appropriate program for the student. The teacher, feeling overwhelmed by the competing needs of 25 to 30 other children, may blame either the parent for not providing adequate support or the child for not trying. In fact, such finger-pointing serves to blame the victim of a dubious and unresponsive system (Reschly & Gresham, 1982).

In other instances, the psychoeducational assessment may clarify global or specific deficits in cognitive functioning. It may indicate that a child or adolescent has a specific learning disability. Typically this is determined by finding a "significant" discrepancy between intellectual ability and academic performance. While some type of a discrepancy formula is the most commonly used way of identifying individuals with a learning disability (Silver & Hagin, 1993), it is by no means the only method (Reynolds, 1990). For example, an assessment which documents a specific processing deficit may be used to justify a diagnosis of a learning disability.

Assessment of the Family

It is important to assess each adult and each child or adolescent, as well as the couple and the family as a whole. Is each individual (the couple as parents as well as marital partners) and the family functional or dysfunctional? If anyone or part of this system is dysfunctional, is the stress from this problem impacting on the individual who is academically underachieving, possibly causing the school difficulties? Or are the academic difficulties and the resulting stresses on the couple and family causing the difficulties (Silver, 1993c). [Family history and its significance is covered elsewhere (see Chapters II F and II H-4) and will not be discussed here.]

THE INDIVIDUAL ADULT

Where children or adolescents have a learning disability and/or ADHD, a similar familial pattern is present in about 40% of the cases. Thus it is important to learn if either parent had academic or behavioral difficulties and whether these problems still exist. A detailed family history might reveal not only that a particular parent had and still has a learning disability and/or ADHD, but that he has siblings, nephews, nieces, or cousins with the same problems.

If a parent has a psychiatric disorder, it is relevant to clarify how this disorder affects other family members. Might this clarify the academic difficulties of the identified patient? Again, it is possible that the parent's emotional difficulties are secondary to having a child or adolescent with an academic difficulty and to the resulting frustrations and failures experienced by the individual and by the parents.

THE COUPLE

It is important to determine whether the parents share the same concerns about their child being evaluated. Do they agree on parenting and discipline styles? Is one parent more understanding and permissive while the other is more firm

and strict? Is one more informed of the academic difficulties and one less informed or avoiding any awareness or acceptance of the problems?

Is there evidence of marital distress? As with emotional problems, it is important to clarify if these difficulties are primary or secondary. Is the marital dysfunction causing stress that might be contributing to the child's academic difficulties, or are the academic difficulties causing stress with a parent or both parents, resulting in the marital problems? Possibly both issues are relevant.

SIBLINGS

Is there stress between the siblings, resulting in conflict and fighting or in competitiveness and jealousy? Why does this problem exist? Could the family conflicts be causing the academic difficulties? Or might the stress or the extra time needed with the child or adolescent with academic difficulties be causing the family difficulties and sibling conflicts? It is evident that the individual with ADHD who has not been diagnosed can cause significant difficulties within a family.

Evaluation of the Environment and Culture

ASSESSMENT OF THE SCHOOL AND COMMUNITY

As is true for other child or adolescent disorders, academic difficulties can evolve from a complex environmental context. Learning problems tend to be attributed to cognitive or behavioral problems within the individual; however, environmental factors involving the school and/or community can also influence such difficulties. For the practitioner, general conclusions concerning the community's social, cultural, and institutional structures typically evolve over time in the process of conducting one's practice. Interviews with teachers and other school personnel are critical aspects of this enterprise (parental permission for such contacts is essential).

The interview with the teacher can be very informative. It is important to solicit the teacher's perceptions concerning the child or adolescent. In order to clarify the nature of the specific areas of strength and weakness, the clinician should request examples of the child's work which would illustrate both accomplishments and difficulties. A chronology of the academic problems should be examined. Additionally, the teacher should be encouraged to offer her own ideas concerning the causes of the problem. Teachers are particularly valuable in clarifying social problems, deficits, and disruptive behavioral disorders. These perceptions may be supplemented by rating scales to determine the child's relative capabilities in critical aspects of cognitive processing and behavioral functioning (Ostrander, 1993).

The clinician should also review the efforts that have been undertaken to address the academic problems. For example, has the teacher attempted to vary the instructional approach to accommodate the child? Is an incentive program in place? Has the child been considered for retention, suspension, or expulsion? Has the teacher consulted with other specialists concerning the problems (e.g., school psychologist, special education consultant)? The clinician should determine the nature of the classroom (e.g., open or traditional), curriculum (e.g., emphasizes phonics, language experience approaches, or other approaches), and teaching style. The teacher can provide valuable information concerning alternative services available to the child, such as special education, speech/language, tutoring, or vocational services. The range of services can be compared to legislative directives and community standards (Ostrander, 1993).

In addition to information concerning the school structure, the clinician should inquire concerning the social and cultural composition of the community. The teacher can provide some insight concerning the abilities and characteristics of the child when compared to community standards. The teacher can also offer an assessment of the child's social relationships and how they might affect the child's academic characteristics.

In some instances the information provided by the teacher can be supplemented by data offered by key decision makers within the school. In many instances, critical information can be gleaned by consulting with the principal, school psychologist, counselor, nurse, or social worker. Throughout interviews with school personnel, the clinician should be sensitive to any bias and attitudes individuals have concerning the educational enterprise. For example, does the teacher believe that it is the responsibility of the child to adapt to the instructional style of the teacher, or does the teacher believe in altering the mode of instruction to conform to the individual students' learning style? Has the teacher had experience in dealing with children who have similar problems? If so, what has been the typical outcome? As a general rule, teachers who have had a measure of success in the past with a particular type of child, or who have a history of making adaptations, are more responsive to suggestions and new ideas. In contrast, teachers who tend to be more restrictive or rigid in their approach to teaching tend to be less responsive to alternative ways of intervening with a given child. There should be an appraisal of the teacher's knowledge of the particular psychiatric, neurological, medical, and environmental factors that may be impinging on the child (Ostrander, 1993).

If the teacher's lack of skill, limited knowledge, or biased perceptions compromise his ability to deal effectively with a particular child's needs, it is important to determine if the teacher is aware of this, and, if so, if the teacher has access to appropriate institutional supports (e.g., consultants, inservice training). If the appropriate institutional resources are not available, are there alternative programs, teachers, or classroom settings where such resources are available? For example, if it is likely that a student will require a self-contained special education setting, are there such arrangements in place, and what are the possible roadblocks to assessing such services?

Reaching Conclusions Following the Assessment

By following each line of exploration—the child or adolescent, the family, and the environment and cultural issues—the clinician should be able to reach conclusions. By evaluating possibilities, the clinician should be able to establish the probable cause of the academic difficulties. With this understanding and/or diagnosis, an intervention strategy and treatment plan can be developed.

REFERENCES

Ostrander, R. (1993). Clinical observations suggesting a learning disability. *Child and Adolescent Psychiatric Clinics of North America.* Philadelphia: W. B. Saunders.

Ostrander, R., & Silver, L. B. (1993). Psychological interventions and therapies for children and adolescents with learning disabilities. *Child and Adolescent Psychiatric Clinics of North America,* Philadelphia: W. B. Saunders.

Reynolds, C. R. (1990). Conceptual and technical problems in learning disability diagnosis. In C. R. Reynolds & R. W. Kamkphaus (Eds.), *Handbook of psychological and educational assessment of children: Intelligence and achievement.* New York: Guilford Press.

Sattler, J. (1988). *Assessment of children.* San Diego: Author. Sattler,

Silver, A., & Hagin, R. (1993a). The educational diagnostic process. *Child and Adolescent Psychiatric*

Clinics of North America. Philadelphia: W. B. Saunders.

Silver, L. B. (1981). The relationship between learning disabilities, hyperactivity, distractibility, and behavioral problems. *Journal of the American Academy of Child Psychiatry, 20,* 385–397.

Silver, L. B. (1992). *Attention-deficit hyperactivity disorder. A clinical guide to diagnosis and treatment.* Washington, DC: American Psychiatric Press.

Silver, L. B. (1993b). Introduction and overview to the clinical concepts of learning disabilities. *Child and Adolescent Psychiatric Clinics of North America.* Philadelphia: W. B. Saunders.

Silver, L. B. (1993c). The secondary emotional, social, and family problems found with children and adolescents with learning disabilities. *Child and Adolescent Psychiatric Clinics of North America.* Philadelphia: W. B. Saunders.

70 / Observation, Interview, and Mental Status Assessment (OIM): Physically Ill

Lucienne A. Cahen and Michael S. Jellinek

Children and adolescents who face a serious, acute illness or live with a chronic health condition are at increased risk for emotional distress, behavioral dysfunction, and/or academic difficulties (Cadman, Boyle, Szatmari, & Offord, 1987; Gortmaker, Walker, Weitzman, & Sobol, 1990; Nolan & Pless, 1986; Perrin & MacLean, 1988b; Pless & Roghmann, 1971; Stoddard, Norman, Murphy, & Beardslee, 1989). Advances in intensive life support and in the management of prematurity, congenital heart disease, leukemia, and cystic fibrosis have resulted in a generation of children who previously would have died, but who now contend with the complications of their disease or disability. New populations of children are emerging, including those afflicted with human immunodeficiency virus (HIV) or who have undergone organ transplantation. When such children are members of low-income families, they are at increased risk for serious health problems (Starfield, 1991) and bear the double burden of poverty and illness.

These extraordinary changes and demands are occurring at a time when the traditional family unit is being redefined, as reflected in the high prevalence of divorce, single parents, teenage mothers, blended families, and families in which both parents work. These and other family stressors have a profound effect on the care and well-being of the child with either an acute or long-term medical condition (Jellinek and Herzog, 1990).

Such formidable quantitative and qualitative changes present new challenges to the child, family, pediatrician, and mental health clinician. Although varied in the sophistication of their medical knowledge, mental health clinicians contribute a unique expertise in psychodynamics, development, and systems that is applicable and invaluable to medically ill children and their caregivers.

The Characteristic Features of Medical Conditions

The clinician who works with medically ill children and their families should have a basic understanding of the medical principles involved. All children must cope with a series of developmental tasks; in addition, however, the physically impaired child must master his illness or disability. Each illness has its own range of severity, predictability, control, comprehensibility, and degree of disruption in daily life, all of which are subject to change over time and likely to be perceived differently as the child develops. Compliance with care, for example, is affected by multiple variables, including the child's age, psychosocial characteristics, and family environment (Hauser et al., 1990; Jacobson et al., 1990). Although some diseases allow for more control than others (e.g., diabetes in contrast to cancer), the individual responses to the same process differ enormously. Such complexity may partially explain the difficulty of defining characteristic profiles of children with a disease (e.g., the "typical" asthmatic) and predicting the level of psychosocial dysfunction (Fritz, Williams, & Amylon, 1988). If the child is dying or is at risk for death, the intensity of affect and concern is often dramatic; however, many of the issues and approaches are identical to those encountered in any child with a medical condition. Rather than needing to master a fixed constellation of facts for each disease, the clinician can explore the following principles.

ADJUSTMENT TO THE DIAGNOSIS

From the moment a medical condition is suspected and diagnosed, hopes and fears about the future become a daily concern. Whether the condition is mild or severe, the family must cope with the loss of "wellness" and undergo a period of shock, anger, and denial. An uncertain, labile course or prognosis is especially stressful. Initially the threat of death or disability overshadows other considerations. Hope often depends on the predicted "life span" of the condition, such as those which are permanent but stable (e.g., congenital deformities), are likely to resolve (e.g., trauma),

may resolve intermittently or permanently (e.g., asthma), substantially shorten life span (e.g., cystic fibrosis), or are fatal (e.g., AIDS). As the family members adjust to living with a chronic condition, their focus shifts to maintaining as normal a life as possible. Since both the child's development and the fluctuations of the disease process may affect the quality of life, the anticipated impact must be reassessed and discussed repeatedly over time.

MEDICAL VULNERABILITY

The contrast between apparent wellness and a seemingly abrupt transformation into severe illness and/or death is the hallmark of certain conditions, such as seizures (Ziegler, 1981), asthma, or cardiac arrhythmias. These children seem to walk a tightrope every day, and their parents must observe them, never knowing if or when equilibrium will be lost. Thus a decision to go for a swim in the ocean or to take a vacation evokes faith, fear, denial, and anxiety, and requires a balance between promoting normality and being overprotective.

ALTERATIONS OF MENTAL STATUS

The intangible, fluctuating quality of changes in personality and cognitive function is particularly frightening and frustrating. Seizures are anxiety provoking because of their unpredictability, appearance, and potential for injury to the child. Sometimes the alterations are acute, as when mood changes erupt because of steroids; at other times, long-term deterioration is an issue, such as happens following cranial irradiation or chemotherapy. The child may be depressed, confused, and/or terrified. The physician must consider an extensive differential diagnosis; in addition to emotional factors, this would include metabolic abnormalities, infection, tumor, trauma, or medication effects. Faced with a child who alternates between his usual self and a different persona, caregivers need to relate to and discipline him, while concomitantly attempting to distinguish between medical and behavioral factors.

IMPACT ON LIFESTYLE

Despite sometimes heroic efforts to blend into the normal world, many children with medical conditions are constantly reminded of their differences. Medical needs dominate daily routines, mobility, choice, and time, and engender conflicts involving dependence and control. Life is complicated by the constraints of a wheelchair, the need to change a colostomy bag, or the anguish of waiting for the call that a donor organ is available (Slater, 1994). Each encounter with food is a confrontation for the diabetic child, who wishes for true freedom of choice. The "extracurricular activity" of dialysis leaves the child with no time to participate in the school play. When pain intrudes, interests and activities become luxuries relative to attaining relief. Illness and treatment can interfere with both school attendance and performance (Weitzman, 1984).

INTERPERSONAL EXPERIENCES

Many children and families live with the frequently unpredictable risk of being embarrassed, intruded upon, or limited by a medical condition. From infancy to adolescence, they are sensitized by the fear, disdain, or pity their condition elicits. Whether a child was born with a physical deformity (Nolan & Pless, 1986) or has adjusted to an "invisible" condition, he will continue to be affected as his world expands. Experiences with peers are limited for the blind child who cannot play videogames or for the deaf adolescent at a punk rock concert. HIV-infected children encounter myriad prejudices which engender significant emotional and pragmatic repercussions (Krener & Miller, 1989; Stuber, 1990). Conversely, the child may use his illness to manipulate others. Therefore an assessment of "severity" must include others' responses, particularly those of parents, both as they subjectively perceive the child's condition and as their reaction influences the child and family.

Physical Appearance: Congenital deformities, burns (Bernstein, Breslau, & Graham, 1988), amputations, dermatologic disorders (Rauch & Jellinek, 1989) and other such "visible" conditions are bound to elicit interpersonal reactions, which may be more or less concealed. Ambiguous genitalia evoke confusion about the child's basic sexual identity. As the child grows older, particularly during adolescence, his inner concerns may conjure up fantasies of others' responses. However, when an adolescent asks, "Who is going to want to kiss someone with a tracheotomy," the answer must address both the likely reality of the social responses as well as his personal anxiety.

Invisible Conditions: "Invisible" conditions such as diabetes, epilepsy, or gastrointestinal or metabolic disorders at once support the child's denial, yet create tension as he attempts to hide the underlying flaw. Youngsters with inflammatory bowel disease live with the risk of being humiliated if they have uncontrolled diarrhea. There may be a credibility gap until others witness an event, such as a seizure. The child then retreats into a tenuous guise of normalcy, awaiting the next disclosure of his secret.

Developmental Discrepancies: Since most of us rely on visible cues, it is understandable that children with growth or sexual developmental abnormalities are treated according to their external physical characteristics. Consequently, children with short stature tend to be treated as though they are younger, while those with tall stature are often expected to be more mature than their chronological age. Social pressures are exerted on youngsters with precocious or delayed puberty. In fact, the only abnormality may be that their physical or sexual development is temporally "out of synch" with their intellectual, emotional, and social skills. However, these discrepancies can impede the development of self-esteem and age-appropriate behaviors, and are particularly confusing and painful during adolescence.

RELATIONSHIPS WITH CAREGIVERS

Ironically, in their attempt to care for ill children, health care professionals and parents are obliged, directly or indirectly, to contribute to morbidity. As children struggle with disease, they feel angry or betrayed by their treatment. The physician, held in high regard as healer and savior, joins the ranks of the enemy as he inflicts pain or fails to provide a cure. The hemophiliac youngster may learn that the very transfusions that kept him alive, in reality, harbored a deadly virus. The adolescent with an osteogenic sarcoma may have to sacrifice his leg to obtain the only possible cure. Rage against the disease and its treatment understandably may spread to the professional caregivers upon whom the child and family are dependant. Maintaining a therapeutic alliance requires that caregivers both validate the anger and deal with the aggression, as well as attend to their own feelings of anger, guilt, frustration, and sadness (Geist, 1979; Jellinek, Todres, Catlin & Cassem, 1993).

Initial Contact

Although a psychological evaluation may be requested by parents, pediatricians, or subspecialists, the impetus may also emanate from school, church, camp, etc. Assessment may be sought at the time certain conditions are diagnosed (e.g., cancer, diabetes, cystic fibrosis, AIDS, or organ failure requiring transplantation). Most nonemergent referrals arise from five areas of concern:

- Behavioral dysfunction (e.g., noncompliance with medical care, acting out, or poor school performance)
- Affective changes (e.g., anxiety, depression)
- Family conflicts
- Differentiation of organic versus psychological etiologies
- Troublesome interactions with medical providers

The presence of a medical condition, especially if chronic or life threatening, frequently amplifies and distorts what might otherwise be a developmentally appropriate albeit bothersome behavioral deviation, and lowers the threshold for referral. How does a preschool teacher know whether to put a screaming diabetic toddler with a "time-out" or rescue him from hypoglycemia with orange juice? A 10-year-old with severe asthma who refuses to take medication needs help to assume more responsibility. When an adolescent hemophiliac wants to perform dirt bike stunts with his pals, how should his parents respond? The consequences of poor judgment and oppositional behavior range from inconvenient to disabling to potentially life threatening. Pressured by health and safety concerns, the clinician frequently needs to take an active approach within a short time frame, while maintaining psychodynamic and longer-term developmental perspectives.

Managed care approaches such as critical pathways, shift towards outpatient care, and shortened lengths of stay have all had an effect on consultation. Consultants must be especially responsive and often initiate or bridge the consultation evaluation between the short initial workup in the hospital and then follow up in outpatient settings, preferably pediatric. Child psychiatrists have an opportunity to influence critical pathways based on clinical wisdom and research findings regarding the impact of chronic disease on children and their families. Given the highly focused nature and intensity of inpatient care and the pace of outpatient practice, brief questionnaires designed to screen for psychosocial functioning can often be helpful in recognizing which children may benefit from further pediatric assessment and potentially require a consultation (Lloyd, Jellinek, Little, Murphy, & Pagano, 1995; Jellinek, Little, Murphy, & Pagano, 1995).

Assessment

Particularly during the initial interview, the clinician can facilitate communication by posing questions concerning the child's medical condition and expected course. Such an invitation to a familiar narrative offers the patient and family an opportunity to demonstrate their knowledge and competence and may feel safer to them than direct queries about emotions. To assess their perspectives, the clinician should have an understanding of the medical facts, preferably from the patient's treating physician. Discrepancies in accuracy arise from several sources. They can stem from the child or family having been overwhelmed and unable to integrate information, be illustrative of characteristic defensive postures, or reflect poor communication between the physician and family. They can also indicate pivotal issues to pursue. The intensity of the patient's and family's affect (or lack thereof) is also a useful barometer, especially when compared with the reality of the child's condition and how the family members coped with previous pressures and losses.

The clinician may be asked to generate a formulation and recommendations after only one meeting. A rapid assessment of relevant biological, developmental, medical, psychological, and social factors will provide a framework and lead to a therapeutic plan (see Table 70.1). The interview should be constructed to create an alliance, elicit

TABLE 70.1

Factors to Consider in the Assessment of the Patient and Family

BIOLOGICAL AND DEVELOPMENTAL
Biological contributions (physical characteristics, physiological response to pain/anxiety, intelligence, genetically transmitted disease)
Temperament (adaptability, responsiveness, persistence, mood)
Family environment (support, organization, cohesion, expressiveness, conflict)
Developmental stage of the child (cognitive, emotional)
Developmental stage of the family
Phase of response to the condition (shock, anger, sadness, denial, guilt, grief, integration)
MEDICAL
Onset (congenital, acquired)
Severity and limitations incurred (acute, chronic, life threatening; change over time)
Past losses and encounters with illness or death (by the patient or family)
Understanding, fantasies, and fears versus reality of the disease
Expectations about the future; loss of previous hopes
PSYCHOLOGICAL
Coping and defense mechanisms (intellectualization, obsession, fantasy, isolation, denial, locus of control)
Capacity for judgment and insight
Coexisting psychiatric disorder (anxiety, depression)
SOCIAL
Cultural, religious influences
Socioeconomic status
Additional stressors
Supports (family, friends, school, groups, VNA, respite care)

---

complex information, answer questions, and provide a therapeutic intervention. Concepts and vocabulary must be adapted to the child's and family's cognitive capacities. The following questions are designed to meet such challenges, while inviting the patient and/or family members to communicate the uniqueness of their experiences (Jelinek, Catlin, Todres, & Cassem, 1992).

- What is their understanding of the condition? What may have contributed to the child developing the condition? (In addition to eliciting factual information, these questions probe for fantasy, magical thinking, and guilt.)
- What's the worst thing about having the condition? If they could change one thing, what would it be? What do they worry about most? (The responses to these questions may be surprising, but convey the personal meaning of the condition and indicate directions of treatment.)
- How have things changed at home since the illness began (or worsened)? How are the siblings doing? How are the parents getting along? How do they cope with the time and financial demands of the illness? (Descriptions of both interpersonal and pragmatic aspects of everyday life reveal both the level of function and the available resources.)
- Has anything good come about as a result of this

condition? Who or what helps the most? (Even a minor example of a capacity to perceive value and accept support can be reinforced by the clinician during initial and subsequent contacts.)

- Have they ever had to face anything like this before? How did they deal with it? How did it turn out? (These questions may stir memories from the past, reveal value judgments of the current and previous dilemmas, provide clues to defenses, and serve as the best predictor of current and future coping.)
- How often are they angry or sad about the illness? (By assuming they indeed are angry or sad, affect is both elicited and validated.)

The objective severity of and limitations imposed by a chronic disease do not necessarily predict the degree of distress that the patient and family experience (Perrin & MacLean, 1988a). Previous encounters with loss, handicaps, illness, or death will influence responses to the current strife, particularly if past experiences were traumatic or occurred at a developmental age that resonates with the child's current experience. A family's "overreaction" to an uncomplicated leg fracture could well be explained by the fact that the adolescent patient's college education is dependent on a football scholarship, or that his grandfather required a leg amputation. As the child and family relate concrete examples of how the condition has invaded their everyday lives, transformed dreams into nightmares, and marred visions of the future, the clinician must respond to their appeal for relief, whether they are contending with a terminal brain tumor or controllable asthma.

Cultural or religious practices and beliefs can affect the child's care directly, particularly when unusual approaches engender suspicion and hostility in medical personnel. If a Native American family insists that a shaman perform healing rituals on behalf of their ill child, the clinician may actively or unconsciously communicate disapproval. However, if he educates himself about the culture and maintains a supportive role, he will minimize conflict, while respecting and optimizing the comfort offered by the family's beliefs.

Anticipation of Responses to the Medical Condition

Illness in a child or adolescent elicits intense, complicated, and diverse responses in the patient, family members, friends, and caregivers (Drotar & Bush, 1985). All of these influence the child's psychological state and frequently the course of the medical condition. In order to assess and treat the patient effectively, the clinician must consider the experience the illness evokes from multiple perspectives.

THE CHILD

The child's capacity to understand concepts of body functioning and illness parallels cognitive development in other areas (Cerreto & Travis, 1984; Perrin & Gerrity, 1981). However, it turns out that when compared with healthy, comparably aged peers, children with certain chronic conditions have unexpectedly been found to have similar understandings of body functioning and less sophisticated concepts about illness causality (Perrin, Sayer, & Willett, 1991). Given the propensity for regression in the face of illness (Freud,

1952), when the condition imposes new demands, the same child may function at a less mature developmental level (e.g., a 7 year old develops enuresis when hospitalized).

Although it is very difficult to distinguish between neurobiological and emotional etiologies, it is likely that the ill newborn or young infant who has experienced pain, hunger, or disruption of contact with a primary caretaker will incur physiological consequences. Sensory overload or deprivation may disrupt sleep or feeding. Temperamental difficulties can be heightened and complicate attachment. Blind infants are at risk for delays in prehension, gross motor, and language development, as well as for impaired object relations and body and self-image (Fraiberg, 1977). In response to the troubled infant, caretakers may become distant, anxious, or overprotective, setting the tone of their long-term relationship.

The egocentric toddler strives for mobility, autonomy, and control, and tends to interpret pain or deprivation as punishment. When a child with thrombocytopenia jumps off a chair, he may be exploring his world and abilities in an age-appropriate way, not necessarily manifesting oppositional behavior or poor judgment. Struggles around food are intensified if the child has diabetes or must gain weight to avoid hyperalimentation. How does a 2-year-old diabetic child experience his parents giving him an injection before two of his meals, or sticking his finger when he is feeling frustrated and angry? When the clinician reframes a child's behavior for the caregivers as developmentally appropriate and offers management suggestions, frustration and irritation can be alleviated.

Although the preschool child begins to tolerate longer separations, comprehends some explanations of medical procedures, and expresses himself through words and play, cognitive capacities are still limited. He may notice that the word diabetes sounds like "die" (Norman, 1987) or project anxiety-laden fantasies into explanations or onto overheard comments. Fantasy and magical thinking may be self-protective or, conversely, confirm for him that his illness is a punishment. Body integrity is of critical importance. Surgical interventions may be experienced as attacks or mutilation. Clinical experience and psychoanalytic theory would suggest that procedures or attention involving the genitourinary areas are particularly anxiety provoking during this developmental phase. By exploring the child's understanding and offering explanations appropriate for his cognitive capacity, more effective reassurance may be achieved.

By latency, the child should be enlisted in some of his own care, supporting his penchant for rules, order, and most importantly, control. However, as he becomes more socially aware and active, the restrictions and differences imposed by illness generate frustration and anger. Aspects of the illness or treatment which interfere with peer-related activities are especially problematic. For example, a 9 year old with cystic fibrosis might proudly organize his chest physical therapy schedule, but he may then refuse to comply when a friend sleeps overnight.

For the adolescent, conditions which interfere with emerging sexuality and the need for autonomy are particularly difficult. Illness evokes memories of losses and deprivations from the past, as well as confrontations with his present and future limitations. As a youngster enters adolescence congenital deformities which had previously been tolerated, now feel insurmountable. The "ghosts" of previous surgical procedures for hypospadias may be reawakened by the boy's new concerns about his masculinity and sexual functioning. The normal narcissism of early adolescence is threatened, particularly when cultural values reinforce doubts of self-worth, as might be experienced by a short boy or tall girl. The struggle to be "normal," despite the social and physical stigmata of a medical condition, calls forth many defenses (Fritz & Williams, 1988). Rationalization and intellectualization are embellished with the recently acquired cognitive abilities of abstract thinking. Rebellion may take the form of flagrant noncompliance with treatment. Supported by a sense of invincibility, acting out behaviors test the ill adolescent's body in a more profound and dangerous way than if he were healthy. When the ammunition includes medical illness, these attempts at separation and individuation can be life threatening. The clinician thus faces an ill adolescent with evolving characterological difficulties.

THE PARENTS

Regardless of their child's age or the stage of their child's illness, parents live with their own chronic condition: loss. From the first moment of diagnosis, independent of the severity of the illness, their image of a perfect, healthy child is shattered. Struggling to comprehend how such a thing could happen, they cannot avoid their own reflections and memories. Parents are supposed to be guardians, protectors, in charge; what did they do—or fail to do? If they did not ensure safety thus far, how will they be able to in the future? Since present loss stirs echoes of previous losses, defensive patterns emerge; this is particularly likely if the parents had previously encountered illness or death, or if they tend to employ immature defenses or experience characterological problems. Throughout the oscillations of the illness, new hopes and losses are superimposed on the old. Thus past and future are integrated and become linked to the child's condition.

As the parents grieve, their own guilt, anger, denial, and fantasies will affect others, including the ill child, spouse, other children, and caregivers (McDaniel, Hepworth, & Doherty, 1992; Sabbeth, 1984). Although the couple may unite around the illness, marital conflicts are common. If the condition is genetic, congenital, or (theoretically) could have been prevented, guilt and blame will be heightened. As parents are unable to justify the rage they feel toward their ill child and attempt to compensate for all that he (and they) must bear, routine discipline and limit setting are compromised. Loss, guilt, and the complexity of the illness may engender irrational thoughts or feelings. Did their permissiveness about candy cause the diabetes? If their child had not been in day care, he would not have meningitis. As they become sleep deprived with a child in pain, miss work, keep appointments with multiple caregivers, or struggle with unresponsive school or reimbursement systems, the pragmatic burdens of having a child with a medical illness perpetuate the cycles of guilt and anger. Thoughts of having other children need to be reexamined. Since control must be relegated to the medical caregivers, the medical community is at particular risk for being a target of the parents' displaced anger (Beresin, 1990). Denial and fantasies are necessary buffers; if they are too rigid, however, they can jeopardize or block medical treatment. Much of the clinician's contribution is to understand the nature of the parents' guilt and defenses, support their capacity to care for their children, and help them to gain perspective on their feelings.

SIBLINGS

For siblings, the experience of living with acute or chronic illness evokes complex questions and responses (Gogan & Slavin, 1981; Lobato, Faust, & Spirito, 1988; Tritt & Esses, 1988) and is influenced by multiple factors, including their developmental age, sex, birth order, and their own health. Regardless of careful adult explanations, siblings often create a personal version of the illness. They may feel guilty that it was they who caused the illness or that they are themselves not afflicted. Since another child is ill, the identification and fears of "catching" the condition are heightened. Siblings frequently are deprived, not only of adults' time, attention, and patience, but also of the ill child's, who is irritable or unable to play. Shame and embarrassment can affect social interactions. Overt frustration and anger are stifled by the expectations that they be tolerant and generous. How can they be mad at someone who is in pain? Repetitively hearing valid reasons for others being occupied, they may develop somatic symptoms, withdraw, or become oppositional or accident prone. When a younger sibling's accomplishments surpass those of the ill child, roles reverse and both children's identities are altered. If siblings are affected by the same illness, their fears, fantasies, and identification may be intensified, although the shared experience may ease their isolation. Although they are at risk for becoming overprotective and pseudomature, siblings may develop appropriate thoughtfulness, sensitivity, and empathy. By considering the sibling as part of the consultation, the clinician's attention to this family dynamic adds a critical dimension.

RELATIVES AND FRIENDS

In their response to the ill child, relatives and friends have the potential for triggering painful feelings or providing extraordinary support. Their fears, limited understanding, or sense of inadequacy can be manifested as criticism or distancing. Intergenerational conflicts become particularly heated in the arena of medical issues. Grandparents may blame the in-law's side of the family. In an attempt to protect their own children or themselves from the feelings evoked by witnessing an ill child, parents' friends may become less available. Peers are capable of concocting humiliating jokes. Conversely, when these relationships offer a sense of family and the constancy of friendship, they provide a much-needed resource, both pragmatically and emotionally.

MEMBERS OF THE COMMUNITY

Professional caregivers and parents recognize the importance of normalizing the lives of children with medical conditions and integrating them into school, groups, camp, etc. However, the people whom the youngsters encounter in the "outside world" frequently feel uncomfortable in their presence (Eiser & Town, 1987). Typically the parent is the major source of educating the adult who assumes responsibility for the child, and that parent may convey inaccurate or distorted information. It is understandable that a teacher would be terrified that a child with epilepsy might seize. A Scout leader may refuse to take a diabetic child on a camping trip. Babysitters frequently are reluctant to care for a child who has been labeled ill, even if the child functions normally. In addition to feeling inadequate to care for the ill child, the responsible adult may be unprepared to deal with the reactions of the child's peers and their parents. The ensuing apprehension may be manifested as avoidance, anger, or scapegoating. Limited knowledge, misconceptions, and fear thus unintentionally contribute to the child's sense of being different and increase his isolation.

PROFESSIONAL CAREGIVERS

When treating the medically ill child and his family, physicians, nurses, rehabilitation therapists, mental health clinicians, and other professional caregivers face particular challenges. It is difficult enough to accept the limitations of current medical knowledge and treatment, but it becomes infuriating when noncompliance or perceived incompetence adversely affects outcome. The hostile patient or family evokes personal reactions in the caregiver that can thwart alliance and jeopardize treatment. The professional's priorities may not match those of the patient, family, or another colleague. Conflicts can develop among health care providers or disciplines. Comprehensive care requires empathy, humility, introspection, judgment, consideration of ethical issues, and not least of all, a great deal of time. Success is not dramatic, but must be measured in small increments and experienced as limited victories, not necessarily by cure of the illness. However, following a child and family and aiding them to cope with seemingly insurmountable obstacles offers rewards that are indisputable and not uncommon.

Strategies for Intervention

The mental health clinician must assess and prioritize the child's need for counseling, taking into account the limitations of motivation, time, and finances for an already burdened family. Family meetings may be particularly productive. National organizations, self-help, and other groups for children, siblings, or parents can provide invaluable support and education.

The medically ill child often requires specialized resources to address his complicated needs. If psychotropic medication is indicated, given the complexity of some medical regimens, consultation with a child psychopharmacologist is advisable. Psychological testing may facilitate the differentiation between medical and psychological causes of symptoms (Heiligenstein & Jacobsen, 1988). Neuropsychological testing is helpful both to define cognitive impairments and to follow the course of a condition with serial evaluations, such as in the case of a child with head trauma, a central nervous system hemorrhage, or AIDS dementia complex. Many children benefit from the modalities practiced by behavioral medicine specialists, such as biofeedback, hypnosis, or behavioral management (Bush & Harkins, 1991; Cardona, 1994; Gardner & Olness, 1981; Russo & Varni, 1982). Educational needs can include comprehensive evaluations, specialized classes, or home tutoring. A quest for financial support or legal involvement may need to be pursued.

Although the clinician usually delegates or in part shares the responsibility of providing or advocating for services, he must nonetheless interface with other caregivers on an ongoing basis. The mental health clinician has a particular ability to address tensions among caregivers and to suggest how efforts to improve patient care can be better coordinated (DeMaso & Meyer, 1996). The following guidelines, if adhered to, will contribute to making the clinician's role effective and well utilized.

- Be available. Communication is facilitated by (1) using an answering machine or beeper, (2) returning calls rapidly, and (3) attending rounds or meetings of the medical staff.
- Recognizing that some issues may be covert, define the question(s) being asked of the clinician. A brief discussion with the referring physician can be invaluable, particularly since much of the critical information is subjective and usually not documented in the medical record.
- Learn from the experience and expertise of the referring physician. Extrapolate from knowledge of basic developmental issues to pose questions. Ask about the patient's medical and psychological course, and how this patient differs from others with similar conditions. (For example, anticipating the concerns that a 17-year-old adolescent with cystic fibrosis would have about her sexuality, reproductive capacity, and genetic status, the clinician could learn about the patient's potential for and risks of pregnancy from her subspecialist.)
- Be practical. In addition to defining goals, offer specific suggestions on how to attain them. Recommend ways the child can maximize his participation in various arenas of his life and enhance his self-esteem. (These might include that a diabetic child choose the site of his injections, utilize food exchanges so he can eat cake at a school party, alter an insulin dose so he may engage in sports safely, learn about celebrities with diabetes, or role play responses to peers' questions and taunts.)
- Avoid psychiatric jargon. Although psychodynamic terminology conveys rich meaning to other mental health professionals, and *DSM-IV* categorization may be obligatory for third-party payers, the assessment of the child's needs, developmental tasks, and functioning in daily life must be communicated in terms that are relevant to all caregivers.
- Maintain an open forum for communication. A clearly worded letter to the treating physician with copies to other involved caregivers validates their active involvement, demystifies the psychiatric process, and enhances coordination of care. Parents also benefit from a copy of such correspondence, allowing them to review the clinician's impressions and recommendations, share the information with future caregivers, and feel both respected and included.

Challenges of the Future

As medical care systems are forced to become more efficient and contain costs, they generate a flurry of activity that relegates the child with a medical condition to a lower priority. Education, support, and attention to emotional dysfunction are potentially jeopardized by the pressures to avoid hospitalization, shorten lengths of stay, and limit outpatient psychotherapy. A child may be inadequately prepared for day surgery, with an adverse psychological reaction to the procedure remaining unrecognized, while the burden of postoperative care is left to the family. In the crisis surrounding outpatient education when a child presents with newly diagnosed diabetes, it is not unusual for familial conflicts to be initially overlooked, only to be disclosed after the fourth episode of ketoacidosis. The clinician may then inherit an accumulation of problems which might have been avoided or, at least, mitigated with earlier intervention.

At a time in history when quality of life is philosophically valued but insufficiently financed, economic constraints and poverty are both engendered by and contribute to medical illness (Hobbs, Perrin, & Ireys, 1985). The consequences of societal problems such as prenatal substance abuse are already overwhelming the current health care system. While evolving societal expectations and the progressive refinement of case law continue to exert pressures or even to mandate that children with medical conditions be integrated into the community, the financial resources of school systems and social service agencies are being cut back. Although the future of managed care is uncertain, the current trend in allocation of resources is not supportive of child and adolescent services (Fuchs & Reklis, 1992). As the health care environment undergoes frequent alterations, families are forced to change their insurance coverage, and consequently physicians, thereby disrupting continuity of care. It is expensive for families to provide for a child with medical illness. The fact that many associated costs (e.g., medication, special formulas, babysitting for the ill child's siblings, parking at the hospital, loss of work time) are not reimbursed affects a family's ability to follow medical recommendations and may jeopardize the child's care.

Medical progress has only increased the need to integrate biological, psychological, and social perspectives. Much understanding is yet to be gained about the psychological risk factors and family dynamics of both familiar and emerging conditions. Mental health clinicians need to develop creative ways to educate and learn from other professional caregivers, such as participating in seminars or study groups (Schwam & Maloney, 1997) in which didactics and clinical dilemmas are shared. Clinical pathways should support the clinician's involvement in outpatient as well as inpatient arenas to maximize continuity of care. Despite significant obstacles, working with medically ill children and their caregivers provides an intimate entry into the daily experience of living with illness and an exceptional opportunity to integrate psychological, medical, and research skills for the benefit of the medically ill child and his or her family.

REFERENCES

Beresin, E. V. (1990). The difficult parent. In M. S. Jellinek & D. B. Herzog (Eds.), Psychiatric aspects of general hospital pediatrics (pp. 67–75). Chicago: Year-Book Medical Publishers.

Bernstein, N. R., Breslau, A. J., & Graham, J. A. (Eds.). (1988). *Coping strategies for burn survivors and their families*. New York: Praeger.

Bush, J. P., & Harkins, S. W. (Eds.). (1991). *Children in pain: Clinical and research issues from a developmental perspective*. New York: Springer-Verlag.

Cadman, D., Boyle, M., Szatmari, P., & Offord, D. R. (1987). Chronic illness, disability, and mental and social well-being: Findings of the Ontario child health study. *Pediatrics, 79* (5), 805–813.

Cardona, L. (1994). Behavioral approaches to pain and anxiety in the pediatric patient. In: Lewis, M. & King, R. A. (Guest Editors.) *Consultation-Liaison in Pediatrics, Child and Adolescent Psychiatric Clinics of North America, 3,* 3:449–464. Philadelphia: W. B. Saunders Company.

Cerreto, M. C., & Travis, L. B. (1984). Implications of psychological and family factors in the treatment of diabetes. *Pediatric Clinics of North America, 31* (3), 689–710.

DeMaso, D. R. & Meyer, E. C. (1996). A psychiatric consultant's survival guide to the pediatric intensive care unit. *Journal of the American Academy of Child and Adolescent Psychiatry, 34,* 10:1411–1413.

Drotar, D., & Bush, M. (1985). Mental health issues and services. In N. Hobbs & J. M. Perrin (Eds.), Issues in the care of children with chronic illness (pp. 514–550). San Francisco: Jossey-Bass.

Eiser, C., & Town, C. (1987). Teachers' concerns about chronically sick children: Implications for pediatricians. *Developmental Medicine and Child Neurology, 29,* 56–63.

Fraiberg, S. (1977). *Insights from the blind.* New York: Basic Books.

Freud, A. (1952). The role of bodily illness in the mental life of children. *Psychoanalytic Study of the Child, 7,* 69–81.

Fritz, G. K., & Williams, J. R. (1988). Issues of adolescent development for survivors of childhood cancer. *Journal of the American Academy of Child and Adolescent Psychiatry, 27* (6), 712–715.

Fritz, G. K., Williams, J. R., & Amylon, M. (1988). After treatment ends: Psychosocial sequelae in pediatric cancer survivors. *American Journal of Orthopsychiatry, 58* (4), 552–561.

Fuchs, V. R., & Reklis, D. R. (1992). America's children: Economic perspectives and policy options. *Science, 255,* 41–46.

Gardner, G. G., & Olness, K. (1981). Hypnosis and hypnotherapy with children. New York: Grune & Stratton.

Geist, R. A. (1979). Onset of chronic illness in children and adolescents: Psychotherapeutic and consultative intervention. *American Journal of Orthopsychiatry, 49* (1), 4–23.

Gogan, J. L. & Slavin, L. A. (1981). Interviews with brothers and sisters. In Koocher, G. P., & O'Malley, J. E. *The Damocles Syndrome* (pp. 101–111) New York: McGraw-Hill.

Gortmaker, S. L., Walker, D. K., Weitzman, M., & Sobol, A. M. (1990). Chronic conditions, socioeconomic risks, and behavioral problems in children and adolescents. *Pediatrics, 85* (3), 267–276.

Hauser, S. T., Jacobson, A. M., Lavori, P., Wolfsdorf, J. I., Herskowitz, R. D., Milley, J. E., & Bliss, R. (1990). Adherence among children and adolescents with insulin-dependent diabetes mellitus over a four-year longitudinal follow-up: II. Immediate and long-term linkages with the family milieu. *Journal of Pediatric Psychology, 15* (4), 527–542.

Heiligenstein, E., & Jacobsen, P. B. (1988). Differentiating depression in medically ill children and adolescents. *Journal of the American Academy of Child and Adolescent Psychiatry, 27* (6), 716–719.

Hobbs, N., Perrin, J. M., & Ireys, H. T. (1985). *Chronically ill children and their families.* San Francisco: Jossey-Bass.

Jacobson, A. M., Hauser, S. T., Lavori, P., Wolfsdorf, J. I., Herskowitz, R. D., Milley, J. E., Bliss, R., Gelfand, E., Wertlieb, D., & Stein, J. (1990). Adherence among children and adolescents with insulin-dependent diabetes mellitus over a four-year longitudinal follow-up: I. The influence of patient coping and adjustment. *Journal of Pediatric Psychology, 15* (4), 511–526.

Jellinek, M. S., Catlin, E. A., Todres, I. D., & Cassem, E. H. (1992). Facing tragic decisions with parents in the neonatal intensive care unit: Clinical perspectives. *Pediatrics, 89* (1), 119–122.

Jellinek, M. S., & Herzog, D. B. (Eds.). (1990). *Massachusetts General Hospital: Psychiatric aspects of general hospital pediatrics.* Chicago: Year-Book Medical Publishers.

Jellinek, M. S., Little, M., Murphy, J. M., & Pagano, M. (1995). The pediatric symptom checklist: support for a role in a managed care environment. *Archives of Pediatric Adolescent Medicine 149:* 740–746.

Jellinek, M. S., Todres, I. D., Catlin, E. A., Cassem, E. H., & Salzman, A. (1993). Pediatric intensive care training: confronting the dark side. *Critical Care Medicine, 21,* 5:775–779.

Krener, P., & Miller, F. B. (1989). Psychiatric response to HIV spectrum disease in children and adolescents. *Journal of the American Academy of Child and Adolescent Psychiatry, 28* (4), 596–605.

Lloyd, J., Jellinek, M. S., Little, M., Murphy, J. M., & Pagano, M. (1995). Screening for psychosocial dysfunction in pediatric inpatients. *Clinical Pediatrics, 34,* 1:18–24.

Lobato, D., Faust, D., & Spirito, A. (1988). Examining the effects of chronic disease and disability on children's sibling relationships. *Journal of Pediatric Psychology, 13* (3), 389–407.

McDaniel, S. H., Hepworth, J., & Doherty, W. J. (1992). Childhood chronic illness. In S. H. McDaniel, J. Hepworth, & W. J. Doherty, Medical family therapy: A biopsychosocial approach to families with health problems (pp. 211–230). New York: Basic Books.

Nolan, T., & Pless, I. B. (1986). Emotional correlates and consequences of birth defects. *Journal of Pediatrics, 109* (1), 201–216.

Norman, D. K. (1987). Psychosocial commentary on insulin-dependent diabetes mellitus: Infancy to age 5 years. In S. J. Brink (Ed.), *Pediatric and adolescent diabetes mellitus* (pp. 33–41). Chicago: Year-Book Medical Publishers.

Perrin, E. C., & Gerrity, P. S. (1981). There's a demon in your belly: Children's understanding of illness. *Pediatrics, 67* (6), 841–849.

Perrin, E. C., Sayer, A. G., & Willett, J. B. (1991). Sticks and stones may break my bones . . . reasoning about illness causality and body functioning in children who have a chronic illness. *Pediatrics, 88* (3), 608–619.

Perrin, J. M., & MacLean, W. E., Jr. (1988a). Biomedical and psychosocial dimensions of chronic illness in childhood. In P. Karoly (Ed.), *Handbook of child health assessment* (pp. 11–29). New York: John Wiley & Sons.

Perrin, J. M., & MacLean, W. E., Jr. (1988b). Children with chronic illness: The prevention of dysfunction.

Pediatric Clinics of North America, 35 (6), 1325–1337.

Pless, I. B., & Roghmann, K. J. (1971). Chronic illness and its consequences: Observations based on three epidemiologic surveys. *Journal of Pediatrics, 79* (3), 351–359.

Rauch, P. K., & Jellinek, M. S. (1989). Pediatric dermatology: Developmental and psychological issues. *Advances in Dermatology, 4,* 143–158.

Russo, D. C., & Varni, J. W. (Eds.). (1982). *Behavioral pediatrics research and practice.* New York: Plenum Press.

Sabbeth, B. (1984). Understanding the impact of chronic childhood illness on families. *Pediatric Clinics of North America, 31* (1), 47–57.

Schwam, J. S. & Maloney, M. J. (1997). Developing a psychiatry study group for community pediatricians. *Journal of the American Academy of Child and Adolescent Psychiatry, 36,* 5:706–708.

Slater, J. A. (1994). Psychiatric aspects of organ transplantation in children and adolescents. In: Lewis, M. & King, R. A. (Guest Editors.) *Consultation-Liaison in Pediatrics, Child and Adolescent Psychi-* *atric Clinics of North America, 3,* 3:557–598. Philadelphia: W.B. Saunders Company.

Starfield, B. (1991). Childhood morbidity: Comparisons, clusters, and trends. *Pediatrics, 88* (3), 519–526.

Stoddard, F. J., Norman, D. K., Murphy, J. M., & Beardslee, W. R. (1989). Psychiatric outcome of burned children and adolescents. *Journal of the American Academy of Child and Adolescent Psychiatry, 28* (4), 589–595.

Stuber, M. L. (1990). Psychiatric consultation issues in pediatric HIV and AIDS. *Journal of the American Academy of Child and Adolescent Psychiatry, 29* (3), 463–467.

Tritt, S. G., & Esses, L. M. (1988). Psychosocial adaptation of siblings of children with chronic medical illnesses. *American Journal of Orthopsychiatry, 58* (2), 211–220.

Weitzman, M. (1984). School and peer relations. *Pediatric Clinics of North America, 31* (1), 59–69.

Ziegler, R. G. (1981). Impairments of control and competence in epileptic children and their families. *Epilepsia, 22,* 339–346.

71 / Observation, Interview, and Mental Status Assessment (OIM): Traumatized

Lenore Terr

When, in the mid-20th century, trauma was first considered to be a problem in children, most of the emphasis was given to those adults whose difficulties had stemmed from their childhood traumas (Bonaparte, 1945; Greenacre, 1949) and to those parents who were thought to be able to convey traumatic anxiety directly to their offspring (Carey-Trefzger, 1949; Mercier & Despert, 1943). In fact, when the first attempts were made to understand childhood trauma, a number of studies were done without working directly with the children involved [see especially, Bloch, Silber, and Perry (1956), an NIMH study, which included no interviews with the child subjects who had endured a tornado while attending a Saturday matinee movie)]. One notable exception among the early studies, however, was the work of David Levy (1945), whose article on children's postoperative courses included careful observations of the children themselves. It is to Levy, therefore, whom we owe our understanding of the detailed observations of children's behaviors that are required for the assessment of childhood psychic trauma.

The Traumatized or Neglected Infant

Infants and toddlers are generally not capable of retaining full verbal memories of traumas until about the age of 28 to 36 months at the time of the traumatic event (Terr, 1988). A minority may remember a few shards of scenes connected to their original plights. Infants are, however, fully capable of retaining enough nondeclarative memory to harbor some symptoms and signs of their traumas (Terr, 1988). Furthermore, if they are repeatedly abused or neglected, they may develop the symptoms and signs of "reactive attachment deprivation/maltreatment disorder of infancy" (National Center for Clinical Infant Programs, 1994).

Very young children usually require the presence of a parent or guardian while they are being psychiatrically examined. The examination consists, in part, of observing the interactions between the young child and the primary guardian. One watches for mutual attention, mutual engagement (first readily apparent at 3 to 6 months), and interactive intentionality and reciprocity (purposeful initiation and response to another person, first readily apparent at 6 to 8 months). Other more elaborate forms of infant play can be observed with or without a parent or guardian in attendance (National Center for Clinical Infant Programs, 1994). These are representational/affective communication (use of language or pretend play to communicate emotional themes, such as "feeding the baby doll," first readily apparent at over 18 months), representational elaboration (use of language or make believe to convey themes that go beyond simple needs, such as "the trucks are crashing," at over 30 months), representational differentiation I (use of symbolic expression to communicate two or more connected ideas, at over 36 months), and representational differentiation II (use of symbolic expression to communicate three or more ideas, wishes, etc., with "how," "what," and "why" elaborations, at over 42 months). The main forms of reactive attachment disorder in children are (1) the withdrawn, unsocializing child, and (2) the "hail-fellow well-met," indiscriminately interested, but not deeply attached child (Terr, 1970).

In terms of posttraumatic stress disorder, all of the signs and symptoms apparent in adults should be checked in the very young child, bearing in mind that many of these findings will be absent because of the extreme developmental differences between infants and more mature individuals. Those signs of PTSD most likely in the infant or toddler will be repetitive play; reenactive behaviors; psychophysiologic upsets that mimic upsets connected with the traumatic event(s); avoidance of things associated with the trauma; hyperalertness to sounds, sights, etc., that resemble the traumatic stimuli; and personality changes. There are few ways, other than trauma, to permanently change a formerly placid, cuddly infant into an irritable, clinging one. There are few ways,

other than trauma, to change an adventuresome infant into a withdrawn apathetic one. Moving to a new home or having a new sibling may affect such changes in the occasional youngster. But trauma and extreme neglect are the two most likely external conditions that permanently affect such changes in maturing "character."

Among infants and toddlers, some of the classic findings of trauma (for example, posttraumatic dreams) will not be evident. At these youngest stages of life, dreams are not verbal, nor can they be verbally described afterward by the child. Instead, one sees sleep interruptions, fears of going to sleep, crying in the middle of the night, and at times, full-blown pavor nocturnus (Terr, 1987). One is also unlikely to see truly symbolic play in the toddler under the age of 2½, yet one can sometimes observe in the consulting room rudimentary actions that mimic the actions that were connected to the traumatic event(s). In other words, if an infant had been bitten as part of horrible, sexualized adult behavior, the infant might play repeatedly at biting. If someone else sat on an infant's head, as recorded in a confession by a caretaker, that infant might sit on others' heads, as observed in a 1-year-old's behavior with her younger cousin.

Among infants, toddlers, and preschoolers, the clinician can often observe some of the specific fears that were inspired by the traumatic event(s). The child who was bitten feared my nutcracker soldier. The child who was sat upon by a babysitter feared me—in this child's eyes, another potential babysitter. In this regard, although Ainsworth's strange-situation testing (Ainsworth, Blehar, Waters, et al., 1978) is occasionally used in clinical infant evaluations, we do not ordinarily advocate using this tool for trauma evaluations because the traumatized or neglected infant is usually too sensitive to potential abandonment and aloneness to be further stressed by strange-situation testing.

This brings us to a final group of observations about the traumatized infant and toddler. When profoundly stressed, very young children regress into younger behaviors and losses of key developmental facilities. Such infants may lose newly attained speech, becoming mute and soundless. They may regress in bowel training, or even ambulation. Clinging, fears of being left alone, of the dark, of looming objects, and of falling asleep plague the traumatized and/or neglected child.

These regressive behaviors and "fears of the mundane" (Terr, 1979) are fully observable in the consulting situation. Often, however, the child must be seen about three times before the complete extent of the youngster's symptomatology is evident.

The Traumatized Preschooler

In the fourth and fifth years of life, play and symbolic dreams become more accessible to the professional office evaluation. The child's own history of the trauma is also more accessible. Because children of this age are far more fluently verbal than their younger counterparts, they can explain what is happening in their play ("What is that cowboy going to do now?"), their dreams ("What pictures do you see when your eyes are closed and you're sleeping at night?"), and their memories ("What are the best things that ever happened to you?" "What are the worst things that ever happened to you?").

Three-, four-, and five-year-olds are relatively easily led into accepting suggestions from an assessor (Ceci & Bruck, 1995). Three-year-olds are far more prone to receiving suggestions than five-year-olds (Ceci, Leichtman, Putnick, & Nightingale, 1993). As a general rule, it is preferable to ask broad-based, open-ended questions. One can also ask questions about play-displacements of the child's conflicts and concerns. "That princess" or "that dinosaur" remain within the metaphors of pretend, even when the princess suffers from the same auto accident that the little girl being assessed actually did. One cannot accept a historical response from a child as total and absolute "truth," however, without external confirmation from some other neutral source and internal confirmation from the child's own symptoms. One must also realize that even though it is proven that a young child endured a certain event, some of the child's details may be distorted or wrong (Terr, 1996). Details, however, can be distorted at any age.

Sometimes a preschooler has drawn a paper full of scribbles in the consulting room that seem to mean nothing (drawing skills lag behind speaking skills). If the child is asked to tell the story of this picture, however, the child may relate a fully traumatic narrative, complete with symbolic elaboration. Then, too, whereas a traumatized child may fiddle with the therapist's toys, lining up trucks by color and failing to make anything related to the trauma happen, if the child is asked to bring his or her favorite toys from home, these Power Rangers, trolls, or Barbies may play out the child's trauma in an evident fashion. It can be useful to ask possibly traumatized young children to bring their favorite toys at least once to the clinician's office, so that if a posttraumatic game is being played secretly at home, it might be exposed in the consulting room.

School-Age Trauma-Exposed Children

With school age comes the reading and math skills, the report cards, the obvious socialization, the expected conduct, and the teachers' comments that add so much to our knowledge about a youngster. All of these are important to assess in terms of the traumatized child. Traumatized children generally do about the same in school as before, unless (1) they have begun to dissociate a great deal and thus become "absent" mentally; (2) they are being kept up late at night or are being physically injured and worn out by at-home abusers; or (3) they have a specifically traumatic fear that precludes their attending or cooperating with their educational program. By the time a child has reached school age, it is important to include school comments, educational testing, and intelligence testing in the professional assessment of the child. However, school performance in and of itself does not determine the diagnosis of posttraumatic stress disorder.

The school-age traumatized child is usually able to fully cooperate with a psychiatric evaluation. These children can draw decipherable pictures (Pynoos & Eth, 1986). Their explanations and accompanying stories should be written down. The child can also play "pretend" in the psychiatric office and is able to recite a narrative of the events and the accompanying symptoms in "sit down on the couch" fashion. The latency-age child should also be able to separate from parents when coming into the consulting room and should see the clinician alone.

In evaluating the school-age child, the therapist must observe play and listen to a narrative account by the child of the traumatic occurrences. Again, as with the preschooler, having the child bring play objects, drawings, and other art productions from home may be extremely helpful. If any siblings were present during the traumatic occurrences, they also should be seen. Often even when siblings were removed during an occurrence, they require assessment because their lives have been deeply affected by the trauma to their brother or sister (Terr, 1989).

If a traumatic situation was very recent and the resultant symptoms very acute, it is often helpful to include a few simple treatment suggestions to the child in the process of assessment. For example, a school-age child who has recently been bitten by a dog might go to a pet shop to visit puppies. School-age children who have been kidnapped and returned might carry a quarter in the arch of their shoes so that they know they can always make a phone call. The way that such a child takes this kind of suggestion plays a part in the child's assessment. The potential difficulty or ease of treatment may lay itself out in the course of observing a school-age child's response to and utilization of a cognitive behavioral technique. (See the chapters on Clinical Processes, Volume 6.)

The Traumatized Adolescent

Adolescents who have been exposed to traumatic situations are often particularly ashamed and humiliated about their loss of control. Here the interpersonal transactions between therapist and child may become an immediate problem because an adult (the assessing clinician) is holding the adolescent under scrutiny. It is important for the interviewer to set the adolescent at ease by listening to the trauma story nonjudgmentally and with some sympathy. Most adolescents are fully capable of telling their stories entirely in words, but

it is also helpful to ask the adolescent to draw a picture, write a poem, or compose a piece of music that expresses his emotions. It is also helpful to look through photo albums and scrapbooks with the adolescent. All of these elicit fuller expressions of emotion and more details of the trauma story which may be weighing heavily in the adolescent's resultant pathology.

Adolescents respond in interesting ways to any treatment suggestions that are offered as part of the assessment procedure for trauma. Teenagers are fully able to use behavioral modification techniques, such as "corrective redreaming," once these techniques are suggested. A 16-year-old girl who ate a poisoned pizza, for instance, had been repeatedly dreaming that a man's head exploded to bits. She was told that she might will herself to dream this dream, but to correct it with a new ending. On her second assessment visit, she excitedly reported that she had mastered the dream by having the man put all of the exploded pieces of his head back together and walk off. A number of trauma-related problems do not clear as quickly. Upon a second or third assessment visit, the therapist becomes more aware of which of the adolescent's trauma-related symptoms will require more prolonged and more subtle styles of treatment.

The Child's Family

Families require assessment in addition to the traumatized child. Their handling of the anxiety and guilt surrounding their child's trauma must be assessed and managed (Terr, 1989). Often families respond to trauma with the defense of denial (Vaillant, 1992). This response may stop any early treatment efforts before they get started. Families may also discontinue treatment too soon as a result of their intensely negative feelings. Parents and siblings require careful assessment to determine just how much depression, anxiety, and even vicarious trauma (Terr, 1991) they are experiencing in connection with the child's trauma. At times, grandparents, aunts and uncles, and other family members must be assessed in order to utilize them as caregivers and/or cotherapists (Furman, 1957), especially when an immediate family is debilitated through grief, denial, neglect, or criminal prosecution.

Assessing the Adult Who as a Child Was Traumatized

Adults make their way to the professional's consulting room when they realize that they are still suffering the signs and symptoms of a trauma-related childhood condition. This often comes up when adults are raising children of similar ages to the age that they were when they were traumatized. It arises too when adults evaluate their own skills as parents and find that their old traumas are impinging on these skills. It comes up when an adult traumatic response is reawakened by a new event or a new stage of life. It may occur at the same time of year that the original trauma occurred—an "anniversary reaction." It also comes up with newly retrieved memories of old traumas (Terr, 1994).

In assessing previously traumatized adults, it is essential for clinicians not to suggest things. Any preconceived expectations must be held back from exposure, either in comment or in question form. Nonverbal cues must be self-censored as well. When a therapist smiles, nods the head, looks concerned, becomes bored, or interjects, these actions are often taken by patients to signify what is or is not important or "true" to the therapist. Adult patients should tell their stories without any linkages supplied by their assessors. If the story remains fragmented, so be it. If the story is uninterpretable, so it must be.

An adult can aid the process of assessment by doing some of the "detective" work—for instance, asking the police for their report of an old occurrence, asking the prosecutor's office, asking siblings, friends, or parents, or checking out old newspaper files.

The clinician should be prepared to look for "external" and "internal" confirmations to the story (Terr, 1994) in assessing the adult's old childhood traumas. Internal confirmations are those symptoms that flow directly from the event. These should be trauma specific (directly related to fragments of the story that has been told). A woman, for instance, sought my help for extreme fear of elevators, sexual numbing, and a sense of having fallen into a deep, dark hole as a toddler. She was convinced that she had been sexually abused by her father, and without any supporting memories, she had cut off their relationship. I asked if she knew anyone with whom she had played as a very young child. She said she did. The next week the woman returned with an explanation. She had spoken to Margie whom she had known 32 years earlier. Margie remembered their going to a neighbor man's house and repeatedly jumping through his second-floor clothes chute onto the basement laundry table. It was a scary ride. "I have the feeling I was sexually abused on top of a soft pile—maybe clothes," the patient then told her old friend. "Well, he didn't do anything to me," Margie answered, "but my sister has always said that he raped her!"

Often there are only two or three trauma-related findings in a past-traumatized adult. Adults may miss making the criteria cutoff for PTSD diagnoses, yet their symptoms may be bothersome and debilitating enough to merit treatment. Every symptom and sign—present and past—should be considered in such an assessment. The length of time that a symptom lasted should be noted. If adults still have their own childhood products—drawings, scrapbooks, essays, poems—these too should be included in the assessment process.

REFERENCES

Ainsworth, M. D. S., Blehar, M. C., Waters, E., et al. (1978). *Patterns of attachment: A psychological study of the Strange Situation*. Hillsdale, NJ: Lawrence Erlbaum.

Bloch, D., Silber, E., & Perry, S. (1956). Some factors in the emotional reactions of children to disaster. *American Journal of Psychiatry, 113*, 416–422.

Bonaparte, M. (1945). Notes on the analytic discovery of a primal scene. *Psychoanalytic Study of the Child, 1*, 119–125.

Carey-Trefzger, C. (1949). The results of a clinical study of war-damaged children who attended the child guidance clinic, the Hospital for Sick Children, Great Ormond Street, London. *Journal of Mental Science, 95,* 535–559.

Ceci, S. J., & Bruck, M. (1995). *Jeopardy in the courtroom: A scientific analysis of children's testimony.* Washington, DC: American Psychological Association.

Ceci, S. J., Leichtman, M., Putnick, M., & Nightingale, N. (1993). Age differences in suggestibility. In D. Cicchetti & S. Toth (Eds.), *Child abuse, child development, and social policy* (pp. 117–137). Norwood, NJ: Ablex.

Furman, E. (1957). Treatment of under-fives by way of parents. *Psychoanalytic Study of the Child, 12,* 250–262.

Greenacre, P. (1949). A contribution to the study of screen memories. *Psychoanalytic Study of the Child, 3/4,* 73–84.

Levy, D. M. (1945). Psychic trauma of operations in children. *American Journal of the Diseases of Childhood, 69,* 7–25.

Mercier, M., & Despert, L. (1943). Effects of war on French children. *Psychosomatic Medicine, 5,* 226–272.

National Center for Clinical Infant Programs. (1994). *Diagnostic classification: Zero to three.* Arlington, VA: National Center for Clinical Infant Programs.

Pynoos, R. S., & Eth, S. (1986). Witness to violence: The child interview. *Journal of the American Academy of Child Psychiatry, 25,* 306–319.

Terr, L. C. (1970). A family study of child abuse. *American Journal of Psychiatry, 127,* 125–131.

Terr, L. C. (1979). Children of Chowchilla: a study of psychic trauma. *Psychoanalytic Study of the Child, 34,* 547–623.

Terr, L. C. (1987). Nightmares in children. In C. Guilleminault (Ed.), *Sleep and its disorders in children* (pp. 231–242). New York: Raven Press.

Terr, L. (1988). What happens to early memories of trauma? A study of twenty children under age five at the time of documented traumatic events. *Journal of the American Academy of Child and Adolescent Psychiatry, 27,* 96–104.

Terr, L. C. (1989). Family anxiety after traumatic events. *Journal of Clinical Psychiatry, 50,* 15–19.

Terr, L. (1991). Childhood trauma in society: The pebble and the pool. In J. E. Hamner III (Ed.), *The 1990 distinguished visiting professorship lectures* (pp. 71–91). Memphis: University of Tennessee.

Terr, L. (1994). *Unchained memories: True stories of traumatic memories, lost and found.* New York: Basic Books.

Terr, L. C., Bloch, D. A., Michel, B., Shi H., Reinhart, J. A., & Metayer, S. A. (1996). Children's memories in the wake of *Challenger. American Journal of Psychiatry, 153,* 618–625.

Vaillant, G. (Ed.). (1992). *Ego mechanisms of defense: A guide for clinicians and researchers.* Washington, DC: American Psychiatric Press.

72 / Observation, Interview, and Mental Status Assessment (OIM): Violent

Elliot M. Pittel

Clinicians are faced with the need to assess and treat youths who have been or will become affected by violence. The clinician must be skilled at determining whether aggression is caused by psychiatric conditions such as psychosis, mania, delirium, or cognitive impairment. But, the epidemic of violence that has affected youth, is generally not caused by soaring rates of psychosis, mania, or cognitively impaired children. Rather the increased incidence of violence seems to be related directly to intentional conflict between peers.

Early predictors of violent behavior include individual characteristics such as low cognitive ability, poor verbal skills, antisocial behavior, head injury, and poor motor skills development. Other factors important to evaluate include personality variables such as coping style and maladaptive defenses, cognitive distortions, affective arousal, anger dyscontrol, and impulsivity. The psychiatric symptom of paranoia, when combined with neurological impairment and a history of abuse, is considered an important risk factor for severely aggressive behavior (Lewis et al., 1988). Family characteristics such as family criminal behavior and certain parenting practices like abuse, neglect, rejection, absence, or harsh disciplinary practices are also predictors (Buka & Earls, 1993). Adolescent peer violence is a problem that has particularly affected the minority communities of inner cities, and all youth who are coping with poverty, unemployment, and lack of economic and social opportunities.

Clinicians can use a systematic approach based on established risk factors to evaluate a child's risk for interpersonal violence. A thorough assessment of behaviors, thoughts, and feelings associated with interpersonal violence can help us understand and treat children at risk for further violence. Using knowledge of typical developmental paths that can lead to violent behaviors, clinicians can evaluate the effects of violence and the possibility of further violent encounters. Because the risk for violence is also influenced by social, geographic, and economic issues, it is essential that the clinician respect the environment and culture of the youth.

As the story of a violent encounter is being told by a youth, a common assumption is the youth may have been a victim of random violence. We are rarely told that it was random violence, however, because intentional peer violence occurs in the context of interpersonal conflict. Sometimes the youth may defensively offer a euphemism, such as, "I was in the wrong place at the wrong time." Statistics confirm that only 1 out of 10 handgun victimizations results from random violence; the remainder results either from behavioral risk factors (carrying guns, being involved with drugs, or affiliating with people who carry guns) or from environmental risk factors (Sheley, McGee, & Wright, 1992). A task of the clinician should be to help provide a meaning for the incident that makes sense, given the youth's circumstances and any behavioral risk factors. For example, two victims may report being in the wrong place at the wrong time: one youth was robbed and beaten on the way home from basketball practice because of an item of clothing that was worn, whereas another youth was selling drugs and was shot when the deal fell through.

Structuring the Interview

The clinician's goal is to assess the relationship between violence, development, and physical and mental function. The clinician should include information on the child's current involvement in violent behavior, history of exposure, victimization, and perpetration. The interviewer can develop an empathic framework for understanding the youth before building an emotional bridge to more challenging topics, such as assaultive behaviors. Clinicians should start the interview with the least threatening theme, which in most cases will be exposure to violence or victimization. It is easier for children to describe what they have seen first, before revealing what has happened to them or what they have done. This model reflects current opinion about the common causes of youth violence—that violence is learned and is more likely to affect (or occur) those who witness it or who were victims of it, such as child abuse.

Observation of the Child

The clinician can start by observing the youth for visual signs that might suggest involvement with violence. Because a child's behavior can be influenced by social and economic class, and geographic, ethnic, and cultural factors, note these factors at the start. Where does the child live and what is the housing situation? Children who reside in communities that have been chronically plagued by violence may be particularly at risk for traumatic symptoms (Pynoos and Nader, 1988). What is the child's ethnic or racial background and does it differ from the majority of youth in the area, thus making the child vulnerable to bias? Does the child have a tattoo or wear clothes that suggests membership in a gang (Stringham, 1994)? Ask about any bruises or old scars that are visible. Is there evidence of an old injury that could have been caused by a violent encounter? Clinicians, particularly those who work in medical settings, should also be concerned about somatic presentations, such as chronic pain symptoms without apparent etiology, which can occur in situations of abuse.

A History of the Child's Exposure to Violence

Assessing a child's degree of exposure to violence is important, because children who are more highly exposed will report greater symptoms. Exposure to violence includes what children witness in the home or community, including what is directly seen and consumed in the media. Ask about key events such as experiences of knowing about, inadvertently seeing, or purposely watching violent encounters such as stabbings, shootings, or beatings at home, school, or in the neighborhood. Assess the types of experiences, proximity, seriousness of exposures, and the relationship of the child to the victim. Because children take in information through all sensory modalities, we ask whether the child has heard, as well as seen, such violent events as gunshots or verbal threats.

The child may come upon the scene after the incident. Determine how close the child was to any incident, because the closer the proximity, the greater the trauma from the exposure. When interviewing a child after witnessing an acute violent incident, it is important to ask how the violent incident affected them. Can the child describe the scene from memory—what was seen, heard, felt, smelled? While preschool children may have difficulty describing their experiences, school aged children are quite adept [or capable of] at telling what they have witnessed. Putting the experience into words with the support of a clinician can help the child of any age cope with the effects of witnessing violence.

The assessment of children exposed to acute violent events in their community includes evaluation for the presence of acute traumatic stress symptoms that are related to the degree of exposure (e.g., increased arousal, startle response). Other acute symptoms may be unrelated to the degree of exposure; these symptoms include guilt, fear of recurrence, separation anxiety, and grief.

Fear of recurrence of the trauma can be a result of the "symptom contagion" effect (Terr, 1985) in which children who are not directly affected can also experience symptoms of traumatic stress. This effect can occur among any community of children and adults affected by a violent event. Guilt may be the result of "survival, failure to intervene, or protective actions taken on one's behalf" (Pynoos & Nader, 1988). Some children may worry intensely about the safety of their parents or siblings and this anxiety may be very stressful for them. If the child has also suffered a loss of a significant person, then the clinician should also be concerned about the presence of grief reactions.

Chronic exposure to communal violence may affect the child's school performance, learning, and behavior, particularly aggression (Shakoor & Chalmers, 1991). A relationship between chronic violence exposure and frequency of fighting among adolescents has been noted (Durant, Pendergrast, & Cadenhead 1994). Ask about the child's sense of safety and security at home, at school, and in the community, including playgrounds, public transportation, and specific neighborhoods. Children living in violent environments report exposure related fears and worries in their homes or communities.

In the group of refugee children who have lived through situations of war, which may include political oppression, relocation, and loss, clinicians should consider that they have witnessed or experienced multiple acts of horrific violence, and that evaluation of this population involves awareness of unique and complex issues of trauma (Apfel & Simon, 1996). Children who have been chronically exposed to violent situations should be assessed for the presence of posttraumatic stress disorder (PTSD), which may include intrusive reactions or emotional numbing as primary symptoms. A child who does not show feelings, who appears unaffected by violence in the community, should raise the clinician's suspicion of the presence of emotional numbing from traumatic stress.

Stress-related disorders in children can may or be manifested by a broad range of symptoms, because PTSD may actually be too narrow a condition to look for. Children have been found to have depression with symptoms of low self-esteem and worries about death and injury (Freeman,

Mokros, & Poznanski, 1993). Chronic stress-related disorders in children may be suggested by complex symptoms of trauma, such as affect dysregulation, dissociation, somatization, anxiety disorders, brief psychotic reactions, and depersonalization (AAP, 1996). There may be signs of pathological adaptation to a chronically stressful environment, which include reenactment of violent behaviors, fighting to avoid being labeled "a sucker," developing feelings of invincibility or "not caring" about living or dying. Another consequence of chronic exposure to violence is a foreshortened future or sense of hopelessness. Does the child expect to be alive in 5 years? In 1 year? When a child has been exposed to chronic violence, clinicians can also inquire about any adaptive changes in lifestyle. Examples of adaptations to chronic violence exposure might include tighter restrictions by parents. Family responses may include protection of the child by restricting outdoor play in playgrounds located in or near unsafe neighborhoods.

Children may also experience violence by being a bystander. Witnessing a violent incident can stimulate children in different ways, so it is important to ask whether the child became excited or physiologically aroused by seeing violence. Bystanders have an opportunity to make choices: stay and watch, actively encourage a fight, join in, try to stop the events unfolding, or leave (Slaby & Stringham, 1994). Bystanders who support violence do not intervene to stop fights. They tend to actively encourage violence; define aggression between others as not a problem; believe that violence among others is not their problem; and are low in nonviolent assertiveness (Slaby, Wilson-Brewer, & DeVos, 1994). It is helpful to find out what predominant behaviors are chosen when the child watches a fight. Some youth who are bystanders support violence, while others try to stop fights or prevent them from occurring. Bystanders who try to stop a fight are likely to be chosen as friends; are unlikely to be socially rejected; are high in nonviolent assertiveness; are unlikely to choose passive acceptance of violence of others; seek additional facts in solving social problems; reject the belief that behaving aggressively is OK; and give high priority to information seeking (Slaby, Wilson-Brewer, & DeVos, 1994).

A History of Victimization

There are various ways a child can be victimized. A child can be teased, verbally intimidated or harassed, threatened, beaten up, or injured by a weapon. From a developmental perspective, victimization has its roots in teasing. Even young children may experience ridicule or physical intimidation by their peers. Victims of repeated bullying are often anxious, lack self-esteem, socially isolated, and feel afraid to defend themselves (Olweus, 1993). If there are no physical signs of bullying, parents and teachers may not be aware that a child is a victim. The first sign may be the child's refusal to attend school or the onset of somatic symptoms. Subtle forms of bullying, sometimes seen among girls, may include name calling or spreading rumors. Bullying may be ignored in school settings and treated as an acceptable prank behavior, but it is a form of violence that can have serious long-term consequences.

Many children adapt and cope with living in violent communities. Information about the child's coping skills can provide insight into the strengths and resiliencies of a particular child. Does the child consider the neighborhood or apartment building unsafe? Be open to learning about the child's skills for coping with life in a dangerous neighborhood. Does the child engage in increased risk-taking behaviors because of low self-worth? or, to establish machismo, is there a pattern of counterphobic behaviors? Some adolescents may deny their vulnerability by showing they can "take a risk and not pay the price" (AAP, 1996). Identify any individuals the child feels threatened by. Are there certain neighborhoods, streets, buildings, or apartments which the child can identify as a safe place or haven?

The Child After Acute Violent Trauma

Adolescents age 12 to 19 have the highest victimization rates of all age groups for most crimes of violence and theft (Valois, McKeown, Garrison, & Vincent, 1995). Violent injuries among children and adolescents account for increasing numbers of visits to hospital emergency departments. When conducting an evaluation in an emergency setting after an acute injury or assault, clinicians should evaluate the adolescent's acute stress response, coping skills, and family and support systems. Inquire about the child's thoughts and feelings in the midst of the experience. It is helpful to establish the circumstances and context for the injuries, and determine whether the youth has been beaten, jumped, mugged, robbed, or assaulted with a weapon. A clinician should determine what the youth's role was in the fight and whether the fight was related to race, gender, or culture. Ask the adolescent to identify how the interaction became a conflict which turned violent. Ask the victim what form it took—verbal abuse, harassment, threats, or physical intimidation or whether there was an argument. Did the adolescent attempt any technique of self-defense? Have there been any previous injuries from violence? If the injury is severe, assess the incident's long-term consequences such as physical rehabilitation and emotional adjustment, medical complications, or projected long-term disabilities.

After an acute violent incident, regardless of the seriousness of any sustained injuries, it is important to inquire whether the conflict was resolved and the situation settled. The clinician might ask whether the conflict was long-standing or had started recently. If the situation has been resolved, the clinician might ask the youth to explore ways of responding to conflict. However, if the conflict remains, ask how the youth would/could/might peacefully settle the dispute. Talk with the youth about possible consequences of perpetuating a cycle of violence, which can occur if the youth believes in seeking revenge: Adolescents who believe in the code of not "snitching" on someone else, who take matters into their own hands increase the risk for another violent incident. Some may seek justice through the legal system. In each case, assess the safety and security of the youth, and whether the danger still remains to anyone else upon the youth's discharge from the facility. The child may be worried about the safety of friends, so ask about threats to any of the child's peers. Make sure the child has a safety plan before leaving, which might, for example, suggest alternative responses to potential violent confrontations.

The Violent Child

Before moving to the next major part of the violence history, two important risk factors or predictors of violence should be emphasized. The first is the important relationship between exposure to violence, victimization, and violent behavior. The former issues now become major risk factors for violent behavior outcomes. One study found that previous exposure to violence and victimization were the strongest predictors of the use of violence in adolescents living in housing projects (Durant et al., 1995). Another important risk factor predictive of violence later in life is aggressive behavior during early childhood. Clinicians are advised to include early childhood behavioral problems as part of the violence history. For instance, we can start taking a fighting history by inquiring of the family how early the child started showing tendencies to hit or kick other children.

The role of the child's imagination can provide key information about the potential for violence. Consider whether the child connects aggressive impulses or behaviors with feelings. Does a young child act out a violent scene in play without any show/expression of affect? Does the child have aggressive fantasies? For example, does the child wonder what it would feel like to shoot or stab someone with a weapon? Inquire about whether the child played with toy weapons when younger. Some youths may be obsessed with weapons and may fantasize about the power weapons endow on individuals. Find out if the child identifies with violent characters or themes in favorite movies, television programs, or music groups (Walsh, Goldman, & Brown, 1996).

Family attitudes and behaviors toward fighting can provide significant insight into the child's attitudes toward fighting. Children often model the behavior of family members or of characters depicted in the media. Children may witness the fights of older siblings or adults in their families, and because the victor is the person who physically won the fight, they learn the importance of toughness and that power equals strength. Although parents want to protect their children from being hurt, many parents emphasize the necessity of standing up for yourself. Parents may give strong messages to children about violence, such as, "watch your back . . . protect yourself . . .

if somebody messes with you, you got to pay them back" (Anderson, 1994). Some children may learn that fighting is not only acceptable but is strongly encouraged, not only as a way of survival on the streets, but also at home. This may occur if a child loses a fight and the parent responds with a counterthreat such as, "Don't you come in here like a sap, crying that somebody beat you up; you better get back out there and whip his ass. If you don't whip his ass, I'll whip your ass when you come home" (Anderson, 1994). Look also for the parents who reinforce nonviolent approaches to conflict resolution or alternative strategies for avoiding violence (e.g., "it's OK to walk away from a fight").

The clinician should explore the ability of the child to regulate anger. The evaluation of anger includes identifying the external cues that trigger it, the child's ability to control it, the use of anger in socially maladaptive or inappropriate ways, and the consequences the child has suffered due to anger expression. Ask the child to identify the situations that trigger anger and talk about alternative nonviolent ways to manage anger. The ease and speed of losing control of anger is important to establish. If the child seems unsure of this, the child can be asked to "time" how long it takes to lose control.

Besides anger, the clinician should place considerable emphasis on assessing how the child responds to interpersonal conflict. Does the child respond to conflict in a thoughtful, cool-headed way by getting the facts, or in an impulsive, provocative, hot-headed way? The clinician can attempt to draw links between anger, aggression, and violent behavior. For example, a crucial point regarding anger is the importance of identifying youths who become extremely aroused, who need to express anger by acting out and usually committing a violent act. Some children, therefore, describe their tendency to fight as a preferred way to release, and thereby reduce, their level of anger.

Although external cues and internal regulation of anger are important, there is also a cognitive component to aggressive behavior. Thoughts and beliefs about aggression are key factors for clinicians assessing children's response to conflict and whether they are likely to fight. Research has shown that highly aggressive children may lack the cognitive skills necessary for solving social

problems and believe that aggression is a legitimate response, increases self-esteem, avoids a negative self-image, and does not cause suffering in the victim. An aggressive child is more likely to fight for several reasons: the child sees fewer options, lacks the ability to develop alternative solutions and see the consequences of actions, and perceives the world as threatening. Aggressors may also view themselves primarily as victims (Slaby & Stringham, 1994).

Clinicians can help youths identify immediate precipitants to a fight. Common precipitants may include insults or verbal provocation (trash talking), arguments, rumors, mistaken identity, revenge, robbery, drugs, prejudice, or a girlfriend (or boyfriend). However, guard against asking, "Who started the fight?" because the answer may not be reliable. Finding out who threw the first punch does not necessarily explain how a fight started. The aggressive child may find it difficult to take responsibility for starting a fight, may not have seen any alternatives, and will be able to justify the actions taken. The clinicians may encounter a youth who is involved in an ongoing conflict and is planning on a fight. If a youth does not see any alternative to fighting, then when faced with an escalating conflict, the response is to prepare for a physical confrontation. This was found to be the case in a study of more than 400 adolescents in Boston, where only 53% believed there were alternatives to fighting or fleeing. When asked what they did to protect themselves from their last fight, 78% chose to fight back, whereas only 11% tried to reason with their opponent, and only 2% ran away (Hausman, Spivak, & Prothrow-Stitch, 1994). Thus it is common to encounter youths who see no way out of a conflict other than by fighting.

Because fighting leading to serious injury can be a common occurrence among adolescents, ask about the severity of fights. In a cross-sectional survey of high school students in 1990, almost 1 in 12 reported they were involved in a fight during the preceding 30 days in which someone was injured severely enough to require medical attention (Sosin, Koepsell, Rivara, & Mercy, 1995). When asking about peers the youth has had fights with, be aware that fighting among adolescents is more frequent among individuals who know each other (Spivak, Prothrow-Stitch, & Hausman, 1988).

Does the youth have a history of previous conflicts with peers that can't be solved nonviolently? If a youth shows a pattern of behavior that suggests difficulty with avoiding fights, ask about the peer culture. Perhaps the youth lives in an environment where only certain behaviors are effective for avoiding fights, or where one is expected to fight in certain situations. Fighting may seem like the best way to fit in and to become accepted by one's peer group. A phenomenon often seen with adolescents who live in unsafe environments is the avoidance of being labeled as a "sucker." Those who take advantage of a person might perceive that individual as weak. They may come back and "try to walk all over you again, if you don't do anything to protect yourself." Thus, honor, respect, and dignity are important in adolescent culture. Many conflicts arise over the issue of who gets or feels respected and who doesn't. Adolescents can sometimes interpret subtle gestures or glances from peers as signs of disrespect. Those who do not respond appropriately to such challenges may also be regarded as weak and become targets. Adolescents do not want others to think that they are weak and can easily be taken advantage of. Because many fights occur in public settings, in front of others or with others knowing about the fight, acknowledge the importance of the presence of peer pressure to fight, such as the importance of impressing peers or not losing "face" (respect) in front of one's peers.

Many youths report that they don't like to fight although they may be easily provoked to aggression if they feel disrespected. Find out what the youth's threshold is for fighting and what kinds of problems are really worth fighting over. There are secondary gains from receiving respect, too. Someone who is perceived as capable of "taking care of himself" is given a certain respect, which translates into physical and psychological control. Gaining the respect of peers can be very adaptive, because it can translate into survival on the streets. Clinicians can discuss these issues with adolescents by asking about their experience of being respected by others or whether they fear losing the respect of peers.

Another important attitude to explore with adolescents is "nerve." To adolescents who live in dangerous neighborhoods and face the threat of violence daily, the way to survive comes through respect and power on the streets. Nerve is often necessary to achieve respect from peers, because to have "nerve" indicates there is no fear of death. Clinicians should ask the youth about the potential for lethal violence and feelings on facing death. If a youth is not afraid to die, the risks for lethal violence escalate. We can acknowledge with the adolescent that "not to be afraid to die is by implication to have few compunctions about taking another's life—for the right reasons, if the situation demands it" (Anderson, 1994).

A related concept is "shame", which is often experienced by individuals who have suffered from traumas and victimazations. Children who experience shame feel so rotten, their identities so flawed, that sometimes they resort to violence to establish some self-pride (Gilligan, 1996). Shame-based children may feel they have nothing more to lose, so violence is a means of expressing what they may be feeling. Ask a child how he feels after a fight, and whether fighting makes him feel good about himself.

Although most children and adolescents are capable of pinpointing the precipitant to a fight and how it started, they may not be so clear at identifying how a fight usually ends. "Someone usually wins" is a common explanation. However asking who won or who lost focuses the youth on the violent outcome of the conflict. Clinicians can reframe the question in a way that focuses the youth's attention on the resolution of the conflict and, in addition, ask if the child has any skills for stopping a fight once it has started.

An important part of the violence history is a frank discussion about weapon carrying. Weapon carrying has become increasingly common—in one study, 21% of high school students in New York City reported carrying a gun, knife, or club within the previous 30 days (CDC, 1993). After motor vehicle injuries, weapon-related injuries were the second leading cause of death for children age 5 to 19 (U.S. Congress, 1995).

According to the National Center for Health Statistics, injury was the leading cause of death for youth below the age of 20 in 1991, and homicide was second only to motor vehicle accidents as the leading cause of fatal injuries. Approximately 57% of all juvenile homicide victims were killed with a firearm, 8% were killed with a stabbing weapon, and 17% were killed with personal weapons such as fists or feet (Snyder & Sickmund, 1995).

Factors influencing gun carrying in youths include having someone in the immediate family who has been the victim of a shooting and living in a neighborhood with a lot of shootings (Hemenway, Prothrow-Stitch, Bergstein, Ander, & Kennedy, 1996). Boys reporting the most aggressive behaviors (i.e., being more likely than classmates to initiate fights), who believe that shooting someone is justifiable under certain circumstances, and who perceive peer acceptance of violence are more likely to carry handguns (Webster, Gainer, & Champion, 1993).

The clinician should determine if the youth has even considered carrying a weapon. Inquire about the child's beliefs and attitudes about weapon carrying, because these factors may influence weapon carrying decisions. Ask about various kinds of weapons, but pay special attention to firearms and the risk factors associated with handguns. Lack of belief that weapon possession increases one's risk of being injured or killed, evident in 55% of male inner-city middle-school students, was found to be associated with knife carrying (Webster, Gainer, & Champion 1993). Find out about a child's access to weapons, and if a handgun could be obtained. One study indicated that 34% of 11th grade students in Seattle perceived handguns to be easily accessible, and males were twice as likely as females to report easy access to handguns. The highest prevalence of easy access was reported by African American male students. Students said they would obtain a gun from a friend, buy one on the street or a gun shop, or obtain it from home (Callahan & Rivara, 1992). Lending a weapon to someone else is also common, so ask whether the child has ever borrowed a weapon or held it for someone else. One study reported that 30% of adolescent gun owners lend guns to someone else (Ash, Kellermann, Fuqua-Whitley, & Johnson, 1996).

Inquire about situations, places, and reasons for carrying a weapon. Responses can vary from denial and claims of innocence, with explanations like, "I was holding the knife for my friend," to frank acknowledgments that a weapon is necessary for one's protection. Weapon carrying at public schools is increasingly more common. One study indicated that 46% of student handgun owners, 4% of all 11th grade students, and 6.6% of males had carried a handgun to school at some time (Callahan & Rivara, 1992). Determine

whether it is possible to apply the "contagion effect" concept to weapon carrying. Find out whether weapon carrying at school is commonplace and whether the child carries a weapon because peers are doing it.

What feelings does the child have when carrying a weapon? Other youths may decide to carry weapons because of their heightened fear of violence. The clinician can bring up the issue of whether weapons produce feelings of security and safety or power and prestige. Does the child gain confidence and security from carrying a weapon and thus perceive fewer risks during conflicts (Cotten, Resnick, Brown et al., 1994)? The risk of middle-school students starting to carry a lethal weapon were greater among those who demonstrated self-reported fears and worries about their safety (Arria et al., 1997). Find out whether simply holding a weapon makes the child feel safer. In the previously cited study by Ash et al. (1996), responses of juvenile offenders to this question included feeling safer, anxious about being stopped by the police, energized, excited, powerful, or more dangerous—7.5% cited an urge to commit a crime or saw themselves as a magnet for trouble.

A weapons history should also include an inquiry about the child's family. While asking about weapons in the home may be standard practice in the evaluation of suicidal individuals, it is also advisable to include this issue with violence-prone youth. Find out whether other members of the child's family possess or carry weapons, particularly firearms. The availability of handguns in the home is known to increase the risk of firearm death to family members. Does the child have knowledge about the risks and the consequences of carrying a weapon? If a parent is available, the clinician can also inquire about the level of parental supervision in the home, and whether the parents know about the child's potential to use a weapon.

The clinician should ask whether the youth is or has ever been in a gang. Gang involvement can add considerable danger to the youth's life. Since proximity to a gang may be a key factor in joining one, ask if gangs are present in the area. Even if the youth does not live in a neighborhood where gangs are located, the youth may be affected by gangs. The youth may have friends or an older sibling in a gang or may need to pass through the gang's neighborhood on the way to school. Adolescents join gangs for a variety of reasons: to get respect from others, a perceived sense of safety, or a sense of belonging. In some communities, the pressure to join a gang is significant.

Gang activity is dangerous, not only to those in the gang, but especially to younger children who aspire for membership by modeling the behavior and dress of a gang. Some young adolescents may want to give the impression they are gang members for safety or prestige. There is usually a developmental progression of activities, which may include illegal activities and involve the drug trade, that young gang "wannabes" must demonstrate before being initiated as full-fledged members. If an adolescent is trying to join a gang, find out about any dangerous activities [that are being carried out.] or [they are doing]. Being a member may, in some cases, indicate that the youth is willing to put his life on the line. If the youth is gang involved, find out the effect on the youth's family. Being in a gang can endanger the youth's family because the home may become a target for rivals. After becoming a member, it is usually difficult to leave a gang. Inquire if the youth has tried to leave a gang. A youth who leaves a gang may become a target for that very same gang and any former rival gangs. Does the youth know of anyone who has successfully left a gang, and if so, how? Getting out of a gang can be extremely dangerous, and the clinician needs to be aware of security and safety issues.

While exploring the child's feelings about violence, the clinician should also inquire about the child's ability to empathize. One writer has suggested that there is a relationship between the trauma of violence exposure and empathy. "The intense negative emotions from exposure to violence interfere with the development of emotional regulation, which may lead to disruption in the development of empathy" (Osofsky, 1995). The clinician can ask how the youth feels about the thought of shooting another person. Find out if the child is capable of seeing the situation from the perspective of a victim.

Issues involving justice and fairness are important to children throughout development, and some youth may consider further violence the only logical response to an assault. These issues tend to play out when discussing revenge, and can

be particularly sensitive in minority communities. "For some adolescents, the acquisition of material possessions overrides relational concerns.... African American adolescents, seeing themselves ignored and marginalized in society and feeling they cannot find justice anywhere else in their lives, may be viewed as attempting to take justice into their own hands" (Ward, 1995). Clinicians should ask youth who are victims whether they have considered revenge, and how retribution for an assault would make them feel.

In youth street culture, children and adolescents value their ability to survive in their environment. Survival is sometimes in direct opposition with morality. Perhaps, as another author stated, "this behavior can be traced to the sense of alienation from society and institutions by poor inner-city youth. There is lack of faith in the police and the judicial system to protect inner-city people. People feel they must be prepared to take measures to defend themselves (and their loved ones) against those who are physically threatening" (Anderson, 1994). When interviewing violence-prone youth in these situations, clinicians should be aware of how issues of morality, justice, and dignity are played out.

The Child and Family Violence

The realm of family violence encompasses the short- and long-term effects of physical and sexual abuse and the witnessing of domestic violence on the child. Although there have been references to the child's family in earlier sections of this chapter, clinicians can devote a significant portion of the interview to this issue. Because children learn by what they see and hear, exposure to domestic violence and spousal abuse is a major part of the violence epidemic in the 1990s. Studies show that between 3 and 4 million children between the ages of 3 and 17 in the United States are at risk of exposure to domestic violence each year (Carlson, 1984). Although family violence is acknowledged to be common, children and adolescents may find this to be a difficult topic to talk about. Along with family violence comes secrecy, denial, avoidance, or resistance. Sometimes it is not possible to obtain information about family violence directly from the child. Cultural issues also need to be acknowledged, because attitudes and practices of family life, child rearing and discipline may vary with different ethnic or social groups.

The interviewer might start with an inquiry about the child's background and relationship with primary caretakers. Identify whether neglect or physical or sexual abuse ever occurred, or is still occurring. It may be necessary to determine whether the child is in any current danger [or risk] from being abused. The child needs to feel safe to talk about present and sometimes even past abuse. Children raised with inconsistent parenting may need to learn how to survive and fend for themselves. Ask the child to describe how his or her parents handled discipline in the family and whether all children in the home were treated equally. Was corporal punishment, such as spanking, used as the primary form of discipline? Determine whether the discipline was warm and consistent or harsh and unjustified. Inquire about the occurrence of verbal abuse as well. Children will often describe that being "emotionally abused" was a worse experience and more hurtful than the physical abuse associated with spanking or other physical forms of punishment. Also ask about sibling abuse, a question that is commonly omitted when evaluating for child abuse.

A child can witness domestic violence in several ways. Domestic violence exposure can mean having an awareness of tension in the home, such as a mother's display of fear when the man comes into the house; observing the consequences of physical abuse, such as bruises on the mother; hearing verbal threats or fighting noises coming from another room; and seeing actual incidents of verbal, physical, or sexual abuse. Ask the child specifically about knowing of, hearing, or seeing one parent assault the other parent. Try to learn if the child took steps to protect the mother. If the child was unable to protect the mother, the child may experience significant feelings of guilt and self-blame. A child who steps in to protect the mother is also at great risk for being abused. In addition, some children may become so angry that they want to or try to kill their mother's abuser. Clinicians should inquire about the child's anger toward each parent and thoughts about hurting or killing the abusive parent.

There are other consequences of witnessing domestic violence. Clinicians should consider the range of emotional and behavioral problems that can occur when witnessing violence between caregivers. Because the violence occurs in the home between adults whom the child is dependent on, the effects of witnessing domestic violence on children can be terrifying and confusing. The play of traumatized young children can show a lot of risk taking, reenactment of violent themes, and solutions stuck in themes of helplessness and hopelessness. Some children may be drawn to reexperience traumatic memories; ask if the child likes to watch scary movies as a way to master the traumatic experience of family violence. Specific emotional responses, such as anxiety, fear, guilt (particularly if fights are about them), sleep disturbances, depression, distractibility, anger, enuresis, somatic responses including stomachaches or headaches, and interpersonal difficulties such as aggression or socialization problems are possible. Resistance to going to bed, school, or leaving the mother may be symptomatic of separation anxiety, when the child worries about the safety of the mother. In those children who witness or experience fatal family violence, their response is complicated by grief, loss of comfort from their primary attachment, and other losses such as loss of home, school, and friends, when placed with relatives or foster care.

Following the discussion about domestic violence, clinicians can obtain a history of family violence that occurred outside the family. Inquire about family members who have been violent or victims of community violence and whether any relative has been in trouble with the law or been incarcerated for violent offenses. Assess the history of substance abuse and mental illness in the family. Chemical dependency and severe mental illness of caregivers significantly affects their parenting capacity, and can increase the risk of neglect or abuse of the child. Trauma and disrupted attachment, which occur in dysfunctional or disturbed families, can lead to aggression in the child. As part of the family history, the clinician should therefore ask children about their relationships within the family. Does the child have a primary attachment, and is that person capable of nurturing the child? Ask the child if there is a trusted adult to talk to when there is a problem. Identify any positive role models in the immediate or extended family and find out if an adult has

492

been consistently available. Family disruptions such as parental loss, homelessness, foster care, incarceration, or migration add to the demands on the child for secure attachment to family and affect the child's ability to form positive relationships outside of the family. Determine also if the family is connected with the community at large, or isolated and cut off from support or social services.

The Adolescent and Dating Violence

Relationship or dating violence occurs among adolescents. The clinician can ask youths whether dating has begun. Ask how any relationship is going. Find out whether someone is controlling the relationship by threats or intimidation. Determine an adolescent's attitudes and behaviors regarding battering and fighting in a dating relationship by tactfully asking about partner violence. A discussion might focus on both physical and sexual victimization experiences. Look for injuries on the face or torso, and particularly for multiple injuries. These questions can be used when interviewing adolescents about either heterosexual or homosexual relationships. For adolescent boys, a brief screening can be done by asking whether the boy has learned to respect women. Find out how the youth treats the girls he dates. Positive responses to these screening questions suggests that a more detailed inquiry into prior sexual-offending behavior is indicated. For girls, find out if they have experienced abuse within a dating relationship. Remember to provide support and validation to any adolescent who is a victim in an abusive relationship. Make it clear that no one deserves to be abused, and that safety and well-being are the highest priority.

Context of the Violence History in the Overall Assessment

A violence history should be conducted within the context of a comprehensive evaluation (including the child's psychiatric, medical, and neurological history, substance abuse history, and educational background). Pertinent issues from the psychiatric history and mental status to include are assessment of mood, neurovegetative symptoms, suicidality, homicidality, depression, anxiety, and inattention. The clinician should determine whether there is a specific psychiatric condition, whether it relates to violence, and whether the child received treatment for it. When obtaining the history of aggression, conduct, and antisocial behavior, ask whether the child has ever been arrested or picked up by the police, charged with any offenses, or involved with the court system. Ask the adolescent whether drugs or alcohol were involved or caused any fight or violent incident. Violent behavior attributed to alcohol use accounts for a significant number of murders. The clinician can educate the adolescent that people act more aggressively or impulsively when drinking and that over 50% of homicide victims have alcohol in their bloodstream.

For medical history, screen for the presence of head trauma or other central nervous system impairment that might effect cognition, impulsivity, learning, or affect. Exposure to maternal drugs during the prenatal period or lead intoxication are examples of early biological insults that can affect behavior. Ask about access to medical care—the factors that limit access to health care, such as poverty, may also increase the risk for violence. For education history, ask about school attendance, truancy, tardiness, academic performance, special education status, and grade retention. If there have been academic failures, are there vocational or alternative educational programs in which the adolescent can participate? Find out whether the adolescent plans to continue school or drop out and look for a job.

The violence history might also contain a section where the clinician obtains information about the community the youth lives in. Are there community resources available for children and adolescents that provide them with safe recreational and social opportunities? Such programs as Boys and Girls Clubs, Scouts, religious groups, antigang programs, sports leagues, neighborhood centers, mentoring programs, or summer job programs can offer youth opportunities to engage in social activities that promote personal development and nonviolent skills. Ascertain whether the child has a sense of spirituality or community, demonstrated by participation in prosocial activities or groups.

Clinician's Self-Observations

There are several issues to acknowledge during clinical work with youth at risk for violence. An important aspect of engaging the violence-prone child is to discuss the issue of confidentiality—a child may not otherwise feel safe to talk openly. A nonjudgmental approach helps break down barriers and build trusting relationships, particularly when the young person is of a minority culture or class with different values. Be aware of negative media images and stereotypes of youth particularly when interviewing children from diverse backgrounds (Stark, 1993). A violent incident described by a child may sound, at first, like another instance of "senseless" violence, but it might not have been senseless to that person.

Recognize that because violence can be an emotionally charged area both for children and caregivers, there are a variety of barriers that may interfere with providing optimal care. Bringing up issues of violence or abuse with victims can lead to discomfort. As clinicians, we should become aware of our own feelings, beliefs, and attitudes about violence in this society, and ask ourselves whether these interfere with or facilitate our clinical skills. Acknowledge whether there have been any personal experiences with violence or victimization. Prior personal experiences with such issues, or the converse, not having any personal experience with violence, may make it more challenging to empathize with a victim or perpetrator. Clinicians might feel uncomfortable asking questions about issues which may be perceived as too personal or private. It is also important to avoid the tendency to blame the victim of a violent relationship for causing the violence. Some clinicians may worry about their own safety when interviewing violence-prone youth, thinking that youth who are involved with violent incidents are "bad" or "dangerous." Many youth who are involved in violent behaviors want to find ways to avoid further violence. However, safety should not be ignored. When conducting interviews, the clinician should remember to trust her instincts and act to ensure her safety and that of the youth.

Violence is a complex problem that has no easy answers. The increased prevalence of violence among children and adolescents has been receiving attention from officials in fields such as education, law enforcement, public health, and social policy. Clinicians can play an important role in the larger picture of violence prevention by identifying those youth most at risk for becoming victims and perpetrators, developing clinical treatment plans that address violence, and referring them to appropriate community resources. While the clinician needs to focus on each individual child, be cognizant of the social, economic, and political factors that have been related to the increased incidence of violence. Blend professional expertise about the individual child with knowledge of the social ecology of life in a violent society. Taking a violence history is not only a tool that can improve the quality of care of children and help keep them safe, it is also an important component of the campaign to decrease the incidence of youth violence.

REFERENCES

Anderson, E. (1994, May). The code of the streets. *Atlantic Monthly*, 81–94.

AAP (American Academy of Pediatrics), Task Force on Adolescent Assault Victim Needs. (1996). Adolescent assault victim needs: A review of issues and a model protocol. *Pediatrics*, 98 (5), 991–1001.

Apfel, R., Simon, B. (1996). *Minefields in their Hearts: The Mental Health of Children in War and Communal Violence*. Yale University Press, New Haven.

Arria, A., Borges, G., Anthony, J. (1997). Fears and other suspected risk factors for carrying lethal weapons among urban youths of middle-school age. *Archives of Pediatric and Adolescent Medicine*, 151, 555–560.

Ash, P., Kellermann, A., Fuqua-Whitley, D., & Johnson, A. (1996). Gun acquisition and use by juvenile offenders. *Journal of the American Medical Association*, 275, 1754–1758.

Buka, S., Earls, F. (1993). Early determinants of delinquency and violence. *Health Affairs 12:*46–64.

Callahan, C., & Rivara, F. (1992). Urban high school youth and handguns: A school-based survey. *Journal of the American Medical Association, 267,* 3038–3042.

Carlson, B. (1984). Children's observations of interparental violence. In A. Roberts (Ed.), *Battered women and their families* (pp. 147–167). Springer.

CDC (Centers for Disease Control). (1993). Violence-related attitudes and behavior of high school students—New York City, 1992. *Morbidity and Mortality Weekly Report, 42,* 773–777.

Cotten, N., Resnick, J., Brown, D., Martin, S., McCarraher, D., & Woods, J. (1994). Aggression and fighting behavior among African-American adolescents: Individual and family factors. *American Journal of Public Health, 84,* 618–622.

Durant, R., Getts, A., Cadenhead, C., Emans, J., Woods, E. (1995). Exposure to violence and victimization and depression, hopelessness, and purpose in life among adolescents living in and around public housing. *Developmental and Behavioral Pediatrics 16:*4, 233–237.

Durant, R., Pendergrast, R., & Cadenhead, C. (1994). Exposure to violence and victimization and fighting behavior by urban black adolescents. *Journal of Adolescent Health, 15,* 311–318.

Freeman, L., Mokros, H., & Poznanski, E. (1993). Violent events reported by normal urban school-aged children: Characteristics and depression correlates. *Journal of the American Academy of Child and Adolescent Psychiatry, 32,* 419–423.

Gilligan, J. (1996). *Violence: Our Deadly Epidemic and Its Causes.* G. P. Putnam's Sons, New York.

Hausman, A., Spivak, H., & Prothrow-Stith, D. (1994). Adolescents' knowledge and attitudes about and experience with violence. *Journal of Adolescent Health, 15,* 400–406.

Hemenway, D., Prothrow-Stith, D., Bergstein, J. M., Ander, R., & Kennedy, B. (1996). Gun carrying among adolescents. *Journal of Law and Contemporary Problems, 59,* 101–115.

Lewis, D., Pincus, J., Bard, B., Richardson, E., Prichep, L., Feldman, M., & Yeager, C. (1988). Neuropsychiatric, psychoeducational, and family characteristics of 14 juveniles condemned to death in the United States. *American Journal of Psychiatry, 145* (5), 584–589.

Olweus, D. (1993). *Bullying at school: What we know and what we can do.* Cambridge, MA: Blackwell.

Osofsky, J. (1995). The effects of exposure to violence on young children. *American Psychologist, 50* (9), 782–788.

Pynoos, R., & Nader, K. (1988). Psychological first aid and treatment approach to children exposed to community violence: Research implications. *Journal of Traumatic Stress, 1,* 445–473.

Shakoor, B., & Chalmers, D. (1991). Co-victimization of African-American children who witness violence: Effects on cognitive, emotional, and behavioral development. *Journal of the National Medical Association, 83,* 233–238.

Sheley, J., McGee, Z., & Wright, J. (1992). Gun-related violence in and around inner-city schools. *American Journal of Diseases of Children, 146,* 677–682.

Slaby, R., & Stringham, P. (1994). The prevention of peer and community violence: The pediatrician's role. *Pediatrics, 94,* 608–615.

Slaby, R. G., Wilson-Brewer, R., & DeVos, E. (1994). *Aggressors, victims, and bystanders: An assessment-based middle school violence prevention curriculum.* Available from National Technical Information Service, 5285 Port Royal Road, Springfield, VA 22161.

Snyder, H., Sickmund, M. (1995). *Juvenile offenders and victims: A national report.* Washington, DC: Office of Juvenile Justice and Delinquency Prevention, Office of Justice Programs, US Department of Justice publication.

Sosin, D., Koepsell, T., Rivara, F., & Mercy, J. (1995). Fighting as a marker for multiple problem behaviors in adolescents. *Journal of Adolescent Health, 16,* 209–215.

Spivak, H., Prothrow-Stith, D., & Hausman, A. (1988). Dying is no accident: Adolescents, violence, and intentional injury. *Pediatric Clinics of North America, 35,* 1339–1347.

Stark, E. (1993). The myth of black violence. *Social Work 38:*485–490.

Stringham, P. (1994). *Guide to violence prevention and treatment.* East Boston, MA: Department of Pediatrics and Adolescent Medicine, East Boston Neighborhood Health Center.

Terr, L. (1985). Children traumatized in small groups. In R. Pynoos & S. Eth (Eds.), *Post-traumatic stress disorder in children* (pp. 45–70). Washington, DC: American Psychiatric Press.

U.S. Congress. (1995). *Risks to students in schools.* Washington, DC: Office of Technology Assessment.

Valois, R., McKeown, R., Garrison, C., & Vincent, M. (1995). Correlates of aggressive and violent behaviors among public high school adolescents. *Journal of Adolescent Health, 16,* 26–34.

Walsh, D., Goldman, L., & Brown, R. (1996). *Physician guide to media violence.* Chicago: American Medical Association.

Ward, J. (1995). Cultivating a morality of care in African American adolescents: A culture-based model of violence prevention. *Harvard Educational Review, 65,* 175–188.

Webster, D., Gainer, P., & Champion, H. (1993). Weapon carrying among inner-city junior high school students: Defensive behavior vs. aggressive delinquency. *American Journal of Public Health, 83,* 1604–1608.

73 / Observation, Interview, and Mental Status Assessment (OIM): Disabled

Henry T. Sachs, III

In 1801 Gaspard Itard (1775–1838), a French physician, published the first-known accounts of a coordinated assessment and treatment plan for a child with disabilities. Victor "The Wild Boy of Aveyron" made significant gains with relationship-oriented psychotherapy, social skills training, and a carefully planned educational program. This initiated a period of aggressive intervention on behalf of all individuals with disabilities lasting until approximately 1900. Unfortunately, several factors conspired to create a climate of misunderstanding and regressive policies within the helping professions toward those with disabilities during the first half of the 20th century (Harris, 1995).

Psychoanalysis diverted psychiatry's attention from this population deemed unable to benefit from the psychoanalytical approach. Mendelian principles of genetic inheritance were misapplied to support the Eugenic movement's recommendation for institutionalization and sterilization of "morons." Neurology characterized mental retardation as incurable brain pathology.

Physical disabilities became more common in adults as medical advances improved the survival rates of accident and war victims. However, society's acceptance of this population has been significantly delayed. True integration of children with handicaps with nondisabled children is only now becoming a reality. Also, it has only been in the past 20 years that clinicians have appreciated the increased risk of developing psychopathology in children with disabilities (Bregman, 1991).

Assessment

The clinical assessment and treatment planning process for a child or adolescent with disabilities is a demanding and rewarding experience which calls on all of a clinician's skills (See Figure 73.1).

In the care of children with disabilities, many issues may occur simultaneously. Clarification of presenting problems and the goals of the assessment are very important. Children with disabilities often have had numerous evaluations which characterize the extent of their disability. Sensory and physical handicaps, speech and language delays, cognitive delays, and social dysfunction may be previously documented. Foreknowledge of these issues may assist the clinician in preparing an initial clinical session that is highly productive. A competent translator for one who is deaf, enough space for a child in a wheelchair, and the presence of a knowledgeable caregiver for a child with moderate to severe mental retardation are examples of steps that should be taken before the clinician meets the child.

The child and caregiver's initial impression of a clinician's sensitivity to their special needs is crucial in fostering a clinical alliance. A well lit room with adequate space for child and caregivers, developmentally appropriate toys or activities, and minimal distractions create an atmosphere conducive to a useful clinical interview.

Observation

Observing the patient in the waiting room and watching him navigate the distance to the clinician's interview space provides valuable insight for obtaining a thorough clinical history. How is the patient interacting with those accompanying the youngster? Is the patient engaged in a group or isolated activity? Does the child appear to be aware of what is going on around him? How difficult is it both cognitively and physically for the patient to travel from the waiting room to the exam room? A brief review of these issues allows the clinician to develop lines of inquiry for the interview.

Direct observation in the clinical setting, and if

Developmental Disorders: Assessment and Treatment Planning

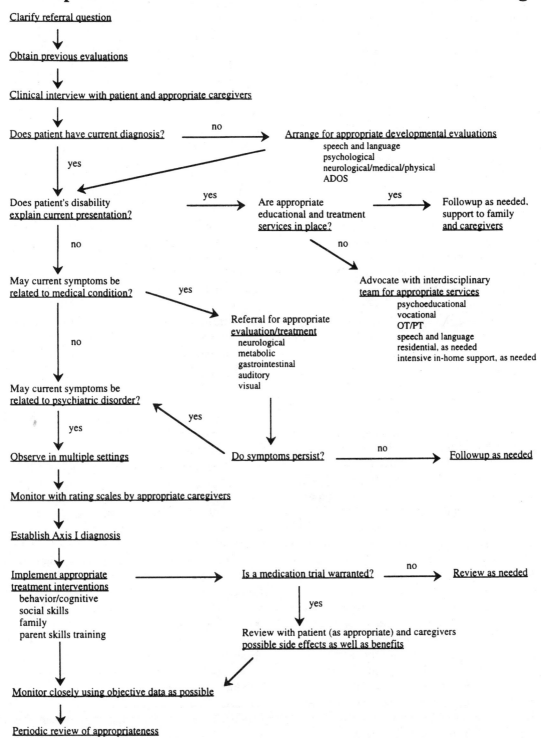

FIGURE 73.1

Developmental Disorders: Assessment and Treatment Planning

497

possible, within the child's daily environment and routine is very helpful. (See chapters 63 and 64 on Home Visits and School Observation.) It is often impossible to appreciate the degree of incapacity caused by a disability. At the same time the extent to which the challenges of a handicap are overcome is also difficult to comprehend if not witnessed firsthand.

The Interview

Most clinical interviews begin with one or more caregivers accompanying the identified patient. It is important to clarify the role these caregivers play in the child's life. If possible, the patient should be encouraged to introduce the caregivers and describe their roles.

It is common for the input of the child with disabilities to be ignored or minimized as caregivers and clinicians speak for them. This is an important trap to avoid. When appropriate, the patient should be addressed directly from the outset. Does the patient understand the purpose of the meeting? Any uncertainties should be addressed. In crisis situations, extra time and effort should be given to orienting the child and making her as comfortable with the situation as possible. Caregivers are often very helpful in this process.

Many children with disabilities have abnormal communication skills. If the child has cognitive or speech and language delays, the questions should be asked at their developmental level without being infantilizing. This usually means short, simple, questions asked after the clinician has made consistent eye contact. The clinician should speak slowly and clearly, avoiding any jargon. Comprehension of questions should not be taken for granted. The patient's understanding of what has been said should be reviewed frequently. For those who are deaf or use sign language as a form of augmentative communication, the interviewer should always address the patient and not the translator. When interviewing those with severe visual impairment, a verbal description of the setting and who is present is necessary.

Many children with disabilities benefit from devices such as hearing aids, glasses, and FM audio amplifiers and yet are hesitant to wear them for fear of ridicule from peers. In the interview setting, they should be encouraged to use these devices.

The technique of facilitated communication involves the patient spelling out words on letter boards or typewriter-like devices with some degree of physical assistance from an aide. Facilitated communication (FC) is very controversial. Initial case reports indicated dramatic improvements in the communication skills of individuals with a wide spectrum of diagnoses including autism and severe mental retardation when FC was employed. Numerous well-designed validation studies have failed to demonstrate that FC is a reliable form of communication (Montee et al., 1995). This controversy has led to resentment and confusion among patients, families, and caregivers (Delmolino & Romanczyk, 1995).

One must allow adequate time to obtain an appropriate clinical history from the patient. The pace of interviewing children with disabilities is often slower than with other children. Children with cerebral palsy may have great difficulty in their articulation. Caregivers are often helpful in clarifying difficult to understand statements. For the hearing impaired, the use of a translator may slow down the pace of the interview. For those with cognitive or speech and language delays, it is often necessary to rephrase questions several times to assist the patient in understanding the issues. The patient may look to caregivers for answers or explanations to questions if they do not understand what has been said. Answers are often tangential or incomplete. Establishing time frames for events is particularly challenging.

The clinician may be tempted to avoid these issues and go right to the caregiver for the "facts." Unfortunately this approach often leads to several unintended consequences. The opportunity for alliance building with the patient is greatly diminished. The amount and quality of information the patient can provide, especially if they are cognitively impaired, is often underestimated. Most importantly, descriptions by any caregiver of a patient's behavior, mood, concerns, or thoughts has gone through a process of interpretation. The caregiver has decided what is important, what something means, or why something has happened. It is not unusual for the patient with disabilities to report as major concerns issues that the caregiver saw as inconsequential. This is most common when the patient's developmental level is not taken into account. Finally, this direct interaction may create a common language for patient and clinician. The clinician's explanations and recommendations will have a much greater impact on the patient if given in the patient's own words and not those of the surrounding adults.

Developing an alliance with a child with disabilities greatly enhances the clinical value of the interview. Often these children have poor self-esteem and have experienced numerous social and academic failures. Questions early in the interview that address school issues and behavioral problems often are answered with increasing withdrawal. The clinician should find areas of patient strength or particular interests (sports, movies, hobbies, etc.) and allow the patient to expound on those topics for several minutes at the start of the interview. Discussing these topics with the child at their developmental level and joining them in their enthusiasm is time well spent. This technique may be especially helpful in children with restricted interests and/or significant social skills deficits. It is important to be patient in allowing the youngster time to communicate and feel comfortable with the clinician.

A 10-year-old boy with a history of language delays, severe social deficits, and restricted interests presents with parents for evaluation and treatment recommendations. After initially being withdrawn and quiet, he mentioned that it was a "happy Windsday." The clinician, demonstrating his limited knowledge of children's movies, asked what the boy meant. Boy and parents answered this was a reference from *Winnie the Pooh*. The clinician commented that he guessed the young man liked movies very much, and the boy's affect brightened immediately. When the clinician asked him to talk about his favorite movie, the boy went into a very animated replay of a scene involving seals. He enthusiastically mimicked the seals and repeated the narration verbatim. He was not redirectable for 10 minutes despite numerous social cues from the adults around him. The parents noted this was the first time any clinician had seen these characteristic behaviors. "Usually he is asked how school is and what problems he is having. He does not care about those topics and always gives just Yes and No answers."

Empathic responses are valuable tools for clinicians in eliciting a history. Often these indications of empathic understanding are facial gestures, nods, or subtle statements. With most children having disabilities, the clinician should use clear, direct statements to convey their understanding of the child's situation. Acknowledge their frustrations and highlight their strengths in overcoming their handicaps.

At the conclusion of the initial assessment several clinical questions must be addressed. What are the current behaviors and concerns that led to the initial referral? What are the child's level of cognitive, physical, and adaptive functioning? Do the child's social and play skills correspond to these developmental levels? Are there additional physical or communication disabilities? Is an undiagnosed medical condition masquerading as the current presentation? Are underlying medical conditions causing or exacerbating the current presentation? What role do environmental and support system issues play in contributing to or ameliorating the ongoing difficulties? Finally, are there any primary psychiatric diagnoses that may explain, at least partially, the child's presenting problems? An initial case formulation should be considered incomplete if these questions are not reviewed.

A detailed developmental history, including language, motor, and social milestones is needed. Family, psychiatric, and medical histories are often essential in differentiating potential etiologies of symptom clusters in nonverbal, nonabstract thinking children. Clarification of the extent of their handicaps and whether they are currently receiving appropriate services is very important. Missing or inappropriate speech and language therapy, educational or vocational services, or physical or occupational therapy may contribute significantly to any presenting problem. (See Chapter 17, Disabilities History.)

Mental Status Assessment

Creativity is an essential ingredient in a useful mental status assessment in a child with disabilities. In the course of contact, the clinician has an opportunity through observation and minimally structured interventions to evaluate most areas of concern. Children with neurological impairment have an increased risk of movement disorders. Children with cerebral palsy often face difficult challenges overcoming otherwise routine environmental obstacles. Dysmorphic features may indicate appropriate diagnostic evaluations.

Social relatedness is often difficult to assess in those with severe impairment. Extent of eye contact should be noted. The child should be given several clear social cues, such as an extended hand or encouragement to start a conversation. If the child engages in conversation, the clinician should evaluate the patient's ability to shift between subjects with verbal cueing and to allow others to lead the conversation. The manner and extent to which the child seeks comfort and support from caregivers during the assessment is very useful information.

Standard attentional and cognitive questions are often inappropriate for children with significant cognitive delays. The manner in which they present the chief complaint and history of the present illness may be most informative. Do they have a concept of time and sequencing of events? Can they stay on topic? Do they accurately recall distant and recent events? Do they understand simple analogies? Only in assessments where uncertainty of cognitive and attentional capacity remain should the clinician employ more formal mental status testing.

Many children with disabilities have great difficulty differentiating their own affective states. They may also have great difficulty assessing the affect state of people around them. Underlying sadness and depression are often masked by aggression in these children, especially those with significant language delays. The association of physical symptoms and affective state is often not appreciated. Many children have had extensive evaluations for neurological or gastrointestinal complaints related to anxiety and depression. Terms describing mood commonly used by children without disabilities may not be meaningful to children with cognitive or language delays. A clinician must carefully explore issues of mood and affect with patient and caregiver. Low self-esteem is a very common finding.

Children with disabilities often describe phenomena interpreted as auditory or visual hallucinations. Limited vocabulary, poor insight, and nonabstract thought processes may contribute to the overdiagnosis of psychotic thought processes. Children removed from the home or who have experienced other losses may report "hearing voices" or "seeing ghosts" or "angels". In periods of anxiety some children relive scenes from movies or television shows. Careful assessment of the child's affective state, the full nature of these events, and the patient's ability to communicate psychological processes will assist in differentiating true psychotic processes from other presentations.

Assessment devices such as the Aberrant Behavior Checklist, the Reiss Screen for Maladaptive Behavior, the Emotional Disorders Rating Scale, and the Diagnostic Assessment for the Severely Handicapped Scale have been developed specifically for the developmentally delayed population. These instruments may assist clinicians in differentiating and clarifying clinical questions.

Treatment Planning

In formulating an appropriate treatment plan, several questions must be addressed. What are the most likely contributing factors to the presenting complaint? Is the child able to engage in individual and/or group therapeutic processes? Is the current living and educational environment safe and appropriate? Are the needed ancillary and medical services being provided? These may include speech and language therapy, occupational therapy, special education services, neurological follow-up, etc. Does the psychiatric diagnosis dictate specific treatment interventions?

Children and adolescents with disabilities will often have a myriad of presenting difficulties. Choosing the most salient issues is essential in developing a reasonable treatment plan. Invariably, multiple clinicians, special educators, and caregivers comprise the child's clinical team. Well-communicated, detailed treatment planning, and measurable goals are critical to a successful clinical outcome. Results of the careful monitoring of targeted behaviors must be routinely reviewed. These data serve as the feedback mechanism for a treatment plan and guides ongoing changes in the plan, as needed. A well-thought-out behavior modification program is often the foundation on which all other interventions can build. Frequently the overlearned problematic behaviors of the patient and the maladaptive responses of the support system must be modified to create long-lasting improvement. (See Volume Six.)

The ability of children with developmental delays to participate in treatment planning and interventions requiring verbal communication is often underestimated. Children can benefit from discussing a lack of social acceptance, loss, disappointment, confusion, and many other topics when given the opportunity (e.g., Hurley, 1989; Sigman, 1985). An inability to verbally express troubling thoughts and feelings often leads to detrimental behaviors and inappropriate treatment interventions.

More frequent, briefer individual intervention may be more accommodating to children with short attention spans, limited ability to process information, and the need to hear topics multiple times before the concepts are incorporated. These children have internal conflicts, but these issues may be better addressed in a cognitive/behavioral therapy format. (See Volume Six.)

Many children with physical, cognitive, or communication disabilities are deficient in age-appropriate social skills. Social skills deficits can often be addressed and taught in both individual and small group settings. (See Volume Six.) For many children, the opportunity to rehearse basic social skills with other equally challenged individuals is very helpful. Finding others with similar issues is often emancipating and empowering.

Family therapy, parent skills training, and/or supportive case management work is essential in many situations. The home environment is often dramatically affected by a child's behaviors and disabilities. Questions about the child's fragility or self-management abilities frequently are confusing to families. These concerns may inadvertently support maladaptive behaviors. Many families need support in creating and maintaining an appropriate behavior modification program. Family stress and guilt may be elevated. Dealing with numerous human service, educational, medical, and legal systems can be confusing and overwhelming.

There are indications for the use of psychiatric medications in children with disabilities (Aman & Singh, 1988). The disability should not distract the clinician from considering the full range of psychiatric diagnoses. In fact, children with disabilities are at greater risk of adjustment, mood, anxiety, and sleep disorders than children without disabilities. Developmental disabilities do not protect children from diagnoses such as schizophrenia and other psychotic disorders. Attentional difficulties and tic disorders are also common in this population.

Only after correctly identifying the etiology of target behaviors can an appropriate medication trial begin. Also, many children with disabilities have known or presumed neurological abnormalities. These impairments may increase the child's susceptibility to drug side effects. Lowered seizure thresholds, disinhibition with benzodiazepines, and increased confusion or lethargy are often encountered. Clinicians must monitor and treat symptoms such as constipation. Akathesia, headaches, or other physical discomfort may be misinterpreted as increased agitation in nonverbal or minimally communicative children.

The basic rule in prescribing psychoactive medications to children with disabilities is "start low and go slow,"—a minimal initial dose and small incremental increases. Improved functioning and not sedation should be the goal of all medication interventions. Careful monitoring for side effects should be continuous and involve caregivers who know the patient well. Deterioration in behavior while on medication raises the possibility of side effects as a possible etiology for the decline. Often unusually low doses of medications are the most efficacious. The risk in such children of multiple medication use is significant. Clinicians should be aware of all the medications the child is taking. The effects of one medication on another should always be considered, even when over-the-counter cold remedies are taken. Medications that are sedating, constipating, or lead to changes in pulse or blood pressure should not be given in combination with other medications with similar profiles, if possible.

Many children with disabilities are incapable of accurately describing internal states. Therefore, objective behavioral data is often the yardstick for evaluating any specific treatment. Decreased frequencies of self-injury, aggression, or destruction may indicate a favorable treatment response. If that information is not available, meaningful assessment of interventions can be difficult.

REFERENCES

Aman, M. G., & Singh, N. N. (1988). *Psychopharmacology of the developmental disabilities.* New York: Springer-Verlag.

Bregman, J. D. B. (1991). Current developments in the understanding of mental retardation. Part II: Psychopathology. *Journal of the American Academy of Child and Adolescent Psychiatry, 30,* 861–872.

Delmolino, L. M. & Romanczyk, R. G. (1995). Facilitated communication: A critical Review. *The Behavioral Therapist, 18* (2), 27–30.

Harris, J. C. (1995). *Developmental Neuropsyhiatry: Assessment, Diagnosis, and Treatment of Developmental Disorders. Vol. II.* New York: Oxford University Press.

Hurley, A. D. (1989). Individual psychotherapy with mentally retarded individuals: A review and call for research. *Research in Developmental Disabilities, 10,* 261–275.

Matson, J. L., & Barrett, R. P. (1993). *Psychopathology in the mentally retarded* (2nd ed.). Boston: Allyn and Bacon.

Matson, J. L., & Mulick, J. A. (1991). *Handbook of mental retardation* (2nd ed.). New York: Pergamon Press.

Montee, B. B., Miltenberg, R. G., & Wittrock, D. (1995). An experimental analysis of facilitated communication. *Journal of Applied Behavior Analysis, 28,* 189–200.

Sigman, M. (1985). Individual and group psychotherapy with mentally retarded adolescents. In M. Sigman (Ed.), *Children with emotional disorders and developmental disabilities: Assessment and treatment* (pp. 259–275). Orlando, FL: Grune & Stratton.

Sturmey, P., Reed, J., & Corbett, J. (1991). Psychometric assessment of psychiatric disorders in people with learning difficulties (mental handicap): A review of measures. *Psychological Medicine, 21,* 143–155.

Szymanski, L. (1985). Diagnosis of mental disorders in mentally retarded persons. In M. Sigman (Ed.), *Children with emotional disorders and developmental disabilities: Assessment and treatment* (pp. 249–258). Orlando, FL: Grune & Stratton.

74 / Observation, Interview, and Mental Status Assessment (OIM): Competence to Testify

Karen J. Saywitz

Increasingly, children are called upon as witnesses in the legal system to report about past experiences—events ranging from kidnaping and molestation to automobile accidents and community violence. Clinicians who work with child witnesses are faced with a multi-dimensional challenge. They must be aware of the child's developmental status and clinical condition at the same time they are satisfying legal requirements and ethical codes. Clinicians must coordinate with other agencies and disciplines. They must integrate a growing body of research into case conceptualization as well.

Frequently there are no adult witnesses to verify children's reports and definitive physical evidence is lacking. Yet, legal professionals and jurors require reliable, uncontaminated information on which to base decisions regarding protection, liability, and punishment. In many cases, a child's statements can be instrumental to the course of justice, not only statements made in court but also out-of-court statements made in pretrial interviews.

Clinicians can occupy a number of roles when children are involved in the legal system, although these roles vary across jurisdictions. Often, clinicians elicit forensically relevant information from children in pretrial interviews to obtain specific statements regarding alleged crimes. In other situations, children may be referred for evaluation of behavioral changes, such as nightmares or imitations of adult sexual activity. Allegations of abuse may arise in the midst of ongoing therapy with an unanticipated need to assess imminent risk of danger to the child if returned to the caretakers. In the United States, clinical evaluations also are relied upon to determine whether or not children are able to testify at trial because testifying might be too traumatic. Clinicians may be called upon to advise the court on a child's need for special courtroom accommodations that are designed to reduce stress and allow the child to testify at her optimal level of performance, such as closing the courtroom to spectators or providing testimony via closed circuit television. Clinicians may be asked by parents or attorneys to prepare children to testify. In American juvenile and family courts, decisions about court-ordered treatment, custody, home and school placements, visitation, or family reunification are often based in part on children's testimony and on clinician recommendations. Also, in the United States, judges frequently consider indicators of reliability documented by the clinician in determining the admissibility of hearsay and other evidence. And, although the determination of competence to testify is a decision made by the judge alone, information documented by the clinician can often be instrumental to judicial decision making (Myers, 1998).

Ethical and Legal Considerations

Although there are many roles for the clinician in the forensic context, ethical and legal considerations drive role definition. For example, ethical dilemmas arise if clinicians engage in dual relationships. When a clinician is both the treating therapist and an evaluator who provides information to the court, there are often competing demands that can undermine confidentiality and therapeutic alliance. Many professional organizations recommend that in a given case, professionals take one role and refer to qualified professionals for the other (Melton et al., 1996).

Another ethical obligation is the clinician's duty to use methods sufficient to provide the necessary substantiation for their conclusions. Sufficiency varies according to context. Clinical impressions may be useful as a working hypothesis in therapy but spurned as an offer of proof in the forensic context. Routine diagnostic and therapeutic procedures developed for one purpose may have unintended ramifications when used for another in the forensic context. Certain clinical techniques, such as hypnosis or play therapy, may distort preschoolers' testimonies when utilized without appropriate precautions, potentially contributing to the pursuit of false allegations (Ceci and Bruck,

1995). Even if contamination does not occur, there is concern that some of these techniques may undermine children's perceived credibility in the courtroom if the specter of contamination is raised. When clinicians fail to consider legal implications, evidence can be rendered inadmissible, child witness credibility can be undermined, and standards of practice can be violated inadvertently. Hence, the clinician must be familiar with relevant ethical and legal issues.

Empirical Considerations

Until recently, there were surprisingly sparse scientific data to guide professionals' efforts to elicit forensically relevant information from children. At the turn of the century there was some research on child witnesses, with legal scholars suggesting that children would make quite unreliable witnesses. Often, however, the studies were flawed. After a long hiatus, research on child witnesses resumed with vigor in the mid-1980s on an international scale (Bottoms and Goodman, 1996; Ceci, Toglia, & Ross, 1987). Studies with increased ecological validity and appropriate control groups were conducted in the laboratory and in the field. Researchers focused on two central questions: Do children remember and relate their experiences in a reliable, trustworthy manner? and Is participation in the legal system unduly stressful for young children? Results have not revealed a simple relation between age and testimony or age and vulnerability. Researchers find that children can provide information that is meaningful and accurate. Yet developmental limitations are barriers to adultlike testimony. Similarly, studies of system-induced stressors suggest that testifying is not necessarily harmful for children, yet some children are vulnerable to adverse effects and benefit from special court procedures to reduce stress.

Despite the rapid expansion of scientific knowledge on this topic, researchers have not produced definitive tests of children's competence, accuracy, honesty, or their ability to withstand the stress of testifying. Instead, studies have identified a wide array of factors that are influential. To evaluate a child's statements, to recommend appro-

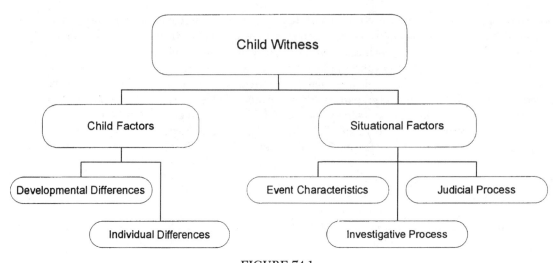

FIGURE 74.1

Factors Affecting the Child Witness

priate courses of action, and to advise both parents and judges, a professional needs to be familiar with the developmental, individual, and situational factors that can affect the child witness.

Factors Affecting Child Witnesses

Children, and their statements, are affected by numerous factors, some internal some external. Figure 74.1 displays one heuristic framework for organizing these factors. Factors to consider that are internal to the child include (1) the child's phase of development in the areas of memory, reasoning, suggestibility, and language, and (2) the child's individual characteristics such as temperament, coping pattern, and clinical condition. There are also situational factors to consider that are external to the child. These factors can undermine or facilitate the child's ability to testify optimally and without adverse sequelae and include (1) characteristics of the events under investigation, such as duration or level of violence associates with the incident, (2) characteristics of the investigative process, such as the use of coercive techniques during investigative interviews, and (3) characteristics of the judicial process itself, such as the extent to which it accommodates to a given child's needs and limitations. The remainder of this chapter discusses these factors and their

application to the work of clinicians with children involved in the legal system.

DEVELOPMENTAL FACTORS

No matter what the reason for referral, a child's stage of development will be a factor in almost every determination. Developmental factors influence the kinds of information to which a child can testify, the level of detail a child provides, and the best methods for eliciting reliable information. A question easily answered by a ten year old, such as "How many times did he do that?" can elicit confusion and misunderstanding when asked of a four year old who answers "five times" aloud and simultaneously raises seven fingers in response. The four-year-old in this case has not yet learned to count but knows enough numbers to guess from, fertile ground for misinterpretation. Stage of development is clearly a factor in assessing whether to rely upon or disregard the child's answer.

Memory: A child's phase of memory development is key to determining the kind of information and the level of detail a child can provide independently. Children at different phases of memory development will perceive, encode, and retrieve different kinds and amounts of information—information elicited with varying degrees of prompting. Developmental limitations on memory are not merely a function of less capacity to store information. As they grow, children are able to use more complex and successful memory jogging strategies to increase the amount of detail they retrieve spontaneously. The way they interpret situations and the kinds of information they notice and earmark as important come to resemble the kinds of forensically relevant information required of witnesses.

Although a 10-, 5-, and 3-year-old who witness the same event can each provide relevant and accurate information, their renditions will take different forms. When asked, "What happened?" the ten-year-old may respond with a highly detailed narrative in chronological order, while the five-year-old may simply say "We played." In this case, the 5-year-old's spontaneous recall, despite its accuracy, is insufficient for clinical and legal decision making (Myers, 1998). When the younger child is prompted with a few simple, direct questions, he or she can describe central actions quite accurately, but the information provided is driven by the questions (e.g., "Where did you play?" "On the playground." "Who did you play with?" "Mary and Bob." "What did you play?" "We went on the swings.").

Unfortunately, the questions used to elicit additional information, if misleading, can undermine the accuracy, relevance, or consistency of children's statements. In the forensic context, this can result in grave consequences if it leads to the accusation or conviction of an innocent adult. The problem is especially true of the 3- to 4-year-old witness. Such very young children are ones who require the most specific questions to trigger recall, but they are the most vulnerable to contamination by misleading questions as well. Their reliability is highly dependent on the way in which they are questioned.

Language Acquisition: In addition to memory differences, children vary in their ability to comprehend the vocabulary and linguistic complexity of questions in and out of court. Miscommunication is responsible for a great many of the inconsistencies in children's testimony, rather than memory failure or dishonesty. At early stages there is a limit to the number of words children can process in a sentence. Children who do not yet comprehend sentences over 5 to 7 words in length should not be asked lengthy questions containing linguistically complex constructions that are typical of adult conversation. In one case, a 4-year-old was asked, "When your mom took you to your uncle's house last Sunday, did you stay the night or did you drive back to San Diego and have dinner with your dad?" "No." This 30-word question is overloaded with embedded clauses, not to mention requests to verify days of the week and locations that a 4-year-old is unlikely to have mastered. In reality, it is several questions under the guise of one. Does the child's response of "No" mean she did not visit her uncle, did not do so on Sunday, did not stay the night, did not drive to San Diego, or did not have dinner with her dad? Several short questions, rather than a single overloaded one, are required to elicit reliable information from a 4-year-old.

Cognitive Development: Besides memory and language, children differ in knowledge, experience, and reasoning ability. To evaluate a suspect's alibi, a child may be asked to pinpoint the time of an event. If a child who has not yet learned to tell time is asked when something occurred, the answer must be heard within that context. Telling time is not fully mastered until second grade. Young children cannot be relied upon to indicate that a question is beyond their ability. Often, they contradict themselves or stretch to explain something that is beyond their understanding. In order to determine jurisdiction, a witness may be asked to establish a location in terms of miles or city or state; to identify a perpetrator, a witness may be asked to describe height in feet and inches, weight in pounds. However, young children learn these conventional systems for measurement gradually over the course of the elementary school years.

When children are asked questions they do not possess the skills to answer, their responses must be interpreted within a developmental framework. Individual responses may need to be disregarded, although they do not necessarily invalidate everything a child has to offer. When a child in a case of alleged sexual assault describes that "white glue came out his penis," this response is not interpreted on the basis of its factual inaccuracy. Instead it is considered with the understanding that young children create their own explanations for what they observe around them. It is developmentally appropriate for a child to liken an unfamiliar substance (semen) to a familiar one (glue) on the basis of its physical characteristics in order to make sense of the unfamiliar experience. Mischaracterization of semen as glue is a developmentally expected reasoning error that highlights the authenticity of the response, not its incredulity.

While these examples have focused primarily on the role of development in questioning children and interpreting their answers, developmental considerations are vital in other areas as well. One last example highlights the child's emotional maturity as a factor in determining the need for special court procedures. Young children possess a limited repertoire of strategies for coping with anxiety provoking situations. Since avoidance is a common one, children are often reluctant or resistant witnesses. Older children can put their feelings in perspective and invoke alternative coping methods to help themselves through an unpleasant experience for the sake of some greater good or delayed gratification. The younger child may be overwhelmed with the feelings of the moment and may not be able to testify without external accommodations to alter the factors causing anxiety.

The way evidence is customarily elicited from adult witnesses is not sensitive to the capabilities, limitations, and needs of children. Often, the reliability of a child's statement has more to do with the competence of the interviewer to conduct a developmentally appropriate interview than the competence of the child to offer reliable evidence. The past fifty years of research on child development provide a framework to guide the clinician in the forensic context. A clinician will need to assess a child's developmental level in order to phrase questions in language that is understood, interpret responses accurately, and formulate meaningful recommendations. Given that clinicians will be called upon to explain and justify their methods and conclusions in the adversarial process, clear procedures and rationales need to be developed. A developmental framework provides a rationale for choosing one technique, interpretation, or recommendation over another. It is a rationale that can be easily articulated when called to testify.

INDIVIDUAL FACTORS

The younger child is not necessarily a less able witness nor the one in need of the most protective measures in the courtroom. Competence and credibility may be dominated by emotional and temperamental factors unrelated to the child's age. A shy, insecure, and withdrawn 5 year old may refuse to testify or may burst into tears. An outgoing, friendly, and self-confident 5 year old may proceed with minimal difficulty. These differences have little to do with age or the truthfulness of their testimony. But often, the former child is judged incompetent or less credible than the latter.

In addition to influencing the perception of the child's competence, emotional factors can influence the memory retrieval process itself. For example, in pretrial interviews with unfamiliar authority figures, or in the courtroom, transient emotional states such as anxiety associated with the fear of the unknown and feelings of inadequacy could divert attention, disorganize mental operations, or reduce the motivation for memory retrieval. Hence momentary feelings, self-perceptions, and coping strategies could facilitate or undermine the memory retrieval process. A recent study suggests that childhood trauma may influence the course of brain development itself (Perry, Pollard, Blakley, & Vigilante, 1995). If replicated, it may show that traumatized children do not always process information similarly to nontraumatized peers.

The different ways in which children of any age cope with the stresses of victimization, parental discord, and violence, can affect their demeanor on the stand and their need for special accommodations. Coping with mastery may lead some children to experience testifying as cathartic; they may want to have their day in court. Other children may cope by using avoidance or denial. These children may refuse to talk without special court procedures, such as closing the courtroom to spectators or the presence of a support person in the courtroom. Clinicians can be called upon by parents, attorneys, or judges to consult on individual cases regarding a child's need for special procedures.

Researchers who study children referred to clinics for suspicion of abuse find that they display certain clinical symptoms at significantly higher rates than nonreferred peers, although many of these symptoms are found among children who are distressed for reasons unrelated to abuse. These symptoms can include anxiety, depression, nightmares, suicidal ideation or behavior, schizoid-like avoidance and social withdrawal, low self-esteem, sleep disturbance, somatic complaints, fearfulness, and dissociation (Beitchman, Zucker, Hood, daCosta, & Akman, 1991; Pynoos & Eth, 1984; Terr, 1990). However, many genuinely abused children fail to demonstrate any measurable psychiatric symptoms. Yet when such symptoms do exist, they can influence a child's demeanor, motivation, ability to concentrate and to recall, as well as their need for special courtroom accommodations. Still, clinicians should be aware that when abuse is suspected, these behaviors indicate that further evaluation is necessary (Melton et al., 1996). Their existence alone cannot be used to determine the occurrence of maltreatment. As well, their absence cannot be used to conclude that a child was not maltreated.

Children of the same age also differ in their ability to cope with the stress of the investigative and judicial process itself. Most studies of the emotional effects of testifying on children suggest that child witnesses of all ages are moderately to highly stressed at the time of initial interviews. However, stress dissipates over time. Still, some children do appear to be more vulnerable to the adverse effects of court involvement than others. These include children with very negative experiences, such as those called to testify several times, those who endure particularly harsh cross-examinations, and those with certain a priori vulnerabilities. For example, children with low levels of social support due to multiple losses of primary attachment figures through placements in a series of foster homes could be at greater risk of adverse effects than children with sufficient parental support and stable, secure attachments.

Psychiatric disorders common among child crime victims include depression, acute stress disorder, posttraumatic stress disorder (PTSD), dissociative disorder, reactive attachment disorder, generalized anxiety disorder, and sleep or adjustment disorders (Beitchman et al., 1991). It is not difficult to speculate how the symptoms of disorders such as PTSD (e.g., flashbacks, hyperarousal, psychogenic amnesia, dissociation) or depression (anhedonia, psychomotor retardation, difficulty concentrating, hopelessness) could dramatically influence children's demeanor and performance on the stand. Such disorders could also render children especially vulnerable to the stresses of the legal system. For example, children suffering from PTSD also strive to avoid thoughts, feelings, and situations associated with the traumatic event.

This can include avoidance of interviews and courtrooms. Such behavior creates an uncooperative, oppositional, or indifferent witness who may be perceived by jurors or interviewers as being dishonest or incompetent. A child who suffers depression may display poor concentration, delayed, one-word utterances, indifference, and indecisiveness that could undermine both memory function and credibility, especially when such symptoms are mistaken for lack of sincerity or evidence of confabulation. In such cases, clinicians may be consulted to determine the need for special courtroom accommodations. Testifying under traditional conditions may be overwhelming and even dangerous for a child with a past history of suicide attempts. Sensitivity to children's individual characteristics is critical to evaluating their needs and capabilities in the forensic context.

Situational Factors

THE EVENT UNDER INVESTIGATION

Other determinants of children's testimony are related to the event under investigation (Goodman and Bottoms, 1993; Zaragoza, 1995). For example, characteristics of the crime can determine the ease or difficulty of recalling the incident. These include the retention interval, type and severity of alleged offense, presence of weapons, coercion, violence and threats, and the familiarity of the location and of the perpetrator. For example, the location of the crime can affect a child's ability to recall details; a familiar environment is easier to describe than an unfamiliar one. A crime that occurred in the distant past involving strangers is more difficult to recall than a recent incident with known participants. It may be more difficult to testify against a parent than a stranger because feelings of ambivalence or guilt interfere with truth telling. A child who has been threatened with bodily harm may possess higher levels of fear that hinder testifying. Generally, studies confirm that a child victim is likely to have a better memory for an event than a bystander. On the other hand, embarrassing information may be less likely to be reported to an unfamiliar interviewer than more neutral information. These types of event factors must be considered in setting expectations for a child's performance and determining whether his statements are credible.

THE INVESTIGATIVE PROCESS

The pretrial investigative process varies greatly across cases and communities. Characteristics of the investigation can influence a child's testimony and stress level (Ceci and Bruck, 1995; Melton et al, 1996; Myers, Saywitz, & Goodman, 1997; Zaragoza, 1995). For example, the level of maternal support, the number of interviews, the interviewer's demeanor, the setting, and the wording of questions have been identified as influential. Most studies suggest that maternal support during the investigative process is associated with improvements in a child's mental health. However, if caretakers are suspected of maltreatment or neglect, children may be removed from their homes and placed in the care of unfamiliar foster families, isolated from their support system for long periods of time. In other cases, even parents who are not suspected of abuse may refuse to entertain the possibility that their child has been abused. Without their parents' support, testifying in court is an onerous task, and these children appear to be more vulnerable to system-related stressors.

In addition, children may be questioned repeatedly, each time telling their story to yet another unfamiliar adult. There is some research to suggest that multiple interviews with unfamiliar authority figures may be more stressful for children than fewer interviews with follow-up conducted by the same person. Moreover, the variations across multiple interviews can create unnecessary inconsistencies in children's statements. Children typically report different information in different settings, depending on the way questions are worded, their familiarity with the interviewer and the setting, how much time has passed since the event, and the consequences to the child of previous disclosure (e.g., removal from home, pressure to recant). Thus the number and nature of investigative interviews can create inconsistencies, even in valid cases of abuse.

Another concern with investigations that involve too many interviews is the concern that if suggestive techniques were used repeatedly, then the child's testimony will be distorted (Ceci & Bruck, 1995). Recent studies highlight the danger when young children are repeatedly questioned week after week with misleading questions about information from the distant past that is difficult to recall. It is important to note, however, that repeated questioning in and of itself is not necessarily problematic; when questions are not misleading, repetition can strengthen and consolidate memory.

Even within a single interview, children's reports are influenced by the psycho-social atmosphere created by the interviewer. An accusatory context in which suspects are referred to as "bad" people who did "bad" things increases the potential for distortion of children's statements. Precautions need to be taken. Accusatory contexts can be avoided without the loss of vital information.

Additionally, children's reports vary depending on characteristics of the interviewers (social status, supportiveness) and the setting (familiarity, formality). In one study, the social status of the questioner was reduced when leading questions were posed by another child rather than an adult. Suggestibility effects were reduced, indicating that children in this study acquiesced to leading questions more frequently when posed by authority figures. In another study, age differences in recall were eliminated when the interviewer created a supportive climate. Three-year-olds in the supportive atmosphere performed at a level comparable to 5-year-olds in a neutral one. Hence the demeanor of the interviewer can influence the quality of children's testimony.

The setting itself can be influential. Studies indicate that children can use certain retrieval strategies to aid recall in their homes that they do not use in the laboratory, presumably an unfamiliar, anxiety-provoking environment. Children are more easily influenced by the context than adults. Children's memory performance can be less than optimal in complex, unfamiliar, settings that possess few cues and stimulus supports, especially on verbal tasks. Inconsistencies across different settings are to be expected, even in genuine cases of abuse. Clinical tools that use consistency as a measure of reliability are being re-evaluated in light of such findings.

Complicating matters further, the wording of questions is critical to eliciting a reliable account from a child. Wording can vary along a continuum of suggestiveness—questions can be open-ended and nonleading (e.g., "Is there anything you want to tell me?") or highly leading ("It was Henry who hurt you, wasn't it?"). Reasonable minds differ on the degree to which questions in the center of this continuum have the potential to aid or distort children's recall, depending on the specific circumstances of the case and the age of the child (Doris, 1991). The spontaneous reports of very young children are woefully incomplete—insufficient for legal decision making. Three- to 4-year-olds are the most in need of focused questions to direct their attention to a particular topic ("Tell me about preschool.") and specific questions ("Was he wearing a jacket?") to tell what they know. They have little understanding of the purpose of the interview, limited ability to judge the forensic relevance of information, and difficulty employing strategies to retrieve details independently. Unfortunately, they are also the most vulnerable to contamination if such questions are misleading.

Although some 3-year-olds are resistant even in the face of relentless interviewers, others acquiesce to adult suggestions, rendering their reliability difficult, if not impossible, to determine. By 6 to 7 years of age studies show a dramatic increase in resistance to suggestive questions. In one recent study, only the most highly leading forms of the questions continued to mislead substantial proportions of children in the 5- to 7-year-old range. Increasing resistance to suggestion has been documented up to the age of 10 to 11 years.

At one end of the continuum of suggestiveness, the thoughtful and judicious use of mildly leading questions can elicit additional information that is not otherwise forthcoming—information that could protect a child from imminent physical danger. At the other end of the continuum, deliberately biased and coercive interviewing, combining several suggestive techniques in one interview, may result in the implanting of fictitious events into a very young child's memory and lead to false accusations.

Further research is needed to examine whether children distinguish between actual and implanted memories or whether they come to believe the fictitious events occurred. Study of the malleability of childhood memory is a relatively new area of research. There is no doubt that conclusions and guidelines will continue to evolve as new data emerge. Based on the available data, it appears to be far easier to change a memory than it is to erase it or implant a fictitious one, although it is not impossible to do so with young children (Leichtman & Ceci, 1995). To date, there is little evidence that it would be easy to implant enduring memories of sexual abuse via interviews by professionals (Pezdek, 1995; Pezdek & Roe, 1997). Typically, errors in response to individual leading questions are omissions of information, not the confabulation of sexual or aggressive incidents. Children, like adults, tend to be more resistant to leading questions about personally meaningful actions in which they participate (undressing, genital touch) than about peripheral details (eye color); although even reports of central events can be distorted by repeated, accusatory, and biased interviewing. To date, much of the research is limited in its ecological validity and applicability to children who are victims of abuse. More research is needed to clarify these important matters. There is no doubt that pretrial interviewing is a powerful influence on children's reports. Young children's suggestibility during the investigative process presents a challenge to which the clinician must respond, but it does not render interviewing impossible if appropriate precautions are taken.

THE JUDICIAL PROCESS

The legal system is a complex network of unfamiliar people, places, and situations for which children are ill-prepared. They can become involuntary participants in a system evolved for the needs of adults (Goodman, Levine, Melton, & Ogden, 1991). The judicial process itself can facilitate or undermine a child's testimony. It can heighten or lessen the stress of an already vulnerable child. System-induced stress can prevent a child from testifying to the best of his or her ability. The quality of a child's testimony is, in part, a function of the degree to which the system accommodates to the child's needs and limitations (Spencer & Flin, 1993). For example, continuances are frequent in the legal context. However, some (although not all) studies have found that delays are associated with slower recovery from depression and higher ratings of stress. Further, people experience forgetting of details over time.

Hence this common legal practice may compromise testimony and interfere with mental health recovery. It has been suggested that continuances and pretrial delays be limited in child witness cases.

On the basis of the available literature it cannot be stated conclusively that testifying is either harmful or beneficial to children. In the United States, there is some evidence to suggest that testifying in criminal court may impede the recovery of some children, while testifying in juvenile court proceedings may enhance the recovery of others. These two contexts differ dramatically. These two courts, criminal and juvenile, have very different mandates and burdens of proof. Criminal proceedings are adversarial with numerous protections for defendants and no constitutional protections for witnesses. Child protection hearings in juvenile court are aimed at developing a plan that is agreeable to all parties, with hearings that are less confrontational and where children are rarely subjected to cross-examination. When they do testify in juvenile court, it is often in the judge's chambers rather than in public. These findings suggest that the relaxed rules of evidence and procedure in juvenile court are beneficial for children.

Although the process is not harmful for most children, some are vulnerable to adverse long-term effects. Extensive delays, numerous interrogations by insensitive authority figures, confronting the accused, harsh cross-examination, lack of preparation, and multiple court appearances are differentially stressful for these children (Spencer & Flin, 1993). Children also express fears of public speaking, humiliation, and rejection, as well as confusion regarding the expectations placed upon them in court. In response, special court procedures have been developed to offset system-related stressors. These include

- The presence of support persons during children's testimony
- Limits on continuances
- Closing the courtroom to spectators
- Testimony via closed-circuit television
- Appointment of an attorney for the child
- Videotaping of pretrial interviews to reduce the number of interviews and to be used in lieu of courtroom testimony when children are unable to testify

- Scheduling changes to ensure that children testify during school hours and receive regular breaks
- Allowing children to take special objects to the stand for security
- Nonverbal demonstrations to supplement limited language skills.

Even the U.S. Supreme Court has considered the potential liabilities and benefits of special courtroom procedures for children. Advocates claim that some child victim witnesses are emotionally vulnerable and might otherwise be unable to testify at all or may provide only single-word responses and fragmentary testimony that invites misinterpretation as inconsistent with prior statements made under less stressful circumstances (e.g., *Coy v. Iowa*, 1988; *Globe Newspaper Co. v. Superior Court*, 1982; *Maryland v. Craig*, 1990). Critics claim that some special accommodations violate the defendant's right to confrontation and due process as well as the public's right to access the trial through the press, and that some techniques are prejudicial. The U.S. Supreme Court has determined that the need for innovations be evaluated on a case by case basis. For example, closing the courtroom to spectators and other alternatives to confrontation can be used only when it can be shown that a child would suffer serious emotional trauma if she had to testify under traditional circumstances. Clinical evaluations may be relied upon on a case-by-case basis in judicial decision making on these matters.

Available research studies of mock courtroom trials and field studies of actual child witnesses suggest that interventions limiting children's involvement in legal proceedings and shielding them from the defendant can reduce stress. Although legal professionals agree that such innovations are useful in decreasing a child's stress, these are rarely employed in the United States. Survey studies suggest that only those innovations that are inexpensive, easy to implement, and those unlikely to be challenged by the defense are employed. In other countries (e.g., Great Britain) reforms, such as videotaped testimony and closed-circuit television during cross-examination, are frequently used. These examples illustrate the ways in which the judicial process itself can impair or enhance a child's ability to provide the best testimony she is capable of providing.

A Case Illustration

A comparison of two cases will illustrate the interaction among the developmental, individual, and systemic factors discussed above. First, consider the testimony of a 6-year old alleged victim of sexual abuse by a teacher's aide 6 weeks earlier. A girl with strong parental support, showing no signs of serious psychological distress, could be expected to provide a meaningful account of what happened to her, testifying about a known person, a familiar place, and a salient personally meaningful event in the recent past, providing the examiner takes into account her level of knowledge and suggestibility. She should be able to respond accurately to direct questions about major actions in the absence of repeated, highly leading suggestions. A 6 year old may also need age-appropriate preparation, the presence of support persons, and the comfort of a favored object, such as a doll or teddy bear, in order to talk freely from the witness box.

Consider, on the other hand, a 13-year-old alleged victim of sexual abuse, suffering from posttraumatic stress disorder, testifying in a high-profile case to charges of forcible rape by a well-respected member of the community. Her age suggests accurate, detailed memory of the event, with a level of resistance to suggestion that may be comparable to that of an adult. But her age also suggests that she will experience acute levels of embarrassment and self-consciousness that could render her testimony incomplete or inconsistent, especially if she fears public exposure, peer rejection, and injury to self-esteem. Moreover, the severity of her abuse, the use of threats and force, and her current emotional disturbance may make it more difficult to obtain testimony in open court than is the case for the younger child. Testifying under such conditions of emotional distress could stimulate even more serious psychological reactions, such as flashbacks, dissociative episodes, or suicidal thoughts. In such a case, it may be necessary to consider more significant protective measures, such as closing the courtroom to spectators. Clinicians involved in these cases need to consider the developmental, individual, and situational factors that may affect children's testimonies to make recommendations to attorneys, judges, or parents.

Enhancing a Child's Testimony

ELICITING RELIABLE INFORMATION

Experts tend to agree on a general approach to questioning children based on our understanding of their memory and suggestibility. Most guidelines recommend beginning by offering children an opportunity to make a spontaneous statement as close in time to the event as possible to stem forgetting and lessen the need for leading questions (Bull, 1995; Lamb, 1994; Saywitz & Goodman, 1996; Yuille, et al. 1993). In general, authors recommend creating an opportunity for children to provide the most independent and complete description possible in their own words (Jones & McQuiston, 1986; Lamb, 1994; Yuille, et al., 1993). There is solid evidence to endorse the practice of beginning the interview with the most open-ended and nonleading approaches first, even when interviewers anticipate such efforts will be fruitless (Lamb, 1994). Many children do respond to open-ended questions with relevant and meaningful information. A number of experimentally derived protocols, such as cognitive interviewing (e.g., Saywitz, Geiselman, & Bornstein, 1992) and narrative elaboration (Saywitz & Snyder, 1996; Saywitz, Snyder, & Lamphear, 1996), advocate this approach as do clinically derived approaches that have been field tested, such as the step wise approach (Yuille et al., 1993), and the protocol developed by Lamb and his colleagues (Lamb, et al., 1994).

If open-ended questions are not fruitful, introducing the topic of interest (e.g., sexual abuse) seems to be the step in the interview where empirical research offers the least guidance. There are a number of approaches that have been recommended in the clinical literature but have not been tested empirically (Jones & McQuiston, 1986). There is consensus that once a child begins his description of the event, he should be allowed to proceed at his own pace, without interruption. Adults can prompt children to elaborate with statements such as, "and then what happened," or "tell me more," when the child pauses (Lamb et al., 1994; Yuille, et al., 1993). Following the child's narrative, the interviewer moves to relatively open-ended "wh" questions (e.g., "Who was there?" "What did he look like?" "What did she do?" "What did they say?" "Where did it happen?"). Becoming progressively more specific, interviewers proceed to short-answer questions with queries that help children elaborate in their own words.

REDUCING SUGGESTIBILITY

Recent studies of young children's suggestibility highlight the importance of a clinician maintaining an objective, neutral stance toward the veracity of any allegations that arise (Ceci & Bruck, 1995). In every decision, clinicians should strive to minimize both false allegations and failure to detect genuine abuse to the greatest degree possible (e.g., Lamb, 1994; Lamb, Sternberg, & Esplin, 1994; Lyon, 1995; Myers, Saywitz, & Goodman, 1997). Biases need not be intentional or explicit, they can be conveyed inadvertently in tone of voice, facial expression, or in an intimidating, accusatory context.

The clinician must generate alternate hypotheses and explanations for children's statements, and continually revise hypotheses as new facts emerge (Yuille, et al., 1993). For example, if a young child states that she was touched on her "pee pee," the clinician must consider the explanation of routine toilet training or bathing and explore the circumstances leading to the touch. One study suggested that when clinicians carry inaccurate presuppositions about what happened, they are more likely to use leading questions. Clinicians must refrain from drawing conclusions prematurely on the basis of leading questions that confirm their presuppositions. Another precaution to reduce the potential for distortion is to refrain from inquiring about information obtained from other sources (e.g., parents) until elaboration of the material provided by the child is exhausted.

Laboratory studies of young children's suggestibility indicate that leading questions are to be avoided whenever possible (Doris, 1991). On the other hand, studies of memory development have long documented the incompleteness of children's spontaneous reports and the value of prompts and focused questions to elicit additional information (Fivush and Hudson, 1990; Goodman and Bottoms, 1993). Interviewers can limit the use of leading questions by rephrasing yes-no questions into "wh" questions that have less potential for distortion (e.g., "Did he hit you?" be-

comes "What did he do with his hands?"). If yes-no questions are used, they can be followed by queries that require children to elaborate, justify, or clarify their responses in their own words ("Tell me more." "What makes you think so?" "I'm confused."). This ensures that a child's "yes" or "no" means what the interviewer assumes it means.

Given the variability case to case, the use of progressively more specific questions might be justified under certain conditions but not others. In a case with corroborative evidence indicating that an older child is in imminent risk of physical danger, and when the child seems reluctant to complain, the cautious use of leading questions is justified. In another case, where the child is very young and no longer in contact with the alleged perpetrator, the same questions may not be justified or necessary to make an appropriate plan. Clinicians will need to be aware of local and professional protocols and to develop their own guidelines for considering each case on its own merits. In general, studies to date find that when interviewed in a relatively straightforward manner, school-age children are capable of providing quite useful testimony. On the other hand, the testimony of 3 and 4 year olds can be heavily influenced by the interview process, and precautions must be taken to avoid undue influence and misinterpretation of the child's statements.

REDUCING MISCOMMUNICATION

Arriving in the courtroom, a child resembles the traveler in a foreign land who has little knowledge of its language, culture, or laws. In court, professionals speak legalese. Incomprehensible rules of evidence dictate every interaction. Transcripts of child witness examinations are replete with questions poorly matched to the child's level of comprehension. Such discrepancies can create unnecessary inconsistencies, misunderstandings, and omissions. For example, the vocabulary used can be critical. Studies show that young children are unfamiliar with many legal terms. In one study, children asked to define legal terms typically gave the familiar meaning and denied the term could possess an alternate meaning in a court of law (e.g., "court is a place to play basketball," "charges are what my mom does with her credit card") or they demonstrated auditory discrimination errors, assuming an unfamiliar word (jury) was a familiar one (jewelry) (e.g., "a jury is that stuff my mom wears on her fingers & ears,").

In court, young children who comprehend one- to two-syllable words are often asked questions containing three- to four-syllable words. In one instance a child was asked to *identify* (a four-syllable word) someone in the courtroom. She said that she could not, but when she was asked to *point to* (two one-syllable words) the person in the hall, she did so accurately. The phrasing created unnecessary inconsistencies. Another preschooler denied seeing a *weapon* at the scene of the murder, but later agreed there was a gun present. The abstract, hierarchical, and categorical term *weapon* was either unfamiliar or insufficient to trigger recall of the specific, concrete, visualizable object *gun* that had been perceived, encoded, stored, and was potentially accessible to retrieval, depending on the way the question was worded.

In addition to sophisticated vocabulary, courtroom questions often involve a level of linguistic complexity beyond the child's understanding. Compound sentences with embedded clauses and double negatives are common in and out of court. Unfortunately many of the grammatical constructions which abound in the courtroom are not mastered by children until 7 or 8 years of age. Overloaded questions that ask several questions under the guise of one and limit a child's responses to yes or no are plentiful in the courtroom—fertile ground for misinterpretations on both sides of the communicative interchange. Complicating matters further, young children are not adept at detecting noncomprehension (Dickson, 1981). They rarely request clarification. Children may try to answer questions they do not fully understand. Their response is an association to a part of the question that was understood or remembered. Unfortunately adults often perceive the response as the answer to their intended question.

To minimize miscommunication, clinicians must evaluate a child's level of language acquisition and then match the vocabulary and grammar of the question to the child's language level. This can be accomplished by listening to the child's speech during rapport development, asking the child to describe the room or to tell what happened that morning. Is the child's speech intelligible? On average, how many words are there in a sentence? How many syllables? How complex is the grammar? How sophisticated is the vocabu-

lary? As a general guide, children ought to understand if interviewers phrase questions in utterances of comparable length, complexity, and vocabulary. Younger children will require shorter utterances and fewer syllables per word.

Recently researchers have begun to develop innovative techniques to improve children's testimony. In one study, barriers to communication were reduced by preparing children for questioning. These children were warned that they may not understand all the questions in order to disabuse them of the notion that they should provide a substantive response to every question. Children were given permission to ask for clarification and rephrasing. School-age children were quite successful at eliciting a simpler version of the question and providing accurate responses.

USING SPECIAL TECHNIQUES

Special tools are sometimes used to question allegedly abused children. These include gender-neutral line drawings and anatomically detailed dolls. Body drawings are used by asking children to name each body part, its function, and whether it has been injured, and if so, under what circumstances. In evaluations of suspected maltreatment, such activities can reveal developmentally inappropriate knowledge of sexual activity and/or descriptions of physical or sexual abuse.

The use of anatomically detailed dolls has been surrounded by more controversy. Critics claim that the dolls are unnecessarily suggestive if used improperly and taint a child's statements, fostering false allegations. Proponents claim that when used with appropriate caution, dolls help children with limited language ability and emotional reticence to show (in addition to tell) what happened to them, promoting discovery of genuine abuse. Research studies show that the dolls are not a test of abuse. Sexually explicit doll play, in and of itself, although rare in the normal population, cannot be used to diagnose or prove a child has been molested. When dolls are introduced according to semistandardized protocols, and children clearly state that "this is what happened to me," while demonstrating with dolls, additional, information may be forthcoming. However, recent studies suggest that the use of dolls may be contraindicated for 3 to 4 year olds. Children in this age range have difficulty using dolls for self-representation. At the very least, additional precautions are necessary with young children (Koocher et al., 1995). More research to illuminate the costs and benefits of using dolls with young children is clearly needed and is under way.

ASSESSING COMPETENCE TO TESTIFY

In the forensic context, competence refers to whether or not a child is qualified to be a witness and testify. In the United States, most states follow the Federal Rules of Evidence which state that every person is qualified to be a witness, regardless of age. A witness is presumed to be competent unless there is a showing to the contrary. However, if a child's competence is challenged, a judge must determine competency. This is generally accomplished with a hearing outside the presence of the jury. States differ in the criteria used for determining whether a witness is incapable and must be disqualified. Historically, four areas of competence have been highlighted in U.S. courts (*Wheeler v. U.S.*, 1865). These include the abilities (1) to perceive the event accurately, (2) to remember the event without coaching, (3) to communicate memories verbally, and (4) to differentiate truth from falsehood and understand the duty to tell the truth in court. In most modern courts, the focus is on the last of these four considerations.

It is important to distinguish between a child witness' competence and his credibility. A witness who is legally competent may nonetheless be judged unbelievable. The average child under 3 years of age would be unlikely to possess the verbal skills necessary for testimony, yet there is no minimum age for competency. On occasion, 3 year olds have taken the stand and cases in which 3 year olds testified have been affirmed on appeal. In general, the developmental literature suggests that children 4 years of age and older are likely to have the minimum level of competency necessary to testify. Most children this age have the ability to recall some autobiographical events and to describe them verbally, albeit succinctly. They understand that it is wrong to lie and important to tell the truth (Goodman and Bottoms, 1993).

Although many states have relaxed their competence requirements, allowing anyone to testify, the Federal Rules of Evidence still maintain that any person who testifies must take the oath. Alternate wordings, such as promising to tell the truth, are frequently used with child witnesses. The law assumes that a promise to tell the truth has an effect on the witness. In fact, some researchers have found that children will keep secrets when asked to do so, concealing the truth and suggesting that they view a promise as a commitment.

Recent research suggests that by 5 years of age even abused and neglected children with serious delays in verbal ability from disadvantaged and ethnically diverse backgrounds can demonstrate a good understanding of the meaning and morality of truth telling and lying. This understanding is apparent, however, only if sufficiently sensitive procedures are used to assess competence. In one study, delayed, disadvantaged, and allegedly maltreated 5 and 6 year olds appeared incompetent when asked to define or explain the difference between the truth and lies (a skill not mastered until 7 years of age in this sample). However, these 5 year olds were able to demonstrate competence when asked to identify truthful statements and lies as such. Hence it is probably best to give children age 5 and over sample statements that can easily be verified visually (e.g., the color of the interviewer's clothing) and ask them to identify if the statement is in fact true or false.

With 4 year olds, especially those who may be maltreated, neglected, developmentally delayed, or economically disadvantaged, another method may be best. While 4 year olds in one study were extremely good at identifying truthful statements as such, they were no better than chance at identifying lies as lies. They avoided calling the experimenter a liar. However, in a series of studies they were able to demonstrate adequate competence when assessed in a very specific way. They were presented with two fictional child characters depicted on a page. One made a true statement, the other a false statement, about an object also depicted on the page. The 4 year olds were able to identify when the fictional character lied, even though they had not been able to do the task when it involved the experimenter. In fact, for children whose verbal abilities were not delayed and have not been environmentally deprived, 3 year olds have demonstrated competence when assessed with this simple picture task.

Some clinicians believe it is helpful to assess and document a child's legal competence at the time of the pretrial interview. This can be important. The information can be used in advising attorneys who are trying to determine whether a child witness is capable of testifying and should take the stand. In addition, some types of hearsay statements are admissible in U.S. courts only if the child was legally competent to testify at the time the hearsay statement was made, that is, at the time of the interview. Some clinicians believe that it is helpful in their own determination of a child's reliability or credibility if they can be certain that the child does, in fact, understand the obligation to tell the truth.

Clinicians should refrain from using a child's ability to count, recite the alphabet, tell time, state their address, or provide birth dates as methods of evaluating competence. In fact, such questions could inadvertently result in discrimination against children from disadvantaged backgrounds. Similarly, admissions of belief in fantasy figures, such as the tooth fairy or Mickey Mouse, are not relevant to competency determinations. Inconsistency does not necessarily disqualify a child witness. As mentioned previously, certain types of inconsistencies are to be expected from child witnesses in certain stages. Similarly, factual mistakes do not render a child incompetent. In one case, a 4 year old was qualified as a witness despite the fact that she insisted she was only 5 months old, since otherwise she gave a coherent and plausible account of molestation. In another case, even though a 5 year old did not know her address, how long she had lived at that address, how long since she had gone to school, or the name of her church, the trial judge's determination of competency was sustained on appeal because of that judge's ability to observe her demeanor and because the record reflected the child gave a credible account of molestation. These judges took the children's limited knowledge base into account when evaluating competence.

PREPARING CHILDREN FOR COURT

Children are ill-equipped to enter the adversarial system. Fear of the unknown and unrealistic expectations may influence a child's memory performance and their experience of stress. Children have a limited context for understanding the purpose of questioning, the functions of the various professionals, or the rules by which people interact in the legal setting. Their misunderstandings

can result in heightened and unrealistic fears, failure to recognize the significance or consequences of their testimony, and failure to use the "big picture" to put their feelings in perspective and cope with the stress of testifying.

Studies generally find that children under 10 years of age have somewhat limited knowledge of the legal system. For example, in one study, many 4 and 5 year olds did not know that the judge is in charge of the courtroom or that the judge has decision-making responsibilities. They described the judge's function in terms of appearances ("He wears a robe, bangs a gavel, and sits up high," "He listens"). They expressed the belief that the judge is omniscient (e.g., "He knows if you are telling the truth or not"). Young children expressed the belief that jurors were mere spectators. Many did not understand that they were impartial but assumed these unfamiliar adults must be friends of the defendant. Some children believed they would go to jail if they made an inadvertent mistake on the stand. Many children did not understand the flow of information from the police officer to the attorney to the judge, expressing surprise or betrayal when they learned that strangers had knowledge that had been disclosed in private.

Typically preparation of child witnesses involves a brief tour of the courtroom. This is helpful to desensitize children to the setting, but insufficient. Court schools have arisen in many countries to educate children and demystify legal process and procedure. Recent studies of preparation programs in the field and in the laboratory stress the need for more extensive preparation that includes the use of anxiety reduction techniques such as deep breathing and stress inoculation training, as well as efforts that prepare children for the unique memory and communication demands placed upon them in court. However, preparation must be distinguished from coaching children on the facts of the case. More studies are needed to demonstrate that preparation approaches are free of contaminating effects on children's memory.

When clinicians are involved in preparing child witnesses, there needs to be close coordination with the attorney calling the witness. At the very least, children may benefit from understanding the functions of the various professionals in the courtroom. Children need to be instructed not only that the judge is in charge, but that she will ensure that no one gets hurt, that the proceeding is fair, and that the bailiff will keep order. Children need to understand why they are in court and how the proceeding relates to the previous investigation. They need to understand the flow of information from the investigation to the trial, so they are not surprised when information provided in perceived confidence is now public information in court.

Children need to know what will happen in the courtroom. Advance education makes the unfamiliar less threatening. It keeps children from operating under misplaced perceptions. Children may benefit from a brief outline of what will happen, including instructions about the mechanics of testifying (e.g., "Talk into the microphone. You cannot nod your head; you must say yes or no out loud"). Even so they may need reminders throughout their testimony if it extends over hours and days rather than minutes.

Children need to understand their own role as a witness, that they will be questioned regarding events they have seen or heard. Children also need to be instructed in language they can understand regarding the obligation to testify truthfully. The specific explanation will differ depending on the type of case.

Children need to understand that they are a team player, that their testimony is only one piece of information to be considered in juror and judicial decision making. They need to understand that many factors are beyond their control. Children should not be made to feel responsible for the outcome of the case. A child needs to hear that the adults, and not the child, have the responsibility and authority to make decisions.

IDENTIFYING CHILDREN IN NEED OF SPECIAL COURT PROCEDURES

Identifying children in need of special courtroom accommodations is a case-by-case determination. Children at risk for adverse effects of testifying tend to be found in cases involving severe abuse, physical injury, weapon use, threats of retaliations against the child or family, little corroborative evidence, and little family support. As previously mentioned, children who testify multiple times or children who encounter particularly lengthy or harsh cross examination may experience more stress. In realistic mock trials, children who refused to testify tended to be younger children, children of lower verbal ability, children with poorer memory in pretrial questioning, and children with greater pretrial anxiety. Although there are no data bearing directly on the relation between psychiatric disorder, developmental delay, social history, and courtroom stress, it is reasonable to assume that children with uncomplicated pasts, in stable, nurturing environments, without signs of prior psychopathology, dysfunction, or delay may be less vulnerable to system-induced stressors than other children.

History is often a good predictor of future behavior. Children who have shown maladaptive patterns of coping with past stressors may be in greater need of accommodation. Prior reactions to court appearances, questioning, and threats of retaliation can be good indicators of who may be in need of special accommodations to testify. For example, a child who was threatened that a sibling or parent would be injured if the child ever told what happened may develop suicidal ideation after pretrial questioning. This child is an obvious candidate for special accommodation when the time to testify arrives. Additionally, children may be vulnerable to system-induced stress if they become so anxious they can not speak, blame themselves, feel stigmatized, or fear humiliation and rejection by loved ones if they testify.

To determine the necessity for special accommodations in a given case, judges labor to balance the rights of the defendant, the needs of the child, and the demands of society for a child's testimony. Clinician's can aid judges to be more informed decision makers by providing an assessment of the clinical, developmental, and systemic factors operative in a given case. Although the available research is insufficient to prove that special court procedures reduce anxiety and promote reliable testimony from children, judges are often in the unenviable position of making decisions on the basis of incomplete information. Clinicians who stay abreast of the latest research in the area and who conduct developmentally sensitive evaluations of individual children can offer judicial decision makers an additional source of valuable information to consider.

Past studies have revealed considerable information about child witnesses' capabilities, limitations, and needs. Devoting similar resources to improving the quality of children's testimony and reducing their distress should be rewarded with a greater protection of both children and adults in the forensic context. The clinician can play a unique role in enhancing the reliability of children's testimony and reducing children's distress. Such efforts should forward the course of justice and children's well-being.

REFERENCES

Beitchman, J. H., Zucker, K. J., Hood, J. E., daCosta, G. A., & Akman, D. (1991). A review of the short-term effects of child sexual abuse. *Child Abuse & Neglect, 15* (4), 537–556.

Bottoms, B. L., & Goodman, G. S. (Eds.). (1996). *International perspectives on child abuse and children's testimony.* Thousand Oaks, CA: Sage publications.

Bull, R. (1995). Innovative techniques for the questioning of child witnesses, especially those who are young and those with learning disability. In M. S. Zaragoza, G. R. Graham, G. C. N. Hall, R. Hirshman, Y. S. Ben-Poroth (Eds.), Memory and testimony in the child witness (pp. 179–194). Thousand Oaks, CA: Sage.

Ceci, S. J., & Bruck, M. (1995). *Jeopardy in the courtroom.* Washington, DC: American Psychological Association.

Ceci, S. J., Toglia, M. P., & Ross, D. F. (Eds.). (1987). *Children's eyewitness memory.* New York: Springer-Verlag.

Coy v. Iowa, 487 U.S. 1012 (1988).

Dickson, W. (Ed.). (1981). *Children's oral communication skills.* New York: Academic Press.

Doris, J. (1991). *The suggestibility of children's recollections.* Washington, DC: American Psychological Association.

Fivush, R., Hudson, J. V. (1990). *Knowing and remembering young children.* New York: Cambridge University Press.

Globe Newspaper Co. v. Superior Court, 457 U.S. 596, 73 L. Ed. 2d 248: §50 (1982).

Goodman, G., & Bottoms, B. L. (Eds.). (1993). *Child victims, child witnesses.* New York: Guilford Press.

Goodman, G. S., & Bottoms, B. (1993). *Child victims, child witnesses: Understanding and improving testimony.* New York: Guilford.

Goodman, G. S., Levine, M., Melton, G. B., & Ogden, D. W. (1991). Child witnesses and the confrontation clause: The American Psychological Association brief in *Maryland v. Craig. Law and Human Behavior, 15* (1), 13–29.

Jones, D. P. H., & McQuiston, M. (1986). *Interviewing the sexually abused child* (2nd ed.). Denver, CO: The C. Henry Kempe National Center for the Prevention and Treatment of Child Abuse and Neglect.

Koocher, G. P., Goodman, G. S., White, C. S., Friedrich, W. N., Sivan, A. B., & Reynolds, C. R. (1995). Psychological science and the use of anatomically detailed dolls in child sexual abuse assessments. *Psychological Bulletin, 118* (2), 199–222.

Lamb, M. (1994). The investigation of child sexual abuse: An interdisciplinary consensus statement. *Child Abuse & Neglect, 18,* 1021–1028.

Lamb, M. E., Sternberg, K. J., & Esplin, D. W. (1994). Factors influencing the reliability and validity of statements made by young victims of sexual maltreatment. *Journal of Applied Developmental Psychology, 15,* 255–280.

Leichtman, M., & Ceci, S. J. (1995). Effects of stereotypes and suggestions on preschoolers' reports. *Developmental Psychology, 31,* 568–578.

Lyon, T. (1995). False allegations and false denials in child sexual abuse. *Psychology, Public Policy, & Law, 1* (2): 429–437.

Maryland v. Craig, 110 S.Ct. 3157 (1990).

Melton, G., Goodman, G., Kalichman, S., Levine, M., Saywitz, K., & Koocher, G. (1996). Empirical research on child maltreatment and the law. *Journal of Clinical Child Psychology.* 24 (Suppl.), 47–77.

Myers, J. E. B. (1998). *Legal issues in child abuse and neglect* (2nd ed.). Newbury Park, CA: Sage Publications.

Myers, J., Saywitz, K., & Goodman, G. (1997). Psychological research on children as witnesses: Practical implications for forensic interviews and courtroom testimony. *Pacific Law Journal, 28,* 3–91.

Perry, B., Pollard, R., Blakley, W., & Vigilante, D. (1995). Childhood trauma, the neurobiology of adaptation, and "use-dependent" development of the brain: How "states" become "traits." *Infant Mental Health Journal, 16* (4), 271–291.

Pezdek, K. (1995, July). *Childhood memories: What types of false memories can be suggestively planted?* Paper presented at the Society for Applied Research in Memory and Cognition Meetings, Vancouver, Canada.

Pezdek, K., & Roe, C. (1997). The suggestibility of children's memory for being touched: Planting, erasing, and changing memories. *Law and Human Behavior, 21* (1), 95–106.

Pynoos, R. S., & Eth, S. (1984). The child as witness to homicide. *Journal of Social Issues, 40,* 87–108.

Saywitz, K., Geiselman, R. E., & Bornstein, G. (1992).

Effects of cognitive interviewing and practice on children's recall performance. *Journal of Applied Psychology, 77* (5), 744–756.

Saywitz, K., & Goodman, G. (1996). Interviewing children in and out of court: Current research and practice implications. In J. Briere, L. Berliner, J. Bulkley, C. Jenny, & T. Reid (Eds.), *APSAC handbook on child maltreatment* (pp. 297–318). Newberry Park, CA: Sage Publications.

Saywitz, K., & Snyder, L. (1996). Narrative elaboration: Test of a new procedure for interviewing children. *Journal of Consulting and Clinical Psychology, 64,* 1347–1357.

Saywitz, K., Snyder, L., & Lamphear, V. (1996). Helping children tell what happened: A follow up study of the narrative elaboration procedure. *Child Maltreatment, 1,* 200–212.

Spencer, J., & Flin, R. (1993). *The evidence of children: The law and the psychology* (2nd ed.). London: Blackstone.

Terr, L. (1990). *Too scared to cry: Psychic trauma in childhood.* New York: Harper & Row.

Wheeler v. U.S., 158 U.S. 523 (1865).

Yuille, J. C., Hunter, R., Joffe, R. & Zaparnuik, J. (1993). Interviewing children in sexual abuse cases. In G. S. Goodman & B. L. Bottoms (Eds.), *Child victims, child witnesses: Understanding and improving testimony.* (pp. 95–115). New York: Guilford.

Zaragoza, M. (1995). *Memory and testimony in child witnesses.* Newberry Park, CA: Sage Publications.

75 / Observation, Interview, and Mental Status Assessment (OIM): Competence for Independent Decision Making

Peter Ash, Gregory Jurkovic, and Saul Isaac Harrison

The assessment of a youngster's decision-making capacity and right to privacy can pose a challenge for clinicians. A young patient may be considering a decision, such as whether to attend college, to get involved in a sexual relationship, or to have an abortion. Parents may ask the clinician for advice: should they defer to a youngster's preference about going or not going to camp, or what schedule should be used in visiting a divorce parent. Courts may want to make use of expert opinion on such questions as whether a youngster is a "mature minor" and so is legally competent to consent to an abortion, whether a child can form a "reasonable preference" which should be given weight in deciding custody postdivorce, or whether an adolescent was competent to waive his Constitutional right not to incriminate himself when talking to the police following arrest.

Whether or not a child has the capacity to make a decision is not determinative of who has the authority to make the decision. In some cases, such as those which typically involve courts, there are legal rules which determine who decides. In many arenas, parents hold the reins of decision making but may defer to their child's wishes. In many day-to-day activities, children make their own decisions, such as the mundane (who should be their friend, choice of activities) and in those activities which youngsters typically do not bring to adult attention (e.g., drug and sexual behavior). Decisions in all these arenas may be brought to clinicians for their advice as to whether the youngster has developmentally achieved the requisite capacity.

Age Guidelines

As children mature, their ability to reason increases. Other capacities relevant to decision making, such as general knowledge, appreciation of risk, social judgment, readiness to seek and accept consultation, and accumulated experience, also develop. Because many of these capacities are complex to assess individually, but do correlate roughly with age, chronological benchmarks have evolved as the predominant way of providing communal rules. Historically, ages that approximate multiples of seven have tended to be encoded in both civil and religious law, with the age of 7 being considered the end of infancy, 13 to 14 as marking the beginning of adult responsibilities, and 21 (now often 18) as the age of majority and the granting of all adult rights and privileges. Seven and 14 correspond also with Piagetian notions of important shifts in cognitive developmental level. A comprehensive exploration of these issues can be found in *How Old is Old Enough?* (Group for the Advancement of Psychiatry, 1989).

Research has provided a number of general findings to keep in mind. In most studies, normal children 15 years old and older have been found to have cognitive decision-making capacities not significantly different from those of adults, and in some studies the threshold age has been placed at 14. This has been determined by posing hypothetical situations to youngsters, asking about their choices, probing for the reasons for their choices, and comparing their responses to those of adults. Specific capacities which have been studied include competency to waive the right to remain silent and the right to an attorney following arrest (Grisso, 1981), decisions about consenting to health care (Weithorn & Campbell, 1982), and decisions about psychoeducational interventions (Adelman, Lusk, Alvarez, & Acosta, 1985).

The limited research on preadolescent decision making suggests that for decisions on issues *within their experience,* preadolescents tend to choose reasonable outcomes when compared with older youngsters or adults. However, preadolescents are typically unable to cite the reasoning underlying their decisions. Children as young as 5 to 12 have been found to make reasonable decisions on issues of minor health care (Lewis, Lewis, Lorimer, & Palmer, 1977), 9 year olds in one study made reasonable preferences about custody in hypothetical divorce situations (Garrison, 1991), and 7 to 13 year olds were found to make useful contributions to psychoeducational placement decisions (Taylor, Adelman, & Kaser-Boyd, 1985).

It is in the age range of normal 10 to 14 year olds that questions of decision-making capacity are especially problematic. Also problematic are those children with developmental delays and psychopathology which render general age guidelines inappropriate. Particularly in these two classes of youngsters, case-by-case assessment is necessary.

Components of Decision Making

Assessment of a youngster's capacity to make a decision involves exploring the following components:

- Awareness of the existence of a choice and the nature of the decision being made
- Voluntariness of choice
- Knowledge of alternatives and their consequences
- Reasoning in weighing alternatives
- Having a preferred outcome

To assess capacity we should focus on the *process* of making a decision rather than on the content of the chosen outcome. As is the case with competent adult decision making, the clinician's disagreement with the decision itself does not necessarily bespeak the underlying decision-making capacity. But the selected outcome does provide a context for assessing the decision-making process: a decision to refuse treatment which will lead to death, for example, requires greater scrutiny than a decision to accept conventional life-saving treatment, although the formal decision process is identical.

Assessment Techniques

AWARENESS AND VOLUNTARINESS OF CHOICE

A contaminating factor in assessing this capacity is children's experience that their parents have made virtually all of their major decisions for them. Thus children may assume a choice is not theirs to make. In consequence, even in situations in which they do have a say, it is not uncommon for children to assume they do not. They may believe their assent is being sought to rubber stamp a decision already made, or that their task as decision maker is to second-guess their parents. Finally, they may defer to parental pressure (Scherer, 1991). A familiar example is the adolescent brought for inpatient psychiatric admission in a jurisdiction that allows adolescents to veto voluntary admission. The reluctant adolescent whose parents want admission may be subject to powerful pressure, pressure that may include threats of negative consequences if the adolescent refuses admission. The tendency for youngsters to believe they have no choice may also be influential in the presence of nonparental authority figures. Thus Grisso (1981) found that many younger adolescents did not appreciate that they had the option of refusing to answer questions asked by the police. In his study, practically no adolescents younger than 15 elected to remain silent even after being read the standard *Miranda* warning which advises them of their right not to answer questions asked by the police.

The issues of awareness of the right to decide and voluntariness are complicated most when a decision is being assessed in retrospect. Prospectively, clinical exploration with youngsters can serve to clarify their understanding of their role. Such discussion can also be used to educate the child as to what that role actually is.

KNOWLEDGE OF ALTERNATIVES AND THEIR CONSEQUENCES

Experience is a great teacher, and youngsters have had less than adults. The amount of *relevant* experience, however, needs to be assessed. In some instances a youngster has had more relevant experience than those adults endowed with the power to decide. An 8 year old will have had considerably more experience with each of his divorcing parents caregiving skills than the court-appointed evaluator who has spent an hour discussing with each competing parent their parenting skills and observed each parent and the child interacting. While the child may be able to articulate little in response to generalized questions, such as "Who do you usually go to when you're feeling bad?", a child's strong preference gains weight by virtue of the child's wealth of experience, particularly in the absence of recent attempts to curry the child's favor (has Dad been giving him presents every time Jimmy comes over?). If a child has had experience with the consequences of a particular event, the child can take those consequences into account without having the more abstract reasoning ability of being able to consider himself in a hypothetical situation which has never been experienced. When asked to consider what they would do in hypothetical treatment dilemmas, 9-year-olds have been shown

to make reasonable choices regarding routine medical interventions (Lewis, 1981), but they have a more difficult time with choices outside their range of experience (Weithorn & Campbell, 1982). Thus the clinician should explore the youngster's background of experience.

In cases in which the child does not know the range of alternatives or their likely outcomes, the clinician must also assess whether education will remedy the situation by providing information of value to the youngster. The youngster may be in a position analogous to that of an adult patient facing a decision about medical treatment: the patient may not know the range of treatments or their probable outcomes, but may be able to make an informed decision when provided with information.

REASONING IN WEIGHING ALTERNATIVES

The most complex aspect of the assessment tends to be the assessment of the youngster's reasoning process. This assessment involves four aspects:

- The youngster's ability to think and reason generally
- The child's reasoning about the particular issues involved
- The presence of developmental tendencies which affect reasoning
- Emotional conflicts which interfere with the utilization of existing capacities

Assessment of General Reasoning: Key cognitive processes in decision making involve the capacities of

- Imagining oneself in a future situation
- Understanding causal connections (causal reasoning)
- Hypothesizing about a variety of consequences associated with different choices (consequential reasoning)
- Evaluating various alternatives and their outcomes (evaluative reasoning) (*cf.* Spivack, 1976).

To evaluate a child's reasoning capacity, it is not sufficient to refer them for IQ testing with the traditional psychometric instruments. Although intelligence and achievement tests reflect what children have learned and their capacity to achieve in school, they do not specifically assess their ability to apply their knowledge in making real-life decisions. A youngster, for example, may be fully aware of certain consequences of a course of action, particularly if prompted or informed, but may fail to exercise awareness and consider a range of consequences when faced with a new decision.

Naturalistic Observations: One way to assess a child's reasoning is to observe and to probe the child's spontaneous behaviors, comments, questions, and conceptualizations for signs of mature causal, consequential, and evaluative reasoning. With regard to causal thinking, the clinician should observe whether the child spontaneously links his actions to consequences in the decision-making process. If not, the clinician can ask how the child decided on a particular course of action. What did the child think? Did the child consider the effects of the choice?

CASE EXAMPLE

When 11-year-old Johnny was asked why he had stolen the wallet out of a schoolmate's purse, he merely said, "I wanted some money to buy a Coke." Because of a number of more serious offenses that he had committed earlier, he was placed in detention. The judge had explained to him that one more violation of any kind would result in placement. Johnny was confused. He said, "I don't get it. I didn't get locked up for stealing that car. I take two bucks and I'm thrown in here."

This interaction points to limitations in Johnny's understanding of cause and effect. Although most children his age are able to engage in simple causal reasoning, that is, to connect A and B, such as a particular misbehavior and its punishment, they may have difficulty incorporating mediating events into their thinking about the causal relation of A and B. Johnny did not understand the role of the mediating event: he did not grasp the implications of the judge's warning, that his history of delinquency would result in a stiffer consequence for a minor offense than would have been the case if his record were clean. If questions were being asked about his capacity to enter into a decision involving several interrelated variables (e.g., about a life-threatening surgical procedure), information gleaned from the quality of his thinking about an unrelated decision, his decision to steal a wallet, would be important to consider.

When evaluating consequential thinking, the clinician should note whether the youngster spontaneously considers a range of outcomes in the effort to explain the rationale for a choice. If such consequential thinking is not spontaneous, the child can be asked to speculate about possible consequences. The more prompting that is required, the less likely the youngster is able to engage in such thinking. Illustrative of a well-developed capacity to think both causally and consequentially are the spontaneous remarks of 14-year-old Mary who was experiencing increasing peer pressure to become sexually active.

I decided not to. *Why?* Well, I just started thinking about what could happen. I mean, well, I might get pregnant. But that's not all. I don't know, it scares me. I'm just not ready, you know. And all this stuff about AIDS and diseases and safe sex. What if he didn't want to be safe? You know what I mean? It'd be hard for me to deal with that—like say something.

Not only does Mary exhibit the ability to project into the future and to generate various hypothetical outcomes but she also shows signs of evaluative thinking. For example, imagining how she would respond to pressure to engage in unsafe sex helped her to decide to abstain.

Areas in which to question children regarding evaluative thinking (weighing the pros and cons of alternatives) include How do they decide which alternative is best? Do they spontaneously compare and contrast various decisions and their consequences? Are they able to do so with minimal prompting?

CASE EXAMPLE

Because of an attention deficit disorder, 15-year-old Cliff had been prescribed stimulant medication. Although it helped significantly, he questioned the need to continue medication. He said, "I just don't want to take that stuff. I know it helps me calm down in school and stuff. My grades are better. I just don't like taking pills." When asked what might happen if he discontinued his medication, Cliff said, "I don't know. School will probably get hard again. Maybe zeros in math and stuff. I guess my teachers will be on me. I don't know. I'm not taking that stuff anymore."

Expressive of his difficulty in evaluative thinking, Cliff resisted efforts to encourage him to weigh the different outcomes.

Questions About Hypothetical Situations: Along with evaluating spontaneous responses, questions regarding hypothetical dilemmas can reveal a child's ability to exercise causal, consequential, and evaluative reasoning.

CASE EXAMPLE

Twelve-year-old Jack was presented with a health-related dilemma. *Let's say that you had a rare medical condition that surgery might help. But the surgery is risky. Would you want to help decide whether to have the surgery?* Well, yeah. *What would you think about in making the decision?* I guess whether it'd hurt. *Hurt?* Yeah, you know, the operation. *Would you think about anything else?* Not really. I'm not going to let some doctor hurt me. *But what if you might die without the operation?* I don't know. I just wouldn't think about that.

Jack's responses reflect limited causal, consequential, and evaluative thinking. If evidence from other sources (such as his thinking about real-life problems) is consistent, then it is likely that his general decision-making capacity is limited.

The answers of 14-year-old Jane to a different dilemma illustrate a more sophisticated cognitive orientation to making decisions.

What if some of your best friends were planning to skip school one day and asked you to skip with them? How would you decide what to do? I'd see what I had to do in school that day. And the chances of getting into trouble. *Anything else?* You can imagine what problems might come up. You might end up with a lot of homework. You may have to deal with your Mom, like convincing her you went to school. You might not do as well on a test later in the week. If you skip, you might keep doing it. It won't matter to you. You could drop out of school. Not go to college.

Jane demonstrates a good ability to understand cause and effect and to generate consequences.

Assessment of Reasoning Concerning the Particular Issues of the Decision: In addition to questioning a child's responses to real-life and hypothetical situations to assess their general decision-making capacity, questions that tap the specific issues of the decision being addressed can be constructed. For example, 14-year-old Henry decided that his placement in a self-contained classroom for behavior disordered students was no longer helpful and he asked to be mainstreamed. Administrators and teachers at his school were ambivalent about his request. Although his behavior and grades had improved, he was again experiencing problems. Henry's therapist was contacted by school officials to help decide on the best course of action. School personnel wondered if Henry's input should be considered. His therapist queried him about his decision.

Tell me how you decided that you no longer needed special education. I just don't need it anymore. You know I was doing much better. I was paying attention in class, doing homework. My grades came up. *But you've not been doing so well lately.* Yeah, I haven't. I thought when I improved, they'd move me to regular classes. It's kind of depressing to work so hard and then nothing happens. *Has that affected your school work?* Yeah, it has. I started thinking, why do the work if I'm just going to be left in those classes. *Has anything else happened to affect your work in school lately?* Well, yeah. I've made some new friends. They're in the regular classes and keep asking me why I'm in special ed. It's embarrassing. It's getting to me. But, I guess, I know if I start messing up again, I'll never get back to regular classes. So I decided to ask to be moved. *What if you're moved and you still have problems?* I've thought about that. I'm not going to mess up if I'm moved. If I did, then I'd be back in special ed forever. What would my friends think? And the teachers wouldn't ever take me seriously again. I know I can do the work now.

Two qualities of Henry's reasoning support a recommendation to school officials that they seriously consider his request: (1) his appreciation of cause and effect, and (2) his consideration of various consequences of alternative choices and actions.

In assessing whether a youngster has the capacity to make decisions, the nature of the decision in question must be considered. More complex decisions require more advanced reasoning abilities. For instance, a juvenile offender may be presented with the apparently uncomplicated option of naming his accomplices to avoid incarceration. In doing so, a simple understanding of cause and effect appears sufficient. However, if the youngster is unable to imagine and to compare various consequences of a choice to maintain loyalty to his peers versus the consequences of incarceration on his education, family relationships, and general well-being, then questions should be raised about his capacity to make this decision.

DEVELOPMENTAL INTERFERENCES WITH REASONING

Reasoning encompasses not only cognitive factors, psychosocial factors also contribute to mature judgment (Scott, Reppucci, & Woolard, 1995; Steinberg & Cauffman, 1996). Several expected developmental proclivities need to be considered as potentially interfering with judgment in reaching a decision. As a group, adolescents are often perceived as egocentric, risk taking, impulsive, and susceptible to peer pressure. These characteristics need to be evaluated in each individual instance. With increasing age, adolescents show increased awareness of risk, appreciation of future consequences, and comprehension of vested interests (Lewis, 1981).

Egocentrism in young adolescents often reflects a cognitive limitation in considering one's actions from the perspective of others, which leads to a view of oneself as invulnerable (Elkind, 1967). For example, it is not uncommon for 13 and 14 year olds who are sexually active to decide not to practice safe sex and birth control because they egocentrically think that unlike others, they are special, that they will not become pregnant or contract a sexually transmitted disease. The extent to which adolescents take undue risks is unclear (Furby & Beyth-Marom, 1992). Some of the limited research on adolescent risk taking (see, e.g., Quadrel, Fischhoff, & Davis, 1993) suggests that for decisions not made impulsively, adolescents, when compared to adults, do not see themselves as significantly more invulnerable to bad outcomes. The nexus between risk taking and impulsivity is complex. A particular youngster's risk taking and impulsivity can best be assessed by his history of other risky and impulsive behavior, including a previous history of accidents, and by discussion of the risks involved in a particular decision. The clinician should be on the lookout for aspects of the discussion process, such as inattention, rapid shift of focus, or an adolescent's wish to reach premature closure, which may indicate

impulsivity. The consistency over time of the child's choice should be assessed. If a child's preference changes from day to day or from week to week, the preference is not solidly grounded, which may reflect an impulsivity born of varying feeling states or a cognitive style of focusing on the most recently obtained information. Some clinical conditions, such as ADHD and certain organic brain syndromes, generate impulsivity as a symptom, and we need to pay special attention to this issue when dealing with youngsters with such conditions. For those decisions in which a clinician's input is sought, the process of assessment usually alters the decision-making process by making it considerably more deliberate, and this discussion can counterbalance the youngster's inattention. The clinical situation also allows for interventions which can often slow down impulsive tendencies, such as focusing the youngster's attention on the decision or discouraging premature closure. When the decision-making process is being reviewed retrospectively (e.g., in determining whether a youngster is to be held responsible for having waived a right or for possessing a particular level of criminal intent at the time of a crime) the question of impulsivity is more difficult. Generally it requires a detailed reconstruction of the adolescent's mental processes at the time of the relevant act.

Early adolescents are especially concerned with conformity to peers. This tendency peaks at age 11 to 12, then decreases (Grisso & Vierling, 1978). Here again, discussion with the youngster can illuminate whether the decision is perceived as consistent with the values of his peers. To what extent are friends actively encouraging a particular choice?

EMOTIONAL INTERFERENCES WITH REASONING

A youngster's cognitive capacity can be compromised by emotional conflict.

CASE EXAMPLE

Joanne, 14, was seen in consultation because she was refusing surgery for removal of a suspicious ovarian cyst. The surgeon anticipated the surgery to be a relatively uncomplicated and probably curative procedure. Two years previously, Joanne's father had died unexpectedly while undergoing surgical removal of a cerebral aneurysm. Joanne was still grieving for her father, and had repeated fantasies that she too would die during surgery.

Clinical work with Joanne should try to help her achieve a realistic assessment of her medical condition, help her distinguish the risk of her surgery from what happened to her father, and explore the extent to which her own depression was coloring her view of her prognosis. While clinicians may identify the interfering effects of emotional conflict, the fact that many issues have to be decided in a fairly short time calls for only a brief, albeit intensive intervention.

HAVING A PREFERRED OUTCOME

A youngster may have the capacity to make a decision, but may not *want* to make the decision, thereby avoiding thinking through the issues and formulating a choice or, alternatively, keeping the choice secret. In these cases the clinician should consider carefully whether to push the issue. For example, it is not uncommon for children in parental custody disputes to signal that they have either not formed a preference as to which divorcing parent they wish to live with, or that they may have a preference but do not want to express it, often out of fear (sometimes well-founded) of alienating one parent or of being caught up in the acrimony of marital strife. In other types of decisions, a youngster may feel so overwhelmed by the emotional conflicts associated with the issue or have regressed in conjunction with medical illness that they prefer to feel taken care of by parents. While youngsters' appropriate strivings for autonomy merit support, childhood and adolescence simultaneously entail the right to be taken care of. Pushing a responsibility on an unwilling child can cause significant trouble. Since for most issues a parent stands by ready to make the decision for the youngster, those youngsters can usually defer to parental choice.

Intervention

The assessment of decision-making capacity is a deliberative process which, by its nature, affects the decision-making process. For each of the decision-making steps, it is likely that discussion with an empathic clinician will help a youngster clarify preferences, consider new possibilities, become aware of areas of incomplete information, etc. As these issues are discussed, the clinician has many opportunities for maximizing a youngster's capacity to make a good decision. Further, the youngster's ability to make use of the clinician's input provides additional data regarding decision-making capacity. By highlighting the limitations in a youngster's decision-making process, assessment provides direction for ameliorative interventions. These can encompass clarification and the provision of new information, or may entail more extensive interventions to work through emotional conflict or bolster a youngster's immature reasoning process.

A second arena for intervention centers on helping a youngster and parents come to a joint decision. For many decisions, parents have the authority to decide yet wish to include their child in the decision, but they are unclear how to do so or what weight they should give the youngster's choice. Family-oriented interventions can be quite useful in helping family members feel comfortable with whatever decision is reached.

Finally, when assessments are requested by agencies or courts, the clinical recommendation that the youngster be found legally incompetent to decide should be accompanied by information to assist the adult decision maker (judge, parent, etc.) to better understand the child's thinking and preferences. Such information can be invaluable when the decision maker must ascertain what is in the youngster's best interest or exercise "substituted judgment" by deciding in accordance with how the child would decide if the child were competent.

REFERENCES

Adelman, H. S., Lusk, R., Alvarez, V., & Acosta, N. K. (1985). Competence of minors to understand, evaluate, and communicate about their psychoeducational problems. *Professional Psychology Research and Practice, 16,* 426–434.

Elkind, D. (1967). Egocentrism in adolescence. *Child Development, 38,* 1025–1034.

Furby, L., & Beyth-Marom, R. (1992). Risk taking in adolescence: A decision-making perspective. *Developmental Review, 12,* 1–44.

Garrison, E. G. (1991). Children's competence to participate in divorce custody decisionmaking. *Journal of Clinical Child Psychology, 20,* 78–87.

Grisso, T. (1981). *Juveniles' waiver of rights: Legal and psychological competence.* New York: Plenum Press.

Grisso, T., & Vierling, L. (1978). Minors' consent to treatment: A developmental perspective. *Professional Psychology, 9,* 412–427.

Group for the Advancement of Psychiatry, Committee on Child Psychiatry (1989). *How old is old enough?: The ages of rights and responsibilities.* New York: Brunner/Mazel.

Lewis, C. C. (1981). How adolescents approach decisions: Changes over grades seven to twelve and policy implications. *Child Development, 52,* 538–544.

Lewis, C. E., Lewis, M. A., Lorimer, A., & Palmer, B. (1977). Child initiates care: The use of school nursery services by children in an "adult free" system. *Pediatrics, 60,* 449–507.

Quadrel, M. J., Fischhoff, B., & Davis, W. (1993). Adolescent (in)vulnerability. *American Psychologist, 48,* 102–116.

Scherer, D. G. (1991). The capacities of minors to exercise voluntariness in medical treatment decisions. *Law & Human Behavior, 15,* 431–449.

Scott, E. S., Reppucci, N. D., & Woolard, J. L. (1995). Evaluating adolescent decision making in legal contexts. *Law & Human Behavior, 19,* 221–244.

Spivack, G. (1976). *The problem-solving approach to adjustment: A guide to research and intervention.* San Francisco: Jossey-Bass.

Steinberg, L., & Cauffman, E. (1996). Maturity of judgment in adolescence: Psychosocial factors in adolescent decision making. *Law & Human Behavior, 20,* 249–272.

Taylor, L., Adelman, H. S., & Kaser-Boyd, N. (1985). Minors' attitudes and competence toward participation in psychoeducational decisions. *Professional Psychology Research and Practice, 16,* 226–235.

Weithorn, L. A., & Campbell, S. B. (1982). The competency of children and adolescents to make informed treatment decisions. *Child Development, 53,* 1589–1598.

76 / Observation, Interview, and Mental Status Assessment (OIM): Pregnant Adolescent and Teen Parent

Lucile M. Ware

The Scope of the Problem

One in every 10, or more than a million teenage girls become pregnant every year. The United States has the highest rate of adolescent pregnancy of all the developed countries (DeRidder, 1993; Guttmacher Institute, 1991). These teenagers come from all strata of society, all races, all faiths, and all parts of the country.

Adolescents are increasingly sexually active. It is estimated that one-fourth of 15-year-old girls have had premarital sex, escalating to one-half by age 17, and three-fourths by age 19 (DeRidder,

1993; Guttmacher Institute, 1991). Poor contraceptive use makes it quite likely that the sexually active teen exposes herself to pregnancy (Brooks-Gunn & Furstenberg, 1989). Almost half of these girls either miscarry (13%) or terminate the pregnancy (40%). Of the half million who do give birth, an estimated 90 to 96% elect to keep their children. Only a small percentage opt for adoption (Resnick, Blum, Bose, Smith, & Toogood, 1990). We thus have children raising children, which poses many risks and challenges for both the young mothers and their offspring (Dryfoos, 1990; Osofsky, Hann, & Peebles, 1993). Although teenage pregnancy is not by itself evidence of psychopathology, any clinician who sees adolescent girls will surely confront the sexually active or pregnant teen.

Assessment of the Adolescent's Risk of Becoming Pregnant

MOTIVATIONAL FACTORS

Even though sexual intercourse may be irregular and infrequent, the sexually active teen is at great risk of becoming pregnant. Young people experiment sexually at increasingly younger ages. The clinician evaluating sexually active adolescents should try to explore and arrive at some understanding of the level of their sexual knowledge. The goal of such inquiry is to correct misinformation, to identify beliefs and values, and to help the youngsters focus on the consequences of their behaviors. The teenager receives mixed and distorted messages about sexuality and "risky behaviors" from peers, the media, and even family members. The extent and quality of sex education provided by schools is quite variable and altogether unpredictable in terms of its ability to get through meaningfully to the youngsters. Also, drinking, smoking, and drug use frequently accompany sexual activity (Dryfoos, 1990).

Despite rising concern about AIDS and sexually transmitted diseases, contraceptive practices are notoriously underutilized. The clinician must learn whether or not birth control measures are acceptable, available, or effectively used.

CASE EXAMPLE

Linda, 16, remarked to her therapist how courageous it was that a well-known athlete had spoken out about AIDS. She felt his statements would send a clear message to young people to protect themselves. Yet within days she reported having unprotected sex.

If they are to be of help, family planning resources for the adolescent should be highly individualized. In statistical studies, the regular use of contraception is correlated with a positive relationship between the girl and her mother and the presence of the girl's father in the home (Miller, Card, Paikoff, & Peterson, 1992).

Studies of adolescents who become pregnant show that the majority of such conceptions are unintended; only a minority are "wanted." The clinician should be alert to the motivational forces that put the teen at risk. Although the sexual activity of adolescents often seems unplanned and unprotected, it may psychologically be far from an "accident" (Noshpitz, 1991). Even desired and planned pregnancies by older, married teens may be ill considered. The responsibility of a baby born to a young couple beginning their careers can interfere with the couple's adjustment. A longer delay would have allowed them to cement their relationship and get better established so that they could more comfortably welcome a new arrival (Furstenberg, Brooks-Gunn, & Morgan, 1987).

When girls get pregnant, there is a complex mix of conscious and unconscious factors that play a role. Some may seek to have a baby in identification with their mother or with a mothering role. Some may be motivated by conflicted or competitive feelings about their mother. Some want a baby to "love them," in effect, to compensate for feelings of deprivation. Other girls enjoy taking risks or respond to the crude sensuous component of sexuality and feel excited about "having fun." Misinformation supports behaviors: "You can't get pregnant the first time;" "As long as it's far away from your period;" "You can't get pregnant standing up." The girl may yield to feelings of being "in love;" she may be responding to peer pressures; or she may experience a sense of invulnerability. Some girls may naively experiment sexually because of misinformation about their bodies, fertility, or contraceptives.

The meaning of the sexual relationship should be evaluated. A girl might try "to keep" a boyfriend by having sex or use sex as an antidote for loneliness or emptiness. Sometimes the important aspect is not sex per se but being held or cared for. Several girls in our study had experienced significant loss, such as death or abandonment by their mother (Osofsky, Culp, & Ware, 1988; Osofsky, Eberhart-Wright, Ware, & Hann, 1992). Sexual favors are "exchanged for closeness." Some pregnancies serve to satisfy, placate, or spite a parent or to ape a parental model. Pregnancy may serve as a distorted step to "facilitate" separation or repeat an abusive sexual relationship. More unfortunately still, pregnancy can result from rape, incest, or sexual exploitation.

ACTUAL AND DEVELOPMENTAL AGE

The clinician needs to evaluate the cognitive, emotional, social, and developmental aspects of the adolescent as these interact with all the other forces that affect her.

The teen years span almost a decade. Accordingly, the moment in the teenage range matters a great deal, that is, whether the girl is barely 11 or 12 years old, on the one extreme, or is a high school graduate of 18 on the other. The early teen (12–14) has an immature body, less knowledge and experience, less capacity for abstract thinking, is dependent on her family and needs to remain in school. The mid-teen (15–16) can likely rely on a greater sense of who she is, strives toward independence, tends to place great reliance on peers, and has more ability to think abstractly. She is closer to being able to drop out of school. The older teen (17–19) by contrast is usually more comfortable with her body and has a more consolidated sense of identity. She is likely to be capable of abstract thinking, has clearer life goals, and is developing a sense of values which allows for greater coherence in her sexuality. She may be near completion of high school.

LEVEL OF MATURITY

The clinician needs to evaluate an adolescent's level of maturity. Does she swing from adultlike to childlike behaviors, or is there a greater degree of coherence to her overall functioning? How competently does she plan and consider future consequences? How rooted is she in the immediate? How well does she apply her reasoning skills and reflect upon her emotional life? Can she articulate her goals, values, and moral beliefs? How well does she take the needs, feelings, and motives of others into account? (Gordon, 1990)

RELATIONSHIP TO SELF AND OTHERS

It is vital to measure the adolescent girl's level of self-esteem. Girls who lack belief in their competence or skills, and see few options for themselves, are at greater risk. Family risk factors include having a mother who was herself a teen mother, a sister who has become pregnant, or a milieu that views motherhood as the primary role for a girl. Children from families that are chaotic, disorganized, nonsupportive, or from lower SES groups are more at risk.

Adolescents normally have to deal with issues of separation and individuation from their family of origin. A pregnancy which propels the teen back to her family for help and support compromises this process. A pregnancy may also push the girl into a premature independence for which she may be ill prepared.

LOCUS OF CONTROL

The concept of "locus of control" refers to whether the person sees herself as a victim of forces outside her control (externally controlled) or as the agent of control of her life (internally controlled) (Dunn, 1988). Investigators show that adolescents who consider the locus of control to be within themselves are much more likely to set priorities, opt for staying in school, use contraceptives effectively, and seek abortions when pregnant. These girls are more likely to view early parenthood as bad for both them and their child. They consider themselves not ready for the burdens of parenthood (Dunn, 1988). Although the significance of this characteristic has been questioned by some, experience with numerous failed appointments despite reminders and bills speaks to impulsive behaviors which indicate that for many, the locus of control is external (Osofsky, Culp, & Ware, 1988; Ware, Osofsky, Eberhart-Wright, & Leichtman, 1987).

CONCURRENT PSYCHOPATHOLOGY

Certain troubled adolescents are at risk for getting pregnant. Psychiatric conditions that come with a propensity for acting-out behaviors (such as borderline conditions), oppositional behaviors, poor judgment, impulsivity, and risk taking all place the girl in greater jeopardy. Both depressive disorders and manic hypersexuality could plunge a vulnerable girl with poor self-esteem into ill-considered sexual activity. High self-esteem is a protective factor that may indirectly reduce childbearing by fostering higher educational aspirations (Kovacs, Krol, & Voti, 1994).

The lack of structure and supervision characteristic of dysfunctional families or unavailable parents may increase the likelihood of premature pregnancy. Sexual abuse, incest, or a family pattern of early childbearing also leads to more risk. Negative life events are modestly correlated with poorer psychological adjustment. The clinician needs to be aware of the negative life stressors that are so frequent among the poor, the uneducated, and deprived youngsters. They live from day to day, often from crisis to crisis, with little hope and few aspirations. Other important risk factors include living in a single-parent family with little contact with father, having many siblings, and perceiving limited opportunities (Resnick et al., 1990).

contraceptive information, and counseling can be obtained (DeRidder, 1993; Miller et al., 1992).

For the vulnerable adolescent, useful programs have been devised that emphasize promoting self-esteem, discovering life options, maintaining school attendance, and facilitating family communication. They offer involvement with wholesome role models, constructive after-school activities, and career exploration. Big Brother/Big Sister, girl's clubs, Y programs, church and other youth groups, and school counselors are examples of helpful support systems.

Intervention Strategies for the Adolescent at Risk

Most schools offer primary prevention efforts in the form of family life or sex education programs. They traditionally cover such topics as human reproduction, family planning, contraceptive methods, and abortion. Often these efforts are too short and too late, that is, after intercourse has been experienced. Many do not help adolescents understand the impact that pregnancy will have on their lives (Brooks-Gunn & Furstenberg, 1989; DeRidder, 1993). Clinicians who see children should familiarize themselves with the availability and quality of sex education programs in their community. Indeed, the clinician's input may help in ensuring that they are comprehensive. Age-appropriate programs can start as early as the preschool and kindergarten level and continue through all the school years. In this way meaningful learning can occur well before the teen is sexually active. Any effective curriculum should have a focus on acquiring, processing, and retaining information, along with clarification of attitudes and values, assuming responsibility, and learning to problem solve and understand consequences. An effective program will help the teen "say no" or delay until she can act responsibly.

For the adolescent, some communities have health clinics linked to or near schools, special clinics associated with medical facilities, YWCA programs, or specially designed public health services. Here health checkups, family planning,

Assessment of the Pregnant Adolescent

DISCOVERING THE PREGNANCY

The realization that she is pregnant is a crisis in the life of a young girl. She may be shocked, excited, dismayed, disbelieving, or frightened. Whether she suspects the pregnancy early or late, she is likely to have gone through a varying period of denial. She may attempt to conceal the pregnancy.

CASE EXAMPLE

Celeste, 16, was a heavyset high school student. During her pregnancy, she wore loose-fitting clothes, said nothing to anyone, and continued with school. Not even her best friend suspected when she was "out with the flu" at her aunt's home. After the birth, Celeste did not identify the father and signed adoption papers.

The clinician can help the adolescent explore her reactions, fears, conflicts, and confusions. The girl can then begin to form a coherent plan for herself and how she will deal with the pregnancy. There will be much to process. Eventually she will need to decide who to tell (e.g., the baby's father, her parents, family, or friends). She will need to decide whether to carry the baby to term or to become one of the 400,000-plus teens who each year have abortions. She will need to think through the consequences of her decisions.

The pregnant teen will struggle with her own feelings, and what she imagines will be the reactions of those around her. The changes in her body will be new, possibly mysterious, to her. She will have important feelings about the baby growing within her and about the father of the child. When she does let others know, she may face a range of intense responses including shock, condemnation, rage, rejection, abandonment, acceptance, understanding, and moral and practical support.

CASE EXAMPLE

Latoya, 16, finally decided she had to tell her parents. They were furious with her and the young man and crushed that this might prevent her from going to college. Latoya felt pressured but refused to seek an abortion; she also did not think marriage was right for her. She decided to move in with her sister and have the baby. She was pleased when her parents relented, forgave her, and became supportive of her and her daughter.

It is important that the clinician remain nonjudgmental and help the adolescent sort through conflicting advice and messages. The girl may need to deal with interference by others—pressure to abort or carry to term, give the child up for adoption, get married or break up with her boyfriend. Any of these possibilities may run counter to her own desires or values—which may themselves be ambivalent. The girl's biggest need is to be able to comprehend her options, sort through and clarify her wishes, and understand consequences.

For some girls, pregnancy is a cause for celebration, an initiation rite that welcomes the girl into a peer group marked by extended abdomens and babies. Early pregnancy may have occurred in the family for generations and be part of the cultural heritage. In one study I visited homes where baby pictures covered the walls, and each new baby was a sign of hope—a new beginning for a family that had little. These girls dressed their babies in beautiful clothes and spent hours fixing their hair in elaborate braids. They did not experience a loss of peers since all their peers were having babies. They could be seen at the local mall proudly displaying their babies. For these girls, the pregnancy may not be planned, but it is expected and considered positive.

The clinician must learn about family influences and cultural values in order to comprehend the girl's milieu. Further information about family, kinship, and cultural, and religious factors are contained in other chapters.

DECISIONS ABOUT THE PREGNANCY

Once the pregnancy is confirmed, the adolescent will need to decide whether to carry to term or to terminate the pregnancy. The interviewer can assist her to arrive at the best decision for her. For girls with a family heritage of having babies that the whole family raises, there is less of an issue. One can explore whom she plans to include in her decision making and what resources she can envision. Will she be obligated to tell a parent whom she fears? What does an abortion mean to her, to her family, or to her milieu? Will she need to plead for an exception to parental notification in the legal system? She may have meager knowledge of the medical or legal system, even less knowledge of community resources, health professionals, or clinics, and only a vague idea of her options. Again, she may be in a peer group that has abortions and thinks very little about the implications of what they are doing.

The pregnancy may be too far along for termination to be an option. Whether the decision to go to term is a positive one or is arrived at by default, the girl will need to be told about the importance of prenatal care for both herself and the baby and be given an appropriate referral. In cases where the pregnancy is denied or concealed, prenatal care is obviously not sought. Poor nutrition, smoking, drug or alcohol ingestion, and sexually transmitted diseases are all common among the teen population and require education and referral when encountered.

Intervention Strategies for the Pregnant Adolescent

Lack of or inadequate prenatal care and its attendant risks are more likely a function of poverty and a lack of education than of age per se. A number of communities have health clinics geared to the pregnant teen. Public health nurses and social workers provide a coherent program that addresses medical, nutritional, educational, social, emotional, and family needs. These clinics can refer pregnant youngsters to an obstetrician, have them visit the hospital delivery room, and teach them what to expect when the baby arrives. In smaller communities, visiting public health nurses are more likely to be available. It is important to note that with proper prenatal care, healthy outcomes for teens are on a par with those for older mothers (Osofsky et al., 1988, 1993).

The clinician who helps the adolescent get adequate prenatal care, whether public or private, relieves stress and increases the likelihood of a satisfactory outcome for mother and baby. Emotional bonds to the baby can be promoted by having the mother listen to the heartbeat, see the sonogram, and learn about the fetus's reactions to sounds, music, and exercise.

A study of appointment keeping among pregnant teenagers shows that the greater the discrepancy of the perceived need and risk between the girl and the health professional, the greater the likelihood of missed appointments. Community-wide educational campaigns, information targeted specifically at adolescent groups, as well as individual efforts, are all necessary for getting knowledge to the teen. Unfortunately a number of girls still go the hospital only for the delivery or medical complications. This lack of preparation coupled with emotional immaturity, instability of relationships, poverty, and lack of education form a morbid constellation which inevitably sets the stage for subsequent difficulties (Miller et al., 1992; Osofsky et al., 1992). For girls who cannot stay in their own homes due to abuse, incest, abandonment, or loss, group homes or foster homes may be appropriate.

Assessment of Adolescent's Early Parenting

THE YOUNG MOTHER'S EARLY ADJUSTMENT

After the adolescent has given birth, the mental health professional can continue to help her clar-

ify her feelings about keeping or relinquishing the child. Only 4 to 5% of adolescents choose to place their babies for adoption. Those girls who do relinquish have often had family experiences with adoption (Resnick et al., 1990).

CASE EXAMPLE

Cheryl had just turned 16 and was the younger of two adopted children living with her parents. Since she turned 13 she was rebellious and impulsive. She was particularly angry at her adoptive mother, who was often depressed and whom she felt had not protected her from an episode of abuse in her childhood. One night she ran off with a group of friends she'd been told not to frequent, drank a lot, and got pregnant. She refused to get an abortion, insisted on carrying the baby to term, and then gave the child up for adoption.

Most adolescents now elect to keep their babies. A mother's sense of competence is the strongest predictor of good adjustment to motherhood, and an internal locus of control is the major factor correlated with positive involvement with the infant (Moroz & Allen-Meares, 1991).

If at all possible, the clinician should see the mother and baby together. The new mother's feelings and attitudes about her infant can be explored not only through what she says but by observing how she attends to the baby. Inquiring about her social support network provides valuable information. Teens who are negative about the baby and lack support are vulnerable to maladaptive efforts at child rearing as well as future neglect or abuse of the child (Moroz & Allen-Meares, 1991).

Bonding and attachment may be problematic if the baby is male, premature, temperamentally difficult, or handicapped. The adolescent's own background, if she has been deprived, poorly parented, abused, neglected, or abandoned, can seriously impair her mothering ability. She is especially at risk for reenacting the past when her own childhood emotions are poorly remembered, that is, when she experiences a "ghost in the nursery" phenomenon (Fonagy, Steele, & Steele, 1991; Fraiberg, Adelson, & Shapiro, 1975). On the other hand, some adolescents become quite proud and effective mothers.

CASE EXAMPLE

Maria, 16, was outspoken. "I know he needs me. I'm proud of him and feel that I can really give him what he needs. We just figured out our schedule together."

Competing and conflicted feelings can strain coping skills. A mother's excited, happy feelings may falter under the realities of caring for a baby around the clock. Not only sleep deprived, she may feel incompetent and frightened by the intensity of her emotions.

CASE EXAMPLE

Vivian, 15, reported, "It was awful when she'd start up crying. I'd get to where I couldn't stand to pick her up—I'd want to walk out I'd get so upset. Like I couldn't do nothing right."

Normal adolescent self-centeredness may make it hard for some young mothers to understand the baby empathically. Other teens may blossom as they gain experience, feel competent, and glow as the child thrives.

EVALUATION OF PARENTING AT RISK

A mother's depression can interfere with the attachment process and predispose the infant to develop "depressed" behavior quite early. Estimates of the incidence of depression in teen mothers vary from 47 to 63% (Osofsky et al., 1988, 1992; Field, 1989). Research indicates that the incidence of avoidant attachment is more common in adolescent mother-infant dyads than in adult mother-infant dyads. A baby with disorganized avoidant attachment may have experienced a depressed mother (Field, 1989). Secure attachments exert a protective function. The attachment paradigm is a laboratory measure of the baby's reaction to the reunion with mother after a brief separation.

A baby's insistent demands produce intense feelings. Sometimes this very intensity is masked by a cover of apathy or nonresponsiveness on the mother's part. The young, immature, adolescent mother may find it hard to think beyond the immediate or the concrete and to envision the future and the implications of her current decisions.

Should this be coupled with less than adequate educational experiences, little incentive for learning, distrust of authority, and limited experience in child development, she may find it hard to anticipate what her baby will need.

Commonly adolescent mothers overestimate developmental milestones (e.g., they assume an infant should be toilet trained at 6 months). Thus judgment can be affected by needs, limited experience, and inaccurate beliefs.

CASE EXAMPLE

Trisha, 16, showed her 6 month old how to dial a play telephone. She got angry when he wouldn't pay attention and copy what she was showing him. She persisted, he cried, and mother felt defeated.

When low self-esteem is part of the picture, the young mother may make decisions that are not in her own or her baby's best interest. She may be easily pressured by those around her. It can be hard sometimes for her to separate out her needs from those of the baby.

CASE EXAMPLE

Annie, 15, repeatedly interrupted the feeding of her eagerly nursing 4 month old to feed herself juice and a cookie. Her baby became increasingly frustrated and started to cry.

ASSESSMENT OF THE MOTHER-INFANT DYAD

The clinician evaluating mother-baby pairs should observe how much the mother talks to the baby, cuddles it in the en-face position (especially during feedings), and is attuned to the baby's needs. Attunement measures the mother's responsiveness to the baby's cues without imposing one's own agenda or teasing. Teasing is typical of teenagers. If a mother is depressed or preoccupied, this may further diminish her responsivity, expressivity, availability, and energy to interact with the infant. Studies show that by age 1, many infants with such a parent show insecure and/or disorganized attachment. Children of depressed mothers are at greater risk for later problems in affect regulation, subdued emotional expression, depression, or inappropriate aggression (Field,

1989; Osofsky et al., 1992, 1993; Zahn-Waxler, Iannotti, Cummings, & Denham, 1990).

CASE EXAMPLE

Donisha, 17, sat and rocked with a distant sad look. Her 6-month-old son was placed on the floor at some distance from her holding his own bottle. Although the baby kept trying to look at his mother and get her attention, she was oblivious to his appeals.

ASSESSMENT OF SUPPORTIVE RELATIONSHIPS

The clinician should help the young mother evaluate her available, trustworthy sources of support (Moroz & Allen-Meares, 1991). Adolescents living alone, or even with partners, can easily feel quite isolated and away from the mainstream of activities. Such a youngster may envy her peers their carefree existence. The girl's relationship to her own mother is of paramount importance. How supportive is the baby's maternal grandmother? What are the family problems? The grandmother's concrete involvement can vary from occasional babysitting to becoming a major caretaker. Whether the teen lives at home, with a partner, or on her own, her mother's level of constructive support is a protective factor rather than a specific service rendered.

CASE EXAMPLES

Ester, 14, cared for her baby all the time she was at home, including all his night feedings. She went to school every day and helped with chores. Her mom cared for the baby while she was at school. Ester thought there was nothing difficult about parenting.

Nancy, 17, married the baby's father after she learned she was pregnant. She competently cared for her infant daughter and completed her high school education. When she eventually decided to divorce, she returned home for a few months until she could get her bearings. She appreciated her family's support until she could locate a job, a day care center, and a new apartment. She protected her daughter and their relationship in spite of the external stress.

Whether or not they are married, the mother's relationship to the father of the child is of critical importance. Sometimes the father's family is more involved (Moroz & Allen-Meares, 1991).

CASE EXAMPLE

Shirley, 17, came from a family long affected by her father's drunken episodes of physical abuse. When she found herself pregnant by her high school boyfriend, his family took her in, helped her get prenatal care, and supported the couple in completing high school.

The essential ingredient seems to be the availability of support from someone. For an isolated mother, there may be community support groups, home visitors, or teen programs that can be helpful.

TEEN FATHERS

Adolescent fathers have been much less studied than teen mothers. Teen fathers account for about one-fifth of the children born to adolescent girls. Whenever possible, it is quite useful to include the young father in an evaluation, as many express a desire to be involved in their child's life. Often they find themselves limited by poor educational and job opportunities with which to support the baby, even when they want to. Teen couples often believe they love and care for each other. Currently, teen marriages are less often embarked on than in the past and still suffer from a high divorce rate; nonetheless, many fathers do maintain some contact with their children. In some cases, fathers have fought for and won custody when the mothers did not perform well (Parke & Neville, 1987).

Intervention Strategies for Adolescent Parents

Mother-infant dyads may benefit from a variety of programs that can provide support, developmental information, and child-rearing guidance. Such programs can also help parents continue with their education or training, assist the mother in understanding her feelings, and provide peer relationships. These resources include teen mother groups which include the babies, drop-in centers, special teen school programs, infant development centers with strong parent components, and vocational and technical schools that have infant day care or home visitor programs (Ware, 1988).

Other resources for young parents include infant day care with a strong parenting component (sometimes organized through churches, schools, community resources) and group homes or foster homes where baby and mother live together. Sometimes specialized groups for mother-infant pairs are organized around special needs—drug rehabilitation, mental health treatment, or abuse issues. Home visitor programs may address special needs and may vary in intensity and staff expertise. They may combine with health clinics or teen outreach programs. Volunteer efforts such as mother-to-mother programs can probably be organized in any community.

For teen fathers, the most successful intervention efforts are directed by energetic men who can help the young parents get past their feelings of not needing help. Through these groups they can learn to delight in their children, feel responsible for them, share feelings that are difficult to express, and build their self-worth through feelings of attachment to their babies (Parke & Neville, 1987).

A Look to the Future

The major focus of primary prevention efforts should be toward helping reduce the incidence of teenage pregnancy. As described above there are many such undertakings, and they need to approach their targets differently depending on the community (Miller et al., 1992).

Most programs attempt to reduce the number of repeat pregnancies, but few have documented a reduction in teen birth rates (Dryfoos, 1990). In fact, 30 to 50% of first-time mothers get pregnant again within 2 years (Seymore, Frothingham, MacMillan, & Durant 1990). Studies show that repeat pregnancy is more likely to occur in the context of poverty, low educational aspirations, disorganized family life, and absent fathers.

Even though there may be rough beginnings, longitudinal studies such as Furstenberg's 17-year follow-up of 300 primarily African American mothers show many patterns that can lead to eventual success. A substantial number of girls, even those with large families, do eventually return to school and obtain regular employment. They do this despite the fact that they must be on public assistance for a time. This is, however, at a certain cost to the children. Their offspring are at greater risk for school problems, delinquency, and psychopathology (Furstenberg et al., 1987; Osofsky et al., 1992). The challenge is to help the teen find and pursue opportunities for educational, economic, and personal development and help their children develop normally through appropriate supportive, preventive intervention programs.

REFERENCES

Brooks-Gunn, J., & Furstenberg, F. F., Jr. (1989, February). Adolescent sexual behavior. *American Psychologist*, 249–257.

Dryfoos, J. G. (1990). *Adolescents at risk: Prevalence and prevention.* New York: Oxford University Press.

Dunn, S. K. (1988). A model of fertility decision-making styles among young mothers. *Human Organizations, 47* (2), 166–175.

DeRidder, L. M. (1993). Teenage pregnancy: Etiology and educational interventions. *Educational Psychology Review, 5,* 87–107.

Field, T. M. (1989). Maternal depression effects on infant interaction and attachment behavior. In D. Cicchetti (Ed.), *The emergence of a discipline* (pp. 139–163). Hillsdale, NJ: Lawrence Erlbaum.

Fonagy, P., Steele, H., & Steele, M. (1991). Maternal representations of attachment during pregnancy predict the organizational infant-mother attachment at one year of age. *Child Development, 62,* 891–905.

Fraiberg, S., Adelson, E., & Shapiro, V. (1975). Ghosts in the nursery: A psychoanalytic approach to the problems of impaired infant-mother relationships. *Journal of the American Academy of Child Psychiatry, 14,* 387–422.

Furstenberg, F. F., Jr., Brooks-Gunn, J., & Morgan, S. P. (1987). *Adolescent mothers in later life.* New York: Cambridge University Press.

Gordon, D. E. (1990). Formal operational thinking: The role of cognitive-developmental processes in adolescent decision-making about pregnancy and contraception. *American Journal Orthopsychiatry, 60* (3), 346–356.

Guttmacher Institute. (1991). *Some answers to commonly asked questions about teenage sexuality and pregnancy.* New York: Author.

Kovacs, M., Krol, R., & Voti, L. (1994). Early onset psychopathology and risk for teenage pregnancy among clinically referred girls. *Journal of the American Academy for Child & Adolescent Psychiatry, 33* (1), 106–113.

Moroz, K. J., & Allen-Meares, P. (1991). Assessing adolescent parents and their infants: Individualized family service planning. *Families in Society: Journal of Contemporary Human Services, 7,* 461–468.

Miller, C., Card, J. J., Paikoff, R. L., & Peterson, J. L. (Eds.). (1992). *Preventing adolescent pregnancy.* Newberry Park, CA: Sage Publications.

Noshpitz, J. D. (1991). Disturbances in early adolescent development. In S. I. Greenspan & G. H. Pollock (Eds.), *The course of life* (Vol. 4, pp. 119–180). International Universities Press.

Osofsky, J. D., Culp, A. M., & Ware, L. M. (1988). Intervention challenges with adolescent mothers and their infants. *Psychiatry, 61* (3), 236–241.

Osofsky, J. D., Eberhart-Wright, A., Ware, L. M., & Hann, D. M. (1992). Children of adolescent mothers: A group at risk for psychopathology. *Inf. Mental Health Journal, 13,* 119–131.

Osofsky, J. D., Hann, D. M., & Peebles, C. (1993). Developmental risk for adolescent mothers and their infants. In C. Zeanah (Ed.), *Handbook of infant mental health.* New York: Guilford Press.

Parke, R. D., & Neville, B. (1987). Teenage fatherhood. In S. L. Hofferth & C. D. Hayes (Eds.), *Risking the future: Adolescent sexuality, pregnancy and childbearing* (pp. 145–173). Washington, DC: Wat. Academic Press.

Resnick, M. D., Blum, R. W., Bose, J., Smith, M., & Toogood, R. (1990). Characteristics of unmarried adolescent mothers: Determinants of child rearing versus adoption. *American Journal of Orthopsychiatry, 60* (4), 577–584.

Seymore, C., Frothingham, T. E., MacMillan, J., & Durant, R. H. (1990). Child Development knowledge, child-rearing attitudes and social support among first and second time Adolescent Mothers. *Journal of Adolescent Health Care, 11* (4), 343–350.

Ware, L. M., Osofsky, J. D., Eberhart-Wright, A., & Leichtman, M. L. (1987). Challenges of home visitor interventions with adolescent mothers and their infants. *Journal of Infant Mental Health, 8* (4), 418–428.

Zahn-Waxler, C., Iannotti, R., Cummings, E. M., & Denham, S. (1990). Antecedents of problem behaviors in children of depressed mothers. *Development and Psychopathology, 2,* 271–292.

77 / Observation, Interview, and Mental Status Assessment (OIM): Adopted

Arthur D. Sorosky and Bonnie L. Sorosky

In most situations the adopted child is brought for psychiatric evaluation or treatment without the adoptive status being presented as a primary issue or concern. It is not until a routine inquiry is initiated into developmental history, especially the nature of the pregnancy and delivery, that the child is acknowledged to be adopted. Once this fact is known, the evaluation must determine whether the psychodynamics of the adoption have any bearing on the presenting symptomatology. In order to make such a determination, however, a basic understanding of adoption-related issues is essential.

History

Initially adoption was a way of protecting young children who lacked parents or an extended family to nurture them. As the nuclear family began to assume greater importance, adoption became a way of ensuring the continuity of the family line, especially for couples who were infertile or who had a high likelihood of transmitting serious genetic disorders. During the 1970s and 1980s, changes were effected by liberalized abortion laws, improved methods of contraception, and an increasing tendency for single mothers to keep and raise their children. Infertile couples with an intense desire to adopt have had to compromise by turning to older, harder-to-place children, including those that are handicapped, retarded, international, or transracial. There has also been a growing trend toward adoption by biological relatives and stepparents. These events have resulted in a marked shift from agency to privately arranged adoptions.

In the United States, by the end of the 1930s, there was a successful campaign to seal an adoptee's original birth certificate and replace it with an amended one, tying the child legally and psychologically to the adoptive parents. It has been assumed that the original reason for sealing the records was both to protect the adoptee and adoptive parents from a disruption by the birth parents, and to allow the birth parents to make a new life for themselves, free of the responsibility for the child and safe from the disgrace associated with an out-of-wedlock pregnancy. In actual fact, the original purpose was neither of the above, but merely a way of protecting the adoptive family from intrusion by uninvolved persons.

Beginning in the 1970s and continuing to the present, there has been intense pressure nationwide to unseal or open original birth records. This has been sought by adult adoptees who insist they have a constitutional right to information about their birth parents. These adoptees have joined together in activist groups to provide assistance for searching adoptees, to pressure the various state legislatures to enact new laws, and to institute legal court challenges. Although these movements have resulted in minimal legal reform, there has been significant policy change, with extensive nonidentifying information now being provided to the adoptive parents or the adult adoptee.

Because many birth parents are unwilling to give up all ties to the child, the innovative "open adoption" was created in which the birth parent meets the adoptive parents and participates in the adoption process (Baran, Pannor, & Sorosky, 1976). Although she relinquishes all legal, moral, and nurturing rights to the child, the birth mother nonetheless retains the right to continuing contact and to have knowledge of the child's whereabouts and welfare. In order to understand the true sig-

nificance of these events, one must view adoption as a multifaceted process involving each of the members of the "adoption triangle": the birth parents, the adoptive parents, and the adoptee. Each group in the triad has its own unique concerns and areas of vulnerability (Table 77.1).

Birth Parents

The majority of adopted children who are alive today were conceived out of wedlock. However, there are some who were given up by married birth parents who were unable to care for them due to the death of one parent, divorce, mental illness, physical illness, or poverty. Other children were given up because they were handicapped, retarded, or affected by maternal substance abuse during the pregnancy. Still others were taken away from their families of origin because of abuse and neglect.

Typically the relinquishing birth parents are young and not mature enough to handle the responsibility of parenting. The commonly held assumption that the birth parents want to block out the memories of the adoption and begin life anew appears to be erroneous. Although they have relinquished all rights to and responsibilities for the child, their feelings of grief and loss do not disappear. Many continue to experience anniversary reactions on the child's birthday. Not only do they remain concerned about the child's welfare, but they often carry a sense of guilt that the child will never understand the reason for the relinquishment (Roles, 1989). They may also live in fear that someday they will be confronted by a hostile birth child. Contrary to public opinion, the birth father (when aware of the pregnancy) is also very concerned about the child's welfare. In most cases the birth parents are open to the idea of a reunion with the relinquished child if he so desires after reaching maturity.

Adoptive Parents

Although some adoptive parents adopt because of genetic considerations or for altruistic reasons, the

TABLE 77.1

The Adoption Triangle: Areas of Concern and Vulnerability

Birth Parents	Adoptive Parents	Adoptees
• Shame, embarrassment, and guilt over the relinquishment	• Fear of intrusion, or loss of the child, by the birth parents	• Stigma of being different or feeling innately defective
• Concern about the child's welfare and outcome	• Discomfort in discussing the birth parents	• Perpetuation of the family romance fantasy with a splitting into good and bad parents
• Fears of being confronted by a hostile birth child	• Need to accept themselves as different	• Anxiety associated with separation, rejection, and abandonment
• Receptive to the idea of a reunion if pursued by birth child upon reaching maturity	• Ambivalence regarding the revelation or disclosure	• Propensity for disinhibiting behavior problems, including ADHD
	• Threatened by the child's separation-individuation	• Genealogical bewilderment
	• Frightened by the child's instinctuality	• Identity lacunae
	• Insecurity in the parental role with resulting overprotectiveness	• Concerns about dating, with fears of an incestuous union
	• Disappointment with the child's abilities and accomplishments	• Sexual conflicts
	• Concerns about "bad seed"	• Desire for more information or to search for the birth parents

majority do so because of infertility. Some couples will choose to adopt early on, avoiding the numerous high-tech fertility correction options. Others will make the decision only after everything else has failed. For most the discovery of sterility is extremely traumatic, with accompanying psychological reactions characteristic of grief and mourning. The ensuing feelings of envy, self-incrimination, anger, and mutual blame must be explored or the couple will have difficulty in helping the adopted child with his own feelings of loss and abandonment created by the adoption experience.

Once the couple has decided to adopt, they must go through rigorous screening by the agency, private attorney, or the relinquishing birth mother. Even after the adoption is consummated they must endure a mandatory waiting period (usually 6 months) during which there is a persistent fear of the birth mother changing her mind. If she does, the parties may become involved in a contested adoption litigation.

Adoptive parents find themselves confronted with many issues for which they have little background, experience, or preparation. For example,

they are placed in the uncomfortable double bind of trying to make the child feel like she is their own, but telling her that she is not. They are told that they must accept themselves as different from biological parents rather than denying that such a difference exists; that within this context they will be better able to communicate openly with their children regarding their adoptive status and deal more effectively and supportively with any of the problems that may arise (Kirk, 1964). It also stands to reason that the adoptive parents' nurturing experiences by their own parents affects their parenting of the adopted child.

Another growing population of adoptive parents is single women, who choose to adopt because their "biological clocks" are running out and they haven't established a relationship with a man whom they would want to father a child. In these families, in addition to the typical adoption issues, there is the early persistent questioning of "Where is my Daddy?" For all adoptive parents, support groups, whether designed for adoption or for parenting skills in general, can be very helpful.

BONDING AND ATTACHMENT

Bowlby (1969) introduced the notion of mother-infant bonding and attachment as the cornerstone of healthy child development. More recent evidence suggests that the attachment of the mother to the infant begins before fetal movement, and that it grows throughout the pregnancy, peaking during the first hours and days after birth (Brazelton & Cramer, 1990; Kennell & Klaus, 1983). During this initial postnatal phase, the "maternal sensitive period," the mother is especially affected by physical contact with the baby. The earlier this contact, the more affectionate their relationship is likely to become. In cases where the contact has been prolonged or disrupted, as in C-section or prematurity, there may be a breakdown in the bonding process. Recent studies have established the link between early attachment problems and later psychopathology (Biringen, 1994; Fonagy et al., 1996; Rosenstein & Horowitz, 1996).

Stern (1985) has shown how almost from birth, and especially after 2 months of age, the infant plays an active role in evoking responses from the mother. Thus, after birth, the attachment process is a reciprocal, complementary experience in which the infant and mother have the immediate potential of eliciting in each other behaviors that are bonding. This mutual interaction can be further affected by the similarities or differences in the innate temperaments of each. The "goodness of the fit" or the "poorness of the fit" determines healthy or disturbed psychological functioning in the child (Chess & Thomas, 1986).

In the adoptive family there is a delayed connection between the mother and infant; typically a few days after birth. The mother has had limited opportunity during the gestation period to commence bonding, and the initial contact occurs at the tail end or even beyond the "maternal sensitive period." Breast-feeding, although attempted in some cases, is another bonding experience which is usually lacking in the adoptive mother-infant dyad. For the adoptive mother, the child was once part of someone else. This may cause her to perceive him as an "alien child," and can give rise to difficulties of attachment (Derdeyn, 1991). During the mandatory waiting period, there is also a fear on the part of the adoptive mother of getting too close to a child who might be taken away from her if the birth mother should change her mind. Furthermore, there may be a greater likelihood of a "poorness of fit" when there is no genealogical link to influence compatibility of temperaments.

The many obstacles occurring in the adoption process do not preclude healthy bonding, but they do make the process more difficult. One of the best preventive measures is early professional intervention with mother-infant dyads, either individually or in a group setting. These experiences can significantly mitigate the effects of disrupted bonding and attachment, as well as increase maternal confidence.

REVELATION OF ADOPTION

Although some would disagree (Donovan, 1990), most adoption experts believe that children must be told of their adoptive status early on in order to establish an honest, trusting relationship with the parents and to avoid the trauma of the child finding out from someone else. The typical approach is to begin the disclosure at an early age, around 2 to 4, and then gradually to increase the depth of discussions according to the child's maturity level in a manner similar to imparting sexual matters. Not only should the child know he's adopted, but he should be provided with considerable (albeit nonidentifying) information about the birth parents and their reason for relinquishing their baby (MacIntyre, 1990).

If the child asks few questions or shows little interest in his birth parents or his adoptive status, it is a mistake to assume that there is a lack of interest. This seeming indifference may actually mask a fear of hurting the adoptive parents by questioning. If the parents bring the subject up from time to time, it will keep the lines of communication open and will enable the child to share his feelings or concerns as they arise.

OVERPROTECTION

In general adoptive parents have a deep sense of gratitude that their lives have been enriched by their adopted youngster. However, feelings of insecurity may cause many adoptive parents to become controlling and overprotective with their children. In his classic study of overprotection, Levy (1943) discovered that many of these excessively concerned mothers (like adoptive mothers) had undergone a longer period of anticipation before the child's birth due to periods of infertility, miscarriages, still births, etc. Overprotection can also evolve as an overcompensation or reaction formation against unconsciously felt parental rejection, unconsciously felt hostility toward or envy of the child, or because of anxiety arising from circumstances surrounding the child's birth or health.

Maternal overprotection reflects an inability by the mother to develop a synchronous relationship with her infant. The overprotected child tends to be insecure, has low self-esteem, and is not likely to develop a sense of control or to believe he can have a meaningful influence over his environment. Ultimately he has a choice of regressing to a position of helpless dependence or responding with retributive aggression. Parental overprotectiveness has an inhibiting effect on the child's attempts at separation and individuation. This is a process that normally occurs between 4 and 36 months of age, a developmental step which enables the youngster to evolve a sense of being a separate person (Mahler, Pine, & Bergman, 1975). Blos (1967) views adolescence as a second individuation process, necessary for developing extrafamilial love relationships. Others have conceptualized human psychological development as a lifelong process of recurrent separation-individuation experiences.

Adoptive parents often have difficulty dealing with their child's separation-individuation process, especially during adolescence, because it forces them to reexperience their own preadoption feelings of rejection and abandonment. For the infertile mother, as she watches her daughter develop into a woman, there may be a revival of envy for women who are capable of having children. For the infertile adoptive father, his son's emerging sexuality may be viewed as a personal threat because of father's unconscious association of infertility with a lack of virility.

There is also a tendency for adoptive parents to pressure their child academically because of a fear that she will turn out to be the failure they imagine the birth parents to have been. Such a fear of "bad seed" can also cause the adoptive parents to overreact to their child's expressions of instinctuality in many dimensions, that is, soiling, sexual curiosity, aggression, and eating. At the same time, the adoptive parents have the unique ability to use the "bad seed" ideation to avoid feeling the typical parental guilt over their child's emotional problems.

Many adoption placements break down, especially in adolescence, because of the phenomenon of "unmatched expectations" (Reitz & Watson, 1992). The adopted child often suffers from the belief that he was rejected by his biological parents and consequently feels innately defective. Unfortunately this belief becomes reinforced by disappointed adoptive parents. Their overly critical attitude leads to acting out on the part of the children, thus exacerbating the parental anger. The vicious cycle mounts and can lead to the dissolution of the adoptive family relationship, often through long-term residential placement— a tragic repeat of the original parental abandonment.

Adoptees

Throughout his life the adoptee is confronted with reactions from others which tend to reaffirm his sense of being different. Some describe feeling like a "fraud" because of being "taken in" and being expected to fit in with adoptive parents with whom they had little in common, both physically and emotionally. A particularly stressful experience for adopted youngsters occurs around the fourth or fifth grade when they encounter a standard social science assignment of preparing a "family tree." Reactions of discomfort or pity from peers upon learning that they are adopted intensifies stigmatic feelings which make for isolation and alienation. It is most helpful if the adopted child is provided an opportunity to associate with other adoptees so that mutual concerns and interests can be shared.

THE CHILD

Freud (1950) described a "family romance fantasy" occurring in elementary school-age children in which a nonadoptee fantasizes that he really had been adopted. This is most likely to occur when the child feels angry or frustrated with his parents. He typically will create dreams of families of great power or wealth in which he will be showered with endless love and recognition. The family romance fantasy usually represents a brief stage; once the child works through his ambivalent feelings toward the parents it is abandoned.

In the case of the adoptee, however, there really *are* two sets of parents, which allows the child to prolong the family romance fantasy, resulting in a splitting of the two sets of parents into good and bad roles. This splitting can lead to problems in personality development. The adoptee has an additional romance process which presses him to continue gathering facts about his biological origins (Rosenberg, 1992). Conversely, in some cases the adopted child will do everything she possibly can to deny the adoption and to establish a fantasy blood tie to the adopted parents in an attempt to erase the inherent insecurity of the adoptive state.

Many adopted youngsters display a special interest in the nature of their conception, the reasons for the adoption, and their genealogical history. Unfortunately this healthy curiosity is often construed by the adoptive parents as an indication that they have failed in their role as parents or as a sign of their child's lack of love for them. Their discomfort with these issues forces the child into a feigned compliance beneath which lurks unexpressed rage and resentment.

Adoptive parents may also become concerned about the expression of negative genetic factors; indeed, they may view any behavioral aberration as a consequence of constitutional factors transmitted by promiscuous, impulse-ridden birth parents. Thus behavior is mobilized in the child by the suggestive force of the parents' suspicions, and the child is driven into compulsive acting out through an unconscious identification with the birth parents. These family conflicts can be dealt with most effectively when the adoptive parents can be helped to realize that many of their youngster's behaviors are typical of children, adopted or not.

THE ADOLESCENT

The age-appropriate identity conflicts of adolescents are complicated by the knowledge that an essential part of the self has been cut off and remains on the other side of the adoption barrier. Adoptees appear to be particularly susceptible to identity confusion and the development of "identity lacunae" (Sorosky, Baran, & Pannor, 1975). The lack of family background knowledge in adoptees can lead to confusion about what has been inherited. The adoptees' preoccupation with such matters has been referred to as "genealogical bewilderment" (Sants, 1965).

Some adopted youngsters have been observed to run away or to roam around aimlessly, as if they are seeking the fantasized about good, real parents. This "roaming phenomenon" can be interpreted as enactment of a search for stable relationship ties that were not provided by adoptive parents. In other cases, adopted adolescents become dreamy and inaccessible, with preoccupying fantasies about their forebears.

THE YOUNG ADULT

The psychological needs of the adult adoptee have been seriously neglected. One of the common complaints of adopted adults is that they continue to be treated by society as adopted children. They feel that they are never allowed to grow up and assume adult status. Other areas of concern are the dating experience and consideration of marriage. Adoptees are often concerned about being rejected because of their adoptive status. Some have reported a fear of an incestuous union with an unknown biological relative. Furthermore, feelings of an original rejection by their birth parents, especially if reinforced by a poor relationship with their adoptive parents, can cause adoptees to be more anxious and less effective in established intimate relationships as adults.

For adopted women, pregnancy brings fears and concerns of unknown hereditary illness and about the complications of delivery and birth. On the positive side, the birth of a baby is the first opportunity for an adoptee to experience an encounter with a blood relative. As parents, adoptees may become embarrassed and frustrated because they are unable to transmit genealogical information to their own children.

Evaluations of older adoptees show that certain factors are correlated with a good adult adjustment: adoption at a young age, an early awareness of being adopted, open channels of communication with the adoptive parents and being able to discuss the birth parents, and the presence of siblings in the adoptive home. The most frequently encountered problems in adult adoptees have to do with genealogical and identity concerns. In a growing number of cases, the desire for more extensive knowledge has led adoptees to seek contact with their birth parents.

It is difficult to determine what percentage of young adult adoptees are interested in pursuing a reunion with their birth parents. It is clear that such a need is not necessarily related to underlying emotional problems. For some, interest in searching for the birth parents becomes a burning issue, either because they have an intense desire to fill an hereditary void, or because they simply have curious minds and approach all of life's problems in an inquisitive manner. Reunions also provide the opportunity for adoptees to see their birth parents as real people. Now they can better understand the circumstances surrounding their adoption and realize that any imagined deficiency within themselves was not the cause of the adoption. The reunion of adoptees and their birth parents is generally a positive experience, satisfies years of questioning and concerns on the part of the birth parents, and usually results in a closer relationship with the adoptive parents (Sorosky, Baran, & Pannor, 1978).

PSYCHOLOGICAL PROBLEMS

It has long been known that adopted youngsters are overrepresented in mental health facilities. It has been argued that this is not an accurate portrayal and that it is in fact because of the adoptive parents' higher socioeconomic status, their earlier association with mental health and social service facilities (i.e., the adoption agency), and/or their readiness to disassociate themselves from their youngster's problems by blaming genetic factors. However, adopted children appear to be more vulnerable to experiencing loss, separation anxiety, and fear of abandonment and rejection. It is as if they have a socially unrecognized loss of their sense of origin. This loss is viewed as even more complicated to work through than the losses experienced by a child whose parents divorce or die (Brodzinsky, Schechter, & Henig, 1992). The adoptee may also take the blame for being relinquished, resulting in chronic feelings of worthlessness and low self-esteem. At the same time, the adopted child can use his adoption as an excuse to feel victimized or manipulated.

Most studies have shown that adopted children who are seen in psychotherapy are more likely to be referred for behavior problems or personality disorders than anxiety, mood disorders, or psychosomatic problems. They are especially prone to acting out behaviors such as lying, stealing, and running away. There is also a higher incidence of learning problems, which may result either from a passive resistance to parental pressures or from neurological difficulties secondary to poor prenatal care and delivery complications. There also appears to be a greater incidence of genetic disinhibition syndromes, such as attention deficit hyperactivity disorder (ADHD). It has been suggested that the birth parents are at higher risk for having children with impulse control problems because they themselves may have suffered from similar problems (Deutsch et al., 1982).

In adopted adolescent girls, a particular form of acting out may have special significance. Promiscuity may result from an identification with the image of an immoral birth mother; retaliation against rigid, sexually inhibited adoptive parents; or a compulsive urge to procreate a blood relative; or, indeed, from any combination of these.

Overall, the adoptee and his family would appear to be at relatively high risk for the development of psychological problems, especially during adolescence and young adulthood. In some cases these conflicts will be resolved through psychotherapy, in others, after a reunion with the birth parents, and in still others through the passage of time, maturation, and reattachment to more stable love relationships, that is, a spouse and one's own biological children.

Adoption as a Lifelong Process

Working with members of the adoption triangle has helped us to appreciate the unique effects the adoption experience has on adoptees, adoptive parents, and birth parents. Areas of special concern are the problems encountered in the attachment process between the adoptive parents and the adopted infant; the deleterious effects of strained communication or secrecy in dealing with vital but sensitive issues, that is, the nature of the conception and reasons for relinquishment;

the identity conflicts experienced by many adoptees because of an unknown genealogy; and the intense pain and lifelong grieving experienced by the birth parents as a consequence of giving up a child for adoption.

It is obvious that adoption is a lifelong process, deeply affecting each of its participants. It involves the experience of loss at three levels: the birth parents lose a child, the child loses his birth parents and the extended biological family, and the adoptive parents relinquish their dream for a biological child. Each has his/her own areas of concerns and vulnerability which are probably inevitable and unavoidable. However, educated awareness on the part of mental health professionals can result in early and effective therapeutic intervention. This can serve to prevent or contain the emotional damage that might otherwise erode the basic fiber of the adoptive family.

IMPLICATIONS FOR ALTERNATIVE PARENTING

The lessons learned from the adoption experience can also help us in dealing with recent developments in reproductive technology which have led to a wide range of assisted pregnancy possibilities. These techniques, including donor insemination, surrogate parenting, in vitro fertilization, and other related procedures, have created a host of unsettling psychosocial, moral/ethical, and legal issues (Golombok, et al., 1995). It is generally conceded that there is no such thing as a "family secret," and that at some level the family system is adversely affected by attempts at concealing vital issues from certain of its members. For example, when subjected to clinical observations, some donor-inseminated youngsters, who have been told nothing about the nature of their birth, display fantasies and behavior that suggest an awareness of an unknown genealogy.

It is the authors' opinion that none of these alternative birth methods should be withheld from the child. The only real issue in question then is the proper timing for such disclosure. In cases where a number of other people have been made aware of the procedure, the parents must be cognizant of the traumatic effect it would have on the child if she learned about her conception from someone other than the parents.

There has been little research aimed at developing a timetable for discussions about an alternatively conceived pregnancy with the child involved. Unless the child is mature enough to understand the complexities of the reproductive procedure, full disclosure could be very confusing and possibly overwhelming. Thus it may be necessary to wait until she has reached puberty, or even later.

The child who will have the most difficulty with such disclosure is the one who has to deal with the fact that the true identity of the donor parent is unknown. Such a complete and final thwarting of genealogical curiosity is likely to cause immeasurable frustration. Consequently there is a growing movement to require that donors provide their name and identifying information which can be made available (like in adoption) to the donor offspring, if he so desires it, upon reaching maturity.

In order to avoid the many problems that developed throughout the history of the adoption experience, there must be an ongoing forum for the brainstorming of issues related to alternative reproduction and its unique effects on each of the family members. Such communication must be encouraged among pediatricians, family physicians, infertility specialists, and all of the various mental health specialists. Only in this way can the potential problems be recognized and protocols established for dealing with these highly complex psychosocial phenomena.

REFERENCES

Baran, A., Pannor, R., & Sorosky, A. D. (1976). Open adoption. *Social Work, 21,* 97–100.

Biringen, Z. (1994). Attachment theory and research: application to clinical practice. *American Journal of Orthopsychiatry,* 64, 404–420.

Blos, P. (1967). The second individuation process of adolescence. *Psychoanalytic Study of the Child,* 22, 162–186.

Bowlby, J. (1969). *Attachment and Loss: Vol. 1, Attachment.* New York: Basic Books.

Brazelton, T. B., & Cramer, B. G. (1990). *The earliest relationship.* Reading, MA: Addison-Wesley.

Brodzinsky, D. M., Schechter, M. D., & Henig, R. M. (1992). *Being adopted: The lifelong search for self.* New York: Doubleday.

Chess, S., & Thomas, A. (1986). *Temperament in clinical practice.* New York: Guilford Press.

Derdeyn, A. P. (1991). Psychological issues in adoption. In M. Lewis (Ed.), *Child and adolescent psychiatry* (pp. 1099–1107). Baltimore, MD: Williams & Wilkins.

Deutsch, C. K., Swanson, J. M., Bruell, J. H., Cantwell, D. P., Weinger, F., & Baren, M. (1982). Over-representation of adoptees in children with attention-deficient disorders. *Behavior Genetics, 12,* 231–237.

Donovan, D. M. (1990). Resolved: Children should be told of their adoption before they ask: Negative. *Journal of the American Academy of Child and Adolescent Psychiatry, 29,* 828–833.

Fonagy, P., Steele, M., Steele, H., Leigh, T., Kennedy, R., Mattoon, G., Target, M. & Gerber, A. (1996). The relation of attachment status, psychiatric classification, and response to psychotherapy. *Journal of Consulting and Clinical Psychology, 64,* 22–31.

Freud, S. (1950). Family romances. In J. Strachey (Ed. & Trans.), *Collected papers* (Vol. 5, pp. 74–78). London: Hogarth Press.(Originally published 1909.)

Golombok, S., Cook, R., Bish, A., & Murray, C. (1995). Families created by the new reproductive technologies: quality of parenting and social and emotional development of the children. *Child Development, 66,* 285–298.

Kennell, J. H., & Klaus, M. H. (1983). Early events: Later effects on the infant. In J. D. Call et al. (Eds.), *Frontiers of Infant Psychiatry.* New York: Basic Books. pp. 7–16.

Kirk, H. D. (1964). *Shared fate.* New York: Free Press.

Levy, D. M. (1943). *Maternal overprotection.* New York: Columbia University Press.

MacIntyre, J. C. (1990). Resolved: Children should be told of their adoption before they ask. *Journal of the American Academy of Child & Adolescent Psychiatry, 29,* 828–833.

Mahler, M. S., Pine, F., & Bergman, A. (1975). *The psychological birth of the human infant: Symbiosis and individuation.* New York: Basic Books.

Reitz, M., & Watson, K. W. (1992). *Adoption and the family system: Strategies for treatment.* New York: Guilford Press.

Roles, P. (1989). *Saying goodbye to a baby, Volume 1: The birthparents' guide to loss and grief in adoption.* Washington, DC: Child Welfare League of America.

Rosenberg, E. B. (1992). *The adoption life cycle: The children and their families through the years.* New York: Free Press.

Rosenstein, D. S. & Horowitz, H. A. (1996). Adolescent attachment and psychopathology. *Journal of Consulting and Clinical Psychology, 64,* 244–253.

Sants, H. J. (1965). Genealogical bewilderment in children with substitute parents. *Child Adoption, 47,* 32–42.

Sorosky, A. D., Baran, A., & Pannor, R. (1975). Identify conflicts in adoptees. *American Journal of Orthopsychiatry, 45,* 18–27.

Sorosky, A. D., Baran, A., & Pannor, R. (1978). *The adoption triangle.* Garden City, NY: Anchor Press/Doubleday.

Stern, D. N. (1985). *The interpersonal world of the infant.* New York: Basic Books.

78 / Observation, Interview, and Mental Status Assessment (OIM): Single-Parent Homes

Julie A. Larrieu and Charles H. Zeanah

Over the past 20 years, one of the most dramatic changes in family demographics has been the increase in the number of children raised by single parents. For example, in 1970, 12% of all children in the United States lived with one parent, whereas by 1990 this proportion had increased to 26% (National Commission on Children, 1991).

The causes of this change are multiple and complex. In 1987, of all female-headed households, 24.1% were due to parents never marrying, 16.6% due to separation, 34% due to divorce, and 23.5% due to death. Every year more than one million children in the United States experience the divorce of their parents (U.S. Bureau of the Census, 1989); indeed it is estimated that 50% of the children born in the late 1970s and early 1980s will experience their parents' divorce. Such children will then spend an average of 5 years in a single-parent home before their custodial parents remarry (Glick & Lin, 1986). Projections indicate that 38% of white children and 75% of black children born to married parents will experience divorce before the age of 16 (Bumpass, 1984).

The principles guiding the clinical assessment of children of single parents are not so different from those guiding the assessment of children of two-parent families. However, what *is* important are the general and specific risk factors associated with being the child of single parents. Therefore, in this chapter, we will identify and discuss the potential psychosocial risks that children of single parents may manifest in order to highlight salient areas of concern for clinicians. While a single stressor often carries no significant risk for a child, when multiple stressors are experienced, negative effects often increase substantially (Rutter, 1980). Research indicates that single parenthood often occurs in conjunction with multiple risk factors.

General Risk Factors for Children of Single Parents

Although single parenthood is on the rise, it is still the case that for most of their lives, the majority of children have two parents. This means that the child of single parents may feel both different from and distant from the mainstream. When compared to children who have known only one parent, this feeling of estrangement may be even more intense in children who experience the loss of a parent. Among single-parent families, economic disadvantage may increase isolation by diminishing opportunities for supportive relationships outside the family and inviting overreliance on children in the family. In addition, if economic disadvantages require a family to occupy public housing in high crime areas, further isolation may well ensue, since parents will purposefully isolate themselves from their neighbors in an effort to protect their children from dangerous influences. Single mothers also tend to return to work earlier after the birth of their children, and as a result, in their early infant years, the children experience separation for longer periods during the day.

A variety of psychiatric disorders and symptoms have been documented in children of single parents than in children in 2-parent homes (Moilanen & Rantakallio, 1988). Steinhausen, von Aster, and Göbel (1987), for example, found that children of never-married, divorced, or separated mothers or fathers had more conduct problems than children living with both their biological parents. These investigators also documented that among children of single parents, developmental delays are significantly higher. If single parenthood has resulted from the loss of a parent, then unresolved mourning becomes a risk for the child and family. In a study by Lindblad-Goldberg and Dukes (1985), less adaptive single parents whose children were referred for mental health services were significantly more likely than adaptive single parents whose children were not in need of mental health treatment to list deceased individuals as important sources of support.

The loss of a parent, regardless of how it comes about, typically results in emotional distress and behavioral symptomatology in children (Black & Urbanowicz, 1987; Felner, Ginter, Boike, & Cowen, 1981; Hetherington, 1989; Nelson, 1982; Van Eerdewegh, Bieri, Parilla, & Clayton, 1982; Van Eerdewegh, Clayton, & Van Eerdewegh, 1985). To be sure, there is great variability in children's responses to the loss of a parent, but in most cases depression, anxiety, guilt, anger, and resentment, individually or in various combinations, may all be demonstrated. Children with family histories of death and divorce have greater overall school difficulties than children from intact families.

For clinicians evaluating and treating children in single-parent families, it is important to examine within-the-child risk and protective factors. Rutter (1980) suggests that the child's personality and coping responses be addressed. A temperamentally more difficult child may elicit more adverse reactions from the custodial and noncustodial parents and may have fewer resources to draw on in order to cope with these negative responses. Such stressors may result in the appearance of behavior problems, which in turn may escalate the negative reactions in the home, and thus exacerbate existing difficulties in the single-parent household. On the other hand, temperamentally easier children may elicit fewer negative reactions and may have better coping mechanisms and stronger support systems to help mediate the stress.

Specific Risks Related to the Nature of Single Parenthood

Children of single-parent households are subject to several psychosocial risks. Some of these risks are common across all single-parent families; others are specific to the unique nature of each single-parent family. These results are summarized below for three categories: divorce, loss through death, and homosexuality of a parent. A fourth category, which has not yet been the subject of much research, is single parenthood by choice. This topic will be discussed briefly.

LOSS OF PARENT THROUGH DIVORCE

Research indicates that compared with those who grew up in a continuously intact family, children who experience parental divorce are at risk for lower educational attainment, earning less income, being welfare dependent, being more likely to bear a child outside of marriage, being more likely to get divorced, and being more likely to be the head of a single-parent family (Amato & Keith, 1991). Although loss through divorce may have a relative rather than an absolute character, it is not unusual for a child to lose significant involvement with one parent following divorce.

After divorce, boys exhibit more difficulty in social adjustment than do girls, especially in the 8 to 12 year old range (Hetherington, Stanley-Hagan, & Anderson, 1989; Hetherington, 1989). In particular, for the first 2 years following divorce, conduct problems are apparent. Beginning the third year after divorce, these problems become less pronounced. It is sobering to note that children of divorce have lower levels of well-being than children who experience parental death.

This has been evident outside the home as well. Children who experienced divorce have been judged by their teachers to have fewer competencies than children who experienced loss of a parent through death. They are reported to have difficulties in following rules, they have lower frustration tolerance, and they are regarded as less sociable by their peers (Felner et al., 1981).

Parental conflict has been demonstrated to be more deleterious to a child's adjustment than ab-

sence of a parent, and another specific risk for children of divorce is their exposure to such conflict (Hetherington, Stanley-Hagan, & Anderson, 1989). Children caught up in conflicting loyalties toward their divorced parents may well exhibit behavior problems (Rutter, 1987). If parental conflict continues, such children are likely to have less contact with the noncustodial parent (Hetherington et al., 1989). Most children desire to maintain relationships with both parents. Indeed, the opportunity to maintain relationships with each parent has been demonstrated to be an important factor in a child's successful adjustment to divorce (Santrock & Sitterle, 1987). Thus a child's well-being is inversely correlated with the level of post-divorce conflict that persists between parents. However, the data overwhelmingly support the observation that children in divorced families appear to have a higher level of well-being than do children in high-conflict intact families. Longitudinal studies demonstrate that following divorce, children's functioning improves with the passage of time (Hetherington, 1989).

In addition, children of divorce may experience absence of a parent, reduced availability of the custodial parent, changes in the custodial parent's emotional adjustment, unstable household routines, and fewer economic resources in the home. The particular losses of the individual child and the meaning of those losses are central to understanding the child's single-parent experience.

LOSS OF A PARENT THROUGH DEATH

Children who are living in single-parent homes due to the death of one parent appear to be at lower risk for psychiatric symptoms or disorders than those who are living in single-parent homes due to separation or divorce. While the pattern is heterogeneous in one study (Felner et al., 1980), reactions of school-age children or adolescents to the death of a parent tended to be short-lived and mild as compared to reactions due to divorce. The nature of the reactions differ, of course, according to the type of loss the child experiences. Children of widowed mothers displayed significantly more anxiety, hysteria, phobias, obsessive-compulsive disorders, depression, depersonalization syndrome, hypochondriasis, and disturbances of emotion specific to childhood and adolescence. Children who experienced the death of a parent showed more shyness and anxiety than children who experienced separation (Felner et al., 1980).

In a recent study, preschool children, who were compared to their nonbereaved counterparts, showed more emotional and behavioral problems following the death of a parent (Kranzler, Shaffer, Wasserman, & Davies, 1990). It is noteworthy that these children's levels of problems were highly correlated with those of their surviving parent, underscoring the importance of the caregiving environment after death.

HOMOSEXUAL SINGLE PARENTS

Green, Mandel, Hotvedt, Gray, and Smith (1986) discovered that boys and girls raised from early childhood by a homosexual mother without an adult male in the household do not appear to be appreciably different in psychosexual or psychosocial development from children raised by heterosexual mothers without an adult male present. Children of both sexes display similar levels of "masculine" behavior and more "androgenous" behavior than do children from intact heterosexual families. Golombok, Spencer, and Rutter (1983) conclude that being raised in a lesbian household does not lead to atypical development or constitute a psychiatric risk factor. Nevertheless, one investigator (Javaid, 1993) has suggested that some children raised with one homosexual parent may feel that they must keep the homosexual relationship a secret from the peer group because they are aware of their own and certain others' prejudice regarding homosexuality.

SINGLE PARENTHOOD BY CHOICE

Currently a dearth of research exists regarding the characteristics of children whose parents have chosen to be single. However, our clinical experience suggests that certain areas may be potential causes of concern. These include lack of or little emotional and instrumental support for the parent and indirectly, the child, and inappropriate expectations of the child on the part of the parent (e.g., the child having excessive caretaking responsibility in the home, expecting the child to operate as the confidant or emotional supporter of the parent, and/or the child having less freedom to develop outside friendships). The child of

a single parent may also find that the parent is less available due to her need to work.

On the other hand, there may be certain advantages to being raised by a single parent who has chosen such a course as opposed to one who has not (i.e., due to abandonment, divorce, or death of a spouse). When no conflict exists in the home due to divorce, for example, the child is more likely to adapt well. Thus, given that divorce did not occur, a more harmonious environment may exist. In addition, the child did not experience a loss directly, in that he did not get to know a parent whom he then lost. The increased demands for maturity made on the child may enhance his competence in a variety of areas. Thus, while these suggestions are speculative, they have been confirmed by our clinical experience. Further verification, or lack thereof, awaits large-scale research investigations.

Important Areas to Address in Assessment of Children of Single Parents

In evaluating the child of a single parent, perhaps the first question to ask is whether the single parent's status is new or old. The child of an always single mother, for example, will require different approaches than a child whose parents are locked in a custody battle or a child whose parent has recently died. There has been little research on children of never-married, single parents. As a result, it is not clear the extent to which possible risks to their development are related to the social class factors, or whether they experience increased risk within socioeconomic levels when compared to children of two-parent families. If the child's single-parent status is related to separation, divorce, or death of a parent, then a series of questions about the loss become salient for the clinician assessing the child.

HOW OLD WAS THE CHILD AT THE TIME OF THE LOSS?

The developmental level of the child is related both to the child's coping mechanisms and to the types of emotional and behavioral difficulties he may display when he finds himself in a single-parent home. Young children's reactions are predicated upon the immaturity of their social and cognitive competencies, their dependency on their parents, and their lack of autonomy. Children 5 years and younger are less able to understand the implications of marital breakup—the separation experiences, the affective responses of their parents, their own role in the divorce or death, and the implications of the separation. Infants who experience the loss of a primary caregiver may experience significant symptomatology (Bowlby, 1980), and preschoolers' symptoms tend to correlate highly with those of the surviving parent (Kranzler et al., 1990).

Older children and adolescents often experience a variety of painful emotional reactions at the loss of a parent. Daniels (1990) outlined several reactions that are common to adolescents who have experienced parental separation and divorce. These include anger, sadness, anxiety, grief, depression, emotional and social withdrawal, and pseudomaturity. Anger and blame are common reactions. Adolescents frequently form alliances with one parent, which in turn facilitates emotional and often physical separation from the other parent. However, adolescents' cognitive maturity enables them to assess responsibility for the separation more accurately to understand the motives of their parents in the cases of divorce and separation, and to work through grief reactions and cope with multiple stressors such as economic deprivation and changes in availability of time with the custodial parent.

Adolescents may assume greater role responsibilities. One risk is that they become detached and disengaged from their parents at an early point. It is important to assess the nature of the peer group and extrafamilial relationships they develop. Adaptive prosocial peers may result in strengthened coping mechanisms for the adolescent. Conversely, involvement in antisocial groups may lead to destructive outcomes (Hetherington et al., 1989). For any age child one should not expect more mature behavior than he is capable of performing. Needy parents may perceive their elementary school-age children as more mature than they are, and thus may burden them with inappropriate choices and requests for support; later, such children will report that they missed out on childhood and experience a unique sense of loneliness. When adolescents are elevated to the role of support person, nurturer, confidant, or partner, the process may result in conflicted feelings as the adolescents attempt to separate from the parent. It is important that the parent guard against such expectations for pseudomaturity or role reversal in the remaining children.

WHAT IS THE EFFECT OF THE CHILD'S GENDER?

Following a divorce, approximately 90% of children live with a custodial mother. In a single-parent family where the mother has custody, the effects of divorce and the ensuing life pattern are more evident for boys than for girls (Hetherington et al., 1989; Jackson, 1994; Rutter, 1987). In general, both inside the home and in the school setting, boys living with single mothers show more behavioral disruptions and problems in social relationships. Conduct disorders are more often found in boys; single mothers may experience difficulty monitoring and supervising the activities of boys. In one study, single mothers consistently expected less age-appropriate independent, mature, responsible behavior from their sons than did married mothers (Weinraub & Wolf, 1983). Never-married mothers were more nurturant toward their children than were divorced mothers. For girls, problems with social and behavioral adjustment usually disappear by 2 years after the divorce, although during adolescence difficulties may reemerge in the form of disruptions in heterosexual relationships.

There is some evidence that school-age children adapt better when in the custody of a same-sex parent (Camara & Resnick, 1988). Boys in the custody of their fathers are more independent, mature, less demanding, and have higher self-esteem than do girls in their father's custody. However, these boys are usually less communicative and affectionate. Girls in the custody of their fathers are more aggressive and less prosocial than girls in the custody of their mothers (Furstenberg, 1988).

Boys are more likely than girls to respond to stress with externalizing, noncompliant, oppositional, antisocial behaviors (Hetherington et al., 1989). Concurrently, boys are less able than girls to discuss their feelings and to ask for and obtain support from others. Girls may also demonstrate behavioral disruptions following divorce, and some internalizing behaviors have been noted as well (Hetherington & Clingempeel, 1988). Reduced economic resources in a mother-custodial home may result in poor quality housing, schools, neighborhoods, and child care, and a loss of familiar friends and adults in the child's life. Preschool children may feel abandoned, particularly if a mother works and is uncomfortable with her new employment; in such instances, the child may be adversely affected by interactions with an unhappy mother. Since both noncustodial and custodial fathers typically maintain or improve their economic standing following divorce, those children who reside with their fathers following divorce rarely encounter stressful financial resources (cf. Hetherington, 1989). Boys, particularly adolescents, tend to experience severe depression following the death of their fathers (Van Eerdewegh et al., 1982).

HOW LONG AGO DID THE LOSS OCCUR?

Research indicates that in general the more time that passes after the loss, the better the child's adjustment. In the case of death, as time goes on, children are more likely than not to complete the grieving process (Van Eerdewegh et al., 1985). In the case of divorce, particularly if the parents are committed to resolving the issue for themselves and for the child, the initial pain and conflicts around loyalty diminish. This progresses as time passes, as parents settle their differences, or as the children and parents become involved in new relationships (Hetherington, 1989).

WAS THE CHILD EXPECTING THE DIVORCE, DEATH, OR SEPARATION?

In general, even for young children, having an unexpected event occur is more stressful than anticipating a loss. If there was a high level of conflict between parents before a divorce, the breakup of the marriage may be met with some relief on the part of the child. In the case of death, if the parent had a long and painful illness, there may also be a degree of relief when death finally occurs. It is important to explore how the child copes with both expected and unexpected losses (Owusu-Bempah, 1995).

WHAT BEHAVIORAL SYMPTOMS IS THE CHILD DISPLAYING? WHAT ARE THE CHILD'S EMOTIONAL REACTIONS TO THE LOSS?

It is, of course, important to note the child's behavioral presenting problems. In general, research indicates that children with histories of loss through death and divorce evidence more school problems than children from intact families (Felner et al., 1981). Separation and divorce often result in more acting out and behavioral problems than does separation due to death. Children who experience the death of a parent more often display anxiety and affective disturbances than do children whose parents separate or divorce (Felner et al., 1981).

IS THE REMAINING PARENT DISPLAYING SYMPTOMS OR ADJUSTMENT PROBLEMS?

Divorce and death often cause a parent to demonstrate psychological, emotional, or physical changes. It is during these times that children are most likely to need stability and support, and the wounded parent may be unable to provide that support. Thus parents and children may exacerbate each other's problems (Lipman, Offord, & Boyle, 1997).

Stable, supportive environments are important for children of all ages. For young children who are less able to be autonomous, it is particularly important that the parent have a well-organized household, show nurturance, and make only reasonable demands on the young child. For older children and adolescents, while greater household and child care responsibilities may be expected, it is important for the parent to monitor the emotional requirements made on the child to prevent the child from experiencing feelings of incompetence and resentment (Hetherington, 1989; Hetherington et al., 1989; Randolph, 1995).

WHAT IS THE NATURE OF SIBLING RELATIONSHIPS?

It is important to assess the nature of sibling relationships among children in single-parent households. Female siblings have been found to act as buffers and emotional support for each other (Hetherington & Clingenpeel, 1988). Among male siblings of divorced mothers, however, relationships are often more antagonistic than among those with nondivorced parents (Hetherington et al., 1989).

HAS THE HOUSEHOLD ROUTINE CHANGED?

Weinraub and Wolf (1983) demonstrated that, compared to married mothers, single parents work longer hours and tend to face more stressful life changes. Such single women tend to be more isolated and less consistent in their social contacts, less involved in organizations and parenting groups, and less supported, both emotionally and in their parenting roles (Murata, 1994).

The child of a single parent is likely to spend a greater number of hours in alternative child care arrangements. At home, the single-parent child may have less frequent and less consistent contact with adults than the child from a two-parent household. The single mothers' life tends to be characterized by frequent changes in work, housing, and social concerns. The associated changes in living arrangements, schedule, and time with mother may directly affect the child. However, Weinraub and Wolf (1983) found that single parents reported no more difficulties in their overall coping ability than did married mothers; indeed, only in the area of household chores did single mothers report more difficulty. Household chores, therefore, may be the most easily neglected responsibility.

Weinraub and Wolf (1983) demonstrated that, in single-mother homes, increased employment was related to increased control and demands for greater maturity. Many single parents feel that they have no choice but to work, and this, therefore, justifies their exercising more control and placing higher demands on their children.

Fergusson, Dimond, and Horwood (1986) investigated children who had experienced a marital breakdown due to separation and divorce. They discovered that those children whose parents had reconciled and those who had entered further two-parent families were more prone to behavior problems than were those who remained in a stable single-parent family. The greater the number of changes in the child's family history during early childhood, the more likely it was that the child would display behavior difficulties by age 6. The apparent correlation between childhood be-

havior problems and family placement history appears to be explained by the effects of social and contextual factors related to the child's family placement history. In particular, increased instability of the child's family situation was associated with social disadvantage, economic deprivation, and higher rates of marital discord. Collectively this combination of social and economic disadvantage, coupled with family discord and stress, appear to be the major reasons that children who experience broken homes show poor behavioral adjustment.

Other Considerations

VIOLENCE IN SINGLE-PARENT FAMILIES

Gelles (1989) emphasizes that single parents tend to be more likely to use abusive forms of violence toward their children than are parents in dual-caretaker households. This study demonstrates that single parents are no more likely to use any particular form of physical violence toward their children than parents in dual caretaker homes, but the rates of severe and very severe violence toward children are substantially higher in single-parent households.

Gelles (1989) reported that single fathers were much more likely to use acts of severe and very severe violence toward their children. In particular, single-parent fathers and mothers were equally likely to use violence toward their children, but single fathers had higher rates of severe and very severe violence than did single mothers. Having other adults present does little to reduce the apparent stress experienced by some single parents. Rates of severe and very severe violence were actually slightly higher in homes with more than one adult, although the differences were not significant. Living alone, as opposed to living with other adults, does not in itself explain the high rates of violence and abuse found in single-parent homes.

Gelles (1989) concluded that economic deprivation was the reason why single-parent mothers in his study were more likely to abuse their children. He concluded that poverty exacerbates the greater risk that single fathers will abuse their children, but poverty alone does not seem to explain why single fathers are so much more likely to use abusive violence than fathers in dual-caretaker homes or than mothers in general.

ROLE INAPPROPRIATE BEHAVIOR

Although little research has addressed the question directly, clinical experience suggests that children of single parents are at risk for various kinds of role inappropriate behavior. This might include the child acting as a peer, spouse, or even the caregiver of the parent. Especially in families disrupted by divorce or death, children may experience changes in boundaries and roles which may be developmentally inappropriate. In our experience, the probability of these patterns emerging may be increased if the single parent is subject to depression or alcoholism. Research has identified a number of these patterns in school-age children (Main & Cassidy, 1988; Solomon, George, & Ivins, 1987), but whether they are truly increased in the children of single parents remains to be demonstrated. The major issue for the clinician is whether there is evidence that the child is being relied upon by the single parent to function in ways that are excessively burdensome to the child's own psychological development.

In order to give the reader an idea of what an actual interview and clinical assessment of a child of a single parent may entail, what follows is a description of a clinical case. The details are elaborated, particularly the process the psychiatrist uses to conduct the interview. The psychiatrist's internal deliberations, intuitions, and emotional responses to the situation are outlined to clarify how he determined the questions he asked of the mother and the child.

CASE EXAMPLE

A mother called an outpatient psychiatry clinic about her 8-year-old daughter. She told the receptionist that she was very concerned because her daughter had been sexually abused 2 weeks before by three adolescent boys. They had fondled her and had forced her to perform fellatio on them in a vacant apartment in the same building where the girl lived. The girl had been under the care of a neighbor when the abuse occurred. Mother said that she wanted her daughter seen as soon as possible for evaluation.

The psychiatrist who agreed to pick up the case won-dered as he read the intake form about what sort of neighborhood the family lived in and how the 8-year-old girl could have been so poorly supervised. He wondered how the mother felt about having failed in her protective function, and about the strengths of her supports, given the lapse in supervision of her daughter. He also realized that the mother had called for help relatively soon after the event, and he made a note to credit her for having acted promptly. In addition to this information, the psychiatrist noted from the intake form that the mother was divorced and lived alone with her daughter. The mother worked in a clerical position and had no mental health coverage under her medical insurance policy.

As he dialed the mother's phone number to arrange an initial appointment, the psychiatrist noted the implicit urgency in the mother's reaction that came across on the intake sheet. He wondered what it was about the girl's behavior that had prompted the call and what had transpired in the 2 weeks since the abuse had occurred. Realizing that the mother was a single parent increased his concerns about the adequacy of her supports.

The mother answered the phone and made it clear that she was indeed quite concerned about her daughter. Nevertheless, she was not aware of any symptoms or unusual behavior in the girl, other than that she seemed a bit more sober and perhaps more withdrawn than usual. The mother thought that such an "absolute tragedy" deserved an evaluation. The poetic phrasing of "absolute tragedy" caught the psychiatrist's ear, and he remembered his earlier fleeting question about whether the mother had been sexually abused herself when she was a child. After confirming the demographic information that had been obtained previously, the psychiatrist arranged a time to meet with mother and daughter together. Before hanging up, he asked the mother if she had discussed the referral with her daughter. She said that she had told the girl that she planned that they "go and talk to someone about what happened." The girl had not said anything in response, but her mother felt that she would be agreeable to the visit.

At the first appointment, the psychiatrist met initially with mother and daughter together. In addition to gathering details of the abusive incident and the girl's reaction to it, the psychiatrist also made a number of observations about the dyad's interaction. He noticed that the girl, who ostensibly busied herself with toys as he talked with her mother, carefully monitored her mother's behavior and affect. He also noticed that the girl seemed unusually familiar with details of her mother's childhood history and recent relationship history with men. This was apparent because the girl corrected details of her mother's story on several occasions in a matter-of-fact way. When corrected by her daughter, the mother seemed a bit embarrassed, giggling nervously, but she usually accepted her daughter's version of the events. When her mother seemed to become emotional, the girl interrupted to show her something or to look coyly at the psychiatrist.

The mother was unaware of any problems at home, although she did report that the girl had had some conduct problems in school with oppositional behavior toward her teachers. She also had a few friends, who sounded more like acquaintances, but no best friend. Mother seemed oblivious to or at least untroubled by the girl's somewhat controlling behavior toward her. In fact, when asked, she described her relationship with her daughter as "close—she's the closest friend I've got."

All of this suggested to the psychiatrist that role reversal was a clinical concern in this mother-daughter relationship. It was less the girl's somewhat precocious responsibilities around the house that led to this impression (she fixed her mother breakfast almost every morning), but rather her monitoring of her mother's moods and her overinvolved and controlling interaction with her. It seemed as if the emotional burden of the relationship had shifted excessively and detrimentally to the daughter's side. Other relevant parts of the story were that the mother and girl had been abandoned by two men. The girl's father had left the state during her infancy and had maintained only minimal and sporadic contact with her after that. In addition, the mother's subsequent long-term boyfriend, who had taken a real interest in the girl, had died in a motorcycle accident 2 years before.

As he noted again the girl's flirtatious behavior with him, the psychiatrist wondered about whether she had been previously abused, whether she had witnessed any of her mother's sexual encounters, and whether her losses had anything to do with the way she related to him. He remembered that when a parent leaves the family, there is often pressure for another family member (especially a child) to step into the role of the lost parental figure and attempt to fill the void that is created.

In meeting with the mother alone, the psychiatrist took care to explore the mother's emotional reactions to the abusive episode and attempted to ascertain the mother's experience of her daughter's exploitation. He was relieved to learn that the mother held her daughter in no way accountable for the event, and that she seemed to accept a share of culpability for having failed to protect her daughter. On the other hand, she maintained a clear and appropriate concern for her daughter rather than for herself.

Still, all of the concerns about her lack of supports had been well-founded, as the mother had few dependable friends and no extended family in the area. And most concerning, she seemed unaware of the degree to which she sought and accepted support from her daughter, as well as the developmental burden it seemed to be imposing.

The psychiatrist also spent part of the initial session with the girl alone. Her mental status exam was unremarkable, except that she seemed to be somewhat sexually preoccupied. She told the psychiatrist that she had kissed two boys, one of them a 12 year old. She also mentioned that she had "French kissed" the 12-year-old boy three times, but her mother only knew about the first time. She mentioned the kissing at several different points in the interview, which led the psychiatrist to convey less interest in the details. She seemed notably uncomfortable when asked about the incident with the teenage boys, and the psychiatrist commented on her discomfort but did not insist that she discuss the incident further.

The psychiatrist made other observations in the joint part of the session as well as in his interview of the girl, but they tended to amplify his initial impressions rather than to change them substantively. The initial strategy that he envisioned was to obtain information from the girl's school directly by speaking to her teachers and principal and by obtaining a standardized teacher's rating of her behavior. He was interested both in the girl's relatedness with her teachers, but also with peers.

In addition, because he had many questions for her mother, he decided that it might be useful to spend an entire session with her. In that session he hoped to learn more about how much awareness the mother had about their role-inappropriate interaction and about how amenable she might be to seeing some aspects of her "closeness" with her daughter as potentially compromising. At the same time, he felt that he needed to affirm the mother's concern about her daughter's well-being following the abuse. He also felt that a full session with the daughter alone might allow him to make some preliminary clarifications and interpretations to test her response to a "dose" of insight-oriented psychotherapy.

The major treatment decisions that these additional data might lead to were whether he might recommend individual psychotherapy with the girl along with parental guidance for the mother, dyadic mother-child sessions, and/or group psychotherapy with age-mates, perhaps with a social skills training focus. He also considered the possibility that the mother might be interested in treatment for herself.

Conclusion

Being the child of a single parent does not define a specific set of risks for the child. Rather it raises the probability that the child will be subject to other risk factors and to a variety of psychiatric disorders. Wide variability is the rule rather than the exception; the details of the child's particular history, strengths and weaknesses, and current situation are all important. Further, beyond the facts themselves, the meaning of all of these factors to the child are likely to be central in determining a specific plan for intervention. Nevertheless, much more information about the nature and interaction of risk factors for children of single parents may help us to understand better the challenges faced by these children.

Clearly, much work needs to be done in outlining special considerations for children of single-parent homes. Research focused on the unique aspects, if any, of being raised by a single parent is sorely needed. This is true for parents electing to have or adopt a child, never-married single parents, homosexual single parents, parents who are temporarily absent due to educational and military commitments, and parents who are absent due to desertion. In addition, it would be beneficial for future empirical work to assess whether the parent and child were expecting the separation, no matter what the reason, and the effects of forewarning or lack thereof. Longitudinal studies which compare those who experience loss due to separation, divorce, death, homosexuality, and temporary absence of the parent need to be conducted so that the nature and dynamics of the symptomatology can be assessed over a long period of time. In addition, studies which identify any differential effects of the child's gender as related to the gender of the absent parent need to be conducted.

Ultimately, large-scale studies which address the multiplicity of factors associated with single-parent households and investigate the salient variables are recommended. These variables include type of loss, sex of the lost parent, age and sex of the child, length of time since the death or separation, number of people remaining in the home, relationship among the people remaining in the home (i.e., extended family, siblings, cohabitating adults), developmental maturity of children, expectation of the loss, and the personality characteristics of both the children and the remaining parent. Clearly this field is open to researchers who wish to investigate the acute and long-term outcomes of being raised in a single-parent home. With such data available, intervention can be tailored to address problematic outcomes, and such intervention may result in optimal adjustment and development for children who experience life with a single parent. In any case, all these salient variables need to be evaluated in the interview and assessment of children of single parents.

REFERENCES

Amato, P. R., & Keith, B. (1991). Parental divorce and the well-being of children: A meta-analysis. *Psychological Bulletin, 110* (1), 26–46.

Bumpass, L. (1984). Children and marital disruption: A replication and update. *Demography, 21,* 71–82.

Bowlby, J. (1980). *Attachment and loss: Loss.* New York: Basic Books.

Camara, K. A., & Resnick, G. (1988). Interparental conflict and cooperation: Factors moderating children's post-divorce adjustment. In E. M. Hetherington & J. D. Arasteh (Eds.), *Impact of divorce, single-parenting, and stepparenting on children* (pp. 169–196). Hillsdale, NJ: Lawrence Erlbaum.

Felner, R. D., Ginter, M. A., Boike, M. F., & Cowen, E. L. (1981). Parental death or divorce and the school adjustment of young children. *American Journal of Community Psychology, 9* (2), 181–191.

Furstenberg, F. F. (1988). Child care after divorce and remarriage. In E. M. Hetherington & J. Arasteh (Eds.), *Impact of divorce, single-parenting, and stepparenting on children* (pp. 245–261). Hillsdale, NJ: Lawrence Erlbaum.

Gelles, R. J. (1989). Child abuse and violence in single-parent families: Parent absence and economic deprivation. *American Journal of Orthopsychiatry, 59* (4), 492–501.

Golombok, S., Spencer, A., & Rutter, M. (1983). Children in lesbian and single-parent households: Psychosexual and psychiatric appraisal. *Journal of Child Psychology and Psychiatry, 24* (4), 551–572.

Green, R., Mandel, J. B., Hotvedt, M. E., Gray, J., & Smith, L. (1986). Lesbian mothers and their children: A comparison with solo parent heterosexual mothers and their children. *Archives of Sexual Behavior, 15* (2), 167–184.

Hetherington, E. M., Stanley-Hagan, M., & Anderson, E. R. (1989). Marital transitions: A child's perspective. *American Psychologist, 44* (2), 303–312.

Jackson, A. P. (1994). Psychological distress among single, employed, Black mothers and their perceptions of their young children. *Journal of Social Service Research, 19,* 87–101.

Lipman, E. L., Offord, D. R., & Boyle, M. H. (1997). Single mothers in Ontario: Sociodemographic, physical and mental health characteristics. *Canadian Medical Association Journal, 156(5),* 639–645.

Murata, J. (1994). Family stress, social support, violence, and sons' behavior. *Western Journal of Nursing Research, 16(2),* 154–168.

Nelson, G. (1982). Coping with the loss of Father: Family reaction to death or divorce. *Journal of Family Issues, 3,* 41–60.

Owusu-Bempah, J. (1995). Information about the absent parent as a factor in the well-being of children of single-parent families. *International Social Work, 38,* 253–275.

Randolph, S. M. (1995). African American children in single-mother families. In B. J. Dickerson (Ed.), *African American single mothers: Understanding their lives and families* (pp. 117–145). Thousand Oaks, CA: Sage Publications.

Steinhausen, H., von Aster, S., & Göbel, D. (1987). Family composition and child psychiatric disorders. *Journal of the American Academy of Child and Adolescent Psychiatry, 26,* 242–247.

Van Eerdewegh, M. M., Clayton, P. J., & Van Eerdewegh, P. (1985). The bereaved child: Variables influencing early psychopathology. *British Journal of Psychiatry, 147,* 188–194.

Weinraub, M., & Wolf, B. M. (1983). Effects of stress and social supports on mother-child interactions in single- and two-parent families. *Child Development, 54* (5), 1297–1311.

79 / Observation, Interview, and Mental Status Assessment (OIM): Divorce

Neil Kalter

Professionals specializing in work with children and adolescents must pay increasing attention to the potential impact of parental divorce on youngsters. Current estimates are that over 40% of all children growing up in the United States will see their parents divorce prior to the children reaching the age of 18 (Furstenberg, 1990). Since youngsters whose parents divorce are referred for mental health services more frequently than those from nondivorced households (Zill, Morrison, & Coiro, 1993), clinicians are likely to encounter many such young patients.

Increasingly divorce is conceptualized as a process extended in time and associated with a great many life changes and challenges to healthy social, emotional, and cognitive development (Emery & Kitzmann, 1995; Kalter, 1987, 1990; Pearson & Anhalt, 1994; Wallerstein, 1991). The professional literature focused specifically on how children fare when their parents divorce is barely 25 years old; nonetheless, there has been considerable progress in describing the psychiatric sequelae for such youngsters.

Postdivorce adjustment is associated strongly with the child's current age, the age at the time of the decisive parental separation, the child's gender, and the custody arrangements. Generally, younger children have more difficulty than older children and, at the time of the marital separation and divorce, boys display more problems than girls. This outcome persists up until adolescence when both genders may experience significant difficulties. In general, youngsters do best when both parents continue to be constructively involved in their lives. [The interested reader is referred to Chase-Lansdale & Hetherington (1990) and Emery & Kitzmann, 1995) for a detailed review of the empirical research literature, and to Kalter (1990) for an in-depth treatment of pivotal clinical issues for youngsters whose parents divorce.]

It is widely agreed that children of all ages experience significant distress in the immediate aftermath of their parents' separation. The specific ways in which this is manifested depend in part upon the age and gender of the youngster. Common reactions are anxiety, loss of previously attained developmental accomplishments, aggressive behavior problems, sadness/depression, and a decline in academic performance (Chase-Lansdale & Hetherington, 1990; Guidubaldi & Perry, 1985; Emery & Kitzmann, 1995; Wallerstein & Kelly, 1980).

It is especially important for clinicians to be attuned to the possibility that a youngster's presenting complaints may be linked to divorce-related individual and family dynamics, even when "the divorce" occurred years in the past. Long-term effects of parental divorce include aggressive behavior problems, poor academic performance, depression, and physical health problems (Bray & Berger, 1993; Chase-Lansdale & Hetherington, 1990; Guidubaldi, 1988; Peterson & Zill, 1986). Additionally, in adolescence, impulsive behavior problems, precocious and/or promiscuous sexual activity, and other delinquent-like behaviors may emerge (Kalter, 1990; Newcomer & Udry, 1987).

These clinical and research findings address the central tendencies of youngsters' reactions and adjustment to parental divorce. They do not account for the substantial variability in how divorce affects the lives of the children involved. An examination of both the psychosocial stressors often associated with divorce and the specific psychological stresses and conflicts engendered by parental divorce can aid clinicians' assessment of their young patients. It is useful to conceptualize psychosocial stressors as external stimuli that impinge on children, and to regard psychological stresses and conflicts as the internal reactions of youngsters to these stressors. Objectively, the fewer the psychosocial stressors and the less chronic and intense they are, the more likely it is that youngsters will adapt well to their parents' divorce. However, a youngster's subjective experiences do not correlate in a predictable fashion with the array of psychosocial stressors to which she has been exposed. In the aftermath of divorce, the child's temperament, developmental stage, gender, quality of relationships with each parent and overall predivorce adjustment will contribute in major ways to the nature and degree of internal stresses and conflicts, and to any behavioral expressions which may ensue.

Psychosocial Stressors and Internal Stress and Conflict

The many contributors to the clinical and research literature are in substantial agreement regarding the nature and relative importance of divorce-specific psychosocial stressors for youngsters. These are, in order of importance, (1) hostilities between parents; (2) the presence of an emotionally distraught parent, especially the primary custodial parent; (3) loss of the relationship with the noncustodial parent; (4) downward economic mobility of the primary postdivorce household; (5) the primary custodial parent's dating activities; and (6) the primary custodial parent remarrying. It is essential for the clinician to evaluate each of these factors in order to assess the array and intensity of psychosocial stressors with which the young person has had to contend.

Each of these psychosocial stressors not only burdens youngsters and taxes their defenses and coping resources, but each is also associated with both specific internal stresses and conflicts and the behavior problems they often give rise to. Warfare between parents is experienced by young children primarily as extremely frightening and confusing and by older children and adolescents as scary and enraging. It also produces intense loyalty conflicts over which parent to side with. Thus younger children tend to display anxiety symptoms (e.g., separation anxiety, phobias, and regressive behavior) and somatic expressions of tension, while older children and adolescents tend to feel anxious and guilty over loyalty issues and develop aggressive problems with peers and family members. Alternatively, they may manage their anger defensively through inhibitions and turning aggression inward, with ensuing depression.

When a custodial parent is emotionally distraught (e.g., depressed, anxious, enraged), young children feel unprotected and fearful. Since they are very much dependent on their parents for emotional sustenance, they tend to become anxious, displaying such symptoms as separation anxiety and phobias, or they fall into a depression characterized by feelings of hopelessness, withdrawal from peers and previously pleasurable activities, sleep and eating disturbances, and suicidal thoughts. Older children and adolescents often assume new and inappropriate family roles in order to cope with the stress of having a distraught or less capable parent. They may become allies in a vendetta against the other parent, coparent to younger siblings, and parent or confidant to their distressed parent. The pseudomature, somewhat depressed, "parentified" child emerges. Some teenagers withdraw from their family, seeking refuge in their peer group; they then become especially vulnerable to peer pressure.

Maintaining a close emotional relationship with a parent is nearly impossible from the distance of biweekly or even sparser contact. Hence, the loss of the relationship with the noncustodial parent, typically the father, may be substantial and obvious (although its effects can be more subtle). Youngsters of all ages experience a pronounced sense of loss and may develop depressive symptoms. Preschoolers and older children are likely to experience this loss as a narcissistic injury which assaults their feelings of self-worth. As they view it, father left, or does not see me much, because I am unlovable or unworthy.

Downward economic mobility tends to affect youngsters indirectly, yet nonetheless powerfully. It often precipitates residential shifts which mean multiple losses for children: they must give up the familiarity of home, neighborhood, caregivers, and school, and say good-bye to friends and classmates. Fewer economic resources also curtail opportunities for cultural and academic enrichment. The custodial parent may become anxious or depressed by similar losses. Younger children resonate to their primary parent's distress, often becoming anxious, fearful, and withdrawn. Older children and especially adolescents react with anger as well as sadness over these losses, and their academic performance may decline. When they move, not only is their family disrupted, but they lose the comfort afforded by familiar routines, caring teachers, caregivers, and significant peers.

Unlike the other psychosocial stressors, parents most often experience dating and remarriage positively. Parents find new sources of social support and pleasure, and have a sense that they are putting "the divorce" behind them and getting on with their lives. At that point, parents frequently become less distraught and may reduce the level of conflict with their ex-spouse. However, children and adolescents generally are less pleased by parent dating and remarriage, at least initially. Younger children often view their parent's dating partner or new spouse as a competitive threat, fearing that their parent will be less loving or committed to them. Older children and adolescents have these same competitive feelings, but are just as likely to become curious and excited about the sexual overtones of their parent's intimate relationships, while also condemning them. Young children tend to become whiny and cling to their parent in a hostile-dependent manner, as they express simultaneously their anxieties and anger over possibly losing their parent to the new partner. Older children and adolescents often express their anger by becoming rebellious and uncooperative at home. Adolescents may become sexually active and/or engage in delinquent-like activities, as they both identify with their "immoral" parent and also angrily punish the parent by getting into trouble. For school-age youngsters, academic performance can decline as these emotional agendas absorb their time, energy, and commitment.

The interplay between psychosocial stressors and the common internal stresses and conflicts they elicit in youngsters at different developmental stages provides a crucial guiding framework for evaluating children and adolescents. Within the context of parental divorce, the matrix of external stressors, the developmental stage of the youngster, and internal stresses and conflicts helps define the expectable emotional, behavioral, and academic difficulties that may develop.

Structuring the Evaluation

In the course of psychiatric evaluations of youngsters whose parents are together, the first telephone contact and the initial parent sessions are important. Where the parents are divorced, this initial contact is crucial to a successful assessment and intervention. The threats to a clinically useful evaluation include beginning the process without a custodial parent's consent, failure to invite participation of the nonreferring parent, and insufficient attention to the motives of the parents for initiating an evaluation of their child.

In the initial telephone call, the parent typically

indicates the status of the marriage: that they are anticipating a marital separation, have already separated or filed for divorce, or that they are divorced, and perhaps remarried. If this information is not volunteered, it is important for the clinician to ask who is in the household and what is the marital status of the parents. Once it is clear that a divorce is in progress or has occurred, the evaluator needs to ascertain the current custodial arrangements.

CASE EXAMPLE

Professor A. called an outpatient psychiatry department clinic to schedule an evaluation for his 10-year-old son, Matthew. He stated to the intake worker that he and Matthew's mother had been divorced for 3 years, and that his son appeared increasingly sad, lonely, and socially withdrawn. The case was assigned to Dr. R., a resident in child psychiatry, for evaluation. He saw Professor A. and Matthew in back-to-back appointments the following week. Matthew had arrived 2 weeks earlier for a 6-week stay with his father during the summer. He appeared clinically depressed. Several days later, Dr. R. received a telephone call from the attorney representing Matthew's mother. She had learned of her son's contact with Dr. R. during her weekly telephone visit with Matthew. The attorney told Dr. R. that Matthew's mother had sole legal custody and that medical treatment, including assessment, without her client's authorization was in conflict with the provisions of the divorce decree and, further, was illegal in that state. The evaluation was terminated immediately.

The clinic's intake worker and Dr. R. had failed to inquire about custody. The result was an aborted evaluation, no possibility of beginning treatment for this depressed boy, and the likelihood that tensions between Matthew's parents had been escalated. Clinicians need to be alert to this issue and may wish to have the referring parent bring a copy of the divorce judgment to the first parent session so that a parent's possible confusion about legal custody does not determine what happens.

Even when the referring parent has full or joint legal custody of the youngster in question, it is important to ask whether the other parent is aware of the potential evaluation and whether he might welcome the opportunity to participate. Most of the time the other parent has been informed of the plan to seek a psychiatric assessment of the youngster. However, it is useful for the clinician to ask the referring parent's permission to contact the other parent "to begin to get his input about how your child is doing."

CASE EXAMPLE

Ms. B. called a public child and family agency about her son, Michael, who was 8 years old. She spoke with Dr. S., a staff psychologist, about Michael's difficulties with aggressive behavior. He had been in trouble at school over the past 6 months for lashing out physically at other children and taking their possessions. Michael also had been displaying aggressive behavior at home. Ms. B. had joint legal and full physical custody of her children, who visited their father regularly. Dr. S. had Ms. B. bring a copy of the divorce judgment to confirm these facts. An evaluation was completed, and once weekly individual psychotherapy with Michael was begun. Michael's father had never been contacted by Dr. S., who had been told by Ms. B. that her ex-husband was "not interested in psychological stuff and wants nothing to do with it." Three months later, Mr. B. called bitterly accusing Dr. S. of excluding him from his son's treatment. Michael became increasingly resistant to coming for his appointments, saying that "my dad doesn't think I should go and it's all bull." This treatment terminated prematurely and unsuccessfully after 5 months.

Dr. S. had colluded unwittingly with Ms. B.'s uneasiness about having her ex-husband involved in the evaluation and treatment of her son. She never invited Mr. B.'s participation nor informed him of the evaluation and the recommendation for psychotherapy. Dr. S. simply took Ms. B. at her word regarding Mr. B.'s opposition to psychiatry. Even when a parent holds this view, failure by the clinician to extend an invitation directly to the nonreferring parent is fraught with problems. Feeling devalued and excluded, the nonreferring parent may derogate the child and/or his psychiatric involvement, pit his relationship with his child against the clinician-child alliance, and thus bring the clinical process to an untimely end. Conversely, inviting the nonreferring parent's participation early in the evaluation process establishes the clinician's view that both parents are important in the youngster's life and that both can contribute to understanding and helping their child.

While some parents cannot bear to be in the same room together, many others are quite capable of putting aside old or current animosities in the service of helping their child. I find that during the initial telephone call, it is best to ask the referring parent whether separate or conjoint parent meetings would be most constructive. The response to this question yields diagnostic information about the coparenting relationship as well as guidance for how to arrange for parent participation in the evaluation. In most instances, when one parent is not living at a great distance, conjoint parent sessions are possible.

When structuring the evaluation, it is especially helpful to ask the referring parent about the reasons for seeking a psychiatric evaluation of the child. As is the case generally, the primary impetus for the referral typically comes from the youngster's school, child care provider, pediatrician, or parent(s). However, most parent motives fall into one or more of three categories: a wish to provide prophylactic help for their child, treatment for a child who has become symptomatic, or to acquire ammunition or support in an ongoing or anticipated legal battle. In a parent's mind, these need not be mutually exclusive, and at times are not clearly thought through. For mental health professionals these are important distinctions. The majority of clinicians agree that if the primary aim of an evaluation is to provide information to be used in court, it is structured differently than a clinical evaluation. It also is best not to engage directly in either parent guidance or treatment of the child.

CASE EXAMPLE

Mr. C. contacted Dr. T., a psychiatrist in private practice, seeking an evaluation of his 4-year-old daughter, Jenny. In the first telephone call Dr. T. determined that Mr. and Mrs. C. had separated 6 months earlier, had temporary joint legal custody, and that Jenny spent every other Thursday through Sunday with her father. Mr. C. described Jenny as having become a fearful child over the past several months. She had trouble going to sleep alone and cried when being dropped off at her nursery school. Because Jenny was a young child, Dr. T. set up a first parent meeting without scheduling a session for Jenny. Dr. T. suggested that Mr. C. tell his wife of the evaluation and let her know that Dr. T. would call her to discuss it. Dr. T. contacted Mrs. C. the next day, and she agreed to participate in the evaluation by meeting separately with Dr. T. Based on his initial session

with Mr. C., Dr. T. had the impression that Mr. C. saw Jenny's problems as related to her mother's distress over the divorce and her parenting style. Also, Mr. C. had asked what Dr. T. thought about joint physical custody or fathers being the primary parent for young girls. Dr. T. began to question, in his own mind, what Mr. C.'s motives were for seeking an evaluation of Jenny. Did he want a diagnostic assessment and treatment for Jenny? Parent guidance for himself and/or Jenny's mother? Or was Mr. C. seeking an ally in a possible custody battle? Mrs. C., in her session, described Jenny as doing reasonably well given the abrupt and unexpected nature of the marital separation. Though she did seem more clingy and tearful at separations, she had maintained her developmental progress in other areas. Mrs. C. did not think Jenny needed to be seen by a psychiatrist, but that divorce-focused parent guidance for her and her husband, separately, made good sense. In Dr. T.'s second session with Mr. C., he noted Mrs. C's willingness to proceed with the evaluation, with the primary aim being separate parent guidance for each. As a precaution, Dr. T. explained to Mr. C., as he had to Mrs. C., that because of the nature of their work together, Dr. T. would not be available to provide information to either parent's attorney or to the court. Mr. C. questioned the need for Dr. T. to stay out of the legal arena and remained unconvinced by Dr. T.'s further explanations. Mr. C. stopped coming after the following session, and the evaluation as well as the subsequent parent guidance continued successfully with Mrs. C.

The care with which Dr. T. conducted his first telephone contact with Mr. C., and his sensitivity to Mr. C.'s potential multiple agendas, permitted this evaluation and intervention to serve Jenny well. While Mr. C. genuinely was concerned about his daughter's separation anxieties, his solution appeared to be to gain joint or full physical custody of Jenny, thus reducing her exposure to what he perceived as her mother's problematic parenting and distress. When Dr. T. articulated his clinical role and excluded the possibility of providing information for use in court, he avoided the likely disruption of a useful intervention on Jenny's behalf.

Lack of care in properly structuring an evaluation can cause it to end badly. Uncompleted assessments, rejection of recommendations, parentally undermined treatments, or clinical efforts being disrupted by unanticipated demands for the clinician to become involved in legal matters are common.

Conducting the Evaluation

When conducting evaluations of children and adolescents in the context of divorce, clinicians proceed much as they would in cases where families are intact. That is, the evaluator obtains a developmental history of the young patient from parents, interviews the youngster directly, collects diagnostic data from relevant sources such as the patient's pediatrician and school, and orders further diagnostic assessments (e.g., a hearing test, an EEG, psychological testing, etc.) when indicated.

Of course, it may be that the youngster's difficulties are not centrally related to her parents' divorce. Many children of divorced parents suffer from biologically based affective disorders, attentional problems, learning disabilities, or psychoses. The fact of a parental divorce by no means rules out the possibility that an unrelated psychiatric disorder is primarily responsible for the observed symptom picture. Therefore the clinician is actually conducting two simultaneous evaluations, one focused on the divorce context and the other more broadly attentive to the full range of potential child or adolescent psychopathology.

A child or adolescent may develop a diagnosable mental disorder which can be caused by ongoing intrapsychic and family conflicts directly tied to parental divorce. This is especially likely when numerous, divorce-related, psychosocial stressors are present that have been chronic as well as intense. Disorders which commonly arise include internalizing disorders such as separation anxiety disorder, generalized anxiety disorder, phobias and dysthymia, externalizing disorders such as oppositional-defiant disorder and conduct disorder, and the range of adjustment disorders.

When a parental separation or divorce is imminent or has occurred, it is wise to obtain a detailed history of the circumstances surrounding the divorce from the parents before scheduling an appointment with the youngster. This includes special attention to risk factors, along with information about the timing of the decisive parental separation in the child's life, what the custody and visitation arrangements have been, the nature of the coparenting relationship, the parents' adjustment to the divorce, and whether either or both parents are dating or have remarried. This helps the evaluator gain a sense of the psychosocial stressors confronting the child.

After assessing these factors, the evaluator must decide whether or not to see the child or adolescent. It is important to bear in mind that young children, in the context of divorce, often form rapid and intense attachments to caring adults. This object hunger makes short-lived relationships hard on many children who experience an acute sense of loss when the contact in over. Evaluations, without further therapeutic involvement, can cause undue pain for younger patients. Generally the age of the child, the nature of the presenting complaints, and the number and intensity of psychosocial stressors help the clinician make this decision.

CASE EXAMPLE

Mr. and Mrs. D. each contacted Dr. U. regarding their two children, Mark, age 4, and Stacy, age 2. The parents had separated 2 months earlier, and had agreed to joint legal and physical custody of their children: Mark and Stacy spent 3 days of the week and alternate Saturdays with each parent. Mr. and Mrs. D. wanted to discuss how they could be helpful to Mark and Stacy. Mark was exhibiting aggressive behavior with peers at nursery school and toward his sister, while Stacy was manifesting several regressive behaviors. Dr. U. met with the D.'s twice together and once each separately. She determined that the parents had an excellent coparenting relationship, were adjusting well to their marital separation despite occasional angry flare-ups, were both lovingly involved with their children, had agreed to maintain the original family home in which Mrs. D. lived, and were not dating other people. Dr. U. elected not to see Mark or Stacy. Instead she recommended weekly joint parent guidance sessions. In these meetings Dr. U. helped the parents understand the nature of the children's internal stresses and conflicts which were giving rise to their observed problems, and how they could talk with Mark and Stacy. The youngsters' difficulties gradually resolved after 4 months and the parent sessions were discontinued.

Dr. U. reviewed Mark's difficulties managing his rage toward his beloved parents over the loss of his sense of family and Stacy's regressive behaviors in the face of confusion and anxiety-laden fantasies over losing her parents as well as her family unit. He felt they were developmentally normative reactions to their parents' separation. The joint physical as well as legal custody arrangement that the parents had voluntarily entered into underscored their respect for the value of the "other" parent to their children's development and their mutual capacity for constructive coparenting. Such arrangements occur relatively infrequently, perhaps because cooperative coparenting so often is undermined by unresolved conflicts between divorced parents or animosities still held by one or both parents. In this case the evaluation and subsequent intervention were accomplished by working exclusively with these parents.

This parent-centered approach can work well with children of all ages and with adolescents. However, it is most effective when the identified patient is young (under 6), the problems are expectable and stem from divorce-related internal stresses and conflicts, they are not severe, and there are few significant psychosocial stressors present.

We turn now to evaluating children and adolescents directly. In the case material that follows, the clinicians structured the evaluations appropriately in the ways described earlier.

EVALUATING PRESCHOOL AND GRADE SCHOOL CHILDREN

After obtaining information about divorce-related issues, general child development, and family relationships from parents, the clinician usually elects to see the child. It is most helpful to have one, and preferably both, parents present during the first few minutes of the initial child session. The evaluator can state the confidentiality rule in the presence of all concerned and have the parent(s) tell the youngster why she is there. (Parents of course will have been prepared for this meeting, and will have been helped to prepare the child, in the previous parent session.) When parents attend this first child session, even if only for a few minutes, it underscores for the child the presence of a coparenting alliance.

After the parents leave the session, the clinician may begin by empathizing with the child's likely distress over the family's circumstances: "You know that I've talked with your mom and dad about your family. So I know things haven't been easy. When parents split up, most kids have questions, special feelings, and even worries. Well, since I know a lot about how divorce works, and how boys and girls feel about divorce, I think I

can help. Some kids even call me a worry doctor, because I can usually help make worries a lot smaller for kids." This approach quickly communicates to the child that divorce is stressful for all children, that children have important inner experiences of divorce in the form of thoughts, feelings, and worries, and that there is hope that the psychiatrist can help things get better. By placing the child's presenting complaints in the context of divorce and divorce-related issues, the evaluator normalizes the youngster's difficulties and intimates that they are probably reactive to the divorce.

Some children respond immediately and directly to these introductory comments. One 8-year-old boy blurted, "Oh, you mean worries like my mom and dad will get in a big fight and kill, I mean, hurt each other!." Another boy, a reserved, somewhat intellectualized 10 year old confessed, "I have some real big worries when my dad's late coming to get me for a visit. I start thinking like maybe he's been in a car wreck or maybe some crazy person shot him on the expressway." In these examples, the evaluator began thinking of how angry a youngster must be to develop fantasies in which parents wind up getting hurt or killed. Interestingly, neither boy presented with anxiety problems; each had been referred for problems with aggressive behavior at school. This led the clinician to a preliminary hypothesis that these boys were wrestling with intense rage at one or both parents, and that this was being defensively displaced to the peer arena in order to avoid the pain and guilt of feeling so powerfully angry at much loved parents.

Most children do not verbalize their inner concerns so quickly. Thus, after the introduction, it is helpful for the evaluator to invite the child to explore the play materials and pick something he likes. In addition to the usual stock of materials in a child mental health professional's office, it is a good idea to have two doll houses and enough puppet or play figures to constitute two families. This permits children to represent each of their parents' homes and allows play activities to include references to stepparents and/or parents' dating partners.

CASE EXAMPLE

Ms. E. called to set up an evaluation for her son, David, age 4, who was becoming increasingly angry and noncompliant in nursery school and at home. Ms. E. and her ex-husband had separated a year earlier, and the divorce became final after 8 months. She and her former husband had joint legal custody, and David saw his father every other weekend and Tuesday and Thursday evenings. Both parents were agreeable to a conjoint appointment. In assessing the psychosocial stressors, Dr. V. noted that there was a great deal of anger between the parents, characterized by each being verbally explosive. The remaining psychosocial stressors were absent or minimal. Both parents reported that David had been an easy baby, had progressed through developmental milestones well and slightly early, was physically healthy, and had seemed well-adjusted prior to the marital separation. About 8 months before the evaluation, David had begun being noncompliant at home. A few months after that he became aggressive with other children at nursery school, pushing and hitting them with little or no provocation. Reasoning with David, giving him "time outs," and withdrawing television as a punishment had not been helpful.

After the first several "introductory" minutes of David's appointment, and following Dr. V.'s empathic comments about the difficulties divorce brings to families, Dr. V. invited David to play or draw. David picked the army figures and quickly set up two opposing forces. They soon killed each other off. Dr. V. noted that, "Those armies sure seem angry at each other." David set up another battle, and Dr. V. wondered what the armies were so angry about. David replied, "They hate each other's guts!" After this play was repeated, Dr. V. commented, "Looks like there are no survivors—everyone's been killed." David continued this play with increasing energy and sound effects. Dr. V. then introduced the idea of "civilians" who were not part of any army but were people who lived near the battlefield. She wondered aloud how these people felt about the war. David continued his play. Dr. V. then asked if the "civilian people were scared by all the fighting." David designated some dollhouse figures as "those civils people" and had them killed by stray bullets. In the next battle the "civils" became angry, built a huge bomb, and killed all the soldiers. Dr. V. talked with David about how boys are like the "civils" when a divorce war starts: they are frightened, worried about parents hurting each other, and then they become furious at "both sides." David became sad and quietly stated that he wished he could be the king who could order all fighting in the world to stop.

Dr. V. quickly saw the warfare David portrayed as a representation of his parents' ongoing hostilities. She sensitively introduced the idea of nearby civilians to provide a displacement figure for David to represent himself in the play. David made use of this addition by showing his worries about getting hurt by the rage that swirled around him and his anger over his parents' behavior. Dr. V. stayed within the play metaphor to facilitate David's expression of his concerns. Many young children, and even older children, do best in this format and retreat from communicating if problems are addressed directly. Even when Dr. V. talked with David about the meaning of his play, it was done in the verbal displacement of boys and divorced parents generally.

David's noncompliance at home and his aggression at nursery school could be understood as reactions to his parents' warfare: he identified with their mode of relating and simultaneously expressed his anger at them while protecting himself from feeling worried about his parents' and his own safety. This child's developmental progress had been excellent until he was caught in his parents' bitter divorce. And in many ways he continued to do well. Most of the time he related well to others, including Dr. V., and was on course in many areas of development. However, without a therapeutic intervention that addressed the key external stressor, intense interparental hostilities, and David's reactions to it, this patient's adjustment disorder could, within a short time, evolve into an oppositional-defiant disorder pervading many aspects of his life and interfering with subsequent development.

As noted earlier, it is also important that clinicians be attentive to the possibility that a youngster's problems may, in part or in whole, be the result of a psychiatric condition unrelated to the divorce.

CASE EXAMPLE

Ms. F. called an outpatient department of psychiatry to have her son, Barry, age 10, evaluated. The case was assigned to Dr. W., a fellow in child and adolescent psychiatry. Dr. W. saw Ms. F. and her former husband separately the following week. The F.'s had been divorced 4 years earlier after a year-long separation. Burdened by their continuing animosities, they had not been able to coparent well, despite having joint legal custody and a mutually satisfactory visiting arrangement for Barry and his father (two Saturdays per month). Mr. F. had remarried 2 years earlier and had a new baby boy. Ms. F. was single, held a good job, and dated casually. Thus all divorce-related psychosocial stressors were present in moderate degrees except for downward economic mobility.

Both parents described Barry's current difficulties as primarily school related: he was doing poorly academically, often failing to complete in-class or homework assignments; in addition, he had become the class clown, disrupting lessons frequently. He had one friend whom he saw regularly at school and with whom he occasionally played. Barry's main love was video games of all types, which he played for hours at a time. Developmentally Barry had achieved all milestones in a timely manner. However, his parents described him as having been a difficult baby and young child: he had had colic for the first 6 months of his life; he was "always into things" as a toddler; slept poorly; and seemed "stubborn" about following directions. Barry's pediatrician described him as a healthy child. His current teacher said that Barry impulsively talked out in class, had trouble completing assignments, and was difficult to "keep on task."

In the two evaluation sessions with Barry, Dr. W. noticed Barry's tendency to go quickly from one activity to another. He began by competing with Dr. W. using plastic race cars. Soon Barry tired of this game and suggested they have a puppet show with the hand puppets. Barry was a hungry bear and Dr. W. a kitten, who presently became the meal. After a few minutes Barry wanted to draw. He drew a small boy in the lower corner of a large piece of paper, erasing frequently because he "couldn't get it right." During the various play activities, Dr. W. commented from time to time about what was occurring, but Barry rarely responded. After Barry had struggled with his drawing for awhile, Dr. W. noted that "sometimes it's real frustrating for a guy when he feels he can't get something to turn out just right." Barry sadly stated that he really was not good at drawing, and then asked if Dr. W. had any video games in the office.

Dr. W. was puzzled. There were several divorce-specific psychosocial stressors present, but no thematic play developed around any of them. Nor was Barry responsive to verbalizations about divorce and the difficulties it can cause boys. What was most striking was Barry's rapid movement across play materials and themes; competition, oral aggression, and self-criticism were all present, but no coherent play developed. Dr. W. put these observations together with the parents' report of Barry's developmental history, the teacher's description of his classroom behavior, and his long-standing difficulties at home and at school in following directions. They pointed collectively to attention deficit hyperactivity disorder (ADHD).

Dr. W. also noted that Barry's prolonged emotional distance from his father and the birth of his half-brother may also have been contributing subtly to this boy's problems. Barry had a depressive quality which may have reflected his experiencing his father's distance from him as a narcissistic rejection. He was at once feeling unworthy of his father's love and assaulted by the academic failures and behavior problems associated with ADHD. Together these could have been responsible for his chronic, moderate depression, and the defensive avoidance of school work through clowning. Dr. W. thought that a trial of methylphenidate for ADHD and individual psychotherapy to address the underlying depression would be in Barry's best interest.

EVALUATING ADOLESCENTS

Adolescents usually require different evaluation approaches than children. Teenagers typically do not respond well to play materials, experiencing them as insultingly infantile and as a regressive threat. On the other hand, gentle humor can go a long way in helping establish an alliance with adolescents who often do not wish to be in a mental health professional's office. Teenagers frequently externalize their difficulties and view their parent(s) as the source of their problems. Because many adolescents are quick to perceive the clinician as an adult who is likely to be aligned with the parent(s), it is often useful to gather preliminary information from the parents during the initial telephone contact and then to schedule the first appointment with the youngster.

CASE EXAMPLE

Ms. G. called Dr. X., a psychiatrist in private practice, because ever since a marital separation 9 months earlier, tensions between her and her 14-year-old daughter, Lindsay, had been increasing. Ms. G. and her husband had temporary joint legal custody. She and Lindsay fought over how Lindsay kept her bedroom, how much telephone time Lindsay should have, and the like. Lindsay's grades had recently dropped from A's and B's to mostly B's. Ms. G. also described her daughter as being irritable with her much of the time. She reported that Lindsay's relationship with her father, with whom she lived Wednesday through Friday each week (a physical custodial schedule that was nearly equally divided) was "all right, but a little emotionally distant." Ms. G. tearfully recounted how close and loving her relationship with her daughter had been until the marital separation. Dr. X. spoke by telephone to Mr. G., who reported that he and Lindsay were getting along well, but was supportive of the evaluation.

In order to underscore his commitment to her and avoid her perceiving him as an agent of her mother, Dr. X. decided to see Lindsay first. After Dr. X.'s introductory comments, he asked how Lindsay thought things had been going for her. Lindsay quickly said that she was fine, but that her mother was upset about the divorce: "It really freaked her out when dad decided to leave—she's been crying a lot and she's always on my case." She recounted problems similar to those reported by her mother. Lindsay went on to talk about several girlfriends whom she described as "good kids who are all doing good in school" and her continued involvement in figure skating and field hockey. She spoke calmly, related well to Dr. X., and appeared genuinely enthusiastic about her social relationships and interests. In her second appointment, Lindsay emphasized that "the problem is my mom—she's having trouble with the divorce, not me." Dr. X. underscored the differences between an adult getting a divorce and a teenager having her parents split up. Then he gently wondered what the stresses were for teenagers. Lindsay looked sad and noted that sometimes it was hard to be "up for school;" she spent more time talking on the telephone than she used to. Dr. X. noted that when a teenager's family is changing, it can be important and good to spend more time talking with friends. He added that Lindsay seemed to be doing reasonably well, but that her mother was very worried about her. He suggested that a few meetings with Lindsay and her mother, together, "to get some agreements in place about how things can work between you" might take some pressure off both of them. Lindsay agreed stating, "I'm just a normal teenager who's having some ups and downs—mom needs to chill."

When assessing adolescents, it is especially important to separate normative developmental conflicts, perhaps exacerbated by divorce-related family dynamics, from psychopathology in the youngster. The former frequently can be resolved by conjoint sessions between the parent(s) and teenager.

Dr. X. viewed Lindsay as progressing well in the face of her parents' divorce. She related well to Dr. X., had a circle of friends whom her mother also saw as "good kids," and had maintained her interest and involvement in appropriate extracurricular activities. She did not appear to be suffering from a psychiatric disorder, her behavior was not out of control, and her development prior to her parents' separation had been excellent. It was apparent that Lindsay needed to see her mother as very different from her in their reactions to the impending divorce. Dr. X. perceived this as partly an expression of the developmentally normative task of adolescent girls to separate emotionally from their mothers. He sensitively highlighted that difference and reframed the presenting problem as a communication difficulty between mother and daughter. After 3 months of conjoint sessions with Lindsay and her mother, Ms. G. came to understand that her anxieties about Lindsay were not well-founded, and mother and daughter were able to agree on ground rules for Lindsay's behavior at home. They resumed their previously healthy mother-daughter relationship, but with Lindsay appropriately having greater independence.

When "the divorce" has occurred years prior to the referral, it is important for the clinician to be attuned to its possible long-term effects.

CASE EXAMPLE

Mrs. H. called Dr. Y., a clinician in private practice, in a panic about her 15-year-old daughter, Melanie. Over the past few months Melanie had come home drunk several evenings and had recently left her birth control pills on the dining room table. In that initial telephone call, Dr. Y. learned that Mrs. H. had been divorced from Melanie's father when her daughter was 3 years old, and that soon thereafter he had moved out of the state never to be heard from again. Mrs. H. had raised Melanie and her older brother, Greg, on her own until she had begun dating Mr. H. 2 years earlier; they married within a year. Dr. Y. explained the reasons some teenagers are more comfortable having the first appointment with a clinician, and scheduled an appointment for Melanie.

Melanie came to the first session dressed all in black; a tight scoop-neck tank top, jeans, and "Doc Martin" shoes. She entered the office sullenly, sat down crossing her arms tightly across her chest, and looked out the window with an air of bored indifference. After a few seconds, Dr. Y. wryly said, "I see that you're happy about being here, sort of like you're looking forward to having a good time." Melanie giggled briefly, despite herself. Dr. Y. told Melanie about his telephone conversation with her mother, and stated the confidentiality rule. Because "the divorce" had taken place so long in the past, Dr. Y's introductory comments focused on the recent marriage between Melanie's mother and Mr. H. and the family tensions that remarriage can stimulate. Melanie snorted and said, "I don't know why she married that asshole. He's gross! All Hank does when he gets home from work is sit around doing crossword puzzles." As she silently fumed, Dr. Y. empathized with her saying, "It's hard having a man around the house after so many years with just mom there." Melanie went on angrily to list all the reasons that Mr. H. was "a loser," and stated that everything would be fine if her mother had never met him. Dr. Y. quietly asked what it was like "B.H.—you know, Before Hank." Melanie became sad and wistful as she painted a picture of warmth and closeness between her and her mother (which Mrs. H. confirmed in a subsequent appointment). However, she quickly returned to her angry derogation of her stepfather: "He's not my real father, but he tries to act all nice and stuff." Dr. Y. noted that, "Some teenagers are also pretty mad at their moms for picking someone to marry who seems to be 'a loser.'" Melanie agreed and went on to characterize her mother as a "wuss," always acting so loving and happy around Hank.

In the course of the next two sessions, Melanie admitted to using alcohol on weekends, becoming intoxicated two or three times a month, and being sexually active with a 19-year-old young man who worked at a nearby supermarket. She angrily insisted that she could do as she wished, and if her mother objected, well, that was her problem. Her pattern of angry self-destructive behavior suggested a chronic underlying depression.

Dr. Y. also met with Mr. and Mrs. H. to gather developmental information about Melanie, a history of divorce-related psychosocial stressors, and to share with them his preliminary understanding of Melanie's difficulties. He recommended twice weekly psychotherapy for Melanie, the possibility of a trial of antidepressant medication, and biweekly parent guidance sessions.

Adolescents whose parents divorced years in the past, and who have shown good adjustment,

may begin to evidence significant difficulties as teenagers. Often this is related to an interaction between divorce-related psychosocial stressors and the normative developmental needs and conflicts of adolescence. In Melanie's case, the prolonged, total absence of her father dealt a depression-inducing blow to her feminine self-esteem. She had been protected from experiencing this during her preschool and elementary school years by enjoying a close and loving relationship with her mother. However, her mother's marriage to Mr. H. rather precipitous had served to push Melanie away emotionally. Melanie turned to peers to seek validation of her self-worth. For Melanie, the key psychosocial stressors were the ongoing absence of a caring relationship with her father and her mother's recent marriage. Her drinking and her sexual relationship with an "older man" can be understood as a need to separate from her mother, to punish her, and to seek a sense of being loved by a man.

Conclusions

Conducting evaluations of children and adolescents whose parents have separated or divorced requires attention to divorce-specific factors as well as general issues of child development and family dynamics. As with any major life stress, for example, death of a parent, a youngster's chronic illness, or child abuse, it is incumbent on the clinician to be aware of the external stressors and of the youngster's internal responses to them. Long- as well as short-term patterns need to be understood and evaluated within the context of a comprehensive understanding of child and adolescent psychiatry.

REFERENCES

Bray, J. H., & Berger, S. H. (1993). Developmental issues in the stepfamilies research project: Family relationships and parent-child interactions. *Journal of Family Psychology, 7,* 76–90.
Chase-Lansdale, P. L., & Hetherington, E. M. (1990). The impact of divorce on life-span development:

Short and long-term effects. In P. Baltes, D. L. Featherman, & R. M. Lerner (Eds.), *Life-span development and behavior* (Vol. 10, pp. 105–150). Hillsdale, NJ: Lawrence Erlbaum.
Emery, R. & Kitzmann, K. (1995). The child in the family: Disruptions in family functions. In D. Cic-

chetti, & D. Cohen (Eds.), *Developmental Psychopathology, vol. 2.* New York: John Wiley & Sons. pp. 3–31.

Furstenberg, F. F., Jr. (1990). Divorce and the American family. *Annual Review of Sociology, 16,* 379–403.

Guidubaldi, J. (1988). Differences in children's divorce adjustment across grade level and gender: A report from the NASP-Kent State nationwide project. In S. A. Wolchik & P. Karoly (Eds.), *Children of divorce: Empirical perspectives on adjustment* (pp. 185–231). New York: Gardner Press.

Guidubaldi, J., & Perry, J. D. (1985). Divorce and mental health sequelae for children: A two-year follow-up of a nationwide sample. *Journal of the American Academy of Child Psychiatry, 24,* 531–537.

Kalter, N. (1987). Long-term effects of divorce on children: A developmental vulnerability model. *American Journal of Orthopsychiatry, 57,* 587–600.

Kalter, N. (1990). *Growing up with divorce.* New York: Free Press.

Newcomer, S., & Udry, J. R. (1987). Parental marital status effects on adolescent sexual behavior. *Journal of Marriage and the Family, 49,* 235–240.

Pearson, J., & Anhalt, J. (1994). Examining the connection between child access and child support. *Family and Conciliation Courts Review, 32,* 93–109.

Peterson, J. L., & Zill, N. (1986). Marital disruption, parent-child relationships, and behavior problems in children. *Journal of Marriage and the Family, 48,* 295–307.

Wallerstein, J. S. (1991). The long-term effects of divorce on children: A review. *Journal of the American Academy of Child and Adolescent Psychiatry, 30,* 349–360.

Wallerstein, J. S., & Kelly, J. B. (1980). *Surviving the breakup.* New York: Basic Books.

Zill, N., Morrison, D. R., & Coiro, M. J. (1993). Long-term effects of parental divorce on parent-child relationships, adjustment, and achievement in young adulthood. *Journal of Family Psychology, 7,* 91–103.

80 / Observation, Interview, and Mental Status Assessment (OIM): Homosexual

Richard R. Pleak and Dennis A. Anderson

Although few clinicians report any experience in assessing and treating homosexual adolescents, most probably have at least unknowingly dealt with gay/lesbian teenagers. With growing numbers of adolescents realizing their homosexual orientation at earlier ages, and choosing to disclose this to others, more and more clinicians will have the opportunity to work with these adolescents in the coming years. Also, with more open discussion about homosexuality within Western societies, more teenagers and preteens will have more explicit questions to pose to professionals about sexuality. This chapter presents information about gay and lesbian adolescents that the clinician should find useful for guiding assessment and intervention strategy planning and suggests ways to better assess this population. For the purposes of this chapter, the terms "homosexual" and "gay and lesbian" are used synonymously, even though some prefer to reserve the latter terms for those who are acculturated within gay and lesbian communities.

Background and Developmental Considerations

Homosexual sexual behavior among adolescents is quite common in most societies. In the United States, most adults report some homosexual sexual experiences prior to or after puberty. The prevalence of predominate or exclusive homosexuality in the general population is currently disputed, with figures ranging from 1 to 10%. Adding the prevalence of less predominant homosexuality and nonexclusive heterosexuality makes this figure much higher. Hence a great number of adolescent patients with whom professionals work have had or will have homosexual experiences. For those adolescents who have already identified or will later identify their sexual orientation as homosexual or bisexual, same-sex sexual activities during adolescence are likely to be qualitatively and quantitatively different than for their heterosexual peers. The onset of homosexual romantic attachments, erotic imagery, and sexual arousal is reported to have occurred prior to 14 years of age by most homosexual adults. Homosexual adolescents begin same-sex sexual activities earlier and with greater frequency and variety than heterosexual adolescents who engage in same-sex sexual activities.

An organized awareness of homosexual orientation may be lacking in adolescents whose cognitive development has just begun to allow longitudinal understanding of their personal history and its implications for their future. For other adolescents, there may be a self-awareness of their sexual orientation which may include self-labeling as homosexual or bisexual, and even disclosure to others about their homosexual orientation.

Oftentimes homosexual adolescents or even preadolescents come to a seemingly sudden realization of their sexual orientation for a variety of reasons. Many adolescents gain the capacity for abstract thought and are able to consider their history, recognize current feelings, and imagine themselves in the future. With the onset of puberty, masturbation with its accompanying erotic imagery, sexual arousal to particular stimuli, and romantic attachments all increase dramatically. Gay and lesbian teens see their peers become more interested in opposite-sex relationships and heterosexual activities. Some homosexual adolescents who had engaged in sexual activities with same-sex peers may find their former partners no longer interested. Today adolescents are more likely to see information on homosexuality and portrayals of homosexual people in the media, which may assist their own self-realization. There are some indications from research and clinical findings that adolescents who come to terms with their own homosexuality early on may be better adjusted and more integrated with the gay/lesbian community than those who do not accept their homosexuality until their adulthood. However, too early can also be a problem, especially in light of underdeveloped cognitive abilities to deal with dissonance between internal erotic realizations and societal homophobia—an unreasonable or irrational fear or hatred of homosexuals or homosexuality.

EFFECTS OF HOMOPHOBIA

Many gay and lesbian adolescents report feeling sexually different for many years, but they did not relate these feelings to their—or society's—concept of homosexuality. Most teenagers who acknowledge a homosexual or bisexual arousal pattern quickly realize that "gay," "lesbian," "homosexual," and other terms are applied in derogatory ways to those thought to have such feelings. Intense anxiety about belonging to a group vehemently despised by many others can jeopardize their positive self-regard and their vision of a happy and productive future. An ego crisis occurs that can best be understood as the conflict produced by the juxtaposition of the negative ideas about homosexuality which have been learned previously with the incipient ego-identity that is developing. These negative ideas are the result of societal homophobia, which is generally internalized by children at a young age. The individual's management of this perceived stigma and the nature and effect of the internalized and external homophobia are crucial to the gay/lesbian adolescent's development, and are crucial for the clinician to appreciate. This homophobia is most often responsible for the difficulties adolescents have in discussing their homosexuality with professionals, which will be addressed below.

Most gay/lesbian adolescents go through a period when they attempt to change their sexual orientation, sometimes by accentuating gender-typical behaviors (for young persons, the incorrect notion that all or most homosexuals manifest traits of the opposite gender is particularly prevalent). Boys may tape their wrists at night, walk with an exaggerated swagger, and engage in compulsive body building, while girls may dress in very feminine clothes, use exaggerated gestures, and wear excessive amounts of makeup. Both sexes may join their peers in deriding homosexuality and may frantically pursue heterosexual dating and sexual activities. This compensatory pseudoheterosexuality can result in pregnancy, which adolescents find is a powerful way of maintaining their claim of being heterosexual. Attempts are made to use sheer will and self-recrimination to suppress homoeroticism. Masturbation may be avoided due to increased guilt over homosexual fantasies. Associations with same-sex peers may be terminated because of the erotic feelings that are aroused or because of the anxiety which accompanies fear of discovery.

During this time some gay/lesbian adolescents may seek professional assistance in changing their sexual orientation to heterosexual or in "diminishing their homosexuality." Some professionals will accept this goal and promise results of heterosexuality to the parents and the adolescent (e.g., Nicolosi, Socarides, & Kaufman, 1993), even though there are no documented cases of actual changes in sexual orientation regardless of treatment modality. Such an approach views homosexuality as a "choice of lifestyle," whereas most current research indicates that homosexuality is determined at a very early age or prenatally with genetic and/ or biologic determinants. This treatment approach to homosexuality has generally been discarded by the medical profession, and is thought to potentiate delayed development and iatrogenic problems. Depending on support from others, access to information, and the age and ego strength of the individual, the period of wanting to change one's homosexual orientation may last weeks to decades, but usually within a few months to a year the adolescent has little desire to change his/her orientation, although still remaining fearful of anyone finding out about it.

This can be an extremely lonely time for gay/ lesbian adolescents. The developmentally normal egocentrism of early adolescence can cause teenagers to feel that others are observing them and can read their thoughts or "find them out" through their interactions and body language. Gay/lesbian adolescents are forever monitoring themselves: "Am I standing too close? Is my voice too high (low)? Do I seem too happy to see him (her)?" What should be spontaneous expressions of affection or happiness become moments of agonizing fear and uncertainty. For many, the most painful moments are when they hear antigay jokes or when they see someone else being harassed or ridiculed or called some epithet for being homosexual. The experience of the teenager whose homosexuality becomes suspected or known varies: name-calling and baiting are the rule, and physical assault is not uncommon. Ostracism of the adolescent and the peers who associate with her are also frequent. Homosexual adolescents feel very vulnerable to rejection and homophobia, and they spend a great deal of energy guarding themselves against expressing the flood of emotions which they experience, and which they see their heterosexual peers openly expressing. Many will effectively defend against any conscious awareness of their homosexuality until much later in adolescence or adulthood. Thorough assessment of these factors will give the clinician a much better idea about gay/lesbian adolescents' day-to-day lives and the stressors which impact on their functioning and development.

DERAILED DEVELOPMENT

A derailment of healthy adolescent development may occur in homosexual teenagers secondary to homophobia. A dual life begins to develop, where homoerotic imagery and arousal, and even homosexual sexual activity, occur secretly and in a world completely separated from the social milieu of peers. Clandestine trips to the library occur to seek information on understanding homosexual feelings, but most of the material available in public and school libraries is inaccurate and portrays homosexuality negatively, which is a further assault to the adolescent's self-esteem. Expression of homosexual feelings within the dominant peer group, where there is tremendous pressure to conform to heterosexual norms, is likely to result in alienation at least, or violence at worst. Suppression of the gay/lesbian adolescent's proclivities results in the elaboration of false personas in order to gain peer acceptance. This psychosexual duality exacts a high cost in vigilance, self-loathing, and the expansion of defenses to contain the chronic anxiety produced. This state inhibits a variety of important social interactions, the most destructive of which is the restriction of activities which promote the capacity to engage in nonerotic and erotic intimate relationships. For those adolescents in this situation who do not have the luxury of a prolonged adolescence (such as those in college), a premature foreclosure of identity development during a period where much internalized homophobia has not been worked through can result in a very long and unnecessarily painful coming-out process. Maylon (1981) has identified three common adaptations of homosexual adolescents: (1) repression of same-sex desires; (2) suppression of such desires with a developmental moratorium, which can result in a biphasic adolescence with accommodation to expectations of heterosexuality, followed, sometimes years later, by psychological integration of previously rejected sexual and intimate capacities; and (3) disclosure to others, which for the homosexual adolescent often leads to alienation and neglect in a "hostile and psychologically impoverished heterosexual social environment," especially so for the younger adolescent. Troiden (1989) has proposed a four-stage model of identity development: sensitization, identity confusion, identity assumption, and commitment. In evaluating where an adolescent is in this process, the clinician can anticipate the adaptations (and complications) to follow.

Gay and lesbian adolescents experience much of the heterosexual and explicit or implicit homophobic effects of adolescent life as exceedingly isolating. They may become enraged watching boys and girls walk hand-in-hand down the hallway and openly display other signs of affection while their own desires must be kept "in the closet." Low self-esteem, academic inhibition, rejection by peers, social withdrawal, sexual inhibition, truancy, substance abuse, depressed mood, self-destructive acts (including unsafe sex) and suicidal ideation or attempts are not unusual and can be better differentiated from depressive disorders by the evaluator with careful assessment for this derailed development.

THE SEARCH FOR HOMOSEXUAL PEERS AND ROLE MODELS

Gay and lesbian adolescents, desiring involvement in a peer group that accepts them and offers the possibility of establishing meaningful and even intimate relationships, often begin to search for other gay or lesbian people. In large cities, they may frequent areas where they believe gay and lesbian people are to be found. This search may take teens into areas where they are placed at risk for violence, sexual victimization, and prostitution (Roesler & Deisher, 1972). Although most large cities have a variety of gay and lesbian services, most of these are directed toward adults and sometimes discriminate against youth because of their fear of societal reprisals if they serve, and thereby could be charged with "recruiting," young people. When gay and lesbian adolescents meet other gay and lesbian people, it is not unusual for

them to become involved in a sexual relationship. The teenager who is lonely and sexually frustrated may prematurely experience the release of tension, the supportive environment, and the affection of another person as love. Asking about their search for social contacts—with both peers and adults—can bring to light these problems the adolescent may be having.

Part of the difficulty gay/lesbian teens have in coming to terms with their homosexuality and knowing how to deal with their feelings in adaptive ways is the lack or absence of positive role models. They go wanting for the same diversity of adults to identify with as heterosexual teens. As more gay/lesbian adults acknowledge their sexual orientation publicly, they can serve as mentors and role models for adolescents, showing them that there are gay/lesbian people leading productive and healthy lives. Positive fictional gay/lesbian characters on television, in the movies, in comic books, and in other media can provide sources of identification important for the adolescent's identity formation and consolidation, although very few of these characters to date have been adolescents. A discussion in the assessment of who the adolescent looks up to, admires, and wishes to be like often reveals an absence of adults known to be homosexual, and can be broadened by inquiries about which homosexual adults the teen is aware of. This provides insight into the identification and self-esteem of the individual.

FAMILY ISSUES

Gay and lesbian adolescents are faced with the conundrum of whether or not they should tell their family, and will sometimes seek professional advice on this question. They realize that their parents are raising them not as they really are, but as heterosexual children, predicating they be something they are not (Borhek, 1988). Some teens may collude with this and try to maintain a "cover" by flaunting ersatz heterosexual relationships; the gay boy quickly learns that discussing or introducing a "girlfriend" to his parents or therapist limits their overt questions regarding his sexuality. Despite the strong desire for their families to accept their sexual orientation, most gay/lesbian adolescents spend enormous amounts of time and energy hiding it. They dread that their families will think them contemptible, so they typically

566

evade questions regarding their romantic or sexual interests and often painfully and silently endure their family's disparaging remarks about homosexual people. It is not surprising that most homosexual adolescents fear that they will be rejected, punished, physically assaulted, or perhaps thrown out of their homes if their sexual orientation were known. Those working with gay/lesbian adolescents have seen all of these consequences actually happen; in fact, a great number of teenagers who have been thrown out of their homes and expelled from their families are those whose homosexuality has been divulged. Homosexual teenagers may try to avoid these potential consequences by withdrawing emotional investment in the family as a way of diminishing the impact of possible rejection. Even in families who may be accepting of the adolescent's homosexuality, the adolescent's internalized homophobia is likely to be projected onto family members and others. Teens whose peer group includes other gays and lesbians often hide from their families the most prosaic social activities that heterosexual adolescents would easily share. Even the most innocent and healthy social activities become tainted by this need to dissemble from their families. This deceit is frequently ego dystonic and at odds with the pattern of communication and intimacy adolescents have learned to expect and desire within their families.

Adolescents may come out (disclose) as homosexual to their families in a variety of ways: after careful consideration and planning with a gradual introduction of the topic, in an impulsive confessional, by being found out via diaries, letters, or magazines, by telling more distant relatives or siblings first, and so on. Siblings may react to disclosure with an intensification of sibling rivalry as well as sudden rejection, and family alliances may be disrupted (Borhek, 1988).

The reactions of parents to the disclosure or discovery of homosexuality in their sons or daughters proceed in somewhat predictable stages. Initially there is shock and denial, with an acute sense of loss of the hoped-for future and of grandchildren, as well as the sense of losing the child they had known. Their fears and prejudices regarding homosexuality are brought to the surface, and the adolescent may be in danger of being assaulted, thrown out, or running away. Parents may entreat their child to consider homosexuality as

only a phase, to never talk about it again, to pray for "salvation," or demand that the adolescent see a therapist. This denial may be protracted into years, but usually gives way to a second stage of anger and guilt. The parents—and teenagers—are likely to hold the issue of homosexuality responsible for all difficulties in the family (Borhek, 1988), a trap the clinician should keep in mind. The parents try to discover proximate causes for their child's homosexuality, and may blame and attack the child's teachers, school, peers, themselves, other family members, and the therapist. The parents may make frantic and at times ludicrous attempts to alter their parenting style, often becoming repressive and regressive in imposing rules, searches, limits on peer interactions, and disciplinary practices in an attempt to "turn back the clock." As these attempts fail, and the anger and guilt subside, they can give way to the third stage of acceptance. Parents who are or become well-educated about homosexuality, those who seek therapists and counselors who can give accurate advice and information, and those who redevelop trust with their child may or may not approve of homosexuality, but recognize that their child is the same child as before disclosure and that the child's sexual orientation is an enduring characteristic.

The clinician can assist the adolescent with disclosing to others by exploring the need to do so with the adolescent, discussing the degree of preparedness of the family and/or friends, reviewing the potential consequences of disclosure and alternatives for the adolescent, and considering various ways to disclose. Adolescents, especially younger ones, often feel they can accurately predict their parents' reactions, and the clinician can point out pitfalls in this belief. These discussions can help avoid impulsive coming out, optimize the timing of disclosure, and prepare the teen for how to react if unexpectedly found out. Referral to a hotline or to the many books now available on coming out can also be very beneficial.

ETHNIC DIVERSITY

The ethnicity or cultural milieu of the adolescent can have diverse effects. For example, in an ethnic minority which is marginalized in a society, the homosexual adolescent will likely be at the margins of their ethnic group (Monteiro & Fuqua,

1995), that is, multiply marginalized. To maintain their status and comfort within an ethnic minority, the adolescent may downplay or deny his homosexuality. Or the adolescent may downplay his ethnicity to better fit in the majority gay/lesbian community, which can make the individual feel "in a cross fire" (Sears, 1995). For African Americans, this has led to a distinction by some between "gay blacks" and "black gays" (Sears, 1995), which can make the black teen confused and lost in search of identity, and vulnerable to a fragmentation of his/her sense of ethnic and sexual identity (Monteiro & Fuqua, 1995). Most ethnic minorities do not place emphasis on the homosexuality of major figures in their history who are gay or lesbian, so, for example, role models for black adolescents such as Langston Hughes or George Washington Carver do not readily become role models for gay black adolescents if their homosexuality is unknown (Pleak & Anderson, 1995). Further, some ethnic leaders, educators, or historians may ignore or actively deny even the existence of homosexuality in the ancestry of a people, claiming homosexuality as an import or contaminant or by-product of oppression (Monteiro & Fuqua, 1995) or even as a diabolical plot or conspiracy by other groups. This lack of acceptance makes homosexuality appear unnatural and alien in an ethnic group, complicating the gay adolescent's development even more.

Even within ethnic minorities, differences in socioeconomic status may result in diverse reactions to homosexuality. Sears (1995) has shown that in middle-class black families, adherence to the norm may be so closely watched that departing from the norm may result in ostracism within the family, and the gay/lesbian may not come out in such a family. In contrast, in the majority of working-class black families, gay lovers and friends are accepted by or into families, and coming out is more routine.

In assessing the homosexual adolescent who is also an ethnic minority within a society, the evaluator should be aware of this multiply marginalized status and investigate the adolescent's conflict in this area. The teenager's role models can also be examined as to whether they are from the same ethnic group, or the majority ethnic group, in attempting to better assess identity formation.

Psychiatric Aspects

Most readily available textbooks of psychiatry (including child and adolescent psychiatry) for the clinician at the time of this writing contain dated and inaccurate information about homosexuality, if it is mentioned at all (Herbert and Womack, 1995). Few adult or child and adolescent psychiatry residency programs provide much education about gay/lesbian adolescents, and even that small amount is dated and does not address the special issues and needs of this population (Townsend, Wallick, Pleak, & Cambre, 1997). Thus, many graduates of psychiatry residency programs are not optimally trained and educated for working with gay/lesbian teens. Revisionist approaches to homosexuality as nonpathology have come about in more recent years, following the declassification of homosexuality as a disorder by the American Psychiatric Association in 1973 and exemplified by newer psychoanalytic perspectives (Isay, 1985, 1989; Lewes, 1988; Friedman, 1988). Despite this, older views of homosexuality as being pathological still continue to influence some clinicians and sometimes fuel homophobia. This perspective is dissipating, as seen by the 1991 reversal by the American Psychoanalytic Association of its discrimination against homosexual applicants for training and by the decisions of the American Medical Association in 1993 to bar discrimination against homosexual physicians and in 1995 to repudiate attempts to change sexual orientation.

POSSIBLE ASSOCIATIONS WITH PSYCHOPATHOLOGY

When considering to what extent psychopathology may be found in lesbian and gay adolescents, developmental factors such as those discussed above must be taken into account. These complications place the homosexual adolescent at increased risk for acute adjustment reactions, and may lead to relatively transient symptoms which, when seen acutely, may lead the clinician to misdiagnose or overdiagnose the adolescent as having major depressive disorder, anxiety disorders, personality disorders, and the like. This is especially so if, as is often the case, the adolescent does not

568

disclose concerns about and/or reaction to homosexuality to the clinician. In some adolescents these complications may culminate in more severe consequences such as failure in school, running away or being thrown out of the home, prostitution, substance abuse/dependence, and suicide attempts. In these cases, criteria for psychiatric diagnosis will often be met. The clinician who acknowledges the fact that adolescents may be homosexual, and who realizes homosexuality in adolescence is not a "passing phase," and who does not attempt to convert the lesbian/gay adolescent to heterosexuality or push the adolescent into heterosexual behavior will avoid potential iatrogenic disorders.

What *is* known about psychopathology—particularly psychiatric diagnoses—in lesbian and gay teens is unfortunately very little. Part of this dearth of knowledge has to do with the difficulty of doing studies with this population, which is hard to identify and recruit for study, although it is also due to the reluctance of many investigators to specifically target these teens for study. The few studies on adolescents have conflicting findings, with some reporting no important differences between homosexual and heterosexual adolescents in personal adjustment, self-esteem, and psychological health (*e.g.,* Savin-Williams, 1990; Thompson, McCandless, & Strickland, 1971), while others with possibly biased samples report elevated rates of behavior problems and psychiatric symptomatology (Kremer & Rifkin, 1969; Remafedi, 1987a,b,c; Roesler & Deisher, 1972). There are no studies to date which systematically assess psychiatric diagnoses in this population, nor which include representative samples or adequate control groups, so we are left with no clear conclusions other than knowing of the potential developmental complications and possible psychiatric morbidity.

To understand more about what psychopathology may afflict lesbian and gay teens, one must look at the literature on homosexual adults. In summaries and reviews of research findings, no associations between homosexuality and psychopathology have been found (Friedman, 1988; Lewes, 1988; Stoller, 1980). Although some studies suggest that there may be elevated rates of major depression, substance abuse/dependence, and perhaps anxiety disorders in homosexual sub-

jects, with onset frequently during adolescence, the results are conflicting among the studies and they have not been replicated (Atkinson et al., 1988; Saghir & Robins, 1973; Siegelman, 1972; Williams, Rabkin, Remien, Gorman, & Ehrhardt, 1991). Insufficient data are available from these studies to determine the incidence of onset of these disorders in adolescence. None of these adult studies have included evaluation for childhood-onset disorders, such as attention-deficit/hyperactivity disorder, conduct disorder, gender identity disorder, and separation anxiety disorder. From the available data, we can only speculate that lesbian and gay adolescents may possibly be at increased risk for major depression, substance abuse/dependence, and perhaps anxiety disorders.

SUICIDALITY

The most studied and controversial area of psychopathology in lesbian and gay teens has been suicide. Early reports indicated that gay men and women were much more likely to attempt suicide, especially during adolescence, than heterosexual men and women (Bell & Weinberg, 1978; Saghir & Robins, 1973; Schneider, Farberow, & Kruks, 1987; Swanson, Loomis, Lukesh, Cronin, & Smith, 1972). Turning to reports specifically on homosexual adolescents, high rates (21–36%) of suicide attempts have also been reported (Hunter & Schaecher, 1990; Kremer & Rifkin, 1969; Martin & Hetrick, 1988; Remafedi, 1987b, 1994; Roesler & Deisher, 1972). Many times these attempts follow the adolescent's self-disclosure as being homosexual. Several centers for gay youth across the country report that more than 50% of clients have had suicidal ideation, with much higher rates for those who are homeless (Gibson, 1989). These reports are striking for the rates of suicide attempts and ideation, although the findings must be taken with some caution, as these reports did not use heterosexual comparison groups or representative homosexual samples.

Such information led authors in the U.S. Department of Health and Human Services' (HHS) *Report of the Secretary's Task Force on Youth Suicide* (Alcohol, Drug Abuse, and Mental Health Administration, 1989) to conclude that homosexual youth of both sexes are much more likely to attempt suicide than are heterosexuals and are more at risk of attempted and completed suicide during late adolescence and early adulthood (Gibson, 1989; Harry, 1989b). The HHS report prompted Remafedi, Farrow, and Deisher (1991) to specifically study suicide attempts in young gay and bisexual males: most of their subjects had received mental health care, and thus this sample was probably biased toward more disturbed youths. Thirty percent had attempted suicide at a mean age of 15, and half of these attempted more than once. Three-quarters of attempts followed self-labeling as homosexual. Attempters were no more likely than nonattempters to be depressed or hopeless, although they were more feminine or undifferentiated in gender role, were more likely to report sexual abuse, had more illicit drug abuse, had been arrested more often, saw themselves as homosexual at younger ages, and engaged in homosexual sex at younger ages. From these studies and clinical reports, it is probable that lesbian and gay teens are at higher risk for suicide than reported for their heterosexual counterparts. Psychological autopsy studies to date have failed to find significantly increased rates of completed suicide for gay/lesbian teenagers (Shaffer, 1993), although the methods to elicit homosexual sexual orientation in these studies appear to have been inadequate, and thus new research strategies from the U.S. Centers for Disease Control and Prevention have been proposed to deal with this dilemma.

GENDER IDENTITY AND CROSS-GENDER BEHAVIOR

Contrary to popular stereotypes, most homosexual adolescents do not exhibit cross-gender or gender-deviant behavior, and probably have not in their childhood. This popular notion of homosexuality being strongly associated or equated with gender identity disorders has been reinforced by misinterpretation of various studies (e.g., Green, 1987; Zuger, 1984). Although the majority (three-quarters) of children who have gender identity disorders are homosexual or bisexual in young adulthood in these studies, the reverse is not true. Such data has often been misconstrued to mean that the majority of gays and lesbians have histories of childhood gender identity disorder; how-

ever, this is shown not to be the case when the data is examined more closely (Green, 1987; Isay, 1985, 1989; Saghir & Robins, 1973). It is important to note that childhood cross-gender behavior is also associated with later heterosexuality.

It is not known what the later sexual orientation is of children with minor or lesser forms or gender-atypical behaviors (e.g., most "tomboys"). Those gay and lesbian adolescents who do have an early childhood history of gender-atypical behavior may later display extreme cross-gender behavior, including cross-dressing, in a defiant and openly provocative manner, especially in situations they perceive as being hostile to their homosexuality such as when confronting or rebelling against social institutions and authorities. This is a defense against threatened self-esteem and can be viewed as an identification with the societal gender-role expectations (stereotypes) of lesbians being "butch" or gay men "effeminate." Similar adaptations have been noted in individuals from extremely strict religious backgrounds where cross-dressing or even transsexualism may be a defense against homosexuality. In some ethnic minority groups, especially Latino cultures and others with rigidly dichotomized sex-role differences between the feminine and the machismo, there appears to be a greater tendency for homosexual adolescents to display more extreme cross-gender behavior. In fact, those homosexual male adolescents who conform to the social role of the "maricon" (butterfly, an effeminate male) are more likely to be tolerated and less subject to violent harassment than homosexual youth displaying more typical gender behavior. Many gay/lesbian adolescents who cross-dress will gradually drop this behavior once they are exposed to a gay/lesbian peer group where the dominant cultural or subcultural expectations for cross-gender role behavior for homosexual adolescents are not encountered (Martin & Hetrick, 1988). However, some adolescents, especially those who can socialize with lesbian/gay peers, may feel freer or even compelled to explore and experiment with gender-atypical behaviors as part of their adolescent identity rehearsal and formation (Pleak & Anderson, 1995).

The clinician may observe and/or elicit reports of cross-gender behavior when evaluating homosexual adolescents. Such adolescents may have ongoing childhood gender identity disorders or confusion; more likely, however, are the alternative explanations above. Thus cross-gender behaviors in homosexual adolescents may not necessarily be a manifestation of psychopathology in gender identity.

SEXUAL BEHAVIOR

Very few detailed data on the sexual activities of adolescents exist, especially for homosexual behaviors. The professional needs to be mindful of the diversity in sexual behaviors; for example, many gay male teens do not engage in anal intercourse, but prefer masturbation and oral sex. In obtaining a history, the evaluator should first assess the pubertal development of the adolescent by asking about such milestones as growth spurts, changing of the voice, breast development, pubic and axillary hair, and menarche/adrenarche. Then the evaluator can inquire about a variety of romantic and sexual activities in all patients, including dating, kissing, fondling, self and mutual masturbation, fellatio, vaginal and anal intercourse, and the use of condoms and birth control for these activities. In males, condoms may be used more consistently in homosexual sex than heterosexual sex, based on the perceived risk for HIV (human immunodeficiency virus) transmission, while the reverse may be the case for females. It is also important to ask about sexual abuse, forcing others to have sex, substance abuse during sex, payment for sex or prostitution, and history of sexually transmitted diseases. It is not known if rates of sexual abuse in childhood or adolescence are higher in the homosexual than heterosexual population, although gay males report higher rates of physical abuse in adolescence by parents (Harry, 1989a), and this should also be asked of all adolescents. Sexual dysfunctions in lesbian and gay adolescents, about which almost no reports exist, may include impotence and hyposexuality more commonly than promiscuity and hypersexuality, and are especially important areas to assess in adolescents who are taking psychotropic medications which can have sexual side effects.

HIV/AIDS

The AIDS epidemic has clouded the picture of psychopathology. Homosexual adolescents with HIV infection, HIV spectrum disease, or AIDS may show cognitive impairments, including organic brain syndromes, and they may be at greater risk for suicide. The data from adult studies, however, do not support the hypothesis that HIV-infected individuals or people with AIDS have increased rates of psychiatric disorders exclusive of organic brain syndrome (*e.g.*, Williams et al., 1991).

Gay male adolescents at the time of this writing are engaging in more unsafe sexual practices than their adult counterparts and have higher than expected rates of HIV infection. Gay youths seem to see little relevance in the massive and effective AIDS prevention programs developed by and for adult gay men in the early 1980s, and they are engaging in much more unsafe sex than the next older generation of gay men. What took such great effort to achieve by the latter group is being lost by the newer generation, with its resentment of growing up and becoming sexual in a world already racked with AIDS, with its different beliefs, mores, and values, and with the nature of adolescents to rebel and consider themselves invulnerable. The clinician needs to take thorough sexual histories repeatedly on all adolescents, rather than only at the initial assessment, as behavioral intervention/prevention is currently the only effective strategy against HIV.

General Clinical Issues in Assessment

DISCLOSURE TO THE CLINICIAN

Most gay and lesbian adolescents do not come in for a psychiatric evaluation of their own accord. Those who are brought in or are in treatment are ostensibly there for other reasons, and their homosexuality may never be disclosed or asked about. The gay/lesbian adolescent may see this as irrelevant, or more likely fear that disclosure will result in rejection by the clinician or that the clinician will inform the parents. The gay/lesbian adolescent is very attuned to statements and questions (and the tone of such) by the clinician which indicate whether the clinician will be receptive to disclosure. We all have been socialized to reflexively employ noninclusive language in asking about romantic and sexual interests, so clinicians have to actively guard against exclusionary questions such as asking a girl, "Do you have a boyfriend?" or a boy "Do you have a girlfriend?" Such restrictive questioning immediately signals the adolescent that the clinician is making the assumption that she is heterosexual and the adolescent becomes more anxious, less able to disclose, and more likely to fabricate to placate and fulfill the expectations of the clinician. The authors have observed this kind of limiting questioning in many professional trainees as well as in established clinicians, even though they may have had experience with gay/lesbian adults. The clinician without explicit training in interviewing about sexuality may shy away from this topic with adolescents, asking only a few perfunctory questions before darting off to a "safer" area of the history. A negative countertransference to the homosexual adolescent may be due to the clinician's own internalized homophobia, and this is unlikely to go unnoticed by the adolescent.

The avoidance of such exclusionary history taking and defending against negative countertransference opens up an enormous amount of material for the clinician and permits a better understanding of the particular developmental issues discussed above. This facilitates assessment, promotes a positive transference, fosters appropriate family interventions, and helps prevent misdiagnosis.

CASE EXAMPLE

A 15-year-old homosexual boy seen by the authors had been diagnosed by a psychiatrist as psychotic and placed on a neuroleptic due to his egocentric fears that others could "read his mind" (*i.e.*, tell he was homosexual) and that they would harm him (as he had seen in violent antigay incidents in his school and in the media). His previous therapist had apparently assumed he was heterosexual and never discussed homosexuality with him, and he naturally felt inhibited in disclosing to the therapist. He became depressed, truant, and suicidal, and began abusing alcohol and drugs. With appropriate discussion about his homosexuality with sensitive clinicians, his fears subsided; he was able to discuss his feelings with his parents and several peers; his depressive symptoms, suicidal ideation, and substance abuse resolved without neuroleptics or other psychotropic medication, and he made a good adjustment back to his

family and school with referral to a gay and lesbian youth services organization.

The clinician who has developed knowledge and sensitivity about homosexuality should use caution in not pushing the adolescent to disclose to the clinician prematurely. Although an adolescent's homosexuality may sometimes be evident to the parents or therapist, the adolescent may not have come to the point of viewing himself/herself as homosexual or may not have developed the trust necessary to disclose. The optimal approach is to ask questions in a gender-neutral, nonjudgmental way, and to assure the adolescent that the clinician is ready at any time to hear more about the adolescent's feelings. Questions in the initial evaluation such as, "Have you been in a romantic relationship?," "Tell me about your sexual relationships," or "Have you been sexual with anyone?" allow the adolescent a better opportunity to discuss same-sex or opposite-sex relations. If the adolescent provides information about one or more heterosexual relationships, the clinician must still not assume heterosexuality, but should follow up with questions such as, "What about relationships with girls?" for girls, and likewise for boys. Even if given an emphatic "NO!" and other negative reactions to such questions, the clinician still should not assume heterosexuality but rather should consider the possibility that the adolescent is testing the clinician. The clinician should, at the appropriate time, assure the adolescent that some teens and adults do indeed have romantic and sexual relationships with same-sex partners and that this is considered normal. Such an intervention may need to wait until the adolescent is ready to hear it. The clinician should further question the adolescent and discuss sexuality in future sessions in a similarly nonexclusionary and gender-neutral manner.

Some adolescents may voice to the clinician same-sex crushes or attractions and may express uncertainty about sexual orientation. This type of internal questioning is often seen in homosexual adolescents and should be considered seriously. Discussing the adolescent's and the adolescent's perceptions of her family's and society's feelings and fears about homosexuality in these cases can be more productive than attempting to get direct information about the adolescent's sexual orientation.

Conclusion

Gay and lesbian adolescents face unique developmental tasks. Their healthy development may be derailed by homophobia, resulting in maladaptive behaviors and psychopathology. Gay and lesbian teens face and deal with these tasks and derailments in diverse ways, and the responses to the adolescent by peers, families, institutions, and health care workers may also be diverse. It is important for clinicians (and researchers) to consider these developmental issues in guiding assessment rather than relying on stereotypes and generalizations about this population. In this way a more accurate picture of gay and lesbian adolescents can emerge, they will be treated equally, and overall assessment will be enhanced.

Clinicians should be alert to the possibility that symptoms of mood and anxiety disorders and substance use may represent adjustment difficulties or disorders in overtly or covertly homosexual youths. The clinician evaluating gay and lesbian adolescents may elicit symptoms reflecting their developmental complications, but diagnoses should not be made unless diagnostic criteria are clearly met. Even so, the clinician's index of suspicion for suicidality should be high. Clinicians should evaluate homosexual interests and activities in *all* adolescents, and should routinely assess these factors in any adolescent with suicidal ideation or attempts, major depression, anxiety disorders, or substance abuse. Cross-gender behaviors in homosexual adolescents are more likely to be associated with cultural expectations, identity formation, and rebellion than with true gender identity disorders. Sexual behavior frequently may be unsafe and place the gay adolescent at high risk for HIV infection, requiring continual reassessment and behavioral intervention. There is great need for studies on homosexuality in adolescence which include rigorous assessment of psychopathology and of coping skills. Studies on suicide, such as psychological autopsy studies after suicide completion, must take into account homosexuality as a possible risk factor. Risks for suicide and other psychopathology may be greater for adolescents who self-identify as homosexual at younger ages.

Herdt (1991), who has studied hundreds of lesbian and gay teens, estimated that homosexual youth will be coming out around the age of puberty by the year 2000. If Herdt is right, we may be faced with younger, possibly more-troubled lesbian and gay teens in the near future, unless more radical changes occur in society's—and mental health professionals'—acceptance of homosexuality, particularly in youths. As Gibson (1989a) has advocated, we must do better at providing information, acceptance, and support to gay youth, while continuing to confront homophobia in society and within our professions.

Further assistance for the clinician, patient, and family to assist in assessment and intervention strategy planning can be provided by local, state, and national gay/lesbian youth groups (cf. Greeley, 1994), some of which have toll-free hotlines, and by the national and local chapters of P-FLAG, Parents and Friends of Lesbians and Gays. A variety of specialized books for the gay/lesbian adolescent can also be of great help (*e.g.,* Fricke, 1981; Heron, 1983, 1994; Miller and Waigandt, 1990; Rench, 1990).

REFERENCES

Alcohol, Drug Abuse, and Mental Health Administration. (1989). *Report of the Secretary's Task Force on Youth Suicide, Volume 1: Overview and Recommendations.* DHHS Pub. No. (ADM)89-1622. Washington, DC: U.S. Government Printing Office.

Atkinson, J. H., Grant, I., Kennedy, C. J., Richman, D. D., Spector, S. A., & McCutchan, A. (1988). Prevalence of psychiatric disorders among men infected with human immunodeficiency virus. *Archives of General Psychiatry, 45,* 859–864.

Bell, A. P., & Weinberg, M. S. (1978). *Homosexualities: A study of diversity among men and women.* New York: Simon & Schuster.

Borhek, M. A. (1988). Helping gay and lesbian adolescents and their families: A mother's perspective. *Journal of Adolescent Health Care, 9,* 123–128.

Fricke, A. (1981). *Reflections of a rock lobster.* Boston: Alyson Publications.

Friedman, R. C. (1988). *Male homosexuality: A contemporary psychoanalytic perspective.* New Haven, CT: Yale University Press.

Gibson, P. (1989). Gay male and lesbian youth suicide. In Alcohol, Drug Abuse, and Mental Health Administration, *Report of the secretary's task force on youth suicide, Volume 3: Prevention and interventions in youth suicide.* DHHS Pub. No. (ADM)89-1623. Washington, DC: U.S. Government Printing Office. pp. 3-110–3-142.

Greeley, G. (1994). Service organizations for gay and lesbian youth. In T. DeCrescenzo (Ed.), *Helping gay and lesbian youth: New policies, new programs, new practice.* New York: Harrington Park Press.

Green, R. (1987). *The "sissy boy syndrome" and the development of homosexuality.* New Haven, CT: Yale University Press.

Harry, J. (1989a). Parental physical abuse and sexual orientation in males. *Archives of Sexual Behavior, 18,* 251–261.

Harry, J. (1989b). Sexual identity issues. In Alcohol, Drug Abuse, and Mental Health Administration, *Report of the secretary's task force on youth suicide, Volume 2: Risk factors for youth suicide.* DHHS Pub. No. (ADM)89-1622. Washington, DC: U.S. Government Printing Office. pp. 2-131–2-142.

Herbert, S. E., & Womack, W. (1995). *Textbook equality for lesbian, gay, and bisexual adolescents: Resources for professionals in pediatrics and psychiatry.* Paper presented at the annual meeting of the American Psychiatric Association, Miami Beach, FL.

Herdt, G. (1991). *The well-being of gay and lesbian youth.* Paper presented at the annual National Lesbian and Gay Health Conference, New Orleans, LA.

Hunter, J., & Schaecher, R. (1990). Lesbian and gay youth. In M. J. Rotheram-Borus, J. Bradley, & N. Obolensky (Eds.), *Planning to live: Evaluating and treating suicidal teens in community settings.* Tulsa: University of Oklahoma Press.

Heron, A. (ed.). (1983). *One teenager in 10.* Boston: Alyson Publications.

Heron, A. (ed.). (1994). *Two teenagers in twenty.* Boston: Alyson Publications.

Isay, R. A. (1985). On the analytic therapy of homosexual men. *Psychoanalytic Study of the Child, 40,* 235–254.

Isay, R. A. (1989). *Being homosexual: Gay men and their development.* New York: Farrar Straus Giroux.

Kremer, M. W., & Rifkin, A. H. (1969). The early development of homosexuality: A study of adolescent lesbians. *American Journal of Psychiatry, 126,* 129–134.

Lewes, K. (1988). *The psychoanalytic theory of male homosexuality.* New York: Simon & Schuster.

Martin, A. D., & Hetrick, E. S. (1988). The stigmatization of the gay and lesbian adolescent. *Journal of Homosexuality, 15,* 163–183.

Maylon, A. K. (1981). The homosexual adolescent: Developmental issues and social bias. *Child Welfare, 60,* 321–329.

Miller, D. A., & Waigandt, A. (1990). *Coping with your sexual orientation.* New York: Rosen Publishing Group.

Monteiro, K. P., & Fuqua, V. (1995). African-American gay youth: One form of manhood. In G. Unks (Ed.), *The gay teen: Educational practice and theory for lesbian, gay, and bisexual adolescents.* New York: Routledge. pp. 152–187.

Nicolosi, J., Socarides, C., & Kaufman, B. (1993). A diminished homosexuality [letter to ed.]. *Psychiatric Times, 10* (5), 6.

Pleak, R. R., & Anderson, D. A. (May, 1995). Diversity in gay & lesbian development. Paper presented at the annual meeting of the American Psychiatric Association. Miami Beach, FL.

Remafedi, G. (1987a). Male homosexuality: the adolescent's perspective. *Pediatrics, 79,* 326–330. *American Medical Association, 258,* 222–224.

Remafedi, G. (ed.). (1994). *Death by Denial: Studies of Suicide in Gay and Lesbian Teenagers.* Boston: Alyson Publications.

Remafedi, G., Farrow, J. A., & Deisher, R. W. (1991). Risk factors for attempted suicide in gay and bisexual youth. *Pediatrics, 87,* 869–872.

Rench, J. E. (1990). *Understanding Sexual Identity: A Book for Gay Teens and Their Friends.* Minneapolis: Lerner Publications.

Roesler, T., & Deisher, R. W. (1972). Youthful male homosexuality: homosexual experience and the process of developing homosexual identity in males aged 16 to 22 years. *Journal of the American Medical Association, 219,* 1018–1023.

Saghir, M. T., & Robins, E. (1973). *Male and Female Homosexuality: A Comprehensive Investigation.* Baltimore: Williams & Wilkins.

Savin-Williams, R. C. (1990). *Gay and Lesbian Youth: Expressions of Identity,* New York: Hemisphere Publishing Co.

Sears, J. T. (1995). Black-gay or gay-black?: choosing identities and identifying choices. In: G. Unks (ed.) *The Gay Teen: Educational Practice and Theory for Lesbian, Gay, and Bisexual Adolescents.* New York: Routledge, pp. 135–157.

Schneider, S. G., Farberow, N. L., & Kruks, G. N. (1987). Suicidal behavior in adolescent and young adult gay men. Paper presented at the annual National Lesbian and Gay Health Conference, July, Los Angeles, CA.

Shaffer, D. (1993). Shouts and murmurs: political science. *New Yorker.* 23 April:116.

Siegelman, M. (1972). Adjustment of homosexual and heterosexual women. *British Journal of Psychiatry, 120,* 477–481.

Stoller, R. J. (1980). Problems with the term "homosexuality." *Hillside Journal of Clinical Psychiatry, 2,* 3–25.

Swanson, D. W., Loomis, S. D., Lukesh, R., Cronin, R., & Smith, J. A. (1972). Clinical features of the female homosexual patient. *Journal of Nervous and Mental Disease, 155,* 119–124.

Thompson, N. L., McCandless, B. R., & Strickland,

B. R. (1971). Personal adjustment of male and female homosexuals and heterosexuals. *Journal of Abnormal Psychology, 78,* 237–240.

Townsend, M. H., Wallick, M. M., Pleak, R. R., & Cambre, K. M. (1997). Gay and lesbian issues in child and adolescent psychiatry training as reported by training directors. *Journal of the American Academy of Child & Adolescent Psychiatry, 36,* 764–768.

Troiden, R. R. (1989). The formation of homosexual

identities. In: G. Herdt (ed.) *Gay and Lesbian Youth.* New York: Harrington Park Press.

Williams, J. B., Rabkin, J. G., Remien, R. H., Gorman, J. M., & Ehrhardt, A. A. (1991). Multidisciplinary baseline assessment of homosexual men with and without human immunodeficiency virus infection. *Archives of General Psychiatry, 48,* 124–130.

Zuger, B. (1984). Early effeminate behavior in boys: outcome and significance for homosexuality. *Journal of Nervous and Mental Disease, 172,* 90–97.

81 / Observation, Interview, and Mental Status Assessment (OIM): Cult Involvement

Louis Jolyon West

It has been estimated that there are some 5000 cultic groups in the United States. Some are large, powerful, and international in scope (e.g., Unification Church or "Moonies," Hare Krishnas, Church of Scientology, Children of God, etc.); others are as small as a dozen members. There are many of intermediate size. All of them pose an immediate or potential psychiatric risk to children and adolescents. Overviews of the problem have recently been published: two brief (West, 1993a & b), one comprehensive (Singer, 1995).

In 1985 an international conference on cultism sponsored by the Johnson Foundation, the American Family Foundation, and UCLA, defined the term as follows:

Cult (totalist type): a group or movement exhibiting a great or excessive devotion or dedication to some person, idea, or thing, and employing unethical, manipulative or coercive techniques of persuasion and control (e.g., isolation from former friends and family, debilitation, use of special methods to heighten suggestibility and subservience, powerful group pressures, information management, promotion of total dependency on the group and fear of leaving it, suspension of individuality and critical judgment, etc.), designed to advance the goals of the group's leaders, to the possible or actual detriment of members, their families, or the community. (West, 1989)

A more recent but compatible definition was derived from a study employing factor analysis of 308 former members of 101 groups (Chambers,

Langone, Dole, & Grice, 1994). This study produced the Group Psychological Abuse Scale, which identified four factors associated with cultic environments (induction of "anxious dependency," compliance, exploitation, and mind control) and generated the following definition:

Cults are groups that often exploit members psychologically and/or financially, typically by making members comply with leadership's demands through certain types of psychological manipulation, popularly called "mind control", and through the inculcation of deepseated anxious dependency on the group and its leaders.

Cults are best identified by the authoritarian fashion in which they function; by their de facto value systems usually based on power, money, and aggrandizement of the leaders; by their secretive practices, jealously guarded boundaries, and tough rules about the flow of information. Most, if not all, have the possibility of becoming deadly, as did the People's Temple of Jim Jones, the Branch Davidians of David Koresh, Aum Shinri Kyo of Shoko Asahara, Heaven's Gate of Marshall Applewhite, and the mysterious Solar Temple with its group suicides in Switzerland, Canada and France. Many other cults that superficially appear harmless have done serious damage to members and their families. While hard data regarding morbidity and mortality rates are impossible to gather because of the general secrecy and defensiveness of totalist cults, cumulative clinical observations make it clear that potentially or actively harmful cults pose a serious and growing problem.

Children and adolescents may be involved with cults either as primary recruits or through the participation of family members (usually parents). When children become cult victims because of their parents' involvement, they may be subject to neglect or abuse. The signs and symptoms of abuse and mistreatment of children whose parents are members of cults are often similar to those found in abusive homes. When cult-related ritual abuse is involved, the findings may be so bizarre as to inspire disbelief in the clinician. Cult-related neglect may include failure to provide adequate education, nutrition, and medical care. Some cults deliberately injure children through harsh punitive practices or ideologies. Approximately one-third of the 913 people who died in Guyana at Jonestown on November 18, 1978, were the children of Jim Jones's followers in the People's Temple. Children and adolescents also accounted for nearly a third of the victims of the fire that destroyed the Branch Davidian cult's compound outside of Waco, Texas, on April 19, 1993.

While these are extreme examples of how serious damage can be done to children of cult members, they do reflect the total disregard cult leaders generally have for the welfare of their members, and especially of the young. Langone & Eisenberg (1993) and Markowitz and Halperin (1984) have reviewed the psychological dynamics that make cultic groups prone to neglect, abuse, and mistreatment of children. The reader is referred to these publications for thorough discussions of the environmental factors, the child-rearing practices, and the types of harm that have been documented.

One tragic example is the Ecclesia Athletic Foundation. It was founded by Eldridge Broussard, Jr., in South-Central Los Angeles as a haven for inner-city African American youngsters (and a few adults) to discipline their bodies in a program of athletic training and gospel study. The group subsequently moved to Oregon for a more communal life. There they lived in tents, worked at farming, and engaged in strenuous physical workouts. The discipline became increasingly strict, harsh, and punitive. One day, ritual punishment by beating was responsible for the death of Brous-

sard's 8-year-old daughter. (Broussard was away at the time.) The subsequent investigation revealed that 55 children were malnourished and had been routinely beaten with a paddle or electric cord up to 800 blows while other youngsters were required to chant the strokes. The children, whose families had turned them over to Broussard in the hope of better lives for them, were then placed by Oregon authorities in foster homes.

Unfortunately, until a child dies, or there is clear and convincing legal evidence of maltreatment, there is often little that can be done to remove children from the cult environment. In 1992 police and welfare officials in Australia took into protective custody approximately 140 children whose parents were members of the Children of God (later known as the Family of Love, and other pseudonyms). The Children of God is a pseudo-Christian fundamentalist cult that encourages extensive sexual activity among members, including sex among children as young as 3 or 4 years and between children and adults. Unfortunately a week after the children were rescued, a court temporarily returned them to their parents on an interim accommodation order. While the matter was being further adjudicated, many of the children—and some whole families—vanished from that jurisdiction.

Ritual abuse is another, more controversial, dimension to cultic mistreatment of children. It is controversial because the allegations are often hard to verify and may be so horrific that when they become public (which happens all too rarely) they are disbelieved by the average person. The symptoms of such abuse are essentially similar to those generally found in the sexually assaulted child, except that there are more and varied episodes of abuse. Children who have been victims of ritual abuse are also generally subjected to greater intimidation and threats (e.g., of death or mutilation) than are victims of other types of abuse. As a result, like all torture victims, they have more persistent fears and more behavioral problems usually consistent with a diagnosis of posttraumatic stress disorder (Hudson, 1990; Kelley, 1993; Nurcombe and Unützer, 1991).

Satanic cults are occasionally decried when such criminal activities as child kidnapping, pornography, egregious abuse, and even human sacrifice are reported. Although a number of apparently well-organized satanic groups are "public" religions (e.g., they worship Satan, their beliefs are protected by law, and it has not yet been proved that they engage in illegal activities), most satanic groups are underground, and it is difficult to estimate how many people are involved. There is also a good deal of satanic nonsense in the drug abuse subculture, in certain types of music (e.g., "heavy metal"), and in rebellious youth groups and violent street gangs which engage in aberrant behavior but do not meet the definition of totalist cults (Tucker, 1993).

Clark (1992) and Wheeler, Wood, and Hatch (1988) have developed assessment strategies that assist in determining a young person's involvement with such deviant subcultures. Adolescents who are involved in satanism or violent gangs demonstrate various symptoms. They may become secretive, withdraw from family and school activities, change friends, use mysterious words and phrases, decorate their rooms or bodies with cabalistic symbols, etc. Others may exhibit such dysfunctional behaviors as drug and alcohol abuse, sexual promiscuity, or truancy. Many have difficulty in expressing anger appropriately and are prone to act out impulsively and violently. They may become depressed, make suicidal gestures, or engage in self-mutilation. Substance abuse, sexual deviance, and promiscuity are common. Horrific tatoos may be seen. Satanists tend to use hallucinogens, while gang members are more likely to abuse alcohol, heroin, or stimulants such as crack cocaine or amphetamines. Many adolescents involved in satanism are "dabblers" who are really not deeply committed to satanic practices (Steck, Anderson, & Boylin, 1992); but others may display profound psychopathology such as multiple personality disorder, other dissociative disorders, or even psychoses. The families of these adolescents are frequently chaotic and there may be a significant family history of abuse and neglect.

Youngsters are often targeted for recruitment by cults. In my experience, most of those who join cults do not come from unusually disturbed families or broken homes and they are not psychiatrically disturbed to begin with. They may have become more open to recruitment at a time of life change, loneliness, or disorientation after a move to a new city, or to a new school, or simply while traveling. Cults seek out such people precisely because they are known to be more vulnerable in these circumstances. Once identified, the target is subjected to powerful recruitment techniques which include many elements similar to "brainwashing" or coercive persuasion (Schein, 1961; West, 1993b; West and Singer, 1980).

Often the cult victim's family members (usually the parents) are the first to seek help, advice, or even psychotherapy in their anguish over the apparent loss of—or rejection by—a loved one. There have been a few agencies, such as the Los Angeles Cult Clinic, available to provide specialized services and support for these indirect victims of cults (Addis, Schulman-Miller, & Lightman, 1984). However, the L.A. clinic is now defunct, and other such services are rare indeed. Many families in desperation have been driven to kidnapping (or from their point of view rescuing) their own children in order to extract them from cults, and then to have them "deprogrammed." This is a procedure involving intensive discussions of the cults' practices, including hard facts about the leadership.

As more and more people (mostly adolescents and young adults) have emerged or been rescued from cults, some are joining the growing ranks of those who now act as "reentry counselors." Most of those who are "deprogrammed" never go back to the cult, even though they are usually free to do so in a matter of days or weeks. Nevertheless, some return to the cult either temporarily or permanently (Langone, 1984). A number of parents and/or their agents have been charged with kidnapping as a consequence of such failed rescue efforts, but they are virtually never convicted. For individuals who were not forcibly removed, but rather escaped or were ejected from cults, reentry counseling or voluntary "deprogramming" is available, which represents a relatively effective, legal, therapeutic approach in helping cult members to cope with the many problems involved in resuming a normal life. The former cultists must assimilate information previously denied them by the cult, perhaps for years, and in the case of some children, all their lives up to the point of rescue. Mental health professionals who work with cult victims are well advised to contact such reentry counselors, and to identify appropriate self-help groups of former members, for adjunctive treatment.

The psychiatric symptoms seen in people emerging from totalist cults often meet the criteria for posttraumatic stress disorder (PTSD).

Dissociative features are usually prominent, with findings likely to include disturbances or alterations in the normally integrative functions of identity, memory, or consciousness. Symptoms such as trance states, depersonalization, partial amnesia, feelings of unreality, emotional numbness, or an altered sense of identity may occur. Such disturbances or alterations may be sudden or gradual, transient or chronic, immediate or delayed. Dissociative disorders in cult victims were recognized by the DSM III-R (p. 277) which described "dissociated states that may occur in people who have been subjected to periods of prolonged and intensive coercive persuasion (e.g. brainwashing, thought reform, or indoctrination while the captive of terrorists or cultists)." DSM IV, for some reason, ends that sentence after the word "captive" (p. 490), thus regrettably eliminating any specific reference to cult-related psychopathology. A recently defined concept describes a type of dissociative disorder called "pseudoidentity," which differs in several ways from multiple personality disorder (West and Martin, 1994). The pseudoidentity phenomenon is commonly seen in cult victims, and should be understood if best results are to be achieved in their psychotherapy and rehabilitation.

Many people in cultic organizations are at risk. Many are already sick. Some have been permanently damaged. The stress on their families generates additional psychiatric casualties. There is also physical morbidity to consider, as well as the danger of fatalities. The casualties are steadily mounting. Unfortunately mental health professionals in general have been relatively ignorant of these issues. Some actually minimize or even reject the dangers posed by cults. Nevertheless, more and more children are emerging as victims of totalist cults—either directly or through the involvement of family members, or both—and are being referred to psychiatrists who specialize in the treatment of children and adolescents. It is essential that these specialists prepare themselves to understand the nature and extent of the problem, to recognize cult-related psychopathology for what it is, and to employ appropriate methods of treatment utilizing both traditional psychiatric techniques and special adjunctive therapies such as reentry counseling and self-help groups of former cult members.

REFERENCES

Addis, M., Schulman-Miller, J., & Lightman, M. (1984). The cult clinic helps families in crisis. *Social Casework, 65,* 515–522.

American Psychiatric Association. (1987). *Diagnostic and statistical manual of mental disorders* (3rd ed., rev.). Washington, DC: Author.

Chambers, W. V., Langone, M. D., Dole, A. A., & Grice, J. W. (1994). The Group Psychological Abuse Scale: A measure of the varieties of cultic abuse. *Cultic Studies Journal, 11,* 88–117.

Clark, C. M. (1992). Deviant adolescent subcultures: Assessment strategies and clinical interventions. *Adolescence, 27* (106), 283–293.

Hudson, P. S. (1990). Ritual child abuse: A survey of symptoms and allegations. *Journal of Child and Youth Care* [Special Issue], 27–54.

Kelley, S. J. (1993). Ritualistic abuse of children in daycare centers. In M. D. Langone (Ed.), *Recovery from cults* (pp. 343–355). New York: W. W. Norton.

Langone, M. D. (1984). Deprogramming: An analysis of parental questionnaires. *Cultic Studies Journal, 1,* 63–78.

Langone, M. D., & Eisenberg, G. (1993). Children and cults. In M. D. Langone (Ed.), *Recovery from cults* (pp. 327–342). New York: W. W. Norton.

Markowitz, A., & Halperin, D. A. (1984). Cults and children. *Cultic Studies Journal, 1* (2), 143–155.

Nurcombe, B., & Unützer, J. (1991). The ritual abuse of children: Clinical features and diagnostic reasoning. *Journal of the American Academy of Child and Adolescent Psychiatry, 30* (2), 272–276.

Schein, E. H. (1961). *Coercive persuasion.* New York: W. W. Norton.

Singer, M. T. *Cults In Our Midst.* San Francisco: Jossey-Bass, 1995.

Steck, G. M., Anderson, S. A., & Boylin, W. M. (1992). Satanism among adolescents: Empirical and clinical considerations. *Adolescence, 27* (108), 901–914.

Tucker, R. (1993). Teen satanism. In M. D. Langone (Ed.), *Recovery from Cults* (pp. 356–381). New York: W. W. Norton.

West, L. J. (1989). Persuasive techniques in contemporary cults. In M. Galanter (Ed.), *Cults and new religious movements* (pp. 165–192). Washington, DC: American Psychiatric Association Press.

West, L. J. (1993b). A psychiatric overview of cult-related phenomena. *Journal of the American Academy of Psychoanalysis, 21* (1), 1–19.

West, L. J.(1993a). Cults. *Directions in Psychiatry, 13* (7), 1–7.

West, L. J., & Martin, P. R. (1994). Pseudo-identity and the treatment of personality change in victims of captivity and cults. In S. J. Lynn and J. W. Ruhe (Eds.), *Dissociation: Clinical and theoretical perspectives.* New York: Guilford Press (pp. 268–288).

West, L. J., & Singer, M. T. (1980). Cults, quacks, and nonprofessional psychotherapies. In H. I. Kaplan, A. M. Freedman, & B. C. Sadock (Eds.), *Comprehensive textbook of psychiatry* (Vol. 3, pp. 3245–3258). Baltimore, MD: Williams & Wilkins.

Wheeler, B. R., Wood, S., & Hatch, R. J. (1988). Assessment and intervention with adolescents involved in satanism. *Social Work, 33,* 547–550.

---

82 / Physical Examination

Janice M. McConville and Brian J. McConville

This chapter describes those processes of physical examination of infants, preschoolers, grade-school children, and adolescents with which practicing child and adolescent psychiatrists should be familiar. The authors, a pediatrician and a child and adolescent psychiatrist, have focused on common events that occur when the child psychiatrist first meets the patient. We also have taken into account that in contrast to earlier practice, many child and adolescent psychiatrists are now called upon to do physical examinations, especially with inpatient children and adolescents. Hence this chapter refers not only to outpatient observational assessments but also to inpatient evaluations. The details of the assessment will first be described in relation to the appearance of the child in the office, inpatient, or residential unit and will then proceed to those aspects of physical examination that should be done by child and adolescent psychiatrist. We will also discuss when the child should be referred to the pediatrician or other relevant specialist. It will be assumed that if the child and adolescent psychiatrist is not experienced in delivering preventive and primary care, then a pediatrician or family doctor will be involved with the child. Hence, any physical abnormalities which are detected can be discussed with the other physician collaboratively.

Child and adolescent psychiatrists examining infants and young children should be aware that it is not always possible to proceed through a detailed physical examination in the way the examiner was originally taught. Small children can be examined adequately when they are held by their parents, especially if they are comfortable and not crying. Hence, examination of the heart and abdomen should be done early, when the child is relaxed; examination of other organ systems, such as the lungs, ears, throat, and neurologic system, may be done subsequently, even if the child is distressed. (It is possible to perform an adequate examination on the lungs when the child is crying, by listening to the breaths taken in between cries). The examiner needs to be flexible and able to adapt to the child's state rather than adhere to a rigid predetermined sequence. With toddlers and preschool children, it is helpful to introduce each step of the examination with a positive statement. For example, the examiner might say, "Now I am going to listen to your heart" rather than, "Please will you let me listen to your heart?" Preschoolers are inherently prone to say "no" and should not be given this opportunity, since this can lead to a battle of wills. In contrast, grade school and high school children should be treated with the same degree of politeness, respect, and request for cooperation as is used with adults. Prior to each step, some degree of explanation, especially in terms of whether the particular examination procedures will hurt, should be given, for example, "I am going to listen to your heart and lungs. The stethoscope may feel cold" or "I am going to feel your abdomen. It should not hurt you, but if it does, please tell me."

Examiners should also be concerned about issues which relate to a particular child's fears or transference reactions. For example, a child who has been physically abused may well be extremely frightened during the process of physical examination, or a teenager who has experienced sexual abuse may be extremely anxious during examination and refuse to allow examination of the genital area or even the abdomen.

Finally, a great deal of information can be obtained by observation of the child or adolescent while obtaining information either from the parents or from the patient. For example, the child's capacity for speech, general development level, relatedness to others, anxiety, muscle development (including motor coordination), activity level, and neurologic problems such as inability to move or clumsiness moving any part of the body may easily be observed without the child feeling that she is being examined. This information can be very helpful, especially if physical examination later proves to be difficult. The examiner should be able to think "in parallel;" while taking a history from the parent or child, the examiner should observe the patient closely in order to pick up whatever findings may be available on inspection. These will be commented on as we move through the various age groups in this chapter.

All evaluations have to be done against the background of normal growth and development for the child and adolescent. An excellent summary is given in the section on Growth and Development by Needlman in Nelson: *Textbook of Pediatrics* (Nelson, 1996).

When examining children, the examiner should be friendly at a level appropriate to the patient's age, and, if possible, should involve the child as a willing participant in the examination process rather than assuming (as with adult patients) that the patient will cooperate with the examiner's wishes. This is both an art and a skill; it can be learned with practice, but it is helpful if the examiner has the correct attitude to begin with.

Examination of the Infant/Toddler (Birth–2 Years)

GENERAL OBSERVATION

Size: The most important initial impression is related to the size of the patient. Is the youngster's size appropriate for his chronologic age? With infants, this relates to the baby's birthweight and period of gestation. Most full-term infants regain their birthweight by 10 days, double it by 5 months, and triple it in 1 year. The length of the normal infant, which is 19 to 21 inches at birth, increases during the first year by 10 to 12 inches. Head circumference, which is ordinarily 34 to 35 cm at birth, increases to 44 cm by 6 months and to 47 cm by 1 year. The central incisors erupt at 6 to 8 months, and by 1 year, six to eight deciduous incisors are present. The ranges given are normal clinical variations. Height, weight, and head circumference charts are available for both boys and girls for the period between birth and 36 months of age. It is suggested that these be used routinely as needed.

During the second year, there is deceleration in the rate of growth; the average child gains 5 lb. and grows about 5 inches. The brain growth also decelerates, with head circumference increasing only 2 cm during the entire year. The plump infant changes into the leaner toddler and develops the lordosis and protuberant abdomen which are characteristic of the second and third years of life. During the second year, 8 more deciduous teeth erupt (the first molars and canines) with a total of 14 to 16 teeth by age 2 years.

By definition, the premature infant is born at less than 37 weeks gestation and weighs less than 2500 g; those with very low birthweight are less than 1500 g. A baby's birthweight may be appropriate for gestational age (AGA), or may be small for gestational age (SGA) due to intrauterine growth retardation (IUGR). A newborn maturity rating and classification scale are shown in the tables.

Height, weight, and head circumference data are usually plotted on appropriate charts as noted above and growth is followed longitudinally. A measurement at any point in time will show where the child is compared to the percentiles for normal children at that chronologic age. The rate of growth will also indicate whether the growth is normal, accelerated, or delayed over time. Correction needs to be made for the gestational age, as distinct from the chronologic age of the premature infant. It must be remembered that a baby born at 30 weeks gestational age who appears small for his chronologic age may be average in size when correction is made for his gestational age. For example, a 3-month-old infant weighing 8 lb. would appear very small for his chronologic age, but when correction is made for 10 weeks prematurity, he would fall within the normal range. Many preterm infants grow at an increased rate during the first 2 years, ending up in the normal range for their chronologic age (2 years) without correction for prematurity. Others, particularly those with IUGR, may continue to grow at a slower rate than the normal full-term infant, and may never catch up to the normal range. The premature baby may be recognized for many months, even up to the second year, by the characteristic narrow bifrontal, and elongated anteroposterior diameters of the head.

The body proportions of an infant are very different from those of older children and adolescents. The head is relatively large, the face is round, and the lower jaw appears small. The chest is rounded, the abdomen is prominent, and the arms and legs appear relatively short. During the first year of life, the infant becomes more chubby in appearance, and should appear well nourished. When a child is malnourished for any reason, height will increase fairly normally but weight will lag, so that there is a drop in percentile position. Although the baby may not lose weight, weight gain will not occur in the expected fashion. The failure to gain weight is most noticeable in the arms and legs, particularly the thighs and buttocks; in contrast, the abdomen may remain prominent. Nutrition needs to be assessed in terms of both the adequacy of what the child is offered to eat and what the child actually eats. Starvation, as in famine, inadvertent inadequate caloric content of the diet, neglect, emotional deprivation, lethargy or anorexia associated with infections, congenital heart disease, chronic renal disease, or intestinal malabsorption may all affect the nutritional status.

Mental Status: The child's capacity to make eye contact, interest in surroundings, social skills, including the ability to show a social smile, language development, shyness, friendliness, or, alternatively, avoidance of eye and physical contact are all easily observed during history taking. The developmentally handicapped child will often appear less alert than normal children of the same age. Motor and psychosocial development and early language development have been covered in other chapters. In contrast to the physical exami-

nation of the adult, developmental assessment is a routine part of assessment of the child. A fundamental decision that is part of every assessment is whether the child's development is appropriate for its age, with correction for prematurity if necessary.

Motor Development, Gait and Coordination: Generally speaking, control of the body in the first year of life proceeds from head to foot. Head control is gained by 2 months of age. Hand control, including the ability to reach for, grasp, and place objects in the mouth is achieved by 4 months. Control of the trunk, including rolling over (both from front to back and from back to front) is attained by 5 to 6 months. Sitting alone, initially in a tripod position, is attained by 6 months, with crawling ability occurring by 8 months, pulling to a standing position by 9 to 10 months, and walking by 12 to 15 months. Hence, if the examiner remembers the head to foot sequence, and also remembers that more complex movements such as sitting, crawling, pulling up, and standing must follow earlier more basic movements, it will be seen that simple sequences precede more complex ones with each step being the precursor of the next. (This will, we hope, make the understanding of motor developmental sequence more logical to the examiner.) The sequence of emerging patterns of behavior during the first year of life are contained in Table 82.1. When the infant starts to walk, it is with a wide-based unsteady gait. This improves until, at 18 months, he can run stiffly and climb stairs with one hand held. At 2 years of age he walks with a normal gait, runs well, and has usually outgrown the tendency to fall. Hand coordination improves during the first year from grabbing objects in the fist and putting them in the mouth at 4 months, to transferring them from hand to hand at 6 months. By 9 months the infant can pick up small pellets or pieces of food between thumb and forefinger and by 12 months can give the object into the hand of the parent or examiner when asked. At 15 months he can place a pellet in a small bottle. Cubes can be piled into a tower of three by 18 months and a tower of six by 2 years. A simplified schema showing acquisition of motor skills and the variation in age of acquisition is found in Table 82.2 (Sayley, 1969).

Language Development: Language development also follows a logical developmental sequence. By 1 to 2 months the infant should be

TABLE 82.1

Emerging Patterns of Behavior During the First Year of Life

Neonatal Period (First 4 Weeks)	
Prone:	Lies in flexed attitude; turns head from side to side; head sags on ventral suspension
Supine:	Generally flexed and a little stiff
Visual:	May fixate face or light in line of vision; "doll's eyes" movement of eyes on turning of the body
Reflex:	Moro response active; stepping and placing reflexes; grasp reflex active
Social:	Visual preference for human face

At 4 Weeks	
Prone:	Legs more extended; holds chin up; turns head; head lifted momentarily to plane of body on ventral suspension
Supine:	Tonic neck posture predominates; supple and relaxed; head lags on pull to sitting position
Visual:	Watches person; follows moving object
Social:	Body movements in cadence with voice of other in social contact; beginning to smile

At 8 Weeks	
Prone:	Raises head slightly farther; head sustained in plane of body on ventral suspension
Supine:	Tonic neck posture predominates; head lags on pull to sitting position
Visual:	Follows moving object 180 degrees
Social:	Smiles on social contact; listens to voice and coos

At 12 Weeks	
Prone:	Lifts head and chest, arms extended; head above plane of body on ventral suspension
Supine:	Tonic neck posture predominates, reaches toward and misses objects; waves at toy
Sitting:	Head lag partially compensated on pull to sitting position; early head control with bobbing motion; back rounded
Reflex:	Typical Moro response has not persisted; makes defense movements or selective withdrawal reactions
Social:	Sustained social contact; listens to music; says "aah, ngah"

At 16 Weeks	
Prone:	Lifts head and chest, head is approximately vertical axis; legs extended
Supine:	Symmetrical posture predominates, hands in midline; reaches and grasps objects and brings them to mouth
Sitting:	No head lag on pull to sitting position; head steady, held forward; enjoys sitting with full truncal support
Standing:	When head erect, pushes with feet
Adaptive:	Sees pellet, but makes no move to it
Social:	Laughs out loud; may show displeasure if social contact is broken; excited at sight of food

TABLE 82.1

(Continued)

At 28 Weeks

Prone:	Rolls over; may pivot
Supine:	Lifts head; rolls over; squirming movements
Sitting:	Sits briefly; with support of pelvis; leans forward on hands; back rounded
Standing:	May support most of weight; bounces actively
Adaptive:	Reaches out for and grasps large object; transfers objects from hand to hand; grasp uses radial palm; rakes at pellet
Language:	Polysyllabic vowel sounds formed
Social:	Prefers mother; babbles; enjoys mirror; responds to changes in emotional content of social contact

At 40 Weeks

Sitting:	Sits up alone and indefinitely without support, back straight
Standing:	Pulls to standing position
Motor:	Creeps or crawls
Adaptive:	Grasps objects with thumb and forefinger; pokes at things with forefinger; picks up pellet with assisted pincer movement; uncovers hidden toy; attempts to retrieve dropped object; releases object grasped by another person
Language:	Repetitive consonant sounds (mamma, dada)
Social:	Responds to sound of name; plays peekaboo or pattycake; waves bye-bye

At 52 Weeks (1 Year)

Motor:	Walks with one hand held; "cruises" or walks holding on to furniture
Adaptive:	Picks up pellet with unassisted pincer movement of forefinger and thumb; releases object to other person on request or gesture
Language:	A few words besides mamma, dada
Social:	Plays simple ball game; makes postural adjustment to dressing

able to listen to a voice, coo responsively, and smile socially. By 4 months the baby should laugh aloud and by 6 months should be able to produce syllabic babbling. By 9 months, though not yet meaningful, repetitive consonants (mama, dada, baba) can be heard, and the child should respond to the sound of her name. A 9-month-old baby can also play patty-cake and peekaboo. By 12 to 15 months the child should have at least three meaningful words, usually including mama and dada. (It should be pointed out that these are minimal expectations; many children have a larger vocabulary than this at 1 year of age, but the examiner is probably less interested in evidence of early linguistic proclivity than in finding out if the child has substantive areas of developmental delay. By 18 months the toddler has gained many more words, with a lower limit of 10 words. Usually these words have to do with needs or actions and are used singly. By the age of 2 years, the child is able to connect words into simple three-word sentences, again usually related to simple, often action-oriented needs. In assessing toddlers, it should be remembered that 2 year olds are famous for their difficulty in dealing with frustration; this can result in temper tantrums, sometimes including breath holding. Thumb sucking is common when the child is fearful or stressed.

TABLE 82.2

Median Age and Range in Acquisition of Motor Skills

Motor Skill	Age in Months	
	Median	Range°
Transfers objects hand to hand	5.5	4 to 8
Sits alone 30 seconds or more	6.0	5 to 8
Rolls from back to stomach	6.4	4 to 10
Has neat pincer grasp	8.9	7 to 12
Stands alone	11.0	9 to 16
Holds crayon adaptively	11.2	8 to 15
Walks alone	11.7	9 to 17
Walks up stairs with help	16.1	12 to 23
Walks up stairs both feet on each step	25.8	19 to 30

°*5th to 95th percentile*
Adapted from Bayley (1969)

Table 82.3 indicates emerging patterns of cognition, play, and language from birth to 2 years of age.

Appearance: Skin tone obviously depends on genetic factors, both familial and racial. The appearance of the skin may also be related to nutrition and hydration. For example, wrinkling may indicate recent weight loss, in contrast to smoothness of skin, which is usually an indication of good nutrition. However, the skin may appear shiny and smooth in the presence of edema.

Cyanosis may take the form of peripheral acrocyanosis, which is normal in the hands and feet during the newborn period. It may also be transient, as in the deep red or purplish color of the screaming infant, or confused with mottling, which is transient and related to skin temperature, as when the infant or toddler is undressed in a cool room. (Persistent mottling may also be a sign of peripheral vascular impairment due to serious illness. Again, the general appearance and activity level of the child are important; sick children generally look lethargic and are irritable when handled, whereas children showing normal physiologic mottling are normally active, responsive, and well.) In contrast to children with mottling caused by severe illness, physiologic mottling disappears when the skin is covered or warmed. True cyanosis is ordinarily a sign of either cyanotic heart disease or severe pulmonary disease; it is more commonly central, and most obvious in the lips and in the mucosae, as well as peripherally in the nail beds. Pallor of the skin may indicate anemia.

Bruising may at times be confused with cyanosis, but true cyanosis blanches temporarily with pressure, whereas bruising does not. Bruising is uncommon in children before they are able to stand, and if seen in a child who is unable to stand and move around in an exploratory fashion, it should always be assessed critically. In the mobile, actively exploring child, bruising from falls is usually confined to the knees, shins, and extensor surface of the forearms. Bruises in other areas should be regarded with suspicion because of the possibility of bleeding disorders or physical abuse or neglect. Bite marks or burns may also be an indication of physical abuse.

Mongolian spots are irregular, often large, blue-grey stained areas in the skin on the buttocks, the back, and, less frequently, the arms and legs. These commonly fade during the first year but may persist even into adult life. Distinguishing Mongolian spots from bruises can sometimes be difficult, but in contrast to bruises which fade and change color with time, their color persists unchanged. These spots are uncommon in white children and are more likely to occur in black, oriental, and East Indian infants.

Jaundice in infancy is very common and may be

TABLE 82.3

Cognition, Play, and Language

Piagetian Stage	Age	Object Permanence	Causality	Play	Receptive Language	Expressive Language
I	Birth to 1 month	Shifting images	Generalization of reflexes		Turns to voice	Range of cries (hunger, pain)
II	1 to 4 months	Stares at spot where object disappeared (looks at hand after yarn drops)	Primary circular reactions (thumb sucking)		Searches for speaker with eyes	Cooing Vocal contagion
III	4 to 8 months	Visually follows dropped object through vertical trajectory (tracks dropped yarn to floor)	Secondary circular reactions (recreates accidentally discovered environmental effects drops)	Same behavior repertoire for all objetcs (bangs, shakes, puts in mouth)	Responds to own name and to tones of voice	Babbling Four distinct syllables
IV	9 to 12 months	Finds an object after watching it hidden	Coordination of secondary circular reaction	Visual motor inspection of objects Peekaboo	Listens selectively to familiar words Responds to "no" and other verbal requests	First real words Jargoning Symbolic gestures (Shakes head no)
V	12 to 18 months	Recovers hidden object after multiple visual changes of position	Tertiary circular reactions (deliberately varies behavior to create novel effects)	Awareness of social function of objects Symbolic play centered around own body (drinks from toy cup)	Can bring familiar object from another room Points to parts of body	Many single words uses words to express express needs Acquired 10 words by 18 months
VI	18 months to 2 years	Recovers hidden objects after invisible changes in position	Spontaneously uses nondirect causal mechanisms (uses key to move wind up toy)	Symbolic play directed toward doll (give doll a drink)	Follows series of two or three commands Points to pictures when named	Telegraphic two-word sentences

physiological or due to blood group incompatibility. It usually fades by 7 to 10 days of age, but for some breast fed infants, jaundice may persist for up to 3 to 4 months. Jaundice persisting beyond the expected time should be further assessed for the possibility of hemolytic or liver disease.

Flat hemangiomata (nevus flammeus) are very common in newborn infants, especially on the eyelids, forehead, and nape of the neck. These hemangiomata generally fade during the first year of life and have no clinical significance. In contrast, the port wine stain occurring on the face, neck, or mucous membranes, usually in the distribution of the fifth cranial nerve (especially the ophthalmic division) may be a manifestation of Sturge–Weber syndrome. Port wine stains, wherever they are present, are permanent.

Small areas of hyperpigmentation (nevi) are not unusual in infants and small children. Unless these are large or extremely black, they usually are quite benign. The giant pigmented nevus, most commonly situated on the trunk or proximal limbs, usually involves large areas of the body surface and is of concern because of its association with leptomelanocytosis and a predisposition to development of malignant melanoma. Hypopigmented skin lesions may be oval or irregular in shape and vary from a few millimeters to several centimeters in diameter. They may occur on the arms, legs, or trunk and are commonly associated with tuberous sclerosis. The yellow-orange nevus sebaceous may be seen on the scalp in infants. Because of the risk of secondary malignancy, these lesions are usually removed prior to adolescence.

During the first and second years, the rashes of such infectious diseases as chicken pox, roseola, impetigo, may occur.

Appearance of the Eyes: A general assessment of the eyes can be done with the child in the mother's arms. Hypertelorism, which is an increased distance between the eyes with apparent broadening of the nose, may be associated with mental deficiencies or other congenital disorders, but mild forms occur in perfectly healthy children.

Ptosis, or droopiness of the upper eyelid, may be congenital and frequently occurs in otherwise healthy children, but it also occurs in a large number of congenital syndromes. Acquired ptosis of childhood requires ophthalmologic assessment because of the likelihood of serious underlying disease.

Epicanthal folds are vertical or oblique folds of skin which extend on either side of the bridge of the nose and cover the inner canthus. They are present to some degree in most young children and become less apparent with age. They are also a common feature of many syndromes including chromosome abnormalities, for example, Down syndrome.

Nystagmus, which is a rhythmic oscillation of one or both eyes, may be congenital or acquired. Congenital nystagmus is commonly associated with abnormalities of the eye and vision, as in the wandering eyes of the blind child, but may be benign and familial. Acquired nystagmus necessitates prompt evaluation because it can indicate severe intracranial disease. Spasmus nutans is the triad of pendular nystagmus, head nodding, and torticollis. It is a benign and self-limited condition.

Strabismus (squint) is due to malalignment of the eyes. The two principal types are heterophoria, which is a latent tendency to malalignment (where the eye deviates with fatigue, illness, or stress) and heterotropia, where the malalignment is constant. Early diagnosis and correction are very important because the child learns to suppress the incoming image from the deviating eye and becomes effectively and permanently blind in that eye.

Physical Examination

Having gained as much information as possible by observation of the child, the clinician would ordinarily start the physical examination at this point. As mentioned previously, the order of the examination elements may be varied from that described here depending on the age and cooperation of the child. With the infant and toddler the clinician would ordinarily proceed to examination of the heart and abdomen first while the child is quiet. As a rule, the clinician examines the child from the top down, because this allows for undressing in stages rather than complete undressing, and is accordingly better tolerated by young children.

EXAMINATION OF THE HEAD

Upon examining the head, the clinician first notices the size of the head, which may appear to be normal, obviously large (macrocephaly), or small (microcephaly). The head circumference should be measured and plotted on the growth chart to confirm the initial impression. Ordinarily, macrocephaly is defined as two standard deviations above the mean (95th percentile), and microcephaly as two standard deviations below the mean (3rd percentile). However, if there is a marked discrepancy between the child's height and weight percentile and the size of the head, this may represent an abnormality. In infants, the anterior fontanelle is normally open and softly rounded. The fontanelle progressively becomes smaller and closes between 6 and 18 months of age. Macrocephaly associated with a bulging fontanelle may indicate hydrocephalus or some other intracranial lesion. Microcephaly is commonly associated with congenital malformations and developmental delay. A sunken fontanelle may be associated with dehydration.

The premature infant is distinguished for many months by the narrow bifrontal and elongated anteroposterior diameters of the head. Craniofacial abnormalities are frequent components of congenital disorders, for example, craniosynostosis (premature closure of one or more sutures). Abnormalities of the facies are common aspects of many congenital syndromes, for example, flat facies in achondroplasia and Down syndrome, round facies in Prader–Willi syndrome, broad facies in Crouzon syndrome or Sotos syndrome, triangular facies in Turner syndrome, masklike facies in Moebius anomaly, and coarse facies in Hurler syndrome. More details on these syndromes can be found in Smith's Recognizable Patterns of Human Malfunction (1996).

EXAMINATION OF THE EYES

Along with those features noted in the general assessment, the physical examination includes assessment of the iris for color. Heterochromia, where the two irises are of different color or a portion of the iris is a different color from the remainder, may occur alone, as a feature of Waardenberg syndrome, or with other diseases of the eye. Coloboma of the iris (defect in the iris) may occur alone or in association with other abnormalities. It is a common component of chromosomal abnormalities, for example, trisomies 13 and 18.

Examination of the pupils includes estimation of size and reaction to light. During the first weeks of life the pupils may be unequal (but remember that the most common cause of unequal pupils is a brighter intensity of light on one side of the patient than the other, as from a window). This can be easily distinguished by moving either the light or the patient. In the infant and toddler the pupils usually react briskly to light. Assessment of the fundi is not ordinarily done as part of the physical examination at this age; however, with the ophthalmoscope set on +5, the clinician should shine the light at the infant's pupils in order to obtain a red reflection, thus indicating that there is no cataract present. A white pupillary reflection can also be caused by retrolental fibroplasia, retinal detachment, and retinoblastoma. This finding always warrants prompt examination by a pediatrician or an ophthalmologist. Ocular motility is tested by having the child follow a light or toy through the various directions of gaze.

EXAMINATION OF THE EARS

The external ear should first be assessed for size, shape, and position, since malformation and displaced ears are common in many congenital syndromes. Low-set ears are common in trisomies 13 and 18 and malformed ears are common in Down syndrome, fetal hydantoin syndrome, Turner syndrome, trisomies 13 and 18, and Klinefelter syndrome.

Preauricular tags and sinuses are commonly first observed in normal infants; however, they may be associated with congenital malformation syndromes and early infantile autism. These persist throughout life.

The most common disease process of the ear at this age is otitis media. This is obvious on examination because of redness or injection of the tympanic membrane, sometimes associated with bulging. Serous effusion, with a normal-colored dull, nonmotile, sometimes bulging tympanic membrane, is a common sequela of otitis media, and if persistent is of concern because of possible hearing loss and delayed speech development.

EXAMINATION OF THE MOUTH

Examination of the mouth includes observing the presence of the deciduous teeth. The central incisors normally appear first between 6 and 8 months of age, and by 1 year the child usually has 6 to 8 teeth. By 2 years of age, the child usually has 16 teeth.

A protruding tongue may be associated with Down syndrome or other craniofacial malformation syndromes. Drooling is common at this age, with its associated teething.

Central cyanosis is sometimes most easily detected by examining the oral mucosa. Cracked lips and dry tongue and oral mucosae are indicative of dehydration.

Assessment of the mouth includes examination of the palate for the presence of cleft palate involving either the soft palate alone or the hard palate. Cleft lip may vary from a small notch to a complete separation extending into the nose.

It may be unilateral or bilateral. Cleft lip and/or palate may be an isolated malformation, but may also form part of several congenital malformation syndromes.

EXAMINATION OF THE NECK

Examination of the neck may be difficult in infants, because the neck is very short and the chin tends to rest on the upper chest. Congenital torticollis in which the sternomastoid muscle on one side is shortened, is not uncommon in infancy. Cysts and sinuses in the neck may be formed along the first and second branchial clefts due to incomplete closure during embryonic life. Thyroglossal cysts occurring in or close to the midline of the neck may occasionally be found. Rotation of the neck should be possible for a full 90 degrees from the midline in each direction, and complete flexion and extension should also be easily achieved. Movement has to be tested passively in the first months of life until the infant gains head control at around 4 to 6 months of age.

EXAMINATION OF THE CHEST

Young infants ordinarily use their diaphragm for breathing, so respirations are mainly abdominal. The sternum and lower ribs retract during breathing. Supernumerary nipples are not uncommon and occur along a line from the nipple to the inguinal area. They may have an areola and frequently are mistaken for congenital nevi. Examination of the heart includes the heart rate, which is rapid and very variable in infancy (average 120–140 beats/minute, but during vigorous crying it may increase to 170 or more, and may drop to 80 or 90 during sleep). Sinus arrhythmia is a common finding in young children. Persistent tachycardia, bradycardia, or irregular heartbeat requires assessment by a cardiologist. Evaluation of the femoral pulses is important to make sure that coarctation of the aorta is not overlooked. Because the heart rate is very rapid in infants and toddlers, assessment of heart sounds may be difficult, as is evaluation of a cardiac murmur. Any murmur heard during this age should be considered abnormal and referred for evaluation because of the likelihood of congenital heart disease, for example, ventricular septal defect, coarctation of the aorta, or other congenital conditions. Examination of the lungs is easy in this age group because the breath sounds are very clearly heard through the thin chest wall. Breath sounds are bronchovesicular and should be heard equally in all areas. (Remember that upper airway sounds are readily heard and are sometimes felt as a vibration in the chest of the young child). Rales, rhonchi, stridor, or wheeze (as distinct from upper airway sounds) are caused by respiratory disease and should be referred to the pediatrician for assessment.

EXAMINATION OF THE ABDOMEN

The abdomen of the infant and toddler is prominent and rounded. Umbilical hernias are not uncommon and are usually of no significance. The liver and spleen are frequently palpable at or below the costal margin. In a sleeping infant it is easily possible to palpate the kidneys. Inguinal hernias are not uncommon, especially in males. Because of the increased risk of strangulation of the hernia due to the narrow neck of the hernia sac compared with the adult inguinal hernia, they require referral to a surgeon.

EXAMINATION OF THE GENITOURINARY SYSTEM

Examination in the male includes observation of the penis, which may be circumcised, and, in a plump infant, not infrequently it appears to be partially buried in the pubic fat. Assessment of the length of the penis can be made by pushing on the surrounding fat with resultant extrusion of the penis. Hypospadias (opening of the urethral meatus on the under, or ventral, surface of the penis) is not uncommon. It varies in severity from minor displacement to severe failure of urethral fusion and genital ambiguity. It is often associated with chordee (ventral curvature of the penis). The testes should be present in the scrotum at birth; however, in about 5% of term infants and about 30% of low birthweight infants, they are undescended on one or both sides. It is important not to confuse normally retractile testes with undescended testes. Hydrocele due to persistence of the processus vaginalis is very common during the first months of life, but it should resolve by 1 year. Hydroceles persisting beyond this age or those associated with inguinal hernias should be referred to a specialist.

At birth the female genitalia, especially the clitoris, may be prominent and there may be considerable mucoid discharge due to stimulation from the maternal hormones crossing the placenta. During infancy the labia majora frequently are not completely apposed, and the vaginal orifice is usually easily seen. There is considerable variation in appearance, but bleeding, tears, or bruising in this or the anal area should arouse suspicion of sexual abuse.

EXAMINATION OF THE EXTREMITIES

This includes assessment of spontaneous movement which is usually readily observed and should be symmetrical. In the newborn, nonmovement of one limb compared to the other suggests either trauma, including fracture (usually clavicle), or paralysis, such as brachial palsy (Erb's palsy). In later infancy, trauma or abuse should be suspected. Assessment of tone and reflexes is important because hypotonia or hypertonia and hypo- or hyperreflexia may occur with cerebral palsy or various other neurological conditions which are described elsewhere.

The hands should be inspected for Simian creases, syndactyly, or disproportion between the length of the fingers and the total hand. These features may be associated with congenital abnormalities (Smith, 1996). Common orthopedic problems of the lower limbs would include metatarsus varus, where the forefoot deviates medially relative to the hind foot, overlapping toes, syndactyly of the toes, club foot, and congenital displacement of the hip or more rarely the knee.

Examination of the Preschool Child (2–5 Years)

Although for purposes of convenience the preschool years are lumped together as one group, nevertheless, there is a distinct pattern of behavioral change and maturation during this period. The 2 year old typically has difficulty separating from the parent and is very negative about the examination. The 3 year old may be timid, but with reassurance from the parent, will allow physical examination. At 4 the child can separate more easily from the parent and may participate in talking and playacting the roles of doctor or patient. By 5 years of age the average child can carry on a conversation and participate in the physical examination after reassurance that it will not hurt.

During years 3 to 5, growth is relatively steady at about 4 to 5 lb. and 2 to 4 inches per year. Most children are relatively lean, and the lordosis and protuberant abdomen of the 2 to 3 year old is lost. By age 2½, all 20 deciduous teeth have erupted. During this time the head appears to be less large relative to the total body, and by 5 years of age, head and body more closely approximate adult proportions. The fontanelle is ordinarily closed, and the head circumference increases very slowly. Previously unrecognized macrocephaly, microcephaly, or other craniofacial abnormalities may be detected at this age. The association of these with other disease entities has already been mentioned. Nutrition is assessed in a similar fashion to that of the infant, but children of this age are more lean than chubby.

The normal preschooler appears bright and alert and very interested in her surroundings, although she may be fearful of separation from the parent or of being undressed and examined. Most will vigorously explore their environment and may at times have to be restrained for safety. By age 3, most children respond to their name, know their age, and know whether they are a boy or girl. Thumb sucking and temper tantrums, which are common in the 2 year old, become much less typical as the child ages. Some 4 to 5 year olds revert to thumb sucking when under stress or if fatigued. A summary of emerging patterns of behavior from 1 to 5 years of age is given in Table 82.4. (Neeldman, 1996) The 4- to 5-year-old child is frequently very shy during examination of the abdomen and genital area and may be reluctant to remove pants or underwear; accordingly, this is usually deferred until the end of the examination. Hopefully, by that time, the child has relaxed and will allow a quick examination of these areas.

Speech and language develop very rapidly during this period. From a vocabulary of 50 words at 18 months, the child has 800 words by 3 years and 2000 by 5 years of age. Sentence structure becomes more complex, and the child is able to express ideas and feelings. Transient stuttering is not uncommon. (A simple but useful summary of milestones from 1 month to 5 years as used by our

TABLE 82.4

Emerging Patterns of Behavior From 1 to 5 Years of Age°

15 Months

Motor:	Walks alone; crawls up stairs
Adaptive:	Makes tower of 2 cubes; makes a line with crayon; inserts pellet in bottle
Language:	Jargon; follows simple commands; may name a familiar object (ball)
Social:	Indicates some desires or needs by pointing; hugs parents

18 Months

Motor:	Runs stiffly; sit small chair; walks up stairs with one hand held; explores drawers and waste baskets
Adaptive:	Piles 3 cubes; imitates scribbling; imitates vertical stroke; dumps pellet from bottle
Language:	10 words (average); names pictures; identifies one or more parts of body
Social:	Feeds self; seeks help when in trouble; complains when wet or soiled; kisses parent with pucker

24 Months

Motor:	Runs well; walks up and down stairs, one step at a time; opens doors; climbs on furniture
Adaptive:	Tower of 6 cubes; circular scribbling; imitates horizontal stroke; folds paper once imitatively
Language:	Puts 3 words together (subject, verb, object)
Social:	Handles spoon well; often tells immediate experiences; helps to undress; listens to stories with pictures

30 Months

Motor:	Jumps
Adaptive:	Tower of 8 cubes; makes vertical and horizontal strokes, but generally will not join them to make a cross; imitates circular stroke; forming closed figure
Language:	Refers to self by pronoun "I"; knows full name
Social:	Helps put things away; pretends in play

36 Months

Motor:	Goes up stairs alternating feet; rides tricycle; stands momentarily on one foot
Adaptive:	Tower of 9 cubes; imitates construction of "bridge" of 3 cubes; copies a circle; imitates a cross
Language:	Knows age and sex; counts 3 objects correctly; repeats 3 numbers or a sentence of 6 syllables
Social:	Plays simple games (in "parallel" with other children); helps in dressing (unbuttons clothing and puts on shoes); washes

48 Months

Motor:	Hops on one foot; throws ball overhand; uses scissors to cut out pictures; climbs well
Adaptive:	Copies bridge from model; imitates construction of "gate" of 5 cubes; copies cross and square; draws a man with 2 to 4 parts besides head; names longer of 2 lines
Language:	Counts 4 pennies accurately; tells a story
Social:	Plays with several children with beginning of social interaction and role-playing; goes to toilet alone

TABLE 82.4

(*Continued*)

60 Months	
Motor:	Skips
Adaptive:	Draws triangle from copy; names heavier of 2 weights
Language:	Names 4 colors; repeats sentence of 10 syllables; counts 10 pennies correctly
Social:	Dresses and undresses; ask questions about meaning of words; domestic role-playing

Data are derived from those of Gesell, Shirley, Provence, Wolf, Bailey, and others. After 5 years the Stanford–Binet, Wechsler–Bellevue, and other scales offer the most precise estimates of developmental level. In order to have their greatest value, they should be administered only by an experienced and qualified person

pediatric group is shown in Table 82.5. This may well be useful for child and adolescent psychiatrists requiring a brief schema for developmental assessment.)

EXAMINATION OF THE SKIN

This includes the same features that were relevant for the infant and toddler. The common hemangiomata of the eyelids, occiput, and forehead have ordinarily disappeared by this age. Port wine stains, however, are permanent and will still be present.

Cyanosis is uncommon in this age except in the child who is known to have cyanotic congenital heart disease or severe pulmonary disease. Mongolian spots may still be obvious. Bruising is very common because of the increasing activity level and exploration that occur with this age group. During years 2 and 3, the child frequently falls or bumps into furniture, whereas by 5 years of age the child commonly acquires bruises and scrapes by falling from bicycles, playing with bat and ball, and other activities.

Jaundice is uncommon in this age group and indicates the need for assessment of liver function. The combination of pallor, bruising, and petechiae is very suggestive of leukemia or other neoplastic disease.

Pigmented nevi continue to develop at all ages, and some "birth marks" may appear during the preschool years. Café-au-lait spots are commonly identified at this age. These are flat, irregular, pigmented lesions; the presence of more than six, measuring more than 1.5 cm each, is highly suggestive of neurofibromatosis. The hypopigmented lesions of tuberous sclerosis may be identified during this period, as may the small bright-red or brownish nodules (known as adenoma sebaceum) in a butterfly distribution over the nose and cheeks, which are the most characteristic skin manifestation of tuberous sclerosis.

Rashes of the various infectious diseases of childhood are common at this age, for example, chicken pox, scarlet fever, or impetigo. Measles and rubella are now uncommon in North America because of widespread immunization. As the child moves into a larger environment and is exposed to more potential irritants, such as poison ivy, allergic rashes and contact dermatitis become increasingly common.

Once again, unusually placed bruises, bites, and burns should be assessed as possible indicators of physical abuse.

EXAMINATION OF THE EYES

This includes those features mentioned in the previous section. Strabismus is more commonly identified at this age, and with a cooperative child it may also be possible to examine the fundi if that seems clinically indicated.

EXAMINATION OF THE EARS

This is the same as that detailed previously. Otitis media is very common due to the frequency of respiratory infections. Many children in this age group may already have had pressure equalizing tubes put in place for recurrent otitis media or persistent effusions. These tubes will appear as round brightly colored plastic tubes in the lower posterior quadrant of the tympanic membrane. If a pressure equalizing tube has been extruded, it

TABLE 82.5

Name_____   Date of Birth_____

Developmental Screen

1 mo	2 mo	4 mo	6 mo	9 mo	12 mo	15 mo	18 mo	24 mo	30 mo	3 yr	4 yr	5 yr
Social smile	Coo	Localize voice	Babbles	Paired consonants	Mama, dada specific	Other words	Names body parts	Two words together	Names pictures in book	Three words together	Knows colors	Counts to 10
Head up	Chest up	°Rolls over	Sits	Pulls to stand	Cruises	Walks	Walks up steps with hand held	Kicks, throws ball	Jumps in place	Pedals broad jump	Hops one foot	Stands one foot
		Reaches	Transfers hand to hand	Looks for dropped toy	Pincer grasp	Uses cup	Tower of 3 cubes	Scribbles	Tower of 8 cubes	Draws O; potty trained	Draws +	Draws person with body prints name

x—if achieved   o—if not achieved; place age of attainment
°if infant sleeps in supine position this may not be achieved till 6 mo.

may be visible as a brightly colored, small, spool-shaped object often embedded in cerumen in the external auditory canal.

EXAMINATION OF THE MOUTH

This includes the same features that were mentioned earlier regarding hydration, color, etc. The full quota of deciduous teeth remain in place at this age, with the first shedding occurring at about age 6 or 7 years. Defects in the enamel may be noted, indicating prior nutritional deficiencies. Dental caries are an increasing problem for children of this age. Permanent orange discoloration of teeth due to tetracycline is very rare these days because the association of this antibiotic with permanent discoloration of the teeth during tooth formation is well known.

Examination of the throat will often reveal very prominent tonsils or posterior pharyngeal lymphoid tissue. This is usually the result of respiratory infections but is sometimes due to an active disease process, for example, streptococcal throat infection. If the tonsils appear actively infected (as indicated by redness and pus), the child should be examined by a pediatrician.

Usually a cleft palate would have been diagnosed at an earlier age. However, it is possible, unless examination has been careful, for a small cleft in the hard palate immediately behind the upper teeth to be missed.

EXAMINATION OF THE NECK

Thyroid enlargement is rare at this age but may be caused by goiter or thyroiditis. Graves disease is very uncommon prior to 15 years of age, but has been described as causing emotional disturbances and hyperactivity in younger children.

On palpating the neck of preschool children, the most common finding is enlarged lymph nodes, usually under the angle of the mandible or down the anterior border of the sternomastoid muscle. These small, mobile nodes are usually a reaction to viral respiratory infections and may persist for weeks or months.

EXAMINATION OF THE CHEST

This includes observation of the chest wall. Development of breast tissue (premature thelarche) is uncommon and, when present, should be referred to a pediatrician or endocrinologist for assessment.

During respiration, children of this age use their rib cage as well as their diaphragm and breath sounds are easily heard. Wheezing caused by narrowing of the small airways may be associated with viral illnesses or caused by allergic processes. Rales or rhonchi are caused by infections. Any abnormality in examination of the lungs should be assessed by a pediatrician.

Examination of the heart should include the heart rate which may vary from 80 to 130 beats/minute in the 2 year old and 75 to 115 in the 5 year old. Blood pressure should be measured in the arm, using a cuff that covers approximately ⅔ of the upper arm. A cuff that is too large will give a false low reading, and a cuff that is too small will give a false high reading. Blood pressure varies with the age of the child and is related to height and weight. Exercise, excitement, anxiety, or coughing can all raise the systolic pressure as much as 40 to 50 mm. The average blood pressure of a child of this age is about 95/60. Both first and second heart sounds are easily heard in this age group. The second sound is normally split during inspiration and closed with expiration. Significant murmurs (whether continuous, systolic, or diastolic) may be heard at this age and may be associated with a palpable thrill over the area of maximum intensity of the murmur. Many murmurs are not associated with significant cardiac abnormality and are referred to as functional, innocent, or benign murmurs. It is estimated that during routine, random examination, over 30% of children will have an innocent murmur. They are most frequently heard between 3 and 7 years of age. The murmur is brief, systolic, and musical. It may be intensified by fever, excitement, or exercise. It is suggested that any murmur should be referred to a pediatrician or cardiologist for assessment. Sinus arrhythmia is frequently obvious in this age group and is normal. Any other arrhythmia is probably abnormal and should be assessed by someone skilled in cardiac examination.

EXAMINATION OF THE ABDOMEN

In the preschool child the abdomen appears more thin and less protuberant than in the toddler. Umbilical hernias have usually resolved spontaneously, although those that were very large may still be visible. Liver and spleen are usually not palpable during this period, or are palpable only at the costal margin. Inguinal hernias may develop at any age, so an inguinal swelling should

prompt referral to a pediatrician or surgeon for assessment. Abnormal masses may sometimes be detected on random examination, for example, Wilms tumor.

EXAMINATION OF THE GENITOURINARY SYSTEM

In the male, examination of the penis is identical to that of the infant, although excessive pubic fat giving the appearance of a small penis is less common at this age. The testes should be descended bilaterally, but retractile testes are very common. Examining the child in the standing position may help in assessment. Hydroceles have ordinarily resolved by his age, so any swelling in the scrotum is suggestive of an inguinal hernia. Sudden severe pain, tenderness, and swelling of the testis may indicate torsion; this is an emergency and should be assessed as quickly as possible by a urologist.

Examination of the female external genitalia is the same as that described earlier, and the examiner should always be alert for signs of sexual abuse.

EXAMINATION OF THE LIMBS

This includes assessment of movement, coordination, tone, power, reflexes, and sensation. This will have been described in detail in the neurological assessment. Common concerns of parents for children of this age include flat feet and in-toeing, both of which are normal until 4 to 5 years of age. Sometimes a child will limp with no history of injury and vague complaints of pain. This needs to be assessed for a possible greenstick fracture or the irritable hip of transient synovitis. Limp associated with pain in the hip or knee must be assessed for Legg–Perthes disease, rheumatoid arthritis, or septic arthritis, although many will be found to be due to minor trauma or overuse.

Examination of the Grade School-Age Child (6–12)

The grade school years are a time of relatively steady growth, ending in the preadolescent growth spurt which occurs in girls at about age 10 years and in boys at age 12 years. The average weight gain per year is about 7 lb. and the increase in height is about 2 to 3 inches per year. Head circumference increases very slowly during this period from 51 cm to 53 to 54 cm, at which time the brain has virtually reached adult size. At this age, children are increasingly able to be independent of their parents, and this is reflected in the physical examination. Frequently they like to answer questions in the history taking and participate in the physical exam independent of their parent, although most prefer to have her in the room. The examiner can expect the child to cooperate with the physical exam, although some maneuvers such as examination of the throat are still dreaded by many children. Total undressing is often difficult for children at this age, as they are shy about their bodies, particularly as pubertal changes become apparent. It is preferable to allow them to keep their clothing on and just remove a segment at a time or examine the child under the cover of a gown or loose-fitting shirt. Engaging the child in conversation about sports, hobbies, school, or other interests often will help ease the embarrassment or shyness they are feeling during the physical exam.

GENERAL EXAMINATION

Having determined the child's position on the growth charts for height and weight, it is possible to see whether they are well nourished and large or small for their age. If previous measurements are available, linear growth can be followed. Head circumference growth charts are not generally available for this age group, and as long as there are no other abnormalities on examination of the head, just knowing the size of the normal head is usually adequate. Assessment as to the adequacy of nourishment is important. During the grade school years most children are relatively tall and lean with increasing development of muscle strength for the motor activities and sports in which these youngsters tend to be involved. Obesity is a common problem in North American children, and although it may have been identified at an earlier age, socially it becomes an increasing problem for these children. The child who appears underweight may merely be following family patterns of growth or may have some chronic,

underlying disease process. A series of measurements made over a period of months or years can be very helpful in assessing whether the child is just small but growing steadily or truly failing to thrive.

MENTAL STATUS

Most children in this age group are accustomed to functioning away from home and away from their parents; although they may be shy, they are usually able to converse and participate in the physical exam with no difficulty. A child of this age who still clings to the mother or whose mother is very overprotective and has difficulty letting the child function independently is outside the norm. Most children can converse about their school performance, although the clinician may need to question the parent directly about grades and attainments. Most children do not like to admit that they are doing poorly in school and, surprisingly, those on the honor roll are often equally reticent. Grade school children can carry on a conversation, particularly about topics in which they are interested. They can also answer questions about their general health and activities and are often more accurate than their parents. The child who has a developmental handicap will increasingly diverge from other children the same age, and deficits that were previously unnoticed may now become very obvious. The child with a short attention span or hyperactivity will also stand out in this age group, whereas in the preschool group it is usual for children to be very restless when confined to an exam room. Determination of mental functioning is ordinarily done by inquiring about the child's school performance and social skills.

MUSCULAR COORDINATION AND DEVELOPMENT

This can usually be assessed by inquiring into the child's participation in sports, gym, music lessons, etc. Fine motor skills can be quickly assessed by having the child write her name and address, and draw pictures. The way in which they hold the pen or pencil and their handwriting can also contribute to this assessment. A box of crayons for use while the clinician is talking to the parent can turn the paper covering the examination table into a work of art.

SKIN

The coloring of the child is usually determined by familial or racial factors. Assessment of hydration can be done by noting the moistness of the oral mucosa. The normal child will have no evidence of cyanosis either at rest or on exercise; if this is present, it should alert the examiner to an underlying problem with the cardiovascular or pulmonary systems. The clinician might check for digital clubbing in order to determine whether this is a long-standing problem.

Bruising in this age group is uncommon unless it is related to a specific trauma, and the child will usually be able to detail exactly how a bruise was obtained. A vague response or "I don't know" should alert the clinician to the possibility of parental abuse.

Anemia is not common in this age group but it can be detected in the conjunctivae or oral mucosa. A combination of pallor, bruising, and petechiae is highly suggestive of leukemia or other neoplastic disease.

Mongolian spots have ordinarily faded by this age, but some pale or faint residual spots may be noted on the buttocks or back. Most hemangiomata except port wine stains or very large strawberry lesions have faded by this age. Café-au-lait spots of size and number to suggest neurofibromatosis may be detected along with freckling in the axillae. Subcutaneous nodules along the course of the large peripheral nerves or cutaneous soft pedunculated tumors may appear in late childhood.

Oval or irregularly shaped hypopigmented macules on the skin of the arms, legs, and trunk may be noted for the first time at this age. Like adenoma sebaceum on the face, they are one of the skin lesions of tuberous sclerosis. Burns, bruises, or bites should raise a suspicion of physical abuse. It should be noted that the child will often be evasive about how these were incurred, in contrast to the ready explanation for the true accidental bruise. Rashes such as psoriasis may present at this age. Some infectious diseases, for example, chicken pox or scarlet fever, are common, as is contact dermatitis, for example, poison ivy.

A common disorder during school age is alopecia, or hair loss; this usually starts in a localized area and sometimes enlarges quite dramatically.

The most common cause is traction resulting from tight braiding, ponytails, or rubber bands. Circumscribed areas of alopecia may also develop in areas of the scalp infected by fungi, for example, tinea capitis. Alopecia secondary to radiation or drugs such as chemotherapeutic agents is usually diffuse and generalized. Trichotillomania (compulsive pulling or twisting of the hair resulting in breakage close to the scalp) may be denied by the child and parent, yet may be readily observed during history taking. Localized or widespread alopecia may result, sometimes even involving eyelashes or eyebrows.

EXAMINATION OF THE EYES

Hypertelorism is less evident at this age, although in certain families it may persist throughout life.

Epicanthal folds, which were a common finding in infancy and toddlers, are much less frequent at this age, and their appearance is likely due to race or to some chromosomal syndrome.

Nystagmus may be congenital or acquired. If of recent onset, it requires prompt and thorough evaluation because of the possibility that it indicates serious cerebral disease.

Strabismus usually appears prior to school age; however, accommodative esotropia sometimes presents in the early grade school years. Strabismus is usually tested for by observing the corneal light reflex while the child fixes on a small light source. The corneal reflex should be in the same position in each eye.

Redness of the eyelid margin is not uncommon in the school-age child. If localized, it may represent a hordeolum (stye); if diffuse, blepharitis.

Cataracts would ordinarily have been detected prior to school age but will present as a white retinal reflex. Visual acuity should be tested using the Snellen chart. At this age the clinician can check the iris more carefully for evidence of coloboma, Brushfield spots, general loss of color, or heterochromia as mentioned earlier. The pupils will ordinarily constrict rapidly to light and to accommodation.

Assessment of the range of movement of the extraocular muscles is easily achieved at this age. Palsy of any of the muscles indicates the need for further assessment. All cranial nerve palsies in children are highly suggestive of serious pathology such as intracranial tumor or other causes of increased intracranial pressure. But of note, benign sixth nerve palsy is a painless acquired palsy which resolves spontaneously; it usually develops 2 to 3 weeks after a nonspecific minor febrile illness.

Assessment of binocular function is done as mentioned above by assessing the corneal light reflex or by the cover, uncover, cross-cover test, where the eyes are observed for compensatory or adjustive refixation movement.

Examination of the fundi, though difficult with the younger child, should be attempted at this age, especially if there is complaint of headache or blurring of vision. Blurring of the disk margin, loss of spontaneous venous pulsation, and hemorrhages or exudates around the disc indicate papilledema secondary to increased intracranial pressure. The common causes of this in childhood are intracranial tumors, obstructive hydrocephalus, encephalopathies, and pseudotumor cerebri. Any suspicion of papilledema should be referred to a pediatrician or ophthalmologist for further assessment.

EARS

A hearing screen should be part of the general physical examination. As at earlier ages, abnormalities of shape, size, or position of the external ear should be noted. Examination of the tympanic membrane may reveal evidence of otitis media or serous effusion. Inflammation of the skin lining the external auditory canal (swimmer's ear) is not uncommon in this age group and should be suspected when manipulation of the pinna to insert the otoscope is unduly painful. It should be noted that scarring or perforation in the lower posterior quadrant of the tympanic membrane may persist for prolonged periods following extrusion of pressure equalizing tubes.

EXAMINATION OF THE MOUTH, TEETH, AND THROAT

Examination of the mouth for pallor or cyanosis of the mucosa and assessment of hydration should be carried out quickly because many children fear a tongue blade in the mouth.

The first permanent teeth, the 6-year molars, appear during the seventh year of life, followed shortly by the beginning of shedding of the decid-

uous teeth at a rate of about four teeth per year over the next 5 years. They are replaced by the permanent teeth.

Lymphatic tissues are at their height of development during the grade school years; accordingly the tonsils will frequently appear large compared with those of an adult but they are within the normal range for a child of this age. Similarly, small, mobile lymph nodes may be palpable at the angle of the jaw and down the anterior border of the sternomastoid muscle. They are usually reactive to the many respiratory infections that beset children of this age, and unless they are hard, matted together, or inflamed, they have no ominous significance.

EXAMINATION OF THE NECK

This should include palpation of the submandibular anterior and posterior borders of the sternomastoid and occipital area for lymphadenopathy. This will ordinarily be reactive and have no pathologic significance. Palpation of the thyroid gland is best undertaken from behind, asking the patient to swallow in order to identify the thyroid. Swelling of the thyroid may occur in either hyperthyroidism, endemic goiter, or most commonly in this age period, thyroiditis. Any enlargement of the thyroid should prompt evaluation by a pediatrician or endocrinologist.

EXAMINATION OF THE CHEST

This should begin with inspection, checking for supernumerary nipples, pectus excavatum, and symmetrical movement of the chest with respiration. The breath sounds are usually easily heard, but if necessary the child can be asked to breathe through the open mouth. The heart rate of children of this age gradually becomes slower, ranging from 75 to 115 in the 6 year old to 65 to 100 in the 12 year old. The blood pressure should be measured using a cuff of correct size, as described earlier. The systolic pressure will vary from 80 to 110 at 6 years of age to 95 to 130 at 12 years of age. The diastolic pressure varies from 50 to 80 at 6 years of age to 60 to 90 at 12 years of age. Exercise, anxiety, and excitement may all raise the systolic pressure in children; hence if hypertension appears to be present, serial measurements need

TABLE 82.6

Classification of Sex Maturity Stages in Boys

Stage	Pubic Hair	Penis	Testes
1	None	Preadolescent	Preadolescent
2	Scanty, long, slightly pigmented	Slight enlargement	Enlarged scrotum, pink texture altered
3	Darker, start to curl, small amount	Longer	Larger
4	Resembles adult type, but less in quantity; coarse, curly	Larger; glans and breadth increase in size	Larger; scrotum dark
5	Adult distribution, spread to medial surface of thighs	Adult size	Adult size

TABLE 82.7

Classification of Sex Maturity Stages in Girls

Stage	Pubic Hair	Breasts
1	Preadolescent	Preadolescent
2	Sparse, lightly pigmented, straight, medial border of labia	Breast and papilla elevated as small mound; areolar diameter increased
3	Darker, beginning to curl, increased amount	Breast and areola enlarged, no contour separation
4	Coarse, curly, abundant but amount is less than in adult	Areola and papilla form secondary mound
5	Adult feminine triangle, spread to medial surface of thighs	Mature; nipple projects, areola part of general breast contour

to be obtained. Heart sounds should be checked as described previously. Arrhythmia is uncommon at this age. Murmurs, whether systolic or diastolic, should be assessed by a pediatrician or cardiologist; many children will have an innocent murmur as described previously. Examination of the breasts should include an estimate of the Tanner staging (Tables 82.6 and 82.7). Some normal girls will have evident breast development as early as 8 or 9 years of age. They are usually of chubby build, and there is usually a family history of early puberty.

EXAMINATION OF THE ABDOMEN

The abdomen should be inspected for obvious masses, then palpated for tenderness, guarding,

rebound, nonvisible masses, and checked for liver or spleen enlargement. Umbilical hernias are uncommon at this age, having already resolved spontaneously or been repaired surgically. Inguinal hernias may present at any age, and any swelling in the inguinal area other than a small lymph node should be assessed by pediatrician or surgeon. The renal area and flank should be palpated for tenderness (which would suggest urinary tract infection, though this would be unlikely unless suggestive symptoms were also present).

EXAMINATION OF THE GENITOURINARY SYSTEM

In the male, the external genitalia at this age will ordinarily appear immature, with both testes descended into the scrotum. Relatively little change in the size of the penis, scrotum, and testes occurs until around age 12 when the testes start to increase in size along with early development of pubic hair. The anal area should be inspected for signs of sexual abuse.

Examination of the genitalia in the female will show little change from the preschool appearance until around age 10 to 11 years when pubic hair may start to develop. A breast bud behind the areola will commonly be noted at around the same time. Once again, inspection of the genital and anal area should include checking for findings suggestive of sexual abuse—tears, scarring, bruising, herpetic lesions, and/or purulent discharge.

EXAMINATION OF THE LIMBS

This includes inspection for bruising, pigmentation, asymmetry, or swelling. Cysts around the knee joints are not uncommon and, being painless, are seldom noted unless looked for. Assessment regarding muscle tone and power should be carried out, and each joint should be tested for range of motion. Reflexes at the elbow, wrist, knee, and ankle are readily obtained. Minor infections—paronychia, ingrown toenail and rash—are not uncommon at this age. Many children have complaints of pain in the legs, usually around a joint and usually related to the overuse syndromes brought on by vigorous activity or participation in sports. "Growing pains" in the legs are felt at night by a child who is active and painfree during the day. More serious diseases of the joints—Legg-Perthes disease or arthritis—are associated with pain and limitation of movement, often observable as a limp or refusal to bear weight. Sprains and even fractures are not uncommon in this age group, reflecting the child's increased strength, power, and participation in more rigorous exercises or games. Examination of the spine should be carried out with the child standing erect with feet together, viewed first from the rear, checking for symmetry of shoulders, scapulae, and hips, then from the side to check for abnormal curvature, and finally from the rear with the child bending forward, checking for asymmetry of the paraspinal muscles.

Examination of the Adolescent

At the doctor's office, the adolescent usually functions independently of the parent. The adolescent can often give a very good history and usually prefers to have the physical examination done without the parent being present. However, some younger adolescents may like to have the moral support of a parent in the room. If the adolescent elects to be examined without the parent present, it is prudent to have a nurse present when examining those areas of the body normally covered by clothing, in particular, the chest and breasts in girls and the abdomen and genital area in both sexes. One should treat the adolescent with the courtesy and respect shown an adult patient, discussing areas of concern to the patient and showing flexibility when necessary rather than attempting to overwhelm the teenager with the authority of the doctor. Once again, if the doctor has found areas of interest to the patient during the history, it is helpful to discuss these during the examination in order to distract and relax the patient.

The teenager's height, weight, and blood pressure should be recorded at the beginning of the physical examination along with the relevant percentiles from the appropriate growth chart. The growth spurt, which may begin at about 10 years of age in girls and about 12 years in boys, is variable in onset, so that teenagers of the same chronologic age show a wide divergence in physical development and maturation. This often follows a family pattern, so that if the child appears to be earlier or later in development than might be expected, it is helpful to check with the parents as to when they themselves or the patient's siblings had their growth spurt and pubertal development. Girls who go through puberty early, culminating in early menarche, tend to have much greater growth velocity occurring over a shorter period of time and are likely to have a higher weight-to-height ratio in adult life than do girls who mature more slowly.

Accompanying the growth spurt are the signs of sexual maturation. Physical changes in adolescents follow a definite sequence, though the onset, velocity, and age at completion vary greatly. The growth spurt begins in boys at between 13 and 15½ years; in girls the growth spurt begins at around 11½ years and is finished by 13½ years. Following the spurt, height growth decelerates and by 18 years is virtually complete. In both sexes, lengthening of legs is followed by widening of the shoulders and growth in the length of the trunk. In girls, muscular strength normally increases until the time of menarche, whereas in boys it continues to increase for about 18 months after the year of most rapid growth.

Sexual maturity ratings are part of the physical exam of an adolescent. These scales assess the changes of the breasts and the pattern and amount of pubic hair in girls, and the size and appearance of the penis, testes, and scrotum, plus the amount and pattern of pubic hair in boys. Sex maturity ratings range from stage 1 to 5, with a score of 1 representing the prepubertal child and 5 representing adult status. The Tanner scale is widely used for assessment of sex maturity in both sexes (Tables 82.6 and 82.7). Usually genitalia and pubic hair in boys and breast development and pubic hair in girls are rated separately. If the two ratings differ, they are averaged. If there is significant pubertal delay, it may be necessary to have an endocrine evaluation. However, the great majority of adolescents with delayed onset of puberty have merely a constitutional or genetically determined delay.

ASSESSMENT OF NUTRITION

In an age group where anorexia nervosa has a relatively high incidence, it is important to assess nutrition. Obesity is another common disturbance of nutrition and warrants evaluation of caloric intake and physical activity. If these appear to be age appropriate, further consultation is desirable, particularly if the obesity is combined with delayed sexual maturation.

MENTAL STATUS

The average adolescent will appear mentally alert and can participate fully in the interview and physical examination. Inquiry about school performance will indicate any significant lags in mental capacity or learning disabilities. Assessment of affect and mood is an integral part of the physical exam but is discussed in detail elsewhere.

EXAMINATION OF THE SKIN

This should include assessment of those items previously mentioned in other age groups. In addition acne is a common problem for adolescents and often impacts significantly on the teenager's self-esteem and socialization. The appearance of facial hair, though desirable for boys, may cause great distress for adolescent girls. If present to a significant degree, it warrants further consultation, as does excessive hirsutism of the remainder of the body. Infectious rashes are less common at this age, except for fungal diseases. These, however, are very common due to increased sweating and participation in strenuous activity. Folliculitis of legs or axillae is common in teenage girls who shave these areas.

EXAMINATION OF THE HAIR

This includes inspection of hair and scalp. Fine, thin hair, especially if combined with sparse eyebrows may be suggestive of hypothyroidism. Alopecia may be present at this age as mentioned in the school-age section. Fungal infections of the scalp are not uncommon and seborrhea (or dandruff) is very common.

EXAMINATION OF THE EYES

This includes all aspects previously detailed. Abnormalities of refraction and accommodation are not uncommon, and myopia has a tendency to increase during adolescence. Visual acuity is easily measured by the standard Snellen chart. At this age it is usually possible to examine the fundi without dilation of the pupils.

EXAMINATION OF THE EARS

Inspection of size and shape should be carried out along with assessment of the tympanic membrane and external auditory canal as mentioned for grade school children.

EXAMINATION OF THE MOUTH

The mouth, oral mucosa, and teeth should be inspected. The deciduous secondary molars are usually shed between 10 and 13 years and the eruption of the second permanent molars occurs between 12 and 13 years. The third molars, or wisdom teeth, usually appear (often with problems) toward the end of adolescence. Examination of the throat will reveal that the tonsils have usually shrunk and approach adult size.

EXAMINATION OF THE NECK

This should include assessment of lymph nodes and the thyroid gland. An enlarged thyroid, particularly in girls, may occur during early adolescence. Thyroid function should be assessed by appropriate laboratory tests.

EXAMINATION OF THE CHEST

This includes assessment of the lungs, which should be clinically clear with symmetrical breath sounds in all areas.

The heart rate during adolescence varies from 55 to 100 beats/minute. The systolic blood pressure varies between 90 and 130 and the diastolic pressure between 55 and 80. As with the school-age child, any elevation of blood pressure should be evaluated in serial fashion over time, as anxiety or exercise can increase the systolic pressure quite markedly. The heart sounds are usually easily heard. Murmurs are relatively less common than in the younger age groups.

Assessment of the breasts should be done at this stage of the examination. Gynecomastia of varying degrees occurs in approximately ⅔ of boys during early puberty. It may involve only one breast, both breasts, or one after the other. It usually regresses spontaneously over a period of months. Gynecomastia also occurs in Klinefelter syndrome and with other types of testicular failure or hormonal problems. In girls, assessment of the breasts is part of the Tanner or sexual maturity rating. Occasionally a lump will be felt in the breast; the majority are cysts or benign fibroadenomas that vary in size throughout the menstrual cycle. If the lump does not disappear, referral to a surgeon for assessment is appropriate. Symmetrical enlargement of the breasts with development of the nipple and venous dilation may be an early sign of pregnancy.

EXAMINATION OF THE ABDOMEN

As for previous age groups, this includes inspection then palpation for tenderness, guarding, rebound, and masses; for example, in girls, the pregnant uterus, and in either sex, hernias.

EXAMINATION OF THE GENITOURINARY SYSTEM

This includes inspection for sexual maturity rating and for the skin and mucosal lesions of sexually transmitted disease, particularly herpes. In the sexually active female, the presence of vaginal discharge should be checked for and, if present, an appropriate pelvic exam performed and cultures taken. Inspection of the anus and perianal area should be made for evidence of sexual abuse, particularly in the younger teenager. In addition, the buttock crease should be inspected for evidence of cysts or abscess, for example, pilonidal.

EXAMINATION OF THE LIMBS

This includes inspection for evidence of wasting, such as one might see in anorexia nervosa, or atrophy of muscle groups or hypertrophy of calf muscles as might be seen in muscular dystrophy. Assessment of tone, power, and reflexes should be carried out as described previously.

Pain and swelling in joints is common during this age of rapid growth, especially when combined with vigorous participation in sports. The tender enlargement of the anterior tibial tubercle in Osgood–Schlatters disease is very common, especially in the younger adolescent male. (Pain in the knee associated with limp may be the presenting sign of slipped femoral epiphysis, especially in the obese boy.) Minor trauma, such as sprains, and more serious traumatic events, such as torn ligaments or menisci in the knee joint, are not infrequent.

The examination may be completed with observation of the spine for asymmetry of the paraspinal muscles, symmetry of the scapulae or hips, and, on forward bending, assessment for a paraspinal hump. These findings are evidence of scoliosis, which is common in minor degrees, and can sometimes be rapidly progressive during the period of rapid adolescent growth. Significant asymmetry indicates a need for evaluation by a pediatrician or orthopedic surgeon.

Conclusion

This chapter is written for child and adolescent psychiatrists who are increasingly called on to perform aspects of the physical examination of infants, children, and adolescents. Although this is in some ways a new departure for the field, it is nonetheless necessary and important. This mode of practice reflects our growing interdependence with the general field of medicine. Child and adolescent psychiatrists are physicians, and many will enjoy this partial return to their primary identity.

REFERENCES

Bayley, N. (1969). *Manual for the Bayley Scales of Infant Development.* New York: Psychological Corporation.

Behrman, R. E., Kliegman, R. M., & Arvin, A. M. (1996). In *Nelson Textbook of Pediatrics,* R. D. Needlman, (Ed.) 15th ed., Philadelphia: W. B. Saunders, pp. 30–72.

Levine, M. D., Carey, W. B., Crocker, A. C., & Gross, R. T. (1983). *Developmental-Behavioral Pediatrics.* Philadelphia: W. B. Saunders. pp. 89–91.

Tanner, J. M. (1962). *Growth at Adolescence,* 2nd ed. Oxford, England: Blackwell Scientific Publications.

83 / **Neurological Examination**

Joel D. Bregman

Neurological disorders that arise during childhood frequently present with changes in affect, behavior, and thought process. When such symptoms develop, referrals for psychiatric evaluation are often made. Accordingly, child and adolescent psychiatrists should be familiar with the principles of neurological assessment, and during the course of their evaluations should consider potential neurological factors which may underlie the development of psychiatric symptoms in their patients.

Referral for a formal neurological examination should be considered in the following situations (Touwen, 1987, 1979):

- When the signs or symptoms are indicative of a neurological disease (abnormalities of gait, focal weakness, diplopia, severe headaches, etc.). Note: the indications for neurological referral would be stronger in the presence of a positive family history of neurological disease (e.g., movement disorders such as Huntington's disease, muscle diseases, migraines, etc.);

- When the assessment of an identified neurological disorder would help to clarify factors that affect prognosis and treatment;
- When a systemic illness has been diagnosed which is known to have neurological manifestations (e.g., collagen-vascular disease, leukemia, etc.); and
- When there is an acute onset of serious learning or behavioral problems that cannot be explained by psychosocial factors alone.

Neurologic referrals also should be considered when the pattern of presenting psychiatric symptoms is suggestive of a primary neurological condition. For example, paroxysmal neurological disorders (e.g., seizures, migraines, and syncopal episodes) are often associated with affective and behavioral symptoms (Fenichel, 1993; Wallace, 1988). Complex partial seizures can include stereotyped mannerisms, dissociative features (e.g., depersonalization, deja vu sensations), and perceptual distortions (e.g., illusions, hallucinations). Benign occipital epilepsy is characterized by visual illusions and hallucinations in conjunction with restrictions in visual acuity and visual fields. Migraines can present with unusual visual and sensory symptoms which may be mistaken for somatoform disorders. In view of this, psychiatrists should consider potential neurological factors in their etiological formulations of psychiatric symptom clusters and refer for more extensive examinations when indicated.

History

A careful and complete history will help to organize and focus the neurological study. A thorough history is particularly important in the evaluation of complex or chronic neurological symptoms, and should include developmental, medical, psychosocial, family, and educational histories. In eliciting the present history, special attention should be paid to several aspects of the symptom pattern: onset, progression, and localization (Huttenlocher, 1987; Swaiman, 1989). The onset of symptoms can be acute, subacute, or gradual. An acute onset suggests a vascular or traumatic etiology; a subacute onset suggests a toxic, electrolytic, or infectious etiology; and a gradual or insidious onset suggests a degenerative, neoplastic, or inborn metabolic etiology. Once manifest, symptoms can remain static (and allow for ongoing functional development) or become progressive (and result in losses of previously acquired abilities). A static neurological condition is suggestive of a congenital malformation or perinatal lesion, whereas a progressive disability is suggestive of a degenerative, neoplastic, or chronic infectious disease (uncompensated hydrocephalus also leads to progressive impairment). Some neurological diseases proceed in a pattern characterized by exacerbations and partial remissions (e.g., demyelinating diseases), whereas others exhibit a paroxysmal pattern (e.g., seizure disorders, migraines). Determination of the breadth of the symptom pattern can help to guide etiological diagnosis. Circumscribed symptom patterns suggest focal neurological conditions. For example, isolated symptoms such as uncharacteristic clumsiness or unsteadiness of gait suggest motor system dysfunction. Focal conditions are often caused by vascular, neoplastic, or traumatic insults, while generalized or multifocal conditions are often caused by metabolic, toxic, or degenerative processes.

Neurological Examination

GENERAL PRINCIPLES

The childhood neurological examination is a dynamic process, since the nervous system in childhood is in a state of rapid development. During the growth years, some neurological phenomena arise, others disappear, while still others undergo qualitative change. An appreciation for these features is important in differentiating structural and functional abnormalities from normal developmental changes and maturational delays.

A systematic, yet flexible approach to the neurological exam is necessary. The examination should be based on reliable and objective measures that assess all major areas of neurological functioning. Since accurate assessment depends on cooperation and compliance from the patient, the exam should proceed in a nonthreatening, gentle manner. For younger children, the presence of a parent or guardian often is essential. The exam should be conducted in stages, beginning with general observations of motor, communicative, and social behavior, followed by items requiring responses or maneuvers from the child, and concluding with the more intrusive procedures (e.g., examination of the eyes, mouth, etc.). Touwen (1979) suggests the following order of examination:

1. In the sitting position, assessment of spontaneous motility and posture, visual tracking, motor functioning (strength, tone, range of movement), and reflexes.
2. In the standing position, assessment of posture, balance, motility, coordination, and observation for the presence of involuntary movements.
3. While walking, assessment of gait and elicited motor movements (walking on tiptoes, heels, hopping, etc.).
4. While standing and undressed, examination of the skin, and testing of abdominal and cremasteric reflexes.

5. In the lying position, examination of the spine, extremities, and joints.
6. In any position, examination of the head (eyes, ears, mouth, and cranial nerve functioning).

In order to maintain the cooperation of younger children, it is often necessary to modify the sequence of examination items. Such flexibility on the part of the examiner enhances the reliability of the examination. However, at the conclusion of the assessment, the examiner should organize the findings in a systematic manner.

The following sections review the broad categories of the neurological examination. The mental status examination (which includes assessment of speech and language functioning, cognition, orientation, etc.) is covered in detail in other chapters and will not be discussed here.

GENERAL OBSERVATIONS

The exam should begin with careful observation and measurement of the child's head shape and position, anthropomorphic features (weight, stature, head circumference), skin, and musculoskeletal characteristics. The skull should be examined for abnormalities in contour (De Vivo, 1991). For example, a narrow anteroposterior contour may reflect scaphocephaly (premature closure of sagittal suture), and a broad biparietal contour may reflect brachycephaly (premature closure of the coronal suture). The position of the head should also be noted. A head tilt may reflect an abnormality of contralateral superior oblique muscle function (cranial nerve IV) or of vestibulocerebellar function (posterior fossa).

Occipital-frontal head circumference (OFC) measurements are relatively accurate in reflecting cranial volume, although they are affected to some degree by head shape and skull thickness (Fenichel, 1993). Microcephaly is defined as OFC < 2 standard deviations (SD) below the mean for age. Primary microcephaly (inadequate brain development) is caused by a genetic or chromosomal abnormality or a malformation syndrome. Neuroimaging reveals either a normal-appearing brain or one with a characteristic malformation pattern. Secondary microcephaly is abnormal brain growth caused by a disease process, such as a congenital infection, perinatal brain injury, or postnatal dis-

ease. Neuroimaging reveals a variety of abnormalities, such as ventricular enlargement, porencephaly, calcifications, etc. Macrocephaly is defined as OFC ≥ 2 SD above the mean for age. It may be caused by hydrocephalus, intracranial hemorrhage, thickening of the skull, or by an enlargement of the brain itself (megalencephaly). Megalencephaly may be due to abnormal accumulation of a metabolic substance (inborn error of metabolism), tumors (neurocutaneous disorder), or an increase in brain tissue. The latter can represent a normal familial variant, result from a neurological disorder, or if associated with large stature, reflect pituitary or cerebral giantism (Sotos syndrome). Sotos syndrome is usually sporadic and is associated with cognitive impairment (learning disability or mental retardation).

Examination of the skin is very important, since a number of congenital neurological disorders (e.g., neurocutaneous syndromes) present with cutaneous manifestations, such as hyperpigmentation, depigmented nevi (ash leaf), café-au-lait spots, fibromas, telangiectasis, etc. Examination of the hair and nails is also important.

Integrity of the musculoskeletal system should be assessed by examining for limb asymmetries, kyphosis, scoliosis, and lower extremity abnormalities [e.g., pes planus (flat feet), genu valgum (knock-knee), genu varum (bowleg), and clubfoot deformities].

THE MOTOR EXAMINATION

There are two major components of the motor system (Huttenlocher, 1987). The pyramidal system originates in the motor cortex, where the cell bodies of the upper motor neurons (UMN) lie. The UMNs traverse the internal capsule and brainstem (crossing over in the medulla) and synapse in the spinal cord with the anterior horn cells (lower motor neurons, LMN), which then innervate the muscles. The other major component of the motor system is the extrapyramidal system, which includes the basal ganglia and the cerebellum. The pyramidal system largely controls voluntary motor activities, and suppresses involuntary, reflexive movements. The extrapyramidal system controls repetitive motor behaviors and influences the coordination of movement. Lesions of the UMNs of the pyramidal system lead to disruption of voluntary movement (and a release of inhibi-

TABLE 83.1

Rating of Muscle Strength

Rating	Criteria
0	No movement
1	Trace movement not against gravity
2	Active movement but not against gravity
3	Active movement against gravity
4	Active movement against resistance
5	Normal strength against resistance

tory influences on reflexes and involuntary movements); whereas, lesions of the LMNs interrupt both voluntary and involuntary movements.

Examination of the motor system includes assessment of muscle strength, tone and mass, spontaneous and involuntary movements, fine and gross motor coordination, and posture and locomotion.

Muscle Strength: The strength of proximal/distal and flexor/extensor muscle groups should be tested. Arm and shoulder strength can be tested most easily by having the patient lean against the wall, with support from the palms. Alternatively, the child can be lifted by supporting her under her arms. Strength of the back, hips, and proximal leg muscles can be assessed by asking the patient to arise from a supine position. The gastrocnemius and soleus muscles can be tested while the patient walks on toes, and the tibialis anterior muscle can be assessed while the patient walks on heels. Ratings are typically based on a five-point scale (Table 83.1).

Generalized weakness can result from systemic illnesses, malnutrition, or metabolic disturbances. Muscle weakness (particularly weakness of the proximal flexors) may be due to intrinsic muscle disease, such as progressive dystrophy or inflammatory disorders (e.g., polymyositis, dermatomyositis) (Swaiman, 1989). Weakness of neuromuscular origin can be of central (UMN) or peripheral (LMN) etiology. UMN lesions typically result in weakness of the extensors of the upper limbs and the flexors of the lower limbs. Peripheral nerve lesions often lead to distal weakness (Huttenlocher, 1987).

Muscle Tone and Mass: Muscle tone refers to resistance to passive movement. This can be tested by having the patient extend his arms in a supinated position. Decreased tone (hypotonia) is likely if there is a subsequent downward and inward drift of the arms. Hypotonia may be secondary to cerebellar or LMN disorders. Rigidity may be due to lesions of the basal ganglia, and spasticity (clasp-knife pattern) to lesions of the corticospinal tract (UMN) (Huttenlocher, 1987; Swaiman, 1987). Muscle mass or bulk is assessed by palpation. Muscles and nerves should be examined for tenderness and/or hypertrophy. Myotonia can be assessed by tapping on the deltoid muscle and the thenar eminence. Muscle atrophy with fasciculations suggests anterior horn cell disease. Pseudohypertrophy with weakness (most obvious in the gastrocnemius and deltoid muscle groups) may be secondary to muscular dystrophy or storage diseases.

Spontaneous and Involuntary Movements: In both the sitting and standing positions, the child should be observed for spontaneous and involuntary movements (Fenichel, 1993; Huttenlocher, 1987; Touwen, 1979). The level of activity and the quality (e.g., smoothness, speed) of spontaneous motility should be assessed. Careful observations should be made for the presence of involuntary movements (Table 83.2). Involuntary movements often become more pronounced when the patient stands with feet together, arms extended, fingers spread apart, eyes closed, and tongue protruded. Choreiform movements can be intensified by asking the patient to raise her hands above her head or tightly grip the examiner's fingers.

Posture and Gait: Muscle tone, cerebellar and proprioceptive functioning, and skeletal integrity contribute to posture and locomotion (Huttenlocher, 1987; Swaiman, 1989; Touwen, 1979). The patient should be observed for the symmetry of shoulders, back, and pelvis, and examined for the presence of hemisyndromes (hemihypertrophy, hemiparesis, lateralized hyper- or hypotonia, etc.), head tilt, and skeletal abnormalities.

The child's gait should be observed for width of base, arm swing, and symmetry. It is often useful to observe the child during routine walking and running, toe walking, heel walking, and tandem walking. There are several pathological types of gait, including a spastic gait (UMN lesion), an

TABLE 83.2

Abnormal Involuntary Movements

Movement°	Description and General Clinical Correlates
Tremor	Rapid, rhythmic, regular, oscillatory movements, usually manifest in the distal extremities Coarse tremor: benign hereditary trait Fine tremor: hyperthyroidism, anxiety Intention tremor: cerebellar dysfunction Proximal tremor: Wilson's disease
Chorea	Irregular, jerky, arrhythmic, nonstereotyped movements (choreiform movements are less pronounced and usually of lesser clinical significance); present in basal ganglia disease
Athetosis	Slow, writhing, continuous, irregular, arrhythmic movements; usually occurs with chorea as choreoathetoid movements, particularly if secondary to perinatal injury; present in striatal and basal ganglia disease
Ballismus	Abrupt, vigorous flinging of a limb from shoulder or pelvis; in children, usually associated with chorea
Myoclonus	Rhythmic, rapid jerking movements in a focal, multifocal, or generalized distribution; random, intermittent, and cannot be suppressed
Fasciculations	Irregular, coarse, twitching movements, representing contraction of entire motor units; occur in lower motor neuron diseases
Fibrillations	Vermicular movements whch are difficult to visualize (except in the tongue), secondary to contraction if individual muscle fibers; present in diseases which involve denervation of the muscle

°*Tics, dyskinesia, and dystonia are discussed in other chapters.*

ataxic gait (cerebellar dysfunction), a waddling gait (pelvic girdle weakness), and a steppage gait (secondary to peripheral neuropathy, with exaggerated elevation of the knee and a slapping down of the foot) (Swaiman, 1989). A narrow gait may be due to hypertonicity of the adductor muscles of the leg, while a wide gait may be secondary to cerebellar or sensory disorders, hypotonicity of pelvic or leg muscles, or an orthopedic problem (e.g., subluxation of the hips).

Fine and Gross Motor Coordination: Both fine and gross motor coordination involve an intricate interplay of corticospinal, cerebellar, and sensory proprioceptive functioning. Coordination can be assessed by observing the child while walking, running, manipulating toys and other objects, and during the performance of particular stress maneuvers, such as diadochokinesis (rapidly alternating movements, such as rapid pronation and supination of the forearm), the knee-heel test, the finger-to-nose test, and the follow-a-finger test (Touwen, 1979). The Romberg maneuver (standing with eyes closed for 15 to 20 seconds) is useful

for assessing vestibular and cerebellar integrity. During this and other coordination maneuvers, observations should be made for the presence of ataxia, a sign of cerebellar dysfunction. Ataxia with consistent falling to one side is indicative of a cerebellar hemisphere lesion, whereas ataxia with falling to either side is indicative of a midline cerebellar vermis lesion (Huttenlocher, 1987). An acute onset suggests an infectious or inflammatory etiology, while a gradual onset suggests a degenerative or neoplastic etiology. Intermittent ataxia is often secondary to a metabolic derangement (De Vivo, 1991).

EXAMINATION OF REFLEXES

The deep tendon reflexes (DTRs) reflect the functional integrity of the corticospinal tract (Table 83.3). In young children the briskness of the reflexes varies considerably, and therefore the range of normal is quite broad. Many healthy young children have brisk reflexes bilaterally (Touwen, 1979). However, pathology is likely if

TABLE 83.3

Innervation Pattern for Deep Tendon Reflexes (DTR) and Skin Reflexes

DTR	Innervation
Jaw jerk	Cervical nerve V (Trigeminal N.)
Biceps	Cervical nerves V–VI
Triceps	Cervical nerves VI–VIII
Patellar	Lumbar nerves II–IV
Achilles	Sacral nerves I–II

Skin Reflexes	Innervation
Abdominal	Thoracic VII–Lumbar I
Cremasteric	Lumbar nerves I–II

neurological abnormalities are also present. For example, if the clinical presentation includes brisk reflexes, problems swallowing, impaired speech, and affective lability (e.g., inappropriate laughter, crying), corticobulbar disease should be suspected (e.g., pseudobulbar palsy). This condition can occur in conjunction with spastic cerebral palsy (Huttenlocher, 1987).

In assessing the reflexes of children, particular attention should be paid to the symmetry of responses. For example, unilateral hyperreflexia often indicates corticospinal tract dysfunction, particularly if lateralized abnormalities of tone and strength are present. Other positive findings have a pathological significance similar to that found in adolescents and adults. For example, hyporeflexia may reflect LMN involvement (e.g., anterior horn cell disorders). In addition, abnormal distal reflexes which occur in conjunction with sensory abnormalities suggest the presence of a peripheral neuropathy. DTRs can remain relatively preserved, however, in the early stages of a myopathy (e.g., muscular dystrophy).

In children, the DTRs are examined in a manner similar to that used for adolescents and adults. However, in young children, the examiner may need to place one or two fingers over the child's tendon before tapping with a reflex hammer. The plantar response is also conducted in a different manner. The lateral aspect of the sole is scratched from toes to heel, rather than from heel to toes, since the latter maneuver would serve as a stimulus for the grasp reflex (Touwen, 1979). After the age of 4 or 5, dorsiflexion is usually abnormal, especially if it is asymmetrical and associated with other lateralizing signs. Another sign of corticospinal tract involvement is a pathological Hoffman reflex. This reflex is elicited by flicking the second or third fingernail downward. Brisk or asymmetrical flexion of the distal phalanx of the thumb constitutes an abnormal response.

The threshold of response for reflexes should be recorded and based on the intensity of the examiner's tapping stimulus. Although the range of normal is quite broad in young children, an exceptionally high threshold may reflect disease of the UMN, whereas an exceptionally low threshold may reflect disease of the LMN, peripheral nerve, or muscle. In addition, the presence of sustained clonus should be noted, since this is a sign of abnormal hyperreflexia.

Skin reflexes should be elicited. The abdominal reflexes are tested during the latter stages of the examination by scratching the abdomen laterally toward the midline, just below the umbilicus. Contraction of the abdominal muscles should follow. The cremasteric reflex is elicited by scratching the inner thigh in a downward direction. Elevation of the testis results.

EXAMINATION OF THE SENSORY SYSTEM

The sensory examination is more difficult to conduct in children than it is in adults, since several aspects of the assessment require a degree of understanding and cooperation beyond the capability of younger children. The more objective and reliable parts of the exam include sensory functions which involve motor movement, such as oculomotor and pupillary responses, nystagmus, pain perception, and proprioception. Other sensory tests include light touch, two-point discrimination, and posterior column functions (e.g., vibratory sense, joint position). Several cortical sensory functions (predominantly parietal lobe) include graphesthesia (recognition of numbers, letters, or other symbols traced on the palm), and stereognosis (the tactile identification of common objects placed in the hand).

EXAMINATION OF CRANIAL NERVE FUNCTION

Cranial nerve (CN) function is assessed in the standard manner (Swaiman, 1989; Touwen, 1979).

Olfactory Nerve (CN I): The olfactory nerve is rarely impaired in children. It is tested by presenting several pleasant aromas to each nostril, such as chocolate, vanilla, peppermint, etc. Younger children may not be precise in their identifications, but they should be able to discriminate among the different aromas. Lack of smell (anosmia) can be secondary to Kallmann syndrome, neoplasms, or head trauma. Unilateral anosmia is of most concern.

Optic Nerve (CN II): Visual acuity is tested using the Snellen letter charts, or the E chart with older children. With younger children, shape and color identification and letter matching can be used. Visual fields are tested by asking the child to fixate on a small object held 15 to 18 inches ahead and to identify or grasp a moving object as soon as it enters her visual field from a lateral position. The object should be moved in a temporal to nasal direction. Normal visual fields include an angle of approximately 60 to 80 degrees laterally and 45 degrees upward. Visual field defects are more sensitive indicators of increased intracranial pressure and papilledema than are abnormalities of visual acuity.

Homonymous hemianopsia is one of the most common visual field defects in children and is usually caused by an optic chiasm tumor. Bitemporal hemianopsia is often caused by a craniopharyngioma. The pupils should be examined for size, contour, and responsiveness. A reduced or absent pupillary response suggests the presence of a lesion between the retina and the lateral geniculate body. The absence of a direct light response in the presence of a preserved consensual response of the other eye is referred to as a Marcus Gunn pupil. The fundoscopic examination should be reserved for the end of the examination and should include observation for signs of optic nerve atrophy, papilledema, abnormal pigment, etc.

Oculomotor, Trochlear, and Abducens Nerves (CN III, IV, VI): CN III, IV, and VI innervate the extraocular muscles which are responsible for eye movements. The innervation patterns and functions of the muscles that control eye movements are detailed in Table 83.4. The child is asked to track a small object visually; the object is moved in all planes by the examiner while the child's head is stabilized. During these visual pursuit maneuvers, the range and quality of the eye movements are evaluated. The eyes should move in a conjugate and smooth fashion in all planes. Heterotropia is present when eye deviation occurs during binocular vision (esotropia for adduction or convergence, and exotropia for abduction or divergence). Diplopia results in older children and adolescents. It is rare in young children because of cortical suppression of one of the images (Touwen, 1979). Heterophoria is present when eye deviation occurs while one eye is covered and the other is fixating (esophoria for convergence and exophoria for divergence).

The eyes should be observed for convergence and accompanying pupillary contraction, a test of lens accommodation. Lesions of the nucleus of CN III or of the ciliary ganglion result in internal ophthalmoplegia (a dilated pupil, unreactive to light, and accommodation in the presence of preserved EOMs (extra-ocular movements) when the eyes are tested separately) (Swaiman, 1989).

Dysfunction of extraocular eye movements may be caused by a brainstem tumor, myopathy, myasthenia gravis, ophthalmoplegic migraine, or cavernous sinus thrombosis (Swaiman, 1989). Lesions of the midbrain or pons (e.g., demyelinating disorders, vascular disease, etc.) may cause disruption of the medial longitudinal fasciculus, resulting in internuclear ophthalmoplegia (weaknesses of the medial rectus muscle, with nystagmus and absence of abduction) (Swaiman, 1989).

The quality of eye movements should be noted and the presence of nystagmus, choreiform, or ataxic movements should be recorded. Nystagmus is an oscillatory movement of the eyes with an involuntary drift and a jerky compensatory component. Vertical nystagmus is usually secondary to medication (e.g., barbiturates, carbamazepine, phenytoin) or brainstem dysfunction. Horizontal nystagmus is usually of cerebellar or brainstem origin. Nystagmus of labyrinthine etiology has a rotatory component and changes with head position.

Trigeminal Nerve (CN V): The trigeminal nerve has two components, a motor component, which innervates the muscles of mastication (and can be tested with the jaw jerk reflex), and a sensory component, which innervates the face and the anterior

TABLE 83.4

Innervation and Function of the Extraocular Muscles

Muscle	Innervation	Function	Paralysis
Medial rectus	CN III, Oculomotor	Moves eyes medially	Paralysis of CN III results in lateral and somewhat downward deviation of the affected eye at rest, poor adduction, ptosis (secondary to paralysis of the levator palpebra superioris mm.), and a large pupil which responds sluggishly to light
Inferior rectus	CN III, Oculomotor	Moves eyes downward and slightly outward (depresses globe when eye is abducted)	
Superior rectus	CN III, Oculomotor	Moves eyes upward and slightly outward (elevates globe when eye is abducted)	
Inferior oblique	CN III, Oculomotor	Moves eyes upward and slightly inward (elevates globe when eye is adducted)	
Superior oblique	CN IV, Trochlear	Moves eyes downward and slightly inward (depresses globe when eye is adducted)	Paralysis of CN IV results in no change or slight upward and outward deviation at rest, and a failure of downward gaze when the eye is adducted; a head tilt may occur toward the opposite shoulder
Lateral rectus	CN VI, Abducens	Moves eyes laterally	Paralysis of CN VI results in medial deviation at rest, failure of abduction, and a turning of the head in the direction of the affected muscle

half of the scalp. The corneal reflex is also mediated by the sensory limb of CN V.

Facial Nerve (CN VII): The facial nerve mediates the following functions: innervation of the facial muscles, taste for the anterior two-thirds of the tongue, and innervation of lacrimal and salivary gland secretion (via parasympathetic fibers). A peripheral lesion (affecting the nucleus, pons, or the peripheral nerve), results in complete facial paralysis, whereas a central lesion (involving the supranuclear region) results in preservation of forehead movement (because of bilateral innervation).

Auditory Nerve (CN VIII): The auditory nerve subserves hearing and vestibular function. It is tested in the usual manner. It may be necessary to conduct brainstem auditory evoked potentials to assess functioning in young children.

Glossopharyngeal and Vagus Nerves (CN IX and X): These CN nerves innervate the larynx, pharynx, and palate and are tested in the usual fashion. Symptoms of dysfunction include nasal speech, inability to swallow fluids, hoarseness, stridor, etc.

Spinal Accessory Nerve (CN XI): CN XI innervates the trapezius and sternocleidomastoid muscles. Shoulder and lateral neck strength and movement are tested.

Hypoglossal Nerve (CN VII): Tongue position, tongue movements, atrophy, fasciculations, and the quality of speech are tested.

SOFT NEUROLOGICAL SIGNS

During the past 50 years, clinicians and investigators have sought to identify a cluster of examination findings which are specific for children without serious neurological conditions who, nonetheless, manifest behavioral and learning disorders of presumed neurological etiology. Most of these children exhibit some combination of hyperactivity, attention deficits, impulsivity, and specific learning disabilities. In the past, diagnoses such as minimal brain dysfunction, minimal brain damage, or minimal cerebral dysfunction were used to describe these children, since their symptom pattern was thought to be similar to that experienced by children known to have suffered definitive brain injury (e.g., trauma, infection).

Examination findings were sought which were capable of reflecting subtle, nonfocal aspects of neurological dysfunction. The predominant view was that the standard or "hard" signs (which directly reflect underlying neuropathology) were not sensitive enough to identify manifestations of less severe forms of neurological dysfunction. Various terms have been used to describe such examination findings, including soft, minor, and nonfocal neurological signs (SNS, NFNS) (Hertzig & Shapiro, 1987; Tupper, 1987). These signs typically reflect maturational lags, or subtle but deviant functioning that is independent of age. Taylor (1987) suggests that SNS may assess particular dimensions of behavioral functioning, such as temporal-spatial integration, motor planning, and impulse control. Touwen (1987) suggests that it may reflect vulnerabilities of the nervous system which stem from variations in interneuronal connectivity. Since a single abnormal soft sign generally has little clinical significance, it has been suggested that a test battery should be performed. Soft or nonfocal neurological examination batteries have been described by a number of clinical investigators (e.g., Birch et al., 1970; Touwen, 1979). In addition, the National Institute of Mental Health (NIMH) developed an instrument, the Physical and Neurological Examination for Soft Signs (PANESS, 1985). Most of the batteries include examination items from the following general categories (Deuel & Robinson, 1987; Taylor, 1987; Touwen, 1979):

- Gross motor coordination, persistence, and steadiness [e.g., balance during the Romberg stance and other sustained postures and stations (standing with feet together, arms held out with fingers spread, tongue out, and eyes closed), accuracy and dexterity while standing on one leg, hopping, tandem walking, toe or heel walking, walking on sides of feet]
- Motor speed, accuracy, and facility [e.g., finger tapping, sequential finger-to-thumb opposition, finger-to-nose touching, follow-a-finger (examiner's) maneuver, diadochokinesis (rapid alternating

movements, arm pronation-supination, heel-toe tapping]
- Presence of associated and adventitious movements [e.g., motor overflow, mirror movements (synkinesis), mild asymmetries, choreiform movements, athetoid-like movements, tremor]
- Sensory and somatosensory ability [e.g., double simultaneous stimulation (identification of two body areas lightly touched, while eyes are closed), stereognosis, graphesthesia]
- Manual dominance and right-left discrimination [e.g., hand, foot, and eye preferences; laterality and cross-laterality identification (identification of lateralized body parts on patient and examiner]

Taylor (cited by Yule and Taylor, 1987) conducted factor analytic studies of frequently used soft signs. The largest factor within an epidemiological sample reflected measures of lower limb coordination (standing, hopping, and heel-toe walking), whereas the largest factor within a clinical sample reflected measures of fine finger coordination, mirror movements, and the presence of athetosis. In a 4-year follow-up study, Hertzig (1982) found high within-subject consistency for double simultaneous stimulation, stereognosis, choreiform movements, finger opposition, and balance.

During recent years, the validity, significance, and usefulness of SNS has been questioned. The conceptualization and classification of behavioral and learning disorders has changed appreciably, and terms such as minimal brain disfunction are now rarely used. In addition, SNS batteries have not been adequately standardized for potentially confounding variables, such as IQ. The signs and examination batteries themselves have been criticized. For example, Rutter, Graham, and Yule (1970) noted that some frequently used SNSs are not due invariably to CNS dysfunction (e.g., strabismus, nystagmus), and others are so subtle that reliability is low and validity is questionable. The presence of SNS does not necessarily indicate the presence of neuropathology or behavioral dysfunction. In the Isle of Wight study, 7% of control children without evidence of neurological, behavioral, or learning impairment had at least one prominent SNS (a higher percentage did so when the severity of the sign was not considered). This finding has been replicated by other investigators. In addition, the presence of SNS did not discriminate reading-impaired children from normal controls. Questions also have been raised regarding the discriminant validity of SNS in differentiating among various neuropsychiatric disorders. Finally, the interrater and test-retest reliabilities and the internal consistencies of the various assessment batteries vary considerably.

Despite their shortcomings, there is support for the use of SNS batteries. SNS (especially when multiple) are uncommon among normally developing children. Hertzig & Birch (1968) found that less than 5% of normal children had two or more nonfocal neurological signs. In addition, when they are present, SNS appear to be consistent over time. For example, Hertzig (1982) reported that 8- to 12-year-old children with two or more signs continued to manifest these signs when tested 4 years later (despite the fact that many of these signs tend to disappear with age). There also is evidence that SNS reflect underlying neuropathology. For example, numerous studies have shown that children who have suffered neurological insults (e.g., CNS infections) have more SNS than the general childhood population (including age-adjusted sibling controls) [see Taylor (1987) for a review]. In addition, children who exhibit SNS are more likely to have histories of perinatal complications than children without SNS (see Taylor, 1987). A biological etiology for SNS is further supported by the absence of a relationship with sociofamilial characteristics.

There also is evidence in support of a relationship between SNS and both learning disorders and psychopathology. Children with behavioral disorders (e.g., hyperactivity syndromes), learning disabilities, and academic underachievement are significantly more likely to exhibit SNS than control populations. In addition, among children with complicated perinatal histories, those with SNS are more likely to be referred for treatment of behavioral and learning problems than those without SNS (despite equivalent IQ). Furthermore, within a general early school-age population, the presence of neuromotor soft signs appears to be related predictively and concurrently with achievement measures, independent of IQ (Wolff, Gunnoe, & Cohen, 1985). There is less consistent support for a relationship between specific soft sign profiles and particular types of learning and behavioral disorders. Some studies have reported higher rates of SNS (especially motor overflow)

among children with hyperactivity syndromes than among those with other types of psychopathology (e.g., aggressive conduct disorders); however, the studies lack adequate control (e.g., IQ, diagnostic specificity, uniformity of SNS exams, etc.). Further study is necessary.

Several investigators support future studies of SNS and have offered methodological suggestions (Hertzig & Shapiro, 1987; Taylor, 1987). A range of signs should be studied, including those that reflect motor, sensory, and cortical-integrative functions. The items should have adequate prevalence within the childhood population and should be appropriately operationalized with regard to administration and scoring. They should be objective, observable, and quantifiable. Several groups of items should be excluded, including those that are too subtle to be reliable, those that may be of nonneurological origin, and those that are affected to an appreciable degree by motivation, learning, verbal ability, and other similar factors. The individual items and the entire test battery should be reliable. Interrater and test-retest reliability should be demonstrated. In addition, the battery should be parsimonious and have acceptable internal consistency. Appropriate multivariate procedures should be conducted to determine the relationship between individual signs and social, cognitive, and environmental variables. The test batteries should be able to discriminate accurately children with learning and behavioral disorders from normally developing children. Finally, studies should be conducted to determine which soft signs tend to cluster together, and which clusters (or individual items) are associated with specific patterns of psychopathology and learning impairment. These studies should lead to findings which guide differential diagnosis, treatment, and prognosis.

Conclusion

It is important for child and adolescent psychiatrists to be familiar with the neurological assessment, since childhood neurological disorders often present with psychiatric symptomatology. In addition, children with established neurological conditions experience a particularly high rate of psychopathology. It is essential that their neurological status be considered when planning psychiatric treatment.

A careful history is central to the neurological assessment of children and adolescents. Particular attention should be paid to the onset, progression, and localization of neurological symptoms. The neurological examination includes general observations and measurements and assessment of the motor, sensory, cranial nerve, and reflex systems. Assessment of mental status is also essential. Although the validity and significance of nonfocal (or "soft") neurological signs has been questioned, they can provide valuable information regarding temporal-spatial integration, motor planning, and impulse control.

REFERENCES

Birch, et al. (1970). Cited in Hertzig, M. E. & Shapiro, H. G. (1987). The assessment of nonfocal neurological signs in school-aged children. In D. E. Tupper. (Ed.), *Soft Neurological Signs* (pp. 71–93). Orlando, FL: Grune & Stratton.

De Vivo, D. C. (1991). A clinical approach to neurologic disease. In A. M. Rudolph, J. I. E. Hoffman, & C. D. Rudolph (Eds.), *Rudolph's pediatrics* (pp. 1681–1691). Norwalk, CT: Appleton & Lange.

Deuel, R. K., & Robinson, D. J. (1987). Developmental motor signs. In D. E. Tupper (Ed.), *Soft neurological signs* (pp. 95–129). Orlando, FL: Grune & Stratton.

Fenichel, G. M. (1993). *Clinical pediatric neurology: A signs and symptoms approach* (2nd ed.). Philadelphia: W. B. Saunders Company.

Hertzig, M. E. (1982). Stability and change in nonfocal neurologic signs. *Journal of the American Academy of Child Psychiatry, 21*, 231–236.

Hertzig, M. E., & Birch, H. G. (1968). Neurologic organization in psychiatrically disturbed adolescents. A comparative consideration of sex differences. *Archives of General Psychiatry, 19*, 528–537.

Hertzig, M. E., & Shapiro, T. (1987). The assessment of nonfocal neurological signs in school-aged children. In D. E. Tupper (Ed.), *Soft neurological signs* (pp. 71–93). Orlando, FL: Grune & Stratton.

Huttenlocher, P. R. (1987). Evaluation of the child with neurologic disease. In R. E. Berhman, V. C. Vaughan, & W. E. Nelson (Eds.), *Nelson textbook of pediatrics* (13th ed., pp. 1274–1283). Philadelphia: W. B. Saunders.

PANESS (Physical and neurological examination for soft signs). (1985). In: Rating scales and assessment instruments for use in pediatric psychopharmacology research. *Psychopharmacology Bulletin, 21* (4).

Rutter, M., Graham, P., & Yule, W. (1970). A neuropsychiatric study in childhood. *Clinics in Developmental Medicine, Vols. 35 & 36.* London: Heinemann Medical Books.

Swaiman, K. F. (1989). Neurological examination of the older child. In K. F. Swaiman (Ed.), *Pediatric neurology: Principles and practice* (pp. 15–33). St. Louis: C. V. Mosby.

Taylor, E. A. (1985). Cited in Yule, W. & Taylor, E. (1987). Classification of soft signs. In D. E. Tupper. (Ed.), *Soft Neurological Signs* (pp. 19–43). Orlando, FL: Grune & Stratton.

Taylor, H. G. (1987). The meaning and value of soft signs in the behavioral sciences. In D. E. Tupper (Ed.), *Soft neurological signs* (pp. 297–335). Orlando, FL: Grune & Stratton.

Touwen, Bert, C. L. (1979). Examination of the child with minor neurological dysfunction. *Clinics in Developmental Medicine No. 71.* London: Heinemann Medical Books, 141 pp.

Touwen, Bert, C. L. (1987). The meaning and value of soft signs in neurology. In D. E. Tupper (Ed.), *Soft neurological signs* (pp. 281–295). Orlando, FL: Grune & Stratton.

Tupper, D. E. (1987). The issues with "soft signs." In D. E. Tupper (Ed.), *Soft neurological signs* (pp. 1–16). Orlando, FL: Grune & Stratton.

Wallace, S. J. (1988). Seizures in children. In J. Laidlaw, A. Richens, & J. Oxley (Eds.), *A textbook of epilepsy* (pp. 78–143). Edinburgh: Churchill Livingstone.

Wolff, P. H., Gunnoe, C. E., & Cohen, C. (1987). Cited in Taylor, H. G. (1987). The meaning and value of soft signs in the behavioral sciences. In D. E. Tupper. (Ed.), *Soft Neurological Signs* (pp. 297–335). Orlando, FL: Grune & Stratton.

Yule, W., & Taylor, E. (1987). Classification of soft signs. In D. E. Tupper (Ed.), *Soft neurological signs* (pp. 19–43). Orlando, FL: Grune & Stratton.

84 / Behavioral Assessment

David B. Goldston and Katherine Kirkhart

Systematic behavioral assessment methods are used to help identify specific problematic behaviors of youths, to formulate interventions based on observations of the environment, and to assess outcomes of interventions (Nelson & Hayes, 1986). The primary differences between the general clinical observations and the behavioral assessment methods to be discussed in this chapter are threefold. First, behavioral assessment methods are predicated on the assumption that specific, identifiable, objective environmental factors determine the probability of a behavior occurring and may have played a causative role in its etiology. Therefore, behavioral assessment focuses on identifying those aspects of the environment which influence the likelihood of a behavior, and which may be modified by intervention. Second, behavioral assessment methods depend upon the systematic identification of both objective antecedents and the objective consequences of youths' behaviors. Third, behavioral assessment methods emphasize the measurability or quantification of problematic behavior to a greater extent than is characteristic of general behavioral observations. More specifically, in behavioral assessment, the clinician typically focuses on objective characteristics such as the duration, intensity, or frequency of problematic behavior.

Behavioral assessment is used to examine behaviors that are problematic to determine if too much of the behavior is being exhibited (behavioral excesses), too little of the behavior is being exhibited (behavioral deficits), or the behavior being exhibited is inappropriate for the situation or context (behavioral anomalies) (Walker, Hedberg, Clement, & Wright, 1981). A child who is constantly running at home and at school and climbing on the furniture is exhibiting a behavioral ex-

cess. An anxious, shy child who will not join peers in play activities is exhibiting a behavioral deficit. A child initially encouraged to talk with friends of his parents in the home who begins indiscriminately to talk with strangers at the shopping mall or the park is exhibiting a behavioral anomaly.

In examining these behavioral excesses, deficits, and anomalies, it is essential to understand the context or setting within which the behavior occurs. For example, a child may throw temper tantrums only at school, at certain times of the day, with certain individuals, when being confronted, or after being frustrated with certain tasks. Assessment of those environmental cues which are associated with an increase or decrease in the likelihood of the target behavior is crucial to the design of effective interventions.

In a similar manner, it is important to assess the consequences of the problematic behavior. The consequences in response to a behavior can affect whether the behavior is more or less likely to recur. For example, a child may not receive positive attention for complying with the parents' requests in the home, but when he exhibits inappropriate behavior, the parent may spend a great deal of time trying to talk and reason with him. The parent may become increasingly frustrated as the child exhibits increasingly oppositional behavior despite repeated "discussions." In this circumstance, it is possible that the consequence of the attention paid to the noncompliance is inadvertently contributing to the behavior's recurrence. Likewise, a child at school may find that when he fights with another child, he receives much social attention from his peers. The consequence of attention from peers may then increase the likelihood that the child will be aggressive in the future. Hence, behavioral assessment helps to identify those aspects of the environment which are associated with an increase or decrease in the problematic behavior.

Finally, continued behavioral assessment of problematic behavior is necessary to evaluate the success of the intervention. For example, the cli-

Preparation of this chapter was supported in part by a Faculty Scholar Award to Dr. Goldston by the William T. Grant Foundation. We thank Richard Brunstetter, M.D., Stephanie Daniel, Ph.D., Margot Homan, Ph.D., Arthur Kelley, M.D., Jeffrey A. Smith, Ph.D., and Lyn Treadway, M.A., for their helpful comments regarding this chapter.

nician may determine that the parents of a child who demonstrates oppositional behavior need to increase the frequency of praise when their child complies with requests. However, without continued assessment of the target behaviors, the clinician as well as the parents will be unable to say definitively whether the intervention has had the desired effect in improving compliance.

In sum, the primary objectives of formal and systematic behavioral assessment are threefold. First, the primary purpose of a behavioral assessment is to define and describe the behavior(s) of interest. Second, an objective of behavioral assessment is to identify aspects of the environment—both antecedents and consequences—which serve to increase or decrease the likelihood of target behaviors. Third, the process of behavioral assessment is used to evaluate the impact of interventions.

The SORC Model

Environmental variables are presumed to function as the decisive elements controlling the occurrence of the target behaviors. Hence, formal behavioral assessment is often referred to as a functional analysis. The systematic framework used as the basis of functional analysis is summarized by the acronym SORC (stimulus-organism-response-consequence; Goldfried & Sprafkin, 1976) and includes all of the variables that are considered and evaluated when a practitioner completes a behavioral assessment. It is assumed that behavior is the result of a combination of both environmental variables—stimuli and consequences—and organism variables—physiology and past learning history.

STIMULUS

The stimuli of importance refer to the antecedent aspects of the environment that reliably evoke the problematic behavior. Therefore, a major task of behavioral assessment is to identify those stimuli that are associated with a greater or diminished likelihood of a behavior occurring. Specific effort should be made to identify aspects of the environment which serve as a cue for a behavior, and in

whose absence, the behavior is less likely to occur. Conversely, the clinician seeks to identify facets of the environment which are present when appropriate behavior occurs, and which are absent when appropriate behaviors are not being demonstrated. For example, a child may anxiously avoid speaking to or maintaining eye contact with people with whom he is not familiar. However, this same child may start conversations with and interact spontaneously with family members and children who are his neighbors. The presence or absence of strangers in this example is an environmental condition (stimulus) which is reliably associated with the presence or absence of avoidance behavior on the part of the child.

Implicit in this part of the SORC model is an emphasis on understanding the situation specificity of behavior (Nelson & Hayes, 1986). The problematic behavior may not be present across all situations; it is therefore important to assess the behavior across different situations or environmental settings. That is, it is important to assess behavior not in isolation, but in the context of factors which are associated with a greater likelihood of the problematic behavior occurring. Although it is often not practical to assess the behavior(s) of interest in all environments in which they might occur, it is important that the behavioral assessment be performed in as wide a sampling as possible of the environments in which the problem behavior is exhibited.

ORGANISM

The "O" part of the SORC model represents the differences among individuals which influence the likelihood that a behavior will occur in the presence of environmental stimuli. It is evident that not everybody reacts in the same manner to the same environmental stimuli. Organism factors refer to these differences among individuals and include both factors related to the physiology and constitution, as well as to the learning history of the individual. Some of these individual differences may be modifiable and some may not. For example, it may not be possible to change a factor such as intelligence, but other factors such as level of fatigue are potentially modifiable. In addition, some of these factors (e.g., learning history) may help to explain why an individual exhibits one behavior more often than another in a specific setting. For example, a child who has observed adults using assaultive behavior as a way of resolving conflict may be likely to deal with conflict by means of aggressive or assaultive behavior. Although some of the organism factors (e.g., neurologic disease) may complicate or present limits to therapy, others simply represent variables that need to be considered in the formulation of interventions. For example, interventions focused on reducing temper outbursts are likely to differ depending on the intellectual or maturational level of the individual.

RESPONSE

The response in the SORC model is the target behavior. The target behavior is the behavior that is problematic and needs to be modified. Behaviors should be targeted (1) when they pose a potential danger to the child or adolescent or to other individuals with whom the child or adolescent interacts, (2) when the behaviors, because of their unpredictability or because of prevailing norms, are aversive to others or unacceptable in the setting in which they are displayed, or (3) when modification of the behaviors results in greater flexibility in the child or adolescent's coping ability better able (Nelson & Hayes, 1986). It is imperative that behaviors not be targeted for assessment and intervention unless they are causing difficulties. To use a common-sense example, a teenager may not have attempted suicide despite exposure to multiple suicide attempts in his family and among his friends. Despite the prevalence of suicidal behavior among the youth's family and peer group, the absence of suicidal behavior is adaptive and obviously should not be targeted for intervention.

The target behaviors should be defined in such a manner as to make them readily identifiable by different observers. For example, telling a child to "be good" might not evoke a satisfactory response because the target behavior description (i.e., "being good") is a subjective judgment that may not be consistently identified in the same way by different people (including the child). On the other hand, telling a child to "complete his math homework before dinner" is a command that refers to a specific behavior which different people will identify in similar fashion.

In addition to being specifically and objectively defined, target behaviors should also be amenable to change. Clear definitions of behavior allow for the behavior to be measured, first in order to determine the extent of the problem, and later, to evaluate treatment effectiveness. Target behaviors are generally defined in quantifiable terms, such as duration, frequency, or intensity. The goal of an intervention is either to reduce certain behaviors (e.g., behavior excesses), to increase other behaviors (e.g., behavior deficits), or to change the situations in which the behaviors occur (e.g., behavioral anomalies). In addition, whenever possible, it is usually desirable to select target behaviors that will maximize the opportunities for the child or adolescent to be rewarded in the natural environment (Nelson & Hayes, 1986).

Behaviors whose elimination or alteration would lead to increased difficulty for the child are not appropriate targets for intervention. For example, although crying behavior may easily be identified by a parent, efforts to achieve a dramatic decrease in the crying of an infant would usually not be appropriate because an infant has no other effective means of communication at his disposal. On the other hand, an 11-year-old's tantrum behavior would be a reasonable target behavior because developmentally that youth should have a richer repertoire of alternative and less disruptive ways of communication than the younger child.

Among some individuals, there also may be a constellation of related behaviors that are problematic (Evans, 1986; Nelson & Hayes, 1986). For example, in some cases, covert, physiological, and overt behavior (e.g., the arousal associated with conflict, aggressive self-talk, and aggressive behavior) may occur together because they are components of the same overall response, and interventions may focus on any or all of the component behaviors. In other cases, discrete behaviors may occur together because they comprise a psychiatric syndrome (e.g., the impulsivity, overactivity, and inattention of the attention deficit hyperactivity disorder child). In these cases, the clinician may try to target what is considered to be the "core" symptom of the response cluster, may try to intervene with several behaviors at once, or may try systematically to intervene with the separate target behaviors one at a time.

CONSEQUENCES

Consequences refer to the environmental conditions or changes that occur after the occurrence of the target behavior. These consequences may be either positive or negative, with this valence suggesting that something is either added or subtracted from the environment following the response or target behavior of interest. For example, if praise is given after a child has completed her homework, praise is a positive consequence. A child who is not allowed to go on a field trip with her class at school because of failing to complete her homework the night before is receiving a negative consequence.

In addition to consequences being added to or subtracted from the environment following a response, consequences also can be either reinforcing or punishing. A reinforcing consequence will increase the likelihood that the same response will occur again under the same circumstances, whereas a punishing consequence will decrease this likelihood. With these considerations, there are four types of consequences that can occur in response to behavior. *Positive reinforcement* (also referred to as reward) is the application of a consequence that results in an increase in behavior. *Negative reinforcement* is the withdrawal of a consequence that results in an increase in behavior. *Positive punishment* is the application of a consequence that results in a decrease in behavior. *Negative punishment* is the withdrawal of a consequence that results in a decrease in behavior.

Consequences and their impact are sometimes difficult to detect. A teacher ignoring quiet, task-oriented behavior and scolding children who are off task and getting out of their seats in the classroom may actually increase the amount of off-task and out-of-seat behavior because of her attention to these behaviors. Similarly, a mother smiling when she sees her daughter combing her hair may notice an increase in grooming behavior by her daughter.

Some consequences normally occur in the child's environment and influence the target behavior. In a classroom setting, for example, children often will pay attention to youths who are disruptive and make silly or sarcastic remarks instead of focusing on assigned work. Other consequences do not naturally occur in the child's environment, but are potentially controlling of the target behavior. For instance, a parent may introduce a system for earning points and privileges in exchange for compliant behavior or completion of chores. The clinician treating a child's behavior may either try to identify the naturally occurring consequences that influence the likelihood of the behavior, or instead may introduce a previously unused consequence into the environment (e.g., a new reward or punishment).

Example: Functional Analysis of a Child's Oppositional Behavior

An 8-year-old child is brought to a clinician's office by her mother because of frequent noncompliance with the mother's requests. The mother states that the child is more compliant with her grandmother and with her father during their weekend visitations, and has not had major compliance problems at school. The mother states that she is unaware of why the child is so defiant in the face of her requests.

STIMULUS

In evaluating the antecedent environmental stimuli that seem to trigger the noncompliance, the clinician might first follow up on the mother's observation that her child is defiant primarily in her presence, but is more compliant with other adults. This may be done by asking the mother about her approach to parenting her child and how this differs from that of other adults. Other relevant adults such as the child's father, grandmother, or teacher could be interviewed to determine how they elicit compliance from her. Efforts would be made to discern if the mother actually differs from other adults in the manner in which her child is asked to do things, or if the mother simply expects more from the child and places more demands on her, thereby giving her more opportunities to be noncompliant. In this manner, both the consistencies and inconsistencies among caretakers in the degree to which they place demands on the child, and the different caretakers' perceptions of the child would be evaluated. In addition, the assessment would include a focus on determining whether there is pattern to the child's noncompliance at home, that is, whether the child is noncompliant to all requests at home or simply noncompliant with a certain subset of requests.

In trying to determine the specific situations in which the child is most likely to be noncompliant, the mother may be asked to record on a daily basis the specific situations or requests with which the child is noncompliant. Conversely, if there appear to be certain situations in which the child is compliant, the mother may be asked to record or document those requests or situations as precisely as she can. In the office, direct observation can be utilized during free play to examine how the parent and child interact, and how the mother responds to the child when demands are not being placed on the child. In addition, the clinician may structure the playroom interaction by instructing the mother to ask the child to complete certain tasks in the course of play. The way in which the mother tries to elicit compliance from her child can then be observed. Specifically, the playroom situation may be used to determine whether the mother is using vague commands ("Be good"), multiple commands ("Pick up the toys, move the chair over here, and come to the table"), or questions ("Could you please help your mother?"), which are less likely to elicit compliant behavior from children than are simple, direct commands ("Put the toys in the toy chest") (Forehand & McMahon, 1981).

ORGANISM

In assessing "organism" variables, the clinician tries to obtain as complete a history as possible about the emergence of the current behavioral problems. The perspectives of multiple informants in describing the child's history are often especially instructive. Issues that would be of particular importance might include how other children are parented in the home, how this child differs from other children, whether the child is exhibiting new behavior, and whether the child is simply exhibiting behavior that has become more problematic recently because of its increasing frequency. The clinician's assessment would also explore whether the child has any developmental delays, physical problems, or is taking any medications which may make a difference in the treatment approach. In addition, the behavioral assessment would focus on whether the noncompliant behaviors are associated with fatigue or other states which can be modified. Other circumstances potentially associated with an increased likelihood of noncompliance in the home, such as exposure to increased animosity between the mother and an ex-husband or exposure to conflict or disagreement between the mother and grandmother, also would be important to assess.

RESPONSE

A primary objective in assessing the target behavior (response) of interest is to assess its frequency, duration, and intensity so the current extent of the problems can be determined. This original "baseline" level of problematic behavior can serve as a point of comparison against which the efficacy of any interventions can be judged. In this example, the behavior that has been identified as most problematic is noncompliance. Hence one of the goals of assessment would be to track the frequency or the proportion of time that the child is noncompliant prior to the intervention (baseline) and subsequent to any intervention. Ideally, the clinician would be able to observe and monitor the child's noncompliant behaviors in the home. However, because of practical considerations, the assessment typically would be accomplished by asking the mother to monitor those instances in which the child is noncompliant in the home. If the frequency of the target behavior is great enough, the mother may be asked to use a sampling strategy wherein she records the child's behavior only during certain predefined periods of time, rather than attempting to record its every occurrence. In addition, the relationship of the target behavior to other behaviors exhibited by the child would need to be examined. Of particular interest would be whether or how often noncompliant behavior escalates into temper outbursts, or whether the child's noncompliant behavior in the home is preceded by certain other behaviors that can be identified (e.g., complaints about not being able to spend time with the father and grandmother).

616

CONSEQUENCE

Finally, the clinician is interested in ascertaining the consequences of the child's noncompliance in the home. The assessment should focus on the attention the mother gives to the noncompliant behaviors, whether she tries to punish noncompliance, how the mother tries to set limits or punish the noncompliance, and the consistency with which the mother administers consequences for noncompliant behavior. The clinician would specifically assess whether the parent gives attention to the child when she is noncompliant that she would not otherwise be giving the child, and the degree to which the parent attends to the child when the youngster is compliant. Also of interest would be whether the parent has tried to utilize time-out from positive reinforcement strategies, utilizing a "time out" chair or room in which the child receives no parental attention, or whether the parent has tried to establish any type of reward or point system in which the child is given privileges or rewards contingent upon compliant behaviors. The clinician also would be interested in the different approaches and the consistency among different caretakers in how they respond to the child's noncompliance. Whether the frequency of the child's noncompliance has varied as a function of any of the different strategies experimented with by the mother would be of particular interest, since this may suggest what intervention should be utilized.

Considerations in Behavioral Assessment

MULTIPLE INFORMANTS

In child psychiatry, dating back to the Child Guidance Movement, there has been an emphasis on using multiple informants in the assessment of emotional and behavioral problems. As was illustrated in the above example, the use of multiple informants (e.g., grandparents, mother, father, teachers) regarding a child's behavior is also desired. By using multiple informants, the clinician can often obtain useful information that is not available or obvious to a single caretaker about the environmental variables which cue problematic behavior. By dint of using such multiple sources, the clinician also obtains data regarding the cross-situational consistency or the situation specificity of behavioral problems. For example, comparison of parent and teacher reports may reveal that a child displays markedly different behaviors in the classroom and in the home. Moreover, the use of multiple informants is important in that it can shed light on the different perceptions of the adults who deal with the child. When there are significant differences among adults in their perceptions of a child, the clinician needs to determine (1) whether the behavior actually differs in the presence of different individuals or in different settings, (2) whether the demands placed upon the child and the consequences of his behavior differ significantly in different settings, and/or (3) whether the same behavior is being observed by the different informants but is being interpreted as more problematic or pathological by one set of observers relative to another. Differences in the perceptions of the two parents, or in the perceptions of parents and grandparents, can belie significant inconsistencies in parenting styles, inconsistencies that can exacerbate a child's behavioral problems.

RECIPROCAL INFLUENCES

In constructing a functional analysis of behavior, there is an assumption of unidirectional influence. That is, there is an assumption that the environment affects behavior, but there typically is no consideration of how the child affects his environment. However, in actuality, individuals interact with each other, and there are reciprocal interchanges between an individual and others in the environment (Lerner, Hess, & Nitz, 1991). Referring to the aforementioned example of a child's noncompliance in the home, a typical interaction might involve the parent asking the child to do a household task, the child refusing to comply, and the parent in turn becoming angry and more demanding. In response to the anger and increasing demands, the child might become even more angry, more defiant, and exhibit even more oppositional behavior. In such a case, it is possible to conceptualize the parent's response (expressions of anger, increasing demands) to the child's behavior as a "consequence" of that behavior. However, it also is possible to focus on the parent's behavior, and conceptualize the child's defiance as a stimulus which cues the parent to respond with more demands. If the manner in which the parent makes demands on the child is construed as a "target behavior," then it can also be said that the response of the child (the consequence to the parent) will either increase or decrease the likelihood of the parent making additional similar demands.

To capture the degree to which the child and parent affect each other, it is often useful to conceptualize the task of behavioral assessment in terms of two functional analyses—one focusing on the child's behavior, and the other on the parent's. The two complementary conceptualizations have implications for treatment design. First, with a functional analysis focusing on parental behaviors, it is possible to determine what behaviors of the child are most likely to affect parental behaviors. Second, although behavioral therapies often focus on the parent as the agent of change (the intervention) when trying to modify a child's behavior, it also should be possible to conceptualize the child as the agent potentially able to control the parent's behavior. For example, it should be possible to teach children to "reinforce" their parents when they spend free time with them and attend to their compliant behaviors.

BEHAVIORAL ASSESSMENT AS AN INTERVENTION

Behavioral assessment is usually thought of as a means to an end. That is, the purpose of behavioral assessment is to help in the formulation of an appropriate intervention and to help in evaluating the efficacy of that intervention. However, behavioral assessment can be thought of as having therapeutic properties in and of itself. For example, monitoring of behavior can sometimes produce changes in the behavior being observed. This change in behavior being observed is referred to as reactivity, and is sometimes viewed as a source of measurement error and bias in the behavioral assessment. However, if a child exhibits a reduction in problematic behavior because he is being observed and recorded, from the perspective of the clinician, the change is desirable and therapeutic. In such cases, the observation of behavior

becomes a new environmental stimulus associated with an increase in appropriate behavior, and a decrease in inappropriate behaviors. If the behavioral monitoring results in such a desirable change, the clinician may advise that the behavioral monitoring continue as a simple intervention.

In addition, behavioral assessment can be used to redirect attention from the behaviors that are problematic to behaviors that are desired. For example, there are occasions in which parents are so frustrated with their child's inappropriate behaviors that they spend a great deal of time attending to the inappropriate behavior and little time focusing on appropriate behavior. The clinician may hypothesize that the child would exhibit more appropriate behavior if the parents attended more to these appropriate behaviors. In part to focus the parents' attention on the appropriate behaviors that the child exhibits, the clinician may ask the parents to monitor the frequency of the child's appropriate behaviors rather than focusing on the inappropriate behaviors.

PSYCHOMETRIC CONSIDERATIONS

In the development of new psychological assessment instruments, there typically is considerable attention given to the demonstration of acceptable reliability, internal consistency, validity, and the clinical utility of the instrument. However, there have been differences of opinion as to the applicability of typical psychometric test standards for behavioral assessment (Ollendick & Hersen, 1993). As Ollendick and Hersen (1993) have pointed out, in behavioral assessment, the focus or target of the assessment is often chosen because of convenience or practicality. There often is little consideration of what constitutes adequate reliability and validity for an analysis which focuses on the individual and presumably reflects situation specificity in the occurrence of the behavior (Ollendick & Hersen, 1993).

Nonetheless, behavioral assessment is limited by the degree to which observations of a behavior can be made reliably and the degree to which behavior assessed is predictive of future behavior (Ollendick & Hersen, 1993). In a behavioral assessment, the target behaviors, the antecedents, and the consequences of the behavior should be identified in identical or highly similar situations in a reliable manner by a single observer (test-retest reliability), or by different individuals observing the same behavior at the same point in time (interrater reliability). In addition, the utility of the functional analysis of behavior will depend upon its ability to be predictive of later behavior and the contingencies controlling behavior (Ollendick & Hersen, 1993). In the practical application of behavioral assessment and behavioral methods, there is little assessment of the psychometric properties of the assessment utilized. As a result, an increasing number of child clinicians augment functional analyses with behavior checklists such as the Achenbach Child Behavior Checklist (Achenbach & Edelbrock, 1983). These assessment methods have demonstrated reliability and validity, and typically have normative data based on large numbers of individuals; they therefore complement the idiographic approach of the functional analysis. Further discussion of behavior checklists is contained in a separate chapter in this volume.

DEVELOPMENTAL CONSIDERATIONS

Despite its extensive use with children and adolescents in educational and clinical populations, behavioral assessment has generally not involved a developmental approach; that is, the mechanics of assessing behavior and developing a functional analysis have generally been the same regardless of age. Nonetheless, Ollendick and Hersen (1993) have argued that behavioral assessment methods should consider developmental differences in understanding the expression of behavior, in considering youths' reactivity to behavioral assessment, and in choosing which behavioral assessment methods to employ. For example, self-monitoring behavioral assessment procedures may be appropriate for adolescents, but are inappropriate for younger children (Ollendick & Hersen, 1993). Clinicians should also consider normative data regarding behaviors, particularly when target behaviors are selected on the assumption that they reflect either behavioral excesses or deficits (Ollendick & Hersen, 1993). As mentioned above, behavioral clinicians now often complement their functional analyses of behavior with data from behavior checklists, which may provide data about age and gender differences in a wide variety of behaviors. Finally, from a developmental psychopathology perspective, it has been suggested that the same psychiatric disorders may have different behavioral manifestations at different ages, and that certain behaviors (e.g., aggressive behaviors) may exhibit more continuity over time than others (Ollendick & King, 1991). Therefore, in conducting behavioral analysis and constructing a functional analysis, the practitioner should be alert to developmental differences in the covariation among problematic behaviors, and should devise interventions with consideration for what is known about continuities and discontinuities in problematic behavior over time (Ollendick & King, 1991). For example, Kazdin (1987) has advocated family and behavioral intervention and long-term follow-up for youths exhibiting conduct disorder behaviors because of the chronicity of those behaviors and their resistance to change over time.

History of Child and Adolescent Behavioral Assessment and Current Trends

In the final section of this chapter, an effort is made to provide a historical context for the development of child and adolescent behavioral assessment methods and to provide an overview of the current trends in the area. Historically behavioral assessment with children and adolescents has been associated primarily with operant conditioning models of learning. Operant models focus on the learning of behavior in response to environmental consequences. This approach follows in the tradition of Thorndike's (1913) Law of Effect (i.e., behavior with rewarding consequences will tend to occur more frequently than behavior with unsatisfying consequences) and Skinnerian psychology, as described in his book, *Science and Human Behavior* (1953).

The literature focusing on the use of behavioral assessment and operant procedures with children did not begin to grow in earnest until the 1960s and 1970s. During that time period, a number of articles appeared focusing on clinical applications of operant methods with children, including mentally retarded and autistic youths. In early studies, research demonstrated control of children's behavior in experimental or laboratory settings. Subsequent studies focused on assessment and modification of behavior in natural settings such as the home. In this context, behavioral assessment often was used to demonstrate the baseline (pre-intervention) proportion of time that the child exhibited problematic behavior and the desired decrease in these behaviors following introduction of an intervention. In an effort to examine the extent of environmental "control" over the behaviors of interest, behavioral assessment was used to demonstrate that the frequency of problematic behaviors would increase again following the withdrawal of the intervention and decrease with the reintroduction of the intervention.

In the 1970s and 1980s, an increasing emphasis in behavior therapy and behavioral assessment was on the measurement of long-term or durable change (Hersen & Ammerman, 1989). This presented an extension of the scope of the early studies that had focused primarily on short-term changes, typically in the presence or absence of an intervention. Studies also began to explore the generalizability of change. That is, researchers began to examine the degree to which behavior learned in one setting generalized to new settings.

Many of the early behavioral assessment strategies and intervention designs contrasted the frequency of behavior prior to an intervention (or during its absence), and the frequency of behavior in the presence of that intervention. Most of these studies used what is referred to as an A-B or A-B-A-B study design. In this type of study design, A refers to the assessment of behavior in the absence of an intervention or prior to the intervention, and B refers to the assessment of behavior when an intervention is present. However, a problem with the A-B design is that it is difficult to argue definitively that changes in behavior over time are actually due to the interventions as opposed to, for example, maturation. A problem with the A-B-A-B design is that it is sometimes difficult to interpret desirable changes that occur following the introduction of an intervention but persist after the intervention is withdrawn. Another question focuses on the ethics of withdrawing interventions once problematic behavior has started to decrease (particularly self-destructive behavior) in an effort to demonstrate the environmental "control" over the target behaviors.

Hence, intervention designs and behavioral assessment strategies became more sophisticated, including those that use "multiple baseline designs" to examine the effects of interventions on multiple behaviors, in different individuals, and/or in multiple settings (Baer, Wolf, & Risley, 1968). With the multiple baseline design, the clinician is able to focus an intervention on behavior in a single setting, while continuing to assess behavior in the absence of an intervention in other settings. The clinician is able to introduce the intervention systematically in additional settings, observing not only the differences in target behavior prior to and after the intervention, but also in settings with and without the interventions. In a similar manner, clinicians are able to use multiple baseline designs to assess the effects of interventions on multiple individuals, or to assess the effects of interventions on multiple behaviors of the same individual.

In the 1980s and 1990s, a number of additional issues came under discussion. These included the reliability and validity of behavioral assessment methods, developmental factors affecting behavior, and the degree to which exhibited behavior constituted normative or developmentally inappropriate behavior. In response to these concerns, many behaviorally oriented clinicians increasingly began to rely upon psychometrically sound behavior inventories with normative data to complement their individual functional analyses. Additionally, in a continuing trend, there have continued to be an ever-increasing number of settings in which behavioral assessment and behavioral methods have been applied over the years. Of particular note is the increasing use of behavioral assessment and interventions in pediatric settings, for example, in the targeting of such behaviors as adherence to medical regimens. In recent years, behavioral assessment and intervention strategies also have been used increasingly in the design of preventative health strategies. In particular there have been efforts to reduce behaviors that have potential long-term deleterious consequences for health, such as high-risk sexual behavior and cigarette smoking.

Finally, it is worth noting that, historically, behavioral assessment has been linked to behavioral therapy interventions. However, clinicians not trained as behavioral therapists have increasingly begun to apply some of the methods of behavioral assessment. For example, it is not uncommon for clinicians in contemporary practice to judge the efficacy of medication trials in part by examining behavioral ratings completed by several different observers of a child's behavior over a given period of time. Over the last several decades, there has been increasing emphasis in child psychiatry on both the objective measurement of behavior and the objective measurement of the outcomes, as well as a greater understanding of the manner in which aspects of the environment can affect the behavior of children. It is now evident that behavioral assessment methods can be used in tandem with other evaluative methods and interventions to achieve a richer understanding of the impact of the environment on children and adolescents, and well as the impact of children and adolescents on their environments.

REFERENCES

Achenbach, T. (1991). *Manual for the Child Behavior Checklist 14–18 and 1991 Profile.* Burlington, VT: University of Vermont Department of Psychiatry.

Baer, D., Wolf, M., & Risley, T. (1968). Some current dimension of applied behavior analysis. *Journal of Applied Behavior Analysis, 1,* 91–97.

Evans, I. (1986). Response structure and the triple-response-mode concept. In R. Nelson & S. Hayes (Eds.), *Conceptual foundations of behavioral assessment* (pp. 131–155). New York: Guilford Press.

Forehand, R., & McMahan, R. (1981). *Helping the noncompliant child: A clinician's guide to parent training.* New York: Guilford Press.

Goldfried, M., & Sprafkin, J. (1976). Behavioral personality assessment. In J. Spence, R. Carson, & J. Thibaut (Eds.), *Behavioral approaches to therapy* (pp. 295–321). Morristown, NJ: General Learning Press.

Hersen, M., & Ammerman, R. (1989). Overview of new developments in child behavior therapy. In M. Hersen (Ed.), *Innovations in child behavior therapy* (pp. 3–31). New York: Springer Publishing.

Kazdin, A. (1987). Treatment of antisocial behavior in children: Current status and future directions. *Psychological Bulletin, 102,* 187–203.

Lerner, R., Hess, L., & Nitz, K. (1991). Toward the integration of human developmental and therapeutic change. In P. Martin (Ed.), *Handbook of behavior therapy and psychological science: An integrative approach* (pp. 13–34). New York: Pergamon Press.

Nelson, R., & Hayes, S. (1986). The nature of behavioral assessment. In R. Nelson & S. Hayes (Eds.), *Conceptual foundations of behavioral assessment* (pp. 1–41). New York: Guilford Press.

Ollendick, T., & Hersen, M. (1993). Child and adolescent behavioral assessment. In T. Ollendick & M. Hersen (Eds.), *Handbook of child and adolescent assessment* (pp. 3–14). Boston: Allyn and Bacon.

Ollendick, T., & King, N. (1991). Developmental factors in child behavioral assessment. In P. Martin (Ed.), *Handbook of behavior therapy and psychological science: An integrative approach* (pp. 57–72). New York: Pergamon Press.

Skinner, B. (1953). *Science and human behavior.* New York: Macmillan.

Thorndike, E. (1913). *Educational psychology: The psychology of learning.* New York: Teachers College Press.

Walker, C., Hedberg, A., Clement, P., & Wright, L. (1981). *Clinical procedures for behavior therapy.* Englewood Cliffs, NJ: Prentice-Hall.

85 / Psychodynamic Assessment

David I. Berland

Fourteen-year-old Zack was a handful. Over the past 3 years he had been suspended from school four times and seemed to be spending more time serving detention and in school suspensions than attending class. One of his fights spilled over into a fast-food restaurant and the police were called. He had no wish to be evaluated and made clear his preference to be thought of as bad, not sick. He was brought against his wish to the assessment and lived up to his billing—he was nasty, rude, and communicated with many expletives. What should the clinician do? The youth could be taken at face value and told there is nothing to be done except wait for legal action. An alternative approach could look beyond the behavior and wonder if something else may be going on. Are there other ways of understanding Zack's tough, aggressive demeanor? (We will return to Zack at the end of the chapter to present his psychodynamic assessment.)

Introduction

Organizing information from an encounter with another person can be overwhelming. One may be tempted to narrow one's focus to another's appearance, smile, friendliness, warmth, or conversational ability. When a parent brings a child or adolescent for help, the evaluator confronts a multitude of observational data. An assessment of psychodynamics, the child's psychologically motivating factors, provides the clinician with the tools necessary to collect, organize, and understand these data of observation—the child's actual or manifest behavior and the underlying thoughts, feelings, and motivations behind the youngster's words and deeds.

This chapter explains the psychodynamic aspects of clinical assessment: its components (defenses; ego, id, and superego functions; transference and countertransference), its usefulness, and its organization into a coherent formulation.

Contextual History

Psychodynamics stems from the clinical reports and theorizing of Sigmund Freud, a Viennese neurologist starting in the late 19th century. He encountered patients whose sensory or motor dysfunction did not conform to known patterns of innervation. To explain these clinical discrepancies, Freud invoked unconscious mental functioning: those thoughts, wishes, beliefs, values, feelings, or sensations that occur within an individual, but are inaccessible to the person's awareness, that is, unconscious. A person may feel uneasy about a wish

or desire and not know the source of the uncomfortable feeling. The discomfort could come from a conscious wish coupled with an unconscious conflict, and the underlying dynamics might result in a symptom such as hand numbness, as a patient of Freud's era experienced. She had used her hand for sexual stimulation, which was forbidden in Victorian Europe. Hence she experienced a tension or conflict between the pleasure and her acceptance of the prohibiting cultural values. The unconscious solution to this woman's internal conflict was anesthesia of her hand. The dynamics of unconscious and conscious mental functioning—the internal mental interplay of various tensions, thoughts, feelings, fears, and desires—produced the physical symptoms that could not be explained neurologically.

Freud continued to explore models of the mind as well as internal conflicts and the individual's responses to them. He delineated what has been designated a structural model of the mind, dividing mental functions into id, ego, and superego (Freud, 1961). Freud employed vivid literary metaphors. He compared ego to a rider on horseback and id to the forces and power of the horse. Id functions represented biological drives, the source of the person's hypothesized psychic energy. Ego functions experience and interpret the person's internal and external worlds as part of executive decision making about one's life. Superego functions represent conscience and ideals; what one should do and strive to become.

Understanding a person in terms of id, ego, and superego functioning retains utility in organizing data from a clinical encounter. Such an approach yields a living person struggling with inner tensions, as well as relationships with others and the environment, to enrich and sometimes explain the categorical diagnostic classification.

Formulating the child's psychodynamics facilitates intervention planning. John, an 8-year-old diabetic, refused insulin. Appearing oppositional and defiant, John's psychodynamic assessment revealed superego conflicts. His ego ideal, derived from his father, entailed his being independent, self-reliant, and self-sufficient. Further, his teacher and peers were completing a unit on the dangers of drug use. For John to accept the injections violated his ego ideal and peer values. Once the clinician understood the motivation for his refusal, efforts could be directed to modify the superego and ego functioning to be more flexible and adaptive. John learned to administer the injections himself (self-reliance) and led a class discussion on the distinction between drugs that help and drugs that harm.

The Beginning: Sources of Data and Hypotheses

The data for the psychodynamic assessment are derived from observations of the youngster's world along with clinicians' awareness of our own thoughts and feelings. As clinicians, we must be in touch with our own feelings in the course of clinical encounters. The goal is to utilize our self-observations to help understand the patient, instead of acting on our feelings. Despite the expanding numbers of valuable strategies and aids created to enhance the clinical assessment, as professionals our understanding of our own feelings remains a vital ingredient of clinical assessment. Am I feeling annoyed at this agreeable appearing patient because of what underlies the smile or is it something in my personal feelings that generates my irritability?

The child's world includes both internal experience (psychological and biological) and interaction with the environment. The assessment process begins with the initial telephone contact. Did mother, father, school, parent's secretary, or social agency initiate the clinical contact? What is the presenting problem?

The clinician generates and tests hypotheses as the assessment proceeds. If the school counselor calls to request an appointment because the child is withdrawn and doing poorly in school, the clinician may hypothesize that the child feels badly about himself. The clinician must take care to assess whether the parents are sufficiently involved with the youngster; why didn't they initiate the contact? This hypothesis is tested initially when the patient and parents are greeted in the waiting area. If both parents have arrived on time and the child appears sad, yet comfortable with them, the hypothesis may need to be modified.

Henry, 10, arrives with his foster parents, sits between them, and appears comfortable. On closer observation, the clinician notices the boy has a cleft lip and expands the hypothesis to encompass concerns about self-image and whether peers accept him. The clinician generates, tests, and modifies hypotheses about the child from the first contact. Here, the clinician has generated and modified clinical ideas even before meeting the family preparatory to formal interviews. These hypotheses should tie together the child's inner experience and outer behavior in a way that contributes to understanding the problem for which help is sought.

The evaluation continues with interviews of the parents, family, teachers, and others to obtain more information about the patient. The biological life of the child is assessed through the developmental history and physical examination, as well as information from the primary care physician and other relevant care providers.

To learn about the child's psychological life, the clinician interviews the child in a developmentally appropriate context (e.g., with or without parents, with or without appropriate play equipment); and draws inferences regarding the child's inner experiences and interactions with others. While avoiding eye contact and mumbling inaudibly, Henry draws a tiny person with a prominent mouth stuck in the lower corner of the paper. On closer examination, Henry's clothes don't fit and are mismatched. Which hypotheses do these data of observation support?

Acquainting ourselves with this child's external world may involve interviews with caregivers (Henry's foster parents), teachers, and other concerned adults such as Henry's social worker. Review of the medical history reveals multiple ear infections and out-of-date immunizations.

Assembling all this information enables the clinician to assess Henry's psychodynamic functioning: his internal or psychodynamic conflict involves his feeling unloved (his birth parents were unable to provide adequate parenting, so the state assumed responsibility) and he feels unlovable in spite of appearing comfortable with his foster parents. Wanting to feel cared for, while simultaneously believing that is impossible, Henry presents himself as small, insignificant, and undeserving of adult attention. Peers tease him because of his facial appearance and he conveys the impression of possessing neither the confidence nor social skills to cope with the teasing. In addition, his chronic earaches confuse sensory input, further isolating him. He has difficulty concentrating and does not seek help from teachers at school.

In addition to these observations, the clinician has another source of data: his own feelings, which may be used to help understand the patient. Seven-year-old Linda exerts a lot of energy to please the clinician. She addresses the doctor as "Ma'am," sits up straight, asks permission to draw on each piece of paper she uses and offers to help pick up play equipment. Yet the clinician may experience a vague discomfort with this polite prosocial child. Silently attending to this feeling, the clinician senses annoyance and wonders what might cause it. Is the feeling coming from within? Did I sleep well the night before? Did I have an argument with family or colleague? Or could the sense of annoyance reflect something about Linda? Is there something else beneath the surface of her pleasing compliance? The youngster may be angry or hurt and attempting to conceal it—perhaps outside of Linda's conscious awareness.

Utilizing our internal feelings to enrich clinical assessment mandates knowledge of ourselves. Are we confident that the source for the puzzling annoyed feeling does not stem from something like unconscious rivalry or competition with the patient's parent? As clinicians we need to know ourselves well enough to identify reliably the sources of our own feelings. Each of us as individuals represent a vital clinical instrument—akin to our reliance on laboratory findings, imaging, and other valued sources of clinical data.

There are multiplicity of approaches to enhance self-understanding. Clinical supervision followed by peer group consultation suffice for some. Many find personal psychotherapy to be especially useful. Enhanced self-understanding should be a life-long professional goal. See also the section on transference and countertransference below.)

Defenses

A challenge facing clinicians is how to understand the patient's manifest activity—what we observe. Is there something important lying beneath the child's behavior? Is Linda covering anger with pleasantries or is she truly in a genuinely pleasant mood? If the child's activity during the assessment differs markedly from what might be expected from the history gathered from parents and teachers, the clinician should be alert to the possibility of the child's being defensive in the clinical setting—obscuring deeper worries or conflicts. The frightened child acting tough or the worried child acting cocky represents the effects of psychological defenses, those intrapsychic maneuvers outside our consciousness which protect us from awareness of personally uncomfortable feelings and conflicts. Thus defenses help preserve psychic equilibrium, they help maintain self-esteem, permit us to function without undo anxiety, and help us deal adaptively with internal and external reality (see Table 85.1).

Defensive operations may be stratified from the developmentally immature, rigid, less adaptive ones (e.g., projection, projective identification, splitting, and denial) to the more flexible and adaptive defenses (e.g., repression, identification, reaction formation, rationalization, sublimation, and intellectualization). Between those extremes are mechanisms like identification, undoing, and conversion. In general, children and adolescents who utilize immature or rigid defenses are less likely to join with the clinician in a collaborative effort to find help. Many will blame their circumstance on others—parents, school, even the clinician whom they have just met. Hence, being able to recognize defenses may help the clinician predict the alliance with the patient as well as the patient's response to interventions. In addition, understanding defenses helps us achieve an important goal: the tying together of the child's inner world and outer behavior in order to understand the problems and devise ameliorative strategies (Bleiberg, Fonagy, & Target, 1997). Further, this understanding may be the only way to make sense out of symptomatic behavior which otherwise may be perceived as psychotic or delinquent. Endeavoring to understand maintains the humanity of those with whom we consult. Perceiving others as like us, trying to make the best of life, enriches the process of planning therapeutic intervention strategies.

Defensive operations are likely if the child's words and deeds are different from what might be anticipated. An illustration is the child who has just experienced parental separation but talks

TABLE 85.1

Defense Mechanisms

More flexible and adaptive:

Intellectualization imposes thought to control an emotionally charged situation and avoid feeling. After finding out that a friend has developed a potentially fatal illness, a teenager feels nothing while retreating to the library to devour books and periodicals about the illness.

Isolation of affect refers to the separation of feeling from thinking. A child whose pet died expends a lot of thought and energy preparing for the funeral in an unconscious effort to avoid experiencing sadness.

Reaction formation allows a person to handle contradictory competing impulses by acknowledging the more acceptable side of the conflict. For example, children enjoy messing, finger painting, mud pies; mixing together recipe ingredients delight them. But society rewards cleanliness and orderliness. Thus a child may be troubled by simultaneous wishes to be both clean (superego) and soiled (id), which might be resolved, so to speak, by the child emphasizing cleanliness to the point of fastidiousness. The meticulousness represents a reaction formation against the wish to experience pleasure by soiling.

Rationalization involves conceiving justifications to explain an otherwise unacceptable thought or action. The child stated that cheating was okay because the exam was unfair, illness precluded studying, and besides, no one liked the teacher anyway.

Repression is a fundamental defensive operation. It banishes unacceptable wishes, thoughts, actions, and feelings from awareness. Unselective repression, via a yet unidentified biological mechanism, is the fate of virtually all cognitions in the first two or so years of life. Elementary school-age children who suffered the death of a parent during their toddler years may berate themselves for their inability to generate a memory of the deceased parent in contrast to the memories recalled by older siblings and the surviving parent. With maturity, repression becomes selective and often needs the help of additional defensive maneuvers to maintain unawareness of those memories unconsciously selected for repression.

Sublimation entails the substitution of an accepted acitvity for one that is not acceptable. Angry aggression can be sublimated into contact sports.

Mid-level:

Conversion refers to developing a somatic symptom that represents an unconscious wish or impulse. The child who wishes to strike an abusive stepparent and run away from home develops a paralysis of the legs which precludes acting on the feeling.

Dissociation refers to a temporary loss of identity or sense of reality. When Michelle was hit, she stopped feeling the blows and lost all sense of time while remaining fully conscious. Later she realized that she had been walking for a long time, but had no memory of being hit or her walk.

Identification is a developmentally more mature version of introjection and incorporation which children and adolescents use to grow and develop. Frank, 16, develops a swagger like his coach and denounces cigarettes in spite of the fact that he occasionally sneaks one (as does the coach).

Undoing refers to the child's efforts to reverse imagined damage caused by thoughts, feelings, or wishes. After disrupting mother's coffee with friends, Jenny, 5, is sent to her bedroom where she arranges her dolls in a tea party in which the baby doll helps the mommy doll, who praises the baby for her help.

Less adaptive, more immature:

Denial refers to the negation of a thought, feeling, or wish. The child appears psychologically blind to internal feelings or external events. In spite of the fact that the teen repeatedly gets into trouble—drinking, failure to complete homework, curfew violations—while with certain peers who have betrayed him, he tells his parents and he believes that these peers are "friends" who exert no bad influence on him. On the other hand, adaptation may require denial when armed intercontinental missiles target where we live.

Introjection and *incorporation* are mental mechanisms employed to adopt the characteristics of someone in an effort to control an overpowering fear of the other person. Initially frightened of the students at his new school, William dyed his hair black, donned a tongue stud, and bullied smaller students.

Projection renders feelings tolerable by attributing them to another person. The child who misses an absent parent and is angry at the parent for leaving may perceive the anger as intolerable. The same anger can be rendered tolerable by *projecting* the anger onto the parent and feeling that parent left because the parent was mad. By

TABLE 85.1

(*Continued*)

attributing this feeling and impulse to the parent, the child maintains the sense of being good without awareness of the unacceptable anger.

Projective identification is a defensive maneuver whereby the child projects unconsciously unacceptable feelings onto another person so that the feelings are perceived as the other person's feelings. The child then feels a kinship with the other person. This process may permit intrapsychic change in the child if the child experiences the projections as neither alienating nor destroying the other person. For example, after a particularly frustrating day at school, Alice exploded at her father when he asked her to end her lenghty telephone conversation so that others might use the phone. She screams, "I hate you. You hate me. Everyone hates me." and storms off to her room. Father examines his feelings, realizes he is annoyed about the unavailability of the phone, but does not feel hateful. He wonders what he can he do to help his daughter. To go to her room would risk prolonging and escalating the tantrum. Aware of feeling helpless and powerless (the feelings his daughter projected), Dad elects to contain his feelings, master them, and trust his daughter to do the same. He waits and talks to Alice later. Via identification, she adopts her father's mature neutralization of the anger.

Regression entails renouncing age-appropriate wishes for those of an earlier developmental period. A fourth grader, experiencing trouble with homework and beginning to feel dumb, gets out his younger sister's second grade work and breezes through it.

Somatization involves developing physical symptoms as a way to manage psychic pain. Carl complained of severe abdominal pain when his parent's separated and he could only see his father twice a month.

Splitting refers to the simplification and reduction of other people into all good or all bad categories to facilitate either idealization as all good or devaluation as all bad. Cliques may be based on this phenomenon. Kathy's boyfriend breaks up with her and starts to go with another girl. Kathy tells her friends what a creep he is. Even though he was wonderful last week, he is now a rotten human being.

Turning against the self refers to youngsters doing to themselves what they would like to do to another person. Tom, 4, becomes furious when another child takes away a toy. He clenches his fist, turns red, then sticks his fist in his own mouth and bites himself.

More detailed discussion of defenses can be found in A. Freud (1937) and Vaillant (1977).

about everything and anything except the family disruption. Similarly, if the child demonstrates incongruities such as punching walls and claiming not to be angry, the clinician is probably observing defenses in operation. Delineating the patient's predominant defensive style contributes to shaping assessment interviews (e.g., Gothelf, Apter, Ratzoni, et al., 1995). A fruitful strategy for discerning a child's defensive style is to employ displacement by interacting with the child in play. For example, while a child when asked directly about mother's death may demonstrate isolation of affect and undoing, that same child may be able to integrate sad thoughts, feelings, and actions as long as it is the puppet or doll who has experienced the death of a mother puppet or doll. The child may feel safe only when allowing "someone else" to experience the intolerable feelings.

Throughout the history-taking and interview process, the clinician is constantly assessing defensive style. What does the child do or report thinking at a time of stress? When Grandma died,

Mom mourned her mother's loss and became less available emotionally to Jim. How did Jim respond? Did he regress to wetting or soiling? Did he deny mother's unavailability by stating that nothing had changed? Did Jim attempt to care for his mother (might that be reaction formation?)? Jane's parents are undergoing divorce, but during the play interview Jane sets up a family in the dollhouse with mother and father living together. If we note that differs from Jane's family and suggest or move one doll to a different location, how does Jane react? Does she sadly acknowledge her wish to change reality or does she regress and insistently reunite the parents (denial)? Or does she effect a reunion and remarriage (undoing)? Or does she . . . ?

Kevin, 16, was referred because of repeated violent outbursts. Recently while playing pool with friends, he missed a shot and became enraged. He splintered his cue on the table and began cursing. His friends left and when his parents tried to calm him, Kevin struck his mother and kicked his father. The next day he went to school, returned home, and never mentioned anything about the previous evening's events. His parents complained to the clinician that Kevin has never shown remorse following such outbursts. Not only were they concerned about his violence, but also the absence of remorse, suggesting a deficiency of conscience. After interviewing Kevin, the clinician stated that he perceived things differently. Kevin set nearly perfectionistic standards for himself. He would have felt devastated had he continued to think about his actions and their impact on his friends and family. Unable to tolerate such unacceptable feelings, he used the primitive defense mechanisms of projective identification and denial and acted as though the troubling events had never occurred. His defensive operations helped protect him from uncomfortable feelings and conflicts, while making those around him anxious, distraught, and frightened. The clinician can distinguish the defense of denial from a psychotic deficiency of reality testing by asking the patient about the events. The psychotic patient will maintain it never occurred, whereas the nonpsychotic patient who had maintained denial will acknowledge the event's occurrence and become either anxious or blame others, which is what Kevin did. Hence, while the clinician believed that Kevin did have a conscience and beneath the surface felt terrible about what had happened, the clinician simultaneously recognized Kevin's reliance on immature defenses to support his perfectionist high standards. Along with addressing the underlying cause of the outbursts, these psychological mechanisms were the focus of therapeutic interventions.

Melody, 11, was brought for assessment because she was not learning in school. The examining clinician wondered about a specific learning disability and preformed a series of tests and collected information from the school. Melody possessed high average intelligence, but seemed unable to learn math and history. She read well, paid attention, finished her projects, and was well behaved. The clinician was puzzled. This patient met no criteria for any attention or learning disorders, yet she was not learning. Could something be occurring beneath the surface to explain the behavior? Additional interviews were arranged to explore underlying dynamics.

Melody drew some pictures of a family with two fathers, not one. When asked about the second father, she explained that there was only one father, the other figure was a mistake and she erased it. She seemed nervous and the clinician hypothesized that defenses were operating to protect her from this anxiety. Was there something she should not learn? In addition to the expected behavior of a child with a biological learning and/or attention problem, there is the anxiety regarding an extra man in the picture. Did the anxiety reflect maladaptive defenses? Indeed, explorations with the patient and her family uncovered a family secret. The defensive maneuvers manifested by learning problems served to avoid illuminating that Melody's father was different from that of her two younger siblings. Melody had been born 7 months after her mother's marriage, but was told she was premature. Yet mother told the pediatrician her birthweight was greater than her younger sister's who was not premature. The numbers and history did not add up per her mother's elaborate subterfuge. So Melody adopted a defensive style utilizing denial, rationalization, and identification with the mother that permitted her to avoid learning the secret but also impeded desired learning.

Returning to 14-year-old Zack, who presented in an aggressive, nasty fashion, the clinician addressed two facts in the clinical history that suggested something else underlay the aggressive surface. First, Zack had done okay until 3 or 4 years ago—he passed his courses, had friends, and enjoyed soccer and basketball. Second, losses occurred in the family. Mother's mother, who died recently, had been diagnosed with breast cancer 4 years earlier. Downsized, father had to find a new job which necessitated much travel and a family move. The clinician hypothesized that beneath Zack's aggression was a sense of loss, depression, and dysphoria, and that neurological studies being contemplated might be postponed in favor of getting to know Zack via a series of clinical assessment interviews. When the clinician spoke with Zack about getting to know people, Zack commented that it was not worth the effort because "they were never around when you needed them." The aggression was easy to understand as a defense against loss, depression, and loneliness. As the assessment progressed in subsequent interviews, Zack demonstrated not only the capacity for relationships, but also a desire for them, in contrast to his initial protest. If the clinician had not wondered whether something lay beneath Zack's abrasive surface, this youth might have been investigated neurologically and in the absence of a remedial problem been referred to juvenile authorities and placed in a correctional facility.

Ego Functions

Ego functions encompass those psychological activities regulating the relationship to self, others, and the environment. These functions may be conscious (decision making, organization), unconscious (perception, memory, involuntary motor activity), and preconscious, that is, outside of awareness, but available to consciousness (voluntary motor activity, cognitive functions, self-esteem). Sharp and Bellack (1978) delineated 12 ego functions that can facilitate organization of the massive data of clinical observation (see Table 85.2).

Assessment of ego function provides a particularly useful model to describe the strengths and weaknesses of a child. By carefully examining these abilities, the clinician is able to delineate not only what needs improvement, but the strengths the patient brings to the clinical setting which can be utilized therapeutically. For example, the clinician might enlist a patient's sense of reality and autonomous functioning to help gain better regulation of drives, affects, and impulses that would consequently improve interpersonal relations and mastery competence. Evaluation of ego functions helps assess risk in suicidal children (Pfeffer, Hurt, Peskin, et al., 1995).

Drives

Drives refer to what Freud designated as id functioning in his tripartite model of the mind. Unfortunately, some otherwise valuable English language literature mistranslated Freud's concept of drives as "instincts," creating English linguistic confusion. Freud hypothesized sexual and aggressive drives as inherent, reflecting the energy the child possesses either to seek joy and positive interactions or to display destructive and perhaps self-defeating behavior.

A second way to think about drives is that they serve to organize experience. In lieu of emerging from a seething id cauldron, drives can be compared to Chomsky's deep structures (Pinker, 1994) or processes that energize ego functioning. Life events are experienced as pleasurable or painful through these structures and organized in the mind as memories or representations of experience with the world. Libido, the sexual or pleasurable drive, then becomes a way of representing and experiencing the world, as opposed to a force propelling one through the world. This model helps the clinician understand children who become involved in repetitive situations, whether helpful or destructive. The achieving children who assimilate information, seek others who help them, and feel satisfied somehow end up eliciting positive efforts even from less achieving peers. The capacity to organize experience and internalize representations of interactions consistent with their experience (and constitute the deep structures) may be responsible for this ability. Historical reports as well as the child's response in the clinical setting will inform the clinician how the child internally represents experience. In the most basic model, is the child's predominant organization positive and rewarding or negative and defeating? The implications of this model are crucial for any intervention: if a child does not possess structures geared to assimilate positive helpful experience, they must first be developed through positive interactions with the therapist and other important people in the child's life. On the other hand, if those structures exist, the clinician must empathically tap them to help the child.

Superego

Superego refers to the youngster's ideals, goals, and conscience. Clinicians can assess superego functioning through inquiry regarding the child's aspirations, heroes, and standards. What is the child's concept of fair play? This idea can be inferred directly from playing board games with the child or less directly by posing moral dilemmas

TABLE 85.2

Ego Functions

Adaptive regression in the service of ego functioning is the capacity to act younger than one's age for a specific purpose (e.g., fun, spiritual experience) accompanied by the capacity to return to acting one's actual age when appropriate. Joy, 16, while babysitting, genuinely enjoyed finger painting and modeling clay with her preschool charges. But the pleasure did not interfere with her providing supervision when appropriate. She also engaged the children in cleaning up.

Autonomous functioning may include activities (e.g., athletic, scholastic, artistic) that are free from psychological conflict. Whatever else occurred in her life, Susan always attended her dance lessons and performed well. For Robert, sports were initially an outlet for aggression, but he began to enjoy them for their own sake and became a skilled basketball player. Dancing and playing competitive basketball had become autonomous functions.

Defensive functioning (see Table 85.1) are those unconscious psychological maneuvers which protect us from awareness of disagreeable feelings.

Judgment entails recognizing that one has options, weighing them, and deciding what to do in a given situation. Molly, 14, complains of boredom, leaves a group of peers, and wanders off in an unfamiliar area. Strangers confront her and she becomes frightened and worried. After finding her way back, she questions her judgment in leaving the group.

Interpersonal relations (which have unfortunately been referred to as *object relations* in valuable psychodynamic literature) calls upon the clinician to assess the quality of the youngster's relationships with others via two clinical channels. First is what the child and people who know him report about relationships with others, both peers and authority figures. Are they mutual or is one exploiting the other? Is a teenage boy sexually using a girl or the girl using the boy to gain status with peers? Is a current relationship a repetition of an earlier destructive one? The second source of information derives from our interaction with the youngster. How are we treated? The child's reaction to the clinician may provide valuable clues to understand how the child views other adults. This concept is discussed in more detail under the heading of transference later in this chapter.

Mastery competence is meeting and overcoming new challenges. Matt, 16, is scheduled to begin classes at a new school. To prepare, he visits the school to learn the location of his classes and initiates arrangements to meet other students who will help him with his new challenge.

Reality testing refers to the accurate perception of the external world, that is, the ability to distinguish internal processes from external events. Delusions and hallucinations, which are not as common in children as in adults, represent impaired reality testing. We should endeavor to delineate the circumstances in which reality testing becomes impaired. Are there emotionally charged topics or situations, such as separation, loss, perceived rejection from peer group, etc., in which the capacity to test reality suffers and the world is perceived as more arbitrary and capricious than it really is?

Regulation and control of drives is the capacity to control impulses and not act reflexively on urges. Thought is interposed between wish and action. Sexually excited Jason delays contacting his 14-year-old classmate until he finds out if she will be receptive. The growing child resists the urge to take candy from the store.

Sense of reality involves an altered experience of reality without frank misperceptions. For example, one may see a menacing, threatening person, but not feel fear. That feeling is separated or dissociated from the event, which is accurately perceived. Disassociative phenomena may refer to a person's sense of something not being quite real (derealization) or not really happening to oneself (depersonalization). The experience of violence may elicit a change in a child's sense of reality. If a child witnesses a shooting, that child may ignore the danger and act as though he were never in danger, while not denying the event. The abused child may not experience the pain and may feel it is not really he who is being hit. Another child may experience no pain immediately after an accident and only experience hurt on seeing blood and reactions of others in the vicinity.

Stimulus barrier refers to the child's ability to focus on an important sensory input and ignore extraneous stimuli. The child with a less selective threshold is readily distracted by peripheral, even repetitive stimuli and experiences difficulty sustaining attention. This factor assumes increasing importance with the ever-increasing cultural stimulation impacting on teens with their propensity to seek thrills.

Synthetic integrative functioning involves the capacity to pull together contradictory feelings, thoughts, and experiences into a united whole. Steve feels left out of friendships and lonely. Part of him would like to make friends, but he feels anxious and uncomfortable when he meets other children. He realizes that he wants to be

TABLE 85.2

(*Continued*)

with and to avoid peers at the same time. Thinking about the contradiction, he compartmentalizes the reason for his discomfort as his being bullied by a tiny group of classmates. But that hasn't occurred in several months. Steve then integrates the bullying experience with different, satisfying acquaintances and decides on a plan to talk and play with peers. He has synthesized disparate experiences, integrated them, and developed an adaptive plan.

Thought processes and content are formal aspects of cognition like memory, concentration, attention, and abstraction.

Sharp and Bellack (1978) originally described these ego functions.

(e.g., if your family is starving and has no money, is it all right to steal bread?) and listening to the child's response. The clinician may also ask the child about heroes and what the child wants to do after finishing school. The child's conduct during the interview will yield information about superego functioning. How does the young patient respond to directions to draw a person, clean up, or answer a question? Among other possibilities, the child's actions may reflect views toward authority or a wish to please. Does the child ever feel shame or guilt? If so, under what circumstance? If not, what does the child feel after hurting a peer's feelings?

Assessment of superego function helps determine how much external control will be required for therapeutic intervention: inpatient, residential, partial hospitalization, or outpatient. Children with immature superego functioning are more likely to experience the clinician's comments as criticism than the child with a more forgiving conscience. How the child experiences the clinician is discussed under the rubric of transference and countertransference.

Transference and Countertransference

A central component of psychodynamic assessment is understanding the interpersonal interaction in the clinical context. When two people interact with each other, past experiences with people in similar roles influence the process. Transference refers to those interpersonal responses which are based on past experiences. In the clinical context, transference is shaped by earlier experience with helpers, teachers, authority figures, older people, and/or parents. The child whose parents were harshly critical and abusive may reflexively experience the clinician similarly. The superego, derived in part from identification with parents, contributes to this set of beliefs. This child may experience an invitation to draw or to play as a criticism that the child has done something wrong by not playing. The child does not react to the reality of the clinician as a helper.

The child's unconscious experience of past relationships in the presence of the clinician has been designated as transference, and the clinician's responses to the child's transference, as well as to the totality of the child and family, has been designated countertransference. In addition to the clinician's countertransference responses to the child's transference, we experience our own individualistic transference responses to the youngster as well. Both clinician and child have past experiences and problems. Consequently, it is vital that we understand our own past and our propensities for experiencing certain feelings regarding children. If assessment of a certain type of child results in the clinician feeling a specific emotion, that should be used to enhance understanding. For example, one clinician may experience annoyance with passive dependent children; whereas another may feel an overwhelming wish to rescue. Neither feeling is "correct" or "incorrect," but both should be used to inform us about the child as we factor in the possible influence of our past and our personal mood that day.

Dynamic Formulation

In the course of the assessment, the clinician determines the adaptiveness of the defensive style, the relative strength and weakness of the youngster's ego functioning, the child's superego functioning, and transference and countertransference paradigms. The child's energy level and experience of the clinical interaction helps the clinician to assess the strength of the child's drives and/or the child's internal representation of experience.

Endeavoring to identify the patient's inner forces and tensions generates hypotheses about intrapsychic conflicts and possible resolution. Conflicts can be conceptualized as unconscious struggles between urges for pleasure and social prohibitions or autonomy and interpersonal closeness or even competing prosocial values. Examples include the teen torn between two superego values—the wish to obtain additional education and the sense of obligation to work as many hours as possible to contribute to the family's limited resources. In another youngster the clinician may identify the internal conflict of anger at one parent for not understanding and fear of reprisal if the anger is exposed; or the wish to steal and shame if caught; or the wish to succeed at school and fear of exceeding one's peers.

In summary, psychodynamic assessment provides a link between the youngster and problem: what is occurring within the child that results in the symptomatic behavior? (Toews, 1993) The dynamic formulation provides links between assessment and treatment as it summarizes and synthesizes the data of observation. Shapiro (1989, 1991) delineates the following four-step process which we illustrate by returning to our angry, rude, help-rejecting, 14-year-old, Zack.

- Global identifying summary: a brief description of the patient including age (date of birth), year in school, current living arrangements, and reason for clinical consultation. For example, Zack is a 14-year-old (DOB 8/29/86), eighth-grade student earning C's, D's, and 1 F in regular courses. He lives with his 42-year-old mother, an artist; 45-year-old father, a corporate manager; 17-year-old sister; and 10-year-old brother. His sister has achieved well in school, but the younger brother is diagnosed with learning problems and attention deficit disorder. The parents brought Zack to obtain help with his aggressive outbursts and deteriorating academic performance.
- Life events: a summary of significant life events such as deaths, changes of school, divorce, and

other verifiable occurrences in the child's life. Zack's mother reported the pregnancy with Zack had preceded smoothly, unlike that with his younger brother. Zack's developmental milestones unfolded within normal limits. He had no prolonged or unusual medical illnesses and no surgery. The family lived in the same house until 4 years ago, when two important events occurred. First, father had to find a new job which necessitated a family move and his having to be away a great deal on business travel. Second, Mother's mother, who died recently, had been diagnosed with breast cancer about the time of the move. At this time, father acknowledged a drinking problem. The parents disclosed they had experienced a marital separation 2 years earlier.

- Dynamic summary: the patient's response to the life events. Here the clinician applies the psychodynamic framework. The clinician reviews the components (id, superego, ego functions including defenses, transference, and countertransference) and states her hypothesis which links the child's inner and outer worlds to the presenting problem. Zack had been involved with school and sports until the move, suggesting he once had the capacity to organize his experience positively. He had a strict and at times punitive conscience that would not permit him to integrate his explosions into his self-concept. Hence he denied the severity and impact of the explosions. Further, his aggression seemed to be a response to distressing inner feelings of loss (old friends, school, father with the travel, and mother because of her mother's death and the demands of helping Zack's younger brother adjust). The world that had been so supportive and friendly was now experienced as hostile, arbitrary, and capricious. Zack would fight against it. His sense of reality and interpersonal relations were disrupted and disturbed. His not yet having turned to substance use was a strength, but how long would it last?
- Predictive response: How will the child respond to the people who treat him and to subsequent interventions? Because of experience with the child in assessment, the clinician can anticipate transference paradigms. While Zack initially rejected the clinician's comments and the very notion that he might be having some problems, with empathic statements about the numerous changes he experienced over the past 4 years, followed by acknowledgment of the losses, Zack demonstrated not only a capacity but also a desire for relationships consistent with the parent's reports of his functioning prior to the move. The therapist must be sensitive to the patient's wish for autonomy and not become

another teacher or parent, lest the therapeutic process repeat the failure at school or home and result in interruption of treatment processes. Simultaneous interviews targeted the parent's dysfunctional transactions as a couple, father's drinking, and Zack's brother's school and learning difficulties. Tutoring to help remediate Zack's academic deficits will also be considered.

Summary

The components of a psychodynamic assessment include sources of data, defenses, ego function, drives, superego functions, and transference/ countertransference paradigms. The clinician uses psychodynamics to generate hypotheses that link the patient and the problems. The hypotheses are honed and modified through the course of the assessment. The dynamic formulation may be conceptualized as the link between the assessment and the treatment. Here, one can understand the youngster who has a specific problem and how that child may respond to proposed interventions. The clinician's conceptualization of a psychodynamic formulation should add to maintaining the whole child as the central focus in helping children.

Readers seeking more detailed discussion of psychodynamic concepts should access the works of Brenner (1973), Erikson (1963), A. Freud (1937), Lichtenberg (1985), and Waelder (1960), as well as the more recent contributions of Grotstein and Rinsley (1994), Kernberg (1992), and Ogden (1986).

REFERENCES

Bleiberg, E., Fonagy, P., & Target, M. (1997). Child psychoanalysis: Critical overview and a proposed reconsideration. *Child and Adolescent Psychiatric Clinics of North America, 6,* 1–38.

Brenner, C. (1973). *An elementary textbook of psychoanalysis.* New York: International Universities Press.

Erikson, E. (1963). *Childhood and society.* New York: W. W. Norton.

Feldman, S. S., Aroujo, K. B., Steiner, H. (1996). Defense Mechanisms in adolescents as a function of age, sex, and mental health status. *Journal of the American Academy of Child and Adolescent Psychiatry, 34,* 1344–1354.

Freud, A. (1937). *The ego and the mechanisms of defense.* London: Hogarth Press.

Freud, S. (1961). The ego and the id. In J. Strachey (Ed. and Trans.), *The standard edition of the complete psychology works of Sigmund Freud* (Vol. 19, pp. 3–66). London: Hogarth Press. (Original work published 1923.)

Gothelf, D., Apter, A., Ratzoni, G., Orbach, I., Weizman, R., Tyano, S., Pfeffer, C. (1995). Defense mechanisms in severe adolescent anorexia nervosa. *Journal of the American Academy of Child and Adolescent Psychiatry, 34,* 1648–1654.

Grotstein, J., & Rinsley, D. B. (Eds.) (1994). *Fairbairn and the origins of object relations.* New York: Guilford Press.

Kernberg, O. F. (1992). *Aggression in personality disorders and perversions.* New Haven, CT: Yale University Press.

Lichtenberg, J. (1985). *"The talking cure" A descriptive guide to psychoanalysis.* Hillsdale, NJ: Lawrence Erlbaum.

Ogden, T. (1986). *The matrix of the mind: Object relations and the psychoanalytic dialogue.* Northvale, NJ: Jason Aronson.

Pfeffer, C., Hurt, S., Peskin, J., Siefker, C. (1995). Suicidal children grown up: Ego functions associated with suicide attempts. *Journal of the American Academy of Child and Adolescent Psychiatry, 34,* 1328–1325.

Pinker, S. (1994). *The language instinct.* New York: William Morrow and Co.

Shapiro, T. (1989). The psychodynamic formulation in child and adolescent psychiatry. *Journal of the American Academy of Child and Adolescent Psychiatry, 5,* 675–680.

Shapiro, T. (1991). Diagnosis and diagnostic formulation. In J. Weiner (ed.) *Textbook of child and adolescent psychiatry* (pp. 128–135). Washington, DC: American Psychiatric Press.

Sharp, V., & Bellack, L. (1978). Ego function assessment. *Psychoanalytic Quarterly, 47,* 52–72.

Toews, J. A. (1993). Editorial: Case formulation in psychiatry: Revitalizing an ailing art. *Canadian Journal of Psychiatry, 38,* 344.

Vaillant, G. E. (1977). *Adaptation to life.* Boston: Little, Brown.

Waelder, R. (1960). *Basic theory of psychoanalysis.* New York: International Universities Press.

86 / Rating Scales

Jacquelin Goldman and James R. Rodrigue

Parent and child report measures were developed to ensure that topics of interest to clinicians would be surveyed or screened comprehensively. However, such measures were not constructed and should not be conceived of as diagnostic in themselves. They are meant to be used as one of several different sources of data, in particular, to supplement interview data and data provided by standardized tests. All of these methods are commonly employed approaches used in psychological evaluations as well as in research.

Psychological evaluations are performed for assessment of a wide range of problems and requests for such assessments arrive through many types of referral channels. Many evaluations are performed for descriptive purposes rather than because a problem has been detected. These referrals for descriptive purposes are generally used in everyday decision making, for example, to determine school placement, for preadoption, or before other legal action takes place.

Referrals for evaluation regarding dysfunction often come from schools, physicians, and social agencies. These referrals are prompted because the child is having difficulty in maintaining an adequate level of achievement, because behavioral problems have become obvious, or because the child appears withdrawn or unhappy. Either the parents or school officials refer the child to clarify the nature of the problems and seek counsel in making decisions about how to treat the child.

Neuropsychological evaluations often aid neurologists in determining the degree to which brain dysfunction has affected cognitive and motor function. In some settings, pre- and postsurgical or pre- and posttreatment testing is done to determine the effects of the intervention. Researchers are particularly interested in the effects of some aggressive treatments (radiation and chemotherapy) on a broad range of cognitive and affective functions.

Probably the most frequent reason for evaluation by psychologists is because the child is behaving in a way that has distressed some adult caretaker, impaired the child's interpersonal relationship, or made management difficult. Children are thus referred to determine the nature of the problems and the type of treatment that might be indicated.

Even though a referral may have been prompted by a set of presenting complaints or for what seems a purely administrative reason, the clinician should keep an open mind as to the possibility of other alternatives. For this reason, even when the referral question seems straightforward, it is sometimes helpful to use screening instruments because they can provide information on important issues that may not have been obvious to the referral source.

Given the nature of the referral for the assessment, the psychologist must decide which clinical methods and instruments to employ. Chapter 87 on psychological testing includes an overview of the measurement issues involved in the use of tests. In this chapter the material will center on parent and child reports. These measures, largely rating scales and checklists, are not intended nor should they be used as a substitute for interview and other assessment procedures (Goldman, L'Engle Stein, & Guerry, 1983).

Clinical assessment by means of checklists and rating scales implicitly involves many of the same measurement issues that are encountered in the use of psychometric tests. One major issue is that of validity, specifically which information about a child is most valid. Retrospective data from parents, for example, may reflect bias, inaccurate observation, and defensiveness. This is more likely to be true in families with significant problems than in families without major dysfunction. Likewise self-reports by children may also be biased. Children may attempt to please an examiner by saying what they believe the examiner would like to hear. An example would be when the child believes that feeling depressed is devalued. In such cases the child may avoid expression of depression (Cytryn & McKnew, 1974). Children who suffer from conduct disorders, on the other hand, are often resentful of having to come to an evaluation. Their self-reports often suffer from biases that spring from other motivations, either not revealing any psychological distress or not wanting to admit to problem behavior which may be used for dispositions that they want to avoid.

Since these several types of bias may influence both self-reports and reports by parents and other caretakers, the consideration of such factors has stimulated research. The question that is addressed through studies is essentially, What is the best source of data with respect to a given aspect of a child's functioning? Not surprisingly, different sources of data are better for one purpose than another.

Research has shown that parents are the best source of some types of information about children, particularly behavior problems (Achenbach & Edelbrock, 1978). Some data also exists which indicate that the parents' psychopathology is associated with the parents' perceptions of child behavior problems. However, parents are still generally considered to be the primary sources of information regarding child behavior problems (Chamberlain & Reid, 1987).

On the other hand, teachers are the best sources of information about a child's social functioning (Hughes, 1990; Milich & Krelbiel, 1986). Many children who are reported to manifest conduct disorders may also suffer from less obvious internalizing problems. Other children who do not present behavioral problems may suffer from internalizing problems. For these reasons, self-report measures should be included in the assessment of children's problems (Kendall, 1987). Children themselves are the best sources of information about internalizing problems such as depression, anxiety, and poor self-esteem (Hughes, 1984; Reynolds & Richmond, 1985; Saylor, Finch, Furey, Baskin, & Kelly, 1984; Semrud-Clikeman, 1990).

Children's self-reports are especially important because of the stability of these self-perceptions and because they are often incongruent with external indicators of adjustment, including parent and teacher reports (Bierman, 1990). Nor are parents and teachers the only caretakers who may have difficulty in forming accurate estimates of a child's problems and abilities. Child therapists should exercise caution in making judgments of how bright children are, particularly when school problems have been reported. Studies in this area report that therapists rarely are able to make accurate judgments of a child's level of cognitive functioning (Sattler, 1988).

Rating scales and checklists are used by psychologists as a way of collecting data in a systematic manner and often in a brief format. The psychometric properties of rating scales and checklists may vary widely, depending upon whether they were standardized with regard to the measurement principles discussed in Chapter 87 on psychological tests. Many times rating scales and checklists are devised so that there are several forms available, depending upon who is the desired respondent.

Psychologists have created instruments that can be divided into those requiring self-reports and those which are based on the observations of caretakers who know the child well. Both rating scales and checklists have been employed within these categories. In the sections that follow, parent and child report instruments are included which are either psychometrically among the best that can be found or are so widely used as to come to the practitioner's attention.

Checklists

Checklists require the respondent to indicate whether a behavior, a problem, a feeling, or some other type of response occurs. Many checklists are designed for screening or other special purposes by practitioners or in institutional settings. Usually the object of these instruments is to ensure that no important area of interest is overlooked by the clinician, and they typically require the respondent to check all items that apply. Focused interviews or specialized testing may then follow to determine the nature, depth, and breadth of items that have been checked.

Rating Scales

Rating scales provide more information than do checklists. Because rating scales quantify the extent as well as identify the presence of a problem or behavior, the clinician can both highlight an area of interest and determine something about the importance of the area. A child whose parent identifies oppositional behavior as a problem area but indicates that it is seldom a problem suggests a different level of concern than does a parent who both identifies oppositional behavior as a problem and indicates that the problem is severe.

In the following discussion self-report measures will be described first, with parent and teacher report measures reviewed in the next segment.

CHILD AND ADOLESCENT SELF-REPORT MEASURES

In administering self-report measures to children, one of the first concerns is the degree of literacy that they possess. Many children are unable to read or to read at age level because they suffer from learning disabilities or attentional problems. Because many of these children are referred to clinics and practitioners, this is a problem of some consequence. Problems with reading may not be apparent, even when they are of moderate level. If the child is in the appropriate grade for age level, the clinician may assume that all is well. However, many children are assigned to special classes for learning disabilities. When these children and their parents come to the clinic or office, these special classroom placements may not be mentioned. Many times children who cannot read well do not report this fact spontaneously, either because they are embarrassed or suffer from feelings of poor self-esteem when confronted with written material.

Clinicians should never assume that the child can read well enough to complete the self-report measures. In the psychological evaluation, an interview usually precedes formal testing. During the interview some attention should be paid to the cognitive developmental history of the child, including school performance. If this is done, relevant information about learning problems will often surface in the discussion, even though no previous mention of the difficulties may have been made.

Although a cognitive developmental history is gathered from the parent, important facts may be omitted, particularly when the parent is a poor informant or a poor observer. At other times, evaluations are requested when parents are not available for interview, for example, in psychiatric inpatient settings. In fact, a thorough cognitive assessment of the child may reveal unsuspected problems. A very well socialized and attractive child is often seen as bright, probably part of the social halo induced by the other positive aspects of the child's personality. However, some of these children and adolescents will be found to be of low intelligence and with learning problems which prevent them from reading at grade level. As a consequence, these cognitively impaired children and adolescents may be viewed as much more seriously ill psychiatrically than many of them are. Poor judgment can result when children or adolescents who are of borderline intelligence live in unstructured or chaotic living situations. If there is insufficient information to help the clinician make the distinction, the adaptive behavior exhibited by these children may give a superficial impression of major thought disorder. Interpretation of self-report instruments may be faulty if the mental health professional does not have an accurate appraisal of the patient's cognitive level of functioning.

For the reasons cited above, particularly if a major psychiatric diagnosis is entertained, it is wise to have a thorough psychological evaluation, including an assessment of cognitive and scholastic functions. Such an evaluation ordinarily would include individually administered intelligence and achievement tests. The most frequently used instruments of these types with good reliability and validity are the Wechsler intelligence tests and the Woodcock–Johnson Psycho-Educational Battery Revised, Tests of Achievement. The latter instrument will give estimates of reading level.

The norms for self-report instruments indicate the age and/or grade levels for which they are appropriate. If the child's IQ or achievement level is significantly depressed and the child's age is at the lower end (or floor) of the level for the self-report instrument, it is unlikely that reliable information will be obtained through written self-report instruments. In such cases it is better to have extensive interviews, perhaps structured so as to include the scope and nature of the material ordinarily covered in the self-report instrument. It is also possible to derive the reading level of any instrument by means of computerized programs which can assess the vocabulary employed.

Traditionally self-report measures have been used to survey symptoms of internalizing problems in children and adolescents. Whereas many externalizing problems such as conduct disorders, hyperactivity, and oppositional behaviors are obvious to parents and teachers, internalizing problems are much less obvious. In fact, it is likely that many children who are referred because they are behavior problems may have either primary or secondary problems with self-esteem, anxiety, or depression. As a consequence it is desirable for the clinician to assess the child or adolescent for these otherwise often undetected affective problems.

A number of self-report instruments have been developed and are widely used. Many of the instruments that have been published are designed to be employed with special or esoteric populations. Others have little psychometric development and depend almost entirely upon face validity. The instruments of most interest to psychiatrists are those that reveal attitudes and feelings of children, adolescents, and parents with regard to behavioral and affective problems affecting the individuals in a family as well as the family as a whole. The instruments reviewed in this chapter are frequently employed when psychiatric problems are encountered and have known psychometric properties.

Child Depression Inventory (CDI): This is a 27-item instrument designed for children 7 to 17 years old. The CDI elicits information about mood, somatic symptoms, self-evaluation, and interpersonal relationships. The CDI is an adaptation of an adult instrument (the Beck depression inventory) and is written in language understandable by first graders. Cutoff scores have been derived by Carlson and Cantwell (1980) and by Kovacs et al. (1978) for different levels of depression from none to severe. Various aspects of the psychometrics have been studied and found to be reasonable, for example, reliability (Friedman & Butter, 1979) and validity (Kovacs & Beck, 1977). However, the norms are based on a restricted geographical sample. Because the instrument depends heavily upon face validity, it is easy for a child either to deny or to exaggerate symptoms.

Self-Perception Profile for Children: Developed by Harter (1982, 1985), this is a 36-item self-report measure designed for children 8 to 13 years old and who possess at least a third-grade reading level. A pictorial version for younger children and a version for adolescents are also available (Harter & Pike, 1981). The items tap five specific domains and also provide a global estimate of self-worth. The domains that are surveyed include scholastic competence, social acceptance, athletic competence, physical appearance, and behavioral conduct. There are norms for each sex by grade. While the instrument suffers from a restricted geographical sample (the data were collected in a single state), the reliability estimates for internal consistency and for test-retest seem reasonable. Two studies of the instrument (Harter, 1982; Marsh & Governet, 1989) reported good construct, content, and discriminant validity.

Revised Children's Manifest Anxiety Scale (RCMAS): The RCMAS (Reynolds & Richmond, 1978) has 35 items, 28 of which are anxiety related items. The scale is also called "What I Think and Feel" (WITF) and has been factor analyzed (Reynolds & Richmond, 1979) and found to yield three factors consisting of a physiological manifestations of anxiety factor, a worry and oversensitivity factor, and a fear/concentration factor. The measure has been used with children in grades 1 through 12. There are means and standard deviations for total scores and for factor scores for both white and black boys and girls ages 6 to 19. Additionally there are data for a lie subscale which is included in the instrument. There is also a separate kindergarten sample for boys and girls, although no ethnic data are provided. Tables are provided for converting scores to percentile equivalents and to t scores for all of the school-age subjects by race and age.

Reynolds Adolescent Depression Scale (RADS): The RADS (Reynolds, 1987) consists of 30 questions describing symptoms associated with depression for respondents who are 13 to 18 years of age. The symptoms include cognitive, motoric-vegetative, somatic, and interpersonal problems. The subject uses a four-point Likert scale to respond to each item. (Likert scales are based on an ordinal level of measurement, for example, none, a little, a moderate amount, a fairly large amount, a large amount. An ordinal level of measurement permits the application of many statistical techniques unavailable when categories are used, but not as many as when interval levels of measurement are employed.) It is introduced as a questionnaire concerning feelings about oneself and

636

things in general rather than as a depression questionnaire. Because the questions are face valid, it is both possible and easy for a subject to deny symptoms if a response bias of this nature is utilized. For this reason this instrument is best used as a screening device. When denial or oppositional behavior are suspect, if the scores are within normal limits for an adolescent suspected of being depressed, they may not reflect the true level of depression. The mean score on the RADS is 60. Clinical levels of depression are based on the entire standardization sample, but subsample percentile ranks can also be obtained. Different mean score levels have been established for males and females and there is a cutoff score that denotes a clinical level of depression.

The RADS was standardized on a large sample from three schools in one midwestern city; most of the adolescents came from lower middle-class backgrounds (Reynolds, 1987). Reliability estimates are generally .90 or better for α and split-half coefficients. Test-retest reliabilities are reported and adequate, and content, concurrent, and convergent reliabilities have also been studied.

PARENT REPORT MEASURES

Parent report measures are designed to elicit parental viewpoints about a range of child and family related issues. Some parent report measures focus directly upon the child. In effect, these checklists and rating scales require the parents to describe the child's behavior. While some measures ask only for narrowband descriptions of specific problem areas, others are broader in scope. For the purposes of this chapter we will focus on the broaderband instruments. Other measures elicit parents' descriptions of the family structure and of their own degree of stress in relation to the parental role.

It should be stressed that parent report measures are subject to the biases discussed earlier in this chapter, and that some of these biases are likely to be greater in dysfunctional families. Thus when assessment of a child's behavioral problems is desired, multiple sources of information are necessary to ensure that either situational factors or bias have not resulted in a distorted assessment of the child's problems and adjustment. It is commonplace to find situations where parents perceive few problems at home, but teachers note all too many problems at school. If the home environment is permissive and does not demand high levels of achievement and concentration, problems with attention and learning may not be obvious to a parent. Similarly, when there is a disturbed parent-child relationship, overly permissive or overly rigid parenting problems may occur at home, but the child may have little problem in a well-structured school setting.

Child Behavior Checklist (CBCL): The CBCL (Achenbach & Edelbrock, 1983) is a standardized measure that assesses children from 4 to 14 years old for both behavioral deviance and social competence as seen by parents. The behavioral deviance scales were derived through factor analytic methods that yielded two broadband factors: internalization and externalization. There are also narrowband subscales: schizoid/anxious, depressed, uncommunicative, obsessive-compulsive, somatic complaints, social withdrawal, hyperactivity, aggressive, and delinquent. The social competence scales assess the amount and quality of the child's participation in activities, school, and social situations.

One limitation of the CBCL is that the standardization used only outpatient clinical samples. The total number of items is 138, which are answered on a three-point scale. It should be noted that a teacher's form of the same instrument has been developed, as well as a self-report version for older children. The parent form requires a fifth-grade reading level. Norms are supplied for three age levels by sex. The reliabilities are quite good and validity studies comparing clinic and nonclinic children have been reported favorably (Buros, 1972; Goldman et al., 1983; Sattler, 1988).

Conners Rating Scales: These rating scales include both long and short versions of parent and teacher rating forms; the scales are designed to evaluate reported problem behavior of the child. The various forms yield scores for hyperactivity, conduct problems, learning problems, antisocial behavior, anxiety, obsessive-compulsive behavior, and psychosomatic problems, although the exact content varies with the form used. Versions of the Conners rating scales first appeared in 1969. The initial form consisted of a 39-item teacher version (CTRS-39) designed to study the effects of medication administered for inattention and hyperactivity on children's behavior. Unfortunately the majority of items are related to conduct disorder problems, obscuring discrimination of conduct disorder from problems related to hyperactivity and inattention. Subsequently a 28-item version of the teacher scale (CTRS-28) and a 48-item parent scale (CPRS-48) appeared. Unfortunately both forms were based on a sample that was almost exclusively white and drawn from one geographical location. The CPRS-93 norms are based on 1970 data.

Despite the widespread use of these scales, they are rife with psychometric problems. Poor sampling in the CTRS-28, CPRS-48, and CTRS-39 versions make the norms of questionable value. The CTRS-28 and CPRS-48 also have very small numbers of children at each level of gender and age. The CPRS-93 was published in 1989 but used the limited 1970 sample and did not present basic psychometric data. Even the 1989 10-item hyperactivity index contained within the longer 1989 version does not report data supporting construct validity. As a result, while there has been some support for the scales' ability to demonstrate behavior change in response to medication, the diagnostic value of the scales is highly questionable. Recent reviewers (Martens, 1992; Oehler-Stinnett, 1992) strongly caution practitioners to be aware of newer measures that may be more useful instruments for children who have problems of inattention, hyperactivity, and impulsivity.

Family Adaptability and Cohesion Scales (FACES-III): This is the third version (Olson, Portner, & Lavee, 1985) of a measure of family functioning that describes families on two dimensions: adaptability and cohesion. Family adaptability refers to the ability of the family system to change role relationships, relationship rules, and power structure as the family encounters stress, which may be either situational or developmental. Cohesion refers to how closely the family members are bonded to each other and what manner of boundaries, shared activities, time, and support characterize the family.

Because a circumplex model underlies this instrument, there is a curvilinear relationship postulated for each of these factors, with the middle levels describing optimal family adjustment. This self-report measure consists of 20 items rated on a five-point scale.

Reliability estimates are acceptable and the scales are independent. The standardization sample was described as nonproblem families. Joan-

ning and Kuehl (1986) have criticized the FACES III for imposing its model on families, particularly minority and underprivileged families whose structures may differ from the model and the standardization sample.

Family Environment Scale (FES): The FES (Moos, 1974) is included here under parent report measures, but it is actually a self-report measure that can be completed by both parents and adolescents. It consists of 90 true/false items covering three areas: relationships, including cohesion, expressiveness, and conflict; personal growth, including independence, achievement orientation, intellectual/cultural orientation, and moral/religious emphasis; and system maintenance including organization and control. There are two forms available for real and ideal family environment concepts.

The norms for this measure were based on 1125 normal and 500 distressed families which are not described in terms of age, race, socioeconomic status, or other variables. However, the sample did include some single-parent, multigenerational, and ethnic minority families which are reported national in distribution. Validity is based on the ability of the subscales both to discriminate between normal and distressed families and to detect change in treatment. However, construct validity studies, such as factor analyses, have not been reported. While reliability is reported for test-retest (generally in the .70s), some questions about concurrent validity have been raised (Bagarozzi, 1984; Busch-Rossnagel, 1985; Lambert, 1985).

Minnesota Child Development Inventory (MCDI): The MCDI (Ireton & Thwing, 1974) was designed to identify children from 1 to 6 years of age who suffer from developmental delays. The parent or other primary caregiver reports the behavior of the child on a 320-item questionnaire. Eight areas are surveyed: general development, gross motor, fine motor, expressive language, comprehension/conceptual, situational comprehension, self-help, and personal social skills. The scales are based on the child development literature. The reading level of the informant should be eighth grade. However, caretakers who cannot read at this level can respond very well when the items are read aloud to them.

The standardization sample is small and suffers from an attenuated socioeconomic and geographical range. Despite these limitations, it should be noted that the behaviors represented are primarily motor and neurologically based developmental items; these are probably less affected by the sample limitations than might be the case if the items were more culturally dependent. The most internally consistent scale is the general development scale, which is quite high. Face and content validity are excellent. Motor and expressive language scales correlate closely with intelligence estimates (Ireton, Thwing, & Currier, 1979), and a number of other studies indicate the inventory does discriminate between various clinical samples of developmentally delayed children and normal children.

Parenting Stress Index (PSI): The PSI (Abidin, 1983) was developed to aid early identification of children up to 10 years of age who are at risk for behavioral or emotional disturbance. The instrument assesses the nature and magnitude of stress in the parent-child relationship as seen by the parent. The current version (Loyd & Abidin, 1985) consists of 101 items on a five-point Likert scale. These items are used to obtain a total stress score as well as two broad domain scores: child domain and parent domain. Within each domain are several subscales. The child domain includes adaptability, acceptability, demandingness, mood, distractibility, and reinforces parent. The parent domain includes depression, attachment, restriction of role, sense of competence, social isolation, relationship with spouse, and parent health. High scores usually arise from high levels of stress; very low scores probably indicate defensiveness (Loyd & Abidin, 1985).

The standardization sample was drawn from one location. It is skewed toward the more affluent and better educated rather than representative of the general population. However, the α coefficients for the domains and the total scores are quite good, as are the test-retest reliabilities. Validity measures are not well described but do appear promising.

Revised Behavior Problem Checklist (RBPC): The revision of the behavior problem checklist (Quay & Peterson, 1987) is helpful in obtaining descriptions of children and adolescents for screening purposes. The checklist consists of 89 items forming six scales: conduct disorder, socialized aggression, attention problems/immaturity, anxiety/withdrawal, psychotic behavior, and motor excess. The checklist is designed for children 6 to 18 years old and may use parents and teachers as respondents. The checklist employs a three-point scale. While the standardization of the revised version is problematic (Cancelli, 1985) the internal consistency, interrater reliability, and test-retest reliability, as well as a number of validity estimates, appear adequate (Sattler, 1988).

EXAMINER RATING SCALES: PERVASIVE DEVELOPMENTAL DISORDERS

In addition to self-report and parent report measures, there are a variety of rating scales that are designed to be completed by the examiner as part of the diagnostic assessment. Perhaps the most common childhood condition associated with examiners' use of rating instruments is autism. Indeed, clinicians involved in the assessment of pervasive developmental disorders have several rating scales from which to choose (Morgan, 1988; Parks, 1983). The clinician's use of rating scales in this area is prompted by the fact that pervasive developmental disorder presents a unique diagnostic challenge because symptoms associated with conditions such as autism may vary considerably both in nature and degree. The three scales reviewed below are often used together with some of the parent report scales described above. The tests reviewed in Chapter 87 also assist in diagnosis as well as in differentiating autism from other related disorders (e.g., mental retardation, developmental language disorder).

Behavior Observation Scale (BOS): The BOS (Freeman, Ritvo, Guthrie, Schroth, & Ball, 1978) is an observational checklist developed for use with autistic, mentally retarded, and normal children. The child is placed in an examination room containing age-appropriate toys. One clinician remains in the examination room with the child and varies her interactions with the child according a standardized sequence. The child is simultaneously observed through a one-way mirror and the frequency of 67 objectively defined behaviors during nine 3-minute intervals is recorded. Interrater reliability is acceptable, although internal consistency and test-retest reliability are unknown (Morgan, 1988). There is some evidence for construct (Freeman, Schroth, Ritvo, Guthrie, & Wake, 1980) and discriminant (Freeman, Guthrie, Ritvo, Schroth, Glass, & Frankel, 1979) validity, but additional studies are needed to determine how well the BOS distinguishes between children with autism and those with other behavioral disturbances (Morgan, 1988; Parks, 1983).

Behavior Rating Instrument for Autistic and Atypical Children (BRIAAC): Developed by Ruttenberg and his colleagues (Ruttenberg, Dratman, Fraknoi, & Wenar, 1966; Ruttenberg, Kalish, Wenar, & Wolf, 1977), the BRIAAC comprises eight scales that are completed by the clinician from direct observation of the child. The scales include relationship to an adult, communication, drive for mastery, vocalization and expressive speech, sound and speech reception, social responsiveness, body movement, and psychobiological development. Behavioral descriptions on each scale range from behavior typical of a normally developing child to behavior more characteristic of severe autism, yielding a possible total of 10 points for each scale.

Derived from observations of autistic children in intervention programs, the BRIAAC has good internal consistency for the eight scales (.54–.86), and it can successfully discriminate among children with autism, early psychosis, mental retardation, developmental aphasia, and normal development (Morgan, 1988).

Childhood Autism Rating Scale (CARS): The CARS (Schopler, Reichler, DeVellis, & Daly, 1980) closely parallels current diagnostic criteria for autism and was developed out of the widely known TEACCH program in North Carolina. Ratings [1 (normal) to 4 (severely abnormal)] along 15 scales are made by the clinician based on observations of the child across various structured activities and situations. Examples of behaviors noted by the clinician include the child's relationships with people, body awareness, affect, adaptation to change, relation to nonhuman stimuli, and verbal and nonverbal communication.

Empirical studies have demonstrated that the CARS is the most psychometrically sound rating scale for autism. It has excellent interrater reliability and internal consistency ($\alpha = .94$) with a substantial sample. In addition, the CARS has adequate content and construct validity, high concurrent validity (with independent clinical ratings), and excellent discriminant validity in distinguishing children with autism from those with mental retardation (Morgan, 1988).

Additional and Developing Measures

Researchers and clinicians construct parent and child report measures as new needs arise. Frequently at the first appearance of these instruments their psychometric characteristics are weak or practically nonexistent. Despite the lack of adequate standardization, reliability, and validity, however, many instruments do find their way into use. Some of these instruments are refined later and become psychometrically sound, that is, reliable, valid, and standardized or field tested on representative samples. This permits a clinician to have confidence that performance on the instrument will describe or predict important patient characteristics and behavior. Some instruments, such as the Conners scales, achieve some utility on a limited basis (e.g., determining response to psychostimulant medication) but do not help much in other respects (e.g., elucidating the etiology of the behavior described). Similarly, some instruments are constructed to offer a number of factors or scales (e.g., the Tennessee self-concept scale; Archambault, 1992; Dowd, 1992), yet it is only their total score that is reliable and reasonably valid. In the latter case, the clinician should only use the total score, otherwise the unreliability of the factors and their scores will lead to overinterpretation which is not supported by the psychometrics of the instrument. Thus the clinician may be able to talk about the child's self-esteem in general, but will not be able to describe a specific aspect of the self-esteem with any confidence.

Sometimes parent and child report measures yield helpful information even though they do not meet minimum psychometric criteria. The limit of confidence in this information is that it functions in the same manner as would a single verbal statement obtained in an interview. The material elicited by measures with insufficient psychometric properties has no higher quality than that which would occur in a structured clinical interview, that is, we do not know its reliability or validity.

Important ethical issues should be considered when employing parent and child measures. Before a clinician uses an instrument, it is obligatory that psychometric information about the instrument be obtained and considered. If this is not done, the clinician is essentially practicing a form of pseudoscience. Information is readily available in manuals, mental measurement yearbooks, and psychological literature that reviews psychological instruments. There is one other important aspect of child assessment through parent and child report measures. Since parents and children frequently disagree on perceptions of the problem, the clinician should obtain data from both sources when making an assessment and recommendations for treatment.

Conclusion

This chapter focused on issues related to the use of child and parent report measures as well as examiner rating scales. The nature of the instruments was discussed and reviews of frequently used measures offered brief descriptions and discussions to acquaint the reader with the type of measures that psychologists often employ. It should again be emphasized that the types of reports (child, parent, examiner) and the measures based upon them are subject not only to the specialized perceptions of the reporters, but to various types of bias which may cause, result from, or interact with the problems that have prompted a referral. No single source of data, whether based on self-report, parent perceptions, or examiner ratings, is sufficient to give a comprehensive and accurate impression of the child's or adolescent's diagnosis or treatment needs. The checklists and rating scales reviewed must not be used independently to determine a diagnostic impression. While they may provide excellent screening functions, they can and should only contribute to a multimethod, multimodal assessment process. This comprehensive assessment ideally includes interviews (which may be structured or unstructured), intellectual assessment, and personality assessment through a variety of means, as well as the use of measures based on child, parent, and examiner perceptions.

REFERENCES

Abidin, R. R. (1983). *Parenting Stress Index: A manual.* Charlottesville, VA: Pediatric Psychology Press.

Achenbach, T. M., & Edelbrock, C. S. (1978). The classification of child psychopathology: A review and analysis of empirical effects. *Psychological Bulletin, 85,* 1275–1301.

Achenbach, T. M., & Edelbrock, C. S. (1983). *Manual for the Child Behavior Check List and the Revised Behavior Profile.* Burlington, VT: University of Vermont Press.

Archambault, F. X. (1992). Review of the Tennessee Self-Concept Scale (Revised). In J. J. Kramer & J. C. Conoley (Eds.), *The eleventh mental measurement yearbook* (pp. 929–932). Lincoln: University of Nebraska Press.

Bagarozzi, D. (1984). Family measurement techniques. *American Journal of Family Therapy, 12,* 59–62.

Bierman, K. (1990). Using the clinical interview to assess children's interpersonal reasoning and emotional understanding. In C. R. Reynolds & R. W. Kamphaus (Eds.), *Handbook of psychological and educational assessment of children: Personality, behavior, and context* (pp. 204–219). New York: Guilford Press.

Buros, O. K. (1972). *The ninth mental measurement yearbook.* Highland Park, NJ: Gryphon Press.

Busch-Rossnagel, N. (1985). Review of Family Environment Scale. In J. Mitchell, Jr. (Ed.) *The ninth mental measurements yearbook* (pp. 573–574). Lincoln: University of Nebraska Press.

Cancelli, A. A. (1985). Review of Revised Behavior Problem Checklist. In J. Mitchell (Ed.), *The ninth mental measurement yearbook* (pp. 1274–1276). Lincoln: University of Nebraska Press.

Carlson, G., & Cantwell, D. (1980). A survey of depressive symptoms, syndromes, and disorders in a child psychiatric population. *Journal of the American Academy of Child Psychiatry, 18,* 587–599.

Chamberlain, P., & Reid, J. (1987). Parent observation and report of child symptoms. *Behavioral Assessment, 9,* 97–109.

Cytryn, L., & McKnew, D. H. (1974). Factors influencing the changing clinical expression of the depressive process in children. *American Journal of Psychiatry, 131,* 879–881.

Dowd, E. T. (1992). Review of the Tennessee Self-Concept Scale (Revised). In J. J. Kramer & J. C. Conoley (Eds.), *The eleventh mental measurement yearbook* (p. 933). Lincoln: University of Nebraska Press.

Freeman, B. J., Guthrie, D., Ritvo, E., Schroth, P., Glass, R., & Frankel, F. (1979). Behavior Observation Scale: Preliminary analysis of the similarities and differences between autistic and mentally retarded children. *Psychological Reports, 44,* 519–524.

Freeman, B. J., Ritvo, E. R., Guthrie, D., Schroth, P., & Ball, J. (1978). The Behavior Observation Scale for Autism: Initial methodology, data analysis, and preliminary findings on 89 children. *Journal of the American Academy of Child Psychiatry, 17,* 576–588.

Freeman, B. J., Schroth, P., Ritvo, E., Guthrie, D., & Wake, L. (1980). The Behavior Observation Scale for autism (BOS): Initial results of factor analysis. *Journal of Autism and Developmental Disorders, 10,* 343–346.

Friedman, R. J., & Butter, L. F. (1979). *Development and evaluation of a test battery to measure childhood depression.* Unpublished manuscript, Ontario Institute for Studies in Education.

Goldman, J., L'Engle Stein, C., & Guerry, S. (1983). *Psychological methods of child assessment.* New York: Brunner/Mazel.

Harter, S. (1982). The perceived competence scale for children. *Child Development, 53,* 87–97.

Harter, S. (1985). *Manual for the Self-Perception Profile for children.* Denver, CO: University of Denver.

Harter, S., & Pike, R. (1981). *The Pictorial Perceived Competence Scale for Children.* Unpublished manuscript, University of Denver.

Hughes, H. M. (1984). Measures of self-concept and self-esteem for children ages 3–12 years: A review and recommendations. *Clinical Psychology Review, 4,* 657–692.

Hughes, J. (1990). Assessment of social skills: Sociometric and behavioral approaches. In C. Reynolds & R. Kamphaus (Eds.), *Handbook of psychological and educational assessment of children: Personality, behavior, and context* (pp. 423–444). New York: Guilford Press.

Ireton, H., & Thwing, E. (1974). *Minnesota Child Development Inventory manual.* Minneapolis, MN: Behavior Science Systems.

Ireton, H., Thwing, E., & Currier, S. K. (1979). MCDI: Identification of children with developmental disorders. *Journal of Pediatric Psychology, 2,* 18–22.

Joanning, H., & Kuehl, B. (1986). A review of FACES-III. *American Journal of Family Therapy, 14,* 163–165.

Kendall, P. (1987). Ahead to basics: Assessments with children and families. *Behavioral Assessment, 9,* 321–332.

Kovacs, M., Betof, N. G., Celebre, J. E., Mansheim, P. A., Petty, L. K., & Reynek, S. T. (1978). Childhood depression. In E. A. Petti, Depression in hospitalized child psychiatry patients. *Journal of the American Academy of Child Psychiatry, 17,* 49–59.

Kovacs, M., & Beck, A. T. (1977). An empirical-clinical approach toward a definition of childhood depres-sion. In J. G. Schulterbrandt & A. Raskin (Eds.), *Depression in childhood: Diagnosis, treatment, and conceptual models* (pp. 1–25). New York: Raven Press.

Lambert, N. (1985). Review of the Family Environment Scale. In J. Mitchell, Jr. (Ed.), *The ninth mental measurements yearbook* (pp. 574–575). Lincoln: University of Nebraska Press.

Loyd, B. H., & Abidin, R. R. (1985). Revision of the Parenting Stress Index. *Journal of Pediatric Psychology, 10,* 169–178.

Marsh, H. W., & Governet, P. J. (1989). Multidimensional self-concepts and perceptions of control: Construct validation of responses by children. *Journal of Educational Psychology, 81,* 57–68.

Martens, B. K. (1992). Review of Conners Rating Scales. In J. J. Kramer & J. C. Conoley (Eds.), *The eleventh mental measurement yearbook* (pp. 233–234). Lincoln: University of Nebraska Press.

Milich, R., & Krelbiel, G. (1986). Issues in the assessment and treatment of socially rejected children. In R. J. Prinz (Ed.), *Advances in behavioral assessment of children and families* (Vol. 2, pp. 240–270). New York: Plenum Press.

Moos, R. (1974). *Family Environment Scales.* Palo Alto, CA: Consulting Psychologists Press.

Morgan, S. B. (1988). Diagnostic assessment of autism: A review of objective scales. *Journal of Psychoeducational Assessment, 6,* 139–151.

Oehler-Stinnett, J. (1992). Review of Conners Rating Scales. In J. J. Kramer & J. C. Conoley (Eds.), *The eleventh mental measurement yearbook* (pp. 234–240). Lincoln: University of Nebraska Press.

Olson, D. H., Portner, J., & Lavee, Y. (1985). *Faces-III: Family Adaptability and Cohesion Evaluations Scales.* In D. H. Olson, H. I. McCubbin, H. Barnes, A. Larsen, M. Muxen, & M. Wilson (Eds.), *Family inventories: Inventories used in a national survey of families across the family life cycle* (pp. 1–42). St. Paul, MN: Family Social Science, University of Minnesota.

Parks, S. L. (1983). The assessment of autistic children: A selective review of available instruments. *Journal of Autism and Developmental Disorders, 13,* 255–265.

Quay, H. C., & Peterson, D. R. (1987). *Manual for the Revised Behavior Problem Checklist.* Coral Gables, FL: University of Miami.

Reynolds, W. (1987). *Reynolds Adolescent Depression Scale: Professional manual.* Odessa, FL: Psychological Assessment Resources.

Reynolds, C. R., & Richmond, B. O. (1978). What I Think and Feel: A revised measure of children's manifest anxiety. *Journal of Abnormal Child Psychology, 6,* 271–280.

Reynolds, C. R., & Richmond, B. O. (1979). Factor structure and construct validity of "What I Think and Feel": The revised Children's Manifest Anxiety Scale. *Journal of Personality Assessment, 43,* 281–283.

Reynolds, C. R., & Richmond, B. O. (1985). *Revised*

Children's Manifest Anxiety Scale (RCMAS) manual. Los Angeles: Western Psychological Services.

Ruttenberg, B. A., Dratman, M. L., Fraknoi, J., & Wenar, C. (1966). An instrument for evaluating autistic children. *Journal of the American Academy of Child Psychiatry, 5,* 453–478.

Ruttenberg, B. A., Kalish, B. I., Wenar, C., & Wolf, E. G. (1977). *Behavior rating instrument for autistic and other atypical children* (rev. ed.). Philadelphia: Developmental Center for Autistic Children.

Sattler, J. M. (1988). *Assessment of children* (3rd ed.). San Diego, CA: Jerome M. Sattler.

Saylor, C. M., Finch, A. J., Furey, W., Baskin, C. H., & Kelly, M. M. (1984). Construct validity for measures of childhood depression: Application of multitrait-multimethod methodology. *Journal of Consulting and Clinical Psychology, 52,* 977–985.

Schopler, E., Reichler, R. J., DeVellis, R. F., & Daly, K. (1980). Toward objective classification of childhood autism: Childhood Autism Rating Scale (CARS). *Journal of Autism and Developmental Disorders, 10,* 91–103.

Semrud-Clikeman, M. (1990). Assessment of childhood depression. In C. Reynolds & R. Kamphaus (Eds.), *Handbook of psychological and educational assessment of children: Personality, behavior, and context* (pp. 279–297). New York: Guilford Press.

87 / Psychological Testing

James R. Rodrigue and Jacquelin Goldman

The purposes of this chapter are multifold. It will highlight the roles and objectives of psychological testing as well as the applicability of testing for diagnosis and treatment of children and adolescents. In addition, the decision-making process involved in determining the nature and scope of psychological testing will be considered. This chapter will summarize important psychometric constructs, including test standardization and the various types of reliability and validity. Moreover, differences in test structure, stimulus properties, and response demands (e.g., "objective" versus "projective" testing), as well as factors that can affect test selection, performance, and interpretation will be discussed. Finally, the material will present and selectively review the most commonly used psychological tests for assessing the cognitive functioning, academic achievement, and personality of children and adolescents.

Roles, Objectives, and Models of Psychological Testing

Numerous changes in psychiatric practice during the past decade have paralleled recent develop-ments in psychological assessment (Sattler, 1988; Wetzler & Katz, 1989). Indeed, since Magnussen's (1979) chapter on psychological testing in the first *Basic Handbook of Child Psychiatry* (Noshpitz, 1979), the roles of biological and psychological factors in the etiology and treatment of psychopathology have multiplied, brief (versus extended) hospitalization periods are preferred, and third-party payers and patient advocates have led efforts to "economize" on psychological testing. As a result of these changes, the demand is for psychological testing to be more focalized or to answer a specific question, for example, the presence of neurological or neuropsychological dysfunction, differential diagnosis (ADHD versus oppositional defiant disorder), suicidal or homicidal potential, or likely response to various treatment alternatives. Nevertheless, psychologists continue to conduct assessment procedures that include both clinical methods and psychometric evaluation. Indeed, the "traditional" psychological test battery has been articulated by many authors (Lourie & Rieger, 1974; Rieger & Baron, 1991; Siegel, 1987) and typically includes a labor-intensive and time-consuming evaluation of cognitive, developmental, behavioral, and personality functioning. This comprehensive battery allows for the examination of complex diagnostic and treatment issues, including the delineation of learning difficulties, developmental disorders, and psychopathology in children and adolescents.

Several models or clinical approaches have been used to conceptualize and formulate assessment decisions. Such models include but are not limited to the traditional medical diagnostic model, the behavioral model, the decision-making model, and the operations research model (Arthur, 1969). In addition, Sloves, Docherty, and Schneider (1979) detailed a scientific problem-solving model involving six sequential and interrelated phases of psychological assessment. The six phases included problem clarification (the problem is articulated), planning (hypotheses are generated), development (tests are selected), implementation (the assessment is conducted), outcome determination (data are reviewed in light of initial hypotheses), and dissemination of findings to the referral source.

Another model used to conceptualize the assessment process is one in which the testing situation is viewed as a single-case experiment using probabilistic inferences (vanReken, 1981). This hypothesis testing model provides an avenue for exploring hypotheses that may assist in better understanding the individual being evaluated. As with experimental research, in clinical hypothesis testing, the clinician must not rigidly adhere to only one method of assessment. Indeed, adjustments to various hypotheses and methods of evaluation are often necessary to determine the adequacy of their "goodness of fit" for the child or adolescent.

Within the hypothesis testing model, there are several elements that are important in delineating the nature and scope of psychological testing. Perhaps the most important determinant is the referral question or hypothesis. Testing is typically initiated by a referral question which serves as the focal point for the entire assessment. The relative importance of a clearly articulated referral question cannot be overstated. Indeed, Levine (1981) noted that the lack of a clear understanding of the referral question is one of the more frequent sources of error in test interpretation. In the event that it is poorly expressed, it is the psychologist's task to clarify the referral question and to rephrase it into a workable hypothesis. Considering the vagueness of many testing referrals and the hidden agendas or unspoken expectations that sometimes accompany such referrals, this is not always an easy task. For instance, referrals for a "psychological," "psychological testing," "test battery," "projective testing," or "IQ and personality testing" are vague and do not adequately represent the issues the referral source is facing or the relevance of the psychological evaluation in regard to diagnosis or treatment. Furthermore, these types of referral questions make it difficult for the clinician to determine the advantages, usefulness, and potential limitations of psychological testing.

In a psychiatric setting, the psychiatrist often must simultaneously assume the role of administrator, therapist, and physician, and it is important for the clinician to understand the contextual issues associated with testing referrals. Each of the hats worn by psychiatrists carries unique responsibilities and may sometimes determine the type of referral question for which psychological testing is being sought. As an administrator, a "psychological" may be requested to assist with decisions regarding the patient's suicide risk, admission, discharge, or custody. As a therapist, a psychological may be requested to delineate disturbances in thinking or to determine whether the patient is suitable for therapy. In this instance, an evaluation that elaborates on the patient's cognitive style, affect, capacity for insight, diagnosis, and problems that may surface during therapy might be particularly useful. Or there may be a concern regarding appropriate educational placement which might be addressed using standardized intelligence tests and measures of academic achievement. As a physician, a psychological may be requested to identify and delineate factors that may be affecting the patient's compliance with a particular medical regimen. Clearly the types of referral questions differ significantly as a function of the psychiatrist's role in the referral setting. Nevertheless, it is the appropriately articulated referral question or hypothesis that ultimately guides the clinical investigation within the hypothesis testing model.

The method of the clinical assessment involves the selection of psychological procedures and tests that will be used in data collection. What is important to recognize at this point is that the particular methodology to be used should always be determined by the psychologist, whose training and expertise in psychometric issues and standardized instrumentation give breadth and depth to the assessment process. Competency in the administration and scoring of tests is clearly not sufficient to yield an effective assessment. Knowledge and awareness of psychopathology, personality theory, developmental psychology, and in-depth knowledge regarding the constructs they are measuring and the tests they are selecting are essential possessions for the clinician.

As noted above, once clarified, the referral question provides the basis for guiding the particular methodology used in an assessment. However, there are several other factors which may influence the selection of assessment procedures. These include the theoretical orientation of the tests, practical considerations, the psychometric properties of the instruments, and their appropriateness for the individual being evaluated. Regarding theoretical orientation, it is important to determine what theoretical construct the test is purported to be measuring and whether the test items correspond to the theoretical description of the construct (Groth-Marnat, 1984). In addition, there are a number of important practical considerations that have less to do with the psychometric components of a test and more to do with individual or contextual factors. For instance, the nature of any time constraints that have been placed on the evaluative process, the reading ability match between the examinee and that required by the test, and the availability of family members or school teachers will determine the types of tests that can be administered. In most instances a battery of assessment tools is preferred over a single test in order to generate a broad range of data from which inferences about the individual being evaluated can be drawn. Although such a battery typically is multidimensional, assessing primary areas of functioning (e.g., cognitive, achievement, personality) across several testing situations (e.g., structured, unstructured, interactive), it is time intensive and not always possible to administer.

Of course, instruments selected for use in an assessment should possess a high degree of validity and reliability for the particular hypothesis being investigated. These constructs and issues are reviewed elsewhere in this volume (see Chapter 8) and will not be discussed in much detail here. Suffice it to say that there are a number of questions that psychologists ask about the psychometric properties of a test before it is considered for use with a particular child or adolescent. For instance, how high are the reliability estimates?

What methods were used to estimate reliability? What criteria and techniques were employed to validate the instrument? Has the test been used and proven to be valid for the purpose and in the context for which it is now being considered? How appropriate is the test for the individual being examined? This last question is one of the more fundamental questions involved in selecting a test. The examinee's age, developmental level, cultural background, socioeconomic status, ethnicity, and the presence of any motor or sensory impediments must all be considered. Whether the examinee shares the demographic characteristics of the test's standardization sample is important to determine at the outset.

Tests also differ with respect to their structure, stimulus properties, and response demands (Rieger & Baron, 1991). Some tests are structured (or "objective") and provide information about the examinee relative to a criterion group. Such tests generally elicit scorable responses to specific verbal questions or performance tasks that have been standardized on regional or national samples. Other tests are more open-ended and less structured. So-called projective tests are designed to provide information regarding the examinee's perception, interpretation, and reaction in response to environmental and interpersonal stimuli by placing more emphasis on the examinee's idiosyncratic response pattern. It is important to emphasize that many tests are viewed as either objective or projective when, in fact, the two categories of tests are not mutually exclusive. Indeed, many quantifiable objective tests provide qualitative information about the examinee's response style to external stimuli. Similarly some projective techniques now have formalized scoring systems with normative data to which comparisons can be made.

In addition to the use of particular tests, the clinician will usually collect information from a wide variety of other sources. These sources might include the clinical interview, behavioral observations, parents, school teachers, school records, previous psychological evaluations, and juvenile justice records, among others. Information obtained from these sources is critical and allows the clinician to place test findings in an appropriate context. Indeed, test scores alone are usually not sufficient to answer the referral question adequately and responsibly.

In summary, the roles and objectives of psychological testing are multifarious, and many models of assessment have been advanced throughout the past several decades. In general, the hypothesis testing approach to assessment is preferred because it serves as a good compromise for the scientist-practitioner by allowing the clinician to capitalize on the scientific method of formulating a hypothesis, designing an appropriate methodology to evaluate the hypothesis systematically, and then applying the findings within a clinical context (vanReken, 1981).

Psychometric Considerations

Wells provides an excellent discussion of psychometric concepts related to the psychological assessment of children and adolescents. Other thorough reviews of these important issues are provided in texts by Anastasi (1988), Reynolds and Kamphaus (1990), and Sattler (1988). Nevertheless, below are a few brief definitions of key statistical and measurement concepts that are referred to repeatedly throughout this review of psychological tests.

In order to be considered psychometrically sound instruments, tests constructed to measure aspects of a child's intellect, academic achievement, or personality must meet a few basic criteria. Indeed, most tests are evaluated in terms of how well they fulfill the criteria of adequate standardization, reliability, and validity as set forth in the American Psychological Association's *Standards for Educational and Psychological Testing* (APA, 1985). The primary objective of the standardization process is to provide a normative base to which the individual being evaluated can be compared. Ideally standardization samples are representative of the general population and stratified according to several important variables including age, gender, socioeconomic status, ethnicity, and geographical location. In addition, the number of individuals included in the standardization sample must be sufficiently large to obtain adequate estimates of reliability and validity.

Although there are several types, reliability in general refers to the degree to which an instrument is consistent in measuring the property that it measures, that is, the degree to which it assesses the same thing time after time and item after item. Of course, any time a test is administered to an individual more than once, variability or variance in the scores should be anticipated. The magnitude of this "error" is determined by calculating the standard error of measurement, which is the difference between an examinee's true score (e.g., examinee's average score if it were administered 100 times) on a given test and her obtained or measured score. The less error in a test, the greater its reliability. The specific types of reliability usually considered in evaluating a psychological instrument are test-retest reliability (temporal stability of the results), internal consistency (homogeneity of items within the test), and interrater reliability (agreement of results between examiners of the same child or adolescent).

There are three types of validity that should be considered when using or selecting a test—content validity, construct validity, and concurrent validity. Content validity refers to the degree to which the items of a particular instrument are representative of the broader domain of attributes of behaviors that are being sampled. Construct validity may be defined as the extent to which a test measures the theoretical or psychological construct of interest (e.g., intelligence, visual-motor integration, personality); that is, how well do the scores of a particular test correlate with other tests to which we can expect it to be related? Concurrent validity refers to the agreement of the test findings with an independent, already available criterion. A variant of concurrent validity that is important in diagnostic assessments of children is discriminant validity, or the ability of a test to differentiate among independently defined diagnostic groups or categories. One final and major aspect of psychological assessment is a test's ability to predict future performance. This is referred to as predictive validity and it is especially important in psychoeducational assessments of children when the clinician is being asked to make predictions about future academic performance.

There are several factors which potentially affect the validity of a person's test results or which may serve as sources of test variability. These include lasting and general characteristics of the child, such as prior testing experiences and attitudes generally operating in testing situations, and temporary characteristics of the child, including health, fatigue, emotional strain, motivation, rapport with the examiner, and fluctuations in attention or concentration. In addition, environmental factors (effects of heat, light, ventilation, etc.) may account for sources of errors in measurement. In general, such factors should be noted at the time of testing and interpretations of test findings should not be made without careful consideration of possible sources of test variability.

Another important statistical concept that relates to psychological tests is factor analysis. This concept has evolved into a significant tool in assessment research during the past fifteen years. It is an important statistical concept to understand because it is directly related to issues of test validity. Many psychologists believe that results obtained on several tests or scores from items within a particular test (e.g., WISC-R) are most meaningful when grouped into "factors." For instance, as is discussed in greater detail below, Kaufman (1979) suggested that the 12 WISC-R subtests could be meaningfully regrouped into three factors: verbal comprehension, perceptual organization, and freedom from distractibility.

By conducting exploratory factor analysis, it is possible to group together those items, scales, or instruments that correlate highly with each other (i.e., they measure something in common) and thereby determine the underlying structure of a test or group of tests. However, it is critical to understand that because there is a great deal of subjectivity in the criteria used to select and interpret factors, the fact that the developer of a test reports a specific factor structure does not mean that these factors are indeed reliable or valid.

Methods of Child and Adolescent Assessment

Numerous volumes have been written on the psychological assessment of children and adolescents (e.g., Anastasi, 1988; Goldman, L'Engle Stein, & Guerry, 1983; Johnson & Goldman, 1990; Reynolds & Kamphaus, 1990; Sattler, 1988). The purpose of the following sections is not to review all that is known about child assessment instruments. Rather it is intended to provide the reader with an overview of the tools used most frequently by

psychologists in evaluating infants, children, and adolescents.

Prior to reviewing the various instruments, it is important to emphasize that the tests described below should be used only as part of a comprehensive approach to assessment. This approach should include evaluations of development across several areas, the nature of the caregiver-child relationship, environmental and cultural influences, and the range of previously discussed factors that may affect test performance. Culbertson and Gyurke (1990), for instance, emphasize that in addition to a thorough knowledge of childhood development, clinicians should strive to meet six basic goals as part of the child assessment process: (1) assessment of a broad spectrum of developmental skills (e.g., cognitive, motor, linguistic, adaptive, behavior); (2) know the strengths and weakness of the various tests used with children and recognize that repeated assessments over time (especially with infants and young children) are likely to be more accurate than one assessment at a given point in time; (3) obtain information about the child's developmental (timing and sequence of early milestones), behavioral (activity level, affective development), medical (course of pregnancy, postnatal status, illness), and family background from a knowledgeable and reliable source; (4) rule out sensory deficits (i.e., auditory, visual, or motor impairments) prior to beginning the evaluation; (5) use a hypothesis testing approach (as described previously) where tests are selected on the basis of the referral questions and presenting problems; and (6) use the results of testing to generate a profile of strengths and weaknesses that can assist in guiding early intervention efforts, future educational planning, or therapeutic intervention.

ASSESSMENT OF COGNITIVE AND MOTOR DEVELOPMENT IN INFANTS

The Bayley Scales of Infant Development (Bayley, 1969) is the most widely used instrument for establishing an infant's current developmental status and for delineating the nature and extent of any deviations from normative development. Administered individually (usually with the child's caregiver present) to children 2 to 30 months of age, the Bayley scales contain 163 items that comprise the mental scale, motor scale, and infant behavior record. Mental scale items are designed to assess sensory-perceptual abilities, the acquisition of object permanency, memory, problem-solving skills, and early verbal abilities (e.g., vocal imitation), which are thought to be precursors of intelligence (Culbertson & Gyurke, 1990). Motor scale items tap fine and gross motor coordination, including degree of head and trunk control, rolling, grasping objects, sitting independently, walking, and balance. The infant behavior record allows the examiner to rate the child's behavior across 11 domains: social orientation, cooperativeness, fearfulness, tension, general emotional tone, object orientation, goal directedness, attention span, endurance, activity, and reactivity.

Raw scores on the mental and motor scales yield two normalized standard scores ($M = 100$, $SD = 16$), a mental developmental index and a psychomotor developmental index, respectively. It should be emphasized that these standard scores are considered "developmental quotients," not "intelligence quotients" (Bayley, 1969). Mental developmental indices extrapolated below 50 have been reported (Naglieri, 1981). A standardized score cannot be obtained from the infant behavior record. Administration of the Bayley takes approximately 45 to 60 minutes and requires intensive training and experience.

Strengths of the Bayley include its excellent standardization (1262 infants/children stratified across several demographic variables) and psychometric properties (moderately high reliability, good predictive validity at upper age levels and for children scoring significantly below average) and the availability of a developmentally defined observational component. Limitations include poor predictive validity for younger children and for children scoring in the average range; no provisions for subscale analyses within the mental or motor scales; and exclusion of premature infants and infants with sensory or physical limitations, which necessarily limits applicability and interpretation of test findings with such populations (Culbertson & Gyurke, 1990; Goodman, 1990).

The Cattell Infant Intelligence Scale (Cattell, 1960) is frequently reported by authors discussing tests of infant development. Designed to yield a standardized measure of mental development, the Cattell is appropriate for use with children ranging in age from 2 to 30 months. It provides a single score, namely, a mental quotient that can be con-

verted into a ratio IQ. Although its development in the 1930s reflected an improvement over tests available at that time, it has not maintained its status as a widely used infant measure of mental development. The standardization sample is unnecessarily narrow (middle-class only; children at 3, 6, 9, 12, 18, 24, and 30 months only) and not stratified according to important demographic indices (e.g., SES, ethnicity, geography). Although the Cattell was initially thought to be a downward extension of the Stanford–Binet, research has not supported its use in this manner (Culbertson & Gyurke, 1990; Hooper, Conner, & Umansky, 1986; Whatley, 1987).

Other procedures designed to assess cognitive and motor development among infants include the Gesell Developmental Schedule (Ilg & Ames, 1965), the Infant Psychological Development Scale (Uzgiris & Hunt, 1975), the Apgar score, and the Neonatal Behavioral Assessment Scale (Brazelton, 1973). For descriptions and critiques of these measures, the reader is referred to Sattler (1988).

ASSESSMENT OF COGNITIVE DEVELOPMENT: PRESCHOOL CHILDREN

The cognitive and motor abilities of preschool-age children are generally assessed using one of four widely used instruments: the Wechsler Preschool and Primary Scale of Intelligence-Revised (WPPSI-R), the Stanford–Binet Intelligence Scale: Fourth Edition (SB-IV), the Kaufman Assessment Battery for Children (K-ABC), and the McCarthy Scales of Children's Abilities.

The WPPSI-R (Wechsler, 1989), like its predecessor (WPPSI; Wechsler, 1967), is a norm-referenced test of children's intelligence. It contains 12 subtests comprising two principal factors—verbal (information, comprehension, arithmetic, vocabulary, similarities, sentences) and performance (object assembly, geometric design, block design, mazes, picture completion, animal pegs). Each subtest yields a raw score that is then converted into a scaled score ($M = 10$, $SD = 3$). The scaled scores loading on the verbal or performance scales are then transformed into a verbal IQ ($M = 100$, $SD = 15$) and a performance IQ ($M = 100$, $SD = 15$), respectively. The aggregate scaled score (verbal scale + performance scale) is then converted into a full scale IQ ($M = 100$,

SD = 15). Full scale IQs range from 41 to 160, thus allowing for discrimination among children with very low and very high intellectual abilities.

The original WPPSI was developed to provide a measure of cognitive development during the transitional preschool period. The recent revision expands the effective age range. Whereas the WPPSI was appropriate for children 4 years to 6 years, 6 months of age, the WPPSI-R may be used with children ranging in age from 3 years to 7 years, 3 months. Now there is overlap with the WISC-R (Wechsler, 1974), thereby providing the clinician with a choice of tests for some younger children. In addition to the expanded age range, the revised version has more appealing stimulus materials (colorful artwork), more contemporary content (50% new items), and new normative data. There is also one new subtest (object assembly).

The standardization sample for the WPPSI-R comprised 1700 children (200 in eight age groups, 100 in the 7-year-old age group) stratified by gender, ethnicity, geography, and parents' education and occupation. Reliability is high at the scale and subtest levels; construct and concurrent validity data are promising, although predictive validity has yet to be determined. Clearly its technical standards are very high. Further empirical study will undoubtedly substantiate its clinical utility with young children.

The Stanford–Binet Intelligence Scale: Fourth Edition (SB-IV; Thorndike, Hagen, & Sattler, 1986) also measures various aspects of intellectual functioning and is appropriate for individuals 2 to 23 years old. There are 15 subtests, although most children are administered only 8 to 13 of them, depending on their chronological age and basal level. All subtests appear to be good indices of general intelligence or "g" (Sattler, 1988). Scaled scores ($M = 50$, SD = 8) are computed from raw scores, and these are then converted into four area scores ($M = 100$, SD = 16): verbal reasoning, abstract/visual reasoning, quantitative reasoning, and short-term memory. A composite score ($M = 100$, SD = 16), which is the best estimate of general reasoning and comparable to the deviation IQ common to the Wechsler scales, is subsequently derived. Sattler (1988) reports the results of a factor analysis which may prove useful for interpreting SB-IV results. A two-factor solution—verbal comprehension and nonverbal reasoning/visual-

ization—characterizes the scale for children 2 to 6 years old, whereas a three-factor solution—verbal comprehension, nonverbal reasoning/visualization, and memory—is best for individuals 7 to 23 years old.

The SB-IV standardization sample comprised 5013 individuals stratified across gender, ethnicity, geographic location, community size, and parental education and occupation. Although only a handful of psychometric studies have been published since the revision was released, the findings are quite promising. Excellent internal consistency has been reported for the composite score. Subtest scores are somewhat less reliable, particularly for younger children. Indeed, as with most individual subtests assessing the cognitive abilities of younger children, the SB-IV subtests should not be considered very stable measures of ability for children younger than 6 years of age. Validity studies indicate that the SB-IV composite score compares favorably with the WPPSI, WISC-R, and K-ABC overall indices of cognitive functioning, although these findings are more consistent within the average intellectual range (Spruill, 1987).

In summary, the SB-IV is clinically useful in delineating particular learning problems a child may be having in school. Its transition from an age-scale format to a point-scale format makes it more comparable to the Wechsler scales. Unlike the previous version, the revised edition permits the examiner to examine a child's performance across several areas (i.e., use of area scores or factors) rather than provide only a single index of overall cognitive development. However, Glutting and Kaplan (1990) have suggested that clinicians should exercise caution in using area scores because their existence has not been adequately substantiated by factor analytic studies. In fact, the authors suggest that all interpretations and placement decisions be made on the basis of the composite score only. The SB-IV boasts an expanded and more representative standardization sample. Indeed, there was a concerted effort to ensure that the revision was culturally sensitive by assembling a panel of ethnic minorities to review and evaluate test items for content bias. However, clinicians should be aware that African American children and children of lower SES obtain composite scores approximately one standard deviation lower than White children and children of higher SES, respectively (Sattler, 1988). Finally, perhaps the SB-IV's most serious limitation pertains to low-functioning preschool children. Because of the difficulty in obtaining a basal level for low-functioning preschool children, the SB-IV demonstrates a minimum capacity to detect moderate to severe mental retardation or developmental delay in this population of children (Glutting & Kaplan, 1990; Sattler, 1988). Thus preschool children referred by psychiatrists for evaluation of possible cognitive deficiencies will likely be evaluated using instruments other than the SB-IV (e.g., WPPSI-R).

Another individually administered intelligence test is the K-ABC (Kaufman & Kaufman, 1983). The K-ABC comprises 16 subtests that assess the abilities of children age 2 years, 6 months to 12 years, 5 months of age across four scales ($M = 100$, SD = 15): sequential processing scale, simultaneous processing scale, achievement scale, and nonverbal scale. As primarily nonverbal measures of problem-solving and information processing abilities, the sequential and simultaneous processing scales are combined to yield one index of overall intelligence—the mental processing composite. The achievement scale comprises subtests designed to tap children's factual knowledge and academic-related skills (e.g., vocabulary, arithmetic, reading). The nonverbal scale comprises those items on the sequential and simultaneous processing scales that do not require verbalizations by either the examiner or the child. The primarily nonverbal nature of the K-ABC reflects the developers' decision to obtain fair assessments of children who are bilingual, who have speech or language difficulties, who are of ethnic minority status, or who have learning disabilities by placing less emphasis on verbal expression or comprehension skills.

The K-ABC standardization sample was adequately stratified across age, gender, geographical location, community size, SES, and ethnicity. It included 2000 children; 200 to 300 at each of nine age levels. The K-ABC seems to be reliable and valid, although the existence of the two factors—simultaneous processing and sequential processing—have not been supported by research (Anastasi, 1988; Sattler, 1988).

The K-ABC is a very popular instrument among school psychologists, in spite of the considerable controversy surrounding its use (Merz, 1984; Miller & Reynolds, 1984). For instance, Glutting and Kaplan (1990) reported the findings from one study that this test is used nearly as often as the Wechsler scales and considerably more frequently than the Stanford–Binet (Form L-M and the fourth edition). Despite its apparent popularity, recent critiques have noted several serious limitations of the K-ABC and its use as a measure of intelligence and achievement. The relative exclusion of items assessing verbal expression, comprehension, and reasoning on the mental processing composite may reduce cultural bias, but it necessarily precludes the measurement of verbal skills that are considered by many to be an integral component of intelligence. The use of predominantly verbal items on the achievement scale (and ones that also rely heavily upon mental processing abilities) further complicates interpretation of K-ABC findings. Bracken (1985) further noted that the K-ABC's culture fairness has not been supported by research demonstrating that African American children score nearly one standard deviation lower than their White peers.

In addition, like the SB-IV, the K-ABC is not the instrument of choice for classifying mental retardation, especially among preschool children, because even children who fail all items obtain high mental processing composite scores (e.g., a 2-year, 6-month-old child who fails all items would earn a mental processing composite of 79). Although the K-ABC appears to be a good instrument for measuring nonverbal cognitive abilities, its use with special populations or as a primary measurement of intelligence is not generally recommended. In his concluding remarks, Sattler (1988, p. 303) emphasized that the serious limitations of the K-ABC should preclude its use as "the primary instrument for identifying the intellectual abilities of normal or special children, including the mentally retarded, gifted, or learning disabled."

One test of children's intelligence that has received several favorable reviews is the McCarthy Scales of Children's Abilities (McCarthy, 1972). The McCarthy is appropriate for children 2 years, 6 months to 8 years, 6 months old. It comprises 18 subtests which yield six scales: verbal, perceptual-performance, quantitative, memory, motor and general cognitive index (GCI). The sixth scale—GCI—is an estimate of the child's global level of intellectual functioning and is determined by summing the child's scores on the verbal, perceptual-performance, and quantitative scales. McCarthy (1972) attempted to avoid using of the term "IQ," yet the GCI is widely accepted as an index of intelligence and as an IQ analogue (Kaufman & Kaufman, 1977; Valencia, 1990). The GCI has a mean of 100 and a standard deviation of 16, while the other five scales have means of 50 and standard deviations of 10.

Nagle (1979) cited the McCarthy as a test that employed comprehensive sampling techniques. It employed a national standardization sample stratified by age, gender, ethnicity, geographic region, urban/rural residence, and father's occupation. Overall there were 1032 children (516 boys, 516 girls), with approximately 50 boys and 50 girls at each of 10 age levels. Valencia (1990) provides an updated review of the psychometric properties of the McCarthy. Overall the McCarthy possesses very good reliability (i.e., internal consistency), with the GCI and verbal scale demonstrating excellent accuracy in several studies and adequate stability over time. High concurrent and predictive validity are supported by several empirical studies. Construct validity is very good for the GCI as well as the verbal, perceptual-performance, and motor scales, but has been mixed for the remaining scales.

Reviewers have criticized the McCarthy for its lack of items measuring social comprehension, social judgment, verbal reasoning, and abstract problem solving; problems in assessing school-age children (i.e., 6 years, 6 months to 8 years, 6 months old); and the restricted range of GCIs when examining the cognitive abilities of children with mental retardation. Notwithstanding these few relative weaknesses, the McCarthy is considered by many psychologists to be the instrument of choice for assessing the cognitive abilities of preschool children. In particular, Valencia (1990) concluded in his review that the McCarthy is especially useful as an instrument for early detection of children likely to experience later learning difficulties.

ASSESSMENT OF COGNITIVE DEVELOPMENT: SCHOOL-AGE CHILDREN AND ADOLESCENTS

The most widely used test of cognitive functioning or intelligence in school-age children is the Wechsler Intelligence Scale for Children-Revised (WISC-R; Wechsler, 1974). Sattler (1988) and Reynolds and Kamphaus (1990) provide recent detailed discussions and reviews of the WISC-R. Appropriate for children 6 years to 16 years, 11 months old, the WISC-R comprises 12 subtests (two are optional) which, like the WPPSI-R described previously, yield a verbal IQ ($M = 100$, SD $= 15$), performance IQ ($M = 100$, SD $= 15$), and full scale IQ ($M = 100$, SD $= 15$). Subtests loading on the verbal scale include information, similarities, arithmetic, vocabulary, comprehension, and digit span. Subtests comprising the performance scale include picture completion, picture arrangement, block design, object assembly, coding, and mazes. Factor analysis findings summarized by Kaufman (1979) suggest three principal factors: verbal comprehension, perceptual organization, and freedom from distractibility.

The WISC-R was standardized on 2200 children, with 200 in each of 11 different age categories. The sample was stratified by age, gender, urban/rural residence, and SES. Also, unlike its predecessor (WISC), the WISC-R included minority children in its standardization sample. The WISC-R has adequate criterion and concurrent validity and high internal consistency reliabilities. Several short forms of the WISC-R have been developed, but most carry significant disadvantages and their usage is not advised. Sattler (1988) criticized the WISC-R largely on the basis of its limited applicability for children younger than 6 years, 4 months and older than 16 years, 8 months, limited floor and ceiling, and nonuniformity of scaled scores (i.e., highest possible scaled score differs according to age group).

In 1991, the long-awaited revision of the WISC-R was published. The WISC-III (Wechsler, 1991) retains the essential features of the previous Wechsler tests while providing up-to-date normative data, test materials, content, and administration procedures. Like its predecessor, the WISC-III standardization sample included 2200 children, with 200 in each of 11 age groups ranging from 6 to 16 years. Stratification of the sample was based on age, gender, race/ethnicity, geographic region, and parent education, and the sample appears to have been very representative of the U.S. population based on 1988 census data.

Subtest improvements include the minimization of bias in content, refinement and updating of artwork, and the adding of items to several subtests to address the issue of high basals and low ceilings. Regarding bias, the content of several subtests was revised to include a comparable number of references to males and females, as well as more ethnically diverse references to individuals, names, and topics. Refinement and improvement of the artwork includes the enlargement of stimulus materials and more colorful artwork on performance subtests to enhance the attentiveness of children. Also, new items were created on the arithmetic, similarities, picture arrangement, and mazes subtests to extend measurement both downward and upward, as necessary. Finally, other minor modifications include reordering the administration sequence of the subtests (ostensibly to allow rapport to be established more easily), revision or deletion of dated items, reordering items within a few of the subtests to account for changes in item difficulty, changes in scoring criteria based on the new norms, and the addition of a new optional performance subtest (symbol search).

In addition to verbal, performance, and full scale IQ scores, the WISC-III yields four-factor, analytically based scores which have a mean of 100 and a standard deviation of 15. These factors, and the subtests which comprise them, include verbal comprehension (information, similarities, vocabulary, comprehension), perceptual organization (picture completion, picture arrangement, block design, object assembly), freedom from distractibility (arithmetic, digit span), and processing speed (coding, symbol search). Confirmatory factor analysis has demonstrated that these four factors can be generalized to children with learning disabilities, reading disorders, attention deficit disorders, high ability (e.g., gifted), and mental retardation. Future research will provide additional information regarding the diagnostic utility of these factors.

Finally, numerous studies reported in the manual provide evidence for the convergent and discriminant validity of the WISC-III (Wechsler, 1991). Of particular note and interest is the relationship between the WISC-R and WISC-III IQ scores. The magnitude of the correlations between the WISC-R and WISC-III IQ scores (.81–.90) provides strong evidence that the two tests measure the same constructs. However, the WISC-III verbal, performance, and full scale IQ scores are all lower than those of the WISC-R

(two, seven, and five points lower, respectively). As noted by Wechsler (1991, p. 197), this finding suggests that "when a child's performance is referenced to an outdated standardization sample [i.e., WISC-R], rather than to a contemporary sample, the IQ score will be inflated."

There is some overlap between the WISC-R/WISC-III and the WPPSI-R for younger children and between the WISC-R/WISC-III and WAIS-R (described below) for older adolescents, and there is some evidence to suggest that the three scales do not yield interchangeable IQs (Sattler, 1988). Consequently the clinician must often decide which Wechsler scale to administer to a child. This is not a decision that is made hastily or without consideration of the possible long-range implications for the child. Indeed, the decision should be made not on the basis of personal preferences but rather on the strengths and weaknesses of the particular test in answering the referral question. For instance, if the clinician is referred a 6½-year-old child for evaluation of delayed cognitive development, it would be best to administer the WPPSI-R because this test would allow the examiner to obtain a greater sampling of ability by administering more items. The same is true for a 16½-year-old adolescent, that is, the WISC-R/WISC-III would provide a more comprehensive sampling of ability than the WAIS-R.

As described above, the SB-IV and the K-ABC are also used to assess the cognitive abilities or intelligence of school-age children. The SB-IV and WAIS-R are also the instruments of choice for measuring intelligence in older adolescents. Like the other Wechsler scales, the WAIS-R has excellent standardization procedures (1880 individuals, 16 to 74 years old, stratified by age, gender, race, education, and geography) and possesses very good psychometric properties. Like the WISC-R, its primary limitation is its limited floor and ceiling; this renders it insufficient as a measure of moderate to severe mental retardation or of extreme giftedness (Sattler, 1988).

OTHER TESTS USED TO ASSESS COGNITIVE FUNCTIONING

In addition to the tests described above, there are several other tests that are used by psychologists to measure various aspects of cognitive and motor development. These include the Peabody Picture Vocabulary Test-Revised (PPVT-R), the Test of Nonverbal Intelligence (TONI), the Cattell Culture Fair Intelligence Tests, the Hiskey–Nebraska Test of Learning Aptitude, and the Leiter International Performance Scale. Of these tests, perhaps the two most commonly used, and those with which the psychiatrist should have some familiarity, are the PPVT-R and TONI. Consequently they will receive brief mention here.

Originally developed in 1959 and revised in 1981, the PPVT-R (Dunn & Dunn, 1981) measures the hearing vocabulary or receptive knowledge of individuals ranging in age from 2 years, 6 months through adulthood. It is a relatively brief test (10 to 15 minutes) and requires no special reading ability on the part of the examinee. The examiner states a word and the examinee is asked to indicate which of four pictures best represents the meaning of the word. Standard scores range from 40 to 160 ($M = 100$, $SD = 15$) and an age equivalent can be obtained. Sattler (1988) notes that the PPVT-R represents a significant improvement over its predecessor, both in terms of its standardization and psychometric properties. It is a useful assessment tool with children who have verbal expression deficits. However, the PPVT-R should not be viewed as a measure of intelligence and is best used as a supplement to other tests of cognitive ability.

The TONI (Brown, Sherbenou, & Dollar, 1982), and its successor (TONI-2, published in 1990), is a test that is frequently used with children for whom language or hearing difficulties are known or expected. This instrument was developed for individuals age 5 years through adulthood and is administered in a manner that requires no listening, speaking, reading, or writing skills. Gestures and pantomime are used to instruct the examinee in responding to a series of 50 pictures. The examinee is required to examine the similarities and differences among the various figures, identify one or more problem-solving rules that define the relationship among the figures, and then select a correct response. A TONI quotient ($M = 100$, $SD = 15$) is derived from raw scores. Although this is a very useful instrument for assessing the problem-solving skills of children with language impairments or bilingual or non-English-speaking children, the TONI (like the PPVT-R) should not be used as a screening device

for assessing intellectual level of functioning (Naglieri & Prewett, 1990).

ASSESSING THE ACADEMIC ACHIEVEMENT OF SCHOOL-AGE CHILDREN AND ADOLESCENTS

In addition to standardized measures of cognitive ability, a psychological evaluation typically includes a test of academic achievement that measures a wide variety of achievement domains, including reading, spelling, mathematics, written language, and general factual knowledge. The administration of individual achievement tests increased following the passage of P.L. 94–142 and is central to the diagnosis of specific learning disabilities in children and adolescents. Concomitantly we have witnessed a burgeoning of tests of academic achievement during the past decade. As a result, psychologists are no longer restricted to one or two achievement tests; now there are many other achievement instruments with sound standardization and psychometric data. The more commonly used individually administered instruments of academic achievement are reviewed below. The reader is referred to Kamphaus, Slotkin, and DeVincentis (1990) for a more comprehensive review of the "state of the art" in individual assessment of academic achievement.

Wide Range Achievement Test-Revised (WRAT-R): The WRAT-R (Jastak & Wilkinson, 1984) measures basic skills in reading, spelling, and arithmetic and is appropriate for use with individuals ranging in age from 5 to 74 years. There are two forms: level I is for children 5 to 11 years, 11 months old and level II is for adolescents and adults 12 to 74 years, 11 months old. The test was developed to assess whether the examinee has mastered the basic mechanics of the three domains. Reading items tap the individual's ability to recognize and recite letters and pronounce words; spelling items assess the ability to copy symbols, write one's own name, and accurately spell single words from a dictated sentence; arithmetic items measure counting, oral computation, and written calculation skills. The WRAT-R is relatively brief (20 to 30 minutes), easy to administer, and yields a variety of scores (standard scores, percentile ranks, grade equivalents, *t* scores, normal curve equivalents).

Although one of the more widely used measures of achievement in educational and inpatient psychiatric settings, the WRAT-R unfortunately possesses many significant drawbacks. Among its particularly important limitations are its very inadequate psychometric properties (poor reliability, concurrent and content validity not established) and the omission of socioeconomic status as a stratification variable in its standardization. This test does not assess reading comprehension or understanding of complex arithmetic processes (Sattler, 1988). Consequently the WRAT-R should be not be used for diagnostic or placement purposes, and any references to such usage should be viewed skeptically (Kamphaus et al., 1990; Sattler, 1988).

Peabody Individual Achievement Test-Revised (PIAT-R): Originally developed in 1970 (Dunn & Markwardt, 1970) as an achievement screening instrument, the recently revised PIAT-R (Markwardt, 1989) measures academic functioning across six domains: mathematics, reading comprehension, reading recognition, spelling, written expression, and general information. Intended for use with children 5 to 18 years old, the PIAT-R has an administration time of approximately 50 minutes and yields standard scores ($M = 100$, $SD = 15$), stanines, and normal curve equivalents. The norms are relatively current (based on 1985 census figures), reliability data are impressive and vastly improved compared to the earlier version, and content validity has been established. Although construct and concurrent validity are weak, the PIAT-R has received favorable reviews, and future research will likely demonstrate that it is a useful test of academic achievement.

Woodcock–Johnson Psycho-Educational Battery-Revised (WJ-R): The WJ-R (Woodcock & Mather, 1989) is a widely used, individually administered series of tests measuring cognitive abilities, scholastic aptitudes, and achievement of individuals 2 years old through adulthood. The WJ-R represents a revision and expansion of the 1977 version. It is organized into two major components—tests of cognitive ability and tests of achievement—which are both subdivided into a standard battery and a supplemental battery. Although the tests of cognitive ability have been expanded and are purported to be more representative of intellectual processing, their use as a replacement for other well-standardized intelligence instruments is not encouraged. Conse-

quently most psychologists administer only the tests of achievement which, in its standard battery, consist of nine tests. These tests include letter-word identification, passage comprehension, calculation, applied problems, dictation, writing samples, science, and social studies. Raw scores from these tests can be combined to yield cluster scores across five domains: broad reading, broad mathematics, broad written language, broad knowledge, and skills. A child's performance also can be presented in terms of percentile rank, standard score ($M = 100$, $SD = 15$), grade level, or age equivalent.

Regarding the tests of achievement, the major differences between the original WJ and the WJ-R are the addition of four new tests, a significantly modified organizational format, and the extension of the normative sample to include children as young as 2 years old. It has adequate reliability and is related to other measures of achievement; however, its ability to predict future academic achievement (especially that of young children) has not been fully established. Also, considering that factor analytic studies failed to support the use of cluster scores in the previous version (Sattler, 1988), use of the WJ-R cluster structure awaits empirical validation. Despite these limitations, the WJ-R appears to have utility in the diagnosis of learning difficulties and in preparing individual educational programs.

Kaufman Test of Educational Achievement (K-TEA): The K-TEA (Kaufman & Kaufman, 1985b) is a recent addition to the achievement test compendium, and its use is becoming increasingly popular. Appropriate for children 6 to 18 years old, the K-TEA comprehensive form is designed to measure academic achievement across five domains: reading decoding, reading comprehension, mathematics application, mathematics computation, and spelling. An abbreviated version of the comprehensive form is also available (Kaufman & Kaufman, 1985a) and provides information about reading, mathematics, and spelling skills. Raw scores on the individual subtests are converted into standard scores ($M = 100$, $SD = 15$) which then yield a composite score. Norms are available for both age and grade. Overall this instrument demonstrates very good validity and reliability. However, its use is limited with high-achieving older students and with younger children who are well below their age or grade level (Kamphaus et al., 1990).

TESTS OF VISUAL-MOTOR COORDINATION AND INTEGRATION

Tasks of visual-motor coordination and integration are often included in the assessment of children's abilities. The major tests of intelligence include subtests that provide information regarding a child's visual-motor perception and motor proficiency (e.g., WISC-R block design, object assembly, coding). There are times, however, when additional tests of visual-motor integration are used. For instance, in a child with possible learning difficulties or neurological complications, tasks involving fine and gross motor coordination might provide important information about the child's sensory and motor modalities and assist the clinician in developing appropriate remedial instruction (Sattler, 1988).

Observations of the child throughout testing are always of critical importance. This is especially true during the administration of visual-motor tasks. Of particular relevance is the child's handedness, degree of deliberation or impulsivity, reliance on memory, rotation of designs, reproduction quality, use of space, use of time, recognition of errors, frustration tolerance, level of fatigue, and need for encouragement. Because there are many possible reasons for poor visual-motor performance—misperception of stimulus, execution problems, central processing difficulties, maturational delay, limited intellectual stimulation, poor motivation, neurological impairment, fatigue, and affective disturbances—observations of the child's response tendencies will assist the clinician in formulating hypotheses that can be used to account for the child's performance.

Extreme caution should be exercised in interpreting the results of visual-motor integration tests obtained from children with visual or motor limitations and from children with certain medical conditions (e.g., cerebral palsy, advanced HIV infection) that might affect performance on such tasks. Furthermore, these tests should not be used as indices of intellectual prowess. Two of the more popular tests of visual-motor development that are frequently employed as part of a larger battery of tests are the Bender Visual-Motor Gestalt Test

and the Developmental Test of Visual-Motor Integration.

Bender–Gestalt Test: Developed as a measure of perceptual motor maturation for children and adults, the Bender–Gestalt test (Bender, 1938, 1946) is unquestionably the most frequently used instrument for this purpose (Goh, Teslow, & Fuller, 1981). The child is asked to reproduce nine geometric designs presented one at a time on 4-inch × 6-inch white cards. Although several scoring systems have been developed over the years, the Koppitz Developmental Bender Scoring System (Koppitz, 1964, 1975) has emerged as the most widely used scoring system for children 5 to 11 years old. This system comprises both a developmental scoring component and scoring of emotional indicators. There are 30 developmental scoring items for which errors in design reproduction are scored as either 1 (present) or 0 (absent). Four major types of errors are recorded: distortion of shape, rotations, integration problems, and perseveration. A total Bender developmental score is obtained by summing the errors. Age equivalent scores, percentile ranks, and standard scores based on the 1975 restandardization sample are available and applied most appropriately to children between 5 and 8 years of age.

As indicated, Koppitz (1964, 1975) believed that the Bender–Gestalt test could be a useful projective technique for identifying emotional difficulties in children. Indeed, there is some empirical evidence that the Total Bender Developmental Score and Emotional Index Score measure different aspects of functioning. Examples of the 12 emotional indicators include

- confused order: poor planning, difficulty organizing information
- increasing size: poor ability to tolerate frustration, possible explosiveness
- expansion: impulsive, acting-out behaviors
- spontaneous elaboration or additions to designs: high anxiety level, intense fears, preoccupation with inner thoughts

Generally the Bender–Gestalt test is a reliable and valid measure of perceptual motor functioning and should be used for this purpose. Although it has some utility as a projective assessment tool, it should not be considered a definitive diagnostic tool for brain damage, intellectual development, or personality functioning.

Developmental Test of Visual-Motor Integration (VMI): Although originally designed to screen learning and behavior problems in preschool children, the VMI (Beery, 1989) can be used with children 2 to 15 years old. The short form of the VMI has 15 geometric figures arranged sequentially from simple to complex and is appropriate for children 2 to 8 years old. The long form uses 24 figures to assess visual-motor integration in examinees 2 to 15 years old, and can be used with adults suspected of developmental delays. The child attempts to reproduce each figure until three consecutive failures have been recorded. The VMI is more structured than the Bender–Gestalt test in that three stimulus designs are presented on each page and the child is instructed to reproduce them in square boxes immediately below the design. Raw scores (number of correct reproductions) are converted to developmental age equivalents and standard scores ($M = 10$, $SD = 3$). The VMI has been found to correlate with reading ability and developmental age. Future research is needed to establish its reliability and validity.

ASSESSING PSYCHOPATHOLOGY AND PERSONALITY DEVELOPMENT

Tests of psychopathology and personality structure have historically been divided into two categories: objective and projective tests. Objective tests are characterized by discrete, scorable responses to specific questions presented verbally or in a written format. The child's performance on such tests is usually compared to a criterion group. Examples of clinical objective personality tests include the Minnesota Multiphasic Personality Inventory (MMPI) and the Millon Clinical Multiaxial Inventory (MCMI). The most common reasons for using objective personality tests are for psychiatric diagnosis and the identification of abnormal personality traits. Projective personality tests, on the other hand, are characterized by their relatively unstructured, open-ended format that focuses more on the child's idiosyncratic response pattern. As noted by Goldman et al. (1983, p. 223).

All projective devices rest upon the assumption that the manner in which the person is organized psychologically will determine the content and style of the person's perceptions. The nature of personal symbolism is assumed to be determined by the characteristics of that person and not to be random in nature. This assumption of the deterministic nature of symbolism and perception is called the projective hypothesis. Specifically, symbolism and perception are assumed to be shaped by the needs, fears, defenses, and coping mechanisms of the person and to be revealed in projective data whether the product is stories a person tells, perceptions of inkblots, or responses to incomplete sentences or other ambiguous stimuli.

Although projective tests have often been criticized for their poor standardization and inadequate psychometric properties, more recent developments in this area allow for normative comparisons in addition to their more idiographic aspects of interpretation.

Prior to reviewing a few common tests of psychopathology and personality development and their use with children and adolescents, two general points must be made. First, the traditional distinction drawn between objective and projective tests is tenuous at best. While the words "objective" and "projective" may adequately define the stimulus properties of a particular test, they should not be construed to mean that the skill level of the clinician is necessarily greater for the one over the other. Indeed, the interpretation of information obtained from both objective and projective techniques requires considerable training and experience in order to place such information in its appropriate clinical context. Second, the use of personality tests, whether considered objective or projective, should not be viewed as yielding a definitive blueprint of an individual's personality structure. It is not uncommon for a psychologist to receive a referral for "personality testing" to assist with differential diagnosis or treatment planning. It is important to emphasize that personality tests are incapable of making a diagnosis. They are best used in conjunction with multiple other aspects of the CA/ISP and OIM processes to generate diagnostic and trait hypotheses about an individual. It is the convergence or divergence of the data arising from these multiple sources of information that is prerequisite to formulating diagnostic impressions and treatment recommendations.

Minnesota Multiphasic Personality Inventory

(MMPI): Numerous volumes have been written on the MMPI (Hathaway & McKinley, 1943) and its use in the clinical setting. This section will focus on the use of the MMPI with adolescents and offer a brief discussion of the recently restandardized version of the MMPI, the so-called MMPI-2 (University of Minnesota, 1989).

The MMPI is the most widely used and researched instrument for the assessment of personality functioning. Originally developed as a diagnostic tool and as a means for objectively, assessing therapeutic change, the MMPI consists of 566 statements to which the examinee responds true or false as they apply to him. It is self-administered and requires that the examinee have at least a sixth-grade reading level. There are 10 clinical and 3 validity scales. The original MMPI items were empirically selected based on their ability to discriminate between psychiatric diagnostic groups; accordingly, the names of the scales reflect psychiatric syndromes common to the 1940's era. The eight original scales include hypochondriasis (1-Hs), depression (2-D), hysteria (3-Hy), psychopathic deviate (4-Pd), paranoia (6-Pa), psychasthenia (7-Pt), schizophrenia (8-Sc), and hypomania (9-Ma). The masculinity-femininity (5-Mf) and social introversion (0-Si) scales were added at a later date. Four validity scales—"cannot say," L, F, and K—were developed to detect deviant test-taking attitudes. In addition, many special research scales and lists of "critical items" have been elaborated and extensively reviewed elsewhere (e.g., Graham, 1977). Raw scores are converted to *t* scores, which are then used in the analysis and interpretation of the MMPI profile. The skilled clinician relies on the configuration or pattern of scores (e.g., two- and three-point codes) in guiding interpretations of the MMPI; interpretations made solely on the basis of individual clinical scales should be viewed with extreme caution.

Because the original MMPI normative sample was based entirely on individuals residing in Minnesota during the 1930s, it was desperately in need of an expanded normative base that more accurately reflected the current U.S. population and culture. In addition, many of the items had become obsolete, obscure, or objectionable. Consequently several major revisions were made and are reflected in the MMPI-2 including (1) editing or eliminating outdated items, deleting duplicate items, and adding items with new content, so that the resulting test employed a total of 567 items (basic scales in items 1–370), (2) obtaining a new, larger, and more representative national sample of 2600 adults, and (3) the addition of three new validity scales. Furthermore, there is some evidence that the most noticeable difference will be a general decrease in *t*-score elevations across normal and clinical samples (Finn & Butcher, 1991).

Although originally considered to be inappropriate for individuals under 16 years of age, the MMPI has been successfully employed with adolescents as young as 14 (Graham, 1977). Several early studies found that adolescents' responses to the MMPI yielded general elevations on many of the clinical scales. Consequently special adolescent norms were developed to avoid this problem of false positives (Archer, 1987; Marks, Seeman, & Haller, 1974). At the time of this writing, an adolescent form of the MMPI-2 is being prepared for publication. This new version addresses more age-appropriate issues of peer relations, behavioral difficulties, and family conflict. Williams (1989) offers the most current interpretation guidelines for use of the MMPI-2 with adolescent populations.

Millon Clinical Multiaxial Inventory (MCMI): The MCMI (and its successor, the MCMI-II) (Millon, 1983, 1987) is a self-administered, 175-item true-false inventory designed to assess psychopathology. Developed in response to the shortcomings of the MMPI, the MCMI is based on Millon's theory of personality structure and is in turn closely related in structure to current diagnostic nosology. It consists of one validity scale and several clinical scales designed to assess the presence of specific personality disorders and other clinical syndromes. Several recent reviewers (Finn & Butcher, 1991; Hess, 1985; McCabe, 1987) have suggested that the MCMI, though demonstrating reasonable concurrent validity with the MMPI, has only moderate correspondence with *DSM-III* personality disorders. Furthermore, there is evidence that because of its neglect of common vegetative symptoms of depression, this test underdiagnoses clinical depression among inpatients and outpatients. On the other hand, it overdiagnoses personality disorders (Finn & Butcher, 1991).

657

An adolescent version of the MCMI, the Millon Adolescent Personality Inventory (MAPI), was developed in 1977 and can be used with adolescents 13 to 18 years old. In addition to more specific personality traits, it is designed to measure adolescent coping styles, expressed concerns, and behavior. It comprises 150 items that yield two validity scales and 20 clinical scales. However, the psychometric components of this test are virtually unknown, and its use with various adolescent populations has been limited (Rieger & Baron, 1991).

Rorschach Inkblot Test: Perhaps better than any other instrument of personality, the Rorschach epitomizes what is meant by projective testing. It is unquestionably one of the most unstructured projective techniques available. Use of the Rorschach is based on the premise that unconscious processes (e.g., needs, motives, conflicts, etc.) determine a person's responses to ambiguous stimuli. Therefore, when presented with amorphous, nonspecific stimuli such as inkblots, an individual must call upon internal images, ideas, and relationships in order to generate a response (Groth-Marnat, 1984). Considerable formal training and experience are needed to administer, score, and interpret the Rorschach properly.

The Rorschach consists of 10 bilaterally symmetrical inkblots (5 achromatic, 5 with color) that vary in complexity and organization. The examinee is presented with one inkblot at a time and asked to tell the clinician what it might be. Responses are recorded and a subsequent inquiry phase allows the examiner to obtain information regarding the location and determinants (color, shape, etc.) of the inkblot elements used by the examinee as well as the general content or class of objects to which the response belongs (Groth-Marnat, 1984). Interpretation is then based on the relative percentage of responses in each of these categories.

Of the six Rorschach scoring systems that have emerged over the past 70 years, Exner's (1986) "comprehensive system" is the one most frequently used today. Exner's scoring system overcomes many of the problems inherent in previous systems and attempts to enhance the reliability and validity of the Rorschach procedure. In addition to location, determinants, and content, Exner's structural summary allows for the coding of organizational activity, developmental level, form quality, and deviant verbalizations. Furthermore, the structural summary yields considerable information about the examinee's perceptual accuracy, thought processes, quality and modulation of affect, coping style, stress tolerance, self-perceptions, and defense mechanisms. The development of this system has renewed research interest in the Rorschach.

Although the Rorschach has been used to assess the personality structure of children and adolescents (Ames, Metraux, Rodell, & Walker, 1974; Ames, Metraux, & Walker, 1971; Exner & Weiner, 1982; Groth-Marnat, 1984), its clinical utility with this population has not been extensively evaluated. As summarized by Goldman et al. (1983, p. 245), the most consistent findings across studies are that "younger children give fewer responses than adults, while adolescents approach the lower limit of adults in terms of number of responses." Furthermore, given the decreased numbers of responses typically obtained, its use with children and adolescents with low intellectual abilities is not advised.

Perhaps the most often cited criticism of the Rorschach is its questionable validity. Indeed, studies designed to establish the validity of the Rorschach have yielded negative, inconclusive, and often contradictory findings. To a large degree, this pattern of results can be attributed to the many different ways the instrument is administered and scored. Such variability in administration and scoring not only affects validity studies but also makes it extremely difficult to establish adequate levels of reliability. However, Exner's comprehensive system provides increased opportunity for empirical examination of the instrument's psychometric properties. Indeed, its emphasis on the quantitative and structural aspects of the Rorschach, rather than on its qualitative features, makes it even more likely that it will continue to be the preferred tool for assessing individuals' unconscious processes.

Apperception Tests: Apperception tests offer the clinician another avenue for pursuing information about an individual's needs, perceptions, goals, defenses, and interactions with the environment. Although several have been constructed, we will briefly review only two of the most commonly used: the Thematic Apperception Test and the Tasks of Emotional Development.

The Thematic Apperception Test (TAT) is perhaps the most extensively used apperception test and has served as the model for the development of similar types of tests. Based entirely on Murray's (1943) theory of personality, the TAT allows the trained interpreter to assess an individual's inner drives, conflicts, and emotions, even when these psychological characteristics are not apparent to the examinee. The TAT differs from other projective instruments, like the Rorschach, in that its stimuli are more structured and require the examinee to produce more complex and organized verbal responses (Groth-Marnat, 1984). Test stimuli include 19 cards with relatively ambiguous pictures on them of people in varying poses and relationships and 1 blank card. Half of the cards include scenarios that are related to everyday life situations, whereas the others are extremely ambiguous. The actual number of cards presented to the examinee depends on several factors, including the examinee's age, gender, relevance to the presenting problem, and/or information derived from the clinical interview; however, usually between 8 and 10 cards are administered. Upon presentation of each card, the examinee is instructed to make up a dramatic story with the following components to the story: a beginning that leads up to the picture, what is happening at the time of the picture, the thoughts and feelings of the characters, and an ending.

Murray's (1943) original scoring system requires the examiner to identify the hero of the story, the forces arising from the hero, and the environmental forces which pressed (i.e., impinged) upon the hero. Twenty-six needs are classified for valence and strength based on frequency, intensity, duration, and relative importance in the story's plot. Interpretations are made based on the foregoing "needs assessment" and the thematic aspects of the stories. The attributes of the hero are thought to reflect the personality characteristics of the examinee and attributions made about the environment are thought to mirror the examinee's view of his world (Goldman et al., 1983). Many subsequent approaches to scoring and interpretation have been advanced over the past 40 years (e.g., Bellak, 1975), but none has achieved universal appeal.

One popular derivative of the TAT is the Children's Apperception Test (CAT) which offers both animal (Bellak & Bellak, 1974) and human (Bellak & Bellak, 1965) figures. Both sets contain 10 cards and are appropriate for children between 3 and 10 years of age. It is generally believed that children more readily identify with these more age-appropriate pictures and therefore reveal more information about relevant developmental issues (e.g., separation, dependency, fantasies, fears and anxieties, inhibitions and impulses, etc.). Other outgrowths of the original TAT that have been used with children and adolescents include the Michigan Picture Test (Hartwell, Hutt, Andrew, et al., 1953), the Roberts Apperception Test for Children (Roberts & McArthur, 1982), and the recently developed Apperceptive Personality Test (Holmstrom, Silber, & Karp, 1990).

The Tasks of Emotional Development (TED; Cohen & Weil, 1975) is a projective technique designed specifically to assess the mastery of critical tasks of emotional growth and development during childhood and adolescence. The 13 tasks that comprise the test include

- Socialization within the peer group
- Establishment of trust in people
- Acceptance and control of aggressive feelings toward peers
- Establishment of positive attitudes toward academic learning
- Establishment of respect for the property of others
- Separation from mother
- Identification with same-sex parent
- Acceptance of siblings
- Acceptance of limits set by adults
- Acceptance of affection between parents (resolution of oedipal conflict)
- Establishment of positive attitudes toward orderliness and cleanliness
- Establishment of positive self-concept
- Establishment of positive heterosexual socialization

These tasks have been translated into pictures of real-life situations and the examinee is directed to tell a story about what is happening in the picture as well as what the characters are feeling and thinking. Different series of pictures have been constructed for males and females as well as for younger children and adolescents. Responses to each of the tasks are scored across five domains: perception, outcome, affect, motivation, and spontaneity. Standardization was based on 1100 normal boys and girls 6 to 11 years old and 600 children referred to a clinic for suspected emotional difficulties. Cohen and Weil (1975) provide evidence of high interscorer reliability, although important validity data are lacking.

Like other projective techniques, apperception tests are often considered a valuable addition to the clinician's assessment battery for several reasons. They are useful in accessing covert structures of personality, they focus on more global aspects of personality in contrast to the specific trait focus of objective tests, and they are less susceptible to faking on the part of the examinee. However, several criticisms have been leveled at apperception tests, and, indeed, on projective techniques in general. Because interpretations of responses to apperception tests are based largely on qualitative rather than quantitative analysis, establishing reliability is very problematic. Although it might be possible to establish good interscorer agreement on some quantification of responses, this would provide no information about whether clinicians would make the same inferences or draw the same conclusions based on these responses. Establishing test validity is similarly complex and has been the source of considerable controversy and criticism. Furthermore, early development of apperception tests failed to give adequate consideration to cultural differences that might affect such tests.

Sentence Completion Tests and Projective Drawings: Sentence completion tests and projective drawings are two additional projective techniques that are frequently included in the evaluation of children and adolescents. There are numerous variations of these techniques which are not reviewed here. Suffice it to say, however, that such tasks are based on the premise that free associations, either in response to sentence stems or in drawing a picture, will provide relevant clinical information about the examinee's feelings and personality structure. Such procedures gained popularity among many clinicians because examinees could respond in a nonverbal manner to the task demands. Sentence completion tests and projective drawings are usually used with elementary school-age children and adolescents. However, these techniques must be interpreted with caution and in the context of interview information and other test data.

Conclusion

This chapter addressed issues pertinent to the use of psychological tests with children and adolescents. Furthermore, it has attempted to provide the reader with a basic fund of information regarding the many different types of instruments that are used to assess cognitive, motor, achievement, and personality functioning in infants, children, and adolescents. Several conclusions can be drawn from this discussion. First, the increased knowledge base and diverse settings from which clinicians now operate have significantly expanded the roles and objectives of psychological testing. Second, assessments of children should address the specific referral question in as comprehensive a manner as possible. Although there are many models of assessment, the hypothesis testing model offers the most sophisticated approach to evaluating children. Third, single test findings should never be used as a basis for clinical conclusions; rather they should be viewed only within the context of additional assessment information. Finally, there are many tests designed to measure various aspects of children's functioning, and the selection or use of these instruments should be based on detailed knowledge and understanding of their psychometric properties, ability to address the referral questions, appropriateness for the child being evaluated, and clinical utility.

REFERENCES

APA (American Psychological Association). (1985). *Standards for educational and psychological testing.* Washington, DC: Author.

Ames, L. B., Metraux, R. W., Rodell, J. L., & Walker, R. N. (1974). *Child Rorschach responses: Developmental trends from two to ten years.* New York: Brunner/Mazel.

Ames, L. B., Metraux, R. W., & Walker, R. N. (1971). *Adolescent Rorschach responses: Developmental trends from ten to sixteen years* (2nd ed.). New York: Brunner/Mazel.

Anastasi, A. (1988). *Psychological testing* (6th ed.). New York: Macmillan.

Archer, R. P. (1987). *Using the MMPI with adolescents.* Hillsdale, NJ: Lawrence Erlbaum.

Arthur, A. Z. (1969). Diagnostic testing and the new alternatives. *Psychological Bulletin, 72,* 183–192.

Bayley, N. (1969). *Bayley Scales of Infant Development.* New York: Psychological Corporation.

Beery, K. E. (1989). *Manual for the Developmental Test of Visual-Motor Integration* (3rd ed.). Cleveland, OH: Modern Curriculum Press.

Bellak, L. (1975). *The TAT, CAT, and SAT in clinical use* (3rd ed.). New York: Grune & Stratton.

Bellak, L., & Bellak, S. (1965). *Children's Apperception Test (Human Figures).* Larchmont, NY: CPS.

Bellak, L., & Bellak, S. (1974). *Children's Apperception Test* (rev. ed.). Larchmont, NY: CPS.

Bender, L. (1938). A Visual Motor Gestalt Test and its clinical use. *American Orthopsychiatry Research Monograph,* No. 3.

Bender, L. (1946). *Bender Visual-Motor Gestalt test.* San Antonio: Psychological Corporation.

Bracken, B. A. (1985). A critical review of the Kaufman Assessment Battery for Children (K-ABC). *School Psychology Review, 14,* 21–36.

Brazelton, T. B. (1973). *Neonatal Behavioral Assessment Scale.* Philadelphia: J. B. Lippincott.

Brown, L., Sherbenou, R., & Dollar, S. (1982). *Test of Nonverbal Intelligence (TONI).* Austin, TX: PRO-ED.

Cattell, P. (1960). *Cattell Infant Intelligence Scale.* Cleveland, OH: Psychological Corporation.

Cohen, H., & Weil, G. R. (1975). *Tasks of Emotional Development: A projective test for children and adolescents.* Brookline, MA: TED Associates.

Culbertson, J. L., & Gyurke, J. (1990). Assessment of cognitive and motor development in infancy and childhood. In J. H. Johnson & J. Goldman (Eds.), *Developmental assessment in clinical child psychology: A handbook* (pp. 100–131). New York: Pergamon Press.

Dunn, L. M., & Dunn, L. M. (1981). *Peabody Picture Vocabulary Test—Revised.* Circle Pines, MN: American Guidance Service.

Dunn, L. M., & Markwardt, F. C., Jr. (1970). *Peabody Individual Achievement Test.* Circle Pines, MN: American Guidance Service.

Exner, J. E., Jr. (1986). *The Rorschach: A comprehensive system* (Vol. 1, 2nd ed.). New York: John Wiley & Sons.

Exner, J. E., Jr., & Weiner, I. (1982). *The Rorschach: A comprehensive system. Vol. 3: Assessment of children and adolescents.* New York: John Wiley & Sons.

Finn, S. E., & Butcher, J. N. (1991). Clinical objective personality assessment. In M. Hersen, A. E. Kazdin, & A. S. Bellack (Eds.), *The clinical psychology handbook* (2nd ed.). Chapter 21, pp. 362–373. New York: Pergamon Press.

Glutting, J. J., & Kaplan, D. (1990). Stanford-Binet Intelligence Scale, 4th ed.: Making the case for reasonable interpretations. In C. R. Reynolds & R. W. Kamphaus (Eds.), *Handbook of psychological and educational assessment of children: Intelligence and achievement* (pp. 277–295). New York: Guilford Press.

Goh, D. S., Teslow, C. J., & Fuller, G. B. (1981). The practice of psychological assessment among school psychologists. *Professional Psychology, 12,* 696–706.

Goldman, J., L'Engle Stein, C. L., & Guerry, S. (1983). *Psychological methods of child assessment.* New York: Brunner/Mazel.

Goodman, J. F. (1990). Infant intelligence: Do we, can we, should we assess it? In C. R. Reynolds & R. W. Kamphaus (Eds.), *Handbook of psychological and educational assessment of children: Intelligence and achievement* (pp. 183–208). New York: Guilford Press.

Graham, J. T. (1977). *The MMPI: A practical guide.* New York: Oxford University Press.

Groth-Marnat, G. (1984). *Handbook of psychological assessment.* New York: Van Nostrand Reinhold.

Hartwell, S. W., et al. (1953). The Michigan Picture Test: Diagnostic and therapeutic possibilities of a new projective test for children. *American Journal of Orthopsychiatry, 21,* 124–137.

Hathaway, S. R., & McKinley, J. C. (1943). *The Minnesota Multiphasic Personality Inventory.* Minneapolis, MN: University of Minnesota Press.

Hess, A. K. (1985). Review of Millon Clinical Multiaxial Inventory. In J. V. Mitchell (Ed.), *The ninth mental measurements yearbook* (Vol. 1, pp. 984–986). Lincoln, NE: Buros Institute of Mental Measurements.

Holmstrom, R. W., Silber, D. E., & Karp, S. A. (1990). Development of the Apperceptive Personality Test. *Journal of Personality Assessment, 54,* 252–264.

Hooper, S. R., Conner, R. E., & Umansky, W. (1986). The Cattell Infant Intelligence Scale: A review of the literature. *Developmental Review, 6,* 146–164.

Ilg, F. L., & Ames, L. B. (1965). *School readiness: Behavior tests used at the Gesell Institute.* New York: Harper & Row.

Jastak, S., & Wilkinson, G. S. (1984). *Wide Range Achievement Test—Revised.* Wilmington, DE: Jastak Associates.

Johnson, J. H., & Goldman, J. (Eds.). (1990). *Developmental assessment in clinical child psychology: A handbook.* New York: Pergamon Press.

Kamphaus, R. W., Slotkin, J., & DeVincentis, C. (1990). Clinical assessment of children's academic achievement. In C. R. Reynolds & R. W. Kamphaus (Eds.), *Handbook of psychological and educational assessment of children: Intelligence and achievement* (pp. 552–570). New York: Guilford Press.

Kaufman, A. S. (1979). *Intelligent testing with the WISC-R.* New York: Wiley-Interscience.

Kaufman, A. S., & Kaufman, N. L. (1977). *Clinical evaluation of young children with the McCarthy Scales.* New York: Grune & Stratton.

Kaufman, A. S., & Kaufman, N. L. (1983). *K-ABC: Kaufman assessment battery for children.* Circle Pines, MN: American Guidance Service.

Kaufman, A. S., & Kaufman, N. L. (1985a). *Kaufman test of educational achievement brief form manual.* Circle Pines, MN: American Guidance Service.

Kaufman, A. S., & Kaufman, N. L. (1985b). *Kaufman test of educational achievement comprehensive form manual.* Circle Pines, MN: American Guidance Service.

Koppitz, E. M. (1964). *The Bender Gestalt test for young children.* New York: Grune & Stratton.

Koppitz, E. M. (1975). *The Bender Gestalt test for young children (Vol. 2): Research and application, 1963–1973.* New York: Grune & Stratton.

Levine, D. (1981). Why and when to test: The social context of psychological testing. In A. I. Rabin (Ed.), *Assessment with projective techniques.* New York: Springer.

Lourie, R. S., & Rieger, R. E. (1974). The psychiatric and psychological evaluation of children. In G. Caplan (Ed.), *American handbook of psychiatry* (Vol. 2, 2nd ed., pp. 3–36). New York: Basic Books.

Magnussen, M. G. (1979). Psychometric and projective techniques. In J. D. Noshpitz (Ed.), *Basic handbook of child psychiatry* (Vol. 1, pp. 553–568). New York: Basic Books.

Marks, P. A., Seeman, W., & Haller, D. L. (1974). *The actuarial use of the MMPI with adolescents and adults.* Baltimore, MD: Williams & Wilkins.

Markwardt, F. C., Jr. (1989). *Peabody Individual Achievement Test—Revised.* Circle Pines, MN: American Guidance Service.

McCabe, S. P. (1987). Millon Clinical Multiaxial Inventory. In D. J. Keyser & R. C. Sweetland (Eds.), *Test critiques compendium* (pp. 304–315). Kansas City, MO: Westport Publishers.

McCarthy, D. A. (1972). *Manual for the McCarthy Scales of Children's Abilities.* San Antonio, TX: Psychological Corporation.

Merz, W. R. (1984). Kaufman Assessment Battery for Children. In D. J. Keyser & R. C. Sweetland (Eds.), *Test critiques compendium* (Vol. 1, pp. 245–259). Kansas City, MO: Test Corporation of America.

Miller, T. L., & Reynolds, C. R. (1984). The K-ABC [Special Issue]. *Journal of Special Education, 18.*

Millon, T. (1983). *Millon Clinical Multiaxial Inventory manual* (3rd ed.). Minneapolis, MN: Interpretive Scoring Systems.

Millon, T. (1987). *Manual for the Millon Clinical Multiaxial Inventory—II.* Minneapolis, MN: National Computer Systems.

Murray, H. A. (1943). *Thematic Apperception Test manual.* Cambridge, MA: Harvard University Press.

Nagle, R. J. (1979). The McCarthy Scales of Children's Abilities: Research implications for the assessment of young children. *School Psychology Review, 8,* 319–326.

Naglieri, J. A. (1981). Extrapolated developmental indices for the Bayley Scales of Infant Development. *American Journal of Mental Deficiency, 85,* 548–550.

Naglieri, J. A., & Prewett, P. N. (1990). Nonverbal intelligence measures: A selected review of instruments and their use. In C. R. Reynolds & R. W. Kamphaus (Eds.), *Handbook of psychological and educational assessment of children: Intelligence and achievement* (pp. 348–370). New York: Guilford Press.

Noshpitz, J. D. (Ed.). (1979). *Basic handbook of child psychiatry.* New York: Basic Books.

Reynolds, C. R., & Kamphaus, R. W. (1990). *Handbook of psychological and educational assessment of children: Intelligence and achievement.* New York: Guilford Press.

Rieger, R. E., & Baron, I. S. (1991). Psychological and neuropsychological testing. In J. M. Wiener (Ed.), *Textbook of child and adolescent psychiatry* (pp. 104–120).

Roberts, G. E., & McArthur, D. S. (1982). *Roberts Apperception Test for Children.* Los Angeles: Western Psychological Services.

Sattler, J. M. (1988). *Assessment of children* (3rd ed.). San Diego: Jerome M. Sattler.

Siegel, M. G. (1987). *Psychological testing from early childhood through adolescence: A developmental and psychodynamic approach.* Madison, CT: International Universities Press.

Sloves, R. E., Docherty, E. M., Jr., & Schneider, K. C. (1979). A scientific problem-solving model of psychological assessment. *Professional Psychology, 10,* 28–35.

Spruill, J. (1987). Stanford-Binet Intelligence Scale: Fourth Edition. In D. J. Keyser & R. C. Sweetland (Eds.), *Test critiques compendium* (pp. 14–23). Kansas City, MO: Test Corporation of America.

Thorndike, R. L., Hagen, E. P., & Sattler, J. M. (1986). *Technical manual, Stanford-Binet Intelligence Scale: Fourth Edition.* Chicago: Riverside Publishing.

University of Minnesota. (1989). *Manual for the restandardized Minnesota Multiphasic Personality Inventory: MMPI-2.* Minneapolis, MN: Author.

Uzgiris, I. C., & Hunt, J. (1975). *Assessment in infancy: Ordinal scales of psychological development.* Urbana: University of Illinois.

Valencia, R. R. (1990). Clinical assessment of young children with the McCarthy Scales of Children's Abilities. In C. R. Reynolds & R. W. Kamphaus (Eds.), *Handbook of psychological and educational assessment of children: Intelligence and achievement* (pp. 209–258). New York: Guilford Press.

vanReken, M. K. (1981). Psychological assessment and

report writing. In C. E. Walker (Ed.), *Clinical practice of psychology* (pp. 129–160). New York: Pergamon Press.

Wechsler, D. (1967). *Manual for the Wechsler Preschool and Primary Scale of Intelligence.* San Antonio, TX: Psychological Corporation.

Wechsler, D. (1974). *Manual for the Wechsler Intelligence Scale for Children—Revised.* San Antonio, TX: Psychological Corporation.

Wechsler, D. (1989). *Manual for the Wechsler Preschool and Primary Scale of Intelligence—Revised.* San Antonio, TX: Psychological Corporation.

Wechsler, D. (1991). *Wechsler Intelligence Scale for Children—Third Edition Manual.* San Antonio, TX: Psychological Corporation.

Wetzler, S., & Katz, M. M. (1989). *Contemporary approaches to psychological assessment.* New York: Brunner/Mazel.

Whatley, J. L. (1987). Bayley Scales of Infant Development. In D. J. Keyser & R. C. Sweetland (Eds.), *Test critiques compendium* (pp. 14–23). Kansas City, MO: Test Corporation of America.

Williams, C. L. (1989). MMPI profiles from adolescents: Interpretive strategies and treatment considerations. *Journal of Child and Adolescent Psychotherapy, 3,* 179–193.

Woodcock, R. W., & Mather, N. (1989). *Manual of the Woodcock-Johnson Psycho-Educational Battery-Revised: Tests of Achievement.* Allen, TX: DLM Teaching Resources.

88 / Structured Interviews

J. Gerald Young, David Kaufman, and Robert Nadrich

Structured Interviews for Children and Adolescents

THE DEVELOPMENT OF STRUCTURED INTERVIEWS FOR CHILDREN AND ADOLESCENTS

When the first structured diagnostic interviews were developed there was substantial controversy concerning their validity and clinical applicability. Clinicians asked whether a structured interview could fulfill the purposes of a clinical interview without losing essential information from the interview, such as the nuances of the patient's associations, emotional interactions, indicators of underlying emotions, and patterns of behavior and mood. Yet conventional interview techniques were known to be inadequate in some respects, such as the frequent lack of agreement among interviewers about symptoms and diagnoses. Several likely causes of these problems propelled the

development of the structured interview format forward: the content of the conventional clinical interview was variable, the wording of questions for a child was idiosyncratic, variable criteria for diagnoses were used, the training of the interviewer influenced the results of the interview, and the overall validity of the process was an open question. More than 25 years of research using structured interviews has provided new perspectives on these problems.

Structured clinical interviews are used primarily for diagnostic purposes. Nearly three decades of use suggest that they have three principal clinical applications currently: (1) clinical use to ensure that the diagnostic interview covers all major diagnoses and applies the most recent formal diagnostic criteria; (2) clinical research use to ensure uniform diagnostic procedures for epidemiological, pharmacological, biological, and other research protocols; and (3) clinical research use to generate scientific data about the diagnostic interview, informing clinicians about the status of specific features of the clinical interview (e.g., agreement between different informants). These applications indicate that, in reality, the predominant use of structured diagnostic interviews for children and adolescents is for clinical research;

This work was supported by the Medical Fellows Program of the New York State Office of Mental Retardation and Developmental Disabilities.

relatively few clinicians routinely use structured diagnostic interviews in their practices or clinics, although some use them periodically for specific purposes. Nevertheless, the significance of structured diagnostic interviews for clinicians is profound, because they are a major tool for the investigation of our most important clinical procedure, the clinical interview.

CHARACTERISTICS OF STRUCTURED INTERVIEWS

Structured interviews are the most directive of all clinical interviews, because the interview format, topics, and sequence are prearranged. Questions ("probes") for the child are not left to the interviewer to formulate, but are specifically worded to obtain the required information, to be appropriate to the developmental level of the child, and to avoid various distortions of the interview such as subtle unintentional influences on the part of the interviewer. Answers to each question are chosen from a group of specific, pre-coded responses.

Some structured interviews vary somewhat from this format and are identified as "semistructured" interviews. They are intermediate between directed (see below) and fully ("highly") structured interview formats, containing some of the advantages of each. The semistructured interview utilizes a preset sequence of topics, as well as many fully structured sections with specifically worded probes. The latter sections are particularly likely to provide essential diagnostic information, such as the presence or absence of inclusion or exclusion criteria. In the sections not specifying the actual wording of questions, the topics and symptoms are indicated and the clinician is left to use his clinical judgment about the best methods for eliciting the data. In order to clarify what is intended, clinical examples are provided as anchor points.

Several structured interviews were developed in the early years of this research and have evolved through various versions reflecting the results of research and improvements in their performance. Clinicians intending to use structured interviews should familiarize themselves with the instruments available; it is especially important to examine the diagnostic categories surveyed in each interview. The interviews vary in their specific purposes and characteristics, but each has a form for an interview with the child and another form for an interview with the parent, and each of these forms requires up to 1½ hours to administer. The structured interviews have a branching format which uses additional questions (e.g., items related to the onset and duration of the symptom) only when it is indicated that a symptom or problem behavior is present. Therefore the interviews take more time when the child has more numerous symptoms and problem behaviors. All are designed for use with children and adolescents from about 8 to 18 years of age. Some structured interviews are to be administered by a clinician, while those designed for use in epidemiological surveys use trained nonprofessional ("lay") interviewers. For this reason, fully structured interviews are usually chosen for epidemiological research (Jensen, P. S., Watanabe, H. K., Richters, J. E. et al., 1995). Computer algorithms are generally used to extract the diagnostic data generated by a structured interview.

Interviews do not generate completely accurate information, as there are many sources of misinformation (Young, O'Brien, Gutterman, et al., 1987). For example, there might be problems with the structure of the interview so that the concepts of a section are too complex for a child to understand or the wording of questions is inexact or too nonspecific; the interviewer might have biases or might make recording errors; or the child or parent might alter responses to give socially desirable answers or might have memory lapses or feel that some questions are too stressful to answer accurately. This problem is much greater in children than in adults. First, children most often do not want to be interviewed, and can experience interviews as confusing and difficult. For example, the formality of the approach may amplify the child's sense of boredom and restlessness, and the child may begin to give negative responses upon realizing that this avoids follow-up questions and causes the interview to be finished earlier. Another problem that has been recognized is that the relative rigidity of the preset wording of questions for children increases the chances that children may misinterpret the meaning of questions. This is particularly true for obsessions, compulsions, or psychotic phenomena experienced by children. Each of these experiences is difficult for a child to describe and understand, but descriptions of these phenomena given in a question to a child who has not experienced them can lead to misinterpretation of the meaning of the question by the uncomprehending child. Finally, there was a concern at the time of initial development of structured interviews that they might be harmful to children in some way, but this has not proven to be the case (Herjanic, Hudson, & Kartloff, 1976; Lewis, Gorsky, Cohen, & Hartmark, 1985; Zahner, 1991). Children participate in structured interviews and adapt quite well to them without resulting harm to the child; whether they routinely cooperate fully enough to give adequate responses is another question.

Clinical interviews for children and adolescents are components of the overall clinical assessment. The results of other components of the evaluation (e.g., physical and neurological examinations, psychological testing, etc.) provide the context within which the information of the clinical interview will be understood (Young, Kaplan, Pascualvaca, & Brasic, 1995), and the clinician should not habitually use the clinical interview in isolation. Similarly, it must be recalled that there is no single *type* of interview, according to the objective and content. The clinician must keep in mind the many types of interviews available (psychoanalytic, genetic history, play interview, etc.) and select the proper interview format and procedures prior to seeing the patient. The major interviewing *formats* include nondirective (meaning that the interviewer does not verbally direct the interview, but uses the child's comments and behaviors to help guide the structure of the interview, as in a psychodynamic interview), directed (the interviewer determines the content and pace of the interview, stopping and redirecting the interview as necessary, as in an interview to obtain the developmental history), semistructured, and structured interviews. In practice, of course, the boundaries among these interview types blur. Structured interviews can be developed to elicit information about many topics, but are most often used to determine formal diagnoses. This chapter discusses structured diagnostic interviews for children and adolescents as examples of structured interviews generally.

Specific Structured Diagnostic Interviews

Many structured diagnostic interviews for children and adolescents have been developed. Some cover a relatively broad range of disorders, while others are standardized interview formats for a single disorder or group of related disorders. They generally began to appear in the 1970s and have subsequently been revised several times. The essential structure and characteristics of the interviews remain the same, but the ongoing revision of various elements means that comparability among versions, including future versions, cannot be guaranteed. To complicate the problem further, users also modify the instruments in various ways in response to the needs of a particular study or the views of users about the strengths and weaknesses of the interview. Of course, this is discouraged by instrument developers who want to ensure stability of versions of the instruments in order to maintain comparability of research data across studies using the same instrument. Nevertheless, interview authors themselves contribute to this ambiguity at times; for example, while the interviews are either highly structured or semistructured, their developers often allow the clinician to determine how rigidly the written format is followed.

Clinicians often ask which structured diagnostic interview they should use. There is no simple answer to this question. The Diagnostic Interview for Children and Adolescents (DICA) and the Child Assessment Schedule (CAS) are general diagnostic interviews that might be a first choice, but it is more sensible for the clinician to learn some basic facts about existing instruments that will guide him in the selection of the one best for his purposes. Table 88.1 lists characteristics of structured diagnostic interviews to be considered by clinicians when selecting one.

DICA: A STRUCTURED/DIAGNOSTIC INTERVIEW

The DICA was initially developed around 1969 by Herjanic and her colleagues at Washington University (Herjanic, Herjanic, Brown, & Wheatt,

TABLE 88.1

Interview Characteristics: Considerations when Selecting a Structured Diagnostic Interview for Children and Adolescents

Practical Features

Purposes: Do the structured diagnostic interview purposes match your needs?

Organization: Is the interview organized according to diagnostic syndromes or functional domains?

Informants: Who is interviewed?

Age range: What are the ages of children or adolescents for whom the interview is intended?

Developmental effects: Can a child understand and give information about the topics of the interview?

Time to administer: How long does it take to administer each version?

Qualifications of interviewers: Who interviews the child?

Training for administering structured interviews: Is special training for the structured interview necessary?

Results: What are the products of the interview?

Procedures for scoring and diagnostic assignment: Can diagnoses be generated by computer algorithm?

Feasibility: Is the structured interview practical for this clinical use?

Revisions and new versions: Have recent revisions of diagnostic systems and/or structured diagnostic interviews made a new version of the structured interview preferable?

Diagnostic Information

Diagnostic content: Are the relevant symptoms and diagnoses covered in the interview?

Time frame: What period of time is used for symptom inquiry?

Operational criteria: Are all necessary diagnostic criteria present and has the application of their meaning and intent been reviewed?

Severity ratings: Does the interview permit indication of the severity of a symptom?

Degree of functional impairment: If criteria for a childhood psychiatric disorder are included, are there inquiries about its effects on the child's functioning?

Clinician observations: Does the interview permit the clinician to provide observations beyond answers to the diagnostic questions containted in the interview?

Categorical versus dimensional perspectives: Have available behavior checklists and their relation to the structured interview been considered and reviewed?

Best estimate diagnoses: What procedures have been established to assign final clinical diagnoses?

Performance Data

Measures of accuracy and precision: What quantifiable measures of performance for the structured interview will be used?

Validity: Does the structured diagnostic interview accurately identify the specific psychiatric disorders of interest in children and adolescents, as well as identify those who do not fit the criteria?

Reliability (agreement among raters): Do different interviewers describe symptom status similarly and consistently with this interview?

Reliability (agreement among informants): Do different respondents give related, informative responses?

1975; Herjanic & Reich, 1982). It is designed to fit DSM criteria, is useful for both clinical and epidemiological purposes, and generates both current and past diagnoses. The DICA, with parent and child versions requiring a little more than 1 hour each to administer, is for children 6 to 17 years old. It requires little or no clinical judgment by the interviewer (with some exceptions, such as follow-up questions), because it is designed to be used by nonprofessional interviewers. While it is a highly structured interview, the interviewer does have some flexibility in how to approach certain aspects of the interview.

There is broad coverage of symptoms and diagnoses, generating diagnoses keyed to the major classification systems. The questions are organized partly according to the domains of activity of the child's life (e.g., family, school, friends), but mostly according to syndromes. Emotional and behavioral problems are grouped in relation to the most relevant domain, where possible. The DICA uses a "skip structure," meaning that additional questions are not asked when the informant gives a negative response to the first screening question for a specific syndrome. The focus of the interview is the present, although the absence of a positive response to some items leads to inquiries about past symptoms. Each item is coded as present or absent, so the DICA does not monitor the severity of symptoms. A computer algorithm generates the diagnoses, or the clinician can assign the diagnoses based on clinical judgment.

CAS: A SEMISTRUCTURED DIAGNOSTIC INTERVIEW

The CAS was developed at the University of Missouri by Hodges in the 1970s as a clinical and research tool. The CAS was designed to respond to the clinical and emotional needs of the family by following a familiar, traditional clinical format: it facilitates the development of rapport with the child by organizing the interview items into sections of questions with topics appealing to the child (such as family, friends, school, activities, and hobbies). Similarly, some questions focus on treatment planning instead of diagnosis, such as those about the parents' relationship. The first part of the interview, 75 items grouped by themes related to the child's life, has a scoring structure of positive, negative, ambiguous, not applicable, or no response for each item. Diagnostic symptom items are distributed among them. In the second part of the CAS the onset and duration of selected symptoms is scored in a manner that can generate DSM diagnoses. The third section is devoted to observations by the interviewer. The time frame utilized is the past 6 months.

The CAS is designed for children 7 to 16 years old. There is broad coverage of childhood psychiatric disorders. The original interview was to be

administered to the child, but the 1983 revision produced a parent version (Hodges, Kline, Stern, Cytryn, & McKnew, 1982; Hodges, McKnew, Burbach, & Roebuck, 1987). Each version requires just under 1 hour to complete. The CAS was developed for use by experienced clinicians, as the format anticipates their ability to offer support to children struggling with difficult problems without biasing the interview, to clarify unclear answers, and to use the child's replies to indicate the presence or absence of symptoms. Yet, in spite of its semistructured format, specific training in child mental health and experience with child psychopathology are not required according to the developers of the CAS. However, they do recommend specific training in the use of the CAS.

Diagnoses are generated by computer algorithm or the clinician can assign the diagnoses based on clinical judgment. The CAS has an interesting additional perspective for which scores are generated: "content scales" that give scores indicating the child's functioning in the sectors of her life, such as family, friends, or school.

DISC: A STRUCTURED DIAGNOSTIC INTERVIEW

The National Institute of Mental Health (NIMH) sponsored the development of a structured diagnostic interview for children and adolescents, known as the Diagnostic Interview Schedule for Children (DISC). The specific purpose was to provide a companion to the DIS (used for adults) that would facilitate extension of epidemiological studies to the 6- to 17-year-old age group. The initial version was developed by Herjanic, Puig-Antich, Kovacs, and Conners and was modeled on the DICA and other interviews developed by these investigators. Several subsequent versions reflect continuing refinement of specific questions and the computer algorithms producing diagnoses, as well as the need to conform to changes in the diagnostic nomenclature, by different groups working under contract to NIMH: Costello, Edelbrock, Dulcan, and colleagues at the University of Pittsburgh in the early 1980s (DISC-1), followed by Shaffer, Schwabe-Stone, Fisher, Piacentini, Cohen, and colleagues at the New York State Psychiatric Institute in the late 1980s and the 1990s (DISC-R, the first revision, and DISC-2, the second revision). These studies have benefited from the continuity of effort in response to studies of reliability and validity in both clinic and community samples (e.g., Edelbrock & Costello, 1988; Fisher, Shaffer, Piacentini, et al., 1993). More recent studies indicate the advantageous effects of revisions, as well as some disadvantages (Piacentini et al., 1993; Schwab-Stone et al., 1993; Shaffer et al., 1993). These are the type of comparisons that illuminate basic features of interview procedures with children.

The DISC stands in sharp contrast to the K-SADS, as the DISC is so highly structured that it does not require that the interviewer have clinical skills. It was designed for use by nonprofessional (lay) interviewers in epidemiological research and has not been applied broadly in clinical work. The questions are predetermined, including their exact wording, order of presentation, and recording procedures. The interviewer simply asks the indicated questions, which are worded to distinguish diagnosis-related symptoms and behaviors from similar behaviors in a standardized manner. For some symptoms, notably any positive responses, the interviewer is to ask for more information about the topic the informant is responding about. The interviewer writes down the verbatim response of the informant, making it possible for an experienced clinician to review the ratings later, comparing the lay interviewer's rating for a question with the patient's verbatim response and ensuring that an informant's positive response to a symptom probe reflects a reasonable understanding of the intent of the question. A broad range of behaviors and symptoms are included in the DISC. Most importantly, additional characterization of each symptom is possible, including severity, associated impairment, onset, and symptom duration. Rather than a dichotomous scoring format, the symptom items are coded 0 (no or never), 1 (a little, somewhat, sometimes), or 2 (yes, often, a lot).

The questions are arranged according to the areas of activity of the child's life (e.g., family, school, friends); emotional and behavioral problems are grouped in relation to an associated domain where possible. A skip structure is used. While the DISC is intended for use by children from 6 to 18 years of age, research data suggests reservations about its use with the youngest children. Parent and child versions are available, each requiring about 1 hour to administer; a little longer for the parent version due to the inclusion of additional items children cannot answer. The questions have a time frame of the past year, and interviewers attempt to specify durations for significant symptoms (e.g., 2 weeks or 2 months). While both clinicians and nonprofessional interviewers can administer the DISC, training is recommended. Computer programs for administering the interview and data entry have been prepared. It is even possible for the user to modify the interview if desired. The diagnoses are generated by computer algorithm (Costello, 1996).

K-SADS: A SEMISTRUCTURED DIAGNOSTIC INTERVIEW

Another early structured interview was the Kiddie-Schedule for Affective Disorders and Schizophrenia (K-SADS), developed by Puig-Antich and Chambers at the New York State Psychiatric Institute in the 1970s (Chambers, Puig-Antich, Hirsch, et al., 1985). It was based on the Schedule for Affective Disorders and Schizophrenia (SADS) for adults and systematically developed over the next 15 years: they standardized the wording and format of ratings across all items, provided clear language for each anchor point within an item, broadened the number of diagnoses, and expanded the anxiety, behavioral, and affective disorder section to more directly reflect DSM diagnostic subtyping. The last published revision (by Orvaschel and Puig-Antich) appeared in 1987, and covered a much broader range of disorders keyed to *DSM-III-R*.

Two versions of the K-SADS are typically used, among several available: a present episode version (K-SADS-P) and an epidemiological version (K-SADS-E) that inquires about both past and current diagnoses. The K-SADS is to be administered to the parent first, preparing the clinician for the interview with the child (in which the child's responses are recorded separately). Unlike the procedure in fully structured interviews, the clinician is to attempt to resolve discrepancies between the informants, when they are found, by further discussion with the parent. This is an interesting strategy for understanding differences among informants (Nguyen, Whittlesey, Scimeca et al., 1994).

Clinicians using the K-SADS must be knowledgeable about psychiatric disorders and have sophisticated clinical competence in interviewing techniques, as it is a semistructured interview and the clinician uses her own judgment for formulating some of the questions for the patient and devising follow-up questions. Therefore clinicians (not nonprofessionals) are recommended as interviewers. It's first section is unstructured, focusing on recent problems and symptoms related to the current illness, as well as a treatment history. In the body of the interview a semistructured format is utilized. The items are organized by clustering together the questions related to a specific diagnosis (however, if information is used for multiple diagnoses the probe is not repeated). Questions about symptom groups begin with a definition of the symptom and comments about aspects of the symptoms that might lead to ambiguity or confusion for the clinician. A group of example probes is then given in detail in order to help the clinician determine possible ways of eliciting the data that will lead to indicating that the symptom is present or absent. The clinician decides the order of questions to be used, as well as the choice of the probes he thinks will be most useful for a particular symptom and child. A skip structure is used. Observational data and a global assessment of functioning are included in a subsequent section. The interview does not generate computerized diagnoses. The K-SADS is weighted toward the diagnoses of research interest that prompted its initial development: affective disorders, schizophrenia and related disorders, and anxiety disorders.

ISC: A SEMISTRUCTURED DIAGNOSTIC INTERVIEW

The Interview Schedule for Children (ISC) was developed at the University of Pittsburgh in the 1970s by Kovacs (Kovacs, M., 1985). There are parent and child versions. The mother is interviewed initially, and the child is then interviewed by the same clinician. It was modeled on the K-SADS and has many similarities, but the symptom probes were made more precise and adapted for use as preset interview questions. The ISC initially centered on affective disorders, but was subsequently systematically revised and expanded to survey symptoms of additional diagnoses. The ISC examines current symptoms, while a follow-up version is used to assess symptom changes over

the interim period. There is an initial unstructured section in which the natures of the current problems are established and the clinician builds rapport with the informant. Items are organized by clustering together the questions related to a specific diagnosis. Questions confirming the child's first answer are included before the clinician gives a final score. Observational items are also rated by the clinician, who additionally is required to dictate a clinical summary.

The ISC can be used with children and adolescents 8 to 17 years old. The interview with the parent can take up to 2 hours to administer, while the child interview typically requires 1 hour or less. The items are scored on a 0 to 8 scale and criteria are supplied along this continuum. The ISC includes both severity and functional impairment ratings. This is a semistructured interview that recommends clinicians as interviewers, as it assumes clinical experience and skill on the part of the interviewer, as well as knowledge of diagnostic criteria. For example, the interviewer can vary the order of questions in response to the concerns of the informant. The interviewer uses all available clinical information and then determines the diagnosis based on clinical judgment, similar to the K-SADS. Specific training for the use of the ISC is recommended and the clinician must be knowledgeable about the interview content and rating procedures.

CAPA: A STRUCTURED DIAGNOSTIC INTERVIEW

The Child and Adolescent Psychiatric Assessment (CAPA) is the most recent structured diagnostic interview to be developed. While it appears to have strengths in its design, psychometric data are not yet available, nor is it widely used. It is designed for use by nonprofessional, lay interviewers, and diagnoses are generated by computer algorithm.

Descriptive Characteristics of Structured Diagnostic Interviews

The use of structured diagnostic interviews led to the investigation of the specific characteristics of these interviews that are of special importance, such as who is interviewed, the time frame for symptoms, and other features. In essence, these are fundamental questions about any diagnostic interview, and the answers to them are significant for any clinician who conducts clinical interviews. In particular, they help the clinician recognize that choices are always necessary when interviewing, and there is no single perfect answer: for example, one must decide whether to inquire about symptoms in the past month, past 6 months, or some other time period. A few examples of these characteristics and their related controversies will clarify how this affects the information obtained from a structured diagnostic interview.

DIAGNOSTIC CONTENT: ARE THE RELEVANT SYMPTOMS AND DIAGNOSES COVERED IN THE INTERVIEW?

Structured interviews are keyed to the most recent version of the diagnostic system (e.g., *DSM-IV*) and are revised during the transition to a new system. A single structured diagnostic interview does not necessarily provide symptom probes for all possible diagnoses, and the level of information generated about the included diagnoses varies (Carlson, Hashani, Thomas, et al., 1987; Gutterman, O'Brien, & Young, 1987). For example, only a few screening questions might be included for one diagnosis, while a survey of all specific criteria for another diagnosis might be given. Clinicians need to become familiar with the diagnoses covered and the completeness of criteria surveyed in diagnoses of particular interest. Structured interviews tend to be hand scored early in their development or if judgment in the scoring procedure is required, but computer scoring is now the rule for epidemiological instruments, such as the DISC. However, even when computer scoring is used, it is necessary to review handwritten notes of verbatim responses or interviewer comments in order to ensure that the rating used is sensible and to avoid inflating the prevalence of disorders generated when these comments are ignored. For example, a question in the DICA parent interview asks, "Has he ever had thoughts or ideas that he couldn't keep out of his mind no matter how hard he tried? I don't mean worries, but strange thoughts that just wouldn't go away." The clinician might need to write the following in the margin

next to the coding of "yes": "mother says 'yes' and describes the child's repeated thoughts that he will flunk his exams at the end of the year" because (in spite of the clinician's explanation) the mother answers positively when this is probably not an obsession. This type of misunderstanding is most common in the interview with the child.

INFORMANTS: WHO IS INTERVIEWED?

Among the difficult challenges to clinicians is the need to obtain information from multiple people in the child's life, commonly including the child and his parents, teachers, social worker, guidance counselor, and pediatrician. It is not only time consuming, but it is often not clear how to understand the varying information. How to weigh conflicting reports from these sources, as well as how to put the information from multiple sources to practical use, are clinical challenges that are difficult to examine and answer.

Structured diagnostic interviews for children and adolescents use separate interviews for the child and the parent, but how this is accomplished differs across the various interviews. The development of the CAS, DICA, and DISC included the use of separate interviewers for the child and parent, so that distinct scores are generated. This poses the problem of deciding on an "overall" diagnosis, which, in different interviews, has been accomplished by using all diagnoses from either interview or only consensus diagnoses obtained from both interviews. Obviously the results are quite different (Hodges, McKnew, Burbach, et al., 1987). In contrast, the K-SADS and ISC were developed with a procedure in which a single interviewer interviews both informants, first the parent, then the child. A summary rating for each symptom is derived from all available information. The K-SADS explicitly indicates that the interviewer should clarify discrepancies between the two informants during the child interview. The ISC recognizes the developmental limitations of the child: the interviewer obtains information concerning duration of symptoms and diagnoses from the parent.

With each choice something is gained, something is lost. The use of a single experienced clinician as interviewer for both informants has the obvious advantage that it facilitates the assignment of a single diagnostic rating and increases confidence in the diagnoses because this approach resembles a best estimate diagnosis procedure. This is particularly the case for the K-SADS, whose procedure includes the use of all sources of information (such as the medical chart, school reports, etc.) when formulating the final rating. It is clear, however, that this procedure carries a risk of biasing the child interview by the information obtained from the earlier parent interview, for example (Costello, 1996). At the same time, this same procedure might bias the summary ratings through a recency effect, in which the final interview (of the child) is unintentionally given more weight (Chambers, Puig-Antich, Hirsch, et al., 1985). Finally, much of the focus of research on structured interviews is to determine the contribution of interviews alone, and combining all sources of clinical information prior to assigning diagnoses makes it impossible to sort out the contributions of the interview.

The choice of informants spawns questions about the degree of agreement between informants (Achenbach, McConaughy, & Howell, 1987; Welner, Reich, Herjanic, et al., 1987). At the present time, it might be generalized that the best parent-child agreement occurs for behavioral symptoms such as are found in disruptive disorders, while moderate agreement is often observed for symptoms of depression; symptoms of anxiety continue to be subject to poor agreement (Bird, Gould, & Staghezza, 1992; Hodges, Gordon, & Lennon, 1990). It would seem likely that use of the diagnoses generated from both parent and child interviews would produce more diagnoses than when using either informant alone, and this has been shown to be the case using the DISC-2 (Jensen, Salzberg, Richters, & Watanabe, 1993). The diagnoses that are added by this procedure are largely internalizing diagnoses emerging from the child interview.

Various methods for combining the information obtained from parent and child are possible. First, the clinician might decide to use only one of the versions of an interview (a "single informant" approach), but this is a questionable approach, given that situational variability in reporting is well established and both informants are necessary. Second, the clinician might use the "simple combinatorial rule" that a diagnosis is assigned if either the parent or child interview produces one (Hodges, 1993; Jensen et al., 1993). Third, it is possible to

use an "optimal informant" approach in which it is established, for example, that for certain symptoms reported consistently by parents, but inconsistently by children, the parent report will be used because it is regularly more informative (see, e.g., Bird et al., 1992; Loeber, Green, Lahey, & Stouthamer-Loeber, 1989). Fourth, a "clinical combinatorial procedure" might be preferred, in which information from both sources is examined, with the flexibility of returning to either informant for additional information, followed by assignment of diagnoses by the clinician with full information.

In sum, we recognize that information from both parent and child is necessary. We do not yet know how to combine the information from two different informants, but attempt to do so in a commonsense manner. For example, the agreement between mother and child using the K-SADS varies markedly across symptoms and syndromes (Chambers et al., 1985), and when the diagnoses are derived independently the agreement can be poor (Ivens and Rehm, 1988). The usual strategy of a K-SADS or ISC interview (using parent information in the child interview and returning to the parent to resolve discrepancies) more closely approaches the commonsense clinical means for obtaining accurate information used in the best estimate diagnosis procedures.

TIME FRAME: WHAT PERIOD OF TIME IS USED FOR SYMPTOM INQUIRY?

All interviews include questions to determine the presence or absence of *current* diagnoses, but the definition of "current" or "present" varies. The usual purposes of the instrument determine the time frame. For example, in the DISC, used for epidemiological studies, diagnoses are generated from symptoms present during the prior 6 months; in some instances the diagnoses reflect symptoms and behaviors reported during the previous year. In contrast, the CAS has a less clearly defined concept of "present," although the diagnoses generated must fulfill specific DSM time-frame criteria.

The choice of time frame can be managed by inquiring about two time frames. For example, the K-SADS-P includes symptom ratings for both the past week and for the most severe symptoms during the present episode. Using a short, 1-week interval is unique to the K-SADS, and the intent is to allow assessment of change over time. The K-SADS-E contains ratings for lifetime diagnoses, yet inquires about "the present episode." Overall it focuses on the presence or absence of specific symptoms during the most severe past episode. In some instances, the K-SADS-E rates whether the disorder "ever occurred," but does not record both present and past status; examples are attention deficit disorder and substance abuse. The ISC inquires about emotional symptomatology during the prior 2 weeks, but asks about situation-specific behaviors within the past 6 months. The inquiries in the DICA examine lifetime diagnoses and "present" diagnoses. The "present" is referred to in a rather general way, although specific time criteria for DSM diagnoses must be fulfilled. When the child is 12 years or older, the DICA contains questions to determine if psychiatric symptoms occurred in the past.

Important interview characteristics related to the time frame of symptoms are symptom severity and the sensitivity to change of the ratings. For example, the K-SADS-P and the ISC were designed to rate gradations of severity of symptoms related to the diagnosis of depression. Such ratings are especially useful in short-term treatment studies, defining treatment response by indicating changes in severity missed in simple inquiries about the presence or absence of a symptom. In longitudinal studies the requirements are different, although symptom severity might also be useful in order to demonstrate the natural history of a disorder or its response to earlier interventions. In longitudinal research the simple presence or absence designation is generally sufficient, as indicated by the ratings in any of the structured diagnostic interviews. This requires sufficient intervals elapsing between ratings for a disorder to resolve and for other disorders to begin. A typical time period for these purposes might be 5 years. An additional problem appears in longitudinal research for children and adolescents, because diagnostic changes must be differentiated from developmental changes. Many childhood disorders, such as ADHD, Tourette's disorder, or autistic disorder, can have altered manifestations reflecting a change in developmental status; the ratings must be structured in a way that makes it clear that the diagnosis continues to be present in spite

of these changes, and that this is not the onset of a new disorder or resolution of the old disorder.

DEVELOPMENTAL EFFECTS: CAN A CHILD UNDERSTAND AND GIVE INFORMATION ABOUT THE TOPICS OF THE INTERVIEW?

Clinicians caring for children know how difficult it can be to obtain information from children that is practical and related to the questions asked, and that gives confidence to the interviewer that the answer is accurate. The problem is greater the younger the child. Two general types of challenges are most important, how the age of the child affects the interview style and content, and how the age of the child affects her understanding and ability to give answers.

Altering one's interview style with a child can radically change the quantity and quality of information obtained from the child. After unproductive questions and play techniques with toys, actively intervening with comments and behavior guided by the child's behavior can suddenly make the interview productive; for example, becoming playful and humorous with a child can sometimes disarm a taciturn, oppositional child who has confused parents and clinicians by his lack of response. Children typically have little motivation to be cooperative in an activity that might be intimidating, confusing, frightening, or boring for them. Moreover, in spite of their often adultlike vocabulary, they often do not understand the intent of the questions. A good deal of effort and inventiveness, through direct and indirect methods of inquiry and observation, are necessary to clarify the meaning of many of the child's answers. Only then will the clinician feel confident that he can use the information provided by the child. For a full appreciation of these pitfalls when interviewing, the clinician needs to know the usual developmental capacities of the child at this specific age as he appraises the answer. Greater clinical experience provides the interviewer with the ability to understand the meaning of many behaviors that can be confusing.

At the same time that the interviewer is assessing the child's developmental level to guide how he conducts the interview, he is simultaneously using this information to gauge the likely level of understanding that the child has about the questions and comments of both the interviewer and the child himself. Were words used that the child is unfamiliar with or are conceptually too complex? Was the grammatical structure of the sentence too complicated for the child to follow? Did the question contain an unrecognized abstract concept before the child was capable of abstraction? Was a time reference included that the child misunderstood? Is the child able to identify and describe her own feelings? Are memories of events orderly and retrievable in an older child, or confused and biased by dramatic events or repetitive statements of important adults?

The youngest children included among informants for structured interviews are typically 6 to 8 years of age. It is no surprise that the test-retest (over 1 to 3 weeks) reliability of symptom reports by children increases with age (Edelbrock, Costello, Dulcan, Kalas, & Conover, 1985), so the question is, where is the threshold for obtaining meaningful information? Many clinicians came to doubt the reports of children in the 6- and 7-year age groups, so that 8 to 18 years of age seemed to be practical boundaries for structured interviews. However, more recent studies demonstrate that children up to the age of 11 or 12 years might be unreliable informants (Boyle, Offord, Racine et al., 1993; Breton et al., 1995; Fallon and Schwab-Stone, 1994). This makes it very clear that studies including structured interviews of children within this age range should be cautiously reviewed, and that further research on these developmental effects is imperative (Hodges, 1994; Shaffer, 1994). It will be interesting to see whether the use of an experienced interviewer and a more flexible interviewing format, such as a semistructured interview, might improve the yield of accurate information from a child, or whether it has no effect.

Interviewers need to be attentive to the informant's age when selecting a structured interview for other reasons as well. For example, upon entry into adolescence, the diagnoses covered in the interview must be considered. New diagnostic sectors are essential, such as eating disorders or substance abuse. On the other hand, the clinical symptom patterns characteristic of an illness can change during early adolescence, such as the diminishing importance of hyperactivity in ADHD.

A fundamental controversy remains. How do we understand the meaning of a child's answers to formal, preset questions in a highly structured interview? Even allowing the intervention of the interviewer to clarify uncertainties in a semistructured interview, do we have confidence in the meaning of the child's answer? Or can this understanding be achieved only through a combination of directed and nondirective interview methods for children?

CLINICIAN OBSERVATIONS: DOES THE INTERVIEW PERMIT THE CLINICIAN TO PROVIDE OBSERVATIONS BEYOND ANSWERS TO THE QUESTIONS CONTAINED IN THE INTERVIEW?

Clinicians recognize that the parent's and child's answers to questions are not the only source of information critical to assigning diagnoses. For example, it is not uncommon for behavioral cues in the interview to give an additional meaning to the formal verbal answers provided by the informant. A potential problem for a structured diagnostic interview is that it might lack a structure for indicating these observations, compromising the validity of the diagnoses generated. However, some of the interviews have formats for registering clinician observations. The ISC and the K-SADS base diagnoses on all clinical information available to the clinician, providing the opportunity for the clinician to include such observations. In addition, the CAS, DICA, and ISC include sections for systematically recording information based on the interviewer's observations.

FEASIBILITY: ARE STRUCTURED INTERVIEWS PRACTICAL FOR ROUTINE CLINICAL USE?

Some documented benefits of structured diagnostic interviews suggest that they be used routinely by clinicians, rather than only in research protocols. For example, clinicians obtain more clinically relevant patient information when using structured interviews; the information is not restricted to presenting symptoms and is more reliable. However, clinicians do not commonly use structured interviews in their clinical practices. Structured interviews can be time consuming, as probes pursue unlikely diagnoses. Moreover, this is only one component of an initial assessment for a patient, so that the total time for the overall evaluation becomes formidable. Structured interview scoring may require software and data processing resources in order to generate a diagnostic product, leaving many clinicians disinterested because of the burden of setting up such a system. Some argue that structured interviews interfere with the flow and organization of information needed from the interview, although most clinicians experienced in the use of structured interviews disagree.

There is not yet a convincing argument for the routine clinical use of structured diagnostic interviews. Alternatively, in certain circumstances it might be useful if the two types of interviews, with separate purposes, be individually administered for the benefit of the patient. However, such decisions are now often controlled by nonclinical administrators with little understanding of the matter. While structured interviews might be more time consuming than unstructured clinical interviews at the beginning, experience leads to their administration in a comparable length of time. An additional consideration is the amount of data processing that will be necessary and whether a program for generating the appropriate data is available. Further development of structured interviews, in the context of changes in health care management, will determine whether or not structured interviews find their way into everyday clinical practice.

Diagnosis-Specific and Other Structured Interviews

Structured diagnostic interviews have appeared that refine and organize the diagnostic interview for a group of related disorders, usually for research purposes. These interviews are designed to select homogeneous groups of patients with any of the selected group of disorders, often for longitudinal study, treatment with a specific medication, or other investigative purposes. For example, autistic disorder is a syndrome with many causes whose clinical presentation varies somewhat and can be difficult to discriminate from related diag-

noses at the borders of the symptom profile. Standardization of the interview questions seeking to determine the presence or absence of symptom criteria is very useful for minimizing the heterogeneity of the subject group. For example, the Autism Diagnostic Interview-Revised was shown to be highly sensitive and reliable in the diagnosis of autistic disorder in preschool children, although there was some overdiagnosis of autistic disorder in young children with severe mental retardation (Lord, Storoschuk, Rutter, & Pickles, 1993). Similarly, structured diagnostic interviews for adults with personality disorders were shown to have good interrater reliabilities, while features needing further study were identified (Pilkonis et al., 1995). Related descriptors of behavior that are useful for clinical research can also be examined by structured interviews, as in the Social Adjustment Inventory for Children and Adolescents (John, Gammon, Prusoff, et al., 1987).

Developing Further Knowledge About the Clinical Interview

In spite of such difficulties as developing adequate means for determining validity and establishing high rates of reliability, 25 years of research has opened up our understanding of the clinical interview. Basic questions about the clinical interview now have more complete and specific answers and no longer simply refer to clinical experience as validation for a "fact." Some fundamental questions have been surprisingly neglected, however. The most striking example is the neglect of developmental effects on the child's understanding and responses to structured interview questions. This undermines much of the other ongoing research on interviews, much as the lack of attention to problems with laboratory assays thwarted earlier expensive clinical studies using biological measures. Continuing investigative efforts combined with attention to basic principles promises to continue the gratifying progress in our knowledge about our major clinical instrument, the interview.

REFERENCES

Achenbach, T., McConaughy, S., & Howell, C. (1987). Child/adolescent behavioral and emotional problems: Implications of cross informant correlations for situational specificity. *Psychological Bulletin, 101,* 213–232.

Bird, H. R., Gould, M. S., & Staghezza, B. (1992). Aggregating data from multiple informants in child psychiatry epidemiological research. *Journal of the American Academy of Child and Adolescent Psychiatry, 31,* 78–85.

Boyle, M. H., Offord, D. R., Racine, Y., Sanford, M., Szatmari, P., Fleming, J. E., & Price-Munn, N. (1993). Evaluation of the Diagnostic Interview for Children and Adolescents for use in general population samples. *Journal of Abnormal Child Psychology, 21,* 663–681.

Breton, J. -J., Bergeron, L., Valla, J. -P., Lépine, S., Houde, L., & Gauder, N. (1995). Do children aged 9 through 11 years understand the DISC Version 2.25 questions? *Journal of the American Academy of Child and Adolescent Psychiatry, 34,* 946–954.

Carlson, G. A., Hashani, J. H., Thomas, M. D. F., Vaidya, A., & Daniel, A. E. (1987). Comparison of two structured interviews on a psychiatrically hospitalized population of children. *Journal of the American Academy of Child and Adolescent Psychiatry, 26,* 645–648.

Chambers, W., Puig-Antich, J., Hirsch, M., Paez, P., Ambrosini, P. J., Tabrizi, M. A., & Davies, M. (1985). The assessment of affective disorders in children and adolescents by semi-structured interview: Test-retest reliability of the K-SADS-P. *Archives of General Psychiatry, 42,* 696–702.

Costello, A. J. (1996). Structured interviewing. In M. Lewis (Ed.), *Child and adolescent psychiatry: A comprehensive textbook* (2nd ed., pp. 457–464). Baltimore, MD: Williams & Wilkins.

Edelbrock, C., Costello, A. J., Dulcan, M. K., Kalas, R., & Conover, N. (1985). Age differences in the reliability of the psychiatric interview of the child. *Child Development, 56,* 265–275.

Edelbrock, C., & Costello, A. J. (1988). Convergence between statistically derived behavior problem syndromes and child psychiatric diagnoses. *Journal of Abnormal Child Psychology, 16,* 219–231.

Fallon, T., & Schwab-Stone, M. (1994). Determinants of reliability in psychiatric surveys of children aged 6–12. *Journal of Child Psychology and Psychiatry, 35,* 1391–1408.

Fisher, P. W., Shaffer, D., Piacentini, J. C., Lapkin, J., Kafantaris, V., Leonard, H., & Herzog, D. B. (1993). Sensitivity of the Diagnostic Interview Schedule for Children, 2nd Edition (DISC-2.1) for specific diagnoses of children and adolescents. *Journal of the American Academy of Child and Adolescent Psychiatry, 32,* 666–673.

Gutterman, E. M., O'Brien, J. D., & Young, J. G. (1987). Structured diagnostic interviews for children and adolescents: Current status and future directions. *Journal of the American Academy of Child and Adolescent Psychiatry, 26,* 621–630.

Herjanic, B., Herjanic, M., Brown, F., & Wheatt, T. (1975). Are children reliable reporters? *Journal of Abnormal Child Psychology, 3,* 41–48.

Herjanic, B., Hudson, R., & Kotloff, K. (1976). Does interviewing harm children? *Research Communications in Psychology, Psychiatry, and Behavior, 1,* 523–531.

Herjanic, B., & Reich, W. (1982). Development of a structured psychiatric interview for children: Agreement between child and parent on individual symptoms. *Journal of Abnormal Child Psychology, 10,* 307–324.

Hodges, K. (1993). Structured interviews for assessing children. *Journal of Child Psychology and Psychiatry, 34,* 49–68.

Hodges, K. (1994). Debate and argument: Reply to David Shaffer: Structured interviews for assessing children. *Journal of Child Psychology and Psychiatry, 35,* 785–787.

Hodges, K., Kline, J., Stern, L., Cytryn, L., & McKnew, D. (1982). The development of a child assessment interview for research and clinical use. *Journal of Abnormal Child Psychology, 10,* 173–189.

Hodges, K., McKnew, D., Burbach, D. J., & Roebuck, L. (1987). Diagnostic concordance between the Child Assessment Schedule (CAS) and the Schedule for Affective Disorders and Schizophrenia for School-Age Children (K-SADS) in an outpatient sample using lay interviewers. *Journal of the American Academy of Child and Adolescent Psychiatry, 26,* 654–661.

Hodges, K., Gordon, Y., & Lennon, M. (1990). Parent-child agreement on symptoms assessed via a clinical research interview for children: The Child Assessment Schedule (CAS). *Journal of Child Psychology and Psychiatry, 31,* 427–436.

Ivens, C., & Rehm, L. P. (1988). Assessment of childhood depression: Correspondence between reports by child, mother and father. *Journal of the American Academy of Child and Adolescent Psychiatry, 27,* 738–741.

Jensen, P. S., Salzberg, A. D., Richters, J. E., & Watanabe, H. K. (1993). Scales, diagnoses, and child psychopathology: I. CBCL and DISC relationships. *Journal of the American Academy of Child and Adolescent Psychiatry, 32,* 397–406.

Jensen, P. S., Watanabe, H. K., Richters, J. E., Cortes, R., Roper, M., & Liu, S. (1995). Prevalence of mental disorder in military children and adolescents: Findings from a two-stage community survey. *Journal of the American Academy of Child and Adolescent Psychiatry, 34,* 1514–1524.

John, K., Gammon, G. D., Prusoff, B. A., & Warner, V. (1987). The Social Adjustment Inventory for Children and Adolescents (SAICA): Testing of a new semistructured interview. *Journal of the American Academy of Child and Adolescent Psychiatry, 26,* 898–911.

Kovacs, M. (1985). The Interview Schedule for Children (ISC). *Psychopharmacology Bulletin, 21,* 991–994.

Lewis, S. A., Gorsky, A., Cohen, P., & Hartmark, C. (1985). The reactions of youth to diagnostic interviews. *Journal of the American Academy of Child Psychiatry, 24,* 750–755.

Loeber, R., Green, S. M., Lahey, B. B., & Stouthamer-Loeber, M. (1989). Optimal informants on child disruptive behaviors. *Development and Psychopathology, 1,* 317–337.

Lord, C., Storoschuk, S., Rutter, M., & Pickles, A. (1993). Using the ADI-R to diagnose autism in preschool children. *Infant Mental Health Journal, 14,* 234–252.

Nguyen, N., Whittlesey, S., Scimeca, K., DiGiacomo, D., Bui, B., Parsons, O., Scarborough, A., & Paddock, D. (1994). Parent-child agreement in prepubertal depression: Findings with a modified assessment method. *Journal of the American Academy of Child and Adolescent Psychiatry, 33,* 1275–1283.

Piacentini, J., Shaffer, D., Fisher, P., Schwab-Stone, M., Davies, M., & Gioia, P. (1993). The Diagnostic Interview Schedule for Children—Revised Version (DISC-R): III. Concurrent criterion validity. *Journal of the American Academy of Child and Adolescent Psychiatry, 32,* 658–665.

Pilkonis, P. A., Heape, C. L., Proietti, J. M., Clark, S. W., McDavid, J. D., & Pitts, T. E. (1995). The reliability and validity of two structured diagnostic interviews for personality disorders. *Archives of General Psychiatry, 52,* 1025–1033.

Schwab-Stone, M., Fisher, P., Piacentini, J., Shaffer, D.,

Davies, M., & Briggs, M. (1993). The Diagnostic Interview Schedule for Children—Revised Version (DISC-R): II. Test-retest reliability. *Journal of the American Academy of Child and Adolescent Psychiatry, 32,* 651–657.

Shaffer, D. (1994). Debate and argument: Structured interviews for assessing children. *Journal of Child Psychology and Psychiatry, 35,* 783–784.

Shaffer, D., Schwab-Stone, M., Fisher, P., Cohen, P., Piacentini, J., Davies, M., Conners, C. K., & Reiger, D. (1993). The Diagnostic Interview Schedule for Children—Revised Version (DISC-R): I. Preparation, field testing, interrater reliability, and acceptability. *Journal of the American Academy of Child and Adolescent Psychiatry, 32,* 643–650.

Welner, Z., Reich, W., Herjanic, B., Jung, K. G., & Amado, H. (1987). Reliability, validity and parent-child agreement studies of the Diagnostic Interview for Children and Adolescents. *Journal of the American Academy of Child and Adolescent Psychiatry, 26,* 649–653.

Young, J. G., O'Brien, J. D., Gutterman, E. M., & Cohen, P. (1987). Research on the clinical interview. *Journal of the American Academy of Child and Adolescent Psychiatry, 26,* 613–620.

Young, J. G., Kaplan, D., Pascualvaca, D., & Brasic, J. R. (1995). Psychiatric examination of the infant, child, and adolescent. In H. I. Kaplan & B. J. Sadock (Eds.), *Comprehensive textbook of psychiatry* (6th ed., Vol. 2). Baltimore, MD: Williams & Wilkins. Pp. 2169–2206.

Zahner, G. E. P. (1991). The feasibility of conducting structured diagnostic interviews with preadolescents: A community field trial of the DISC. *Journal of the American Academy of Child and Adolescent Psychiatry, 30,* 659–668.

89 / Laboratory Testing

Jennifer Levitt and James T. McCracken

In many cases in which underlying physical factors cause psychiatric symptoms, the relationship between the underlying physical illness and the patient's psychopathology is unsuspected or occult. Such clinical experiences, bolstered by survey data, have led to the widespread recommendation for screening laboratory tests as a routine aspect of assessment in psychiatric practice. Laboratory tests have other roles as purported diagnostic aids, as safety indicators for implementation of treatment, and for toxicity monitoring of various therapies. Too often child psychiatric practice has largely adopted recommendations developed for adult psychiatry, sometimes without empirical support or a thorough acknowledgement of age differences in the natural history or prevalence of the physical illnesses of concern. This chapter summarizes available information on the role of laboratory testing in general psychiatry, reviews specific reports pertaining to child psychiatry, and puts forth general recommendations for the application of testing in child and adolescent psychiatry.

Occult Physical Illness in Adult Psychiatric Populations

Sternberg (1986) delineated three relationships between physical illness and psychiatric disorder. Physical disease can be causative, or the primary etiology of the observed psychopathology, which is secondary; physical disease can itself, or in concert with other influences, precipitate psychiatric symptoms; and physical illness may be comorbid, but unrelated, to a primary psychiatric disorder. Regardless of the relationship to the patient's psychopathology, the recognition of the existence of physical illness is important in the overall care of the patient. However, research on the frequency of occult medical illness in psychiatric patients does not always clarify the relationship of observed physical abnormalities, making an estimate of the importance of medical screening in psychiatric assessment less clear.

The frequency of occult medical illness contributing to or causing psychiatric symptoms and syndromes in child and adolescent populations is not well researched. Prior recommendations for testing in child psychiatry have relied heavily upon data on the prevalence of medical illness in adult populations. These data confirm the undeniable significance of medical illnesses either causing or contributing to mental disorder in adult psychiatric outpatients and inpatients ranging from 8 to 43% (Bartsch, Shern, Feinberg, Fuller, & Willet, 1990; Hall, Popkin, Devaul, Faillace, & Stickney, 1978; Hoffman, 1982; Koranyi, 1992). The medical conditions most frequently associated with psychiatric symptoms in adults include cardiovascular and endocrine disorders, infection, metabolic and nutritional disturbances, CNS disease, and drug- or alcohol-related toxic reactions (Bartsch et al., 1990, Hall et al., 1978; Sternberg, 1986).

Routine laboratory testing *per se* lacks a high degree of clinical utility in typical psychiatric settings, as documented in a study by Hall et al. (1978) in which only 0.4% of patients without any clinical symptoms of physical illness were found to have significant laboratory abnormalities indicative of disease. In contrast, 60% of those patients with four or more positive physical symptoms from a review of systems evaluation were noted to have laboratory abnormalities. Similarly a true-positive rate of 1.8% for an average of 28 admission tests was noted from a retrospective analysis of 250 adult psychiatric inpatients (Dolan and Mushlin, 1985). These data reflect the reduction of the diagnostic utility of laboratory tests due to the low prevalence of specific disease states in the population. Similarly, Hall & Beresford (1984) point out that laboratory screening tests are cost effective only with high risk populations, defined as those seen in psychiatric emergency facilities, and psychiatric inpatients admitted with diagnoses of acute psychotic or major depressive disorders and/or dementia. These data emphasize a focused role for laboratory screening, as well as the importance of eliciting a careful and structured medical history in psychiatric assessments. The use of standardized questionnaires as an aid is supported (Hall et al., 1978).

Occult Physical Illness in Child and Adolescent Psychiatric Samples

Rivinus, Jamison, & Graham (1975) reported on 12 children with occult organic neurological disease that had been diagnosed as a psychiatric disorder. They noted that symptoms primarily included deteriorating school performance and disturbances of posture and visual loss. Psychiatric diagnoses included anxiety disorder, psychosis, conduct disorder, and hysterical reaction. The final neurological diagnoses included astrocytoma, Addison's disease, congenital syphilis, subacute sclerosing panencephalitis, metachromatic leucodystrophy, idiopathic degenerative CNS disease, polymyositis, Friedreichs ataxia, and dystonia musculorum deformans. The authors emphasized that relatively simple investigations such as serum electrolytes, syphilis serology, and serum creatinine phosphokinase would have prevented the misdiagnoses. These observations demonstrate that some forms of child psychopathology can be related to occult medical illness, but leave open the question of how frequently this occurs.

Though sparse, several published reports have attempted to assess the utility of screening tests in the clinical assessment of child and adolescent psychiatric patients. Gabel and Hsu (1986) reviewed 100 consecutive inpatient adolescents to determine the clinical importance of a variety of routine screening tests (thyroid function, electroencephalogram, chest X ray, chemistry panel, urinanalysis, complete blood count, electrocardiogram, and rapid plasma reagin). Although a relatively high proportion of abnormal test results were obtained (depending upon the test), the authors concluded the screening tests provided "minimal benefit." Indeed, in this series, only one patient of 100 had an initial "functional" diagnosis changed to an organic mental disorder at discharge; no patient had an initial organic mental disorder changed to a "functional" diagnosis at discharge. Furthermore, the abnormalities detected were more often assessed as minor; the majority were not followed up. A high frequency of abnormal EEGs were observed, though apparently without clinical significance in all but one instance.

Similarly, Woolston and Riddle (1990) reported on a sample of 200 consecutive child psychiatry inpatient admissions that received a variety of laboratory diagnostic investigations. Diagnostic testing (EEG, CT, MRI, chromosomal analysis) revealed clinically relevant results in 5% of tests performed, and 3.5% of the sample. In contrast, medication blood level testing, cognitive testing, and chromosomal analysis in selected patients provided higher yields of information of direct benefit to the patient's treatment planning. Additionally, in a prospective evaluation of endocrine and neuroimaging tests in 111 adolescents with first-onset psychosis admitted to a psychiatric inpatient unit, Adams, Kutcher, Antoniw, and Bird (1996) found that none of the results were of diagnostic utility in these patients. In the absence of signs or symptoms from the clinical history and physical examination, there were no laboratory tests that by themselves pointed toward either a medical or psychiatric illness.

Weiss, Stein, Tropmmer, and Refetoff (1993) and Hauser et al. (1993) have investigated the association between thyroid function abnormalities and ADHD. In Weiss' study of 277 children with

ADHD, thyroid function abnormalities were present in 5.4% as compared to <1% in the general population. Hypothyroidism was present more commonly than hyperthyroidism, and both studies recommended thyroid assessment in children with ADHD. However, in a retrospective study of 196 psychiatric inpatient adolescent patients, Leo et al. (1997) found that no patients tested required treatment for thyroid abnormalities. They concluded that thyroid screening should only be carried out in inpatients with signs or symptoms indicative of thyroid illness.

In summary, commonly applied screening laboratory tests have limited utility in child and adolescent psychiatric assessment, presumably due to the low prevalence of physical illness in younger populations. The value of laboratory testing will be greatly influenced by the characteristics of the population, and symptomatic indications for testing. The utility of testing can likely be enhanced by more selective application, as well as an increased emphasis on comprehensive and structured medical history taking.

Screening Laboratory Testing

The following tests are suggested as minimum routine screening tests. In the case of positive clinical histories of symptoms, other tests should be considered. For inpatients, a complete blood count (hemoglobin, hematocrit, white blood cell count, and mean cell volume), serum levels of thyroxine, calcium, aspartate aminotransferase, alkaline phosphatase, syphylis serology, urine toxicology screen, and, in males, a urinalysis are suggested. In female adolescents, a serum pregnancy test should be obtained prior to implementing medications. In the absence of an increased index of suspicion, it is unlikely that screening laboratories for outpatients are of value.

The selection of studies should be based upon information gained from a thorough history with perinatal and developmental history, review of symptoms checklist, and mental status exam. Symptoms indicative of neurologic illness should be carefully reviewed. The family history should include inquiries as to the possibility of degenerative CNS disease (such as Wilson's, Huntington's),

TABLE 89.1

Medical Diseases Associated with Depression

Endocrinopathies and Metabolic Disorder	Infections	Rheumatic	Central Nervous System Disorders	Metal Intoxications	Others
Addison's disease		Rheumatoid arthritis	Epilepsy	Thallium	Disabling diseases of all kinds
Cushing's disease	Infectious mononucleosis		Postconcussion	Mercury	Postsurgical procedures
Hyperthyroidism		Systemic Lupus Erythematosus	Normal pressure hydrocephalus	Lead	Acute intermittent porphyria
Hyperparathyroidism	Influenza				
Hyperthyroidism	Encephalitis		Focal lesions of the nondominant lobe		
Hypoglycemia	Subacute bacterial endocarditis		Subarchnoid hemorrhage		Hypochromic anemia
Hypopituitarism			Cerebrovascular accident		Wilson's disease
Hypothyroidism	Hepatitis				ETOH abuse
	Pneumonias		Multiple sclerosis		Drug abuse/ withdrawal Cocaine Amphetamine Opiates
	Tuberculosis		Huntington's disease		
	Neurosyphillis				
	AIDS				Electrolytic abnormalities Hypokalemia Hyponatremia
					Failure to thrive
					Uremia

heritable metabolic disease (diabetes, porphyria, pernicious anemia), and seizure disorders. Positive findings should alert the physician to the potential for underlying medical disorders. Care should be taken to assess the rapidity of onset of symptoms, history of medication/drug use, toxin exposure, trauma (particularly head trauma), and illness.

Screening Considerations for Child and Adolescent Psychiatric Syndromes

In child and adolescent assessment, specific medical illness comorbidities and causative influences should be considered. In the case of patients with higher risks of physical illness due to the existence of positive physical symptoms or stigmata, specific laboratory investigations should be entertained. The following sections review physical illnesses associated with various forms of psychopathology.

MOOD DISORDERS

Physical disorders associated with child, adolescent, and adult mood disorders are presented in Table 89.1. Common causes of mood disorders in younger patients include infectious diseases, drug/alcohol abuse, and thyroid disease, particularly hypothyroidism. Severe fatigue, rapidity of onset of psychological symptoms, and inability to sustain attention are suggestive of organic illness. If a child with depression or change in cognitive function has a history of sexual abuse or sexual activity, they should be evaluated for sexually transmitted diseases with syphilis serology and HIV assessment.

ANXIETY DISORDERS

Though not common in children and adolescents, a variety of medical illnesses, as described below, may underlie symptoms of anxiety. Similarly, symptoms associated with panic can mimic many medical illnesses (Raj and Sheehan, 1987). Screening for medical disorders in the setting of symptoms consistent with panic should be based on signs and symptoms gathered in the history and physical exam, and could include laboratory screens such as CBC, urinanalysis, renal and hepatic studies, serum calcium and phosphorous, and an electrocardiogram. Raj and Sheehan (1986) note that there is little evidence of a relationship between hypoglycemia and panic disorder. Screening for hypoglycemia should be done for patients with a history of postprandial attacks, panic attacks with accompanying hunger, or patients with past gastric surgery. Furthermore, in the case of pheochromocytoma, somatic complaints dominate cognitive symptoms. Echocardiography is recommended to evaluate the possible presence of mitral valve prolapse (MVP) only when the history, physical exam, or ECG suggest the possibility of MVP. Further screening for illnesses such as thyroid disorders, hypoglycemia, MVP, or temporal lobe epilepsy should occur only if abnormalities in the routine evaluation point to a need for further diagnostic work-up.

PSYCHOTIC DISORDERS

Expansion of the basic screening battery should be based on the results of the history and physical exam. A cerebrospinal fluid (CSF) examination should be done in patients presenting with psychosis accompanied by any combination of symptoms such as altered level of consciousness, headache, cognitive impairment, new onset of seizures, neurologic findings, fever, or peripheral leukocytosis (Koran, Sox, Sox, & Marton, 1987). A psychotic patient presenting with severe extrapyramidal symptoms, confusion, and fever should also be assessed for the possibility of neuroleptic malignant syndrome (NMS) with vital signs, elevated serum creatinine phosphokinase and myoglobinemia, and

serial mental status examinations (Latz and McCracken, 1990). Table 89.2 reviews medical illnesses that the clinician should include in the differential diagnosis for organic causes of psychotic symptoms.

TIC DISORDERS AND OBSESSIVE COMPULSIVE DISORDER

The differential for tic disorders includes a variety of other movement disorders that are usually excluded by careful history and examination (Jankovic, 1993). Other causes of ticlike movements such as Huntington's chorea, Wilson's disease, stimulant abuse, neuroleptic withdrawal, heavy metal poisoning, anticonvulsants, and tuberous sclerosis can be confirmed by specific testing in support of history and physical examination data (Jankovic, 1993; Kurlan, 1989). Recently the importance of autoimmune-induced tic and obsessive-compulsive symptoms has been emphasized, and laboratory screening (streptoccal cultures, anti-streptolysin-O and anti-DNAseB titers) in conjunction with clinical history taking of infection history has been suggested (Allen, Leonard, & Swedo, 1995; Kieslling, Marcotte, & Culpepper, 1993).

PERVASIVE DEVELOPMENTAL DISORDERS

Children and adolescents with clinical histories consistent with pervasive developmental disorders are at higher risk than other child psychiatric populations for associated medical conditions including seizure disorders (20 to 40% by adolescence), chromosomal anomalies (fragile X), and other neurogenetic and perceptual disorders. As a result, a broadened screening test battery is recommended in conjunction with focused history taking and examination pertaining to other disorders. If indicated by exam and family history, fragile X testing, Wood's lamp examination for tuberous sclerosis, hearing testing, and neurological consultation and electroencephalogram should be included (Volkmar, 1991).

TOXIC EXPOSURES

Often ignored in the differential diagnosis of mood, anxiety, developmental, and psychotic dis-

TABLE 89.2

Major Medical Causes of Psychosis

Central Nervous System Disorders	Endocrinopathy	Infectious	Alcohol-Related	Drug-Related	Other
Cerebrovascular accident	Corticosteroid Cushing's Addison's Iatrogenic	Encephalitis Meningitis Neurosyphilis	Chronic alcoholism Intoxication Withdrawal states	Amphetamines Hallucinogen-induced	Acute intermittent porphyria
Hypertensive encephalopathy	Diabetic Ketoacidosis			Iatrogenic Expected side effect Dose-related effect Idiosyncratic drug reaction	Hypoxic and hypoperfusion states
Multiple sclerosis	Hypoglycemia				
Seizure disorders	Thyroid Hypothyroidism Thyrotoxicosis			Adrenergic psychosis Sympathomimetic drugs Sedative hypnotic drug withdrawal	
Subdural hematoma					
Tumor (sphenoidal ridge meningioma)				Anticholinergic psychosis	
Wilson's disease					

Adapted from Wise and Taylor (1990).

orders are the effects of toxic exposures. For example, low-level lead exposure has been reported to be causally related to overactivity, intellectual decline, psychotic symptoms, and other forms of disruptive behavior (Edwards & Forsyth, 1989; McCracken, 1987). Fulton et al. (1987) and Thomson et al. (1989) reported on the Edinburgh lead study of 501 pupils between 6 and 9 years of age. These studies indicated that a dose response relationship exists between blood lead levels and poor performance on tests of ability and attainment (British Ability Scales). This relationship, although small, showed no evidence of a threshold. Moreover, there was an association between lead levels and deviant (hyperactive, aggressive) behavior, even after controlling for cofounders. Based on these data, the Centers for Disease Control considers greater than 25 μg/dl excessive for children. Children living in urban environments not usually contaminated by lead may be expected to have mean blood lead levels in the region of 10 to 25 μg/dl (Graham, 1983). Other heavy metals, such as mercury and thallium, have been reported to elicit psychiatric syndromes of varying types (Fagala & Wigg, 1992).

OTHER MEDICAL ILLNESSES AND PSYCHIATRIC PRESENTATION

Table 89.3 lists some of the other medical illnesses that may present with psychiatric symptoms, and suggested laboratory examinations appropriate if these illnesses may be present.

Laboratory Monitoring in Clinical Practice

Laboratory monitoring in the treatment of a child or adolescent with a psychiatric illness should be driven by the potential abnormalities related to the specific illness. For instance, serum electro-

TABLE 89.3

Other Medical Illnesses and Psychiatric Presentation

Illness	Laboratory	Symptoms May Include:
Acute intermittent porphyria	Porphobilinogen and alphaminolevulinic acid in a 24-hour urine sample	May present with psychiatric symptoms of mood disorder or psychosis.° Boon et al. (1989) reported on 2 children ages 6 and 11, presenting with psychotic behavior.
Encephalitis (particularly Herpes Simplex)	CSF examination	Behavioral disturbances are common and include hallucinations, psychosis, personality change, anosmia.°
HIV	Indications for testing in children include high risk groups or symptoms of AIDs or ARC	Personality change, difficulty concentrating, short term memory loss, chronic mild depression or acute psychosis/mainia (Anderson & Morris 1993).
Meningitis	CSF examination	Headache, confusion, memory difficulties.°
Subacute sclerosiing panencephalitis (in particular after measles vaccination or infection)	CSF examination	Explosive temper, oppositional/defiant behavior, insomnia, hallucinations.°
Systemic Lupus Erythematosus	Diagnosis of SLE requires a constellation of at least 4 of 11 symptoms, and cannot be based simply on the presence of a positive ANA	Depression, mania, anxiety, psychosis, also memory alteration, urinary incontinence (Yancey et al., 1981).
Wilson's disease	Serum copper, serum ceruloplasmin, and slit lamp exam for Kayser Fleischer rings (Walshe & Yealland, 1992)	10–25% present with psychiatric symptoms including psychosis, labile mood, disinhibition, memory abnormalities.° See case series reviews by Dening (1989) and Walshe, J. M. and Yealland, M. (1992).

°*Adapted from Skuster et al. (1992).*

lytes should be monitored in any child with severe bulemia.

When medications will be used in the treatment of a child or adolescent, Green (1991) recommends a full pretreatment laboratory battery including CBC and differential, serum electrolytes, calcium, phosphorus, BUN, and creatinine, AST/ALT/LDH, and total and indirect bilirubin.

However, given the low positive predictive value of these tests, we recommend that the physician base the premedication laboratory work-up on the history, review of symptoms, and the particular medication to be used. Table 89.4 lists the laboratory examinations that the child psychiatrist should obtain prior to starting medication and during the period that the child is being treated.

TABLE 89.4

Recommended Laboratory Testing for Medication Use

Medication	Baseline Labs	Monitoring Labs
Carbamazepine	CBC/platelets/differential, electrolytes, renal and liver function tests	CBC repeated every 6 months. Check CBC, LFTs if rash, sore throat or fever occur. Liver enzyme induction maximal for up to 6 weeks—requires more frequent level check during this time.
Clonidine	EKG	Repeat EKG with dose increase.
Lithium	Thyroid function, electrolytes, renal function, parathyroid function (serum calcium and phosphate) CBC, EKG. Pregnancy test in adolescent girls.	Lithium level twice weekly during med titration, monthly for maintenance. Renal function and CBC/diff every 3–6 months, thyroid function every 6 months. Carbamazepine may increase lithium serum levels.
Neuroleptic	EKG with pimozide	Yearly routine laboratory tests. Repeat EKG with each dose increase of pimozide. WBC if patient reports sudden onset of infection. Green recommends serum levels prior to terminating trial as ineffective.
Stimulants	Liver function tests for pemoline	Liver function tests for pemoline.
Tricyclic antidepressants	EKG	Repeat EKG prior to each dose increase. Medication concentrations useful to avoid toxicity and useful for therapeutic efficacy of imipramine, amitriptyline, and nortriptyline. If patients develop signs of infection, check CBC.
Valproic acid	CBC/differential, serum chemistries and liver function tests. Pregnancy test in adolescent girls.	Sever hepatotoxicity and thrombocytopenia may occur. No clear guidelines exist on monitoring, but if symptoms occur, check LFTs or platelet count. LFTs should be monitored in children 10 and under.**

Adapted from Green (1991).
***Schatzberg and Cole (1991).*

REFERENCES

Adams, M., Kutcher, S., Antoniw, B. A., & Bird, D. (1996). Diagnostic utility of endocrine and neuroimaging screening tests in first-onset adolescent psychosis. *Journal of the American Academy of Child and Adolescent Psychiatry, 35,* 67–73.

Allen, A. J., Leonard, H. L., & Swedo, S. E. (1995). Case study: A new infection-triggered, autoimmune subtype of pediatric OCD and Tourette's syndrome. *Journal of the American Academy of Child and Adolescent Psychiatry, 34,* 307–311.

Bartsch, D. A., Shern, D. L., Feinberg, L. E., Fuller, B. B., & Willet, A. B. (1990). Screening CMHC outpatients for physical illness. *Hospital and Community Psychiatry, 41,* 786–790.

Davies, D. W. (1965). Physical illness in psychiatric outpatients. *British Journal of Psychiatry, 111,* 27–33.

Dening T. R., Berrios G. E. (Dec., 1989). Wilson's disease: Psychiatric symptoms in 195 cases. *Archives of General Psychiatry, 46,* 1126–1133.

Dolan, J. G. M., & Mushlin, A. I. (1985). Routine laboratory testing for medical disorders in psychiatric inpatients. *Archives of Internal Medicine, 145,* 2085–2088.

Edwards, K. S., & Forsyth, B. W. (1989). Lead screening at pediatric teaching programs. *American Journal of Diseases of Children, 143,* 1455–1457.

Fagala, G. E., & Wigg, C. L. (1992). Psychiatric manifestations of mercury poisoning. *Journal of the American Academy of Child and Adolescent Psychiatry, 31,* 306–311.

Fulton, M., Raab, G. M., Thomson, G. O. B., Laxen, D. P. H., Hunter, R., & Hepburn, W. (1987). Influence of blood lead on the ability and attainment of children in Edinburgh. *Lancet, 1,* 1221–1226.

Gabel, S., & Hsu, L. K. (1986). Routine laboratory tests in adolescent psychiatric inpatients: Their value in making psychiatric diagnoses and in detecting medical disorders. *Journal of the American Academy of Child Psychiatry, 25,* 113–119.

Graham, P. I. (1983). Poisoning in childhood. In M. Rutter (Ed.), *Developmental neuropsychiatry* (pp. 56–67). New York: Guilford Press.

Green, W. H. (1991). *Child and adolescent clinical psychopharmacology.* Baltimore, MD: Williams & Wilkins.

Hall, R. C. W., & Beresford, T. P. (1984). Laboratory evaluation of newly admitted psychiatric patients. In R. C. W. Hall & T. P. Beresford (Eds.), *Handbook of psychiatric diagnostic procedures* (Vol. 1). Ch. 1 & 2, pp. 3–45, Tables pp. 276–304. New York: Spectrum Publications.

Hall, R. C. W., Popkin, M. K., Devaul, R. A., Faillace, L. A., & Stickney, S. K. (1978). Physical illness presenting as psychiatric disease. *Archives of General Psychiatry, 35,* 1315–1320.

Hauser, P., Zametkin, A. J., Martinez, P., Vitiello, B., Matochik, J. A., Mixson, A. J., & Weintraub, B. D. (1993). Attention deficit-hyperactivity disorder in people with generalized resistance to thyroid hormone. *New England Journal of Medicine, 328,* 997–1001.

Herridge, C. F. (1960). Physical disorders in psychiatric illness: A study of 209 consecutive admissions. *Lancet, 2,* 949–951.

Hoffman, R. S. (1982). Diagnostic errors in the evaluation of behavioral disorders. *Journal of the American Medical Association, 2,* 964–967.

Jankovic, J. (1993). Tics and other neurological disorders. In R. Kurlan (Ed.), *Handbook of Tourette's syndrome and related tic and behavioral disorders.* Ch. 8, pp. 167–181. New York: Marcel Dekker.

Johnson, D. A. W. (1968). The evaluation of routine physical examination in psychiatric cases. *Practitioner, 200,* 686–691.

Kiessling, L. S., Marcotte, A. C., & Culpepper, I. (1994). Antineuronal antibodies in movement disorders. *Pediatrics, 92,* 39–43.

Koran, L. M., Sox, H. C., Jr., Sox, C. H., & Marton, K. I. (1987). Detecting physical disease in psychiatric patients. *Medical Care, 25* (12 Suppl.), S99.

Koranyi, E. K., & Potoczny, W. M. (1992). Physical illnesses underlying psychiatric symptoms. *Psychotherapy & Psychosomatics, 58,* 155–160.

Kurlan, R. (1989). Tourette's syndrome: Current concepts. *Neurology, 39,* 1625–1630.

Latz, S., McCracken, J. T., Schmidt-Lackner, S. (1990). *Neuroleptic malignant syndrome in adolescence: A review and two cases.* Paper presented at the annual meeting of the American Academy of Child and Adolescent Psychiatry Chicago, IL.

Leo, R. J., Batterman-Faunce, M., Pickhardt, D., Cartagena, M., & Cohen, G. (1997). Utility of thyroid function screening in adolescent psychiatric patients. *Journal of the American Academy of Child and Adolescent Psychiatry, 36,* 103–111.

McCracken, J. T. (1987). Lead intoxication psychosis in an adolescent. *Journal of the American Academy of Child and Adolescent Psychiatry, 26,* 274–276.

Raj, A., & Sheehan, D. V. (1987). Medical evaluation of panic attacks. *Journal of Clinical Psychiatry, 48,* 309–313.

Rivinus, T. M., Jamison, D. L., Graham, P. J. (1975). Childhood organic neurological disease presenting as psychiatric disorder. *Archives of Diseases of Children, 50,* 115–119.

Skuster D. Z., Dirge K. B., Corbette J. J. (June, 1992). Neurologic Conditions Presenting as Psychiatric Disorders. *Psychiatric Clinics of North America, 15* (2), 311–333.

Sternberg, D. E. (1986). Testing for physical illness in psychiatric patients. *Journal of Clinical Psychiatry, 47* (1, Suppl.), 3–9.

Thomson, G. O. B., Raab, G. M., Hepburn, W. S., Hunter, R., Fulton, M., & Laxen, D. P. H. (1989).

Blood-lead levels and children's behavior—results from the Edinburgh lead study. *Journal of Child Psychology and Psychiatry, 30,* 515–528.

Walshe, J. M., Yealland M. (1992). Wilson's disease: the problem of delayed diagnosis. *Journal of Neurology, Neurosurgery, and Psychiatry, 55,* 692–696.

Weiss, R. E., Stein, M. A., Tropmmer, M. D., & Refetoff, S. (1993). Attention-deficit hyperactivity disorder and thyroid function. *Journal of Pediatrics, 123,* 539–545.

Wise, M. G., & Taylor, S. E. (1990). Anxiety and mood disorders in medically ill patients. *Journal of Clinical Psychiatry, 51,* 27–32.

Woolston, J. L., & Riddle, M. A. (1990). The role of advanced technology in inpatient child psychiatry: Leading edge or useful aid? *Journal of the American Academy of Child and Adolescent Psychiatry, 29,* 905–908.

Volkmar, F. R. (1991). Autism and pervasive developmental disorders. In M. Lewis (Ed.), *Child and adolescent psychiatry: A comprehensive textbook.* Baltimore, MD: Williams & Wilkins. pp. 499–507.

---

90 / Genetic Studies

Linda J. Lotspeich

The genetic basis of disease is perhaps the most rapidly growing area of medical knowledge. In the past decade the genes responsible for many human diseases have been identified. Every year new links between specific genes and behavioral disorders are being formed, adding to our fundamental understanding of mind and body. We anticipate that in the next decade our insight into the genetic basis of human disease will increase tenfold, and forward-looking clinicians should prepare themselves for the challenge.

The genetic origins of mental illnesses are of particular interest. Some neuropsychiatric disorders, such as Huntington's chorea, have been traced to specific single genes. The expectation is that within the coming years, genes will be found for a long list of additional major psychiatric disorders. Investigators are currently studying the familial and/or genetic basis for depression, manic depression, schizophrenia, Tourette's disorder, obsessive compulsive disorder, attention deficit

hyperactivity disorder, pervasive developmental disorders, and dyslexia. A review of these studies can be found in Lombroso, Pauls, and Leckman (1994). When the genetic etiologies for some or all of these disorders are identified, benefits to the patient and his family will include genetic counseling, better targeted therapies, and more accurate prognostic information. With increased understanding of how the brain is influenced by specific genes, we may be able to unravel the relationship between nature and nurture in these disorders. However, at present, in spite of our recognition that genes have a clear influence on behavior, we have only a preliminary understanding of how genes influence a child's behavior.

Recognizing that a disorder may have a familial and/or genetic basis can be helpful in making a diagnosis. For example, when evaluating a 4 year old with hyperactivity and poor attention, the evaluator may learn that the family history is significant for Tourette's disorder. A diagnosis of Tourette's disorder then becomes more likely, since it is known that Tourette's has a familial basis and that childhood symptoms of hyperactivity and poor attention often present before the appearance of motor and vocal tics. The clinician can then counsel the parents that while the child's problems may stem from attention deficit hyperactivity disorder, they may actually be secondary to Tourette's disorder. In this way the clinician

This work was initially started with Roland Ciaranello, M.D. who died on December 15, 1994. This author is grateful for Dr. Ciaranello's mentorship. This work was supported by the grant from the National Alliance for Research on Schizophrenia and Depression (NARSAD) and from the Scottish Rite Benevolent Foundation's Schizophrenia Research Program. This author would also like to acknowledge the support of Dr. Athena Milatovich Cherry, Director of the Cytogenetics Laboratory at Stanford, for providing the chromosomal figures and aiding in editing of the manuscript.

prepares the parents for the possible development of motor and vocal tics in the future. When the putative gene(s) involved in Tourette's are eventually identified, a specific test will probably follow, reducing the need for inference of genetic disease based on family history. Thus, as evaluators, we are often informally assessing presumed genetic diseases for which specific tests are not yet available. Until specific tests are available, the clinician must use clues from the family history to ferret out possible genetic disorders.

The past decade of research has been remarkable for the appearance of an increasing collection of genetic disorders that present as cognitive delays and behavioral disturbances. These disorders have a known genetic basis and specific genetic tests are available. Clinicians should be aware of these disorders, so that the appropriate genetic tests may be ordered. If test results are already present in the medical record, the clinician can interpret and explain these tests to the parents. To cite an illustrative example, a 3-year-old child with laryngomalacia and developmental delays presented for treatment of aggressive and self-injurious behaviors. The child had two balanced chromosomal translocations. One translocation [t(7;12)(q32;q22)] was inherited from the father while the other translocation [t(16;17)(p11;q21.1)] was a sporadic (de novo) occurrence. The inherited translocation was most probably unrelated to the child's developmental delays, since the father was normal. The de novo translocation, though balanced, was probably, but not certainly, the cause of the developmental delays. The parents were confused about the significance of the chromosomal abnormalities. The father expressed guilt about having passed a translocated chromosome to his child. The mother was more concerned about her child's uncontrollable and self-injurious behaviors. The clinician was able to help the family by assessing the child's behavioral abnormalities and developmental delays and recommending appropriate treatments. Perhaps equally important, the clinician educated the parents about the probable connection between the translocations and the child's developmental delays; this helped to address the major parental concerns, which included the father's guilt and the parents' struggle to care for their child.

This chapter will first review the various types of genetic testing that are available today. Next we

will present descriptions of a few relatively well-understood genetic disorders that affect behavior: Prader–Willi syndrome, Angelman syndrome, Smith–Magenis syndrome, Williams syndrome, and fragile X syndrome. Several of these genetic disorders illustrate the recently discovered phenomena of genetic imprinting and genomic anticipation.

Specific Types of Genetic Testing

Currently there are relatively few methods of genetic testing in routine clinical use, though the number will undoubtedly increase over time. This section will review the most frequently used tests, including routine karyotype testing, high-resolution banding, DNA testing, and fluorescence in situ hybridization (FISH). For additional information on these types of genetic testing, surveys of medical genetics such as those by Thompson, McInnes, and Willard (1991) or by Jorde, Carey, and White (1995) are suggested.

ROUTINE KARYOTYPE TEST

When ordering routine karyotyping, the lab prepares and photographs nuclei that contain the condensed chromosome material extracted from white blood cells or other living tissues. In the karyotype one can visually identify the 22 pairs of autosomal chromosomes and the sex chromosomes, X and Y (see Figure 90.1). Chromosomes have a centromere (a constriction), and a short and long arm, referred to as p and q, respectively. When stained with a dye, each chromosome pair reveals a characteristic banding pattern that enables each pair to be uniquely identified. For example 3p12.5 refers to the short arm of chromosome 3, at band number 12.5. From this type of visual examination, gross chromosomal abnormalities may be detected; these may include deletions, translocations, fragile sites, and abnormal chromosome number (aneuploidy). Gross abnormalities of chromosome structure are often associated with the clinical characteristics of multiple malformations, dysmorphic features, and cognitive impairments such as mental retardation.

Deletions: Deletions are regions of missing

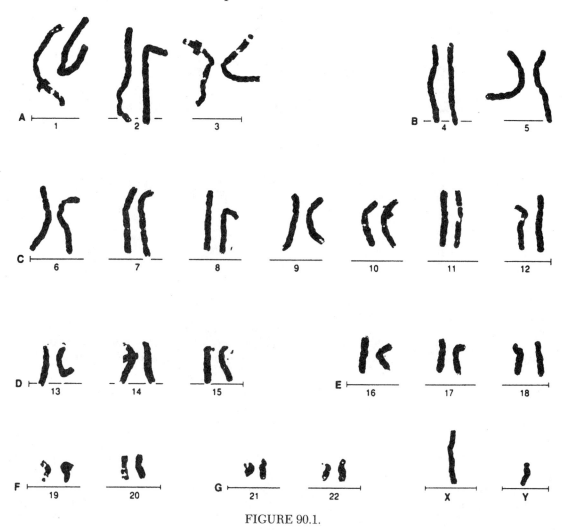

FIGURE 90.1.

A routine G-banded karyotype of a normal male at approximately the 550 band level of resolution.
(Photomicrograph courtesy of Athena Milatovich Cherry, Stanford University, Stanford, CA.)

DNA. They can occur at any location and may be of virtually any size. Terminal deletions are those that occur at the tips of a chromosome, while interstitial deletions occur in the middle of a chromosome. Deletions can be submicroscopic and invisible, such as those caused by loss of one or a few base pairs. Only very large deletions are detectable by karyotyping; these tend to be of the size of millions of base pairs and include a large number of genes. Often a deletion is suspected based on routine karyotyping and then confirmed by high-resolution banding (see below). Small deletions, too small to be picked up on routine karyotyping, are tested for either by high-resolution banding or by FISH (see below).

Translocations: Translocations occur when two (or more) chromosomes break and exchange pieces of chromosomal material. For example, a woman has the distal fragment of the long arm of chromosome 7 (7q32) attached to chromosome 12, and in the same karyotype a distal fragment of the long arm of chromosome 12 (12q22) is attached to chromosome 7. This karyotype is referred to as 46, XX, t(7;12)(q32;q22). This is an example of a balanced translocation; there is no net loss or addition of chromosomal material. Balanced translocations are usually compatible with normal development. Normal development is not guaranteed though, since a critical gene may have been split and inactivated by the translocation. An

Fragile X Syndrome: fra(X)(q27.3)

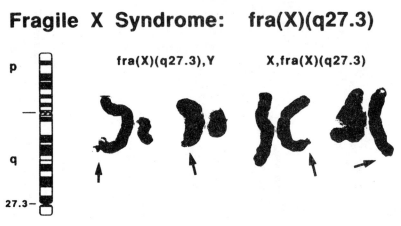

FIGURE 90.2.

A composite demonstrating the fragile X site at Xq27.3 associated with the fragile X syndrome. On the left is an ideogram or graphic representation of a G-banded X chromosome showing the location of the fragile site. In the middle are sex chromosomes from two metaphase cells of an affected male, while on the right are the two X chromosomes of an affected or carrier female. The arrows indicate the observed fragile sites on the X chromosomes. (Illustration courtesy of Athena Milatovich Cherry, Stanford University, Stanford, CA.)

unbalanced translocation involves both deletion and addition of genetic material. Unbalanced translocations are usually associated with abnormal development.

Fragile Sites: A nonstaining gap in a chromosome preparation is known as a fragile site. Fragile sites are heritable variations that tend to occur at specific sites on one or more chromosomes. Most often they have no clinical significance, but in a few cases their clinical significance may be important. For instance, a specific fragile site occurring on the long arm of the X chromosome (Xq27.3) is associated with a form of X-linked mental retardation called fragile X syndrome (see Figure 90.2). The cytogenetic test for the fragile X site involves growing cells in thymidine- and folate-deficient medium prior to chromosome preparation. These conditions induce the expression of this fragile X site in some of the cells analyzed. Recently a specific DNA test for fragile X syndrome became available (see text below). Usually, when one is testing for fragile X syndrome, the DNA test is used in preference to karyotyping, since it is more accurate and less expensive.

Aneuploidy: This is a general term indicating that an individual has either too few or too many chromosomes as compared to the normal diploid number of 46. There are many common types of aneuploidies associated with specific clinical syndromes. The most common is trisomy 21, or three copies of autosome 21 (Down syndrome). Commonly occurring sex chromosome aneuploidies are monosomy X (Turner syndrome) and XXY (Klinefelter syndrome). Some persons can be mosaic for an aneuploidy, meaning that a variable percentage of somatic cells have an abnormal number of chromosomes, while the remaining cells have a normal count. Persons who are mosaic for aneuploidy, such as those with mosaic Down syndrome, are often only mildly affected.

HIGH-RESOLUTION BANDING

In routine metaphase karyotype preparations, about 400 to 500 bands are identifiable. In general this type of analysis is adequate for identifying the majority of chromosomal anomalies. Higher resolution analysis may be required, either to define

Prader-Willi/Angelman Syndromes, del(15)(q11.2q13)

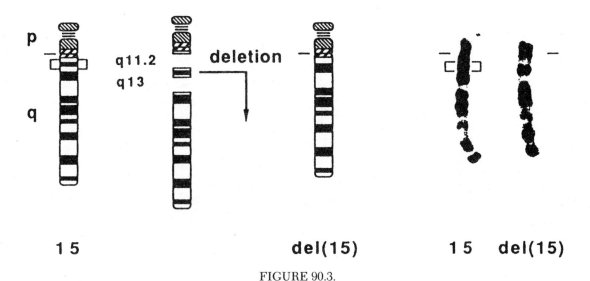

p

q11.2
q13

deletion

q

15　　　　　　　　**del(15)**　　　**15**　　**del(15)**

FIGURE 90.3.

Ideogram illustration and high resolution (≥ 850 band level) chromosome 15 homologs showing the deletion that is commonly described in Prader–Willi and Angelman syndromes. On the left is a graphic representation of how the deletion occurs. On the right are a pair of chromosomes 15 homologs with the deleted chromosome 15 on the far right. (Illustration courtesy of Athena Milatovich Cherry, Stanford University, Stanford, CA.)

breakpoints or to detect microdeletions. High-resolution banding analysis can increase the number of detectable bands to about 800. In high-resolution banding cultured blood cells are harvested early in mitosis. Karyotypes prepared from such cells demonstrate an increased number of bands (high-resolution banding), since the chromosomes are less condensed than in the standard preparations. This allows more subtle changes to be detected and better defined. Some microdeletions, those smaller than about 1 to 3 million base pairs, are not detectable even by high-resolution banding. These can be identified by the FISH technique if appropriate DNA probes are available (see below). Microdeletions have been identified as the cause of a number of important developmental abnormalities. For example, Prader–Willi and Angelman syndromes, clinical syndromes of mental retardation, are known to be due to the

same microdeletion on chromosome 15 (see below under Prader–Willi/Angelman syndromes). In some cases high-resolution banding can detect the microdeletion on chromosome 15 (see Figure 90.3), but in other cases FISH testing is required.

DNA TESTING

DNA testing involves testing for specific DNA sequences using Southern blot analysis or polymerase chain reaction (PCR). Southern blot analysis entails digestion of chromosomal DNA with endonucleases, separation of the fragments by gel electrophoresis, and identification of sequence alterations using specific DNA probes. PCR uses specific DNA primers and the enzyme Taq polymerase to vastly increase the number of targeted DNA sequences, allowing better identification of the targeted DNA. As more and more single-gene disorders are found, there will be greater use of DNA testing for these specific genetic disorders. For example, fragile X syndrome, a single-gene disorder caused by an expansion of repeated base pair sequences (see below), can now be detected with specific DNA tests. These methods of DNA testing allow a more accurate and inexpensive test for fragile X syndrome than is offered by standard cytogenetic testing.

FLUORESCENCE IN SITU HYBRIDIZATION (FISH)

In this test a selected DNA probe is hybridized to a chromosome that was previously fixed to a slide (an "in situ" preparation). A fluorescent molecule is then added to visualize the DNA probe—hence the name fluorescence in-situ hybridization. The probe visually identifies a specific chromosome segment; a duplicated segment can easily be detected as a double fluorescent spot while a deleted segment will be detected by an absence of fluorescence (as in the case of Prader–Willi syndrome). This technique was once a research procedure, but it is now commonly used in clinical labs to identify deletions of a few thousand to a million base pairs (microdeletions) that are not detectable by routine karyotyping or by high-resolution banding. As specific genes for neuropsychiatric syndromes are identified, the need for FISH analysis increases, since in many cases the deletion or duplication is submicroscopic. FISH is particularly valuable at present in testing for the deletion of genes in Williams syndrome (chromosome 7), as well as in confirmation of Smith–Magenis (chromosome 17) (see below).

Examples of Specific Genetic Disorders

There are several rules of thumb that can be put to use when associating a specific set of signs and symptoms with a genetic defect. Most children with chromosomal disorders will present with mental retardation and dysmorphism. Although there are many nongenetic etiologies for mental retardation, many are not associated with dysmorphic features. Also, if there is a history of similar problems in first- or second-degree relatives, this will increase the level of suspicion for a chromosomal disorder or a single-gene disorder. Since some genetic problems are predominately sporadic, there may be no familial history to reinforce a suspicion. The known genetic causes of mental retardation are too numerous to review in this chapter; we refer interested readers to Schaefer and Bodensteiner (1992) for an extensive review.

Autism and other pervasive developmental disorders (PDD) have been associated with a few known genetic disorders. Fragile X syndrome is the most frequent of these, and it is seen in about 2 to 5% of PDD cases. Other autism-related genetic disorders include tuberous sclerosis, neurofibromatosis, Williams syndrome, and chromosomal abnormalities such as translocations. However, these disorders represent only a small percentage of persons with PDD. Refer to Lotspeich and Ciaranello (1993) for a review of known genetic disorders associated with autism.

With the application of more specialized genetic research tools, an increasing number of newly recognized genetic disorders are emerging. In this section we describe a few selected behavioral genetic disorders, including Prader–Willi syndrome, Angelman syndrome, Smith–Magenis syndrome, Williams syndrome, and fragile X syndrome. We anticipate that many more such examples will be available 10 years from now. These newer and more complex genetic disorders often do not observe simple Mendelian inheritance. Genomic imprinting and genomic anticipation, to be described later, are complex genetic mechanisms that effect the inheritance pattern of these disorders.

PRADER–WILLI SYNDROME AND ANGELMAN SYNDROME

Both Prader–Willi syndrome and Angelman syndrome are microdeletion disorders caused by a single-gene or multigene deletion localized at the same position on chromosome 15 (15q11-q13). Phenotypically these two disorders are very different. Children with Prader–Willi have obesity, short stature, mental retardation, polyphagia, and dysmorphic features of hypogonadism, small hands, and small feet. In contrast, children with Angelman syndrome, or "happy puppet" syndrome, characteristically present with microbrachycephaly, ataxia, seizures, mental retardation, and inappropriate laughter. The population frequency of Prader–Willi syndrome is estimated at 1 in 25,000.

Some explanation is necessary to understand how a single deletion can produce two distinct syndromes. This phenomenon, called genomic imprinting, occurs because some genes are chemically different, depending on whether they originate from the mother or father. These "imprinted" DNA sequences have subtle gender-specific chemical differences, and their chemical differences cause them to be expressed differently. While the exact chemical mechanism of imprinting is not known, it has been suggested that addition of methyl groups to the genomic DNA could account for some cases of imprinting; in general, methylated genes are poorly expressed compared to nonmethylated genes. A normal phenotype depends on the balanced, but differential, functioning of the maternal and paternal genes. With this as background, it is at least reasonable that deletion of the paternal gene might result in one syndrome, while maternal deletion could result in a quite different syndrome.

In both Prader–Willi and Angelman syndromes a segment of DNA has been deleted from one copy of chromosome 15; the other chromosome 15 is either inactivated or poorly expressed due to imprinting. If the father donates the chromosome with the deletion, while the mother donates the imprinted copy of the 15q11-q13, the child will have Prader–Willi syndrome. Conversely, if the mother contributes the deletion and the father contributes the imprinted copy, the child will have Angelman syndrome. Because of this gender-dependent chemical imprinting, a child with the 15q11-q13 deletion may have either Prader–Willi syndrome or Angelman syndrome, depending on which parent donated the deletion. About 70% of occurrences of the two syndromes seem to be due to this mechanism, while the remaining 30% have a more complex origin.

When either of these two disorders is suspected, one orders high-resolution chromosomal analysis of chromosome 15 to look for a 15q11-q13 deletion. FISH testing may also be ordered. Once a child is diagnosed with either disorder through genetic testing, the parents can then be tested to determine which parent contributed the deletion. However, the clinical picture alone should determine whether a child with a 15q11-q13 deletion has Prader–Willi syndrome or Angelman syndrome. For additional information we refer the reader once again to texts on medical genetics, including those by Thompson et al. (1991), and Jorde et al. (1995), in addition to the article by Nicholls (1993).

SMITH–MAGENIS SYNDROME

Smith–Magenis syndrome is a microdeletion disorder with an estimated prevalence of 1 in 25,000 births. It affects girls and boys equally. Smith–Magenis syndrome was identified in the 1980s, when a characteristic pattern of dysmorphic features, developmental delays, and behavioral abnormalities were noted in persons with an interstitial deletion on the short arm of chromosome 17. Clinically the majority of individuals with Smith–Magenis syndrome have mental retardation, usually in the moderate range, with early speech delays. Their dysmorphic features typically include brachycephaly, midface hypoplasia, broad nasal bridge, ear malformations, and short hands. Other possible symptoms include myopia, conductive hearing loss, short stature, and cardiac defects. Their behavioral abnormalities can consist of hyperactivity, stereotypic self-hugging, aggressive behaviors, an abnormal sleep pattern (absence of REM sleep is reported in a few cases), and self-injurious behaviors. The self-injurious behaviors are, characteristically, head banging, self-mutilation of fingernails and toenails (onychotillomania), and insertion of foreign bodies into various body orifices (polyembolokoilamania). These children frequently present by the age of 3 years with speech delays.

Persons with this disorder have one normal chromosome 17 and one abnormal chromosome 17 with a microdeletion that spans multiple genes. The specific gene whose absence produces the signs and symptoms of Smith–Magenis syndrome has not yet been positively identified. Most likely it will turn out that the absence of several genes is responsible for the array of signs and symptoms seen in this disorder. The microdeletion on chromosome 17 is usually not present in the parents. Thus most cases are sporadic occurrences, presumably due to errors in chromosome duplication during germ cell development. The abnormal chromosome 17 can come from either parent. The syndrome is identical, regardless of which parent donates the microdeletion, and so genomic imprinting does not appear to be a feature of Smith–Magenis syndrome. Diagnosis is confirmed through genetic testing either by high-resolution analysis of chromosome 17 or by FISH testing. This disorder is described by Colley, Leversha, Voullaire, and Rogers (1990).

WILLIAMS SYNDROME

Williams syndrome is a genetic disorder that has recently been traced to a microdeletion on chromosome 7 (7q11.23). Williams syndrome affects approximately 1 in 20,000 to 1 in 50,000 individuals and affects boys and girls equally. The disorder was first identified in the 1960s as a behavioral syndrome consisting of dysmorphic features, developmental delay, early skin aging, and infantile hypercalcemia. Children with Williams syndrome have characteristic facial dysmorphism referred to as "elfin" facies. The dysmorphic features consist of an elongated face, periorbital fullness, up-slanting palpebral fissures, epicanthal folds, small and anteverted nose, elongated philtrum, thick lips, open bite, auricular asymmetry, and prominent ears. Most children with Williams syndrome have mental retardation, but some have normal IQs; verbal abilities tend to be more developed than visual-spatial abilities. Many are unusually talkative and friendly, while others have been reported to meet diagnostic criteria for autism. Many of these children also have supravalvular aortic stenosis (SVAS) and narrowing of other large elastic arteries.

Since SVAS alone is also a distinct vascular autosomal-dominant disorder that had been traced to the elastin gene on chromosome 7, researchers were led to examine chromosome 7 for possible abnormalities in Williams syndrome. They found that the majority of patients with Williams syndrome have a microdeletion spanning the elastin gene on chromosome 7 (7q11.23). Since the absence of one elastin gene may not account for all the symptoms of Williams syndrome (such as cognitive delay), it is hypothesized that other adjacent genes are also deleted. Since a normal chromosome 7 is present in every cell, it seems surprising that loss of just one copy of the elastin gene and possibly other genes could lead to such drastic developmental consequences. Williams syndrome is one more example of the importance of precise gene dosage for normal development.

Most cases of Williams syndrome are sporadic events, due to errors in germ cell development. However, in some cases the disorder is inherited in an autosomal-dominant fashion—in these cases both parent and child are affected. As with Smith–Magenis syndrome, Williams syndrome is the same regardless of which parent contributes the deletion, and thus there is no evidence of genomic imprinting.

The microdeletion is too small to be detected by routine karyotyping and in most cases too small to be detected by high-resolution mapping. Thus the recommended test is FISH analysis. There are a few children who have the clinical features of Williams syndrome but who do not have a 7q11.23 microdeletion. In these cases a point mutation might produce the syndrome. Therefore a negative FISH test does not rule out Williams syndrome. For more detail we refer the reader to the study of Ewart et al. (1993).

FRAGILE X SYNDROME

Fragile X syndrome is considered to be the second most common known genetic type of mental retardation—Down syndrome being the most common. The estimated prevalence of fragile X syndrome is 0.5 to 1 per 1000 in male births and 0.2 to 0.6 per 1000 in female births.

Fragile X syndrome is an X-linked disorder caused by mutations in the fragile X mental retardation-1 gene (FMR-1). The specific genetic defect of the FMR-1 gene is an abnormal expansion of CGG trinucleotide repeats. Normal individuals have 5 to 50 CGG trinucleotide repeats, while persons with fragile X syndrome have more than 200. CGG trinucleotide repeats in the range of 50 to 200 are referred to as premutations. Usually individuals with premutations are asymptomatic. The name fragile X comes from the fragile site observed on karyotype studies when the cells are first grown in thymidine-deficient medium. Since 200 or more CGG repeats are required to produce the characteristic gap on the X chromosome, normal persons and those with premutation (fewer than 200 CGG repeats) are cytogenetically normal.

The best way to understand the genetics of fragile X syndrome is to review the three-generation pedigree of a typical fragile X family. If a boy is positive for fragile X syndrome (i.e., has 200 or more CGG repeats), the disorder can be traced to his maternal grandfather. The maternal grandfather will generally be found to harbor a premutation of 50 to 200 CGG repeats. This premutation is inherited by his daughter and then passed on to her children, in this example to her son. During oogenesis the premutation is amplified to more than 200 repeats. Her son thus inherits an X chromosome with 200 or more CGG repeats and he expresses the phenotype of fragile X syndrome. Her daughter, who also inherits the full mutation, will have a variable expression of the disorder, since she has a normal X chromosome to balance the abnormal one. It should be recalled that in females, only one of the two X chromosomes in a given cell is active while the other is condensed and inactive. Thus the severity of the daughter's disorder will depend on the percentage of cells that harbor an active mutated X chromosome. The progression of clinical and genetic findings of fragile X syndrome over successive generations is known as genetic anticipation.

Clinically the vast majority of boys with the full mutation present with mental retardation. Other symptoms of fragile X syndrome include learning disabilities, behavioral abnormalities, and, usually, dysmorphic features, including an elongated face, prominent mandible, enlarged ears and enlarged testicles after puberty. Not all children with fragile X syndrome have dysmorphic features. Approximately 30 to 50% of girls heterozygous for the full mutation develop mental retardation, while others may develop learning disabilities. Some children with the full mutation meet diagnostic criteria for one of the PDD. Fragile X syndrome is the most common known genetic disorder associated with PDD. Person's with premutation are usually asymptomatic; however, current research is revealing that some individuals have certain personality traits. The current trend in testing children for fragile X syndrome is to order a specific DNA study for fragile X syndrome. For additional details on fragile X syndrome, we refer the reader to Baumgardner, Green, and Reiss (1994) and Hagerman, et al. (1994).

Conclusion

Familial syndromes involving behavioral and developmental problems can increasingly be traced to defects in specific genes. Examples of syndromes in which symptoms appear in childhood include fragile X syndrome, Prader–Willi syndrome, Smith–Magenis syndrome, and Williams syndrome. As genome sequencing and mapping accelerate, the number of genetically determined behavioral syndromes is sure to increase. These syndromes are recognized clinically by delays in maturation, mental retardation, and somatic features. In general they are caused by deletions and/or additions of genetic material, or, in the case of fragile X syndrome, by expansion of a specific nucleotide triplet repeat. When the clinician's suspicions are raised either because of symptoms or family history, a variety of tests are available to rule out specific syndromes. Testing is guided by clinical judgment. In general, routine karyotyping will pick up gross deletions and translocations of chromosomal fragments. When a deletion is very small, high-resolution banding may be required, in addition to a fluorescence-based DNA probe test known as the FISH technique. In the case of fragile X syndrome, a specific DNA probe test is generally required for diagnosis. To help parents and patients understand these gene-based syndromes, the competent clinician needs to be familiar with standard methods of genetic testing, with the spectrum of symptoms characteristic of the syndrome, and with the specific mode of inheritance.

REFERENCES

Baumgardner, T. L., Green, K. E., & Reiss, A. L. (1994). A behavioral neurogenetics approach to developmental disabilities: gene-brain-behavior associations. *Current Opinion in Neurology, 7,* 172–178.

Colley, A. F., Leversha, M. A., Voullaire, L. D., & Rogers, J. G. (1990). Five cases demonstrating the distinctive behavioural features of chromosome deletion 17(p11.2 p11.2) (Smith-Magenis syndrome). *Journal of Paediatric Child Health, 26,* 17–21.

Ewart, A. K., Morris, C. A., Atkinson, D., Jin, W., Sternes, K., Spallone, P., Stock, A. D., Leppert, M., & Keating, M. T. (1993). Hemizygosity at the elastin locus in a developmental disorder, Williams syndrome. *Nature Genetics, 5,* 11–16.

Hagerman, R. J., Wilson, P., Staley, L. W., Lang, K. A., Fan, T., Uhlhorn, C., Jewell-Smart, S., Hull, C., Drisko, J., Flom, K., & Taylor, A. K. (1994). Evaluation of school children at high risk for fragile X syndrome utilizing buccal cell FMR-1 testing. *American Journal of Medical Genetics, 51,* 474–481.

Jorde, L. B., Carey, J. C., & White, R. L. (1995). *Medical Genetics.* St. Louis: Mosby-Year Book.

Lombroso, P. J., Pauls, D. L., & Leckman, J. F. (1994). *Journal of the American Academy of Child and Adolescent Psychiatry, 33* (7), 921–938.

Lotspeich, L. J., & Ciaranello, R. D. (1993). The neurobiology and genetics of infantile autism. In R. Bradley (Ed.), *International review of neurobiology* (pp. 87–129). New York: Academic Press.

Nicholls, R. D. (1993). Genomic imprinting and uniparental disomy in Angelman and Prader–Willi syndromes: A review. *American Journal of Medical Genetics, 46,* 16–25.

Schaefer, G. B., & Bodensteiner, J. B. (1992). Evaluation of the child with idiopathic mental retardation. *Pediatric Clinics of North America, 39* (4), 929–943.

Thompson, M. W., McInnes, R. E., & Willard, H. R. (1991). *Thompson & Thompson: Genetics in medicine* (5th ed.). Philadelphia: W. B. Saunders.

91 / Speech, Language, and Hearing

Christiane A. M. Baltaxe

The assessment of a youngster's speech and language skills is complex. It requires knowledge of what can be expected of a youngster, given normal development. The clinician must recognize developmental language delay and deviant linguistic behaviors when they occur and interpret their significance in the context of overall assessment.

The clinician who observes or interviews a child or adolescent must listen carefully not only to what the child says but also how it is said. In order to assess the child's linguistic behavior, it is useful to divide communication into its 3 basic components: speech, language, and social communication or pragmatics. Delays or deviances can occur in any 1 or all 3 of these domains. *Speech* is the motor component, *language* the symbolic component, and *pragmatics* or *social communication* the interactive component of linguistic behavior.

Recognizing the Differences Among Speech, Language, and Communication and Their Functions

THE SPEECH COMPONENT

Speech, or the motor component, includes *articulation* (production of sounds and their combination into words and sentences), *fluency* (smooth flow of speech), *voice* (quality, resonance features, loudness, and pitch characteristics), and *prosody* (stress and intonation patterns). The characteristics of speech also can provide important information about a speaker's age, sex, emotional state, and general well-being.

THE LANGUAGE COMPONENT

The language component is the symbolic component. It consists of a linguistic code governed by the system of rules that a speaker has to acquire in order to communicate. Language consists of a receptive and an expressive component. It includes semantics (vocabulary and its selectional rules) as well as a grammatical component (phrase and sentence formation and their transformations). Language also provides information about the speaker's educational level, social class, gender, and membership in a particular speech community, such as an ethnic or dialect group.

THE PRAGMATIC COMPONENT

The pragmatic or social component is the interactive component that relates to language use in a social context and is governed by a system of socially related linguistic rules. Social communication also has a nonverbal component. Variations in social communication also provide information about the age, sex, education, occupation, mental or physical health, dialect, and social group of the speaker. Variations can occur in the same speaker depending on the social situation, the specific function, and listener identity. Social communication assumes a speaker, a topic, a listener, and a setting in which the interaction takes place.

The speaker's communicative behavior, at the speech, language, and pragmatic levels, also tells us whether he or she has nativelike competence in the language or whether the language has been acquired later in life.

The clinician, when talking to the child and observing the child speak, must be able to consider all 3 domains and tell whether the child uses speech and language appropriately and whether the youngster adheres to the rules of social communication.

The clinician must assess the child's linguistic behaviors in their own right. A youngster's linguistic behaviors during a clinical interaction provide a picture of his or her linguistic strengths and weaknesses and are indicators for linguistic intervention planning when problems are identified. In addition, language is also the primary vehicle through which a variety of information essential to the assessment process is passed between child and clinician and for which all 3 domains, speech, language, and social communication, provide major clues.

Careful listening to the speech, language, and communication characteristics of the child helps the interviewer tune in to the youngster's state of mind. These characteristics assist the clinician in formulating an overall clinical assessment and help to interpret the patient's cognitive state, mood and affect, as well as orientation, judgment, and reasoning. For example, the type and speed of linguistic response provide the clinician with clues about a youngster's cognitive and emotional state. A cognitively delayed youngster may have a slower linguistic response, one that also may be different in quality from that of a youngster with superior cognitive function. Similarly, a depressed youngster may be slow in linguistic response, and the briefness of responses may show a lack of interest in the interaction.

The youngster's linguistic behavior also can provide the clinician with information about memory and recall abilities. For example, recalling events in time and space can provide clues on the youngster's memory. The clinician also can observe the youngster's ability to formulate and understand abstract ideas and metaphors and to draw inferences from what is said. Clues on mood and affect are provided through observations of verbal, vocal, and nonverbal communication. All these observations take place simultaneously, and all provide building blocks in the clinical assessment.

In interaction with the child, the clinician observes the child's speech: articulation, voice quality, modulation and pitch, fluency and response time; the child's language: vocabulary choice and grammatical structure (use of simple and complex sentences, negatives and questions); and the child's nonverbal and verbal social communication: eye contact, facial expression, body posture and gestures, and appropriateness of verbalization, and turn-taking behavior. The clinician takes note of whether nonverbal and verbal communication are in agreement or send conflicting messages to the listener, and whether speech, language, and communication are age appropriate.

The clinician also must watch for possible neurological signs in the child's or adolescent's responses and interactions. For example, if the child gropes for words or is inconsistent in the pattern of articulation of words, there may be a verbal apraxia, a motor speech impairment (Hodge, 1994).

Intact language function helps establish rapport between clinician and child and develops the natural rhythm of the interview. Language delay or dysfunction may hamper and/or interfere with both as well as with the overall ease with which the clinician-child interaction takes place. The language-delayed or impaired child or adolescent may become more stressed than the subject matter warrants and may have difficulty responding to the finer points of the interview, or may not be able to respond adequately to the social cues provided by the interviewer. Such a child also may be self-conscious about his or her linguistic disability and refuse to talk or become silly in his interactions. The youngster may have developed personal strategies in order to give the impression that his or her communication is adequate.

Language-impaired children or adolescents may have developed verbal and nonverbal mannerisms that may make it appear as if the interview flows smoothly. The youngsters may provide continuation gestures, such as nodding the head or shrugging the shoulders, and continuation indicators, such as "hm-hm, yeah," as part of a response to signal the clinician to continue to speak. By echoing the clinician's questions in the affirmative or negative or with slight modification, the youngsters may appear to be in command of their verbalizations. By refusing to yield the floor or by abrupt topic changes, language-impaired children may try to redirect the interview to more familiar ground in an attempt to take command of the situation and relieve the stress experienced because of the linguistic disability. The children's responses may be abrupt due to an inability to make a smooth transition from one topic to another, and the connections between what is said may not be self-evident to the clinician. Furthermore, there may be a lack of clarity in their response because of difficulty with finding the right word or difficulty with auditory processing, or referencing problems. Word-finding problems reveal themselves through the youngsters' groping for words,

long hesitations, and using almost, but not the right, word as well as reformulations.

Auditory language processing refers to the ability to process language taken in through the auditory channel. It covers such phenomena as discrimination, identification, speed of processing, and short-term memory for spoken language (Kelly, 1995; Stark & Bernstein, 1984). Auditory language processing should not be confused with the understanding or auditory comprehension of language. *Language comprehension* refers to the ability to interpret and make sense of spoken and written language (Miller & Paul, 1995). The clinician must suspect auditory processing problems if children do not respond to the whole question but only to a part or a word within the question in the presence of apparently normal language comprehension for their age level. Youngsters also may have auditory processing problems if they cannot respond to serial 2- or 3-step commands, or do not remember all verbally presented objects in a series, or are unable to repeat longer and more complex sentences, as expected for their chronological age. Referencing problems may reveal themselves when youngsters use only noun forms or only pronoun forms, or when plural forms are used to refer to singular forms (Haliday & Hasan, 1976). Temporal relationships may be disturbed or jumbled, and word order may be reversed. New topics may be introduced without sufficient backgrounding. In telling a story or recounting an event, there may be difficulties in the sequential ordering of the beginning, middle, and end of a story. Language-impaired children or adolescents also may lack the linguistic flexibility to express themselves. They may have a limited vocabulary and not be able to reformulate ideas and may have difficulties with synonyms, the multiple meanings of words, word choice, and shades of meaning (Wiig & Semel, 1984).

Assessing patients' cognitive processes, orientation, insight, and judgment is more difficult when language is delayed or impaired. Youngsters' underlying problems with abstract language and social communication may affect the clinician's assessment of their judgment and orientation. A major question that the clinician must keep in mind is whether youngsters understand or process auditorily all that is said in the clinical interaction and whether they have the expressive linguistic capability to cooperate fully with the clinician. Therefore, the preparation for the clinical interaction itself becomes essential for adequate linguistic assessment of the child.

Obtaining an Adequate Language Sample

INTERVIEW STRATEGIES

In order to assess linguistic skills of youngsters, the clinician must obtain an adequate sample of their language. From a linguistic perspective, 50 to 100 utterances or a half-hour of verbal interaction with the youngsters is considered an absolute minimum (Hubbell, 1988; Miller, 1981).

Because the clinician has to interact with and observe the youngsters and interpret their linguistic behaviors, audio or video recording of the interaction for later replay and analysis is recommended for greater accuracy of assessment.

Children and adolescents may have intervening behaviors such as hyperactivity, distractibility, poor attention span, a low frustration tolerance, behavior problems such as oppositionality, and emotional problems such as high anxiety or depressed mood. They also may have developmental inadequacies or physical problems, such as a cognitive delay or a hearing impairment. All of these factors may make it more difficult to collect an adequate language sample. Similar difficulties may arise with youths who are language delayed or impaired. To reward and ensure adequate cooperation, it may be important to use reinforcers in the form of social praise or food and allowing children to engage in a favorite activity or play with a favorite toy. It may be a good idea to include the mother in the interaction when a child has difficulty separating from the mother and in order to maximize language output. The mother's interaction with the child may be a useful cross-check on the linguistic skills the child exhibited with the clinician. Observation of children's linguistic interaction with siblings or other children also can provide important information about their level of linguistic functioning. Accuracy of assessment of linguistic functioning improves when the clinician takes into consideration youngsters' language un-

der different conditions and with different speakers. Obtaining a sample in multiple environments (e.g., clinic, play, school, and home) is useful to assure the accuracy of the assessment. In young children, language often accompanies play and other activities, even when the children do not interact with another person. Observations of what children say at this time is informative to the clinician.

In order to collect a sufficient language sample from younger children, it is useful to introduce a variety of age-appropriate activities and toys. Pictures also can be helpful for eliciting language samples. Pictures should illustrate a variety of objects, actions, and activities to which children can relate. Another way to elicit a language sample in somewhat older children is to tell them a story and then have them repeat the story back or draw a picture and talk about it. It is useful if the clinician focuses on the "here" and "now" with young children—what they see and experience during the time of the clinical interaction. This is particularly important with children who may be language impaired. Visual stimulation provided to children of any age, such as pictures, will assist the clinician in assessing their linguistic skills.

A sufficient language sample from youngsters with better language skills may be obtained by asking about a favorite movie, TV show, video game, or book. Another way to elicit language is in the context of a pretend activity, such as talking on the phone, baking a cake, or asking children how to spend a million dollars, what they would do if they were president, or asking directly what makes them sad, happy, or angry.

Children with language impairment tend to do more poorly on listening to auditory questions alone. They do better when questions are supported by visual stimuli, such as pictures or objects.

Activities that require joint attention are important for both younger and older children. As with younger children, the activities used with older ones should be appropriate to their developmental age. Such activities should require sufficient language interaction between them and the clinician. For example, a game of checkers does not require a lot of language interaction, whereas the game 20 Questions does.

The verbal interaction alone between the clinician and youngster may be a good starting point to assess their linguistic skills (Miller & Paul, 1995; Shipley & McAfee, 1992; Stewart & Cash, 1991).

When collecting a language sample, regardless of children's ages, the clinician should use open-ended questions and avoid questions requiring a yes or no response. When interacting with children, the clinician must take into account their age, linguistic level, and auditory processing capacity. For example, a 3-year-old youngster will understand "what," "who," and "where" questions, asking for or about things, persons, and places. A 3-year-old will not understand "when" and "why" questions, asking about temporal and causal relationships (Miller & Paul, 1995). He or she also will have a short auditory language processing capacity. Therefore, long and complex sentences may not be fully understood or processed. In interacting with youngsters, the clinician must adapt language behavior to that of the children, taking into account the children's ages, what they are expected to understand, and their auditory processing capacity.

One of the things that makes an interview complicated is that the clinician has to assess language productions as well as language comprehension. Children's level of language production is roughly, but not totally, equivalent to their language comprehension. In the early years, language comprehension generally precedes production by about 6 months. Therefore, normally developing children generally are able to understand slightly more than they are able to produce (Miller & Paul, 1995).

TECHNIQUES TO ASSESS LANGUAGE SKILLS

Language Expression: The clinician can assess language production in young children in several ways (Gleason, 1989; Miller, 1981):

1. By counting and averaging the morphemes or words that occur in an utterance based on a language sample of 50 to 100 or more utterances. (Morphemes are the smallest meaningful units of a language and include words, but also grammatical markers, such as plural markers. A word such as "apple-s" will have 2 morphemes—apple and the plural morpheme /-s/).
2. By repeating short sentences and linguistic analysis of the sentences produced. Both of these tech-

niques will provide the approximate age level of the child.
3. A third way is to linguistically analyze the language sample collected using 1 of 3 techniques, the averaging technique, the repetition technique, or formal linguistic analysis.

When using the *averaging technique,* certain restrictions apply to averaging morpheme or word counts; for example, repetitions, stereotypic utterances, and yes/no responses are not counted. Thus a child, with sentence length varying from 1 to 6 words and a total of 175 words distributed over 50 utterances, should have an average word count for all sentences of 3.5 words. This places the child roughly at the level expected for a 3-year-old. A 5-year-old youngster producing an average of 3.5 words has not achieved his or her chronological age level. This averaging technique has shown that up to about 5 years of age, the average word or morpheme count in the normal child roughly corresponds with chronological age. Thus a mean length of utterance of 1.0 to 2.5 morphemes corresponds to a developmental level of 8 to 24 months; and a mean length of utterance (MLU) of 2.5 to 4.5 morphemes corresponds to a developmental level of 24 to 60 months; and an MLU of 4.5 morphemes and up represents a developmental level between 5 to 10 years. Different stages of lexical and grammatical development are associated with each of these stages, as is discussed later.

Because repetition has been shown to reflect level of language skill in normal children, the way children repeat an utterance represents their expressive level of language development (Gleason, 1989; Wiig & Semel, 1984). Thus when a child repeats "baby eat cookie" to the clinician's modeling "the baby is eating a cookie," the child's response reveals his or her productive language level. The clinician must keep in mind that a repetition technique requires more than 1 utterance for repetition, since consistency strengthens the assessment (Gleason, 1989; Wiig & Semel, 1984). The repetition technique uses linguistic complexities or levels associated with the child's developmental stages of expressive language.

Language production also can be assessed by using language sampling as just described and identifying the types and levels of grammatical structures, morphological markers, and type and range of vocabulary used. In this *formal linguistic analysis,* the sample is then compared to what is expected for the chronological and/or mental age of the child (Miller, 1981).

While the averaging and the repetition techniques can provide us with a child's developmental level (i.e., normal or delayed), these techniques do not tell us whether the child has normal or deviant grammatical development. For example, the child may have consistent problems with word order in a sentence. This is an indication that the youngster's expressive language is deviant despite an age-appropriate mean length of utterance.

The quality of the language sample obtained ultimately depends on the rapport between the interlocutor and the child and the skill of the interlocutor to engage the child, including the types of activities used and the types of questions asked.

Language Comprehension: Often it is possible to judge whether the child has understood the speaker by analyzing the child's verbal or "action" response. But it is also easy to think of situations where a listener may give an apparently appropriate response although little or no understanding has occurred. While it seems more straightforward to assess language production in the clinical interaction, assessing the child's language comprehension is more difficult without the use of standardized or formal measures. Children may rely on the nonlinguistic context or only small aspects of what is said to provide a response. Even though children appear to demonstrate comprehension, it is difficult to know what aspect of the communication they are responding to. For example, when the clinician asks a child to give him the shoe, in a series of 3 items, with an outstretched hand, the child may respond to the outstretched hand with the object closest in proximity. When assessing the child's comprehension, the clinician also must be aware of differences in comprehension of literal versus implied meanings. Miller and Paul (1995) present an example in which a 4-year-old is asked when he is supposed to go home. The child's lack of comprehension as seen from the response indicated that the child actually did not know the concept of time and, therefore, could not produce an adequate answer. The child did not know the actual time and furthermore did not understand the implied meaning, which was that it was time for him to go home. There are basically 2 types of language impairment in children, impairment of only

language production and impairment of both language production and comprehension. In only a small number of cases is there impairment in comprehension only. Assessing the child's level of language comprehension is important since it will affect the intervention strategies chosen. Assessment procedures will vary depending on the child's age.

Children at the emerging language stage, between 8 and 24 months, understand very little of the language spoken to them. At this level the clinician should try to assess whether children understand any labels for objects and any action words and whether they understand words only in the context of familiar routines. A minimum of 2 or 3 correct responses should be elicited to ascertain whether children really understand what is heard. Also, can the children identify objects only within view or out of sight? The clinician should use familiar objects in the assessment process, such as toys, familiar clothing, eating utensils, names of familiar persons. For children between 18 and 24 months, person, object, and action words combined to express the following semantic relations should be presented: possessor-possession (i.e., Mommy's shoes); action-object (i.e., kiss the baby); agent-action with the child as the agent (e.g., Briana, eat); agent-action-object (i.e., Briana, drink your milk). Natural behavioral compliance and familiar routines and joint reference activity are suggested. In conversation a minimum of 10 to 15 minutes are necessary to interact with children in order to assess their age-appropriate comprehension of social communication and whether they understand the conversational obligation to correspond.

During the early period—ages 2 to 3½ years— of the 2- to 5-year age range, some additional and new options become available. Children also can be asked to answer questions, point to pictures, and manipulate objects. During the later stage (3½ years to 5 years), question-answer exchange with and without toy manipulation, pretend play, story retelling, and picture pointing tasks should all be used for assessment of children's comprehension.

From age 2 and up until the age of 4, picture pointing tasks may be unreliable, however. Several responses must be elicited to be sure that the response is stable and not correct by chance. Children may be asked to manipulate toys in the context of "show me" (e.g., show me "the baby is drinking milk" in the context of toy manipulation). The clinician also may ask children to act out agent-action combinations (e.g., show me: horse eat, cow drink, doll come, horse run, doll eat) and agent-action-object combinations (e.g., doll kiss dog, horse eat sugar, doll push cup, horse hit cup). Comprehension testing for prepositions, such as "in," "on," "under" for the younger group and "behind," "in front of," and "beside" for the older group should be added. While the prepositions "in," "on," and "under" are understood by 50 to 85% of children at 30 months of age, most children do not comprehend "in front of" and "beside" until 42 months of age. The assessment also should include asking questions of the children. In assessing comprehension, the clinician may want to use requests using familiar vocabulary. For 2- to 3-year-olds, "yes/no," "what," "what (X) doing," "where (place)," and "where (direction)" are developmentally appropriate questions. Starting with the age of 3, "whose," "who," "why," and "how many" questions should be included. Starting with 4 years, "how," "how much," "how long" (duration), and "how far" are appropriate questions. Starting at about 4½ years, "how often" and "when" questions are appropriate.

Toward the end of the later period (3½ to 5 years), word order as a grammatical clue in English also becomes increasingly understood. Word order is important, for example, in understanding the difference in meaning between "the baby kisses the daddy" and "the daddy kisses the baby." Because word order becomes a primary clue, declarative sentences such as "the boy pushes the girl" and passive constructions such as "the boy is pushed by the girl" may be interpreted to be identical in meaning. At this level children understand their obligation to speak when spoken to in a conversational setting. Children begin to maintain a topic by the age of 3½ to 4 years, and politeness forms in conversation gradually emerge between the ages of 4 and 8 years of age.

SPECIFIC GUIDELINES FOR ASSESSING THE DEVELOPMENTAL LEVEL OF EXPRESSIVE AND RECEPTIVE LANGUAGE

The developmental levels discussed here crosscut or dovetail with the preceding and provide more specific information about the child's expected language levels.

Developmental Level 7–12 Months: Between the ages of 7 and 12 months, infants have an expressive vocabulary of 1 to 3 words and use a songlike intonation pattern when babbling and babbling. The babbling includes a large variety of sounds. Children understand "no" and "hot" and respond to simple question intonation. They understand and respond to their names and recognize words for common items such as "cup," "shoe," and "juice," and also begin to understand simple commands.

Developmental Level 13–18 Months: Between the ages of 13 to 18 months (MLU 1.0) children have an expressive vocabulary of 3 to 20 words, mostly nouns. They also begin to use intonation patterns and repeat sound combinations, combine gestures and vocalizations, and make requests for more of desired items. Receptively, children follow simple commands and identify 1 to 3 body parts. At 15 months children can be expected to have a receptive vocabulary of 50 words and at 18 months a vocabulary of 100 to 150 words.

Developmental Level 19–24 Months: Between 19 to 24 months (MLU 1.5 to 2.5), children's expressive vocabulary can be expected to grow to between 50 and 100 words. Children are expected to name a few familiar objects accurately. At this stage, children use true words more frequently than jargon. During this time, they also begin to combine nouns and verbs and begin to use pronouns. Although there is unstable voice control, children may use appropriate intonation for questions. Receptively, children have a vocabulary of 300 or more words, can answer "what's that?" questions, knows 5 body parts, and enjoys listening to stories.

Developmental Level 2–3 Years: Between 2 and 3 years (MLU 2.5 to 3.5), children are able to ask 1- and 2-word questions and use 3- and 4-word sentences. Children can request items by name and use words that are general. Their expressive vocabulary is between 50 and 250 words. They also use some prepositions, articles, present progressive verbs, regular plurals, contractions, and irregular past tense forms, and also are able to use some regular past tense verbs, possessive morphemes, pronouns, and imperatives. Their sentences exhibit multiple grammatical errors, primarily because of omissions of function words and morphological markers.

Receptively, children understand "one" and "all," identify several body parts, point to pictures in a book when named, follow simple commands, answer simple questions, and enjoy listening to short stories and rhymes. Children have a receptive vocabulary of 500 to 900 words and understand the general gist of most things said.

Developmental Level 3–4 Years: (MLU 3.0/3.5–4.0/4.5). Between the ages of 3 and 4 years, children frequently ask questions and demand details. They also use sentences 4 to 5 and even 6 words in length, and use nouns and verbs most frequently. They start to use "is," "are," and "am" in sentences appropriately. They ask questions using "who," "what," and "where" as well as "why." Children can tell 2 events in chronological order and engage in long conversations, and have an expressive vocabulary of between 800 to 1,500 words. Sentence grammar improves, although some errors may still occur.

At this stage, children also use language to express emotion; they begin to manipulate peers and adults through the use of language and can produce simple verbal analogies.

Receptively, children understand object functions and differences in meaning between such concepts as "come-go," "in-on," "big-little." They are able to answer simple questions—who, what, where, as well as why (although without fully understanding why-responses). Children are also conscious of past and future, and have a receptive vocabulary of between 1,200 to 2,000 words.

Developmental Level 4–5 Years: (MLU 4.5/5.0 and 5.0 and up) Between the ages of 4 and 5 years, expressive vocabulary has grown to between 900 to 2,000 or more words. Children make sentences of 4 to 8 words and up, ask for word definitions, and have grammatically correct sentences. They also are able to count to 10 by rote and use language to talk about experiences at school, at friends' homes, and the like. The 4- to 5-year old also can accurately tell a long story and use some irregular plurals, possessive pronouns, future tense, reflexive pronouns, and comparative morphemes in sentences.

Receptively, children understand the concept of number up to 3, begin understanding spatial concepts, and recognize 1 to 3 colors. They an-

swer questions about function as well as more complex 2-part questions and enjoy rhymes, rhythms, and nonsense syllables. Their receptive vocabulary should be 2,800 words or more, and they understand word order cues to sentence comprehension. Youngsters also are able to pay attention to a story and answer questions about it.

Developmental Level 5–6 Years: At this developmental level, youngsters can name 6 basic colors and 3 basic shapes, and can ask "how" questions. They can use past tense and future tense appropriately and conjunctions such as "and" and "but," can name opposites, and sequentially name the days of the week. Children also can understand passive constructions and word order cues as well as "when" questions. Youngsters should be able to count to 30 by rote. Surprisingly, sentence lengths may be reduced to between 4 to 6 words, although expressive vocabulary continues to increase drastically. Youngsters use language to exchange information and ask questions, sentences show detail, and stories are accurately relayed. At this stage children use accurate grammar in most cases. Communication with adults and other children is done with ease.

Receptively, children can follow instructions given to a group as well as 3-step commands. Their receptive vocabulary should be about 13,000 words.

Developmental Level 6–7 Years: Between 6 and 7 years of age, youngsters use most morphological markers (past tense, etc.) appropriately, have a sentence length of approximately 6 words, and use the passive voice appropriately. Children can count to 100 by rote; name some letters, numbers, and currencies; recite the alphabet, and sequence numbers. They also are able to engage in different types of conversation and use increasingly more complex descriptions.

Receptively children understand "left" and "right" and the content of a conversation to which they are a partner. At this stage children should understand most concepts of time (Miller & Paul, 1995; Shipley & McAfee, 1992).

MODIFICATION OF INTERVIEW STRATEGIES

Awareness of possible disturbances in speech, language, and communication may allow the clinician to change interview strategies more readily

701

and adjust his or her own language to the level of that of the child in order to be better understood and facilitate rapport. For example, a language-delayed child may not understand certain concepts used by the interviewer. The clinician must be prepared to reformulate questions keeping in mind the potential level of the child's disability. A language-impaired youngster may need more help or time to express himself. Also, the clinician may have to simplify his or her vocabulary and sentence structure and also may have to speak more slowly or repeat questions.

When communicating with a hard-of-hearing child, knowledge of sign language is useful. Deaf interpreters also may be used to facilitate a clinical interaction. The presence of a significant other, familiar with the child's speech pattern, may be useful. When an interview is conducted with a hard-of-hearing child, it is useful to signal before speaking. Body space should be reduced. The interviewer's speech should be at a normal rate. The interviewer should face the child so that the child has access to all of the verbal and nonverbal aspects of speaking (Estabrook, 1994).

Recognizing Speech, Language, and Communication Impairment and Associated Conditions

RECOGNIZING SPEECH IMPAIRMENT

Speech impairment includes impairment in articulation, fluency, prosody, and voice. It also includes apraxia and dysarthria. An apraxia of speech is a disturbance in the motor patterns of speech resulting from neurological damage and an inability voluntarily to select, direct, organize, and/or sequence the speech musculature. It is characterized by an inability to execute volitional (purposeful) movements despite normal muscle tone and coordination (Hodge, 1994; Rosenbeck, 1985). Dysarthria represents a group of speech disorders that result from the disruption of the motor patterns of speech due to paralysis, weakness, or incoordination of the speech musculature (Rosenbeck & LaPointe, 1985).

Recognizing Articulation Impairment: The clinician must ask whether a youngster has adequate use of the sounds of the language and whether the child combines them into words in an age-appropriate fashion.

A delay or impairment in articulation is recognizable by the production of speech sounds that is inaccurate or delayed compared with that of other speakers of the same dialect at the same age level (Creaghead, Newman, & Secord, 1989; Stoel-Gammon & Dunn, 1985). The earliest sounds developmentally are the nasals /m, n, and ng/, voiced stops /b, d, g/ and some continuants /h, w/, followed by voiceless stops /p, t, k/, followed by additional continuants /f, y/, which should be present by 3½ years of age. Sounds that may not be present earlier but are still within the normal range of development by the age of 4 to 6 years are the continuants /r, l, and s/. Sounds that can be expected to develop still later, between the ages of 4½ to 6 or even 7 years, are the sibilants /ch, sh, z/ and even later /j, v/, and voiced and voiceless /th/. The production of sound clusters such as /spl/ or /str/ in English as well as placement of sounds within a word—whether word initially, medially, or finally—are all developmental aspects of speech sound production.

General signs of faulty articulation include omissions, substitutions, additions, or distortions of speech sounds. The clinician must observe whether these occur. Are there reversals of speech sounds in a word? Is intelligibility poor? Does the youngster have slurred speech (dysarthria), or is there inaccurate and/or inconsistent repetition of words (apraxia)? Frequent otitis media and/or hearing loss also may compromise articulation and other features of speech. The most frequent cause for articulation problems is a specific developmental speech delay. Articulation errors tend to decrease as children mature. When problems occur, these should be analyzed for delay or deviance or both. Problems in articulation are the most frequent in the general child population. It is not to be confused with a foreign accent, nor does it imply a language disorder (Bernthal & Bankson, 1988). Dysarthria and apraxia are specific neurological conditions affecting motor speech and articulation. Apraxia of speech occurs with reasonably high frequency in children (Creaghead et al., 1989; Love, 1992).

Specific Signs Associated with Apraxia: When an apraxia is present, the child generally misarticulates words and the number of misarticulations

702

increases as word length and sentence length increase. While misarticulations occur in both consonants and vowels, sounds in word initial position are affected more than in the middle of a word or word finally. The most frequent type of misarticulations are sound substitutions, omissions, syllable transpositions, and reductions of motorically complex words. The child can be observed to struggle with words, a struggle that becomes greater with longer words and sentences. The child may misarticulate the same word differently on 2 different occasions. One of the hallmarks of a verbal apraxia therefore is the variable nature of the production of the same word. When the clinician attempts to model a word, the child generally is also unsuccessful in repeating the model. Another indicator is that automatic and overused speech are produced better than creative speech. Further, the child is conscious of his or her disability. Apraxia of speech can occur with an oral apraxia, an inability to execute nonspeech–related motor movements volutionally, and less commonly with a limb apraxia (Hodge, 1994).

Specific Signs Associated with Dysarthria: Articulation errors, consist primarily of omissions and distortions, are the most common features of dysarthria, followed by impairments of voice, resonance, and fluency. Consonant production is consistently imprecise, and vowels may be neutralized. Voice also may be affected, and sound hyper- or hyponasal or breathy or harsh. There also may be excessive variation in pitch and loudness or insufficient variation in pitch or loudness, as well as an excess of stress, equal stress, or reduced stress. Furthermore, depending on which system is involved, there may be short rushes of speech as well as long pauses (Darley, Aronson, & Brown, 1975).

Specific Signs Associated with a Hearing Problem: The clinician must ask him- or herself whether the characteristics of speech and articulation observed may suggest a possible hearing loss. A youngster with fluctuating hearing loss due to chronic otitis media will have a delay in speech development, including the development of sounds. The clinician may be able to identify a hearing loss as well as its severity from the child's articulatory pattern and the nonverbal communicative behavior. The faulty pattern of articulation in hearing-impaired youngsters is consistent, since they cannot produce the sounds that they cannot hear. Children with a mild hearing loss (25–40 decibels) miss many specific consonant sounds /f, s, th, z, v, p, h, g, k, ch, sh/. Youngsters with a moderate hearing loss (40–65 decibels) can hear no speech at normal loudness levels and have a speech language delay with deviant articulation and language patterns. Children with a severe hearing loss (65–95 decibels) will have a severe aural-oral speech-language handicap. When hearing loss is profound (more than 90 decibels), the voice and speech sound like that of a deaf person, with features of loudness, pitch, resonance, and articulation as well as language seriously compromised. The clinician should look for distortions, substitutions, and omissions that characterize the articulatory pattern of hearing-impaired children. Most hard-of-hearing children have less difficulty with vowel perception. Consonants have higher-frequency components than vowels and are more difficult to discriminate perceptually. The most common errors are consonants that differ by place of articulation, such as /b,d,g/ and /p,t,k/. These errors are more frequent with consonants in word-final position since sounds in that position are acoustically weaker. Deaf and hard-of-hearing children have less difficulties perceiving voicing, nasality, and manner of articulation. Characteristics such as high pitch, nasal resonance, or a voice that is too loud or too soft also may be an indication of a hearing loss (Stoker & Ling, 1992; Wolk & Schilbroth, 1986).

Disorders of articulation can occur independently or in association with developmental language disorders. In young children, speech disorders frequently co-occur with language impairments. They are likely to occur with any type of psychiatric condition. Articulation also may be delayed or impaired, however, as part of a general cognitive delay. The presence and severity of articulation disorders increase with severity of cognitive delay. While most articulation problems in children cannot be associated directly with an organic or physical problem, faulty articulation occurs with structural abnormalities, such as dental problems, cleft palate or cleft lip, sensory deficits such as a hearing loss, other cranial nerve involvement, or other central nervous system dysfunction.

A verbal apraxia can occur independently or with an oral apraxia and less frequently with a limb apraxia. Children with a verbal apraxia usually demonstrate normal hearing, adequate intelligence, possible use of gestural language, and a lack of demonstrable oral motor weakness, and paralysis or incoordination of the speech musculature to account for the delay in speech-language development. Children usually are aware of their disability.

When dysarthria is present, there also tends to be difficulty with voluntary and involuntary motor acts such as swallowing, chewing, and licking. It differs significantly from apraxia and also from aphasia, the loss of language skills through neurological disease or trauma. Dysarthria may involve lower or upper motor neurons, the cerebellar system, or the extrapyramidal system (Rosenbek & LaPointe, 1985).

Some common conditions and causes associated with a hearing loss include childhood diseases such as measles, mumps, chicken pox, and meningitis. Infections accompanied by a high fever can damage the hearing system at any age. A child's hearing can be damaged before birth—for example, as a result of certain diseases contracted by the mother or ototoxic drugs taken by her during pregnancy. A blow to the head or exposure to excessive noise can physically damage the hearing structures. Certain inherited characteristics can make a person more susceptible to diseases and defects of the ear and hearing system. Children with Treacher Collins syndrome, Goldenhar syndrome, and Waardenburg syndrome may suffer a hearing loss. There are more than 150 types of genetic deafness. Other causes include syphilis or anoxia contracted during birth delivery, presbycusis associated with the effects of aging, Meniere's disease, a unilateral disease characterized by vertigo (dizziness), and tinnitus (noise in the ear) (Northern & Downs, 1991).

Recognizing Fluency Impairment: Fluency is a speech pattern that is rhythmic and smooth. Dysfluencies are disruptions or breaks in the smooth flow of speech. The clinician has to observe the fluency aspect of speech. What is the youngster's fluency like? Impairment in fluency exists when there is a disruption in the smooth flow of speech. Dysfluency is also a phenomenon in normal language acquisition. For example, children between 2 and 4 years of age may exhibit repetitions of speech, especially with first syllables but also with the pronoun "I." Children also may repeat their own sentences, and exhibit hesitations often associated with disturbed breathing and facial grimacing. In normal language development, dysfluencies steadily decrease after the age of 4 (Adams, 1980; Shipley & McAfee, 1992).

Impairment in fluency can be recognized from repetitions or prolongations of words or sounds, hesitations or pauses within or between utterances. There also may be repetitions of parts of or whole utterances. Such problems are also referred to as stuttering. Youngsters may have apparent difficulties with saying some words or may avoid specific words. There may be long latencies before responding as well as secondary characteristics, such as facial grimacing. Children also may have other fluency problems, such as speaking too slowly or too fast or speaking with an uneven rhythm. There may also be starts into false patterns and reformulations of sentences.

Rapid rate of speech can be associated with intoxication, compulsive thinking as well as psychosis, schizophrenia, or mania (pressure of speech). Revisions and reformulations are associated with apparent deficits in cognitive-linguistic planning and are seen in pervasive developmental disorders, schizophrenia, and schizotypal personality disorder as well as in bipolar disorder. However, this type of fluency problem also can be seen in children with attention deficit hyperactivity, where speech productions sometimes appear fragmented. Long latencies that disturb the rhythmic flow of speech often are associated with depression. Fluency also is affected by word-finding difficulties, by an apraxia of speech, and in dysarthric speech. Fluency problems in young children often are associated with anxiety disorders as well as with family dysfunction (Adams, 1980; Baltaxe, 1997; Cantwell & Baker, 1991).

Organic as well as environmental theories as to the etiology of stuttering have been suggested. Organic theories include those associated with defective cerebral dominance for language; problems with interhemispheric processing; defective neural control for speech; and genetic predisposition. Environmental theories include those associated with conditioned response including avoidance behavior, with conditioned response secondary to anxiety, and with anticipatory struggle, that is, with stuttering as a response to tension and fragmentation.

Although generally no obvious physical reasons are found for problems in fluency, they may be related to neurological disorders and central nervous system dysfunction. Problems in fluency also may be genetic or familial (Starkweather, 1987).

Recognizing Prosodic Impairment: Impairment in prosody relates to impairment in the melody of speech or intonation. When assessing prosody, the clinician must consider the child's sentence intonation and word stress pattern, whether he speaks in a monotone or with exaggerated intonation. The clinician also must consider whether the youngster can express himself emotionally through intonation and the pitch of voice. Can he express anger, joy, surprise, and sadness through intonation? Child also should be able to interpret the expression of emotions in the speech of others. Anger is expressed through overloudness and wider excursions of the loudness parameter in the speech melody, sadness through a narrowed pitch range and some lengthening in duration of speech, and happiness through larger pitch excursions and a widened pitch range (Baltaxe, 1991; Scherer, 1981a, b; Williams & Stevens, 1981).

While stress and sentence intonation are directly observable from children's speech, emotional tone may be more difficult to assess. One way for the clinician to approach assessing emotional tone is through role playing, telling a story that has emotional content, or asking children to describe a picture with emotional content. For example, in order to elicit angry intonation, the clinician might show the child a picture of a woman scolding a dog that has soiled a rug and then ask the child what he would say under these circumstances. Similarly, showing the youngster a picture of a girl opening a present with an expression of happiness or surprise on her face, or a picture of a car crashed against a tree, may help to elicit intonation indicating surprise, happiness, or sadness.

A problem with prosody may be present when the child's pitch range is consistently too narrow or too wide, and loudness patterns associated with intonation and stress are consistently exaggerated. Disturbances in the rhythmic pattern of speech also indicate problems with prosody. A prosodic problem also exists when the youngster's speech prosody does not signal emotional expression or coloring or when prosody is incongruent with verbal content. Also, the youngster may not understand the emotions as they are expressed in the prosodic patterns of others.

In psychiatric practice, problems with prosody

are an important parameter. For example, an adolescent with autism may be unable to produce adequate prosodic contouring of words and sentences. Word stress may not be present or may be misplaced. All syllables in a word may receive equal stress or no stress at all. Similarly, sentence stress and intonation patterns may not differentiate statements from questions. The autistic child's pitch range may be narrowed or her speech overloud. In addition, the child may have problems with the durational characteristics of the prosodic contour, and her words and sentences may be either too long or too short. Further, the child may not understand the secondary meanings expressed through intonation. This may critically affect her understanding of what is said. The adolescent going through a major depressive episode may show a slowing of speech rhythm and a narrowed pitch range as well as insufficient loudness, while during a manic episode an adolescent with bipolar disorder may have exaggerated excursions of pitch as well as loudness (Baltaxe & Simmons, 1985). A monotonous voice (narrow pitch range) can be associated with depression, schizophrenia and, autism, while deficits in word, sentence, and emphatic stress, and lack of prosodic emotional coloring are seen in autism and, schizophrenia (Alpert, 1981; Baltaxe & Simmons, 1985; Darby, 1981).

Although the relationship of prosody to brain function is complex, prosodic functions appear broadly related to the right hemisphere (Monrad-Krohn, 1957). An adolescent with a right-hemisphere lesion may have a narrowed pitch range and be unable to produce or understand pitch patterns that characterize sentence intonation and emotions.

Recognizing Voice Impairment: A problem with voice is characterized by deviations in voice quality, pitch, loudness, and/or resonance (Aronson, 1985; Boone & McFarlane, 1988). In assessing children's voices, the clinician also needs to assess youngsters' vocal characteristics. The clinician must observe whether the voice is nasal, breathy, hoarse, or creaky and whether the child has excessive glottal fry and consistently speaks overly loud or overly low (whisper). The clinician also should consider whether youngsters have normal habitual pitch for gender or age, or if it is always too high or too low.

When the vocal quality in speech production is

harsh, breathy, hoarse, creaky, or has excessive glottal fry, voice quality is impaired. Hypo- or hypernasal speech is a sign of impaired voice resonance. A habitual pitch that is too high or too low, or frequent pitch breaks, indicates a pitch problem. Similarly, a voice that is too loud (more than 86 decibels) compared to normal amplitude (76 decibels) or speech produced at too low an amplitude (less than 46 decibels) or whispered indicates that vocal behavior needs attention (Wilson, 1987).

An abnormally loud voice may be associated with angry mood, emphatic speech, intoxication, disinhibition, mania, or autism. A soft or low voice may be associated with anxiety or depression. A whispered voice—a normal use of voice often associated with secretiveness—also can occur with autism and types of schizophrenia as well as laryngitis and vocal cord pathology. A high-pitched voice may be associated with fetal alcohol syndrome, autism, or a hysteric personality disorder (Alpert, 1981; Baltaxe & Simmons, 1985; Boone & McFarlane, 1988; Darby, 1981).

Youngsters' voices may be altered because they have vocal nodules or contact ulcers, due to vocal strain and abuse. Voice also may be impaired due to endocrine disorders, structural abnormalities such as nasal obstruction and velopharyngeal insufficiency, a hearing impairment, neurological disorders such as vocal cord paralysis, and tumors of the larynx. Pitch and/or volume that is too low or too high may be indicators of physical and psychiatric conditions (Boone & McFarlane, 1988).

Velopharyngeal insufficiency is associated with "cleft palate" speech. Inadequate velopharyngeal closure characterizes nasal speech. Nasality in speech may indicate hearing loss. A hearing problem also can be signaled by habitual pitch that is too low or too high, or a voice that is too loud or not loud enough (Love, 1992).

RECOGNIZING LANGUAGE AND AUDITORY LANGUAGE PROCESSING IMPAIRMENT

To assess language competence, the clinician must analyze the child's vocabulary and grammatical skills. Are they age appropriate? Are there features relating to vocabulary or grammar that are not age appropriate at any age?

Language function can be delayed or impaired in the comprehension and use of the semantic and grammatical structures necessary to express ideas. In youngsters who have reached 6 to 8 years of age, language problems can include problems in the use abstract language. Auditory language processing is a language-related problem. *Auditory language processing* refers to the ability to process language taken in through the auditory channel. It covers such phenomena as discrimination, identification, speed of processing, and short-term memory for spoken language (Kelly, 1995; Stark & Bernstein, 1984).

Recognizing Vocabulary Impairment: To assess vocabulary, the clinician should ask whether the youngster's vocabulary is age appropriate and has linguistic flexibility, that is, can he use a variety of vocabulary items in different communicative situations and on different topics?

When a youngster has problems at the semantic level of language, the following indicators may occur in their spoken language. The youngster may have a limited vocabulary. Limitations may occur both in number and the kind of words used as well as the frequency or repetition of words. Does the child have a limited understanding of word meaning? At the age of 18 months, does the youngster have a vocabulary of between 100 and 150 words, and at an age of 24 months to 42 months, a vocabulary size of 300 to 1,000 words, and between 42 and 48 months, a receptive vocabulary of between 300 to 8,000 words?

A youngster may overuse nonspecific vocabulary (this, that, thing, stuff, you know) and frequently misname items, using related but incorrect words, using words belonging to the same lexical category. The child may say "apple" instead of "pear," both belonging to the category of fruit, or "fork" for "knife," both utensils for eating. The child may mispronounce a word, similar to a slip of the tongue (e.g., life for knife), or provide the function of a word in the form of a circumlocution (e.g., intending to say "knife," the child may say "it is for cutting." Communications may show hesitations, and self-corrections, and he may overuse gestures. The older child may have difficulties with the abstract aspect of semantics, such as with the secondary and multiple meanings of words, and synonyms (Murdoch, 1991; Wiig & Semel, 1984).

Recognizing Grammatical Impairment: In order to evaluate the child's grammatical structures, the clinician must look at phrase and sentence formation and sentence types and the way the child understands sentences of others.

When observing spoken language, the clinician should ask whether youngsters have adequate control of spoken language to express their thoughts and ideas and facility with using different sentence types such as questions, statements, commands, and negation. Do youngsters have an age-appropriate level of syntactic complexity?

The clinician also must assess children's comprehension. The clinician must determine whether their understanding of language is age appropriate. Between the ages of 18 and 24 months, does the child understand words in a situational context. Between the ages of 2 and 3, if the child does not understand the meanings associated with 3-word combinations and more he is language impaired in comprehension. If the child does not understand "who," "what," "where," and "whose" questions by the age of 2 to 3½ years or who, by the age of 4, do not speak in simple sentences and/or understand "how" questions and cannot interpret the basic syntactic cues (sequential order) for sentences the child is impaired in language comprehension. Also, if between the ages of 4 and 8 years, the child does not begin to understand passive sentences and respond to "when" questions, there is a problem (Miller & Paul, 1995).

Youngster may use the sentence forms and grammatical structures of younger children. The youngster may use limited verbal output and limited sentence types. Their grammatical structures may consist of only simple questions, statements, commands, and negatives, but complex sentences are absent. There may be omissions of words from utterances, and his language may sound like telegraphic speech. For example, a youngster may use "boy go school" for "the boy is going to school." Also, the youngster may use incorrect grammatical forms (e.g., I no like you). There also may be difficulty sequencing words to form sentences (e.g., the children the bear saw) and understanding longer or more complex sentences (e.g., the girl was pushed the boy). The youngster may make errors in the grammatical features such as noun/verb agreement (the dogs is), tense and plural markers such as the substitution of regular verb tense markers for irregular ones ("eated" for "ate"), and/or regular plurals for irregular ones ("childs" for "children"), features appropriate only

for very young children. Despite an older age, such as pre- and early teens, the youngster may not produce complex sentence formations, such as compound sentences and those containing embedded, relative, subordinate, or conjunctive clauses (i.e., "the dog the boy loved ran away," "The boy left home, but the girl did not"). Also, the older language-impaired child may not have the grammatical skills to express more complex linguistic relationships such as analogies and causal relationships in grammar.

The youngster's verbal interactions and language may show difficulty with metaphors, figurative language, idioms, and proverbs, and difficulty detecting and understanding ambiguity. Abstract language skills emerge between 6 and 8 years of age (Bashir & Scavuzzo, 1992; Lahey, 1988; Wiig & Semel, 1984).

Recognizing Auditory Language Processing Problems: Can the youngster process the language taken in through the auditory channel?

In assessing auditory language processing problems, the clinician has to assess whether the child has difficulty in perceiving the relevant acoustic cues for speech. Does the youngster have difficulty retaining sequences of auditory stimuli such as sentences, words, or digits? Does she have difficulty organizing speech sounds into accurate sequential patterns both in perception and in production? Does she use the temporal patterns of language to facilitate recognition and retention?

When auditory processing problems are present, the youngster will have difficulty processing auditory information and retaining it. His responses in the communicative interaction may be to words in a sentence rather than to a full sentences. He may be unable to follow directions or 2- and 3-step commands. Are there problems recalling names, dates, times, and so on? Is a child easily distracted by auditory stimuli? Does a child have difficulty with background noises, or give inappropriate responses to simple questions or in conversation? Does a child ask for repetitions of what is heard? Is a child slow to respond to questions and directions? Does he or she sometimes appear to confuse one sound with another? Visual information assists in processing, understanding, and retaining verbal information processed auditorily (Kelly, 1995; Levinson & Sloan, 1980; Stark & Bernstein, 1984).

Semantic or lexical deficits frequently are associated with deficits or impairment in grammar, but they may occur in isolation as well and thus be an aspect of the child with specific language impairment. These deficits may be seen in autism, schizophrenia, and the affective disorders as well as hearing impairment. They also are related to specific and general brain pathology, such as an expressive aphasia, Alzheimer's disease, and learning disabilities. However, lexical problems also may occur in bilingualism.

Grammatical deficits can occur independently as a category in themselves. However, more generally they are associated with additional semantic problems. Together they represent a general language problem. Grammatical or syntactic disturbances occur in pervasive developmental disorders. In addition, they can occur in attention deficit hyperactivity disorder, the behavior disorders, and the emotional disorders. They also occur with a hearing impairment. Language delay as expressed in semantics and grammar is part of the picture when general cognitive delay is present. Language impairment also can occur with seizure disorders, psychosis, schizophrenia, the affective disorders, Tourette's disorder, and elective mutism. Language impairment is closely associated with learning disabilities. Limited verbal output and simplified grammatical structures also are seen in depression and catatonia. Deficits in abstract language function are associated with language disorders in adolescents with learning disabilities, schizophrenia, psychosis, affective disorders, the pervasive developmental disorders, the aphasias, and traumatic brain damage (Baltaxe, 1997; Baltaxe & Simmons, 1995; Beitchman et al., 1996; Cantwell & Baker, 1991; Murdoch, 1991; Tuchman, 1994).

Bilingual children and adolescents also may experience difficulties in grammar. Their difficulties should not be considered an impairment (American Speech-Language-Hearing Association, 1985; Taylor, 1986).

RECOGNIZING PRAGMATIC IMPAIRMENT

Often it is easier for the clinician to recognize when the child does not communicate effectively or violate the rules of pragmatics than to evaluate more complex grammatical and abstract language skills.

When the clinician assesses the pragmatics of language, the obvious question is whether children use language in context appropriately and age appropriately. The clinician may ask whether a child can communicate effectively. Is she able to put herself into the listener's shoes when providing information? Is she able to provide relevant background information? Is the youngster aware when she has provided sufficient information to the listener? Does she use correct and appropriate linguistic forms and conventions to do so? Can she adjust conversations to topic, situation, and listener? Does the youngster initiate and maintain topics in the interaction? Does she follow the rules of turn-taking in the communicative interchange? What are the youngster's referencing skills?

One important aspect of social communication is the nonverbal communication that accompanies spoken language. In assessing social communication, the clinician also should note eye contact, facial expression, body language, and speech prosody (Arwood, 1991). Bilingual children and children from minorities with a different linguistic code may experience difficulties with the pragmatic rules of the dominant code (Taylor, 1986).

The youngster's pragmatics may be inadequate or impaired along a number of parameters, including backgrounding the listener, situational variations in language use, turn-taking behaviors, behaviors relating to topic of a conversation, nonverbal vocal behaviors, and nonverbal behaviors. The youngster may start a conversation without first seeing that the listener has sufficient information to follow what is said. There may also be difficulties in using language differentially depending on conversational setting. The youngster may sound too formal when more informal language use would be more appropriate, or too informal when more formal language is required. Turn-taking rules may not be observed in the communicative interchange. The youngster may not respond to the listener or may respond only with sparse verbalizations. Also, the youngster may refuse to yield the floor, or initiate or maintain the communicative interaction with the listener, when required. Responses may be off target (inappropriate, bizarre), and children may use words and sentences idiosyncratically. The youngster also may have difficulty maintaining a topic; there may be inappropriate and abrupt topic changes. And there may be poor referencing skills. For example, a youngster may use only nouns, avoiding pronouns, and therefore sound very literal. He may not signal old and new information linguistically—new information usually is signaled by nouns and noun phrases and old information by pronouns. The youngster may overuse pronouns so that it is difficult for the listener to know what he is referring to. The melody of speech may be incongruous with the content of what is said. Nonverbal communication, such as eye contact, facial expression, or body language, also may not be in agreement with what is said.

In psychiatric conditions, communication in a social context is significant both verbally and nonverbally. In nonverbal communication, a lack of eye contact may indicate avoidance, shyness, hostility, or anxiety. A lack or poor eye contact also may be indicative of autism and may be seen in depression. Children may have greater control over verbal communication than the nonverbal aspects of communication, such as eye gaze and facial expression. Incongruence between what is said and how it is said are important aspects of psychiatric diagnosis. Incongruence between verbal and nonverbal communication may signal conflict, avoidance, anger, or the presence of specific psychiatric disorders. Speech and its subcomponents of prosody, fluency, and voice are the other components that affect social communication. In almost all psychiatric disorders of childhood and adolescence, rather typical problems in social communication can be identified; specific problems in social communication may predict for specific psychiatric illnesses (Baltaxe, 1993, 1997). Social communication also is impaired when there is a hearing impairment (Trychin & Busacco, 1991).

When assessing the speech, language, and communication behavior of the youngster, and because thinking is inferred from spoken language, the clinician should be alert to the effects of abnormal thought processes (Andreason, 1979a, b). When considering the presence of a thought disorder, the clinician must first rule out a language disorder. For example, such indicators of a thought disorder as pressure of speech and thought blocking must be differentiated from fluency disorders, in which rate of speech may also be speeded up or disrupted incoherence from a language disorder; poverty of speech and poverty of content of speech must be distinguished from language disorders as well as pragmatic disorders. Similarly, the linguistic characteristics such as those seen in derailment, tangentiality, and circumstantiality where quantity and quality of language may also be affected, may be seen in youngsters violating the relevancy principle of social communication (Grice, 1975), while stilted speech can be interpreted pragmatically in terms of referencing problems and problems adjusting language to conversational partner or setting.

Conclusion

A wealth of linguistic information emerges from the clinician's observation or interview with a youngster that allows him or her to make judgments on their speech, language, and communication skills. When speech, language, and communication delays or impairment or a hearing loss is suspected, referral to professional speech language and hearing services is essential for a more thorough assessment and implementation of intervention services.

REFERENCES

Adams, N. (1980). The young stutterer. Diagnosis, treatment, and assessment of prognosis. *Seminar in Speech, Language, and Hearing, 1,* 289–299.

Alpert, M. (1981). Speech and disturbances of affect. In J. Darby (Ed.), *Speech evaluation in psychiatry* (pp. 358–368). New York: Grune & Stratton.

American Speech-Language-Hearing Association. (1985, June). Clinical management of communicatively handicapped minority language populations. *ASHA, 27* (6), 29–32.

Andreason, N. C. (1979a). Thought, language, and communication disorders: I. Definition of terms and their reliability. *Archives of General Psychiatry, 36* (2), 1325–1321.

Andreason, N. C. (1979b). Thought, language, and communication: II. Diagnostic significance. *Archives of General Psychiatry, 36* (2), 1322–1330.

Aronson, A. E. (1985). *Clinical voice disorders: an interdisciplinary approach* (2nd ed). New York: Thieme-Stratton.

Arwood, E. L. (1991). *Semantic and pragmatic language disorders* (2nd ed.). Gaithersburg, MD: Aspen Publishers.

Baltaxe, C. (1991). Vocal communication of affect and its perception in three- to four-year-old children. *Perceptual & Motor Skills, 72,* 1187–1202.

Baltaxe, C. (1993). Pragmatic language disorders in children with social communication disorders and their treatment. *Neurophysiology and Neurogenic Speech and Language Disorders, 3* (1), 2–9.

Baltaxe, C. (1997). Communication behaviors associated with psychiatric behaviors. In T. Ferrand & R. L. Bloom (Eds.), *Organic and neurogenic disorders of communication* (pp. 51–83). Boston: Allyn & Bacon.

Baltaxe, C., & Simmons, J. Q. (1985). Prosodic development in normal and autistic children. In E. Schopler & G. B. Mesibov (Eds.), *Communication problems in autism* (pp. 95–126). New York: Plenum Press.

Baltaxe, C., & Simmons, J. Q. (1995). Speech and language disorders in children and adolescents with schizophrenia. *Schizophrenia Bulletin, 21* (4), 125–140.

Bashir, A., & Scavuzzo, A. (1992). Children with language disorders: Natural history and academic success. *Journal of Learning Disabilities, 25* (1), 53–65.

Beitchman, J. H., Brownlie, E. B., Inglis, A., Wild, J., Ferguson, B., Schachter, D., Lancee, W., Wilson, B., & Mathews, R. (1996). Seven-year follow-up of speech/language impaired and control children: Psychiatric outcome. *Journal of Child Psychology and Psychiatry and Allied Disciplines, 37* (8), 961–970.

Bernstein, D., & Tiegerman, E. (1985). *Language and communication disorders in children.* Columbus, OH: Charles Merrill Publishing.

Bernthal, J. E., & Bankson, N. W. (1988). *Articulation and phonological disorders* (2nd ed.). Englewood Cliffs, NJ: Prentice-Hall.

Boone, D. R., & McFarlane, S. C. (1988). *The voice and voice therapy* (4th ed.). Englewood Cliffs, NJ: Prentice-Hall.

Cantwell, D. P., & Baker, L. (1991). *Psychiatric and developmental disorders in children with communication disorder.* Washington, DC: American Psychiatric Press.

Creaghead, N. A., Newman, P. W., & Secord, W. (1989). *Assessment and remediation of articulatory and phonological disorders* (2nd ed.). Columbus, OH: Charles Merrill Publishing.

Darby, J. (1981). Speech behaviors associated with psychotic disturbances. In J. Darby (Ed.), *Speech evaluation in psychiatry* (pp. 253–284). New York: Grune & Stratton.

Darley, F. L., Aronson, A. E., & Brown, J. R. (1975). *Motor speech disorders.* Philadelphia: W. B. Saunders & Co.

Estabrook, W. (1994). *Auditory-verbal therapy for parents and professionals.* Washington, DC: A. G. Bell Association for the Deaf.

Gleason, J. (1989). *The development of language* (2nd ed.). Columbus, OH: Charles Merrill Publishing.

Grice, H. (1975). Logic & conversation. In Cole, P. & J. L. Morgan (Eds.), *Syntax and Semantics* (Vol. 3): New York: Academic Press.

Haliday, M. A. K., & Hasan, R. (1976). *Cohesion in English* London: Longmans.

Hodge, M. (1994). Assessment of children with a developmental apraxia of speech: A rationale. *Clinics in Communication Disorders, 4* (2), 91–101.

Hubbell, R. (1988). *A handbook of English grammar and language sampling.* Englewood Cliffs, NJ: Prentice-Hall.

Kelly, D. (1995). *Central auditory processing disorders.* San Antonio, TX: Communication Skill Builders.

Kent, R. D., & LaPointe, L. L. (1984). Apraxia of speech: An overview and some perspectives. In J. C. Rosenbek, M. R. McNeil, & A. Aronson (Eds.), *Apraxia of speech: Physiology, acoustics, linguistics, management* (pp. 1–72). San Diego: College Hill Press.

Lahey, M. (1988). *Language disorders and language development.* New York: Macmillan.

Levinson, P., & Sloan, C. (Eds.). (1980). *Auditory processing and language.* New York: Grune & Stratton.

Love, R. J. (1992). *Childhood motor speech disability.* Columbus, OH: Merrill/Macmillan.

Miller, J. F. (1981). *Assessing language production in children.* Baltimore, MD: University Park Press.

Miller, J. F., & Paul, R. (1995). *The clinical assessment of language comprehension* Baltimore: Paul Brookes Publishing Co.

Monrad-Krohn, G. (1957). The third element of speech: Prosody in the neuropsychiatric clinic. *Journal of Mental Science, 103,* 326–333.

Murdoch, B. (Ed.). (1991). *Acquired neurological speech/language disorders of childhood.* London: Taylor & Francis.

Northern, J. L., & Downs, M. P. (1991). *Hearing in children* (4th ed.). Baltimore, MD: Williams & Wilkins.

Rosenbek, H. (1985). Treating apraxia of speech. In D. F. Johns (Ed.), *Clinical management of neurogenic communicative disorders* (2nd ed.) (pp. 267–312). Boston: Little, Brown.

Rosenbek, J. C., & LaPointe, L. L. (1985). The dysarthrias: Description, diagnosis, and treatment. In D. F. Johns (Ed.), *Clinical management of neurogenic communicative disorders* (2nd ed) (pp. 97–152). Boston: Little, Brown.

Scherer, K. R. (1981a). Speech and emotional states. In J. Darby (Ed.), *Speech evaluation in psychiatry* (pp. 189–220). New York: Grune & Stratton.

Scherer, K. R. (1981b). Vocal indicators of stress. In J. Darby (Ed.), *Speech evaluation in psychiatry* (pp. 171–188). New York: Grune & Stratton.

Shipley, K., & McAfee, J. (1992). *Assessment in speech-language pathology*. San Diego: Singular Publishing Co.

Stark, R., & Bernstein, L. (1984). Evaluating central auditory processing in children. *Topics in Language, 4* (3), 57–70.

Starkweather, C. W. (1987). *Fluency and stuttering*. Englewood Cliffs, NJ: Prentice-Hall.

Stewart, C. J., & Cash, W. B. (1991). *Interviewing: Principles and practices* (6th ed.). Dubuque, IA: William C. Brown.

Stoel-Gammon, C., & Dunn, C. (1985). *Normal and disordered phonology in children*. Austin, TX: Pro-Ed.

Stoker, R., & Ling, D. (1992). Speech production in hearing impaired children and youth [Monograph]. *The Volta Review*.

Taylor, O. L. (1986). *Treatment of communication disorders in culturally and linguistically diverse populations*. San Diego: College Hill Press.

Trychin, S., & Busacco, D. (1991). *Manual for mental health professionals, part I*. Washington, DC: Gallaudet University.

Tuchman, R. (1994). Epilepsy, language, and behavior: Clinical models in childhood. *Journal of Child Neurology, 9* (1), 95–102.

Wiig, E. H., & Semel, E. (1984). *Language assessment and intervention for the learning disabled* (2nd ed.). Columbus, OH: Charles Merrill Publishing.

Williams, C. E., & Stevens, K. N. (1981). Vocal correlates of emotions. In J. Darby (Ed.), *Speech evaluation in psychiatry* (pp. 220–242). New York, NY: Grune & Stratton.

Wilson, D. K. (1987). *Voice problems in children* (3rd ed.). Baltimore, MD: Williams & Wilkins.

Wolk, S., & Schilbroth, A. M. (1986). Deaf children and speech intelligibility: A national study. In A. N. Schildbroth & M. A. Karchmer (Eds.), *Deaf children in America* (pp. 139–159). San Diego: College Hill Press.

92 / Brain Imaging

Monique Ernst and Lucie Hertz-Pannier

For the first time in the history of medicine, brain structure and function can be studied in man *in vivo*, using brain imaging technologies. These technologies hold great potential for furthering the understanding of the neural substrates of human behavior and psychopathology. To date, most of our knowledge comes from inferential hypotheses drawn from research in animals, and in humans with brain lesions.

Images of the brain obtained through imaging techniques, while visually fascinating, are difficult to interpret. Indeed, their assessment depends on complex mathematical models. With regards to the study of children and adolescents, additional problems emerge. These problems include ethical considerations and issues of stability of data in a developing organism.

Along with advances in other scientific fields such as genetics, neurobiochemistry, and neuropsychophysiology, brain imaging studies promise to significantly contribute to the understanding, diagnosis, management, and prognosis of psychiatric disorders. For example, findings of specific brain abnormalities in genetic disorders can help narrow the search for the defective genes to those that control the development of the identified abnormal brain structure or function.

This chapter is divided into four sections, including presentation of the various brain imaging techniques, discussion of the issues pertaining to the study of children, clinical and research applications, and conclusions.

Definitions and Characteristics of Brain Imaging Techniques

Brain imaging techniques provide data on the anatomical structures and/or function of the brain. Anatomical data are mainly derived from computerized tomography (CT) and structural magnetic resonance imaging (MRI), and functional data from single photon emission computerized tomography (SPECT), positron emission tomography (PET), and more recently functional MRI (F-MRI).

STRUCTURAL BRAIN IMAGING TECHNIQUES

Computerized Tomography (CT): Computerized axial tomography was introduced in 1973 by Godfrey Hounsfield (for a review see Kuperman, Gaffney, Hamdam-Allen, Preston, & Venkatesh, 1990). The basic physical principle is based on the fact that the structures of a two-dimensional object, such as a plane or a slice, can be reconstructed from multiple projections of the slice. Beams of X rays are directed at many angles toward the brain. After crossing the brain, these rays are picked up by X-ray detectors, which generate small electrical impulses proportional to the intensity of the X-ray beams.

The intensity of the beams depends on the X-ray attenuation produced by the tissues that have been traversed. The denser the tissue, the greater the attenuation, and the "whiter" or brighter on the image. Tissues, in descending order of density, include bones and calcifications, gray matter, white matter, fluid, fat, and air. The electrical impulses generated by the sensors are digitized. The image is then reconstructed in serial, cross-sectional views using filtered back-projection algorithms.

Given the low intrinsic contrast of soft tissues, intravenous nondiffusible iodinated contrast agents are often used to improve the visibility of vascular structures and of pathologic tissues where there is disruption of the blood-brain barrier.

Despite the very rapid development of MRI, CT scanners are still more accessible and less costly than MRI. Although MRI is the method of choice to assess brain structures, CT continues to hold a privileged place in the assessment of specific conditions, particularly those involving detection of brain calcifications and bone abnormalities.

With recent progress in CT technology, acquisition times of brain images have been dramatically reduced. This improvement reduces the incidence of motion artifacts and the need for sedation in children and uncooperative patients.

CT is used when MRI is contraindicated. These cases include patients who carry ferromagnetic foreign bodies, such as a pacemaker, recent vascular clips, dental braces, or intraocular metallic foreign bodies, and patients who are connected to various apparatuses such as respirator, pumps, or drainage devices. Also claustrophobia is a relative indication of CT when the patient cannot handle the MRI scanner.

Risks include potentially lethal, although very rare, allergic reactions to the iodinated contrast agents often used in CT studies. In addition, minor adverse effects to these agents are frequent (such as nausea, vomiting, or rash). Exposure to radiation (40 to 60 mGy) represents a significant disadvantage compared to MRI which involves electromagnetic fields and no radiation exposure. It is important to note that certain structures, particularly the posterior fossa and the spinal cord, are poorly imaged because of the presence of bone artifacts. Also, CT images are obtained only in transversal planes. However, sagittal and coronal reconstructions can be obtained but do not achieve the same resolution as transverse planes.

Structural Magnetic Resonance Imaging (MRI): (See Figures 92.1 and 92.2.) MRI has now become the technique of choice to study most brain pathologies because of its exquisite spatial resolution and the absence of ionizing radiation exposure. The physical and mathematical principles underlying MRI technology are complex. For the sake of completeness, a succinct presentation of these principles is provided below. The reader can easily skip this section without interfering with the rest of the chapter.

Nuclear magnetic resonance (NMR) was discovered by Purcell and Bloch in 1946 (for a review see Keshavan, Kapur, & Pettegrew, 1991). The principles of NMR are based on the fact that atoms with uneven numbers of protons act as small spinning magnetic dipoles. The spinning of these magnetic dipoles produces a microscopic magnetic field analogous to those of microscopic bar magnets. In the absence of an external magnetic field, all atoms (magnets) are randomly oriented, with their vectorial sum being null. When submitted to an external magnetic field (B_0), these microscopic magnets line up in the direction of the external field (z axis). When an appropriate second field (B_1) is applied in an orthogonal plane to the z axis, the magnets are "tipped" (flip angle) along this second plane (plane x-y). This B_1 field is created by a radio frequency pulse (RF) whose frequency is accorded to the spinning frequency of the targeted atoms (phenomenon of resonance).

During the radio frequency pulse (second

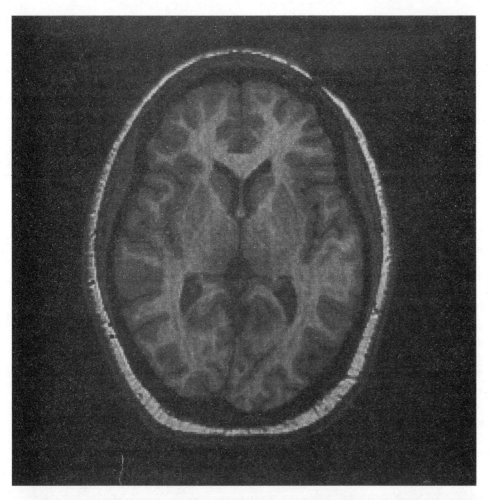

FIGURE 92.1.

T1 weighted image (gradient echo, TR = 400 ms, TE = 15 ms, flip angle = 90°). Clear gray-white matter delineation, with excellent visualization of the cortical ribbon. The CSF is dark, and the white matter is brighter than the gray matter.

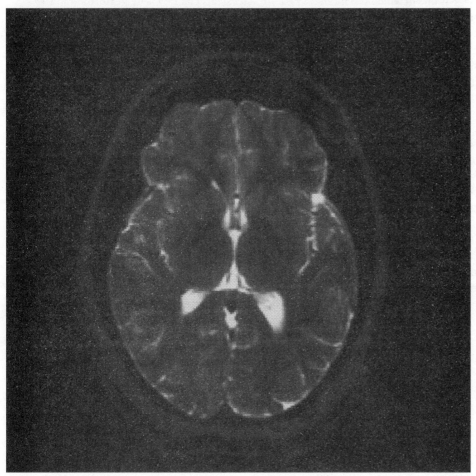

FIGURE 92.2.

T-2 weighted image (spin echo, TR = 2300 ms, TE = 100 ms). The contrast between the gray and the white matter is inversed as compared to the T1= weighted image (the white matter is now darker than the gray matter). The CSF is very bright, as any pathologic process would be with increased water content.

field), the spins build up energy. At the discontinuation of the radio frequency pulse, this energy is released as an "MR signal," when the spins return to their original position (relaxation). When the energy is released, that is, during the relaxation time, the signal increases along the z axis (recovery) and decreases along the xy plane. As the MR signal is collected on the xy plane, relaxation leads to a signal decay. A combination of magnetic field gradients in the x, y, and z axes allows spatial localization of the signal after Fourier transformation.

As a convention, T1 refers to the relaxation time along the longitudinal z axis (T1 = time of recovery of 63% of the initial magnetization along the z axis), T2 to the x-y transversal plane (T2 = time of decay to 37% of the initial magnetization on the transversal plane), and ρ refers to proton density. In MRI, the proton used is the hydrogen nucleus of the water molecules. T1, T2, and ρ are characteristic of a given tissue.

The contrast between tissues can be modulated by choosing the type of sequence (i.e., spin echo, gradient echo, inversion recovery), or adjusting the time when the RF pulses are repeated (TR = repetition time), the duration of the RF pulse (flip angle), and the time when the signal is collected (TE = echo time).

A T2-weighted image is one in which the intensity contrast between any two tissues is due mainly to the T2 relaxation properties of the tissues. This is typically achieved with spin echo sequences (TR: 1800 to 2500 ms, TE: 80 to 120 ms). T2-weighted images generate strong contrast between normal brain tissue and tissues with high water content, namely CSF and pathologic processes (i.e., tumors, inflammation, cysts, demyelinating processes). Conversely, high iron content decreases MR signal, especially on T2-weighted images. Gradient echo sequences do not permit true T2 weighing (because of the absence of refocusing the RF pulse), but rather T2° contrast which corresponds to spontaneous signal decay along the xy plane, and depends on magnetic field inhomogeneities. T2° contrast is widely used in functional MRI (see below).

A T1-weighted image is one in which the intensity contrast between two tissues is due mainly to the T1 relaxation properties of the tissues. This can be obtained with spin echo sequences (TR: 400 to 600 ms, TE: 10 to 30 ms) or with gradient echo sequences. T1 contrast is best to delineate anatomical structures, differentiate white and grey matter, and detect subacute hemorrhage.

The third factor influencing image contrast is the tissue proton density (ρ). A spin density weighted image (i.e., spin echo, TR = 1800 ms, TE = 20 to 40 ms) has a low contrast, since hydrogen content differences between tissues are small.

In all types of images (T1 weighted, T2 weighted, ρ), bone and calcifications give essentially no signal, as their water content is very low. In addition to these parameters, it is possible to highlight the effects of flow (MR angiography, CSF flow) to create images of microscopic molecular movements (diffusion) or to increase contrast between tissues (magnetization transfer).

Despite the high intrinsic contrast of cerebral structures in MR images, the use of exogenous paramagnetic contrast agents (chelates of gadolinium) is sometimes needed, especially in tumoral pathologies.

MRI has numerous advantages which explain its popularity. MRI does not involve ionizing radiation, and appears to be a very safe method of investigation. To date, no adverse effects have been reported, except in the cases of the presence of a foreign ferromagnetic body. For this reason, repeated MRI scans can be easily performed in the same subject. Although data are lacking regarding safety during pregnancy, there are no reports of harmful effects on embryos or fetuses. The incidence of adverse effects related to MR contrast agents is extremely low.

Because of the reduction of bone artifacts and the possibility to explore brain structures in all possible planes, MRI is the best method to visualize the middle and posterior fossa, the temporal lobes, the cranio-cervical junction, and the spinal cord. MRI also produces superb gray-white matter contrast with a high in-plane resolution up to 0.1 mm², which allows excellent visualization of the cortical ribbon, as well as easier detection of subtle pathologic processes (i.e., multiple sclerosis). Given the low MR signal produced by calcium, MRI is not an appropriate method for visualizing brain calcifications or bone abnormalities.

An important recent application of MRI includes its use as an aid to anatomical localization in functional imaging by SPECT or PET. For example, a subject's MRI can be superimposed on her SPECT or PET scan (colocalization), which improves the reliability and validity of the identification of structures.

Definite MRI contraindications include patients with ferromagnetic foreign bodies, such as dental braces, pacemakers, recent neurovascular clips, and metallic intraocular foreign bodies. Bone prostheses are often nonferromagnetic; though they can create local artifacts, they usually do not interfere with brain imaging.

Given that the shape of the MR scanner is like a narrow tunnel, claustrophobic patients should not be examined without being sedated. However, open MRI scanners are being developed.

At the present time, the shortest duration required for an MRI scan of the whole brain is in the order of a few minutes. Because motion artifacts generally invalidate MRI data, sedation or anesthesia may be necessary for some subjects to remain absolutely still, particularly for young children or children with neuropsychiatric disorders. Of note, anesthesia requires adapted nonmagnetic equipment.

Finally, the cost of MR studies is still relatively high and may be an issue in public health.

FUNCTIONAL BRAIN IMAGING

Functional neuroimaging uses various indices of brain function, depending on the methodology and the goal of the studies. Cerebral blood flow is the first and most widely studied variable. Brain oxygen or brain glucose metabolism is also commonly used. These measures reflect neuronal activity (Devous, 1992). Functional brain imaging permits assessment of global as well as regional brain activity. Neurotransmitter systems can also be studied with specific tracers. The qualitative and quantitative visualization of the activity of specific neurotransmitter systems, as well as the assessment of brain activation by functional MRI, are probably the most promising areas of functional brain imaging.

Single Photon Emission Tomography (SPECT): The first SPECT scanner was introduced in the early 1960s (Kuhl and Edwards, 1963; for a review see Cohen & Nordahl, 1988). SPECT scanners are gamma-ray devices used in nuclear medicine. SPECT measures radionuclide activity, such as ^{99m}Tc or ^{123}I. These nuclides, which emit one pho-

ton per disintegration, have fairly long half-lives ($t_{1/2}$) and can be obtained from commercial radiopharmacies.

SPECT scanners are available in most radiology and nuclear medicine departments in the United States. These scanners detect photons emitted during the radioactive decay of the administered radionuclide. They record the light scintillations produced by the collision of the photon (gamma ray) with a scintillation crystal (usually enhanced sodium iodide). The original source of the photon determines, in part, the intensity of the energy of the ray, and its trajectory. The level of radioactivity at any given point in the tissue of interest is proportional to the number of light scintillations during a given period of time. Previous methods used a single detector rotating around the head. Present approaches employ multiple detectors, which improve image sensitivity and therefore decrease scanning time.

Several radiopharmaceuticals have been developed. The radioactive gas ^{133}Xe ($t_{1/2} = 5.25$ days) measures cerebral blood flow. Other radionuclides include ^{123}I ($t_{1/2} = 13$ hours) and ^{99m}Tc ($t_{1/2} = 6$ hours). These radionuclides are attached to organic molecules like HMPAO (hexamethylpropyleneamine) to measure specific functions like blood flow. Markers of neurotransmitter systems are also available, labeled with the same commonly available radionuclides.

The spatial resolution for single-photon devices can generally reach 11 mm with good sensitivity. With increased scanning time, spatial resolution may reach up to 8 mm.

Brain SPECT scanning procedures can be delayed up to 24 hours after the administration of the tracer, if necessary, depending on the biological and physical half-life of the radiopharmaceutical agent injected. Theoretically a patient could receive the agent while acutely psychotic, and be scanned as long as 24 hours after the administration of the tracer, when better able to cooperate with the scanning procedure. The image obtained shows the state of the brain at the time of injection.

SPECT is easily available, because of its relatively low cost and because the radiopharmaceutical need not be made on the premises. This represents a significant advantage over PET. The image residence time of some SPECT radiopharmaceuticals in the brain can also be used for special protocols, allowing some flexibility in the design.

The major drawback is the limited sensitivity and spatial resolution which preclude precise analysis of several important brain structures, and restrict the interpretation of data from neuroreceptor systems. It is also not possible to do rapid sequential tasks or acute drug challenge studies to look for changes in cerebral blood flow or regional metabolism.

Another limitation is the fact that SPECT does not provide absolute quantitative data (except for SPECT with ^{133}Xe because of the poor corrections for attenuation and for scatter. Also, like CT and PET, SPECT exposes subjects to ionizing radiation.

Positron Emission Tomography: This approach takes advantage of radionuclides that have an excess of protons in their nuclei (for a review see Cohen & Nordahl, 1988). This unstable state is relieved by the emission of a positron, that is a particle with a positive electric charge. When the positron collides with a tissue-atom electron, after a trajectory of 1 to 2 mm, two annihilation photons (gamma rays) are emitted in opposite directions. The PET scanner detects the presence of the gamma rays as they coincidently strike crystals 180° apart in the detector ring. The information is converted into a time-dependent quantitative measure that reflects the amount of radionuclide present at a point of origin at a given time.

Available PET tracers include those for measuring blood flow (H_2O^{15}), glucose utilization (18-fluorodeoxyglucose, ^{18}FDG), and a large number of compounds marking various neurotransmitter and neuromediator systems, at different levels of functional units (e.g., presynaptic, postsynaptic, receptor site, and storage).

The spatial resolution with PET, up to 5 mm, permits the *in vivo* studies of small discrete anatomical structures. PET is the only technique that provides consistent quantitative data (absolute values of functional parameters; i.e., blood flow in units of nl/min/gm, or metabolic rates in mgm/sec/gm).

A large number of tracers have been developed, which permit the study of acute changes of cerebral blood flow (^{15}O), steady state of glucose brain metabolism ([^{18}F]fluorodeoxyglucose), and activity of various neurotransmitter systems, such as dopamine ([^{18}F]fluorodopa, ^{11}C-WIN 35,428),

or opiate serotonin (18F-alpha methyl tryprophane) ([^{18}F]Cyclofoxy).

A number of tracers have been developed, but in some instances the interpretation of the data depends on the validity of the mathematical model used to convert the behavior of the tracer into a meaningful index of physiological activity. Much work has been devoted to generate these models, but their applicability may be limited when the biological behavior of the pharmaceutical being studied is poorly understood.

Because of their short half-life, PET radiopharmaceuticals have to be produced in close proximity to the PET scanner, and most facilities using PET possess a cyclotron on their premises. PET instruments are expensive, on the order of $1 to $2 million. These considerations make the cost of a single PET scan $500 or more, depending upon the complexity of the study.

Finally ionizing radiation exposure is a serious limiting factor in designing intraindividual repeated studies.

Functional MRI (F-MRI): Functional MRI was developed in the early 1990s and is still in its infancy. The advantages of F-MRI over other functional brain imaging techniques explain its rapid development and its particular value as a promising tool for functional brain studies in children.

Functional MRI is based on the detection of variations of cerebral blood flow (CBF), blood volume (CBV), and blood oxygenation during cerebral activation. The first approach (Belliveau et al., 1991) used the injection of a paramagnetic contrast agent before and during visual activation, clearly demonstrating an increase in local CBV in the calcarine fissure (primary visual cortex). A more recent approach uses the deoxyhemoglobin as an endogenous paramagnetic contrast agent (blood oxygenation level dependent contrast or BOLD contrast). Contrary to oxyhemoglobin, which essentially does not influence a magnetic field (diamagnetic), deoxyhemoglobin is paramagnetic and modifies local microscopic magnetic fields. The decrease of deoxyhemoglobin concentration (i.e., increase of blood oxygenation) leads to an increase of MR signal, especially on T2°-weighted images (gradient echo). During activation, local net increased oxygenation leads to higher MR signal in activated areas.

The first studies were performed on sophisticated equipments using either very high magnetic

716

fields (4 Tesla) to improve the sensitivity (Kwong et al., 1992) or echo planar imaging (EPI) which produces images in less than 100 ms (Bandettini, Wong, Hinks, Tikofsky, & Hyde, 1992). More recently, standard gradient echo sequences have been used on conventional equipment (1.5 or 2 Tesla) with good results but lower temporal resolution.

The technique is noninvasive, devoid of radioactive exposure, and allows repeated experiments. F-MRI brain imaging yields higher temporal resolution (less than 100 ms in EPI, 5 to 10 sec for gradient echo sequences) and higher spatial resolution (in the order of 1 to 4 mm²) than the nuclear medicine techniques. In addition, functional MR images can be superimposed on structural MR images acquired during the same study, increasing the accuracy of anatomical localization.

F-MRI is a new methodology that is still being developed. Presently findings from F-MRI studies are often variable and difficult to reproduce.

F-MRI carries the disadvantages and contraindications of structural MRI in addition to those outlined below. Motion artifact sensitivity is increased, compared to SPECT and PET, in part because of MRIs higher spatial resolution. Postprocessing algorithms to correct for motion artifact are often required.

Other artifacts specific to MRI, including distortion of magnetic fields related to various degrees of magnetic sensitivity of different tissues may limit the analysis of some brain regions (temporal, frontal lobes). For example, the temporal lobe is difficult to image because of the proximity of the petrous bone.

Recent studies have shown that the primary effect in F-MRI studies may be located in small drainage veins rather than in capillaries, raising the issue of anatomical accuracy of the activation site (Lai et al., 1993). However, F-MRI and PET findings show high concordance of localization of the activated areas for similar tasks (McCarthy, Blamere, Rothman, Gruetter, & Shulman, 1993).

Because of the complexity of underlying physiological processes, and the current lack of experimental models, F-MRI data provide only qualitative information, in contrast to the quantitative data obtained with PET. Furthermore, F-MRI is limited to activation studies and does not provide information on steady states. Results in F-MRI are usually expressed in percent changes of signal

upon activation. Also, the potential use of F-MRI for the study of neurotransmitter systems is not foreseeable in the near future.

F-MRI places constraints on the type of equipment needed in experimental designs involving activation tasks, because ferromagnetic and electronic devices cannot be in the magnet room. Also, inherent to MRI techniques is the production of noise (due to the switching of the gradients) that can create artifacts in specific studies (e.g., auditory or sleep studies).

Adverse effects secondary to exposure to high magnetic fields (2 to 4 Tesla) have not been reported. However, safety data are still lacking. Given the recent development of F-MRI, many technical limitations are likely to be overcome in the future.

Issues Specific to the Child and Adolescent Population

The clinical care of children and adolescents raises specific legal and ethical issues. Methods have to be adapted to accommodate for the physical and psychological vulnerabilities of youngsters. Also, the study of a growing and maturing organism requires special considerations.

With regard to research, studies of adults are easier to carry out. However, assessment of children cannot be replaced by that of adults. Although collecting data on adults is recommended before enrolling children in research, knowledge of functional abnormalities in the developing brain is pivotal for the understanding of childhood disorders.

ETHICAL CONCERNS

The use of functional brain imaging techniques such as PET, SPECT, or F-MRI is not yet recommended for psychiatric assessments. At present, the purpose for using such technologies is research oriented, which raises ethical issues specific to research in children and adolescents (for a review see Arnold et al., 1995; Jensen et al., 1996).

The first issue involves informed consent. The law considers any person under 18 years old to be a minor, and as such, not legally competent to give consent to treatments or procedures involved in research. Children can agree to participate in research by giving their assents. Assent is sought only after full discussion of the research study with the child, in language appropriate to her mental age. When children reach a mental age allowing them to understand an invitation to participate in a study, it is essential to obtain their assents, especially when no direct benefits are expected. However, assents do not replace parental consents, which have to be sought to proceed with the research.

The second issue involves the evaluation of the risk/benefit ratio. In most cases, brain imaging research does not hold out the prospect of direct benefit to the subjects. The benefit expected is the acquisition of knowledge that may lead to improved diagnoses, treatments, and accuracies of prognosis. The level of risk varies according to the imaging technique being used. Risks associated with MRI are considered minimal when standard procedures are used. Radiation exposure in CT, PET, and SPECT is of much concern to human research committees/institutional review boards (IRBs) (Ernst, et al., in press). Strict guidelines for research involving ionizing radiation have been established by the National Institutes of Health's Radiation Safety Committee, a group of experts on radiation matters. The doses of radiation considered to be a "slight" risk for subjects under 18 years old are 0.3 rem to any tissue in a 13-week period and 0.5 rem in a 1-year period, or $1/10$ of the adult guidelines. Within these guidelines, the risk can be estimated minimal, that is, no greater than the risk of harm or discomfort encountered in daily life or in routine medical examinations.

The placement of an arterial line in PET procedures is critical for the collection of valid absolute quantitative data. The level of risk of the placement of an arterial line was investigated at the National Institutes of Health (NIH) (Jons et al., 1997). The true incidence of complications from arterial line placement for PET research was found to be 2 in 6045 from three research centers, including NIH. Both complications were successfully treated with local surgery. The majority of patients in the above survey involved adults.

The study of disorders such as autism or Lesch–Nyhan disease may require that the child be anesthetized to be able to comply with the scanning procedure (Ernst et al., 1996). In these cases, the risk of the procedure is increased and relates to the type of anesthesia. However, these disorders are so pervasive and so devastating to the individuals and their families that the gained knowledge may represent a higher benefit compared to that of studies of less severe disorders. Then, the risk/benefit ratio remains acceptable.

The third issue involves the collection of normative data. The use of age-matched normal controls in brain imaging research is prohibited by most IRBs. The issue remains on how to obtain developmental norms of brain function. Some researchers have applied themselves to developing techniques with decreased radiation exposure and which do not require invasive procedures such as the placement of an arterial line. Others use medical controls whose pathology is restricted to one side of the brain, allowing the healthy side to serve as a control. The use of unaffected siblings has also been an alternative since siblings may benefit indirectly from the knowledge acquired through research.

TECHNICAL/PRACTICAL PROBLEMS

The prerequisite of stillness imposed on subjects to complete the scanning can be difficult or impossible to fulfill for certain children.

In structural brain imaging, sedation is not so problematic since it does not affect anatomy; the choice of the type of sedation depends on the time constraints rather than on the type of study. Sedation can occur naturally, waiting for the child to be tired enough to fall asleep, or be induced by the administration of sedating drugs.

In functional brain imaging, however, sedation may alter brain function and introduce artifacts in the results. The choice of the type of sedation depends on the neural system under study and the paradigm of the experiment. For example, a study of the dopamine system would prohibit the use of dopamine blockers such as droperidol. Activation studies where the subject is asked to complete certain tasks during the uptake of the tracer prior to scanning require the sedation to be initiated after the completion of the task, and therefore to have a very short onset of action.

Another important factor involving sedation is flexibility of scheduling. The onset of action of mild sedative drugs, such as chloralhydrate or midazolam can vary greatly among individuals and be unpredictable. In fact, paradoxical reactions seem to be more common among children than among adults. In general, it is difficult for an imaging facility to accommodate delays greater than half an hour. In addition, the physical characteristics of the radioactive tracers, mainly decay, impose their own temporal limits. PET studies use tracers of relatively short half-life ($t_{1/2}$ ^{11}C $= 20.4$ minutes; ^{18}F $= 110$ minutes; ^{15}O $= 2.03$ minutes), and the tracers are synthesized for a specific time of injection. Any delay in the time of injection allows for decay to progress, resulting in decreased specific activity of the tracer. In these instances, it is critical to be able to predict with precision the onset of action of a sedative. A fairly new agent, propofol (diprivan, 2,6 diisopropylphenol) is gaining more and more popularity for its use in brain imaging because of its short onset and offset of action and low incidence of side effects.

ISSUES OF BRAIN DEVELOPMENT AND MATURATION

Knowledge of developmental norms of brain anatomy and function are essential for the interpretation of data from children with brain pathology. Anatomical and functional changes accompany brain development. As a function of time, these changes are nonlinear. They vary according to the brain structures and according to gender, and are influenced by experience (Thatcher et al., 1996).

For MRI studies, the state of myelinization is an important factor as it influences T1 and T2 relaxation times. Most of the myelinization is a process which continues up until 2 to 3 years of age. Reiss (1993 NIH workshop, "Frontiers in Neuroimaging: Challenges in Mapping Brain-Behavior Relationships in Children") presented normative MRI data on 55 children and adolescents. White matter was found to increase between 5 and 18 years of age, while gray matter was found to decrease between 11 and 18 years of age. No changes were reported in total CSF volume, nor in the CSF/brain ratio in youngsters between 5 and 18 years old. In this same age range, the size of the caudate nucleus as well as the caudate/brain ratio was constant.

The formation of synapses in humans seems to follow a predictable pattern. In a study of 21 postmortem normal human brains of subjects 0 to 90 years old, synaptic density was found to increase to twice the adult values from 0 to 2 years old, then decreased to reach adult levels around 16 years of age (Huttenlocher, 1979). In this study, neuronal density was also found to change with age, particularly in the first 6 months of age. Generalization of these findings should be made with caution because of the small sample size and the lack of data in the 7 to 16 year age range. The question of how developmental changes in synaptogenesis and neuronal density affect brain imaging data is not entirely clear.

In SPECT/PET studies, where neural activity parallels the number of nerve terminals excited, the issue of neuronal packing density can give spurious results. Small brains may be associated with increased neuronal density which would be interpreted in PET data as increased activity. Changes in the head size of children with age adds to the variability of the data, interindividually in cross-sectional studies and intraindividually in longitudinal studies.

Ogawa, Sakurai, Kayama, and Yoshimoto (1989) using SPECT with ^{133}Xe measured blood flow in 16 children between 1 and 15 years old and in 14 adults. They reported a sharp decrease of the gray matter cerebral blood flow between 1 and 10 years of age, followed by a mild decrease to late adulthood. The time course of developmental changes of the gray matter cerebral blood flow closely paralleled that of neuronal density calculated from data by Brody (1955). In contrast, the blood flow in white matter showed little change after the age of 4 years. Chiron et al. (1992), using SPECT and ^{133}Xe, reported age-related changes of regional cerebral blood flow (rCBF) in 42 neurologically normal children (18 boys; 2 days to 19 years old) and 32 adults (age 19 to 29 years). In contrast to Ogawa et al.'s (1989) findings, cortical values of rCBF were lower in newborns than in adults; these values increased to reach a maximum 70% higher than adult levels at ages 5 to 6 years, and finally decreased to adult levels at age 15 years. The regional distribution of cerebral blood flow also changed with age: children younger than 5 years old showed a decreased anterior/posterior ratio of cerebral blood flow pattern compared to that of adults (Ogawa et al., 1989).

Millner (1967) presented a general timetable of regional brain development. The parietal and occipital cortices developed between the ages of 1 and 6 years, followed by the development of the temporal cortex. The frontal association areas matured between the ages of 7 and 11 years. Cortical development was essentially completed by age 13 years.

There is a differential gender-related effect of aging on brain activity. Developmentally determined sex differences in brain structure, neuronal connectivity, and neural responses to circulatory hormones begin to be recognized, as evidenced by the symposium on "Gender and the Brain" chaired by Andreasen at the 23rd Annual Meeting of the Society for Neuroscience (1993).

The issues raised by the critical influences of brain maturation in the conduct of neuroimaging research, design of experiments, and interpretation of findings need to be addressed. Chugani, Phelps, and Mazziota (1987) studied a group of 29 infants and children with PET and FDG, ages 5 days to 15.1 years, selected from a population of 100 infants and children referred for neurological evaluation. These 29 children were considered to be "reasonably" representative of the normal population. They found the changes with age of local cerebral glucose metabolic rates to follow those of initial overproduction and subsequent drop in the number of neurons, synapses, and dendritic spines that accompany normal development.

Finally, developmental processes affect neurotransmitter systems. Much evidence has been collected with regard to effect of age on the dopaminergic system. Wong et al. (1984) assessed age-related changes of D2 receptor density through measures of D2 receptor binding in the basal ganglia by means of PET and ^{11}C-labeled 3-N-methylspiperone, a neuroleptic ligand, in 22 male and 22 female subjects. The authors showed a reduction of dopamine receptor concentration in the putamen and caudate nucleus between 19 and 73 years of age, greater in men (up to 46%) than in women (25%). Seeman et al. (1987) demonstrated dopamine receptor density increases from birth to 2 years of age, and then decreases to adult levels by adolescence. Scarth, Lainus, and Shaw (1993) reported in vitro changes over time in both the amount and direction of D2 receptor regulation by sulperide, a specific D2 antagonist, or by a combination of veratridine and glutamate (increase cellular depolarization) in the neocortex of the rat. Finally, Volkow et al. (1996) estimated the dopamine D2 receptor loss per decade to approxi-

mate 7.9% for the study using 11C-raclopride tracer and 7.8% for the study using a similar tracer, [^{18}F]-N-methylspiroperidol. Both ligands documented significant age-related decreases in dopamine D2 receptors that occurred relatively early in life (40 years of age).

Clinical and Research Applications of Brain Imaging in Child and Adolescent Psychiatry

Results of brain imaging studies vary widely for several reasons. First and most importantly, the multidimensional, phenomenologic, biochemical, genetic, and physiologic heterogeneity of most psychiatric disorders requires the selection of homogeneous samples in a given diagnostic group for a given study. Even in the ideal conditions of access to patient population and of unlimited financial resources, the selection of homogeneous diagnostic groups is hampered by the quality of our assessment tools.

Second, results can be difficult to compare among studies because of differences in (1) population characteristics (gender, age, severity of disorder, history of pharmacological treatment); (2) methodologies (MRI: type of scanner, MRI sequence; PET: cerebral blood flow versus glucose brain metabolic rates; different neurotransmitter markers; CT versus MRI; PET versus SPECT); and (3) experimental paradigms (rest with various degrees of sensory deprivation, activation with various attention or cognitive tasks).

Third, the statistical power of brain imaging studies to detect significant effects is often limited. The variance introduced by sample heterogeneity could be corrected by statistical means, at the expense, however, of the statistical power. Furthermore, because of the general high cost of brain imaging research, particularly functional brain imaging, studies are often limited to small sample sizes.

Finally, most studies used adult subjects. Because of the ethical and legal issues discussed above, there is a paucity of studies in minors. In addition, when minors are studied, control groups are usually suboptimal, consisting of "medically stable patients."

To demonstrate the potential yield of brain imaging techniques for studying psychiatric disorders, examples for each category of findings will be provided. These categories include findings of (1) structural brain imaging; (2) functional brain imaging of integrated neuronal activity (global, regional, interregional correlations), neurochemical systems, and activation tasks; (3) effects of age and gender; (4) drug treatment influences; and (5) correlations between clinical variables and brain abnormalities. Results are taken out of context and serve only an illustrative purpose. Their interpretation and discussion are outside the scope of this chapter. Lastly, only positive findings are selected, and many results are still controversial.

Individual studies are not referenced. However, readers may access them through the bibliographic citations provided in the text.

STRUCTURAL BRAIN IMAGING STUDIES IN PSYCHIATRY

The brain is the most complex organ to study. It is composed of about one trillion cells, including one hundred billion neurons. These neurons are organized into circuits coding cognition, emotion, and behavior. Very schematically, the brain is a dual lateralized structure with a left and right side interconnected at the cortical level principally by the corpus callosum. The base of the brain consists of structures governing physiological processes, that is, medulla for respiration, circulation and digestion and cerebellum for motor coordination. Central structures include those associated with emotion processing and memory (limbic system) and gating of sensory-motor input (striatum and thalamus). Finally, the cortical hemispheres are divided by deep sulci into frontal, parietal, temporal, and occipital lobes, which, in addition to association areas, contain motor, somatosensory, language (left side) and auditory, and visual cortices, respectively.

Cerebral Atrophy: Enlarged ventricles is one of the most consistent findings in CT and MRI studies of psychiatric disorders, and is interpreted as evidence of cerebral atrophy. Enlarged ventricles have been reported in children and adults with autistic disorder, fragile X syndrome, obsessive compulsive disorder (OCD) (for a review see Kuperman et al., 1990), schizophrenia (for a review see Shelton and Weinberger, 1986, 1987),

and mood disorder (for a review see Schlegel et al., 1991).

Abnormalities in Size or Shape of Brain Structures: Structural brain imaging studies showed a reduction in size of specific cortical regions in various disorders. Reduction in size might reflect abnormal developmental neural processes, such as cell migrations, dendritic arborisations, or pruning. Various factors, such as the type of the deviant structure given the timetable of its organogenesis and the evolution of the deviance over time, might inform about the period of vulnerability when the pathological process was likely to have been active, and about the potential subsequent compensatory mechanisms reflecting brain plasticity. Changes in the ratio of right to left size of any structures may provide similar information, in addition to furthering our knowledge of the functional significance of hemispheric lateralization.

Most studies report reduction in size of various cortical structures or loss of normal right or left assymetry. For example, frontal lobe reduction was reported in Rett syndrome and mood disorders, decreased temporal areas in schizophrenia and mood disorders, and temporal symmetry or reversed normal asymmetrical pattern in dyslexia.

Subcortical structures have also been found deviant in various disorders. Cerebellar abnormalities were reported in autism. The basal ganglia was found smaller in Rett syndrome, attention deficit hyperactivity disorder (ADHD), OCD, and mood disorders. Decreased asymmetry between right and left caudate nucleus has been described in Tourette's disorder.

These findings illustrate how unspecific the reported structural brain abnormalities are. However, as mentioned above, these abnormalities can help formulate hypotheses of the mechanisms of action of the pathological processes responsible for the disorders. Implication of specific neurotransmitter dysfunction can also be inferred when the deviant structures contain specific receptors. For example, the basal ganglia is predominantly dopaminergic and any disorders associated with an abnormality in this structure probably present some dopaminergic dysfunction.

FUNCTIONAL BRAIN IMAGING STUDIES

Before focusing on findings directly related to psychiatric disorders, it is important to mention the use of functional brain imaging for unraveling the neural substrates underlying mental operations and emotional states. This research is critical to the interpretation of results in psychiatric research. For example, the identification of the various structures and pathways involved in attention processes are clearly needed to understand the significance of findings in ADHD. Attention is not a unitary concept and has been divided into components hypothesized to be processed by discrete neuronal networks. Neuroscience has provided theories and models of the localization of these networks. This research strategy also holds true for understanding mood disorders. Investigators are trying to localize brain structures and networks processing emotions such as happy, sad, or anxious states. Mood or anxiety disorders would result from dysfunction of these systems.

Posner, Petersen, Fox, and Raichle (1988) summarize assumptions underlying the conduct of research in brain imaging of cognitive function. In brief, a cognitive task can be analyzed functionally and dissected into elementary operations. These elementary cognitive operations are subserved by discrete localized neural networks. The performance of the cognitive task results from the coordination and integration of the activity of these discrete functional units. Most importantly, the activity of these neural networks are functionally independent. Therefore, subtraction of maps of brain activity produced by a cognitive task from those produced by the same task minus a selected elementary cognitive operation should expose the neural circuit subserving that elementary cognitive operation. For example, the subtraction of brain activity produced by the repetition of words from that produced by the generation of words should isolate brain activity associated with the process of semantic association.

General Brain Neuronal Activity: Cerebral blood flow and glucose brain metabolism give an estimate of neural activity. Measures include global and regional (cortical and subcortical) brain activity. Regional data are reported in absolute or relative values. Relative values correspond to the ratio of the regional to global value and are used to decrease the influence of interindividual variability in global brain activity on regional measurements. The choice of the global values varies according to the study, for example, mean value of all gray matter regions of interest, or global

value of the plane that includes the given regions of interest.

Compared to normals, global brain activity was found increased in adults with autism. It was decreased in adults with ADHD, mood disorders, and high anxiety states. The significance of differences in global brain activity is unclear. Functionally, investigators seem to agree on the concept of reduced activity associated with improved efficiency. As a correlate, training in the performance of a task reduced brain activity associated with that task. Simplistically this could be translated as decreased neuronal recruitment during a given state or a given task. Another interpretation of abnormally low global brain activity in disorders such as ADHD invokes the reduction of inhibitory cortical activity leading to excess motor activity and loss of modulatory control on behavior and emotions.

Regional measurements as well as measures of left-right asymmetry of relative CBF and glucose metabolic rates have been assessed. Various cortical regional activities have been reported abnormal. Frontal lobe dysfunction has been implicated in mood disorders with a relative decreased activity predominantly on the left side, in schizophrenia with decreased relative hyperfrontality, and in obsessive compulsive disorder with increased orbitofrontal activity. Cerebral blood flow was found reduced in the left parietal region in dyslexia, and bilaterally enhanced in obsessive compulsive disorder. Low activity in the temporal lobe has also been reported in mood disorder patients. Given the role of the prefrontal cortex in cognition, particularly in attention, abnormalities in frontal regions might be expected in a number of psychiatric disorders.

The basal ganglia are the subcortical structures most frequently examined in brain imaging studies of psychiatric disorders, partly because of their relatively large size compared to other subcortical structures, and because of the role of dopamine dysfunction in many behavioral problems. The association of abnormalities in basal ganglia and in frontal cortex suggests a role of striatocortical connections in psychopathophysiology. Decreased activity in the caudate nucleus has been reported in studies of ADHD, Tourette's disorder, generalized anxiety disorder, unipolar and bipolar mood disorders.

Investigators have been interested in the identification of neural "networks" involved in various functions, behaviors, or disorders. They hypothesize that correlations of neural activity among brain structures represent functionally linked brain regions. For example, Horwitz, Rumsey, Grady, and Rappaport (1988) showed loss of interregional correlations of glucose metabolic rates in autistic subjects compared to normal subjects, suggesting deviant functional organization. In contrast, clinical improvement in obsessive compulsive disorder patients after treatment with either fluoxetine or behavioral therapy was associated with loss of significant interregional metabolic rate correlations between the orbitofrontal cortex and both the caudate nucleus and thalamus, suggesting abnormal functional connections between brain regions in the pathophysiology of this disorder.

Neurochemical Systems: Both PET and SPECT provide a way to measure receptor density as well as concentration and distribution of neurotransmitter turnover and enzymes, depending on the choice of the tracer. So far, results have been somewhat disappointing. D2 dopamine receptor density in schizophrenia has yielded mixed results when quantified by PET (increased D2 density or no deviance) (Tune et al., 1996; Kapur, et al., 1996). Presynaptic dopamine accumulation in Tourette's disorder has been found normal and dopamine D2 receptor binding has also been inconclusive. However, in a recent study of adult monozygotic twins discordant for Tourette syndrome severity, Wolf et al. (1996) showed differences in D2 dopamine receptor binding in the head of the caudate nucleus that predicted differences in phenotypic severity (r = 0.99).

Other neurotransmitter systems have also been investigated. For example, benzodiazepine receptor binding has been reported decreased in the cerebellum of autistic children. Studies of opioid receptors are being conducted in eating disorders.

Substance abuse disorders are of particular interest in studying the function of neurotransmitter systems, particularly when challenged by drugs of abuse. Effects of abused drugs (such as cocaine, nicotine, marijuana) on brain function and neurotransmitter systems, such as the dopaminergic system in the case of cocaine, have been explored. Relationships between pharmacokinetics and behavioral responses have been examined in an attempt to clarify mechanisms of reinforcement, toxicity, and addiction (Ernst and London, in press).

Activation Tasks: An important application of functional brain imaging consists of the judicious use of activation tasks which hypothetically should unveil neural dysfunctions not detectable in a resting state. Several examples attest to the usefulness of this research strategy.

In subjects with dyslexia, neural dysfunction of the left temporoparietal region (failure to be activated) was selectively elicited during a phonologic task and not during rest or a nonphonologic task. Similarly, the triggering of anxiety in obsessive compulsive disorder with "imaginal flooding" (anticipatory anxiety) resulted in the relative increased blood flow in the temporal region, while exposure to the phobic stimulus itself ("obsessional anxiety") was associated with a general blood flow decrease, particularly in the temporal regions.

Studies of cerebral blood flow with ^{133}Xe inhalation indicated relative hypometabolism and reduced blood flow in the dorsolateral prefrontal cortex of patients performing a psychological task of working memory (the Wisconsin Card Sorting Task, WCS) which activates this brain region in normal subjects. When patients worked on tasks not specific to this brain region (simple number matching), no cerebral blood flow abnormalities were observed.

Pharmacological challenges can also be used. Using ^{133}Xe-computed tomography, a serotonin agonist (chlorophenylpiperazine) administration to 10 patients with obsessive compulsive disorder (OCD) produced increased CBF, particularly in the frontal lobes, which correlated with increased severity in OCD symptoms.

AGE AND GENDER EFFECTS

Age and gender affect the anatomy and the function of the brain in normal development and in psychopathology. For example, ventricular enlargement in autism was found to correlate with age. In Rett syndrome, cerebellar atrophy increased with age.

A differential effect of ADHD on brain metabolism was observed as a function of gender. Brain metabolism in male adolescents with ADHD did not differ significantly from that of normal male adolescents. In contrast, brain metabolism in

ADHD girls was significantly reduced compared to normal girls.

DRUG TREATMENT EFFECTS

Changes in brain activity as a function of drug treatment and clinical improvement have been assessed in various psychiatric disorders. The acute or chronic oral administration of stimulants to ADHD adults produced only few changes in glucose metabolic rates compared to drug-free states, despite significant clinical improvement. In OCD, trazodone hydrochloride treatment was associated with increased relative glucose metabolic rates of the caudate nuclei in drug responders. In contrast, decreased relative glucose metabolic rates was reported in the right head of the caudate after treatment with fluoxetine hydrochloride or behavior therapy in patients who responded to therapy. In generalized anxiety disorder, benzodiazepine decreased brain metabolism in the occipital lobes, particularly the right side limbic system and basal ganglia compared to placebo. In schizophrenia, neuroleptics seemed to further decrease dorsolateral prefrontal cortex cerebral blood flow compared to never-medicated and normal subjects.

CLINICAL CORRELATES

Structural changes have been associated with severity and biological correlates of psychiatric disorders. In depression, ventricular brain ratio correlated with postdexamethasone cortisol level was greater in the nonsuppressor than in the suppressor group.

In functional brain imaging, neural function also correlated with clinical measures. In normal adults and adults with childhood dyslexia, cerebral blood flow in the left superior temporal region correlated positively with accuracy of performance on a spelling task. With regard to OCD, increased orbitofrontal, cingulate, and caudate metabolism was associated with baseline symptom severity, as well as with treatment response. In schizophrenia, prefrontal cerebral blood flow activated by the Wisconsin Card Sort Task (WCS) was correlated with cerebral ventricular size on CT and with reduced hippocampal volume. In

mood disorder, decreased cerebral blood flow of the left hemisphere correlated with severity of depression.

Conclusion

Research based on brain imaging techniques is rapidly evolving. However, the number of exploratory studies still exceed the number of hypothesis-driven studies. Part of the reason is that norms need to be established to guide questions and interpretation of results. Functional brain imaging techniques have not yet been exploited to their full potential.

The critical issue of knowledge of the course of a disorder for diagnosis and prognosis is very familiar to psychiatrists. Longitudinal studies need to be performed to increase the validity of the findings. Inclusion of children in functional brain imaging research will have to occur more systematically. Technological improvement will permit further reduction of radiation exposure, allowing the participation of minors in research studies. Functional MRI, still being developed, has the great advantage of not involving radiation exposure.

Besides the implementation of longitudinal studies, the selection of several diagnostic groups within the same investigation can offer vast advantages. In this chapter, our review of brain imaging research in psychiatry illustrates how comparisons among various studies are difficult and how the same brain structures, though not surprisingly, are implicated in different disorders. It seems important to contrast diagnostic groups and assess how the abnormalities of the similar targeted structures differ among groups using the same equipment, methodology, and design within the same time frame.

One of the major roles functional imaging has already accomplished is to validate the neuropsychiatric basis of psychiatric disorders, such as ADHD or OCD. This is just the beginning of a potentially extraordinary explosion of a new understanding of brain functions and dysfunctions and the exploration and design of new treatments.

REFERENCES

Arnold, L. E., Stoff, D. M., Cook, E., Cohen, D. J., Kruesi, M., Wright, C., Hattab, J., Graham, P., Zametkin, A., Castellanos, F. X., McMahon, W., & Leckman, J. F. (1995). Ethical issues in biological psychiatric research with children and adolescents. *Journal of the American Academy of Child and Adolescent Psychiatry, 34,* 929–939.

Bandettini, P. A., Wong, E. C., Hinks, R. S., Tikofsky, R. S., & Hyde, J. S. (1992). Time course EPI of human brain function during task activation. *Magnetic Resonance in Medicine, 25,* 390–397.

Belliveau, J. W., Kennedy, D. N., McKinstry, R. C., Buchbinder, B. R., Weisskoff, R. M., Cohen, M. S., Vevea, J. M., Brady, T. J., & Rosen, B. R. (1991). Functional mapping of the human visual cortex by magnetic resonance imaging. *Science, 254,* 716–719.

Brody, H. (1955). Organization of cerebral cortex. III. A study of aging in the human cerebral cortex. *Journal of Comparative Neurology, 102,* 511–556.

Chiron, C., Raynaud, C., Maziere, B., Zilbovicius, M., Laflamme, L., Masure, M.-C., Dulac, O., Bourguignon, M., & Syrota, A. (1992). Changes in regional cerebral blood flow during brain maturation in children and adolescents. *Journal of Nuclear Medicine, 33,* 696–703.

Chugani, H. T., Phelps, M. E., & Mazziota, J. C. (1987). Positron emission tomography study of human brain functional development. *Annals of Neurology, 22,* 487–497.

Cohen, R. M., & Nordahl, T. (1988). Brain imaging techniques. In J. G. Howells (Ed.), *Modern perspectives in clinical psychiatry* (pp. 102–129). New York: Brunner/Mazel.

Devous, M. (1992). Comparison of SPECT applications in neurology and psychiatry. *Journal of Clinical Psychiatry, 53* [Suppl. 11], 13–19.

Ernst, M., Freed, M. E., Zametkin, A. J. (1998). Health hazards of radiation exposure in the context of brain imaging research: Special consideration for children. *Journal of Nuclear Medicine* (in press).

Ernst, M., London, E.D. (1998). Brain imaging studies of drug abuse: Therapeutic implications. *Seminars in Neuroscience* (in press).

Ernst, M., Zametkin, A. J., Matochik, J. A., Pascualvaca, D., Jons, P. H., Hardy, K., Hankerson, J. G., Doudet, D. D., Cohen, R. M. (1996). Presynaptic dopaminergic deficits in Lesch-Nyhan Disease. *New England Journal of Medicine, 334:* 1568–1604.

Hoagwood, K., Jensen, P. S., & Fisher, C. B. (1996). Ethical Issues in mental health research with children and adolescents. Lawrence Erlbaum Associates, Inc.

Horwitz, B., Rumsey, J. M., Grady, C. L., & Rappoport, S. I. (1988). The cerebral metabolic landscape in autism: Intercorrelations of regional glucose utilization. *Archives of Neurology, 45,* 749–755.

Huttenlocher, P. R. (1979). Synaptic density in human frontal cortex—developmental changes and effects of aging. *Brain Research, 163,* 195–205.

Jons, P. H., Ernst, M., Hankerson, J., Hardy, K., Zametkin, A. J. (1997). Follow-up of radial catheterization for positron emission tomography scans. *Human Brain Mapping, 5:* 119–123.

Kapur, S., Remington, G., Jones, C., Wilson, A., DaSilva, J., Houle, S., Zipursky, R. (1996). High levels of dopamine D2 receptor occupancy with low-dose haloperidol treatment: a PET study. *American Journal of Psychiatry; 153:* 948–950.

Keshavan, M. S., Kapur, S., & Pettegrew, J. W. (1991). Magnetic resonance spectroscopy in psychiatry: Potential, pitfalls and promise. *American Journal of Psychiatry, 148,* 976–985.

Kuhl, D. E., & Edwards, R. Q. (1963). Image separation radioisotope scanning. *Radiology, 80,* 653–661.

Kuperman, S., Gaffney, G. R., Hamdam-Allen, G., Preston, D. F., & Venkatesh, L. (1990). Neuroimaging in child and adolescent psychiatry. *Journal of the American Academy of Child and Adolescent Psychiatry, 29* (2), 159–172.

Kwong, K. K., Belliveau, J. W., Chesler, D. A., Goldberg, I. E., Weisskoff, R. M., Poncelet, B. P., Kennedy, D. N., Hoppel, B. E., Cohen, M. S., Turner, R., Cheng, H.-M., Brady, T. J., & Rosen, B. R. (1992). Dynamic magnetic resonance imaging of human brain activity during primary sensory stimulation. *Proceedings of the National Academy of the Sciences, USA, 89,* 5675–5679.

Lai, S., Hopkins, A. L., Haacke, E. M., Li, D., Wasserman, B. A., Buckley, B., Friedman, L., Meltzer, H., Hedera, P., & Friedland, R. (1993). Identification of vascular structures as a major source of signal contrast in high resolution 2D and 3D functional activation imaging of the motor cortex at 1.5 T: Preliminary results. *Magnetic Resonance in Medicine, 30,* 387–392.

McCarthy, G., Blamere, A. M., Rothman, D. L., Grueter, R., & Shulman, R. G. (1993). Echo-planar magnetic resonance imaging studies of frontal cortex activation during word generation in humans. *Proceedings of the National Academy of Science, USA, 90,* 4952–4956.

Millner, E. (1967). *Human neural and behavioral development. A relational inquiry, with implications for personality.* Springfield, IL: Charles C Thomas.

Ogawa, A., Sakurai, Y., Kayama, T. (Sept., 1989). Yoshimoto Regional cerebral blood flow with age: changes in rCBF in childhood. *Neurological Research, 11*(3): 173–6.

Posner, M. I., Petersen, S. E., Fox, P. T., & Raichle, M. E. (1988). Localization of cognitive operations in the human brain. *Science, 240,* 1627–1631.

Scarth, B. A., Lainus, R. A., & Shaw, C. A. (1993). Age-dependent regulation of dopamine D2 receptors to antagonist and depolarizing stimuli. *Society for Neuroscience Abstracts, 19,* 101.5.

Schlegel, S. (1991). Computed tomography in affective disorders. In: Brain imaging in affective disorders. *Progress in Psychiatry, 34,* 1–24.

Seeman, P., Bzowej, N. H., Guan, H. C., Bergeron, C.,

Becker, L. E., Reynolds, G. P., Bird, E. D., Riederer, P., Jellinger, K., Watanabe, S., & Tourtellotte, W. W. (1987). Human brain dopamine receptors in children and aging adults. *Synapse, 1,* 399–404.

Shelton, R. C., & Weinberger, D. R. (1986). X-ray computerized tomography studies in schizophrenia: a review and synthesis. In H. A. Nasrallah & D. R. Weinberger (Eds.), *Handbook of schizophrenia, Vol. 1: The neurology of schizophrenia* (pp. 207–250). Elsevier Science Publishers B.V.

Shelton, R., & Weinberger, D. R. (1987). Brain morphology in schizophrenia. In H. Meltzer, J. Cowl, & K. Davis (Eds.), *Psychopharmacology: The third generation of progress* (pp. 773–781). New York: Raven Press.

Thatcher, R. W., Lyon, G. R., Rumsey, J., Krasnegor, N. *Developmental Neuroimaging.* Academic Press Inc., 1996.

Tune, L., Barta, P., Wong, D., Powers, R. E., Pearlson, G., Tien, A. Y., Wagner, H. N. (1996). Striatal dopamine D2 receptor quantification and superior temporal gyrus: volume determination in 14 chronic schizophrenic subjects. *Psychiatry Research* 31:67:155–158.

Volkow, N. D., Wang, G. J., Fowler, J. S., Logan, J.,

Gatley, S. J., MacGregor, R. R., Schlyer, D. J., Hitzemann, R., Wolf, A. P. (1996). Measuring age-related changes in dopamine D2 receptors with 11C-raclopride and 18F-N-methylspiroperidol. *Psychiatry Research 31;* 67:11–16.

Wolf, S. S., Jones, D. W., Knable, M. B., Gorey, J. G., Lee, K. S., Hyde, T. M., Coppola, R., Weinberger, D. R. (1996). Tourette syndrome: prediction of phenotypic variation in monozygotic twins by caudate nucleus D2 receptor binding. *Science 30;* 273:1225–1227.

Wong, D. F., Wagner, H. N., Dannals, R. F., Links, J. M., Frost, J. J., Ravert, H. T., Wilson, A. A., Rosenbaum, A. E., Gjedde, A., Douglass, K. H., Petronis, J. D., Folstein, M. F., Toung, J. K., Burns, D., Kuhar, M. J. (1984). Effects of age on dopamine and seratonin receptors measured by positron emission tomography in the living human brain. *Science, 23,* 1393–1396.

Zametkin, A. J., Schwartz, D. J., Ernst, M. E., Cohen, R. M. (1996). Is research in normal and ill children involving radiation exposure ethical? Letter to the Editor (in reply), *Archives of General Psychiatry,* 53:1060–1061.

93 / Electrophysiological Studies

Steven R. Pliszka

What is the role of the electroencephalogram (EEG) and event-related potentials (ERPs) in the assessment and treatment of child and adolescent psychopathology? The question has embedded in it many complex issues: What does the EEG measure in terms of brain functioning? If the EEG detects an abnormality, is this related to a mental disorder, a neurological condition, or is it simply a normal variant? What is the relationship between epilepsy and mental disorder? The use of EEG also involves boundary issues between mental health clinicians and neurologists. Do we use EEG to shift the responsibility for difficult clinical cases to our neurologist colleagues? Are we naive in what we believe an EEG will tell us about a child's condition? Do neurologists overextend their use of EEG, drawing conclusions about EEG findings in psychiatric disorders that are

not justified from the extant data? These issues have become more acute with the advent of new technologies in EEG such as quantitative EEG (QEEG), often referred to as brain mapping. While clinicians may have heard of these new techniques, many are unsure of basic EEG concepts. QEEG, with its results expressed as colored maps of the brain, seems to be a technique that makes psychiatry more scientific and/or medical. In lieu of collaborating with neurologists, there is the risk that clinicians may allow EEG findings to drive their clinical thinking. Doing so may include framing the child's diagnosis in terms of brain damage, encephalopathy, or organic factors (Pliszka, 1991). This chapter reviews the relevant data surrounding a number of clinical issues involving neurophysiological techniques:

- What basic principles of EEG, QEEG, and ERP should a clinician know?
- Contrary to much prevailing opinion, there is no indication for routine or screening EEGs as part of a workup of a child with psychiatric symptoms. In the vast majority of cases, the EEGs are normal; abnormal EEGs may not have clinical significance.
- EEG is indicated as part of a neurological workup only if there are certain signs of neurological disease. These include delirium, changes in or loss of consciousness, or specific symptoms of epilepsy, including absence spells, tonic-clonic movements, or automatism. Sudden onset of visual or gustatory hallucinations in a child with no prior psychiatric disorder indicates the need to rule out seizure activity. The more common forms of childhood psychiatric symptoms, such as inattention, hyperactivity, mood disturbance, and oppositional or antisocial behavior, are virtually never symptoms of epilepsy and are not indications for an EEG.
- Aggression and impulsivity are not symptoms of temporal lobe or other forms of epilepsy. EEG will rarely add useful information to the workup of aggression in the absence of signs of neurological disease.
- QEEG does not have the capacity to diagnose mental disorder or learning disabilities. QEEG is a highly useful research tool and may have promise as a means to elucidate the underlying neurophysiology of psychiatric disorder, but the technique is not ready for clinical use at this time. It is important for clinicians to be familiar with QEEG principles, however, since this technology may have important clinical applications in the future.
- Childhood and adolescent psychiatric disorder should not be formulated as organic problems, encephalopathy, or neurological disorders based on abnormal EEG or QEEG findings alone. That is, if 2 children have an identical clinical presentation of attention deficit hyperactivity disorder or major depression, the fact that 1 of those children has an abnormal EEG in the absence of clinical seizures would not change the clinical management of that child.
- While anticonvulsants often are useful as a psychotropic agents, EEG is not a predictor of behavioral response in children with psychopathology. Certain conditions, such as bipolar disorder, may respond quite well to anticonvulsants even in the presence of a normal EEG. An abnormal EEG in a child with attention deficit hyperactivity disorder does not mean that child will be more responsive to an anticonvulsant than to a stimulant.

What Is the EEG?

In 1929 Hans Berger, a psychiatrist at the University of Vienna, first reported that electrical waves could be recorded from the scalp; his findings initially were rejected by the medical community until confirmed and extended by others (Shepherd, 1988). What produces the EEG waveform? Clinicians often assume that action potentials from neurons are responsible, but actually excitatory postsynaptic potentials (EPSPs) from neurons that are perpendicular to the skull generate EEG phenomena. (See Figure 93.1.) Thalamic neurons make contact with cortical neurons primarily in layer IV. When they release excitatory neurotransmitters, ion channels open that allow sodium to flow into the neuron, producing the EPSP. If enough EPSPs are generated, they will sum to bring the neuron to threshold and an action potential will ensue. Before this occurs, however, the outside of the neuron at the synaptic junction will become more negative relative to the inside, due to inflow of positive sodium charges. Simultaneously, the extracellular area around the axon of the cortical neuron will become more positive than the body, creating a dipole perpendicular to the skull. An electrode on the skull will pick up this positive charge. By convention, this is recorded as a downward stroke of the EEG pen. The situation is reversed for input to the axon, but the reasoning is the same. This time the dipole will be negative at the area closest to the scalp, resulting in an upward stroke of the pen.

Andersen and Andersson (1974) proposed the basic model for the EEG. The thalamic cells of the brain stem have pacemaker properties. As they discharge, they excite cortical neurons as well as inhibitory interneurons within the thalamus. As a result, different thalamic neurons have different frequencies of bursting; this results in the various background rhythms, which range from delta (0.5–4 Hertz [Hz]), to theta (4–7 Hz), alpha (8–13 Hz), and beta (13–30 Hz). The total frequency range for the EEG is from 1 to 70 Hz. It is important to note that most, if not all, of what is observed during the EEG is background thalamocortical activity. In terms of this background rhythm, the 8- to 13-Hz alpha rhythm is seen most prominently in adult EEGs in the relaxed state,

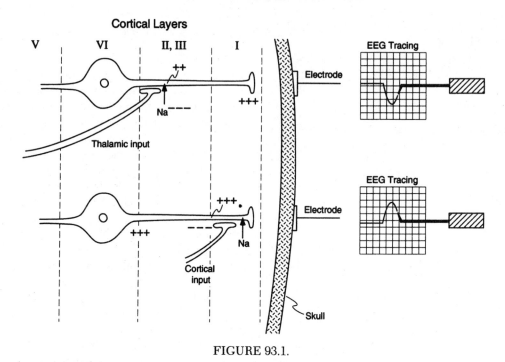

FIGURE 93.1.

Basic principles of the electroencephalgram (EEG).

primarily over the parietal and occipital areas; it is referred to as the posterior dominant rhythm. Adults should have only trace amounts of theta activity during wakefulness. Children are most different from adults in that the posterior dominant rhythm is slower. In children ages 4 to 6, the dominant rhythm may even be slower than the 8- to 12-Hz frequency range that defines alpha waves. By age 8, 95% of children have an 8-Hz posterior dominant rhythm (Duffy, Iyer, & Surwillo, 1989). Children also have "posterior slow waves of youth," waves that appear like sails on the EEG tracing; they also are more likely to show fronto-central theta activity. Delta and theta waves are the most synchronous and are associated with sleep, presumably because there is little mental activity superimposed on the background rhythm (except during rapid eye movement sleep). Alpha is seen primarily in the parietal and occipital areas during relaxed wakefulness, while beta is seen over the frontal lobes during mental activity. Thus the changes in mental status that the EEG can detect reliably are fairly gross, consisting principally of those changes induced by sleep, major structural abnormalities, diffuse encephalopathies, and epilepsy. Psychiatrists order EEGs not infrequently to "screen for neurological disorder," to "rule out seizures," or to "assess organic factors." What are the abnormalities the EEG can detect?

Abnormalities in EEG consist of either paroxysmal activity or abnormalities of background activity. Spike discharges consist of "transients" (i.e., change in wave form) that can be distinguished from the background activity and have durations of 20 to 70 milliseconds, whereas sharp waves have duration of 70 to 200 milliseconds. Spikes may occur together (polyspikes) or in combination with sharp waves (spike and wave complexes). The latter occurs most commonly in absence (petit mal) seizures. It is important to note that epileptiform patterns can occur on EEGs in children who have no clinical signs of epilepsy. Cavazzuti, Cappella, and Nalin (1980) performed EEGs on over 3,500 children without epilepsy; 131 (3.54%) showed epileptiform discharges. This included the whole range of spike, polyspike, and spike and wave complexes. Follow-up 8 years later showed that only 7 of the 131 individuals developed seizures; the EEG normalized for most subjects. Eeg-Olofsson (1971) found a 15% prevalence of abnormal activity in children carefully screened for an absence of neurological disorder of any kind. Clearly, EEG abnormalities should not by themselves be taken as evidence of epilepsy.

Event Related Potentials: Basic Principles

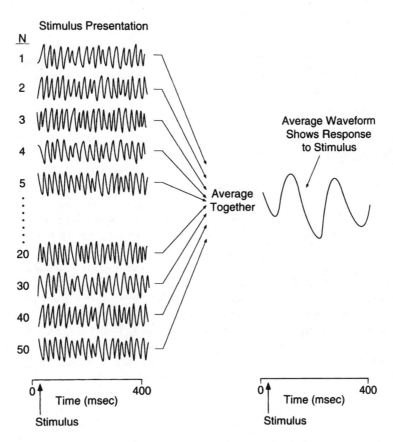

FIGURE 93.2.

Basic principles of the event-related potentials (ERP).

What Is QEEG?

QEEG is a potentially useful research tool used primarily to qualify the proportion of different frequencies recorded at the various electrodes. A segment of the EEG is subjected to a mathematical technique called the Fast Fourier analysis. This breaks the EEG wave down into simple sine waves of differing frequency and amplitude and gives the proportion of delta, theta, alpha, and beta waves that "constitute" the original wave. Note that this analysis is not performed on all of the EEG tracings, but only on one particular segment of each pair of electrodes. It is critical that the segment selected be artifact free. The patient must be alert and not sleeping or drowsy.

As shown in Figure 93.2, the amount of alpha, beta, delta, and theta can be graphed. The value on the *y*-axis is referred to as the *absolute power* for each of the frequency. The *total power* is found by summing the absolute power of the 4 frequencies. Relative percent power (RPP) for each of the frequency is found by dividing the absolute power for that frequency into the total power and multiplying by 100. It is not at all clear what the relationship of power, either absolute or relative, has for actual cognitive functioning. Most QEEG machines contain a large normative sample for power in each lead. Thus the patient's proportion of frequencies can be compared to the normal population. Suppose Figure 93.2 represents the mean RPP results from a group of normal controls. For this pair of leads the normal population has a mean alpha RPP of 31.25 with a standard deviation of 20. Suppose the patient has an alpha RPP of 58. The QEEG machine, after some statistical transformations, calculates a z score. This is done according the following formula:

$$z = \text{(Patient score − Normal population mean)}/\text{Standard Deviation of the Normal Population}$$
$$z = (58 − 31.25)/20 = 1.3$$

This means the patient's alpha RPP in that one lead is 1.3 standard deviations above the normal population mean. That pair of scalp electrodes is shown in a different color on the video display. The more standard deviations from the mean the lead is, the brighter the color on the display. This process must be repeated for each of the 4 frequencies (alpha, beta, theta, and delta) in each of the 24 or so EEG sites. A number of methodological problems with QEEG have not been resolved. Burgess (1990) lists these as follows: (1) The topographic maps produced by QEEG are derived from 16 to 32 points (the EEG leads) with the intervening points on "map" obtained from interpolation; (2) the mathematical techniques used to transform the data involve a variety of assumptions that may not be valid and lead to erroneous maps. In particular, the performance of such a large number of z-tests on a patient's data (one for each pair of leads, for each frequency) may lead to a large number of abnormal findings by chance alone; and (3) the color used may make artificial distinctions.

What Are Event Related Potentials?

Event-related potentials (ERPs) are a variant of EEG. (The term *event-related potentials* has replaced the previously used term, *evoked potentials*.) In ERP, a stimulus is repeatedly presented to the patient, and the EEG is measured for several seconds before and after the stimulus. The stimulus may be as simple as a click presented thousands of times (auditory ERP) or a flashing checker board (visual ERP). As shown in Figure 93.3, the EEGs from each presentation of the stimulus are averaged together. The random variations in EEG waveforms cancel out, leaving a tracing that represents the brain's processing of the information. The ERP waveform is divided into 3 major components: early, midlatency, and processing components (Hillyard & Picton, 1987). The early waveforms, which occur 0 to 10 milliseconds after the stimulus, represent the activity in the brain stem. The early phase is broken down into 6 components representing various structures in the brain stem. Neurologists examine this portion of the ERP for evidence of brain stem disease (i.e., multiple sclerosis), but it has little relevance in psychiatric disorder. The midlatency components represent early sensory processing in the cortex and also have not been the focus of study in mental disorders.

Studies of psychopathology and cognition have focused on the N100, Nd, and the P300 waves. (The N refers to negative, P to positive, and the number represents how many milliseconds the wave occurs after the stimulus.) The N100 wave grows larger when the subject is told to focus on a particular stimulus. For instance, a subject may be presented auditory clicks to both ears but told to mentally count only the clicks delivered to the right ear. The N100 wave when the right ear clicks are presented will be much larger than that when the left ear clicks are presented. (See Figure 93.3.) An Nd wave can be calculated by subtracting the N100 to unattended stimuli from the N100 to the attended stimuli. The Nd is also referred to as the "processing negativity" wave.

ERPs often utilize an "oddball" paradigm. The subject listens to a series of identical tones, with a tone with a different frequency presented occasionally. On the presentation of the rare tone, subjects will generally produce a large positive wave, the P300. The P300 is larger the more alert the subject is and the greater the difference between the rare and common stimuli. P300 is frequently used in studies of attention and has been examined in children with attention deficit hyperactivity disorder. I review these results later. Most QEEG machines also can perform an ERP study and assess P300.

EEG/QEEG in Child and Adolescent Psychiatric Disorder

The study of EEGs in behaviorally disordered children began not long after the clinical use of EEG in the 1930s. Ellingson (1954) reviewed this

Waveform of Event Related Potential

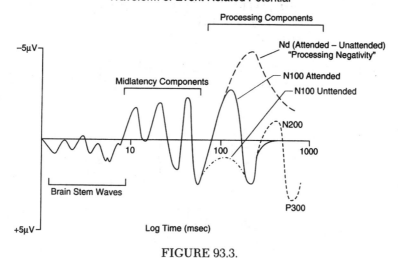

FIGURE 93.3.

Idealized waveform of the event-related potential.

early work, mostly studies performed in the 1940s. He reviewed 18 studies; the rate of abnormal EEGs in clinical populations ranged from 2 to 92%, with most studies showing an abnormality rate of about 50 to 60%. These early studies seem to form the basis of the clinical practice that EEG is useful in the workup of the psychiatrically disturbed child, so it is important to examine them more closely. Only 2 of the studies he reviewed used a concurrent control group and performed a statistical analysis; the rest merely stated the abnormal EEG rate for the clinical group. Ellingson pointed out that many of these studies used very heterogeneous subject populations, even by the standards of that time. Paine, Werry, and Quay (1968) found that 41% of EEGs were abnormal in a heterogeneous group of children with minimal brain dysfunction. EEG abnormalities were weakly associated with "neuroticism," lower performance IQ, and abstracting difficulties. Arid and Yamamoto (1966) examined the EEGs of 100 children with heterogeneous psychiatric disorder. While 49% of EEGs were abnormal, there was no relationship between the EEG and psychiatric findings. There were *fewer* abnormal EEGs in children with a family history of neurological disease, and EEGs tended to be abnormal in children with a "neurological history" (i.e., history of perinatal complications) and in those with abnormal neurological examinations. Using psychometric and mental status examinations, Loomis,

Bohnert, and Huncke (1967) found little correlation of EEG findings in 100 delinquent girls.

These studies found high rates of abnormal EEGs in groups of children with heterogeneous psychiatric disorders, but none of them showed any specific relationship of EEG to a given psychiatric disorder. The relationship between EEG abnormality and childhood psychiatric disorder becomes even more tenuous in the more carefully controlled studies. Ritvo, Ornitz, Walter, and Hanley (1970) examined the prevalence of abnormal EEGs in psychiatrically disordered children with neurotic, behavior, and psychotic reactions. Importantly, in this study EEGs were read blind to subject's clinical status. In addition to categorizing psychiatric diagnoses, subjects were further classified as to the presence of "organicity." A subject was classified as having definite organicity if there existed a specific central nervous system pathology. Probable organicity was defined as the subject having a history of perinatal complications and/or central nervous system infection or injury. EEGs were abnormal in 21 to 33% of all three psychiatric diagnostic groups. Organicity was equally prevalent in all 3 groups, and EEGs were twice as likely to be abnormal in the "organic" subgroups. No specific psychiatric symptoms were linked to the subgroup with temporal lobe abnormalities.

EEGs did not distinguish boys with mental retardation, reading disorder, or psychiatric disorder

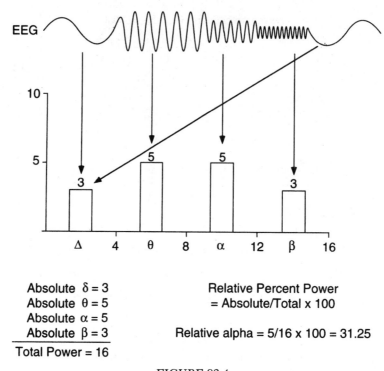

FIGURE 93.4.

Assessing EEG power using quantitative EEG.

from controls (Fenton, Fenwick, Dollimore, Rutter, & Yule, 1974). Hsu, Wisner, Richey, and Goldstein (1985) examined EEGs in 4 groups: inpatient juvenile delinquents, outpatient juvenile delinquents, nonadjudicated adolescent conduct disorders, and adolescent with psychiatric diagnoses other than conduct disorder. There was no excess of any type of EEG abnormality (diffuse, focal, or paroxysmal) among the diagnostic groups, even without excluding subjects with epilepsy (i.e., epilepsy was equally disturbed among the groups). Four male subjects with temporal lobe foci all had histories of violent outbursts, a point I return to later in examining the specific relationship of violence to the EEG. Sixty-nine EEGs obtained in a group of psychiatrically hospitalized children did not yield any new medical diagnosis or lead to a change in treatment (Woolston & Riddle, 1990).

Has the advent of QEEG improved this situation? Early reports (Ahn, Prichep, John, Baird, & Trepin, 1980; Duffy, Denckla, Bartels, & Sandini, 1980; Duffy, Denckla, Bartels, Sandini, & Kiessling, 1980; John, Prichep, Firdman, & Easton, 1988) seemed to indicate that QEEG could dis-

criminate children with learning disabilities from controls with a reasonable degree of accuracy. Ahn et al. reported QEEG data from 2 control groups, a neurologically "at-risk" group and 2 learning disabled groups. The neurologically at-risk group was not defined but contained at least "a few" children with epilepsy; these children were on anticonvulsant medication during the test. The first learning-disabled group had IQ scores between 65 and 84, and thus constituted a mentally retarded group. The second learning-disabled group had IQs above 85 but standard achievement scores in either language or arithmetic below 90. It can be seen that the groups are highly heterogeneous, and this limits any conclusions that can be made from this study. As described earlier z tests were used to determine how far from a normative sample each subject was for various EEG features. Specifically, a z test was performed for the delta, theta, alpha, and beta frequency bands in 8 different regions of the scalp. That is, 32 z tests were performed on each subject's EEG, and there were 1,177 subjects for a total of 37,664 z-tests. The authors reported their data as the percentage of "significant" z tests for each of the frequencies in each of the regions. They found that the control groups had low rates of "abnormalities" (2–6%) in each of the 32 features, while all of the clinical groups had "abnormality" rates that varied from 4 to 34%. Several points need to be made. First, the rate of EEG abnormality in this unselected clinical population is comparable to that found 3 decades ago with standard EEG. Second, QEEG did not detect different patterns among the neurologically at risk, retarded, and learning disabled group. Finally, their clinical groups have "abnormal" proportions of every frequency in every brain region. When they compared the different groups statistically, differences were primarily found in the amounts of alpha, delta, and theta in parietal-occipital region. Yingling, Galin, Fein, Peltzman, and Davenport (1986) pointed out that this is a common finding in individuals with brain damage and may have resulted from the inclusion of so many children with low IQs as well as those with sensory deficits.

Duffy, Denckla, Bartels, and Sandini (1980) used QEEG to compare evoked potential and EEG data in 8 dyslexic and 10 controls. Unlike the study populations of Ahn et al. (1980), which were highly heterogeneous, Duffy's group studied "pure" dyslexics—children who meet criteria for reading disorder but who did not show other psychiatric disorders or neurological disorders. EEGs were obtained under 10 different conditions ranging from resting to performing cognitive tasks. Visual and auditory evoked potentials were obtained during an alert state; auditory potentials were also obtained during a language task. Rather than z-tests, t-tests were used to compare the groups. As is a chronic problem in QEEG studies, multiple tests must be performed. Duffy et al. suggested that EEG was abnormal in dyslexics in multiple areas. Excess alpha was found in the medial frontal areas, left midtemporal areas, and left anteriofrontal region. Which areas were different varied according to the task being performed. The dyslexic groups had higher mean theta, particularly in the left anteriofrontal, midtemporal, and medial frontal regions.

In a follow-up study, Duffy, Denckla, Bartels, Sandini et al. (1980) selected 183 EEG features (based on the earlier work) and through a complex statistical procedure further selected 10 EEG features to do a discriminant function analysis in attempt to predict whether a new set of subjects (n = 24) could be classified accurately as dyslexic or control. The authors found that the discriminant function correctly identified 90% of the subjects, but the number of subjects was too small relative to the number of variables to place great faith in the analysis. Through further statistical analysis, the authors concluded that they could just as accurately diagnose the subjects using only 2 of the many EEG features: the posterior occipital area auditory evoked potential during the language task and the resting auditory evoked potential in left parietal area. The authors suggested that QEEG might be useful in the clinical assessment of dyslexia, but subsequent studies have not replicated their work.

Yingling et al. (1986) studied a larger sample of 38 dyslexic and 38 control boys. The groups were equivalent in IQ, free of neurological disease with normal neurological exams, and were different only in reading grade level (10.6 grade for normals vs. 3.3 for dyslexics). Of the controls 5.3% showed "abnormalities" on the QEEG; only 10.5% of the dyslexics did so, a difference that was not statistically significant. Visual and auditory potentials did not differentiate the groups. This study is particularly striking because the dyslexia of these subjects was much more severe than the learning disabilities in the subjects studied by Ahn et al. (1980).

QEEG has been obtained in a number of studies comparing attention deficit hyperactivity disorder. These studies have varied widely in diagnostic criteria for attention deficit, the degree to which other psychiatric disorders were controlled for, and the type of task used. QEEG has been used mainly to examine for differences in relative or absolute power between controls and children with attention deficit hyperactivity disorder. While there is a trend for these children to have increased beta frequency power, there are too many inconsistencies across the small number of studies for this fact to be useful clinically. One group (Mann, Lubar, Zimmerman, Miller, & Muenchen, 1992) has found increased beta power in attention deficit, a result not confirmed by any of the other groups. Nonetheless, this finding has been the basis of claims that training children with the disorder to increase the amount of theta power via biofeedback can ameliorate symptoms. These claims are dubious even at theoretical level. No controlled studies of biofeedback have been performed, and it should not be recommended for the treatment of attention deficit. It should be clear that QEEG is not ready for routine clinical use in child and adolescent psychiatric disorders.

A distinct pattern seems to emerge from the EEG studies in child and adolescent psychiatric populations: (1) EEG is abnormal in 25 to 40% of unselected clinical psychiatric populations, as opposed to 15% of control populations; (2) EEG abnormalities do not relate to any specific psychiatric disorder or symptoms; and (3) abnormal EEG are correlated (although not always strongly) with neurological disease or with a history of neurological risk factors. As Fenwick (1985) has pointed out, this is not particularly helpful in a mental health workup. In a group of children with epilepsy or hemiplegia, 100% may have abnormal EEGs regardless of the presence of psychiatric disorder. In a more subtle example, a clinician might see 2 children with conduct disorder—1 has a history of anoxia at birth and is poorly coordinated, the other has a normal neurological history and exam. The child with the neurological history has a greater probability of having an abnormal EEG, but the clinician is not justified in concluding that the child has an "organic" etiology to the conduct disorder. Why? Because if a group of children with a history of anoxia at birth are followed, many will be found with "abnormal" EEGs and neurological soft signs who do not have conduct disorder. The neurological and psychiatric findings are relatively independent.

The question remains, however, if the EEG can be useful to answer specific clinical questions, even if it cannot diagnose mental disorder. In particular, there is a fascination with the supposed relationship among EEG abnormality, epilepsy (particularly that of the temporal lobe), and violence. Is impulsive aggression in childhood and adolescence related to epileptiform activity? Do EEG abnormalities help identify children who might have a behavioral response to anticonvulsants?

The EEG and Aggression

The idea that aggression may be related to epileptiform activity in the brain is a long-standing part of clinical lore, despite the fact that an association between aggression and epilepsy is not put forward in modern neurology textbooks (Ashbury, McKhann, & McDonald, 1992; Gummit & Leppik, 1992). The first published account of this association occurs in the 19th century, in discussions of the "epileptic character." During this period the concept of "degeneracy" dominated the work of both neurologists and psychiatrists; both epilepsy and mental illnesses were seen as heritable disorders that not only worsened during an individual's lifetime but worsened as they passed from one generation to another (Temkin, 1971). Temkin further points out that many 19th-century clinicians worked at large insane asylums or "colonies" for epileptics. There they saw patients who coincidentally had major mental illness in conjunction with epilepsy, and they often falsely concluded that the epilepsy caused the mental disorder. These patients today would be regarded as schizophrenic or bipolar. Their aggressive behavior was most likely secondary to psychosis. Second, the causes and course of epilepsy of that era were quite different from today. Untreated meningitis and crude obstetrical practices resulted in large numbers of brain-damaged patients who also had epilepsy. Epilepsy also went untreated, and years of frequent seizures lead to further brain damage. Naturally, such severely organic patients showed high levels of aggression. In more modern times, Gibbs, Gibbs, and Fuster (1948) put forward the hypothesis that patients with temporal lobe epilepsy had higher incidence of interictal psychopathology (including aggression) than patients with other forms of epilepsy. It is important that clinicians understand the crude beginnings of the epilepsy-aggression hypothesis, for rarely has a hypothesis maintained such a hold on clinical thinking in spite of a lack of data to support it.

Hermann and Whitman (1984) reviewed the literature regarding the interictal aggression, particularly in temporal lobe epilepsy. Early studies that did find a relationship between aggression and temporal lobe epilepsy used samples of epileptics referred for temporal lobectomy (Serafetindes, 1965; Taylor, 1969). As Hermann and Whitman (1984) point out, this constituted less than 1% of the population with temporal lobe epilepsy of the time, and such patients who were aggressive were more likely to be referred for lobectomy in the first place. A review of 7 studies that compared epileptics with and without temporal lobe epilepsy did not reveal an excess of aggression in the patients whose temporal lobes were affected (Hermann & Whitman, 1984). While epilepsy of all types appears to have an increased incidence in adult prison populations (Gunn & Fenton, 1993), epileptic prisoners are not more violent than nonepileptic prisoners. Hermann and Whitman found in their review that epileptics who are aggressive share the same risk factors (low socioeconomic status, sex, early environmental stress, and abuse) that are related to aggression in the nonepileptic population.

A number of studies have addressed this issue in children and adolescents. Ounsted, Lindsay, and Norman (1966) reviewed the records of 100 children with temporal lobe epilepsy and found a 26% prevalence of hyperkinesis, while 36% had catastrophic rage, but Stevens (1975) pointed out that this sample was highly contaminated with retarded and severely brain-damaged subjects. In the 12 cases without evidence of gross neurological insult, there was not a single case of hyperactivity or pathological aggression.

Recently Lewis and colleagues (1979, 1982, 1987, 1989) have explored the role of neurological factors as well as family violence in severe delinquency. Lewis et al. (1979) performed neurological exams and EEGs on a group of incarcerated delinquents that was divided into a more violent and less violent group. None of the less violent group had an abnormal EEG, while about 30% of the more violent group had EEG abnormalities, a difference that approached statistical significance ($p = .108$). The more violent group also had more neurological "soft signs" and a much higher incidence of physical abuse. In this study it is impossible to untangle the effects of EEG abnormalities (which did not exist in the majority of violent subjects) and the effects of abuse. In a later, similar study, Lewis et al. (1982) divided a group of 74 incarcerated delinquents on whom EEG data was available into 2 groups: 1 group of 65 with histories of severe violence, 1 group of 9 with lesser histories of violence. Again, 29% of the "more violent" sample had abnormal EEGs (EEGs were all normal in the less violent group), but most of the EEG findings were nonspecific. Only 3 of the subjects had temporal lobe abnormalities.

Lewis et al. (1987) further explored neurological and abuse factors in the genesis of violence.

They compared the above sample of 97 boys (along with 22 delinquent girls) to a community sample of nondelinquent adolescents. EEGs were not a part of this study, but seizures and "hard" neurological signs did not distinguish the groups. Delinquents did have a significantly higher incidence of various soft signs and "psychomotor" symptoms. Psychomotor symptoms were defined as staring episodes, impaired memory, dizzy spells, episodes of unprovoked anxiety, olfactory/gustatory hallucinations, déjà-vu, visual changes, or automatisms. It is clearly problematic that these symptoms are not unique to psychomotor epilepsy and that the examining neurologist eliciting these symptoms was not blind to group membership. Delinquents showed more psychomotor symptoms than nondelinquents, but abuse and family psychopathology were far more effective in distinguishing delinquents from nondelinquents than were the neurological variables. The authors performed a discriminant function analysis using psychopathology, cognitive dysfunction, neurological variables, psychomotor symptoms, and abuse-family violence to determine group membership (delinquency-nondelinquency). Family violence predicted group membership over 80% of the time, while the neurological and psychomotor variables did not significantly contribute to the prediction. The results of this study argue persuasively for the role of family violence and abuse in the genesis of aggressive behavior, but the data do not support the role of neurological factors in the *general* violence of delinquents.

Data from the same sample of incarcerated adolescents was further analyzed to attempt to separate the effects of abuse and "intrinsic vulnerabilities" (Lewis et al., 1989). The latter were defined as psychotic symptoms, "neurological/limbic dysfunction," or cognitive impairment. A child had to have just 1 of the 3 to be scored as intrinsically vulnerable. Within the neurological/limbic category, a child had to have psychomotor symptoms, a history of seizures, or an abnormal EEG. A loglinear analysis showed that neither intrinsic vulnerabilities by themselves nor family violence predicted delinquency but that the 2 interacted to predict more violent offenders. The intrinsic vulnerability factor confounds the variables of psychosis and abnormal EEG, and thus it is impossible to extract from this study the unique role of EEG or seizures in predicting violence.

Essentially, no study has conclusively shown a relationship among abnormal EEGs, epilepsy, and violence, and considerable negative evidence exists (Hermann & Whitman, 1984; Stevens & Hermann, 1981). Unselected groups of aggressive individuals may have an increased incidence of abnormal EEGs, but it is unclear what this means. In terms of treatment or prognosis of an aggressive child or adolescent, does an abnormal EEG have any implications?

The EEG and Anticonvulsants as Psychotropics

EEG would have clinical utility if it predicted drug response in some fashion. Clinical tradition often dictates the use of anticonvulsants in children with behavior disorder and neurological abnormalities (Lewis, 1990). There is a paucity of data on the effectiveness of anticonvulsants as therapeutic agents in childhood behavior disorder. Phenytoin has been shown ineffective in children and adolescents with behavior disorder (Conners, Kramer, Rothschild, Schwartz, & Stone, 1971; Lefkowitz, 1969). Egli and Graf (1975) followed up 76 behaviorally disordered children with spike discharges on their EEGs (but no seizures). Fifty-six of these children were treated with anticonvulsants, some for years, yet none was felt to have benefited. Puente (1976) carried out a small double-blind, placebo-controlled crossover study of carbamazepine in a heterogeneous group of children with behavior disorders. Eleven of the 27 subjects had mental retardation; most had abnormal EEGs. Each subject served as his own control; the sample was randomized to receive either the active drug or the placebo first. Seventeen of the subjects improved on carbamazepine, while only 5 improved on placebo. There was an order effect, with the subjects who received carbamazepine first appearing to get a greater benefit. More recently, a well-designed double-blind, placebo-controlled trial of carbamazepine in aggressive children has been performed (Cueva et al., 1996). Twenty-two preadolescent children with histories of severe aggression who did not re-

spond to inpatient milieu treatment alone were randomized to receive placebo or carbamazepine. None of the subjects was psychotic or had bipolar disorder. The mean dose of carbamazepine in the treatment group was 683 milligrams per day (range 400 to 1,000 milligrams) per day. The mean plasma carbamazepine level was 6.81 µg per milliliter; all of the children in the study had therapeutic levels of the drug. After six weeks of treatment, there was no difference between the placebo and carbamazepine groups in term of aggression. This study does not support the use of carbamazepine to treat aggression.

Would an abnormal EEG predict response to anticonvulsant medication or other psychopharmacological interventions? The data of Elig and Graf (1975) suggest not, and an adult psychopharmacology study sheds some light on this issue. Cowdry and Gardner (1988) performed a double-blind, placebo-controlled trial of an antianxiety drug, carbamazepine (an anticonvulsant), a neuroleptic drug, and an antidepressant in patients with borderline personality disorder, which is often associated with episodic dyscontrol. The antianxiety drug appeared to worsen symptoms (according to physicians' global ratings), while the other 3 drugs were superior to placebo in enhancing global improvement. Neither neurological soft signs nor EEG changes in response to procaine administration predicted specific drug response. Thus an abnormal EEG is not a prerequisite for drug response to anticonvulsant medication when behavior is the target symptom. Halperin, Gittelman, Katz, and Struve (1986) found no relationship among neurological soft signs, EEG findings, and stimulant responsiveness in a sample of 80 ADHD children.

Does an EEG have prognostic value? Are psychiatrically disturbed children with abnormal EEGs more "organic"? Would this imply a poorer prognosis? Only limited data address this issue. Cavazzuti, Cappella, and Nalin (1980) found that 3.54% of their sample of nonepileptic children had epileptiform patterns on EEG; half of these children did show behavior problems. The EEG normalized with age, however, while the psychiatric problems persisted, suggesting a lack of a direct association between the 2. Satterfield and Schell (1984) obtained EEGs on 65 normals and 76 hyperactive children. The hyperactive group was then divided into a delinquent group and nondelinquent group based on whether they had an arrest by age 18. The authors attempted to see if the EEG predicted antisocial outcome. Surprisingly, delinquent hyperactive subjects had childhood EEGs that were similar to normals. The nondelinquent hyperactive subjects EEGs' were significantly different from controls in a number of different EEG power bands. In short, the "good outcome" group had more abnormal EEGs as children. Clearly the relationship between EEG and prognosis is complex. The EEG is not a simple indicator of "organicity" that foreshadows a poor outcome for a patient.

ERP Studies in Attention Deficit Hyperactivity Disorder

Most ERP studies have focused on the measurement of the P300 during an "oddball" task. The child is presented many stimuli to which no response is required and occasionally a rare stimulus is presented. The child may asked to press a button in response to the rare stimulus (also called the target) or to count them mentally. ERPs are measured to both the common and rare stimuli; both types of stimulus will produce a P300. The P300 to the rare tone generally is much larger than that to the common tone. Studies have consistently shown that children with attention deficit show a much smaller difference between the common and rare P300 response to the stimulus (Holcomb, Ackerman, & Dykman, 1985; Klorman, Salzman, Pass, Borgstedt, & Dainer, 1979; Kuperman, Johnson, Arndt, Lindgren, & Wolraich, 1996; Loiselle, Stamm, Maitinsky, & Whipple, 1980; Satterfield, Schell, Nicholas, Satterfield, & Freese, 1990). These differences emerge only when the hyperactive children do more poorly on the task than controls. If the test conditions can be adjusted such that the hyperactive children perform as well as controls, the differences in P300 also disappear (Klorman, 1991). In a review, Klorman (1991) also noted that reduced P300 target-nontarget differences have also been found in learning-disabled children without atten-

tion deficit hyperactivity disorder, in autism, and in schizophrenia. The differences in P300 between the hyperactive group and controls are interesting from a research perspective but are too small to be useful clinically. For instance, the mean P300 to the rare tone was found to 5.8 μV $\pm$ 3.7 for the controls, while the hyperactive group P300 mean was 2.5 μV $\pm$ 3.3. Substantial overlap between the groups can be seen. ERP in children remains a highly valuable research tool. It is the only technology with the ability to detect neural events at the millisecond level. With more sophisticated paradigms and advanced in technology, ERP may increase our understanding of neurophysiology of the major childhood mental disorders.

Conclusion

Nearly a century has passed since the invention of the EEG, and for 50 years standard EEG has been obtained in large samples of children with mental disorders. The ability of the standard EEG to yield useful clinical data in evaluation or treatment of mentally ill children is quite limited. Rarely is the ordering of a "routine" EEG necessary in children with behavioral or emotional problem—only if a child shows evidence of clear cut neurological signs and symptoms should an EEG be considered necessary. These include seizures, loss of consciousness, or focal signs on neurological exam. QEEG allows the examiner to determine how the power (percentage of alpha, beta, delta, or theta frequencies) differs in each of the patient's scalp leads relative to a "normal" population. The relationship of these power differences to cognitive functioning or psychopathology is unclear. Until further research is done, there is no clinical indication for QEEG or "brain mapping" as lay persons often refer to it. Further research is also needed into the role of ERP in childhood psychopathology. Ultimately, these electrophysiological techniques must be integrated to other neuroimaging methodologies such as functional magnetic resonance imaging to give us a complete picture of the neurology of child and adolescent mental disorders.

REFERENCES

Ahn, H., Prichep, L. S., John, E. R., Baird, H., & Trepin, M. (1980). Developmental equations reflect brain dysfunction. *Science, 210,* 1259–1262.

Andersen, P., & Andersson, S. A. (1974). Thalamic origin of cortical rhythmical activity. In A. Ramond (Ed.), *Handbook of electroencephalography and clinical neurophysiology* (pp. 90–114). Amsterdam: Elsevier.

Arid, R. B., & Yamamoto, T. (1966). Behavior disorders of childhood. *Electroencephalography and Clinical Neurophysiology, 21,* 148–156.

Ashbury, A. K., McKhann, G. M., & McDonald, W. I. (1992). *Diseases of the nervous system: Clinical neurobiology.* Philadelphia: W. B. Saunders.

Burgess, R. C. (1990). The scientific basis of computed neurophysiologic topography. *Journal of Clinical Neurophysiology, 7,* 457–458.

Cavazzuti, G. B., Cappella, L., & Nalin, A. (1980). Longitudinal study of epileptiform EEG patterns in normal children. *Epilepsia, 21,* 43–55.

Conners, C. K., Kramer, R., Rothschild, G. H., Schwartz, L., & Stone, A. (1971). Treatment of young delinquent boys with diphenylhydantoin sodium and methylphenidate. *Archives of General Psychiatry, 24,* 156–160.

Cowdry, R. W., & Gardner, D. L. (1988). Pharmacotherapy of borderline personality disorder. *Archives of General Psychiatry, 45,* 111–119.

Cueva, J. E., Overall, J. E., Small, A. M., Armentos, J. L., Perry, R., & Campbell, M. (1996). Carbamazepine in aggressive children with conduct disorder: A double-blind and placebo-controlled study. *Journal of the American Academy of Child and Adolescent Psychiatry, 35,* 480–490.

Duffy, F. H., Denckla, M., Bartels, P. H., & Sandini, G. (1980). Dyslexia: Regional differences in brain electrical activity by topographic mapping. *Annals of Neurology, 7,* 412–420.

Duffy, F. H., Denckla, M. B., Bartels, P. H., Sandini, G., & Kiessling, L. S. (1980). Dyslexia: Automated diagnosis by computerized classification of brain electrical activity. *Annals of Neurology, 7,* 421–428.

Duffy, F. H., Iyer, V. G., & Surwillo, W. W. (1989). *Clinical electroencephalography and topographic brain mapping.* New York: Springer-Verlag.

Eeg-Olofsson, O. (1971). The development of the electroencephalogram in normal children and adolescents from the age of 1 through 21 years. *Acta Paediatrica Scandinavica* (Suppl.) *208,* 1–46.

Egli, M., & Graf, I. (1975). The use of anticonvulsant treatment of behaviorally disturbed children with bioelectric epilepsy. *Acta Paedopsychiatrica, 41,* 54–69.

Ellingson, R. J. (1954). The incidence of EEG abnormality among patients with mental disorders of apparently nonorganic origin: A critical review. *American Journal of Psychiatry, 111,* 263–275.

Fenton, G. W., Fenwick, P. B. C., Dollimore, J., Rutter, M., & Yule, W. (1974). An introduction to the Isle of Wright study. *Electroencephalography and Clinical Neurophysiology, 37,* 325.

Fenwick, P. (1985). The EEG. In M. Rutter & L. Hersov (Eds.), *Child and adolescent psychiatry: Modern approaches* (2nd ed., pp. 280–303). Oxford: Blackwell Scientific Publications.

Gibbs, F. A., Gibbs, E. L., & Fuster, B. (1948). Psychomotor epilepsy. *Archives of Neurology and Psychiatry, 60,* 331–339.

Gummit, R. J., & Leppik, I. E. (1992). The epilepsies. In R. N. Rosenberg (Ed.), *Comprehensive neurology* (pp. 311–336). New York: Raven Press.

Gunn, J., & Fenton, G. (1993). Epilepsy in prisons: A diagnostic survey. *British Medical Journal, 4,* 326–328.

Halperin, J. M., Gittelman, R., Katz, S., & Struve, F. A. (1986). Relationship between stimulant effect electroencephalogram, and clinical neurological findings in hyperactive children. *Journal of the American Academy of Child Psychiatry, 25,* 820–825.

Hermann, B. P., & Whitman, S. (1984). Behavioral and personality correlates of epilepsy: A review, methodological critique, and conceptual model. *Psychology Bulletin, 95,* 451–497.

Hillyard, S. A., & Picton, T. W. (1987). Electrophysiology of cognition. In V. B. Mountcastle (Ed.), *Handbook of Physiology: Section 1. The Nervous System: Volume 5. Higher Brain Functions* (pp. 519–584). Baltimore, MD: American Physical Society.

Holcomb, P. J., Ackerman, P. T., & Dykman, R. A. (1985). Cognitive event-related potentials in children with attention and reading deficits. *Psychophysiology, 22,* 656–667.

Hsu, L. K. G., Wisner, K., Richey, E. T., & Goldstein, C. (1985). Is juvenile delinquency related to an abnormal EEG? A study of EEG abnormalities in juvenile delinquents and adolescent psychiatric inpatients. *Journal of the American Academy of Child Psychiatry, 24,* 310–315.

John, E. R., Prichep, L. S., Firdman, J., & Easton, P. (1988). Neurometrics: Computer-assisted differential diagnosis of brain dysfunctions. *Science, 239,* 162–169.

Klorman, R. (1991). Cognitive event-related potentials in attention deficit disorder. *Journal of Learning Disabilities, 24,* 130–140.

Klorman, R., Salzman, L. F., Pass, H. L., Borgstedt, A. D., & Dainer, K. B. (1979). Effects of methylphenidate on hyperactive children's evoked responses during passive and active attention. *Psychophysiology, 16,* 23–29.

Kuperman, S., Johnson, B., Arndt, S., Lindgren, S., & Wolraich, M. (1996). Quantitative EEG differences in a nonclinical sample of children with ADHD and undifferentiated ADD. *Journal of the American*

Academy of Child and Adolescent Psychiatry, 35, 1009–1017.

Lefkowitz, M. M. (1969). Effect of diphenylhydantoin on disruptive behavior: Study of male delinquents. *Archives of General Psychiatry, 20,* 643–651.

Lewis, D. O. (1990). Conduct disorders. In B. D. Garfinkel, G. A. Carlson, & E. B. Weller (Eds.), *Psychiatric disorders in children and adolescents* (Vol. 12, pp. 193–209). Philadelphia: W. B. Saunders.

Lewis, D. O., Lovely, R., Yeager, C., & Femina, D. D. (1989). Toward a theory of the genesis of violence: A follow-up of study of delinquents. *Journal of the American Academy of Child and Adolescent Psychiatry, 28,* 431–436.

Lewis, D. O., Pincus, J. H., Lovely, R., Spitzer, E., & Moy, E. (1987). Biopsychosocial characteristics of matched samples of delinquents and nondelinquents. *Journal of the American Academy of Child and Adolescent Psychiatry, 5,* 744–752.

Lewis, D. O., Pincus, J. H., Shanok, S. S., & Glaser, G. H. (1982). Psychomotor epilepsy and violence in a group of incarcerated adolescent boys. *American Journal of Psychiatry, 139,* 882–887.

Lewis, D. O., Shanok, S. S., Pincus, J. H., & Glaser, G. H. (1979). Violent juvenile delinquents: Psychiatric, neurological, psychological, and abuse factors. *Journal of the American Academy of Child Psychiatry, 18,* 307–319.

Loiselle, D. L., Stamm, J. S., Maitinsky, S., & Whipple, S. C. (1980). Evoked potential and behavioral signs of attentive dysfunction in hyperactive boys. *Psychophysiology, 17,* 193–201.

Loomis, S. D., Bohnert, P. J., & Huncke, S. (1967). Prediction of EEG abnormalities in adolescents delinquents. *Archives of General Psychiatry, 17,* 494–497.

Mann, C. A., Lubar, J. F., Zimmerman, A. W., Miller, C. A., & Muenchen, R. A. (1992). Quantitative analysis of EEG in boys with attention-deficit-hyperactivity disorder: controlled study with clinical implications. *Pediatric Neurology, 8,* 30–36.

Ounsted, C., Lindsay, J., & Norman, R. (1966). *Biological factors in temporal lobe epilepsy.* London: Heineman.

Paine, R. S., Werry, J. S., & Quay, H. C. (1968). A study of minimal cerebral dysfunction. *Developmental Medicine and Child Neurology, 10,* 505–520.

Pliszka, S. R. (1991). Anticonvulsants in the treatment of child and adolescent psychopathology. *Journal of Clinical Child Psychology, 20,* 277–281.

Puente, R. M. (1976). The use of carbamazepine in the treatment of behavioral disorders in children. In W. Birkmeyer (Ed.), *Epileptic seizures-behavior-pain* (pp. 243–247). Baltimore, MD: University Park Press.

Ritvo, E. R., Ornitz, E. M., Walter, R. D., & Hanley, J. (1970). Correlation of psychiatric diagnosis and EEG findings—a double blind study of 184 hospitalized children. *American Journal of Psychiatry, 126,* 988–996.

Satterfield, J. H., & Schell, A. M. (1984). Childhood brain function differences in delinquent and nondelinquent hyperactive boys. *Electroencephalography and Clinical Neurophysiology, 57,* 199–207.

Satterfield, J. H., Schell, A. M., Nicholas, T. W., Satterfield, B. T., & Freese, T. E. (1990). Ontogeny of selective attention effects on event-related potentials in attention-deficit hyperactivity disorder and normal boys. *Biological Psychiatry, 28,* 879–903.

Serafetinides, E. A. (1965). Aggressiveness in temporal lobe epileptics and its relation to cerebral dysfunction and environmental factors. *Epilepsia, 6,* 33–42.

Shepherd, G. M. (1988). *Neurobiology* (2nd ed.). New York: Oxford University Press.

Stevens, J. R. (1975). Interictal clinical manifestations of complex partial seizures. *Advances in Neurology, 11,* 85–107.

Stevens, J. R., & Hermann, B. P. (1981). Temporal lobe epilepsy, psychopathology, and violence: The state of the evidence. *Neurology, 31,* 1127–1132.

Taylor, D. C. (1969). Aggression and epilepsy. *Journal of Psychosomatic Research, 13,* 229–236.

Temkin, O. (1971). The falling sickness: A history of epilepsy from the Greeks to the beginnings of modern neurology (2nd ed.). Baltimore, MD: John Hopkins University Press.

Woolston, J. L., & Riddle, M. A. (1990). The role of advanced technology in inpatient child psychiatry: Leading edge or useful aid? *Journal of the American Academy of Child and Adolescent Psychiatry, 29,* 905–908.

Yingling, C. D., Galin, D., Fein, G., Peltzman, D., & Davenport, L. (1986). Neurometrics does not detect "pure" dyslexics. *Electroencephalography and Clinical Neurophysiology, 63,* 426–430.

94 / Computers and Assessment

Milton P. Huang and Norman Alessi

The computer as a tool is growing in power and ubiquity at an exponential rate. As it has become able to do more, the computer has found many applications in clinical assessment. This growth has proceeded from the computerization of easily automated, simple tasks to the design of more complex computer-based assessment tools and systems. In this chapter, we briefly describe some of these developments, then explore the impact they may have on the assessment process, and review the software currently available.

The Computerization of Assessment

The first uses of computers in assisting with assessment involved the automation of particular assessment techniques: the computerization of assessment. Before looking at this process of computerization, we briefly review the use of current techniques. This use can be broken down into 3 parts: test administration, test scoring, and data interpretation.

The first part of test administration refers to the administration of questionnaires or rating scales such as the ACTeRS or the Child Behavior Checklist-CBCL. These are basic pencil-and-paper tasks where a rater familiar with the patient's behavior makes numeric judgments in response to questions and writes them down. Then comes the second part of test scoring. Scores are obtained from the test sheets by adding up the responses to questions relevant to a particular scale. The scales are desired measures like "hyperactivity" or "uncommunicative." The final part is the "interpretation" of the results and development of a formulation which will guide decisions of intervention. At this point, the clinician makes decisions about the relevance of the calculated measures. This same process occurs with the use of structured interviews like the Diagnostic Inter-view of Children and Adolescents (DICA) or the NIMH's Diagnostic Interview Schedule for Children (DISC). Such instruments guide the interviewer to ask a set of questions directly of the patient or their parents (see Chapter 88). They generally attempt to comprehensively cover symptoms involved in making DSM diagnoses. Some administration booklets allow the interviewer to skip questions that are irrelevant or to ask more questions on a particular subject if there is a suspicious answer to a previous question. A scoring process following a flowchart of choices creates a report summarizing the results. The following section explores what is currently known about the computerization of these processes.

TEST ADMINISTRATION

There has been extensive automation of the administration of many preexisting questionnaires and rating scales. In most cases, the same questions from the earlier pencil-and-paper versions are presented on a computer screen and either the rater or patient enters the answers with a keyboard. Although the process is similar, we need to question the impact that interaction with a computer might have on test results. This impact could affect parent and patient, as well as the physician. Parents and patients may react differently to the process of diagnosis and treatment depending on their perceptions of a lack of human contact or because of attitudes towards computer technology. In studying this question using a computerized version of the CBCL, Sawyer found that parents judged it less friendly (on a Semantic Differential Scale), than a clinical interview, but more friendly than the equivalent written questionnaire version (Sawyer 1990). Once parents were familiarized with the computer-interview procedure, there was a significant increase in their preference, and they provided significantly more ancillary information for the computer than for the comparable written instrument (Sawyer

1991). Other studies suggest patients themselves can also find computer interviews more comfortable. In one study of six Kaiser pediatric clinics involving 3327 adolescents, patients felt more comfortable in answering questions on topics such as alcohol and drug use, and sexual behaviors when questioned by a computer (Paperny et al. 1990). They gave more honest answers, and 89% reported preferring the computer interview over questionnaire or personal interview for answering sensitive questions. When compared to the questionnaire version, the computer interview identified significantly higher reported rates of family problems, chronic sadness, and weekly alcohol consumption. Thus for some of the questions in psychiatry, this study suggests that a computer administered questionnaire may obtain more accurate results than a written one. Finally, there is evidence that these instruments also affect the clinician's diagnostic process. In one study using the CBCL and the Family Assessment Device, clinicians who had computerized reports available tended to shift their diagnoses away from developmental delay and academic difficulties towards enuresis, encopresis, and family problems (Sawyer 1992). This bias seems to have arisen from the specific information provided by the computer, relevant to these last three diagnoses. Thus computerized questionnaires can help in gathering information from parents and patients that we might not otherwise have access to, but at the same time can create biases in the diagnosis made by the clinician.

Because of the personal effects that interaction with a computer has, we need to be sure of their reliability and validity. Because of their close correspondence to the original instruments, it is likely that the broad number of pen and paper questionnaires will be valid in their computer versions. Studies have specifically shown the reliability and validity of computerized versions of the Child Behavior Checklist (Sawyer 1991) as well as the Piers-Harris Children's Self-Concept Scale (Simola 1992). Whether such validity will also apply to the large number of other computerized tests (see review below) is still in question and will require specific testing of each instrument. The process of computerization introduces new variables into test administration. In some implementations, subjects may be allowed to skip question items or go back and review previous questions. Other implementations may not be as flexible. These differences may result in discrepancies from the original instruments. Different software implementations of the same questionnaire can produce differences in results just as changes in wording can change the response to written tests. Furthermore, some computerized tests are "adaptive," altering the set of questions asked depending on the responses to previous questions (Wise 1989). Such options allow for more complex and efficient testing, but again may change the original instrument so that the original reliability and validity studies no longer apply. As we modify tests to take advantage of the storage capacity and cross-referencing abilities of the computer, we will be creating new instruments, requiring further tests of reliability and validity and perhaps reevaluation of our constructs.

The ability to store large numbers of questions and present them in an "adaptive" fashion naturally lends itself to using the computer to administer structured interviews. Different computerized versions of the NIMH's highly structured Diagnostic Interview Schedule (DIS) have been created by Griest and his colleagues at the University of Wisconsin (Mathisen et al. 1989) and by researchers at the Ottawa Civic Hospital (Levitan 1991). Both versions have been shown to be valid in tests of general psychiatric inpatient populations, and the first of these two has been examined in a comparative sample of adolescents admitted to a nonresidential psychiatric hospital day school (Kight-Law et al. 1989). The latter study found that although they were less comfortable with the test than the associated group of adults, the adolescents reported more frequently that they would feel more embarrassed answering the questions for a person. This study also showed concurrent validity for the DIS with the SCL-90 for the areas of depression, panic, and phobia although it did not for obsessive-compulsive symptoms and psychosis. Since the DIS is not designed to assess the full range of DSM adolescent syndromes, its validity is already suspect for this population. The Diagnostic Interview Schedule for Children (DISC) is available on computer, and the Diagnostic Interview for Children and Adolescents (DICA) has been computerized as well, yet specific reliability and validity studies have yet to be performed. We suspect they would generally correspond to their paper and pencil based equivalents. They are already being used by groups at Columbia (personal communication) and the University of Toronto (Stein 1987) respectively, and appear to be useful instruments for clinicians. The computer interview gathers a complete database of information that sometimes includes areas missed by a busy clinician. In two cases examined by the Toronto group, the computer discovered incidents of sexual abuse that were not reported to the clinician. Although not a substitute for clinical exam, computerized assessment instruments can serve as a time saving adjunct in assessment.

TEST SCORING

There is little to comment on the computerization of test scoring. Scoring methods for rating scales have generally been mathematical formulas or other structured calculations that were easily adapted to the computer. Some of these calculations can also include information from other databases or population norms. MMPI scoring programs, for example, often include data from research and adult/adolescent samples in generating written reports. Computerization of scoring is expanding to include more than just calculations. As described above, the Yes-No decision algorithms incorporated into the construction of DSM-IV lend themselves to computerization in the DICA and the DISC. The process of scoring is moving to include more complex correlations among patient data, exam findings, and epidemiological research.

The Computer as an Assessment Instrument

Beyond its use in administering or scoring questionnaires, the computer is now being employed as a more active diagnostic tool. Computers have the ability to present a variety of stimuli and then time the subject's responses. This allows the computer to be used as an actual test instrument itself,

assessing particular measures previously performed by paper and pencil tasks. Several systems exist that measure continuous performance in responding to auditory or visual stimuli (Conners 1985). In the Continuous Performance Test, a series of letters appears on a computer screen. The patient is instructed to press a key in response to a target letter, say "T," only when it follows the presentation of a particular stimulus letter, such as "S." The program monitors the length of time to respond and records errors of omission and commission. The Gordon Diagnostic System is one electronic device that uses this last paradigm to test vigilance and also includes tests designed to evaluate ability to delay or amount of distractibility. This instrument showed good test-retest reliability (Gordon et al. 1988) as well as concurrent validity with the freedom from distractibility factor of the WRAT-R (Grant 1990). In fact, the vigilance and distractibility tasks significantly also correlate with the Finger Recognition subtest of the Halstead-Reitan Neuropsychological Battery and the Raven's Coloured Progressive Matrices, suggesting that the computer test is a more unique measure which assesses abilities in a fashion that has not been accomplished by traditional attentional tests.

Current Software

Above we reviewed the literature on the current state of computerized assessment, moving from simple questionnaires to more complex test instruments. We will now touch on the nuts and bolts issue of the software currently available, which can be practically used by the clinician. Table 94.1 summarizes our review of the various software packages currently marketed, divided into diagnostic categories.

We have purposely excluded the wide array of psychological testing packages available (Rorschach, Wechsler Adult Intelligence Scale [WAIS], Wechsler Preschool and Primary Scale of Intelligence [WPPS], etc.) as we feel they are not generally used by the practicing psychiatrist. For a similar reason, we have also purposely excluded the wide range of speech and language, motor skills, neuropsychological, and other ancillary tests that can provide helpful information (Bender, TOLD, WCST, etc.). We have not specifically tested all of the packages and therefore make no specific recommendations. In general, these packages represent the translation of more familiar paper and pencil questionnaires into computer form. (e.g. the ACTeRS, the Children's Depression Inventory, etc.) Note that in accordance with licensing restrictions, some of these programs only administer a limited number of tests before you need to purchase another copy. This list includes structured interviewing programs based on the DICA and the DISC where the program can prompt an interviewer with questions or directly examine the parent or child. There are also programs that test for attention deficit using the Continuous Performance Task (e.g. Conner's CPT, TOVA). For more specific details, we recommend contacting the manufacturers who are listed in Table 94.2.

The Computer as Assessing Instrument

The above summary of studies suggests that computerized assessment and computer assessment instruments may expand the kinds of data we can acquire. Although we need to monitor reliability and validity, computer interviews may pick up information we might not otherwise obtain, and computer assessment tools can measure useful variables that can not be easily measured with traditional tests. Other advantages of using computers include rapid analysis of information, automation of report writing with no problems of legibility, and the possibility of lowering costs. In evaluating computer-assisted clinical assessment compared to traditional narrative reports and form-style reports, Yokley found computer-assisted assessment to be as effective as the others but only 20–45% as costly (Yokley et al. 1990). Yet, despite these advantages, there are several difficulties that currently face computerized assessment. These can be divided into two parts: machine issues and man-machine issues. Machine issues are problems inherent in the use of computers. These include the limitations of programming. Computers

can only be used for tasks they are programmed for. There are many techniques of evaluation that could be useful but have not been programmed. Conversely, any particular program is limited to the specific instructions that the computer is programmed to ask. To the extent that this inflexibility exists, there will be a decrease in validity compared to clinical judgement (Krol et al. 1990).

Man-machine issues refer to the difficulties in the interface between computer and human being. The primary difficulty that exists here is in clinician use and acceptance of computers. Current interfaces are too cumbersome and hardware set-ups are too complex for most physicians to feel the investment of time and effort is worth the potential benefit. The vocabulary of bytes and discs is not too complex, yet the "hassle factor" that this separate vocabulary implies has limited the use of computers to the enthusiastic.

The future of computerized assessment will be dictated by the boundaries set by the above two problems. Increased computational power and decreasing price are reducing the effect of both of these problems. Increased power has now allowed computers to juggle ever larger databases and question sets so that programs can be broader in their range of inquiry. More recent modifications of the DISC have included measures of impairment that are scaled to population norms to increase validity (Cohen et al. 1987). Neural network technology is allowing computers to simulate some of the flexibility of human intelligence so that computers can learn to make more decisions based on general pattern recognition rather than pre-programmed expectation. The problem of clinician acceptance is a more restricting limitation. Graphical user interfaces and other techniques are slowly developing and disseminating. This use of pictorial representation instead of abstruse computer commands can make the computer less intimidating and more accessible. The recent popular fanfare on "multimedia" reflects the use of video and sound to simplify explanation and interaction through computers (Huang et al. 1996). As computing power expands and is devoted to making a simpler interface, assessment tools will eventually become easy enough to use that the level of specialized knowledge and vocabulary will no longer be an obstacle to adoption of this technology.

TABLE 94.1

Listing of currently available software

Name	Platform	Vendor
General		
Diagnostic Interview for Children and Adolescents (DICA): child/adolescent version (DSM-IV)	IBM	MHS
Diagnostic Interview for Children and Adolescents (DICA): parent version	IBM	MHS
Columbia Diagnostic Interview Schedule for Children (C-DISC)	IBM, Mac	Lynn Lucas
Developmental History Checklist: Computer Report	IBM	PAR
Personal History Checklist - Adolescent: Computer Report	IBM	PAR
Personal History Checklist - Children: Computer Report	IBM	PAR
Mental Status Checklist - Adolescent: Computer Report	IBM	PAR
Mental Status Checklist - Children: Computer Report	IBM	PAR
Attention Deficit Hyperactivity Disorder		
ACTeRS Rating Scale	IBM	MetriTech
Conner's Parent Rating Scale - Revised	IBM	MHS
Conner's Teacher Rating Scale - Revised	IBM	MHS
Conner's Continuous Performance Test	IBM	MHS
Test of Variables of Attention (TOVA)	IBM, Mac	MHC
Mood		
Children's Depression Inventory	IBM	MHS
Piers-Harris Children's Self-Concept Scale	IBM	WPS
Anxiety		
Children's State-Trait Anxiety Inventory Computer Program		MHS
Yale-Brown Obsessive Compulsive Scale (YBOCS)	IBM	MHC
Personality		
Personality Inventory for Children - Revised (PIC)	IBM	WPS
Jesness Behavior Checklist	IBM	MHS
Jesness Inventory of Adolescent Personality	IBM	MHS
Substance Abuse		
Chemical Dependency Assessment Profile	IBM	MHS

Conclusion

In summary, the computer currently can serve as an easily accessible aid to the clinician in making assessments. A wealth of programs are available that gather data on mood, anxiety, or can run through an entire structured interview. Programs are also available that can test variables like attention. As computing power increases, these types of tools will become easier to use and more ubiquitous with time.

TABLE 94.2

Listing of Contacts for Obtaining Software

Lynn Lucas 3 Wood Street Katonah, NY 10536 888-814-DISC (888-814-3472) disc@worldnet.att.net	MetriTech, Inc. P.O. Box 6479 Champaign, IL 61826-6479 800-747-4868 http://www.metritech.com
MHC (Mental Health Connections, Inc.) 21 Blossom St. Lexington, MA 02173 1-800-788-4743 http://www.mhc.com	Psychological Assessment Resources, Inc. (PAR) P.O. Box 998 Odessa, FL 33556 800-331-8378 http://www.parinc.com
MHS (Multi-Health Systems) 908 Niagara Falls Blvd North Tonawanda, NY 14020-2060 1-800-456-3003	Western Psychological Services (WPS) 12031 Wilshire Blvd. Los Angeles, CA 90025-1251 800-648-8857

REFERENCES

Cohen, P., Velez, N., Kohn, M., Schwab-Stone, M., Johnson, J. (September 1987). Child psychiatric diagnosis by computer algorithm: Theoretical issues and empirical tests. *Journal of the American Academy of Child and Adolescent Psychiatry, 26* (5): 631–638.

Conners, C. K. (1985). The computerized continuous performance test. *Psychopharmacology Bulletin, 21* (4): 891–892.

Gordon, M., Mettelman, B. B. (1988). The assessment of attention: I. Standardization and reliability of a behavior-based measure. *Journal of Clinical Psychology, 44* (5): 682–690.

Grant, M. L., Ilai, D. (1990). The relationship between continuous performance tasks and neuropsychological test in children with attention-deficit hyperactivity disorder. *Perceptual and Motor Skills, 70:* 435–445.

Huang, M. P., Alessi, N. (1996). Tools for Developing Multimedia in Psychiatry. In *Mental Health Computing.* Miller, M., Hammond, K., and Hile, M. (eds.) pp. 322–341. New York: Springer-Verlag.

Kight-Law, A., Mathisen, K. S., Calandra, F., Evans, F. J., Salierno, C. A. (1989). Computerized collection of mental health information from emotionally disturbed adolescents. *Computers in Human Services, 5* (3/4): 171–181.

Krol, N. P. C. M., De Bruyn, E. E. J. (Nov. 1990). Validity of the CBCL. *Journal of the American Academy of Child and Adolescent Psychiatry, 29* (6): 986–987.

Levitan, R. D., Blouin, A. G., Navarro, J. R., Hill, J. (Dec. 1991). Validity of the computerized DIS for diagnosing psychiatric inpatients. *Canadian Journal of Psychiatry, 36:* 728–731.

Paperny, D. M., Aono, J. Y., Lehman, R. M., Hammar, S. L., Risser, J. (Mar. 1990). Computer-assisted detection and intervention in adolescent high-risk health behaviors. *The Journal of Pediatrics, 116* (3): 456–462.

Sawyer, M. G., Sarris, A., Baghurst, P. (1992). The effect of computer-assisted interviewing on the clinical assessment of children. *Australian And New Zealand Journal of Psychiatry, 26:* 223–231.

Sawyer, M. G., Sarris, A., Baghurst, P. (July 1991). The use of a computer-assisted interview to administer the child behavior checklist in a child psychiatry service. *Journal of the American Academy of Child and Adolescent Psychiatry, 30* (4): 674–681.

Sawyer, M. G., Sarris, A., Quigley, R., Baghurst, P., Kalucy, R. (1990). The attitude of parents to the use of computer-assisted interviewing in a child psychiatry service. *British Journal of Psychiatry, 157:* 675–678.

Simola, S. K., Holden, R. R. (1992). Equivalence of computerized and standard administration of the Piers-Harris children's self-concept scale. *Journal of Personality Assessment, 58* (2): 287–294.

Stein, S. J. (1987). Computer-assisted diagnosis in children's mental health. *Applied Psychology: An International Review.* 36(3/4):343–355.

Wise, S. L., Plake, B. S. (Fall 1989). Research on the effects of administering tests via computers. Special Issue: Computer applications to testing: Review of recent research and developments. *Educational Measurement: Issues & Practice, 8*(3): 5–10.

Yokley, J. M., Coleman, D. J., Yates, B. T. (Spring 1990). Cost effectiveness of three child mental health assessment methods: Computer-assisted assessment is effective and inexpensive. *Journal of Mental Health Administration, 17* (1): 99–107.

Yokley, J., Reuter, J. M. (1989). The Computer-assisted child diagnostic system: A research and development project. *Computers in Human Behavior, 5* (4): 277–295.

SECTION VI
Concluding the Assessment Process

95 / Clinical Formulation

Barry Nurcombe

Definitions and Premises

The term *diagnosis* comes from the Greek (*dia*, meaning "through"; *gnosis*, meaning "knowing or discernment") and denotes a distinguishing, resolving, or deciding. Today the term applies both to the process of medical decision making and to its product or conclusion. This chapter concerns the manner in which the conclusion is expressed.

A consideration of the process and product of diagnosis raises philosophical and technical questions that involve many controversies. What is the purpose of diagnosis? Can diagnosis be harmful to patients? What defines psychiatric abnormality? Are the concepts of "mental disease" or "mental disorder" viable? What is the difference, in psychiatry, among "syndrome," "disorder," and "disease." Should diagnosis be framed in categorical or in dimensional terms? Is diagnosis primarily the classification of or the detailed understanding of people?

This chapter is based on the following premises. Diagnosis has several purposes, among them communication and scientific prediction. However, its clinical purpose is to acquire sufficient understanding of a patient to make those decisions concerning treatment that are both judicious and individualized. In the hands of those who are inept, or who do not have patients' interests at heart, diagnosis can indeed cause harm. Diagnostic errors lead to improper treatment and diagnostic labels, to injustice or to the creation of barriers between clinicians and their patients. Nevertheless, the fault is not in the process itself but in those who apply it negligently or inhumanely.

Mental disorder can be defined as a clinically significant behavioral or psychological pattern associated with present distress or impairment (experienced by the patient, by those in his or her milieu, or by both) or with a significant risk of future suffering or impairment (American Psychiatric Association [hereafter APA], 1994). Disorder or disease, therefore, conveys biopsychosocial disadvantage (Scadding, 1967). Controversies arise when the boundaries of disorder so impinge on social phenomena (e.g., personal eccentricity or homosexual behavior) as to have sociopolitical implications.

Some "disorders" (e.g., as defined in the fourth edition of the *Diagnostic and Statistical Manual of Mental Disorders* (1994)) probably are truly categorical and distinctive, whereas others are dimensional, merging seamlessly with their diagnostic surrounds. When a number of behavioral disturbances are present and the "cutoff points" between disorders are obscure or merely arbitrary, it is difficult to know whether polymorphous dimensionality or categorical comorbidity is involved. This debate is not a trivial one. To the extent that a syndrome is truly categorical, it probably has a distinctive biological basis, at least in part. To the extent that it is dimensional, it probably is composed of a variable mix of polygenesis, temperament, and learned maladaptive coping strategies. If a distinguishing biological cause can be found, a "disorder" becomes a "disease." "Disorder," therefore, can be seen as a temporary way-station in the theoretical conversion of a neutral "syndrome" to a distinctive, biologically based "disease." Not all syndromes or disorders will prove to be categorically distinct; furthermore, some entities in the current taxonomy of disorders will be found to be heterogeneous and to require a fresh classification.

The clinician, therefore, combines nomothetic classification (aware that much of the taxonomy is provisional) with idiographic understanding, relating a given patient's psychological and behavioral patterns both to those of other patients and to the unique influences that have precipitated the disequilibrium in question, rendering the individual vulnerable in the first place. Diagnosis, therefore, is an amalgam of empathy, existential understanding, and objective analysis.

The Dimensions of Diagnosis

The diagnostic formulation has 3 dimensions: biopsychosocial, developmental, and temporal.

THE BIOPSYCHOSOCIAL DIMENSION

Imagine that the patient is in a freeze-frame and that the clinician is analyzing him or her with regard to physical health or development, psychological status, and adaptation to family and society.

No single theoretical system can unify these different levels of functioning. Biological or psychosocial reductionism (e.g., explaining psychopathology exclusively in terms of synaptic derangement, behavioral reinforcement, unresolved psychodynamic conflict, or family boundary pathology) will not work. The well-prepared clinician has mastered an array of different theoretical paradigms and applies them as appropriate to the various biopsychosocial levels.

The clinician analyzes the following levels and sublevels in order to determine whether they are dysfunctional or impaired, and, if so, what is the pattern of dysfunction:

1. *Physical level*
   1.1 Peripheral organ systems
   1.2 Immune system
   1.3 Autonomic system
   1.4 Neuroendocrine system
   1.5 Sensorimotor system
   1.6 Overall physical attributes, such as height, beauty, grace, etc.
2. *Psychological level*
   2.1 Information processing (orientation, attention, memory, comprehension, judgment)
   2.2 Academic achievement
   2.3 Communication
   2.4 Attitudes and emotions toward self and others
   2.5 Social competence
   2.6 Symptoms, signs, and patterns of psychopathology, including categorical diagnosis
   2.7 Unconscious conflicts, ego defenses, and coping style
   2.8 Honesty, ethical stance, dependability, values, ideals
3. *Social level*
   3.1 Family structure, complexity, and dynamics (e.g., what is the family's level of functioning with regard to communication, emotional sensitivity, the sharing of emotion, boundary

and role definition, behavior control, problem solving, crisis resolution?)
   3.2 Relationship to social groups (e.g., peers, adult authority) and social institutions (e.g., school)

THE DEVELOPMENTAL DIMENSION

In deciding whether the patient is dysfunctional or impaired, the clinician scrutinizes the different systems within the biopsychosocial axis, relating each to the range of normal development expected at the patient's age. A knowledge of normal development will allow the clinician to know if a particular function (e.g., height, weight, organ growth, coordination, language, intelligence, reading, social cognition, moral development, coping style) is at the level expected, accelerated, decelerated, deficient, hypertrophied, or deviant in relation to the normal range for that age.

Families, too, develop proceeding from childless couples or single young womanhood, through pregnancy, the care of infants, children, adolescents, and young adults, to grandparenthood. The birth of a baby to a family whose other children are about to leave home, for example, is likely to have significant implications for all concerned.

THE TEMPORAL DIMENSION

How did the patient and family arrive at their present disequilibrium? What is its prognosis? Essentially, how did they get here, and where are they headed?

It is convenient to divide the temporal dimension into sequential way-stations marking the gradual evolution of psychopathology, as follows: predisposition, precipitation, presentation, present pattern, perpetuation, prognosis, and potentials.

Predisposition: Essentially, the clinician searches for genetic, physical, or psychosocial factors that could have rendered the patient vulnerable to later disequilibrium. In particular, Is there evidence for genetic factors, or for physical insults or deprivations that affected the patient during the intrauterine or perinatal periods? What were the sources of stress during the formative stages of infancy and childhood? Is there evidence of psychosocial deprivations, traumata, or distortions during the formative period?

Precipitation: Is there evidence for a physical or psychosocial stressor (e.g., an acute physical illness, a loss, or other trauma) operating at the onset of the current pattern that could have tipped the dynamic scales toward disequilibrium? Not all current patterns have an onset; some (e.g., pervasive developmental disorder) have a long, gradual evolution without specific precipitants. In other cases the precipitant is more of an *aggravant* to some preexisting disorder or impairment. Some precipitants, in themselves apparently minor (e.g., a calendar date), represent recapitulations or symbolic reenactments of an unresolved but hitherto dormant trauma. Other stressors (e.g., repeated exposure to combat, coercive sexual abuse, and some instances of civilian catastrophe) probably would cause the strongest personality to crumble.

Presentation: Often it is useful to ask: Why now? Why are the family presenting the patient at this time? Frequently the answer is obvious: the patient's behavior has become so disruptive, distressing, or dangerous that the family or community can no longer cope with it. Do the family present the child because they perceive a problem, or is it because someone else thinks the child has one?

Sometimes, especially in psychiatric hospitals, a patient presents because an external community system has failed (e.g., the leader of a group home becomes ill, the staff cannot cope with a particular child's resultant behavior, and vicious cycles of rule-testing and ineffective response overwhelm them), or because of poor communication between external institutions (e.g., a juvenile court judge orders a delinquent adolescent to be admitted to a psychiatric hospital for evaluation, because in that jurisdiction, the judicial system and the community mental health system are at odds).

Pattern: The current pattern of biopsychosocial phenomena has been discussed already. They make up the biopsychosocial dimension. Broader questions arise, however. What does the biopsychosocial pattern represent? The breakdown of prior adaptation with the emergence of more primitive coping patterns? Impending decompensation, with resultant anxiety, somatization, or tension discharge? The residue of a past decompensation? The unevenness and deviance in development associated with a pervasive develop-

mental disorder? Psychotic disintegration? The reemergence, following trauma, of previously dissociated memories? An attempt to repair a defensive breach with secondary defenses and neurotic compromise? Do the symptoms serve a communicative purpose of somatoform nature? If so, what is being communicated, and to whom? Are the symptoms related to a psychogenic aggravation or perpetuation of physical illness? If so, what is the secondary gain?

Perpetuation: Why has the disequilibrium not abated? What physical, psychological, or social factors keep it going? Most stressors precipitate a temporary condition from which the individual recovers without professional help, sometimes stronger than before, sometimes with scars that predispose to subsequent breakdown. Often the identification of perpetuating factors must be conjectural. Disequilibrium can be prolonged by physical illness, malnutrition, exhaustion, or substance abuse. The biochemical derangements associated with posttraumatic stress disorder, melancholia, or bipolar disorder may be reversible only with special means; the pessimism and self-derogation associated with some dysthymic patients may require psychotherapy; while the inadvertent reinforcement of psychopathology by disturbed families indicates the need for psychosocial intervention. Have the family so adapted to the patient's disturbance as to perpetuate it? Does the patient's psychopathology maintain the homeostasis of a dysfunctional family? Hypothetical explanations of perpetuation, thus, require the clinician to refer to biochemical, behavioral, psychodynamic, and family systems theory. No single approach will suffice.

Prognosis: What is the likely outcome or range of outcomes with and without treatment?

Potentials: It is helpful, at this point, to balance the catalog of defects and problems considered heretofore with an inventory of biological, psychological, familial, and social strengths. Physical strength, beauty, athletic ability, artistic talent, intelligence, social skills, and family resources are all examples of personal assets that can be incorporated in a treatment plan and fostered so as to circumvent defects or compensate for them.

The diagnostic formulation, therefore, is derived from a matrix that combines a vertical, *biopsychosocial* axis, a longitudinal, *temporal* axis, and a *developmental* axis that intersects the other 2 at the point of the biopsychosocial pattern.

CASE EXAMPLE: A DIAGNOSTIC FORMULATION

Patricia is a 13-year-old white female, referred to a psychiatric hospital by her psychotherapist, after she had frightened the staff of another hospital by behaving in an apparently psychotic manner. Patricia was the oldest of 3 siblings. She is adopted; her 2 young siblings are the biological children of the parents, and were born when she was 3 and 8 years of age. The family is intact. Her father is an affluent businessman, and her mother works at home. This is their first marriage.

There was no clear precipitant to Patricia's current disorder, although the onset of adolescence (menarche at 12 years) probably has accentuated it. As a younger child, she was contrasuggestible, negativistic, and prone to severe tantrums. Her negativism, irritability, and storminess continued throughout middle childhood to the present. At the age of 8 years, she began to pull out her eyebrows, eyelashes, and scalp hair. This has continued to the point that she now has a large bald spot on the frontal region and no eyelashes or eyebrows. In middle childhood she began to exhibit bed-time rituals and other compulsive behavior. These continue to the present. One month prior to admission, during a family argument, she threatened suicide, as a result of which she was admitted to the psychiatric ward of a general hospital where she was uncooperative and disruptive to the treatment program. Eventually she simulated "craziness" (claiming to hear voices and behaving in an apparently disorganized manner) and was transferred to this hospital, where she at once confessed that her "psychosis" was bogus.

Her predisposition to the current illness probably is associated with the following factors: She was born out of wedlock to a woman who is said to have taken a suicidal overdose of sedatives during pregnancy; she was subjected to severe neglect and possible physical abuse during the first year of her life; when adopted at 12 months she was physically and mentally delayed in development. Her adoptive mother had had several miscarriages before deciding to adopt. By 18 months of age Patricia exhibited insecure attachment to her adoptive mother, with severe separation and stranger anxiety, which continued until she was about 4 years of age. Otherwise, after 3 years of age, she showed no evidence of physical or mental delay.

The current pattern of her disorder involves the following: compulsive eyelash, eyebrow, and hair pulling, at least once per day, especially in the aftermath of conflict with her mother; obsessive-compulsive rituals that are not resisted; low frustration tolerance; explosive

tantrums; and an undercurrent of chronic depression and suicidal ideation arising from frustrated rage. She has low self-esteem (defended against by a superficial air of superiority). Her relationship with her mother is characterized by insecure, disorganized attachment, hostile dependency, and constant limit testing; she is rivalrous with her mother for her father's attention; she is resentful that the birth of 2 siblings has diverted her parents' attention from her, and she is openly envious and spiteful toward her brother and sister. She perceives her father as unreachably distant. Her current defenses involve projection, displacement, intellectualization, isolation, idealization, and the introversion of aggression. Her unconscious conflicts involve frustrated dependency needs and abandonment anxiety in regard to the mother, oedipal rivalry in relation to the father, and unresolved sibling rivalry. Her psychopathology represents the neurotic shoring up of failing repression against aggressive impulses by the use of obsessional defenses.

Physically she is in good health, with normal physical development. Her sensorimotor system is intact. Her intelligence is superior and her school achievement above average (despite a recent deterioration in effort). She exhibits no defects in communication or information processing other than when conflictual issues are impinged upon, at which time her judgment is poor, and she can act in a self-defeating or even self-destructive manner.

Patricia's present condition is perpetuated by her own provocative, self-defeating attitudes and behavior, by her depreciated self-image, and by significant family dysfunction. Her parents are emotionally estranged; the father is emotionally unavailable, frequently absent, and preoccupied with business; the mother is chronically depressed, socially isolated, and emotionally unresponsive. The family members communicate poorly, are emotionally insensitive to each other, and share feelings poorly (except when they are enraged). Both parents have difficulty controlling the patient's disruptive or limit-testing behavior. They vary inconsistently from ignoring it to being excessively and explosively punitive toward Patricia, which they subsequently regret and renounce. It is possible that the patient's behavior is, in part, an attempt to ward off parental separation or abandonment by keeping the parents focused upon her. It also represents a compulsive need to test the limits of their tolerance by goading them to reject her.

The categorical diagnosis is:

Axis I
1. Trichotillomania
2. Oppositional defiant disorder
3. Depressive disorder Not Otherwise Specified
4. Parent-child problem

Axis II
1. Obsessive compulsive traits
Axis III
No diagnosis
Axis IV
3
Axis V
40

The prognosis without treatment is poor. The condition may evolve into a fully fledged obsessive-compulsive disorder or borderline personality disorder. Prognosis with treatment is fair but dependent on whether both parents can be fully engaged in the treatment plan.

The child's potentials and strengths are as follows: above-average intelligence; artistic ability (writing); good financial resources.

Conclusion

The biopsychosocial formulation guides treatment planning by helping the clinician identify the foci of treatment, which are the pivots around which the treatment plan will revolve. (See Chapter 95.)

Other systems have been introduced to aid diagnostic formulation and treatment planning, including those of Amchin (1991); Faulkner, Kinzie, Angell, Uren, and Share (1985); Leigh and Reiser (1993); Perry, Cooper, and Michels (1987); Sperry (1992); Shapiro (1989); and Sperry, Gudeman, and Faulkner (1992). Only Shapiro's work, which is designed for children and adolescents, gives adequate weight to psychodynamic, developmental, and family factors.

REFERENCES

Amchin, J. (1991). *Psychiatric diagnosis. A biopsychosocial approach using DSM-III-R.* Washington, DC: American Psychiatric Press.

American Psychiatric Association. (1994). *Diagnostic and statistical manual of mental disorders* (4th ed.). Washington, DC: American Psychiatric Press.

Faulkner, L. F., Kinzie, J. D., Angell, R., Uren, D. C., & Share, J. H. (1985). A comprehensive psychiatric formulation model. *Journal of Psychiatric Education, 9,* 189–203.

Leigh, H., & Reiser, M. F. (1993). *The patient: Biological, psychological, and social dimensions of medical practice* (2nd ed.). New York: Plenum Press.

Nurcombe, B., & Gallagher, R. M. (19). *The clinical process in psychiatry.* New York: Cambridge University Press.

Perry, S., Cooper, A. M., & Michels, M. D. (1987). The psychodynamic formulation: Its purpose, structure, and clinical application. *American Journal of Psychiatry, 144,* 543–550.

Scadding, J. G. (1967). Diagnosis: The clinician and the computer. *Lancet, 2,* 877–882.

Shapiro, T. (1989). The psychodynamic formulation in child and adolescent psychiatry. *Journal of the American Academy of Child and Adolescent Psychiatry, 26,* 675–680.

Sperry, L. (1992). Demystifying the psychiatric case formulation. *Jefferson Journal of Psychiatry, 10,* 12–19.

Sperry, L. T., Gudeman, J. E., & Faulkner, L. R. (1992). *Psychiatric case formulations.* Washington, DC: American Psychiatric Press.

96 / **Clinical Decision Making**

Barry Nurcombe

THE PURPOSE OF DIAGNOSIS

Diagnosis has 4 aims: It aids research, facilitates administration, summarizes information, and guides treatment. By diagnosing subjects, the researcher hopes to collect comparable groups. Diagnostic terms enable administrators and insurers to count heads and decide, for example, whether people should be reimbursed for the costs of illness. But for clinicians, the chief purposes of diagnosis are to summarize information and to guide treatment.

Philosophical questions bedevil diagnosis. Are the familiar syndromes of medicine (e.g., rubella, subacute bacterial endocarditis, schizophrenia) things in themselves ("entities"), or are they hypothetical constructs of more or less utilitarian value? Is it helpful to classify patients into taxonomic pigeonholes (even if such pigeonholing were clearly reliable and valid)? Woodruff, Goodwin and Guze (1974) have no doubts. They assert that psychiatric disorders should be precisely defined and that each will prove to have a predictable cause. On the other hand, it could be argued, each patient is an individual, subject to different influences. To ignore uniqueness would deplete the information required to design individualized treatment plans.

Few clinicians today would subscribe to one of these approaches to the exclusion of the other. Most seek generic patterns, such as the syndromes of the fourth edition of the *Diagnostic and Statistical Manual of Mental Disorders,* while at the same time individualizing treatment in accordance with the unique temporal and biopsychosocial configurations of each patient. (We also discuss this matter in Chapters 95 and 97.)

CLINICAL REASONING VS. STATISTICAL PREDICTION

Diagnosis is a risky business. No one gainsays the errors with which it is fraught or doubts that error can have serious consequences. How could it be improved? This question has generated a continuing controversy. On the one hand are clinicians who make observations, interpret them, and combine their findings, intuitively, to form diagnostic patterns—patterns that are formed by and then matched against their memory of textbook syndromes. Opposing them are the psychological actuaries who regard the intuitive clinical approach as obsolete, compromised as it is by unreliability, and who see it as ripe for replacement by statistical formulae and machine logic.

Research into the way clinicians think is *normative;* the researcher attempts to capture, analyze, and reproduce the actual processes by which a clinician makes decisions. Actuarial research is *prescriptive:* The researcher aims to replace intuitive

ratiocination with probabilistic formulas. Both kinds of research are cited in this chapter.

As will be seen, a considerable amount of actuarial research purports to demonstrate the error of clinicians' ways. Why has this research had so little impact? There are several explanations. First, some of the experimental situations described are so artificial that clinicians are inclined to disregard them. Second, actuarial work typically deals with the kind of diagnostic reasoning that converges on categorical entities or single decisions, when it is apparent that, in the real world, clinicians usually deal with dynamic networks. Third, clinicians tend to concede that others may make mistakes but to believe that errors of that sort do not apply to them. Last, it is likely that, in order to survive in such a risky environment, clinicians develop a defensive overconfidence that is relatively impervious to criticism. Otherwise, awash in self-doubt, they would become dangerously indecisive.

One facet of clinicians' overconfidence is an immense respect for the flexibility, efficiency, and mercurial nature of their own thought processes. It is not uncommon for clinicians to resist research into diagnostic reasoning for fear that, if tampered with, the mystical skill will evaporate. Their fear contrasts with researchers' evident scorn for the value of clinical ratiocination. A deeper concern is the specter of the machine advancing inexorably to replace human frailty with actuarial formulas of cast-iron reliability.

This chapter deals with the natural process of diagnostic reasoning, discuss its flaws, and suggest that machine logic could complement the clinician's skill rather than replace it.

Research into Clinical Reasoning

Elstein and Bordage (1988) classify research in clinical reasoning into 3 types: clinical judgment, decision theory, and information processing.

In the first type, the researcher attempts to identify the criteria used in reaching a decision. In the second, the flaws inherent in clinical reasoning are unveiled as the clinician struggles to make sense of incomplete information. In the third, the researcher traces the natural process of reasoning by analyzing its progressive elements. The first 2 types are prescriptive; the third is normative. Each is discussed herein.

CLINICAL JUDGMENT

One theoretical model of clinical judgment was derived by Hammond (1955) from Brunswick's (1955) concept of a determinative "lens." According to the lens model, each patient presents a set of symptoms and signs that the clinician weighs and combines to reach a decision. Researchers attempt to "capture the policy" of the decision maker in order to ascertain how decisions are reached. This model applies best to convergent problems (e.g., concerning the risk of suicide or violence, the advisability of hospitalization, or the need for electroconvulsive therapy). Mathematical models then can be constructed and incorporated into computer programs that replicate clinical judgment.

DECISION THEORY

Given the often incomplete and "fuzzy" nature of clinical phenomena, medical decision making is probabilistic. Decision theorists recommend that, to be efficient, clinicians should understand Bayes' theorem, which states that $P(D/F)$ (the probability of a disease being present when a particular finding or set of findings is elicited) is a function of $P(F/D)$ (the probability of the finding being present in that disease), $P(D)$ (the base rate of the disease in the particular population) and $P(F)$ (the probability of the finding in that population), such that:

$$P(D/F) = \frac{P(F/D) \times P(D)}{P(F)}$$

The intuitive clinician tends to gauge $P(F/D)$ from theoretical knowledge and clinical experience. However, $P(F/D)$ should be combined with local base rates for both the disease and for the findings. Actually, heuristic errors of a systematic nature are endemic to clinical reasoning (Arkes, 1981; Faust & Nurcombe, 1989; Kahneman, Slovic, & Tversky, 1982; Tversky & Kahneman, 1974, 1981) as follows:

1. If a set of clinical features resembles a textbook syndrome, clinicians tend to diagnose it without considering $P(F/D)$ and $P(D/F)$, forgetting that sparrows are much commoner than canaries.
2. Since base rates are often unknown, clinicians fall back on subjective estimations. They are likely to be overconfident concerning the accuracy of their estimations.
3. Clinicians tend to overestimate PD as a result of previous salient or recent experience. Thus exotic or dangerous diseases may be overdiagnosed. It should be pointed out, however, that there is a point to entertaining the diagnosis of uncommon diseases (e.g., brain tumor). First, the consequences of missing a dangerous disease are serious, and second, an exotic diagnostic hypothesis keeps the mind from closing too soon on the most probable candidate.
4. Clinicians are conservative thinkers; that is, they are slow to correct subjective base rates in the light of new information (Edwards, 1968).
5. Clinicians rely too much on positive evidence (that supports their impression) and too little on negative evidence that would tend to challenge it. In fact, the more powerful strategy is to search for information inimical to a pet hypothesis.
6. Early preference for a given diagnostic hypothesis can impede the collection of evidence to disprove it.
7. Clinicians have difficulty controlling for the placebo effect and allowing for the tendency of extreme findings to regress toward the mean.
8. Unaided, clinicians have difficulty separating the utility of a treatment (e.g., longevity) from its value (e.g., quality of life).
9. Preconceptions, particularly stereotypical ones, bias the collection of data and the recall of information.
10. Hindsight is easier than foresight.

INFORMATION PROCESSING

Using experts as subjects, cognitive psychologists have attempted to trace the steps of naturalistic reasoning in such fields as chess (De Groot, 1965), physics (Larkin, McDermott, Simon, & Simon, 1980), neurology (Kleinmuntz, 1969), family practice (Feightner, Norman, Barrows, & Neufeld, 1975), and internal medicine (Elstein, Shulman, & Sprafka, 1979). Process training research is derived from the pioneering work of Newell and Simon (1972). A chess expert, for example, has an experiential memory for thousands of meaningful board patterns. The retrieval of these patterns from long-term memory gives the expert access to strategic options. Similarly, the memory of a diagnostic syndrome is linked to tactics for eliciting, evaluating, and assembling the missing elements of a diagnostic puzzle. It also is linked to strategic therapeutic options.

Elstein and Bordage (1988) describe clinical reasoning as a form of "bounded rationality" in which the clinician converts an open problem (i.e., one with no clear end point) into a series of closed problems (each with a hypothetical end point). Thus, presented with a child of 3 years who has not yet spoken (open problem), the clinician may hypothesize deafness, mental retardation, autism, developmental language disorder, and cerebral palsy (5 closed problems). By this means, the search for evidence is organized.

Feinstein (1967) regards diagnosis not as an end in itself but as the means to an end. Naturalistic diagnosis is best considered as an interrelated causal explanation rather than a static entity. Furthermore, the decision pathway toward that end is a series of hypothesized graduated steps:

1. Perceive salient data.
2. Verify data.
3. Decide whether data are deviant.
4. Select a pertinent data set.
5. Refer the data to clinical domains (e.g., "infectious process") or disorders within the domain (e.g., "pyelonephritis").
6. Assemble a set of domain/disorder candidates that best explains the data set.

Support for Feinstein's thesis has come from Elstein, Shulman, and Sprafka (1978), who presented clinicians with simulated patients and patient management problems, and then compared the performance of expert internists to that of medical students. These researchers identified 3 elements of reasoning, cues, hypotheses, and information search units.

Cues are elicited from history and direct examination. From sets of cues, diagnostic hypotheses are generated. Diagnostic hypotheses dictate and organize the subsequent search strategy. These hypotheses appear early in the interview, despite the fact that only a limited data base has been elicited. The hypotheses are progressively refined, deleted, or supported on the basis of subsequent diagnostic cues and information search strategies.

Due to limitations of short-term memory, only about 5 diagnostic hypotheses can be created. From the outset, an array of diagnostic candidates may consist of specific alternatives, or it may be organized in a hierarchical fashion. Hypothetical structures of hierarchical nature are highly efficient.

Hypothetical reasoning of this type prevents premature closure on 1 diagnosis. It also spares short-term memory by separating the information derived from cues and inferences into meaningful units, out of which a systematic search for evidence can be designed. Moreover, hypotheses are open to revision in the light of new evidence cycled back from the inquiry process.

Tactically, diagnostic reasoning involves cue elicitation, pattern recognition, hypothesis generation, information search, probability estimation, and decision making. The key features in the incomplete pattern of cues are linked to prototypic syndrome configurations in long-term memory, from which the hypotheses are generated. The subsequent search plan yields further information to complete, fail to complete, or disconfirm each hypothesis. The array of hypotheses represents a "problem space" that converts the open problem to a series of closed ones. Elstein, Shulman, and Sprafka (1978) found little consistency across problems: faced with a neurological problem, an expert dermatologist is likely to regress to the level of a novice.

Feightner et al. (1975) and Barrows (1979) have corroborated the findings of Elstein, Shulman and Sprafka's regarding early hypothesis generation and a limitation to the number of hypotheses generated.

Psychiatric Reasoning

Gauron and Dickinson (1965), Kendell (1973), and Sandifer, Hordern, and Green (1970) conducted early investigations of psychiatric reasoning. Their findings are consistent with Elstein, Shulman, and Sprafka's theory that clinical reasoning is hypothetico-deductive in nature; however, their stimulus materials (narrative case histories) lacked face validity.

Studies at the University of Vermont (Nurcombe & Fitzhenry-Coor, 1982, 1986; Fitzhenry-Coor & Nurcombe, 1983) used videotaped cases as stimuli presented to subjects of varying experience (medical students, residents, and psychiatrists). Each videotape was divided into six 5-minute segments. From the raw material of reasoning (the subjects' verbal or written productions produced after each segment), units of analysis were identified—phrases or sentences each of which contained a single idea. Content analysis allowed each unit to be parsed into one of the following categories:

1. Salient cue (e.g., "He says he hears voices")
2. Clinical inference (e.g., "He has auditory hallucinations")
3. Preliminary hypothesis (e.g., "schizophreniform disorder")
4. Inquiry plan (e.g., "Order projective testing")
5. Diagnostic conclusion (e.g., "schizophrenia")
6. Management plan (e.g., "hospitalization")

SALIENT CUES

Salient cues are recognized from the documentation provided, from the history given by the patient, or from other sources, as well as from the physical and mental status examinations. The experienced clinician is alert to particular phenomena (e.g., the complaint of hearing voices) that are likely to be important to diagnosis (i.e., salient). An internist, for example, is likely to be more interested in blue lips than in freckles.

CLINICAL INFERENCES

A clinical inference is a salient cue (e.g., "hears voices") that has been weighed and interpreted (e.g., "auditory hallucinations"). Some inferences combine cues; for example, "slow thinking," "slow movement," and "delayed responses to questions" become "psychomotor retardation".

PRELIMINARY HYPOTHESIS

A preliminary hypothesis is a hunch derived from a cue or from an inference, from a set of cues and inferences, or from inferred discrepancies, inconsistencies, gaps, contrasts, and parallels in the history and examination. Hypotheses organize the subsequent search plan.

INQUIRY PLANS

In accordance with each hypothesis, the clinician generates systematic probes in order to gather secondary cues that will complete the initial diagnostic pattern and refine, confirm, fail to confirm, or challenge the hypothesis in question. Uncorroborated or unconfirmed hypotheses are discarded.

DIAGNOSTIC CONCLUSION

Thus the clinician reaches a diagnostic conclusion and decides whether a unitary diagnosis is appropriate or whether multiple diagnoses are required.

The following profile of diagnostic competency was derived from the content analysis of the subject's protocols:

1. *The onset-of-hypotheses score.* The proportion of all hypotheses generated during the first segment of the videotape.
2. *The hypothesis-tracing score.* The number of times each hypothesis is reevaluated.
3. *The tactical justification score.* The frequency with which each hypothesis or enquiry plan is justified.
4. *Diagnostic accuracy.* The relative concordance of the subject's diagnosis with a model diagnosis (provided by a panel of experts).

Compared to students and residents, experienced psychiatrists generated hypotheses earlier and were more accurate diagnostically. Compared to students, residents and psychiatrists were more likely to trace their hypotheses consistently and to offer justifications for their inferences, hypotheses, inquiry plans, and management plans.

Nurcombe and Fitzhenry-Coor (1986) implemented a course that aimed to promote the following diagnostic competencies:

TACTICAL OBJECTIVES

1. Recognize and evaluate salient cues.
2. Interpret cues when appropriate.
3. Assemble clusters of cues and inferences.
4. Generate an array of categorical and dynamic hypotheses.
5. Design an inquiry plan that searches for confirmatory disconfirmatory evidence.
6. Weigh the evidence and reach a conclusion.

757

7. Formulate a biopsychosocial diagnosis.
8. Design a goal-directed treatment plan.

STRATEGIC OBJECTIVES

1. Separate cue and inference.
2. Tolerate uncertainty, avoid premature closure, and consider alternatives.
3. Be aware of personal reactions to the patient.
4. Be alert for fresh evidence.
5. Value negative evidence. Revise interpretations or hypotheses if the evidence demands it.
6. Do not go on interminably. Be prepared to commit oneself.

The instructional technique involved exposing students to the same segmented videotapes as were used in the original research and fostering the objectives through small-group teaching. Contrasted to controls in terms of pretest and posttest, the experimental group at posttest generated more hypotheses, tested their hypotheses more accurately, tended to offer rationales for their reasoning, and were more accurate in their final diagnoses.

Diagnostic Reasoning in Child Psychiatry

Child psychiatrists encounter their patients in outpatient clinics, pediatric units, community agencies, forensic settings, inpatient units, and private offices. Each setting has its advantages, drawbacks, and constraints, and each is associated with a particular range of cases. Nevertheless, certain principles apply whatever the setting.

The clinical process is a sequence of steps commencing with referral and ending with termination (Nurcombe, 1986a). The duration of the process varies from 30 minutes (e.g., a brief consultation in an emergency room in order to determine the need for hospitalization) to months or even years (in long-term psychotherapy or medication maintenance). It is important to note that the process has "feed-forward" and "feedback" characteristics: Each step presupposes and anticipates the steps ahead; and information provided from each step may be cycled to influence prior steps. For example, the initial array of hypotheses may be discarded, modified, refined, or accepted in accordance with later inquiry.

In child psychiatry, the process involves a clinician, a child, and a family (or surrogate family). In the case of more severely disturbed children (e.g., in inpatient psychiatry), the clinician is replaced by a clinical team (e.g., psychiatrist, nurse, social worker, psychologist, mental health worker). The team leader—the psychiatrist—coordinates the eyes and ears of the team.

The clinical process commences with referral (e.g., from a pediatrician, an emergency room physician, a school counselor, an attorney, or a friend). Referral is a point of heightened vulnerability. It progresses to the initial contact (often by telephone) and the diagnostic encounter (which varies in extent from 1 interview to several days of multidisciplinary, biomedical, and psychosocial assessment). At the end of the diagnostic encounter, the clinician (or team) formulates the biopsychosocial diagnosis from which the treatment plan is derived. (See Chapter 97.)

Diagnostic formulation and treatment planning mark the end of the diagnostic phase, after which the therapeutic phase begins. Actually, therapy begins with referral, even before the initial contact, and diagnosis ends with termination; the best clinicians are alert for information that might appear at any point during treatment, and that would then necessitate a change, modification, or addition to diagnosis.

At the beginning of the diagnostic encounter, based on referral information and interview, the clinician begins to note the cues and make the inferences that are the grist of diagnostic reasoning (Nurcombe, 1986c).

CASE EXAMPLE

Jane is a belligerent 14-year-old white female adolescent from an impoverished background who has been charged with aggravated assault of a female peer. She presents herself as unremorseful and justified in what she has done. From her language development, I would estimate her to be of low verbal intelligence (but I must take cultural factors into account before I make up my mind about that). She does not sound psychotic, but I wonder if there is some depression beneath her bravado.

The cues and inferences are assembled into a pattern that forms the basis of hypothetico-deductive reasoning; for example, after the first 5 minutes:

- Fourteen-year-old white female adolescent referred from a juvenile detention center.
- Accused of beating up another female adolescent in the company of 2 female peers.
- Was "on the run" from a group home at the time.
- Had been placed in the group home as a status offender because she was uncontrollable at home.
- Said to have no history of other criminal offenses.
- Father died 3 years ago.
- Mother had a stroke 2 years ago and is partly paralyzed.
- Mother's boyfriend smelled strongly of alcohol when the patient was admitted.
- Patient refuses to accept the authority of her mother's (possibly alcoholic) boyfriend.
- Belligerent, self-justifying, with apparent bravado.
- Hint of depressive affect when discussing father's death.
- No evidence of thought disorder.
- Uses "street" language and African American phraseology.
- Poor language development.
- Not obviously hyperactive or fidgety.

The clinician is already generating an array of hypotheses:

1. Conduct disorder (This diagnosis must not be accepted without careful investigation for other conditions.)
2. Oppositional defiant disorder (Probably an understatement.)
3. Affective disorder (Could she have a covert depressive disorder expressed in aggressive acting out?)
4. Impulse control disorder (This is an unsatisfying diagnosis, more a description than an explanation.)
5. Postabuse syndrome (Has she experienced physical or sexual abuse? Could she have a hidden posttraumatic stress disorder?)
6. Developmental disorder (Could she have a language abnormality? Is she culturally disadvantaged?)

This array of hypotheses (which are not mutually exclusive) alerts the clinician during the standard investigation (history, mental status, physical examination, laboratory testing, social history), directs discretionary emphases within and diver-

sions from the standard investigation, and calls for special investigations or data gathering of discretionary nature (Nurcombe, 1986b). For example, the clinician would seek the following information:

- A detailed history of the offense (from the patient and, if possible, from an independent observer)
- A record of past legal involvement (from the patient, Department of Social Services, and parent)
- A developmental and family history
- Detailed mental status examination (particularly regarding posttraumatic and depressive phenomena and cognitive performance)
- Physical examination (for sexually transmitted disease and evidence of substance abuse)
- Educational history (any psychoeducational testing done previously?)
- Past mental health and pediatric history (documentation?)
- Interview with mother (possibly, also, interview with mother's boyfriend)
- History of alcohol intake, illegal substance abuse (from patient and mother)
- Psychological testing (intelligence; language development; school achievement; personality; evidence for depression, unresolved trauma, organicity)

Based on further history, physical examination, and psychological testing, it is possible (although unlikely) that electroencepholography or other neurological testing could assist diagnosis. In a case of this sort, documentation concerning previous legal and child welfare contact is likely to be of great importance.

Note that these hypotheses are not static tags but dynamic pointers in the direction of further standard and discretionary investigations. The hypotheses also are taking form as a combination of categorical diagnoses and dynamic interactions, in preparation for the biopsychosocial diagnosis (See Chapter 95.)

Cues and inferences are derived from the factual data elicited and also from the patient's dress, demeanor, eye contact, emotion, and spontaneity with which he or she recounts his or her story. Cues also are present in the gaps and discrepancies, if any, within the patient's story, or between the patient's account and information provided by other informants or documents.

The *standard inquiry* plan gathers generic information and screens for conditions or situations of diagnostic importance in that age group. For example, among adolescents, the clinician should routinely screen for suicidal ideation or attempts, homicidal or assaultive ideation or behavior, self-injurious behavior, antisocial behavior, alcohol or substance abuse, sexual activity, and physical or sexual abuse. Physical examination screens for general health, neurological status, and signs of alcohol or substance abuse, sexually transmitted disease, and physical or sexual abuse. Laboratory tests should probe for any evidence of liver, kidney, hematological, electrolytic, endocrine, and nutritional abnormality, and, in adolescent females, for pregnancy.

Discretionary probes are based on the array of hypotheses. They are ordered only if they are likely to disconfirm or corroborate the hypotheses in question. For example, in this case, language testing would be ordered only if standard psychological tests (intelligence and school achievement) suggested that receptive or expressive communication were impaired. The expert clinician aims to knock down his or her own pet hypotheses: Disconfirmation is more powerful than corroboration. The value of a probe is linked to its capacity to disconfirm.

When sufficient positive and negative information is available, the clinician discards inoperative hypotheses, refines those that need polishing, and accepts those that withstand testing or are corroborated by the search plan. Having converged upon the categorical diagnosis, the clinician then opens up to a biopsychosocial and temporal diagnosis. (See Chapter 95.) A number of presentations can be associated with specific discretionary protocols, as follows.

PERVASIVE DEVELOPMENTAL PROBLEMS

The child manifests severe arrest or delay in language, intellect, and social development. The condition may have evolved gradually, or it may have its onset after a period of relatively normal development. There may be associated signs suggesting infantile autism (e.g., unexplained panic, resistance to change, stereotyped movements, and deviant speech). The following protocol is recommended.

- Hearing
- Speech and language evaluation
- Neuropsychological testing
- Electroencephalography

- Magnetic resonance imaging
- Chromosomal analysis
- Thyroid function
- Amino aciduria

Additional tests (e.g., immunologic studies) may be ordered if there is reasonable cause for suspicion.

ACUTE OR SUBACUTE DISINTEGRATION

After normal or near-normal development, the child fails to attain or loses development attainments in one or more of: speech, language, memory, attention span, intellect, school performance, sphincter control, and social competence. The following should be checked:

FOR GENERAL SYSTEMIC DISEASE

- Thyroid function
- Adrenal function
- Urinary porphyrins
- Disseminated lupus erythematosis
- Serum ceruloplasmin

TOXIC FACTORS

- Exclude systemic infection, electrolytic abnormality, or physiological toxins (electroencephalography, specific biochemical, bacteriologic, or virologic tests)

DISEASES OF THE CENTRAL NERVOUS SYSTEM

- Seizure disorder (electroencephalography)
- Space occupying lesion (skull X ray, magnetic resonance imaging, computed tomography scan)
- Herpes encephalopathy (lumbar puncture, virology)
- Metabolic or subacute viral infection (electroencephalography, lumbar puncture, virology, immunology)
- Degenerative disease (electroencephalogram, urine amino acids, biopsy)
- Demylinating disease
- Leukemic infiltration of central nervous system (hematology of blood and lumbar puncture fluid)

ATTENTION DEFICIT HYPERACTIVITY

- Thyroid function (thyroid function tests)
- Plumbism (urine lead, hematology, X rays of long bones)

- Seizure disorder (electroencephalography)
- Sleep apnea (otolaryngology consult, sleep electro-encephalogram and observation)
- Sydenham's chorea (blood antistreptolysin-O antibody titre, neurology consultation)

DEPRESSION

General Systemic Disease

- Malignancy (pediatric consultation)
- Chronic infectious disease (pediatric consultation)
- Viral infection (pediatric consultation)
- Hypothyroidism (pediatric endocrinology)
- Hypoadrenalism (pediatric endocrinology)
- Chronic anemia (hematology)
- Subnutrition (hematology, pediatric consultation)

Toxins

- Excessive dosage of anticonvulsants or sedatives (urine drug screen and blood levels)

Central Nervous Disease

- Neurological examination
- Specific tests

APPARENT SOMATOFORM DISORDER

General Systemic Disease

- Disseminated lupus (LE cells)
- Hypocalcemia (laboratory tests)
- Hypoglycemia (glucose tolerance)
- Porphyria (blood and urine porphyrins)

Central Nervous Disorder

- Multiple sclerosis (neurology consultation)
- Movement disorder (neurology consultation)
- Spinal cord tumor (neurology consultation)
- Intracranial space occupying tumor (especially brain stem, cerebellum, frontal lobe, or parieto-occipital cortex; neurology consultation, skull X ray, computed tomography scan, magnetic resonance imaging)
- Seizure disorder (neurology consultation, electro-encephalography)
- Migraine
- Dystonic reaction to neuroleptic drugs

ANOREXIA

- Chronic systemic infection (especially tuberculosis)
- Systemic malignancy (especially pancreatic, medi-astinal, intraperitoneal, pulmonary, lymphatic, leukemic, ovarian)
- Hypothalamic or pituitary tumor (skull X rays, brain imaging)
- Diabetes mellitus (urinalysis, glucose tolerance test)
- Hyperthyroid (thyroid function test)
- Drug addiction (history and blood screen)

SLEEP DISTURBANCE

- Seizure disorder (electroencephalography and pol-ysysmenography)
- Delirium (acute febrile or toxic state)
- Narcolepsy (neurology consultation)
- Intoxication with sedative, opioid, anticonvulsant, antidepressant or neuroleptic drugs (drug screen)
- Hypoglycemia (glucose tolerance test)
- Any debilitating disease, especially those associated with chronic hypoxia (congenital heart disease, pulmonary disease, anemia)
- Sleep apnea (sleep encephalography)

DELAY IN SPEECH AND LANGUAGE DEVELOPMENT

- Deafness (acoustic testing)
- Palatal abnormality (otorhinolaryngolocial consultation)
- Cerebral palsy (neurology consultation)
- Mental retardation (psychological testing)
- Seizure disorder (neurology consultation)
- Aphasia (speech and language consultation, neuro-psychology)
- Developmental articulatory dyspraxia (speech and language consultation, neuropsychology)
- Pervasive developmental disorder

LEARNING PROBLEMS

- Visual defect (ophthalmoscopy, visual acuity, visual fields, ophthalmology consultation)
- Deafness (acoustic testing)
- Inability to attend in class (e.g., due to illness, fatigue, hunger, pain, or drug use)
- Cerebral palsy (neurology consultation)
- Mental retardation (psychological testing)
- Seizure disorder (electroencephalography, neurology consultation)
- Dementia due to intracranial space–occupying lesion or to cerebral degeneration (neurology consultation, electroencephalography, skull X rays, computed tomography scan, magnetic resonance imaging, neuropsychological testing)

ABNORMAL MOVEMENTS

- Attention deficit disorder (neuropsychological testing)
- Tourette's disorder (neurology consultation, neuropsychological testing)
- Sydenham's chorea (neurology consultation, anti-O-streptolysin titer)
- Huntington's chorea (neurology consultation, magnetic resonance imaging)
- Wilson's disease (neurology consultation, serum ceruloplasmin)
- Paroxysmal choreoathetosis (neurology consultation)
- Dystonia musculorum deformans (neurology consultation)
- Cerebellar tumor or degeneration (neurology consultation, skull X rays, computed tomography scan, magnetic resonance imaging)
- Drug effects (e.g., caffeinism, neuroleptic medication)

EPISODIC LAPSES OF AWARENESS

- Seizure disorder (electroencephalography)
- Cardiac arrhythmia (electrocardiography, pediatric consultation)
- Narcolepsy (electroencephalography, neurology consultation)
- Migraine (neurology consultation)
- Hallucinogenic drugs (urine drug screen)
- Posttraumatic stress disorder (detailed history)

EPISODIC VIOLENCE

- Temporal lobe seizure (electroencephalography)
- Herpes encephalitis (electroencephalography, immunologic study, examination of cerebrospinal fluid for viral culture and immunology)
- Drug effects (urine drug screen for alcohol, phencyclidine, hallucinogens, amphetamine)

Sometimes, after thorough inquiry, it is still unclear which diagnostic hypothesis is correct. If so, a clinician should consult with a colleague. If the diagnostic hypothesis is still unclear, the clinician should treat the patient vigorously for the most likely condition.

CASE EXAMPLE

Lou, a 14-year-old female, was referred to a psychiatric inpatient unit because, over the past 5 weeks her behavior had undergone a marked change. Formerly an outgoing, argumentative child, over the past 5 weeks she had become withdrawn, depressed, anxious, extremely dependent on her mother, and unwilling to go to school. The mother related the onset of her social withdrawal to her having contracted a sexually transmitted urethritis following consensual sexual intercourse with a boyfriend, supposedly her first sexual experience.

At interview, she was fully oriented, and looked preoccupied and perplexed rather than depressed. She spoke only in response to questions, and her answers were impoverished in content. She said she felt "confused" but was unable to elaborate upon it. On several occasions she remarked that sounds seemed "louder" than before; once she put her hands over her ears. She denied hallucinations, delusions, obsessions, compulsions, or panic attacks. She had lost about 10 pounds in weight over the past 6 to 8 weeks and had little appetite. She had difficulty falling asleep and often awoke during the night, but could not account for why she did so.

The diagnostic hypotheses entertained by the psychiatrist were: (1) schizophreniform disorder, (2) severe major depressive disorder, (3) posttraumatic stress disorder, and (4) organic dementia. Hypotheses (1) and (2) seemed the most likely. Physical examination, neurological examinations, routine laboratory tests (kidney, thyroid, hematological, electrolytic), electroencephalography and magnetic resonance imaging were not contributory.

Despite consultation, the psychiatrist still could not decide between hypothesis (1) and (2). However, she decided to treat the patient vigorously for major depression, while keeping a weather eye open for the appearance of more clearly schizophrenic phenomena (disorganized or tangential thinking, odd associations, frank delusions, hallucinations, affective incongruence).

Flaws in Clinical Reasoning

Flexible, wide-ranging, and mercurial though it is, the natural process of clinical reasoning is fraught with errors. These errors are a consequence of the inherent limitations of the human computer and its vulnerability to interference from other psychological systems.

First, despite the best intentions, a clinician's concentration can be disrupted by fatigue, illness, or emotion. Judgment can be impaired by stereotyping or countertransference, for example, when the patient (inadvertently or deliberately) stirs up conflicted issues in the clinician. The patient may, for example, elicit anger, boredom, erotic arousal, or the need to provide nurture. Whenever the clinician feels strong like, dislike, or identification with the patient, errors of judgment are possible. Consultation should be sought from a colleague.

Since the capacity of short-term memory is finite, there is a limit to the number of alternative hypotheses that can be mentally juggled. Four to 5 is usual; 6 is about the limit. Hierarchical organization helps, but is still limited. What if there are more than 6 reasonable diagnostic candidates?

The human computer tends to be more impressed with information appearing early in the diagnostic encounter and relatively less efficient in eliciting or accounting for later information, especially if it runs counter to first impressions (a primary effect).

Clinicians seem better at positing alternatives concerning categorical diagnosis (e.g., schizophrenia versus affective disorder) than at generating hypotheses for psychodynamic diagnosis (e.g., acting out unresolved grief following loss of father vs. reenactment of unassimilated physical abuse trauma). This is probably due to the fact that the relatively greater complexity of dynamic hypotheses puts additional strain on short-term memory.

Other problems (e.g., ignorance of Bayesian statistics, "hindsight bias," the "availability" heuristic, illusory correlations, and preference for positive rather than negative evidence) are described by Faust and Nurcombe (1989), Kahneman et al. (1982), and Schwarz and Griffin (1986).

Remedies

Unfortunately, too little time is devoted to the teaching of clinical reasoning. Good teaching and self-reflection can help aspiring and experienced clinicians to think critically about the cues they elicit, to be cautious about the inferences they make, to generate alternative hypotheses, to be consistent about testing them, and to seek negative evidence.

Nevertheless, even after good teaching and honest self-scrutiny, clinical reasoning is not perfectible—capacity limitations, system interference, and heuristic fallacies dictate the need for assistance. It is here that computers can help. No contemporary computer can match the ability of a good clinician to identify and weigh cues, form tentative patterns, and match them to prototypical syndromes. However, computers can store diagnostic information, generate extensive arrays of hypotheses, calculate probabilities based on base rates of disorders and symptoms, and avoid the biasing effects of primacy and recency. One day they will be essential for the comparative prediction of outcome following different treatments, given different combinations of age, sex, class, intelligence, family structure, diagnosis, severity, acuity, and economic and clinical resources.

Self-report questionnaires and structured interviews can improve the reliability and thoroughness of data gathering. Standard and discretionary search protocols can enhance the reliability of the inquiry plan (Nurcombe, 1986). The monitoring of treatment progress could be greatly assisted by computerized ratings of progress toward focal objectives.

Although machines, questionnaires, structured interviews, and search protocols can bolster human reasoning, today they cannot replace it. Whether they ever will be able to do so is an interesting question. At this time, the machines are promising aide-mémoire and actuarial predictors rather than true rivals.

REFERENCES

Arkes, H. R. (1981). Impediments to accurate clinical judgment. *Journal of Consulting and Clinical Psychology, 49,* 323–330.

Barrows, H. S. (1979). *An overview of medical problem solving.* Paper presented at the conference on the role of problem solving in medicine, Smugglers Notch, VT.

Brunswick, E. (1955). Representative design and probabilistic theory. *Psychological Review, 62,* 193–217.

De Groot, A. D. (1965). *Thought and choice in chess.* The Hague: Mouton.

Edwards, W. (1968). Conservation in human information processing. In B. Kleinmuntz (Ed.), *Formal rep-*

resentations of human judgment. New York: John Wiley & Sons.

Elstein, A. S., & Bordage, G. (1988). Psychology of clinical reasoning. In J. Dowie & A. Elstein, *Professional judgment: A reader in clinical decision making* (pp. 109–129). New York: Cambridge University Press.

Elstein, A. S., Shulman, L. S., & Sprafka, S. A. (1978). *Medical problem solving: An analysis of clinical reasoning*. Cambridge, MA: Harvard University Press.

Faust, D., & Nurcombe, B. (1989). Improving the accuracy of clinical judgment. *Psychiatry, 52,* 197–208.

Feightner, J. W., Norman, G. R., Barrows, H. S., & Neufeld, V. R. (1975). *A comparison of the clinical methods of primary and secondary care physicians.* Paper presented at a symposium sponsored by the Association of American Medical Colleges, Washington, DC.

Feinstein, A. R. (1967). *Clinical judgment*. Baltimore, MD: Williams & Wilkins.

Fitzhenry-Coor, I., & Nurcombe, B. (1983). Assessing clinical reasoning: The development of a new test in psychiatric education. *7,* 183–196.

Gauron, E. F., & Dickinson, J. K. (1965). Diagnostic decision making in psychiatry: I. Information usage. II. Diagnostic styles. *Archives of General Psychiatry, 14,* 225–232.

Hammond, K. R. (1955). Probabilistic functioning and the clinical method. *Psychological Review, 62,* 255–262.

Kahneman, D., Slovic, P., & Tversky, A. (1982). *Judgment under uncertainty: Heuristics and biases.* New York: Cambridge University Press.

Kendell, R. E. (1973). Psychiatric diagnoses. A study of how they are done. *British Journal of Psychiatry, 122,* 437–445.

Kleinmuntz, B. (1969). *Clinical information processing by computer.* New York: Holt.

Larkin, J., McDermott, J., Simon, D. P., & Simon, H. (1980). Expert and novice performance in solving physics problems. *Science, 208,* 1335–1342.

Newell, A., & Simon, H. A. (1972). *Human problem solving.* Englewood Cliffs, NJ: Prentice-Hall.

Nurcombe, B. (1986a). The clinical process. In B. Nurcombe & R. M. Gallagher (Eds.), *The clinical process in psychiatry* (pp. 101–111). New York: Cambridge University Press.

Nurcombe, B. (1986b). The diagnostic inquiry in child psychiatry. In B. Nurcombe & R. M. Gallagher (Eds.), *The clinical process in psychiatry* (pp. 510–525). New York: Cambridge University Press.

Nurcombe, B. (1986c). The tactics and strategy of clinical reasoning. In B. Nurcombe & R. M. Gallagher (Eds.), *The clinical process in psychiatry* (pp. 112–126). New York: Cambridge University Press.

Nurcombe, B., & Fitzhenry-Coor, I. (1982). How do psychiatrists think? Clinical reasoning in the psychiatric interview. *Australian & New Zealand Journal of Psychiatry, 16,* 13–24.

Nurcombe, B., & Fitzhenry-Coor, I. (1986). A review of research into clinical reasoning. In B. Nurcombe & R. M. Gallagher (Eds.), *The clinical process in psychiatry* (pp. 635–662). New York: Cambridge University Press, 1986.

Sandifer, M. G., Hordern, A., & Green, I. M. (1970). The psychiatric interview: The impact of the first three minutes. *American Journal of Psychiatry, 126,* 968–973.

Schwarz, S., & Griffin, T. (1986). *Medical thinking: The psychology of medical judgment and decision making.* New York: Springer.

Tversky, A., & Kahneman, D. (1974). Judgment under uncertainty. Heuristics and biases. *Science, 185,* 1124–1131.

Tversky, A., & Kahneman, D. (1981). The framing of decisions and the psychology of choice. *Science, 211,* 453–458.

Woodruff, R. A., Jr., Goodwin, D. W., & Guze, S. B. (1984). *Psychiatric diagnosis.* New York: Oxford University Press.

97 / Intervention Strategy Planning

Barry Nurcombe

Models of Treatment Planning

THERAPY-ORIENTED PLANNING

The natural mode of treatment planning is therapy oriented. Given a particular configuration (e.g., 7-year-old boy; only child of motivated middle-age parents; average intelligence; attention deficit disorder of moderate severity; learning problems; discipline problems at school), the clinician will fit it to a pattern of treatment derived from experience and training (e.g., parental education, education of school authorities, behavioral programs at home and school, psychoeducational testing for possible remedial teaching, stimulant medication). A sophisticated clinician might nominate target symptoms (e.g., attention span, activity level) to be monitored by special means (e.g., behavioral checklists). Often, however, the child's progress is assessed in a global manner, treatment proceeding until parents and clinician are satisfied that sufficient improvement has been attained, or until it is evident that the plan has failed. At that point, the plan will be changed, the parents will seek help elsewhere, or the family will drop out of treatment.

Although therapy-oriented planning is efficient of time and facility in its practice is acquired naturally, such a method of treatment planning has serious defects. The absence of stipulated objectives (and of an estimation of how long it will take to reach them) leads to vagueness. Family and clinician often are unclear about both how much improvement to expect and how to assess it. As a consequence, too often therapy will drift; the therapist is not held responsible for deciding whether the treatment is working and what to do if it has not been effective. When a clinical team is involved in planning and monitoring treatment, all these problems are magnified. Indeed, lacking a common and explicit logic for role assignment and decision making, the group is likely to become discoordinated.

PROBLEM-ORIENTED PLANNING

Weed (1969) introduced the problem-oriented medical record to overcome such difficulties. The problem-oriented system begins with the assemblage of a data base from which a set of diagnostic or treatment problems is extracted. Subsequently, when sufficient data have been gathered, diagnostic problems either become inoperative or are restated as categorical diagnoses for which therapy is prescribed. Subsequent therapeutic problems remain active, become inactive, or are resolved.

The explicit logic of this system fosters teamwork and enhances communication. Furthermore, the definition of a master problem list prevents the patient—particularly the hospitalized patient—from slipping through the cracks between organ specialists. Indeed, Weed's system has revolutionized hospital medicine. Why then has it failed in psychiatry?

A psychiatric patient presents problems from every level of the biopsychosocial axis; categorical diagnosis is seldom a useful guide to individualized treatment. Recognizing this, early workers (e.g., Grant & Maletzky, 1972) recommended that psychiatric problems be stated in the form of deviant behaviors in need of extinction or deficient behaviors in need of enhancement. No guidelines were offered as to how problems should be extracted from the data base or how they might be integrated. When this method was used, master problem lists degenerated into fragmented, trivialized inventories of a dozen items or more. Worse still, the clinician or clinical team, focused as they were on the writing of purely behavioral objectives, often missed the gist of the problem. Consequently, problem-oriented plans became mere paper formalities relegated to the chart in order to satisfy external reviewers, while the clinicians reverted to the tried (if not true) technique of therapy-oriented planning.

GOAL-DIRECTED OR FOCAL TREATMENT PLANNING

Focal treatment planning was introduced by Nurcombe and Gallagher (1986) and further expounded by Nurcombe (1987a,b,c; 1989). Its essence is the extraction from the diagnostic formulation of pivotal treatment foci. Each of these then gives rise to a behavioral objective with a target date, and for each, a treatment or set of treatments is designed. No attempt is made to list all the patient's problems, since treatment is impracticable or impossible for many of them. Within the existing therapeutic context, given the nature of the patient's psychopathology and the time, funds, and treatment resources available, the clinician decides what is changeable and what needs to be changed for treatment to terminate. Focal treatment planning is described in detail later in this chapter; but, initially, since foci, objectives, target dates, and modes of treatment vary according to the opportunities, resources, and constraints that present in different clinical situations, different treatment contexts are discussed.

The Contextually Determined Aims of Treatment

Treatment contexts are defined by intensity and duration. These dimensions can be classified respectively as low, intermediate, and high intensity, and ultrabrief, brief, intermediate, and extended duration. Intensity has to do with the closeness of the observation of the patient, and varies, for example, from outpatient treatment less frequent than once per week, through home-based treatment, to 24-hour-a-day hospitalization. Duration varies from ultrabrief (less than 2 weeks), brief (2 to 4 weeks), and intermediate (1 to 3 months), to extended (longer than 3 months).

Depending on the intensity and duration of treatment, different aims are possible. In ultrabrief treatment, no more than crisis alleviation is possible. In brief treatment, it may be possible to stabilize the patient sufficiently to allow treatment elsewhere at a less intensive level of care. In extended contexts, for example, day treatment or long-term outpatient therapy, the more ambitious aims of reconstruction, remediation, reeducation, or compensation are possible. Psychodynamic psychotherapy, for example, is reconstructive in aim, whereas behavior therapy is reeducative, special education is remedial, and the fostering of latent talent is compensatory in nature. Intractable difficulties arise when the treatment setting is designed for a different aim than funding resources will permit—for example, when a psychiatric hospital is forced by economic pressures into a brief-stay mode but retains diagnostic and therapeutic approaches appropriate to extended stay.

The different aims of treatment dictate the treatment foci, objectives, and modalities appropriate to a given patient in a particular context. The purpose of brief hospitalization is as follows: protection; rapid, comprehensive diagnosis and treatment planning; treatment; stabilization; and discharge to a less intensive setting. Stabilization foci and objectives vary considerably from those suitable for reconstruction, for example. The purpose of stabilization is to address those foci that prevent the patient from being treated outside of hospital. The next section discusses the principles of stabilization planning, with particular reference to hospital treatment. Then treatment planning in extended care is discussed.

The Steps of Focal Treatment Planning

1. THE DIAGNOSTIC FORMULATION

Seven days after a patient is admitted to a hospital, and following multidisciplinary assessments, the clinical team holds a diagnostic and treatment planning conference. The key is biopsychosocial diagnosis, a matter discussed in detail in Chapter 95. In summary, a diagnostic formulation should integrate the physical and psychosocial factors involved in the predisposition, precipitation, presentation, and perpetuation of the current biopsychosocial pattern, together with an appreciation of the patient's potentials.

Most important to treatment planning are:

- The physical or psychosocial factors that might predispose the patient to developing psychiatric disturbance in the future.
- The kind of stresses—physical or psychosocial—that might precipitate another emotional crisis in the future.
- The factors—physical, psychosocial, social, and/or legal/administrative—that occasioned the patient's presentation to hospital.
- The physical, psychological, or social factors that perpetuate the current biopsychosocial disturbance.
- The current biopsychosocial pattern; that is, physical and neuropsychological dysfunctions, symptomatic behaviors (considered in terms of coping style), dysphoric emotions, pathogenic dispositions toward the self and others, disordered family and social functioning, and their mutual effects on one another.
- The patient's potentials; that is, those physical and psychosocial strengths and resources that could be fostered in such a way as to circumvent or compensate for psychopathology.

2. STABILIZATION FOCI AND COMPENSATORY POTENTIALS

Stabilization foci are abstracted from the diagnostic formulation by asking the following questions:

- Which symptoms, signs, impairments, behaviors, emotions, dispositions, or dysfunctions in the current biopsychosocial pattern must change if the patient is to be treated at a less restrictive level of care?

- Which of the precipitating, perpetuating, or presenting factors must change if the patient is to be treated at a less restrictive level?
- Which potentials could be enhanced in order to circumvent or compensate for the patient's problems?

In general, 4 to 6 foci and 1 potential represent an array of convenient size; for example, in the case of a suicidal patient, the following problem list might apply.

Focus 1 Depressive mood/suicidal impulses

Focus 2 Unresolved grief reaction related to separation from father

Focus 3 Conflictual relationship with mother

Focus 4 Oppositional behavior toward authority figures

Focus 5 Artistic ability

Generally speaking, treatment foci can be categorized as behavioral (e.g., aggressive outbursts toward peers), psychological (e.g., unresolved conflict concerning past sexual abuse), familial (e.g., mother-child enmeshment), social (e.g., oppositional behavior), educational (e.g., retardation in reading), or medical (e.g., unstable juvenile diabetes mellitus). Further examples of treatment foci are provided in Table 97.1.

Each focus represents what the clinical team members propose to address—or, more correctly, what they aim to help the patient or family address—in order to allow the patient to be safely discharged from hospital.

3. THERAPY

For each focus, the team can select a therapy or set of therapies appropriate to the patient's needs, using the following criteria:

- In this kind of case, for which form of therapy is there the greatest empirical support?
- Which therapy is the least risky?
- Which therapy best matches the clinical resources available?
- Which therapy is the most economic of time and expense?
- Is the therapy under consideration appropriate to the values and expectations of the family?
- Can the therapy be continued after discharge (if continuation is appropriate)?

The nursing and milieu staff then can design a focal milieu plan that reflects the team's master treatment plan. Therapists sometimes use the term *objective* to refer to treatment maneuvers. For example, a therapeutic objective might be stated as "To develop an identificatory relationship with the patient." As this use of the word *objective* differs from the convention employed in the focal planning system, it is recommended that the terms *therapeutic strategy* or *therapeutic tactic* be used instead to apply to therapeutic interventions.

4. TARGET DATE

The team next should estimate how long it will take for treatment to be effective. This date functions as a benchmark against which the progress of therapy can be gauged.

5. OBJECTIVES

Many authorities recommend the use of specific treatment objectives, but few advise the clinician as to what form they should take. Undoubtedly, specificity is desirable, but a premature emphasis on "measurable" behavior may cause the clinician to miss the gist of the patient's disorder as he or she pursues trivial or superficial issues. A specific objective without a goal is stuck in the mud; a focus without an objective is in danger of floating off like an untethered balloon. The clinician should aim at abstract foci but anchor them with clear objectives.

Objectives represent what the patient (or family) should be like (do, say, feel, exhibit . . .) in order to allow safe discharge. To reiterate, a focus is what the team is trying to address; an objective is what the patient will be like at the end of treatment. For example:

Focus 1.   Suicidal impulses.
Objective. (At the time of discharge, the patient will _____) Express no suicidal ideation or risk-taking impulses to milieu staff or peers; express no suicidal ideation on mental status examination; and have articulated a plan for what he will do if he feels suicidal in the future.

Written thus, objectives represent behavioral samples that can be used to monitor goal achieve-

TABLE 97.1

Examples of Treatment Foci

Behavioral Foci
Self-injurious behavior (e.g., wrist slashing, wall punching, head banging) (e.g., in borderline personality disorder)
Hair pulling (e.g., in trichotillomania)
Assaultive behavior (e.g., in posttraumatic stress disorder)
Inappropriate sexual behavior (e.g., in dissociative disorder)
Incapacity to care for self (e.g., in schizophrenia)
Opposition to authority (e.g., in oppositional defiant disorder)
Noncompliance with medical treatment (e.g., in oppositional defiant disorder)
School refusal (e.g., in separation anxiety disorder)
Stealing (e.g., in conduct disorder)
Lying (e.g., in conduct disorder)

Psychological Foci
A. Affect and Attitude
    Depressive mood (e.g., in unipolar depressive disorder)
    Elevated mood (e.g., in bipolar affective disorder)
    Dysphoric mood (e.g., in dysthymic disorder)
    Episodes of anxiety or panic (e.g., in anxiety disorder)
    Hostile mood (e.g., in conduct disorder)
    Suspicious mood (e.g., in schizophrenia)
    Specific phobia (e.g., of attending school, in separation anxiety disorder)
    Interpersonal hostility, toward a specific person (e.g., in paranoid disorder)
    Excessive dependence on a specific person (e.g., in borderline personality disorder)
    Unresolved grief (e.g., in complicated grief reaction)
    Unresolved psychic trauma (e.g., in posttraumatic stress syndrome)

B. Thinking ideation
    Disorder of thought process (e.g., in schizophrenic or dissociative disorder)
    Hallucinosis (e.g., in schizophreniform disorder)
    Illusions (e.g., in hysterical pseudodementia)
    Delusional thinking (e.g., in paranoid disorder)
    Obsessive-compulsive thinking (e.g., in obsessive-compulsive disorder)
    Depersonalization or derealisation (e.g., in dissociative disorder)
    Confabulation (e.g., in histrionic personality disorder)
    Cognitive limitation, general (e.g., mental retardation)
    Cognitive limitation, focal (specific learning disorder)

C. Impulsive ideation
    Suicidal impulses (e.g., in borderline personality)
    Assaultive impulses (e.g., in conduct disorder)
    Destructive impulses (e.g., in conduct disorder)
    Impulses to set fires (e.g., in pyromania)
    Impulses to take risks (e.g., in conduct disorder)
    Impulses to engage in specified, unacceptable, sexual behavior (e.g., in psychosexual disorder)
    Impulses to commit other specified antisocial acts (e.g., in conduct disorder)
    Compulsions to check, to touch, to count

Family Foci
Untreated (specified) physical disorder in family member (e.g., father with untreated cardiovascular disorder)
Untreated (specified) psychiatric disorder in a family member (e.g., maternal alcoholism)
Marital discord between parents
Episodic parental abandonment
Conflict between other family members (specified)
Poor communication between family members in regard to role-taking, problem solving, or the sharing of affection
Emotional insensitivity between family members

768

TABLE 97.1

(*Continued*)

Pathological disengagement, coalition, enmeshment, or detouring of conflict between family members
Parental or familial reinforcement of patient's symptomatic behavior (e.g., in school phobia)
Inadequate parental or familial understanding of patient's physical or psychiatric disorder
Parental ignorance of (specified) appropriate methods of child rearing (e.g., in regard to hygiene, health, nutrition, education, recreation, the reinforcement of positive behavior, the limitation of negative behavior, or the provision of appropriate models)
Parental social pathology (e.g., in prison, media condemnation)
Parental explosiveness or excessive punitiveness towards patient
Parental physical or sexual overstimulation of patient
Parental physical or sexual abuse of patient
Parental rejection of patient (subtle, overt, episodic)
Parental emotional abuse of patient

Social Foci
Opposition to authority (e.g., in oppositional defiant disorder)
Manipulativeness (e.g., in conduct disorder or borderline personality disorder)
Excessive dependence on peers (e.g., in anxiety disorder)
Histrionic exaggeration of symptoms (e.g., in histrionic personality disorder)
Social isolation (e.g., in schizoid personality disorder)
Fear of mixing with peers (e.g., in social phobia)
Provocativeness toward peers (e.g., in conduct disorder)
Assaultiveness toward peers (e.g., ??????)

Medical, Physical, and Sensorimotor Foci
(Specified) physical disease or disorder (e.g., epilepsy, diabetes mellitus)
Weight loss or malnutrition (e.g., in anorexia nervosa)
Dehydration or electrolyte imbalance (e.g., in bulimia nervosa)
Refusal to eat (e.g., in catatonic schizophrenia)
Lack of sphincter control (e.g., in functional encopresis)
Vegetative signs (e.g., insomnia, hypersomnia, anorexia, psychomotor retardation and agitation, in melancholia)
(Specified) sensorimotor dysfunction (e.g., motor paralysis, anesthesia or blindness, in somatoform disorder of conversion type)
(Specified) abnormal movements, phonation, or coprolalia (e.g., in Tourette's disorder)
Delirium confusion, obtundation (e.g., in organic delirium)
Memory loss (e.g., in psychogenic amnesia)
Hyperactivity (e.g., in attention deficit disorder)
Attention span (e.g., in attention deficit disorder)

ment. They also express the extent, degree, or level of goal achievement required. For a simple focus (e.g., "low weight"), a simple objective (viz., a target weight) suffices; but in most instances a more complex objective is required. In general, the more inferential the focus, the more complex the objective needed to validate it.

6. EVALUATION

Child and adolescent psychiatry currently is in the process of developing reliable and valid techniques for assessing psychosocial functioning. Although these efforts are still in their early stages, much progress has been made. Standard ques-
tionnaires, systematic mental status assessments, and neuropsychological testing, for example, may all prove useful. For physical parameters numerous measures (e.g., heart rate, electrocardiogram, laboratory tests) are available. This is a large topic that deserves further attention; at this point, suffice it to say that the team members should design an evaluation plan coordinated with the objectives. Whenever possible, they should employ measurement or ratings rather than qualitative judgment. For example, if the focus "Unresolved conflict about sexual abuse trauma" is associated with an objective that involves a reduction of the number of major and minor dissociative episodes, then a daily count and description of such epi-

sodes is required. If, on the other hand, the behavioral issues involve sexualized speech or inappropriate erotic behaviors, these become the items to be so indexed.

7. DISCHARGE PLANNING

The team should decide where the patient will be discharged, into whose custody, and with what treatment arrangements. Having done so, it is necessary to decide who is responsible for the discharge plan, what are the external obstacles to it, how these obstacles will be overcome (actions), and by whom (clinician responsible). A fallback plan also is required if the initial plan cannot be effected.

8. NEGOTIATION

Focal treatment plans provide an excellent framework for explaining the purpose and nature of treatment to parents and patient, in order to allow them to contribute to the plan, give truly informed consent, and form a genuine alliance with the treatment plan.

9. IMPLEMENTATION AND MONITORING

Coordinated by the foci of their treatment plan, the team members then should implement the different therapies they have selected, with a particular clinician responsible for each. The psychiatrist convenes regular meetings of the treatment team, which, guided again by the foci, objectives, evaluation, and target date, evaluates the progress of the treatment plan.

10. REVISION

If progress stalls, if the patient deteriorates, or if unacceptable complications arise, the master plan may have to be revised. In these circumstances, all aspects of the plan should be scrutinized. Do the foci truly reflect the essence of the patient's disorder? Given the time and clinical resources available, are the foci or objectives practicable? Are the therapies appropriate to this patient? Is the target date realistic? Do the objectives adequately reflect the foci? Are the therapies being faithfully or effectively implemented?

11. TERMINATION

When the foci are stabilized, the patient will exhibit the stated objectives. If discharge planning has kept pace with treatment, the patient will be ready for discharge. Clearly, the collaboration of appropriate external clinicians or agencies is required from the day of admission (if not before). It is very desirable that external clinicians attend the master planning conference.

Table 97.2 provides an example of a treatment plan is provided.

Focal Treatment Planning
in Other Contexts

CRISIS ALLEVIATION

When the aim of crisis management is not to stabilize a patient but to alleviate a specific crisis (e.g., during ultrabrief hospitalization), the number of foci will be reduced and the objectives will be less ambitious. Hospitalization, then, becomes a temporary shelter intended to achieve security, rapid diagnostic evaluation, treatment recommendations, and early discharge (still unstable) to a less intensive setting. Psychodynamic, family system, or complex behavioral foci are less frequently appropriate to crisis alleviation (although they can be recommended for aftercare). Foci and objectives of the following type are most often required.

Foci	Crisis Alleviation Objectives
Suicidal ideation	The patient will express no active suicidal ideation for 1 day and will have made a suicide contract with staff.
Self-injury	The patient will exhibit no self-injury for 1 day.
Assaultiveness	The patient will have assaulted no one for 2 days. The patient will identify what triggers anger outbursts and undertake to talk to staff before exploding.

TABLE 97.2

Example of Focal Treatment Planning

Chapter 95 provides the case example of a diagnostic formulation for this patient. The formulation has to do with Patricia, a 13-year-old female admitted to a psychiatric hospital because, during a family quarrel, she threatened to commit suicide. The diagnostic evaluation revealed trichotillomania, depression, and long-standing oppositional and limit-testing behavior in the context of conflict with her parents and unresolved sibling rivalry.

Foci	*Stabilization Objectives by the Time of Discharge*
B1 Hair, eyebrow, and eyelash pulling	• Hair, lash, or brow pulling no more than twice per week in the week prior to discharge.
P1 Depression/suicidal ideation	• Significant decrease in depressive mood and no suicidal ideation (as evidenced by mental status examination and observation in milieu) for 2 weeks prior to discharge.
P2 Unresolved rivalry with mother for father's attention	• The patient will have become aware of her rivalry and its manifestations and identify this as a focus for outpatient treatment.
P3 Unresolved sibling rivalry	• The patient will have become aware of her rivalry with her siblings and identify this as a focus for outpatient treatment.
F1 Conflictual, punitive, testing mother-daughter relationship	• The mother and daughter will trace the origins of their conflict and identify this as a focus for outpatient treatment.
F2 Paternal inaccessability to patient and mother	• The father will explore his emotional distance from his wife and daughter and identify this as a focus for outpatient treatment.
S1 Oppositional behavior	• The patient will cooperate with the treatment plan and comply with unit rules for at least 2 weeks prior to discharge.

Target Date: Four weeks

Treatment Modalities

B1: Medication (chlorimipramine), behavior therapy (e.g., self-monitoring, substitution)

P1: Individual psychotherapy, family therapy, medication (see P2)

P2: Individual psychotherapy, group therapy, family therapy

P3: Individual psychotherapy, group therapy, family therapy

F1: Family therapy, individual psychotherapy

F2: Family therapy

S1: Milieu program, individual psychotherapy

Evaluation

B1: Self-monitoring (journal). Measurement of bald spot and observation of hair length

P1: Mental status examination and milieu observation

P2: Observation in individual psychotherapy

P3: Observation in individual psychotherapy

F1: Observation in family therapy

F2: Observation in family therapy

S1: Daily report by primary nurse

Refusal to eat or drink	The patient will have taken normal amounts of food and fluids by mouth for 3 consecutive days.
Noncompliance with medical treatment for a potentially lethal condition (e.g., diabetes mellitus)	The patient will have been compliant with medical treatment for the condition during 3 consecutive days.

The concept of ultrabrief hospitalization is derived from acute medical or surgical care and has been imposed on psychiatry by external economic forces. Clearly, it is associated with serious risks to the patient. It should be undertaken only if the continuity between hospital and aftercare is satisfactory, and if the aftercare setting is capable of handling the particular form of psychopathology that the patient is likely to exhibit.

INTERMEDIATE AND EXTENDED CARE

In some forms of day treatment, and in outpatient and residential treatment, remedial, reconstructive, reeducative, and compensatory foci are required. The objectives applied to these foci are more ambitious than in briefer types of care, and it is possible to incorporate into the objectives many symptoms and behaviors (that during brief hospitalization may be separate foci). Consider the following example.

Foci	*Extended Objectives*
1. Mother-child enmeshment	1.1 The child will attend school regularly without anxiety and perform as expected for her grade level.
	1.2 The child will have several friends and be a member of at least 1 extracurricular organization.
	1.3 Mother and child will be capable of disagreeing with each other without decompensating into tears or panic.
2. Unresolved conflict concerning past sexual abuse	2.1 The patient will have recovered in detail all memories of past sexual abuse and be capable of recounting them without terror or dissociation.
	2.2 The patient will exhibit no evidence of minor dissociation (vagueness and discontinuity of thinking) or major dissociation (trances or audiovisual hallucinosis).
	2.3 The patient will demonstrate a reasonable choice of boyfriends, avoiding those who are likely to exploit her.
	2.4 The patient will be able to cope with appropriate heterosexual relationships without dissociating or allowing herself to be exploited by her partner.
	2.5 The patient will have decided on a career and be working appropriately toward it.
3. Hair pulling	3.1 The patient will be aware of the emotional situations in which the compulsion to pull hair arises. She will have identified alternative tactics that counteract hair pulling and be able to implement them without subjective disruption.
	3.2 Episodes of hair pulling will have changed from the current level (twice per day) to completely absent (for the

772

past 3 months).

3.3 Scalp, hair, eyebrows, and eyelashes will have completely regenerated.

3.4 The compulsion to pull hair will be occasional (no more than once per week) and weak in intensity.

3.5 The patient will show an appropriate interest in using cosmetics and in personal grooming.

When the objective is likely to be long term, it is helpful to articulate an intermediate objective, with target date, in order to ensure that treatment is on the proper course, as is shown in the next example.

Focus	*Intermediate Objective*
1. Unresolved grief concerning loss of father	1.1 The patient will be able to attend to tasks (e.g., homework) without intrusive memories of his father disrupting his concentration (3 months).

Terminal Objective

1.2 The patient will be able to remember his father without breaking down, to discuss problems in their relationship, and to be less idealistic in his description of the father (12 months).

Remedial foci of an educational nature are best incorporated into the general and specific objectives of an Individualized Educational Plan. Educational plans can be coordinated effectively with reconstructive and compensatory plans. In fact, focal treatment planning is derived from the planning by objectives that originated in educational psychology (Mager, 1962).

Disadvantages, Flaws, and Advantages of Focal Planning

Focal treatment planning is not easy to master. Those who wish to adopt it will encounter numerous obstacles and objections. Focal planning does not build on the more familiar process of therapy-oriented reasoning, and it requires the clinician to be explicit about matters that are customarily blurred or ignored. Many clinicians are very uncomfortable with target dates, for example, as they are reluctant to make educated guesses about how long it will take to reach a therapeutic objective (or even to pin down the objective itself).

Clinicians properly value most highly their contact with patients. Other things are likely to be relegated to the category of "paperwork." Implemented without understanding, focal treatment planning is likely to deteriorate into pro forma perfunctoriness (as was the sad fate of the psychiatric problem-oriented medical record). Some clinicians object, claiming that the explicitness of objectives will stifle creativity. On the contrary, implemented with imagination, foci actually are liberating, for they provide the team with an intellectual scaffolding whereby alternative therapeutic approaches to the same problem can be considered.

A serious problem in focal planning is the difficulty of framing psychodynamic and family system objectives. Since medical, educational, and behavioral objectives are much easier to articulate, there is a danger that treatment plans will deteriorate into problem-oriented laundry lists—that is, unless the conceptual difficulties inherent in psychodynamic treatment planning can be addressed.

On the other hand, the advantages of focal planning are several. They may be summarized in educational, communicational, regulatory, medicolegal, efficiency-related, and investigative terms.

Focal planning lends itself to teaching by workshop. Practicing clinical teams can be asked to tackle an actual case introduced by narrative history, videotape, or interview and to design a treatment plan. The benefits and difficulties of foci and objectives then can be discussed.

Once mastered, focal planning provides an intellectual scaffolding that promotes and enhances communication between team members, between clinician and community, and between the clinician and regulatory bodies. With clear justification for treatment and monitored goal-directed treatment, the clinician is in an advantageous position to avoid or appeal denials of payment by third-party insurers, to argue for longer hospitalization when stabilization objectives have not been attained, or to clarify with health maintenance organizations why ultrabrief hospitalization might be inadequate for a particular case.

The focal medical record, furthermore, provides potential medico-legal advantages. It reminds the team to record matters that might be otherwise overlooked, and it provides a clear framework for following progress notes that might otherwise be poorly organized.

Finally, focally planned records lend themselves to research. We do not know the relative benefits and costs for particular patient groups of intensive ambulatory treatment, partial hospitalization, brief hospitalization, and extended hospitalization. If these questions are to be addressed, the goals of treatment and the extent to which they have been attained will provide invaluable data.

REFERENCES

Grant, R. L., & Maletzky, B. (1972). Application of the Weed system to psychiatric records. *Psychiatric Medicine, 3,* 119–129.

Houts, P. K., & Scott, R. A. (1976). *Individualized goal planning.* Hershey, PA: Mental Health Rehabilitation.

Kiresuk, T. J., & Sherman, G. E. (1968). Goal attainment scaling. *Community Mental Health Journal, 6,* 443–453.

Mager, R. F. (1962). *Preparing instructional objectives.* Palo Alto, CA: Fearson.

Nurcombe, B. (1987a). Diagnosis and treatment planning I. *Australian & New Zealand Journal of Psychiatry, 21,* 477–482.

Nurcombe, B. (1987b). Diagnosis and treatment planning II. *Australian & New Zealand Journal of Psychiatry, 21,* 483–487.

Nurcombe, B. (1987c). Diagnosis and treatment planning III. *Australian & New Zealand Journal of Psychiatry, 21,* 490–500.

Nurcombe, B. (1989). Goal-directed treatment planning and the principles of brief hospitalization. *Journal of the American Academy of Child and Adolescent Psychiatry, 28,* 26–30.

Nurcombe, B., & Gallagher, R. M. (Eds.). (1986). *The clinical process in psychiatry: Diagnosis and treatment planning.* New York: Cambridge University Press.

98 / Interpretive Interview with Children and Adolescents and Their Parent(s)

L. Eugene Arnold and Peter S. Jensen

The interpretive interview is a medium for giving the parent(s) and child or adolescent feedback about the diagnostic profile, the prognosis, and the recommended treatment plan. The word *interpretive* implies that the clinician is translating concepts and terms from one language (the technical/medical terms of psychiatric jargon) into another (the vernacular). This yields the first of 12 guiding principles for interpretive sessions:

1. Use the language and idiom of the family.
2. Address the child or adolescent.
3. Review the concerns.
4. Decide if intervention is needed.
5. Use clinical "salesmanship"

6. Begin with "where the family is" and redirect or reframe as needed.
7. Play the "heavy" when needed.
8. Consider the child's/adolescent's age.
9. Accentuate the positive, qualify the negative.
10. Solicit questions.
11. Informed consent.
12. Build therapeutic alliances.

Alone or Together

Before discussing these guiding principles in more detail, we first need to consider whether the interpretive interview should be held with the parents alone or with the parents and child or adolescent together. There are several arguments on each side. The main arguments for a joint interview include:

1. It reassures youngsters that the doctor is not conspiring with parents behind their back.
2. It is more efficient; things do not need to be repeated separately with the youngster and with the parents.
3. It facilitates checking a few last items of information that may have been overlooked during the preceding history, examination, and tests.
4. It helps cement the idea of a therapeutic team, including clinician, patient, and parents, all working together.
5. It facilitates the clinching of a tripartite therapeutic contract.
6. It may help "detoxify" affect-laden issues that have been hard to talk about in the family setting.

The clinician's ability to discuss such issues openly in the presence of both child and parents often provides great relief to the entire family. There are 2 arguments for holding the interpretive interview with the parents alone: It is unnecessary for the child, at least a younger one, to hear all of the details about the problems; indeed, hearing them might be hard on the child's self-esteem. Moreover, with the child present, the parents may feel inhibited from asking questions or bringing up problems they anticipate in the treatment program.

By and large, the arguments for the joint interpretive session seem to outweigh those for the parents-alone session, especially for older children and adolescents, but to some extent even for younger children. Consequently, many clinicians who favor a parents-alone session often follow it with a joint session for parents and child together. In most instances, it is expeditious to have a joint interpretive session, perhaps preceded by some opportunistic discussion with either patient or parents or both during their private history taking—or perhaps followed by individual sessions at subsequent appointments. Therefore, the following discussion of guiding principles assumes a joint session. Many of the points made can be applied, with little change, to a parents-alone or adolescent-alone interpretive interview.

Translate into the Family's Idiom: Clinical Formulation and Treatment Plan

The evaluator must necessarily think in psychiatric concepts and make appropriate diagnoses with standard nomenclature. The family needs to be informed of the technical terms but also should be told what these mean in plain language. Many psychiatric terms have come into common usage; sometimes they are understood correctly, sometimes not, and in many cases the family may employ a term very similar to official diagnostic terminology, such as depression, anxiety, or hyperactivity.

When a family uses such a diagnostic or quasi-diagnostic term, it is appropriate to inquire what they understand by it. If they understand it correctly, the correctness of that understanding can be confirmed; if the term fits the child's diagnosis, communication is easy and straightforward. If they understand the term correctly but it is not the correct diagnosis for the child's condition, they can be given the correct diagnosis and an explanation of it. If the term is wrong for the child's condition but their understanding of the term does fit the correct diagnosis, they can be given the correct terminology. This can be done in a way that reinforces their understanding of the problem. For example: "You're absolutely right that the difficulty sleeping, worry, jitteriness, daytime fatigue, loss of interest in sports, games, and school, difficulty concentrating, and loss of appetite are all connected and form part of a single diagnosis. The best diagnosis in this case is major depression rather than anxiety. Anxious symptoms sometimes come as part of depression."

In a similar manner, a family may correctly understand a diagnostic term that is wrong for their child. They can be reinforced for the accuracy of their knowledge but must then be supplied with the correct diagnosis and its explanation. For example:

"You have a very good understanding of attention deficit hyperactivity disorder, and I can understand why you think John has it, with his restless sleep, wandering around the house, pacing, difficulty concentrating on his work, and emotional outbursts. However, John, it appears that your main problem is actually anxiety—technically, adjustment disorder with anxious mood. Remember that the problems started after the burglars broke into your house 2 years ago. After that you no longer felt safe and started worrying about a lot of things, especially about dangers, and got into safety checks of all kinds in a big way. Now you have trouble concentrating because of all your worries, you have trouble sleeping because of your nightmares about burglars breaking in again, and you get frustrated and lose your temper with playmates because they neglect the safety checks you feel you need in order to be safe."

CLINICAL FORMULATION

The forgoing example illustrates not only the translation, interpretation, and clarification of technical terms and concepts but also a bit of the all-important explanation of causal sequence, for which we use the technical term *clinical formulation*. It is not enough merely to name and confirm the problems—after all, the family already knows there is a conduct disorder or depression or anxiety or short attention span. The clinician also must make sense of the problem for the family: What caused it? How did it happen? What circumstances or events are making it worse or keeping it going? How do the facts fit together to make a logical story? It may be appropriate to mention (in the family's vernacular) such things as genetic vulnerability, stressors that have been identified, precipitating events, vicious cycles, normal developmental tendencies that have been sidetracked,

and even good-intentioned but erroneous parental responses that unwittingly aggravate the problem. (Of course, in the latter case, the clinician needs to be careful not to appear to be blaming the parents, who already may be blaming themselves unproductively and do not need aid and reinforcement in that waste of energy.)

Naturally, there will be some uncertainty in the formulation because of the imperfect state of clinical science and because the clinician, after only a few hours of information collecting, cannot fully understand every ramification of a child's or adolescent's life. Nevertheless, by dint of training and experience, the clinician's synthetic and causal understanding of the problem will usually far surpass the family's. The clinician owes it to the family to share this wealth of understanding while acknowledging the limits of scientific knowledge about such problems.

TREATMENT PLAN IN PLAIN LANGUAGE

Not only diagnosis but treatment too should be couched in understandable, defined terms. Most people have some concept of psychotherapy, ranging from accurate to a stereotyped conception of the psychoanalytic couch. The popular term *counseling* may be closer to modern psychotherapy, especially of the cognitive-behavioral type. What is important is to give a succinct description of what will take place: "I'll be teaching and rehearsing some techniques to use when the scared feelings come." Parent guidance might be explained as: "I'd like to meet with both of you a few times to talk about what you can do at home to help Lisa get the most out of her treatment sessions." Or "I'd like to teach you a few techniques for those heated arguments you mentioned, so you can get them settled in a friendlier way, and Brenda won't be so worried that you might get a divorce." Family therapy requires an explanation that makes it clear that other family members, especially the parents, will not be blamed for the identified patient's problems. Naturally, any proposed medication should be fully explained in plain language regarding intended benefit, rationale, and side effects. Such explanations can lay the foundation for informed consent (to be discussed later), for enhancing placebo benefit for the welfare of the patient, and for psychologically detoxifying common, harmless side effects (Arnold, 1973).

Address the Child or Adolescent

To a great extent, the preceding clinical examples seem addressed to the parents. It is appropriate to address the parents intermittently throughout the interview; with younger children, most of the clinician's comments may well be addressed to the parents. However, it is important to establish from the beginning that the interpretive session is for the benefit of the child or adolescent, and that the treatment contract includes him or her as well as the parents.

This kind of understanding actually needs to be established at the very beginning of the evaluation, prior to the interpretive session. For example, youngsters may be first asked, in the presence of the parents, what their understanding is about the visit. If they have some understanding, they can be invited to talk about it, thus getting a chance to "tell their side of the story first." Frequently youngsters will shrug their shoulders or otherwise indicate lack of knowledge. Then they can be asked whose idea it was to come. They will usually indicate their parent(s), providing an opportunity to ask "What do you think is the reason your mom and dad brought you?" "I don't know" is a common response, but often this can be followed up with "What did they say about why you had to come?" If youngsters persist in denying knowledge about the purpose of the visit, the clinician can express empathy for this confusing state of affairs and offer to help them find out from the parent the reason for the evaluation. This makes it clear that the clinician's primary relationship is with the child or adolescent but that the parents are also important players who can be used as resources in helping the youngster. With this preparation, the interpretive session provides another natural opportunity to address the child first. The clinician may say, for example:

"Well, I've had a chance to get some information from you, from your parents, and from some tests. Now I'd like to tell you what I think about your situation. It ap-

pears that you have two different sets of problems. First let's talk about the bad thoughts that keep coming into your head, which we call obsessions. Then there is the fact that you feel like you have to make everyone count to 100 three times before you can eat to make sure the food is safe; that is something we call compulsions. So these things together make what is called obsessive-compulsive disorder. It seems to be caused by an imbalance of brain chemicals, which usually can be corrected with medicine, but it also can be made worse by stress in your life.

"That brings us to a second set of problems. You've been worried that your parents might be planning to get a divorce. I know there is some reason for that concern, because they told me that even though they don't really plan a divorce, they have been having quite a few arguments. There have been other worries as well. You've been worried that your father might be laid off from work like your neighbor's father, and of course you've been concerned about your best friend's injury in the auto accident. All of these things are stressful for you and have probably been making your symptoms worse. Fortunately, there is something we can do about these stresses. How would you feel about coming back several times and meeting with me to talk about some of these things and learning how to keep them from bothering you?"

(Of course, this is not the whole treatment plan; for example, the parents also would be offered marital therapy or conflict resolution training to reduce their arguments, but this offer need not be made in the child's presence.)

While telling this to the child, the clinician can glance occasionally at the parents. When making treatment recommendations, the clinician can solicit the parents' agreement. For example: "Would you be willing to bring him in for those sessions?" or "Would you also be willing to meet a few times to talk about some ways to reduce the stresses in his life?" After the initial explanation, the conversation may drift to more of an interchange between the clinician and parents, especially in the case of younger children. However, even during this interchange, an occasional comment should be directed back to the child. For adolescents, such youth-directed comments should be more frequent and more extensive.

In some cases, youngsters may indicate a lack of interest in the exchange and show more interest in pursuing some book or toy. In that event, clinicians can gracefully accept the fact that the youngster does not wish to acknowledge hearing the information and can comment that he or she and the parents will go ahead and discuss the recommendations while the child plays or reads. The child certainly can listen in if he or she wishes.

On other occasions, issues may arise that need to be discussed with the parents alone. In such a case, the clinician can say "Now that I have explained what I think about your problems, there are some grown-up problems that I need to talk about alone with your parents. Do you have any questions before you go back out to the waiting room? Can you find your way okay by yourself?" In most cases it is not necessary to dismiss a child; usually the things that need to be discussed alone with the parents can be taken care of beforehand during the history taking from the parents alone. (It should have been established at the initial joint meeting that each party will have a chance to talk with the clinician alone.)

Review the Concerns

It is advisable to check whether the complaints expressed at the beginning of the evaluation have been embellished, denied, or otherwise changed by the time of the interpretive interview. Such changes are possible even during the 2 to 4 hours elapsing from the beginning to the end of a marathon same-appointment evaluation and interpretation. In fact, the evaluation process itself is likely to nudge the family into thinking about the problems in new ways. Changes in chief complaint(s) become more likely when several weeks elapse between the beginning of an evaluation and the interpretive session. These can reflect actual changes in symptoms or merely changes of perception, and can result from spontaneous remission, denial, resistance to therapy, "flight into health," natural complication, or aggravation by the evaluation process.

In a same-appointment evaluation/interpretation, in the interests of time saving, it is acceptable for the clinician to summarize the originally stated complaints briefly, and ask if that is correct and whether the family has thought of anything else that should be mentioned. For an extended evaluation or delayed interpretive session, however,

Greenspan (1981) recommends a more unstructured, leisurely approach facilitated by an invitation to bring the clinician up to date.

Decide If Intervention Is Needed

One of the commonest pitfalls for a novice examiner is to assume without reflection that there really is a problem that needs treatment beyond the interpretive session. In most clinical situations, of course, this assumption is valid; parents do not bring their children for mental health evaluation for no reason, and treatment usually is indicated. However, clinicians sometimes have the happy opportunity to evaluate a child where no further intervention is indicated. In some cases an anxious, inexperienced parent mistakes normal developmental phenomena (e.g., preschool sex interest) for a sign of disturbance. In other cases there may be an actual problem, but it is amenable to a "therapeutic consultation" at the interpretive interview without further indication for therapy. In some special situations, children are not showing any symptoms or maladjustment but may be evaluated "to be safe" following a trauma; if a well-functioning child objects to rehashing the trauma and wishes to just forget it, forced treatment focused on the trauma might actually be contraindicated. However, parents should always be invited to come for re-evaluation if problems appear later.

CASE EXAMPLE

A 4-year-old is brought by a harried young mother with the complaint that he lies, fights, and is messy and sneaky. Developmental history was normal, with the usual Terrible Twos, which the mother had expected, followed by good behavior at age 3. The current complaints began 5 months ago shortly after his fourth birthday. He is in general good health. There is no family history of mental disorder or antisocial behavior on either side. The mother was an only child; she quit her job when the boy was born so she could be a full-time mother; she will do this until he starts kindergarten. The father often has to be away on business, but he spends a lot of time with his son when he can. The child's behavior is no different whether father is home or not. Such a mother could be told: "It appears that he is going through a normal stage. You already knew about the Terrible Twos and you saw how that stage passed. A much less well-known stage is the Fearsome Fours, which he seems to be enjoying now. Continue to be firm and set reasonable limits and look for a chance to reward him when you catch him being good, but don't take it too personally when he acts his age. I know it's exhausting, but this stage should pass in a few more months. If you need some relief for yourself, try a preschool a few half days a week; he should fit right in with the other 4-year-olds, and you've probably noticed that most kids behave better for other adults than for their own parents. If he's not tolerable by age 5, though, check with me again and we'll do something about it."

Clinical "Salesmanship"— The Therapeutic Alliance

As far back as 1975, Lazare and colleagues (Lazare, Eisenthal, & Wasserman, 1975; Eisenthal & Lazare, 1976) described a "customer approach to patienthood." They pointed out that in each clinical presentation there are at least 3 distinct issues: the chief complaint, the diagnosis, and the patient's or parents' request. These may enjoy harmonious confluence, as with a patient who says: "I've been hearing voices threatening to kill me, and, since there is schizophrenia in my family, I thought I'd better come and get a tranquilizer." In many cases, however, the chief complaint may be misleading; the patient may offer an erroneous tentative diagnosis as the chief complaint; or the patient may make a request that is inappropriate for either the diagnosis or the chief complaint. For example, a boy who is restless, inattentive, impulsive, and otherwise meets the diagnostic criteria for attention deficit hyperactivity disorder may be brought by parents who describe him as "nervous and bad-tempered," who request a tranquilizer for him, or who describe him as lazy and want the clinician to "motivate" him.

If the comprehensive treatment plan is to enjoy an effective therapeutic alliance, the clinician must pay attention to all 3 areas (complaint, diagnosis, and request). The clinician must make sure that the chief complaint is adequately addressed in the summation, make sure the correct diagnosis is understood by all parties, show how the treatment plan will help the chief complaint, and either grant the request or show how what is being

offered is better than what was requested. Sometimes it is possible to grant the request even though it may not be the most important treatment in this particular case or, had it not been requested, would not have been tried until later in the course of treatment. In agreeing to a requested treatment as the secondary or tertiary part of a treatment package, it is best to state first the requested treatment, then add the others even if the others are considered more important. For example, the clinician may say:

"You mentioned that you wanted Jack to have some counseling, and I agree that that's a good idea. Jack, I'd like to see you for an hour a week for several weeks to talk about some ways that I think you can help yourself. Even more important, we need to arrange some tutoring to help you catch back up with your schoolwork, because I know that it's very discouraging for you being behind like this through no fault of your own. Also, there is very good research evidence that a certain kind of medicine can make it easier for you to pay attention and to overcome those distractions that have been bothering you when other kids shuffle their papers and feet. I'm willing to prescribe that for you if you and your parents are willing. . . ."

The evaluator is in many ways "selling" the family a diagnosis and treatment plan. The "selling" is not entirely metaphorical, because the patient's parents do indeed pay for the treatment, and many treatment compliance problems stem from the patient or parents not being "sold" on what they are paying for. Like a good salesperson, the clinician needs to be alert for what the "customers" are interested in, what their motivation for purchase is, and what they can afford, both in terms of money and in terms of time and emotional investment. Sometimes a less ambitious treatment regimen that the family can tolerate will be more efficacious than an ideal regimen that they "do not buy." Although this may smack of charging what the traffic will bear, it represents reality orientation for the clinician. The clinician who would sell mental health needs to respect the realities of the marketplace, the limitation of the family's resources, and the right of the family to cancel the order if the price seems too steep or the product unattractive.

Although the child or adolescent is the patient to whom much of the communication should be directed (in the case of older adolescents, the pa-

779

tient is the one who most needs to be sold), with younger children usually the parents are most essential to sell, because it is they who control of the situation (or who should).

CLINCHING THE DEAL — THE THERAPEUTIC CONTRACT

To be worthwhile, sales virtuosity, by definition, must end in a contract. In other words, some kind of commitment must be elicited from the family to clinch the deal. This might be an agreement to return for another appointment at a given time and date, an agreement to accept a referral for specialized treatment or diagnostic procedures, or an agreement to call back the next day with a list of times that the whole family could be available for family therapy. Sometimes it is necessary to settle for a commitment to think over the recommendations and call back next day or at a given time and date to discuss the next step. In no event should things merely be left hanging with a vague notion of "getting in touch."

will be able to carry out this parental duty, or do you want some help for a while until you get used to it?"

The clinician can strengthen the therapeutic alliance by accepting the reality of the parent's or other family member's difficulties, and by actively empathizing with the frequent dilemmas that therapy for the child may pose for the parent. Further, the therapist's pointing out the potentially difficult and painful impact of the therapeutic process on parents and other family members (especially in family therapy) can strengthen their commitment to remaining in therapy even after their anxiety heightens.

Of course, any treatment plan that does not take into account the capabilities of both child and parents is bound to fail. In some instances, the parents or the child may not be able to work within the constraints of an ideal treatment plan, so the clinician must determine whether some less than ideal treatment is better than no treatment at all.

Begin With "Where the Family Is"

To be effective in "closing the deal" one must begin where the family is and reinterpret or reframe their natural, sometimes countertherapeutic, tendencies into a therapeutic direction. This is a sort of psychological judo, in which the parent's personality tendency or sometimes even psychopathology is used as the driving force for a therapeutic impact. For example:

An anxious parent feels too guilty about sending a daughter with separation anxiety disorder to school when she seems in so much distress. The vector of this guilt can be changed in direction by statements such as "I know it really hurts you to see how distressed Mary is when you force her to go to school and she clings to you, but you can't think about your own comfort. It's your duty as a parent to see that she goes to school no matter how bad it makes you feel. If you make yourself feel better by letting her stay at home, you are relieving your own pain at her expense. Now, Mary knows how I feel about this (smile warmly at the child). She knows that I think you have no choice but to make her go to school no matter how miserable she is and how miserable it makes you to have to send her. Do you think you

Play the "Heavy" When Needed

In addition to redirecting the parent's concern for the child's well-being in a constructive direction, the last clinical example also demonstrates the principle of shifting the onus of "being the heavy" to the clinician. The parent can simply blame the clinician for having to make the child go to school ("doctor's orders"). In general, any instruction to the parent to do something that the child will not like should be given in front of the child, so that the parent-child relationship is not strained unnecessarily. It should be clear to the child that the parent is doing it on instructions from the doctor. (Of course, the child should not be expected to verbalize this or agree to it.) Usually the parent is the most important person with whom the child must maintain a relationship. Professionals are expendable and, if they do their job well, transient. Therefore, the strategy should be to strengthen the rapport between parent and child, even at the expense of rapport with the clinician. Interestingly, though, rarely does this tactic seem to hurt the rapport between the child and clinician. More often than not, it seems to improve it.

One of the times it is necessary to see the parents alone is when instructing them to do something the child wants or likes. It is desirable for the parents to take credit for such action; and if they decide not to follow the advice, then the child will not have occasion to be disappointed or angry with them for their refusal. More discussion and examples of these principles can be found in Chapter 1 of *Helping Parents Help Their Children* (Arnold, 1978).

Consider the Age of the Patient

Allusion already has been made to the fact that for younger children, more of the interpretive interview may be directed toward the parents. The converse, of course, is that for adolescents, the clinician must be scrupulous about directing most of the communication to the patient. In fact, it is often desirable to discuss the diagnosis and treatment plan briefly first with the adolescent and then suggest that it should be presented to the parents as well, along with some additional details. Sometimes it is useful to introduce the suggestion for bringing in the parents with a question such as "Do you think your parents will agree with this?" Thus the stage is set for the adolescent to view the clinician as an ally who will help persuade the parents to cooperate with the treatment plan that the adolescent and clinician have negotiated. In the case of older adolescents, it is often useful to think of the parents as interested friends and supporters who have accompanied the adolescent, and whom the adolescent wishes to be informed about the diagnosis a nd treatment.

Accentuate the Positive; Qualify the Negative

In formulating a comprehensive treatment plan, it is important to consider the patient's and family's strengths. Moreover, it is equally important to mention these in the interpretive feedback. Families coming to a clinician typically feel weak, vulnerable, damaged, or incompetent/unable. It is important for them to learn that someone also can see their strengths and how these strengths can be used to resolve the problems. For example: "Fortunately, Joe, you have pretty good intelligence, and we can take advantage of that in the treatment program by teaching you some alternate ways of coping. For example, you can learn some ways of making up for your auditory memory problems by using visual memory, which you're good at." Another example is: "One of the things Joe has going for him is your dedication and persistence in trying to help him. All you need is a little guidance in channeling all that effort in the most productive direction, which the parent training group that I'm recommending will be able to offer."

Not everything is positive, of course, and the problems do need to be described. However, the explanation of the problem areas should be couched in terms that make it clear that neither child nor parents are being blamed and that the problem is being defined in order to match it with the most effective solution. Perhaps most important still, the explanation needs to be clothed with empathy for the plight of the child (and parents). For example:

"Jill, I can see from your Bender Gestalt why you've had trouble getting your written work done. As I watched you do this, it was obvious you were trying very hard. (Turning to the parents) The problem is not lack of motivation or laziness or stubbornness, because this test proved that she really was trying hard and doing her best. (Turning back to Jill) Even though you were doing your best, I think you realized you were having some problems with it, didn't you? (Turning back to parents) You can see the difference between the figures she was trying to reproduce and what she actually put on paper. Now, we don't expect picture-perfect reproductions, but the average child her age would be able to make figures that would be recognizable as the same ones on the card. (Turning back to Jill) This must be very frustrating for you, trying so hard and not being able to do it quite right. (Turning back to parents) This is called visual-motor dysfunction, which just means eye-hand coordination problem, and the things that can be done to help it are. . . ."

Solicit Questions and Recapitulate

Several times through the interpretive session, questions should be solicited. Often it is enough just to ask if there are any questions. However, sometimes it is necessary to read the nonverbal look of consternation, puzzlement, or fear of appearing ignorant or stupid that betrays an unspoken question. In some cases the patient and parents, too bewildered and/or intimidated to ask questions, may even try to appear knowledgeable by nodding knowingly. In extreme cases, it may be necessary to guess at the questions, based on nonverbal feedback during the explanation. For example: "I noticed that you looked a little puzzled when I mentioned the possibility of using antidepressant medicine. Were you wondering why we would use an antidepressant to treat anxiety?"

To ensure that all questions will be asked, it is important to reinforce the first few questions. For some patients and parents it is reinforcing enough merely to give a clear answer to the question. For others, it may be necessary to make a comment such as "That's a good question" or "I'm glad you asked that."

After soliciting questions, it may be useful to ask the family to recapitulate. Too often clinicians unwittingly use terms that they assume—erroneously—are well understood by the family. Sometimes the family members share the mistaken belief that they do understand the misunderstood term and therefore do not inquire about it. In such a case, the only way to discover the misunderstanding is to ask them to restate their understanding. After completing the summary of diagnosis and recommendations, the clinician should ask the patient and family to summarize back what they understood about the nature of the child's problems, the causes, and the steps that must be taken to remedy the problems. Even if they understood correctly, this recapitulation will not be wasted, because it will help them remember. The clinician can even preface the request with a statement like "I've found that it helps people to remember if they restate it right away."

Developing Informed Consent

During the last several decades, significant changes have taken place in the nature of doctor-patient relationships. These changes have necessi-

tated more patient involvement in decision making. Certain circumstances render fully informed consent particularly important, namely: when a treatment is hazardous (as with some psychoactive drugs), when it may have both positive and negative effects (as with practically all treatments in the psychiatric armamentarium), or when one treatment is not necessarily greatly superior to another (as with different types of psychosocial treatment or different drugs in the same class). In addition to strengthening the therapist-patient relationship, informed consent can provide patients a cognitive preparation for some of the struggles that lie ahead.

To establish trust early in the therapeutic process, it is advisable to discuss openly with the family the various competing "best interests" of the different family members and to try to anticipate the potential hazards that the therapy may pose for various members. Ideally, such issues are addressed during the interpretive interview. In this context, informed consent can be viewed as: (1) an opportunity to describe some of the difficulties and hazards of the therapeutic process; (2) an opportunity to collaborate with patient and parents in the decision-making process about how the therapy should proceed; (3) an aid in establishing a therapeutic alliance and an empathic therapist-patient relationship; and (4) a means of blunting or preventing the patient's projection of omniscience and omnipotence onto the therapist, thus preventing later disappointment and anger.

Build Therapeutic Alliances

This principle of building therapeutic alliances has been implicit—sometimes explicit—in most of the other principles discussed and needs no elaboration. It is listed separately to emphasize its importance. The term *alliances* is deliberately pluralized to emphasize that for treatment to succeed, the clinician should develop alliances with all relevant parties, not just the patient or just the parents. These alliances constitute the main goal of the interpretive interview: an informed agreement between clinician and patient/family as to what the problem is and what will be done about it.

REFERENCES

Arnold, L. E. (1973). The art of medicating hyperkinetic children. *Clinical Pediatrics, 12*, 35–41.

Arnold, L. E. (1978). Strategies and tactics of parent guidance. In *Helping parents to help their children.* New York: Brunner/Mazel. L. E. Arnold, ed., pp. 3–21.

Eisenthal, S., & Lazare, A. (1976). Evaluation of the initial interview in a walk-in clinic. The patient's perspective on a "customer approach." *Journal of Nervous and Mental Disease, 162* (3), 169–176.

Greenspan, S. I. (1981). Interviewing the parents. In *The clinical interview of the child* (pp. 172–192). New York: McGraw-Hill.

Lazare, A., Eisenthal, S., & Wasserman, L. (1975). The customer approach to patienthood. Attending to patient requests in a walk-in clinic. *Archives of General Psychiatry, 32* (5), 553–558.

99 / Report Preparation

Barry Nurcombe

The Purpose of Report Writing

A clinical report interprets the findings of a clinical assessment and provides a clinical formulation. Often the report conveys recommendations for treatment and discusses the possible outcome of the case. An administrative report analyzes a problem, identifies causes, and recommends solutions, with estimates of time, cost, and the likelihood of success. Reports become documents to which authorized people can refer. They are thus both records of work done and evidence for the writer's thoroughness, balance, discernment, and lucidity.

Psychiatric reports are prepared for psychiatrists and other mental health clinicians and for medical practitioners, attorneys, judges, government agencies, administrators, insurers, and educators. Medical reports may be available to parents and patients, to third-party utilization reviewers, and to lawyers acting on behalf of patients, or, after subpoena, to other parties in a lawsuit.

Before preparing a report, the clinician should clarify what it is that the recipient wants to know. The report should be written with the recipient's professional background in mind and with an awareness that it could be available to others in the future. Thus a forensic evaluation concerning a custody dispute will focus on the elements of "the best interests of the child" (as defined in the local jurisdiction), in such a manner as to help a judge reach a decision in the case. A hospital discharge summary, on the other hand, records the diagnostic evaluation, diagnostic formulation, and treatment provided to a patient, and offers predictions and recommendations for future management. It is desirable, therefore, for the clinician to ask referring agents how they want him or her to help them. For example, is the clinician requested to retain and treat the patient, or asked for an opinion that will help the referring agent to provide treatment?

Types of Report

There are 4 chief types of report: clinical, forensic, educational, and administrative. Each type contains several varieties.

Clinical reports give opinions concerning diagnosis and treatment, or they form a record of diagnosis or treatment with recommendations for future treatment.

Forensic reports contain expert opinions concerning:

- Diagnosis and recommended disposition
- Competence to waive Miranda rights
- Competence to stand trial
- Mental state at the time of the offense
- Waiver to adult court
- Civil commitment
- The validity of an allegation of abuse
- Termination of parental rights
- Custody disputes
- Educational rights
- Civil liability
- Malpractice
- The quality of other experts' reports

Educational reports present expert opinion concerning appropriateness for special education.

Administrative reports consist of evaluations of existing mental health programs, recommendations for new service programs, analyses of administrative problems with recommendations for their solution, or analyses of future trends and recommended responses.

The content, organization, and style of the report will change in accordance with its purpose, the issue involved, and the audience for whom it is intended.

Content and Style

The watchwords are directness, simplicity, freshness, logic, organization, and respect for the audience.

DIRECTNESS

Scientific and technical reports traditionally are written in the third person. False modesty, the wish to eschew bias, and the desire of scientific editors to suppress personality are at the root of this practice. Thus a writer will say "The patient was examined on . . ." instead of "I [we] examined the patient on . . ." Nevertheless, the rhetorical purpose of the passive voice is to emphasize the object of an action, not to permit the writer to hide behind a compound verb. By using "I" or "we," the writer takes responsibility for an evaluation, analysis, opinion, or recommendation, thus avoiding vagueness, tortuosity, and clumsiness.

SIMPLICITY

Simplicity is the foundation of elegance. Prolixity must be avoided. Two sentences may be better than one. In writing and editing, the clinician should rake out the pomposities, prune the redundancies, and weed out the clichés, "buzz words", vogue usages, and unnecessary jargon that infest technical prose. Clinicians should use verbs rather than abstract nouns and shun verbal nouns unless the particular usage is accepted.

Example	*Alternate Version*
The test that was selected in order to measure intelligence was the Bellevue Wechsler Test.	To measure intelligence, I selected the Bellevue Wechsler Test.
The results of the test are not known at this time.	The results of the test are not known.
A total of 14 items was endorsed	He endorsed 14 items.
He has a schizoid-type personality.	He has a schizoid personality.
His personality was impacted by the marital disruption between the parental figures.	His parents' constant quarreling upset him.
Enmeshed with his mother figure, Timmy adopted the role of parental child, resulting in his obsessive compulsive personality traits.	Timmy is closely tied to his mother. He often cares for her. As a result, he has become . . .
Living in a dysfunctional family, she became codependent and enabling.	(Untranslatable)
Their emotionally abusive relationship escalated in consequence of his extramarital relationship, and . . .	After he was unfaithful to her, they argued even more heatedly.

Appendix 99.1 provides a further sample of frequently encountered mental health pomposities.

FRESHNESS

To those who understand their meaning, technical terms convey complex ideas in an abbreviated manner; others may draw a blank or be misled. It is at best discourteous and at worst dangerous to use specialized language when the audience does not comprehend it. Moreover, Graeco-Roman abstractions can sterilize the ideas they represent, muffling the power of the Anglo-Saxon words they replace. Take the following:

Example	*Alternate Version*
He experiences nocturnal auditory hallucinations. The hallucinations consist of instructions to . . .	Lying alone at night he hears voices. The voices tell him to . . .

This is not to say that technical terms should be avoided at all costs; but writers must keep the audience in mind, and consider whether what they want to say is better captured by a technical abstraction or by a plain description. If it is necessary to use the technical term that the audience is unfamiliar with, the term should be defined. For example:

Mrs. B. has a borderline personality: She has an uncertain sense of identity, difficulty controlling her emotions, a prevailing sense of loneliness, and a terror of being abandoned. Mrs. B. has great difficulty sustaining close relationships: She becomes emotionally volatile, suicidal, and self-injurious when those to whom she seeks to be close are repelled by the intense demands she makes of them.

LOGIC AND ORGANIZATION

Writers should construct their reports sequentially, separating observation from inference, inference from opinion, and opinion from recommendation.

For example, a medico-legal report can begin with the circumstances of referral and the purpose of evaluation, then proceed in logical manner through the sources of information and the means by which the clinician got it (e.g., review of specified documents, interviews, psychological testing, special investigations), to a description of what he or she found, an analysis of its meaning, the clinician's opinion concerning the legal elements at stake (short of the ultimate issue), and recommendations. (See Appendix 99.2.)

Numbered and alphabetized headings enhance the clarity of a lengthy report. For example, a hospital discharge summary can be organized by the following headings:

I. Identifying Data and Dates of Admission and Discharge
II. Justification for Admission
III. History of Present Illness
IV. Past Medical and Psychiatric History
V. Family and Developmental History
VI. Mental Status on Admission
VII. Physical Examination on Admission
VIII. Laboratory Findings and Special Investigations
IX. Psychological Test Results
X. Categorical Diagnosis
XI. Diagnostic Formulation
XII. Treatment Plan
XIII. Progress in Hospital
XIV. Status at the Time of Discharge
XV. Prognosis
XVI. Arrangements for Aftercare
XVII. Recommendations for Aftercare

Even in a report sent to a colleague who is a friend, when headings might seem pompous, a logical flow can be sustained.

Dear Bill,

Thank you for referring John Doe and his parents to me.

I interviewed John on three occasions, took a history from the parents, and arranged for [psychologist] to test him.

As you described, Johnny is extremely hyperactive. Neither his mother nor I could prevent him from getting into places in my office where he didn't belong. He was not bothered when I attempted to set limits and soon returned to the activity from which he had been redirected. No wonder his teachers regard him as "headstrong."

Psychological testing assessed his intelligence as average, but he exhibited marked distractibility and impairment of concentration. The test results were in line with the school's educational achievement evaluation. He does not have a learning disorder; nor was there evidence of depression, anxiety, or abnormal hostility.

Mr. Doe has recently had problems at work and is

fearful that he might be laid off. The parents say that this has strained their relationship, but that they have tried to keep their differences from John. Despite their good intentions, I doubt if they could have done so.

In summary, I agree with you that Johnny has attention deficit disorder. However, his temperamental problems have been aggravated by family tension. Mrs. Doe has been preoccupied and inconsistent in her management of him, and has recently had little support from her worried husband. I counseled the parents in this regard, suggesting how they could present a calmer, less irritable, more united front. You and I should talk about how the parents can follow up on my discussion with them. I also recommended that Johnny start on methylphenidate 2.5 mg p.o. at 7 a.m. and 1 p.m., increasing every seven days by 2.5 mg, to a maximum of 20 mg b.i.d. in divided doses. I would predict that 10–15 mg per day will be sufficient. Please let me know in a month how he does on this medication, or earlier if there are any problems. If it doesn't work, we could switch to dextroamphetamine. I think we should inform the school about this evaluation. I have the parents' permission to send the school a report, and I think it would be useful if I could discuss behavioral management with the school staff.

Sincerely,

RESPECT FOR THE AUDIENCE

Psychiatrists and other mental health clinicians are familiar with the technical terms of the behavioral and social sciences. Teachers and educational psychologists have a limited knowledge of psychiatric or psychodynamic terminology but are at ease with cognitive and developmental psychology. Nonpsychiatric physicians probably have forgotten much of what they learned in psychiatry, aside from patchy recollections of the major psychiatric disorders, psychotropic drugs, and mental status phenomena. These considerations guide the writer in the extent to which technical terms should be incorporated in the report and whether the terms should be defined. For example:

The patient reports intense feelings of depersonalization and derealization, particularly during episodes of hyperventilation.

The patient feels peculiar and unreal, as if estranged from the external world. These symptoms worsen when he pants to excess.

Lawyers often regard psychiatrists as muddle-headed gulls, obfuscating bleeding hearts, hangmen's helpers, or the functionaries of a corrupt state that seeks to deprive eccentrics of their liberty. Nevertheless, the psychiatric report can be a crucial factor in a trial, particularly when issues such as competence, mental state at the time of an alleged offense, future dangerousness, or psychological injury are at stake. A forensic report should describe the circumstances of a referral and the purpose of the evaluation. The clinician must list the sources of the information upon which the conclusions are based, weigh the relative significances of different findings, and converge upon the elements of the legal issue at stake. Purpose, technique, observation, interpretation, and opinion are kept separate as the logical sequence of the report unfolds. It is particularly important to state the degree of certainty with which particular opinions can be given yet to stop short of the ultimate conclusion (which is the province of the judge or jury). For example:

Therefore, it is my opinion, with reasonable medical certainty, that A. comprehends both the nature and implications of the charges against him and the pleas available to him; that he has a reasonable grasp of the function of the courtroom personnel; that he is able to collaborate with his attorney, in his own best interests; and that he will be able to comport himself properly in the courtroom.

A judge is certainly interested in the clinician's opinion. However, he or she is more impressed by the reliability and thoroughness of the clinician's information-gathering, the impartiality of the reasoning, the appropriate caution with which he or she states your opinion, and the good sense and professionalism that shape the recommendations. Good writing is clear thinking.

BREVITY

The clinician should try not to bore the reader with interminable details, lest the wood be obscured by the trees. Yet the report is the record of an important transaction that has uses beyond communication with the addressee. If consent is given, reports may be sent to other clinicians. Negative findings can be significant in later diagnostic evaluations. Reports also can be submitted or subpoenaed in legal disputes. Finally, a report is a record of a clinician's work to which the clinician (or others) may refer at a later date. (See Appendix 99.2.)

786

Legal Issues

The psychiatrist is bound by a duty of confidentiality not to disclose the contents of a report to unauthorized third persons. The obligation of confidentiality arises from the implied fiduciary relationship between doctor and patient—a duty imposed by law in order to promote the revelation of intimate matters during psychotherapy. Private matters may be disclosed to third parties only if the patient (or legal guardian) gives full and free consent. The prudent clinician will, therefore, obtain written consent setting out the scope of permissible disclosure.

Clinicians are not liable if they entrust confidential material to their private secretaries; but secretaries are bound by the same obligation as clinicians. If a secretary breaches confidentiality, the clinician could be held vicariously liable.

Testimonial privilege is a form of confidentiality in which the clinician is enjoined from testifying in court, for example to the contents of a report. However, information generated in a doctor-patient relationship has no special privilege in some states; in others it is bestowed by statute. Testimonial privilege belongs to the patient, not the clinician.

A subpoena may compel a clinician to bring records and reports to a court; however, without the patient's express permission, it does not compel the clinician to reveal the contents of the record. The clinician who receives such a subpoena should inform the patient and consult his or her own attorney. At the very least, the clinician should ask the judge to instruct him or her concerning the propriety of testifying to sensitive, confidential matters.

The psychiatric record may be the property of the psychiatrist, but the information therein belongs to the patient. Indeed, many states mandate patients' access to their records. Careless, disrespectful, emotional, or disparaging remarks have no place in a professional report. They could attract legal action on the grounds of defamation or the intentional infliction of emotional distress.

Conclusion

How do you see yourself? Do your reports reflect the kind of person you would like to be? Your style is you—lean and logical, limpid and elegant, or cluttered, murky, pompous and dull.

Imagine you are speaking to someone as you write. That way you are less likely to grasp for the dreary phrases (". . . on the basis of . . ."), barbarisms ("these behaviors were consequated by . . ."), and vogue usages ("hospitalization was impacted by . . .") so dear to us all. Edit your reports. Prune away unnecessary phrases; split up tedious sentences; weed out the rubbish.

Keep a dictionary nearby, and make liberal use of a thesaurus. For general stylistic advice, consult Barzun and Graff (1977), Fowler (1965), Gowers (1973), Strunk and White (1979), and Zinsser (1985). For technical writing, Brogan (1973) and Steinberg (1988) are recommended.

REFERENCES

Barzun, J., & Graff, H. F. (1970). *The modern researcher* (rev. ed.). New York: Harcourt, Brace & World.

Brogan, J. A. (1973). *Clear technical writing.* New York: McGraw-Hill.

Fowler, H. W. (1965). *A dictionary of modern English usage* (2nd ed.). Oxford: Clarendon Press.

Gowers, E. (1973). *The complete plain words.* Baltimore, MD: Penguin.

Steinberg, R. J. (1988). *The psychologist's companion. A guide to scientific writing for students and researchers* (2nd ed.). New York: Cambridge University Press.

Strunk, W., Jr., & White, E. B. (1979). *The elements of style* (3rd ed.). New York: Macmillan.

Zinsser, W. (1985). *On writing well. An informal guide to writing non-fiction* (3rd ed.). New York: Harper & Row.

APPENDIX 99.1 / Lincoln's Gettysburg Address

(As delivered by a contemporary mental health care provider)

Approximately 87 years ago, parties acting in the role of first-degree relatives to this population generated an innovative nationalistic process based on the conceptualization that, as a whole, it behooves male and female individuals to operate on the basis of nondiscriminative equality, at least opportunity-wise.

At this point in time, the nation is engaged in a military operation the purpose of which is to determine whether a nation-state grounded on the above parameters has sufficient capacity to cope, given the vicissitudes of Realpolitik. Accordingly, this congregation has been assembled at a significant location upon which an impactful military collision occurred. The objective of the congregation is to perform a religious ceremony in order to section off a portion of the location that will function as a final resting place for military staff members who have become deceased in the course of fulfilling their military duties.

From a protocol-oriented point of view, the current operation is deemed to be entirely appropriate. Such considerations notwithstanding, it is beyond the ultimate capacity of the individuals assembled at this location at this point in time to prepare the said location sufficiently to allow the pursuance of ritualistic, ceremonial, and/or religious purposes. Indeed, the location has already prior to this time been spiritually transformed by the deceased personnel to a degree or extent impossible to recreate at any subsequent point in time. Although memory traces of the verbal communications emitted at this time have a significant probability of decaying, long-term encoding/storage/retrieval of the specific event that transpired at this location is not subject to mnemonic extinction. Therefore, there is a greater than 50% probability that the individuals who were not lost to attrition or unengaged in the specific military operation should survive as providers and/or consumers of governmental operations. Thus, it is incumbent upon the individuals assembled at this point in time, plus others of the surviving population base, to cooperate in a combined effort of substantive nature in order to achieve the following objectives:

(1) The regeneration of this discrete political entity; and

(2) The maintenance of democratic-type representative government beyond this day and age.

Finally, it should be noted that the above opinions are of a personal nature and not necessarily referable to those by whom this address was originally sponsored.

APPENDIX 99.2 / Review of Medical Record Concerning Justification for Hospitalization

This report illustrates a review of a medical record of an adolescent with regard to the justification of hospitalization and length of stay. The patient's father, who had accused the hospital of improperly admitting his daughter, was withholding payment.

In the case of *Metropolitan Hospital v. William Toohey*

REVIEW OF MEDICAL RECORD
Re: Tania Toohey
Admitted to Metropolitan Hospital
from 04/25/85 to 07/16/85

I. *Purpose of Review*
I was asked by Messrs. Smith & Jones, attorneys

788

at law, to review the medical record of Tania Toohey's admission to Metropolitan Hospital (4/25/85–7/16/85) with regard to the following issues:

1. Was hospitalization necessary and reasonable?
2. Was the treatment provided adequate?
3. Was the length of stay in hospital (82 days) appropriate?

II. *Review of Record*

This 13-year-old single white female was admitted to and discharged from Metropolitan Hospital with the following diagnosis: conduct disorder of adolescence, socialized, nonaggressive. The behavior that occasioned her admission was stated to be: rebelliousness at home; drop-off in school performance; truancy from school; running away from home; and alcohol and marijuana abuse.

Reportedly, her parents had been divorced 5 years before and she was in the custody of her mother. The second of 3 children, she had been closer to her father prior to the divorce than to her mother. However, her relationship with both parents had deteriorated after the divorce, when she fell in with bad company and began to drink alcohol and smoke marijuana. She is reported to have blamed her mother for the divorce and to have wavered about whether to leave her mother and live with her father.

The master treatment plan (04/26/85) is not adequately individualized. Nowhere in the records could I find a diagnostic formulation other than "conduct disorder." The essentials of treatment appear to have been group therapy with regard to her conduct problems and substance abuse, and individual psychotherapy with regard to her family problems and oppositionalism. Several interviews were undertaken with both mother and patient but only one involved the father and the patient.

Progress during hospitalization was slow. Initially and sporadically throughout the entire hospitalization, the patient was avoidant and noncommunicative. At various times she was openly oppositional, flouting unit rules. On 05/06/85 it was noted that her father was antagonistic to hospitalization and that she did not want him to interfere with her treatment. By mid-April 1985 she was often excluded from group therapy because she had been restricted to her room for misbehavior. A previous suicidal attempt (undated) was

noted on 05/14/85. At that time she began to speak about difficulties of communication between her mother and herself. By late April-early June, 1985, she continued to be resistant to hospital rules and to refuse to address her personal problems. This deterioration may have followed a family therapy meeting with her mother on 05/26/85. Her participation in group activities was minimal through the early part of June, and the patient became resistant to the unit point system. On 06/14/85 she stated that she felt rejected by her parents if "she stood up to" them. She described feeling "used" by her parents. She also began to express ambivalence toward living with her father. From mid-June until discharge in mid-July 1985, she made no apparent progress.

III. *Discussion*

The admission of this patient to hospital was justified on the basis of her drinking and marijuana use and her running away from home and school. As she was out of the control of her mother, outpatient therapy would not have been proper at that time.

Unfortunately, no adequate diagnostic formulation was presented (or at least documented) during hospitalization. The treatment foci ("abuse of THC and alcohol" and "conduct disorder") do not capture the essence of the patient's problem. As a consequence, the thrust of therapy—at least as documented—was superficial.

In my opinion, the patient suffered from both oppositional defiant disorder and substance use disorder, secondary to unresolved conflict concerning the separation and hostility between her parents. From time to time, references are made to the patient's lack of communication with her mother, blaming of the mother for the divorce, protective feelings toward her father, and ambivalence about going to live with him. It is likely that her oppositionality, drinking, and marijuana use stem from her psychological inability to resolve these conflictual issues.

Given the reported opposition of the father to hospitalization and the apparent inability of the staff to arrange conjoint family therapy, it is unlikely that hospitalization could have been successful. Had intensive individual psychotherapy focused on the patient's unresolved conflicts been instituted, it might have been possible to justify hospitalization for a period of 4 to 5 weeks. However, if the patient had remained uninvested in psychotherapy, as occurred during this hospitalization, earlier discharge should have been considered.

IV. *Opinion*

1. Hospitalization was justified on the basis of the patient's out-of-control behavior, substance use, and truancy.

2. The diagnostic formulation and treatment plan, as documented, are inadequate.

3. Failing a more successful engagement of both parents in the treatment process, it is unlikely that hospital treatment could have succeeded. However, the attending physician could not have known this on admission.

4. Given the lack of investment of this patient in therapy and the lack of parental support for it, discharge should have been considered at 4 weeks.

EPILOGUE / The Paths to the Bright Future of Clinical Child/Adolescent Psychiatry (CAP)

Saul Isaac Harrison

At the outset, the reader should be assured that the quirky quality of this epilogue differs from preceding chapters. The other chapters delineate today's best available clinical knowledge. This chapter, in contrast, conveys the observations, thoughts, and predictions of one individual. My purpose is to contribute an epistemologic perspective to the accompanying chapters and to the new knowledge and skills we will read about in tomorrow's journals. Also, this chapter is phrased as a collegial chat between the senior editor and the reader. An advantage of the written format over us meeting face to face is that you can tune out my long-windedness at will without expending a whit of energy on civility. Indeed, the zigzags in my thinking may make it advantageous for you to

In formulating this chapter, I have borrowed from so many sources that I regret, with apologies, that bibliographic citations are undoubtedly incomplete. But I am obliged to acknowledge 2 important sources: my friend and historical mentor, the late Joseph Noshpitz, the editor of these 7 volumes, and the late Dennis Cantwell, with whom I collaborated initially in conceptualizing and outlining the Clinical Processes sections of the *Handbook* until family illness obliged Denny to withdraw. In their absence, I am grateful to the following who conveyed advice: Norman Alessi, Irving Berlin, Henry Burks, Albert Cain, Justin Call, Donald Carek, Charles Davenport, Janet Demb, Taheo Doi, Elle Erteman, Spencer Eth, Joseph Fishoff, Kenneth Gordon, Richard Harrison, John Kemph, Boyd Krout, Serge Lebovici, John McDermott, Klaus Minde, Rocco Motto, Barry Nurcombe, Charles Popper, and Jack Westman.

read this chapter in a series of sittings. (An abbreviated summary can be constructed by combining the paragraph that follows with the 14 Clinical Truths listed at the end of the chapter. Be alerted, however, that the many words in between bespeak five decades of observation and thought. Not always linear. Which leads to my regret that this idiosyncratic epilogue may not lend itself to quick reading. Thus, to follow my cognitive paths, I suggest a series of separate readings. Each sitting with pauses for reflection. Personal thoughts will be in smaller print to facilitate triage.)

My prediction is that sometime before the passing of another millennium, child and adolescent psychiatry (CAP) will achieve the pinnacle of being perceived widely as the ultimate paradigmatic helping professional process. Other helping professionals will strive to emulate us. This prognostication is predicated on CAP's future curve of clinical progress continuing in the direction I observed toward the end of the 20th century. A curve that resembles general medical progress a few decades earlier. That we eventually will achieve that acme on the foundation of CAP's commitment to humane delivery of scientific biopsychosocial multidimensionality is a certainty. The timing is less certain. There are obstacles.

A peripheral sidebar that contributes to the confidence of my prediction is the burgeoning epidemiological evidence of the importance of *behavior* in morbidity and mortality—for example, tobacco-related cancer, a variety of pulmonary and cardiac pathology, AIDS, driving under the influence of alcohol, patient compliance with effective treatments. A startling example of the effects of compliance is to be found in the mid-1990s reversal of the curve of tuberculosis from increasing to decreasing frequency. The effective intervention was 100% behavioral. Directly observing treatment compliance for 6 to 8 months worked. It has generated hopes of eradicating TB from our planet, even including Africa, where one-third of the population is infected.

A compilation of more than 100,000 surveys and other data sources (Murray & Lopez, 1996) notes that Unipolar Depression was the world's fourth leading cause of death and disability in 1990—causing more disability than the combination of arthritis, diabetes, hypertension, and back pain. The leading killer was lower respiratory infections, followed by diarrheal diseases, perinatal conditions, Depression, and Ischemic Heart Disease in fifth place. Projections for 2020 elevates Unipolar Depression to the second most lethal disease in the world, preceded only by Ischemic Heart Disease. Also, the overall burden in years of healthy life lost for selected neuropsychiatric disorders is projected to rise from 145 million Disability-Adjusted Life Years (DALY) in 1990 to 204 million DALYs by 2020.

For CAP, the significance is in the potential to contribute child developmental and detection measures designed preventively to decrease the estimate by the World Health Organization that depressive and anxiety disorders are responsible for approximately one quarter of all visits to health care centers worldwide (Ustun & Sartorius, 1995).

Although it is not vital to fulfill the prediction of CAP's bright future, an external boost may come from the future possibility that increasing numbers of students will pursue professional skills entailing people-to-people involvement. Fewer students will be needed for the growing number of long-valued professional skills that are being translated into binary digits. If a computer can beat the world's best chess player, the demand for engineers' skills, for example, probably will diminish. Vivid documentation is the marked diminution in the numbers of bank tellers, gas pumpers, and the like.

***

The major uncertainty in the prediction pertains to the amount of time we and those who follow will require to achieve those heights. Both the speed and the height are predicated on:

- The firmness of our commitment to and enrichment of developmental biopsychosocial integration. *Caution:* Economic influences will encourage and reward biological unidimensionality. If we submit to the temptations, CAP's clinical future will flicker and resemble America's mid–20th-century unidimensionality, which is described subsequently. But there will be a difference: Morality. America's 1950s psychodynamic unidimensionality did not ignore the tiny number of effective therapeutic agents, which are noted later.
- Refinement of clinical assessment/intervention strategy planning (CA/ISP) processes, to which this volume is dedicated.
- New therapeutic interventions.
- Reliable outcome data about existing and future treatments.
- Expanding access to continua of clinical services that are organized and reorganized on the basis of communal needs and clinical knowledge/skills with decreasing concern about economics.
- Rational reconceptualization, as noted in the Reader's Guide, of professional boundaries, interactions, educational preparation, certification, posthoc assessment of professional performance, recertification.
- Societal progress in shedding the legacies of deeply rooted Judaeo-Christian-Muslim insensitivity toward children's suffering (templated in Genesis 22).
- Freeing society from the burden of hallowed traditions that do not fit 21st-century technological reality. The sainted 18th-century concept of freedom of expression was never intended to license media bombardment of developing neurons with toxic pollutants. Similarly, the American public education system, a central child developmental institution, persists in following the agrarian rhythm of 7-hour school days and closing school during the months children were needed on the farm. With most parents working away from home, shouldn't schools be open and actively engaging and supervising children a minimum of 12 hours a day?

Will modification of counterproductive child rearing traditions require serious assessment in the light of day of childrens economic value? That sounds harsh and cold. But might such discussion represent improvement over today's calculation by self-serving secret ballot? Isn't that what distributes American health care liberally to senior citizens like me while neglecting millions of American children without ready access to health care?

In terms of national interest, children's welfare and health should be the third millennium's crusade. Excessive language? Not more than those who see America headed for demographic disaster and intergenerational war.

- The pace at which humanity progresses to the humane goal of every child being a wanted child. Should we challenge scientists to create a reversible immunization against conception to be administered to all newborns? Deimmunization could be a celebratory commitment to the child by the couple standing fully clothed in front of family and community. It would represent a biological mandate for the concept of licensure for parenthood elaborated by one of my former students (Westman, 1994).
- Enhanced parenting knowledge and skills accompanied by growth in adult capacity to cope with the disagreeable biological reality that children are preparing to exceed and replace us.
- Scientific and technological progress, including contributions from clinicians like us. Read on.

∗∗∗

Over the last half of the 20th century, an unfortunate prevailing tendency has evolved that virtually dismisses any expectation that clinicians can contribute to the field's knowledge base, an unwelcome side effect of scientific triumphs. However, that discouraging perspective ignores the host of serendipitous observations that have benefited humanity over the ages. Roentgen stumbled on the X ray. Sir Alexander Fleming's (1929) thought processes transformed a damnable green contaminant into the miracle of penicillin. In psychiatry, Donald Klein's discovery of imipramine's panic prevention potential was an example of planned serendipity (Klein & Fink, 1962). In other words, the observations are there to be made if we are open to them. We do not have to think of ourselves as stereotypic "scientists" to advance knowledge. We need to be open and to constantly refine and integrate the basic clinical skill of keen observation.

Four perspectives on science merit clinician's consideration. They are inspired by Sir Charles Snow, the physicist, known better as the novelist C. P. Snow; Hans Selye, who identified the hypophyseal-adrenocortical pathway that connects feelings with the physical body; Albert Szent-Gyorgi, Nobel laureate biochemist; and Louis Pasteur, who established the validity of the germ theory of disease. Snow characterized science as the refusal to believe on the basis of hope. Selye defined the real scientist as one who is always ready to be amazed. Szent-Gyorgi described science as seeing what everyone has seen and thinking what no one else has thought. And Pasteur noted that chance favors the prepared mind.

In other words, clinicians should be open. The seeds of new knowledge are there to be harvested if only we recognize them. What can we learn from Albert Einstein's child developmental answer to an inquiry about the source of his achievements: Every day when he came home from school, his mother asked if he had asked good *questions* . . . not answers. Questions!

Even Bruno Bettelheim (1948), some of whose behavior has since been reported as reprehensible, recognized the seed Anna Freud handed him in Vienna. The care of one child from another community during Miss Freud's psychoanalytic treatment blossomed over time into notions about therapeutic milieu taken for granted today. Thus lovability is not a prerequisite for harvesting seeds.

I learned about the availability of seeds during a visit home while I was in medical college more than 50 years ago. At dinner I related the saga of Fleming's creation of an antibiotic out of the annoying green mold. My father's color changed. When I heard what my father related, I shared his "goose bumps." He referred to his primitive late-19th-century boyhood when the state-of-art treatment for cuts in the skin were spiderwebs. But if the cut resisted healing and produced pus, the most therapeutic cobwebs were those in the darkest corners with green mold.

An experience of microscopic proportion when juxtaposed to the discovery of antibiotics occurred to me in the course of a social telephone conversation decades later. I mentioned to the woman I had known throughout her 30ish years of life that she sounded "zippy." She responded that she was out of "hibernation." Her word replicated Lewy, Kern, Rosenthal, and Wehr's (1982) pioneering report about seasonality. Then I recalled her parents' concern about the intermittence of her childhood and adolescent school performance. I called back to ask a few clinical questions. Then I told her about the recently described seasonality and phototherapy and proceeded to recommend a clinician in her community. Several years later, after she had benefited from phototherapy, I shared with clinical colleagues via a letter to the editor (Harrison, 1997) the nonaffective nature of her childhood school pattern and the reported benefits from phototherapy.

❖❖❖

The most worrisome prerequisites for future progress are the prospects for overcoming societal resistance to acceptance of children evidenced by inadequate communal access to preventive and clinical resources. When will these be enhanced, made accessible, and organized into a rational continuum of care predicated on the combination of current knowledge/skills and community needs? For example, in 1966 Pittman, Langsley, and their colleagues demonstrated the efficacy and cost effectiveness of family-oriented crisis intervention as an alternative to emergency psychiatric hospitalization. But access to such services mandates that professional teams be organized in sync with the community and ready to respond when needed. Unfortunately, such capacity remains rare.

Another concern pertains to internal obstacles, such as the anti-integrative divisive forces between CAP's several professions. As noted in the Reader's Guide, those so-called professional traditions we inherited are more precisely identified as politics, economics, and elitism and are ill-suited for today's clinical knowledge/skills and community needs. As some of the 14 clinical truths listed at the end of this chapter note, some traditional relics of the past are worth preserving, while some belong only in museums and in historical memory to guard against repeating past mistakes.

Whether or not the future will render economic considerations less consequential akin to the American public acceptance of military spending during World War II and the Cold War, rational CAP services will be refined increasingly in the future into organized (which most assuredly does not mean "managed") systems of care. CAP clinicians with discrete foci of expertise will function as flexible clinical teams because CAP's accumulating knowledge and skills are expanding beyond the capacity of solo practitioners.

The collaborative knowledge and skills inherent in the team will more reliably distinguish neurobiological-based hyperactivity associated with attentional deficits from the restlessness of hunger or from some children's mode of experiencing and expressing fear and anxiety or from behaviors that

have been and/or are being rewarded or from medication side effects. Won't several heads tend to be better than one in assessing whether the depression is endogenous, reactive, learned helplessness, and/or something else?

Further, the communication revolution will make those clinical teams accessible to all geographic locations. The solo practitioner is en route to becoming a relic of the past like the horse and buggy.

❖❖❖

Lest that sound excessive, ponder that we do not have to go back very far in human history to recall when CAP's interventions encompassed infanticide, magic, demonology, religion. Indeed, a variant of religion is what I experienced in the middle of the 20th century at the outset of my clinical career, which I will describe subsequently in tiny print.

As CAP advances through art and developmental biopsychosocial clinical sciences, is it outrageous to spin a futuristic fantasy of punching developmental biopsychosocial data into a machine that dispenses the correct color and dose of psychomycin? That doesn't sound as silly as my boyhood's wild comic-strip fantasies of Buck Rogers's space travel and Dick Tracy's wristwatch telephone.

Maybe the machine is a wild fantasy, but since childhood, I have learned the fate of what Thomas (1979, p. 140) aptly designated as "the most complicated, multicell, multitissue and multiorgan diseases." Each malady has been conquered by finding an unanticipated single switch to turn off "the whole array of disordered and seemingly unrelated pathological mechanisms." Thomas was referring to tertiary syphilis, chronic tuberculosis, and pernicious anemia.

Who knows what will be produced from future intercourse between the barely begun biological and information processing revolutions integrated with our expanding psychosocial knowledge and skills? Will it propel us beyond the biology of memory processes to the biology of individual memories, which Kety considered impossible in 1960? If that evolves, it will be more complex than the spirochete, tubercle bacillus, and liver/B-12? But if a machine can defeat the world's best chess player, who knows?

Change happens. Could that be what the Book

of Genesis intended in describing humans as created in God's image? Would the authors of the scriptures merit being considered sages if their intent coincided with the concrete interpretation we assigned to those words when we first heard them during childhood? Surely the authors of the scriptures must have realized that their ancestors' lifestyles had been far more primitive than what the sages themselves experienced. Human cognition and communication had enabled each generation of humans to evolve—in contrast to nonhumans.

In my youth, Booth Tarkington's popular book about puberty was entitled *Seventeen!* The tallest on the University of Michigan basketball team was 6 foot 3 inches. On April 15, 1997, I heard Bill Walton describe a seven footer as a "small forward"; of the 4 others on the team, 2 are taller! The average weight of that legendary American football line in the late 1930s immortalized as the Seven Blocks of Granite was a shade under 191 pounds. Last fall I heard a football line that averaged 100 pounds heavier described on TV as "puny." A vivid nonbiological documentation that change happens is the persisting validity of Moore's Law, which states that computing power will double—or halve in price—every 2 years.

∞∞∞

In the brief time between those startling reports of evidence of life on Mars and the cloning of primates in 1996, John F. McDermott, Jr., the colleague who over the decades taught me more than any other single individual, envisioned 30 years into CAP's future. It was on the occasion of my former student and valued collaborator's retirement address at the end of a fruitful decade as editor of the *Journal of the American Academy of Child and Adolescent Psychiatry*, during which he had read almost 4,000 submitted manuscripts. Although the 2 of us had not discussed the future for decades, McDermott (1996) envisioned great strides by 2026:

Longitudinal studies have pinpointed specific risk factors for all the disorders. And made them operational. That's right. Quantified for clinical use. Now you can measure precise patterns of individual and family style, corrected for cultural and socioeconomic data, even corrected for changing societal norms like divorce. *You* input the data and your computerized DSM-7 program develops a specific patient profile. Then matches it with

the different pathways to symptom development and symptom resolution. And *then* suggests a treatment plan. A *comprehensive* plan. Not just delivering medication to a genetic marker. Not just new techniques for strengthening areas of the brain to compensate for structural impairment. That's right. Your *psychotherapy* is research-based, too. You focus on the child's specific dyadic relationships, a payoff from research on shared and non-shared family factors. And your home treatment module is an important part of the plan. You're not just reversing behavioral risk factors. Yours is a prescription to boost protective factors, too. Like experimenting with simulated peer relationships. An interactive video program.

∞∞∞

How confident is my prediction about the richness of our field's future? Probably not as confident as Albert Einstein was in 1925 when he predicted a fifth form of matter in addition to solids, liquid, gas, and the plasma in the stars. But CAP will experience immense progress in less than the 70 years required for the inconceivably cold superatom to validate Einstein's prediction. I am confident, however, that my accuracy exceeds those flawed public health forecasts after World War II when penicillin first became available to civilians that the growing number of paralyzed polio survivors would exceed health care capacities, a terror that did not anticipate the Salk vaccine in 1953.

My personal confidence about our field exceeds, by far, the sense of confidence I experienced in the mid-1980s when I told Dr. Boyd Merrill Krout that proliferation of communications technology would render totalitarianism incompatible with economic and lifestyle progress. Some time in the future, I predicted, it would become impossible to prevent citizens from exceeding the threshold of information required by dictatorships. Extending my rationale, I hypothesized that the changes would begin in Eastern Europe, the technologically most advanced. While I do not recall that we discussed a time frame, I confess that I harbored little hope of living long enough to witness the changes I foresaw. In other words, I was utterly amazed when the Berlin Wall tumbled before the end of the decade. What is pertinent is that my global political prediction was predicated on a rational foundation.

Is it not rational that we are the helping professions most committed to developmental biopsychosocial integration? Is it not true also that historians of science perceive the scientific knowledge accumulated in the last decade of the 20th century as exceeding the total accumulated earlier in the century? Thus, I am confident that when unpredictable advances in knowledge and skills are blended with refinement of our CA/ISP capacities, credible outcome data, and accessible continua of care, CAP's curve of progress will be mind-boggling.

With science's capacity to create novel life forms (transgenic species such as plants with human proteins, bacteria that produce medication, synthetic chromosomes), how long will it be before what we imprecisely designate today as stimulants, antidepressants, and neuroleptics are perceived as relics of an earlier stage of empiricism? Epistemologists note wisely that empiricism at one stage of a field's history is perceived as ignorance subsequently in the field's development.

It seems like barely yesterday that CAP was excited by possible linkages between the innate reflexive smile in infants and the subsequent evolution of social smiling. It was as recent as the 1980s that Volume III of the *Basic Handbook of Child Psychiatry* was credited with driving the final nails in the coffin of the earlier prevailing CAP therapeutic parochialism. In the 1960s and 1970s CAP resembled what had prevailed in general medicine decades earlier when physicians had been identified as bleeders, purgers, cuppers, infusers, and the like.

In the 1980s and 1990s American psychiatry residency programs questioned the merit of including supervised psychotherapy as an educational experience for psychiatric physicians. Juxtapose that with the prevailing reality 2 and 3 decades earlier when the prerequisite for the practice of psychotherapy in America was state licensure as a physician and surgeon. Change happens.

My confident prediction is not shaken by vivid recollections of the certainty of those 1950s and 1960s predictions, when computers were in their infancy, that the days of print media and libraries were numbered. Yet as I write these words decades later, bookstores are the fastest-growing retail enterprise in my computer-literate part of the world. Libraries have grown also, albeit more slowly. More books were sold last year than any previous year in American history and the largest market in America was Los Angeles. Tinseltown!

The eternal skeptic might question if I know enough to be pessimistic. Of course I am less than objective; however, I imagine that since 1949 I have learned enough about CAP to be pessimistic. Indeed, it is the amount I have learned which points to our soaring future.

Historical evidence suggests that the less humanity knows, the more narcissistic our self-concept. Before Copernicus, our ancestors were confident we were the center of the universe. When our planet's status in the universe came to be accepted, humanity was comforted by the consolation that humans were uniquely singular—until Darwin's evolutionary hypothesis of our descent from other species pointed to linkages subsequently supported by shared DNA. After Darwin, the major consolation was human rationality. Until Freud.

You and I will share the cognitive underpinnings of my view of our future by meandering in tandem via the printed word, to note similarities in the epistemological paths traveled by general medicine and by CAP. These convoluted printed trails will document that the major difference in the 2 paths is that CAP is a few decades behind.

An earlier draft of this epilogue dedicated many pages to acquainting the reader with my idiosyncratic proclivities. The goal was to assist you in assessing inevitable conative contributions to the printed cognitions. Another goal was to highlight the importance for all of us as clinicians to be aware of and to discuss with trusted colleagues our personal inclinations and their propensity for influencing our clinical observations and thinking. For example, am I inclined to perceive pathology or strengths first among a host of other personal individualistic factors with the potential to influence clinical processes? Although I have edited out all save one particularly relevant personal inclination, if a reader wishes to know more, I am easy to locate.

The self-descriptor I retained pertains to my global outlook. With age, my tendency to perceive the big picture optimistically increases. (Former students may rest assured that buoyancy is independent of my well-honed skills identifying negatives. Simultaneously, the big glass is half full.) I am persuaded that if we were to draw a line globally charting the ups and downs of the history of humanity over the ages on a huge 100-meter chart, the slant of the historical line would be upward. Of course, there would be downward blips. Designating humanity's tragedies as blips should not be misinterpreted as trivializing calamitous disasters. Blip bespeaks the size of the graph. World War II and the Holocaust affected me deeply and intimately. Nevertheless, if the chart were 100 meters long, those destructive years would be represented by no more than a blip despite the depths.

If that mythical chart is less than persuasive, consider the striking differences in 3 millennia between the rules of engagement Moses issued to his troops and the victorious Allies' behavior to our defeated and hated enemies after World War II. Contrast the status of Germany and Japan today with the words of blessed Moses to whom we are grateful for trumpeting the concept of the rule of law to Western civilization. In the 20th chapter of Deuteronomy, Moses tells his troops to kill all those who resist and to enslave those who surrender. That humane elevation would encompass a significant portion of the imaginary graph. That President Truman et al. were influenced by Cold War geopolitics does not diminish the prosocial results, nor the template it established for the future, just as hypotheses about Moses' leadership motivations do not tarnish the concept of the rule of law established by the ten commandments.

Indeed, I perceive the imagined graph taking a sharp upturn in the late 1940s. That stems from the assumption that virtually all boys born prior to World War II had been socialized to think of war as noble and glorious. Personally, I experienced that indoctrination despite considerable explicit pacifist maternal input. Such a militaristic spirit overshadowed my childhood experience that, every time I asked my friend's affable father about World War I, he deftly changed the subject or left the room. Such male indoctrination started to change when Hiroshima conveyed an unavoidable message about the future prospects of military conflict resolution. The modification was implanted deeper when television defied the dictum about the public not being allowed to see either sausage or war being made. The televised news image of the naked Vietnamese girl running desperately after a napalm attack started to change notions of war's long-trumpeted nobility.

In CAP, when the American physician William Healy espoused in 1915 the idea that children should be thought of as individuals, it was not the banality it sounds like today. Although King Solomon had recommended the same 3 millennia earlier, Healy wrote it in an authoritative medical text. It marked the beginning of a revolutionary concept for helping professionals. Paradigm shifting.

Change happens. Fast-forward several decades: Today CAP's biological knowledge is barely beyond the primer level. Yet the psychopharmacology chapters are the longest in Volume VI. And every day takes us further along on the threshold of a knowledge explosion. Read tomorrow's journals.

∘∘∘

Despite our fields' virtually exclusive focus on psychosocial influences in the half century following Healy's text, the *fact* of child abuse was virtually a secret until 1962. That sounds improbable in today's climate in which all know that abuse and neglect are the leading causes of death in American preschoolers. But until 1962 abuse had been hidden in Western civilization's dark closet.

A vivid early documentation of abuse in the Book of Genesis was long ignored. Responding to a voice only he heard, Abraham presumably terrified his son Isaac by standing over him with a knife as poor Isaac was bound on a sacrificial funeral pyre. The scriptural passages that follow delineate Abraham's itinerary and extol his faith. Abraham is praised for his readiness to sacrifice his son. Not a single word about Isaac's presumed travail. Readers tempted to dismiss these observations by recalling Isaac's mature-sounding age, please contemplate his mother's reported age at his birth. Either human biology has changed drastically in the past 4,000 years or they calculated time differently.

Why shouldn't we assume a template of tolerance for child abuse was established when the best-selling book of all time ignored Isaac's feelings in one of the Bible's most frequently cited chapters?

Fast-forwarding 2 millennia, consider the argument articulated in the Middle Ages by church fathers to persuade European men not to visit prostitutes. The clergy warned about the possibility of incest (Boswell, 1988)! Child abandonment was that common, and apparently more acceptable than sex with whores. The common practice of extruding children was not defined as evil perhaps because child abandonment seemed more humane than infanticide.

Moving ahead to the 19th century, the first *publicly acknowledged* American victim of child abuse was brought to the Society for the Prevention of Cruelty to Animals. The animal shelter was then the most prosocial resource for abused children in my beloved country.

Not until 1962 did a spark of attention begin to illuminate humanity's secret. The Denver pediatrician Henry Kempe and his colleagues published an attention-focusing article in the *Journal of the American Medical Association*. Searches of earlier medical literature is reported to reveal only one prior mention of child abuse. That single reference in the 1930s was in an X-ray journal in which abuse was mentioned as one of the several differential diagnostic possibilities in a case report. A major deterrent for our field was Freud's (1935, pp. 62–64) perception that he had been in "error" to believe his patients' reports of abuse.

Resuming the predictive mode, I do not know how long it will be before humanity follows Sweden's lead in outlawing corporal punishment consistent with the reality that spanking is culturally approved violence against children (Straus, 1994). But I am confident that in oncoming millennia, Kempe and his colleagues will be popularly credited for precipitating a historical discontinuity of cosmological magnitude, to borrow Freud's phrase. Kempe will be remembered in the company of the others in humanity's Hall of Fame, side by side with Abraham and his awareness that our planet is an integrated global village; Moses getting the message out about the rule of law; the moral philosophical legacies of Confucius, the Buddha, Hillel, Jesus, Mohammed; Copernicus's demonstration that the earth is not the center of the universe; Newton's physics; Darwin's evolutionary hypothesis; Lister's practical application of Pasteur's demonstration of the validity of Van Leeuwenhoek's concept of microorganisms; Freud chronicling that we harbor thoughts, feelings, and motivations outside of our awareness; Einstein, Watson and Crick and other seminal contributors to 20th-century scientific and technological miracles; Gandhi's demonstration that it is possible to achieve victory in major geopolitical conflicts without employing violence; Truman as the first conqueror in the history of humanity to treat defeated and hated enemies constructively.

It is inconceivable to me that, in retrospect, what Kempe et al. contributed will not be recognized eventually as belonging in that company, unless humanity should sadly regress to the status in which child abuse is once again socially acceptable. Would slavery and infanticide be far behind?

While I know of no reason to predict such reversion, one should never underestimate the risks inherent in coupling today's technology with our triune brain. MacLean (1973) noted that the human brain combines into 1 what are essentially 3 chemically and structurally different cerebrotypes. Apparently derived from phylogenetically discrepant evolutionary levels, there persists between our ears the potential for dyscoordination and perhaps antagonism between our reptilian brain stem, our paleomammalian limbic system, and our neomammalian cerebral cortex on top.

Such a sociocultural regression is not what I had in mind in noting repeatedly that change happens. What I was thinking comes closer to the speculation by Alvin Toffler, who alerted humanity to change in his 1970 book, *Future Shock*. In August 1996, on the day following NASA and Stanford scientists reporting the hint of extraplanetary life on Mars, Toffler estimated that the number of people who consulted NASA's Web site in a single day probably exceeded the total population of humans who for centuries had even heard of Copernicus. It's not a testable hypothesis. But if it were, it would be one on which to wager.

Returning to terra firma, a significant challenge for clinicians and for all of humanity is to illuminate our shared invisible motivations, resentments, and other hidden vestiges of turning a blind eye to child abuse. Isn't it time to discuss and evaluate in the light of day societal attitudes toward and low expectations of the young, as recorded by each successive generation throughout thousands of years of written history? Eveoleen Rexford, the late second editor of the *Journal of the American Academy of Child and Adolescent Psychiatry*, spoke eloquently and persuasively about an unconscious societal prejudice against the young.

Further evidence of the primitiveness of the psychosocial aspects of our clinical knowledge and skills is documented by the quality of that dimension of multiaxial nosological systems. Noting that nosological primitiveness should not be misconstrued as being dismissive of our promising progress in accumulating knowledge and skills about psychosocial factors in child development and pathology. The point is that we have just begun. Please recall that I credit our commitment to developmental biopsychosocial integration as the foundation of my certainty about CAP's future status.

⁂

Another uncertain factor in CAP's future is the daunting challenge to devise, create, and implement reliable systems for (1) post hoc assessment of both the quality and effectiveness of delivered clinical care and (2) overall periodic assessment of professional performance and competence.

I find it easier to articulate the goal than to suggest methodologies. The best I can offer is a global epistemological model and identification of potential enemies. Others will have to address how to get from here to there. But I sense there are strategies and methodologies that are both more rational clinically and less destructive to professionalism than the recent American infatuation with managed care. That pendulum has exceeded rationality in its swing away from costly fee-for-service compensation. The intrusion of economically mandated approval *in advance* of clinical service from a disembodied voice at the other end of a telephone is not prosocial. The voice seems to focus on money without a clue as to what the patient and family even look like.

Please be assured that my relative ignorance about economic details does not bespeak dismissiveness of its importance. Indeed, the comparison of health care *access* and expenditures in my beloved country between our youth and my geriatric demographic group lends credence to the notion of an unconscious societal prejudice against the young. The chaotic irrationality of America's health care nonsystem was epitomized when duration of hospital stay was legislated into law and signed by the president.

My global vision of a rational goal entails economic capitation. It would be agreeable also if it were less stingy, as if children's health were the equivalent of World War III. Most important, however, is that the strategy encompasses post hoc monitoring of our clinical performance. I may not love it, but it will help me grow as a clinician. And I will love that! What I envision is systemization via information technology in the rich tradition of the goals of medicine's CPC, the clinical pathological conferences that followed autopsies. After the fact, CPCs reviewed what had transpired before the patient expired. That second postmortem was not fun but it was educational.

I would wager that the combination of modern technology and sensitive confidential collegial review triggered by performance and outcome thresholds will prove to be far less toxic than those reports by pathologists in front of colleagues on the hospital staff. The bottom line is that we learned and we grew. It is a clinical truth that the mark of a professional is the ready capacity to acknowledge mistakes and to learn from them.

◦◦◦

This clinical assessment volume of the *Handbook* began to germinate in 1949. In retrospect, 2 seeds were planted, which evolved over the decades into Volume V. Unrelated seminal events in 1949 preordained collecting and nurturing the foregoing CA/ISP building blocks to launch us into the future.

The seminal macrocosmic event was Cade's (1949) publication in an Australian medical journal suggesting the utility in treating what we now call Bipolar Disorder with the chemical element lithium, discovered in 1817. Then it was called Manic-Depressive Psychosis. In 1952 the first *Diagnostic and Statistical Manual of Mental Disorders* (*DSM-I*) designated it Manic-Depressive Reaction and categorized it as a Disorder of Psychogenic Origin despite the incontrovertible evidence of genetic factors. That reflected the quasi-religious fervor of the era.

The availability of lithium mandated eventual recognition of the central role of CA/ISP in psychiatry. Prior to Cade's discovery and its subsequent replication and eventual acceptance 2 decades later in the adult psychiatric mainstream, it was a matter of clinical indifference whether a patient was diagnosed as suffering from Schizophrenic or Manic-Depressive Reactions. Without an effective treatment for either, accuracy of diagnosis was perceived as an irrelevant intellectual exercise. Indeed, in America it was demeaned as "descriptive" psychiatry, in opposition to the then prevailing American enthusiasm for psychodynamics. To underscore that this view represents more than my personal perspective, confirmation can be found in both the National Institute of Mental Health's retrospective review of its own initial 25 years (Research Task Force of NIMH (1975) and the Group for the Advancement of Psychiatry's (1962) survey of North American academic psychiatry chairs.

My reference to the adult psychiatric mainstream reflects the fact that CAP has tended to lag behind psychopharmacologically, with 1 notable exception. Bradley's (1937) report on stimulants initiated what is now the longest-running continuous psychopharmacological intervention in history. Benzedrine, however, did not send a message about CA/ISP as lithium eventually did.

CA/ISP was so dissed that several years after my involuntary 1949 entry and subsequent seduction into psychiatry, respected mainstream teachers recommended postponing "diagnosis" in adults until after several years of "treatment." In that era of American unidimensionality, treatment was psychodynamic psychotherapy or psychoanalysis. The only alternative CAP intervention I recall hearing about in the early 1950s was "environmental manipulation," which was the alternative to "treatment."

Half a century later, the central importance of enhancing CA/ISP knowledge and skills is documented vividly by the survey of people diagnosed as bipolar conducted in the mid-1990s by the National Depressive and Manic Depressive Association (NDMDA). The survey revealed that adult respondents had not been diagnosed accurately until an average of 8 years after initially seeking help. Retrospectively, 59% of the bipolar patients reported experiencing their first symptoms during childhood or adolescence.

In my personal path, 1949 happened to be the year in which I became convinced of the central importance of CA/ISP in psychiatry. The conviction was serendipitous and against the stream of the then-prevailing clinical wisdom. Retrospectively, seduced is a more accurate descriptor than convinced. Without a moment of regret since then, I was hooked by psychiatry in 1949 in the course of what could be characterized as a blind date arranged, so to speak, by my commanding officer. The lifelong infatuation overcame me in the context of the greatest therapeutic triumph I have witnessed, heard, or read about in the ensuing decades. Literally.

I had just completed a rotating internship and stood with another young physician in front of the executive officer of Philadelphia's Naval Hospital in 1949. I was in uniform a second time to pay back, as it were, for the 80% of my World War II soft military assignment attending school in the V-12 unit at the University of Michigan. That educational assignment in uniform reflected America's uncertainty about the war's duration. Preparing for the worst, the military created units to educate men—there were no women in V-12 or ASTP—to ensure a continuing supply of vital expertise for however long the war lasted.

The executive officer solicited each of our individual preferences for clinical assignment. The other guy requested surgery and I named internal medicine or neurosurgery. (The combination sounds odd. After my rotating internship, those were the 2 areas in which I was most motivated to learn more.) Ignoring our individual requests, the executive officer offered both of us assignments to psychiatry. The other young physician replied emphatically "Anything but." I acquiesced and, a few weeks later, serendipity generated the startling therapeutic triumph that impressed on me indelibly the centrality of meticulous clinical assessment and therapeutic prescription. Simultaneously, I was seduced. An involuntary assignment was transformed into a multidecade career and this CA/ISP volume. Here's what happened.

In that peaceful interim between World War II and the Korean conflict, in the absence of those wartime "90-day wonder" educational programs that transformed physicians into psychiatrists in 3 months, the navy afforded me a leisurely opportunity to learn psychiatry by examining chronic patients on what was then called a "back ward." Ward 2D housed navy and marine personnel who had previously been hospitalized, by contractual agreement, for years and years at St. Elizabeth's Hospital in Washington, D.C. In the postwar period, with excess hospital capacity, the navy transferred those chronic patients to their direct care in Philadelphia. Most descriptive is the dehumanizing metaphor describing 2D as a virtual museum of pathology. Several patients demonstrated Huntington's disease at differing stages of deterioration. Senile dementia seemed endemic.

It was the rapid and presumed impossible cure of one of those senile patients, hospitalized for more than a decade, that impressed upon me the seminal importance of precision in assessment, diagnosis, and treatment prescription. Over the years of hospitalization, according to the elderly gentleman's chart, he had become increasingly mute and unresponsive. My unproductive efforts to examine him one morning were confirmatory. Later that day, serendipity struck while I was examining the patient in the next bed.

I heard a subdued voice behind me whisper "Philadelphia," consistent with the medical chart's notation that the man I had examined earlier occasionally mumbled irrelevancies. Continuing to examine the patient in the next bed, I subsequently heard the elderly gentleman whisper "Truman." Eventually it dawned on me that those apparent irrelevancies constituted correct answers to those formal mental status questions I had gone through the motion of asking him hours earlier. If that assumption was accurate, it suggested that his problem was not access to knowledge. Rather, those mumbles suggested it was the slow rate of communication of available knowledge.

To test that clinical hypothesis, I arranged to examine him again in the absence of concerns about time. Under ordinary circumstances, waiting 10 minutes for a verbal response can feel virtually interminable. Hence I arranged for plenty of time and brought a book to read to eliminate my impatience. Apologetically, I explained to the blank stare that, without discourteous intent, I would read while he collected his thoughts. Assuming his blank stare signified acquiescence, I proceeded. With time, it became evident that he was indeed knowledgeable albeit with extreme psychomotor retardation.

I persuaded my supervisor to arrange sufficient time and to bring reading material. He replicated my clinical findings and endorsed my assumption that the dementia diagnosis was inappropriate. Al Zuska agreed that depression was a more logical explanation.

In consequence, we instituted electroconvulsive therapy. Less than 3 weeks later, this mute, blank-appearing human vegetable was transformed back to the crisp premorbid military careerist I had read about in the chart. When the head nurse and I made our daily medical rounds, he would snap to attention as we approached his bed and respond with precision to our inquiries, followed by his respectfully polite reciprocal inquiry about our welfare.

The phenomenal therapeutic effect stemmed directly from diagnostic precision. That it was serendipitous did not diminish the lesson's imprint. Only insignificant unanswerable questions persisted. If I had been examining a patient other than the man in the very next bed, would I have heard him identify his location, the president of the United States, and the like? Would I have been attracted to psychiatry? Would I have been indelibly impressed with the importance of CA/ISP? Would I have devoted the latter half of the 20th century to thinking about its refinement, against the tide of those clinical supervisors and colleagues convinced of CA/ISP's unimportance for at least the 2 decades preceding mainstream cognizance of lithium's specificity?

More important than those questions is for you to be alerted to my personal biases. Does attributing my choice of psychiatry to serendipity and seduction interfere with the objectivity and rationality of my prediction about our paradigmatic future? To what extent has my judgment been influenced by the reality that prior to being seduced into psychiatry, my pattern had been to affiliate with what is best described as "winners"? That was my boyhood perception in choosing De Witt Clinton High School and the University of Michigan. In the hierarchy of medical specialties, psychiatry and winner were not linked. Is it conceivable that this geriatric editor is trying to elevate my medical specialty (pediatrics is not a subspecialty of internal medicine) via this long-winded prediction about a future higher status among the perceived hierarchy of medical specialties?

While I hope that is not a factor, I must acknowledge with embarrassment that my selection of psychiatric residency in 1950 was influenced by such immature cognitions. My choice of Temple University Hospital had nothing to do with Philadelphia. Indeed, the navy had transferred me to Michigan shortly thereafter, where I met and became engaged to my late wife, en-

hancing Michigan's appeal. I elected Temple because of the then celebrated internist-psychiatrist team who coauthored Weiss and English's landmark 1943 book *Psychosomatic Medicine*. By becoming a resident in both departments, I could retain an affiliation with my infantile concept of winners.

The reality evolved differently. In the absence of forethought on my part or, to my knowledge, by either department's faculty, the challenge of residency in 2 separate departments exceeded my capacity. It was more than the considerable quantity of time. (I was cursed with excess time because my late wife did not move to Philadelphia until the middle of my first year of residency.) The issue was the risk of being a mediocre resident in 2 departments. Winners prefer to be top notch in 1 field. Fortunately, I overcame my immature cognitions before burning any nonexistent bridges. I departed internal medicine constructively and committed full time to the learning process that was more fun . . . without regret.

Please be assured that displaying the foregoing immature soiled linen in print is less than agreeable. But I learned from my mistakes and it may be relevant. My conscious cognitions doubt that there is any winner motivation fueling my prediction. Not only has self-scrutiny failed to perceive it, but the reality is that I won't survive to enjoy the achievement. It would be agreeable if my grandchildren lived that long. This is not the Berlin Wall. What I knew about Eastern Europe was global and sketchy. I would not characterize my knowledge of CAP similarly.

What is more conceivable to me is that my 23-year-old silliness about being identified exclusively as a psychiatrist may have offered the younger me a broader perspective, a quasi-outsider's vantage enriching my reflexive insider competitiveness. I was fully committed to becoming the best possible psychiatrist and psychoanalyst, to quote the descriptors Temple University's psychiatric faculty employed. Indeed, a significant number of my teachers would have cited psychoanalyst first.

In the interim, I experienced psychiatry and psychoanalysis as simultaneously intellectually stimulating and frustrating. The frustration stemmed from the discrepancy between effort invested and clinical results. Indeed, the intellectual stimulation was not always good news.

Two factors had attracted me to child psychiatry. First, working with children was more fun than working with dreary adults. Also attractive were the preventive promises of the Mental Hygiene Movement: Raise children correctly and eliminate mental illness. The more I learned, the more it became evident those ideas were primarily intellectual. Attractive ideas without evidence. That was midcentury, decades before anyone's wildest preventive dreams imagined gene modification.

A clinical example of the handicaps posed by midcentury intellectual stimulation was my conceptual evaluation of my next surprising therapeutic triumph. After 3 or 4 exploratory clinical sessions, a young adolescent's unremitting debilitating abdominal pain disappeared. I was hailed by family and the host of physicians who had seen the patient before my "cure." But I dismissed the startling outcome as a "flight into health" with the several physicians who telephoned.

In retrospect with subsequent "descriptive" psychiatric enrichment, I suspect I had been consulted just before the end of the young adolescent's lengthy extended depressive episode. But this was the era before children experienced depression. While all celebrated my "cure," I criticized myself for having explored too aggressively and precipitating the "flight into health" from what I had interpreted as the youngster's masturbatory concerns. I had conceptualized the abdominal pain as the "displacement upward" of the youngster's obvious uncertainty about sexual maturation.

As noted earlier, change happens. Not only was that before depression was recognized in children but it was also in the Victorian 1950s, a time in America still exemplified by Balzac's story about youngsters in a museum looking at a nude painting. One asks if it is boy or girl, to which the other responds that you can't tell because they aren't wearing clothes.

In that climate boys—except for one with deficient reality testing—volunteered disbelief, at the start of their clinical sessions with me, about what they had seen on TV news. The first man in space, the cosmonaut Yuri Gagarin, had embraced and exchanged a kiss with Nikita Khrushchev! American boys were startled by physical intimacy between the world's most macho hero and most macho menace. That was before it became acceptable for American men to hug.

Although the forgoing illustrations are male and American, females were not immune and the pathogens were imported. Four decades before Masters and Johnson (1966) courageous paradigm-shifting observations, psychoanalytic ideas from the other side of the Atlantic permeated toxic notions about the clitoris as a second-rate penis. Thus "mature" women derived no pleasure from the clitoris and hoped for "vaginal orgasms." I kid you not. If you have clues about the database for Helene Deutsch's (1925) notions, I would welcome edification.

I am grateful that by the time it dawned on me that the mental hygiene promises were founded on unsubstantiated hopes, CAP was just beginning to be enriched by the intellectual and clinical ferment contributed by the emerging biological, family, behavioral, and cognitive domains. Before then my mentor, the late O. Spurgeon English, was dubbed wild and unorthodox because his clinical efforts sometimes included family members in addition to the identified patient. Spurge, you have my eternal gratitude for the model you provided for me. For several years, you served as my CA/ISP guide. When challenged, I tried to envision what Spurge would think and do.

Prior to lithium and the French discovery three years later of chlorpromazine (Delay & Deniker, 1952), originally synthesized as an antihistamine, the only available somatic psychiatric treatments had been electroconvulsive therapy, insulin coma therapy, lobotomy, and the stimulants' "paradoxical" effects on hyperactive children. Effective treatments were available in the first half of the 20th century for central nervous system syphilis and the psychosis accompanying pellagra. But the bulk of the few psychopharmacological treatments available midcentury served to control patients rather than treat them.

Shortly thereafter, behavior modification started to emerge from the laboratory to fulfill the clinical promises suggested decades earlier. In 1920 Watson and Raynor had reported conditioning the development of a phobia in an infant. Then Mary Cover Jones (1924) demonstrated that such a conditioned phobia could be relieved by social imitation and direct reconditioning. But it required 4 decades to begin to enter the clinical mainstream! Concurrently, the family therapy "movement," as it was called in the 1960s and 1970s, evolved to enrich assessment and treatment processes with systems concepts and strategies. Shortly thereafter, cognitive data and therapeutic interventions started to enrich our armamentarium.

Although American CAP psychodynamic unidimensionality *began* to recede in the 1960s, the designation "eclectic" continued to be pejorative well into the 1970s. Although I do not recall it articulated in so many words, it was as if it would be inappropriate to try to target the treatment to the patient's problem. The emphasis continued to seem to be on the selection of an ideal patient for the several treatments now organized in separate clinical encampments, noncommunicating therapeutic parishes in which clinical assessment was not needed. Treatment had been preordained by which threshold the patient crossed. A single unidimensionality was being replaced by multiple balkanized unidimensionalities. In rare instances of communication across the boundaries of different therapeutic perspectives, hostility seemed to prevail.

That treatments prescribed in those days depended on the orientation of the clinician consulted seemed no different from a homeowner inadvertently summoning an electrician for flooding. The electrical wiring might be upgraded while the water persisted. Another metaphor is the old joke about the apocryphal Jew shipwrecked alone on a comfortable lush island well endowed with physical needs and comforts. While waiting to be rescued, the lonely man consumed the decades by constructing a community. When rescuers arrived, he told the rescuers that he had built one of everything. Proudly, he showed them the city hall, fire station, synagogue, hospital, school, synagogue, police station. The rescuers interrupted to express puzzlement about the duplication of synagogues. He responded that one was for prayer while the other was the one whose threshold he would not cross! Most of CAP felt that way in the 1960s and 1970s, moving me to address "reassessing eclecticism" and "therapeutic choice" (Harrison, 1977, 1978, 1979; McDermott & Harrison, 1977).

***

Since then I have learned that epistemologists of science note that for many disciplines, there exists what they designate as an "antidiscipline." The antidiscipline usually is narrower in scope than its parent discipline and serves to stimulate generative tension within the parent discipline by questioning aspects of its methodology and knowledge. Often it succeeds in reorienting and revitalizing under the rubric of the parent discipline. In 1979 Kandel noted that for the parent discipline of psychology in general, and psychiatry in particular, cellular neurobiology functioned then as an antidiscipline. At more fundamental levels, cellular neurobiology had molecular biology as an antidiscipline, which, in turn, had physical chemistry as its antidiscipline.

In the decades when American psychiatry's principal intellectual stimulus stemmed from psychoanalysis, the most potent antidisciplines were other types of psychology, the social sciences, and philosophy. The challenge then was what it is today and will be always: neither to reject antidisciplines nor to abandon the truths of our parent discipline in favor of focusing *exclusively* on the antidiscipline's creative contributions. The goal is to integrate.

***

Let's take a by-path to glance at the practice of medicine earlier in the 20th century. Physicians then tended to be identified by their preferred treatment modality: bleeders, homeopaths, purgers, cuppers, infusers. It is my understanding that the orientation and allegiance of the consulted clinician determined the therapeutic prescription. Those nonrational clinical prejudgments were not as toxic then as they would be today. In those days, there were no better medical treatments available. Indeed, the balkanized treatments available in CAP in the 1960's had far more therapeutic potential than bleeding and purging. Medicine at the turn of the century had available only a handful of useful specific therapies: mercury for syphilis, digitalis for cardiac failure, cinchona bark for malaria. But there was no insulin for diabetes or antibiotics for infections. Not even hand washing between patients. In America's deadliest war, a few decades earlier, the mid-19th century Civil War, more deaths were due to illness than to wounds.

But in the course of medicine's elevating path from alchemy to today's medical marvels, major diseases have been conquered: Smallpox, typhus, cholera, yellow fever, poliomyelitis. The World Health Organization (WHO) and UNICEF report that we are on the threshold of vaccines for currently unpreventable childhood killers such as diarrheal diseases, acute respiratory infections, and malaria. And it appears TB can be conquered via treatment monitoring. The major obstacle is economic, provided we aren't overwhelmed by mutating viruses and antibiotic-resistant bacteria to add to WHO's mid-1990s estimate of nearly 50,000 daily deaths due to infections. In the interim we can root for the efforts to deliver to specific cells in vivo what was created in a laboratory in 1997: synthetic genes able to disarm bacteria in the lab of their antibiotic-resistant weaponry.

In the face of that many fatalities, experts nevertheless perceive us as on the threshold of conquering premature death. As early as 1979 the eminent physician and self-proclaimed biology watcher Lewis Thomas envisioned a relatively disease-free society, a notion that would have been unthinkable a half century earlier. Thomas points out that what astonishes us in science today can turn out to be usable and useful tomorrow. That was true for the beginnings of chemistry; also electricity. He notes that with surprise as our guide, knowledge has progressed from Newtonian physics, to electromagnetism, to quantum mechanics, contemporary geophysics, and cosmology.

Since mid-18th century, life expectancy has tripled in advanced countries. Even in poor countries life expectancy doubled in the second half of the 20th century. Antibiotics was the first of biomedical advances that accelerated the progress initiated earlier by sanitary engineering and the mass production of soap. In advanced countries today a child's death is a rare tragic catastrophe. A century earlier in those same countries it was a rare family that did not experience a child's death.

Consider also the change in the meaning of the word *pollution* between the two halves of the 20th century. In my youth it meant feces in the river and air that couldn't be breathed without coughing. Everyone recognized pollution when confronted. Today I learn about it in news reports of sophisticated measures.

Juxtapose (1) the progress CAP has made since 1915 when the pioneering William Healy advanced the novel idea of considering difficult children as individuals side by side with (2) the advances in medical knowledge about children's rashes in the 20th century. At the beginning of the century, childhood rashes were identified by roman numerals. What was called I then is called measles today, II is today's scarlet fever, III is rubella, IV is epidemic pseudoscarlatina, V the equivalent of erythema infectiosum, VI roseola. For whatever it is worth, in the course of a century we have come full circle, so that erythema infectiosum today is commonly referred to as Fifth Disease. Far more important is that in the course of that century, we have learned that Fifth Disease is caused by parvovirus B19, a small DNA virus belonging to the family *Parvoviridae* that infects many animal species, including humans.

In lieu of burdening you with the mountains of detailed knowledge since accumulated about Fifth Disease, let us try to imagine instead the probable accumulation of neuroscientific knowledge 100 years after CAP's primitive mid-20th century unidimensionality. With the maintenance of CAP's commitment to developmental biopsychosocial integration, isn't the major uncertainty how soon our curve of progress will seem comparable to the 20th century doubling of the American life span?

Even my optimistic half-full perspective perceives obstacles and unwelcome side effects. For example, increasing life expectancy creates more than geriatric specialists/subspecialists. It has generated previously unreported family dynamics. For the first time in history, many senior citizens, primarily female, devote as much time to caring for their parents as they did decades earlier caring for their children. Increasingly, one hears about resentment. Are the simultaneous observations of apparent increases in alienation between younger adults and their middle-age parents related? To what extent is that alienation propelled by our startling advances in transportation and communication technologies? And to declines in societal ethical standards?

It was changes in society's threshold of evil that evoked my earlier fantasy about neonatal immunization against fertility. Also related is the extent to which changes in ethical standards contribute to the increased visibility on American streets of homeless people. During the Great Depression of the 1930s, census data document a much higher incidence of homelessness than today. Most Americans of my vintage express disbelief when confronted with those data. They have to be reminded how many homeless people they knew well and with whom they interacted closely in the 1930s. The difference was that the homeless then lived with extended family. They were in my home and in virtually all of my friends' homes. For my mother and father to allow her brother's children to live on the street would have been unthinkable. As we have noted, change happens.

A clinical illustration of change is that in the late 1940s, I was taught authoritatively at the University of Michigan Medical College that the physician who knew syphilis thoroughly knew all of medicine. I relish even less recalling the ill-informed teacher who taught at that Harvard of the West that children could not be diagnosed as psychotic because of their normal difficulty distinguishing reality. A few years later in Philadelphia, some taught that "diagnosis" required 5 psychoanalytic sessions per week for years.

The third edition of Leo Kanner's (1957) classic *Child Psychiatry* text includes a graphic representation of the growth of our field over the course of the 20th century. Kanner was centered on the fourth decade when his first 1935 edition had been published. The achievement he celebrated in the 1930s was "Working *with* Children." It represented the "advance" of including the child "personally" in treatment processes.

Kanner characterized the 20th century's first decade as "Thinking *About* Children" to acknowledge the emergence of cultural trends favorable for children. He cited psychometry, separate juvenile courts, psychoanalysis, and the mental hygiene movement. He characterized 1910 to 1920 as "Doing things *to* Children," referring to the development of community facilities for problem children such as special classes, probation, and organized foster home care. The 1920s progressed to what Kanner designated as "Doing things *for* Children" via family and school. In Kanner's words, this represented "the efforts, made in the third decade by the child guidance clinics, to study family relationships and to work constructively with parents and teachers on behalf of the emotionally upset children" (p. 15). Which brings us to the 1930s, the fourth decade, when the advance Kanner highlighted was including the child "personally in the therapeutic program" (p. 15).

Four decades later, the introductory words I wrote for Volume III of Noshpitz's *Basic Handbook of Child Psychiatry* (1979) asserted: "Currently, the child psychiatric clinician's greatest challenge stems from the widespread demand for treatment. Consequently, more professional time and energy is devoted to therapeutic intervention than to all other child psychiatric clinical activities combined" (p. 3). The closing paragraph of that introductory chapter says: "There is much to be learned about how to prescribe treatment. The goal is specificity and therapeutic differentiation, and the method by which to achieve them are based on careful, meticulous diagnostic assessment" (p. 19).

A few years after writing that chapter, I learned that 84 years earlier the uniquely esteemed physician Sir William Osler (1859) had identified as the major problem in medical education and practice the excessive emphasis on therapeutics of questionable efficacy. Eighty-four years later, in the same year I wrote of the "demand for treatment," Lewis Thomas (1979) looked back and recalled the skepticism about therapeutics pervading his earlier medical education. Effective treatments like insulin for diabetes were "regarded as anomalies." Sulfanilamide and penicillin were greeted with "flat disbelief."

I cannot emphasize too much that my earlier reference to the diminishing future competence of CAP solo practitioners bespeaks continuing progress. That prediction represents the polar opposite of CAP's relative ignorance in the 1950s and the intertherapeutic hostilities of the 1960s. The courageous clinicians who pioneered the eventual end of that balkanized CAP era were characterized vividly in a 1975 GAP Report as functioning like "split brain preparations." We might be competent with each modality when considered individually, but combining and integrating both frames of reference simultaneously resulted in what some aptly described as peek-a-boo prescriptions. From a psychoanalytic perspective, those pharmacological interventions were perceived negatively under the rubrics of "contamination of the transference" and "parameters." And those outdated characterizations neglected to address burgeoning psychosocial knowledge and skills. No single clinician will be able to do it all.

❖❖❖

Absent tiny print, it is worth noting that my direct involvement with this edition of the *Handbook* was initiated via declining the late Dr. Noshpitz's invitation to edit the section on diagnostics. My declination was followed immediately by volunteering to edit "Clinical Assessment." That distinction is the premise to which this volume is dedicated. Eventually CAP will progress so that future editions of the *Handbook* will not have to differentiate between diagnosis and clinical assessment. General medicine has evolved to that status. But, unlike today's general medicine, CAP diagnostic categorization and CA/ISP tend to be processes of markedly different complexity. CAP today resembles the practice of medicine decades earlier.

When we diagnose the elementary school-age youngster as Disruptive Behavior Disorder and/or Learning Disorder, the diagnostic process poses minimal challenge. Indeed, it is likely that the child's concrete operational classmates long ago determined the correct diagnosis. Their descriptors may be less dispassionate than *DSM*'s, but they are precise. The clinical challenge that child presents is not diagnostic. The challenge is to determine what contributes to the disruptive behavior and/or learning problem and what to do about it. CA/ISP searches for contributing factors in a host of realms: genetic, neurobiological, familial, social, attentional, cognitive, learned behaviors, abusive, deprivational, loss, conscience, unconscious conflicts, and the host of other factors addressed in the preceding chapters.

Please be assured that the foregoing in no way minimizes the importance and increasing value of the processes represented by the *Diagnostic and Statistical Manual* and *International Classification of Disease* (ICD). I perceive those processes as major advances. Only since 1980, when *DSM-III* was published, has it become possible for American clinicians, who do not communicate regularly, to assume in the course of dialogue that we are talking about the same description. Prior to *DSM-III* in the absence of a *universal* descriptive standard, there was a repetitive need to agree mutually regarding definitions of each diagnostic word. Needless to say, universal does not mean perfect.

The process that began with *DSM-III* has matured but it remains *conceptually* immature. Primitive. That is not a criticism. It is a descriptor and a prediction about future evolution akin to general medicine.

As a consequence of *DSM*'s wise commitment at our current level of knowledge to avoid theory and etiology, the *DSM* process is a commitment to empiricism. We should remember also that empiricism represents only one stage of a field's growth and that in a field's mature stages, empiricism tends to represent ignorance. Change happens.

Harsh-sounding words like primitive and ignorance mandate clarification. They refer to the fact that the *DSM* and *ICD* nosological systems include categories that are the *conceptual* equivalent of the common early 20th-century medical diagnosis of Fever. At that time the most frequently recorded death certificate diagnosis was Indigestion. With no intent to offend, comprehensiveness obliges asserting the obvious: Indigestion and fever are not what we would call *diagnoses* by contemporary standards. Both are *symptoms* with a host of possible etiologies, which in turn will contribute to identifying the correct medical *diagnosis*, which may point in the direction of specific therapeutic interventions.

Decades ago, medical diagnoses could be made with comparable reliability by the most esteemed physicians and by elementary school-age children. Isn't it easy to imagine a concrete operational 8-year-old diagnosing Indigestion with precision: "Grandpa vomited, turned blue, coughed, choked, fell over, and stopped breathing"? Knowledge and time were required before it was discovered that the indigestion was a symptom. The cause of death was myocardial infarction caused by coronary occlusion secondary to a host of risk factors with probable genetic . . .

Just as less than a century ago when the most prominent symptoms/behaviors were mislabeled as diagnoses, today's valuable *DSM* and *ICD* are similar. We have just begun. The future will be different, however. In our clinical microcosms today it is probable that categorical diagnoses will be evident at the *outset* of the assessment process. Indeed, the diagnosis often is determined accurately before clinical contact.

Informally, I tested that hypothesis by observing the diagnostic accuracy of a clerical person assigned to respond to initial telephone calls. Her sole *clinical* responsibility was to distinguish which calls mandated *immediate* professional involvement. The majority of her calls were nonemergent as the psychiatric emergency room had separate telephone lines at Harbor UCLA, the municipal hospital serving southern Los Angeles County, in whose CAP outpatient clinic she had worked 3 years. Her responsibilities also included handling clinical charts and inputting data including categorical diagnoses.

Hence I asked her, as a personal favor, to record her best guess of the diagnosis after she had telephonically accessed and recorded the identifying information on behalf of the intake clinician, who would in turn telephone to initiate the clinical information gathering process on the phone.

It evolved that the clerk was rarely incorrect in identifying the then relevant major *DSM-III-R* diagnostic category after her initial telephone communication whether she spoke with a parent, foster parent, a referring clinician, or the representative of an educational, social or legal agency. There were some instances in which the clerk declined to guess. But when she guessed, mistakes were the exception. I cannot convey percentages because the methodologic rigor of the game, as she perceived it, did not require calculations to be persuasive that *DSM-III-R* diagnostic categorization required clerical skills and job-acquired knowledge. Diagnosis preceded CA/ISP.

Recalling the diagnostic accuracy of the bereaved 8-year-old who witnessed Grandpa's death in the context of general medicine's earlier noso-logical system, isn't it evident that, with the accumulation of knowledge, CAP *eventually* will evolve a complex, useful diagnostic system akin to general medicine's? Do you doubt that our diagnoses eventually will encompass etiology, onset, development, biopsychosocial factors, course, mechanism, treatments, responses, outcome? Then this volume can be entitled "Diagnostics."

Until then, we are obliged to function within the immature conceptual limits of today's nosological *systemization*. Simultaneously, our abundance of accumulated knowledge and skills mandate that each CA/ISP process search individually to identify etiological and maintaining factors to be targeted in formulating treatment interventions. CA/ISP has to run the gamut from determining the extent to which observed abnormalities represent deficiencies in positive adaptive behaviors and the extent to which they represent behaviors in all children at that stage of development but which have been perceived as abnormal by significant adults. And we have to determine whether the conduct-disordered youngster's aggression is phenomenologically and neurobiologically categorizable as impulsive-reactive-hostile-affective aggression or is the controlled-proactive-instrumental-predatory variety (Vitiello & Stoff, 1997). And then there are so many other contributory factors to explore clinically. It is uncertain how far into the future until we are blessed with a reliable complex developmental biopsychosocial subcategorization of aggression. But isn't it certain that we will achieve it just as general medicine subcategorized fever?

What I have seen CAP accomplish in the last quarter of the 20th century reminds me of the general medical progress I have observed up close since I started paying serious attention as a military corpsman in the early 1940s. That was the threshold of the antibiotic era. A guy in my naval unit at the University of Michigan in 1943 developed meningitis and needed penicillin. It had to be flown in to the medical center. Jack was lucky he was in the military. There was no penicillin for civilians.

It has been hypothesized that hygiene, penicillin, and what followed generated a public health/longevity advance rivaled in the history of humanity only when our ancestors adopted tables instead of eating on the ground. And as noted earlier, the epidemiologic effects of longevity will enhance CAP's future importance in preventive early detection and intervention.

∗∗∗

A few *cautions* before listing Clinical Truths: As CAP progresses, all of us would be prudent to exercise vigilance about inevitable intellectual temptations. Many of us are attracted to rational-sounding lures. It is tempting to mistake data as information, information as knowledge and to think of knowledge as wisdom. For example, we are obliged never to forget that knowledge of the mechanisms of action of effective interventions does not necessarily constitute evidence of etiology. Sometimes it does. But at other times identifying etiology by mechanism of action will be no more than a reductionistic logical fallacy. A mistake. For instance, knowing the mode of action of diuretics on renal tubules contributes little to understanding the etiology or pathophysiology of the congestive heart failure helped by those diuretics. Similarly, comprehending how salicylates affect prostaglandins will not identify pneumococci as the etiology of the symptoms caused by pneumonia. In CAP, we have a lot to learn before we will know how much, if anything, we can learn about *etiology* by knowing the mechanisms of action of today's less than precisely labeled stimulants, antidepressants, psychotropics, and whatever tomorrow brings.

∗∗∗

Caution: It is easy to neglect a vital ingredient in both CA/ISP and treatment processes. We have to train ourselves to search for the youngster's and the family's strengths. Many of us have created millions if not billions of neurons focused on pathology in the course of our education and clinical socialization. Experientially, pathology is head-lined at the outset of clinical processes. However, if we attend only to what is emphasized, that poses the risk of neglecting the search for strengths for potential therapeutic use. That youngsters' developmental achievements may be uneven renders it fruitful to search actively.

∗∗∗

The preceding building block chapters contain a host of indicators regarding which individuals and systems should be included to enrich CA/ISP processes. Time and experience were required before I realized the merit of what I now

❊❊❊

perceive as an absolute mandate: *Every CAP CA/ISP should include family group assessment in an interview context.*

Early in my career the practice was to rely on reports from the parents and from the identified patient. Of course, those are valuable clinical data. But those reports do not substitute for direct observation of actual transactions in the course of participating in discussion with the entire family. In 1884, the novelist, Helen Hunt Jackson commented eloquently about the value of individual's descriptions of ones own family: "There cannot be found in the animal kingdom a bat, or any other creature, so blind in its own range of circumstance and connection as the great majority of human beings are in the bosoms of the families" (p. 186).

I assume you know, as I do, from personal family experiences that individuals within a family may perceive family functioning and history differently. Are there any who have grown up in a family setting who would not endorse the virtually universal notion that I can supply accurate family information while others distort?

Unhappily, in an economic context, it may require more than 1 family assessment interview to overcome initial family discomfort in unfamiliar clinicians' presence. At least a second family assessment session, if not more, may be needed to identify the social forces within the family that the family does not recognize and therefore could never describe for us in individual clinical sessions.

I could describe several ancient clinical illustrations documenting therapeutic ineffectiveness until family assessment exposed intrafamilial forces perpetuating symptoms. At times it was parents unconsciously using their shared focus on the youngster's symptoms to avoid addressing their own dyadic marital difficulties. In other instances, siblings benefited from perpetuating the identified patient's symptomatic behavior.

Caution! Scheduling and other difficulties render it tempting to skip family assessment interview(s). I have been obliged to discipline myself to avoid that temptation. There may indeed be rare specific contraindications to family assessment. When I perceive contraindications, I consider those factors seriously. If they persist in my judgment, I consult with colleagues. It is axiomatic that clinical assessment include family sessions as soon as is feasible.

Like the people and clinical ingredients that should comprise each individualized CAP/ISP process, the duration of the process with current knowledge, skills, and instruments has to be individualized. Economic forces dislike that inherent truth. Nevertheless, clinical quality mandates individualization. Sometimes CA/ISP requires only a few minutes. Yet I recall instances in which CA/ISP required many hours over the course of several months. And it was worth it, clinically and economically. The investment of a few dollars in CA/ISP can save a huge amount of treatment expenditures.

A startling example of the clinical benefit inherent in flexibility in the duration of assessment unfolded after it required only minutes for me to confirm the obvious autistic diagnosis conveyed by clinicians elsewhere. But it required weeks that grew into months to formulate and implement what proved to be a relatively inexpensive but amazingly effective therapeutic strategy. Over the course of CA/ISP, it became evident that the 4-year-old's bizarre behaviors and impaired social reciprocity were far more prominent in the presence of parents and less when alone with me in my office. Subsequently, without being informed of my clinical hunch, support for that observation was supplied by the therapeutic nursery day treatment staff whom I had persuaded temporarily to admit the child for assessment. Their extensive report communicated a great deal more about brief interactions with parents than about the autistic child with whom they had spent the bulk of their time.

Fortunately, it was easy to implement referring the youngster to a single clinician who was knowledgeable about and interested in autism, and who also was experienced with conjoint marital psychotherapy. I suggested that the clinician assess the youngster's development every few months and institute weekly conjoint marital therapy. Simultaneously, I was able to arrange a normalizing 5-day-a-week socializing educational experience in a quality community nursery school setting. (The qualitative judgment had been made earlier when my late wife and I had selected it for our children.) When the autistic 4-year-old attended, he was the only student at that time with identified pathology.

A dozen years later, the outcome in terms of the

adolescent's documented academic and social achievements represented the most positive extreme imaginable in the range of conceivable outcomes of Autistic Disorder. At the same time, his parents virulently communicated displeasure with the changes in their marital transactions "created" by that "beastly cruel" doctor to whom I had referred them and "our normal child." How could I have referred them to such a brute?

The point is that this phenomenal clinical outcome was a direct product of being able to devote many many hours over the course of months to assessment and intervention planning.

Another dramatic illustration of the advantage of flexibility in duration of CA/ISP is the first published report of psychosocial interventions changing gender identity in a postpubertal female transsexual (Davenport & Harrison, 1977). In that instance, the CA/ISP process consumed several months of weekly outpatient individual exploratory clinical interviews with the adolescent. The extreme length reflected that she was the first person in my clinical experience with transsexuals (mostly adult biological males) in which I observed clinical evidence of what had only been hypothesized in the past. I detected phobic aspects in the adolescent's reaction to her biology. Cautiously I elected not to explore in depth those clinical hints in our weekly outpatient contacts while the youngster lived in a less-than-ideal home. But that extended CA/ISP process was fruitful because in that era, before economic limits captured our attention, it was possible to arrange an open-ended hospitalization on the Adolescent Service of the University of Michigan's Neuropsychiatric Institute. For 20 months she received intensive individual exploratory psychotherapy in a full-time inpatient therapeutic milieu, followed by continued outpatient psychotherapy and family interventions. The clinical outcome justified the extreme length of the assessment.

⁂

In advance of reading my justification for the continuing indispensability of vital clinical assets that some colleagues denigrate as no more than clinical relics of CAP's psychodynamic era (communication skills and clinician's self-knowledge), it might help you assess my objectivity to recall my perception of the change I observed in the American CAP ideal. When I started in the field it was considered holistic for physician-clinicians to select patients suitable for psychoanalysis. Decades later I perceive psychoanalysts as specialized clinical technicians. The word *technician* bespeaks linguistic precision and should not be misinterpreted as dismissive of the extensive knowledge, skills, and sensitivities required of valued psychoanalytic practitioners. The foregoing specification is intended to dismiss in advance any assumption that what I am about to assert might be influenced emotionally by the reality of my life membership in both the American and International Psychoanalytic Associations.

The fact is that some relics possess inherent value. Others are no more than souvenirs or mementos. There is a lot about CAP's past that we rejoice as no longer relevant—except in historical memory to guard against repeating history's mistakes. And there are also elements of the past that remain an integral ingredient of today's clinical quality.

For clinicians today and tomorrow, self-knowledge and clinical communication skills are requisite. Subsequently I will document the indispensability of clinician's self-knowledge for orthopedic surgeons. Before that I will endeavor to persuade you that in the absence of demonstrated superiority of alternative teaching methodologies, the delivery of our expanding clinical armamentarium has to be via the seminal generic communication skills that evolved over time from psychodynamic exploratory psychotherapy with subsequent cognitive and behavioral enrichments.

I don't know how far in the future those valuable relics will need to persist. Will those skills be vital when we master the molecular chemistry and physics of individual memories as well as of memory processes (Kety 1960), which will facilitate the fantasied psychomycin dispensing machine? In contrast, I am confident that self-knowledge and communication skills will continue to be seminal for CAP clinicians when we achieve the evolutionary-oriented predictions articulated by Randy Nesse, another former student (Nesse & Williams, 1996), when many of the genes that predispose to mental disorders might be demonstrated to have fitness benefits and when many of the more unfortunate aspects of human psychology may be perceived as design compromises and not as flaws. (Randy Nesse and his coauthor articulate those predictions after they assert that akin to the rest of medicine, many psychiatric symptoms will turn out not to be diseases but to be "defenses akin to fever and cough" [p. 209].) Are their genetic predictions comparable to what Levy et al. (1997) conclude in their study of twins, that Attention Deficit Hyperactivity Disorder is an extreme in behavior that varies genetically throughout the population, not a disorder with discrete determinants?

Whatever the future, clinical communication is responsible for more than generating a lot of relevant data. The quality of our communication should contribute to the youngster and family perceiving that something important is trying to be understood by someone who is reliable, caring, and willing, with their collaboration, to try to help. The art of interviewing entails the ability to elicit relevant information and keen observations while conveying sincere interest and concern.

Not everyone agrees with that. Some able colleagues believe the days of unstructured CA/ISP interviewing are numbered. They predict that structured interviews reducible to Xs and Os will routinize CA/ISP. The word *routinize* is not my editorial choice. The word is borrowed from colleagues who predict the demise of unstructured CA/ISP interviewing. But should the concept of routinization alert us to risks inherent in Webster's definition of the word? Lengthy lists of unvarying questions have the potential to bore, irritate, alienate. And structure does not generate data about emotional tone, coping, and the like that less structured clinicians sense.

Structured interviewing tends to contribute in the areas of diagnostic categorization and identifying comorbidities. Those can be valuable epidemiologic and research data. But diagnostic categorization is insufficient for planning clinical interventions for the individual disruptive youngster with learning difficulties. It is not that I cannot imagine routinization some time in the future. But it is nowhere near the horizon. It will be programmed into the psychomycin dispensing machine.

I learned a powerful lesson about clinical communication as an embarrassed intern on a surgical ward. In that Victorian era preceding the sexual revolution, I learned about the potential for pathogenicity inherent in words not being limited to psychosocial clinical activities. The lesson followed my return to the ward after surgical rounds. The teacher was an elderly immigrant anticipating cancer surgery. He summoned me and in-

troduced me to his wife sitting at his bedside. He then asked me to define some of the words he and his wife overheard in the surgical discussions.

"Impotence" was one of the words. I recall the discomfort of my clumsy response far better than I recollect what I actually said. Whatever I said registered as evidenced by his heavily accented challenge to my definition of impotence: "Don't I still got ten fingers and a tongue?" He and his wife smiled. Hers was accompanied by blushing and a quick glance at him. I remember most vividly my prayer that a nurse would call me away stat.

Impotence is imprecise and also potentially toxic for those less resilient than that patient 50 years ago. Since then I have learned that *Erectile Dysfunction* is more accurate and inheres a prosocial potential for expanding and enriching the anatomic foci of subsequent clinical communication. Thank you, sir, for that valuable lesson in 1948.

CAP should celebrate that we outgrew those toxic Mental Hygiene Movement sentiments asserting "No problem children. Only problem parents." Perhaps it could be attributed to the eye of the beholder, but that bias had extensive toxic tentacles. Neither I nor the colleagues I consulted recall any who read Kanner's (1943) landmark report without assuming the etiology of autism resided in parental personality and behavior. In retrospect, Kanner's cluster of parental qualities probably represented a demographic accident. But that was not the message the clinical community received at the time. Parents were perceived as pathogenic in autism.

° ° °

Although it is rarely noted explicitly, there are instances in which the most powerful CAP therapeutic intervention is the authoritative pronouncement that the *identified patient is normal and healthy*. No treatment needed!

Frances and Clarkin (1981) delineated a range of adult psychiatric indications. In my CAP experience, the most common instance has been the otherwise well-developing youngster who commits an isolated bad deed, like 15-year-old Kathryn, one of less than a handful of Asian-Americans in her high school. She was a superb student, popular and a leader among peers. Her parents consulted me about their firstborn in the era when computers were rare. They described Kathryn as knowing more about the high school's lone computer than the entire faculty and student body combined. And her high school served a university community where knowledge was the coin of the realm.

Her father was an esteemed professor in one of the sciences. Kathryn's mother and father had married while both were in graduate school. Her mother reported in the parents' initial clinical interview that she had terminated her promising academic pursuits as a consequence of her perception that her success in the laboratory generated tension at home. While her husband remained silent and appeared to avert both his wife's and my glances, she described assigning priority to family. She had proceeded to create a successful retail enterprise.

They consulted me after Kathryn had been expelled from school for using her special access to the school's offices to supply friends with examination questions. Kathryn was in the process of being enrolled in a private school and grounded from activities. Her parents wanted her "cured," whatever that might require. After eliciting developmental, family, and other relevant historical information from the parents, I scheduled separate assessment interviews with Kathryn and with the 3 family generations living in their home.

My clinical conclusion was that Kathryn was a healthy youngster who had thoughtlessly made a significant mistake and sincerely regretted it. Both cognitively and temperamentally, my global qualitative assessment perceived her at the high extreme of each bell-shape curve. But before communicating my clinical conclusion to the family, I thought it might be judicious to generate quantitative data for the benefit of Kathryn's father. Thus I arranged for a colleague to administer a comprehensive Minnesota Multiphasic Personality Inventory (MMPI) in the hope that it would generate what Kathryn's father would perceive as objective data to complement clinical judgment, which he might demean as subjective.

In addition to Father's quantitative outlook, he had signaled potential resistance to such a conclusion via a bit of family lore he related in the course of the family assessment. He told me and his family—although it was unlikely his mother's limited English enabled comprehension—that during the war in the old country, his starving emaciated father passed an orchard but took none of the food because "stealing was wrong."

I inhibited my urge to blurt out my thoughts lest Father be embarrassed and, for him, devastated in front of his family. Instead, I scheduled a separate session with both parents to reexamine thoughtfully his father's reported hierarchy of values while people were killing on all sides. I highlighted undernutrition's cerebral effects and asked the parents to commit to Father convening and chairing a total family "seminar" to reexamine contextually his father's reported moral judgment. With his wife's and my help, Father could not dispute that the context of destruction, death, famine, and terror enabled categorization of Grandfather's story as impaired nonadaptive reflexive cerebral functioning. Even his younger children would appreciate the marked contrast with their current circumstances.

Last, we scheduled a brief family session for me to pronounce Kathryn as healthy, subjectively and objectively. Unequivocally, she had made a huge mistake and was suffering the consequences. Kathryn told her younger siblings she had learned from the mistake and would never again be that dumb. I added that no treatment was indicated and bade the family farewell.

What informal follow-up information I have gleaned suggests that "no treatment" was a powerful clinical intervention for the entire family, for Kathryn, and for family mythological information processing.

***

Now for the other indispensable relic: Clinician's self-awareness. The inscription "Know Thyself" on the Delphic Oracle and attributed also to Plato is the CAP equivalent of the scriptural "Physician Heal Thyself." It is a basic clinical truth, as the subsequent orthopedic anecdote will document powerfully.

The range of self-knowledge is extensive. There are external factors, such as putative influences of the monetary reward incentive system on our clinical thought processing. Fee-for-service tends to risk overutilization of interventions. Capitation, on the other hand, tends to encourage underutilization of our clinical knowledge and skills.

And there are a host of private individualistic internal factors, such as our personal proclivities to perceive positives or negatives, and my nonobjective reactions when faced with a youngster who resembles that teacher's pet I disliked in elementary school. If we are not committed to trying to understand ourselves, how will we process the irritation we feel with a smiling patient? How will we differentiate whether our irritation is responsive to the rage underlying the patient's superficial smile? Or did we get up on the wrong side of the bed that morning? Or does the smile remind me of Miss McElroy's face when she snapped her wooden ruler on a classmate's knuckles? Or do I react this way frequently? Does it reflect *my* hidden anger? Or does this suggest something to search for in the patient?

My fear is that, if we allow our quintessential communication and self-knowledge skills to atrophy, CAP's bright future will never achieve paradigmatic status. In an effort to persuade you that there will never be an alternative for us as clinicians to endeavor to know our idiosyncratic selves, I will relate a clinical anecdote documenting the centrality of self-knowledge in that highly biological, objective, and mechanical subspecialty of *orthopedic surgery*. I was the victim and the beneficiary.

While on summer vacation with family in a rural area, in my 40s, I reinjured the knee in which my 19-year-old anterior cruciate ligament tear ended Heisman Trophy dreams. (A relevant example of change is that if my original injury occurred today, surgical intervention and rehabilitation would have me playing ball again in a matter of months. But when I was 19, the osteomyelitis terror precluded surgery. The multiplicity of amputees offered vivid testimony to the risks.) But 15 years after the original injury, I was obliged to undergo surgery in which the by-then tattered ligament had to be excised. And then approximately 10 years postarthrotomy on vacation I was obliged to consult with the nearest orthopedist, whose practice focused on acute ski injuries. After examination, he recommended additional surgery. Ugh.

Returning to Ann Arbor, I consulted John Hayes, the highly regarded orthopedist who knew my knee inside and out—before, during, and for the decade after surgery. He disagreed with his northern Michigan colleague. He perceived no indications for surgery. He acknowledged that he was at a loss to explain the injuries that had beset me recently. He had no better explanations than "bad luck" and/or "getting sloppy in your old age." Quickly, he added that he assumed I would welcome a third opinion.

Thus I consulted the revered, recently retired professor emeritus of orthopedics who had just moved into an office in the virtually empty reclaimed building housing retired medical professors. The distinguished consultant spent a great deal of time with me preparatory to conveying what truly was a third opinion. He recommended cessation of all physical activity. Forever! Al-

though this was before the cardiorespiratory benefits of regular exercise were recognized widely, my only hobbies (other than CAP scholarship) were recreational tennis, squash, golf, and whatever games my children and their friends elected.

I argued at length. I succeeded in having the newly retired orthopedist permit golf if I wore flat shoes without cleats. Further arguing proved fruitless and I left deeply dejected. My quest for a third opinion had devolved into what at that moment felt like a life sentence of confinement.

My disconsolate departure from the building was interrupted by a voice from behind calling my name. I turned to face the orthopedic resident who was assigned part time to accompany the emeritus professor to glean pearls of wisdom. From my perspective he had been little more than part of the furniture. Facing him as he walked toward rapidly aging me in that dreary lobby, he looked like a child. He commented that he had noticed that I did not like Dr. Emeritus's recommendation. My dispirited agreement was followed by the orthopedic resident driving the final nail in the coffin of those misguided opinions about the decreasing utility of that ancient Greek and modern clinical maxim: Know Thyself.

The surgical resident commented that he thought I might like to know his observation that it seemed amazingly easy for a man his professor's age to recommend to a man my age giving up all physical activity. Suddenly I felt transformed. The resident turned and disappeared before I could thank him sufficiently or even read the name on his white coat. Enriched with the resident's insight about Dr. Emeritus's deficiency in self-knowledge and probable clinical bias, I proceeded to follow John Hayes's advice and dedicated myself to being less sloppy until the Lenox Hill brace was invented.

In CAP jargon, my orthopedic experience 3 decades ago documents convincingly that countertransference in the absence of self-knowledge can be destructive in orthopedic CA/ISP. And the phenomenal orthopedic progress since then has not changed that inherent clinical truth: Know Thyself.

As clinicians we are inevitably involved in hypothetico-deductive reasoning that obliges us to strive for knowledge about our individualistic information processing characteristics. To what extent are we prone to confirmatory bias—the tendency to assign importance to data of observation consistent with expectations? Many of us are, as when we apply our awareness of the frequent linkage between suicide attempts and depression by overperceiving depression. Or, what bears repeating, does our focus on pathology risk ignoring strengths? Do we tend to identify more with children or parents? Many of us experience a change in our generational loyalties over the years. The bottom line is that those economic and clinical forces that perceive self-knowledge as nothing more than a relic of America's unidimensional psychodynamic past are flat-out wrong. It is an eternal clinical truth.

Clinical Truths

While privileged over the decades to participate in the education and graduation of more CAP resident physicians than any professor in history, I articulated the following clinical truths repeatedly. The first 3 apply to all professionals and perhaps to all humans:

- The mark of a professional is readiness to *acknowledge mistakes* and to learn from them.
- The most basic professional skill to learn is how to learn and to commit to *lifelong learning*.
- We should be *prepared to unlearn* truths. Until 1997 it was a universal axiom that nerve tissue could not be regenerated. And then the severed spinal chord of a rat regrew 90% in 6 months at Sweden's Karolinska Institute.
- Clinically, do not "rule out" prematurely. Until actively proven otherwise, we should consider *etiology* to be *multifactorial*. The seizure disorder with a temporal focus may erupt only under certain conditions, such as fatigue, anxiety, rage, excitement, and the like.
- The component system attracting the most attention is not necessarily the source or locus of the problem. Recall that, in the beginning of the 20th century, Indigestion was the most common cause of death. The gastrointestinal symptom was obvious. The cardiac problem was not evident. Similarly, as noted earlier, a child's misbehavior may serve to distract the parents from their conflicts. Depression may be hidden beneath a host of presenting problems: behavioral, somatic, learning.
- Search diligently for *perpetuating forces* that had nothing to do with starting the problem. Secondary gain? Are the reprimands and punishments for symptomatic behavior the youngster's major source of attention?
- Ascertain that all *define words* similarly. The 12-year-old "runaway" may reflect the rigid phraseol-

ogy of parents whose child does not come home directly from school. Or it may bespeak an abusive home, or point to a conduct-disordered youngster who poses the challenge of determining which of the host of possible etiologies and interventions might be appropriate. As bizarre as it sounds, I was consulted by the parents of a 2-year-old in diapers about "running away." The recommended therapeutic interventions were (1) installing a hook on the screen door so the toddler couldn't push it open to join the older children playing outside, and (2) parental education about child development and parenting skills.

At the opposite end of the developmental spectrum, please recall what the elderly surgical patient taught me about linguistic precision and the constructive power of language. Erectile dysfunction need not be sexual impotence.

- The *conceptual* frameworks underlying the systems we employ to organize our massive quantities of data of clinical observation contributes inevitably to shaping our clinical observations and thinking. It is our responsibility to exercise *self-vigilance*.
- A CA/ISP process is *incomplete* without devoting special attention to:

  - The explicit question as to what might occur *without intervention*.
  - Searching for *strengths* on which to build.
  - Arranging at least one *family interview* except when the colleagues with whom we consult agree the powerful contraindications should prevail.

- It is exceeding unlikely that there is such a thing as a secret within a family under one roof. There may be varying levels of awareness of the secret; however, empirical evidence is persuasive that it is never truly a secret to anyone. To avoid knowledge of the *family "secret,"* developing children have unknowingly gone to the tragic extreme of learning nothing. I am not the only clinician who has seen children who became mentally retarded to sustain ignorance of a family secret (Skeels & Dye, 1938–1939).
- Each assessment and intervention strategy planning should be designed individually. When King Solomon, 3 millennia ago, recommended *individualizing each child's* education, he bespoke a *clinical* truth 500 years before Hippocrates was born.
- When treatment interventions are indicated, our written plan should define precisely not only clinical methodologies but also *targets and goals*. And we should schedule *periodic reviews* of progress, strategies, and future plans. We should not rely solely on economic forces to counter those proso-

cial protective inclinations many of us share inclining us toward the risk of keeping some children in the sick role longer than necessary.

- The next-to-last truth borders on being almost too obvious to say. Every clinical history should include explicit inquiry about *variability in symptoms.* What merits noting is that if there appears to be a

seasonal pattern, phototherapy might be an amazing remedy even for non-affective symptomatology.

- And prerequisite whether orthopedics or CAP: *Clinician, Know Thyself.*

To reciprocate this collegial chat, I hope I can look forward to learning your thoughts.

REFERENCES

Bettelheim, B. (1948). A therapeutic milieu. *American Journal of Orthopsychiatry, 18,* 191–206.

Boswell, J. (1988). *The kindness of strangers: The abandonment of children in Western Europe from late antiquity to the Renaissance.* New York: Pantheon.

Bradley, C. (1937). The behavior of children receiving benzedrine. *American Journal of Psychiatry, 94,* 577–585.

Cade, F. (1949). Lithium salts in the treatment of psychotic excitement. *Medical Journal of Austria, 36,* 349.

Davenport, C. W., & Harrison, S. I. (1977). Gender identity change in a female adolescent transsexual. *Archives of Sexual Behavior, 6,* 327–340.

Delay, J., & Deniker, P. (1952). *Le traitement des psychoses par une methode neurolytique derivee de l'hibernotherapie. Congres des Medicins Aliensites et Neurologistes de France,* vol. 50. Luxembourg.

Deutsch, H. (1925). *Psychoanalyse der weiblichen Sexualfunktionen.* Vienna: International Psychoanal. Verlag.

Fleming, A. (1929). The antibacterial action of cultures of a penicillium. *British Journal of Experimental Pathology, 10,* 226.

Frances, A., & Clarkin, J. F. (1981). No treatment as the prescription of choice. *Archives of General Psychiatry, 38,* 542–545.

Freud, S. (1935). *An autobiographical study.* New York: W. W. Norton.

Group for the Advancement of Psychiatry. (1975). *Pharmacotherapy and psychotherapy: Paradoxes, problems, and progress* (Vol. 9, Report 93). New York: Group for the Advancement of Psychiatry.

Group for the Advancement of Psychiatry. (1962). *The preclinical teaching of psychiatry* (Vol. 5, Report 54). New York: Group for the Advancement of Psychiatry.

Harrison, S. I. (1977). Reassessment of eclecticism in child psychiatric treatment. In M. F. McMillan & S. Henao (Eds.), *Child psychiatry: Treatment and research* (pp. 85–115). New York: Brunner/Mazel.

Harrison, S. I. (1978). Child psychiatry perspectives: Therapeutic choice in child psychiatry. *Journal of the American Academy of Child Psychiatry, 17,* 165–172.

Harrison, S. I. (1979). Child psychiatric treatment: Status and prospects. In J. D. Noshpitz et al., *Basic handbook of child psychiatry* (Vol. 3, pp. 3–20). New York: Basic Books.

Harrison, S. I. (1997). Nonaffective seasonality [Letter to editor]. *Journal of the American Academy of Child and Adolescent Psychiatry, 36,* 163–164.

Healy, W. (1915). *The individual delinquent: A textbook of diagnosis and prognosis for all concerned in understanding offenders.* Boston: Little, Brown.

Jackson, H. H. (1884). *Ramona,* Little, Brown & Co. Boston.

Jones, M. C. (1924). The elimination of children's fears. *Journal of Experimental Psychology* 7:382–390.

Kandel, E. R. (1979). Psychotherapy and the single synapse: The impact of psychiatric thought on neurobiologic research. *New England Journal of Medicine, 301,* 1028–1037.

Kanner, L. (1943). Autistic disturbances of affective contact. *Nervous Child, 2,* 217–250.

Kanner, L. (1957). *Child psychiatry* (3rd ed.). Springfield, IL: Charles C Thomas.

Kempe, C. H., Silverman, F. N., Steele, B. F., Droegemueller, W., & Silver, H. K. (1962). The battered child syndrome. *Journal of the American Medical Association, 181,* 17–24.

Kety, S. (1960, June 7). The true nature of a book: An allegory. *NIH Record.*

Klein, D. F., & Fink, M. (1962). Psychiatric reaction patterns to imipramine. *American Journal of Psychiatry, 119,* 432.

Kleinman, A., & Cohen, A. (1997, March). Psychiatry's global challenge. *Scientific American,* 86–89.

Levy, F., Hay, D. A., McStephen, M., Wood, C., & Waldman, I. (1997). Attention-deficit hyperactivity disorder: A category or a continuum? Genetic analysis of a large-scale twin study. *Journal of the American Academy of Child and Adolescent Psychiatry, 36,* 737–744.

Lewy, A. J., Kern, H. A., Rosenthal, N. E., & Wehr, T. A. (1982). Bright artificial light treatment of a manic depressive patient with a seasonal mood cycle. *American Journal of Psychiatry, 139,* 1494–1498.

MacLean, P. D. (1973). A triune concept of the brain and behavior. In T. J. Boag & D. Campbell (Eds.),

The Clarence M. Hincks memorial lectures (p. 4). Toronto: University of Toronto Press.

Masters, W. H., & Johnson, V. E. (1966). *Human sexual response.* Boston: Little, Brown.

McDermott, J. F. (1996). Looking at the future through orange colored glasses. Plenary Address, *American Academy of Child and Adolescent Psychiatry.* Philadelphia.

McDermott, J. F., & Harrison, S. I. (1977). *Psychiatric treatment of the child.* New York: Jason Aronson.

Murray, C. J. L., & Lopez, A. D. (Eds.). (1996). *The global burden of disease.* Cambridge, MA: Harvard School of Public Health.

Nesse, R. M., & Williams, G. C. (1996). *Evolution and healing.* London: Orion Books.

Osler, W. (1895). Teaching and thinking: The two functions of a medical school. *Montreal Medical Journal, 25,* 561–573.

Pittman, F. S., Langsley, D. G., et al. (1966). Family therapy as an alternative to psychiatric hospitalization: Family structure, dynamics and therapy. *Psychiatric Research Reports of the American Psychiatric Association, 20,* 185–195.

Research Task Force of the National Institute of Mental Health. (1975). *Research in the service of mental health.* Rockville, MD: National Institute of Mental Health.

Skeels, H. M., & Dye, H. B. (1938–1939). A study of the effects of differential stimulation on mentally retarded children. *Journal of Psychoasthenics, 44,* 114–136.

Straus, M. A. (1994). Beating the devil out of them: Corporal punishment in American families. New York: Lexington Books.

Toffler, A. (1970). *Future shock.* New York: Random House.

Thomas, L. (1979). *The medusa and the snail.* New York: Viking Press.

Ustun, T. B., & Sartorius, N. (1995). *Mental illness in general health care: An international study.* Chichester: John Wiley & Sons.

Vitiello, B., & Stoff, D. M. (1997). Subtypes of aggression and their relevance to child psychiatry. *Journal of the American Academy of Child and Adolescent Psychiatry, 36,* 307–315.

Watson, N. B., & Raynor, R. (1920). Conditional emotional reactions. *Journal of Experimental Psychology, 3,* 1.

Weiss, E., & English, O. S. (1943). *Psychosomatic medicine.* Philadelphia: W. B. Saunders.

Westman, J. C. (1994). *Licensing parents: Can we prevent child abuse and neglect?* New York: Insight/Plenum.

SUBJECT INDEX

Subject Index

816

AUTHOR INDEX

824

Author Index